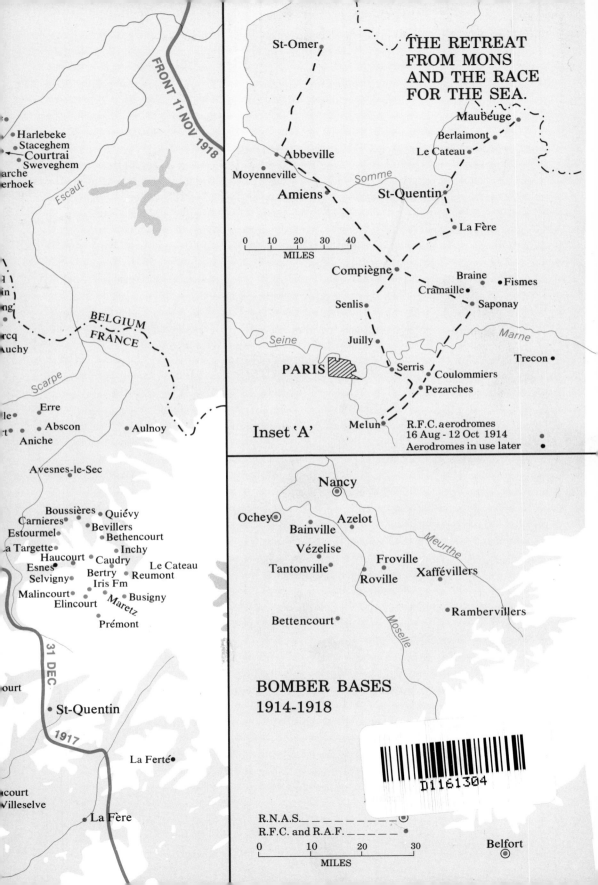

THE RETREAT FROM MONS AND THE RACE FOR THE SEA.

St-Omer

Maubeuge

Berlaimont

Le Cateau

Abbeville

Moyenneville

Somme

Amiens

St-Quentin

La Fère

0 10 20 30 40
MILES

Compiègne

Braine

Fismes

Cramaille

Saponay

Senlis

Marne

Seine

Juilly

Trecon

PARIS

Serris

Coulommiers

Pezarches

Melun

R.F.C. aerodromes
16 Aug - 12 Oct 1914
Aerodromes in use later

Inset 'A'

FRONT 11 NOV 1918

Harlebeke
Staceghem
Courtrai
Sweveghem
erhoek

Escaut

BELGIUM
FRANCE

rcq
uchy

Scarpe

Erre

Abscon
Aniche

Aulnoy

Avesnes-le-Sec

Boussières
Carnieres
Estourmel
La Targette
Haucourt
Esnes
Selvigny
Malincourt
Elincourt

Quiévy
Bevillers
Bethencourt
Inchy
Caudry
Le Cateau
Bertry
Reumont
Iris Fm
Busigny
Maretz
Prémont

31 DEC

St-Quentin

1917

La Ferté

ourt
illeselve

La Fère

BOMBER BASES 1914-1918

Nancy

Ochey

Azelot

Bainville

Vézelise

Meurthe

Froville

Xaffévillers

Tantonville

Roville

Rambervillers

Bettencourt

Moselle

R.N.A.S. _ _ _ _ _ _
R.F.C. and R.A.F. _ _ _ _ _

0 10 20 30
MILES

Belfort

CANADIAN AIRMEN
AND THE FIRST WORLD WAR

THE OFFICIAL HISTORY OF
THE ROYAL CANADIAN AIR FORCE
VOLUME I

S.F. WISE

Canadian Airmen
and the First World War

The Official History of
the Royal Canadian Air Force
Volume I

Published by University of Toronto Press
in co-operation with the Department of National Defence and
the Canadian Government Publishing Centre,
Supply and Services Canada

© Minister of Supply and Services Canada 1980
Reprinted 1981
Printed in Canada
ISBN 0-8020-2379-7
Government catalogue number D2-63-1980

Canadian Cataloguing in Publication Data

Wise, Sydney F., 1924-
    The official history of the Royal Canadian Air
    Force

    Contents: v.1. Canadian airmen and the first World
    War.
    Includes indexes.
    ISBN 0-8020-2379-7
    1. Canada. Royal Canadian Air Force – History.
    I. Title.

    UG635.C3W57   358.4'00971   C80-094480-1

Unless otherwise noted, illustrations in this book come from the Public Archives of
Canada and the Imperial War Museum; acknowledgment is hereby given for permission
to reproduce them.
Codes appearing at the end of captions represent negative numbers at the PAC.

Note: In the writing of this volume the author has been given full access to relevant
official documents in possession of the Department of National Defence; but the
inferences drawn and the opinions expressed are those of the author himself, and the
department is in no way responsible for his reading or presentation of the facts as stated.

Contents

Contents

Conclusion

Appendices

Maps and Illustrations

illustrations

Black and white photographs are placed following pages 1, 19, 121, 229, 329, 577, 621.

Preface

This book, the first in a series of four planned volumes on the history of the Royal Canadian Air Force, has been a long time in the making. It is about what might be called the pre-history of the RCAF, for it is mainly concerned with a part of our aviation experience which is still almost unknown to Canadians: the First World War. The idea that such a book ought to be written, at least so far as the record shows, first belonged to an administrative officer with the Canadian War Records Office. Captain J.N. MacAdams had the job of collecting and organizing the service records of Canadians who had flown with the Royal Air Force and its predecessors during the First World War. He was surprised and impressed by what these records disclosed, and recommended to his superiors in the headquarters of the Overseas Military Forces of Canada that an official history of what Canadians had done in the air should be written.

Nothing came of his suggestion. The very notion of official military history was unfamiliar to Canadians, since they had had little previous requirement for the product. Moreover, if official history was to be written, the Canadian Expeditionary Force was the obvious subject. By far the largest military formation Canada had ever put into the field, it had been commanded in its final years by a Canadian. Its numbered battalions, anonymous though they might at first appear, had in fact been based upon a regional militia system with roots deep in the country's past. The travails of the CEF had brought anguish to tens of thousands of homes; the support it required had strained the political system to an unparalleled degree. Its spectacular victories, and the visible part it had taken in the final victory, had aroused deep and rightful national pride, and won for Canada a place in the councils of the empire, the treaty settlements, and the League of Nations that otherwise she would not have enjoyed. Unquestionably the CEF merited whatever resources the government of the day was disposed to devote to official military history. As for Canadian airmen, it was perhaps believed that their part in the war could safely be left to the historians of the British services for which they had flown. If that was in fact the view, it was a regrettable, if understandable, error.

The British official history, *The War in the Air*, was published in six volumes between 1922 and 1937. It is a landmark of aviation history and has been an indispensable guide in the preparation of this book. Since it was written perspectives have changed and much new information has become available. Many of its

judgments can now be challenged, as from time to time they are in this volume;
many passages are polemical in nature, strongly favouring the Trenchardian view
of strategic air power. From a Canadian perspective there is another deficiency in
War in the Air of which its authors, Sir Walter Raleigh and H.A. Jones, were
probably quite unconscious. British air forces of the First World War – the Royal
Naval Air Service, the Royal Flying Corps, and the Royal Air Force – were multinational in composition, drawn mainly from the British Isles but also, and to a
substantial extent, from many parts of what was then the British Empire. Raleigh
and Jones may have assumed, with Sir David Henderson, a wartime commander
of the RFC, that 'the more people of British origin are mixed up together in this
war the better'; at any rate, little attention is given in *War in the Air* to the contributions made by airmen from the colonies. In 1934 the Australians corrected
this oversight, so far as their own airmen were concerned, with the publication of
F.M. Cutlack's *The Australian Flying Corps in the Western and Eastern Theatres of
War, 1914–1918*. There is recorded, in meticulous detail, the work of the four
Australian squadrons and other units which operated under British control. As it
happens, many more Canadians than Australians served as airmen during the war,
but until its last days there were no formations that had a specifically Canadian
identity. In the indexes to *War in the Air* there are six references to Canada.
Though Canadians are mentioned by name in the text, their national origin
usually is not. Yet Air Ministry records show that by 1918 the Canadians had
become a vital component of the fighting strength of the RAF, just as the RAF
itself had become an essential element in the war on land and at sea.

If there was little the Canadian public could learn of the part their airmen had
played during the First World War from the British official history, they were no
better served by their own authors. One excellent book about the RAF training
organization, *Aviation in Canada, 1917–1918*, by Alan Sullivan, was published at
the end of the war. It was not written in a form that would capture public attention,
however, and even the fact that a large-scale air training scheme was in operation
in Canada during the last years of the war has passed from public memory. Most
material published about the Canadian air effort between the wars was of an
ephemeral character, and almost all of it was about a handful of remarkable fighter
pilots. That many thousands of Canadians flew operationally during the First
World War; that their services were not confined to the fighter role but embraced
the entire range of aerial activities; and that they were present in every theatre,
from Archangel to East Africa, and not solely on the Western Front – none of
these facts ever got home to Canadians at large.

An impression was created that Canadian involvement in the air war could be
summed up in the exploits of a small number of 'aces,' an impression cemented
by George Drew's popular *Canada's Fighting Airmen* (1930). It was a notion that
carried over to the Second World War, and distorted the reality of Canada's air
effort in that struggle quite as much as it had for the First World War.

Survival, not history, was a chief preoccupation of the Royal Canadian Air Force
between the wars. Not until January 1940 was Flight Lieutenant Kenneth B.
Conn, then employed in the Directorate of Staff Duties, given the additional task
of collecting historical records. By the end of the war he was the Air Historian

(since 1944) in the rank of Group Captain with a staff that included thirty-two officers. His establishment published the first two volumes of *The RCAF Overseas*, a popular account of operations prepared while the war was still on. In addition, the Air Historian envisaged a complete official history of the RCAF in nine volumes, to be written and published after the end of hostilities.

After the war, however, the historical establishment was cut to two members, Wing Commander Fred H. Hitchins (Group Captain Conn's successor) and a secretary. The third volume of *The RCAF Overseas* was published, but the ambitious project for an official history was cancelled. The postwar Air Historical Section was, therefore, unable to do much more than maintain the records already held, add to them the current unit historical reports, carry out a limited amount of research on early aviation history, and publish a few small contributions to RCAF history, notably *The RCAF Logbook*, a chronology that appeared in 1949. In 1960 Hitchins was succeeded by Wing Commander Ralph V. Manning, who retired in 1965 when the historical establishments of the three services were merged as the result of integration.

Colonel C.P. Stacey, first director of the unified historical establishment of the three services, quickly obtained authority for an official history of the Royal Canadian Air Force much reduced in scale from that Group Captain Conn had planned. After I had succeeded Colonel Stacey and had begun detailed planning for the series in conjunction with Lieutenant-Colonel D.J. Goodspeed, then Senior Historian in the Directorate of History, we decided that the First World War phase of the history should be treated in a separate volume.

We took that decision for three reasons. Preliminary work already done by the former Air Historical Section and continued by historians in the Directorate of History had demonstrated that the Canadian part in the air history of the First World War was of significant dimensions. Second, it was apparent that much of the Canadian story was utterly unfamiliar, since Canadian activities, so far as the public was concerned, had been telescoped into the activities of a dozen or so fighter pilots. Finally, it was evident that the First World War aviation experience, in all its complexity, was basic to the later history of the RCAF. Nearly all the senior officers of the RCAF between 1924 and 1945 had been directly involved in the First World War; every aspect of modern military aviation had its origins in the 1914–18 period; and so had the beginnings of Canadian air policy. Moreover, an understanding of the relationship of the RCAF to other services, and to the RAF, must derive partly from an understanding of the way in which the air arm evolved during the First World War.

Canadians in large numbers, substantially more than 20,000 of them, were present at the creation of military air power in this century.* An account of their

---

* Air history deals in a scale of numbers much different from army history, partly because of the large ground organization necessary to maintain a relatively small number in the air. The fighting component of an RAF squadron in 1918 was thirty men or less, a figure that may be compared to the one thousand all ranks that constituted the fighting strength of a Canadian infantry battalion of the same period. It is worth noting, however, that at the end of the war there were 188 operational squadrons, plus fifteen independent flights (the equivalent of another five squadrons), in the RAF, and that the total strength, ground and air, of that service was about 300,000.

service experience poses a problem not customarily faced by official historians, although it is one that recurs with respect to many members of the RCAF during the Second World War. Ordinarily, official histories have as their subject the armed forces of Canada, whether the Canadian Expeditionary Force of the First World War or the Canadian Army and the Royal Canadian Navy during the Second. In the present case, however, our subject is the work of many individual Canadians in three British services; in other words, this is essentially a study of the colonial phase of the history of Canadian military aviation. Not until late in the First World War were distinctive Canadian air units formed: the Canadian Air Force and the Royal Canadian Naval Air Service. Until these small organizations were created, Canadians were scattered unevenly through the many units of the RAF and its precursors.

This volume is not simply a collective biography of the thousands of Canadians who fought in the air, or aspired to do so, but is primarily an attempt to restore a phase of our military history – and, indeed, of our national history – that has been all but lost. The aim has been to keep the Canadians to the fore, but at the same time to ground their work in the many contexts that give pattern and meaning to what they were doing. Thus the manner in which Canadians entered the flying services and underwent flying training has been set within the context of the general state of aviation in the country, the shift of public and governmental attitudes towards aviation and the gradual evolution of a Canadian air policy. In theatres of war Canadians, with a few exceptions, did not rise to important command positions. At one level, therefore, much of this history is about the operational tasks of pilots and observers. These operations, however, make little sense by themselves, and it has been necessary to connect them to the evolution of aircraft, weapons, and tactics, to the operations of land and sea forces, and to the policies and organization of the British flying services. So well represented were the Canadians in every aspect of military and naval air operations, especially after 1915, that it has been possible to recount every important stage in the air war by drawing upon the experiences of individual Canadians.

To reconstruct the 1914–18 air war from a Canadian perspective has been a research task of some complexity. The starting point was the thousands of record cards compiled by Captain MacAdams and his clerks in 1919 from records of the RAF and the headquarters of the Overseas Military Forces of Canada in London. On each card was written the name of the airman, his rank, trade, decorations, place of origin in Canada (or place of enlistment), record of service, and, occasionally, occupation prior to enlistment. This invaluable record was brought home to Canada, and for many years found a resting place in the Army Historical Section in Ottawa. The vicissitudes of time, the irrelevance of the card file to the work of the Section, and even the domestic habits of its members (if one is to judge from the coffee rings on some of the cards) resulted in many losses, particularly from the latter part of the alphabet.

Eventually the file was taken over by the Air Historical Section and became a particular concern of Fred Hitchins. Dr Hitchins' scholarly interest in First World War aviation long predated his RCAF service, and it was singularly fortunate that he was given the task of investigating the work of Canadians in the RFC, RNAS, and RAF. He successfully argued that 'a purely statistical account of Canada's aerial contribution in 1914–1918 would be comparable to a pie crust without any filling,' and in 1941–2, therefore, he spent a good part of his time, while working at the National Library of Wales, Aberystwyth, where RAF records were then held, in accumulating notes and documents having to do with First World War aviation. From the point of view of the present history, Dr Hitchins' work had two important consequences. In the first place, he was able to begin the reconstitution of the card file, to add new names to it (MacAdams never claimed to have produced a complete inventory of Canadians), and to annotate many of the cards. Secondly, many of the rough notes and narratives he compiled were based upon documents that no longer exist, since unfortunately a number of RAF files referring to Canada were destroyed before or during the transfer of RAF records to the Public Record Office in London.

Gradually, as the result of Hitchins' work, later carried on by the Directorate of History, there was accumulated a large body of documentation of the most varied kind: logbooks, diaries, letters, photographs, and taped interviews with former airmen. Most of this collection was organized into biographical files, and included papers of such notable airmen as W.A. Bishop, Ray Collishaw, W.G. Barker, Lloyd Breadner, and R.H. Mulock.

The next stage in the research process was to link this mass of biographical evidence with the totality of the record of First World War aviation. At the Public Archives of Canada there were both governmental and private collections having to do with the formation of Canadian aviation policy, the recruiting and training of airmen in Canada, and the establishment of a Canadian aircraft manufacturing industry. The major sources for this volume, however, were in the Public Record Office in London, and comprised not only the massive collection of RAF records grouped under the Air Series but also supporting materials from Admiralty, War Office, Colonial Office, and Cabinet records.

It was a relatively straightforward task to examine these various collections for important evidence dealing with air policy, organization, and the general development of the air war in relation to other services and the many theatres in which aviation played a significant part. It was much more difficult to extract from them evidence which bore on the actual work that the Canadians were doing in the air, if only because the Canadians were rarely identified.

In order to approach the British records effectively, a volume listing every RNAS, RFC, and RAF unit was prepared. Under each unit heading were listed alphabetically the names of every Canadian known to have served with the unit, together with the dates of service whenever that was known. This listing, rather cumbersome to use though kept in loose leaf form (and constantly updated, since new information kept turning up), became the key to the war diaries, record books, bombing and combat reports which constitute the basic operational records of the British flying services in the First World War. With this guide in hand, it was then possible to identify units in which, from time to time, sizeable numbers of Canadians served. Few unit records were copied in their entirety for any given period, but in all cases sufficient copying was done to ensure that the work of the whole unit, and not just of the Canadians in it, became clear in order to maintain a proper balance between the contribution of the Canadians and that of the unit as a whole. All the records collected in this way were indexed and organized to make them accessible for research and to link them to the biographical collection. In sum, the body of evidence ordinarily immediately available for the writing of Canadian service history had first to be generated before a history could actually be written. Only the reader can judge whether the result justifies the effort expended.

Since this book is about Canadians rather than a Canadian service, a working definition of 'Canadian' was a necessity. The term 'Canadian National' had no legal status until legislation of 1921 and prior to that date persons living in Canada and exercising the rights of citizenship were, in law, British subjects, whether native-born or naturalized. Before 1914 people in Canada knew very well what a 'Canadian' was, but their definitions were apt to vary remarkably according to region and ethnic origin.

There was a further complication. The decade prior to the outbreak of war was one of heavy immigration to Canada, a movement that included many thousands of young men from the British Isles. For rather a longer period, there had been a significant emigration of native-born Canadians to the United States. From both groups came many members of the British flying services, recruited either in Canada or through the agency of the Royal Flying Corps in the United States. We have deemed immigrants from the British Isles to be 'Canadian' if they had been resident in Canada for some length of time before the war, could be shown to have established genuine roots in the country, or, above all, if they returned to Canada after the completion of their flying service.* For those resident in the United States who were born in Canada or, through parental or other ties, had some close association with Canada, judgment was made on a case-by-case basis. It is likely that in both these categories were many who, in their own minds, were Canadian but who have been overlooked simply because evidence does not exist to justify their inclusion. The reverse situation also holds: many native-born Canadians joined the RAF or emigrated to the United States after completing their war service. Such persons were undoubtedly Canadian at the time they performed war service. Despite much care, it is probable that a number of individuals have been identified as Canadian who were, at most, mid-Atlantic in affiliation. Nor will the actual number of native-born Canadians who flew during the war ever be known because of the absence of documentation.

Their numbers were indeterminate and the precise status of some of them was unclear, but from their first appearance the Canadians were recognized as a distinctive element in the flying services by those who led them or flew with them. Most of the Canadians who were first on the scene favoured a service in which particular national identities were subordinated to an imperial whole; most of those who came after them were entirely satisfied to be merged with others in a British ser-

---

* Under the Immigration Act of 1910 any person born in Canada (who had not become an alien) or any British subject domiciled for three years in Canada (provided that he had not since left Canada for a period of one year or more) was categorized as a Canadian citizen. This definition was the basis of the Canadian Nationals Act of 1921.

vice. A substantial proportion of their RCAF successors who served with RAF units during the Second World War felt the same way.

Yet as their numbers rose, especially after the beginning of 1917, the Canadians began to develop a consciousness of themselves as a distinct group within the air services. Many of them had transferred to flying duties from the Canadian Expeditionary Force, were undoubtedly nationally-minded, and were confident of the Canadian capacity to sustain an effective military organization. While valuing their comradeship with airmen from the rest of the empire, they were increasingly sympathetic to the idea of a separate Canadian air force. One of these was W.A. Bishop. As a young pilot officer I passed under the cold blue reviewing eye of Air Vice-Marshal Bishop, VC, DSO, MC, DFC, Croix de Guerre, an experience shared with many thousands of graduates of the British Commonwealth Air Training Plan. His presence was a visible demonstration to us that our service, young as it was, had a tradition of high accomplishment.

Those of us who have worked on this history had as our aim the establishment of a foundation for the later history of the RCAF. In assessing the part taken by Canadians we endeavoured to give them their due and, we trust, no more than that. The qualification is necessary because we came to admire greatly this remarkable company. We met some of them, and corresponded with others. I wish to thank them, and the families of other Canadian airmen, for all the advice and assistance patiently and generously given.

When this history was begun, the Directorate of History was made up of former members, military and civilian, of the three historical establishments of the armed services. Other historians joined them in subsequent years. Aviation history was strange and even forbidding territory to all but a few of them. The process of conversion is always difficult, but it was eased by the sense of teamwork which developed among us, a sense that to a great degree came from a mutual conviction of the importance of what we were doing. I must take responsibility for all that follows, but I must say as well that this book is the result of a collective effort sustained over several years, the product of much discussion, heated debate, and mutual criticism and instruction. To the present director, Dr W.A.B. Douglas, and to all members of the Directorate, past and present and too numerous to list, I wish to express my thanks, both for their work and for the experience of having worked with them. They, and the secretaries and typists who coped with early drafts, will understand the particular thanks I wish to extend to Gloria McKeigan and Elsie Roberts for their calm efficiency at all stages of the manuscript.

A number of institutions have helped greatly in the preparation of this history. I wish to thank the Dominion Archivist and the staff of the Public Archives of Canada, the Keeper of the Records and many kind officials of the Public Record Office, London, the Director and staff of the Imperial War Museum, the Curators and staffs of the Canadian War Museum and the Aviation and Space Division of the National Museum of Science and Technology, the staff of the National Aeronautical Collection, the Archivist of the University of Toronto, and the Superintendent and staff of the Alexander Graham Bell National Historic Park at Baddeck, NS. The advice of the Operational Research and Analysis Establishment's Director of Mathematics and Statistics, Dr Marcus Weinberger, was invaluable in preparing Appendix C. My thanks are also due to the many individual researchers in the field of Canadian aviation history who have contributed their expertise.

S.F. WISE

Institute of Canadian Studies
Carleton University

Abbreviations

2/Lt Second Lieutenant
AA anti-aircraft
a/c aircraft
AEG *Allgemeine Elektrizitäts Gesellschaft*
AFC Australian Flying Corps
AFC Air Force Cross
AG Adjutant-General
AGO *Aerowerke Gustav Otto*
AGS School of Aerial Gunnery
Air Air Ministry records in the Public Record Office, London
app. appendix
A/S anti-submarine
BASF *Badische Aniline und Soda Fabrik*
BCATP British Commonwealth Air Training Plan
BEF British Expeditionary Force
BHP Beardmore-Halford-Pullinger
BI Baby Incendiary [Bomb]
Cab Cabinet Office records in the Public Record Office, London
CAF Canadian Air Force
CAL Canadian Aeroplanes Ltd
CAS Chief of the Air Staff
CB Confined to barracks
CEF Canadian Expeditionary Force
CFS Central Flying School
CGS Chief of the General Staff
CIB Wireless Central Information Bureau
CIGS Chief of the Imperial General Staff
C-in-C Commander-in-Chief
CMB coastal motor boat
CMR Canadian Mounted Rifles
CO Commanding Officer
CTS Canadian Training Squadron
DAD Director Air Division, Naval Staff

DAO Director of Air Operations
DCAS Deputy Chief of the Air Staff
DHist Directorate of History, National Defence Headquarters, Ottawa
DFC Distinguished Flying Cross
DFO Director of Flying Operations [in Air Ministry]
DFW *Deutsche Flugzeug-Werke*
DSC Distinguished Service Cross
DSD Director Signal Division
DSM Distinguished Service Medal
DSO Distinguished Service Order
EA enemy aircraft
FAI *Fédération aeronautique internationale*
FBA Franco-British Aviation
F/C Flight Commander
FK *Fliegerkompagnie*
F/S Flight Sergeant
F/S/L Flight Sub-Lieutenant
GAE *Groupe des Armées de l'Est*
GAF German air force
GF fleeting target ('fleeting target at ...')
GHQ General Headquarters
GOC General Officer Commanding
HA hostile aircraft
HAG Heavy Artillery Group
HD home defence
HE high explosive
HM His Majesty's
HMCS His Majesty's Canadian Ship
HMS His Majesty's Ship
hp horsepower
HQ headquarters
hrs hours
HSF [German] High Seas Fleet
IAF Independent Air Force
IAIAF Inter-Allied Independent Air Force
IF Independent Force
IMB Imperial Munitions Board
KB kite balloon
KIA killed in action
kg kilogram(s)
L *Luftschiff*
lbs pounds
LFG *Luftfahrzeug Gesellschaft*
LL 'All available batteries to open fire' [very important target]
Lt Lieutenant
LVG *Luft Verkehrs Gesellschaft*

LZ *Luftschiff Zeppelin*
MC Military Cross
MD Military District
MG [or mg] machine-gun
MIA missing in action
mm millimetre(s)
MP Member of Parliament
mph miles per hour
MT mechanical transport
N 'guns in position at ...'
N Naval
NCO non-commissioned officer
nd no date given
NF 'guns firing in position at ...'
np no place of publication [given]
OBE Officer of the (Order of the) British Empire
OC Officer Commanding
OMFC Overseas Military Forces of Canada
PAC Public Archives of Canada
PC Privy Council [Order-in-Council no]
POW prisoner of war
PPCLI Princess Patricia's Canadian Light Infantry
RAF Royal Air Force
RCAF Royal Canadian Air Force
RCHA Royal Canadian Horse Artillery
RCN Royal Canadian Navy
RCNAS Royal Canadian Naval Air Service
RCNVR Royal Canadian Naval Volunteer Reserve
RE Royal Engineer(s)
RFC Royal Flying Corps
RG Record Group
RHA Royal Horse Artillery
RMC Royal Military College [of Canada, Kingston]
RN Royal Navy
RNAS Royal Naval Air Service
RNCVR Royal Naval Canadian Volunteer Reserve
RNVR Royal Naval Volunteer Reserve
rpm revolutions per minute
SAA small arms ammunition
SE southeast
Set set of notes and translation
SGR Steiger Collection
SL *Schütte-Lanz*
S/M submarine
SN steel-nosed
S of S Secretary of State [for War]

ss Sea Scout [non-rigid airship]
Tech Technical Officer
USA United States Army
USAF United States Air Force
USN United States Navy
VC Victoria Cross
vol. volume
WIA wounded in action
WPNF 'many batteries active at ...'

Introduction

The first aerial photograph in Canada was taken by Capt. E. Elsdale, RE, using a clockwork-operated plate camera from a captive balloon at Halifax, NS, in 1883. (RE 12378-1)

The Aerial Experiment Association: Glen W. Curtiss, Alexander Graham Bell, J.A.D. McCurdy, F.W. Baldwin (C 28213)

The *Silver Dart*, J.A.D. McCurdy at the controls on 23 Feb. 1909 (RE 74-217)

The first all-Canadian 'aerodrome.' *Baddeck No 1* at Petawawa in early August 1909
(AH 170)

William Frederick Nelson Sharpe of Ottawa, one of the two founding members of the short-lived Canadian Aviation Corps, and Canada's first fatal casualty of the air, died in an accident in England, 4 Feb. 1915. This photo was taken at the Curtiss Flying School, San Diego, which Sharpe attended in December 1913 and January 1914. (PL 39933)

The Lohner 'aerodrome' in Ottawa during the winter of 1910 (RE 15360)

Brig.-Gen. David Henderson chaired the
Aeronautical Committee set up to establish the form and direction of Britain's
RFC in 1912. In 1918 he was to play a
major role in the negotiations which
accompanied the formation of the CAF.
(PMR 21-520)

Brig.-Gen. Duncan Sayres MacInnes,
CMG, DSO, of Hamilton, Ont., was a
major in the Royal Engineers in 1912,
when he was appointed secretary to the
War Office's Advisory Committee on
Aeronautics. (RE 67-471)

1
Military Aviation before the
First World War

The first phase of the history of the Royal Canadian Air Force is inevitably a history of the part taken by Canadians in the British flying services. Or almost inevitably. There was a moment before the First World War when it appeared that as a result of the work of some distinguished Canadian air pioneers and of an air-minded staff officer in the Department of Militia and Defence the idea of a distinct Canadian air force might take hold. That moment passed quickly enough and, although the idea of a Canadian service never lacked supporters, it was not until after the war's end that a permanent organization took shape.

To blame particular ministers or civil servants for want of foresight would be easy but mistaken. In 1914 the air age was in its infancy. Very few Canadians had ever seen an aeroplane and only a handful had become pilots. A Canadian air force would have seemed to most Canadians an expensive and useless absurdity. Many had experienced difficulty enough swallowing the idea of a separate navy: the military applications of the invention of powered flight could well be left to Britain and other major nations.

All the great powers had, in fact, interested themselves to one degree or another in the potential military uses of aircraft before the beginning of the First World War. Long before powered flight the balloon had extended the dimensions of war. Its principal military role was reconnaissance, but it was also used for artillery ranging, transportation, and bombardment. As early as 1794 the armies of revolutionary France employed a balloon corps, and the French had also resorted to balloons in military campaigns in Algeria in 1830, in Italy in 1859, at the siege of Paris in 1870–1, and in Indo-China in 1884. In the American Civil War both sides had used balloons.[1]

Until the last quarter of the nineteenth century the British, concerned mainly with small wars of empire, had displayed little interest in the military balloon, and the British colonies even less. Although a civilian aeronaut conducted some trials for the Royal Engineers in 1863, it was not until 1878 that they really became interested. One of the earliest successful balloon experiments in Canada occurred during August 1883 when Captain H. Elsdale of the Royal Engineers succeeded in taking aerial photographs of the Halifax Citadel, using a tethered balloon fitted with a clockwork-operated plate camera. A year later Elsdale commanded one of the first operational balloon sections in the British Army on an expedition to

Bechuanaland. By 1890 army estimates provided for a balloon section as a unit of the Corps of Royal Engineers. Its two balloons gave useful service in the Boer War; more important, the section trained a small number of officers and men who kept alive service interest in military aeronautics.[2]

The first controlled sustained flight of a powered heavier-than-air machine is generally accepted to have been made by Wilbur and Orville Wright at the North Carolina Kill Devil sand hills on 17 December 1903, when their aeroplane, the *Flyer*, flew 852 feet in fifty-nine seconds.* The Wright brothers' breakthrough had come because they daringly abandoned aerodynamic stability for an inherently unstable machine that could make a banked turn by the simultaneous use of wing warping and rudder. For a time, however, few believed that the Wright brothers had actually flown. It was not until the summer of 1908, when Wilbur Wright made more than one hundred successful flights from two fields near Le Mans, France, that it began to be accepted that a new age was dawning.[3]

The first serious aeronautical research in Canada had been undertaken by Wallace Rupert Turnbull of Saint John, NB, who built a wind tunnel in 1902. In October 1907 Alexander Graham Bell, together with two young Canadians, J.A.D. McCurdy and Frederick Walker Baldwin, and two Americans, Lieutenant Thomas E. Selfridge, USA, and Glenn Curtiss, formed the Aerial Experiment Association at Baddeck, NS, aimed at getting a man into the air with a heavier-than-air flying machine. Their early flights were made at Hammondsport, NY, as well as Baddeck. Following experiments in 1908 with a large man-carrying kite named the *Cygnet*, the association built a biplane, the *Red Wing*, which made two short flights before it was destroyed in a crash landing. Bell and his associates went on to build the *White Wing* and the *June Bug*, both of which were flown successfully, and then the *Silver Dart* which was powered with a water-cooled, 8-cylinder engine. In September Selfridge became the first fatality of the air age in a crash near Washington. He had been a passenger in an aircraft Orville Wright was test flying for the United States Army. Despite the setback, the association continued its work at Baddeck where McCurdy made the first Canadian aeroplane flight in the *Silver Dart* on 23 February 1909. The Aerial Experiment Association dissolved at the end of March, having put four machines in the air.[4]

In the next few years the design and performance of aeroplanes improved with astonishing rapidity. By 1914 the official record for altitude was almost 20,000 feet, the speed record 126 mph, and the non-stop endurance record more than twenty-one hours. These performances, of course, were achieved by specialized aircraft designed for specific test purposes and it was not for several years that such capabilities could be incorporated in military aircraft.[5]

British military flying had a relatively slow start, initially being confined to experiments carried out at the Balloon School, Farnborough. Its most notable member was a civilian, S.F. Cody, who designed and tested kites, airships, and, later, aeroplanes. Cody's activities were makeshift: in 1908, for example, construction of *British Aeroplane No. 1* was delayed for several months because the only

---

* Oliver Stewart, however, makes a case for the Frenchman Clement Ader flying a powered heavier-than-air machine in 1890, 1891, and 1897. *Aviation: the Creative Ideas* (London 1966)

available engine was being used in the army's first airship, *Nulli Secundus*. At the same time more extensive experiments were being conducted by A.V. Roe, Horace, Eustace, and Oswald Short, Claude Grahame-White, T.O.M. Sopwith, and C.S. Rolls. Civilian development was so swift and vigorous that there appeared little need for the military to be in the vanguard. In April 1909 the War Office prohibited further aeroplane trials because of the expense – to that point, expenditure amounted to 2500 pounds sterling.[6]

Field Marshal Sir W.G. Nicholson, Chief of the Imperial General Staff from 1908 until 1912, regarded aviation as a useless fad. Even the Master-General of the Ordnance, whose responsibilities included aviation, had no strong belief in its military value. Such views were not so short-sighted as they now seem: balloons had been only of limited utility and in these early days airships and aeroplanes were singularly prone to spectacular mishaps. But a general opposition to innovation played a part as well. The extreme position was held by cavalry officers who claimed that aircraft would frighten their horses, an argument still heard in the 1930s. The Admiralty was not much more enthusiastic, but it had as a stimulus the potential threat posed by German airships. Defence against them, and the beginnings of its own airship programme, were its chief aerial concerns. The airship programme suffered a disastrous setback, however, when a large dirigible built by Vickers, and sardonically named *Mayfly*, broke her back in September of that year without having once been untethered.[7]

Despite official coolness, some progress had been made. In April 1908 a group of British members of parliament had formed an *ad hoc* Parliamentary Aerial Defence Committee, although it does not appear to have had much influence since more than three years later the War Office still had only fifteen aeroplanes. In 1909 an Advisory Committee on Aeronautics was created as a sub-committee of the Committee of Imperial Defence. This body, which included scientific, naval, and military representatives, had no policy function but was concerned solely with the technical side of aviation, supervising research into such matters as aerofoils, engines, lubricants, and aircraft stability.[8] In October 1910 a division of the Balloon School, the Balloon Factory, was authorized to experiment with aeroplanes and to train aviators to co-operate with field troops. Early the following year the Balloon School became the Air Battalion of the Royal Engineers; its small establishment of fourteen officers and 176 other ranks was the forerunner of the British air service. In addition, a small number of individual officers learned to fly – either at the government's expense at places like the Royal Aero Club's Eastchurch grounds or through private tuition.

It would have been strange if young officers had not been attracted to the military possibilities of the aeroplane. In those early days powered flight had an irresistible glamour for the bold and the imaginative. Looking down from their open cockpits at the panoramic world spread out below, it must have seemed that they were the heralds of a new and tremendous dawn. The winds that tore at their goggles, the clouds through which they passed, the sweep and soar and dip of their flight brought a joyous exultation, so that even the mundane requisites of their calling – the exposure to vile weather, the smell of engine oil, the dirty work of maintenance and repair – were romanticized. At army manœuvres in Britain and

India in 1911 a number of flights were made by such pioneering officers, and in January of the same year Captain William Sefton Brancker had put a Bristol Box-kite through its paces before a group of senior officers which included Lieutenant-General Sir Douglas Haig.[9]

At this juncture, nevertheless, British military aviation was lagging behind that of other countries. In 1911 the Americans employed aircraft for communications and reconnaissance during the Mexican Revolution.* In September 1910, at the French military manœuvres in Picardy, aeroplanes piloted by both civilian and military flyers were used for reconnaissance and communications. In Germany the thoughts of the General Staff had also turned to aeroplanes; during the summer of 1910 the first steps were taken to form a corps of military airmen, with seven officers undergoing military flying training, and many more obtaining their pilot's certificates at private schools.[10]

Such continental developments, particularly the appearance of German military airships, the French use of aeroplanes in manœuvres, and Italy's employment of both in the Libyan campaign of 1910–11, generated some public concern in Britain. In November 1911 Prime Minister Asquith asked the Advisory Committee on Aeronautics of the Committee of Imperial Defence to study the role and organization of military aviation. After an investigation conducted by Colonel J.E.B. Seely, the committee reported in February 1912 and its recommendations formed the basis of a government white paper of 11 April. The paper took note of foreign advances in aviation, but pointed out that the tactical and strategic uses of aircraft were still uncertain. It went on to say:

... it is clear that this country cannot afford to incur the risk of dropping behind other nations in this matter, and that every facility must be given for experiment and progress.

There are admittedly advantages in a policy of postponing the development of aeroplanes for naval and military purposes, and of leaving the pioneer work to private enterprise and to foreign nations, but it is clear that aeroplanes have now to a great extent passed out of the experimental stage as regards their employment in warfare, and an active and progressive policy has therefore become imperatively urgent.[11]

The committee proposed that an aeronautical service called the Royal Flying Corps be formed, consisting of a Military Wing to be administered by the War Office and a Naval Wing under the control of the Admiralty. The government responded quickly. On 13 April 1912 the Royal Flying Corps was constituted by Royal Warrant. The regulations to govern the new body, which had been drafted by an informal committee composed of Brigadier-General David Henderson, Captain F.H. Sykes, and Major D.S. MacInnes,† were promulgated by special army order two days later.[12]

---

* In 1914, however, the United States would have only thirteen military aeroplanes. Arthur
   Sweetser, *The American Air Service* (New York 1919), 27
† Major Duncan Sayre MacInnes was a Canadian, a native of Hamilton, Ont. He had graduated in
   1891 from the Royal Military College, Kingston, winning the Governor General's Gold Medal
   and the Sword of Honour. He was commissioned in the Royal Engineers, served with distinction
   in the Ashanti Expedition of 1895–6 and in the South African War, and held staff appointments

The 1912 white paper set forth the role of the Military Wing as reconnaissance, prevention of reconnaissance by the enemy, communication between head-quarters, observation of artillery fire, and infliction of damage on the enemy. *Field Service Regulations*, however, limited the role somewhat, specifying only the first two. The air service was to work in co-operation with the cavalry, but because night and weather might frequently ground its aircraft, the Military Wing was conceived as a supplement to cavalry reconnaissance and not as a substitute for it. The Naval Wing was to have a broader range of tasks. Reconnaissance was its chief function as well, but naval aeroplanes and airships would also be armed with bombs or machine-guns to attack enemy submarines and airships.[13]

The two wings of the Royal Flying Corps began to drift apart almost imme-diately. They were to be co-ordinated by an Air Committee, established as a permanent sub-committee of the Committee of Imperial Defence, but the sub-committee lacked executive powers and could offer advice only upon such matters as were referred to it. It was in no position to object when the Naval Wing started to give primary training at the Naval Flying School at Eastchurch next to the Royal Aero Club. Neither could the committee act when an Air Department was formed within the Admiralty, the term 'Naval Air Service' was adopted, and the correct name of the organization vanished from its official letterhead. From the outset naval ratings at air stations wore on their caps the name *Actaeon* (the ship on whose books they were borne) rather than that of Royal Flying Corps. On 23 June 1914 the Admiralty unilaterally issued regulations which established the Royal Naval Air Service. The regulations prescribed ranks, uniforms, flying badges, and pay and provided for direct recruitment into the RNAS, thus making it the exclu-sive naval air arm and a separate branch of the navy administered in much the same manner as the Royal Marines. As a result, by the outbreak of the First World War, Britain possessed two distinct air forces whose uneasy relationship could – and would – easily turn into acrimony.[14]

There is a sense, even so, in which all airmen and air forces belonged to the same community in the era before the coming of war. All were testing themselves against the unknown. Experimentation was the rule, but all concerned with mili-tary aviation tended to pose the same questions and, on the whole, to come up with similar answers. Every air force sought the ideal aircraft, not realizing, in those more innocent times, that constant change was to be the permanent condi-tion of military aircraft design. The British, for example, issued specifications for the exemplary military aeroplane even before the establishment of the RFC, characteristically offering a prize for the best design. Trials held in August 1912 resulted in the victory of an aircraft designed by S.F. Cody but, though his *Cathedral* met all the formal requirements, its boxkite construction made it

in Canada between 1905 and 1908. In 1910 he was gazetted to the General Staff and in 1912 was secretary of the Advisory Committee on Aeronautics, a post which he held until the following year, when he was posted to the Staff College at Camberley. During the war he became Assistant Director and then Director of Aeronautical Equipment. He had served briefly and been wounded in France in 1914 and returned there in March 1917 as Commanding Royal Engineer to the 42nd Division. After nine months he was posted to headquarters as Inspector of Mines with the rank of brigadier-general. He was killed on 23 May 1918 while on active service at the front.

useless for military purposes. Indeed, the design subsequently proved fatal to its inventor.

A much superior design, the BE2, was also flown in the trials, but it was excluded by the rules because the Royal Aircraft Factory, a government organization that had grown out of the old Balloon Factory, had produced it. It later became the standard aircraft of the RFC. In addition, the Avro 504* and the Sopwith Tabloid, a machine originally designed for racing, were accepted. All these aircraft were tractors (that is, with the propeller mounted in front of the engine and generally in front of the main planes), with enclosed fuselages and a minimum of external bracing. Pusher aircraft with rear mounted propellers also had a future, primarily because of the field of vision they offered the pilot and the unrestricted field of forward fire open to a machine-gun. The Royal Naval Air Service took advantage of the development of practical flying boats, mainly the products of the designing skill of Glenn Curtiss in the United States and T.O.M. Sopwith in Britain, while both British and German naval aircraft were fitted with floats well before 1914.[15]

There was general awareness at this time that the value of aircraft would be much increased by equipping them with wireless. As early as 1908 the Balloon School had received signals from free balloons from up to twenty miles away. By 1912 airships equipped with two-way wireless were taking part in the annual British army manoeuvres, although engine interference cut down their ability to receive transmissions. In aeroplanes the wireless problem was more complex. Contemporary radio equipment was not light, power had to be provided by batteries, and aircraft had a very limited lifting capacity. The first message from an aeroplane to be received by a ground station was sent by the Canadian, J.A.D. McCurdy, during an air meet at Sheepshead Bay, NY, on 27 August 1910. With assistance from H.M. Horton of the De Forest Company, McCurdy fitted a 25-pound transmitter to a Curtiss biplane. A telegraphic key was attached to the control wheel and fifty feet of wire dangled from the machine as antenna, the aeroplane's guy wires being used as a ground. McCurdy circled Sheepshead Bay and tapped out 'Another chapter in aerial achievement is recorded in the sending of this wireless message from an aeroplane in flight.' Two miles away, on top of Sheepshead Bay grandstand, Horton picked up the message. During British Army manoeuvres a month later, Robert Loraine, flying a Bristol Boxkite, transmitted simple messages over a distance of a quarter of a mile. Particularly after 1912 progress was made employing generators driven off the aeroplane's engine. In 1913 a set was designed which screened off magneto interference and enabled the aeroplane to receive as well as to transmit signals. Meanwhile, the weight that aircraft could lift was steadily increasing.[16]

The development of aerial communications appeared to bring the direction of artillery fire from aeroplanes within the realm of the possible. As early as August 1911 the French carried out a number of experiments in observing, from an altitude of 4000 feet, garrison artillery firing at a range of 8000 yards. The Germans,

---

* Later versions of the Avro 504 were in use with the RCAF until 1934. J.A. Griffin, *Canadian Military Aircraft Serials and Photographs, 1920–1968* (Ottawa 1969), 4

too, were impressed with the possibilities of using aeroplanes to observe the fall of shot; in 1912 airmen were assigned to artillery practice schools. The British Army acknowledged the utility of wireless, *Field Service Regulations* stating that 'When sufficient aircraft are available they can be employed for the observation of artillery fire.' In practice, however, aircraft equipped with transmitters were so few that they were retained for reconnaissance and the guns had to be directed by flares and written messages dropped to the gunners.[17]

The first tests with machine-guns in aircraft took place in the United States in 1912. That same year Germany experimented with machine-guns fitted in dirigibles, and British and French pilots fired against ground targets from heights up to 3000 feet. No nation had yet solved the problem of firing through the propeller arc: aeroplanes engaged in these experiments were either pusher types or, if tractors, had a movable machine-gun installed on a mount in the cockpit and a pilot acutely aware of the danger of shooting off his own propeller. At Bisley, in November 1913, extensive air-to-ground firing was carried out from a Grahame-White Boxkite with an air-cooled Lewis gun during which excellent results were achieved against stationary targets from a height of 500 feet. The Lewis gun was chosen as the standard armament for the RFC, but no operational aircraft was fitted with it until September 1914.[18]

Prior to the First World War there was a good deal of visionary writing about the effects of bombing from aircraft, but there was little connection between theory and reality. The earliest recorded instance of bombing experiments occurred in the summer of 1910 in the United States, when Glenn Curtiss dropped a number of dummy bombs on a target representing a battleship before a group of American naval and military officers. The first aerial bombardment took place in Libya in 1911, when an Italian pilot, a Lieutenant Gavotti, attacked a Turkish camp with four small bombs carried in a leather bag. Gavotti laid a bomb on his knees, fitted a detonator, and threw the bomb out, apparently causing some panic among the Turkish troops. In France, in 1912, the Michelin Tire Company offered a cash prize for accuracy in bombing. At the first trial, held at Châlons in April, only two bombs out of twenty-three hit the target. The same summer Geoffrey de Havilland demonstrated at Aldershot that the release of a 100-pound weight had no adverse aerodynamic effect on the aeroplane. The Admiralty experimented with the dropping of dummy bombs, although none of their trials was particularly impressive, and the enthusiasm of bombing advocates was further dampened by the ineffectual results of bombing in the Balkan Wars of 1912 and 1913.[19]

A number of other experiments were conducted at the same time. The air-launched torpedo, which an Italian airman apparently first demonstrated in 1911, was being developed by several countries in the years before the war. In Britain the Admiralty did not seriously tackle the problem until 1913. By July of the following year, however, a Short seaplane had been experimentally equipped to carry a fourteen-inch torpedo. Attempts were also made to fly aeroplanes from ships. An American, Eugene Ely, was able to land on and take off from a special deck on a warship in January 1911, when the ship was at anchor in San Francisco Bay. In 1912, when floatplanes began to alight successfully on rough water, it became possible for warships to launch and retrieve them at sea.[20]

These developments had an impact, but on the eve of war no nation's aircraft were far from the experimental stage. Air forces were small and not one was a formidable military instrument.[21] In Canada, where war seemed a remote and improbable eventuality, governments had given little thought to military aviation. Although Joseph L'Etoile of Ottawa wrote to the Department of Militia and Defence in 1886 offering to establish a balloon corps to be attached to the Active Militia, his credentials seem not to have impressed the authorities and his offer was rejected.[22] Not until 1908 did the department begin to think seriously about the use of military aircraft, when Major G.S. Maunsell, the Director of Engineering Services, requested two weeks' leave in the United States in order to study various developments in military engineering, including 'ballooning and airships.' What recommendations he may have made on his return are not known, but Maunsell's superior, Colonel R.W. Rutherford, the Master-General of the Ordnance, proposed to the Militia Council in March 1909 that the Department of Militia and Defence adopt an aviation policy. One factor prompting his submission was probably the increasing number of proposals that the department was receiving from inventors and aircraft manufacturers who wished to sell their ideas, products, or services to the government. Rutherford submitted a list, commenting that 'this branch of engineering science has not hitherto been taken up by the Militia Department owing to the lack of specialists in the art, for although the number of inventors who have offered their services and their inventions to the Department is increasing, the nature of the majority of their proposals is so indefinite that no action could be taken with regard to them and therefore up to the present no application for funds for the purpose has been made.'[23] The Militia Council's response did not reflect great enthusiasm but at least it left the door open: 'It was decided that while the Department would do everything in its power to facilitate the work of experiments in aerial navigation by placing at the disposal of the inventors the assistance of men and equipment, no financial assistance could be rendered owing to there being no appropriation available.'[24]

In the meantime, the survivors of the Aerial Experiment Association had gone their separate ways. Glenn Curtiss had returned to his home and engine plant at Hammondsport and begun making aircraft on his own. Baldwin and McCurdy had stayed at Baddeck where, with help from Bell, they formed the Canadian Aerodrome Company. Bell did his best to give the two young men a boost by speaking to the Canadian Club in Ottawa on 27 March 1909, before an audience that included the Governor General, the Duke of Connaught, and the Minister of Finance. The country, he said, should have 'the benefit of these Canadian boys ... The nation that controls the air will be the foremost nation of the world.' There was no official reaction to Bell's plea, but Baldwin and McCurdy continued with their experiments and began building their new company's first aeroplane, the *Baddeck 1*.[25]

Even before Bell's Canadian Club talk, the *Silver Dart* had received a good deal of attention in the British, Canadian, and American press and the Governor General had officially drawn the attention of the British government to the flying being done at Baddeck. Such services 'should be retained for Empire.' Bell's speech and the *Silver Dart*'s widely-publicized flights may have been responsible for Rutherford's next move. In a second submission to the Militia Council he suggested that Baldwin and McCurdy be given an opportunity to demonstrate their machines. Rutherford stressed the reports of successful trials and the interest shown by the Governor General. He suggested that, because Baldwin and McCurdy were Canadians carrying out their experiments in Canada, it should 'be ascertained on what terms and conditions they would be willing to give their services to the Department as specialists, also their views as to what funds they consider should be provided for the purpose of pursuing their studies on the Government's behalf.' They should also be asked what aeroplanes they had and whether they would be prepared to carry out demonstrations or experiments at Petawawa. The Department of Militia and Defence, after all, was the proper place for such work.[26]

Rutherford's submission, which apparently aimed at an arrangement similar to that which the British had worked out with S.F. Cody in 1907–9, was studied by the Militia Council. Consideration was given at the same time to a proposal by M.D. Baldwin & Company Ltd of Montreal, which wished to demonstrate the military use of balloons. The council, acting on Rutherford's recommendation, declined the latter offer but decided to ask Baldwin and McCurdy to conduct flying trials at Petawawa, reiterating that no financial assistance would be given.[27]

Early in June McCurdy informed the department that the *Silver Dart* had been shipped to Petawawa. He proposed to stop in Ottawa for talks with the engineering branch of the department – presumably Maunsell, who had pressed for the trials – before proceeding to Petawawa, while Baldwin would go there directly, to be on hand for the *Silver Dart*'s arrival. On 14 June the Petawawa camp engineer, Captain H.H. Bogart, was informed of the plans and told to assist the flyers in any way possible.[28]

Baldwin arrived at Petawawa on 16 June and three days later Bogart asked the approval of Militia Headquarters to build a T-shaped shed to house the *Silver Dart*. Most of the materials were already on hand, but headquarters did approve the expenditure of $5 for laths and tarred paper, instructing Captain Bogart to proceed 'provided it does not interfere with the artillery ranges.' This lavish investment represented Canada's first official expenditure in connection with military flying. When McCurdy arrived in July the two airmen began assembling the *Silver Dart*, which had been fitted with a new engine for the trials. They had the help of two engineer officers, Captain W.G. Tyrrell and Lieutenant G. St C.A. Perrin, as well as their employee, William McDonald. There were also interested spectators, among them a provisional militia lieutenant named A.G.L. McNaughton.[29]

The preparations for the trials were widely publicized, and reporters and photographers gathered at Petawawa to witness the flights, their curiosity heightened by Blériot's conquest of the English Channel on 25 July. Of particular interest was the disclosure that, in addition to the *Silver Dart*, a new 'aerodrome' built by the two airmen at Baddeck would be flown at Petawawa. This was the *Baddeck 1*, which was now on its way from the Nova Scotia plant.[30]

The *Silver Dart* was assembled with its new engine and ready for test flights on 31 July. Before sunrise on 2 August the aeroplane was wheeled out of its hangar and McCurdy took his place at the controls. Weather conditions were perfect. Baldwin swung the propeller, the engine caught, and the *Silver Dart* began to move over the ground. McCurdy took off and flew about half a mile at a height of about ten feet before landing. The machine was turned around, and with Baldwin as a passenger, McCurdy flew back in the direction of the hangar. A third flight, towards the aircraft shed, was made with the workman McDonald aboard. The new engine performed well and the *Silver Dart*, which was carrying a passenger for the first time, achieved speeds estimated at between 45 and 50 mph, the fastest speed they had yet recorded.

The fourth flight, which proved to be the *Silver Dart*'s last, was made with Baldwin again aboard as a passenger. The aircraft covered three-quarters of a mile. As McCurdy prepared to land he was bothered by the rising sun, which was shining directly into his eyes. The front of the tricycle undercarriage struck the edge of a sandy knoll, causing the aircraft to bounce and then crash on its starboard wing. The centre section and the elevators were shattered and the wings badly damaged. Only the engine remained intact. Baldwin and McCurdy, however, escaped with only minor cuts and bruises. The two airmen now began assembling the *Baddeck 1*. 'Undaunted Aeroplanists Will Fly Again This Week,' the headline in the next day's *Toronto Star* trumpetted, 'McCurdy's Nose Still Bleeds From Cut and Baldwin Is Limping ...' 'The two flyers,' added the *Globe*, 'will have the sympathy of a host of well-wishers who will eagerly await their recovery and their further attempts to keep Canada abreast of the times in aviation.'[31]

Militia headquarters had been kept informed of developments by Captain Bogart and an official party from Ottawa arrived at Petawawa on 11 August. The party included Colonel Eugène Fiset, the Deputy Minister, Major-General W.D. Otter, Chief of the General Staff, Brigadier-General D.A. MacDonald, the Quartermaster-General, Rutherford, and Maunsell. That evening the *Baddeck 1* made a taxi run of about 800 yards to test the engine, but no attempt was made to take off. According to Maunsell, 'the engine worked beautifully and was easily started and controlled.'[32]

Baldwin and McCurdy spent most of the next day working on their machine, tightening stays and making improvements, while enthusiastic reporters talked to the members of the official observer party. Nevertheless, one story, filed before the first flight of the *Baddeck 1*, indicates that the Deputy Minister may have already made up his mind before leaving Ottawa:

I think the aerodrome [sic] too expensive a luxury for Canada to indulge in at the present time ... It is largely in an experimental stage as yet ... the government has offered no inducement to them [Baldwin and McCurdy] in the way of money. We have merely given them attendant and camp privileges ... You cannot expect a young country like Canada to strike out and adopt a military aeroplane policy. We will probably follow in the footsteps of England along that line. It is, however, too early to speak of anything ...

Who knows what these aeroplanes can do? ... Can they lift a great weight? What protection would the canvas planes offer? I think they must find something of a more stable nature than canvas to cover the great wings with. We must wait a great many years yet and experiment much more before the true use of these machines can be demonstrated.[33]

According to the same report, Rutherford could foresee a valuable scouting role for the machine but he doubted that Parliament would authorize the purchase of any 'aerodrome.' General MacDonald was non-committal, saying only that the observers were there to see the aeroplanes fly, but also to assess Petawawa's suitability for artillery work.[34]

Baldwin and McCurdy were in an awkward position. They now had an opportunity to show the authorities what they and their aircraft could do but although the *Silver Dart* had made more than three hundred successful flights, *Baddeck 1* had never flown. The first test flight would be the crucial one. Early in the evening of 12 August the craft was wheeled from its shed before the observer party, press, and a large crowd of artillerymen who had arrived for training. McCurdy climbed into the pilot's seat and McDonald swung the propeller. The engine ran smoothly and the aeroplane accelerated quickly. After a run of two hundred yards *Baddeck 1* became airborne and flew about one hundred yards, at a height of ten to fifteen feet. Then, because of a fault in the engine switch, further flights were postponed until the next day. Whatever reservations he may have had, Fiset was impressed by McCurdy's nerve in trusting himself to such a contraption. Rutherford expressed satisfaction with the test flight, despite its brevity, while General MacDonald added that 'if she can hop like that, she can fly.'[35]

Having seen a single, brief flight, the official party returned to Ottawa, leaving Maunsell at Petawawa. Baldwin and McCurdy worked on the aeroplane the following day, strengthening the bow elevator controls and installing a new engine switch. The *Baddeck 1* was ready by 0600 hours but the wind delayed tests. An hour later the wind died and McCurdy took his place at the controls. Again, after running about two hundred yards, McCurdy lifted the nose and the aeroplane climbed very gradually. Unfortunately, after flying another hundred yards and gaining speed, the aircraft suddenly nosed up, climbed to thirty feet, stalled, and fell to the ground, landing hard on its after section. McCurdy was only slightly bruised, but his machine was badly damaged.[36]

The trials were finished for the time being. The two airmen shipped what remained of both machines back to Baddeck, with the intention either of repairing the *Baddeck 1* and returning with it to Petawawa or of installing the undamaged engine in a second machine. As it turned out, however, they did not return to Petawawa, although they completed the *Baddeck 2* and kept Maunsell informed of their progress. He in turn maintained his interest in their activities and placed their reports on Militia Headquarters files.[37]

Questions regarding the government's aviation policy were raised in the House of Commons in late November and early December 1909 by Thomas Chisholm, MP for Huron. Sir Frederick Borden, Minister of Militia and Defence, explained on 25 November that the assistance provided for the Petawawa trials had not included financial aid.[38] Three weeks later, in reply to further questions by Chisholm concerning government policy on constructing aeroplanes in Canada for military purposes, he said that the matter was being 'closely followed' but that no definite action had been decided upon. Borden then added: 'The government is being largely guided by the action of the War Office, in England, in this respect. It is thought that the question has hardly reached the stage that it is desirable for the Dominion government to spend money in assisting inventors, but all reasonable facilities will be afforded to persons, possessing satisfactory credentials, in the way of giving the use of government land for the purpose of experiment.'[39]

The liaison between the two airmen at Baddeck and Militia Headquarters continued. At the instigation of the Duke of Connaught, the Directorate of Intelligence sent the pair a series of short digests of news items on aviation developments in North America and Europe. Many of the experiments were notably less successful than those of Baldwin and McCurdy. The first précis sent to the two flyers, covering the period from November to mid-December 1909, contained news, for example, of a German inventor, George Lohner, who was building a machine at the Exhibition Grounds, Ottawa, 'under conditions of secrecy.' The Ottawa *Evening Journal* described the 'drome' as about forty feet long and twenty feet high. It was constructed on the kite principle (Lohner was reputed to be a balloonist of note) and had 'many features new to airship construction.' 'The front portion from which a stick protrudes is known as the controller and is designed for raising and lowering the drome when in the air. There are two big triangular canvas surfaces, set horizontally, the front one being higher than the rear one.' The device was set on steel runners but had no engine, the inventor and his backers wishing to wait before taking that expensive step 'to see if it [the machine] will rise when pulled rapidly along the ground.'[40]

In subsequent digests Baldwin and McCurdy learned of delays in Lohner's progress, and then of the failure of the first trial on 14 March 1910. The *Evening Journal* elaborated:

After they had got the aerodrome out of the shed and in such a position that the fierce wind did not strike directly against the surfaces of the canvases, something went wrong with one of the steel runners.

Mr. Lohner tightened up a couple of bolts and then the machine was attached to a rope drawn by Mr. E. Code's automobile. In some way the two steel runners at the sides, and the steel upright braces that supported them, did not seem to be strong enough, and when the wind blew from one direction and then from another, they weakened and gave way, first at minor points and later on at important ones ...

At one place the drome came in contact with a telegraph wire and the canvas of the controller was ripped up. Then when entering a gate that leads directly into the race track at the grounds, the drome struck the side of it and several sections were loosened, including many of the guy wires.

At this stage of the game a fierce gust of wind hit the machine so heavily that it could not be kept balanced, and it keeled right over on its side, the tips of the triangular shaped surfaces touching the ground and the strain doing considerable further damage to the steel and wooden sections of the framework.

Inventor Lohner got up on the side of the fence to ease the drome through the narrow space in a fence, but several wires just grazed the top of his head.

There were only about a dozen people on hand,* but several of them took great fun out of the doings. Although the portion of the race track where it was intended to pull the aerodrome at a high rate of speed to see if it would 'take to the air' had been reached, no attempt was made, because it was quite apparent by this time, that the machine was too badly wrecked – the runners being all bent and twisted.[41]

---

* Some four to five hundred spectators, 'including many ladies,' had been at the abortive trial two days before, on a Saturday. *Evening Journal*, 14 March 1910

In the summer, an automobile was able to raise the ungainly contraption two feet off the ground after dragging it for about a hundred yards at a speed of five miles an hour, an experiment that Lohner claimed as a 'highly successful' vindication of his design. Lohner seems to have disappeared soon afterwards, however, leading to a rumour in 1914 that he had been a German spy.[42]

Meanwhile, Baldwin and McCurdy had completed some fifty flights with the *Baddeck 2* by November 1909. When Bras d'Or Lake froze they had transferred their flying to the ice and in March 1910 the militia department sent Maunsell to Baddeck to observe and report on the progress of the flyers. Although weather and mishaps restricted much of the flying to short hops, McCurdy was able to make several good flights during Maunsell's four-day stay, including one of six-and-a-half minutes' duration. Maunsell himself was carried as a passenger on two brief flights in the *Baddeck 2*, becoming the first Canadian officer to fly in a heavier-than-air machine while on duty.[43]

A week after his return to Ottawa, Maunsell suggested three possible options. The first, establishment of an aviation section of the Royal Canadian Engineers, appeared to him to be wasteful because it might require years of work to attain the expertise already possessed by Baldwin and McCurdy. A second possibility was outright purchase of the aeroplanes. On 10 March, indeed, while Maunsell was at Baddeck, Baldwin and McCurdy had offered the two *Baddecks* to the government for $10,000 and said they would give flying instructions to one or two officers. This would provide the government with the nucleus of a flying service and would enable Baldwin and McCurdy to carry on with their own development work at Baddeck. The third suggestion, and the one favoured by Maunsell, called for the department to offer the two airmen an annual grant to carry on their research; in return they would hold one aeroplane for instructing militia officers.[44]

Rutherford summarized Maunsell's report and passed it to the Militia Council for consideration. He pointed out that the main troubles encountered by Baldwin and McCurdy in their flights with the *Baddeck 2* appeared to have resulted from an unsatisfactory engine and that better power plants were on order. He also explained to the council the approach of the British War Office towards aviation: 'to encourage experiments, but to buy nothing.' He, too, favoured Maunsell's third option: 'If we can retain Messrs McCurdy and Baldwin next year by giving them money for experiments – and Sir Frederick Borden believes he can get a vote – the War Office think we shall do quite right, but they would not advise us to merely buy a machine.'[45]

The Militia Council agreed. Rutherford was told to prepare a report for submission to the Privy Council requesting approval of the policy, and to arrange to have an item included in the supplementary estimates for 1910–11. The report was passed to the Cabinet on 7 April, accompanied by a further supplementary estimate of $10,000 for the flyers. It recommended that the grant be renewable annually at the discretion of the government, 'to enable them to pursue their studies in aviation, the said grant to be subject to such conditions as this Department may consider necessary to protect its interests, but to include provisos that they shall train such officer or officers in the use of their machines as the Department may desire.' Baldwin and McCurdy were to place a machine at the department's disposal whenever required and to give the department the right to accept or refuse any invention or machine which they might produce, on terms to be arranged. They were also to carry out trials as required and open their factory to inspection. It was stipulated that the grant of $10,000 was not to be used for the production of machines intended for public sale.[46]

The Cabinet rejected the proposal. Rutherford went back to the Deputy Minister, Fiset, asking whether a grant of $5000 could be made from the funds voted for the Engineer Services (Headquarters Reserve). 'If this is not done,' he pointed out, 'it is evident that we shall lose the services of this firm, and their experiments will cease. In fact they have already shut down their works awaiting assistance.' He was told to bring the matter up before the Militia Council, although Fiset added that 'I doubt very much if we have the power of dividing part of our vote for such purposes.' The Militia Council supported Rutherford and a request to use the $5000 from the Engineering Service's vote was made to the Cabinet. This also was turned down. On 10 June Maunsell admitted defeat, if only temporarily. He cabled Baldwin and McCurdy that he was 'very sorry Department is unable to make you grant towards aviation this year.' Fiset confirmed the disappointing news in a letter to the flyers but he still held out some slight hope, promising that if they continued their work and still wished to associate themselves with the government, the matter would be brought up again the following year. Baldwin and McCurdy closed their plant and separated. Baldwin turned from aircraft construction and active flying to hydrofoil experiments; McCurdy went to the United States. Though their unique combination of engineering ability and flying experience was lost to Canada permanently, McCurdy would later make further contributions to Canadian aviation.*[47]

However, Maunsell had by no means given up the fight to establish a footing for aviation within the Canadian military structure. In August 1910 he recommended to his chief that $10,000 be included in the 1911–12 estimates as a grant to Baldwin and McCurdy along the lines of previous suggestions. The Militia Council considered the proposal on 13 September, but perhaps fearing yet another rebuff from Cabinet, did not approve it. The same day that Maunsell submitted his proposal McCurdy wrote from New York telling of his latest accomplishment of sending wireless messages from an aircraft to the ground and inviting Maunsell to witness further tests. Maunsell was unable to attend but he asked McCurdy to keep him advised of developments.[48]

Maunsell continued to press his case. In late October 1911 he and Fiset visited Atlantic City, NJ, to inspect the Vaniman-Seiberling dirigible *Akron*, which was being built for an attempt at an Atlantic crossing. In a joint report to the Minister, Maunsell and Fiset recommended against the department's buying or building a dirigible: 'It is thought that, for the present, it will be sufficient for this Department to secure say two aeroplanes, which have proved of such value in reconnaissance work, and train a few aviators at next year's training.'[49]

The following month, at Maunsell's request, the British War Office was asked to provide information and advice 'relative to the best method of commencing the

---

* In 1928 McCurdy formed the Reid Aircraft Company with an airport near Montreal. A year later he became president of Curtiss-Reid Aircraft Company Ltd. He was Assistant Director General of Aircraft Production in the Department of Munitions and Supply, 1939–47, and Lieutenant-Governor of Nova Scotia, 1947–52. He died in 1961.

study of Aviation in the Canadian Militia, on a small scale, the best aeroplanes for instructional purposes and also the best for military purposes.' The War Office was also asked to advise on the staff and organization required to start a small (two machine) aviation corps. Maunsell, now a lieutenant-colonel, pointed out that the information would enable the department 'to make a start in the organization of the aviation section, which has become so important in Military operations.' In February 1912 the War Office replied that the employment of aircraft required both skilled military pilots and relatively large ground staffs. It recommended that a two-seater biplane with dual controls and 'plenty of spare parts' be used as a trainer aircraft. The trainer should be able to land at slow speeds and have controls similar to those on the machines selected for service use. The British included their latest specifications for a military aircraft.[50]

Having obtained this information, Maunsell proposed that the department purchase one or two McCurdy machines at an estimated cost of $5000 each and that McCurdy's services be obtained to train a few selected officers as pilots. The important thing, he felt, was to make a start: 'I am strongly of the opinion that it is not particularly important what design of aeroplane is chosen as a first step, as all the present designs will be obsolete within a few years, but the point is to make a start in the direction of training a few officers who would be capable of taking up the practical side of the question and not only learn to handle a machine but build them on the designs that develop from time to time.'[51]

The new Chief of the General Staff, Major-General G.J. Mackenzie, agreed, observing that 'a military organization which does not keep pace with the latest scientific developments must be hopelessly left behind by organizations which are alive to that necessity.' He pointed out, however, that the first thing to do was find if there were any funds available. The proposal was passed to the Deputy Minister, with the comment that money was available in the 1912–13 Engineer Stores vote for the purchase of an aircraft, and possibly for training, although the instruction might be charged to the training vote. Colonel Sam Hughes, now Minister of Militia and Defence, rejected the proposal and, Fiset reported, 'does not want any steps taken this year – neither towards training nor purchase of aeroplanes.'[52]

When Hughes went to England to view the 1912 summer manoeuvres, Maunsell accompanied him to observe the operations of the new Royal Flying Corps. In his report Maunsell described the existing organization of the RFC, its tactical doctrine and equipment, and urged once more that training begin.[53] Maunsell's report went to General Mackenzie, who again agreed:

For the purpose of strategical reconnaissance, in particular, an army unprovided with aeroplanes will be severely handicapped.

The advisability of either commencing instruction in aviation, or of eventually adding aeroplanes to the organization of the Canadian Militia, is a question of policy.

If there is a probability of a Canadian Force being thrown entirely on its own resources, and having to act independently, the arguments in favour of inaugurating an aviation service are strong. If, however, a Canadian Force was acting with an army already provided with aeroplanes, the necessity would not be so pronounced.

Generally speaking, it can be no disadvantage for the Canadian Militia to keep abreast of other countries in the knowledge and application of this branch of military science, and although funds for 1913–14 may not be available, I would recommend that provision be made in the estimates for 1914–15 for this service, even though it be commenced on a small scale.[54]

Although no action was taken, some interest in aviation had taken root in the army. In July 1912 Militia Headquarters had received an application for pilot training from a young Royal Canadian Engineer, Lieutenant B.M. Hay.* He was told that 'the question of Military Aviation in this country is under consideration, but until a definite policy ... has been reached it is not contemplated to send any officers to attend courses at the present time.' In early December 1912 Captain P.S. Benoit, Lieutenant R.H. Irwin, and Lance-Corporal F.S. Brown, all of the Royal Canadian Engineers, applied to take aviation training, but Maunsell explained that 'the Minister does not wish Aviation taken up, at any rate, at present.' The following year the 6th Field Company, RCE, at North Vancouver unsuccessfully recommended that an aviation section be formed.[55]

Before 1914 militia policy, in the main, kept in step with Canada's evolution from colony to self-governing dominion. The recall of two British general officers commanding the militia because they challenged the ultimate responsibility of the Canadian government, the creation of the Militia Council, the withdrawal of the British garrisons from Halifax and Esquimalt, and the growth of the Permanent Force were all part of the process by which Canada was to achieve autonomy and national self-respect. It was therefore regrettable that the governments of the day did not share Maunsell's practical and balanced enthusiasm for aviation. Unquestionably they did not because flight itself was new and strange, because of its possible cost, unknown but rightly suspected to be great, because the military importance of aviation had yet to be shown, and, most of all, because Canada seemed to have no more need for aeroplanes than she did for dreadnoughts. Their decision was not, in itself, so much a result of colonial-mindedness as of a cautious and realistic assessment of the country's peacetime military needs.

Some Canadian politicians may have had an intimation of the imminence of a major war in which Canada might be involved. None could conceivably have anticipated the coming importance of air power, nor the extraordinary response of thousands of young Canadians to the opportunity to join in the air war. Yet as a consequence of that decision, to be reaffirmed during the war itself, the history of Canadian airmen and soldiers took strangely different paths. Canadian flyers did not serve as members of a national expeditionary force led by its own officers and supported by the anxious concern both of government and people at home. Instead, they fought their war as colonial recruits for imperial forces; their services were swallowed in the anonymity of a large organization; and their welfare was the charge, not of their own government, but of that of Britain.

---

* Lieutenant Hay, who came from Woodstock, NB, got his wish several years later. After pilot training in England, he joined 25 Squadron in France during May 1916. He was severely injured in a landing accident when his FE2b overturned on 18 July 1916.

PART ONE
Canadian Training and Air Policy

Ernest Lloyd Janney, commander of the Canadian Aviation Corps. In April and May 1915 he operated a private flying-school at Lawrence Park, north of Toronto. (RE 20365)

A Burgess-Dunne No 1 in the air, being flown by Clifford L. Webster, test pilot. (Smithsonian)

The Burgess-Dunne No 1 – first and only aircraft of the Canadian Aviation Corps – being loaded aboard ship for transportation to England with the CEF in October 1914. It was in this seaplane configuration that the machine was flown from the Burgess-Dunne works in Marblehead, Mass., to Quebec City. (RE 17705)

As an RNAS pilot on the Western Front in 1917–18 (and a member of 'Naval Ten's' renowned 'Black Flight'), F/Cdr W.M. Alexander (right) was credited with 18 victories in 131 sorties and rewarded with a DSO. (RE 19247)

William Melville Alexander was an eighteen-year-old Torontonian trying to enlist in the RNAS when this picture was taken in 1915. (RE 19229)

Students and friends, Curtiss School, Toronto, summer 1915 (PMR 71-17)

F/S/L Bert S. Wemp was a Toronto newspaperman who graduated from the Curtiss School and joined the RNAS in 1915. The first Canadian to receive the DFC (instituted when the RNAS and RFC were amalgamated into the RAF), he was a major by the end of the war. In 1930 he was elected mayor of Toronto. (AH 591)

Capt. Robert Dodds, an instructor at Camp Mohawk during the summer of 1918. Dodds (from Hamilton, Ont.) went overseas with the CEF, but transferred to the RFC in October 1916. He destroyed or forced down eleven enemy aircraft, and was awarded the MC for a bombing attack on an enemy aerodrome. (RE 19917)

One of the three Curtiss F-type flying-boats operated by the Curtiss School in Toronto in 1915 flying over Toronto harbour. (Smithsonian)

As an RNAS pilot on the Western Front in 1917–18 (and a member of 'Naval Ten's' renowned 'Black Flight'), F/Cdr W.M. Alexander (right) was credited with 18 victories in 131 sorties and rewarded with a DSO. (RE 19247)

William Melville Alexander was an eighteen-year-old Torontonian trying to enlist in the RNAS when this picture was taken in 1915. (RE 19229)

Students and friends, Curtiss School, Toronto, summer 1915 (PMR 71-17)

F/S/L Bert S. Wemp was a Toronto newspaperman who graduated from the Curtiss School and joined the RNAS in 1915. The first Canadian to receive the DFC (instituted when the RNAS and RFC were amalgamated into the RAF), he was a major by the end of the war. In 1930 he was elected mayor of Toronto. (AH 591)

Capt. Robert Dodds, an instructor at Camp Mohawk during the summer of 1918. Dodds (from Hamilton, Ont.) went overseas with the CEF, but transferred to the RFC in October 1916. He destroyed or forced down eleven enemy aircraft, and was awarded the MC for a bombing attack on an enemy aerodrome. (RE 19917)

One of the three Curtiss F-type flying-boats operated by the Curtiss School in Toronto in 1915 flying over Toronto harbour. (Smithsonian)

The Young Man's Element
—the Air

THE keen eye, the cool clear brain, the courage of youth, have won for the Allies supremacy of the Air. The world-famous aviators are young men.

In the profession of Military Aeronautics the rewards are all for the keen young man. No calling offers greater scope for individual accomplishment and bravery.

The Imperial Royal Flying Corps conducts in Canada its most efficient and most completely equipped training school. Young men of fair education, alert men 18 to 30 years old, are instructed in the highly specialized work of aerial observation and warfare. While training for their commissions, cadets receive $1.10 per day. Class 1 men under the M.S. Act are eligible.

An interesting Booklet "Air Heroes in the Making," describes fully, the R.F.C. course of training. A copy will be sent post-paid to anyone who contemplates entering military life. Write to one of the following addresses.

Imperial Royal Flying Corps

With no air force of their own, Canadians were invited to join the RFC. This advertisement appeared in many Canadian newspapers. (AH 228-5)

Students at the Curtiss School, Toronto, during the summer of 1915. Standing, sixth from left in white shirt, is Clarence MacLaurin of Ottawa who, in early 1919, would wind up the short-lived RCNAS before becoming a founding member of the Air Board. (PMR 71-11)

L.S. Breadner of Ottawa (left) at a Wright Flying School, Dayton, Ohio, or Augusta, Ga. Breadner began his flying training at the Dayton school but flew his tests at Augusta. With him is John Clark Simpson from Guelph, Ont. (PL 14590)

At right, Frank S. McGill of Montreal (later Air Vice Marshal, RCAF) who was one of several Canadian students at the Thomas aviation school, Ithaca, NY, in 1915. Posing with him is Toronto's mayor, 'Tommy' Church, on a visit to the school. (PMR 74-511)

1915 crashes were rarely as disastrous as modern ones. Often the damage could be repaired on the spot – in this case the Wright School at Dayton, Ohio. (RE 18431-7)

The Curtiss School, Toronto, in the summer of 1915. Standing in the cockpit and wearing a lifejacket is the instructor, Guy Gilpatric, who later achieved some literary renown in the columns of the *Saturday Evening Post* as the creator of Colin Glencannon, chief engineer of the SS *Inchcliffe Castle*. (AH 369)

A few miles west of Toronto, on the Lake Ontario shore, Long Branch housed the Curtiss School's land-plane section from July 1915. With three hangars and a prepared landing strip, it was Canada's first true airfield. (RE 19729-1)

Canadians who joined the British flying services in the dominion underwent extensive training overseas before joining an operational squadron. This picture shows RNAS probationary flight officers receiving ground school instruction at the Crystal Palace in England. (AH 456)

In October 1915 Maj.-Gen. Willoughby Gwatkin, the British officer who headed Canada's General Staff, recommended that 'for the present, at any rate, no attempt be made to organize a [Canadian] squadron ...' (PL 117508)

Prime Minister Sir Robert Borden at the Canadian National Exhibition Grounds, Toronto, inspecting Toronto's CEF Contingent, 5 Dec. 1914 (PA 61349)

Maj.-Gen. Sir Sam Hughes, Canada's 'intense, self-dramatizing, and mercurial' Minister of Militia at a Camp Borden review in 1916. Behind him, Brig.-Gen. W.A. Logie, commanding the troops. (PA 66774)

DROPPED FROM MID-AIR BY ▬▬▬▬▬ AVIATOR'S

CANADA NEEDS HER OWN
AIR-SERVICE

500 CANADIAN AVIATORS NOW IN IMPERIAL SERVICE AT THE FRONT. HUNDREDS IN TRAINING . IT IS HOPED THAT THE CANADIAN GOVERNMENT WILL AT ONCE ORGANIZE THESE FLIERS UNDER CANADIAN CONTROL AS CANADIAN CORPS.

Uncle Sam, take notice!
Thousands of these cards were dropped
...m aeroplanes in diff rent parts of
...anada during the past year.

Post card, dated on back August 1916, dropped from aircraft of the Curtiss School, Toronto, urging the creation of a Canadian Air Service. (AH 361)

The air age meets the steam age. (RE 64-433)

RFC Canada cadets outside Burwash Hall, University of Toronto, April 1917 (RE 19008-1)

Pre-flight test of JN4 rigging by instructor, cadet, and ground crew (RE 19715)

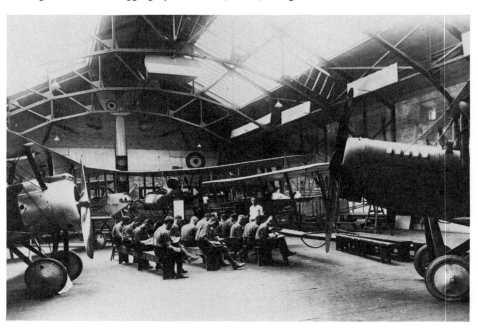

Lecture on aircraft construction at the University of Toronto. The aircraft surrounding the class include, left to right, a Sopwith Camel, a BE2 without engine, an FE2, and a DH4 in the right foreground. (RE 19065-22)

'Hungry Lizzie.' One of the Packard ambulances that were maintained at readiness while flying was underway. (RE 1972-1)

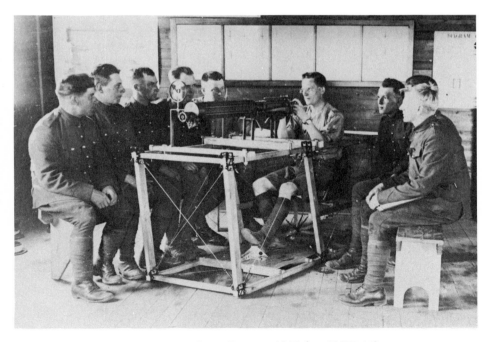

Ground machine-gun instruction, Camp Borden, 1917 (RE 19070-12)

Canadian Aeroplanes Ltd, in co-operation with the Imperial Munitions Board, secured the right to manufacture Curtiss JN4s in Canada. A factory was built on Dufferin St in Toronto, going into operation in April 1917. (RE 19062-11)

Cadets under instruction at the School of Military Aeronautics, Toronto, are shown with a cut-away of a JN4, the RFC's standard trainer in Canada. The facilities of the University of Toronto provided a comparatively luxurious environment for study. (RE 19062-40)

RFC Canada cadets were taught foot and arms drill by men like F/S F. Sedgewick before they graduated to aeroplanes. (PMR 78-613)

Capt. Vernon Castle, half of the famous dance-team of Irene and Vernon Castle, an instructor at Camp Mohawk during summer and autumn of 1917. He was later killed in a crash in Texas. (RE 13533)

Cadets of the US Signal Corps Aviation Section under training at Camp Borden (RE 20055-1)

JN4a and drogue used for aerial machine-gun training at the School of Gunnery, Camp Borden. The drogue was towed further behind the aircraft than as demonstrated in this picture. (RE 20804-3)

Off to work marching behind their own band, RAF recruits at Camp Borden leave their living quarters for the flying field on a summer morning in 1918. (RE 64-505)

This JN4 of RAF Canada carried the first airmail in Canada. (RE 13728)

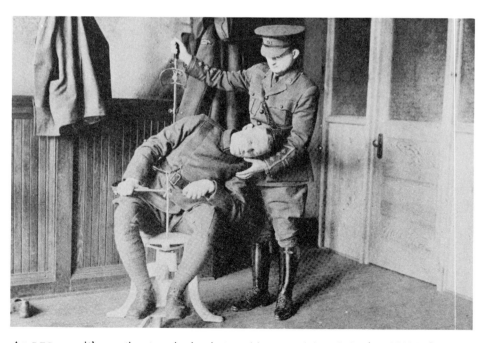

An RFC recruit's reaction to spinning is tested in a revolving chair. (RE 19297-4)

Artillery co-operation instruction RFC Canada scheme. The diagrams on the blackboard illustrate techniques of ranging. (RE 64-507)

Brig.-Gen. Cuthbert Hoare (centre) with his Air Staff. On the right is Lt-Col. A.K. Tylee of Lennoxville, Que., responsible for general supervision of training. Tylee was briefly acting commander of RAF Canada in 1919 before being appointed Air Officer Commanding the short-lived postwar CAF in 1920. (RE 64-524)

Instruction in the intricacies of the magneto and engine ignition was given on wingless (and sometimes tailless) machines known as 'penguins.' (AH 518)

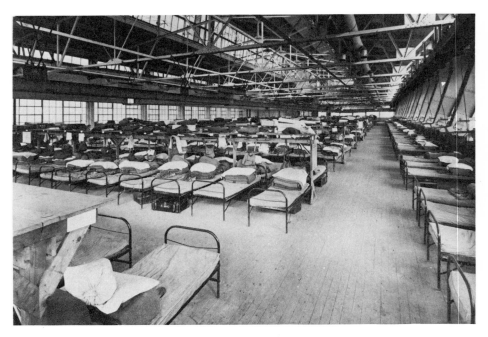

An RFC Canada barrack room (RE 19061-3)

Camp Borden was the first of the flying training wings to become fully organized. Hangars from those days still stand, at least one of them being designated a 'heritage building.' (RE 19070-13)

JN4 trainers of RFC Canada, at one of the Texas fields in the winter of 1917–18 (RE 20607-3)

'Not a good landing!' A JN4 entangled in Oshawa's telephone system, 22 April 1918
(RE 64-3217)

Members of HQ staff, RAF Canada, at the University of Toronto, which housed the School of Military Aeronautics. (RE 64-523)

RFC cadets on their way from Toronto to Texas in October 1917. Canadian winters, it was believed, would prevent or drastically reduce flying training. (RE 20947)

JN4s on skis devised by Canadian Aeroplanes Ltd, probably in February 1918. In an era of open cockpits RFC Canada pioneered winter flying in Canada. (RE 19071-16)

Felixstowe F5 flying-boat under construction at Canadian Aeroplanes Ltd in Toronto. Thirty F5Ls, with American Liberty engines, were built by this company for the US Navy. (RE 15159)

Introduction

During the First World War the policy of the Canadian government towards aviation, and particularly towards the idea of the formation of a Canadian air force, was variously negative, indifferent, inconsistent, and puzzling. It was almost always ill-informed. Yet the behaviour of the government was undoubtedly a faithful reflection of the public mind, or at least of that portion of the public mind that counted politically. For most Canadians there were many subjects of far more importance than aviation; participation in the war brought changes so fundamental that they approached the revolutionary. In the course of the war the Borden government organized and kept in the field an enormous military force, by far the largest in the country's history. To sustain it, in face of the staggering casualties caused by a form of warfare for which Canadians, psychologically as well as militarily, were utterly unprepared, the government had to resort to conscription. In consequence, Borden and his Cabinet had to deal, as best they could, with a political crisis of the most serious nature. And, to meet the insatiable needs of the modern war machine, the government had to give leadership in the transformation of the economy and in the organization of the labour force in ways that were unprecedented. Measured against these great matters, aviation was of small importance, and because the government consistently underestimated the importance it did have, no one made it either a prime concern or a continuing responsibility.

Yet when every allowance has been made for the immense difficulties which beset the Canadian government, there remains a small-mindedness, a species of unimaginative colonialism about its attitude towards aviation, out of keeping with its strong stand over command and control of the Canadian Expeditionary Force and with its political and constitutional thrust for recognition and status within the councils of the British Empire. Until late in the war no Canadian politician (with the quixotic exception of Sir Sam Hughes, the Minister of Militia until the end of 1916) had the faintest glimmering of the potentialities of aviation.

Cabinet ministers, however, being neither military experts nor seers, could assess the value of aviation only in terms of the pressure placed upon them to do something about it. In the opening stages of the war such pressure came chiefly from the few people who wanted very much to fly, and the government therefore did not shift from the essentially negative attitude towards aviation it had displayed in the prewar years. The unhappy and short-lived attempt by Sam Hughes to improvise an air force while the First Contingent was assembling at Valcartier alerted the militia department staff to their minister's propensity for ill-considered and idiosyncratic solutions to military problems and doubtless helps to explain their guarded responses to subsequent proposals concerning aviation, as well as to those having to do with the wide range of other subjects in which Hughes dabbled briefly in the first months of the war.

The efforts of a small number of young men to gain entry to the British flying services through initial training at civilian flying schools in Canada and the United States constitute the modest beginnings of Canadian military aviation. In 1916 their numbers grew as interest spread, and in addition some Canadians for business and patriotic reasons began vigorously to promote a more positive national policy towards aviation. The government's decision in late 1916 to collaborate in the establishment of a domestic aircraft manufacturing industry and in a British pilot training scheme in Canada was taken largely in reaction to the initiatives of these promoters and to the association of some of them with Sam Hughes. That decision inaugurated a period during which the government believed it had done all that could be reasonably expected.

The establishment of the Royal Flying Corps training scheme in Canada in 1917 brought together the need of the RFC for more trained airmen, a need that had become acute towards the latter stages of the Somme battle in 1916, and the rising desire of Canadians to take part in the air war. It is the purpose of the chapters in this section to explain why Canada's first large-scale experience with the air age came about almost entirely under imperial auspices and to show something of what that experience was like for the thousands of airmen who passed through flying training.

In the last year of the war the work of the many Canadians flying in every theatre and the public attention their exploits drew at home compelled the government to reconsider its aviation policy and to take steps to bring into being a distinct Canadian air force. Since this development was closely linked to the rising importance of the air weapon as well as to the scale and quality of the Canadian contribution to the air war, subjects dealt with in later sections, consideration of it is deferred to the concluding chapter of this volume.

2
Recruiting and Training in Canada, 1914–16

In the war that was fought over the battlefronts of Europe, Asia, and Africa and above the adjoining seas Canadians were ultimately to play a prominent part. No one could have foreseen this in August 1914. If most political and military leaders saw flying as a novel specialty best suited to the talents of the light-hearted and light-minded, but scarcely as a crucial element in the serious business of waging war, who can blame them? In time, when the air weapon had proved itself and the British flying services expanded greatly, Canada became a major source of airmen. Even in the beginning, however, and without any substantial encouragement from the federal government, Canadians were attracted to this new field of military endeavour.

It would be speculative to explain this Canadian response, as many were to do, in terms of the national character and situation. Was it really true, as Canadians, in a self-congratulatory fashion, were subsequently to suggest, that there was something about their country – its very newness as a nation, its open spaces, its testing environment – that endowed its people with a kind of immediate air-mindedness and its young men with special aptitudes for military aviation? Most Canadians, after all, chose or accepted military service during the First World War in the various branches of the army. What is demonstrable is that an unconventional minority, in the opening months of the war, were so drawn to flying that they were ready to surmount many difficulties, including some put in their way by their own government, in order to try their wings.

Many Canadians shared the fascination with flying that had swept Europe and North America in the prewar era. Much of this interest was uninformed and faddish, but there is little doubt that aviation had captured the Canadian public imagination. Indeed, the Electric Bean Chemical Company of Albert Street in Ottawa felt sufficiently threatened by the pioneering efforts of such 'aeronauts' as Blériot, after his channel crossing in 1909, to subject the readers of the *Evening Citizen* to a full-page advertisement on 26 July: 'Which is the Greatest Attainment. Dominion over Disease or Dominion over the Air? To have Dominion over the air is something new and wonderful – but, like all great achievements it will be a "nine days wonder" and then be crowded out of the public eye by others perhaps even more wonderful, for people soon tire of their toys and are always craving something new.' The medicines Electric Beans and Electro Balm, the company assured its potential customers, had stood the test of time, conquering sores, cuts, and diseases 'caused by an insufficient supply of blood.' The Electric Bean Chemical

Company's assessment notwithstanding, the aeroplane was here to stay. Reliability and performance rapidly improved. Exhibition flights became major attractions at annual fairs and holiday resorts. The fictional exploits of daring young men operating a wide variety of unlikely flying machines formed a favourite subject of popular literature. Even the songs of the day promoted the cause of aviation: 'Come Josephine, in my flying machine, going UP she goes, UP she goes/Balance yourself like a bird on a beam ...'[1]

Canadian newspapers and magazines speculated freely about the possible military uses of the aeroplane. Such flights of fancy were unencumbered by mundane technical details; it was suggested to a trusting public, for example, that aeroplanes had great potential as troop carriers – for the cost of one dreadnought, it was argued, 25,000 aeroplanes capable of carrying two soldiers each could be constructed. On a more serious level, a small number of Canadian soldiers, notably G.S. Maunsell, now a lieutenant-colonel and Director of Engineer Services at Militia Headquarters, maintained their strong interest in aviation on the eve of the war. There was no reason to suppose, however, that Colonel Sam Hughes, the Minister of Militia and Defence, had changed his attitude; according to his military secretary, Hughes regarded aeroplanes as simply 'costly toys, only as yet in the experimental stage.'[2]

Nevertheless, upon the outbreak of war, Ottawa immediately exhibited an acute sensitivity to the possibility that enemy aircraft might intrude upon Canada. The government, with little appreciation of the limitations of aircraft and airpower, was unduly apprehensive: flights into Canada across the polar region or the Atlantic and Pacific oceans would be technically impossible for a long time to come. It was highly improbable that an air offensive might come from the benevolently neutral United States, although an attack from across the border by a lunatic individual or pro-enemy group was not utterly inconceivable. Flying machines might also be used by enemy agents, Canadian or foreign. An Order-in-Council strictly regulating flying in the dominion was therefore issued on 17 September 1914. It prohibited flying within ten miles of wireless stations and in nineteen stipulated areas, including most main population centres. Aircraft entering Canada were required, after passing over the boundary with the United States, to land at one of eleven designated points extending from Annapolis, NS, to Chilliwack, BC. Aircraft were forbidden to carry mails, explosives, firearms, photographic or wireless equipment, or carrier pigeons. The militia minister was authorized to grant exemptions from certain parts of the order, and this was in fact later done for several of the flying schools that were to come into being and for other legitimate aerial operations. This Order-in-Council gave Canada its first flying regulations.[3]

It was not long after the promulgation of these regulations that reports of suspect aircraft began to arrive at Militia Headquarters. Some of the intruders were undoubtedly American, particularly from New York State,* others were no more

---

* Enough of the reports concerning American aircraft were substantiated to cause the militia department to complain to the Department of External Affairs. The United States government must be asked to prohibit these unauthorized flights. 'Otherwise,' the military warned, 'there may be regrettable incidents; for troops ... mistaking the intentions of trespassing aircraft, may open fire on them.' Deputy Minister of Militia to Under-Secretary of State for External Affairs, 19 July 1915, HQ 6978-2-57, vol. 1, PAC, RG 24, vol. 2036

than the product of overworked imaginations. Fears that Ottawa might be bombed by hostile aircraft caused a partial blackout of sensitive installations in the capital in early 1915. On Sunday evening, 14 February, reports were received from Brockville, Ont., sixty miles to the south, that several unidentified aircraft had flown over the St Lawrence from the American side of the river. As was usual in the case of such reports, these sinister vehicles advertised their presence by displaying powerful searchlights. Upon arriving over Canadian territory they dropped 'fire balls' before continuing in the direction of Ottawa. The House of Commons continued its session, but orders were issued to darken the tower light on the summit of Parliament Hill, to extinguish every illumination on the grounds, and to draw every curtain. Lights were also put out at the Royal Canadian Mint and Government House. The following day, however, the remnants of a hot air balloon were exhibited in the office window of a Brockville newspaper, one of three such devices reportedly sent aloft by youths in Morristown, NY, across the St Lawrence from Brockville, as part of local celebrations upon the hundredth anniversary of the final ratification of the peace treaty ending the War of 1812.[4] The Toronto *Mail and Empire* commented sardonically:

Ottawa today is a little sensitive on the subject, and mention of airships is not regarded as being in the best of taste. Fearful ones this afternoon were still for having the lights [on Parliament Hill] extinguished and the clock face masked, but tidings of the finding of the balloons (one of them in the grounds of an insane asylum) was the last straw. The one concession they obtained was the extinction of the little light on the top of the main tower, a light that signifies a sitting of the House. Hence, if an aeroplane approached it would have a thousand other lights to go by, but would remain in doubt as to whether or not the House had adjourned.

Military authorities assert that they took no stock in the Brockville scare. The few precautions that were taken were more of a polite expression of confidence in the honesty of purpose of the Brockvillians than of anything else. On the other hand, Ottawa people have a weakness for airship raids. For many days last Fall there were earnest eye-witnesses who on various occasions heard and saw a mysterious airship which has never yet come down to earth.[5]

If the outbreak of war produced its moments of farce, it also called forth serious suggestions from across the country concerning military aviation. Letters and telegrams came particularly from young men wishing to serve as pilots, most of them assuming that Canada would be forming a flying service. In the first month of the war Militia Headquarters received offers from at least nine would-be military pilots, among them F.H. Ellis, who would eventually become a noted air historian, and F.F.R. Minchin and T.D. Hallam,* who later distinguished themselves as First World War flyers. These enquiries were referred to Maunsell, who made it clear that he favoured any proposal which would further the cause of military aviation in

---

* Hallam, from Toronto, had trained as a seaplane pilot in the United States. He was later accepted as an armoured-car officer, and went to Gallipoli. There he won the DSC before he was wounded. On his return he took up flying duties at Hendon and then went to Felixstowe, where he twice more won the DSC in anti-submarine flights. Under the pseudonym P.I.X. he wrote *The Spider Web: the Romance of a Flying-Boat War Flight* (Edinburgh 1919).

Canada. But he was again forced to conclude, as he had in late August, that 'the Minister is not favourable to aircraft.' The department was not 'taking up aviation at present.'[6]

In October and November 1914, however, Militia Headquarters engaged in a lengthy correspondence with M.A. Kennedy, vice-president of the Ontario Motor Car Company Ltd, who proposed that members of Toronto's Royal Canadian Yacht Club form a 'civilian aviation corps' and pilot training school. Maunsell argued that the department should encourage Kennedy and his friends: 'at present they do not ask for any financial or military assistance, but they might be a very useful organization in case Aviation is taken up by the Department at a future date.' In the event, the idea received something less than encouragement, the department simply suggesting that Kennedy apply for exemption from the ruling that no person could navigate or be carried in an aircraft of any class or description within ten miles of Toronto. The Chief of the General Staff, who opposed the formation of a Canadian air service throughout the war, indicated privately that he would recommend acceptance of Kennedy's application. The proposal, however, came to nothing.[7]

Nor was the attitude of the Minister himself by any means as clear-cut as it seemed. Hughes had apparently received 'many more' applications for service in the air than the nine names which were listed on headquarters files after a month of war and, although the government had told these young men that 'it was not anticipated the military authorities would have any requirements for the service of aviators,' Hughes did not let the matter end there. On 25 August he sent a wire to Lord Kitchener at the War Office in London: 'Many Canadian and American aviators offering services for the war. Latter offer to come to Canada and enlist here. Have you any suggestions.'[8]

Hughes perhaps overstated the number of applications that the minister and department had received from North American aviators. By this time other Canadians had followed Baldwin and McCurdy into the air, although not in large numbers, and only a very few held the *Fédération aeronautique internationale* [FAI] certificates issued to those having passed certain elementary flying tests under official observation.* Anyone could fly an aeroplane if he was self-taught or if he could find someone to teach him, but the Royal Flying Corps insisted that applicants for pilot service possess proper certificates as evidence of their qualifications.

The War Office, even so, replied on 31 August that it would accept six 'expert aeronauts' at once and that more might be required later. Qualified volunteers would be sent to England to be tested; if accepted, they might be enrolled either as commissioned or non-commissioned officers.[9] No action appears to have been taken to send the RFC its six aeronauts. But early in September two men arrived at Valcartier, Que, where the 1st Contingent of the Canadian Expeditionary Force

---

* Canadians known to have received certificates as pilots before 4 August 1914, in order of certification, were J.A.D. McCurdy, William M. Stark of Vancouver, R.B. Russell of Toronto, Lieutenant F.A. Wanklyn of Montreal, P.H. Reid of Montreal, Ian C. Macdonell of Winnipeg, Jean-Marie Landry of Quebec, and William Fray of North Battleford. In addition, William Sharpe of Prescott, Ont., though not certificated, passed the requisite tests at the Curtiss School, San Diego, in January 1914.

was preparing to sail for overseas and where Hughes himself had gone to supervise activities. Sam Hughes – who up to now had shown himself to be 'not favourable to aircraft' – impetuously granted both of them commissions, authorized the purchase of a secondhand aeroplane, and so improvised a flying corps which sailed with the 1st Contingent. The two airmen, with the ranks given them by Hughes, were Lieutenant W.F.N. Sharpe of Prescott, Ont., and Captain E.L. Janney of Galt, Ont. Neither was gazetted nor attested in the CEF – an omission that was to baffle paymasters and others – but they drew pay for their ranks from 7 and 10 September, respectively.

Shortly after arriving at Valcartier, Janney left to check on aircraft available for purchase at plants in the northeastern part of the United States. Following his return, the Canadian Aviation Corps was born. Many of the details of its birth are unknown, but there seems little doubt of its paternity. A militia department file for the period contains a document bearing the Valcartier Camp stamp, dated 16 September, which reads:

Submitted for the consideration of the Hon'able the Minister

AVIATION CORPS

Mr. E.L. Janney is appointed provisional Commander of the Canadian Aviation Corps with the rank of Captain, and is authorized to purchase one bi-plane, with necessary accessories, entailing an expenditure of not more than $5,000.00
A Burgess bi-plane has been ordered for quick delivery.

The paper is initialled 's.H.' by the Minister and bears, in his handwriting, a bold 'O.K.' The words 'quick delivery' are circled.[10] The author of the document was undoubtedly the energetic Janney himself, who had already gone back to the United States, where he intended to purchase the Canadian Aviation Corps' first aircraft.

Hughes seems to have neglected to inform his headquarters of this startling development. Militia department officials knew nothing of Janney, Sharpe, or the imminent purchase of an aeroplane. The Deputy Minister must have been puzzled to receive a telegram from Hughes at Valcartier on 16 September advising: 'Am arranging for Mr. E.L. Janney to fly from United States to Canada. Please notify authorities.'[11] Janney had crossed the border into the United States packing a pistol on his hip and bearing his written appointment and a government cheque for $5000. His choice of aircraft fell on the first of a number of machines built by the Burgess Company of Marblehead, Massachusetts, to a design produced by Lieutenant J.W. Dunne, a British aeronautical pioneer. It was a tailless, swept-wing float-plane with a pusher propeller and two seats positioned in tandem in an open nacelle mounted on the lower wing. Janney, it appears, had not ordered the aircraft on his earlier visit and he now made it clear that immediate delivery, not safety, was the main consideration.

Captain Janney [an official of the Burgess Company recalled] called here on September 12, took a flight in this machine during a general trip to all the principal factories. He returned on the 17th and made us a spot cash offer for the demonstrating machine as it then stood. We explained to him fully that the motor had been run a great many hours and needed over-hauling and that there were a number of things in the aeroplane which could be put in better shape with a few days' time.

He insisted that to make the sale possible we must ship the machine on Saturday, or less than two days from the time of the sale. We agreed with him that it would be to our advantage as well as his to have the machine at Valcartier and flying, but we did want more time for the overhauling. He wanted to rush the overhauling in order to have the machine flying before the first contingent sailed. The result was that we took the motor down and went over it very hastily, scraping some connecting rod bearings that were tight and regrinding the valves. The aeroplane was knocked completely down, dissembled and shipped in an express car not adapted to it to Isle Le Motte, Vt. We sent men at our own expense up there to assemble the machine in order to help Janney and ordered him the services of Webster [a company pilot] for further training and assistance in delivering the machine to Valcartier.

The aircraft took off for Valcartier Camp on 21 September, with the company pilot at the controls and Janney aboard. 'I don't think anyone shot at us,' Janney's companion reported:

... our altitude varied from 1,000 to 2,000 feet and the wind which had been following at first swung to our port beam and so proved detrimental. Janney drove about a fourth of the time. At the end of an hour and fifty-five minutes we reached Sorel and I decided to land as the gas was getting low.

We managed to get ashore alright and get some gasoline and oil ordered. We started out again at quarter of twelve and made good time to Three Rivers where I expected to land, but Janney signalled me to continue. About ten minutes later I heard a knock in the motor so came down and ran ashore at Champlain (in flight 45 minutes). As the motor would still turn over fairly freely Janney decided (as against my advice) to load it up with oil and chance it for Quebec. I managed to get off and get started down river, but the motor was turning over so slowly that I had to keep damn busy to keep up. I did not get above 15 feet at any time and was often only a few inches clear.

After 18 minutes of this inferno the motor gave up the ghost and I landed with regret but not without relief also. After we had drifted for some twenty minutes a motor boat saw our distress signal and towed us in.[12]

The aircraft was loaded aboard a transport and shipped to Quebec City, where it was embarked, along with the members of the Canadian Aviation Corps, with the 1st Contingent. The corps was now three strong, having added to its number Harry A. Farr, from West Vancouver. Farr had arrived at Valcartier with a Victoria infantry unit. After meeting Sharpe he was able to transfer to the newly-formed aviation corps as a mechanic with the rank of staff sergeant. On arrival in England the three members of the corps accompanied the contingent's headquarters staff to Bustard Camp on Salisbury Plain. The already well-worn Burgess-Dunne aircraft, damaged in transit, appears to have been shipped to the Central Flying School at Upavon.

Having formed an aviation corps, Hughes apparently lost all interest in it. The 1st Contingent was given no indication of the role its three airmen and single aircraft were expected to play. Determined that the aviation corps should be a proper one, Janney took off – with doubtful authorization – on an extended inspection tour of flying fields and aircraft plants in Britain. In early November 1914 he submitted an ambitious proposal for the equipment, organization, and maintenance of a one-flight squadron at an estimated expenditure of over $116,000. Shortly thereafter, however, Militia Headquarters informed the Canadian Contingent that it was 'not intended to form a flight unit' and that 'the intention is to sever Lieutenant [sic] Janney's connection with the CEF.' Janney sailed for Canada on 23 January and was struck off CEF strength on that date. At his own request Sharpe was sent to an RFC reserve squadron at Shoreham for flying training. He was killed on 4 February when he crashed the machine he had taken up on his first solo flight. Farr was discharged from the CEF in May 1915 'in consequence of Flying Corps being disbanded.'[13]

Did Janney and Sharpe represent two of the six pilots that the British War Office had said they would accept? Even assuming that this was the case, why was nothing done about the remaining four? Most of those who wrote to Militia Headquarters volunteering for aerial service possessed no qualifications, it is true, but some did hold FAI certificates or had attended a proper flying school. It was admittedly difficult for the government to separate qualified volunteers from those who possessed nothing but enthusiasm and a venturesome spirit. Maunsell, however, had become sufficiently familiar with flying by this time to have carried out a screening process had he been given the opportunity. Instead, every applicant, regardless of qualifications, was told that his services were not required. The request for six qualified pilots seems to have been shelved or was perhaps left in the hands of the Minister, who moved on to other matters.

The British did not stop trying. On 25 February 1915 the Governor General's military secretary, Lieutenant-Colonel E.A. Stanton, wrote to the Chief of the General Staff explaining that the War Office had asked what arrangements might be made for enlisting 'certain British-born aviators, in Canada or the United States who desire to join the Royal Flying Corps.' He mentioned that the Governor General had also received a similar letter from Major-General Sir David Henderson, then in command of the RFC in France. Stanton enclosed in his letter the RFC conditions of service. Applicants for pilot service were required to hold an aviation certificate of the Aero Club of America or a similar institution issued since 1 January 1913 and to be medically fit with normal vision. No age limit was stipulated. Those accepted would be sent to England as air mechanics, 1st class, and after arrival would be paid £75 as partial reimbursement for the cost of obtaining a certificate. The Governor General's office was to handle the recruiting, although Stanton asked the militia department to assist in locating suitable candidates and in arranging 'to have the men found suitable, duly attested and enlisted and forwarded' to England at imperial expense. A similar arrangement, to be described shortly, was soon established for the Royal Naval Air Service.[14]

It was in this manner, then, that the Canadian recruitment programme for the flying services began. Until the end of 1916, entry for candidates on this side of the

Atlantic was essentially controlled by individuals in Ottawa who, whatever their other duties and lines of responsibility, were for this purpose acting for the Royal Flying Corps and the Royal Naval Air Service with the benign concurrence of the Canadian government. The regulations they enforced for entry were those of the War Office and the Admiralty, and had no relationship to Canadian regulations for recruitment into the dominion's forces. Because recruitment took this form, nothing resembling a broad campaign for enlistment could take place. No authoritative information about the frequent and confusing changes in the regulations was disseminated officially, and publicity about the war in the air and the means by which Canadians might take part in it was left largely to interested newspapers and to private initiative. Despite this situation, the RNAS experienced no difficulty in meeting its small quotas. The number of Canadians who succeeded in entering the RFC in these early years, however, though not insignificant, was probably substantially less than it otherwise would have been had a genuinely national effort been mounted. Moreover, the expense involved in securing the required certification (together with whatever unspoken social requirements were employed) tended to restrict entry, in the main, to young men from families more comfortably situated than the generality of Canadians.

Hughes' cablegram to the War Office in the first month of the war indicating that there were 'many' willing North American aviators may have helped to focus British attention on Canada and the United States as sources of qualified flyers. Most of the credit for the War Office's action, however, must be given to an English electrical engineer living in the United States. In December 1914 Warner H. Peberdy, a recent Oxford graduate, wrote to the War Office from New York, pointing out that there was a supply of young men in Canada and the United States who lacked formal flying experience but who possessed the educational background and other characteristics required of a good pilot. Peberdy suggested that 'an almost ideal combination for an Aviator is that obtaining in a man who has had a British public school education, a good all round engineering training, and has outdoor sporting tendencies.' This proposal gave rise to considerable discussion in the War Office, and it was decided in February 1915 to enlist British-born aviators in Canada, but only those holding certificates.[15]

Militia Headquarters supplied Stanton with names of those who had applied for aviation service and asked the commanders of military districts and divisions across Canada to forward the names of any other suitable candidates. British consular officers in the United States were informed of the plan by the embassy in Washington but were told not to publicize it. Enquiries from suitable British-born persons were to be referred to Stanton, who now applied himself industriously to his task. But only a few enquiries, it transpired, came from qualified aviators in the United States and Stanton had even less luck in Canada: as we have seen, there were few resident Canadians who held FAI certificates. Over the first months of 1915 Stanton was able to send only five men to Britain.[16]

The Royal Naval Air Service, meanwhile, had also begun to recruit in Canada. A private flying school had been established in Toronto to enable embryo naval pilots to obtain their certificates, and the country had acquired an aircraft manufacturing plant. The man responsible in large part for these developments was J.A.D.

McCurdy, who was now associated with the Curtiss Aeroplane Company of Hammondsport, NY. In December 1914 McCurdy had proposed to Sir Robert Borden that Canada form an aviation corps, purchasing machines manufactured by a branch of the Curtiss firm which was to be established in Toronto. The company offered to set up a small school in connection with the proposed Toronto plant and to train, at its own expense, a pilot for each aeroplane ordered by the government. The Canadian government was not interested in another venture into aviation, but Borden did pass the Curtiss proposals to the Admiralty and War Office in February and March 1915, adding that the government would welcome the development of an aviation industry in Canada. The War Office exhibited no immediate interest. On 26 March, however, the Admiralty made an order of additional aircraft from the Curtiss Company, and in so doing asked that as many as possible be built in Canada, provided that no delay resulted.[17]

The Admiralty's proposition came as a direct consequence of a North American visit by Captain William Leslie Elder, Inspecting Captain of Aircraft Building in the Admiralty's Air Department. There seems little doubt that aircraft procurement in the United States was the reason – or one of the main reasons – for his mission. In fact, the Admiralty order of 26 March was probably placed with the Curtiss firm by Elder personally. He then struck an agreement with Curtiss that fifty of the aircraft ordered from his firm would be produced in Canada. After Elder had conferred with Canadian naval officials and Borden himself, arrangements were also made for Naval Service Headquarters in Ottawa to recruit pilots for the RNAS, and for those accepted to obtain their certificates at the Curtiss School in Toronto. Curtiss and McCurdy must have had good reason to anticipate the decision to produce Admiralty aircraft in Canada, because on 18 February 1915 federal incorporation papers were taken out for a Toronto-based company known as Curtiss Aeroplanes and Motors, Ltd. The firm began operations on 12 April with McCurdy as its managing director.[18]

The RNAS call for recruits was publicized in newspapers in mid-April 1915. Recruiting began almost immediately in Ottawa and at the naval establishments on the east and west coasts. It was limited to British subjects of 'pure European descent' and preference was to be given to those between nineteen and twenty-three years of age, thirty being the maximum age limit. Successful applicants, having been interviewed and medically examined, were declared to be 'candidates,' meaning that they had been accepted into the RNAS on the condition that they obtain their pilot certificates. When they reported back to Naval Headquarters with their certification, the young pilots were to be appointed as temporary chief petty officers, 3rd grade, and sent to Britain for service training. Selections for commissions would be made 'in due course.' The Curtiss School charged $400 for its flying training, which involved some 400 minutes of flying time. All training costs were the responsibility of the candidates, although, like the RFC, the RNAS partially reimbursed those accepted by providing a gratuity of up to £75.[19]

Despite the costs involved, there was an immediate response to the call for RNAS pilots. The recruiting programme was geared to quotas set by the Admiralty and although the limited capacity of Curtiss's Toronto school presented a notable obstacle, the Canadian naval authorities had little difficulty in finding sufficient young men to meet RNAS needs. Indeed, active recruiting was suspended at various times, pending the receipt of further quotas. The RNAS recruiters in Canada, headed by Rear-Admiral Charles E. Kingsmill, Director of the Naval Service, could afford to be, and were, highly selective.

The Toronto school began its flight training on 10 May and twenty pupils, some of whom held commissions in the militia, were soon receiving instruction. Although the school had been set up as a result of negotiations with Elder, an Admiralty representative, three RFC aspirants were amongst the first group to begin training and more followed.[20] Most of the school's graduates throughout the two years that it operated went to the RNAS, but RFC candidates were freely admitted.

Shortly after the announcement of the new RNAS recruiting programme, Stanton urged the War Office to send a representative to Canada to look after RFC requirements. He argued that the War Office's envoy should be authorized to grant immediate commissions to suitable candidates or to develop co-operation with the navy. Otherwise the RFC would gain only a few recruits from graduates of the Toronto school or from any similar school that might be formed.

On 20 June Captain Alec Ross-Hume arrived in Canada to oversee RFC recruiting. After a brief survey of the situation he reported to the War Office that there were 'absolutely no trained aviators out here of any kind.' He then visited the Toronto school to see if he could lure recruits into the RFC. Ross-Hume was authorized to offer immediate commissions to suitable certificated applicants (the five that Stanton had sent to Britain having gone as air mechanics, 1st class). Pointing out the advantage of second lieutenant rank in the RFC over that of chief petty officer in the RNAS, Ross-Hume persuaded almost a score of the registered RNAS students to switch their allegiance to the War Office. Not surprisingly, this unedifying development brought harsh words from those handling RNAS recruiting. The RNAS countered by raising the ante, promising commissions to successful candidates, and explaining that as flight sub-lieutenants they would outrank second lieutenants in the RFC and draw more pay. Faced with this counter offer, most of the defectors promptly transferred their allegiance back to the RNAS.[21]

Ross-Hume established his headquarters in Toronto and continued to interview candidates for RFC service. His initial impression of the young Canadian applicants was anything but favourable. During his first ten days in Canada he told the War Office that he had seen 'a great many applicants but the greater number are quite impossible.' Before the end of July, however, he had changed his mind: '... of course the Canadian wants knowing ... [but] take them as a whole the Canadians are a d--d fine lot of fellows.'[22]

The Toronto Curtiss School produced its first graduates on 11 July. By the end of the month a total of eleven had been passed out; eight were commissioned in the RNAS, three in the RFC. Sent to Britain within a week or two of gaining their certificates, they underwent normal service training before being despatched to their operational units. The recruiting programmes of the two British services were rewarded by a small but steady flow of certificated recruits from the Toronto school throughout the summer and autumn of 1915. It soon became apparent, however, that the main problem was not the selection of suitable young men but the limited capacity of the training facilities. The school became hopelessly plugged, with a long waiting list of candidates who had been tentatively accepted by the flying services. Many of the candidates turned south, to flying schools in the United States, but even these had waiting lists and could not accommodate all the Canadians who applied.[23]

There was no thought of the Toronto school trying to carry on through the Ontario winter. As the bad weather approached, concern mounted for the many candidates who had been accepted into training but who were waiting to complete or even to begin their course. McCurdy offered to move the school to Bermuda or to some other warm spot for winter training if the naval service could arrange transportation for the pupils, but this proposal fell through partly because McCurdy subsequently judged Bermuda 'unsuitable for flying.' With the exception of one last student who was tested on 10 December, flying at the school ceased for the winter during the latter part of November. It is estimated that in mid-November 1915 there were some 100 RFC and 150 RNAS candidates waiting for certificate training, most of whom had signed up at the Toronto school. A deputation of RNAS candidates travelled to Ottawa, where, according to one account, Sam Hughes told them 'to forget all about this aeroplane business and join the Army.' The British were more sympathetic. The War Office and the Admiralty authorized the passage overseas of all the candidates who had been accepted into flying training. Both services then temporarily suspended recruiting.[24]

In late September or early October Ross-Hume and Stanton had been informed of changes in the War Office's recruitment policy in the dominions. An FAI certificate was no longer required but candidates were expected to hold a commission in one of their country's armed forces and had to agree to serve overseas with that force should they prove unsuitable for flying duties. So far as Canada was concerned, the new conditions were subject to an important qualification: the requirement for a Canadian commission could be waived in the case of a candidate holding a flying certificate or having progressed far enough at one of the private schools to leave no doubt concerning his suitability as a pilot. These changes in the recruiting regulations eased the problem of dealing with uncertificated RFC candidates whose training had been interrupted by the coming of the Canadian winter. Some already held Canadian militia commissions and others had logged sufficient instructional time in the air to warrant their appointment to RFC commissions before leaving Canada. Three dozen of the RFC candidates went overseas as newly-created second lieutenants in the Canadian militia, hoping to find their way into the RFC after their arrival and indoctrination in England. If they failed to qualify for the RFC, they would be transferred to a Canadian infantry unit overseas. Several others proceeded overseas during the early part of 1916, having attended flying schools in the southern United States. Apart from this group, however, the new RFC regulations were not applied to any other Canadian candidates. Those who were accepted during 1916 entered under new and different sets of regulations.[25]

The uncertificated RNAS candidates, whose passage to England had been authorized by the Admiralty, were given several choices. They could, if they wished, persist in their efforts to obtain a certificate: a large group of candidates completed their instruction at American schools and sailed for England during the early part of 1916. Those who could not or did not wish to continue their pursuit of certificates – and most of these young men simply did not have the financial resources to remain in training – awaited RNAS appointments and overseas passage. The Canadian Department of the Naval Service offered assistance to those for whom delay meant hardship. A special company of the Royal Naval Canadian Volunteer Reserve was formed and the RNAS candidates were invited to join it. Eighteen did so and were given transportation to Halifax, where they boarded HMCS *Niobe* as able seamen in the RNCVR. They received 85 cents a day and underwent elementary naval training pending their RNAS appointments as probationary flight sub-lieutenants and their passage overseas. 'It is highly desirable,' wrote Kingsmill to the *Niobe*'s Commanding Officer, 'without making too many invidious distinctions that this class should be kept to themselves and treated with as much consideration as proper discipline allows.'[26]

Ross-Hume, who yearned for 'real work' and begged not to be left to 'languish here forever,'[27] had been replaced as RFC recruiting officer by Lieutenant-Colonel C.J. Burke, who arrived in Ottawa in the first part of November 1915. Burke served in Canada only a little more than two months. His main legacy was a long and perceptive report, sent to the War Office on 18 December, on aspects of RFC recruiting in Canada.[28] Burke strongly recommended that the RFC establish its own flying school in the dominion. In his view, a false start had been made. The publicity attending the recruitment and elementary training of pilots for the RFC and the RNAS had fostered pressure groups for the construction of additional schools, and public subscription campaigns for that purpose had been organized. 'In fact,' he observed, 'in the language of the country, an aviation boom took place.' Unfortunately, a 'distinct muddle' developed because more candidates were accepted than the existing flying schools could handle. As a result, uncertificated candidates became increasingly apprehensive over their prospects. Burke implied, incorrectly, that this error in judgment had been made, not by RFC recruiters, but by Canadian agencies or individuals. At any rate, much of the public enthusiasm generated for flying had been misdirected. Almost all the schemes for additional flying schools had been faulty in conception, and nothing had come of any of them, leaving 'a feeling of disappointment and of soreness among those who collected money or interested themselves in trying to help.' The War Office, he thought, might well conclude that what had passed was 'a good deal of trouble for a mixed batch of untrained candidates.'

Nevertheless, Burke believed that there were 'great possibilities' in Canada. He was astonished at the number of Canadians of military age not yet in uniform, which he put down to the failure of Canadians yet to realize the grimness of the war. Moreover, because of the heavy immigration of single men, those of military age constituted a higher proportion of the total population than was the case in Britain. Clearly, then, there was a large pool of manpower for the RFC in Canada. Burke, who had begun his career in the Royal Irish Regiment, did have misgivings about the social suitability of most of the potential candidates, and could not accept the blurring of old-world social distinctions which had occurred in Canada. As he wrote to a War Office colleague the day after he submitted his report: 'The R.F.C.

can get a lot out of Canada provided that they retain complete control out here. There are several people who really enjoy giving appointments in the R.F.C. regardless of the suitability of the candidates. Two people I saved you from are examples, one had been a Berkshire farm labourer two years ago and another ran a newspaper stand in Regina. Suitable material for the R.F.C.!!!'[29] In his view, the majority of potential flyers in Canada would be better suited to serve as sergeant pilots than as commissioned officers.

Turning to the Canadian aircraft industry, Burke described it as further advanced than the British air industry was in 1912, and considered that with the right supervision it would repay encouragement by the British government. Moreover, the thriving American aircraft industry was next door, and could provide all the skills needed for an expansion of Canadian plants. International boundaries, he found, meant little in North America: 'a mechanic does not mind whether he works in Toronto or Buffalo, Winnipeg or Minneapolis, Vancouver or Seattle ...' He concluded that Canadian aviation potential could best be tapped by forming an RFC training wing in the dominion, headed by a small RFC detachment but drawing mainly upon Canadian resources for both personnel and material. Six officers and about 150 non-commissioned officers, air mechanics, and civilians would be needed, and all but four or five could be recruited or engaged in Canada. Canadian manufacturers could produce the fifteen aircraft required, presumably obtaining engines in the United States. The wing could handle twenty pilot trainees at a time; each would be given twenty hours' flying time after passing the FAI test. Burke recommended that students should be enlisted as air mechanics and promoted to sergeant the following day. Unlike the Curtiss candidates, then, they would be uniformed members of the RFC, subject to military discipline. A maximum of 10 per cent of them might be recommended for commissions. Some might be held back in Canada as instructors, but the majority would be sent to England for advanced training on service-type aircraft. He estimated that his scheme would cost £50,000 to establish.

In considering a possible site for the training wing, Burke rejected Toronto 'as a centre from which to start aviation in Canada.' Land cost too much, the surroundings were 'indifferent,' and the climate was poor. Winnipeg was his first choice. It was surrounded by a vast 'natural aerodrome,' and though it was somewhat cold in winter, he had been told by the natives that it was 'the halfway house across the Continent and ... the centre of a very wealthy district.' Calgary was his second choice, with its fine terrain and only 'occasional spells of cold weather.' Victoria, he thought, would be a suitable winter flying station.

Burke placed most emphasis upon his recommendation that the school must be under RFC control, and its commander responsible to RFC Headquarters and to no one else. A Canadian-run organization was not in the cards; the Canadians possessed neither the experience nor the expertise. He argued privately that it would be essential to 'keep the fellow in charge free from being pressed on by other interests in Canada – if you *cannot* arrange for him to be directly and only responsible to R.F.C. H.Q., Canada should be left severely alone.'

It was only reasonable that Burke should believe RFC expertise was essential, for his plan called for a much higher level of training than that offered at the

Curtiss School. As it was the Toronto school had had to depend on instructors from the United States. Nor should his desire for direct RFC control be put down entirely to metropolitan condescension. It is true that he feared the possibility of a government takeover should Canada decide to form its own squadrons, which 'cannot expect to be a success,' but he also had become aware of the private interests pressing for advantage in the aviation field. The following year his views were confirmed when a variety of Canadians made a bewildering series of direct approaches to the British government. J.A.D. McCurdy, one of these supplicants, was told, in explanation of his failure to obtain an interview with Lord Curzon, the President of the Air Board, that the board and the War Office 'apparently have not quite understood why so many "different" and "unofficial" persons should desire to see Lord Curzon about a matter which they expect to hear from the Canadian Government.'[30]

Burke's recommendations were considered by the War Office but eventually rejected.[31] This was unfortunate. Burke foresaw the continued growth of the RFC in France and the resultant demand not only for more pilots but also for the means of producing them. He believed – quite rightly as events were to prove – that Canada could help materially in meeting these needs. The proposed school was a realistic project, geared to resources and facilities available or capable of being developed in Canada and the United States and designed for expansion as RFC requirements grew. Had Burke's training wing been established early in 1916 under experienced RFC direction and control, there seems little doubt that it would have evolved into a large-scale training plan along the lines of the scheme that the RFC eventually set up in Canada at the beginning of 1917. A year would have been gained.

Stanton again acted for the RFC following Burke's departure and continued to do so until August 1916. From 1 January the RFC reverted to its original recruitment policy. Pilot certificates were once more required, but no commissions were granted in Canada.[32] During the first eight months of the year no more than twenty RFC pilot recruits were accepted. Most of them had obtained their certificates in the United States; all were sent overseas as air mechanics, 2nd class. The dismal RFC recruiting figures were partly the result of the better terms offered by the RNAS to certificated candidates. RFC officials, however, made no effort to obtain large numbers of pilots in Canada in this period. They seemed content with the trickle of recruits that Stanton was able to despatch. They were only too aware that possession of a certificate meant that a recruit had completed merely the most elementary stage of his training. He would still have to undergo a much longer period of instruction in British schools and training squadrons after leaving Canada – exactly the same training as that given uncertificated candidates accepted at the end of 1915 and those candidates from the CEF who had never attended a private flying school. For at least the first half of 1916 the RFC was concerned with expanding its training facilities in Britain and finding the experienced personnel to operate them. There was no shortage of candidates to fill their training programmes.

The RNAS showed more interest in Canadian pilots. Certificates were still required and candidates having gained them were appointed probationary flight sub-lieutenants. No attempt was made to push RNAS recruiting in the first four months of 1916; nevertheless, a steady stream of naval candidates was commissioned and sent overseas. Some of these were the uncertificated 1915 candidates whose training had been interrupted and whose passage overseas had been authorized late in that year. The last of these men did not leave until February 1916. Others of the new RNAS officers, more than forty in number, had attended schools in the United States during the winter and early spring. The exact source of these pilots is unclear. They may have been accepted under the 1915 quotas and then elected to gain their certificates before being sent to England. It is also possible that the naval service had been authorized at the end of 1915 or the beginning of 1916 to accept a number of additional candidates. Active RNAS recruiting, however, was not begun again until May. The Toronto Curtiss School reopened at this time, with all but a handful of its pupils designated as RNAS candidates.[33] As before, the programme was tied to quotas received from the Admiralty and little difficulty was encountered in finding the required numbers. Admiral Kingsmill again took a strong personal interest and the Canadian naval service continued to act on behalf of the Admiralty in seeking recruits until the programme ceased in January 1918. By this time 635 men had enrolled, of whom fifty-five had transferred to the RFC.[34]

RFC recruiting, by contrast, remained almost dormant until after the arrival in August of Stanton's replacement, Captain Lord A.R. Innes-Ker. He was empowered to offer commissions in the RFC Special Reserve to suitable candidates whether or not they had certificates. Those who held certificates were to be commissioned before leaving Canada; those without were to be sent overseas as civilians and commissioned on arrival in Britain.[35] The new regulations even provided for acceptance of men not considered suitable for commissioning, but this provision does not seem to have been used. These modifications reflected the steady growth of the flying corps and the realization of RFC Headquarters that a flying certificate obtained in Canada or elsewhere meant very little.

Innes-Ker's arrival ended Stanton's long involvement in the RFC's Canadian recruiting programme. He returned to Britain several months later when the Duke of Connaught's term of service as Governor General ended. There is no doubt that Stanton's departure was welcomed by the Prime Minister and some of his Cabinet. Borden was convinced that Stanton was a malign influence at Rideau Hall. 'That gentleman,' he recalled in his memoirs, 'had been Governor of a small Crown Colony or Dependency and seemed to be under the impression Canada occupied the same status as the territory he had governed.' That view was mellow compared to the Prime Minister's fury with Stanton during the war. To his colleagues he depicted Stanton as 'stupid, conceited, maladroit and meddlesome,' and stated that he was 'continually running to the Governor-General with silly tales about administrative matters and unfortunately the Governor-General is inclined to listen to such tales and to attempt unconstitutional interference.' It must be said, however, that although both Stanton and the Governor General had assiduously promoted RFC recruiting and the cause of military aviation in Canada, they had carefully refrained from appearing to commit the Canadian government to action. 'Please ... understand,' Stanton wrote in favourably responding to one of

Colonel W.H. Merritt's training schemes, 'that this has nothing to do with a future Canadian Flying Service, as his Royal Highness understands that the Canadian Government does not contemplate any such department at present.' Moreover, there is no indication of friction between Stanton and General Gwatkin, his chief contact at Militia Headquarters, nor between the military secretary and men like McCurdy, with whom he was closely associated in the search for RFC recruits.[36]

With the requirement for a pilot certificate eliminated, RFC recruiting increased markedly in the autumn of 1916. Twelve or fourteen recruits sailed in late September, followed by a group of thirty-two in mid-October and additional parties at intervals throughout the remainder of the year. This development, as it happens, coincided with a period of heavy RFC losses during the latter stages of the Somme offensive. The RFC regulations were once again altered in mid-November, this time as a result of changes in the flying corps' training organization in Britain. There was, as before, no requirement for a certificate. All candidates for commissions were to be sent to England, there to be attested as air mechanics, 3rd class, and posted to the recently created RFC Cadet Wing, from which they would proceed to other training schools. On completing a preliminary four-month course they would be appointed second lieutenants in the Regular Army for duty with the RFC. Those who proved unsuitable as pilots could be sent to an officer cadet battalion to qualify as infantry officers. Provision was again made for recruitment and pilot training of those not considered suitable for commissioning. The maximum age limit was dropped from thirty to twenty-five.[37]

The RNAS also modified its recruiting regulations during the latter part of 1916. On 25 August the new rank of probationary flight officer – the rough equivalent of midshipman – was introduced. Those who held the new rank were rated as officers but not actually commissioned. Commissioning, in the rank of flight sub-lieutenant, followed successful completion of initial training overseas. Those accepted into the RNAS in Canada were given the new rank after the early part of October. In November the RNAS dropped the requirement for a pilot certificate. This was initially announced as a temporary measure to apply throughout the winter months. The stipulation, however, was not reintroduced.[38]

Although the RNAS and RFC enjoyed the full co-operation of the naval and militia departments in their Canadian recruitment programmes, the recruits themselves received little official assistance. Candidates who were accepted into the flying services were given rail transportation from their homes to Ottawa. From November 1915 onwards, until the requirement for a certificate was dropped, RNAS candidates undergoing instruction at one of the private flying schools qualified for an Admiralty allowance of $1.25 for each day over seven weeks at the school. No such allowance seems to have been available to the RFC candidates. In 1916 the city of Toronto paid a special grant to students at the Curtiss School. This assistance, however, was limited to Toronto men attending the school, who received $8 a week up to a maximum of $64. Payment was made after qualification for a certificate and city records show that a disbursement of $1472 was made to twenty-three students. Some small measure of financial aid was added by the Canadian government from May 1916; those who obtained their certificates in Canada and were accepted by either of the British flying services were given

$100. This payment was not retroactive and did not apply to those gaining certificates at American schools. Only sixty-one recruits qualified.[39]

It is probable that the combined total of 1915–16 RNAS and RFC recruits was in the neighbourhood of 700 – somewhat more than 300 for the RNAS and 350 or more for the RFC. Of these, fewer than 250 were properly certificated pilots. The Toronto Curtiss School contributed slightly over one half of the certificated recruits; almost all the others obtained their qualifications in the United States.[40] The existence of the Curtiss School (and to a lesser extent of schools in British Columbia) seems to have been the major factor determining the provincial origins of the recruits of these early years. In statistical terms, both Ontario and British Columbia were subsequently over-represented among these first entrants. Ontarians alone made up more than half of the recruits to the two flying services in 1915–16. Albertans and Manitobans also enlisted in numbers rather larger than might have been expected. All the other provinces, however, contributed less than their statistical share, presumably because of the absence of flying opportunities and of publicity for flying.*

The Curtiss School had begun its training programme in 1915 with two Curtiss F-type flying boats brought to Toronto from the United States. A third was added a week later. These aircraft were flown from Hanlan's Point, on one of the islands in Toronto harbour, where two hangars were erected. An aeroplane section was opened some weeks later just outside Toronto, at Long Branch on the shore of Lake Ontario, where the initial group of flying-boat students progressed to training on wheeled aircraft on 22 June. A militia department rifle range there was placed at the school's disposal and Curtiss JN3 biplanes were used as training machines. The Long Branch field, where three hangars were built, may justly be called Canada's first proper airfield. During the 1915 season pupils learned to fly at Hanlan's Point, putting in some two hundred minutes of dual time before proceeding to the aeroplane section where they completed their instruction and flew their tests. In 1916 the flying-boat section was closed and the pupils took all their instruction on the JN3s.

With the exception of the FAI examination at the end of the course, all flying at the Curtiss School was dual. The tests called for three separate solo flights. Two involved flying a series of figures-of-eight around two posts 500 metres apart. In these flights the aircraft's engine had to be cut before or at the moment of landing and the machine brought to a stop not more than fifty metres from a predetermined point. On the third flight the student was required to gain at least 100 metres of altitude and then to cut the engine, gliding down without power to a successful landing. The tests were witnessed by official observers and certificates were issued in the name of the Royal Aero Club of the United Kingdom, which then represented all parts of the British Empire in the FAI. Most of the flying was done during the early morning and late afternoon to early evening to avoid windy conditions. With only a few aircraft available, rapid progress was impossible. Operations often slowed to a crawl because of aircraft unserviceability and bad weather. Students spent much of their time waiting and the instruction for many of

* See Appendix C, Tables 1 and 6.

them extended over several months. Little if any technical ground instruction was given and there was no night flying.

The school's activities drew large weekend crowds of spectators. Something of the atmosphere of the school and the boyish enthusiasm engendered by aviation in its early days were captured in a story that appeared in *The Globe* on 15 May 1915, a few days after the opening of the school. 'The roll is called at 5 a.m.,' wrote the reporter assigned to cover the start of the day's flying-boat instruction:

A calm atmosphere is desirable for teaching the novice, and the winds are still asleep for some hours after sunrise. At the same time one has but to meet these young airmen to come into touch with an enthusiasm and earnestness for their calling that would bring them from their beds at a still earlier hour, were that necessary ...

The rendezvous was the foot of Spadina Avenue, where a gasoline launch is moored ...

'All aboard!' was the call and off we went to the Island sandbar. In the gray, calm morning a barque was making sail for the harbor and sea birds flew overhead ...

The boat touched the shore and we leaped out on the sand and entered the hangar. The next stage in the flying was reached – the awakening of George, the mechanic, who slept keeping watch near the flying boat. A few handfuls of sand with sundry odd ends of rope thrown over the wooden partition brought quick shouts from the interior and told that the aim had been true, and in a moment George, thus unceremoniously awakened, emerged and set the engine agoing. This was an operation that required patience till the engine was warmed up ...

'All aboard' again was the call from Instructor Pierce, now clad in a blue coat, with a balaclava helmet on his head and rubber shoes on his feet. Lieutenant Smith* took his seat on the boat, which slipped out over the lake, slowly at first, then faster and faster as the chug, chug of the engine increased in intensity. Sixty miles an hour is the speed the boat is capable of on water and about 65 miles in the air. All gaze after it. 'Thirty,' ... as the boat travels faster; '40,' 'now he's in his swing.' 'Look at her tail rising.' 'She's on the surface of the water.' 'There, she's in the air now.' 'She's going up by bounds.' 'My, that's the highest flight yet.' 'He must be 300 feet up.' 'Compare them with the C.P.R. building.' Then the flying boat swerved round for home, descending gently to the water. Instructor Pierce brought her level a few feet above its surface and she dropped down with a slight splash. A moment more and Lieutenant Smith stepped ashore. He had been away only six minutes ...[41]

The school's standard course remained at four hundred minutes of flying time throughout the 1915 and 1916 seasons. Nevertheless, most of the 1916 pupils received considerably more than the stipulated number of minutes, the extra instruction being subsidized by Colonel Merritt's Canadian Aviation Fund. In January 1916 Merritt had proposed to the War Office that the fund might improve the training given to RFC candidates in Canada by underwriting the cost of thirty hours of flying beyond the certification standard for five to ten pupils a month. The War Office replied that the offer would be 'of material assistance' provided that the extra flying time was given on 'fast machines.' None of the sixty-three pupils who

---

* A number of the students held militia commissions; hence the use of military rank.

obtained certificates during the school's 1916 season logged anything close to the thirty extra hours contemplated by Merritt and almost all were RNAS rather than RFC candidates. But the great majority of pilots did receive additional flying time, though of course there were no 'fast machines.' Nearly three-quarters obtained 480 minutes or more and close to half logged in excess of 540 minutes. Thirteen flew more than 600 minutes while three rolled up over 720 minutes of flying time. None of the Canadian Aviation Fund's cash found its way into the pockets of Curtiss candidates, however. The standard $400 fee remained unchanged. The Curtiss Company presumably was paid directly by the fund for the added flying time.[42]

During the two seasons that the school operated there was neither serious injury nor fatality, a tribute to the corps of excellent instructors, most of them from the United States. The chief instructor was Theodore C. Macaulay and two of his subordinates were Bert Acosta and Guy Gilpatric.* The school produced a total of 130 certificated pilots – sixty-seven during 1915 and sixty-three in 1916. Of these, 106 joined the RNAS and twenty-two went to the RFC.[†] Many others received partial training or were registered on the school's waiting list without ever having an opportunity to fly. The list of pupils, like that of the instructors, contained the names of men who would later become well known, such as Robert Leckie and Wilfrid A. Curtis, both of whom won gallantry awards during the First World War and became Chiefs of the Air Staff in the RCAF in the 1940s.

Although the Toronto Curtiss School was the only truly successful one in Canada during this period, there were a number of other Canadian schools. A company known as the Canadian Aircraft Works in Montreal South, which seems to have constructed two or three Caudron-type aeroplanes, advertised itself as operating a flying school as early as November 1914 and offered to train pilots for the militia department.[43] Little is known of the training, if any, that was given there, but it produced no qualified pilots.

Several new schools blossomed following the news in early 1915 that the RFC – and later the RNAS – were seeking certificated pilots in Canada. E.L. Janney stated his intention to establish a training school upon his return from England in February, the first to be announced following the start of Canadian recruiting. Janney's tiny operation opened and closed later that same year. A small school was also formed in the Vancouver area by the Aero Club of British Columbia, with financial backing from a group of Vancouver businessmen and by public subscription. Training was given to a dozen pupils on a single machine during the summer and autumn of 1915. In the following year a non-profit, patriotic organization known as the British Columbia Aviation School Ltd was formed and stock offered for public sale. The school operated during 1916 from Coquitlam, twenty-five miles east of Vancouver, and when it stopped instruction in October it had two

---

* Acosta became one of Admiral Richard E. Byrd's pilots during the 1927 trans-Atlantic flight of the *America*. Known to his fellow pilots as 'Goggles,' Gilpatric had obtained his pilot certificate before the war at the age of fifteen. After the war he turned to the writing of fiction, creating the popular 'Mister Glencannon,' chief engineer of the *Inchcliffe Castle*.

† Two of the school's 1916 graduates did not enter either of the flying services after having obtained their certificates.

aircraft and twenty-two students. Some of the pupils at the school flew solo but none obtained their certificates there. Most, however, were ultimately accepted by the RFC and RNAS. Other schools were formed in Toronto, Montreal, and Vancouver, but they existed only for brief periods and offered little to those in search of certificates.[44]

We have noted that many who sought to join the RFC or RNAS and were unable to obtain certificates in Canada travelled to schools in the United States.* More than one hundred Canadian candidates for the two British flying services earned certificates in the United States, most of them at the Wright, Curtiss, and Stinson schools. So extensive was the Canadian invasion of the American flying schools that from July 1915 to the same month in 1916 more than half the pilot certificates issued by the Aero Club of America went to Canadians seeking acceptance by the RFC and RNAS.[45]

Since there was no 'recommended list' of flying schools, candidates seeking certificates were very much on their own. Even the best of American schools had only a few aircraft and instructors and the sudden influx of Canadians was almost too much for them. Temperamental engines, the inevitable flying accidents, and spells of bad weather could hold up training for days at a time, when for all the Canadians every day lost was frustrating and for some at least another bite into dwindling funds. The Wright School at Huffman Field outside Dayton attracted many Canadians in this period, among them such prominent pilots of the future as D.M.B. Galbraith and A. Roy Brown of Carleton Place, Ont., J.O. Galpin and C.G. Bronson of Ottawa, Basil Hobbs of Sault Ste Marie, Ont., J. Lindsay Gordon of St Lambert, Que, C.J. Creery of Vancouver, and Kenneth F. Saunders of Victoria, BC. Somewhat exaggerating their affluence, the Dayton *Sunday News* of 3 October 1915 proclaimed that 'Thirty Wealthy Canadian Men Taught Aeroplane,' and quoted one of them as saying that though 'thousands of young men' in Canada wanted to enter the flying service, 'we are among the fortunate ones who are able to obtain sufficient money to pay for the course and our expenses while taking it.' Lloyd Breadner of Ottawa was another member of the group at the Wright School. His letters home show that he was a little concerned about money (his family financed his stay in Dayton), but he chafed at the delays caused by too many students competing for too few aircraft. He decided to go right to the top: 'I went out to see Mr. Wright the other day & he assured me that the school would be run on a different method after this. He said he hadn't been looking after it for the past month & that the instructors weren't doing their work. He told me not to worry, that I'd be finished up before December 1st.'[46] As it happened, at that very time Orville Wright was deeply involved in disposing of his interests in the Wright Company. Breadner did not in fact get his certificate until 28 December, but by January he was bound for England and advanced training with the RNAS.

* Known to have produced certificated Canadian recruits for the flying services during 1915–16 were the Wright Schools at Dayton, Ohio, Augusta, Georgia, Mineola and Hempstead Plains, NY; the Curtiss Schools at Newport News, Virginia, and Buffalo, NY; the Stinson School, San Antonio, Texas; the Thomas School, Ithaca, NY; the Martin School, Griffith Park, Los Angeles, the Burns School, Los Angeles, and the Christofferson School, Alameda, California.

At the same time that Breadner and his fellows were getting their certificates at the Wright school, other Canadians were going even farther afield. Joseph Gorman of Ottawa, J.A. Harman of Toronto, J.E. Walker of Montreal, and H.W. Mackenzie of Victoria, finding the Dayton school overcrowded, travelled in November to the Stinson School at San Antonio. There they became the first four students of Marjorie Stinson, a famous aviation pioneer then still in her teens. Their success, and the excellence of the school, soon attracted other Canadians to San Antonio, but not everyone was so fortunate as to find such a high calibre of instruction. Alfred W. Carter and Thomas R. Shearer, both natives of Calgary who had been classmates at Queen's University, were part of a group of Canadians who attended a very different school in St Augustine, Florida. Having been accepted as RNAS candidates, they borrowed $1000 each and set out in January 1916. Carter has recalled that

On arrival ... we were requested for the $400.00 in advance, which we paid. The whole thing was a promotion by a middle-aged slicker called Benedict. His son was the so-called instructor. There were ten of us Canadians and a few Americans. The money we put up got the Airframe and Engine out of the crates. We were put to work measuring off flying and landing wires from a roll of cable and splicing them and erecting the machine, installing the engine, etc., all under the direction of a hired mechanic who knew damn all about aircraft ... This was all considered to be valuable training ...

After lengthy delays, which included replacing the pontoon landing gear with a wheeled undercarriage, and 'after a lot of threats, some physical,' Carter managed to persuade the reluctant instructor to begin flying.

... we started out one early morning, no wind, low tide, etc., and I got into the seat beside Benedict ... and away we went along the beach. We got into the air and went about a mile swooping from side to side, diving and rising, before he got it in a fairly stable attitude close to the ground and he switched off and plopped on the sand. He was pale as a sheet and shaking. I thought in my complete ignorance that it was great. What actually happened was he got into the air by accident and not knowing how to fly had overcontrolled like crazy, but was committed until he got it down again near the ground and called the whole thing off. We taxied back to the gang who were in great glee that finally instruction would be under way.[47]

The instructor immediately, and understandably, announced that first-time training would be restricted to 'tail up' taxi runs to get some idea of what it was all about. On the first such run, however, the aircraft hit a puddle left by the tide, flipped over, and was smashed. Their borrowed funds nearly depleted, Carter and Shearer 'threatened some money out of Benedict up in his bedroom' and made their way back to Ottawa. Both were appointed to RNAS commissions and sent overseas in the spring of 1916.[48]

Canadian aircraft construction was in the same embryonic stage as flying training. Although there was some scattered activity in this area in different parts of

Canada during 1914–16, the only work of consequence took place in Toronto. In the spring of 1916 the Polson Iron Works, an established shipbuilding and engineering company, designed, built, and test flew an aeroplane known as the MFP machine, a two-place tractor biplane notable for the tubular steel construction of its fuselage. Two of these machines are known to have been constructed, each to a somewhat different design, and others may have been produced. In addition to the test flights out of Toronto, one or more of the aircraft were flown from Hempstead Plains, NY, and the machine was advertised in an American aviation journal during 1916, but no evidence of any sales has been uncovered.[49]

The major producer of aircraft, however, was Curtiss Aeroplanes and Motors Ltd in Toronto. It will be recalled that in March 1915 the Admiralty had arranged for fifty Curtiss JN3s to be made in Toronto. Only eighteen of these were produced and it is possible that six of them may have been diverted to the RFC, which had followed the RNAS lead in placing orders with the American Curtiss Company. In 1915 the Toronto Curtiss plant designed and constructed a twin-engine, three-seater tractor biplane bombing machine for the British services known as the Curtiss Canada. It was intended to serve as a land-based companion to the twin-engined flying boats that the American parent firm was supplying to the Admiralty. The prototype passed its tests early in September 1915 at the Long Branch field and was then delivered to the War Office. Eleven more, known as the Model C1, were built, ten going to the War Office and one to the Admiralty. An additional order of twenty-five was placed by the Admiralty and the contract again went to the Toronto plant. This order was cancelled in June 1916, however, before any of the Admiralty machines had been produced. The Toronto firm continued to make parts for its American parent company, but it does not seem to have produced any further aircraft after the cancellation of the Canada orders in mid-1916. At that time the plant was employing 600 men.[50]

In December 1916 Ottawa loaned the British government $1,000,000 to purchase most of the assets of Curtiss's Toronto plant. The new company, Canadian Aeroplanes Ltd, came under the control of the Imperial Munitions Board* as an essential ingredient in the Anglo-Canadian agreement on a RFC training organization for Canada. The negotiations leading to these developments, which will form an important part of chapter 3, had been proceeding since early 1916, the IMB acting as an intermediary between the two governments. The board had pressed for the diversion of British aircraft orders from the United States to a government-owned operation in Canada. Both Borden and the War Office accepted this argument in principle and, once the agreement to form RFC training squadrons had been completed on 12 December, the accord on a supporting aircraft factory soon followed. Indeed, the IMB had been authorized on 25 November to place an order with a Canadian company for 200 Curtiss-type training machines. The new company quickly acquired the manufacturing rights to an aeroplane based on the

---

* The Imperial Munitions Board was organized 30 November 1915. It served as an agent for British purchases of munitions and other war supplies in Canada and supervised their production. Although responsible to the British Ministry of Munitions, most of its personnel, including management, was Canadian.

Curtiss JN4 two-seater trainer; production of this aircraft and spares, which were to constitute the bulk of Canadian Aeroplanes' output, was designed largely to meet the RFC's needs.[51]

Canadian Aeroplanes Ltd achieved – and with notable efficiency – the first mass production and large-scale export of aircraft in the history of Canadian aviation. The Canadian government, whose attitude towards the development of military aviation had been characterized by the *Toronto World*, among other newspapers, as negative and 'deplorable ... for Canada as a nation,'[52] had supported the establishment of the new aeroplane company and now provided some of the training facilities for the RFC Canada scheme. These were small steps, however, and, perhaps in national terms, even backward ones. Ottawa's critics seemed unlikely to be silenced.

3
Sir Sam Hughes,
the Aviation Lobby, and
Canadian Air Policy, 1914–16

Canadian aviation policy in the years 1914–16 cannot be divorced from the character and personality of Sir Sam Hughes. He was a strange man, intense, self-dramatizing, and mercurial, formidable on the stump or in the House of Commons, a fierce partisan who could excite, amuse, puzzle, or exasperate his fellow Conservatives, not to speak of the opposition. He had been a fine athlete in his youth, a school teacher, and then a newspaper editor who became the most powerful figure in central Ontario's Orange Toryism. He seemed to think of himself primarily as a man of action. From the age of thirteen he had been a member of the militia. His appointment as Minister of Militia and Defence in 1911 was to him a vindication of his militia career – one not lacking in controversy – and he threw himself into his duties with great enthusiasm, enthusiasm redoubled with the coming of the war and its opportunities for action upon a more spacious stage.

Immensely proud of the part Canada was taking in the war, and of his own contribution to it, Hughes jealously guarded his powers as minister, so much so that his Cabinet colleagues, including Sir Robert Borden, usually left him to run his own show. While unquestionably an ardent Canadian patriot, always on the watch for imperial misuse of Canadian troops, at the same time he sought imperial recognition for himself in the way of honours and promotions. Both at home and in the heady atmosphere of the metropolis, he was highly susceptible to praise and flattery. He was not always discriminating in his choice of friends and associates, and some of those whom he appointed to positions of authority or influence in the early days of the war failed the trust he had placed in them, thereby weakening his own political position. In his ministerial style Hughes was unorthodox, preferring to short-circuit established departmental procedures and to run his department as a kind of feudal barony. Since he frequently took advice from persons outside government circles, it was difficult for his officials, as well as his Cabinet colleagues, to ascertain at any given time the extent to which he had committed himself and the government to a variety of schemes.

Hughes' principal military adviser was Major-General W.G. Gwatkin, Chief of the General Staff and, like all his predecessors (with the exception of General Sir William Otter), a British officer. A highly intelligent and long-suffering officer, Gwatkin gave loyal if uneasy service to his volatile Minister, allowing his feelings to surface only in the occasional wry minute, usually written in the course of rectifying the confusion caused by one of Hughes' impulsive initiatives. Gwatkin was both able and orthodox. Unfortunately for those who hoped to see the establishment of a Canadian air force, he took the view from the outset of the war that aviation was not a proper sphere for Canadian involvement, for reasons more fundamental than the chagrin occasioned by his Minister's brief flirtation with the Canadian Aviation Corps. The fact that he held such views made it unlikely that any scheme for a Canadian flying corps would receive support within the militia department itself, despite the presence of such officers as Colonel G.S. Maunsell.

Gwatkin did not express himself at any length about aviation until 1916. Prior to that time, however, his letters and minutes provide ample evidence of his unsympathetic attitude. Towards the end of September 1914 Lieutenant-Colonel P.E. Thacker, a Canadian officer on attached duty at the War Office, sent home information about the equipment, establishment, and cost of raising 'a Flight of Aeroplanes' in Canada. In passing Thacker's notes to Maunsell, Gwatkin merely observed, somewhat ambiguously, that 'of the enclosed documents you are at liberty to make any use you like.'[1]

More explicit evidence about the degree of Gwatkin's hostility to Canadian departures in the field of aviation emerged during discussion of a proposal from the Burgess Company of Marblehead, Mass., an affair that also brought out for the first time Borden's view of the subject. It will be recalled that Hughes had authorized E.L. Janney to purchase from this company Canada's first military aircraft, a Burgess-Dunne machine. Sensing the possibility of further sales, the company approached the Prime Minister and the acting Militia Minister, J.D. Hazen, with the proposition that the government purchase twelve Burgess aircraft, complete with American pilots, and at one stroke acquire an air force. Colonel Maunsell was asked by Borden to draft a cable to Sir George Perley, the acting High Commissioner in London, outlining this novel proposal and requesting the views of the War Office. To Maunsell's draft the Prime Minister added this important sentence: 'We have no aviation service and do not think it desirable [to] attempt organization such service during progress [of] war.' The War Office response made no reference to this statement of policy, but simply advised that Burgess-Dunne aircraft were both expensive and unreliable. In letting Edward Slade, the president of the Burgess Company, know that his proposal had been rejected, Gwatkin saddled the War Office with responsibility for the decision. 'The War Office discourages the organization of a flying squadron,' he wrote, 'and it is our intention, for the present at any rate, to abandon the idea.'[2]

With R.B. Bennett, the Conservative member for Calgary East, the Chief of the General Staff was more direct. Bennett wrote to him in December asking whether he supported the proposed formation of an Alberta flying corps. Gwatkin said flatly that he was 'not in favour of forming a military aviation corps in MD [Military District] 13 or elsewhere in Canada – at present.' There was 'so much else to be done,' he told Bennett. For instance, Alberta had just been asked to produce 'two more regiments of mounted rifles and three more battalions of infantry.'*[3]

---

* Gwatkin was half persuaded that his Minister had encouraged the Albertans. When the Governor General's patronage for the Alberta air force was requested, Gwatkin asked Hughes' military secretary: 'Has the Minister by any chance given his support to the so-called "Alberta Aviation Corps"?' Gwatkin to Winter, 31 March 1915, HQ 6978-2-9, PAC, RG 24, vol. 2033

The truth was that the government, and especially the militia department, was overwhelmed by the tasks confronting it, and had no time and little patience for aviation. The Canadian Expeditionary Force's 1st Contingent sailed for England on 3 October; three days later the government offered a second contingent of 20,000 men. The mobilization and preliminary training of this large force, together with a reinforcement pool of 30,000 also decided upon, demanded the whole attention of Gwatkin and his subordinates, and continued to do so until the 2nd Contingent began its movement to England in April 1915.

In the hectic atmosphere of these months, the many inquiries and suggestions concerning aviation that were received in Ottawa got short shrift. An exception was the proposal made by J.A.D. McCurdy, who had become an executive with the Curtiss Aeroplane Company of Hammondsport, NY. On 21 December he placed before Sam Hughes the outlines of a plan to combine a flying corps with a domestic aircraft industry: 'It has been my desire, as a Canadian, to do what ever in my power lay for Canada. With this object in view, after consultation with my partners, I determined that the establishment of an aeroplane factory in Canada would do much to make easy the inquiring into and purchase of machines by the Canadian Government, should you decide upon the establishment of an aeroplane corps to work in conjunction with the second and subsequent contingents.' What McCurdy wanted most was a guarantee that if a branch of the Curtiss company were established in Canada, 'an order will be placed with us for the manufacture and equipment of an aeroplane squadron ...'[4]

Hughes gave McCurdy an interview, and advised him to see the Prime Minister. In writing to Borden, McCurdy claimed that Hughes gave his proposal 'hearty sympathy and approval.' He saw the Prime Minister at least twice over the next two months and on 3 February 1915 formally summarized his proposal for him. The Curtiss Company intended to start a plant in Toronto capable of producing four aircraft a week. The directors wished a government contract for eight aircraft and for any further aircraft required over the next five years. In addition, 'the Company offers its services to assist the Government in organizing and training an Aviation Corps, and would instruct, for each machine ordered, one Aviator, selected by the Government, at the Company's expense.' This was an offer that Borden could refuse, and he did so, advising McCurdy that 'up to the present time' Canada had 'not decided to order aeroplanes for either military or naval purposes.' Nevertheless, he promised to lay the Curtiss plan before the Admiralty and the War Office. In the event, the Admiralty placed a large order with Curtiss and fifty aircraft from that order were diverted by the parent company to its new branch plant in Toronto. For the time being, McCurdy dropped his advocacy of a Canadian flying corps.[5]

Even as McCurdy was pressing, and losing, his case, the Directorate of Military Aeronautics in the War Office was taking the first step towards a comparable proposal. As we have seen, on 22 October 1914 Gwatkin had mentally crossed his fingers and told the Burgess Company that any idea of a Canadian aviation corps had been dropped by the government because the War Office 'discourages' it. It was, perhaps, a convenient pretext for explaining away E.L. Janney's air force. On 23 October, however, Lord Kitchener himself, the Secretary of State for War, had approved the idea of a Canadian squadron. The unwitting cause of this development was an Englishman with Canadian connections named Griffith Brewer. Brewer had taken his flying certificate with Orville Wright at Dayton, Ohio, in August 1914. On his return to England, having secured a letter from the Aeronautical Society of Great Britain describing him as 'a responsible man and means business,' Brewer obtained an interview with Lieutenant-Colonel Sefton Brancker, Assistant Director of Military Aeronautics. His great plan was that a Canadian squadron should be organized under the cover-name of 'Brewer's Exhibition Flights,' and that Canadian airmen, after training in secret at Dayton and in Florida and California during the winter, should be despatched overseas to form a dominion squadron. 'All this could be done very quietly,' he assured Brancker, 'by the choosing of discreet recruits.' Brancker gave no attention to the notion of smuggling Canadians in and out of the United States for training, but the idea of a Canadian squadron interested him so much that he took it up with Kitchener personally. As a result of that conversation, Brancker noted that 'S of S ... agreed that Canada should be approached with a view to the raising of this Squadron as a part of the Canadian Forces.'[6]

No immediate action followed this interesting conversation with Kitchener, possibly because Borden's cable of 9 October discouraged Brancker and his colleagues. Yet the idea was not forgotten. Lieutenant-Colonel C.C. Marindin, a senior British staff officer who had initially assessed the Brewer proposal, returned to the idea of a Canadian squadron, in quite different context, within a few months. What reawakened his interest was the despatch to England of those members of the South African Aviation Unit who had volunteered for imperial service.* It appeared to Marindin that 'as none of the Dominion forces have their own aviation units, there seems to be an opportunity of making use in the R.F.C. of aviators and mechanics from the different Dominions, and at the same time fostering the spirit of Imperial co-operation.' He therefore proposed converting the Royal Flying Corps into an imperial force.

Marindin's ideas were embodied in a memorandum he circulated to members of the Directorate of Military Aeronautics on 3 August 1915. Canada, Australia, and New Zealand, he suggested, ought to be approached to see whether they would be willing to recruit the officers and men needed for a squadron. Dominion squadrons thus raised would 'form part of the R.F.C., but ... should have a distinguishing designation, e.g. No. 29 (Canadian) Squadron.' Such squadrons would be equipped and maintained by the RFC, and all costs associated with them would be borne from imperial funds. 'Should it not be possible to raise four squadrons,' he thought, 'it might be feasible for South Africa and Canada and for Australia and New Zealand to combine.'

Only the finance officers could see anything wrong with this plan. The imperial government should not be burdened with the entire cost of dominion squadrons, they thought, because the dominions were already paying the expenses of the

---

* This unit, organized before the war, served in the campaign in German Southwest Africa. When that campaign was successfully concluded in July 1915, the air unit was demobilized and most of its officers, and later the other ranks, were sent to England for further training. Eventually the South African Aviation Corps was constituted and became 26 (South African) Squadron of the Royal Flying Corps. It served in German East Africa. H.A. Jones, *The War in the Air: being the Story of the Part played in the Great War by the Royal Air Force*, III (London 1931), 15-16, 19

forces they had sent overseas. As an alternative, they suggested that the Colonial Office, in approaching the dominions, 'might assume that the colonies would bear the pay, but might say that the Imperial Government would provide and maintain, at Imperial costs, all the materiel (other than what is personal to the officers and men).'[7]

Marindin's suggestion, with this amendment and with the addition of information covering the question of recruiting generally for the RFC in the dominions, was passed by the Colonial Secretary to the Canadian High Commissioner, Sir George Perley, on 18 September 1915. After rehearsing the conditions under which Canadians, as individuals, could enter the RFC, the War Office proposal went on: 'It is thought, however, that the Governments of the Dominions might wish to raise complete aviation units, either independently or in conjunction with one another. Should this be the case ... the Army Council would gladly accept the offer of such units ... Such units would take their place in the general organization as units of the Royal Flying Corps, as it would be necessary that they should come under the orders of, and be at the disposal of, the General Officer Commanding that Corps. In order to mark the connection of these units with the Dominions with which they were associated, arrangements would be made to give them a distinguishing designation.' This concept would not necessarily ensure an all-Canadian squadron, however. The RFC reserved the right to post individuals out of the squadrons, or to post in 'officers and men who have no territorial association with them.' High wastage rates might make the second course necessary, and, initially at least, it might not be possible to find dominion officers with sufficient experience for higher appointments. Moreover, if dominion officers were locked within their squadrons, they would have very limited opportunity for promotion. Subject to these conditions, and to dominion responsibility for pay and personal equipment, the War Office invited dominion participation.[8]

Here was an opportunity, then, to establish at relatively small expense the nucleus of a Canadian flying corps within the bounds of the RFC.* It was considered by Major-General Gwatkin, in consultation with Lieutenant-Colonel E.A. Stanton, the Governor General's military secretary, who at that time had responsi-

---

* This was an opportunity seized by the government of Australia, 'mainly for national reasons,' since it had a standing policy forbidding the transfer of personnel from Australian to British forces. On receipt of the War Office's invitation, the Australian official historian records, 'the Australian Government, perceiving the value of an air force for future training as well as for the present emergency, promptly adopted the suggestion.' On 27 December 1915 a commitment was made for one squadron, subsequently formed and trained in Egypt. As 67 (Australian) Squadron RFC and later as 1 Squadron, Australian Flying Corps, it served in the Middle East theatre. Three additional AFC squadrons flew on the Western Front from late 1917 to the end of the war, and a replacement pool of reserve training squadrons was maintained in England. Even before the war the Australian government had established its own Central Flying School at Point Cook, near Melbourne. Its first graduates were despatched to Mesopotamia in response to an appeal from the Viceroy of India. The Australian half-flight there was ultimately incorporated into 30 Squadron, RFC. The AFC, according to its historian, 'was a portion of the Australian Imperial Force, though its squadrons for the most part served separately from each other and under the orders ... of the Royal Air Force.' F.M. Cutlack, *The Australian Flying Corps in the Western and Eastern Theatres of War, 1914–1918*, 3d ed. (The Official History of Australia in the War of 1914–1918, VIII; Sydney 1934), 1–2, 11, 31–2, 175–84, 213, 422–3

bility for RFC recruiting in Canada. Neither of these British officers had any sympathy for the suggestion, though Stanton thought the Canadian government might give some assistance to flying schools. They recommended that 'for the present at any rate, no attempt be made to organize a squadron or any other unit of the R.F.C.' This single sentence, devoid of any supporting explanation, sealed the fate of the British proposal. It was appended to two recommendations for assistance to RFC recruiting in Canada. The whole matter was dealt with summarily – indeed, perfunctorily. On the same day Gwatkin signed this set of recommendations, they were 'approved by the Minister in Council,'* and the document killing the proposal bears the same bold 'OK S.H.' that had called into being the Canadian Aviation Corps. Failing some sudden reconversion of the Minister to the cause of aviation, Gwatkin had had his way.† Only initiative from the Prime Minister and the Cabinet, or strong public pressure, or both, would change the stand of the militia department, and at the end of 1915 neither prospect was at all likely.[9]

Yet within a few months the government was to retreat from its policy, and it was only a few months more before that policy had been drastically revised. The development of aviation was so rapid, and its growing importance so demonstrable, that a policy based on negation alone could no longer be maintained. Pressures built up from a number of directions, none of them sufficiently powerful to bring about a drastic shift of emphasis, but strong enough to cause Canadian authorities to think again about aviation. In 1916 the air war began to expand dramatically in scope and significance, especially on the Western Front. Inevitably senior officers of the RFC were receptive to the ideas of any enterprising Canadian who had plans to push for a more effective use of Canadian manpower. Like it or not, first the High Commissioner in London, and then the government in Ottawa, found it necessary to react to such plans, until finally the hand of the government was forced by the unexpected re-entry of Sam Hughes into the field of aviation.

Before these events took place, however, the government had been impelled to give some ground to a campaign mounted at home for a more positive aviation policy. Its author and leader was Colonel William Hamilton Merritt; his vehicle was an organization he put together in late 1915 called the Canadian Aviation

---

* The phrase 'Minister in Council,' which might suggest some Cabinet discussion of the matter, in fact refers in this case to Hughes' novel method of carrying out his duties as presiding officer of the Militia Council. Since the beginning of 1914 he had ignored the council, and no minutes exist for the period 1914–16, except for those meetings held in 1916 when the Prime Minister, in Hughes' absence, called the council together and presided over its deliberations. The minutes resume in January 1917, shortly after Hughes left the Cabinet.

  Instead of Militia Council meetings, Hughes held what Gwatkin once termed informal gatherings to dispose of business which the council, under other circumstances, would have transacted. It is not suggested that a formal meeting of the council might have adopted another course in the case of the British proposal for official Canadian participation in the RFC. Yet the procedure followed in this case ensured that the deliberation would be confined to a few persons, and, given the predilections of those concerned, also ensured that there would be no discussion of it. It is altogether likely that no Cabinet minister, other than Hughes, had any knowledge that such an approach had been made.

† Ironically, in 1920 Gwatkin would become the first and only Inspector-General of the short-lived Canadian Air Force.

Fund. Merritt, the grandson of the builder of the Welland Canal, was a well-known mining engineer who had also had a distinguished military career. He had served in the North-West Rebellion and the South African War, had commanded the Governor General's Body Guard, and had been president of the Canadian Cavalry Association and the Canadian Military Institute. He had formed the Canadian Defence League before the war to awaken a 'militia consciousness' in Canada, notably by securing the adoption of universal compulsory military service. This cause he pursued with unflagging zeal once war had broken out. But he also discovered a new enthusiasm – aviation.

When war came, Merritt was in Switzerland. As he told Sir Robert Borden, his stay there had impressed him with 'the remarkable change made in warfare by the advent of the Aeroplane.' Having been a cavalry officer for more than thirty years, he readily discerned (as many younger military men in Canada had not) the revolution wrought by the new arm, especially in its reconnaissance function. He was also struck by 'the splendid results obtained in Military Aviation through the Swiss public aiding the government,' particularly in the purchase of aircraft by public subscription. On returning to Canada, Merritt made it his business to discover the state of aviation in the country, and the government's attitude towards it. He travelled from Montreal to Vancouver, talking to anyone who knew something about aviation, or might be encouraged to become interested in it. Among others, he met McCurdy, Gwatkin, Kingsmill, and probably Maunsell, as well as a large number of politicians and businessmen. Merritt found that the government was doing little or nothing. His summation of the official attitude, made at a later date for public consumption, was not unfair. 'The disposition of the Government,' he concluded, 'was that, as so much had been undertaken by Canada in raising the ordinary branches of the service, and the matter of aviation being so new, it was considered best to leave it in the hands of representatives of the Admiralty and the British War Office who were in Canada.'[10]

Having satisfied himself that there was need for his energies, Merritt founded the Canadian Aviation Fund to awaken both the public and the government to the significance of military aviation, and to stir both to contribute to it. His first attempt to win government support won honeyed words from Sir George Foster, the acting Prime Minister, but nothing more. On 3 August 1915 Foster wrote: 'The Government of Canada has no objection at all to the proposal to form a fund and undertake the immediate training of men with a view to the promotion of Aviation in Canada. On the contrary it welcomes every well-based and intelligent effort to stimulate work in that direction, believing that this branch has already demonstrated its great ability for scouting, defensive and offensive work ... In writing the above I am in no way committing the Government as to its policy in relation to the assistance or promotion of Aviation Corps.'[11] Merritt thereupon bypassed Ottawa altogether. During the visit to Canada of the RFC's Lieutenant-Colonel Burke, the two discussed how best the fund might assist in the training of pilots for the RFC. As a result, Merritt proposed to the War Office that the fund would finance the training of 120 pilots a year up to a level of thirty hours in the air (well beyond the certificate standard). This offer, welcomed by Lieutenant-Colonel Marindin on 18 February 1916, was the basis upon which the fund was first organized. The Governor General agreed to act as patron, and eventually Merritt secured every provincial Lieutenant-Governor as a vice-patron. The trustees included Lord Shaughnessy, Sir Henry Pellatt, H. Bell-Irving of Vancouver, and A.G.C. Dinnick, a Toronto investment banker. Merritt served as honorary secretary, but was in fact the real driving force behind what he termed 'the movement.'[12]

Such an assemblage of influence, spearheaded by a person of impeccably Conservative antecedents, would be difficult for the government to ignore. To be certain, however, Merritt laid the groundwork for a newspaper campaign. In late March 1916 an editorial entitled 'Aviation,' clearly based upon information obtained from Merritt, appeared in the *Toronto World*. Its first sentence was sufficiently unpalatable for the acting Minister of Militia and Defence to refer it immediately to his staff:[13] 'Almost daily there is coming to hand the evidence that the Government of Canada is doing less than it ought to do to increase the aviation forces which are of such vital importance to the army at the front.' The editorial continued: 'At Ottawa the authorities who have power appear to be deaf to all representations on the question. The authorities who have no power are precluded by their position from expressing their views.* ... Canada is behind every other place in the world in aviation. Deplorable as this must be felt to be by all patriotic Canadians, there does not at present appear to be any way of remedying it except by private effort ... It is not long since Australia made an offer of a complete squadron for the Royal Flying Corps ... Yet the government will not budge ... as a nation we are not doing as much as the little Island of Mauritius, which raised $25,000 in three weeks by public subscription for the presentation of aeroplanes to the war office.'[14] At the same time that he launched this flank attack, Merritt also wrote directly to the Prime Minister, inviting him to join with the Canadian Aviation Fund in establishing as many as five aviation schools in Canada, the government to contribute $20,000 for every $40,000 raised by public subscription.[15]

The Prime Minister seems to have urged the militia department to find some means of placating Merritt without actually adopting his ambitious programme. After consulting with Stanton, Gwatkin suggested that the government pay $100 to persons qualifying for pilot certificates at Canadian aviation schools, to be paid when the candidate obtained a commission or enlisted in the RFC. This was approved by the Militia Council on 19 April, subject to a further condition contributed by Borden himself that bound every recipient 'to become a member of a Canadian Flying Corps should one be organized in Canada' after the war.† Stanton's opinion that this would 'go a long way towards encouraging aviation, and be the foundation of a Canadian Flying Corps in the future' was surely an exaggeration. The step taken was a small one, and had been wrung from the government only as a result of Merritt's campaign.[16] In the House of Commons on 14 April J.D. Hazen, Minister of Marine and Fisheries and of the Naval Service, speaking

---

* This probably refers to Colonel Maunsell.
† The council met under Borden's presidency. Borden noted that 'Hughes was much exercised.'
  Robert Laird Borden, *Robert Laird Borden: His Memoirs*, Henry Borden, ed. (Toronto 1938), II, 564

on the naval estimates, gave a concise summation of the position of the Cabinet with respect to aviation. In replying to W.F. Maclean (South York), who favoured government encouragement to the aircraft manufacturing industry in Canada, and also 'a corps of flying machines manned by Canadians and men trained in Canada' for coastal defence, Hazen stated: 'So far as Canada is concerned, the opinion of the military experts is that, for its own purposes, there is very little need for a flying corps at the present time. The only service which they could render would be, perhaps, to observe what was going on along the coasts of the Atlantic and the Pacific, and that is not considered very necessary at the present moment.' He went on to outline the assistance the government was giving in qualifying candidates for the British flying services. While he thought the work of Merritt and his friends was 'worthy of all possible praise,' he saw no grounds for large government expenditure unless 'a use might be made of these young men who are being turned out from these aviation schools in large numbers at the present time.'[17]

Merritt recognized that, for the time being, the concession he had won was the most that could be looked for from government. Though he continued to write about aviation to Borden and Gwatkin, he now concentrated upon publicizing the importance of military aviation through press stories, speaking engagements, and newspaper advertisements soliciting contributions to the Canadian Aviation Fund. Merritt was careful in his advertisements not to raise questions about government policy, though readers of them may well have asked themselves why, if aviation was so significant, their government was taking no obvious action in the field. A typical advertisement, featuring a picture of a Zeppelin being brought down in flames by a BE2c, included this message:

FIGHT OR PAY!

HOW YOU CAN HELP THE FIRING-LINE AT HOME

You can help to win the war if you must stay at home! Thousands of good money was poured out for machine guns but it did not add one machine gun to the firing line which would not otherwise have been there! The British War Office has asked for ten expert fliers a month. They want help. They need aviators. Canadian boys are now being trained by the Canadian Aviation Fund to the highest standard yet attempted on this continent. This cannot be done without money. Can you, at home, make better use of money than having a Canadian boy represent you in hurling bombs on German Zeppelins or disclosing the whereabouts of army corps or batteries of the foe?[18]

Merritt's publicity campaign helped stimulate a number of newspaper editorials on the subject of aviation during 1916. Most came from journals hostile to the government, yet they constitute evidence that the public was becoming aware of the air war and of the government's reluctance to take any positive part in it. In the view of the *Toronto Star*, Canadians would have cause to regret 'that Canada did not more fully engage in this arm of war service.' Canadian aviators 'do not form part of our army at the front; they are not attached to our expeditionary forces.' Canada ought to seize the opportunities that would come from building up an aircraft industry 'in a special and sensational new field,' and should also take steps to ensure that she receive 'the credit that will come from the fine deeds of her sons who fly.' The *Star* found it humiliating that the only aircraft owned by Canada had been presented in her name to the RFC by the people of an English city, 'with the proviso that, when war ends, it is to be sent to Canada where, presumably, it is to be viewed with intense interest by the simple natives.' The *Toronto World* was even more critical. It considered that the attitude of the government towards aviation was 'the strangest phenomenon of the war.' The 'unaccountable stupidity' of the government, and the fact that, so far as the militia department was concerned, 'aeroplanes have not yet been invented,' was deeply frustrating to legitimate Canadian aspirations, 'as we have the national spirit to take hold of such work, and we have the national future which cannot ignore the development of the flying machine commercially which will inevitably follow the war.' The *World* anticipated much subsequent editorializing in believing that Canadian aviators were 'an unrivalled class' because of their 'keenness, dash, independence, initiative and native daring,' and in concluding that 'the meagre grants and the cold shoulder of departments that should be interested will remain as historic blots on the record of the war government of Canada.'[19]

Merritt's work was also having some success in encouraging young men to learn to fly. By July the fund had contracted with the Curtiss School to train a number of pilots to the thirty-hour level, and Merritt was considering whether another school should be opened. He therefore asked Gwatkin whether certain newspaper rumours about the formation of a Canadian flying corps or aviation school had any substance and, upon Gwatkin's denial of any such intention on the part of the government, explained that members of the fund wished 'to bring about the creation of a larger school, on a more favourable site for training – such, for example, as on the large plain at Deseronto.' He told Gwatkin that he had been successful in obtaining a commitment from the Ontario government, and had approached other provincial governments, to give financial aid to the establishment of an inter-provincial school, but 'the whole matter is, and has been, held in abeyance by constantly recurring reports that the Dominion Government is about to install a training school and train aviators for the war.'[20]

This was Gwatkin's first clear indication that Merritt and his friends had been putting together a scheme of considerable potential embarrassment to the government, involving as it did the co-operation of provincial and municipal governments, private individuals, and even the imperial authorities:

... under the impression that the Dominion Government did not desire to go further than their grant of $100.00 per man, we approached the Ontario Government and secured from them a promise of substantial assistance, and have been in touch with other Provincial Governments. With this aid, and municipal and private assistance in connection with the raising of a Fund, we feel satisfied that the education of Aviators in Canada can at once be put upon a very much more satisfactory footing than at present exists. This is, of course, contingent on the Imperial authorities being willing to cooperate by allowing an Officer or Officers to come and take charge of a school, or schools, and perhaps further assistance in allowing some trained Officers in the flying services to come to Canada as Instructors, for which work some of them have already applied.[21]

Gwatkin's response was the startling admission that 'the establishment of a Government Aviation School had been the subject of recent discussions.' It was the major change in government policy that this statement presaged that turned Merritt and his committee from their concern with flying training to other aspects of the aviation cause, chiefly the raising of money for the presentation of aircraft to the RFC. Their work, to an extent even Merritt probably did not realize, had had some influence in bringing about the government's change of attitude.[22]

The complex negotiations which, by the end of 1916, had paved the way for the establishment of the Canadian Aeroplane Company and for RFC Canada were set in motion by A.G.C. Dinnick. Like Merritt, Dinnick was an aviation enthusiast who was disgusted by his government's inaction. He found it absurd that young Canadians could gain entry to the flying services only through the inefficient operations of a single private flying school or through the costly expedient of resorting to an American school. Aviation, he thought, was properly the responsibility of the national government; 'it should not be a question of patriotic inspiration.' Since the federal government, chiefly because of the obstruction of the Minister of Militia, refused to take up its proper role in the field, Dinnick was determined to bring pilot training under some alternative form of governmental control. After the War Office had responded positively to the fund's offer to train students to an advanced level, a public meeting of the trustees and others was held in March 1916, at the Canadian Military Institute in Toronto. At that meeting Dinnick was elected chairman of the fund's Ontario committee. Unlike Merritt, he believed that an appeal to the federal government was useless. Instead, he immediately left for England to enlist the help of the imperial authorities.[23]

Dinnick was attentively received in London. On 6 April, through the agency of Marindin who was evidently still intrigued by Canadian possibilities, he had an interview with Sir David Henderson, the Director General of Military Aeronautics. Two days later he saw Admiral Vaughan-Lee, who arranged for him to visit the Royal Naval Air Service training station at Chingford in the company of Captain Elder, an officer who knew the Canadian situation from an earlier visit. At a subsequent meeting at the War Office attended by Brancker and by Captain Vyvyan of the Admiralty Air Department, Dinnick believed that 'an understanding was arrived at' with respect to a Canadian aviation school. At the very least, there was enough interest for Vaughan-Lee to agree to divert twenty training aircraft to the proposed school from those on order in the United States.[24]

The plan Dinnick had unfolded was a simple one, based essentially on the thinking of the Canadian Aviation Fund, but including a role for himself perhaps not contemplated by his colleagues. He proposed that the RNAS and RFC jointly establish an aviation school in Canada, and held out the prospect that financial assistance would probably be forthcoming from the Ontario and other provincial governments. Aircraft for the school would be obtained, at cost, from a factory financed by the British government. Dinnick further proposed that the factory be built upon land he owned in North Toronto, that he manage the enterprise, and that he be given an option to buy the plant at the end of the war. He assured the British authorities that no political objection would come from Ottawa, since the Canadian government would bear no financial burden.[25]

Sir David Henderson immediately referred Dinnick's proposals to R.H. Brand, the representative of the Imperial Munitions Board at the Ministry of Munitions in London. He asked Brand whether, in the view of the board, it was desirable to build aircraft in Canada, and if it was, whether Dinnick or the IMB should supervise their manufacture. Brand relayed these enquiries to Ottawa, and on 5 May J.F. Perry replied that the IMB was 'strongly in favour' of the idea of a factory, that Dinnick, though of sterling reputation, had no manufacturing experience, and that the Canadian government was being approached to find out whether it was prepared to assist. At this point Dinnick ceased to be an important factor, though some weeks were to pass before he was to know it.[26]

The initiative passed to the Imperial Munitions Board, which throughout the course of the ensuing negotiations remained a consistent and even enthusiastic proponent of the idea of a Canadian aviation factory, but to a much lesser extent of a flying school in association with it. As an agency of the British government, charged with the procurement of war materials in Canada on the most favourable terms, the IMB saw financial advantage in building training machines. But for at least some of the board's officials, there were political questions at stake in the issue, particularly with respect to the United States. Both Brand and Perry had been members of Sir Alfred Milner's 'kindergarten' in South Africa, a group largely composed of Oxford-educated young Englishmen with upper-class backgrounds. Though members of the group went their separate ways in business, finance, and government at the close of their South African experience, their tutelage under Milner ripened into a continuing association as the nucleus of the Round Table movement under the guidance of Lionel Curtis. Milner's central belief had been in the superiority of the Anglo-Saxon civilization, or race as he termed it, an idea at the heart of the Round Table mystique of the British Empire. Above all, the movement sought to promote imperial unity and to counter the political, economic, and military threats posed by rivals to British supremacy. Before the war the Round Table had gained adherents in the self-governing dominions, and its members constituted a private network of considerable dimensions and some influence.

The coming of the war provided an opportunity to put into practice at least some of the aims of the movement. The IMB was a case in point. When the Shell Committee, established by Sir Sam Hughes to manufacture munitions for Britain, got into serious difficulties in 1915, the British government despatched W.L. Hichens, chairman of the great Cammell-Laird shipbuilding and manufacturing group, to straighten out the munitions supply organization in Canada. Hichens had been one of Milner's kindergarten and was a prominent member of the Round Table group. He was accompanied to Canada by R.H. Brand. It was upon their recommendations that the Imperial Munitions Board had been established in the first place, and its chairman, the Toronto financier and businessman Joseph W. Flavelle, appointed. Flavelle was already known to Hichens and Brand as a member of the Toronto Round Table group. J.F. Perry became the financial member of the board, based in Ottawa, and Brand its representative in London at the Ministry of Munitions.*[27]

It was natural, therefore, that the approach taken by the IMB to the question of Canadian aviation policy should reflect, in part at least, Round Table views. That approach was first laid out by Perry in a series of telegrams to Brand on 9 May. IMB officials, he reported, had inspected the Curtiss factory in Buffalo and its Toronto branch plant, and had found that the Admiralty had placed orders to the value of $12 million with the American firms. 'We see no reason,' Perry stated, 'why this business should not be largely transferred to Canadian National Factory in the course of 12 months if Admiralty and War Office [are] prepared to cooperate.' If the IMB took over the Curtiss plant in Toronto, it could then be expanded to accommodate fresh British orders.

Perry saw the flying school, in effect, as an appendage to the factory, and was confident that it could be organized without difficulty. There was 'plenty [of] good material available' in the way of young Canadians anxious to fly, and perhaps the Canadian government might be tapped to provide hangars. But the school, like the factory, should be an imperial operation with its entrants 'regularly enlisted and under military discipline.' The Canadian government, he thought, was favourable to the plan, but the IMB view was that it did not seem necessary to rely upon it 'for direct financial assistance.' Perry therefore urged Brand to see Henderson and A.J. Balfour, the First Lord of the Admiralty, and to '... impress on them importance strategically even more than commercially establishment of aeroplane manufacture in Canada now instead of using British orders solely to build up great plants in foreign countries. Curtiss plant have been building up out of our war business and there is no earthly reason why we should not do this in Canada and gain advantage ourselves ... if [the Admiralty] flood American plant with orders without any compensation or previous arrangement U.S. firms will then snap their fingers at us and difficulty of establishing Canadian plant will be enormously increased ...'[28] To Perry the issue appeared an imperial, not primarily a Canadian matter. Indeed, he specifically advised against a factory financed or controlled by the Canadian government, which in his opinion would lead to interdepartmental disputes, delays, and poor management. His argument, that 'it is deplorable' that the British government 'should continue building up industries in foreign countries which could be equally well conducted within the Empire,' might well bring benefits for Canada. But it left no room for such manifestations of national feeling as the creation of a Canadian flying service.[29]

In short order Brand found that the flying school, to which Perry had given little attention, was in fact a major obstacle to any agreement. Neither the War Office nor the Admiralty was prepared to finance and operate one, though they were both willing to supply instructors and aircraft and to absorb the product, for which they were ready to pay a grant to Canada for each pilot enlisted. On turning to Sir George Perley, Brand found the High Commissioner even less inclined to be help-

---

*   It is not known whether the Vice-Chairman, Charles Blair Gordon, a Montreal manufacturer, had any connection with the movement. The most recent study is J.E. Kendle, *The Round Table Movement and Imperial Union* (Toronto 1975).

ful. Perley confirmed that Canada would welcome an aeroplane factory, 'to which no doubt a school would be attached,' but that the government had no intention of launching either. A Canadian-run school would be virtually the equivalent of a Canadian air service, to which Ottawa remained unequivocally opposed. In taking this position Perley was merely relaying a message he had received from Borden on 19 May. He advised Brand, in his dealings with the War Office and Admiralty, not to raise the question of a school at all, at least until a factory had been decided upon. Brand, convinced that the factory and school were inextricably linked, believed that the project was dead.[30]

It could only have been with surprise that Brand learned from Perry that the Canadian Prime Minister had been acting upon the advice of the IMB in Ottawa. According to Perry, Borden 'wants factory started under management of Board. Canadian Government do not wish to be tied up with private enterprise such as McCurdy's, and this is why they have discouraged High Commissioner who recommended McCurdy's scheme and asked him to leave matter in our hands ... We strongly recommend starting factory.'[31] The Canadian government would furnish $75,000 towards the buildings for a flying school. The school itself might be operated by the board, perhaps with instructors from the RNAS and the RFC.[32]

Brand knew that McCurdy was in London trying to obtain new orders for Curtiss, but he seems to have been unaware of the extent of his designs. As well as seeking advantage for his company, McCurdy was trying to get out of the flying school business, a concern that had brought him little profit and much trouble and criticism, especially when student pilots had been left high and dry when the school closed down in the late autumn of 1915. In March McCurdy had told A.E. Kemp, the acting Minister of Militia, that he could no longer accept full responsibility for students who, while waiting their turn to fly, might spend as much as six months in Toronto with meagre financial resources. He had suggested to Kemp that a better alternative would be to establish an aviation branch in the militia department to take over responsibility for flight training. Successful candidates might be given a commission 'in the Canadian Air Corps, from which the British Army or Navy could draw.' Though such a corps would be nothing more than a temporary war measure, amounting to a training organization and a reinforcement pool, it could 'easily be later moulded into a permanent branch of the service.' Naturally McCurdy hoped to sell Curtiss aircraft to the Canadian air arm, but on the face of it his proposal was feasible.[33]

Despite his distinguished contributions to early Canadian aviation, McCurdy in some ways was an unfortunate advocate of the idea of a Canadian flying service. Inevitably his motives in promoting the idea were suspect in the minds of politicians, because he so clearly stood to gain by it. Moreover, his tactics were frequently unwise and not always overly scrupulous. He displayed, in short, a distressing tendency to play both ends against the middle. On 11 April he had a long interview with Sir Robert Borden in which he reiterated the ideas he had put to Kemp and asked for the Prime Minister's support in his quest for new aircraft orders in London. Borden gave him a letter of introduction to Sir George Perley, in which he noted that McCurdy was 'a member of the well-known Nova Scotia family,' and said vaguely that 'he has suggested to us the establishment of a

Canadian Air Service and we have that subject under consideration at the present time.' The government, of course, was considering nothing more than Merritt's proposal for help to flying schools, but McCurdy was able to build much upon Borden's sentence.[34] To Sir George Perley he provided a free interpretation of it, and Perley immediately set about putting his government's new air policy into effect. On 4 May he cabled Borden: 'Regarding establishment air service and complete training by Canadian Government McCurdy thinks you would welcome official suggestion to that effect from Imperial authorities. Am inclined to think they would approve. Am making private inquiries please cable fully your wishes.'[35] While awaiting detailed instructions from Ottawa, Perley took McCurdy on the rounds of London offices. Doubtless British officialdom was perplexed to receive yet another Canadian proposal, but under such auspices, who could question its legitimacy? On 8 May the two met Sir David Henderson, and Perley immediately cabled Borden that Henderson would welcome a Canadian government flying school: 'although he would not be inclined to make a suggestion to the Canadian Government in that direction,' Perley judged, 'it would receive his cordial approval and cooperation if put forward by the Canadian Government itself.'[36]

All this was too much for Borden. He turned Perley's communications over to Loring Christie, legal adviser to the Department of External Affairs, and a man upon whose incisive intelligence he was coming increasingly to rely. As Christie noted, the main question raised by the affair was not McCurdy's tactics, but whether or not 'it is intended to establish a Canadian Flying Corps during the war.' Christie brought a fresh mind to this issue, but little else. He had no special knowledge of aviation, and his only recourse was to turn to General Gwatkin for advice. The Chief of the General Staff's response was pungent and predictable: 'Mr. McCurdy has an axe to grind, and, not without success, he has tried to bluff the High Commissioner.' Gwatkin assured Christie that he had discussed the whole question with the representatives of the RNAS and the RFC, 'and we are all agreed that for the present it would not be advisable to establish in Canada anything in the nature of a Canadian Flying Corps.'[37] Christie fleshed out this judgment with arguments already becoming familiar. Canada, by lending assistance to British recruiting and by granting a gratuity to successful pilots, was already making the best possible contribution. No experienced senior officers were available to command a Canadian air arm. Aircraft for such a force could only come from Curtiss, and 'it is not unfair to say that this consideration points to a prominent motive in [McCurdy's] and the Company's efforts.' Moreover, the Curtiss aircraft was a foreign machine; the 'resources of the Empire' should be used 'for the Empire.'* Christie then summed up his findings: 'In short, the con-

---

* As for McCurdy himself, Christie was damning. 'Mr. McCurdy has apparently conveyed the impression to Sir George Perley that he had reason to believe that the Canadian Government would welcome an official suggestion from the British Government that an air service should be established here. It seems pertinent to recall that Mr. McCurdy has before this displayed a tendency towards misrepresenting or overstating to one Department of the Government statements made to him by another. The file discloses several instances of this and the resultant confusion. A somewhat similar instance occurred last year when in interviews given to the press he intimated that the Canadian Government were responsible for the plight in which certain aviation students at Toronto found themselves when the approach of winter stopped the possibility of training at Toronto and left them in a difficult position.'

clusion of everybody seems to be that the needs of the war are not such as to demand the immediate organization of a distinct Canadian flying service, and that it is therefore better to wait until it has a fair chance of being established on a sound basis when a trained personnel will be available and the conclusions drawn from the experience of the war will have been more carefully considered and formulated.'[38]

Christie's report contained no argument in favour of an air service, for he had no evidence upon which to construct one. Undoubtedly senior officers of the Canadian Expeditionary Force could have provided much information on the role of aviation in war, but their advice was not sought. Nor, probably, was Christie aware of the existence of Brigadier-General D.S. MacInnes, the Canadian officer associated with the RFC from its inception and at that time Director of Aircraft Equipment at the War Office and Henderson's chief aide on the technical side. If Christie knew of the Australian government's decision to look after its own by forming an Australian flying corps, his report was silent on the subject. His advice was conventionally sound, and the Prime Minister accepted it. Borden despatched a curt message to Perley, disavowing McCurdy's statements, reiterating the Cabinet's strong opposition to a Canadian air service, and instructing the High Commissioner to leave the whole matter of aviation in the hands of the Imperial Munitions Board.[39]

At this point, with Dinnick eased out and McCurdy discredited, the IMB ought to have had a clear field. That it did not was owing to the creation in London of the Air Board, whose civilian members knew nothing of the parties involved and little of the objects of the IMB. As a result, the whole charade was run through once more. Under the presidency of Lord Curzon the Air Board held its first meeting on 22 May, and immediately thereafter found itself enmeshed in the complications of the Canadian question.

The IMB was first off the mark. Brand briefed Curzon and Sir Paul Harvey, Secretary to the Air Board, on the nature of the IMB and its interest in Canadian aviation matters, and warned them about Dinnick and McCurdy. Dinnick was able to marshal support from political friends in London, one of whom pointedly stated that he was 'absolutely genuine, and is not simply a representative of an American firm.' For his part, McCurdy proposed to Harvey that Curtiss should be given orders to enable it to expand production to 400 aircraft a year. In addition, he was prepared to manufacture engines as well, provided he could finance the necessary plant with an order for 1000 of them. According to Harvey's notes, McCurdy believed that 'no private company should run a school in war time,' and that Borden was 'interested in flying service & Govt if pushed from here would adopt Canadian Flying Service.'[40]

It did not take the new Air Board long to dismiss the two Canadians. Despite his friends, Dinnick was soon written off as an enthusiast whose plans were 'childishly optimistic and altogether too vague.' McCurdy ruined what slight chance he had of a fuller hearing by an injudicious interview published in the *Daily Mail*. In it he was alleged to have said that Canadians had been agitating for a separate flying corps for some time, and that, though diffident about bringing it before the British government, Borden and a majority of the Cabinet were also in favour. The only obstacle was British officialdom, and therefore he had come to England to lay the whole matter before the Air Board. Though McCurdy apologized for this clumsy attempt to force their hand, board members decided to 'decline to embroil ourselves' in the tussle between the two Canadians, and told them both that future negotiations were to be pursued exclusively with the IMB.[41]

The task of the Air Board was now to co-ordinate the desires of the Admiralty, the War Office, and the Treasury in order to put together a proposal that the IMB could negotiate with the Canadian government. It had accepted the IMB's case that 'it is desirable to foster the aeroplane industry in Canada' rather than in the United States, and was satisfied that the IMB, 'who appear to be a very competent and trustworthy body,' could be relied upon to deal effectively with Ottawa.[42]

More than a month elapsed before the Air Board could secure agreement upon a proposal. The Admiralty had backed away from the factory concept because, from the RNAS viewpoint, 'there would be no advantage in the establishment of a National Factory in Canada.' The War Office, on imperial grounds, supported the factory and was ready to place an initial order for 200 aircraft worth about $1.5 million. But both services, and not solely for imperial reasons, strongly supported a Canadian government flying school, and were willing to provide enough instructors and aircraft for it to make a start. The RFC was particularly anxious. On 30 June Sefton Brancker circulated within the War Office his foreboding that 'our waiting list in England is growing perilously short, and heavy casualties in other arms will make officers increasingly difficult to obtain.' As usual, Brancker was to be proven correct, and in the long run the reinforcement crisis would change drastically the RFC's approach to the Canadian question. For the moment, however, the departments involved agreed that the major responsibilities ought to fall upon the Canadian government. It would be expected to finance the factory, underwrite the capital cost of the school, estimated at $500,000, and meet its estimated annual operating costs of $500,000. The cost of operating the school would be partly offset by British per capita grants of £250 for each graduate of the Canadian school enrolled in the RFC and RNAS. The Treasury, while authorizing the Air Board to enter into negotiations, expressed some concern about the exchange problems anticipated in the financing of the aircraft order.[43]

Curzon outlined this proposal to Brand at a meeting of the Air Board of 7 July. In return, Brand gave the board its first indication that negotiations with Canada were likely to be difficult. As he pointed out, the Canadians were pleased at the prospect of acquiring a factory and an associated school. The Canadian government was prepared to make some contribution, but it also believed that 'the main burden thereof should rest upon this country,' especially because it could see no postwar requirement for either. He also pointed out that the capitation grants would fall short by at least $150,000 a year in meeting the school's operating costs, though he hazarded the opinion that Ottawa might absorb the deficit since 'the Minister of Militia now admitted the importance of aviation.' As we shall see, Brand had some ground for thinking that Hughes was changing his position, but he was badly off the mark about the school. To the Canadian government, a school was a flying corps in embryo, and quite as unacceptable.

Though Brand had sugar-coated his assessment of the likely Canadian position, the Air Board found it unpalatable. Brancker, who throughout these interminable negotiations proved himself the most level-headed and far-sighted of all the participants, had no doubt of the right course for Canada to follow. To him, it was axiomatic that Canada should bear the major cost of the factory, because it was self-evident that she would need an air service after the war. He was not yet sufficiently disturbed by reinforcement prospects for the RFC, however, to propose a larger part in the scheme for Britain, and indeed observed that the project 'was not of vital importance to this country and has been supported by the War Office largely from imperial considerations.' Nor was the Treasury disposed to make concessions to Ottawa; its representative stated that 'the more we could get the Canadian Government to undertake without our being obliged to buy Dollars for payment the better.' Other board members found it incomprehensible that there had not yet been any direct approach from the Canadian government. Brand was thus forced to point out that Canada had taken no initiative in the matter whatsoever; the whole project had started with Dinnick. This appears to have been something of a revelation. Curzon immediately grasped that the situation was a quasi-diplomatic one. Since it was unthinkable that the Air Board could attempt to 'dictate' a solution to Canada, he suggested that representatives of the IMB, in a semi-official way, sketch out to Prime Minister Borden the nature of the British scheme, and obtain his reaction.[44]

Brand, in consultation with the Air Board, prepared a cable to Flavelle giving the details of the British proposal, and emphasizing that 'although school and factory would be valuable from Imperial point of view, it cannot be said that either [is] indispensable to this country.' On receiving this information, Borden asked for further details. On 18 July J.F. Perry outlined for him the history of the factory scheme and argued that British war orders should be used to build up a Canadian aviation industry, partly because of Britain's foreign exchange problems but also 'on general considerations of defence.' Perry suggested that if Canadian financing was available, the IMB could manage the plant, the British government could guarantee sufficient war orders to keep the plant going, and at the end of the war Canada would have recovered its investment and have acquired a national asset. Almost in passing, he observed that a training school for pilots was 'a secondary matter' which need not be considered until the factory was actually in operation.[45]

Thus stated, the case was thoroughly in accord with the thinking of the IMB, but reversed the priorities of the Air Board. Nor had the British proposal been framed in a fashion to impress its urgency upon Canada. Sir Thomas White, the Minister of Finance, was decidedly cool. 'In view of the employment situation,' he advised Borden, 'I think we should not be justified in making advances for the mere purpose of establishing an industry – especially an industry of the unproductive sort – which after the war may not be needed.' Skilled labour was in short supply and it would be an error to direct some of it into an enterprise 'that is not imperatively required by military considerations.' To White, the factory scheme was a small part of a big problem. British difficulties with respect to the financing of munitions orders in Canada had become acute, and he had been asked by the British Treasury to find $1 million a day to help meet their balance-of-payment liabilities. In these circumstances, negotiations concerning the factory were suspended until after White's visit to London in early August to discuss the balance-of-payments question, but the outlook for the scheme, from the Canadian end, was unpromising.[46]

The British air staff was distinctly unhappy with the manner in which the aviation school issue had been shoved to the background by the IMB, and with the constant delays which plagued the whole question. It was therefore resolved to bypass both the IMB and the Air Board, and to approach Canada directly. On 11 August the War Office (through the Colonial Secretary) formally requested the Canadian government to take under consideration the establishment of a training school on a *per capita* grant basis. The basic proposal was unchanged; Canada was still to absorb both start-up costs and operating expenses. But it was now clothed with a new urgency. The school, the Canadians were informed, was a military necessity, 'owing to the difficulty of obtaining and training sufficient numbers of aviators for the Royal Naval Air Service and the Royal Flying Corps in this country.' Here, then, was a deliberate appeal for Canadian assistance. So far as the RFC was concerned, it reflected a sense of genuine emergency. Brancker's appreciation of a possible manpower crisis had been borne out by the enormous casualties of the Somme battle. Already there had been disturbing intimations from RFC Headquarters in France that a vast expansion of the air arm would be vital to military success in 1917. A further indication that a crisis mentality was beginning to take hold in the air staff, and that the Canadian project had assumed a new importance, was the information given to Ottawa that Captain Lord Alistair Innes-Ker was being sent to Canada to discuss the training plan with the government, and to stimulate an RFC recruiting campaign.[47]

On 21 August Innes-Ker met the Canadians in Ottawa. It was 'a somewhat awe-inspiring business,' he reported to Brancker. The meeting was chaired by J.D. Hazen, Minister of Marine and Fisheries and of the Naval Service, and was attended by Sir George Perley, Loring Christie, C.B. Gordon for the IMB, Colonel Stanton, and Commander R.M.T. Stephens. Innes-Ker found Hazen as hot as the Ottawa weather, 'comparable to Mesopotamia, 92–95 in the shade.' What had rendered the Minister 'most antagonistic' was his belief that a flying school financed by Canada would inevitably be run from England. He 'simmered down,' Innes-Ker thought, when he was told that although the school would be staffed by the RFC and the RNAS, the officer commanding would be a Canadian responsible to the dominion government. This explanation, however, did not meet Hazen's real objection. Prior to the meeting he told Borden that Canadian control over the school would be purely nominal, 'as the War Office and Admiralty would have representatives in Canada for the purpose of selecting the pupils, superintending the training and being responsible for the carrying out of the prescribed tests.' It would be far better for the British to finance and control the school, because the illusion of Canadian control 'would lead to a great deal of trouble.'[48]

According to Innes-Ker, the Canadians also objected because the costs of the school would far exceed the proposed *per capita* grants, and because, in their opinion, a factory was unnecessary to support the school and would be useless when peace came. 'I tried to explain that an Imperial Air Service was bound to come,' he wrote, while Gordon argued that the flying-school costs were scarcely more than those needed to raise a new infantry battalion. Neither idea enthralled the committee, which agreed merely to meet again in a week's time, and in the interim to secure the views of the federal departments concerned.[49]

In the interval Admiral Kingsmill dealt a body blow to the project. In a memorandum prepared for Hazen, but which he promptly (and quite properly) sent to Rear-Admiral Vaughan-Lee as well, he forcefully attacked the proposed Canadian flying school and what he saw as its corollary, a Canadian flying service. Because of the Canadian climate and the lack of experienced air officers, he argued, the organization of a Canadian school would be a long and costly process. He predicted that no pilots would be graduated from such a school in less than a year from its inception, and that the British would find that far better results would be obtained by giving financial help to young men to enable them to train in the United States or Canada. For those misguided nationalists who wished a Canadian flying corps, he had no patience: 'A great plea has been made by certain persons in Toronto that we should have a Canadian Air Service because Canadians want to be known as a Canadian Corps. I think that this is an idea only in the minds of those people who are anxious to be busy and who perhaps have some interest in forming an aviation school in this country for various reasons.'[50] Such people had alleged that the British were sympathetic to the idea of a distinct Canadian service. In refutation, he cited a letter written to Perley by Sir David Henderson in June, in which the head of the RFC stated: 'I do not think it would be advisable to form any Canadian Units. Promotion is very rapid, and squadrons are constantly changing, and it would not tend to efficiency if we were obliged to keep Canadian officers in particular squadrons; nor would such squadrons be really Canadian, as there is only a small proportion of Canadian mechanics in the Corps. Further, my personal opinion undoubtedly is that the more all British born people are mixed up in this war the better. When peace breaks out you will have the nucleus of a very fine Canadian Air Service.'[51] For all these reasons, Kingsmill came down strongly against the flying school. 'I think the thing is madness,' he told Vaughan-Lee.[52]

Kingsmill's broadside determined the Admiralty to withdraw altogether from participation in the Canadian scheme and stiffened the Canadian resolve to have nothing to do with an aviation school. The second conference with Innes-Ker was attended by Hazen, Flavelle, White, Gordon, and Kingsmill. The meeting decided that the school would go ahead only if funded by Britain. Should an IMB investigation determine that there was a requirement to have a factory in connection with the school and that its operation in Canada would be technically and financially feasible, then and only then would the Canadian government consider giving some financial assistance towards its establishment. Beyond this highly contingent position the Canadians refused to go.[53]

At this point the entire project had reached an impasse. Significantly, the Canadians had not been sufficiently impressed by the War Office approach to budge from their decided opposition to direct government involvement in air training. They had displayed no enthusiasm for the factory, and the minimal commitment they were prepared to make was unsatisfactory to the Air Board and the ministries for which it was acting. The IMB, by its persistence in promoting the factory because of the imperial benefits expected to flow from it, had thus far managed to keep the whole question alive, despite Canadian passivity. Between them, however, the IMB and the Air Board had mismanaged the approach to the Canadian government in three ways. They had put forward the scheme in a manner that suggested that a boon was being conferred, a gross miscalculation of Canadian official attitudes. They had assumed that Canada would respond positively to an economic arrangement that would assist the empire rather than the United States; the Canadians insisted on viewing the matter as a business proposition. Finally, they had masked the real importance of the scheme to the war in the air, especially as it concerned the training of pilots. This may well have occurred because IMB representatives were insufficiently aware of the military issues at stake, but in the light of their original approach it is scarcely surprising that the Canadians found the change of emphasis by the War Office unconvincing.

Yet within another three months the British and Canadian governments reached an agreement satisfactory to both, and one which was based upon arrangements quite different from those originally suggested. This came about because events external to the negotiations forced both sides to abandon their original positions. The mounting reinforcement problem would eventually compel the Air Board and the Treasury to alter their views. Quite as important were developments which dislodged the Canadian government from its position of virtual immobility. It was the Canadian stance which crumbled first, undermined not by the air situation on the Western Front but by purely domestic political considerations that the British never quite comprehended.

The first hint that there might be a break in the obstructionist tactics of the Canadians came at an Air Board meeting on 24 August, during a discussion of the Canadian flying school. Henderson told the board that 'Sir Sam Hughes was now taking up the matter, so that it was likely to progress.' As a consequence, he thought, the Canadian government would also have to establish a factory. Henderson's information was correct, to a point, but he and the Air Board were mistaken in their conclusion. It was true that Hughes was actively taking up the question of aviation and in a form that would not require extensive British participation. The perfectly understandable mistake made by the board was to conclude that Hughes represented the position of the Canadian government. Because they did, they failed to give proper weight to Innes-Ker's disappointing experience in Ottawa and waited instead for definite proposals from Canada. Thus on 31 August Lord Sydenham, who acted as Curzon's deputy on the Air Board, informed his colleagues that he had seen Hughes the night before and 'tried to impress upon him the importance of a factory & school in Canada.' On 8 September Hughes made a proposal, either to the board or directly to the War Office, and thereafter British officials assumed that a Canadian plan to take full responsibility for pilot training and aircraft supply was in the making. As late as the first week of October, at the time that the board was informed of the Admiralty's withdrawal from the project, Sir Paul Harvey judged that 'at present the best hope of the fruition of the scheme appears to lie in Sir S. Hughes' intervention,' to which Sydenham replied, 'Yes, we must await Sir S. Hughes' proposals.'[54]

In order to explain the surprising behaviour of the Canadian minister, so utterly at variance with his own record on the aviation question as well as with his government's stand, it is necessary to retrace our steps. It was true that Hughes had become a convert to aviation, but not for any of the obvious reasons which, at that juncture in the war, might have prompted an informed politician to cast aside old prejudices and to adopt fresh ideas.

The agent in his conversion was a personal friend, W. Grant Morden* of Montreal, who virtually browbeat the Minister into a reversal of his stand. Hughes had appointed Morden an honorary lieutenant-colonel in August 1914 and had named him to the Remount Committee. As in so many of the appointments Hughes lavished in the first months of the war, friendship seems to have been the chief qualification: Morden had been 'provisional lieutenant in a Militia cavalry unit but had never trained.' He was a Montreal businessman with financial connections in London and on being posted overseas rapidly built up impressive associations in the political, financial, and military worlds of the capital. He was a man of powerful if diffuse ambitions, and when the termination of his brief sojourn with the Remount Committee threatened to cut short his military career, he was fortunate enough to secure from Hughes appointment as his 'Personal Staff Officer Overseas.' Vaguely attached to the Canadian military authorities in Britain, he was given various instructions by Hughes. 'I was specially authorized by him,' he later stated, 'to make a thorough study of Aviation.' The evidence of his subsequent correspondence with the Minister indicates that there is no reason to doubt this assertion.[55]

Early in his aviation studies Morden formed a relationship with Sir A. Trevor Dawson, one of the directors of Vickers. It was with Dawson's help that he organized a 'demonstration' of two Vickers Scouts at Joyce Green on 4 April 1916. Harold Barnwell, the firm's chief pilot, and an RFC aviator put on an aerobatic show for a number of senior Canadian officers, including Major-General J.W. Carson and Brigadier-General David Watson.[56] Morden's purpose, in what otherwise would appear to have been a pointless display, was revealed in a cable from Carson to Hughes. Morden required the Minister's authority to gain access to aviation data held by the Admiralty and the War Office. His aim, Carson said, was to '... draw up a scheme for establishment of Canadian Air Service both in England and in Canada, for submission to you. I naturally refused to take such a serious step without your approval and authority. Morden states that you have decided to go in for an Air establishment in connection with Canadian Expeditionary Force with himself as Director.'[57] Despite repeated reminders from Carson, the only reply received from Hughes was a promise to 'cable later.' No later message appears in the existing record, nor did Morden then obtain the access he sought.[58]

Morden pursued his studies undaunted. In June he was introduced to McCurdy by Walter Long, the British Colonial Secretary. After some discussion, Morden

---

* Walter Grant Morden was born in Prince Edward County, Ont., in 1880, and was educated at Toronto and Harvard. He died in England in 1932. From 1918 to 1931 he was a Unionist MP for Brentford and Chiswick. He was director of many Canadian and British companies, and was a founder of Canada Steamship Lines. Hughes appointed him to the Remount Committee on 21 September 1914; on 21 October he became second-in-command of the Advanced Remount Depot, CEF. Returning to Canada in February 1915 he was appointed staff officer in England to Hughes on 13 August (PC 1838), and later a member of the Pensions and Claims Board. On 3 April 1918 he was seconded from HQ OMFC to the War Office.

and McCurdy decided to pool their interests. Their scheme hinged upon the creation of a Canadian air service. In Canada it would consist of a training organization equipped with a hundred aircraft and staffed by six instructors drawn from the British air services. This organization would produce a thousand pilots within a year; while they were being trained, ten thousand mechanics would be recruited to keep them in the air when they went overseas. On operations they would fly a fleet of one thousand service aircraft, also built in Canada. Within thirteen months this great new air force would take to the skies against the Hun. Its squadrons would serve under imperial command, but would retain their identity as Canadian units. As Director of the Canadian Air Service, Morden would remain in England, 'in constant touch with the Imperial Air Board.'

Manufacture of both training and service aircraft, and the engines they required, would be carried out in Canada, the airframes to be built by Curtiss and the engines by Canadian Vickers. McCurdy estimated the cost of the proposed air fleet at $10,000,000, 90 per cent of which, he later told Borden, might be met by Great Britain. A hundred training machines would cost Canada $750,000, and to operate the training school another $250,000 annually would be required. When he outlined this scheme to the Prime Minister on 10 July, he urged him to act quickly, for otherwise the Curtiss plant with its highly skilled labour force would have to close down for want of orders.[59] At the same time, Morden was warning Hughes that the IMB idea of a government factory was faulty: 'It would be a fatal mistake to commence a Government Factory to turn out machines. The experience of the Royal Aircraft Factory at Farnborough has been a most disastrous one here. It also discourages independent manufacturers, & the results are of the worst description. I would therefore recommend in the strongest way possible that independent manufacturers should build our machines, and not have any Government Factories.'[60]

This rough-carpentered scheme was put before the Air Board, probably on 20 June. Harvey's notes show that in the form it was then presented, Canada was to bear the whole cost. Brancker's comments upon it were scathing. With a hundred aircraft, plus necessary spares unprovided for in the Morden-McCurdy plan, he estimated that perhaps four hundred pilots could be trained in a year, if twenty instructors and five hundred ground tradesmen were available. No Canadian factories were capable of turning out a thousand aircraft and engines, let alone spares, in a year. Under his critical eye the whole scheme became smoke and idle fancy. Yet the Ministry of Munitions was sufficiently disturbed by the proposal (Morden was, after all, Hughes' staff officer) to cable a summary of this 'very ambitious scheme' to Ottawa. On being confronted with it by the Prime Minister, Hughes denied that Morden had his authority to lay the plan before the British, though he admitted having received a copy of it.[61]

Borden, for whom Hughes had provided ample cause for concern during 1916, must have believed that he had scotched at least one potentially damaging situation. He was wrong. When McCurdy returned to Canada he saw both Borden and White and, ever the optimist, came away from these interviews believing that if the British government were to insist that a Canadian flying corps would be 'of great assistance to the Empire in this war,' the Canadian Cabinet would yield. Only

Hughes could bring this about, however, 'as there seems to be a tendency for the Government at the present time to discourage concerns that are regarded as being organized entirely for war profits.' He therefore cabled Morden that 'conditions here require forcing by General from there on imperative grounds. After which Ottawa may fall in.' This was the signal for the start of an extraordinary campaign, devised by Morden, to bring Sir Sam Hughes round.[62]

In mid-July Hughes had been exonerated by the Royal Commission on shell contracts, and assumed once more the ministerial functions he had given up while the Shell Committee was under investigation.* He promptly left for England, and almost upon his arrival was besieged by Morden. The progress of the affair can be traced in cables exchanged during August between Morden and McCurdy.

On 2 August Morden reported that he was doing well with Hughes: 'his ignorance entire subject appalling but am very confident.' The Minister, he found, had no conception of the growth of the flying services, but he was 'driving it in to him by degrees, and our different friends here are also helping.' One of them was General Watson, who was 'arranging that I can have a good go at him at Bramshott on Sunday.' Once the Minister was won over, Morden thought there would be no trouble with the Air Board, 'provided he backs me up in the way I hope he will do.' On 9 August Morden arranged an aerial demonstration for the Minister, during which Captain K.E. Kennedy performed,[†] while a number of Morden's business friends exercised their persuasive talents. In addition, Morden organized a written campaign. He was able to tell McCurdy that 'Sir Frederick Williams Taylor, John Aird of the Canadian Bank of Commerce, Ashe of the Union Bank, G. McL. Brown of the Canadian Pacific Railway, and other prominent Canadians have all written very strong letters to the Minister urging the establishment of our Air Service at once.'[63]

A story in the Montreal *Gazette* on 23 August gave the first indication that Morden's campaign was succeeding. Headlined 'Canadian Flying Corps Now Seems To Be Assured,' the newspaper account gave chief prominence to Morden's part in the 'movement' for a Canadian air service. Canadians serving in the RNAS and the RFC would form 'a splendid nucleus for a Dominion corps,' while the CEF would 'welcome the cooperation of their own fliers.' Besides, there were large industrial benefits to be anticipated. 'The details of the scheme have been fully elaborated and could be inaugurated, Col. Morden asserts, within a week by

---

* On 28 March 1916 G.W. Kyte, a Liberal MP, had charged that American promoters had made enormous profits from fuse and cartridge case contracts awarded by the Shell Committee. He also alleged that another promoter, J.W. Allison, whom Hughes had appointed an honorary colonel at the beginning of the war, had made use of the Minister's influence to obtain lucrative contracts from the Shell Committee. The Royal Commission cleared both Hughes and the Shell Committee, but censured Allison for deception in his relations with them. See G.W.L. Nicholson, *Canadian Expeditionary Force, 1914–1919* (Official History of the Canadian Army in the First World War; Ottawa 1964), 207

† Captain Kennedy, from Sherbrooke, Que., was one of the officers selected by Morden for his air service. An artillery captain with the 1st Contingent, CEF, he had transferred to the RFC after being wounded in April 1915. He qualified as an observer in June and, after service at the front, trained as a pilot in England and qualified in February 1916. He later served as an instructor with RFC Canada.

sending to Canada officers and men already selected, all of whom, with three exceptions, would be Canadians. Col. Morden says the scheme had the support of Sir Robert Borden and Sir Sam Hughes, but the Imperial authorities have not yet approved of the financial proposals.'[64] This newspaper despatch probably caused the Prime Minister some disquiet; a copy of it is to be found in his papers.

Borden would have been much more disturbed had he known of a meeting held at the War Office on 26 August. It was attended by representatives of Australia, South Africa, and Canada; its subject was the arrangements necessary for 'the acceptance of RFC Squadrons from the Dominion Governments.' Grant Morden was the Canadian representative, a status he could only have achieved through Hughes. The dominion spokesmen discussed with Brancker and other RFC staff officers such matters as officers' pay, efficiency badges, and distinctive insignia, but spent more time upon the organization and conditions of service for dominion air units. Morden's remarks show that his earlier plan had been much reduced in scale. The minutes record that 'Colonel Grant Morden stated the ability and willingness of Canada to supply eventually 4 Service Squadrons and 2 Reserve Squadrons.' As he outlined the Canadian proposal, the first two service squadrons would emerge from a Toronto reserve squadron, and they, plus a reserve squadron to replace wastage, would proceed overseas. The next two squadrons would then be formed in a similar manner. Brancker warned him that since wastage in training was 10 per cent and on operations was '240% in pilots,' the manpower demand would be heavy. With respect to the Canadian proposal, the meeting agreed that Canada would supply Curtiss aircraft for the reserve squadrons, but that the British government would equip the service units. Specific financial details were to be settled later.[65]

Clearly Morden had made great strides. He did not, however, relax the pressure upon Hughes. On 29 August he gave an elaborate dinner in honour of the Duke of Devonshire, shortly to go out to Canada as Governor General, with Hughes sharing the place of honour with the Governor General designate. Among the glittering guest list, which included General Sir William Robertson, Admiral Beresford, Walter Long, and a number of peers, were men who had a strong interest in aviation, such as the Earl of Derby, Lord Montagu of Beaulieu, Lord Sydenham, Sir Trevor Dawson, and the Premier of Ontario, W.H. Hearst, who had become one of Morden's backers. Doubtless Morden deployed this company, in part, to persuade the Minister to take the final plunge. On 4 September he told McCurdy that he hoped 'to get things definitely fixed up next week.'[66]

At some point between this date and 8 September Morden's campaign came to fruition. Sir Sam Hughes committed Canada to Morden's scheme, or a version of it (no document is extant). On 8 September the War Office wrote Hughes officially 'in connection with the offer of the Dominion Government to raise certain Royal Flying Corps Squadrons and place them at the disposal of the Imperial Government.' The Minister had clearly taken it upon himself to reverse the standing policy of his government, but he neglected so to inform his colleagues. All he told Borden about aviation was contained in a cable of 9 September, informing the Prime Minister that 'General Sir David Henderson and General Brancker, heads of Army Air Service, have each consulted me urging formation of Reserve Air

Squadron.' He withheld the letter he had received from the War Office, which confirmed that an offer had in fact been made. A copy of this letter was not received in Ottawa until December, through the High Commissioner. As General Gwatkin then commented: 'until I read the attached correspondence I had no knowledge of the fact that the Dominion Government (which in this connection means, I take it, Sir Sam Hughes) had offered to raise Royal Flying Corps Squadrons and place them at the disposal of the Imperial Government.'[67]

Though Gwatkin may have been in the dark, word that Hughes had made some kind of commitment in aviation soon filtered back to Canada. In some trepidation C.B. Gordon, vice-chairman of the Imperial Munitions Board, fearing that his organization had been outflanked by Morden and McCurdy, cabled to London for more information.[68] On 28 September Perry sent him all he had learned: 'General Brancker informs us that Hughes has now made proposal for establishment of Reserve Air Squadron by Dominion Government. This would necessitate school and would probably include it. Brancker thinks it would also necessitate local factory though latter need not be under same control. Of course if it is intention of Dominion Government to establish Reserve Flying Squadron including aviation school there would be no need to proceed with proposals for separate school.'[69] This news transformed what had been a desultory and unpromising set of negotiations into swift action by the IMB to stave off renewed contracts for Curtiss, and an equally precipitate move by the Canadian Cabinet to head off the Minister of Militia.

On 4 October Gordon reviewed the whole course of negotiations for Hazen and told him that C.S. Wilcox, Chairman of the Board of the Steel Company of Canada, had investigated the feasibility of taking over the Curtiss plant and expanding it. Wilcox was convinced that with $1,000,000 of start-up money from the federal government, and a guaranteed British order, an IMB-operated plant was a workable proposition from which Ottawa would be able to recover its investment. In the light of this judgment the IMB therefore recommended proceeding with the factory, and was confident that if Canada moved to do so quickly the Air Board would be able to find the additional monies needed to meet the deficit of a Canadian-run flying school. The next day Hazen passed Gordon's report to Borden, and asked that it be brought before Cabinet for early decision.[70]

While this was going on, Hughes was preparing himself to face his colleagues on the aviation question. On 9 October he and McCurdy had a long discussion. In answer to a series of questions posed by the Minister, McCurdy prepared a report, delivered the same day, which gave a synopsis of the current state of aviation in Canada and Britain, provided a summary proposal for a Canadian air service and a critique of state-controlled factories, and attempted to forecast the probable postwar importance of aviation in Canada. Among other things, McCurdy informed Hughes that Curtiss Aeroplanes Ltd was now wholly Canadian owned and was about to reorganize under dominion charter. In the postwar period this Canadian company, if suitably supported during the war, could take the lead in manufacturing aircraft for timber ranging, fire patrols, air mail, and northern exploration. During the war a Canadian air service, employing Curtiss-built aircraft, would rescue Canadian aviators from the situation they were now in, having 'entirely lost their Canadian identity and Canadian pay.' 'It is a matter of extreme regret among Canadian pilots,' he asserted, 'that they are officered directly by English, and that they do not receive promotions to which they are entitled, and they all feel they would work to much greater advantage if organized into a Canadian Corps, Canadian officered and under Canadian control.' This was, as McCurdy was aware, no more than the principle for which Hughes had stood with respect to the CEF. He therefore concluded: 'I feel, Sir, that if you personally undertake the organization and control of a Canadian Air Service that it will be a success and will be received by the public with great favour.'[71]

It does not appear that Hughes was given an opportunity to fight for a Canadian flying corps. The government made its decision on 12 October not in Cabinet but in a sub-committee of it, probably chaired by Hazen and from which Hughes may well have been excluded. It is unlikely that his presence would have made any difference. His activities in connection with other aspects of his portfolio had already caused great apprehension within the government, especially to Borden, and had fatally undermined his position. His known advocacy of a Canadian air force was, by itself, now sufficient to kill the idea. The fact that Hughes had allowed himself to become involved with individuals in whom the government had no reason to repose confidence made the possibility of an aviation initiative from him doubly dangerous. An open-ended arrangement with Curtiss, and with Vickers in the wings, could conceivably mushroom into the same sort of scandal created by the shell contracts. Hughes could not be trusted, and therefore he must be forestalled.

We learn of the Cabinet's motives from a synopsis that Flavelle found it necessary to give the Air Board on 27 October. In explaining the action taken by the Canadian government, he stressed that Hughes' position was pivotal. When the Minister of Finance had learned that the factory and flying school were indeed considered matters of high importance by the British authorities, he had concluded that it was his duty to find the money for them. He and other ministers, however, had thought it 'undesirable that the School should be placed under the Minister of Militia; they were afraid of the situation which might result.' Even before Hughes returned from England, therefore, they favoured a solution in which Ottawa would advance money for the factory on the understanding that Britain would conduct and administer the school. When Hughes returned to Canada, and appeared about to follow up the intervention in aviation policy he had already made, Flavelle had learned that 'for the purpose of preventing any fresh departure they had passed an order-in-council approving the above scheme.'[72]

From the point of view of the British authorities the Canadian decision had not advanced matters very far. When they first heard of it Flavelle had not yet made his explanation and they were inclined to put their faith in Hughes. As Harvey observed, were Hughes' offer accepted, 'the Canadian government will require a School of its own and would no doubt like to see it constructed at our expense.' In agreeing with this point, Sydenham added that he was opposed to starting an imperial school in Canada for reasons of general policy.[73] Even when Flavelle disabused the board of its reliance upon Hughes, it refused categorically to approve the Canadian plan. Its members were willing enough to guarantee orders for the factory, but they were unwilling to endorse a British-run school. As Sydenham put it, according to Air Board minutes, '... the proposed treatment of the School question was the result of political considerations. He asked whether, apart from these, the Canadian Government really desired that the Imperial Government should construct and administer a School in Canada. Was it a wise step to start an Imperial Institution in the heart of Canada which would remain Imperial property after the war? ... the projected Factory would be run by Canadians; the School on the other hand would be run by Imperial Officers. He pointed out the difficulties and friction which might arise if the discipline of the School were under British authority.' Flavelle unavailingly protested that the situation was 'abnormal' and that it was 'impossible to dissociate the question from the political considerations of the moment.' The Air Board was ready to recommend to the Treasury that the factory proposal be accepted, but Hughes was Canada's problem. Canada must operate the school, by whatever means it chose, and the British government would pay a *per capita* grant that would cover all operating costs.[74]

In this decision the board had the backing of the War Office, or at least of General Henderson. Though he had not been present at the 27 October meeting, Henderson registered his disapproval of the Canadian stand shortly thereafter. He thought the financial terms far too favourable to Canada, and for a somewhat different reason sided with Sydenham about the school: 'He thought it most undesirable that he should be under any obligation to accept the pilots turned out by the school. Local pressure would be brought to bear upon the authorities of the school to accept all sorts of people who might not, in all cases, be desirable members of the Royal Flying Corps.' A Canadian rather than an RFC school was the only proper solution. The RFC should retain the right to weed out rough colonials, or, as Henderson put it, 'the power of requiring the rejection at any stage of any pupil.'[75]

Flavelle was in a quandary. He recognized that the British were reluctant because 'they fear possible conflict with Canadian military authorities,' and especially with Hughes, but at the same time he knew that the Cabinet would never approve a Canadian air service, especially one run by the militia department. In cabling Ottawa a resumé of the British position, he therefore sought from Canada a declaration that would dissolve British scruples and apprehensions: 'This scheme seems ... necessarily to involve further negotiations with Militia Department. Do you know attitude of Hughes towards scheme as it stands and would you think it wise to put these considerations before Prime Minister. If he thinks there would be no difficulties with a school under direct control of British Government please let me know.'[76] His answer came in little more than a week. On 11 November Borden told Gordon that there would be 'no difficulty' with a British-run school. 'So far as we can judge,' Borden wrote, 'there is no probability of any friction with the Department of Militia and Defence in carrying out that arrangement.'[77] There was a good reason. On that day Sir Sam Hughes had defiantly submitted his resignation to Borden.

In the exchange of letters preceding Borden's request for Hughes' resignation, the only specific complaint the Prime Minister had to make with respect to the Minister's recent activities was his establishment of a Sub-Militia Council in

England without Cabinet authorization and without informing his colleagues. Yet the Minister's unilateral initiatives in aviation policy were certainly subsumed under what the Prime Minister described as his penchant for administering his department 'as if it were a distinct and separate government in itself.' Hughes' meddling in aviation had contributed to the final exhaustion of his leader's almost superhuman tolerance of his erratic behaviour.[78]

Lord Sydenham found Borden's blanket assurance insufficient and, indeed, incomprehensible. How could the Prime Minister of a self-governing dominion accept calmly the re-establishment in his country of an imperial command not subject to the control of his own government? Even if the Canadians were negligent with respect to the principles underlying the evolution of colonial self-government, ought Britain to be negligent as well? He wondered, in fact, 'whether, since the withdrawal of the Imperial Garrison from Canada, it was possible for us to exercise command over British troops in Canada at all.' The situation was fraught with dangers. Canadians were notoriously an unruly people, and Canadian pilots had shown themselves less amenable to British discipline than was desirable. 'There had been troubles with Canadians here,' he observed gloomily, 'it would be worse over there.'[79]

It was General Brancker who brushed aside these constitutional niceties and persuaded his chief to grasp the nettle. As early as 20 October, irritated beyond measure by the endless confusions of the Canadian negotiation, and more and more concerned about the prospects for the RFC's order of battle on the Western Front in 1917, he had burst out to Harvey: 'We *must* do something. We have played with this matter for more than 18 months now. If only it had been boldly handled originally we should have obtained much benefit by now.'[80]

The following day Brancker began to apply pressure to Henderson, pointing out that 'increased establishments are being demanded from the Expeditionary Force, and we must start a training establishment in Canada at which the full benefit of the Canadian and American training machines can be reaped.' General H.M. Trenchard was insisting upon an increase of twenty service squadrons and thirty-five reserve squadrons; 'the matter is very urgent, as in order to obtain output both of pilots and equipment by next spring, the work must be put in hand at once.'[81]

As we have seen, Henderson was not yet convinced by these arguments at the time of the meeting with Flavelle on 27 October. Shortly thereafter Brancker drew to his attention the likelihood that twenty of the thirty-five new reserve squadrons would either have to be located in Canada or elsewhere outside Britain, because new training sites at home were no longer readily available. Moreover, given the heavy demands upon British aircraft production, it was vital to make use of North American capacity for the manufacture of training machines. Obviously it would be much cheaper to use these machines in Canada than to pay the costs of shipping them across the Atlantic. These cogent arguments wrought a remarkable transformation in Henderson's views. He was impressed by Brancker's reasoning with respect both to the shortage of British training sites and the economic advantages of employing North American production in Canada, but what he found most persuasive was the very scale of the training operation now deemed essential because of the crisis faced by the RFC on the Western Front. The job in prospect, he thought, was simply too big to be entrusted to the Canadians. At a conference with Air Board members on 20 November he announced his conversion: 'If the proposed training establishment were to be on this scale it would have to be run by the Imperial authorities. We should have to send over so many senior officers that they would work better under the Imperial Government ... If of the proposed dimensions, the school would not be workable in Canadian hands.'[82] When the full Air Board met on 22 November to consider this change in the position of the War Office, nothing further was heard of Sydenham's constitutional scruples. As Lord Curzon observed, 'a new situation had arisen' because of Haig and Trenchard's demand for twenty more service squadrons. The board therefore accepted the recommendation of Henderson and Brancker that it was 'indispensable' that so large a training organization should be under imperial control. By early December Curzon had won over the Treasury by stressing the size of the project and the military emergency which rendered it necessary.[83]

On 23 December the Canadian High Commissioner was officially notified that a large British training organization was about to be established in Canada. This was the inception of the RFC Canada scheme, the single most important development in Canadian air history to that point. Canadians, under British tutelage, were now to be trained for the air war, and for the air age to come, not in hundreds but in thousands. For the future of Canadian aviation, RFC Canada was a priceless benefit. For the Canadian government of the day, it was an expedient that satisfied British military requirements and yet averted the creation of a Canadian air force under unwelcome auspices.[84]

It was in this fashion that the Canadian government arrived at its posture of colonial dependency in the field of aviation. Many factors had brought this about. The government and its advisers were ignorant of the new significance of air power. Nor had the advocates of a Canadian role in aviation been impressive, appearing to Borden and his colleagues either as well-meaning nuisances or as self-seeking promoters. The Imperial Munitions Board, so forthright and aggressive in safeguarding what its members saw as imperial economic interests through the project of a Canadian aircraft factory, had not thought it worthwhile to fight for a Canadian air service. Sir Sam Hughes, both through his tactics and by his association with a scheme that his colleagues understandably saw as politically dangerous, had eliminated what faint possibility existed that the government might reconsider its priorities. The Prime Minister had given no leadership, but had sought instead the least burdensome form of commitment. As a result, the tide of events at the front had overtaken Canadian indecisiveness and Canada became host once again to an imperial military presence, on a scale the Cabinet could hardly have anticipated. Yet, up to the final stage of negotiations, had any minister other than Hughes taken up the idea of a Canadian flying corps with the same vision, determination, and principles that marked the government's attitude towards the CEF, there is no reason to suppose that a Canadian service might not have been inaugurated in 1916. Whatever the preferences of Sir David Henderson, given the Australian precedent and the urgent needs of the RFC, the British were in no position to refuse.

4

RFC Expansion and the
Canadian Air Training Organization

The origins of the large training organization which functioned in Canada for the last two years of the war were unusual, and its status was anomalous, but it was to have a vital influence upon the war in the air and a decisive impact upon the development of Canadian aviation.

RFC Canada (or the 'Imperial Royal Flying Corps' as its stationery and advertisements proclaimed it) enjoyed the co-operation and support of the Canadian government, but was quite autonomous. Though the appropriate Canadian authorities were kept informed of its activities and requirements, the commander of RFC Canada was responsible directly to the War Office (later the Air Ministry) in London. Drawing recruits from across the country and from the United States, the British organization was concentrated in Ontario, with headquarters in Toronto. Never large – its staff and trainees numbered just under twelve thousand at the Armistice – it was certainly sizable in terms of existing military aviation establishments, and rapidly produced an elaborate supporting structure.

RFC Canada's unique situation, the fact that it was competing with the Canadian Expeditionary Force for recruits at a particularly difficult period of the war, and its deep involvement with the United States armed services and American trainees might well have brought tensions with its Canadian hosts. Frictions did occur, but on the whole the relationships between this extension of the British services and the government and people of Canada were remarkably free of difficulties and misunderstandings. The government had gone some way to satisfy critics of its policy towards aviation by providing financial assistance for the aircraft plant and land and facilities for flying schools and airfields, as well as direct help through the militia department. Among the general public there was increasing acceptance of the importance of aviation to the war, and some pride in the part Canadians appeared to be taking in it. The training scheme had its critics, but they were few in number.

A good measure of the success of the RFC Canada undertaking must be assigned to the diplomatic and executive abilities of its commander, Lieutenant-Colonel (later Brigadier-General) Cuthbert G. Hoare. He had received his pilot certificate in 1911, and as a captain was one of a small group of officers belonging to the recently-formed Indian Air Corps (prior to 1911 he had served with the 39th Central India Horse) stationed at Farnborough when war broke out. Posted immediately to an RFC squadron in France, he later commanded 7 Squadron at St Omer and by 1916 had been given command of a wing.

When Hoare was selected to head RFC Canada, many of the details of the Canadian enterprise had already been worked out in a series of meetings of the Air Board, attended by representatives of the Imperial Munitions Board. It was decided that only the preliminary stages of ground instruction and flying training would be given in Canada and that trainees would complete their preparation in Britain. At a meeting on New Year's Day 1917 it was agreed to send out an advance party as soon as possible, to be followed at intervals by groups of experienced officers and men who would form the nucleus of the twenty training squadrons and the supporting ground units. The RFC commander would then be responsible for recruiting not only the cadets he was to train, but also the bulk of the people needed to operate the plan.[1]

Beyond this, Hoare was given virtually a free hand. Though Toronto had been tentatively selected as his headquarters, since the plant to manufacture his training machines was located there, he was free to shift elsewhere if he wished. The Imperial Munitions Board was to handle the building of airfields, but it was Hoare who had to decide how many he needed and where he wanted them. In his hands were left such details as the number of hangars, barracks, messes, and other buildings needed, as well as type of construction. He had to set up accommodations for his staff, to form stores depots and other supporting units, devise a recruiting campaign, and provide for rations, uniforms, medical facilities, and the other multitudinous details demanded by the scheme. All these things he and his staff accomplished with remarkable speed.

The staff Hoare brought with him was almost entirely British. It included Major Dermott L. Allen, formerly a pilot with 3 Squadron, who became Hoare's chief staff officer in Canada. The only Canadian in the initial group was Lieutenant John K. Aird of Toronto. His father, Sir John Aird, general manager of the Canadian Bank of Commerce, had taken considerable interest in air matters; Aird's brother was in the Royal Naval Air Service; and Aird himself had been flying with the RFC since early 1916. He took a leading part in the inauguration of flying training and later commanded a training squadron.[2]

Hoare put his staff to work during the passage to Canada, and together they planned a rough schedule for the development of the training scheme. When the group landed at Saint John, NB, on 19 January, Hoare went to Ottawa while the rest of the party proceeded to Toronto. In the capital Hoare met officials of the militia department, the Imperial Munitions Board, and other agencies. His most important meeting was with General Willoughby Gwatkin. The Chief of the General Staff proved to be one of the best friends that the RFC had in Canada and came to the rescue of Hoare and his staff on several occasions when they found themselves in potentially serious trouble. Hoare's first encounter with Gwatkin, though, was not auspicious: 'My first meeting with General Gwatkin on arrival in Canada ended rather abruptly. He asked me how many men I should require. On my saying 500 for a start he said I couldn't get 500 in six months and added "The best thing you can do, young man, is to turn around, go straight home, and tell them you've been sent on a fool's errand." Somewhat nettled, I replied that the time to go home would be *after* having tried, and not *before*. On that we parted. We subsequently became the best of friends and he helped us in every possible way. Neither of us ever referred again to our first meeting.'[3]

Despite this gruff beginning Gwatkin wasted little time in demonstrating his intentions to help the RFC in Canada. Hoare got to Ottawa on the night of 21 January and on the 23rd Gwatkin advised the commanders of his Military Districts of the RFC commander's arrival and instructed them to be ready to 'render him all assistance' possible. When Hoare left for Toronto on 25 January he took with him firm assurances that the militia department was ready to lend assistance with recruiting, administrative services, and provision of accommodation and other facilities for his men and that government land would be made available for his aerodromes. Headquarters space was obtained in the Imperial Oil Building at 56 Church Street in Toronto and the RFC Canada was in business.[4]

It was hoped that flying training might start by the beginning of April but there was much to do and many problems to solve. The countryside was covered with snow and the ground was frozen, adding to the difficulties of immediate construction work. The only aerodrome in the region was the small field at Long Branch with its several hangars. This was the site that had been used by the Curtiss School during 1915–16 but it was not suitable as a major flying field for the RFC. Other aerodrome sites had to be selected and readied and aircraft had to be obtained. The bulk of the personnel needed to operate the training scheme and to permit its development still had to be recruited, quite apart from the pilot trainees themselves.

Hoare's first job was to select sites for his airfields. The RFC's plans called for the twenty training squadrons to be grouped in four wings, each comprising five squadrons. Three of the wings were to be located in the general area of Toronto and it was tentatively proposed that the fourth would be situated in some part of the country where winter flying was feasible, the west coast being favoured. Each wing was to consist of one or two aerodromes, complete with facilities for the men and the machines.[5]

On 26 January, the day after arriving in Toronto, Hoare went to look at Camp Borden, which had been suggested by the militia department as a possible site for his first wing. The outlook was not promising. As he set out to cover the seventy miles from Toronto, the ground was snow-covered and the temperature well below freezing. Hoare was accompanied by Major-General W.A. Logie, General Officer Commanding Military District No 2 in Toronto, and several other staff officers, and when they reached Angus they found the branch railway line to Borden closed for the winter. The party had to break trail by sleigh and it took nearly two hours to cover the five miles from the rail line. In the circumstances, Hoare was not enthusiastic about what he saw when he arrived at Camp Borden. He inspected the area 'so far as possible' but it was difficult to determine how flat the ground was. Over much of it stumps protruded through the snow. Hoare had heard that the whole district had a 'very bad reputation for sandstorms.' Nevertheless, on the advice of General Logie, Hoare decided to accept the site. The land belonged to the Canadian government, which offered it rent-free to the RFC. It was close to Toronto; a power plant, a sanitation and water system, and a railway siding had already been installed for the thirty thousand troops of the Canadian Expeditionary Force encamped there in 1916. That wintry day in early 1917 was therefore the origin of what was later to become the senior air station of the Royal Canadian Air Force.[6]

Having made his decision, Hoare returned to Toronto and the next few days were busy. On 27 January he wrote several letters to Gwatkin. He wanted to begin recruiting immediately. He wanted accommodation for one thousand men in the Toronto area. He wanted clothing and 'regimental necessaries' for his recruits. He wanted to know whether the militia department could provide medical and dental services for his force and medical examinations for recruits at points across Canada. A cabled request for provision of most of these services on a repayment basis had by this time been received by the militia department and Gwatkin told the British Army Council on 30 January that they would be forthcoming.[7]

The Imperial Munitions Board obtained permission from the militia department to proceed with construction and other work at Borden and contracts for the work were signed on 27 January. Eight days later the rail line into the camp was open and 400 men were at work in freezing weather, clearing stumps from the ground and preparing the area for construction. A week later 1700 men were continuing the work through the night with the help of powerful arc lights. Six weeks after Hoare had inspected the area most of the hangars called for had been finished and enough accommodation was ready to permit a training squadron to form there and start assembling its aircraft. The initial project for the camp was finished on 2 June. Hoare specified that the buildings at Borden were to be of a 'semi-permanent nature' and he arranged for 'the cheapest forms of construction compatible with strength ... giving due consideration for the necessity of heating next Winter.' Despite this and the hectic pace at which the work was carried out, they must have built well, for most of the fifteen hangars put up for the RFC Canada are still in use, serving the Canadian Armed Forces at Camp Borden.[8]

In four months the contractors had erected fifty-seven buildings, cleared and levelled 850 acres and sowed the ground with grass seed, built almost five miles of asphalt road and laid additional sewage pipes and rail sidings. They had installed an electrical system and strung telephone lines to connect the field with Toronto and neighbouring towns. The buildings so successfully developed for the Borden aerodrome served as the standard pattern for subsequent RFC flying fields.[9]

Hoare was much impressed by the manner in which the project had gone ahead. In a report to the War Office he observed that 'work appears to be put through at a speed here which is unknown in England.' The rate at which the work was carried out was the result of efforts by several agencies and individuals, including the militia department, No 2 Military District, Toronto, and Colonel R.S. Low of the Ottawa firm of Bate, McMahon and Co, who had been in charge of the building of Valcartier, Connaught Ranges, and other military camps. Much of the credit must also be given to the Aviation Department of the Imperial Munitions Board, which was created to look after many of RFC Canada's needs, including construction and purchasing. Joseph Flavelle, chairman of the board, had initially selected E.R. Wood to head this department, but ill-health forced his almost immediate replacement by F.W. Baillie in January 1917. When Baillie became president of Canadian

Aeroplanes Ltd soon after, his assistant, G.A. Morrow, took over the Aviation Department.[10]

The Aviation Department, which had its headquarters in Toronto, provided almost all RFC Canada's physical and financial needs, including the aircraft made by Canadian Aeroplanes Ltd. It assisted Hoare and his staff in locating suitable sites for the aerodromes and schools, made arrangements for their use, provided designs for the many types of buildings required, and supervised or carried out the construction work. The department also looked after the arrangements for the many premises that were rented and leased and handled what modifications were needed. Building construction was at first placed by the department in the hands of contractors but from the autumn of 1917 it took over direct control of this work. The construction work force hit a peak of more than 2800 men during the spring of 1917. At the Armistice the department's engineering section still had more than 2200 workers on its payroll.[11]

Even before construction at Borden had begun, other aerodrome sites had been inspected and procured. Deseronto, 130 miles east of Toronto, became the site for a new flying station, with two airfields, one on the Rathbun farm and the other, the Mohawk field on the Tyendinaga Indian Reserve, made available by the Department of Indian Affairs. North Toronto was a third section. Its fields were at Armour Heights and at Leaside, where land was obtained without charge from the town of Leaside and from the York Land Company. On 26 January a contract was signed for the construction of a large new plant in Toronto to house Canadian Aeroplanes Ltd. Before January ended arrangements were also made for RFC Canada to use the Long Branch field.[12]

The progressive establishment of the twenty training squadrons, to be known as 78 to 97 (Canadian) Reserve Squadrons, was undertaken as 'nucleus flights' of experienced officers and men arrived from Britain at intervals determined by forecast availability dates of aerodromes and aircraft. This phased programme unfolded with remarkable smoothness, though Hoare was quite ready to take shortcuts when he felt them necessary. On 24 February, less than a month after his arrival in Toronto, with the new airfields under construction and members of the first nucleus flights still on their way across the Atlantic, Hoare made the sudden decision to start flying. This resolve, taken at a peaceful Saturday lunch, so shook his staff that one member of it was able to recall Hoare's words clearly: 'We have two machines at Long Branch. We have enlisted some cadets and airmen. Why the hell are we not flying? I want flying training started by Monday!' On Monday a party led by Lieutenant John Aird began the assembling of the first JN4 at Long Branch, and on 28 February the unit, called 'x' Squadron, began flying. By the middle of March there were nine cadets undergoing flying training at Long Branch.[13]

Hoare was to deviate from orthodox routine many times during the period of his command, almost invariably with profitable results. At the same time, however, he developed an administrative structure which was both efficient and elaborate – necessarily so because functions carried out by the War Office in Britain for comparable training formations had to be done by RFC Canada itself. The organization was run from its headquarters in Toronto. Two branches reported directly to

Hoare: Air Organization, headed by Major Allen, which was responsible for administration, training, and personnel, and Aircraft Equipment, headed by Hoare's brother, Lieutenant-Colonel F.R. Gurney Hoare, responsible for technical and supply matters.

Out of this headquarters was created a series of units which underpinned the operations of the training scheme and grew with it. The Stores Depot, which acted as the general receiving, distributing, and clearing house for RFC Canada, was formed in February 1917. During that year it acquired or had built a number of buildings close to Canadian Aeroplanes Ltd on Dufferin Street. As well as handling and storing material, its personnel inspected shipments purchased by the Munition Board's Aviation Department and forecast the requirements of the many units within RFC Canada. The depot handled over twenty thousand different items from socks to aeroplane propellers. At the time of the Armistice its staff consisted of seventeen officers, 217 other ranks, and 184 women employees.[14]

The Engine Repair Park was formed in the spring of 1917 and at first occupied the quarters on Atlantic Avenue which had been vacated by Canadian Aeroplanes Ltd. The park was forced to train a large proportion of the men it received and this delayed its output of overhauled and repaired engines received from the training wings. Its production began modestly in July 1917 when four overhauled engines were shipped out but thereafter its output rose rapidly, reaching a monthly figure of sixty before the end of the summer. By the Armistice the unit had carried out complete overhauls of 1325 aircraft engines, all but thirty-five being Curtiss OXs, a monthly average of more than sixty-nine. Each such overhaul represented some three hundred manhours of work. RFC Canada, although enthusiastic about the Curtiss OX, considered the cost of engines and spare parts as 'inordinately high' and at times was worried about deliveries. As a result, the Engine Repair Park turned its hand during 1918 to the production and assembly of the OX. Before the war's end a point had been reached where of the several hundred individual parts of the engine, only twenty or so had to be purchased. The remainder were produced by the park and assembly was carried out with the aid of the purchased spares. The park remained at its Atlantic Avenue premises until September 1918 when it moved into larger and better equipped quarters on King Street in Toronto. Uniformed personnel strength stood at 125 at the war's end.[15]

It had been intended originally that repair of aeroplanes would be carried out at the wings. After flying began at the new airfields, it soon became apparent that the wings could not undertake all repairs, particularly major jobs resulting from serious accidents. By the end of July over fifty aircraft had been 'written off,' and to meet this exigency a centralized repair unit was formed in early August, quartered in the Central Prison buildings. The Aeroplane Repair Park's job was to handle the remains of serious accidents and to carry out major overhauls, required after a machine had logged four hundred hours flying time. This latter task called for a complete dismantling of the aeroplane. All parts were inspected and replaced or repaired as necessary before reassembly of the machine. The unit's formation greatly reduced the number of aircraft 'written off,' all machines damaged beyond the repair capability of the wings being sent to the repair park. Such machines were, like those undergoing a 400-hour overhaul, completely dismantled. All parts were then inspected, feasible repairs were carried out, and the various items were then used for rebuilding machines for issue to the wings. Ultimately a salvage rate of 60 per cent was attained from badly smashed aircraft sent to the park. The Repair Park was able to make many JN4 parts itself and during the early summer of 1918 its salvage and production of components reached a point where the training scheme no longer needed to order complete JN4s from Canadian Aeroplanes Ltd. Instead, the aircraft plant supplied the repair park with only a limited range of parts and the park was able to produce sufficient JN4s to meet the training scheme's requirements. The unit's activities reached a peak in July 1918 when it turned out 130 rebuilt machines during the month. The Aeroplane Repair Park shared to some degree with the flying units the responsibility for aircraft service-ability, which throughout 1917 averaged less than 40 per cent. Thereafter it rose steadily and eventually stood at a highly creditable 79 per cent.[16]

A Mechanical Transport Section was formed in Toronto during March 1917 with a staff of one officer and fifteen other ranks. The section was responsible for providing motor transport services for the entire training scheme, subsections being established at the wings and other outlying units. Normal repair work was handled by these wing and other MT units while the central establishment in Toronto undertook major overhauls. The section's first home was in rented pre-mises in the Wolseley Garage and in August 1917 the unit moved into a new and larger building on Dupont Street. Still larger quarters were obtained on Avenue Road in October 1918, the Dupont Street building being retained as a repair shop. By that time the section operated about four hundred vehicles, including staff cars, trucks of various types, gasoline tank trucks, fire engines, motorcycles, and ambu-lances. The last-named were heavy specially-built vehicles on Packard chassis and they carried axes, saws, heavy wire cutters, fire extinguishers, and other equip-ment for extricating the occupants of a crashed aircraft. Regulations called for one of these ambulances to be positioned on the aerodrome's edge at all times when flying was under way and it was not long before the cadets dubbed the vehicles 'Hungry Lizzies.'[17]

A Royal Engineers' Section was also formed as part of the headquarters in 1917 to look after repair and maintenance of the many buildings and facilities RFC Canada was acquiring. Two engineer officers had already been sent out, shortly after the advance party arrived. Major Osborne C. Macpherson, who was an 1891 Royal Military College graduate from Ottawa, commanded the section in 1918. Ground Tradesmen attached to the section were posted to the several stations of the RFC, where they served under Royal Engineer NCOs. The RE Section, with an authorized establishment of 135, lasted until August 1918 when, because of a shortage of men of military age with the required trades, its duties were taken over by the Aviation Department of the Imperial Munitions Board.[18]

Some prominence has been given to the organizational structure of RFC Canada because its nature reflects not only the normal outlines of any military training establishment, but also the special requirements stemming from the impact of warfare upon a new form of technology. The purpose of the organization was twofold: to teach young men – most of them knowing nothing of aviation – to fly and then to turn them into combat flyers in numbers sufficient to meet the inexor-able demands of the air war.

The instrument chosen for the purpose was the JN4, to be built by Canadian Aeroplanes Ltd. The company began production in space leased from the John Inglis Company, previously occupied by Curtiss Aeroplanes and Motors Ltd. Meanwhile, construction of a new plant on a nine-acre site on Dufferin Street began in February, and Canadian Aeroplanes was in its new quarters by early May. Well before this, in January, the prototype was test flown by Bert Acosta, a former instructor at the Curtiss School, and was formally accepted by the RFC.[19]

The JN4 was a two-seater biplane powered by the Curtiss OX, a water-cooled V-8 engine produced in the United States. It had a maximum speed of about 75 mph and cruised at 60 mph, with an endurance of slightly more than two hours. The aircraft was twenty-seven feet in overall length with an upper wing span of slightly more than forty-three feet, the lower wing being nine feet shorter. The JN4 was a modified version of the American Curtiss JN3, incorporating a number of design changes requested by the RFC. For example, the lower wings were fitted with ailerons rather than relying on wing-warping to provide directional control. Sitka spruce and ash were used for the construction of the fuselage and the wings, the tail assembly was made of tube steel, the engine cowling and cockpit coaming were aluminum.[20]

The designation chosen for the Canadian-built aircraft has caused confusion ever since, because the Curtiss Company in the United States had also developed an aircraft called the JN4. Successive American versions were designated alphabetically, from the JN4A through to the JN4H. To the Americans, the Canadian 'Jenny' was the Canadian JN4D, and the American barnstormers who flew it after the war called it the 'Canuck.'[21]

For the whole period of RFC Canada's operations the JN4 remained the training aircraft. This had not been the original intention. The DH6, specially designed as a primary trainer, had gone into production in Britain early in 1917. Both the Air Board and the Aeronautics Branch of the War Office considered the DH6 superior, particularly since it could be fitted with any of the several types of engines with which pilots had to familiarize themselves during the training process. Moreover, British officials believed that the production costs of the DH6 would be less. As a result, the Imperial Munitions Board was asked to take preliminary steps for the manufacture of the DH6 in Canada.[22] But Canadian Aeroplanes Ltd was not receptive to a production changeover, and Hoare, once he had assessed the qualities of the JN4, preferred it to the DH6. Though Hoare did not regard the JN4 as an ideal trainer, he found it 'fairly suitable.' By the end of July 1917 CAL had produced more than 150 JN4s for RFC Canada.[23]

Important though aircraft, airfields, and ancillary establishments were, the key to the success or failure of RFC Canada lay in recruiting. The scheme could hardly have been launched at a less propitious time. During 1916 Sir Sam Hughes had committed Canada to a fifth division for the Canadian Expeditionary Force, and had spoken rashly of a sixth. By October all thought of a sixth division had disappeared as it became evident that voluntary enlistment would not be sufficient to sustain five divisions in the field. Sir Robert Borden's fateful decision to bring in conscription was not taken until May 1917, but well before then Hoare became aware that enlistments for the CEF were virtually at a standstill. He concluded that the country had been 'worked out.'[24]

Pilot trainees, as it happened, were not hard to get at first. In August 1916 the RFC had dropped the requirement that candidates must have a pilot's certificate, and as a result Lord Innes-Ker, without any real recruiting effort, had been able to secure a large number of recruits, only some of whom had been sent overseas. There was thus a backlog of cadets eager to begin flying training.

The real difficulty lay in finding the required numbers of ground tradesmen. General Gwatkin had told Hoare as much during their initial meeting. Hoare estimated his needs at some three thousand skilled tradesmen, if the full complement of twenty training squadrons and their supporting units was to be achieved. Engine fitters and riggers were most wanted, but altogether the RFC needed men in more than twenty skilled trades. Such men were much in demand by industry and were getting good wages. What the RFC had to offer was enlistment for the duration, including the obligation for overseas service if required, at rates of pay from $1.10 a day for third-class air mechanics to $2.80 for warrant officers, 1st class, plus separation allowances that ranged from $20 to $30 monthly.[25]

The militia department could not be of much help. Hoare reported to the War Office that he had 'attended a Conference of 200 Officers ... and the opinion is unanimous that as far as the Militia is concerned Recruiting has ceased, and nothing short of the introduction of the Militia Act will enable them to supply further drafts.' There was nothing for it but to launch a recruiting programme in competition with industry and the militia department, and Hoare decided to embark upon one, while warning the War Office that 'there will be very great difficulty.' RFC recruiting offices, equipped to give trade tests, were opened in Toronto and Hamilton before the end of January and further offices were later opened in Montreal, Winnipeg, and Vancouver. In the circumstances of the time Hoare's pessimism was understandable but in the event the RFC did remarkably well in the recruitment of ground tradesmen, mustering some six thousand of them by July 1918.[26]

The key unit in the handling of cadets was the Cadet Wing, established on 27 February 1917. As originally constituted, the wing both received cadets and gave them ground school training, whereas in Britain the Cadet Wing, School of Military Aeronautics, and Armament School were quite distinct. Hoare's Cadet Wing was a rough equivalent of the aircrew facilities provided by manning depots and initial training schools in the British Commonwealth Air Training Plan of the Second World War. From the first, a close association was formed between the Cadet Wing and the University of Toronto. The first group of cadets were in fact attached to the Canadian Officer Training Corps at the university. Hoare and Allen visited Sir Robert Falconer, the president of the university, to inquire about the possibility of using university buildings and facilities for the training scheme. 'At first the temperature of the discussion was glacial,' Allen recalled, 'but gradually Sir Robert thawed as he began to get the request into proper perspective. Eventually he agreed in principle. As we walked out Frog [Hoare's nickname] said: "I felt just like I did when I was sent for by the Headmaster at Harrow."'[27]

The Cadet wing began with a class of fifty-two and a small staff, which introduced the cadets to drill and military discipline and taught them such subjects as artillery observation, aircraft rigging, and aero-engines. At this stage the training was severely limited by the lack of instructors and suitable instructional material, though Hoare was promised more instructors both by the War Office and by the Canadian militia department.[28]

Shortly after both ground and flying training had begun, Hoare secured a modification in the programme which drastically altered the nature of the RFC scheme. When he left England he had been instructed to bring his cadets up to seven hours' solo time; they would receive advanced training overseas. In mid-February, after taking stock of his situation, he informed the War Office that once all training squadrons were in operation, their capacity would outstrip the likely supply of cadets. He recommended that a full training programme be instituted, so that graduates of it could go directly to service squadrons after arrival overseas. To get round the lack of an advanced training aircraft, he suggested that Canadian Aeroplanes might be able to manufacture a single-seater of advanced type, using the Curtiss engine. The obvious economies of this proposal found favour at the War Office and Hoare was told to recast his plans so that the entire range of pilot training then being offered in Britain could be undertaken in Canada. It was assumed that Canadians graduating from the scheme would need only a few hours' training on the service machines of the squadrons to which they were posted.*[29]

The new arrangements meant longer and more varied flying training for cadets, as well as a much more comprehensive ground school curriculum. In making the needed changes, Hoare showed his usual administrative flexibility, creating new units at modest levels of staffing and training content which could be rapidly expanded when the promised instructors and material came from England. To train cadets not merely to fly but to become competent in cross-country flying, wireless, aerial photography, aerial gunnery, and artillery co-operation required specialist instructors from Britain. In the interim, the amount of flying time given students was increased. After a group of officer and NCO gunnery specialists arrived in April, a School of Aerial Gunnery was formed on 1 May at Camp Borden. Its beginnings were small. A first class of eighteen cadets did a limited amount of ground range firing on one of the school's two machine guns. As equipment came in from Britain and new instructors were trained, the school expanded. No 80 Squadron was designated as a gunnery unit and aerial firing with Lewis guns started in early June. Camera guns were received in July. By autumn the course was set at three weeks, and cadets were doing aerial firing with fixed Vickers machine-guns after synchronizing gear had been designed for the JN4 so that the gun could be fired forward through the propeller arc.[30]

A similar process marked the expansion of ground training. Since it was impossible to establish immediately a school of Military Aeronautics on the model of Reading and Oxford in England, Hoare formed an interim school at the University of Toronto, under Second Lieutenant Brian A. Peck, a Montrealer who had served

---

* The War Office eventually turned down Hoare's proposal for a more advanced trainer. This meant that the full training programme had to be carried out with an elementary trainer, the JN4. Probably because of this, graduates of the RFC Canada scheme needed more than 'a few hours' of service training. Fifty Canadian trained pilots who arrived in England in late July 1917 underwent at least two months more training before joining service squadrons in France.

with the Canadian Expeditionary Force for two years before joining the RFC and flying briefly on the Western front in the fall of 1916. Only on 1 July, the necessary staff having arrived, was this school designated No 4 School of Military Aeronautics. Henceforth it provided the full range of ground instruction then considered requisite, covering aircraft engines, rigging, wireless, artillery observation, machine-guns, aircraft instruments, and bombs. The school also supervised the trades training given at Lippincott Technical School in Toronto to many of the men who had enlisted for ground duties.[31]

By this time the RFC's use of university accommodation had expanded to include Burwash Hall and the East Residence of Victoria College. To lessen congestion, the Cadet Wing was detached from the School of Military Aeronautics and relocated at Long Branch field, where incoming cadets lived under canvas throughout the summer. In its new form the Cadet Wing introduced recruits to military discipline and law, provided drill instruction and physical training, and gave elementary instruction in topography and wireless.[32]

As we have seen, flying had begun at Long Branch in late February. Though the RFC did not officially take over its new aerodrome at Camp Borden until 2 May, flying there began much earlier. The nucleus flights for three squadrons arrived in early March; on 16 March 79 Reserve Squadron was formed at Camp Borden, and a headquarters staff moved in the same day. The erection of the first JN4s to be shipped to Borden dovetailed neatly with the arrival of the first group of cadets on 28 March; flying began two days later. By 10 April there were five squadrons in being, 78 to 82, much understrength when formed but building up as graduates were retained to serve as instructors and as other officers and men were obtained from British and Canadian sources.[33]

Camp Borden, the largest of the RFC's flying establishments, was the first of the new fields to commence training, but the others were not far behind. At Deseronto, where construction did not begin until 20 April, wing headquarters moved into town on 24 April. On 1 May 'X' Squadron moved from Long Branch to Camp Rathbun; by the middle of the month five squadrons had been formed. 'X' Squadron shared Camp Rathbun with 86 Squadron, while 83, 84, and 87 were at Camp Mohawk. For the summer all ranks slept under canvas.* Flying began at the two North Toronto fields in early July, the squadrons consisting of 'Y' Squadron from Long Branch, 88, 89, and 90 Squadrons, which had been formed at Deseronto before moving, and 91 Squadron.[34]

By the time the first unit moved to North Toronto all cadets under flying training were receiving the extended aerial instruction now demanded of RFC Canada. Deseronto and North Toronto concentrated upon primary instruction, while the squadrons at Camp Borden were assigned specific advanced training tasks. No 80 Squadron continued as an aerial gunnery unit; 78 and 82 Squadrons specialized in wireless and in artillery observation; 79 and 81 Squadrons handled aerial photography and formation and cross-country flying.

---

* They included Captain Vernon Castle who with his wife Irene had made up a renowned dance team in prewar years. Castle, who had Western Front experience, commanded a squadron at Camp Mohawk. He was killed in a Texas flying accident in 1918, but his personality, his pet monkey, and his Stutz Bearcat figure largely in the memories of those who flew at Mohawk in 1917.

As the training scheme moved into high gear it was already producing its first graduates. A group of eighteen had completed training in May and sailed for overseas on 16 June, from which time their appointments as second lieutenants were dated. 'As pilots they are ... far above the average,' Hoare wrote the War Office. 'They have all over 50 hours air experience, a good proportion "loop" well, they have a good general knowledge and I feel sure will be a credit to the Corps.' Five weeks later a second draft of fifty cadets, all of whom had passed through advanced training at Borden, left for overseas, and such sailings soon became routine. Not all graduates departed, however. It was the permanent policy of RFC Canada to retain likely pilots as instructors, and so of the 167 cadets who had completed training by late August, fifty were held in Canada.[35]

RFC Canada had concentrated initially upon the recruitment of ground tradesmen. In May, however, it began what Hoare termed 'a proper campaign' for cadets. Its chief ally was an off-shoot of the Canadian Aviation Fund, the Aero Club of Canada, formed in December 1916 under the presidency of William Hamilton Merritt to 'encourage various forms of aviation, to develop the science of aeronautics and kindred sciences ... to issue pilots' licenses to qualified aviators, and to assist those desirous of taking up aviation with a view of serving in the war.' Through the Aero Club the RFC built a national recruiting organization not dissimilar to that used by the Canadian Expeditionary Force. Citizen committees were eventually established in every community of more than ten thousand (in smaller centres one-man 'committees' were set up) and Canada was divided into five recruiting districts with headquarters at Halifax, Montreal, Toronto, Winnipeg, and Vancouver. Each district had two recruiting officers; candidates were interviewed by the committees and if recommended were examined by the local standing medical board, whose services were made available by the militia department. Those who passed were given transportation to Toronto.[36]

In competing with the army for recruits the RFC had certain distinct advantages. The heavy casualties among military aviators were not nearly so well known as those among subalterns in the CEF. Moreover, military flying still had a glamour that Ypres and the Somme had dispelled for the army. On the other hand, public awareness of the flying services was uneven. There was much truth in Hoare's observation that 'outside of Toronto very little is known of the R.F.C.' Many believed that becoming a pilot was an expensive business, and that it was still necessary to have a pilot's certificate. To dispel misconceptions the RFC launched an advertising and news management campaign with special attention to the colleges and universities. The staff organized press visits to the training camps, prepared press releases and feature stories for the newspapers, and embarked on an ambitious display advertising programme in the press. Whether such advertising was valuable in itself the RFC was unsure, but it 'served to stimulate the newspaper, and thereby helped in the placing of news items.'[37]

RFC correspondence and public pronouncements made clear the kind of recruit sought. Ideally, he should be between eighteen and twenty-five years of age, have matriculated from high school, and have spent a couple of years at university. He should be well grounded in algebra and geometry, be able to 'speak the King's English,' and bear 'the ear-marks of a gentleman.' Above all, he should be 'very keen to join the Royal Flying Corps.' What the RFC was after was a combination of gentlemanliness, educational attainment, mechanical aptitude, and physical excellence, with a measure of recklessness thrown in. As a staff officer told the Toronto *Mail and Empire*, 'the type of fellow wanted as a pilot ... is the clean bred chap with lots of the devil in him, a fellow who had ridden horses hard across country or nearly broken his neck motoring or on the ice playing hockey.' The RFC was to find that not enough of such paragons, whatever their numbers in Canada, were available to sustain the training scheme.[38]

One reason was the counter-attraction of the Royal Naval Air Service. Though its intake in 1917 was little more than three hundred, the RNAS was enlisting first-class candidates and Hoare soon came to believe that the country was too small for both organizations. He was particularly nettled when he learned in April that more naval pilot trainees were being sent to England than RNAS schools could absorb. In a recent draft of sixty-two, only forty were taken, and the remainder were given RFC commissions and sent to the School of Military Aeronautics at Reading.* Hoare feared that such actions would 'put our own cadets' noses out of joint,' especially since the War Office had also agreed to accept, on the same terms, an additional 124 probationary flight officers who were awaiting passage from Canada to England. He agreed with the War Office opinion that the RNAS was recruiting better pilot material in Canada, largely because it could offer immediate appointments as probationary flight officers, rather than the cadetships of the RFC. '... the RNAS take advantage of our publicity campaign,' he said in one of his repeated complaints, 'and without doing a hand's turn themselves can take the pick of our Cadets.' RNAS competition particularly irritated Hoare because for most of 1917 the recruiting of cadets in Canada fell much below his estimates. More and more his thoughts turned to the United States as a possible source, though initially he had rejected any active campaign there because 'there is considerable feeling between Canadians and Americans, and taking American Cadets would not be entirely popular.'[39]

The enlistment of American citizens in the Canadian and imperial forces had been going on since the beginning of the war. The whole subject had been treated with much caution by the British and Canadian governments, since both were wary of displeasing a great neutral power whose friendship was vital and whose adherence to the allied cause was much desired. The policy to be followed had been laid down by Sir Edward Grey at the Foreign Office in the early weeks of the war. It was to respect 'the traditional policy of the United States government.' The statutory basis of that policy was the Foreign Enlistment Act of 1818, which made the recruitment of American citizens on United States soil for service against a friendly state a criminal offence. Not only had the United States strenuously

---

*   Admiral Kingsmill received orders from the Admiralty to halt, until further notice, the shipment of RNAS recruits to England in March 1917. Before receiving the order he had already dispatched the draft of sixty-two referred to, and there remained in Canada a sizable group of accepted RNAS candidates awaiting appointments as probationary flight officers and passage overseas. They were given the choice of waiting in Canada until the Admiralty required more recruits or of going overseas immediately for service as second lieutenants in the RFC. The fifty-five who opted for RFC service were appointed RNAS probationary flight officers prior to embarkation and on arrival in England in May were transferred to the RFC as second lieutenants.

upheld that policy; during the Crimean War it had extended it beyond actual recruiting to the offering of any inducement which would entice Americans to go abroad to enlist. Nevertheless, Grey specifically reserved the right of the British government to accept as a recruit any American citizen who presented himself for enlistment on British territory.[40]

Grey was speaking only for his own government. The Canadian government was informed of the position he had taken when the War Office passed to the Foreign Office an enthusiastic series of cables from Sam Hughes, who reported that 'thousands of Americans' were offering themselves for military service, and that he had 'a plan whereby they may reach Canada voluntarily.' At the same time it was made quite clear that the matter was one which the Canadian government must decide for itself.

The stance Borden adopted was even more cautious than that of the British. He discouraged any enlistment whatever of Americans in Canadian Expeditionary Force units, thus ending Hughes' vision of an 'American Legion' of sixty thousand volunteers. Only when he was assured by Sir George Perley, from London, that Kitchener was anxious to encourage American volunteers did he permit American entry into the Canadian forces. As a result, thousands of Americans entered the CEF in the ensuing years and by 1916 several battalions, exclusively American in composition, were being formed. It was this development, plus the zeal of Canadian recruiters at a number of border points who were undoubtedly luring Americans across the line with a variety of inducements, that brought Borden into conflict with the Governor General in the summer of 1916. The Duke of Connaught believed that any enlistment of Americans was a breach of imperial policy, that in any event it endangered relations with the United States, and that by accepting Americans Canada was putting into uniform untold numbers of German agents. His remonstrances, he complained, had been treated with 'persistent neglect' by the Canadian government.

Responding to the Governor General, the Prime Minister took a high constitutional line. Canada was 'a nation possessing complete powers of self-government,' and its right to enlist American volunteers was incontestable. When Connaught endeavoured to interpose his authority as 'a Field Marshal in His Majesty's Forces,' Borden coolly replied that 'the matters under consideration do not call so much for the exercise of military skill ... as the consideration of international law and the exercise of the common-place quality of common sense.' Nevertheless, he took pains to curb abuses in Canadian recruiting practices which might provoke adverse American reaction.[41] It was into this delicate area that the commander of RFC Canada proposed to venture. The course of action he pursued was a flagrant breach of the policy of both the Canadian government and his own, even though it came after the American declaration of war in April 1917.

In his projections for the air training plan Hoare clearly counted upon American volunteers, who were coming to Canada to join the RNAS and the RFC long before he had arrived on the scene. When the results of Canadian recruiting proved disappointing and when American entry into the war appeared to threaten the end of that source of supply (acceptance of American volunteers might even be forbidden by the War Office), Hoare mounted his own campaign. He had to convince the War Office that the situation was serious enough to give him a free hand and to persuade the right people in the United States not only to allow him to accept American volunteers but actually to recruit them in American territory. He was successful because of his own peculiar position in Canada, his remarkable personal qualities, and the opportunities presented for the exercise of his talents in the enthusiastic and disorganized atmosphere of newly-belligerent Washington.

In June 1917 Hoare told Brigadier-General L.E.O. Charlton, Director of Air Organization and the officer to whom he reported, that the recruiting campaign in Canada was in desperate straits: 'It is essential to take them from the States; this country has been largely drained already, and apart from quality I shall have difficulty about numbers. The fact is that I should have started a Cadet campaign 3 months ago had I known this situation would arise. As it is, owing to my rejections being about 60% and my being debarred from 280 Americans with whom I have corresponded and who were always a blank cheque ready to be filled in, I am short.'[42] Yet a way out of the dilemma was at hand. At the end of May Hoare had received a visit at Camp Borden from Brigadier-General George O. Squier, Chief Signal Officer, United States Army, who commanded the American air service. Squier seems to have fallen under the magnetic spell of Hoare, because during the visit he agreed to the opening of an RFC recruiting office in New York City. On 30 May Hoare cabled the War Office: 'General Squier now staying with me authorizes me to say that there will not only be no objection on the part of the Air Board of the United States of America but he considers it a good arrangement ... If I cannot utilize the admirable material now available in the United States of America the quality of my cadets will deteriorate and I am not yet prepared to say that we can even obtain the quantity sufficient for four Wings in Canada. Colleges are closing down ....'[43] All that was needed, Hoare told Charlton, was the approval of the War Office: 'there is little doubt that if I can be given a free hand I can make all arrangements for Cadets from the U.S. without any friction.'[44]

On the assumption that he would get a free hand, Hoare went ahead with his American arrangements. Working closely with the British Recruiting Mission, established in Washington shortly after the American declaration of war to enlist British subjects domiciled in the United States, he secured quarters on Fifth Avenue in New York City, transferred a recruiting staff there from Canada, posted 'some picked R.F.C. men at the door,' and began quietly to circulate among 'a large number of the best sort of people.' Ostensibly seeking British subjects, Hoare was in fact recruiting American citizens under cover of the British Mission, and with the connivance of American and British authorities. He summed up the position to Charlton in a letter of 28 September 1917: 'The situation is this: the British Recruiting Mission has given a written undertaking not to recruit American subjects; that I can do so is entirely due to personal influence at Washington, and though I think I can carry it through, I cannot possibly give you a definite assurance.'[45]

General Charlton had consented to this scheme at the end of June, but had urged his enterprising subordinate not to relax his efforts to fill the training establishment with Canadians, 'the proper source of supply.' He also requested a forecast of recruiting prospects in Canada. Hoare was not encouraging: 'All estimates break down ... it is a small population in a very big country. I am increasingly doubtful whether they exist in the numbers we require, I do not think it is because they will not come forward. Some of the local committees are excellent, others are lethargic but being voluntary organisations we have to put up with it.'[46] By late September half of Hoare's cadet intake was American. Yet he knew that the New York operation hung by a thread: 'an arrangement which rests on an unofficial and personal basis must be a doubtful factor.' In fact, he had a surprisingly long run. Not until 6 February 1918 did he regretfully report that 'the State Department has been on my track ... I shall have to stop enlisting American citizens as Cadets,' a turn of events he attributed to 'sentiment and Congress.'[47]

It had been a remarkable enterprise. Under the nose of the Canadian government, but apparently without its knowledge, a British officer, with the knowledge and consent of his superiors, had conducted from Canada a quasi-diplomatic operation utterly at variance with Canadian policy, and furthermore, had got away with it. When the Fifth Avenue office closed, the recruiting crisis had passed. Canadians had already begun to enter the RFC in much increased numbers and the need for clandestine measures had ended. It must not be imagined that Hoare had hoodwinked the guileless Americans. His first meetings with General Squier and others concerned with American aviation had been in early April 1917, when he was requested by the British ambassador in Washington to discuss air matters with American officers and government officials. Though the War Office had instructed him not to commit himself, out of these meetings stemmed a number of agreements for mutual assistance, of which the recruiting venture was only a part. For example, Hoare received assurances that there would be no interference with the supply of aircraft engines to Canadian Aeroplanes Ltd. The Americans, for their part, were anxious to profit from RFC training methods. In April Lieutenant-Colonel John B. Bennett, Chief of the Aviation Section, and Major Benjamin D. Foulois, later General Pershing's Chief of Air Service, visited Toronto and Camp Borden to study RFC Canada's structure. They were followed by Major Hiram Bingham, late of Yale and now charged with setting up a preliminary ground training programme, leading a party of eighteen American university professors. After a week in Ontario they returned to the United States burdened with training materials. Shortly afterwards schools of military aeronautics, patterned after the Toronto school, were opened at six American universities.[48]

A much more ambitious form of co-operation arose directly from General Squier's visit in May. For some time Hoare had been concerned that the harsh Ontario winter would severely curtail flying training. He had investigated and rejected New Brunswick as an alternative, because it was 'a wilderness and quite unsuitable, besides being very cold.' British Columbia seemed more promising, despite its heavy rainfall and the scarcity of good airfield sites. After a visit by two RFC staff officers in February, it was decided to lease two properties south of Vancouver, one at Steveston on Lulu Island and the other at Ladner on the south arm of the Fraser River. Though construction was started, the RFC never used either field. A much more intriguing possibility had offered itself.[49]

General Squier had mentioned to Hoare that the military flying schools about to open in the United States were short of instructors and had asked whether RFC

Canada could assist. Hoare leaped at the opportunity for a *quid pro quo*. On 4 June he cabled the War Office for approval of 'a reciprocal arrangement which I can make with Washington by which we would train One Hundred Cadets for them this summer and they will make a winter camp available to us in the States complete with machines.' Hoare's intention was to move the Borden Wing to the United States for a three-month period of training, the wing to use JN4s purchased from Canadian Aeroplanes Ltd by the Americans.* With War Office approval in principle, and support from the Imperial Munitions Board, Hoare left for Washington 'to get everything definitely settled.'[50]

By 22 June Hoare had successfully concluded discussions with Squier and with the Aircraft Production Board, a body of which he was made an honorary member. Hoare had agreed to take a hundred American cadets; in exchange, the Americans agreed to build an airfield in a warm climate to receive an RFC Canada wing. The airfield would be fully equipped according to RFC specifications and would be available for use from December 1917 to the end of February. The only modification made to this plan in the formal agreement reached between the American War Department and the War Office in London was American consent to provide winter training facilities for two wings instead of one.[51]

Hoare's observation of the state of American aviation led him almost immediately to propose a second scheme. The Aviation Section of the Signal Corps, he found, was undoubtedly recruiting excellent material, but the Americans were in no position to train recruits and organize squadrons within a reasonable time. He therefore secured War Office agreement in principle to a proposal that RFC Canada would train sufficient air and ground personnel to organize ten squadrons, that these squadrons would be allotted to work with the RFC in France, and that the United States would be responsible for maintaining them. He assured the War Office that he could so arrange matters that the proposal would appear to emanate from Washington.[52]

On 9 July Hoare placed his proposal before the Aircraft Production Board in Washington. His account of that meeting gives more than a hint of his entrepreneurial style: 'On arrival I was asked to address a meeting of their Signal Officers (as they were called then) and some chief executives of motor industries, etc. I had some ideas of a reciprocal training scheme but had not worked out detail. Before the meeting I had lunch with Col. Hiram Bingham at the Raleigh Hotel, and stimulated with cocktails jotted down some headings on the back of an envelope, Bingham collaborating. This was really where the R[eciprocal] T[raining] scheme originated. This was a great success – everything was agreed in principle and I said on return to Toronto I would elaborate in writing. I may say I pointed out the Scheme would cost them vastly more than us, but they considered that of minor importance.'[53] As finally approved, the scheme provided that the ten American squadrons would be issued with aircraft and other equipment after their

---

* Eventually the United States purchased 680 of the Canadian-built trainers. See K.M. Molson, 'Aircraft Manufacturing in Canada during the First World War,' *Canadian Aeronautical Journal*, V, Feb. 1959, 47–54; M.R. Riddell, 'The Development and Future of Aviation in Canada,' *Journal of the Engineering Institute of Canada*, II, March 1919, 200–8; Hoare to Drew, 26 Dec. 1917, Air 1/721/48/5.

arrival in Britain, and that their establishments would be increased to conform to RFC establishments for service squadrons.* RFC Canada was now committed to the training of three hundred pilots, two thousand ground tradesmen, and twenty equipment officers, in addition to the hundred cadets previously agreed upon. In return, the Americans were to provide three airfields in the southern United States, instead of the one they had previously promised. No evidence has been found to show whether the Canadian government was kept informed of Hoare's transactions, or that it was aware that the first substantial lodgment of American forces upon Canadian soil since 1814 was about to take place.[54]

The first Americans to arrive in Toronto were a small party of United States Navy cadets, included in the programme as a special arrangement.† They arrived on 9 July and were shortly followed by the first drafts of army cadets. Enlisted men did not arrive for more than a month, then drafts of two hundred began to move in at weekly intervals. Before leaving the United States the enlisted men had been organized into squadrons, but the RFC soon discovered that they were raw recruits without basic military training who had been arbitrarily assembled into parties of the required number with scant regard for trade qualifications. Their lack of military smartness, a quality much prized by the RFC staff, dismayed those who met them. On their way from the train to the Recruits' Depot, it was said, they 'just ambled along the road like a baseball crowd.'‡ American cadets presented no particular problem; they were simply incorporated into the training programme, though they were kept together as much as possible. The enlisted men, however, had to be given basic training, trade-tested, redistributed according to the tests among squadrons, and either given on-the-job training or sent to the RFC's technical training establishments.[55]

Meanwhile, preparations had already begun for the move south. RFC staff officers had inspected areas in Florida and Texas even before the first American cadets had arrived in Toronto. Hoare's choice was San Antonio, but American concern about a possible labour shortage there led him reluctantly to accept Fort Worth. Advanced RFC headquarters was established there by a party of ninety-two RFC and American officers who left Toronto on 24 September. They were commanded by Captain Murton A. Seymour of Vancouver, who had begun his aviation career as a student at the Aero Club of British Columbia School in 1915 and had flown with a fighter squadron in France. The first batch of crated JN4s was shipped at the same time. The advance party was followed by the American cadets

---

* It would appear that only two of the ten squadrons flew in France under British control. These two squadrons were attached to the RAF from 20 June and 1 July 1918, respectively, and on 1 November were absorbed into the air service of the American Expeditionary Force. See S.H. Frank, 'Organizing the U.S. Air Service,' *Cross & Cockade Journal*, VII, spring 1966, 66.

† Among their number was Cadet James V. Forrestal, later United States Secretary of the Navy and Secretary of Defense.

‡ Introducing American soldiers to the British Army drill manual had its complications. Major Henry H. Arnold, later commander of the USAAF during the Second World War, was said to have 'exploded with rage when he saw a squadron of good "Dough Boys" doing a very creditable presentation of the British Slow March under one of the Depot Drill Instructors.' A pair of American drill sergeants were shortly posted to the Recruits' Depot. Allen to RCAF Historical Section, 22 July 1962, DHist 76/199

and enlisted men who proceeded in drafts to the Texas fields to continue their training. Grouped into the 17th, 22nd, 27th, 28th, and 139th Aero Squadrons, they left Toronto at weekly intervals commencing on 12 October.* With them went RFC instructional and support personnel, including the staff of the School of Aerial Gunnery. The thirty machines flown by the school were shipped as well, the only aircraft of its own that the RFC took to Texas.[56]

The main RFC move began on 15 November, when the staff and cadets of 42 (Borden) Wing and 43 (Deseronto) Wing pulled out of Toronto aboard six special trains. They arrived in Fort Worth on 17 November. The whole complex there was known as Camp Taliaferro, with three aerodromes, Hicks, Everman, and Benbrook Fields. Everman and Benbrook were occupied by 42 and 43 Wings, respectively, while Hicks Field accommodated the five American squadrons and the School of Aerial Gunnery. As each American squadron completed its training at Hicks Field (the first was scheduled to leave for overseas in mid-December), it was to be replaced by another, formed from American personnel dispersed throughout the RFC units at the other two fields.[†] At the same time, the RFC was to carry on the training of its own cadets in normal fashion, with new drafts arriving from the School of Military Aeronautics in Toronto at phased intervals.[57]

Initially things did not go smoothly. Construction work on the three aerodromes was little more than half completed, the water supply was deficient, one of the fields lacked electrical power, and the sewage systems were not yet operating. Unfinished barracks meant living under canvas. Not until early December were all aspects of the training organization in full swing. Flying, however, began immediately. For example, the School of Aerial Gunnery completed a course at Camp Borden on 30 October, spent two days packing, and left Toronto on 2 November. Its students were in the air in Texas on 5 November, the day after arriving.[58]

---

* Twenty of the US Navy party completed the full syllabus of ground and flying training in Canada. They were the only American pilot trainees to do so.

† The 17th Aero Squadron departed two weeks later than its scheduled date, but the others left on time: the 22nd, 27th, and 28th in January, the 139th, 147th, and 148th in February, and the 182nd, 183rd, and 184th in March. Of these, all but the latter three flew operationally in France: the 17th and the 148th with the RAF and then with the 4th Pursuit Group of the Second US Army and the others with Pursuit Groups of the First US Army. S.H. Frank, 'Organizing the U.S. Air Service,' *Cross & Cockade Journal*, VI, autumn 1965, 267–8. As part of the reciprocal agreement the RFC had agreed to release a number of its experienced American pilots, and five were therefore transferred to the United States Army, where, as majors, they commanded squadrons sent overseas. Curiously enough, two of the five were unquestionably Canadians. Major Harold E. Hartney, given command of the 27th Aero Squadron, was born in Pakenham, Ont., graduated from the University of Toronto and the University of Saskatchewan, and practised law in Saskatoon before going overseas with the Canadian Expeditionary Force. After transferring from the CEF to the RFC, he flew FE2bs and FE2ds in France for eight months before being wounded. Major Laurence C. Angstrom, commander of the 139th Aero Squadron, was born in Toronto. After obtaining his pilot certificate at the Stinson School in San Antonio, he joined the RFC early in 1916 and also flew FE2bs in France. In August 1918 Hartney was promoted to lieutenant-colonel and appointed commander of the 1st Pursuit Group. See correspondence in Air 1/721/48/5; Air 2/166/RU4867; S.H. Frank, 'Organizing the U.S. Air Service in World War I,' *Cross & Cockade Journal*, VIII, spring 1967, 82; Harold E. Hartney, *Up and At 'Em* (Garden City, NY 1971).

For several weeks the flying weather was ideal, and then Fort Worth experienced unusual winter conditions. The student pilots had to cope with 'northers,' high winds combined with sudden temperature drops of as much as 50°F. Heavy rainfalls and even occasional snow turned the surface of the airfields into heavy mud. On a single day forty propellers were smashed by mud flung up and forward from the wheels of the undercarriage, and over a one-month period an average of ten propellers a day were broken, despite wire mesh guards placed over the wheels. Fortunately the periods of bad weather did not last long enough to interfere seriously with the schedule. For the most part, the facilities provided by the Americans were good, and in the case of the School of Aerial Gunnery they were superior. 'The A.G.S. here is a distinct improvement on what we had in Canada,' Hoare told the War Office, 'the U.S. have done everything we asked for in the way of ranges, etc, and in fact have spent a great deal of money for us.' The range, used for live air-to-ground and air-to-air firing, extended over the waters of Lake Worth, northwest of the city. This was the first time RFC Canada had been able to carry out live air-to-air gunnery. There was an advanced landing ground on the lake shore, cutting wasted flying time to a minimum. The school increased its hours of instruction per student from the three hours obtaining at Camp Borden in September 1917 to an average of six and one-half hours before it returned to Camp Borden in the spring, and nearly tripled its output in the same period.[59]

The original agreement had specified that RFC Canada was to quit the Texas aerodromes in mid-February. Hoare had had second thoughts about that, since his training establishments would be returned to Canada with a good part of the Ontario winter yet to come. Since he and General Squier seem to have been at liberty to modify aspects of the agreement as they chose, he secured Squier's consent to an extension to mid-April, at the price of an undertaking to train eight additional American squadrons, comprising 144 pilots, 1200 men, and a number of ground officers. Delays in the arrival of these men meant that when RAF Canada (as it had then become) left Texas, training of the eight squadrons was still incomplete. Nevertheless, RAF Canada had trained or partially trained more than 4800 officers and other ranks of the American services. More than four hundred pilots had been graduated; another fifty were close to graduation. More than 2500 ground tradesmen had been trained; another 1600 had received some instruction. All this had been accomplished in addition to flight training for 1500 of RAF Canada's own cadets, most of them Canadians. Appreciation was expressed by Major-General W.L. Kenly, the new Chief of the United States Air Service, who told Hoare that RAF Canada had 'conferred a great and practical benefit on the United States Air Service.'*[60]

During the winter months, while the Texas experiment was under way, the Cadet Wing moved from its tents at Long Branch into the barracks vacated by the squadrons from Camp Borden and Deseronto. Both segments of the wing continued basic training at these bases until reunited in early April at Long Branch.

---

* The War Office had already expressed its appreciation to Hoare, promoting him to brigadier-general with effect from 1 August 1917. A statistical gauge of Hoare's work is afforded by the summary he sent the War Office on 26 January 1918, the anniversary of the inception of RFC Canada:

There new recruits once more were accommodated under canvas until autumn, when barracks were completed to house twelve hundred cadets and the wing's staff of two hundred officers and other ranks. In the summer the wing was reorganized along the lines of an infantry battalion, with a headquarters company and four squadrons. By the time of the Armistice it had provided training for nearly 6700 cadets.[61]

Even before the Texas move the flight training organization had been substantially altered. When RFC Canada had begun giving advanced or 'Higher' flying training, the Deseronto Wing was confined to elementary or 'Lower' pilot training. In October 1917 each wing became a composite training school giving both elementary and advanced flying training. Five squadrons were allotted to each wing, three to provide elementary training and two to give advanced training. At the same time the wings were recognized as belonging to the overall RFC training structure and were thus numbered as such. The fifteen squadrons then formed were grouped as follows:[62]

42 (BORDEN) WING	43 (DESERONTO) WING	44 (NORTH TORONTO) WING
No 78 CTS*	No 80 CTS	No 88 CTS
No 79 CTS	No 83 CTS	No 89 CTS
No 81 CTS	No 84 CTS	No 90 CTS
No 82 CTS	No 85 CTS	No 91 CTS
School of Aerial	No 86 CTS	No 92 CTS
Gunnery†	No 87 CTS	

A further reshuffling of the wings took place shortly after the return of the Texas contingent. In the spring of 1918 42 Wing was transferred from Camp Borden to Deseronto and 44 Wing from North Toronto to Camp Borden. These wings con-

(con't from 95)	Trained and sent to England	744
	Trained and awaiting transportation	83
	Retained as instructors	138
	Commissioned and killed during instruction	6
	At Recruits' Depot	348
	At Cadet Wing	742
	At No 4 School of Military Aeronautics	753
	At 42nd, 43rd, and 44th Wings	843
	At School of Aerial Gunnery	154
	Discharges	197
	Cadets, fatal accidents	28
	Total enlisted	4036

These figures do not include American cadets trained under the reciprocal agreements. See Hoare to Drew, 6 Feb. 1918, Air 1/721/48/5.
* In June 1917 squadron designations were changed from Canadian Reserve Squadrons to Canadian Training Squadrons.
† The School of Aerial Gunnery was first operated by 80 CTS but in the summer of 1917 this squadron had moved to the Deseronto Wing and the school had been organized as a separate unit.

tinued to give both elementary and advanced training. No 43 Wing, which moved to North Toronto, was given a specialized role to be discussed shortly.

Had the war lasted into the winter of 1918–19 there would have been no need for the repetition of the shift to the United States because of what the 44 (North Toronto) Wing had learned about flying in winter conditions. Its instructors and students had become the pioneers of cold weather flying in Canada. The staff had been pessimistic. 'We had nothing to go on,' Major Allen later recalled. 'The prospect of the 44th Wing sitting on their backsides for months producing no pilots had us scared stiff.' The commander of the wing was Major J. Stanley Scott of Roberval, Que., who had won an MC as a Western Front pilot in 1916.* Under his leadership, and contending with a Toronto winter more severe than normal, the wing demonstrated that flight training in the snow and cold was perfectly feasible.[63]

The chief technical factor in this victory over winter was the adoption of a ski-fitted undercarriage for the JN4s. Its inventor is unknown; probably the idea of replacing undercarriage wheels with skis or toboggan-like devices was one that occurred to many.[†] The real problem was to produce a sturdy mechanism that would stand up to rough landings by inexperienced pilots. A suitable design was achieved by joint experiments carried out by 44 Wing, the Aeroplane Repair Park, and Canadian Aeroplanes Ltd. The problem of taking off, landing, and taxiing on snow-covered airfields had been solved.

Engines and pilots also needed protection. Experiments hit upon the right anti-freeze mixture for the coolant system. On very cold nights the fuel, anti-freeze, and lubricating oil were withdrawn from the aircraft and the coolant and oil heated before being replaced in the morning. Though the electrically heated flying suits just coming into use on the Western Front were not available in Canada, adequate protective gear was devised, including chamois face masks, thigh-length flying boots, and goggles with amber-tinted glass to cut down glare from the snow.

During the winter 44 Wing flew in ground temperatures that dropped as low as 22° below zero Fahrenheit. Normal flying training proved possible at 14° below zero. There were occasional misadventures and a number of minor frostbite cases, but the morale and performance of the wing remained high. Its spirit was characterized by the determination of a student pilot who, after a forced landing in a snowy field, taxied two miles across country to his aerodrome. In the ninety-day period from the New Year to the end of March, the wing was able to fly on seventy-two days; most of its instructors were able to log an average of more than two hours' flying a day.[64]

* Scott later served as Director of the Royal Canadian Air Force from 1924 to 1928.
† The Russians had already flown aircraft fitted with ski-type undercarriages. The principle went back to the beginnings of the air age. The Wrights had flown machines equipped with skids, takeoffs being made from a trolley running on fixed tracks, and most early aircraft continued to use skids. The Aerial Experiment Association's *Red Wing* had used runners for its flight from the ice at Lake Keuka. F.G. Ericson, chief engineer at Canadian Aeroplanes Ltd, had made speed runs over the ice of Lake Superior before the war on propeller-driven vehicles fitted with skis and runners. See Ericson's account in *Aviation News*, II, Dec. 1919.

Winter flying, then, had little effect upon the length of time it took to train a pilot. At this stage of the training scheme's operation, that period, from swearing in to the passing of final tests, was about four-and-a-half months, though the exact duration was determined by weather conditions and individual rates of progress. By late 1918, because of additions to the curriculum, the average period was about six months. A circular prepared by the chief recruiting officer for distribution to the civilian committees outlined clearly the training process experienced by cadets. After tracing the cadet's path from medical examination and swearing-in to the end of his three-weeks' course at the Cadet Wing, where he was 'trained as a soldier,' the circular went on to describe the training at No 4 School of Military Aeronautics. There the cadet '... undergoes instruction in engines, care and maintenance of machines, map reading, cross country flying, and in fact in all branches of aeronautics from a theoretical standpoint. He should be able to detect from the sound of an engine whether it is running correctly or not. It is necessary for him to be expert in the assembling and truing up of the machine. He also learns the first principles of theory of flight and wireless telegraphy. He must be able to read twelve words a minute from the buzzer.'[65] On successful completion of this course, the cadet was sent to a 'Lower Training Squadron' for initial flight training.* 'The average Cadet takes two or three hours' dual control with an Instructor and is then able to go up solo. After five or six hours' solo flying and thirty to forty landings a Cadet is drafted to a Higher Training Squadron for more complete training in cross country flying, wireless telegraphy, photography, bomb dropping, artillery observation, aerial gunnery, etc. He must do at least thirty hours' solo with this Squadron, after which he is sent to a School of Gunnery. This comprises a three weeks' course on fighting in the air, manoeuvring and air tactics.'[66] Only after passing through the School of Gunnery was the cadet 'granted his commission as 2/Lt., given his "Wings" and after a short leave ... sent overseas.'†

This bald outline gives little inkling of the nature of the training process from the viewpoint of the cadets. What struck an American officer who went through the course was the discipline to which trainees were subjected:

All cadets are required to wear white hat or cap bands. This serves to distinguish the cadets from regulars, and makes them easily marked, when 'walking out,' for matters of discipline. There is a healthy fear on the part of the cadets for their officers, not because of any

---

* From May 1918, after completing the School of Military Aeronautics course, cadets were sent to the Armament School, located in Hamilton after 20 June 1918. At the school they were given a four- to five-week ground course on Lewis and Vickers guns, synchronizing gear, ammunition, gun-sights, bombs, bomb-sights, and bomb dropping. Observer trainees were given three weeks' training, chiefly on the Lewis gun. The formation of the Armament School freed the School of Aerial Gunnery (now entitled the School of Aerial Fighting) from most of the ground instruction it had previously given. See Alan Sullivan, *Aviation in Canada, 1917–1918* (Toronto 1919), 159, 166, 170–9.

† RFC/RAF Canada simply published lists of those qualified along with Daily Orders. 'No qualifying ceremony was held and no "wings" appeared,' a former cadet has recalled. 'We didn't know whether to wear them or not. The usual compromise was to have them quickly detachable and out of sight when on duty.' Gibbard to RCAF Historical Section, 8 March 1962, DHist 76/288

injustice on the part of the officers, but rather because of their firmness in all matters of discipline. A cadet failing to stand at attention when an officer enters the lecture room will find himself up for orders. Salutes must always be executed and executed properly. All regulations are rigidly enforced. Disciplinary measures are thorough. Every cadet is accorded thirty units or marks when he enters the School of Military Aeronautics. The loss of these credits renders him liable to discharge. A cadet ... for purposes of discipline may lose any number of these credits ... and be accorded an additional penalty, as 'C.B.' ... There are usually two or three men in the guard house most of the time. This punishment does not of itself render the man liable to discharge. Failure in examinations is cause for discharge, but is seldom used, some men having been given as many as four opportunities to pass them.[67]

The combination of strict discipline and a lenient attitude towards failure in examinations contrasts with the policy pursued in the British Commonwealth Air Training Plan of the Second World War. Unlike the BCATP, RFC Canada cadets deficient in ground school studies or laggard in flight training were given repeated chances to pass. In the first year of RFC Canada's operations the wastage rate among cadets was only 4.9 per cent, a figure far below the 'wash-out' rate of approximately 33 per cent for Second World War pilot training in Canada.[68]

On the whole, cadets gave their instructors, both ground and air, high marks. Some complained of the teaching by rote practised by NCO demonstrator-instructors. 'Some instructors on the Monosoupape engine are in no way acquainted with any other engine,' an American cadet sarcastically observed, 'and their knowledge of the fundamental physical principles of the gasoline engine is fantastic.' Other Americans found gunnery instruction by NCOs highly competent, and 'marvelled at the extent to which the British and the Canadians left the running of everything to these men.' About the officer instructors, there appears to have been no conflict of view. 'Each officer lecturing has had actual and practical military experience in the line he teaches,' one student noted. 'These officers are all returned men ... Their simple practicality and earnestness have a clearly steadying and business-like effect upon the cadets.' Most cadets seem to have found the School of Military Aeronautics a challenging experience. 'I studied harder than I had ever studied in high school and college,' recalled a cadet who had been educated at Massachusetts Institute of Technology before coming to Canada. 'My life, and perhaps the lives of others, might depend on what I learned.'[69]

The promise of flight was the spur that drove most cadets through the hours of lectures and note-taking at ground school. Once posted to a training station, their keenness to fly was intense. William C. Gibbard, of Moose Jaw, Sask., went overseas as a second lieutenant in July 1917 after training at Camp Borden. His recollections of flight training are typical of the enthusiasms of that time:

Our Borden experience was frustrating, too few machines for the over-anxious cadets. Early flying (daybreak) was the rule and I recollect bugles arousing us, not often necessary. Daybreak found each flight's cadets hopefully grouped round its one or two airworthy JN4's. They were taken in turn by the instructor ... He expressed his amazement at the fanatic zeal of Canadians to get flying. Said an aircraft was nothing to get lyrical over – just a mechanical contrivance to carry us through the air ... We lived for flying and were in despair when shortages of machines, sickness, orderly duty, etc. grounded us. Outside social activity was non-existent and was not desired. No time for anything that did not further our aviating.[70]

Gibbard's memories reflect the shortage of serviceable aircraft during the early days of the training scheme. Flying time was really dependent upon deliveries from Canadian Aeroplanes Ltd, and as late as June 1917 only thirty-four Jennies were received. By October, however, the factory was producing at the rate of two hundred aircraft a month, a change that enabled RFC Canada to increase sharply its monthly log of flying hours. Whereas in May only 2164 hours were flown (and only 140 in April), by September the operation was in full stride and 13,000 hours were recorded. Figures for 1918 are somewhat larger; between May and October the monthly totals ranged between 17,000 and 20,000 hours.*[71]

No pilot ever forgets his first instructional flight. William C. Lambert,[†] who was credited with seventeen victories and won a DFC with 24 Squadron in France, remembered every detail:

Compton gave me the controls at about 1000 ft. He told me to climb to 2,000 ft., do some turns, right and left, glide down to 1,000 ft. with throttle back, then climb up again and circle the field several times. He cautioned me about my air speed. My first two or three turns were flat with very little bank and lots of skids. After several attempts, I gained confidence and began to bank as I should. In a few minutes Compton told me to glide down, throttle back, turn into the wind and head in for a landing. I did this and glided down to about 300 ft. before he took over the controls for landing. I had to keep my hands and feet on the controls to feel his actions in landing. We taxied up to the parking line and climbed out. Compton said: 'You did fair.' I thought I had done very well.[72]

Pilots learned to fly by 'feel,' since the JN4's instrumentation consisted of an altimeter and an engine revolution counter. The instructor sat in the rear seat, and communication was sometimes awkward. A story repeated by many cadets was that when a student froze at the controls, 'some instructors were known to stand up and hit the cadet on the head with a monkey wrench or anything available.'[73]

Dual instruction did not last long. J. Sterling Halstead, one of the United States Navy cadets trained in Canada in 1917, stated that the members of his unit soloed 'after periods of dual instruction that ran from a maximum of six hours to a minimum of 45 minutes, compared with the ten hours dual then required in the flying schools of the U.S. Army and Navy.'[74] This was a matter of policy and applied not just to the navy cadets but to all trainees. The object of the elementary training squadrons was to get their pupils flying solo as quickly as possible. Of the five or six hours' dual instruction a student received, only about an hour was away from

---

* The JN4 was a rugged aircraft, and the RFC flew it hard. In September 1917 each serviceable aircraft was flown an average of 105 hours. That was a peak figure; the norm was between 75 and 95 hours per month. Sullivan, *Aviation in Canada*, 20

† Lambert was a chemical engineer born in Ironton, Ohio. He worked in a Montreal explosives plant before joining the RFC in early 1917.

the airfield; most of the time was spent on landing and takeoffs. The ensign in charge of the American naval party was impressed by the system:

Once an instructor is satisfied that the cadet is not going to hurt himself, he sends him solo regardless of what he may think the cadet will do to the machine. It has been found that a man learns far more quickly by teaching himself and the instructor takes far greater chances on the pupils making a rocky take-off or landing. This policy is made possible by having unlimited spare equipment on hand. A broken undercarriage, propeller or wing should not render a machine unserviceable for more than an hour. On all sides of the R.F.C. you will find an indifference to breakage unknown at home, but nowhere more so than at the Preliminary Flying Camps ... At the same time no pupil is ever sent soloing unless the instructor feels confident that he is not going to hurt himself severely.[75]

It was this system which produced the characteristic elementary flying school landscape of 1917–18, as portrayed in many photographs of the period: expanses of rolling grassland, dotted into the middle distance with JN4s in unnatural attitudes – leaning on their propellers, or wingtip to ground and undercarriage buckled, or, much less frequently, in the tangled heap that signalled a serious accident.

Ontario communities close to RFC Canada's training establishments, though at first enthralled by the romance of flight, discovered on further acquaintance that the aircraft, at least in the hands of cadets, was highly accident-prone. Such was the case in Orillia. The first aeroplane to visit Orillia arrived on 20 May 1917, when three JN4s from Camp Borden landed on the town's old racecourse. A large crowd assembled, for as the Orillia *Times* observed, 'While many Orillians are familiar with the aeroplane from photograph and description ... few have ever had the opportunity of examining one at close range.' For readers who had missed the great event the *Times* defined the JN4 as 'a motor car with small front wheels only,' having wings 'cross-wise with the car' and driven by 'motormen' – the latter term shortly to be replaced by 'birdmen.' It had two seats, 'one being for the pilot and the other for the driver.'[76]

The mysteries of aviation were soon dispelled. Within a month the *Times* found that 'the novelty of aerial navigation is rapidly wearing off' since airmen from Camp Borden were making daily use of the racecourse as a practice field. Instead, readers received a steady diet of stories about aircraft from Camp Borden 'coming to grief.' Sometimes these accidents were serious and shocking; on 16 August the *Times* reported the death in a crash of Cadet A. Heyler of Midland, Ont., and on 27 September a mid-air collision in which Lieutenant Arthur Williams of Toronto and a cadet from Venezuela, John Edward Ludford, were killed. Usually, however, the mishaps were minor. On 24 June, for example, 'an immense crowd' watched as a JN4 taking off from the racecourse 'fouled a tree top' and 'hit the ground with a thud,' the pilot emerging unscathed. One of two aircraft sent from Camp Borden to provide help landed on a stump hidden in the grass. Further interest was soon provided by two aircraft which 'had the misfortune to alight head down.'[77] Eventually the passage through town of trucks bearing bent and tattered sections of dismantled aircraft, as well as disconsolate cadets, became a customary sight for Orillians.

For the cadets as well accidents became routine. But the first solo was always an occasion. Gibbard remembered: ''Solo'' was the highest achievement at this stage and the subject of endless discussion in the mess to perfect the mental image of correct procedure. It nevertheless always came without warning. A series of landings ... ended with Russell stepping out and telling the cadet to take it off himself. He was usually airborne before the jitters developed. Every 1st solo had a little something extraordinary to talk about. After mine, the carburettor was found to be hanging by a thread.'[78] Once a student had logged ten solo hours and made thirty landings, including one emergency landing procedure in a field away from the aerodrome, he was ready to proceed to advanced instruction. In the higher training squadrons, and in the specialized schools beyond them, was undertaken the business of converting student pilots into military aviators.

The object of these units was to build upon the ground school instruction already given, to teach the student to become master of his aircraft, and to acquaint him more than superficially with the wide range of skills required of pilots at the front. In 1918, for example, a School of Artillery Co-operation was formed at Camp Leaside under 43 Wing. The three squadrons at the field dealt only with this aspect of air operations. Training techniques were as realistic as possible. The open country which virtually surrounded the aerodrome was turned into an artillery ranging area. Smoke puffs were released on the ground to represent shell bursts and the cadet, flying at 2000 feet, had to locate them on his map, tap out a Morse message giving the map reference of each shell burst to a ground receiving station, and pass adjustments in range and direction to the 'battery.' Since wireless communication was then only air to ground, the student had also to read messages sent from the ground by Aldis lamp, ground strips, and the Popham panel.

This aerial training was bolstered by a number of ground training aids. The school had two huge maps prepared from aerial photographs of sections of the Western Front, each studded with hundreds of light bulbs which could be flicked on singly or in combinations to represent shell bursts from one or more batteries. The cadets sat on elevated benches above the maps, noting shell bursts and passing information by 'buzzer' to the instructor. Similarly, contact patrol instruction was given on a map on which three trench lines, machine-gun emplacements, and other features were represented.

The Artillery Co-operation School also gave instruction in bombing, using the camera obscura method. The student flew towards a designated target, adjusting his bomb sight for the correct altitude, airspeed, and heading of the aircraft, and for estimated wind speed and direction. When he believed the target to be within his sights, he sent down a wireless signal to simulate the dropping of a bomb, while an instructor, watching the aircraft's reflection in a 'target' mirror, could determine from the position of the reflection the accuracy of the student's aim.[79]

An already existing school, the School of Aerial Gunnery, acquired in 1918 a new home, more challenging standards, and a new name. Before the school had been moved to Texas, plans were already under way to find it a new aerodrome. The place selected was the village of Beamsville, a Niagara Peninsula community on the Lake Ontario shore some twenty miles southeast of Hamilton. The Imperial Munitions Board leased a site and carried out construction of an airfield and necessary buildings and facilities during the winter of 1917–18. Apart from British Columbia, Hoare reported to his superiors, this was the warmest part of Canada and he was confident that he would get 'a more complete school' going there in the spring.[80]

On its return from Texas the school moved directly to Camp Beamsville. It then consisted of three squadrons with a total establishment of fifty-four aircraft. From the start the school introduced new training techniques. Shooting at static targets on the range was discarded in favour of travelling targets, so that students could immediately become accustomed to deflection sights and deflection firing. The same approach governed air exercises in which the student, armed with a camera gun, endeavoured to register in his sights a JN4 flown by an instructor while at the same time avoiding being 'shot down' himself. The proximity of Lake Ontario made possible air-to-air firing wth live ammunition at towed drogues. Air-to-ground firing practice included shooting at full-size silhouettes of aircraft mounted on rafts, at a heavily-armoured motor launch, and at dummy trenches. In its last months the school, by this time known as the School of Aerial Fighting, attempted to simulate, so far as the JN4's performance would permit, the conditions of actual aerial combat. The commandant, Major A.E. Godfrey of Vancouver, and the commissioned instructors were all former combat pilots, and their experience was now used directly in the training curriculum.*[81]

In 1918 the whole approach to the training of pilots was similarly influenced by lessons derived from the fighting fronts and the need to bring a new realism to flying instruction. This approach was pioneered by Major R.R. Smith-Barry at Gosport and at the Central Flying School at Upavon in England. After having commanded a fighting squadron in France, he took over a training unit at Gosport on the south coast of England, and there developed the training system which made him the most influential instructor of his time. Too many poor pilots were reaching France, he believed, where they were of no use to their squadrons and sitting ducks for the enemy. The blame for this rested squarely upon the training systems. His prime cure was to dispel the cloud of ignorance about the nature of flight and the capabilities and behaviour of aircraft in which most pilots were enveloped. As he said in his best known training pamphlet, some experienced pilots might consider his methods heterodox, 'but most, it is thought, will consider them quite normal, and indeed rather old-fashioned.'[82]

Until Smith-Barry's time, the mind of the fledgling pilot was filled with taboos about flying. For the student, and often for the instructor, flight itself was unnatural. An aircraft in flight was in precarious balance; any deviation from rote procedures brought sudden, irreparable disaster. Pilots learned to fly by the seat of their pants. Survival of initial flight training and the accumulation of experience brought increasing skills and a greater knowledge of dangers, but no added understanding

---

* RAF Canada began training observers in June 1918. To do so, a fourth squadron was added at Beamsville. The observers worked almost exclusively with Lewis guns on Scarff mountings in the rear cockpits of the JN4s, though they also used camera guns.

of why, in certain attitudes, an aircraft behaved as it did. Smith-Barry's approach was to encourage instructors and students to fly at the limits of their aircraft's capacities, to experiment with the controls of the aircraft when in abnormal or unusual attitudes, and thus to build up the knowledge, confidence, and skill needed to meet any exigency in the air. He put it as follows:

The object has been not to prevent flyers from getting into difficulties or dangers, but to show them how to get out of them satisfactorily, and having done so, to make them go and repeat the process alone. If the pupil considers this dangerous, let him find some other employment, as, whatever risks I ask him to run here, he will have to run a hundred times as much when he gets to France. How can a young officer be expected to do very much in France, if, during the whole of his training in England he has been told of nothing but what it is considered dangerous to do in flying? As most of the supposed dangers are not dangerous at all, but both easy and pleasant, it would seem a simple matter for the pupil to be taught, chiefly by example, to be frightened of nothing connected with flying on this side of the lines.[83]

Smith-Barry placed a much heavier emphasis upon the theory of flight than had previously been the case, and also sought to give practical demonstration of its principles in the air. As one of his staff recalled, 'the gospel he preached was that the aeroplane was a nice-tempered, reasonable machine that obeys a simple honest code of rules at all times and in any weather.' By directly relating the code of rules to the actual behaviour of the aircraft while in flight, 'he drove away the fear and the real danger that existed for those who were flying aeroplanes in the blackest ignorance even of first principles.' Instead of concentrating on dual instruction in the hours before solo and then letting the student virtually teach himself after he had soloed, Smith-Barry extended dual instruction well beyond this stage in order that the instructor might teach difficult manoeuvres and also catch bad flying faults before they became fatal.[84]

Two developments assisted him. The first was the solution to the mystery of the spin. In the first years of the war to spin was almost inevitably to crash. Pilots who had recovered from spins did so by luck or by impromptu experiment, but were unable to explain why they had done so. E.C. Burton of Kenora, Ont., who received his pilot training in 1917 and later became an instructor, was given no aerial instruction whatever in recovery from spins. Instead, spinning was discussed at ground school, and in a fashion that demonstrated both the ignorance of the instructor and the danger to students. 'One lecturer stated,' Burton recalled, 'that not much was known about spins but it was best to keep out of a spin by avoiding a stall.' This officer hazarded the guess that 'If you get into a spin it might be best to keep your hands and feet off the controls and it would come out itself.'[85]

At the time when student pilots in Canada were still being fed such nonsense, the terrors of the spin had been dispelled overseas. By late 1916 a number of pilots had discovered that by moving the stick forward and applying opposite rudder, recovery from the spin occurred. During the same period, experiments at the Royal Aircraft Factory at Farnborough had revealed the aerodynamics of the spin and consequently the measures required for recovery from it. Smith-Barry was thus able to incorporate deliberate spinning and recovery into his training curriculum.[86]

The second development was the introduction of the Avro 504J. This two-seater biplane, fitted with a 100-hp Gnôme Monosoupape engine, was at first used as an advanced trainer. Smith-Barry saw that it was ideal for *ab initio* training. It was a reliable aircraft with the handling characteristics of a single-seater fighter and thus could be used to carry out all the aerobatics in his syllabus. So impressive were the results he obtained by using the 504J that the aircraft was selected as the standard trainer for the RFC.[87]

In August 1917 Smith-Barry's training school became the School of Special Flying, with the task of training instructors according to his new principles. These instructors were then posted throughout the pilot training establishment in Britain to spread the gospel. Word of the 'Gosport System,' however, does not appear to have reached Canada until March 1918. It was then that Hoare complained to the War Office that he was not being sent vital information about new training methods. He had obtained a copy of Smith-Barry's pamphlet unofficially and thought the approach 'so admirable' that he was immediately introducing it to the RFC Canada training system.[88]

This was done at Armour Heights, beginning in April. A special training course for instructors was instituted and the equivalent of an additional squadron of eighteen aircraft was formed to handle the programme. Soon Hoare was able to report that the new course was working smoothly; by the beginning of July ninety-five instructors had passed through it and been sent out to training squadrons. A second squadron had been added to Armour Heights and the new unit was re-formed as the School of Special Flying. By the end of the war the school had trained or retrained 257 instructors.*[89]

---

* The only difference between the Canadian school and Smith-Barry's was, however, an important one: RAF Canada did not have the Avro 504. The JN4's limited performance and handling characteristics diminished the value of the advanced training that could be given on it. Moreover, since it could not be fitted with a rotary engine, pilots trained in Canada were totally lacking experience with an engine type widely used on first-line aircraft. Not only was familiarity required with the running characteristics of the engine, but also with the distinctive aerodynamic effects its rotary action imparted to the aircraft. Canadian cadets were therefore required to take additional training in Britain on service types of aircraft, a fact that put into question the heavy investment made in the Canadian training scheme. Almost from the beginning of the scheme Hoare pressed for a more advanced trainer to supplement the JN4, and saw no reason why such a machine could not be manufactured by Canadian Aeroplanes Ltd, provided suitable engines could be obtained from the United States. During the fall and winter of 1917–18 serious consideration was given to the manufacture of the Sopwith Pup in Canada as an advanced trainer. It was finally decided, however, that the Avro would become the Canadian 'all-through' trainer, and that CAL would produce it. A long delay ensued before CAL was given authority to begin production because of problems with engine supply from the United States. The Avro 504J was therefore modified to take other rotary types – the 110-hp Le Rhône and the 130-hp Clerget – in addition to the 100-hp Mono-Gnôme. The modified version was known as the Avro 504K. The engines for it were to be supplied from England. In July 1918 CAL was given a contract to produce five hundred 504Ks, the intention being to complete re-equipping RAF Canada by April 1919. A number of design changes by CAL, including a distinctive V-type landing gear, further delayed production. At the Armistice parts for about a hundred aircraft had been produced, but only two complete machines were manufactured before the end of the war. The contract was then cancelled. The 504K was the standard trainer of the Canadian Air Force and the RCAF until the late 1920s, but these aircraft were obtained from Britain after the end of the war, as the major part of the British aviation gift to Canada. See Minutes of the Air Board in Air 6; correspondence

For most of its existence, the Armour Heights school was commanded by Major Jack Leach of Toronto, one of the most colourful and popular figures in Canadian aviation history and a particularly fine pilot despite the loss of a leg while flying with 56 Squadron in France. Leach was an RMC graduate who had gone overseas with the First Contingent of the CEF and won an MC before transferring to aviation in 1916. He proved an able Canadian counterpart to Smith-Barry, applying the Gosport methods so effectively that not only were better pilots being produced, but a significant reduction in accidents and flying fatalities occurred.

Accidents had been the bane of the RFC Canada training scheme. As has already been noted, during elementary training accidents were accepted as routine. A cadet who trained at Camp Mohawk in the summer of 1917 wrote at the time that the afternoon he soloed 'there were about ten crashes and several machines were completely wiped out, but no one was hurt.' Another Camp Mohawk cadet recalled that 'there were lots of crashes but relatively few killed; I think there were three planes wrecked the first day we were there.' C.H. Andrews, who trained in the Deseronto Wing, noted in his diary on 21 October 1917 'the results of the day's work: 17 crashes, (three complete washouts) one killed, 5 in hospital. Very cheering.' At the Texas field in the winter of 1917–18 'the death rate was out of all proportion,' another recalled. 'There were no curbs on any type of flying; every good stunt ever heard of was attempted by anyone crazy enough to try it.'[90]

It is true that flying discipline was extraordinarily lax compared with that enforced in more recent times. Students were encouraged to show 'dash,' and practices which would have brought 'washout' and worse during the Second World War earned no more than a reprimand in the First. Frank Ellis recorded one example from his days at Camp Borden:

One practice as far back as the summer of 1917 was for a pilot to wait in the air at the time the Toronto express for Barrie was due, and then to come in from behind at a fast clip, low down above the tracks. As he and his plane swept by over the length of the train, the crazy man at the plane's controls would deliberately bump his wheels on the roofs of several of the coaches before reaching the engine, when he would speed over the top and actually dip down in front of it along the tracks far enough in front to swing away and yet not have his identifying numbers on the rudder seen by passengers or train crew. It was supposed to be great fun along a particular section of the C.P.R. track between Baxter and a small town named Ivy, where the telegraph wires and poles were amply spaced to allow for such mad exploits.[91]

Such escapades undoubtedly contributed to the accident rate and to the toll of injuries and fatalities but the major cause, as Smith-Barry had argued, was insufficient training. J. Sterling Halstead, in assessing his period as a US Navy cadet in Canada during the summer and fall of 1917, had no doubts of the explanation: 'The principal reason for the large number of crashes was insufficient dual instruction. Whether this insufficiency was due to lack of instructors or a studied policy

of Hoare with the War Office and Air Ministry in Air 1/721/48/5; correspondence of General Brancker with the Air Ministry about American engine supply in Air 1/680/21/13/2205; and K.M. Molson, 'Aircraft Manufacturing in Canada during the First Great War,' *Canadian Aeronautical Journal*, v, Feb. 1959, 47–54.

based on the theory that it was more economical in the long run to have the poor material eliminated in this way early in the training course was hard to determine.'[92]

Statistics sent by RFC/RAF Canada headquarters to the War Office exist only for the period April 1917–May 1918:[93]

ACCIDENTS AND FATALITIES BY SECTION, APRIL 1917–MAY 1918

STATIONS	ACCIDENTS	FATALITIES
Fort Worth	74	30
Camp Borden	49	19
Deseronto	30	12
North Toronto	29	12
Beamsville	5	4
Long Branch	3	1

These figures are of limited value, since only those accidents resulting in injury or death were reported. They exclude accidents and casualties to non-RFC and RAF personnel. An analysis of the causes of aircraft accidents is available for the period August-November 1918. During that time there were 174 accidents (not necessarily linked to injury or death). Of these, 110 resulted from errors in judgment, thirty-nine from 'machine trouble,' eleven were assessed, mysteriously, as 'physical or mental,' and the remainder were put down as unavoidable.[94]

Overall, RFC/RAF Canada lost 129 of its cadets in fatal flying accidents, one for every 1902 hours logged by the training scheme. That rate disguises the fact that RAF Canada's performance in this respect improved markedly in its last months. Moreover, statistics compiled for the whole of the RAF's training establishments, both in the British Isles and abroad, show that from January to October 1918 there were 1.34 fatalities per 1000 hours of flying, or about one every 750 hours. Though RFC/RAF Canada plainly had a better record than other RAF training formations, its fatality rate was exceedingly high compared with that of the British Commonwealth Air Training Plan in the Second World War.[95]

HOURS FLOWN PER FATAL ACCIDENT, RFC/RAF CANADA AND BCATP

RFC/RAF CANADA		BCATP	
April 1917	200	1940–1	11,156
May 1917	1000	1941–2	14,001
June 1917	1960	1942–3	17,725
December 1917	1500	1943–4	20,580
July 1918	1560	1944–5	22,388
August 1918	3300		
October 1918	5800		

There seems little doubt that the introduction of Gosport methods of flying training is the chief explanation for the sharp improvement shown by RAF Canada in

August 1918, a date that coincides well with the dispersal of Armour Heights-trained instructors through the system. And despite the improvement, it is evident that learning to fly in 1918 was still a risky business.

Accident rates, and flying training generally, were matters completely under the control of General Hoare and his staff, subject only to the approval of authorities in Britain. In 1918, however, two policy questions arose with which Hoare could not deal unilaterally, since both had to do with the peculiar position of the training organization, an arm of a British service, operating in Canada, a self-governing dominion. The first was the situation precipitated by the creation of the Royal Air Force on 1 April 1918. The British statute which established the RAF, the Air Force (Constitution) Act, provided that no one serving with the RNAS or the RFC could be transferred to the new service without consent. In Britain, those refusing consent were returned to their parent service, either the British Army or the Royal Navy. A period of three months, later extended to six, was allowed for members of the former flying services to exercise this option. In Canada the cutoff date was 10 October.[96]

The problem confronting Hoare was not a threatened exodus of instructors or students; very few officers or cadets chose to leave the RAF. The crisis lay with the other ranks, the backbone of support for the training scheme. When, in July, Hoare protested to the Air Ministry that the extension of the option period from three to six months was 'going to have a paralyzing effect on us,' he did not exaggerate. Over 1600 RAF tradesmen, more than a quarter of those on strength, had applied for discharge and another 1000 were expected to follow suit. The tradesmen were not primarily, or even necessarily, signalling their antipathy to RAF service; rather, they were responding to the high wages to be earned in Canadian war industries. Most of those objecting to RAF service had been without skills at the time of enlistment. Now, having been taught trades, the men were seeking to take advantage of an unusual situation. Many of those wishing discharge were to be found in highly-skilled trades, such as engine mechanics and aeroplane riggers, which were vital to RAF Canada. More than half the other ranks at the Aeroplane Repair Park had asked for release and the proportion in several other units did not go below one in three. Hoare's initial reaction was that discipline was likely to suffer, because 'any man who received a minor punishment or is in any way disgruntled, can walk out as a protest and in most cases will not be liable to further service.'[97]

The last point was the crux of the matter. RAF Canada had little leverage over its other ranks. Had Hoare been commanding a similar unit in Britain, his course of action would have been straightforward: those wishing release would have been paraded for immediate transfer to the Army or the Royal Navy, a sanction formidable enough to discourage all but those opposed root and branch to the formation of the Royal Air Force. But though Canadian tradesmen in the training organization were in fact liable to precisely the same treatment, common sense and ordinary political judgment (apart from other reasons) warned Hoare against the shipping of batches of recalcitrant Canadians overseas to serve in British units.

If the threat of immediate transfer to the British services was ruled out, then why not use the CEF for the same purpose? This was the line that Hoare decided to take, but to make it stick he needed the co-operation of the Canadian government. He got it. With the collaboration of the Department of Militia and Defence and the Military Service Branch of the Department of Justice, Hoare arranged what might be termed a series of 'deterrent parades' throughout the summer and autumn of 1918. Groups of twenty men, all of whom had requested release, were paraded on the drill grounds of the Recruits' Depot, given their final pay and their discharge certificates, and then handed their call-up papers, previously obtained from the Ontario Registrar. They were then turned over to a waiting escort of Canadian military police who took them immediately to a CEF depot.[98]

These draconian tactics served to encourage the withdrawal of a number of applications for discharge, whatever they may have done for morale. Unfortunately for RAF Canada, most of its men were in categories not liable for CEF duty. Many of them, through the co-operation of the militia department, had originally been recruited from the CEF because they were unfit for overseas service. Such men, it was determined, once having been released from the CEF for the purpose of enlistment in RAF Canada, could not legally be conscripted into the CEF upon discharge from the RAF. To stave off the loss of men in these categories, RAF Canada fought for time. Aside from the 'deterrent parades,' RAF Canada adopted the position that no releases would be granted during the option period and successfully obtained an extension of that period until 30 November. At the same time the Canadian government gave every assistance, through passage of a number of orders-in-council as well as orders and instructions from the militia and justice departments, all intended to plug loopholes and extend liability for CEF call-up. When, with a month to go before the expiration of the option period, the RAF appealed to General Gwatkin for legislation rendering *all* men wishing release liable for service with the CEF for the duration of the war, he was quick to oblige. A draft order-in-council was prepared stipulating that '... any man who, having been enlisted in Canada as a soldier of the Royal Flying Corps, has applied ... to annul his transfer to the Royal Air Force and whose transfer is annulled accordingly, shall immediately thereupon become liable to military service with the Canadian Expeditionary Force, and shall report to such unit of the Canadian Expeditionary Force as may be directed by the General Officer Commanding, Royal Air Force.'[99]

This far-reaching order was justified by the militia department on two grounds: first, that its object was to deter men seeking release, not to recruit them for the CEF; second, that since the men involved had voluntarily undertaken military service with the RFC for the duration of the war, a commitment they now could void only because of the 'accident' of the reconstitution of the flying services, no injustice would be done to them by taking them into the CEF. This was an argument which some of those concerned might well have questioned. However, the armistice of 11 November made the order irrelevant and on 23 November the Air Ministry informed Ottawa that all men objecting to RAF service could now be released.[100] RAF Canada had managed to ride out its manpower crisis, but only the help of the Canadian authorities had enabled it to do so.

The training scheme's problems with its ground tradesmen gave rise to another policy consideration, this time originating with the Air Ministry in London. At a meeting of the Air Council on 18 July Major-General Sir Godfrey Paine, Master-

General of Personnel, suggested that the solution to R A F Canada's dilemma was for Canada to take over the training organization. 'This would release our own personnel and instructors,' he argued, 'and make the Canadian government responsible for their own establishment.' At a subsequent Air Ministry conference on 29 July, called primarily to discuss the formation of two all-Canadian squadrons, Paine raised the question again, this time with Major-General S.C. Mewburn, the Canadian Minister of Militia and Defence, in attendance. 'The matter had been brought to a head,' he said, 'by the attitude taken by a large number of the Air Force personnel (rank and file) now in Canada' who 'had refused to transfer to the R.A.F.' Paine went on to tell General Mewburn and his party that the Air Ministry was not satisfied with the output of the training scheme. Its graduates needed a good deal of additional instruction in Britain before being sent to squadrons (because, of course, R A F Canada had no advanced trainer). He alleged, indeed, that only six weeks were saved by training cadets in Canada. Instead, he proposed that Canada take over the training of all cadets recruited in the dominion, that an advanced training element be added, and that complete squadrons of trained pilots, ready for service at the front, be formed and sent to England. Any surplus of trained pilots could be absorbed by other squadrons after their arrival in England. Though he did not make this proposal with a view to the creation of a separate Canadian flying corps, Paine did not rule it out since that question was 'being discussed alongside.'*[101]

That the Canadian government had some ultimate responsibility for the training plan and should answer for its deficiencies must have been news to Mewburn and his associates. The minutes of the conference state that 'the subject having been thus ventilated, the Canadians asked that they might have a memorandum in writing which they can place before their Prime Minister at once. They would like to consider it in the light of their naval defence requirements as well.' This was not the recollection of Major T. Gibson, Assistant Deputy Minister for the Overseas Military Forces of Canada, who was also present. He told his Deputy Minister on 2 October 1918 that after the proposal for a Canadian takeover had been discussed, 'Major-General Mewburn intimated to the Meeting that he could not see his way clear to advise the Government to accede to the proposal.'[102] This seems very likely, not only because of the well-established reluctance of the Canadian Cabinet to make heavy commitments towards aviation, but also because Mewburn had been thoroughly briefed on the proposal by Gibson before the 29 July meeting. Gibson argued that there were two good reasons why Canada should not take over the training scheme. First, there was no connection between it and the proposed Canadian flying corps, since the Canadian Air Force was to be formed from R A F officers already overseas. Second, a Canadian takeover at that time would be an unsound and short-sighted investment:

While some criticism has been offered against the manner in which the Royal Air Force has carried on its work in Canada, the Government would not be justified in response to this criticism, in taking over the plant and activities of the Royal Air Force in Canada on account of the very large expense involved, which would be out of proportion to the benefits that

* The genesis of the Canadian Air Force is discussed in chapter 19.

would accrue. One of the strong reasons for the formation of the Canadian Air Force at this time is that Canada should have at the cessation of hostilities a flying corps trained in all branches of the air service including organization, administration and technical. It will be of advantage to Canada to acquire after the war such of the property of the Royal Air Force as may be needed for the administration and training of the post bellum Canadian Flying Corps. It will then be possible to take over at comparatively small cost such of the plant as Canada may require for the purpose indicated.[103]

Whether Mewburn temporized at the 29 July meeting or not is of little consequence, since there was no likelihood, for the reasons advanced by Gibson, that the Canadian government would accede. The Canadian authorities were saved the necessity of formally rejecting the Paine plan when it encountered heavy weather within the Air Ministry itself. A senior finance official summed up his proposal as tantamount to saying that 'Our training establishments in Canada are not a success; let us therefore hand them over to the Canadian Government,' while Brigadier-General B.C.H. Drew stated flatly that the idea was 'really an impossible proposition.' He prevailed upon Paine to agree to a letter to the Canadian High Commissioner conceding that 'in view of the large financial adjustments necessitated by any such transfer, it would be inadvisable to proceed further with the proposal.'[104]

The Canadian government thus retained its position of benevolent non-commitment towards R A F Canada. General Hoare appears to have taken little part in these proceedings, although he was at the Air Ministry in June and early July, and could hardly have escaped hearing some of the criticisms then circulating about his training scheme.* According to the recollections of Wing Commander D.L. Allen, Hoare then had other plans for the disposition of his Canadians: 'About April 1918, knowing the dreadful shortage of manpower in [the] U.K., we offered the newly-formed Air Ministry to supply the ground crews for five squadrons: ie, 150 N.C.O.'s [and] men per squadron, plus a first reinforcement to 50 per squadron, 1000 in all. We further undertook to keep these squadrons up to strength. We stipulated however, that the five squadrons so formed should be called "Canadian Squadrons" and be clearly identified as such. We did this as we were fully alive to the feelings throughout Canada that greater recognition should be given to the contribution she was making in air warfare.'[105] According to Allen, Hoare pushed this idea at the Air Ministry during his visit, but it was turned down because 'Canadian rates of pay and allowances could not be paid without causing trouble among the other airmen.'† Though no trace of this initiative has been located in

---

* That Hoare was sensitive to criticisms of R A F Canada was indicated by his request for the preparation of statistical data on the relative rates of progress of Canadian-trained pilots and those from other training brigades at advanced training units in Britain. Unfortunately, such statistics do not appear to have been compiled. Hearson to Hoare, 8 Nov. 1918, Air 1/721/48/5

† Allen also claimed to have taken the matter up with General Brancker in September, at the time of his return to England. 'He told me in confidence,' Allen stated, 'that his principal objection to forming Canadian Squadrons at that time was the fact that it was the Canada-trained pilots who were doing the bulk of the actual fighting in France in the R.A.F. squadrons. Suitable pilot material was in such short supply from U.K. sources that the squadrons just could not have carried on without the Canadian-trained element with their high morale and greater number of flying hours to their credit.' Allen to R C A F Historical Section, 22 July 1962, DHist 76/199

the documents surviving in the Public Record Office, it is a fact that by this stage of the war Hoare had become thoroughly committed to what in later years would be called 'Canadianization.'

While he was at the Air Ministry Hoare had proposed that graduates of the RAF Canada scheme be kept together while undergoing advanced training in England. On returning to Canada, he referred to the idea in a letter to the new Master-General of Personnel, Sefton Brancker. 'I think if Canadian pupils can be sent to certain definite Wings and grouped as much together as possible, preferably with officers who understand them, better results would accrue,' he wrote. No evidence exists to show that Canadians going through advanced training in England were encountering difficulties; it is more likely that Hoare's letter reflects both the increasingly nationalist tone of the Canadian press with respect to aviation and a number of complaints of discrimination by Canadians already flying with RAF service squadrons. At any rate, Hoare elaborated on his proposal in a second letter to Brancker. He suggested that one of the 'all-through' training wings in Britain should be allocated solely to graduates of RAF Canada. He could provide instructors for it from his School of Special Flying and augment them with additional staff from his organization, so that eventually the wing would become, except for groundcrew, entirely Canadian and 'practically a branch of the R.A.F. Canada.' Not only would the Canadian wing then have a strong *esprit de corps*, but its formation would find much favour in Canada. To round things off, he suggested that communications would be better on both sides of the Atlantic if the wing were commanded by one of his own officers. He therefore nominated his Inspector of Training, Major Arthur K. Tylee, for the job.*[106]

This modest proposal won no converts at the Air Ministry. Brigadier-General J.G. Hearson, the Director of Training, told Hoare that although the total output of pilots from the Canadian scheme was satisfactory, the rate of supply fluctuated too much to permit the economic utilization of a wing solely for its graduates. Moreover, Hoare's essay at empire-building in reverse was 'most undesirable.' 'The whole object of the organization of the Royal Air Force is to prevent short-circuiting,' he informed Hoare. 'Your proposition would absolutely nullify this organization.' Short-circuitry, at which Hoare had proved so adept in Canada and the United States, could not be tolerated when it affected the structure of the RAF itself. Nevertheless, Hearson gave some encouragement. The Air Ministry had arranged that Canadians receiving advanced training in England would be sent to a selected number of Training Depot Stations and similar units, where they would comprise at least one-third of the students and be grouped in their own flights. A 'certain percentage' of the stations would be commanded by Canadians. In a separate letter Brancker expressed the hope that this policy 'will meet your request to some extent.' 'I am against putting Canadians and nothing else at the one Station,'

* Tylee, from Lennoxville, Que., had graduated from the Massachusetts Institute of Technology in 1907 and taken employment with an American heavy machinery company. Sent to open a company office in Montreal in 1913, he enlisted in the RFC in 1915, served overseas, and joined RFC Canada in 1917. After commanding a training squadron and then a wing, he was appointed Inspector of Training in 1918. After the war, he became the first commander of the Canadian Air Force, formed in Canada in 1920.

he continued, 'chiefly because they are a better type than we are getting in England now, and by distributing them throughout the country we gain by the good leaven they impart to the others.'[107]

Hoare had to be content with this concession, which in any event came too close to war's end to have any noticeable results. That his espousal of Canadianization was genuine, and not motivated merely by stirrings in Canada, can be seen from the transformation which had taken place within the structure of RAF Canada itself. The ground trades, as already noted, were almost wholly Canadian, but at the outset of the training scheme the directing staff was nearly all British. Through the posting home of Canadian pilots and observers with operational experience, the secondment of officers from the CEF in Canada, the retention of graduate pilots as instructors, and the commissioning of technically qualified citizens, RAF Canada's directing staff had become at least two-thirds Canadian by the beginning of 1918. At the time of the Armistice, Canadians commanded two of the three wings and twelve of the sixteen training squadrons, as well as the School of Aerial Fighting and each of its four squadrons, the Cadet Wing, and the Mechanical Transport Section. About 70 per cent of all flying appointments were held by Canadians.* In the improbable event that the Canadian government had taken over the training organization, most of the men required to run it would have already been in place.[108]

RAF Canada in 1918 was a much larger organization than had originally been projected, even though it now consisted of only sixteen numbered training squadrons and three wings, instead of the twenty squadrons and four wings planned.† It was the associated schools that made the difference: there were four squadrons at the School of Aerial Fighting (1 to 4 Aerial Fighting Squadrons), and two more at the School of Special Flying. Nor was it necessary in 1918 to employ the extraordinary methods of the previous year in order to find the recruits to keep the organization going.[109]

The passage of the Military Service Act undoubtedly prompted many young men to choose the RAF rather than be conscripted for infantry service and the upturn in recruiting in the spring of 1918 may in part be attributed to this factor. In addition, the Chief of the General Staff, whose assistance to the training scheme had already been great, took steps to ensure that the RAF would not be starved for

* There were also some anomalies. For example, in February 1918 about one-third of the flying instructors on training squadrons were American.

† H.A. Jones, *The War in the Air: being the Story of the Part played in the Great War by the Royal Air Force*, v (London 1935), 467, notes that 'at the time of the Armistice the full organization of the Royal Air Force in Canada comprised, in addition to the three training wings, another of five squadrons in process of formation,' but this does not appear to have been the case. Much of Hoare's correspondence with the War Office and the Air Ministry throughout the course of the training scheme concerned the question of whether or not a fourth wing should be formed. Had the British Columbia plan been carried through, a fourth wing would have been placed there, but this idea was dropped at the time of the Texas agreement. When the manning picture brightened in late 1917 with the influx of American recruits, Hoare was told to form the five squadrons required to make up the new wing. No 93 Squadron was formed as the nucleus from which the others would emerge, but in the spring of 1918 this squadron was simply added to those already with the Camp Borden Wing.

recruits as a result of the act. Provision was made under the administration of the new act for the creation of a cadet reserve class, in which applicants between seventeen and three-quarters and nineteen years of age were enrolled. Cadets could be held on this reserve for six months. It served the double purpose of protecting RAF applications (under the act a man was required to register on reaching his nineteenth birthday) and providing a guaranteed supply of pilot trainees who could be fed into the training stream at desired intervals and rates. What amounted to a similar reserve of cadets and mechanics was also created within the CEF in Canada. Gwatkin urged commanding officers 'not to deter but to encourage men to volunteer for service in the R.F.C.' Depot Battalions were asked to publicize the existence of vacancies in the air service. Prospective cadets and mechanics were held for up to three months on the strength of the battalion and shown as 'not available for overseas draft.'[110]

In October 1917 Hoare had told Gwatkin that it was essential, were the training organization to continue to operate effectively, that 4500 cadets be obtained over the ensuing twelve months. At that time the intake was 350 cadets a month. The value of the help provided by Gwatkin, in addition to whatever inducement the Military Service Act produced, was demonstrated by the fact that from the end of 1917 to the Armistice 5900 cadets were recruited. At the end of May 1918 RAF Canada had 1200 cadets in the reserve class awaiting notice to report and a surplus of 800 cadets at various stages of ground instruction. Fourteen hundred cadets had been recruited during that one month alone. At that point it was thought wise to 'slow up to some extent.' Over the summer 457 pilot trainees who had finished their ground instruction were sent overseas for flight training because RAF Canada had more cadets than it could handle.*[111]

On Armistice Day there were close to 12,000 men on the strength of RAF Canada, including some 600 officers, 4333 cadet pilots, 444 cadet observers, and 6158 other ranks. As well, nearly three hundred newly-commissioned second lieutenants were awaiting embarkation for overseas when the war ended, but by the end of the year the training organization had been almost completely dismantled. Demobilization began before the end of November, cadets with the least training being the first released. Hoare and British members of his staff departed for England, though RAF Canada continued as a skeleton organization until December 1919.[112]

---

* In 1918 RAF Canada flirted briefly with the notion of recruiting women. It already employed a substantial civilian female work force. Women not only held clerical jobs, but despite local criticism were also employed as transport drivers. In 1918 the manpower shortage drove RAF Headquarters in Toronto to advertise that a wide range of jobs were open to women. About 1200 were hired, and many were given technical training. Six hundred women were working as mechanics at airfields at the end of the war and another 135 were doing engine overhaul work at the repair parks. In May 1918 Hoare obtained the permission of both the Air Ministry and the Canadian government to recruit for a branch of the Women's Royal Air Force in Canada. The idea appears to have been dropped because upon investigation it was discovered that although the cost of barrack accommodation for men was about $235 per capita, for women, because of 'the necessity of special provision,' the figure was $430. See Sullivan, *Aviation in Canada*, 144–5, 283; Hoare to Air Ministry, 28 May 1918, Air 1/721/48/5; Governor General to Colonial Office, 1 Aug. 1918, PAC, RG 7 G22, vol. 9 (2).

The contribution of RAF Canada to the war in the air and to aviation in Canada was significant. Mention might first be made of some of its lesser achievements. One of these was in the field of aviation medicine, a branch of medicine in Canada which dates from the training scheme. The medical and dental staff of RAF Canada came from the Canadian Army Medical Corps and from the Canadian Army Dental Corps, through the co-operation of the militia department. These officers, nurses, orderlies, hospitals, and equipment were paid for by the British government. The medical staff was headed by Major Breffney O'Reilly, before the war a Toronto physician. He and members of his staff became increasingly interested in the physiological and psychological aspects of flying; their reports of their own work and of developments in Britain were the basis for further work in the postwar period.[*][113]

RAF Canada also made the first officially authorized airmail flight in Canada. On 24 June 1918 Captain Brian Peck flew a JN4 from the Polo Grounds in Montreal to Leaside, with stops near Kingston and at Deseronto, in less than seven hours, bearing a mailbag which he then delivered by car to the main Toronto post office. The *cachet* on the letters, authorized by the Deputy Postmaster General, bore the words 'Via Aerial Mail Montreal 23 6 18' (bad weather had forced Peck to delay his flight by a day), and surcharged, misleadingly, by the phrase 'Inaugural Service.' The affair was really a stunt concocted by the Montreal branch of the Aerial League of the British Empire, a body which had been active in publicizing the importance of aviation and in raising funds to donate aircraft to the RAF. Three more such flights between Toronto and Ottawa, again sanctioned by the postal authorities and this time under the auspices of the Aero Club of Canada, were carried out by RAF Canada in August 1918. The flights won some press attention, and served to demonstrate the feasibility of inter-city mail service, but they were not followed up.[114]

More important was the contribution of RAF Canada to the Canadian aircraft industry. Canadian Aeroplanes Ltd produced about 1200 JN4s for the Imperial Munitions Board. If the production of spares is added to this total, the overall output of the company was at least 2900 training aircraft. Of these, 680 were purchased by the American government for use at Fort Worth and in pilot training in 1918. It has been estimated that at least one in five American pilots trained during the First World War received instruction on Canadian-built JN4s.[†] Canadian Aeroplanes Ltd was far from being merely an assembly plant. Though the OX engines for the JN4 came from the United States and radiators, wheels, tires, and instruments were purchased from other firms, all other components, including pro-

---

* RAF Canada also developed the first Canadian flying ambulances. These were devised when it appeared that training might well continue throughout the winter of 1918–19 and some provision might be required for emergency evacuation of casualties from airfields when the roads were blocked with snow. On a number of JN4s the upper part of the fuselage was stripped away aft of the rear cockpit and replaced with an enlarged turtle deck hinged on one side and therefore capable of carrying a stretcher-borne patient.

† It should be mentioned, however, that when CAL production was just picking up in early 1917, and RFC Canada was desperate for aircraft, 150 JN4As were bought from the Curtiss plant at Buffalo, NY. Most of them were used at Deseronto. Hoare to Charlton, 25 April 1917, Air 1/721/48/5

pellers and even turnbuckles, were made within the plant. Almost all the materials used came from Canadian sources. To begin with, Irish linen was used to cover the wings, fuselage, and tail assembly of the JN4, but the successes of the German submarine campaign of 1917, as well as high demands from the British aircraft industry, cut down the amount of linen available to CAL. As a result, cotton produced in Quebec textile plants, after suitable doping, was used instead and proved both satisfactory and much cheaper.[115]

As well as the JN4, and the abortive work on the DH6 and Avro 504, Canadian Aeroplanes also produced flying boats for the Americans. The Felixstowe F5, a large two-engine patrol aircraft, was one of a series of F-boats developed by the RNAS, all their designs having been derived from the Curtiss H4 and H12 flying-boats. The US Navy placed large orders for F5s with a number of American plants, and an order for fifty was given to CAL. This was a large undertaking. The American version of the F5, the F5L, was fitted with 400-hp Liberty 12s instead of Rolls-Royce Eagles. These engines, as well as 'intercom' and wireless equipment, were shipped to Toronto from the United States for installation. The aircraft had an upper wingspan of more than 102 feet, was over 49 feet long, weighed 8250 lbs empty and about 13,000 lbs when fully loaded. It had mountings for as many as eleven Lewis guns and a position in the bow for a Davis quick-firing recoilless cannon.* Altogether the F5L was a much more advanced aircraft than the JN4, and a true test of the capabilities of Canadian aircraft manufacturing.

Canadian Aeroplanes Ltd shipped its first F5L to the Philadelphia Navy Yard at the end of July 1918, and it was successfully test flown the following month. By the Armistice the Toronto plant was producing eight boats a month. With the end of the war, the original order was cut back to thirty. The final F5L was delivered in January 1919. This was the last aircraft to go into production in Canada until 1923, when the aircraft department of Canadian Vickers got under way. Not until 1938, when Vickers began producing the Supermarine Stranraer, was a larger aircraft built in Canada.[†116]

___

* The Davis gun was essentially a tube, open at both ends, which was loaded through a slot in the centre. When it was fired a three-pound projectile was launched at the target through the muzzle and an equivalent weight of small shot took up the recoil energy in being ejected from the rear.
† Aero engine manufacture had a less successful record in Canada during the First World War. The Imperial Munitions Board attempted unavailingly to interest the Wright-Simplex Co in making Hispano-Suiza engines in Canada for use both overseas and in the training scheme in 1916. Canadian Aeroplanes Ltd had the right to make Curtiss OX-5 engines, but found it more convenient to import them from Hammondsport. In early 1917 the IMB concluded an agreement with Willys-Overland to manufacture 240-hp Sunbeam Arab engines in its Toronto plant. The Arab was a V-8 engine with overhead camshafts, designed for lightness. The crankcase, cylinder heads, and engine block were aluminum (the block had hardened steel liners) and the overall weight was only 550 lbs. Unfortunately, while Willys was getting under way, testing of the engine in Britain disclosed cylinder and crankcase weaknesses. Numerous modifications and changes in specifications delayed the adoption of a final design until the end of 1917 and played havoc with the production schedule. Moreover, Willys' workmen were frequently unable to meet the precision machining demanded by the design. An inspector for the IMB reported in 1918 a pile of rejects 'about as high as the first floor of the plant.' By the end of the war only about 150 Arab engines had been shipped overseas from Toronto. All work then ceased. F.H. Hitchins, 'Aero Engine Manufacture,' Hitchins Papers, DHist, 75/514, file G5; C.W. Thomas, 'Sunbeam Arab: Canada's First Production Aero Engine,' *Aircraft*, March 1959, 47–8, 75

The JN4s produced by Canadian Aeroplanes for RAF Canada were to have a usefulness that outlived the training scheme. F.G. Ericson, formerly chief engineer of Canadian Aeroplanes, formed his own company (later Ericson Aircraft Ltd) and bought from the Imperial Munitions Board the whole of RAF Canada's aircraft inventory except for fifty JN4s given by the British government as a gift to Canada. Only ten of the latter were in fact retained; it was decided that the trainers were already obsolescent for military purposes and forty were turned back to the Imperial Munitions Board, winding up in the hands of Bishop-Barker Aeroplanes Ltd of Toronto. Both these and the aircraft acquired by Ericson were used in Canadian commercial aviation during the 1920s, whether for timber surveys in Labrador, for flying passengers and supplies to Northern Ontario gold strikes, or by barnstormers giving flying exhibitions. It was a JN4 that made the first flight over the Canadian Rockies.[117]

The contribution of RFC/RAF Canada to the war in the air was considerable. Of the 9200 cadets enlisted by the training organization, 3135 completed pilot training and over 2500 were sent overseas. Most of the others were either awaiting overseas posting or were serving as instructors in Canada before the end of the war. In addition, 137 observers were fully trained and eighty-five had been sent overseas. There seems little doubt that RAF Canada was just reaching its peak in late 1918. Despite the criticism Hoare had encountered in Britain, the output of the scheme compared favourably with an organization of similar size, the training brigade in Egypt.* The following table compares the pilot output of these two formations with that of training establishments in the British Isles from June 1917 to March 1918, the only period for which data is available:[118]

PILOTS GRADUATING

MONTH	BRITISH ISLES	EGYPT	CANADA GRADUATING	SENT OVERSEAS
June 17	580	51	30	20
July 17	545	37	60	50
Aug. 17	456	59	95	50
Sep. 17	457	52	120	100
Oct. 17	634	39	80	78
Nov. 17	458	47	170	83
Dec. 17	434	49	240	180
Jan. 18	426	139	170	247
Feb. 18	588	79	210	160
March 18	892	136	245	230

Though RAF Canada's monthly average of pilot graduates was about 230 for the whole of 1918, output of pilots was climbing rapidly during the last months of the

* In the comparison period, the training establishment in Egypt attached to Middle East Brigade was larger than RFC Canada. As of January 1918, in addition to No 3 School of Military Aeronautics and a school of aerial gunnery, it contained six training wings and four additional training squadrons. DAO to RFC Records South Farnborough, 4 Jan. 1918, Air 1/1306/204/11/190

scheme. Had the war continued into 1919, RAF Canada would have met about a fifth of the estimated pilot and observer reinforcements needed for the Western and Italian fronts. A statistical summary and operational forecast prepared in the Air Ministry in November 1918 found that the average pilot casualties per month, during 1918, for all overseas operational units was 551, a wastage rate of 32 per cent a month.* Monthly casualties at operational stations in the British Isles averaged 287 pilots a month, for a total of 838. The average output of trained pilots from all training establishments during 1918 was 1200 a month. Given the planned expansion of the RAF for 1919, there was a narrow operating margin, made possible chiefly by the output of RAF Canada. From mid-1917 onwards a considerable and steadily increasing stream of badly needed pilots, the bulk of their training completed, had arrived at British ports and, after final training, had been sent to service squadrons. Their presence and that of the Americans also trained by RAF Canada was crucial to the winning of the air war.[†119]

Much of the credit for the success of RAF Canada belongs to its commander, Brigadier-General C.G. Hoare. His resourcefulness and energy pulled the training scheme through its most precarious stages, his leadership produced an efficient organization and a remarkably loyal staff, and his tact won him the strong support of General Gwatkin and other Canadian authorities, without whose assistance the training scheme could hardly have functioned. Sterling qualities Hoare had in good measure. What is finally so impressive about him is the free-wheeling verve with which he brushed aside impediments insuperable to more orthodox men. International boundaries, national policies, and the hidebound ways of bureaucracies meant little to him; he ran over all of them wearing velvet boots. Certainly he deserves to be regarded as one of the fathers of Canadian aviation.

It is a testimony to Hoare's capabilities that his organization never found itself in trouble with Canadian politicians, and only rarely with the press. While Hoare was in Texas his staff in Toronto became involved in an injudicious attempt to muzzle press criticism of the number of fatal flying accidents occurring at the North Toronto airfields. When the chief press censor, Colonel E.J. Chambers, was drawn into the matter, he told a meeting of Toronto newspaper editors that some of their 'objectionable reports ... indicated a disposition to produce trouble for the Officers of the Flying Corps and ... appeared to have been written without a realization of the injury likely to be done to the service by the publication of statements reflecting upon the administration of the school.' He discovered, however, that the editors had a unanimously unfavourable view of the Royal Flying Corps; 'The Royal Flying Corps Officers do not seem to understand the position of the press on this side of the water and the relation which exists in Canada and the United States

---

* This summary estimated that the average number of operational hours flown per casualty (killed or missing) was 222.

† Because of the heavy recruitment of Americans in the early stages of the training plan, a high proportion, perhaps as much as one-third, of the pilots sent overseas came from the United States. The overall proportion of Americans in the total of cadets recruited by RAF Canada was of course much lower. Of the total of 7463 ground tradesmen enlisted by the RAF, more than 600 were recruited from the United States. RAF Canada HQ to Gwatkin, 30 April 1918, HQ 6978–2–62, vol. 3, PAC, RG 24, vol. 2031; Sullivan, *Aviation in Canada*, 146, 150

between newspaper men and Military Officers and officials generally. They appear to think that as they are Imperial Officers administering a Branch of the Imperial Service in Canada that their actions are entirely beyond criticism and beyond the reach of Canadian laws and Canadian institutions, this notwithstanding that the lives of young Canadians are in their charge. When these gentlemen are asked for news they seem to take pleasure in refusing it, and if any information is forthcoming it is supplied too late to possess any news value.'[120] Gwatkin advised the RFC to temper its attitude towards the press. 'I strongly recommend you not to fight the Press,' he wrote, 'but to conciliate and make use of it; otherwise you will be set upon by masked men with poisoned weapons, and they will do you to death.' This sound advice was accepted. A 'discreet young officer,' Major Murton Seymour, was appointed to work with the press, and, with one exception, appears to have smoothed things over.[121]

The exception was the *Toronto Star*. RAF Canada had fallen foul of the press for understandable reasons. Its staff, or most of it, was accustomed to a more circumspect mode of journalism and in any event was inclined to be overly conscious of security. Such attitudes were bound to irritate newspapermen, and in the case of the *Star*, a paper with a decidedly nationalist outlook, triggered the closest approximation to a campaign against RAF Canada that was to occur during its existence. The *Star*'s hostility focussed first upon an incident in which a seventeen-year-old cadet, after being slightly injured in a training crash at Leaside, was recommended for discharge. Instead of receiving his discharge, the *Star* alleged that he had been ordered to serve as a mechanic. To the Toronto paper, this was arbitrary action against a 'boy volunteer' on the part of the RAF, 'or as it calls itself in Canada, the Imperial Royal Air Force, although why it should be only Royal in England and both Imperial and Royal out here in Canada we do not know, but would very much like to find out.'[122] A subsequent editorial drew attention to the anomalous position of Canadians in the air service, and of the RAF in Canada:

... we have an Imperial Royal Air Force with branches all over this country, enrolling, enlisting, and training Canadian boys for war service under such conditions that they are outside the control of their own Government here at home, are not connected with the Canadian forces when they go abroad, and rely for pensions or any future provision their possible disabilities may require on authorities three thousand miles distant from the capital of their own country. It is curiously inconsistent with the part Canada is playing in the war, both at home and in the field, that both here and in the field there is flying over us an Imperial Royal Air Force and that we are manning a force not officered and administered by us.[123]

In June 1918 the *Star* resumed its attack, the occasion this time being the refusal of the provincial Attorney-General to order an inquest into the death of a cadet at Camp Borden. 'The fact is,' an editorial claimed, 'that the coroner's inquest is the only hold that Canadian authority possesses on the operations of the R.A.F. in Canada.' Neither Parliament nor ministers of the crown could be appealed to for redress of grievance; instead, Canadians who had been injured by this British organization had recourse only to authorities in London, 'as in the days of their grandfathers.'[124] For the *Star*, there was only one solution: 'We should have our own Air Force in Canada, in England, and at the front. Particularly we should have no war-service recruiting and operating here independent of the supervision and control of the Government of Canada. To have such a service operating here is two generations behind the times, and it isn't working and it won't work. It is a plan that did not work in the governing of this country before Confederation.'[125] Though, as will be shown later, there were other voices calling for a separate Canadian air force, the *Star* was all but alone in its attacks upon RAF Canada. Indeed, except for occasional feature stories, the training organization attracted surprisingly little attention in the press, a condition with which its headquarters staff was quite content.

As a result, however, the training organization never received the credit it deserved for contributing to the air-mindedness so much a part of the Canadian outlook since the First World War. Two-thirds of the Canadians who served in the British air arms during the war joined through the training scheme; without it, thousands of them, especially the ground tradesmen, would have had no association with flying. Their exposure to aviation and their knowledge of it permeated the public consciousness in the interwar years and helped foster a climate sympathetic to the role of the aeroplane in Canadian development and communications. It is hardly too much to say that RFC/RAF Canada was the single most powerful influence in bringing the air age to Canada. Without it, both the RCAF and the civil air industry would have been much less solidly based and inevitably Canadian aviation would have been far more dependent upon American flyers and technicians, and upon American innovations. As it was, RFC/RAF Canada, and through it a number of Canadians, had made an impact upon the early history of United States aviation.

PART TWO

The Admiralty and the Air

The intrepid Commander Charles Rumney Samson about to start on one of his excursions over the Turkish lines of Gallipoli. (Q 13542)

Admiral Sir Charles Edmund Kingsmill was born at Guelph, Ont. In 1910 he became the first director of the Canadian Naval Service, playing a notable role in recruiting for the RNAS. (DND RCNO-776-2)

F/S/L R.F. Redpath of Montreal poses in front of a Voisin biplane at RNAS Station Eastchurch in early 1916. A comparison of this machine with a Handley Page V1500 or Sopwith Snipe (illustrated elsewhere) will demonstrate the great strides in aeronautical engineering made during the war. (RE 20959)

A group of Canadians at Felixstowe, 1916. Back row (l to r) F/S/Ls J.L. Gordon of St Lambert, Que., unidentified, F.S. McGill of Montreal, G.R. Halliday of Victoria, BC, and Robert Leckie of Toronto; front row, F/S/L George Hodgson of Montreal, B.D. Hobbs of Sault Ste Marie, Ont., and W.E. Robinson of Winnipeg. (PMR 74-508)

The German submarine U 14 was hit on the stern by an aerial bomb during the night of 1/2 Feb. 1915, while alongside the Zeebrugge mole – the first time in history that an aerial bomb inflicted serious structural damage on a warship. (Q 51410)

British naval airships on coast patrol (Q 18268)

A seaplane version of the Maurice Farman 'Shorthorn' piloted by F/S/L H.A. Peck of Montreal, taking off at Felixstowe, probably in 1915. (RE 19409-3)

An early SS-type coastal airship returning to its base in the Aegean after a patrol over Gallipoli. The combined control car and engine gondola is simply the fuselage and power plant of a BE2c suspended beneath the gas bag. (Q 13498)

Canadians who joined the RNAS in Canada eventually found themselves at the Crystal Palace in London, undergoing basic ground training which included rifle drill. Visiting them, J.B. Brophy of Ottawa (then serving in the RFC) noted that 'The place was alive with Naval youths, whom I scorned ... A useless outfit. They sure have a nice place at the Crystal Palace, but it is not war.' (AH 456)

This reproduction of the painting by Charles Dixon shows F/S/L Robert Leckie of Toronto landing his H12 'Large America' flying-boat in the North Sea to pick up the crew of a downed DH4 on 5 Sept. 1917. With a damaged hull (from landing in the rough seas) and six men aboard, the H12 drifted for three days before being found by a minesweeper and towed to Yarmouth. (RE 17486)

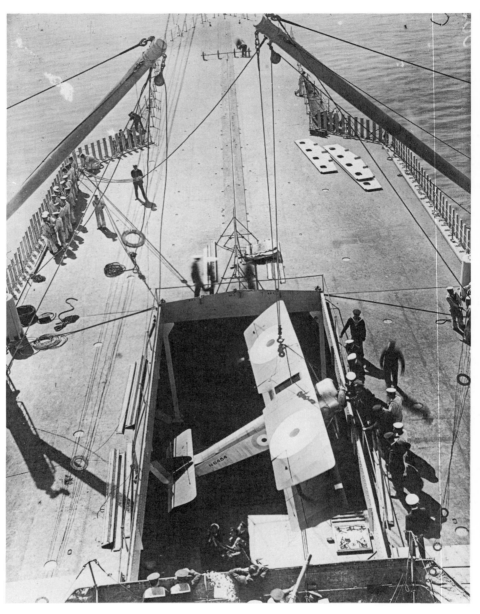

Hoisting a Sopwith Pup from the hangar to the deck. A Pup became the first aeroplane to land successfully on the deck of a ship at sea aboard HMS *Furious* on 2 Aug. 1917. (Q 20638)

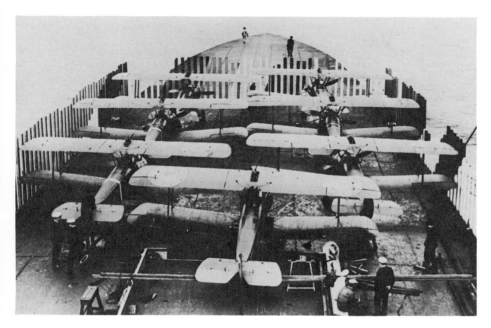

Sopwith Camels lined up on the 228-ft forward flight deck of HMS *Furious*. Originally a heavy cruiser, *Furious* was converted to an aircraft carrier by stages, a longer (280 ft) after flight deck being added later. (PA 6280)

A Sopwith Pup, with skids instead of the usual wheels, lands on HMS *Furious*. Note the longitudinal arrester gear on the deck. (Q 20634)

2/Lt W.S. Lockhart of Moncton, NB, flying a Sopwith Camel off the forward turret ramp of the light cruiser, HMAS *Sydney*, 1918. Machines launched in this manner either had to land on shore or 'pancake' into the sea beside the mother ship. (PMR 71-872)

A Sopwith Camel aboard a lighter at Felixstowe. Towed into the wind at 30 knots by a destroyer, lighters like these provided an adequate take-off platform for the Camel. Landing, the aircraft either had to reach dry land or come down in the sea alongside the lighter. (Q 69367)

A lighter carrying a Sopwith Camel being towed at speed (HC 5066)

A Sopwith Cuckoo drops a practice torpedo, 1918 (RE 22020-1)

Lt S.D. Culley made the first successful take-off from a towed lighter on 31 July 1918. Less than two weeks after this picture was taken Culley shot down zeppelin L 53 over the North Sea, having taken off from a lighter. Born in the United States of a Canadian mother, Culley and his family had lived in Vancouver before the war. (AH 527)

An ss 'z' non-rigid airship escorting a 1918 convoy. One of the crew is semaphoring a message to the airship carrying the cameraman. (Q 20643)

In the foreground an ss 'z' airship ready to lift off on patrol. Behind it (and already in the air) a ss 'c': note the trefoil cross section of the latter. (Q 18263)

An F2a flying-boat with 'dazzle' camouflage on patrol. This machine combined the hull of a Porte flying-boat married to the wings and tail assembly of a Curtiss H12 'Large America.' With its V-shaped, curved hull, the F2a could land or take off in much heavier seas than the H12. (AH 572)

F2b flying-boats waiting to be launched for patrols over the North Sea. Canada was particularly well represented among the crews of these big flying-boats, and many served at the RNAS station at Felixstowe, where this picture was taken. (AH 453)

A Porte Baby flying boat. This machine was distinguished by its three engines, the centre one driving a pusher propeller and the other ones driving tractor airscrews. Only eleven were built before the hull was married to the wings and tail assembly of the Curtiss H12 'Large America' to produce the Felixstowe F2a series. (AH 564)

This rare scene on board an RNAS 'C'-type, non-rigid coastal airship, patrolling the North Sea, gives some idea of how exposed the crew were. (Q 20860)

A Short Type 184 seaplane, flown by many Canadians in the RNAS. The square, box-like object on top of the fuselage, behind the airscrew and in front of the upper wing, is the engine radiator; the vertical pipe in front of that is an exhaust stack. Note the tail float. (AH 574)

An SS 'z'-type airship landing on the after deck of HMS *Furious*. A Sopwith 1½ Strutter can be seen on the forward flight deck. (Q 20640)

A 'c'-type SS airship about to leave its RNAS base on an anti-submarine patrol
(AH 452)

Introduction

Far fewer Canadians served in the Royal Naval Air Service than in the Royal Flying Corps. The naval air arm, however, was itself much smaller than its military counterpart and therefore the Canadians in it formed an important part of its total flying strength. For the first year of the war only a handful flew with the RNAS. One of them, R.H. Mulock of Winnipeg, became the highest ranking Canadian airman of the war. By late 1915 the young men who had received their first taste of flying at the Toronto Curtiss School were reaching England, and from that time on Canadian pilots and observers were entering upon flying operations in increasing numbers. Whether through accident of posting, timing of arrival, or design (though there is no evidence for the latter), certain RNAS units eventually became heavily or even predominantly Canadian. Yet wherever the RNAS flew and whatever it was doing, Canadians were to be found. They flew not only over the Western Front, and deep into Germany, but in many other war theatres as well. They served at Gallipoli, Malta, and Gibraltar, flew over Mesopotamia, the Arabian desert, East Africa, and the Red Sea, or patrolled the Aegean, the Mediterranean, and the Adriatic. Most of them, however, were stationed in the British Isles and at Dunkirk; the waters they knew were the North Sea, the English Channel, and the Atlantic approaches to Britain.

Canadian naval airmen fought a war that, on the whole, was far less intense than the air war over the land battlefronts. The enemy was less frequently encountered, casualties were lower, the chances of survival were better, although even routine patrolling was punctuated with moments of violent action: the sighting of a U-boat, the chase of a zeppelin, sudden and fierce encounters with German seaplanes. Moreover, the RNAS had fighter and bomber formations in Flanders in which many Canadians were concentrated and their war experience was much closer to that of the RFC.

In spirit and structure the RNAS differed in a number of ways from the RFC. As befitted the air arm of the navy, with its diverse and far-flung responsibilities, the RNAS was a loosely constructed and flexible organization not overly preoccupied with establishment tables. No single individual could possibly have made the impression upon it that General Hugh Trenchard made upon the RFC, for its many units and formations were not tied together by a staff system. Overall control was exercised by a designated authority within the Admiralty; operational control lay with the various naval commands, but for most of the war it rested in practice with the senior air officers on the spot. In the RFC standard procedures were laid down for every form of air operations, duly set out in official pamphlets and revised when necessary. In the RNAS each unit worked out its own procedures; the service never made a shibboleth of uniformity. The informal and decentralized character of the RNAS extended to its airmen, who tended to be more individualistic and less specialized than their brethren in the RFC.

Just as the RNAS was more tolerant of organizational diversity, so it was more enterprising and experimental in its approach to the vital matters of aircraft design and supply. The RFC was initially wedded to the designs of the Royal Aircraft Factory, Farnborough, which produced worthy but unremarkable machines. The Admiralty, in contrast, relied primarily upon the resources and ingenuity of private industry and liberally commissioned aircraft and engines from among Britain's best designers and manufacturers. From T.O.M. Sopwith came the Sopwith 1½ Strutter, the Pup, and the Triplane; from Handley Page an outstanding series of heavy bombers culminating in the V1500; from Short Brothers a variety of seaplanes; from Rolls-Royce its splendid engines. So successful was the Admiralty in accumulating stocks of good aircraft and engines that the RFC, hard-pressed for such commodities and locked in a ceaseless struggle with the German air force on the Western Front, protested vigorously. Only a political settlement could finally solve the supply quarrel between the two services.

Both the RNAS and the RFC had to keep constantly abreast of changing aviation technology. A slight improvement in rate of climb, endurance, or handling characteristics spelled the difference between success and failure, between life and death. At the unit level the RNAS was always open to experimental approaches, new designs, and technical innovations. For the naval flyer, technical improvement was not simply a question of aircraft performance but of linking two technologies: that of the aeroplane and the air to that of the ship and the sea. Yet the progress of the RNAS in such matters as torpedo-carrying aircraft or aircraft carriers was disappointingly slow. The Admiralty's conservatism has often been blamed for this state of affairs, but it should also be recognized that, with the exception of the U-boat menace, the RNAS was not exposed to the kind of heavy and constant enemy pressure that speeds technological advance by giving it a vital priority. It was just such an active and innovative enemy that imposed the need for change upon the RFC.

The crucial campaign in which the RNAS was involved was the struggle with German submarines. The mounting danger from enemy underseas forces reached a level in 1917 which threatened the entire war effort, since by this time the maintenance of allied military and industrial strength depended heavily upon shipments from North America. To this point the Admiralty had put its faith in such countermeasures as hunting down submarines with destroyers, mining waters that gave them access to the open sea, and bombing their bases. Finally, in the face of staggering losses of merchantmen, it was compelled to resort to convoy. The part played by the RNAS in the success of the convoy system, though almost completely overlooked by the Admiralty at the time and by historians since, was extremely important. It is ironic that the greatest contribution of naval aviation to the winning of the war came in 1918, when the RNAS itself had ceased to exist.

The RNAS was never content to be a mere auxiliary to the navy. Seeking an offensive role, it pioneered the development of long-range bombing, a form of warfare in which its Canadians played an especially prominent part. It also formed a number of fighter squadrons at its large Dunkirk base which it was forced to lend, from time to time, to the RFC. By late 1917 the friction between the two services over questions of supply, the obvious duplication of operational functions such as bombing and air fighting, and powerful political pressure for retaliatory air attacks upon German cities led to the decision to unify the two air services. On 1 April 1918 the RNAS buried its individuality in the Royal Air Force, a fate brought about in part by its failure to confine itself to a purely naval role. But the Canadians who had served in it, taken part in its extraordinarily diverse activities, flown its many types of aircraft, and become imbued with its prodigious talent for improvisation were to have much to contribute to aviation in postwar Canada.

5

Origins of Naval Airpower

With the exception of a few individuals, Canadians took no part in the air war until the later months of 1915. Even then, their names are scattered infrequently through the war diaries of units on active service. In the Royal Naval Air Service, some divisions of which became virtually Canadian preserves later in the war, significant numbers did not fly operationally before early 1916. Not until the vanguard of recruits from the Curtiss School and other North American flying schools had passed through further training in England did the Canadians begin to make their presence felt.

As latecomers, the Canadians moved into a service which had already been shaped by the exigencies of a year of war. Their duties, and how and where they were to perform them, had for the most part already been determined. By the end of 1915 the chief characteristics of the wartime evolution of the RNAS had already emerged, even though in many respects the service was still in a formative stage and a number of contentious questions had not yet been resolved. For an understanding of the manner in which Canadians were employed in the RNAS, therefore, it is necessary to review its operations during the first year of the war.

The nature and even the spirit of the RNAS differed markedly from its sister service, the Royal Flying Corps. This was not solely because of the contrast between the two forces to which the air arms were attached, but also because the problems confronting the land and sea elements were so different. Three factors governed the development of the RFC during the war: the nature of the land battle, the structure of the British Army, and the principle, virtually unquestioned until late in the war, that the air arm existed solely to serve the ground forces. These factors meant that specialization of function – and hence of airmen and equipment – developed in response to the military situation and to the requirements of the army, and that specialized units were enclosed within a rational hierarchical structure that corresponded to the organization of the army itself and expanded in consonance with it. The RFC was characterized by symmetrical order and subordination of role.

The tasks confronting the British navy during the First World War were far more diverse than those facing the army. The navy's prime duty was, at the minimum, the containment of the German High Seas Fleet by every possible means. But naval responsibilities extended beyond this to the control, not only of home waters but of the oceans, seas, and coasts important to the land campaign and to the protection of the shipping and shipping lanes vital to the prosecution of the war. The ordering of these responsibilities and the allocation of resources among them was the job of the Board of Admiralty and its political head, and their priorities fluctuated with their assessment of the endlessly changing contingencies of the war at sea. Flexibility of response and reliance upon mobility were the hallmarks of the exercise of British sea power. The organization and outlook of the RNAS, so loose and individualistic when compared with the RFC, reflected these principles. The RNAS was never so tightly structured as the RFC and was repeatedly altered to correspond with shifts in Admiralty priorities. Though the RNAS developed specialized functions in conformity with naval requirements, it remained much more elastic in organization and experimental in outlook than the RFC.

Moreover, while both air arms were conceived originally as auxiliaries to the operations of their main forces, the RNAS, to a much greater extent than the RFC, came to be seen as a weapon in its own right both by some policy-makers and by some of its leading members. Almost from the beginning of the war tension arose between those who wished to confine the RNAS to functions closely related to fleet and coastal operations and those who wished, in addition, to exploit its potentialities for offensive action, whether in concert with other naval elements or by itself. This tension was never fully resolved within the RNAS partly because it was so flexible and partly because its manpower and its supply of aircraft and engines made a degree of diversity tolerable: for most of the war it had more men and equipment than it could fully employ on purely naval duties.

Direct co-operation with naval units was never the prime function of the RNAS during the war. When the Grand Fleet steamed to its war station at Scapa Flow on 29 July 1914, not a single aircraft accompanied it. A month later a number of seaplanes, and the men to fly and maintain them, were sent to Scapa to work with the fleet. There was no means of taking them to sea, however, and the Commander-in-Chief, Admiral Sir John Jellicoe, requested a fast seaplane carrier. HMS *Hermes* completed a refit to carry three seaplanes early in October, but she was far too slow (14 knots) to keep station with fleet units, and in any event sank after a torpedo attack at the end of the month. In November the hangars at Scapa blew down in a gale and the Grand Fleet was once more without aircraft until HMS *Campania*, purchased and converted as a result of Jellicoe's representations to the Admiralty, came on the scene in April 1915. Her seaplanes were intended to act as scouts for the fleet.[1]

When the war began Winston Churchill, the First Lord of the Admiralty, had much more aggressive plans for seaplanes. On 11 August 1914 the Admiralty had taken up three fast Channel steamers, the *Empress*, *Engadine*, and *Riviera*, for conversion to seaplane carriers, apparently with the intention of employing torpedo-carrying aircraft in offensive operations. Churchill later stated that he 'ordered immediate preparations for a bombing attack by torpedo seaplanes upon the German Fleet in the Roads at Wilhelmshaven ...' Three Short Folders,* fitted

---

* Squadron Commander Arthur M. Longmore had made the first successful torpedo drop in Great Britain on 28 July 1914 when he released a 14-inch Whitehead torpedo of 810 lbs from a 160-hp Short Folder, one of the earliest aircraft to have folding wings. But this experimental flight was little more than a 'stunt' and a far more highly-powered seaplane was required before an airborne torpedo attack could be attempted under operational conditions. Sir Arthur Longmore, *From Sea to Sky, 1910–1945* (London 1946), 36–7

for carrying torpedoes, went to HMS *Engadine*. But it was to be many months before an aircraft with the endurance and the safety margin needed for the torpedo-carrying role was developed. Nothing more was heard of a carrier-launched torpedo attack after September.[2]

The idea of using seaplanes in a strike role was not abandoned, however, for they could carry bombs if not torpedoes. A major responsibility assigned to the RNAS at the beginning of the war was the defence of Britain against air attack, which in 1914 meant attack by German airships. Rather than await their coming, many at the Admiralty, from the First Lord down, believed that the best defence was attack. On 25 December *Engadine*, *Empress*, and *Riviera*, in company with other naval forces, were directed against the zeppelin sheds at Cuxhaven. Seven of the nine seaplanes launched reached the Cuxhaven area, but none of them could find the sheds, partly because of patches of mist and partly because the sheds were in fact several miles from their assumed positions.[3] While this raid was in progress, the carriers and their escorts were bombed by German seaplanes and zeppelins, without effect.

Much more important than service with the fleet was the patrolling of home waters, a routine but vital duty which the RNAS took up from the beginning of the war. The northern extremity, from Kinnairds Head to the Firth of Forth, and the southern extremity, from Dungeness to the North Foreland of Kent, were patrolled at first by RFC aeroplanes, but after mid-August, when four squadrons had departed for the continent, RFC participation was minimal. As a result, RNAS east-coast stations were greatly over-extended in the first months of the war. When Lord Fisher of Kilverstone became First Sea Lord on 30 October 1914, returning to the office he had left in 1910, he made the strengthening of RNAS patrolling one of his first priorities. Horrified by British shipping losses to mines and submarines, not only did he inaugurate a massive shipbuilding programme but on his second day in office held a meeting of those concerned with air matters that was eventually to result in a non-rigid airship building programme.[4]

The naval air stations in Britain were controlled from the Central Air Office at Sheerness, but control did not mean regimentation. Patrol and other procedures varied greatly from station to station. Many station commanders and pilots in 1914 were naval officers qualified to command small ships and they were given free rein to do their job as they saw fit. Their independent spirit rubbed off on the Royal Marine and direct entry officers serving with them. It was a spirit highly congenial to the Canadians who were to join them. Isolated both from Sheerness and from fleet units, the naval air stations retained their independent character throughout the war. When, in 1915, their rapid increase outgrew the capacity of the Central Air Office to control them, authority over them was assumed by the Air Department itself. This change made no discernible impact on the individualistic tendencies of the naval air stations.[5]

In the first year of the war the capacity of the RNAS to carry out effective patrols in home waters was inhibited not only by shortages of aircraft but by the responsibility it had been assigned for the defence of Britain against air attack. When the war began, Captain Murray Sueter, Director of the Admiralty Air Department, had been ordered to use naval aircraft primarily for this purpose. It was a task for

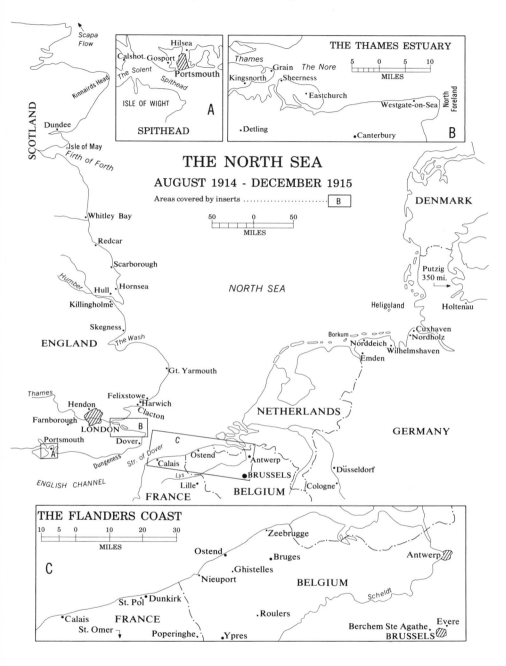

THE THAMES ESTUARY

THE NORTH SEA

AUGUST 1914 - DECEMBER 1915

Areas covered by inserts .... B

SPITHEAD

THE FLANDERS COAST

which the RNAS was unprepared, and certainly not one it had sought. In theory, the War Office was responsible for 'aerial supremacy in the British Isles,' and before the war the General Staff had claimed responsibility for home defence, including the defence of ports and other installations of naval concern. Faced with the realities of war, however, the army authorities 'admitted sorrowfully that they had not got the machines and could not get the money' for home defence. On 3 September 1914, therefore, Lord Kitchener, Secretary of State for War, handed over responsibility for home defence to the Admiralty.[6]

The RNAS was in no better condition than the RFC to discharge this function. In August 1914 it possessed, for all purposes, thirty-one seaplanes and forty aeroplanes, all of very limited range and endurance. Patrols intended to detect the presence of enemy vessels could not be combined with anti-zeppelin patrols. As the RNAS was to discover, the zeppelins waited for nightfall before venturing over land, a circumstance forcing naval pilots to acquire experience in the unfamiliar techniques of night flying. Moreover, German airships normally attacked at heights above the operational ceilings of RNAS aircraft, so that there was little opportunity to build up tactical experience in anti-zeppelin operations. For all these reasons the RNAS was unhappy with its role, but an additional factor caused acute concern to the Admiralty: anti-zeppelin operations took place over the homeland itself, where their inadequacy was spectacularly obvious to the civil population and their conduct was therefore subject to an unwanted amount of public discussion and political comment.

It was not until early 1915 that the RNAS was called upon to come to grips with the zeppelin menace. German army airships were fully occupied over the Western Front in 1914 and the German Naval Airship Division began the war with only one zeppelin, L 3. By the end of the year it had four zeppelins at its new base at Nordholz. On the night of 19–20 January it made its first attack upon England, two airships bombing scattered points in East Anglia. The next visit of naval airships was on the night of 14–15 April when L 9, commanded by *Kapitänleutnant* Heinrich Mathy, bombed an area north of the Tyne. The following night three more zeppelins raided the east coast. No significant damage was done on any of these occasions, nor had the airships encountered any opposition from the RNAS.[7]

Beginning on 29 April 1915 it was the turn of the German army's airship service to carry out a series of raids on southern England from its bases in Belgium. During one of these raids the first interception of an airship over England took place, and a Canadian airman was responsible. Flight Sub-Lieutenant R.H. Mulock, from Winnipeg, had been the first Canadian to join an operational squadron of the RNAS. He had gone overseas with the First Contingent of the Canadian Expeditionary Force, but on 19 January he had been permitted to transfer to the RNAS and had been trained as a pilot at Eastchurch. Flying an Avro, Mulock encountered LZ 38 at the unusually low altitude of 2000 feet on the night of 16–17 May, but after firing one round at her, his Lewis gun jammed.[8]

Two weeks later LZ 38, commanded by *Hauptmann* Erich Lennarz, carried out the first attack upon London. The popular repercussions were disproportionate to the seven fatalities caused. Panic and indiscriminate rioting broke out; for example, on the morning after the raid, the London police reported that a crowd 'raided and attacked a Scotch baker's shop (thinking they were Germans).'[9] When further and more damaging raids followed in June, with no duplication of Mulock's interception, the Admiralty sought to relieve itself of its unwanted burden. On 18 June the War Office was formally requested to take over home defence, but the army authorities, pleading shortage of aircraft and the pre-eminent demands of the Western Front, held out no hope of such a transfer until January 1916. The RNAS had thus to carry on in the face of continued, if sporadic, raiding for the balance of the year. In July new air stations were opened at Redcar, Hornsea, and Scarborough; in August several night-landing grounds were established between The Wash and the Thames estuary. Despite these efforts, the RNAS record of failure in home defence remained unbroken, and was the source of much frustration within the Admiralty and much unfavourable comment outside it.[10]

The Admiralty was particularly aggrieved by this criticism because of its view that offensive action against enemy bases, and not defensive patrolling, was the right policy. It was this thinking that lay behind the pre-emptive strike against Cuxhaven, and had launched much more successful operations from RNAS airfields on the Flanders coast.

The Flanders lodgment, which was to affect greatly RNAS operations during the war as well as the flying careers of many Canadians, had begun fortuitously at an early stage of the war. Shortly after hostilities commenced the aeroplanes at Eastchurch, under Wing Commander C.R. Samson, had been designated a 'mobile squadron' by Sueter. On 24 August 1914 the Admiralty, concerned for the security of the Channel ports, decided to respond to an appeal for help against German cavalry marauders by the Burgomaster of Ostend. Originally conceived as a landing of several hundred men, the project expanded to the commitment of a brigade of Royal Marines, three thousand strong. Churchill aimed at an ostentatious diversion to relieve pressure on Belgian forces near Antwerp and on the British Expeditionary Force retreating from Mons. Samson's mobile squadron was sent to provide the Marines with air reconnaissance. Nine Eastchurch aeroplanes, mostly 'old veteran servants of the Crown,' went to Belgium on 27 August 1914. The Admiralty recalled the squadron together with the marine brigade on 30 August, but by a number of subterfuges Samson, who represented the independent spirit of the RNAS to a quintessential degree, was able to turn a blind eye to repeated orders to return home. On 1 September Admiralty orders arrived for the Eastchurch aeroplanes to operate from Dunkirk.[11]

It was in this manner that the RNAS obtained its toehold on the Continent. From 27 August until the Western Front stabilized at the end of October, Samson's aircraft and the armoured cars he had improvised performed a remarkably varied set of roles in Flanders, operating from Ostend, Antwerp, Lille, Dunkirk, and intermediate points. The chief justification, in the eyes of the Admiralty, for the continued presence of the Eastchurch aeroplanes in Flanders was to find and attack zeppelin bases before the enemy could launch an attack on England. Samson's main effort was therefore directed against the sheds known to exist at Düsseldorf and Cologne. To reach these targets, the attacking aeroplanes had to fly from Antwerp. On 22 September the first raids were launched. Out of four aircraft, one managed to locate the sheds at Düsseldorf, in spite of ground fog, and achieved complete surprise. Unfortunately the pilot glided in so low that the 20-lb bombs did not explode on hitting the shed.* On 9 October, when Antwerp was about to fall to the enemy, the airship bases were again attacked. This time one of the sheds at Düsseldorf and the zeppelin that it housed were destroyed.[12]

After all RNAS aircraft in Flanders were concentrated at Dunkirk in early November, Düsseldorf and Cologne were no longer within range. But on 21 November four newly-acquired Avro 504s were flown to Belfort, behind the French lines, to mount an attack against the sheds at Friedrichshafen, on Lake Constance. Three of the Avros bombed the sheds, but had to be content with near misses. British aircraft made no further attempts on this target until 1916.[13] This was not the end of the RNAS offensive against zeppelins, however. After the German army established airship bases in Belgium and commenced the raiding of England, Dunkirk airmen achieved some notable victories. On the same night that Mulock made his brief interception of LZ 38 over England, pilots from Dunkirk damaged LZ 39 on its return flight. On 6 June 1915 four pilots from Dunkirk took off to raid the Belgian sheds, their attack coinciding with an airship raid on England. Flight Sub-Lieutenant R.A.J. Warneford, flying a Morane Parasol monoplane, intercepted LZ 37, scored hits with his incendiary bombs, and became the first pilot to destroy a zeppelin in the air. Warneford, who won the Victoria Cross for this feat, died eleven days later in a flying accident at Paris. Two other pilots in Henri Farman biplanes bombed the sheds at St Evère and destroyed LZ 38, which had returned early with engine trouble. The commander at Dunkirk used these successes to gain Admiralty approval for an immediate expansion of the forces at Dunkirk, but at the same time the German army closed down its Belgian bases. Most of its future attacks were made from sheds in the Rhineland. Only one more airship was destroyed by RNAS Dunkirk in 1915, at Zeebrugge in August.[14]

Long before this the RNAS had secured acceptance from the Admiralty for the continuance of its presence in Belgium, because of Churchill's belief that 'We would have to concentrate our energies on the Belgian coast, and make every effort to attack Zeppelin bases in case they opened some in Belgium.' After 7 November the RNAS at Dunkirk was placed 'under the general command of the Commander-in-Chief in France, who will authorize them to proceed with their special mission' – that is, surveillance of the Channel coast and action against zeppelin bases.[15]

Dunkirk was to become the largest single RNAS operational base, and to remain so for much of the war. Just why it should have become the favoured child of the Admiralty is not easy to explain, although its strategic position on the left flank of the allied armies and upon the vital artery of the Channel was probably a telling factor. Its very location, however, encouraged a diffuseness of aim and function, a tendency furthered by the relatively loose rein held by the Admiralty on its successive commanders. As a result, virtually every aspect of military aviation was, at one time or another, pursued at Dunkirk, from sea patrolling and work with fleet units to aerial fighting, bombing, and co-operation with ground forces. Partly

---

* For a bomb to be primed for detonation it was necessary to release it at a sufficient height to allow the nosecap to be unwound by the action of airdriven vanes.

because of its versatility, Dunkirk became an experimental arena for the naval air service and its activities often reflected the most advanced and innovative thinking in the Admiralty Air Department.

There was always a fundamental reason for a base at Dunkirk: the need to patrol the Channel. Regular patrolling by 3 Squadron, as the Dunkirk aircraft were designated, began in November 1914. The pilots christened their beat the 'Iron Coast,' in reference to the ever increasing number of coastal and anti-aircraft batteries the Germans constructed. Changeable weather conditions meant a difficult flying environment, particularly with the heterogeneous and obsolescent collection of aeroplanes and seaplanes the Dunkirk establishment flew in 1914 and early 1915.[16]

Dunkirk also became the focus for the strong naval interest in aerial bombing. In December 1914 Sueter laid down the requirement for 'a bloody paralyser' of an aircraft – the origin of the Handley Page bomber. Samson did what he could to implement the clear direction from the Air Department for an aggressive bombing policy, not only against zeppelin bases but also against a reported submarine depot south of Bruges. He also planned night attacks on the coast, primarily for their effect upon morale, for only incidental damage could be hoped for.[17] In March 1915 Samson and 3 Squadron departed for the Dardanelles; their replacements, Squadron Commander A.M. Longmore and 1 Squadron, continued the pattern already established. Indeed, in suggesting the path for future aircraft development, Longmore gave first place to the production of heavy bombing machines, followed by high performance fighters and torpedo-carrying seaplanes, priorities which left no doubt of his offensive-mindedness.

When, on 21 June 1915, consequent upon Dunkirk's solid achievements against German airships, the Admiralty authorized an increase in its establishment to six squadrons of aeroplanes and seaplanes, the tasks allotted reflected the diverse activities of the base. Aeroplanes provided cover for ships bombarding German installations along the coast, escorted seaplanes spotting for the ships, and carried out coastal reconnaissance flights to observe the results of bombardments, to report on activity in Ostend and Zeebrugge, and to watch for German mines and submarines at sea. Offensive roles were given particular prominence. On 26 August near Ostend a British pilot made the first recorded attack by a heavier-than-air machine against a submarine. Eleven days later Mulock, who had joined 1 Wing, as the Dunkirk establishment was now known, in July, made the second recorded attack. On 28 September Mulock was allowed to make a lone bombing raid on the zeppelin sheds at Berchem Ste Agathe: 'a remarkable incident of cross country flying,' wrote Longmore, 'as he had to depend almost entirely on Compass and Time.'[18]

By this time, as the result of a further reorganization in August, Dunkirk had been amalgamated with the RNAS units at Dover under the command of the Vice-Admiral Dover Patrol. Wing Captain C.L. Lambe was in direct command of the eight squadrons. He used the two at Dover for reconnaissance work and for fighter patrols and the six at Dunkirk, which were still in process of formation, he allocated in pairs to the functions of spotting and reconnaissance, fighter patrols and bombing. Like Longmore, Lambe recognized that effective bombing would require aircraft with longer ranges and heavier payloads. Looking forward to the acquisition of the Short bomber and the Sopwith 1½ Strutter, he wrote in November to his commander, Vice-Admiral Bacon, that it would soon be possible to attack 'strategical points such as the lock-gates of canals, railway bridges, cuttings or stations.' He had no doubt about where Dunkirk's priorities should lie, recommending to Bacon the formation of two more wings of four squadrons each to concentrate 'especially on offensive operations.'[19] Admiralty approval of this project came on 13 December, at a time when the Dardanelles campaign was coming to an end and negotiations with the War Office were under way to relieve the RNAS of the home defence burden. The terms of reference given the new wings show the Admiralty's ambivalence over the bombing role, as well as the ambiguities of the Dover-Dunkirk establishment: '... the inland work of the Royal Naval Air Service is to be for the training of personnel in contact with the enemy. The units stationed at these two Aerodromes may be regarded as available in connection with military operations at times *when Naval Air work proper is not required to be carried out*. They will also, if necessary, be drawn upon for completing any Naval Air Service units serving in, or ordered to be dispatched to other spheres of operations, and together with the Naval Air Force at Dunkirk must always be held available for large coast operations when required.'[20]

The evolution of Dunkirk encapsulates Churchill's search for an offensive role for the navy, including the RNAS. Both he and Fisher were concerned that most of the enormous strength of the Royal Navy lay in 'cold storage.' In April 1915 he had enthusiastically endorsed Longmore's priorities for aircraft development. Churchill's main object was not 'reconnaissance and patrolling' but

... the attacking with bombs on the largest possible scale of military points on enemy territory. For this, weight of explosives and numbers of machines are more necessary than skill of pilots or special fighting qualities in the machines. We shall then have passed the stage of daring exploits, and must acquire the power to strike heavy blows which will produce decisive effects on the enemy's fighting strength. The carrying of two to three tons of explosives to a particular point of attack in a single night or day is the least we should aim at as an operation in the future. All possible objectives should be studied and special reports made upon them. The capacities of machines should be considered in relation to these definite tasks.[21]

Churchill's concentration upon offensive roles for the RNAS, and especially upon land-based bombing operations, persuaded many professional naval officers that he had neglected the purely naval side of aviation. It should not be overlooked, however, that he had much professional opinion on his side. A case in point was the response to the rise of the submarine menace. Churchill and many professional officers believed that bombing raids upon submarine installations was the best answer, but others, led by Fisher, held the view that submarines should be attacked at sea, where they were most dangerous and most likely to be found.[22]

Had the two men continued in office, their differing views might merely have produced a healthy tension. When both resigned in May 1915 over the Dardanelles controversy, the RNAS lost its foremost patrons. The comparative lethargy of the new administration is a matter of record.[23] A.J. Balfour as First Lord took a less personal part in making decisions than had Churchill. Admiral Sir Henry Jackson as First Sea Lord was a man of impressive scientific attainments, but he had little of Fisher's drive. The position of Jellicoe as Commander-in-Chief, Grand Fleet, was thus enhanced, and it was his view on air policy that now prevailed.

With Churchill gone the professional sea officers seemed resolved to impose their interpretations upon naval aviation. Jellicoe's memorandum on the functions of the service contrasts sharply with Churchill's pugnacious utterances:

a Observation duties from the coast generally, and from naval bases in particular.
b The attack of enemy aircraft wherever met.
c The aerial defence of all naval centres, such as dockyards, magazines, since the Army who, properly speaking, should carry out this work have apparently turned it over to the navy.
d Scouting for enemy submarines and enemy minelayers, which properly comes under the heading of reconnaissance work.[24]

The further reorganization of the RNAS reflected these aims. In August 1915 RNAS units were absorbed into naval commands. Commanding officers now reported not to the Air Department, but to senior naval officers in their locality. Rear-Admiral C.L. Vaughan-Lee, who had no air experience, was placed in charge of the Air Department in September, over the head of Murray Sueter, whose responsibilities were reduced to aircraft construction. And, in respect to equipment, the rigid airship programme was reinstated. C.R. Samson spoke for many naval airmen when he observed upon his return from the Dardanelles that 'The R.N.A.S. was in the hands of those that knew it not, and the prevalent idea seemed to be that the active pilots were a wild sort of people who should be kept well under.'[25] The fact was, however, that the RNAS itself remained ineradicably stamped with the offensive-mindedness Churchill and Fisher had exemplified and, despite Jellicoe's principles, the new administration, as we have seen, was prepared greatly to expand the land-based bombing role at Dunkirk.

The Churchill-Fisher administration left not only a legacy of offensive-mindedness to the RNAS, but also the Dardanelles campaign, in which the RNAS had been committed almost from the start. After failing to muster War Office support for an amphibious attack upon Zeebrugge, a project that had had Fisher's full support, Churchill persuaded his Cabinet colleagues to undertake an eastern strategy, using the fleet to force access to Constantinople. In what became the largest combined operation of the war, the RNAS provided the air support. *Ark Royal* went to the Eastern Mediterranean with her seaplanes in February. When Samson arrived with 3 Squadron on 24 March, Vice-Admiral J.M. de Robeck had already abandoned his attempt to force the Dardanelles. On 9 April a kite balloon ship arrived and on 19 April it was put to use observing the fall of shot for the bombardment of targets invisible to the guns.

By this time the RNAS had formed another curious organization at the Dardanelles. Based at Mudros Bay, responsible to the Commander-in-Chief, Eastern Mediterranean, was the *Ark Royal*. At Tenedos, on land leased from a local landowner, was 3 Squadron; in July, redesignated 3 Wing, it moved to Imbros. Wing

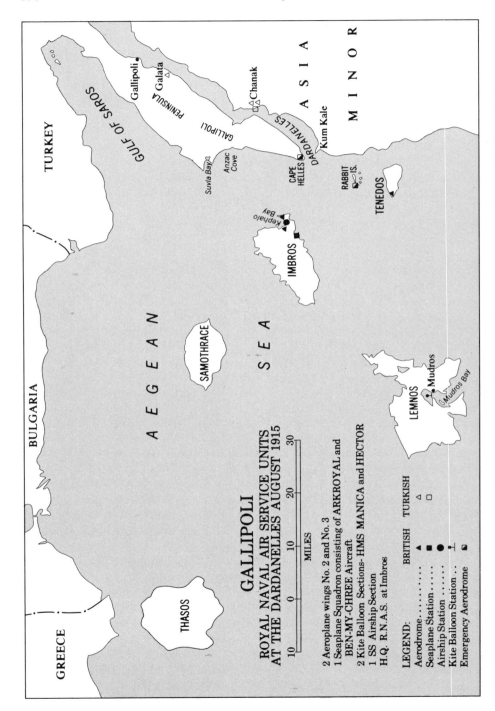

GALLIPOLI
ROYAL NAVAL AIR SERVICE UNITS
AT THE DARDANELLES AUGUST 1915

2 Aeroplane wings No. 2 and No. 3
1 Seaplane Squadron consisting of ARKROYAL and
   BEN-MY-CHREE Aircraft
2 Kite Balloon Sections- HMS MANICA and HECTOR
1 SS Airship Section
H.Q. R.N.A.S. at Imbros

LEGEND:

	BRITISH	TURKISH
Aerodrome.........	▲	△
Seaplane Station....	■	□
Airship Station......	●	
Kite Balloon Station..	⊺	
Emergency Aerodrome	◧	

Commander Samson was responsible to the C-in-C Eastern Mediterranean for operations, but when giving aerial support to the army reported to General Sir Ian Hamilton. There was also a French squadron at Tenedos, working with the French army. The kite balloon ship, *Manica*, was absorbed into the naval chain of command. The nearest RNAS headquarters was the Air Department of the Admiralty. Thus a triad of air units, occasionally reinforced, was to provide all the aerial support for both land and sea operations in the ensuing attempt to take the Gallipoli peninsula.[26]

In a sense, Gallipoli was similar to 3 Wing's earlier experience in Flanders, except that Turkish air opposition did not compare to German strength in Belgium. On the other hand, there was no RFC support, and the RNAS simply did not have enough aircraft to meet its many duties. Of Samson's eighteen aeroplanes, only five were of real use.* Seaplanes could be employed to observe the fall of shot during bombardments, as could kite balloons, but the only way seaplane pilots could gain sufficient altitude was to find one of the notorious thermals or 'up-currents' of the region to give them the needed lift. Kite balloons were excellent for stationary targets, but enemy troops could easily evade them by taking shelter in dead ground. Only aeroplanes could be used for the whole range of flying duties and even they were handicapped by having to fly from an island base to the lines, 'the equivalent oversea flight of crossing the English Channel.'[27] In face of their flying difficulties, it was dispiriting for the RNAS airmen to find that their efforts, particularly in spotting for naval bombardments, were not always appreciated. Ships' gunnery officers were reluctant to believe large spotting corrections. Only when ships began to hold post-mortems on shoots did the seamen come to accept the value of air observation.[28]

Admiral de Robeck managed to persuade the Admiralty to send out additional aircraft in order to ease the strain on Samson's meagre resources.† In June three new pilots arrived; one of them was Flight Sub-Lieutenant H.S. Kerby of Calgary, with fifteen hours of flying experience behind him. These reinforcements were much needed, for the preparations for the Suvla landings created new demands on the air service for information. As at Helles in April, air reports and photographs provided the only reliable intelligence. There were only six pilots available in 3 Wing, and in the days preceding the new landing they 'practically lived in the air.' Bombardment and artillery spotting had almost to be abandoned while reconnaissance was carried out in co-operation with the seaplanes of *Ark Royal* (now anchored in Kephalo Bay because she was too slow to proceed to sea in the face of

---

* Samson says 3 Squadron had twenty-two aircraft, but he only specifically names the same eighteen given in Great Britain, Admiralty Gunnery Division, *Report of the Committee Appointed to Investigate the Attacks Delivered on and the Enemy Defences of the Dardanelles Straits, 1919* ([London] 1921).
† The first batch sent out, obsolete Henri Farmans, were returned. In June five Voisin two-seaters with 140-hp Canton Unné engines were accepted – slow aircraft, and no longer satisfactory in France, but in the absence of enemy air opposition useful for reconnaissance. Eventually they wore out, from having to fly continuously at full revolutions in order to maintain adequate altitude. It was in July that the first really effective reinforcements arrived: six 80-hp Nieuports, excellent aircraft for bombing, single-seater reconnaissance, and aerial combat, and six Maurice Farmans. *Report of the Committee ... on ... the Dardanelles*, 519

the submarine threat) and *Ben-my-Chree*. The latter, the most recently converted merchantman, had arrived on 12 June with 225-hp Short 184 seaplanes and Sopwith Schneider seaplanes, great improvements on the old Wights and Shorts. In torpedo attacks the Shorts scored notable successes in sinking two ships and scoring a direct hit on another that was already aground. There were less successful attempts as well, however, primarily because it required a perfectly running machine and ideal conditions to lift the torpedo.[29]

The Admiralty had realized the need for an assessment of the air situation in June and Colonel F.H. Sykes of the RFC was sent out to report. On 24 July Sykes took command of a central air headquarters at Imbros, with the RNAS rank of wing captain, thus placing Gallipoli and Dunkirk on a similar footing. The reinforcements so badly needed did not appear until late in August. By the time 2 Wing arrived the situation had reverted to static warfare once again, but there was more need for fighter patrols and for bombing, especially on the Turkish line of communications. In addition, in November the Admiralty issued orders for long-distance bombing raids.[30] By then there were about fifty aeroplanes, twenty-three seaplanes, three SS airships (only one was inflated) for anti-submarine patrols, and three kite balloons. But the Admiralty never allocated aircraft to Gallipoli on the scale required by land forces. As Sykes repeatedly stated, his command was hopelessly undermanned by RFC standards. There were two armies on the peninsula, consisting of two corps each plus an independent division. In France such an establishment would have been served by nine squadrons and a flight, or at least 168 aircraft. The Admiralty, however, had not yet adopted any precise table of organization for the RNAS. A squadron of aeroplanes was variously considered at this time to consist of six to ten machines. Seaplanes were sometimes organized into flights, and sometimes into squadrons, presumably according to the capacity of seaplane carriers and to the number of aircraft that could be spared. Not until May 1916 did the Admiralty attempt to lay down exact definitions for units.[31]

On 7 December 1915 it was decided to evacuate Gallipoli, and by 9 January the last troops had gone. No 3 Wing disbanded, Samson's recognition being a censure for a fire in one of his workshops. With a maximum of eleven pilots and an average of seven, and sometimes with as few as four aeroplanes, the wing had logged 2600 hours in the air in exactly nine months.[32]

The navy and the RNAS maintained a presence in the Eastern Mediterranean. No 2 Wing remained at Imbros with three squadrons of ten machines each, eighteen pilots, eight observers, and a photographic section. To the west lay Salonika and the *Ark Royal*, sent in November to provide some air support for a new Anglo-French Mediterranean adventure. At Mudros Bay on the island of Lemnos there were six SS airships. Thus, as 1915 came to an end, the Aegean Sea became a general theatre of operations for the RNAS. To the south, off Palestine, in the Red Sea, and in East Africa there were other units of the RNAS.[33]

A detachment of the RNAS had been drawn into the East African campaign when the German surface raider *Königsberg* went to earth in one of the myriad branches of the Rufiji River delta. In the humid tropical heat, with its lack of lift, and maintenance problems of warping wood, melting glue, and stretching fabric, bombing the *Königsberg* proved impossible. In early June 1915 two shallow draft monitors, *Severn* and *Mersey*, sailed into the Rufiji delta hoping to sink the *Königsberg* with gunfire. Sea and air officers worked out a clock code together, testing it in exercises during which two of the RNAS' four machines were wrecked. On 11 July Flight Commander J.T. Cull and his observer, Flight Sub-Lieutenant H.J. Arnold from the Queen Charlotte Islands, BC, had begun to record hits on the *Königsberg* when shell splinters took away two cylinders from their Henri Farman. As the aircraft planed down, Arnold radioed the final correction that led to the destruction of the German ship. The Farman came down near the *Mersey*, turned over, and trapped Cull. Arnold, who had been thrown clear, swam back and helped his pilot to escape the wreckage.* Cull then took the remaining aeroplanes up-country to participate in the land campaign, while the seaplanes went to Mesopotamia.[34]

The traditional mobility of sea power had played an important part in shaping the roles of the RNAS by the end of 1915. The urgent need to develop and acquire aeroplanes capable of the speed and range for effective bombing had been another consideration, one that had led to the neglect of rigid airships and to some extent of seaplanes and flying boats. Lighter-than-air and seaplane operations became more important with the rise of the submarine threat. These functions, and the varying importance given them, dictated personnel policy which in turn determined the manner in which Canadians were to participate in RNAS operations.

There were three avenues to naval air units for Canadians: by transfer from other forces overseas, by travelling to England to join the RNAS 'from shore,' and by joining through the Naval Service of Canada. In the first category was J.A. Barron of Stratford, Ont. He had joined the Canadian Marine Service as a cadet in 1908 and was one of the Naval Service of Canada's first group of cadets in 1910. In 1912 he received a medical discharge, but managed to get himself accepted as a midshipman in the Royal Navy in 1914. He was the only Canadian among the midshipmen selected for airship service in 1915.† Officers were only chosen for airships and kite balloons if they had naval background or experience. Consequently all the other Canadians in the RNAS in 1915 went to heavier-than-air squadrons. Three transferred from the CEF: R.H. Mulock, T.D. Hallam of Toronto, and W.B. Lawson of Barrie, Ont., a graduate of the Royal Military College of Canada who by the end of the year was taking up an appointment with the seaplane force in Mesopotamia.

At least three Canadians paid their own way to England. H.S. Kerby, already mentioned, who went on to a distinguished career in the Royal Air Force, made his way overseas from Calgary with J.T. Bone, who lost his life in a drowning accident while flying at Dover in November 1915. J.E.D. Boyd, a Torontonian, failed to return from a raid over Zeebrugge on 3 October 1915. He was interned after a forced landing in Holland.

Those who joined in Canada did not become available for operational flying until later in the year. The first two graduates of the Curtiss School in Toronto,

---

* Arnold was awarded the DSO for his part in the proceedings. He was killed in 1918.
† In 1918 he would help J.T. Cull to organize the Royal Canadian Naval Air Service. See chapter 19.

W.H. Peberdy and A. Strachan Ince of Toronto, went to Dunkirk in October, where Ince took part in one of the only two decisive combats recorded by the Dunkirk Wing in 1915. On 14 December, as observer in a Nieuport two-seater, he shot down a large German seaplane. The Nieuport was damaged and had to ditch, but the crew escaped to a nearby minesweeper.[35] Two more of the early Curtiss students went to home stations: C.G. Gooderham of Toronto to Whitley Bay and R.E. Bush, an English immigrant who had enlisted in Canada, to Westgate.

When Squadron Commander Bell Davies returned from Gallipoli to command the naval air station at Killingholme early in 1916, he found that with home defence no longer a prime responsibility of the RNAS there was little for experienced aeroplane pilots to do at coastal stations. He recommended a number of them, including Gooderham (who was now at Scarborough), for service abroad because of their competence in night flying.[36] Gooderham had an active career at Dunkirk. C. MacLaurin of East Templeton, Que., A.J. Nightingale of Toronto, A.T.N. Cowley of Victoria, and F.S. McGill of Montreal,* who had qualified in the United States and then joined the RNAS in Canada, became seaplane pilots at Calshot, Dover, and Westgate and in the new seaplane carrier, HMS *Vindex*. The seven Canadians who sailed for England in September and October and qualified as aeroplane pilots were to form a squadron under Squadron Commander R.L.G. Marix at Detling, the nucleus of the future 3 Wing. R.D. Delamere of Toronto, selected in 1916 to join Cull's aeroplane party in East Africa, was the only one of those who joined in Canada in 1915 to be sent away from the vicinity of home waters.

At the end of 1915 the RNAS had been committed to many theatres and to a large number of functions and was on the threshold of a period of rapid expansion and of considerable improvement in aircraft quality and supply. Though the service had not clearly been directed either towards an offensive policy or towards the pursuit of more conventional naval duties, the Admiralty seemed content to permit it to follow both. It was coincidental that Canadians should begin to arrive in significant numbers at this stage, but the timing of their arrival was crucial in deciding the form their contribution would take. They were soon to be found wherever the RNAS was operating, but the bulk went either to Dunkirk or to coastal air stations in Britain. As a result, in 1916 many Canadians were to be directly involved in the next stage of RNAS experimentation, whether in long-range bombing over the Continent or in the development of the war against the U-boat and in the struggle for air mastery over the North Sea.

---

* Cowley and McGill both later rose to the rank of air vice-marshal in the Royal Canadian Air Force.

6
1916: Diffusion and Misdirection

By January 1916 there were some 120 Canadians in the Royal Naval Air Service, either actively engaged or *en route* from Canada to flying stations.* What they and those who were to join them in the course of the year were to do rested with the Admiralty. The naval officers who struggled to find an air policy 'for all seasons' ran into severe criticisms from many quarters: they were accused of having no imagination (especially about aircraft carriers and torpedo aircraft), of lagging behind the Germans in home waters, and of misusing their forces. The Admiralty, indeed, became embroiled with the War Office and Air Board over undue RNAS concentration on bombing and the inefficient use of forces at Dunkirk – a charge that rendered that command vulnerable to Royal Flying Corps raids upon its strength. Especially damaging was the claim that the navy refused to co-operate in aircraft supply and operational planning. But such great matters, and the shakeup in high command which resulted, were remote from naval airmen on daily flying operations, where the Canadians without exception were to be found.

German naval air policy, meanwhile, was determined by the strategy of *Admiral* Reinhard Scheer, who received his appointment as Commander-in-Chief of the High Seas Fleet on 24 January 1916. Scheer had no wish to bring the enemy's numerically stronger Grand Fleet to battle, but he proposed to keep up 'constant pressure' by provocative sweeps using all or part of the High Seas Fleet, by the harassment of British merchantmen trading with Scandinavia, and by an increased emphasis upon submarine, mine, and aerial warfare. The Royal Navy would be compelled to send out ships to meet these challenges. Sooner or later, Scheer believed, he would find 'favourable possibilities of attack.'[1]

Jutland was the most important result of this strategy. The buildup to it began with the mass airship raid of 31 January. England's home defence system, termed not altogether unfairly 'a screaming farce' by the editor of *Flight*, was swiftly reorganized in the aftermath of this action, and the RNAS as a result was left with only secondary responsibilities.[2] Since its role was now restricted to offshore defence, the naval air arm was presumably in a position to redeploy its strength elsewhere. But where, and in what form?

---

* Total officer strength of the RNAS in December 1915 was 1634. Director, Air Division, 'Appreciation of British Naval Effort RNAS Aircraft Operations,' Nov. 1918, Air 1/308/15/226/91

The Admiralty unfortunately had narrowed the options by according low priority to a plan submitted by Squadron Commander de G. Ireland, commanding officer of Great Yarmouth Air Station, which called for 'between fifty and one hundred' torpedo-carrying aircraft to be ready by summer for a raid on the High Seas Fleet at its bases.[3] The Board of Admiralty, influenced by the poor showing of seaplanes in 1915 and by still unsolved technical problems, placed no urgency upon its order to Short Brothers to design the required aircraft. Not until January 1917 was a production contract let out for twenty-five Short 320s, armed with an 18-inch Mark IX torpedo.*

Instead, the Admiralty was much more interested in a long-range bombing programme, which would employ the high-powered engines the navy virtually monopolized as the result of its agreement with the RFC at the beginning of the war. The Admiralty's preoccupation with strategic bombing heavily biased RNAS operations during 1916; moreover, it brought a confrontation with the RFC on several levels: at the level of high policy, over which service ought properly to carry out this role; at the operational level, over the question of control of air activities on the Western Front; and at the level of production and supply, over how, and according to which priorities, aircraft and engine production ought to be shared between the two services.

It was the strategic bombing argument, combined with strong public dissatisfaction with the apparent failure of the two air services to collaborate effectively against zeppelin attacks, that led the British government to establish the Joint War Air Committee 'for the interchange of ideas and the co-ordination of procedures.'[4] The committee, which consisted of Admiralty and War Office representatives, was established on 24 February 1916. It was short-lived. Its chairman, Lord Derby, proved unable to resolve the main differences between the two services. Over the matter of supply, the Admiralty was intransigent, though it made minor concessions. On the matter of strategic bombing, it was adamant. The paper submitted by the Admiralty in early March for committee discussion laid out the following list of RNAS duties:

1 To attack the enemy's fleets, dockyards, arsenals, factories, air sheds, etc. ...
2 To patrol our own coasts to look out for enemy's ships and submarines, and to meet and repel enemy aircraft. Possibly also to discover minefields.
3 Observation of fire during ships' bombardment of enemy's coasts. Destruction of enemy's coast batteries, means of communication thereto, and material in connection therewith.
4 Scouting for the fleet and reconnaissance work from ships (vide Egypt).
5 To assist the Army whenever and wherever required. (vide East Africa and Mesopotamia).[5]

In early April Derby and Lord Montagu of Beaulieu, who had now joined the committee, decided that it was futile to continue. Derby wrote the Prime Minister

---

* The original version of the Short had the less powerful 310-hp Sunbeam Cossack Engine. By March 1918 the navy had taken delivery of 110 Short 320s. Owen Thetford, *British Naval Aircraft since 1912* (London 1962), 262

that it had been 'quite impossible to bring the two wings closer together,' and that it would not be done 'unless and until the whole system of the Air Service is changed and they are amalgamated into one service as personally I consider they ultimately must be.'[6]

With great difficulty terms of reference for another committee were hammered out. The Air Board's chief architect was Lord Curzon, the Lord Privy Seal; its chief critic was Lord Balfour, at the Admiralty, who feared complications if the proposed board were treated as a 'third fighting department controlling all aerial operations (which is I believe what an unthinking public really want) ...'[7] What emerged was a relatively weak body, with Curzon as its president. Advisory in nature, the Air Board was charged with organizing supply for the two services and was 'free to discuss' matters of general policy. Should the services refuse to follow the recommendations of the president, the War Committee of the Cabinet was the only court of appeal. In May the new board turned warily to a discussion of the problems that had sunk the Derby Committee.

By that time, however, the Admiralty had unilaterally decided upon its own course of action. Nothing Curzon or the RFC representatives could say affected this. It had become clear in February that long-range bombing operations based on Dunkirk were only possible in co-ordination with and under the control of the Commander-in-Chief of the BEF. Nevertheless, the assumption by the RNAS of a strategic bombing role and the establishment of 3 Naval Bombing Wing at Luxeuil was a *fait accompli*. That decision had an important effect upon the capacity of the RNAS to carry out its other duties. Pilots for Luxeuil, and for long-range operations from Dunkirk, had to come from somewhere. By the end of 1916 Luxeuil alone was employing roughly 20 per cent of all RNAS aeroplane pilots.[8]

Most of the pilots for the bombing role came from home stations in the British Isles. Some of the small airfields that had been used for home defence were dispensed with; strength was concentrated at the main coastal and training stations. Cuts in the home establishment were not uniform. The seaplane element, for example, was left untouched. Its chief task remained the hunt for submarines and mines in support of the ship patrol, and it was a task in which Canadians played their part. When the second U-boat campaign against merchant shipping off the British coast began in March-April 1916, Canadians were flying from most of the main seaplane stations.* The small flying boats and seaplanes these men flew – the Short 18, Short 827/830, Sopwith Schneider, and Baby fighters – were slow, poorly armed, and frequently had no wireless equipment. Against submarines they were completely ineffective. However, because the Admiralty was preparing to expand the force with flying-boats when the new Curtiss 'Large America' H12s and more Curtiss 'Small America' H4s were delivered, it was unwilling to make cuts in the seaplane establishment.[9]

Of necessity, then, bomber pilots had to be taken from the pool of aeroplane pilots on home stations. Even here, however, there were both political and military reasons not to go too far. The RNAS still had a secondary responsibility for

---

* Flight Sub-Lieutenants C.N. Geale of Toronto and H.A. Peck of Montreal were at Calshot, while C. McLaurin of East Templeton, Que., was at Bembridge (a Calshot sub-station on the Isle of Wight); J.O. Galpin of Ottawa, B.D. Hobbs of Sault Ste Marie, Ont., and W.H. Mackenzie of Victoria were at Felixstowe, and F.C. Henderson of Toronto was at Killingholme.

home defence, and was vulnerable to public criticism for the manner in which that responsibility was carried out. The weakness of seaplanes against zeppelins, and against German aeroplanes now sporadically raiding coastal towns, meant that defence had to be stiffened by 'fast, rapid-climbing aeroplanes.' Moreover, in the RNAS scheme of things, the home defence establishment was really coterminous with its night-flying training. In April 36 per cent of the 304 aeroplanes on active RNAS duty were being used for this combination of home defence and night-flying duties. By the end of the year the number of aeroplanes on such duties had increased only slightly; more significant, all but ten had been downgraded to the category of second-class aircraft.* In other words, as the Admiralty reordered priorities for its air service, the home aeroplane element lost most of its experienced pilots and its aircraft were allowed to become largely obsolescent.[10]

With the exception of a few veteran pilots retained for night flying, the RNAS used the home aeroplane organization as a graduate course for inexperienced pilots. Flight Sub-Lieutenant L.S. Breadner of Carleton Place, Ont., was a typical example of the young Canadians now being sent for training to operational stations in England. With three other Canadians who had also been at the Wright School at Dayton, he arrived at Redcar in early February; 'a splendid station,' he wrote, 'well-equipped and we will be started flying at once.' The Canadians arrived at their various stations in batches and at first had a tendency to stick together. 'How clannish the Canucks are,' Breadner noted, but 'we are all willing to fly on any kind of a day and that's what pleases the C.O. ... He is tickled with us and is trying to get all the Canadians he can here.'† After train-

---

* In calculating its strength, the RNAS had adopted the practice of distinguishing between first- and second-class aircraft. The former were the most effective combat machines available at the date of assessment; the latter were obsolescent or obsolete machines which were not for use against serious enemy opposition. Some of these second-class aircraft were probably no worse than the aging machines utilized by the RFC on the Western Front.

† Not all station commanders were as enthusiastic. Flight Sub-Lieutenants M.G. Dover of Winnipeg, C.E. Moore of Fort William, Ont., K.M. Smith and Bert Wemp of Toronto figured in a bizarre incident in May in which they clashed with their station commander at Yarmouth. In the words of the investigating officer: 'Squadron Commander Oliver (whom I gathered does not much care for these Canadian Officers) made some remark in the Officers' Mess after dinner about their want of knowledge in the English language and their method of expressing themselves, and said (in what he intended to be a joking manner) that they were to have half-an-hour's [instruction in] English every morning. This was taken literally (or possibly with a view of annoying these officers) by Sub-Lieutenant [S.K.] Reeves, who ordered them to parade in the lecture room the following morning at 9:30. They were all of them (and, in my opinion, quite justifiably so) furious at this reflection on their speech and manners, and agreed together to tender their resignations failing their being removed from the Yarmouth Air Station.' Oliver thereupon called them before him and read them an extract from the Articles of War on 'mutinous assembly.' Oliver was subsequently reprimanded for tactlessness, and the four Canadians were transferred elsewhere. Air 1/416/15/243/pt III. There is some evidence that the arrival of Canadians was not without friction at other stations in 1916, but the period of mutual incomprehension does not seem to have lasted long. The May incident might be seen as the beginning of Bert Wemp's political career. He was later a member of the Board of Education of Toronto, an alderman, controller, and then, briefly in the early 1930s, mayor of Toronto. During the Second World War he travelled to Europe several times as a correspondent for *The Telegram*; one of his bosses described Wemp as 'an exception to the style of dramatic writing that gave *The Telegram* its flavor.' *Globe and Mail* (Toronto), 7 Feb. 1976

ing at Redcar and other stations, Breadner was posted to 1 Wing at Dunkirk in July.[11]

What is particularly notable about his experience is that at Redcar, green though he was, Breadner along with other inexperienced pilots was slated for duty on a roster system in case of air raids. A good many Canadians undergoing final pilot training in 1916 had similar experiences; some of them were actually introduced to the war in the air on anti-zeppelin patrols. Flight Sub-Lieutenant R. Collishaw of Nanaimo, BC, one of the most famous of all Canadian pilots, first flew operationally in this way from Redcar, before joining the Luxeuil bombing wing. Similarly, Flight Sub-Lieutenant Grant Gooderham of Toronto gained his first operational experience against zeppelins before being sent to Dunkirk. Although such training was invaluable for the pilots concerned, it is hardly surprising that the RNAS continued to be criticized for its failings in the home defence role.

The chief beneficiary of the Admiralty's shift in policy was the Dover-Dunkirk Command. During 1916, under Wing Captain C.L. Lambe, it was expanded rapidly. The command operated under Vice-Admiral Reginald Bacon's Dover Patrol, which had three main objectives: to protect the cross-Channel supply routes of the British Expeditionary Force; to harass enemy submarines using Belgian ports; and to take offensive action, by whatever means, against the Channel end of the German lines, manned at their western extremity by three divisions of marine infantry. These objectives dictated the RNAS roles of coastal reconnaissance, wireless spotting for ship bombardment of the shore, anti-submarine and hostile aircraft patrols, and the interception of zeppelins and aircraft returning from raids upon England. To oppose them the German navy had seaplanes at *Seeflugstation Flanders I* on the Mole at Zeebrugge and a growing force of *Marine Korps* aeroplanes in Flanders.[12]

At first Flight Sub-Lieutenants R.H. Mulock of Winnipeg, A.S. Ince of Toronto, and B.C. Tooke, address unknown, were the only Canadians in the command. All but the last had already seen service in the command in 1915.* During the early months of 1916 Mulock was rapidly consolidating his growing reputation as an all-round operational pilot. On 24 January, while carrying out a photo reconnaissance flight to Ostend and Ghistelles, an inland aerodrome to the southeast, he drove down a German biplane to a forced landing. Two days later, while taking part in an operation in which five monitors bombarded shore batteries near Westende, he intercepted a large two-seater biplane heading for the flotilla. Putting his Nieuport Scout under the enemy's tail, he followed his opponent through a cloud bank and then sent his quarry plunging to the ground. Within a week Mulock was taking a prominent part in another of the command's duties. Before dawn on 1 February ten Nieuports were patrolling a line between Nieuport and Zeebrugge at 10,000 feet, hoping to catch zeppelins returning from the first mass raid of the

* By February nine Canadian aeroplane pilots – Flight Sub-Lieutenants E.R. Grange of Toronto, G.E. Hervey of Edmonton, G.C.V. Hewson of Port Hope, Ont., G.N. Hughes of Picton, Ont., H.G. Leslie of Victoria, A.M. Shook of Tioga, Ont., C. Thom of Merritt, BC, A.S. Todd of Toronto, and K. Van Allen of Winnipeg, and two RNVR sub-lieutenants employed as observers, C.L. Hains of Salmon Arm, BC, and A.I. Hutty of Toronto – had joined 1 Wing at St Pol, Dunkirk, while A.T.N. Cowley of Victoria and T.G.M. Stephens of Toronto, flying seaplanes, and an aeroplane pilot, D.A.H. Nelles of Simcoe, Ont., were at the replacement stations at Dover.

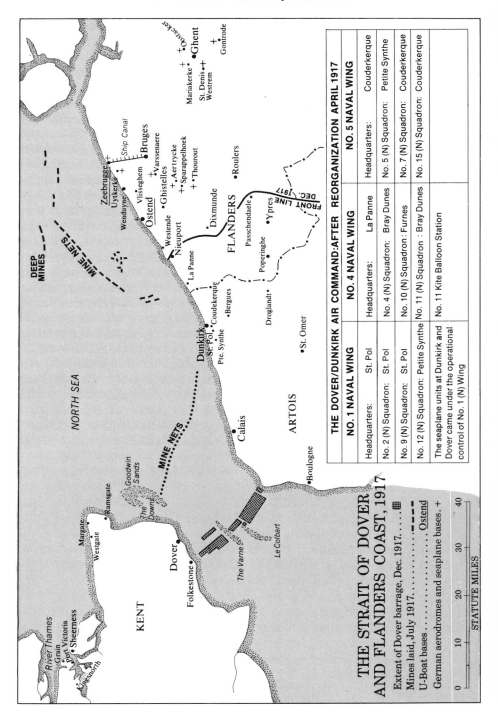

THE STRAIT OF DOVER
AND FLANDERS COAST, 1917

Extent of Dover barrage, Dec. 1917....
Mines laid, July 1917...............
U-Boat bases ....
German aerodromes and seaplane bases. +

THE DOVER/DUNKIRK AIR COMMAND: AFTER REORGANIZATION APRIL 1917						
NO. 1 NAVAL WING		NO. 4 NAVAL WING		NO. 5 NAVAL WING		
Headquarters:	St. Pol	Headquarters:	La Panne	Headquarters:	Couderkerque	
No. 2 (N) Squadron:	St. Pol	No. 4 (N) Squadron:	Bray Dunes	No. 5 (N) Squadron:	Petite Synthe	
No. 9 (N) Squadron:	St. Pol	No. 10 (N) Squadron:	Furnes	No. 7 (N) Squadron:	Couderkerque	
No. 12 (N) Squadron:	Petite Synthe	No. 11 (N) Squadron :	Bray Dunes	No. 15 (N) Squadron:	Couderkerque	
The seaplane units at Dunkirk and Dover came under the operational control of No. 1 (N) Wing		No. 11 Kite Balloon Station				

year. It was they who were caught. With fuel running low after two-and-a-half hours on patrol, the naval pilots discovered, on turning for home, that fog had blotted out land and sea. Only Mulock and one other pilot reached the aerodrome. Mulock then went out with a mechanic in a two-seater Nieuport to help five of the patrol stranded on the sand dunes and guide them home.[13]

The Admiralty's new bombing programme began to affect Dunkirk from February onwards. New bombers were the first sign; most notable were the Caudron G4 and the Sopwith 1½ Strutter. A slow and cumbersome aircraft, the Caudron carried four 65-lb bombs. Dunkirk took delivery of fifty-five, most of them French-built, during the year. The first 1½ Strutters to reach Dunkirk were the two-seater fighter variant, the first British aircraft to enter service equipped with synchronizing gear to permit the pilot to fire his Vickers machine-gun through the propeller arc. This aircraft could carry two 65-lb bombs; later in the year the single-seater bombers arrived, capable of carrying four such bombs.[14] Two-seater Breguets and the Henri Farman F27 were also to be found in the Dunkirk bomber force.

While the two wings that were to use the new bombers were still forming at Eastchurch, the Dover-Dunkirk Command launched its first raid on German bases in Belgium in retaliation for hit-and-run attacks on Kentish towns. Following a protest by General Haig about indiscriminate RNAS target selection in February, Bacon took special pains to control bombing operations. Hence it was with army approval that he ordered an attack on Houttave aerodrome, between Ostend and Bruges on 20 March, in which eight aircraft of 1 Wing joined twenty-one French and Belgian machines in dropping 114 bombs on the target. Simultaneously, seaplanes from HMS *Vindex* and *Riviera* and Dunkirk itself struck at the Zeebrugge Mole. Among the *Riviera* pilots was Flight Sub-Lieutenant G.A. Maclean of Toronto, one of the first Canadians to fly ship-borne aircraft. Whatever the effectiveness of these strikes, the Germans discontinued their own attacks for a month, a period used by the RNAS to adjust and consolidate its organization at Dunkirk.[15]

With two new wings, No 4 at Petite Synthe and No 5 at Coudekerque, ready for operations in late April, flying duties in the command were reallocated. No 1 Wing was divided into two squadrons* and assigned the naval support role. For photographic reconnaissance and fire direction it was given two-seater Nieuports, with BE2cs for night firing. Its single-seater Nieuport fighters patrolled (together with a Belgian squadron) a sector from Ypres to the sea along the Western Front and out over the fleet. The Canadians remaining with this wing were Mulock, Leslie, Hains, and Gooderham. No 5 Wing's main duty was bombing, but it was also to carry out fighter and reconnaissance roles, though on a smaller scale than No 1. It was given a flight of two-seater 1½ Strutters, some Caudrons and Breguets, and a number of Canadians: Grange, Hervey, Hughes, Hewson, Shook, Thom, Todd, and Van Allen, all from 1 Wing. Supply problems spelled a slower rate of expansion for 4 Wing, but it too was to carry out both bombing and fighting duties, and for these purposes it was equipped with an assortment of Caudrons, BE2cs, Avro

---

* From June 1916 a flight consisted of ten aircraft and six pilots; a squadron was made up of two flights and a wing of two or more squadrons. Confidential Admiralty Monthly Order, 268/16, 1 June 1916

504s, and single-seater Nieuports. Among its pilots were two Canadians, Flight Sub-Lieutenants H.R. Aird of Toronto and C.H. Darley of Montreal.

The organization, equipment, and duties of the three wings clustered so closely about Dunkirk fell somewhat short of functional coherence, which is merely to say that the structure of the command reflected the conflicting and competing pulls of its naval responsibilities, its land situation, and the bombing role assigned it by the Admiralty. The same observation can be made about its operations during the spring of 1916. The Dover Patrol had a specific objective in this period – the strengthening of its mine operation to meet the German submarine campaign. Bacon hoped to stop the use of Zeebrugge as a U-boat base by closing the passage between Thornton Ridge shoal and the Flanders coast with a double line of deep mines and mine net barrages. The enlarged Dunkirk air command sought to support this objective by a bombing offensive which was not always clearly related to the aim.

On 23 April, twenty-four hours before the minelayers moved in on the coast, six Caudrons of 5 Wing, including two flown by Thom and Van Allen, battled through heavy ground fire to bomb Mariakerke, a new coastal aerodrome west of Ostend. The next morning Shook in a Caudron was one of twelve pilots from the bombing wings in action over the same target. Meanwhile, fighters and seaplanes flew protective and anti-submarine patrols to seaward. German seaplanes from the Mole reacted by attacking the coal-burning drifters left to watch the nets; one of the Germans was shot down by a Nieuport of 4 Wing, an event prompting the commander of *Seeflugstation Flanders I* to urge the need for fast seaplanes with better combat qualities.

Seaplane pilots from Dunkirk and Dover were very much a part of these operations, making frequent patrols from the Outer Ratel Bank off Nieuport to the Thornton Ridge in order to cover the British ships along the mine barrage line. Of the eighteen seaplane pilots, five were Canadians: Flight Sub-Lieutenants Tooke, Stephens, Cowley, P.S. Fisher, and A.H. Sandwell of Montreal. On 2 May Tooke's bombs forced a surfaced submarine to dive; on 4 May a Short flown by Stephens was damaged by U-boat fire and he was forced to crawl back to base. Cowley was less fortunate. Engine failure forced him down at sea; he and his observer were made prisoners by a German torpedo boat.[16]

Bomb attacks were not resumed until 4 May, when Mariakerke was again hit by thirteen Caudrons and Breguets escorted by Nieuports, all from 5 Wing. Van Allen was shot down over enemy territory during this raid and died of wounds the same day. Not for two weeks was another raid attempted. This time Ghistelles was the target, but it is doubtful that the mixed force of aircraft (Caudrons predominating) caused much damage. For Thom, the lone Canadian taking part, the experience chiefly served to introduce him to the hazards of landing a bomber at night. '... [S]ometimes from 5000 feet one can see the flares beautifully,' a naval pilot wrote, but 'from 20 feet – the most critical time – the light becomes diffused, and one has not the least idea where one is, so one generally lands on a turn and crashes.'[17]

Though these sporadic raids may have had only an indirect effect upon the work of the Dover Patrol, they appear to have aroused the Germans. Between 19 and 22

May German aircraft dropped 372 bombs on the city of Dunkirk, killing thirty-seven people, and *Seeflugstation Flanders I* sent seaplanes to hit Dover and other Kentish towns on 20 May. Dunkirk was immediately drawn into retaliatory action. The fighters of 1 Wing swept over German aerodromes on 21 May. Mulock destroyed one and perhaps two enemy aircraft off Mariakerke while Gooderham sighted five of the enemy near Ghistelles – and engaged a sixth off Westende. Dunkirk's main response, however, was to join in a series of allied counter-blows against aerodromes, ammunition depots, and other targets of military importance. While French and Belgian bombers struck at Ghistelles, Handzaeme, Keyem, and Vyfwegen, and RFC squadrons from Second Army raided Langemarck and the Forêt d'Houthuilst, the RNAS sent sixteen Caudrons and single-seater 1½ Strutters against Mariakerke on 21 May. All pilots encountered poor visibility and had trouble finding the target. Hervey and his observer, bedevilled as well by a jammed bomb rack, were reduced to heaving three 16-lb bombs over the side of their escorting Sopwith from 5200 feet. On Bacon's orders, three pilots were subsequently brought before a court of inquiry to explain why they dropped their bombs on Ostend after failing to locate Mariakerke. He also laid down, in a delphic instruction, that in future bombs not dropped on the designated target were to be jettisoned 'in places other than the main position of the enemy.'[18]

Bacon's order reflected his growing scepticism about the worth of bombing offensives. The obvious German response to them was to bomb French towns; the Allies, at least in the Flanders sector, were in no position to retaliate in kind and, as Lambe pointed out, there was no defence against German night bombing. He considered that a resumption of the bombing offensive against German aerodromes would be valuable only if carried on round-the-clock, and for that he needed more men and aircraft.[19] At this point Bacon reached the same general conclusion about the usefulness of bombing that General Hugh Trenchard, commanding the RFC in the field, had arrived at somewhat earlier. He wrote to Lambe on 6 June:

The chief lesson learned by our airmen in Flanders during the past two months, I hope, is one which the Military have known for some time, namely, that indiscriminate bombing is useless. The point they will eventually appreciate is not only that it is useless, but absolutely harmful to well thought out military operations ... I intend to limit day bombing to such occasions of general attack or a general advance or to the attack of submarines and other vessels at sea. Night bombing may be useful against vessels in a harbour *when present in sufficient numbers* to make success probable, but otherwise bomb-dropping leads merely to the strengthening of anti-aircraft defences without adequate compensation.[20]

Though bombing, for a time, was halted, the command's resources were still being spread over a wide variety of tasks. When the French withdrew their sole squadron from Dunkirk to help with the Verdun battle, the RNAS found itself left with complete responsibility for the aerial defence of the city. On 10 June the two flights of 'A' Squadron, composed solely of Nieuport fighters and therefore the first homogeneous unit in the history of the service, moved to Furnes. Since that aerodrome brought the unit closer to the front, it was agreed that it would furnish

escorts for French reconnaissance and artillery aircraft. All three wings, as a matter
of routine, sent out fighter patrols to prevent enemy spotting over the lines. The
command, then, was charged with the maintenance of aerial superiority over the
French and Belgian lines, and over the fleet as well. The latter task became even
more important with the arrival at Zeebrugge of the 2nd Destroyer Flotilla of the
High Seas Fleet.[21]

To carry out these duties the command had a distinct margin of superiority over
its opponent. The German *Marine Korps* could muster only about eighteen seaplanes at Zeebrugge and twenty-three aeroplanes at land bases, compared to thirty-
seven British seaplanes (of which thirty-two were defined as 'first-class') and 153
aeroplanes (of which 115 were 'first-class'). Even so, with only twenty-seven seaplane pilots and seventy-two aeroplane pilots, Lambe complained that for fleet
support his wings were 'barely over 50% of the approved complement'; and so
high was the priority accorded the command that the Admiralty ordered a speed-
up in supply at the expense of other commands 'whose needs are not so pressing.'
Seven pilots, including Canadians H.H. Arundel of Winnipeg, L.S. Breadner of
Carleton Place, Ont., C.J. Wyatt of Mount Brydges, Ont., and C.B. Sproatt of
Toronto, along with 150 ratings, were drafted immediately to Dover for Dunkirk,
and the Air Department promised quick despatch of twenty-one aeroplanes and
fifteen seaplanes of the latest types.[22] Within three weeks 'A' Squadron had taken
delivery of the first examples of two fine new fighters, the Sopwith Pup and the
Sopwith Triplane.

The high priority given Dover-Dunkirk, particularly when much of the command's work was of no naval value whatever, stood in sharp contrast to the Admiralty's attitude towards the use of aircraft at sea. Here development proceeded at a
more leisurely pace. At the beginning of 1916 the Board of Admiralty placed some
emphasis upon their long-range flying-boat programme, but their main priority was
rigid and non-rigid airships.[23] Carriers came a long way after: only one, *Manxman*, a
former cross-channel packet on the Isle of Man run, came into service during the
year. Few Canadians, therefore, found their way into this branch of the service. Of
the ten who did, three – Flight Sub-Lieutenants W.M.C. Matheson, H.G. Nares,
and L.E. Nicholson, all of Winnipeg – joined *Manxman* in December, when she
was finally commissioned after having spent nearly twelve months undergoing
alterations.

Despite the indifference and conservatism of the navy's senior officers, con-
structive ideas for maritime aviation were not wanting. In 1915 Flight Commander
H.A. Williamson produced a wood model of a vessel bearing a marked resemblance to the 'island type' of aircraft carrier of the postwar era and design drawings
were being considered for a 27-knot light cruiser able to carry five 225-hp Short
and four Sopwith Schneider seaplanes. While these were circulating, the Air
Department organized aeroplane dummy deck-landing trials at Grain Island experimental station to test Williamson's grid scheme* of fore and aft arrestor wires.

---

* In January 1912 Williamson had written a paper for the benefit of an Admiralty committee outlining offensive and defensive measures against submarines which included the suggestion that
  aircraft could utilize a system of wires for operating from the deck of a parent ship.

These trials, though successful, had to be stopped because there was no suitable ship for sea tests. Commodore Murray Sueter, the Superintendent of Aircraft Construction, thought that the 'most satisfactory arrangement would be to so devise the whole scheme that machines could not only fly off the ship, but could also fly back onto it without its having to come to rest, or even slow down.' Backed by his chief, Sueter argued that three such carriers should be approved as urgently needed by the Grand Fleet, and that of those in service only *Campania* was suitable for adaptation.[24]

Nothing came of these plans, so the advocates of specially designed carriers resolved to approach the Commander-in-Chief. Admiral Sir John Jellicoe was much impressed by the idea of aircraft operating from the deck. 'It has ... long been evident to me that the only satisfactory type of seaplane carrier is one from which the machines can rise off the deck,' he wrote to the Admiralty. 'The advantage of being able to land on the deck is, of course, very great and the proposals in this design seem to promise well.'[25] If the new carrier could not be built, he, and some others, thought that some of its features might be embodied in the three large cruisers, *Glorious*, *Courageous*, and *Furious*. Four months, however, elapsed before the Admiralty replied to his letter.

What contribution did seaplane carriers make towards the achievement of naval tactical objectives in 1916? In the Mediterranean and East Africa their work was useful if not spectacular: spotting and scouting for fleet units and, from time to time, providing support for military operations. After the evacuation of the Dardanelles the four available carriers, *Ben-my-Chree*, *Anne*, *Raven II*, and *Empress*, were formed into a composite squadron at Port Said, under the orders of the Commander-in-Chief East Indies Station, whose command extended from Port Said to Singapore. The squadron's pilots, including the Canadians M.G. Dover of Winnipeg, F.C. Henderson, A.J. Nightingale, and T.G.M. Stephens, all of Toronto, flew 225-hp Shorts and 100-hp Schneiders. In April *Empress* was lent to Eastern Mediterranean Command for operations off the Bulgarian coast, and then spent the rest of the year patrolling the Turkish coast south of Smyrna. During this period Sub-Lieutenant D.P. Rowland, RNVR, of Winnipeg served with her as an observer.[26]

If carriers were of some limited but consistent use in secondary theatres, their work in the North Sea was decidedly uneven. There carriers, airships, and seaplanes faced difficult conditions; moreover, they were mere pawns in the great game contested by the two fleets, in which the major pieces were capital ships. From the beginning of 1916 each side engaged in a series of forays intended to isolate, entrap, and destroy unsupported elements of the other. Twice in January Vice-Admiral R. Tyrwhitt's Harwich Force was out, but the launching of seaplanes from *Vindex* against the airship sheds at Hage was thwarted, once by fog and a second time by U-boats.[27]

On 25 March Harwich Force mounted a bombing raid on supposed airship facilities at Hoyer on the Schleswig coast. The force was bait for a trap. It had battle-cruiser support, since it would be working deep in the German Bight. *Vindex* sent out five seaplanes, only two of which returned. After flying some forty miles through a snowstorm, the pilots discovered that Admiralty intelligence was defective. There were no zeppelin sheds at Hoyer, though some were sighted at Tondern. The raid did precipitate some naval action. Two German armed trawlers were sunk near the island of Sylt, a German destroyer was rammed and sunk by Tyrwhitt's flagship, and another was lost after hitting a mine. The British lost the destroyer *Medusa*, also rammed during the confused operations. More important was the fact that the rival main forces both came out. Scheer recalled his battlecruisers, supported by battleships, during the early hours of 26 March. Sir David Beatty and his battlecruisers spent twenty-seven hours in very bad weather off Horn Reefs before giving up hope of enticing the Germans towards the distant Grand Fleet.[28]

To the Admiralty, this operation seemed to promise great things. Why not embark upon an aggressive policy of air and mine-laying sorties in German waters, and thus prod the High Seas Fleet into action? Jellicoe and Beatty were unconvinced, partly because destroyers could not be maintained off a hostile coast for long periods without refuelling, but mainly because they believed that Scheer would risk a major battle only at a time and place of his choosing. Though they were willing enough to support further operations of the kind, they regarded them as minor and the possibilities arising from them as limited.[29]

The initiative then passed to the enemy. To support the Easter rising in Ireland, Scheer despatched eight zeppelins to raid England and bombarded Lowestoft with units of the fleet. The High Seas Fleet had put to sea at noon on 24 April, with L 6, L 7, and L 9 overhead as scouts. At 0410 hrs on the 25th the people of Lowestoft were rudely awakened by the crash of heavy projectiles, delivered by four German battlecruisers hull down on the horizon. After ten minutes the German ships moved north, dropped a few rounds on Great Yarmouth, and then turned away to help the 2nd Scouting Group, by then engaged with the Harwich Force. RNAS pilots at Yarmouth, who had already been up pursuing zeppelins, now became involved in the action. Two of them caught L 9 at 2600 feet, but after fruitlessly expending all their ammunition in a sixty-five-mile chase, had to turn for home. Five other Yarmouth aircraft, one of them piloted by Flight Sub-Lieutenant B.H. Wemp from Toronto, who had only recently qualified as a pilot, flew through the fire of every German gun that would bear to bomb the retiring battlecruisers. Wemp aimed his puny 16-lb bombs at the rear ships of the line. These gallant pin-pricks had nothing to do with *Konteradmiral* F. Boddicker's decision, at 0500 hrs, to pass up the chance to smash the light units of Harwich Force, nor with Scheer's, twenty minutes later, to order the High Seas Fleet back to its bases from its position west of Terschelling. At that moment, far to the north, the Grand Fleet was still bucking heavy seas in an attempt to reach the scene of action.[30]

In assessing the air aspect of the Lowestoft Raid, the Admiralty concluded that the Yarmouth aircraft had been a liability. They had hit nothing. Worse, two Yarmouth submarines had been bombed, apparently by their own aircraft, and forced to dive 'at a particularly unfortunate moment' when they were manoeuvring to attack the enemy. Wing Commander D. Hyde-Thomson, the torpedo expert in the Admiralty's Air Department, was highly critical of the station commanders at both Yarmouth and Felixstowe for not sending up their torpedo-equipped Shorts. Though Hyde-Thomson had ascertained that 'there were many pilots who were willing to run risks to obtain great results' at both stations, their orders had kept them on the ground and 'rendered ineffective the results of two years preparations.' Vaughan-Lee differed; he agreed with the Yarmouth Commanding Officer's assertion that the Shorts would have been 'blown to pieces' before getting into range. In Hyde-Thomson's view, war was about such hazards. If the pilots had 'what is vulgarly known as "guts,"' they should have been employed as intended: 'They would undoubtedly realize that, in company with a large proportion of the British Army, they would be incurring a certain risk.'[31]

The Royal Navy's response was the unsuccessful Tondern Raid. Given the thinking of the two naval staffs, however, a fleet engagement was only a matter of time. Jellicoe had planned an operation similar to the Tondern Raid for 2 June, but with light cruisers as the bait. Scheer anticipated the British and sent two scouting groups of cruisers and destroyers into the Skagerrak, ostensibly to attack shipping but actually intended to bring out the Grand Fleet. On 31 May he ordered all available units to get under way. Jellicoe had already sensed that a major operation was beginning from the mass movement of U-boats to sea and then from the German fleet's signal traffic on 30 May. That evening, at 1910 hrs, the ships in Scapa Flow were ordered to raise steam for full speed. Included in that order was the Grand Fleet's own carrier, *Campania*. She had just been refitted with a longer flight deck and facilities to carry a kite balloon aft.[32] These new capabilities were largely untried, though during her workup programme Sopwith Babys with detachable wheels had been flown off her deck. The Commander-in-Chief, however, had allocated action duties to her in a revised version of the Grand Fleet Battle Orders: 'In suitable visibility, the *Campania* may be stationed in rear of the advanced light-cruiser or cruiser line to enable her to fly the kite balloon for reconnaissance ... The *Campania* if not stationed as above and if the enemy is reported by our advanced cruisers, is to proceed to the front at full speed and prepare to hoist out or to fly seaplanes and fly the kite balloon.'[33] The orders also prescribed that once in the air, *Campania*'s 225-hp two-seater Shorts were to hunt for submarines and minelayers in the vicinity of the fleet, while the Sopwith fighters were to attack zeppelins, 'if these are seen or reported.'[34]

Because she had been allotted a night cruising station in the rear of the whole fleet, *Campania* was to leave harbour last, after the light cruiser *Blanche*. Patiently waiting his turn, Captain Oliver Schwann discovered from the shore authorities, shortly before midnight, that the entire fleet had long since passed out through the boom-gate in accordance with orders signalled throughout the anchorage at 2010 hrs. Had there been a breakdown in the searchlight signal system? The carrier's berth was five miles away from the battleships, over against the north shore of the Flow. Or had she been purposely forgotten? Whatever the reason, *Campania* set off in pursuit of the fleet at 0115 hrs on 31 May. There was every chance that she would make up the forty mile leeway by early afternoon. But at 0437 hrs Jellicoe, who had learned two hours earlier that his unescorted carrier was struggling along behind, ordered her to return to base because she was too easy a target for U-boats and also, he thought, because she would be too late to join in the action.

The first point was valid, for U-boat activity had been reported ahead of *Campania* at 0355 hrs. It seems incomprehensible, however, in view of her length of service with the fleet, that Jellicoe should think *Campania* too slow to catch up, despite his subsequent statement that he found out only in 1926 that she could make 20½ knots. His battle orders supply a hint of the explanation. While he fully accepted the premise that 'the German fleet will not undertake any considerable offensive operations unless the weather is suitable for airships,' he gave his own seaplanes no reconnaissance responsibility for reporting enemy fleet movements and the duties they were assigned could just as easily be carried out by the cruiser screen. To say the least, Jellicoe had little confidence in *Campania*, and it is possible that he regarded her as an encumbrance.[35]

While *Campania* made her disconsolate way back to Scapa Flow, the two fleets approached one another blindly. Commander Peter Strasser, chief of the German Naval Air Division, had ordered five zeppelins 'to be flung boldly out into the distant reaches of the North Sea for the strategic reconnaissance for which they were so pre-eminently suited by virtue of their great range, endurance, mobility and powerful radio equipment.' but they remained grounded by bad weather until afternoon, when it was too late. By dawn the next morning they were back in the sheds at Nordholz and Hage without contributing to the action. Similarly, Beatty made no attempt to use *Engadine*'s four seaplanes on early warning patrols in advance of his battlecruisers. That he did not is scarcely surprising. During the months that *Engadine* had been moored off Rosyth with the Battle Cruiser Fleet, she had been virtually ignored. She had carried out no exercises with the fleet, nor was the training of her observers up to the demands now likely to be made upon them.[36]

At 1415 hrs Beatty's force changed course in accordance with prearranged orders to rendezvous with the Grand Fleet. Five minutes later *Galatea* hoisted battle ensigns and made the electrifying signal 'Enemy in Sight,' having spotted two enemy destroyers fanned out ahead of Admiral F. von Hipper's northward-moving battlecruisers. Beatty, quite unaware of what he was up against, altered course to cut the enemy off from their base. Then at 1440 hrs he ordered *Engadine* to put up a seaplane. Twenty-eight vital minutes ticked by while a Short 184 was assembled and hoisted out. Airborne at 1508 hrs, Flight Sub-Lieutenant F.J. Rutland and his observer found that in the misty conditions the British and German ships could not be kept simultaneously in view. They therefore saw nothing of Hipper's battlecruisers, but they did pass three messages to *Engadine* about the composition and direction of the screen. The second of these, 'Enemy's course is south,' timed at 1533 hrs, would have been useful to Beatty as an early warning of Hipper's movements, but neither it nor the others apparently got further than the carrier, which failed to raise the flagship *Lion* by searchlight. Three minutes after his last signal of 1545 hrs, Rutland had to come down because of a broken fuel line. Although he quickly repaired it himself, the Short was ordered alongside for hoisting in at 1600 hrs.[37]

By this time *Engadine* could no longer keep up with the battlecruisers, rushing towards the German force at 25 knots, and she followed along on the disengaged side. After the first hour of the engagement, destroyer wakes had so disturbed the sea that further flights were impossible, even had they been requested.[38] *Engadine* therefore took no part in the afternoon's battlecruiser action in which *Indefatigable* and *Queen Mary* were blown up, nor in the evening's clash between the battle fleets. Afterwards she took the disabled cruiser *Warrior* in tow until she had to be abandoned and then returned with the survivors to Rosyth. Meanwhile Scheer had managed to break through the destroyer flotillas astern of the British battle line and regain the safety of the swept channel leading home.

In the battle's aftermath searching inquiries were undertaken into the Grand Fleet's command, equipment, training, and tactics. No inquiry was needed to show that the part taken by the RNAS was lamentable, despite the lionizing of 'Rutland of Jutland,' the first aviator to make a sighting report with a fleet in action. The air service, at the moment of crisis, had only 'a comic craft jury-rigged to carry seaplanes'; the performance of the one that flew was little better than Samson's demonstration at the first air-sea manoeuvres in 1913. Jutland, nevertheless, was a turning-point for the air service. The gap between potential and performance bred a new air-mindedness among many officers in the fleet, the fruits of which were to emerge under Beatty's leadership in 1917. The change began with Jellicoe, however; as part of his general shake-up of the Grand Fleet, he held several exercises at sea in the weeks following the battle in which *Campania* was used actively for air reconnaissance. On 3 June 225-hp Shorts were flown off her, initiating deck-flying tests that were to last for five months. Two of the pilots taking part in this work were Flight Sub-Lieutenants Matheson and G.M. Breadner of Winnipeg. Breadner served on *Campania* for the remainder of the war.[39]

If Jellicoe appears to have become somewhat more enthusiastic about the air after Jutland, the same cannot be said for the Admiralty. Thus the Commander-in-Chief's urgent request for eleven kite balloons for his capital ships was refused because it was thought advisable 'to go cautiously experimenting to the full' before laying out money on such expensive devices. Lack of vision was also displayed with respect to carriers. Admiral Vaughan-Lee, for the Air Department, agreed with the estimate that a new carrier would take fifteen to eighteen months to build, and supported a recommendation for the conversion of two large merchantmen then on the stocks.[40] Given his understanding of the current state of the art, he thought a new carrier unwarranted:

Landing on the deck ... has not yet been accomplished but will probably be possible for *aeroplanes*.

The problem of landing seaplanes is more difficult but *may* be evolved and hence it is desirable to consider this possibility in any ship specially designed, as for obvious reasons seaplanes are more suitable than aeroplanes for Fleet scouting.[41]

Vaughan-Lee's judgment, at best, was merely safe. In fact, given the record of seaplanes, it was no longer 'obvious' that they were more suitable than aeroplanes, especially after the success of the Grain Island experiments with aeroplanes using arrestor wires. Tudor went along with this ultra-cautious appraisal, mainly because he still considered that rigid airships were the answer, but he also opposed the conversion of merchant ships. All that he was prepared to recommend was the adapting of *Courageous*, *Glorious*, and *Furious* to aircraft, and so it was in this vein that on 14 July the Admiralty finally replied to Jellicoe's letter of 8 May.[42]

On 19 August the Admiralty got a clear warning that the air element of its sea forces needed bolstering. The High Seas Fleet came out again, with the Naval Airship Division this time taking a prominent part. After Jutland, Scheer had no intention of bringing on another major fleet action, and was convinced that thorough air reconnaissance was the way to prevent one. Provided that it was reliable, he could resume his forays in search of unsupported British naval elements. To this end he attempted a raid on Sunderland beneath a zeppelin screen. Neither side was satisfied with the results of this operation. The zeppelins, Scheer thought, had been too rigid in their patrol patterns and he had also received conflicting and erroneous reports from them. To the British, however, the airships overhead had seemed to give a kind of omniscience to German operations. Jellicoe wrote that they 'hampered us terribly last week and greatly helped their S.M.s [submarines]. One Zeppelin is worth a good many light cruisers on a suitable day.' In contrast, the Royal Navy had had negligble air support. *Campania* was once again left behind, this time with machinery defects. *Engadine* had tried and failed to launch a seaplane to attack a shadowing zeppelin. Naval air stations along the east coast had drawn blanks with patrolling aircraft. By chance, *Campania*'s kite balloon was with the fleet undergoing endurance trials in the battleship *Hercules*. For some twenty-eight hours it soared over the main body without an observer in the basket. As Beatty said in his report, a manned balloon could well have spotted the High Seas Fleet had it been flown from the advanced cruiser line.[43]

Jellicoe, convinced that the Germans now had air superiority for fleet reconnaissance in the North Sea, asked the Admiralty to base ten non-rigid 'coastal' airships along the east coast. Characteristically, the Admiralty agreed only to a test exercise with the fleet to check the navigational accuracy of airships when making sighting reports. The whole matter was too important to be thus shelved. Aware that the aging *Campania* needed another long refit, Jellicoe pressed for a replacement. The Admiralty, reversing itself, had first agreed to convert two merchant vessels and then, with renewed pressure on the shipyards in September, decided instead to convert a 15,750-ton Italian liner, the *Conte Rosso*, renaming it the *Argus*. As well, it authorized the resumption of landing experiments at Grain Island.* At a Scapa Flow meeting on 12 October Jellicoe fought unavailingly for a quicker solution to the carrier problem. On only one matter did he obtain immediate satisfaction – his request for balloons was approved. In December the kite-balloon ship *Canning* (a Canadian, Flight Sub-Lieutenant G.B. Carr, address unknown, was in her company) and *Menelaus* became floating depot ships for the balloons now allocated to Grand Fleet battleships. Thus a few halting steps were taken to improve the Grand Fleet's air arm.[44]

---

* For these experiments the trials team used a wooden platform built to simulate a carrier deck and emulated the technique used by Eugene Ely when he landed aboard USS *Pennsylvania* in 1911. A special hook was fitted to the aeroplane to engage transverse wires stretched across the 'deck.' In 1917 Flight Sub-Lieutenant A.H. Allardyce of Vancouver served with this unit.

In the North Sea the Admiralty's air policy lacked enterprise, but the formidable German presence had forced it, however cautiously, to authorize some innovation. In the Mediterranean, a secondary theatre of operations, there was little pressure for change. The allied naval forces were charged with the protection of communications with the troops in Egypt and Salonika, with immobilizing the Austrian fleet in the Adriatic and the German warships *Goeben* and *Breslau* lying at Constantinople, and with the provision of sea support for military operations. At the Paris naval conference in December 1915 the Mediterranean had been divided into eighteen patrol zones; of these ten went to the French, four to the Italians, and the remainder (the Strait of Gibraltar, Malta and the south coast of Sicily, the Dardanelles-Aegean and Egyptian coast) to the British. These latter responsibilities were extended by the decision of an admirals' meeting in Malta in March to include the Aegean and the routes from Malta and Salonika to Egypt.[45]

RNAS deployment was determined by these arrangements. From Kalafrana Air Station in Malta seven pilots, including J. Gorman of Ottawa, patrolled the transport routes in Short 184s and Small Americas. At Gibraltar Short 184s patrolled the strait; at one point three of the five pilots were Canadians, Flight Sub-Lieutenants J.R. Bibby of Niagara Falls, Ont., M.B. Walker of Hamilton, Ont., and A.G. Woodward of Victoria. But the main RNAS concentration was with the Eastern Mediterranean Squadron, 'a wondrous command – a sort of confederacy of semi-independent nabobs, each of whom had some special duty to perform, and each designated by a grand and resounding title.'[46] The squadron supported allied forces at Salonika, kept a watch on the Dardanelles, patrolled the Aegean, blockaded the coast of Bulgaria, and conducted operations against the Anatolian coast of Turkey.

No 2 Wing, RNAS, served the fleet. In February, when Wing Commander F.R. Scarlett took over, it had three flights of ten aeroplanes each at Imbros; *Ark Royal* lay at Salonika, with five of her seven seaplanes allocated to a shore base at Stavros. Scarlett immediately proposed a second wing and a continuous air offensive. The Admiralty unsympathetically replied that under existing circumstances it was not practicable to expand the air service in the Mediterranean, which was already drawing off too many ships from home waters. The Admiralty did agree, however, to add another flight at once and two more as available. With these resources Scarlett's plans had to be modified.

Scarlett's original proposal had been based on the premise that Salonika could be left 'entirely to the French aviators.' Yet despite the Admiralty's grudging response, 2 Wing increasingly involved itself in military operations, as well as endeavouring to carry out its fleet support duties. The seventeen Canadians with the wing,* more than 25 per cent of its pilot strength, found themselves shifted about from place to place in the Greek islands as Scarlett pursued a vigorous and overly ambitious policy with increasingly obsolete aircraft. In March some flew

---

* The following Canadians were in the Eastern Mediterranean in December 1916: G.S. Abbott of Ottawa (WIA 30 Nov. 1916), H.R. Aird of Toronto (POW 30 Sept. 1917), C.N. Bawlf, address unknown, E.S. Boynton of Toronto, G.T. Bysshe of Ottawa (POW 17 Feb. 1917), J.R.S. Devlin of Ottawa, D.D. Findlay of Carleton Place, Ont., J.A. Harman of Uxbridge, Ont., J.M. Ingham of Toronto (KIA 20 March 1917), G.A. Magor of Montreal (WIA 21 May 1917, MIA 22 April 1918),

from Mitylene to spot for an allied fleet bombardment of Smyrna. After bombing Constantinople and Adrianople with three aircraft on 15 April, Scarlett conceived the idea of a mobile bomber force to hit at points all the way from the Mesta River in Bulgaria around to Cape Alupo. Hence in June elements of the Wing were based on Thasos and at a new aerodrome near Mudros. In August, when the Bulgars advanced towards the Struma River, the RNAS was once more redeployed to assist warships protecting the seaward right flank of the British Army, but also to carry out bombing and reconnaissance missions over the front. All these and other activities were carried out in addition to normal reconnaissance and anti-submarine work for the navy.[47]

By comparison with Dunkirk, 2 Wing at first glance seems to have been handicapped in both aircraft and personnel, as the following table shows:

COMPARISON OF RNAS STRENGTH AT DUNKIRK AND IN THE
EASTERN MEDITERRANEAN, 31 MAY AND 31 DECEMBER 1916
(31 Dec. figures in parenthesis)[48]

AEROPLANES

	CLASS I	CLASS II	TOTAL	PILOTS
Dunk.	77(109)	9(47)	86(156)	72(107)
E.Med.	59(34)	15(42)	74(76)	28(44)

SEAPLANES

	CLASS I	CLASS II	TOTAL	PILOTS
Dunk.	32(23)	5(10)	37(33)	27(24)
E.Med.	17(6)	0(23)	17(29)	11*(15)

In terms of the relative importance of the two theatres, it was proper to favour Dunkirk. The Eastern Mediterranean, in contrast, was becoming a 'forgotten' theatre. While Dunkirk's first-class aircraft strength grew substantially during the year, 2 Wing was making do with aircraft that were rapidly becoming obsolete. As at Dunkirk, the RNAS was permitted to take on too many roles, a commentary both upon the Royal Navy's system of command and control, and upon its flexible, adventurous, and often rash air arm.

An analysis of the work of the Dunkirk Command for the last half of 1916 indicates that the two-way pull of its situation continued to affect its operations. When plans for the Somme battle were first made, the Royal Navy, and hence its air service, were to have an important role. Ten thousand men of the First Division were to have been landed from monitors and lighters to seize the harbour at

F.S. Mills of Toronto, C.E. Moore of Fort William, Ont., and J.L.A. Sinclair and K.M. Smith, both of Toronto. A Canadian warrant officer, J.P. Haworth, address unknown, was on the staff of the airship base at Mudros. H.V. Reid of St John's, Nfld, was also in the Eastern Mediterranean at this time.
* Estimated

Ostend, in conjunction with French and British attacks from Nieuport and Ypres. Until 7 July Haig kept the organizing staff for this venture at his headquarters; lack of progress on the Somme then led him to cancel the operation. From the navy's viewpoint, the feasibility of the landing had already been questioned because the Germans had erected the Knocke Battery of 12-inch guns some thirty thousand yards behind Ostend, commanding its jetties.[49] The role of the Dunkirk Command during the Somme battle was reduced to the task of diverting as much enemy strength as possible through naval and air activity. For this reason Dunkirk's operations were necessarily episodic in character.

Thus in July and early August the command's aircraft worked with naval forces against the Tirpitz Battery, which prevented short-range monitors from bombarding the Ostend dockyard. The destruction of its four 11-inch guns, among the most powerful on the Flemish coast, became the almost exclusive preoccupation of all Dunkirk's available fighters and reconnaissance aircraft, of its seaplanes, and of the Dover Defence Flight. The effectiveness of the enemy battery was to be reduced by the Dominion Battery,* a 12-inch naval gun, and a pair of French 9.2s. Monitors and balloon ships were stationed offshore to confuse the Germans about the direction of fire. During the first two days of the operation, which began on 8 July, RNAS units logged 442 hours of photo reconnaissance and ranging for the Dominion Battery, fighter protection for spotting aircraft, and fighter patrols to interdict German reconnaissance aircraft seeking the source of bombardment.[50] Most of the twenty-five Canadians in the command took part, including some newcomers, Flight Sub-Lieutenants D.M.B. Galbraith of Carleton Place, Ont., and H.R. Wambolt of Dartmouth, NS, in 1 Wing and F.A. Rivers-Malet and A.M. Tidey of Vancouver in seaplanes.

C.B. Sproatt, a 5 Wing pilot from Toronto, became lost and was forced to ditch at sea on 8 July. His experience, insignificant in itself, illustrates the normal hazards of flying at Dunkirk, and also the kind of misadventure that frequently overtook First World War airmen. Returning from an evening patrol off Westende, he let down to 2000 feet before breaking cloud cover. No land was visible, the surface of the sea could barely be seen because of mist, and his compass was 'stuck at North.' Sighting a ship, he let down further in order to get directions. As he reported to his commanding officer: '... we had now come down to 400 feet, and not wishing to run the risk of being found with tracer bullets in our possession,† I instructed my Observer to throw our trays overboard ... unfortunately, the Observer hit the propeller with a tray of ammunition, breaking it, and leaving me no choice but to land in the sea. Believing the machine would float for a few minutes, I tried to pancake gently into the water, but the light being very deceptive

---

* Bacon chose the name because Canadian railway engineers helped in mounting the gun, which
   weighed fifty tons. Sir Reginald Bacon, *The Dover Patrol, 1915–1917* (London nd), I, 183
† The *Declaration of St Petersburg*, in 1868, had established that 'the contracting parties engage
   mutually to renounce, in case of war among themselves, the employment by their military or
   naval troops of any projectile of a weight below 400 grammes which is either explosive or
   charged with fulminating or inflammable substance.' The *Declaration of The Hague* of 1899 ruled
   that 'the contracting parties agree to abstain from the use of bullets which expand or flatten easily
   in the human body.'

I misjudged my distance, and the machine struck a wave, throwing me clear, and my Observer was able to get out quickly.'[51] The vessel, a British monitor, picked them up; the Caudron sank.[52]

In their various tasks the RNAS aircraft seem to have acquitted themselves well. Wireless work with the Dominion Battery went smoothly; before the end of July excellent photographs of the Tirpitz Battery were being obtained from a height of 14,000 feet; and the fighters had destroyed three Fokker monoplanes without loss before weather conditions prevented effective spotting for ten days. During that time Galbraith scored his first victory. Returning in his Nieuport from a seaward patrol, he encountered a German seaplane flying out of Ostend, some five hundred feet below him. Remaining below, the German manœuvred behind the British machine, both aircraft meanwhile executing a steep glide. Galbraith then looped his aircraft (a manœuvre he would not have got away with on the Western Front) and from a position a hundred yards astern opened fire. The German seaplane burst into flames and was 'last seen falling headlong downwards.' Bacon commented favourably on Galbraith's tactics to the Admiralty.[53]

When the bombardment was resumed, it met with no more success. By early August German smoke screens made ranging difficult and in any case the barrel of the British gun was beginning to wear. Bacon chose not to use the bombing weapon at his disposal against the Tirpitz Battery. It is likely that he had little faith in the capacity of bombs to inflict any real damage. Instead, it was General Trenchard who was instrumental in unleashing the long inactive bombers of the Dunkirk Command. At his behest the RNAS took part in an RFC bombing offensive in the northern sector designed to draw off enemy aircraft from the Somme. On 2 August the RNAS attacked St Denis Westrem aerodrome and a large ammunition dump at Meirelbeke, both targets being southwest of Ghent. At St Denis Westrem, ten Caudron G4s, including aircraft flown by Sproatt, Nelles, and Darley, approached the target in wedge formation, led by a single Henri Farman. At a Very light signal from a Sopwith above them they deployed into line ahead and dropped their bombs on parked aircraft and sheds. At Meirelbeke, Sopwith 1½ Strutters dropped thirty-one bombs with no apparent result.[54]

The main efforts of the command were now turned to bombing for the rest of the month. Lambe and Trenchard agreed upon targets for eight more RNAS raids in conjunction with attacks by II Brigade RFC. Targets selected included ammunition dumps, the Hoboken shipyards at Antwerp where submarines were being assembled, aerodromes, the naval airship sheds at Namur, and military airship bases. The airship installations were selected upon the false assumption that they were to participate in the zeppelin assault on London being mounted by the Naval Airship Division from its North German strongholds. Thus in August attacks were made upon such targets as the German army hangars at Evere and Berchem Ste Agathe (both of which were, in fact, empty), the airship sheds at Namur, and ammunition stores at Lichtervede. The offensive continued into September with a raid on the Hoboken shipyards and the Ghistelles aerodrome. Both 4 and 5 Wings were involved in these raids, as they were in separate attacks on St Denis Westrem, Ghistelles, and Handzaeme aerodromes later in the month. On 24 September Sproatt, in company with three other Sopwiths, dropped his twelve Le Pecq bombs along the length of the Evere shed, which, as it happens, was empty.[55]

In mid-September Haig requested, prior to the resumption of the Somme battle, that a diversionary show of naval strength be made off the Belgian coast. Bacon responded with enthusiasm and, as a feint, visible preparations for an amphibious landing were made in Dunkirk harbour. An armada of destroyers, monitors, and a hundred trawlers was assembled off the beaches, and a week-long bombardment was inaugurated upon targets between Middlekerke and Westende.[56] During the whole affair the RNAS was active, culminating its efforts with the bombing of Tirpitz and neighbouring Hindenburg Batteries on the morning that Haig's troops once more moved to the attack.

Did the bombing offensive, including the mid-September demonstration, appreciably alter German air dispositions? It appears that it did not. There was no significant increase in the air arm of the German 4th Army in the northern sector. No reinforcement was provided for the *1st Marine Jagdstaffel* at Handzaeme or the *1st* and *2nd Marine Feldflieger* at Mariakerke and other fields. Indeed, German army air units continued to be sent to the sector for rest and refit, though occasionally they gave assistance to the *Marine Korps* on the coast if the situation warranted. The Germans gave little overt sign that they considered the RNAS offensive important; their reaction was two weak night raids on naval airfields on 8 and 9 September, and another small-scale attack on Dunkirk two weeks later. It is true that German offensive seaplane patrols off the Flanders coast were stiffened in late August by the arrival of the Friedrichshafen FF 33h and Rumpler 6B 1 types, but these new fighters had been requested by the Zeebrugge commander long before. Lambe may well have been somewhat mystified by the enemy failure to respond to what, for the RNAS, had been an all out offensive. He surmised that the enemy 'are concentrating a large force of seaplanes ... since that type of machine could be better spared, and during the next spell of fine weather bomb attacks may be expected on the S.E. coast of England, on the monitors on patrol, and possibly also on Dunkirk.' Admiral Bacon thereupon grounded the bomber force once more, in order to release pilots for anticipated fighter duties.[57]

Now the Dunkirk Command was called upon to assist the RFC in its struggle over the Somme in a more direct fashion by giving up aircraft and men. A naval squadron went to the RFC in October, in the course of which the Admiralty's strong opposition to such a move had to be overcome. Wing Captain Lambe's willingness to co-operate in this, it is clear, was crucial. It reflected not only his good relations with Trenchard, but also the fact that Dunkirk had once more stopped bombing. The reality was that Lambe's fine pilots and first-rate aircraft were under-employed.

Each of the three Dunkirk wings contributed a flight: Sopwith Pups from No 1, Nieuport Scouts from No 4, and Sopwith 1½ Strutters from No 5. All the pilots were volunteers; they included a high proportion of Dunkirk's most experienced and successful airmen. The new squadron, named 8 (N) Squadron,* had six Canadian flight sub-lieutenants among its number. Before leaving Dunkirk three

---

* The RNAS had begun to redesignate its units in a fashion similar to that in the RFC. Previously known by letters – 'A,' 'B,' 'C' in 1 Wing, 'A' and 'B' in 4 Wing, and 'A' and 'B' in 5 Wing – squadrons were now given numbers from 1 to 8. Canadians were founding members of all these squadrons: E. Anthony of Maitland, NS, and G.A. Gooderham of Toronto in 1(N) Squadron; C.J. Wyatt of Mount Brydges, Ont. (KIA 21 Aug. 1917) in 2(N); R.H. Mulock of Winnipeg, H.R.

of them scored victories in aerial combats. In the month from 23 September to 23 October Dunkirk pilots shot down nine enemy aircraft; Thom, Grange, and Galbraith accounted for four of them, all seaplanes. Thom gained his success on 23 September. The next day Grange forced a Sablatnig SF 2 to spin into the sea. The Germans later found it 'completely demolished.' On 27 September Galbraith scored his second victory since arriving at Dunkirk and then on 22 October shot down another seaplane off Blankenberghe, just prior to his departure for the Somme.[58]

Though the command had temporarily lost some of its best pilots, there was no appreciable change in the scale of its operations as the year drew to a close. Admiral Scheer was instrumental in bringing the command back to its naval support role when he moved III and IX Destroyer Flotillas of the High Seas Fleet into Zeebrugge on 24 October. These units fought a night action on 26–27 October with guardships of the Dover Patrol, and sank a British destroyer and six drifters.[59] The Admiralty reinforced the patrol with destroyers from Harwich Force, and when aerial reconnaissance revealed that the Germans remained concentrated at Ostend, Bacon ordered, upon Lambe's urging, the resumption of bombing.

For the last three weeks of November the command attacked Zeebrugge and Ostend, and especially the Slyken Electric Power Station and the Ateliers de la Marine shipyard. Some of the raids were heavy. For example, the Ostend raid of 15 November was delivered by twenty-two bombers, among them four Shorts, a new landplane version of the Short 184 with more than three times the bomb carrying capacity of the Caudron G4. The Shorts had teething problems, however, and while returning from this raid C.H. Darley of Montreal had to make an emergency landing on the beach at Dunkirk. Associated with these raids were bombing attacks by seaplanes on ships, docks, and lock-gates of the Zeebrugge-Bruges Canal. P.S. Fisher and A.H. Sandwell, both of Montreal, were among six pilots in such a raid on 10 November; all experienced heavy anti-aircraft fire.[60]

These November raids were the heaviest of the year, over twelve tons of bombs being dropped. Moreover, they disrupted Scheer's plans for hitting the Dover Patrol. Because of the raids on Zeebrugge he found it necessary to move his torpedo boats up to Bruges, and this meant that there was 'very considerable delay' in getting them back through the locks in order to launch a surprise attack. As he later wrote: 'As soon as they left Bruges harbour it was not possible, as a rule, to conceal the movements of the boats from the enemy.'[61] He decided to withdraw III Flotilla to Wilhelmshaven to await a more favourable opportunity. Here RNAS Dunkirk had made one of its most useful contributions of 1916.

At year's end Dunkirk still enjoyed a favoured status among all RNAS commands. As its older aircraft passed into obsolescence, they were progressively replaced by 1½ Strutters, Pups, and Triplanes. Because of its extremely variable weather, flying at Dunkirk was demanding enough at the best of times, and the

Wambolt of Dartmouth, NS (KIA 4 March 1917), and J.B. White of Vancouver in 3(N); W.E. Orchard of St Lambert, Que. (KIA 3 June 1917), and A.M. Shook of Red Deer, Alta (WIA 21 Oct. 1917) in 4(N); C.B. Sproatt of Toronto in 5(N); C.L. Bailey and G.C.W. Dingwall, both of Toronto, in 6(N); and C.H. Darley of Montreal in 7(N) and J.A. Shaw of Edmonton in 8(N).

station's pilots became highly skilled in meeting the challenge of strong winds, fog, and rapidly changing cloud and ceiling conditions. The reception of more advanced fighter aircraft in late 1916 added another dimension, that of higher altitude flying under extreme conditions. Lloyd Breadner wrote his mother on 21 December: 'It is frightfully cold up high this weather & we are having a hard time of it, from frost bite it is getting to be a serious proposition. You know, we are the first to fly at the height we do, in winter-time. Yesterday one of the boys took a thermometer up with him, the maximum reading was 60° of frost or 28° below as we Canadians speak of it. You can't imagine what it is like up there. When you are shifting through that atmosphere at 100 miles per hour it is certainly cold. We would all be very thankful to anyone that would send a Balaclava or scarf along.'[62] Despite such rigours, combat pilots at Dunkirk, like their counterparts elsewhere, welcomed improved aircraft that would give them, if only temporarily, an edge over their opponents.

What had Dover-Dunkirk Command done to merit special treatment both in personnel and material? Undoubtedly the command had given useful support to the Dover Patrol. More and more, however, it had been drawn into military roles. Thus it had taken up virtually all the fighter work over the northern flank of the Western Front, permitting the French to withdraw aircraft to Verdun. Its bombing record, except for its activities in November against naval forces, had been of questionable effectiveness, lacked a coherent objective, and was at best ancillary to the operations of the RFC. The mission of the command had never been sufficiently defined. Whatever doubts he may have expressed from time to time, Bacon had permitted his airmen considerable leeway and as a result they had fallen increasingly into the military orbit.

Nevertheless, thanks to Admiralty favour and the navy's foresight in aircraft and engine procurement, Dunkirk grew fat; nothing demonstrated this more convincingly than the loan of 8(N) Squadron to the RFC. It is a remarkable fact that the command claimed fifty-two enemy aircraft destroyed during the whole of 1916, yet twenty-five of these were shot down by 8(N) Squadron on the Somme in November and December.[63] No 8's record was testimony to the excellence of RNAS training and aircraft, but it sheds a rather different light upon the activities of the Dunkirk Command.

The size and activities of the command formed part of the indictment marshalled against the RNAS and the Admiralty by the President of the Air Board. Increasingly exasperated by the recalcitrance of the Admiralty on questions of supply and its future air plans, and outraged by his discovery in August that the navy had obtained Treasury approval for an expenditure of £2,875,000 on aircraft and engines without passing the matter through the Air Board, Lord Curzon finally exploded. 'It is our profound conviction,' he wrote in a report of 23 October to the Cabinet War Committee, '... that the addition to the Navy of responsibilities for the air – not in itself necessarily impracticable – has, in the manner in which it has been carried out, been attended with results that have been equally unfortunate for the Navy and the Air Service, and, if persisted in, will be incompatible not merely with the existence of an Air Board, but with the immense and almost incalculable development that ought to lie before a properly co-ordinated and conducted Air Service in the future.'[64] Curzon flayed the Admiralty for its 'indifference or hostility' towards innovative proposals from naval airmen, dwelt upon the 'melancholy illustration of their lack of foresight' about rigid airships, as well as aircraft carriers and kite balloons, and accused the navy of dissipating its air effort upon areas of secondary importance. He was particularly critical of the inflated strength of RNAS Dunkirk. In summing up the indictment, he stated:

... we can draw no other conclusion from the existing situation than that portion of the Air Service which has been subordinated to the Admiralty, and handled on naval lines, has not been the gainer by the connection, but has, on the contrary, failed to make a proportionate contribution to the successful conduct of the war.

A single, instead of a divided, policy, a co-ordination, instead of a dispersion of force, above all, the management of the Naval Air Service by airmen rather than by seamen, would, we believe, have produced very different results.[65]

Curzon's highly charged language betrayed his considerable pique after a long series of heated exchanges with Balfour. Some of his evidence and the construction he placed upon it was erroneous and unfair. But two of his main points were clearly correct: that aircraft supply should be removed from the control of the two services and placed under a single authority, and that the naval air arm should be represented on the Board of Admiralty and on the Air Board by an officer with powers and standing commensurate with those of Henderson for the RFC.*

Personal, political, and inter-service rivalries were further intensified by the revival of the acrimonious dispute over long-range bombing, prompted by the Admiralty's unilateral talks with the French and by an RNAS proposal to the Air Board that 'it should be definitely laid down that the Navy should keep an effective force of at least two hundred bombers in France, to include Dunkirk.'† On 27 and 28 November the War Committee took its first step in resolving these conflicts by agreeing in principle that all responsibility for the design and production of aeroplanes (but not seaplanes or airships) should be placed with the Ministry of Munitions, and that a Sea Lord should be appointed with responsibility for all aspects of naval aviation and a seat on the Air Board.[66]

These important decisions by no means halted this bitter clash. Meanwhile, however, the Admiralty had been encountering equally harsh criticism over a far

---

* Balfour refused to concede either of these points, yet in August he had already agreed with Jellicoe that a change in control of the air service was needed. Jellicoe had then written: 'I have no hesitation in giving my opinion that your proposal to place a naval officer of high standing at the head of the Naval Air Service is the correct solution ... I am also of the opinion he should be a member of the Board ...' John Rushworth Jellicoe, Earl Jellicoe of Scapa, *The Jellicoe Papers: Selections from the Private and Official Correspondence of Admiral of the Fleet Earl Jellicoe of Scapa*, II: *1916–1935*, A. Temple Patterson, ed. (London 1966), 67–9

† The dispute over bombing is dealt with in chapter 10. The main lines of this debate were available to any German intelligence agent who cared to buy a British newspaper. The Admiralty was attacked in the press and publicly urged by the Parliamentary Air Committee to be more co-operative. Much public support was given a resolution of that committee, that 'the Air Board should be given more extensive and immediate executive powers for the development of both air services.' *Flight*, 9 Nov. 1916, 971–2

more vital question – its handling of the new German submarine campaign against merchant shipping. That campaign had been foreshadowed, in September, by an increase in tempo of operations by the small U-boats from Zeebrugge and the movement of large mine-laying submarines to the south of Ireland and the western approaches to the British Isles. This offensive began in earnest on 6 October and, under the restrictions laid down by prize rules,* was to last until the end of January 1917.[67] Against it the Royal Navy employed the methods it had already developed: Q-ships,† a resumption of mine-laying in the Heligoland Bight, and an increase in the numbers of armed merchantmen and small craft on patrol duty. Local commanders were also instructed to make greater use of their air resources.

The state of the Home Commands once again demonstrated that the Admiralty's air priorities were questionable. The overall pilot strength was adequate at 191 (the largest single group in the air service), though some of them were undergoing operational training. Slightly over 25 per cent of them were Canadians. Reflecting the drafts made upon Home Stations by Dunkirk and 3 Wing, the complement of aeroplane pilots had dropped since the end of May. In the same period the number of seaplane pilots had grown to 115, Canadians again forming about a quarter of the total. It was not airmen that were needed, but good patrol aircraft in sufficient numbers. Between May and the end of December seaplanes rated 'first-class' by the RNAS – a more powerful version of the 'soggy' Short 184 and Sopwith Baby fighters – declined from 141 to seventy-four.[68]

Stations operating seaplanes were still all located on the east and south coasts of the United Kingdom.‡ For the western approaches the RNAS relied upon its lighter-than-air organization, one far more effective than it had been in the previous submarine campaign. By December there were thirty-two SS type and twenty-five Coastal airships based not only at the stations opened in 1915 but also

* Under prize rules, submarines could not destroy ships before examining their papers and ensuring the safety of their crews, unless the ships attempted to escape or offer resistance.
† Q-ships were merchant vessels, small enough that an enemy submarine would surface to shell them rather than waste a torpedo. They were equipped with concealed guns, usually 6- and 12-pounders. Q-ship tactics usually included fake attempts to escape, including abandoning ship – except for the gun crews. When the submarine closed, the White Ensign was raised and the concealed guns opened fire.
‡ At the most northerly station, Dundee, there were three Canadians: J.G. Ireland of Montreal, W.R. Kenny of Ottawa, and C. McNicholl of Montreal. At South Shields were G.G. Avery of Toronto (KIA 14 May 1917) and T.C. Wilkinson of Quebec City. Farther down the coast H.H. Arundel of Toronto, M.C. Dubuc of Montreal, F.E. Fraser of Winnipeg, and A.Y. Wilks of Montreal worked out of Killingholme. G.R. Halliday of Victoria, R. Leckie of Toronto, N.W. Leslie of Winnipeg, G.H. Simpson of Toronto, and F.P.L. Washington of Hamilton, Ont., flew from Great Yarmouth. At Felixstowe there were J.L. Gordon of Montreal, B.D. Hobbs of Sault Ste Marie, Ont., G.R. Hodgson and F.S. McGill, both of Montreal, W.H. Mackenzie of Victoria (KIA 25 April 1918), N.A. Magor of Montreal (KIA 25 April 1918), and W.E. Robinson of Winnipeg (POW 8 July 1917). As well, V.H. Ramsden of Toronto and H.A. Wilson of Montreal were under training on Small America H4s. In the Thames estuary and its approaches C.V. Bessette, address unknown, and L.M. Lewis of Montreal were at Grain Island and C.G. Bronson of Ottawa (POW 28 Jan. 1918), F.G. Hellmuth of Allandale, Ont., and R.E. Spear of Winnipeg were at Westgate. At Calshot were the veterans Peck and McLaurin, and the newcomers A.S. Ince of Toronto, W. Lodge of Arnprior, Ont., J.S. Maitland of Montreal, and J.K. Waugh of Whitby, Ont.

at Pembroke, Howden, Longside, and Mullion for coastal patrols, at East Fortune to support Beatty's battlecruisers, and at Caldale adjacent to Scapa Flow.*[69]

Recognition that air dispositions were faulty came when the important coal trade between Britain and France was seriously disrupted in September. Seaplane units began to shift westward. The Commander-in-Chief Portsmouth ordered four Short 184s to join McLaurin's party at the Bembridge sub-station, and a new sub-station was established at Portland to patrol the mid-Channel over a 60-mile radius. Even so, the air weapon was not yet a very effective instrument against submarines. The experiences of two Canadian pilots early in the campaign revealed its possibilities and limitations. A seaplane in which Flight Sub-Lieutenant Spear was a crew member discovered a submarine preparing to sink a Norwegian steamer between Portland and the Channel Islands. The air attack with 16-lb bombs, which did not take place until the submarine had submerged, was quite ineffectual, and yet the presence of the aircraft forced the submarine to break off its own attack. On 9 September Flight Sub-Lieutenant J.A. Barron was on a patrol from Mullion in a Coastal airship. He sighted two sailing ships hove to and on fire, with a submarine lurking near them. Descending to 700 feet, he released his bombs and the U-boat crash-dived out of sight. He then sought help for the blazing vessels, attracting a Norwegian steamship into the area, but Barron was soon too low on fuel to take any further part in the action. As he laid course northeast, he encountered the destroyer he had summoned and at her request signalled the position of the burning vessels. In both these cases aircraft had certainly had their uses, but their shortcomings were also evident. Moreover, the fragmentation of the RNAS under local commands meant that its efforts were largely unco-ordinated, much being left to the initiative of each station commander.[70]

In late 1916 a major shakeup in the Admiralty occurred, closely connected with the events in which Lloyd George replaced Asquith as the head of a reconstituted coalition government. Before this took place Jellicoe had already been brought in as First Sea Lord, with a mandate to organize effective anti-submarine measures. Now Balfour was gone, and Sir Edward Carson was the new Prime Minister's choice as political head of the Admiralty. Carson's naval education proceeded apace. With some chagrin Lloyd George noted that 'the Admiralty had succeeded in kneading its new First Lord into full acceptance of its attitude' in the matter of air supply. Before relinquishing his post at the Air Board to become Lord President of the council and a member of the War Cabinet, Curzon again raised the question of the former War Committee's decision of 27–28 November. The Cabinet, however, having decided that the principles had been agreed upon by its predecessor, approved the draft conclusions without alteration. The unco-operative stance of the Admiralty towards the Air Board during 1916 had in great measure set the Cabinet on a course which would end, in a year's time, with the demise of the RNAS itself.[71]

---

* The Canadians in this branch were J.A. Barron of Stratford, Ont., at Mullion; A.R. Layard of Saanich, BC, at Pembroke; R.F.E. Wickham of Vancouver, at Polegate; and I. Macdonald of Calgary at the navy's main airship base at Kingsnorth.

During this period of naval disarray the Admiralty suffered yet another blow. Haig had given notice that he wanted twenty fighter squadrons for operations in the spring, over and above previously projected requirements. In a forceful appearance before the Air Board Trenchard pressed Haig's request, stating that only eleven squadrons of aircraft (including No 8(N)) 'of a performance equal to that of the new German' would probably be available. As a stop-gap he asked that the navy supply four more squadrons and enough engines to equip six others. The Admiralty, appealed to 'at this moment of great emergency,' was in no state to resist pressure. A new Fifth Sea Lord for Air had not yet been appointed, and all other members of the board, with the exception of Tudor, were new men. It therefore agreed to furnish four complete squadrons, fifty-five Rolls-Royce engines, and, to make up the shortfall, sixty Spad fighters from the 120 on naval order. It was not the sacrifice of material but the loss to the RFC of a large number of its most resourceful and experienced pilots that the RNAS found severe.[72]

It could count, nonetheless, upon mounting numbers of young Canadians. By December the Chief of the Naval Staff in Ottawa was enrolling pilot candidates at the rate of twenty-four a month. There were by this time some 300 Canadians in the RNAS, 230 of them among its total officer strength of 2764.[73] Most Canadian aeroplane pilots were with 3 Wing at Luxeuil, while most seaplane pilots were now on home stations. Some experienced Canadians, notably Mulock, who had become a Flight Commander at Dunkirk, were beginning to attain more responsible positions.

When Balfour and Jackson had taken over in 1915, they had wished the eradication of past heresies in the RNAS and the conversion of its air arm to a more truly 'naval' kind of administration. In the course of this transformation some serious miscalculations were made. The development of ship-borne aircraft had been sacrificed to a reliance upon rigid airships and large flying boats, with disappointing results. The jealousy with which the Admiralty guarded both its material and its authority to deploy that material as it saw fit made it politically vulnerable. Yet undoubtedly much substantial operational work had been done by the RNAS during the year. Some fresh technical approaches, the appointment of a new group, fresh from command at sea, to the Board of Admiralty, the provision for a Fifth Sea Lord for Air, and the creation of an anti-submarine department promised a new purpose and direction for naval aviation, a purpose and direction in which more and more Canadians would join.

7
Alternative Roles, 1917–18

There were 839 fully-trained pilots serving in the RNAS in January 1917; 110 of them were either at Luxeuil or on loan to the RFC in France. Of the 160 Canadians, more than one-third were among those whom the Admiralty reckoned were 'not employed directly in duties in connection with the Navy,' a disapproving phrase which reveals the Admiralty's lack of direction in air matters.[1] But on 11 January Commodore Godfrey Paine had taken up the new position of Fifth Sea Lord responsible for air policy, operations, and training. At last the RNAS would have a spokesman on the Board of Admiralty. Furthermore, Paine had the active support of Beatty who, as soon as he took over from Jellicoe as Commander-in-Chief, Grand Fleet, began to demand from the Admiralty an offensive air capability in the North Sea. Consequently, a new emphasis on training and selection led to 25 per cent of new pilots being directed to fleet work. These were chosen from among those showing the best aptitude in aeroplane handling and on take-off and touch-down.[2] This resulted in three-quarters of the Canadian graduates in 1917 finding their way to anti-submarine and fleet operations, a great change from 1916. There would still be a steady flow of pilots into fighter and bomber units on the Western Front, but naval aviation would acquire increasing importance.*

Technical developments were partly responsible. Early in the year squadrons employed in air defence, offshore fleet support, and anti-submarine patrols used for the most part Short and Sopwith seaplanes. In addition, the FBA, Porte Baby, and Curtiss H4 Small America flying-boats appeared on the station strength of some establishments. In January 1917 Flight Lieutenant J.K. Waugh of Whitby, Ont., took command of the RNAS station at Portland, a patrol base for six thousand square miles in the western reaches of the channel. To patrol this area he found there were only '... three other pilots, three armourers who acted as observers, some thirty odd men and four machines all of different types and in the final stages of dissolution ... morale ... was, to say the least, not at all good.'[3]

---

* Paradoxically, 1917 would also be the year in which the navy lost exclusive control of its own air arm. On 24 August the British Cabinet approved in principle the amalgamation of the two air forces. Parliament passed the Air Force Act, later called the Air Force (Constitution) Act, in November and the Air Council came into being on 3 January 1918. H.A. Jones, *The War in the Air: being the Story of the Part played in the Great War by the Royal Air Force*, VI (London 1937), 22

The news that the long-awaited Curtiss H12 Large Americas were at last coming into service was thus particularly welcome. Manned by two pilots and two
mechanics, H12s had the useful armament for the day of four 100-lb or two 230-lb
bombs, a maximum speed of eighty-five miles an hour, and an operational ceiling
of nearly 11,000 feet. On the debit side they had only two or four Lewis guns for
defence against fighters, and had a tendency to suffer damage on take-off because
of structural weakness in the bottom of the hull. Nevertheless, their six-hour
endurance in the air with a substantial bomb load gave them great advantages in
the anti-submarine war. Flight Sub-Lieutenant Claude C. Purdy of Winnipeg was
among the first RNAS pilots to fly them in May 1917. 'Am here [at Felixstowe]
taking some special work on large sea-planes [sic] which will be able to stay out at
sea on patrol much longer than ordinary ones,' he wrote:

We have not been having a great deal of flying the last few days, as it has been windy and
wet. We have some very fine machines, some of which I should say are the largest in the
world. It seems wonderful that such a large structure can possibly get into the air at all.
Patrols, of course, go on in all kinds of weather and we have to be pretty good at navigation,
as there is very little to go by in the air when it is foggy ... The whole thing has to be done by
instruments by which one can tell the speed through the air, climbing and gliding angles,
and the position laterally. There are also a dozen other things which require attention, and
which help to keep the course and to keep the station at home posted on one's movements.
It is very interesting indeed to go sailing through the air with anything from five hundred to
nine hundred horsepower behind one in the shape of engines.*[4]

Meanwhile, the 'F' (Felixstowe) series were being developed. The prototype,
F1, used the hull of a Porte flying boat married to the wings and tail assembly of
the Curtiss H4, while the F2 combined the same parts of the Porte and H12. From
these evolved the famous F2A. With a 'V' shaped, curved hull this machine had
the advantage of being able to alight and take off in much rougher seas than the
H12. It was also better armed, the high position of the tail enabling two extra
Lewis guns to be fitted at the rear, making a total of up to seven. Both types were
powered by two Rolls Royce Eagle engines and were comparable in performance,
the F2A being slightly faster at 95 mph, but having a lower service ceiling of
9600 feet.†[5]

---

* Purdy's machine was shot down and all four of the crew lost in a running fight between two
   Large Americas and three two-seater German seaplanes (Friedrichshafen FF 33Ls) off the North
   Hinder Light on 15 February 1918. 'Upon sighting our aircraft the Curtiss boats immediately
   turned away to the northwest. The more southerly flying boat was engaged about 1100 [hrs] at
   200 meters and after a brief combat fell in flames. The CO's aircraft then pursued the remaining
   enemy, the other two aircraft being low on gas. The chase was abandoned off Lowestoft. At
   about 1700 the wreckage of the Curtiss boat which was shot down was located, with three survivors clinging to it. Because of heavy seas, however, aircraft were unable to land.' 'The Hornets
   of Zeebrugge: Annotated Excerpts from the War Diary of Seeflugstation Flanders I, 1914–1918,'
   Cross & Cockade Journal, CXI, spring 1970, 23
† The F2A was also superior to the later F3, which had a service ceiling of only 8000 feet and
   though fitted with two 345-hp Rolls Royce Eagle engines could obtain a maximum speed of only
   91 mph.

The Admiralty paid less attention to the development of torpedo-carrying aircraft. Inter-related problems of range and payload suggested that they would usually need to be flown from carriers, but carriers themselves were still at an early stage of development. HMS *Manxman*, the latest addition to the Grand Fleet, had a sixty-foot flight deck forward, a hangar that could take four single-seat fighters in assembled state, and a centre-line cantilever gantry aft for hoisting her four Short 184s over the stern. With a top speed of only sixteen knots she lagged behind the fleet. In March, therefore, Beatty forced through the conversion of the 31-knot battlecruiser *Furious* over the opposition of Admiralty gunnery experts. Instead of the firepower of her forward 18-inch gun, *Furious* was given a hangar on the forecastle; its roof made a flight deck 228 feet long and fifty feet wide. Squadron Commander H.E. Dunning made the first landing on the flight deck while the ship was underway on 2 August; five days later he drowned when his Sopwith Pup stalled and blew over the side. No further deck landings were made until *Furious* received an after flight deck in 1918. Some cruisers were given a flight deck rigged over the forward gun turret from which aeroplanes could fly off at sea when the turret was rotated into the 'relative' or 'felt' wind over the deck. This brought offensive use of aeroplanes at sea closer to realization. Full utilization would only be possible, however, when *Hermes*, laid down in July as the first large carrier to be designed as such, was ready. As a stop-gap *Pegasus* and *Nairana*, converted merchantmen, joined the Battle Cruiser Fleet as seaplane carriers.*[6]

Not surprisingly, therefore, few of the increasing numbers of Canadians selected for fleet operations in 1917 found their way to the carriers or cruisers. The redoubtable 'Rutland of Jutland' in *Manxman* had under his supervision eleven pilots and observers, of whom four were Canadians. One of the five pilots in *Engadine* and two in *Campania*, as well as one kite-balloon officer in the Grand Fleet, were also from Canada.† This amounted to no more than 10 per cent of RNAS personnel in the fleet, but the little contingent played its part in advancing the techniques of heavier-than-air operations at sea. It was hazardous experimental takeoffs from *Manxman*, for example, that paved the way for the equipping of individual ships with Sopwith fighters. Subsequently, the presence of carrier aircraft in the Heligoland Bight helped to force a change in German tactics. Zeppelins had to fly at greater altitudes, and could no longer undertake detailed observation of British minefields. By late 1917 German minesweepers, steaming further out into the North Sea in response to British minelaying activity, had to be accompanied by vessels carrying seaplanes.[7]

The Admiralty's Anti-Submarine Division, which Jellicoe had set up under Rear-Admiral A.C. Duff in December 1916, began immediately to explore strategic and tactical methods to defeat the U-boat. The resulting strategy was at first disjointed, often based upon false assumptions and wishful thinking, and resulted in inappropriate use of naval forces, including the RNAS. The mistaken belief that

* The only Canadians among *Pegasus*' complement of pilots were C. McNicoll of Montreal and G.M. Simpson of Toronto.
† These were, in *Manxman*, W. Lodge of Arnprior, Ont., W.M.C. Matheson, H.G. Nares, and L.E. Nicholson, RNVR, all of Winnipeg; in *Engadine*, M.C. Dubuc of Montreal; *Campania*, George Breadner of Winnipeg and C.V. Bessette, an American citizen of Canadian parentage and recruited in Canada.

convoy was defensive and therefore could not bring about the destruction of enemy submarines lay at the root of the trouble. Several ambitious schemes were put forward, mainly designed to destroy submarines or deprive them of their bases. A military campaign launched to capture Ostend and Zeebrugge was foremost in the planners' minds. It meant laborious preparations for the 'Great Landing' on the Flanders Coast anticipated by Vice-Admiral Bacon and the Dover Patrol.[8]

Offensive operations against destroyers and submarines based on the Belgian ports necessarily involved RNAS squadrons based at Dunkirk. Their aircraft also provided spotting for naval bombardment of the ports and patrols over the vessels which maintained the net and mine barrage across the Straits of Dover. These patrols were designed to give some protection against attack by German surface vessels, as well as to sight and attack submarines. After August the RNAS at Dunkirk was principally concerned, however, with supporting the military offensive which, Jellicoe told the Cabinet, had to succeed, because if the Flanders Coast was not cleared Britain would be out of the war in 1918.[9]

At the end of 1916 the Admiralty had approved Wing Captain Lambe's plan to expand the force at Dunkirk to five fighter, one reconnaissance, and two bomber squadrons. Lambe began this ambitious programme by creating nucleus flights, because initially he was short of fighter aircraft and pilots. The number of Canadians at Dover-Dunkirk in January 1917 had dropped to twenty, since many were with 3 Wing at Luxeuil or with 8(N) Squadron, which had been seconded to the RFC in October. Moreover, as the Luxeuil pilots returned, most were used to staff the additional fighter squadrons promised to the RFC.[10]

These shortages and bad weather kept operations at Dunkirk at a low ebb at the beginning of the year. On 22 January, however, Flight Sub-Lieutenant C.J. Wyatt of Mount Brydges, Ont., flew one of two reconnaissance missions which disclosed that the German Sixth and Ninth Destroyer Flotillas were lying behind the Zeebrugge Mole. Further photographs on 1 February showed that there were eight destroyers, ten to twelve large torpedo boats, and three submarines crammed into Bruges harbour, and that the canals running from the harbour to the coast were frozen. Over the next two weeks bombers struck repeatedly at these targets. Results were disappointing, partly because the aircraft were frequently hampered by low temperatures. In one raid six of twelve bombers made emergency landings because of frozen water or oil, among them the Sopwith 1½ Strutters flown by Flight Sub-Lieutenants Chadwick and Sproatt. Aircraft from the *1st* and *2nd Marine Feldflieger* retaliated with night raids on Dunkirk and RNAS airfields. The chief consequence of this exchange of hostilities was that both sides strengthened their air defences against raids.[11]

The heavy commitment of fighters to the RFC seriously affected the Dunkirk command's capacity to carry out its many tasks. In March and April 1917 Lambe gave his three wings specific roles. No 1 Wing took care of naval co-operation and photographic reconnaissance, with fighter protection from 9(N) Squadron. No 4, the fighter wing, had as its main task offensive patrols 'well over the enemy's lines and from the region of Ypres Sector to ten miles out at sea.' The bomber wing, No 5, had two squadrons to attack German naval bases and 'Military objectives far behind the lines with the object of forcing the enemy to withdraw both Bombing

Machines ... and Fighting Machines ...' Trenchard welcomed the latter objective as being 'in entire agreement with the policy laid down for the Royal Flying Corps by the Commander-in-Chief.'[12]

Only the chief operational duties have been noted; the command was in fact spread too thin to carry out all its duties effectively. The quality of its aircraft was uneven. In the spring a number of DH4s were acquired for reconnaissance and bombing and the Handley Page 0/100s also being delivered were much superior to the Short bombers. Sopwith Triplanes went to the RNAS squadrons committed to the Western Front, however, while Dunkirk had to make do with Sopwith Pups and Nieuport 17s. Moreover, the Dunkirk seaplanes were 'hopelessly outclassed' by their opposition, as developments in the spring and early summer were to prove.[13]

Nevertheless, in early April the seaplanes were of some use as decoys. After a number of raids on the German seaplane station at Zeebrugge Mole, *Seeflugstation Flanders I*, Bacon learned that German destroyers were steaming out to anchor a mile offshore during each raid. On 7 April he sent his seaplanes in once more to bomb; the German destroyer G-88 fell into the trap and was torpedoed by motor-boats. It was their last success. At Zeebrugge the Germans had thirty-seven good aircraft which were now being reinforced by two superior types, the Friedrichs-hafen FF 49 and the Brandenburg W 12. In May the French station at Dunkirk lost six flying boats to the Germans, and on 19 June the RNAS lost two seaplanes and a rescue boat. One of the Sopwith Baby pilots killed was Flight Sub-Lieutenant J.E. Potvin of Midland, Ont. Just before this incident Lambe had told Bacon that the 'Seaplane pilots ... are amongst the best in my command and have constantly applied to transfer to land machines with a view to more active participation in the war.' The first step in this direction occurred in midsummer when the Admiralty scrapped seaplane operations at Dunkirk. Instead, the seaplane pilots, including P.S. Fisher of Montreal, flew Pups as escorts for a Large America flying boat transferred from Felixstowe to carry out anti-submarine patrols. The H12 arrived on 11 July, flown by Flight Sub-Lieutenants C.E.S. Lusk of Toronto and N.A. Magor of Montreal. They were joined by another Canadian, H.H. Gonyon of Chatham, Ont.[14]

Lambe used the bombers of 5 Wing with circumspection in this period. He hoped to attack enemy warships in Flemish ports, but on 21 April the initial attempt was turned back by gale force winds. D.A.H. Nelles of Toronto was forced down during this abortive raid and was interned in Holland.* The newly-arrived Handley Pages were committed to the same targets, but when one was lost in a daylight raid on 26 April, Lambe restricted them to night bombing. The first night raid was not until 10 May, when Flight Sub-Lieutenants J.R. Allen and F.R. Johnson, both of Westmount, Que., flew two of the Handley Pages. It is indicative of the shortage of experienced RNAS pilots that both returned to make their first night landing.[15]

Pilot shortages were even more acutely felt in the fighter wing. The casualties in the naval squadrons on the Western Front, though by no means abnormal for that

_____

* On 19 May he was awarded the DSC 'for conspicuous good work as pilot of a bombing machine.'

theatre, were much heavier than the RNAS ordinarily experienced. As a result, men fresh from flying school were now being sent as replacements to RNAS fighter units, and the naval air service was confronted with the same deadly problem of attrition with which the RFC had coped for so long. Lambe had to take the drastic expedient of reducing fighter squadron establishments to eighteen pilots and then, when 10(N) Squadron was sent to the Western Front in May, of further decreasing establishments to fifteen. At Dunkirk there were never more than twenty fighter pilots (of whom about fourteen might be Canadians at any one time) to maintain the desired offensive posture as well as to provide protection for the fleet. When the Germans began their bombing raids upon England in June, Dunkirk was given the additional task of patrolling the enemy bases at Ghistelles and St Denis Westrem to intercept the bombers on their return from England. In order to carry out Dunkirk's varied fighter duties, Lambe had to press 11(N) Squadron into service, although it was supposed to be a training and manning unit only. Some of the command's wounds were self-inflicted, however. For example, in May 4 Wing was ordered to resume the discredited system of line patrols, which meant that single-fighter patrols had to be maintained for six hours a day to prevent enemy reconnaissance and artillery co-operation aircraft from penetrating British air space.[16]

Just at this point, when Lambe considered the Dunkirk organization stretched to the limit, his command was virtually annexed to the major operation impending on the Western Front. As part of his Flanders offensive Haig planned landings on the Channel coast to collapse the German right wing and free the Allies from the submarine menace. The landing operation, to be directed by Admiral Bacon, was to take place when the Fifth Army's advance had reached Roulers and coincide with an attack by Fourth Army from the Yser bridgehead. To this end General Rawlinson and elements of the Fourth Army, accompanied by IV Brigade RFC, took over the extreme left of the allied line from St Georges to the sea in late June. Air operation orders for the whole sector were issued by Trenchard on 7 July. The RNAS was given a night-bombing area of Dixmude-Thourout-Retrauchement-Nieuport Bains and offensive patrol duties extending from Nieuport to three miles west of Dunkirk. Bacon made Lambe's prime responsibility clear to him on 15 July: 'you are to do what you can to attack hostile machines returning from raids over England; but nothing is to interfere with the efficient protection of the left flank of our army.'[17]

Unfortunately interference had already taken place, as Bacon was fully aware. On the evening of 10 July German infantry assaulted that part of the Yser bridgehead from Lombartzyde to the sea, wiped out two battalions of the 1st Division, and threw the British back across the Yser.* No word of German preparations for

---

* The German assault force included, for the first time, a complete squadron of aircraft in close support. 'The effects of this action on the enemy, both in the form of actual losses inflicted and in the form of its impact on the enemy [ie, British] morale, was so outstanding that the Commanding General of the Air Forces ... immediately proceeded to apply the experience gained and to re-form the existing air units accordingly. From then on ground-attack air squadrons (*Schlachtstaffeln*) supported the army operations ...' Paul Deichmann, *German Air Force Operations in Support of the Army* (USAF Historical Studies No 163; New York 1962), 121–2

this most successful pre-emptive strike had been brought in by RFC or RNAS reconnaissance aircraft. The weather had been poor in the period immediately preceding the attack, though there had been occasional opportunities for observation. In addition, the sector was new to IV Brigade's corps squadrons, and although it was on Dunkirk's front doorstep naval airmen had had little previous experience in detecting those minute but cumulative changes in the enemy's rear that would have spelled 'attack' to an experienced RFC observer. Even so, the episode reflected little credit upon either air service and damaged the prospects for the planned landings.[18]

The main battle opened on 31 July when the Fifth and Second British Armies and the First French Army attacked in Flanders. It had been preceded by a furious RFC air offensive, beginning on 12 July. Before the ground attack commenced, Trenchard complimented his brigade commanders on the 'energy and success' with which the preparatory phase of the air offensive had been secured. He went on: 'It is of the utmost importance that all units keep up the greatest amount of energy in this wearing down process. Bombing should be carried out with vigour, offensive patrols should be out continuously from dawn to dark, and artillery machines must work to the full amount required by the artillery, getting further out over the targets when the visibility is bad. If this is carried out I am confident the final result will prevent the German Flying Corps from taking any important part in the battle.'[19] In accordance with protocol, Lambe received a copy of this characteristic Trenchard exhortation 'for information.' In relaying its substance to his wing commanders, he repeated Trenchard's request for vigorous bombing and dawn to dusk offensive patrols, but added 'as far as possible.' He concluded with a sentence that the RFC commander would certainly have found incomprehensible. 'It is pointed out,' Lambe wrote, 'that the greatest value of the Aerial Offensive lies in the period of time immediately preceding the actual battle, and that once the battle has actually started, the Aerial Offensive can be eased up.'[20]

No mention of this unusual order, nor of the considerations that prompted it, is to be found in the scanty literature on RNAS operations at Dunkirk. Lambe was attempting to deal with an extremely serious morale problem that stemmed from the losses suffered by the RNAS squadrons on loan to the RFC and the consequent strain upon the Dunkirk Command's capacity to carry out its wide range of duties. In reviewing these difficulties for Bacon on 12 July, Lambe had specifically mentioned fighter shortages 'owing to rather heavy casualties of late, and to the fact that many of the pilots – who have been serving for a considerable period – [have been] breaking down.' When Bacon instructed him to make the protection of the army his prime concern, Lambe issued a secret memorandum to his wing commanders which discloses the dimensions of his problem:

Of late there have been rather a large proportion of pilots who state they are unable to fly over the enemy's lines, for various causes. In view of the great shortage of pilots for the forthcoming operations it is essential, as far as possible, that every endeavour is made to eliminate these cases, and I think that the Squadron Commanders can assist very largely if they make every effort to do so. Many of these cases are genuine, and these I will recommend for Seaplanes, but, I am convinced that a large proportion of the officers prefer the comfortable surroundings of an Aerodrome situated near London to the glamour and glory of the battle field. Wing Commanders and Squadron Commanders must make every endeavour to combat this idea.[21]

Instead of following Trenchard's example in holding out the prospect of victory over the German air force as the reward for strenuous effort, Lambe promised a reduction of RNAS strength at Dunkirk in October, with 'promising officers' to be sent for three months to England. 'I hope,' he added, 'that every endeavour will be made by all the pilots to stick it out till then.'[22]

The best explanation for this crisis in morale seems to be a difference in service practice and experience. The RNAS squadrons lent to the RFC performed valiantly, but under conditions for which they were wholly unprepared. Raymond Collishaw, the most successful of all naval fighter pilots and one who rose superlatively to the challenges of the Western Front, put the matter in a nutshell when he spoke of the 'comparatively gentle' operations at Dunkirk.[23] Conducted with relatively few casualties, these operations had permitted the building up of a body of pilots who had developed very considerable skills in the air, but the relentless psychological pressures of the Western Front, with its incessant combats, proved a fearful shock to some of them. Trenchard's driving insistence upon constant offensive was harsh, even cruel, in its effects upon airmen, as many of his critics have said. But it did have one result. Men who were physically or psychologically unable to measure up to the terrible demands of the air war were speedily winnowed out either by being returned to the depot within a few days of joining a squadron, or at the hands of German aviators. Neither RNAS leadership nor airmen had hitherto undergone this stern testing, and it is understandable that at both levels the resolution of some individuals wavered. It is in this context that an incident in September, dealt with later, in which the officer commanding 10(N) Squadron refused to carry out orders issued by his RFC superior, is to be viewed.*

In these circumstances, it was as well for the Dunkirk Command that the Flanders offensive never gained sufficient ground for the Channel coast landings to take place. Consequently, RNAS operations in support of the army never reached a high level of intensity. Nevertheless, during July and August the bombing wing made many night raids against railroad junctions and sidings at Ghent, Thourout, and Ostend and upon the electrical generating stations at Bruges and Zeebrugge, while during the day the DH4s attacked German airfields in Belgium. Many Canadians took part in these raids, the names of Flight Commander C.H. Darley, Flight Sub-Lieutenants H. Allan and F.R. Johnson, all of Montreal, C.B. Sproatt and E.B. Waller of Toronto, W.F. Cleghorn of Ottawa, and J.A. Shaw of Edmonton being among the most prominent.[24]

Dunkirk's fighter effectiveness was greatly enhanced by the return of 3(N) Squadron, with its extremely high proportion of Canadians,† after its service on

---

* See 432–4.
† Canadians in the squadron during July included R.F.P. Abbott of Carleton Place, Ont. (WIA 17 Aug. 1917), M. Allan of Saskatoon, Sask. (KIA 6 July 1917), G.B. Anderson and L.S. Breadner, both of Ottawa, J.S.T. Fall of Hillbank, BC, J.A. Glen of Enderby, BC, N.D. Hall of Victoria (POW 3 Sept. 1917), G.S. Harrower of Montreal (WIA 23 Sept. 1917), H.S. Kerby and L.L. Lindsay, both of Calgary, F.C. Armstrong (KIA 25 March 1918), H.M. Ireland, and A.McB. Walton, all of Toronto, and R.H. Mulock of Winnipeg.

the Western Front, where it had been credited with eighty victories while losing only nine of its own Sopwith Pups. Now re-equipped with Camels, this veteran squadron lost little time in making its presence felt. On 7 July it was despatched to meet the Gothas returning from their spectacular daylight raid on London and became embroiled with German machines acting as a defensive screen for the bombers. Flight Lieutenant J.S.T. Fall of Hillbank, BC, attacked three seaplanes twenty-five miles northeast of Nieuport, sending one down. Later in the day while leading his flight he was credited with another, killing the observer and sending the aircraft crashing into the sea. Flight Lieutenant J.A. Glen of Enderby, BC, opened fire on a third and watched it plummet into the water. The two Canadians then joined in the destruction of yet another enemy seaplane.[25]

In the late summer and autumn of 1917 the naval flyers were periodically involved in activities related to the ground war. For example, in preparation for the Channel landings, naval vessels relaid the 1916 barrage of net mines and deep minefields between Zeebrugge and Ostend. Many combats took place with German aircraft investigating the minelaying. Two Canadians, Flight Commander A.J. Chadwick and Flight Lieutenant R.M. Keirstead, both from Toronto, joined in claiming a seaplane shot down on 26 July. The next day three more, Fall, Glen, and L.D. Bawlf of Winnipeg, were part of a flight that drove off four German seaplanes from the new German torpedo-plane unit at Zeebrugge which were attempting to torpedo destroyers on the barrage line.* RNAS patrols prevented German reconnaissance aircraft from slipping over the allied rear areas from the sea. Occasionally, too, RNAS pilots would initiate individual strafing attacks on enemy airfields. Flight Sub-Lieutenant R.F.P. Abbott of Carleton Place, Ont., sprayed five hundred rounds into the hangars at Uytkerke airfield from fifty feet in the course of one such strike on 16 August.[26]

For the most part, however, operations at Dunkirk maintained their customary pattern and pace, fluctuating with Channel weather, the exigencies of naval warfare, and the changing priorities of Vice-Admiral Bacon and Wing Captain Lambe. In early September that meant the bombing of Bruges and vicinity. The Germans,

---

* German aerial torpedo attacks on merchantmen in the southern North Sea and English Channel between Dover and Yarmouth added further to the responsibilities of British air stations in the summer. The German Naval Air Service had carried out numerous experiments attaching torpedoes to land and seaplanes at a Baltic base in 1916 before developing the twin-engined Brandenburg GW and Gotha WD 11 seaplanes. Following the setting up of the special flight (*T-Staffel*) at Zeebrugge, several attacks by German seaplanes resulted in the sinking of a merchant ship in May 1917. The *T-Staffel* was out in strength again in the afternoon of 9 July, firing torpedoes at three ships between the Sunk and Shipwash Light Vessels; as was usual on such occasions the British air stations were alerted too late. Another party of four seaplanes dropped two more torpedoes off Lowestoft in the evening, also failing to register any hits. One of the attackers was shot down and a second Brandenburg GW trying to rescue the crew had to surrender to a patrol boat. Two months later seven seaplanes made the last sortie, during which three torpedoes were used to destroy a small merchant vessel. Discouraged by the lack of any substantial achievement the Germans disbanded the *T-Staffel* and abandoned the initiative they had taken in torpedo operations, a form of naval aviation of high promise. 'Report of Attacks by German Torpedo Carrying Seaplane,' Air 1/604/16/15/237; Great Britain, [Air Ministry], Aircraft Armament, Torpedo Section, *History of the Development of Torpedo Aircraft* (np, reprinted June 1919), 84; W. von Gronau, 'German Seaplane Stations, 1917,' app. III, Air 1/677/21/13/1901; G.P. Neumann, *Die deutschen Luftstreitkräfte im Weltkriege* (Berlin 1920), 133–4, DHist SGR I 196, Set 65

sensitive to attacks upon this major submarine base, usually responded sharply. Thus after a night raid by Handley Pages on 2–3 September, nine Albatros fighters rose to challenge a Camel formation led by Flight Commander L.S. Breadner and composed of four fellow-Canadians, Flight Sub-Lieutenants W.H. Chisam of Edmonton, L.A. Sands of Moncton, NB, H.M. Ireland of Toronto, and N.D. Hall of Victoria. In the resulting combat Breadner reported shooting down an Albatros D-III with its wings sheared off. Hall, who became a prisoner of war, was lost on the operation. Later the same day a formation of eight DH4s was broken up by German fighters. Attacked by six machines, Sproatt put the nose down to shake off his pursuers and then, he recalled, 'suddenly I pulled up ... turned off my engine and practically came to a stall ... the plane above us was so close my observer could have hit him with a walking stick.' Instead, Petty Officer A. Hinkler used his machine-gun; his bullets found the gas tank of the Albatros which fell away, 'just a black ball of smoke.'[27]

Canadians were involved in two notable successes of this period. On 15 September, during an attempt by British naval monitors to bombard Ostend, thirteen DH4s were over the Channel to catch German warships running to sea. From a group of trawlers and drifters, the team of Sproatt and Hinkler selected what was probably a torpedo boat destroyer and reported a direct hit upon it with a 65-lb bomb dropped from 9000 feet.* The second success, a week later, marked the first (and only) time in the First World War that an aircraft succeeded in sinking a submarine. On 22 September, while the monitor *Terror* was shelling Ostend, Flight Sub-Lieutenants Magor and Lusk were flying a protective patrol in the Large America, some forty-five miles off-shore. They were near the western edge of the North Hinder Bank when '... a long Enemy Submarine, about 200 to 250 feet long, was observed fully blown [surfaced] and attacked, two 230-lb bombs being dropped at about 800 feet and striking just behind [the] Conning Tower as she was half submerged, causing her to keel over on her side and sink. Wreckage, large bubbles and oil were observed subsequently.'[28] The submarine was UB 32, a boat approximately 120 feet long and only about 14 feet wide.[29] To score two direct hits on such a narrow target from a height of 800 feet with the primitive aiming device of the time was a matter of good luck rather than good judgment. (A week later Magor missed another submarine with two more bombs.) But if UB 32 looked twice as long as she actually was, perhaps she looked twice as wide too. In any case, although none of the twenty-three men on board survived there were at least four witnesses to the sinking – Magor, Lusk, and their two crewmen – and UB 32, which had sailed from Zeebrugge on 10 September and sank allied vessels on the 16th and 18th, was never heard from again.† Magor, the captain of the flying-boat crew, received

* Sproatt, who had completed twenty-six bombing raids by this time, and Hinkler, an Australian who became a noted pioneer aviator after the war, were awarded the DSC and DSM, respectively, during this period.
† Much confusion has arisen over Jones' identification of the submarine as UC 72 in *War in the Air*, IV, (London 1934), 73, an error reflected in Vice-Admiral Sir Arthur Hezlet's *Aircraft and Seapower* (New York 1970), 91. Hezlet also follows Jones in wrongly attributing the sinkings of several other submarines to air action. UC 72 was sunk by Q-ship gunfire in the Bay of Biscay on

a DSC before being shot down and killed while at the controls of another machine in April 1918. Lusk and the two non-commissioned crewmen got nothing.

The Germans had not been seriously hurt by the raids upon the Bruges-Ostend-Zeebrugge naval complex, but certainly they regarded these attacks as dangerous. In late September and early October they mounted a strong counter-offensive with aggressive fighter patrols and night-bombing attacks. Two Canadian pilots, Flight Sub-Lieutenants Keirstead and G.S. Harrower of Montreal, both claimed victories in this period. The British were unable to stop the bombing, however. The two Gotha units in Flanders, Nos *1* and *3 Bombengeschwader*, dropped over 120 tons of bombs on Calais, Poperinghe, Dunkirk, and the major RFC base at St Omer in a series of night raids, causing heavy damage. The greatest successes were won at Dunkirk. On the night of 24 September the Gothas raided the Dunkirk depot at St Pol, destroying machine shops, technical records, and 140 aircraft engines. The raids on St Pol were repeated nightly and culminated on 1–2 October with an attack by twenty-four machines from No *1 Bombengeschwader*. They destroyed twenty-three aircraft, damaged another thirty, and gutted a number of sheds and hangars. These concentrated attacks reduced RNAS strength, seriously impaired its operational efficiency, and helped bring 9(N) Squadron back to Dunkirk from the Western Front earlier than had been intended. R.H. Mulock was transferred temporarily from the command of 3(N) to reorganize the supply base; in November he became commander of the Dunkirk Aircraft Depot and Breadner took over command of the squadron.[30]

The attacks were also in response to a joint RFC-RNAS assault against German air bases, which had forced the enemy to shift Gotha operations from St Denis Westrem to Mariakerke, and from Gontrode to Oostacker, north of Ghent. These raids had been ordered because of the resumption of German night bombing against England, but in October Dunkirk began to be affected by the British decision to create a bombing force for long-distance raids against Germany itself. On 4 October Sir Douglas Haig asked Bacon to allocate some of his Handley Pages for long-distance attacks on Belgian rail and road communications and asked that the radius of their attacks be gradually increased to encompass German targets. On 28 October nine bombers were despatched against Germany. Five Canadians took part in this initial raid: Flight Lieutenant C.H. Darley, with Flight Sub-Lieutenant H.L. Webster, both from Montreal, as his observer, and Flight Sub-Lieutenants J.R. Allan of Ottawa, F.R. Johnson of Montreal, and the observer H.H. Costain of Brantford, Ont. Because of bad weather, only one of the nine bombers managed to reach Germany; the rest elected to bomb targets in Belgium. Six of the Handley

20 August 1917, according to R.M. Grant, *U-Boats Destroyed: the Effect of Anti-Submarine Warfare, 1914–1918* (London 1964), 153. Grant also spelt out the causes of the loss of all U-boats, but he complicated the UB 32 issue by reporting her sunk in the vicinity of the Sunk Light Vessel, off the mouth of the River Thames, an error he corrected in his *U-Boat Intelligence, 1914–1918* (London 1969), 186, where the location is recorded in latitude and longitude. Meanwhile, Erich Gröner, in his massive two-volume study, *Die deutschen Kriegsschiffe, 1815–1945* (München 1966), I, 364, located the sinking south of the Isle of Wight, although he accepts that UB 32 was sunk by a flying-boat. See also R.D. Layman, P.K. Simpson, and E.J.L. Malpern, 'Allied Aircraft vs. German Submarines, 1916–1918,' *Cross & Cockade Journal*, XI, (winter 1970), 289–302.

Pages attacked factories at Antwerp. Trenchard, who was responsible for bombing operations along the entire front, was criticized for his action on the ground that large centres of Belgian population, well back from the lines, were not acceptable targets. He gave instructions that in future Antwerp and Brussels were to be spared.[31]

In November poor weather heralded the onset of winter and the curtailment of operations. Bombing was reduced to occasional short-distance forays. On one return flight in December the RNAS bombers were harried by Albatros fighters. Sproatt, leading the escort, plunged at one and reported that 'Machine stalled and then fell spinning rapidly. I then lost sight of it for some seconds and finally saw a number of pieces fall into the sea.' It was the last aerial victory on the coast in 1917.[32]

As operations diminished so, temporarily, did Dunkirk's pilot strength. In a five-week period prior to the end of October, casualties, illness, and transfer saw the loss of sixty-one pilots; only nineteen replacements were sent out. In November, however, 1(N) and 10(N) Squadrons returned from the Western Front and Lambe was able to begin rotating squadrons for rest periods to English bases, as he had promised. In January 1918 Dunkirk activities were further cut back when the seaplane station was turned over to the Americans and the Large America sent back to Felixstowe. Anti-submarine patrols were now to be handled by a new squadron, 17(N), flying DH4s, while the fighter pilots of the former seaplane defence flight became the nucleus of a fighter squadron, 13(N), under the temporary command of Raymond Collishaw.*[33]

These minor organizational changes were overshadowed by greater ones in the naval command and in the relationship of the RNAS with the RFC. One of the initial acts of Admiral Sir Rosslyn Wemyss after he succeeded Jellicoe as First Sea Lord was to appoint Rear-Admiral Roger Keyes to replace Vice-Admiral Bacon, whom Keyes had out-manoeuvred in a dispute over the effectiveness of the Channel barrage. When Keyes arrived at Dover, however, he found that the Air Council, which had come into being on 3 January 1918 under the Air Force Act, was already exerting its authority. Several Dunkirk units were transferred to army control, and then came a major and drastic reduction. The headquarters of 4 and 5 Wings and 3 to 9 Squadrons, inclusive, were removed from Dunkirk and were placed directly under the Commander-in-Chief, BEF. All that remained for naval duties of Dunkirk's once sizeable organization was a reconnaissance squadron, the DH4 anti-submarine squadron, and three squadrons of Camels.[34]

In their correspondence and their memoirs, both Bacon and Keyes seemed genuinely appreciative of the RNAS' work at Dunkirk. Among the achievements they detail were spotting by naval airmen for the bombardments of the Flemish

---

* Flight Sub-Lieutenants H.H. Gonyon of Chatham, Ont. (WIA 30 May 1918) and C.E.S. Lusk of Toronto converted from seaplanes to DH4s to become initial members of 17(N); they were joined shortly by two other Canadians, R.M. Berthe of Montreal and J.A. Shaw of Edmonton. Other Canadians in addition to Collishaw with 13(N) were P.E. Beasley of Victoria, J.E. Greene of Winnipeg (KIA 14 Oct. 1918), G.C. Mackay of Sunderland, Ont. (WIA 15 Sept. 1918), W.J. Mackenzie of Port Robinson, Ont. (WIA 21 April 1918), and G.L.E. Stevens of Peterborough, Ont.

coast, photographic surveys of shipping dispositions and German defence systems from Nieuport to the Dutch frontier, and the dropping of a large tonnage of bombs against strong opposition from German fighters, more than half of it upon railways and aerodromes.[35] For three years Canadians had taken part in these operations. At its peak in December 1917 the command had a strength of 243 pilots, eighty-three of them Canadians. Of the sixty-four pilots killed, interned, or captured between January 1917 and March 1918, twenty-one (30 per cent) were Canadians. In 1915 R.H. Mulock had been the first of his countrymen to arrive at Dunkirk; in 1918, as a wing commander, he was the senior Canadian officer in the RNAS. By March 1918 two Canadians, Collishaw and Wemp, were commanding squadrons and many others were flight commanders.

In retrospect, it must be said that the services of all these men could have been put to better use. Both at Dunkirk and in the Admiralty there was an exaggerated view of the material damage caused by bombing. Dunkirk had launched raids frequently, but they were usually small and rarely concentrated. The enemy was able to repair damaged installations and, in the case of airfields, to switch operations easily from one grass field to another. Though the bombing had caused the Germans to erect a network of ferro-concrete pens at Bruges to protect this major U-boat base, construction work and operations were only slowed, never stopped, by the raiding.[36]

Bombing had not defeated, nor even substantially affected, the submarine campaign. Nor had Bacon's net barrage, over which the RNAS had patrolled so dutifully, prevented U-boats from slipping through the Channel. Some of the most valuable contributions of the RNAS at Dunkirk bore little relation to naval needs. RNAS fighter squadrons played a vital part on the Western Front in 1917, and its bombing in support of army objectives had been of some use, within the limits of the weapon. It was therefore all too easy for the army and the RFC, pleading quite reasonably on grounds of highest military urgency, to take advantage of this naval enclave on their left flank where good pilots and good aircraft were in apparent abundance. Such would not have been the case if the employment of aircraft at Dunkirk had been subordinated to an over-riding strategic objective.

It is now clear that the RNAS should have concentrated on air-sea co-operation to defeat the German attack upon shipping. First World War submarines had a very limited underwater performance and were susceptible to air attack while on the surface. The Admiralty staff, however, had little belief or interest in such an approach. Instead, they relied upon ever more complex routing arrangements for vessels steaming to and from United Kingdom ports, and a substantial enlargement of the surface patrol in home waters. By July 1917 it included 2800 yachts, trawlers, drifters, motor boats, and paddle minesweepers. The endeavour of the RNAS to reorganize its available forces to co-ordinate more effectively with ships, and to make more efficient use of its resources for the anti-submarine campaign, suffered from the lack of any strong lead from the Admiralty.[37]

In the early spring of 1917 the aircraft available for anti-submarine warfare consisted of 176 'Class I' – that is, first-line – heavier-than-air craft and forty-six airships. Seven areas of responsibility on the east coast were centred respectively on Scapa Flow, the Dundee Command, South Shields, the Killingholme Command, Great Yarmouth, the Harwich Command, and the Nore Command. The Dover

Patrol was to cover the eastern Channel; the Portsmouth Group with its main air station at Calshot and two sub-stations at Bembridge (Isle of Wight) and Portland concentrated on the mid-Channel area; and the South-West Group, centred on Devonport with stations at Cattewater, Newlyn, Scilly Isles, Fishguard, Mullion, and Pembroke, covered the Western Approaches.[38]

In July 1917 forty-three of the 147 pilots in British home stations were Canadians.* At various times during the ensuing fifteen months there were Canadians in all these stations with a high proportion of them at Felixstowe (where ten of the twenty-one pilots were Canadian at the start of 1917), Dundee, and to a lesser degree, Killingholme and Calshot. In marked contrast to their colleagues in the Dover-Dunkirk organization who were frequently shifting between squadrons, the 'web-footed boys' often served for anything up to two-and-a-half years with the same unit. While most of the flying in the 1917 anti-submarine campaign was done in seaplanes, the majority of pilots at the larger east-coast stations were also qualified on land-planes and, as at Great Yarmouth, were 'expected to take any of the various types into the air by day and the BE2Cs by night.'[39]

Pilots for Large Americas trained and operated at Felixstowe. In February 1917 two Canadians in the first group of trainees, Flight Sub-Lieutenants F.S. McGill and J.O. Galpin of Ottawa, were among those from Felixstowe who established the 'Porte Boat Flight' on Tresco in the Isles of Scilly where McGill became second-in-command.[40] On 13 April Large America No 8661 inaugurated patrol flights from Felixstowe and the same day Flight Sub-Lieutenant R. Leckie and his crew collected No 8660 for Yarmouth Station. Other flying-boats went to Calshot and Killingholme from the original contract of fifty aircraft, forty-seven of which were delivered by the end of the year.

At the outset of the unrestricted submarine campaign, declared in February 1917, Germany had over a hundred U-boats assigned to operational flotillas. Of these, almost half were based on German North Sea ports, about one-third at Zeebrugge and Ostend, and most of the rest in the Mediterranean. The total rose to a maximum of 139 in September with an average of forty-six on patrol at any time. New tactics required U-boats to attack submerged with torpedoes rather than surfacing to engage with gunfire, and those stationed in the North Sea or Channel ports operated in specifically assigned sectors. Submarines bound for more distant waters normally travelled through the English Channel to and from their stations, but if forced to return by the northern route, because of damage or any other reason, they were 'to let themselves be seen as freely as possible, in order to mislead the English.'[41]

The anti-submarine tactics developed during the year by the RNAS depended principally upon the assumed endurance performances of aircraft.† There was, as

---

* In addition, A.S. Ince of Toronto was flying as an observer from Calshot.
† These were as follows:

Coastal Airships	8–12 hours
SS	4–8
H12 Large Americas	2–6
Short Seaplanes	2–4
Sopwith Seaplanes	1–2
Aeroplanes	1–1¼

yet, no standard doctrine. At Plymouth, however, aircraft were expected to fly routine, emergency, or contact patrols. Routine patrols consisted of search patterns expanding from the air station, flown either on a straight or zig-zag course according to orders issued on a daily basis. Command headquarters would order an emergency patrol if a U-boat sighting or wireless transmission occurred, but airships and seaplanes were to investigate to a distance of no more than fifty miles from shore and aeroplanes were restricted to twenty-five miles. In contact patrols two or three destroyers or motor launches steamed in line abreast while an aircraft flew a zig-zag patrol across the main line of advance, communicating at regular intervals by lamp, wireless telegraphy, or horizontal semaphore. All patrols were supposed to be flown at 1000 feet, because this was the best height for spotting a submarine silhouette as well as for detecting wind changes by reference to the wave caps.[42]

Routine search plans reflected the geographical features of each area and the need to prevent either overlapping or lack of continuity in the air coverage of coastal water. Thus the Admiralty ordered RNAS pilots not to bomb unrecognized submarines outside the limits of their own command. In the South-West Group the seas around each air station were divided into a series of triangular patrol sectors using the station as apex and subdividing each triangle into smaller triangles with bases at 15, 30, 45, 60, and 75 miles out. In the North Sea, Felixstowe developed the famous 'Spider Web' for large flying-boats. Having the Netherlands North Hinder Light Vessel, 52 miles from Felixstowe, as its centre point, the 'web' was an imaginary octagonal figure 60 miles in diameter with eight 30-mile radial arms joined by chords at 10, 20, and 30 miles out. About four thousand square miles of ocean, which it took U-boats up to ten hours to traverse at surface cruising speed (in order to conserve battery power), could thus be systematically searched. With its capability of covering three hundred miles, a single flying-boat could patrol a large segment of the 'web,' the specific sectors for each trip being determined from a master chart at the station which showed the positions of submarines by directional wireless intercepts. This proved more effective than the less patterned patrol which Yarmouth flying-boats carried out along the enemy coast from the Texel to Borkum.[43]

The founder and commanding officer of the Felixstowe 'War Flight' was Flight Commander T.D. Hallam of Toronto, who had entered the RNAS through the armoured car organization which went to Gallipoli in 1915. He was older than most men joining the air services, and because of his wounds he was forbidden to fly. While at Hendon Air Station, however, he disregarded his medical restrictions, qualified to RNAS flying-boat pilot standards, and arrived at Felixstowe in March 1917. This 'thin, dried up' Canadian enjoyed a flying career of great distinction in the subsequent year-and-a-half.[44]

Hallam's description of the first patrol by a Large America on 13 April 1917 tells us much of the nature of this work:

At ten o'clock, on this day, a day with an overcast sky and a twenty-knot westerly wind blowing, I sounded off five sharp taps on the bell, the signal for patrol. The chiefs of the engineer, carpenter, and working parties reported for instructions.

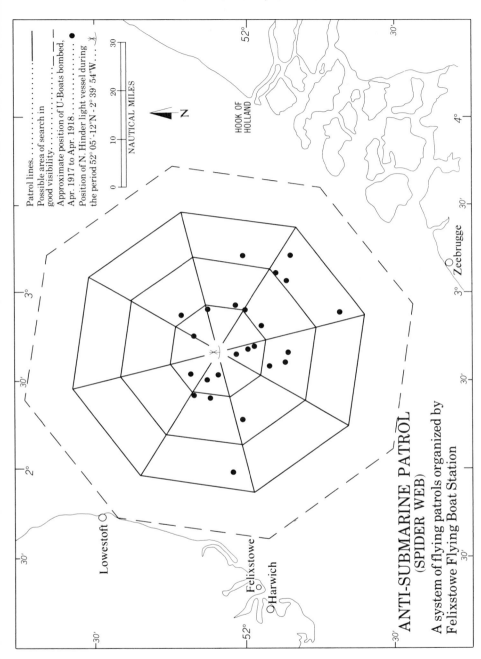

Patrol lines..............
Possible area of search in
  good visibility............
Approximate position of U-Boats bombed,
  Apr. 1917 to Apr. 1918............. ●
Position of N. Hinder light vessel during
  the period 52° 05'·12"N - 2° 39'·54"W....

NAUTICAL MILES

0   10   20   30

HOOK OF
HOLLAND

Zeebrugge

Lowestoft

Felixstowe
Harwich

ANTI-SUBMARINE PATROL
(SPIDER WEB)

A system of flying patrols organized by
Felixstowe Flying Boat Station

The working party of twenty men gathered around *Old '61* and rolled her out of the shed to the concrete area. Here they chocked her up under the bow and tail ... to prevent her standing on her nose when the engines were tested ...

In the meantime the armourers' party had fitted on the four Lewis machine-guns and had tucked up into place under the wing roots, two on each side of the hull, the four one hundred pound bombs.[45]

The crew boarded after all these preparations had been made. The first pilot sat in a cockpit 'covered by a transparent wheelhouse' so that he did not have to wear goggles, since these were thought to interfere with efficient observation. If a submarine was sighted the second pilot was supposed to move to the open forward cockpit with its machine-gun, bomb-sight, and bomb-release levers. The wireless operator sat facing forward on the right-hand side of the boat behind the first pilot, with his wireless cabinet, code books, Aldis signalling lamp, and carrier pigeons. The engineer sat in the cockpit amidships. The working party then rolled the boat out of the slipway:

Here six waders, in waterproof breeches coming up to their armpits, and weighted boots to give them a secure foothold when the tide was running ... steered the boat down into the water, the working party easing her down by tailing on the line ...

As the flying-boat entered the water ... the thrust of the engines urged her forward, and she taxied clear.[46]

Under good conditions the boat would become airborne at about 35 knots, but landing and taking off in bad weather made exceptional demands on the pilot. This was also true of long patrols: 'Coming back against a head-wind, it took so long that I thought somebody had moved England.'[47]

Initially the only other Canadian pilot in the Felixstowe 'War Flight' was Flight Sub-Lieutenant B.D. Hobbs of Sault Ste Marie, Ont. It was on the flight's fourth patrol that Hobbs made the first submarine sighting report. Two days later, on 20 April, two British pilots in No 8661 dropped four 100-lb bombs on a surfaced u-boat, and on the 23rd Hallam made his first bombing attack.* By the end of April the flight's score stood at eight submarines sighted and three bombed. One Large America had been lost, though its crew was rescued by fishermen. For the pilots, who had patrolled for thousands of miles since the beginning of the war with little to show for their efforts, the new turn of events was exhilarating. Volunteers lined up for duty and Hallam noted that his fellow-countrymen were well to the fore: Canadians 'seemed to be best fitted for flying-boat work, and probably as high a proportion as three fourths of the good boat pilots came from that dominion.'†[48]

---

* Awards, including a Bar to Hallam's DSC, were given for the attack of 23 April but records show conclusively that no u-boat was destroyed. Grant, *U-Boats Destroyed*, app. B1, 152

† Early Canadian additions to the flight included H.J. Bat of Oakville, Ont., H.G. Boswell of Toronto, J.O. Galpin of Ottawa, J.L. Gordon, G.R. Hodgson, and N.A. Magor, all of Montreal, and V.H. Ramsden of Toronto. Gordon and Hodgson had previously been in the Nore 'Defence Flight.' On the ground they received advice on the subtleties of bombing from the armament officer, A. Partridge, a former member of the Canadian Army, during his 'continuous performance for their benefit entitled ... Frightfulness for Fritz.' P.I.X. [T.D. Hallam], *The Spider Web: the Romance of a Flying-Boat War Flight* (London 1919), 53–4

In May the Felixstowe 'War Flight' alone reported seven sightings and five bombings. One made on 20 May by Flight Sub-Lieutenant Henry G. Boswell of Cobourg, Ont.,* second pilot to a British officer, Flight Sub-Lieutenant C.R. Morrish, led to the British official historian giving the crew credit for destroying UC 36 'which seems to have been the first direct sinking of a U-boat by aircraft during the war.' The claim has since been discredited, and it is a remarkable coincidence that a British submarine, E 33, was bombed (but not hit) under similar circumstances 'in the same area and about the same time.'[49]

In July two more such claims were made by Felixstowe aircraft, but these cannot be substantiated by the evidence now available. Nevertheless the general increase in submarine sightings and attacks shows that aircraft patrols, particularly from Felixstowe with its monthly average in May, June, and July of six sightings and four attacks, were increasingly effective in harassing the daylight operations of U-boats. Bad weather in August forced a drastic reduction in aerial patrolling, but submarine sightings around the British Isles totalled thirteen for the month, mostly in the western areas. Sopwith 1½ Strutters from Prawle Point and Mullion forced U-boats to dive but never managed to get in an attack because, in the view of one authority, their engines were so noisy. An additional peril of flying these aeroplanes on routine maritime patrols was brought home to Flight Lieutenant W.J. Sussan of Ottawa,† when his engine 'fell to pieces' and he was forced to land in the sea. He and his observer, drifting in life-jackets, were found by purest chance in the gathering dusk when a destroyer stumbled upon them. The problem did not arise again because, fighter pilots being needed on the Western Front, aeroplane detachments were closed down for the winter.[50]

Increasing contact between large flying-boats and submarines in the North Sea and to the south and southwest of the English coast was one of the few encouraging features of the war for the British Admiralty.‡ The problem of how to defend shipping remained, however. The number of allied, British, and neutral vessels sunk by submarines rose steadily from 145 ships totalling 291,459 tons in January to 354 ships totalling 834,549 tons in April. British losses alone reached their peak during 'Black Fortnight' between the 17th and the end of April when 400,000 tons of the British total of 545,000 tons for the month were destroyed by mine or sub-

* Boswell had come over early in the war in the Princess Patricia's Canadian Light Infantry and served in the trenches. Invalided home, he had recovered and joined the RNAS in Canada in June 1916. He was awarded the DSC for his part in this attack of 20 May 1917.
† Invalided in October 1916, Sussan had recently rejoined the RNAS after recuperation in Canada. C.A. Maywood of Winnipeg was also at Prawle Point; he was found unfit for further flying in August and had to resign. A third Canadian to join Prawle Point early in its history was H.L. Crowe of Toronto, who was on his first active service appointment. Returning from an emergency submarine patrol on 22 June, he crashed on the foreshore and was killed.
‡ There was in this period one noteworthy sighting and attack by Flight Sub-Lieutenant C. McNicoll of Montreal, one of the Canadians at Dundee, on 12 March 1917. The attack was unsuccessful, but McNicoll was awarded the DSC in June 1917. Two other Canadians were at Dundee at this time: J.G. Ireland of Montreal and W.R. Kenny of Ottawa, who became an Air Vice-Marshal, RCAF, in the Second World War. By early December they had been joined by F.C. Cressman of Peterborough, Ont. (lost at sea on Christmas Eve, 1917), S.A. Grant of Montreal, J.D. Guild of Kemnay, Man., C.W. Lott of Brussels, Ont. (KIA 20 July 1918), and A.H. Sandwell of Montreal. Seven out of fifteen pilots were Canadian. See McNicoll to CO Dundee, 13 March 1917, Air 1/659/17/122/607.

marine, a high proportion of these sinkings occurring some two hundred miles off the southwest Irish coast and in the western approaches to the English Channel. On 1 May, therefore, the First Sea Lord demanded ruthless control of shipping activity. The Admiralty at last began to resort to the ancient system of convoy.[51]

Coasters plying to the Hook of Holland had been crossing in convoy since July 1916. Large Americas from Felixstowe searched the route beforehand and accompanied the 'beef ships,' as the pilots called the cattle trade, from April 1917. The Anglo-French coal trade had been in convoy from February 1917 and convoys also ran from the Orkneys to Norway from the end of April. The anti-submarine division now recommended ocean convoy; the Admiralty accepted, not without misgivings. Although a convoy leaving Gibraltar on 10 May and met by a Large America from the Scilly Isles arrived without loss, this did not become a regular routine for another two months. On 24 May the first convoy for Britain left Hampton Roads, Virginia, but not for two months did trans-Atlantic convoys begin to sail on a regular schedule. Losses fell off initially, but because so much shipping was still routed independently and so much faith was still placed in the patrol system for detecting and destroying U-boats, the amount of tonnage sunk remained unacceptably high throughout the summer months. Pilots of seaplanes and flying-boats (except for those meeting the inwardbound convoys in the Western Approaches or those escorting the 'beef trade') simply had instructions to carry out their normal patrol, but, should they sight a convoy, to consider its protection 'as their prime task.'[52]

Because of the difficulty of locating the inward-bound convoys, long-range U-boats had moved in to attack outward-bound shipping, which was still independently routed. As a result the first outward convoy was organized to sail on 13 August. Indeed, it was between the fall of 1917 and the spring of 1918 that the convoy system finally turned the tide of the German submarine offensive. The RNAS played its part in this triumph. Kite balloons gave such a good view that submarines could not get into an attacking position without being sighted; non-rigid airships provided the same sort of protection and could also attack submarines, although not with great effect.

At no time did statistics appear from the Admiralty that related the tonnage of shipping arriving safely in port to number of hours flown on convoy escort. The naval staff preferred to place its emphasis on the number of submarines sighted and attacked each month. It was left to an American commanding the USN Aviation Force in European Waters to observe, in a paper of February 1918, that 'The statement ... that the positive effect of patrol is measured best by the submarines that have been sunk, I cannot agree with, as it seems to me the best measure of patrol is the amount of protection afforded our shipping.' As he pointed out, 'the reason of failure to destroy is because a submarine gets ample warning and submerges; this protects friendly shipping – the object of patrol.'[53] There can be no doubt that the sighting of U-boats kept the adrenalin flowing and morale high, and the airmen would not likely have appreciated the possibility that the very absence of sightings might be proof that they were doing their job effectively. Seaplanes, flying-boats, and aeroplanes in the Home Stations flew 3779 patrols from July to December 1917, 362 of which were escorting convoys. During 7592 hours in the air, eighty-six submarines were seen and fifty-eight attacked. Airships had a some-what lower ratio of sightings to hours flown.[54]

On 18 August 1917 the sole Canadian at Cherbourg, Flight Sub-Lieutenant R.T. Eyre of Toronto, sighted a submarine but was unable to attack before the U-boat submerged. A month later Flight Sub-Lieutenant W.A.N. Davern of Belleville, Ont., bombed a submarine with no apparent result during a patrol off Yarmouth. Flying out of Felixstowe, B.D. Hobbs and R.F.L. Dickey carried out an unsuccessful attack on 28 September. Another Felixstowe flying-boat bombed a submarine the next day and in October the 'War Flight' recorded three sightings, including an attack made by a machine with Flight Sub-Lieutenant H.S. Wilson of Westmount, Que., in the second pilot's seat.[55]

Flight Lieutenant McGill attacked two submarines off the Isles of Scilly in October, both with inconclusive results. Flight Lieutenant Leckie at Yarmouth sighted a periscope while searching for a lost seaplane on 29 October, but was unable to make an effective attack. Four days later one of the Felixstowe pilots, J.O. Galpin, flying in broken cloud, caught sight of a submarine and carried out an unsuccessful attack. On 3 December 1917 one of the two Canadians in HMS *Riviera*, Flight Sub-Lieutenant N.I. Larter of Toronto,* unsuccessfully bombed a surfaced submarine thirty miles west-northwest of Cap de la Hague. In December Galpin and his crew made the only attack that month by a Felixstowe aircraft when they sighted two U-boats and were able to release bombs on one. At Cherbourg, just before Christmas, Eyre attacked and thus diverted a U-boat lying in wait for a French convoy off Cap de la Hague. On 20 February 1918 Leckie found two submarines and managed to attack one about thirty miles northeast of Great Yarmouth. He reported seeing the stern rise out of the water, turn over and disappear at a 60-degree angle, but once again, there is no record of a U-boat destroyed by air action. In March there were two more attacks, one by Eyre from Cherbourg and one by Flight Sub-Lieutenant H.B. Kerruish of Fergus, Ont., flying from the aircraft carrier *Campania*.[56] Naval airmen were finding enemy submarines and subjecting them to harassment, and no enemy aircraft was able to stop them.

Air supremacy in the North Sea bore some relation to home defence activities. After the long-range Large Americas started arriving they were kept in readiness at Felixstowe, Yarmouth,† and Killingholme to intercept zeppelins within 150 miles of the British coast. On 14 May 1917 Leckie and his co-pilot began a new and decisive phase in the campaign against German airships. Wireless intercepts had pinpointed a zeppelin on a mine-spotting patrol near the Terschelling Light Vessel and at 0500 hrs the flying boat's crew sighted their quarry fifteen miles ahead at about 3000 feet. Leckie was at 6000 feet and, ordering three of his 100-lb bombs dropped to lighten his aircraft and improve its performance, he went into a shallow dive at 90 knots, levelling out slightly astern of the airship. Twenty feet below the

---

* The other Canadian was B.N. Harrop of Indian Head, Sask., who served in the carrier from November 1916 to July 1918. Larter and his observer disappeared without trace on 9 December 1917.

† Canadians at Yarmouth in the summer of 1917 included G.R. Haliday of Victoria, R. Leckie and N.W. Leslie of Winnipeg, and G.H. Simpson of Toronto.

gondolas on the starboard quarter, his English co-pilot fired incendiary bullets into the airship's envelope, until his gun jammed. But as the flying-boat veered hard to starboard a small glow started to spread inside and within seconds L 22, her number clearly visible, had become a blazing torch plunging tail first into the sea. Soon all that remained was a 'mass of black ash on the surface from which a column of brown smoke about 1,500 feet high sprang up and stood.'*[57] For a time the fate of L 22 remained a mystery to the Germans because Leckie had maintained wireless silence from eighty miles to seaward of his base.

In the foggy early hours of 24 May Galpin and Leckie were out again in the same aircraft to catch the zeppelins returning from a raid on England. This time they suddenly found themselves below L 40 which climbed hard to gain altitude and, according to Galpin, 'threw out a smokescreen under cover of which he gained the main bank of clouds.' By chance the episode was repeated with the same actors on 5 June when they attacked L 40, while flying the westerly patrol off Terschelling Light Vessel. Once more the Germans failed to appreciate that a new type of aircraft was involved.[58]

They were still in ignorance on 14 June when L 43 went on patrol with L 23 to cover minesweepers dealing with a British minefield forty miles north of Terschelling. Following a wireless intercept, a Large America piloted by Hobbs and Dickey set out to find them. At 0840 hrs they spotted L 43 at an altitude of 1500 feet off the Dutch coast at Vlieland. 'We at once proceeded [the pilots recorded] to attack at full speed climbing to 2,000 feet ... Hobbs was piloting machine ... As we approached the Zeppelin we dived for her tail at about 100 knots. Her number L 43 was observed on the tail and bow, also Maltese Cross in black circle. Midship gun opened fire with tracer ammunition and when about 100 feet above Sub-Lieut Dickie [sic] opened fire with Brock and Pomeroy ammunition as the machine passed diagonally over the tail from starboard to port. After two bursts the Zeppelin burst into flames. Cutting off engines we turned sharply to starboard and passed over her again; she was by this time completely enveloped in flames and falling very fast.'[59]

To the German command L 43 had simply vanished, but L 46 later the same day revealed what must have been the fate of the lost airship. It encountered Galpin and Leckie, who were following up the lead given by the airship's wireless messages. The zeppelin escaped by dumping water ballast and rapidly climbing to 18,700 feet off the North Hinder Light Vessel leaving the flying-boat to fire ineffectually at her from its operational ceiling, several thousand feet below. *Fregattenkapitän* Peter Strasser, Chief of the German Naval Airship Division, concluded that L 43 had been shot down by the same plane which had attacked L 46. New precautions and a minimum flight altitude of 13,000 feet were ordered for all future patrols. The result for the crews was 'that each scouting flight became as strenuous as a raid on England.' In tactical terms, the flying-boats had sharply reduced the effectiveness of the airship in its prime function, reconnaissance for British submarines and mines.[60]

---

* All four members of the Large America that destroyed L 22 were decorated: Galpin and Leckie each got a DSO, and the two ratings received DSMs.

In the early hours of 26 July Naval Intelligence recorded the wireless transmissions of L 44, L 45, and L 46 on patrol in Heligoland Bight, giving Leckie and
Galpin an opportunity to finish off their old opponent L 46. At 0935 hrs they
were on the tail of the unsuspecting airship which, despite orders, was flying at
10,000 feet. The sudden realization in the airship that she had unwanted company
and her sudden and violent evasive action produced an electrifying spectacle for
the onlookers. Leckie yelled out in amazement, 'Look Galpin! My God! She's
stalled!' as L 46 threw out ballast and shot upwards with her nose at an angle of
15–20 degrees, thus escaping her attackers.[61]

To meet the changing pattern of air activity over the North Sea in 1917 German
naval aviation was reorganized and expanded under the centralized control of a
chief of naval aviation. The four main operational stations, all located on coastal
islands, had their effective strength increased: List to thirty-two seaplanes, Heligoland to twenty-four. Norderney to forty-eight, and Borkum to twenty.[62] Scouting
areas of each station were divided into nine sectors with the main emphasis early
in the year on surveillance and the protection of minesweeping flotillas.* When
Large Americas appeared off Borkum itself, the station took on the task of providing fighting echelons while Norderney assumed responsibility for reconnaissance
and guarding the minesweepers. Most of the stations' work was carried out by
miscellaneous variants of the *Friedrichshafen* FF 33 seaplane; from May onwards
they began to take delivery of the two-seater *Friedrichshafen* FF 49C equipped with
the more powerful 200-hp Benz engine and armed with two machine-guns.
Another new arrival in 1917 was the two-seater *Brandenburg* W 12 fighter seaplane
designed by Ernst Heinkel, whose 150-hp Benz engine gave it a top speed of 100
mph, faster than any of its British counterparts. An excellent climber, fitted with
guns fore and aft, the W 12 was designed specifically with the ability to fire rearwards in contrast to the earlier single-seat Rumpler, Albatros, and Brandenburg
types which made up the bulk of fighter defence forces.[63]

In May German fighter seaplanes began to launch attacks on Large Americas.
N.A. Magor figured in one of these incidents on the 19th. On 4 July the Germans
introduced a more effective alternative by bombing Felixstowe with fourteen
Gothas. They successfully gutted a flying-boat, seriously damaged another, and
killed eight of the personnel, but once surprise had been lost a second raid on the
22nd failed to make any impact.[64]

The RNAS, no longer able to reach the higher flying zeppelins with Large
Americas, in early September tried using a DH4[†] and a flying-boat in mutual
support. On 5 September Leckie was the pilot of a Large America, taking with him
Squadron Commander V. Nicholl, the overall commander of the experiment.
They made contact with L 44 and L 46 but had to break off the engagement when

---

* General allocation of responsibilities was divided up regionally: List was responsible for regions in
   front of the Danish coast; Heligoland and Norderney for the open sea to the middle of the North
   Sea; and Borkum for regions in front of the Dutch coast. G.P. Neumann, *The German Air Force
   in the Great War* (London 1920), 267–8
† Two DH4 bomber reconnaissance aircraft (powered by a Napier-built 200-hp RAF engine and
   fitted with extra large tanks to give a fourteen-hour endurance) had been sent originally to
   Yarmouth for a photographic reconnaissance flight west of the Kiel Canal.

the DH4's engine faltered, and as they did so their own machine received shrapnel damage from the anti-aircraft fire of a German naval force of cruisers and destroyers below. The engine of the DH4 soon stopped entirely, and eventually the aircraft 'pancaked' heavily onto a breaking sea some fifty miles from home. Nicholl and Leckie were also having trouble with an engine that promised, at best, a hair-raising trip back. Despite the certainty of not being able to get airborne again, 'Bob Leckie simply shoved the nose of 8666 down and went straight for Gilligan and Trewin.' For the next three-and-a-half hours Leckie taxied towards Yarmouth before running out of fuel. Half-a-dozen seasick men without food and short of water were now adrift in a damaged flying-boat that required constant bailing to stay afloat. As Nicholl tersely described it in his official report: 'We then drifted from 7 p.m. on the 5th to 2 p.m. on the 8th ... when we were picked up by HMS *Halcyon* and towed to Yarmouth.'[65] Nicholl and Leckie were each awarded the DSO.

Another example of determined seamanship occurred on 1 October. After Hobbs* skilfully manœuvred a Porte flying-boat for twenty minutes off the North Hinder in a running fight with two seaplanes and an aeroplane, both engines stopped, forcing him to come down. After being raked once more by the departing Germans, the crew of the Porte was left to patch up and start a laborious crawl back on the surface. They were taken in tow close to the English coastline nine hours after the action.[66]

Although naval forces concentrated for the most part in British home waters and RNAS activities (especially for Canadians) were largely centred there, important naval and air elements in the Mediterranean were committed, also, to the Italian, Balkan, and Turkish war zones and to the maintenance of the direct sea route to the East. Canadians in the Mediterranean were less numerous and formed a smaller proportion of aircrew,† but were to be found in every phase of operations. Throughout the period the naval air service in this theatre was somewhat of an orphan, receiving equipment and even some personnel that were not wanted in France or England. Wing Commander Samson, for example, had been sent to Port Said in 1916 under a cloud. Using the seaplane carriers *Ben-my-Chree* (sunk in February), *Empress*, *Anne*, and *Raven II*, his aircraft flew bombing, reconnaissance, and spotting sorties mostly in the army support role until November 1917.‡ Commodore Murray Sueter, who in December 1916 had proposed a carrier-borne raid by torpedo seaplanes on Wilhelmshaven or an attack from Italian land bases on the Austrian fleet in the Adriatic, received an appointment in January 1917 to command the new 6 Wing, which included British aircraft in the Adriatic. This not

---

* Hobbs was well recognized for his work at Felixstowe: he was awarded the DSC on 22 June 1917, the DSO on 20 July 1917, a Bar to his DSC on 30 November 1917, and Mentioned in Despatches on 17 November and 19 December 1917. He was chief instructor in flying-boats for many British, Canadian, and, later, United States naval pilots.

† Only in the Aegean did figures compare with the northern theatre. At the beginning of 1917 14 of the 52 pilots there were Canadians. By April 1918 there were 22 of a total of 100. Great Britain, Admiralty, *Navy List* (London 1917–18), I, 431–1X, IA, 1119–53

‡ At various times in the year pilots M.C. Dover of Winnipeg, F.C. Henderson and T.G.M. Stephens, both of Toronto, and observer D.P. Rowland of Winnipeg flew under Samson. For the army support role in Macedonia, see chapter 15.

only removed Sueter from the Admiralty, where he had become something of an embarrassment, but also gave him a chance to put his ideas into practice.[67]

The chief concern in the Adriatic was to prevent German submarines getting out into the Mediterranean from Austrian ports, principally Cattaro. As they did in the Straits of Dover, the naval forces available laid down a mine barrage outside the enemy base (in this case across the Straits of Otranto), patrolled by trawlers and drifters. But the Otranto barrage was even less successful than that in the Straits of Dover. Under the 1917 air establishment, six Canadian pilots and one engineer were among the personnel sent to form 6 Wing. The wing was given a dozen Short and Sopwith Baby seaplanes for barrage work, twelve torpedo-carrying Shorts, six two-seater aeroplanes as escorts, and six Shorts for the torpedo training school at Malta. In June Flight Lieutenant John A. Barron of Stratford, Ont., brought out a special detachment to rig and test six SS airships sold to the Italians and to give flying instruction. He remained in command of the detachment at Grottaglie Aeroscalo near Taranto until January 1918. Another five Canadians joined the wing towards the end of 1917.* The results, however, were not spectacular. By the end of the year the Otranto air patrols had sighted eight submarines and attacked six of them, but U-boats continued to navigate the Straits, particularly by night. In the autumn Sueter's plan to raid Cattaro failed because of bad weather, and all efforts thereafter went towards patrolling the barrage, there being only six operational aircraft left by 15 December.[68]

In the Aegean, 2 Wing, with seventy-six aeroplanes, continued the tasks developed in 1916. 'A' and 'D' Squadrons based on Thasos and Stavros were employed on reconnaissance and bombing in southern Bulgaria and the Lower Struma; 'C' Squadron, based on Imbros, flew similar missions over Turkish territory; 'B' Squadron at Thermi on the island of Mitylene flew anti-submarine patrols and harassed the Smyrna area. In the spring 'B' and 'C' Squadrons were reduced to half strength to create 'E' Squadron (four two-seater Sopwith 1½ Strutters and a Sopwith Triplane) based on Hadzi Junas and 'F' Squadron (single-seater Sopwith 1½ Strutters) on Amberkoj and later Marian aerodrome to support the army on the Macedonian front. By mid-summer 'G' Squadron (Henri Farmans) was established at Mudros for night bombing and A/S patrols. The seaplanes of 2 Wing flew from Stavros, Thasos, and HMS *Ark Royal* until a slipway was constructed at Mudros. The SS airships were based on Kassandra and Mudros. In February a four-seaplane unit was established at Suda Bay, Crete, both for submarine patrols and to watch for any attempt by the *Goeben* to break out of the Dardanelles.† During the year there

---

* Canadians who went to 6 Wing during the year included J.R. Bibby of Niagara Falls, Ont., who went from Gibraltar (KIA at Malta, 11 June 1917), M.G. Dover of Winnipeg and F.C. Henderson of Toronto, after the sinking of *Ben-my-Chree*, W.C. Ault of Toronto, G.H. Boyce of Ottawa, F.E. Fraser of Winnipeg, E.G. Hellwith of Allandale, Ont., W.H. Mackenzie of Victoria, H.G. Raney of Ottawa, and E.C.R. Stoneman and F. Wood of Toronto. A.R. Layard of Saanich, BC, the wing engineer, was later awarded the OBE for his work at Taranto. By April 1918 five of forty-one pilots were Canadians.

† Some of the Canadians who have been identified in these squadrons and units were: 'A' Squadron, G.T. Bysshe of Ottawa (POW 17 Feb. 1917), J.M. Ingham of Toronto (KIA 30 March 1917); 'C' Squadron, J.R.S. Devlin of Ottawa, A.G. Woodward of Victoria; 'G' Squadron, D.M. Ballantyne of Montreal, Angus D. Macdonald of Ottawa; Seaplane Unit Suda Bay, R.E. Spear of Winnipeg and F.P.L. Washington of Hamilton.

were various modifications to these arrangements, particularly when a Handley Page 0/100 arrived in July. The Handley Page carried out several long-distance flights under the control of its regular first pilot, J.N.W. Alcock, who later made the first non-stop trans-Atlantic flight. On the night of 30 September, with Flight Sub-Lieutenant Hugh Aird* of Toronto as his second pilot, Alcock failed to return from a trip to Constantinople. The two become prisoners of war.[69]

By far the most significant event in 2 Wing's history in this period was the breakout of *Goeben* and *Breslau* from the Dardanelles on 20 January 1918. The situation offered a golden opportunity for the RNAS to launch air attacks on a capital ship. Although *Breslau* was sunk by mines, *Goeben* had gone aground on a sandbank while under air attack by DH4s from Imbros and Mudros and presented a tempting target. For eight days and nights, therefore, under generally poor weather conditions, there were 270 sorties in which over fifteen tons of bombs – some of them 112-pounders – were unsuccessfully dropped.[†] On 25 January HMS *Manxman* arrived from England with two 320 Shorts and 18-inch aerial torpedoes. The next day, however, before the weather cleared and torpedoes could be launched against her, the *Goeben* was towed off the sandbank.[70] The failure to do any significant damage did nothing for the reputation of the RNAS in the Mediterranean theatre.

The *Goeben* episode represents rather well the problem of the naval air service. In its dying days the RNAS had begun to establish the importance of the air in naval warfare, but resistance to innovation was still to be found among senior officers, who rightly pointed out that the capacity of aircraft to achieve the destruction of enemy ships and submarines had yet to be proven. Beatty, commanding the Grand Fleet, and Wemyss, the First Sea Lord, were willing to experiment, but they were the victims of events. In taking on all sorts of unrelated tasks in almost every theatre of war, the RNAS had sown the seeds of its own destruction. Nevertheless, by the time that it was incorporated into the new Royal Air Force it had grown from its handful of men and planes in 1914 to a force of 55,066 personnel[‡] with 2949 aeroplanes and seaplanes.[71]

The demise of the RNAS was regretted by the aircrew rank and file, to whom the Canadians belonged, but principally for sentimental reasons. 'It was a sad

---

* The son of Sir John Aird, General Manager Canadian Bank of Commerce, Hugh Aird was one of two brothers in the British air services, the other serving in the RFC.

† Canadians involved in this episode included C.G. Bronson of Ottawa (POW 28 Jan. 1918), A.S. Girling, address unknown, W. Johnston of Quebec (shot down in flames, 20 Jan. 1918), F.J. Mackie of Winnipeg, C.E. Moore of Fort William, Ont., and D.F. Murray and A.G. Woodward, both of Victoria. Bronson, flying a seaplane from HMS *Empress*, was shot down but won the DSC for his efforts on 28 January in creating a diversion to permit a submarine to get through the Nagara, before it was realized *Goeben* had been towed off.

‡ It has been established that 807 Canadians enlisted in the RNAS and 279 were killed, died, or were released during the war. There were therefore at least 528 Canadians (about 10 per cent of the officers) in the service as of 1 April 1918, but it has been possible to identify by name only 341 who were on the strength of operational or training squadrons. Canada, National Defence Headquarters, DHist, 'Statistical Printout of File by Province, by Year of Enlistment, by Service, in Computer Programme of Biographical and Service Information Concerning Canadians in the British Flying Services, Canadian Forces Computer Centre, TCAA-2.'

moment,' wrote Raymond Collishaw, 'when my squadron had to strike the Royal Navy ensign ... which we had proudly flown even when we were serving with the army on all its fronts.'[72] Sentiment aside, the airmen were still in their element. The RNAS experience would make its mark on them, the Royal Air Force, and the future Royal Canadian Air Force.

8

Aviation and the Victory
over the Submarine

A German naval policy that gave top priority to the U-boat campaign against allied shipping forced the British in 1918 to divert their principal efforts to counter-measures. For the majority of Canadian pilots and observers on maritime flying this meant that they would be involved in operations concerned directly or indirectly with the defeat of the submarine in all theatres, whether by offensive air patrolling, convoy escort, or tactical bombing. The maximum force was to be deployed against the enemy's submarines.

Airmen in ships of the Grand Fleet or in carriers, which remained under complete naval control, were largely unaffected by the change. Those ashore at air stations became part of a new air structure subdivided by area, group, wing, and squadron. Outwardly there were few signs of the new régime. The daily routine went on as before, under the same leadership. All were allowed to wear out their old RNAS and RFC uniforms, a ruling which was freely interpreted by the airmen of the period, giving most RAF units a motley and impromptu appearance.

For the Royal Navy the creation of the RAF meant that it was now dependent upon the Air Ministry for the design and supply of aircraft to meet its commitments. Airships were excepted, through a private arrangement between the First Lord of the Admiralty, Sir Eric Geddes, and the Secretary of State for Air, Lord Rothermere. Although the appointment of Fifth Sea Lord had been abolished, the Admiralty still required an establishment to deal with air policy and organization and to work with the Air Ministry. Captain F.R. Scarlett was appointed Director of the Air Division with the rank of brigadier-general. Since Scarlett was under Rear-Admiral Sydney Fremantle, the Deputy Chief of the Naval Staff, the air arm once more had no direct voice on the Board of Admiralty. By 1918, however, aviation had become an integral part of naval planning. At this stage the Admiralty's attitude toward the RAF was co-operative; it was clearly interested in making the new service a success.

By the end of April the Air Ministry was in disarray, Rothermere and most of his Air Council already having resigned. Admiral Mark Kerr's departure because of 'certain differences on matters of strategy' with General Trenchard, briefly Chief of the Air Staff, and the temporary abolition of the post of deputy chief, were of particular significance to the navy. The Master-General of Personnel, Major-General G.M. Paine, was now the only council member with a naval background. The new Air Minister, Sir William Weir, and the new Chief of Air Staff, Major-

General F.H. Sykes, were both strong advocates of a strategic bombing policy for the RAF, and that role received prime emphasis in Weir's first policy statement on 23 May. The navy could take some comfort from Weir's promise that forces operated independently by the Air Ministry would be allocated to the army or navy should the need arise, and more particularly from his recognition of 'the necessity of quickly strengthening the anti-submarine aircraft patrols.'[1]

Grand Fleet operations in 1918 were dictated primarily by the anti-submarine war. Beatty reluctantly abandoned his policy of 'seek out and destroy' for his main units and reverted to one of 'watching and waiting,' as earlier practised by Jellicoe. As Beatty explained it:

... the correct strategy ... is no longer to bring the enemy to action at any cost, but rather to contain him in his bases ...

This does not mean that an action should be avoided if conditions favour us or that our role should be passive.[2]

Beatty and the Admiralty agreed to build up existing mine programmes in order to curb the High Seas Fleet and help in destruction of U-boats. The Heligoland Bight fields were to be extended; the Northern Barrage between Scotland and Norway was to be completed; the mine barrier across the Strait of Dover was to be strengthened. The relation of these plans to overall strategy was outlined in the naval policy statement approved by the War Cabinet on 18 January: '... these mine fields will, in the opinion of the Board, very materially hamper the movements of enemy submarines and surface craft ... At the same time, the consequent release of destroyers and auxiliary craft at present employed ... in the Dover Channel, will enable minor offensive operations to be undertaken, will release forces for submarine hunting, will ease the strain on the destroyer forces of the Grand Fleet, and will materially improve the shipping situation between England and France.'[3] The naval planners also hoped that the continuous movement of patrolling aircraft and minelayers with their escorting ships would generate action with German mine-sweeping forces. In addition, they envisaged renewed air-sea attacks on enemy-held Flemish ports.

In mid-April Beatty brought the Grand Fleet south to the Firth of Forth to shorten the steaming time to the southern reaches of the North Sea. Rear-Admiral R.F. Phillimore, the Admiral Commanding Aircraft, exercised full administrative control over heavier-than-air units ashore and afloat, and was adviser and deputy to the Commander-in-Chief for aviation. He himself was in the newly-commissioned *Furious*; the other units in the carrier squadron at Rosyth were *Pegasus, Nairana*, and *Campania*.*[4]

The Grand Fleet was changing from seaplanes to aeroplanes for reconnaissance. On 3 November successful flights from *Campania* by the two-seater Sopwith 1½

---

* At this time only eight Canadian RAF officers were on the establishment of the Grand Fleet: two as aeroplane pilots, three as seaplane pilots, and the others as balloon observers. The aeroplane pilots, G.W.J.G.J. Dunn of Winnipeg and H.D. Jack of Toronto, were taking advanced training at East Fortune. George Breadner of Winnipeg and H.B. Kerruish, of Fergus, Ont., both on the books of *Campania*, and F.G. Hellmuth of Allandale, Ont., at Rosyth, were seaplane pilots. G.B. Carr and L.G. Gallwey, addresses unknown, and A.B. Hopper of Ottawa, were balloon observers

Strutter had paved the way for its replacement of the Short seaplane as a shipborne reconnaissance aircraft. *Furious* received a squadron of fourteen 1½ Strutters in March. When on 4 April a fully-loaded Sopwith was flown off the forward turret of the battlecruiser *Australia*, the Operations Committee decided to supply battlecruisers, and later two ships in each division of a battle squadron, with a reconnaissance aeroplane forward in addition to a fighter aft.[5]

The rest of the carrier squadron lagged behind *Furious* in the switch to aeroplanes.* The aging *Campania*, while undergoing refit at Scapa Flow, was at the bottom of the pecking order and retained her Fairey Campania seaplanes. These aircraft had been specially designed as carrier-borne reconnaissance machines and were still capable of useful work. Operating with the Northern Patrol off the Orkney Islands in March, H.B. Kerruish of Fergus, Ont., and his observer spotted the wash caused by the conning tower of a surfacing U-boat about eight miles ahead. Increasing to the Fairey Campania's full speed of 80 knots, they dropped two 100-lb bombs from 800 feet ahead of the swirl made by the target as it crash-dived. Kerruish 'considered the bomb exploded either directly over or very close to the submarine.'[6] But nothing came up. German records show that no submarine was either sunk or damaged anywhere in the area during this period.

Unless they were drafted directly to the three older carriers, aeroplane pilots joining the fleet were appointed on paper to *Furious*. Many were recent graduates chosen for their good landing records during initial training. The route followed by Lieutenant G.W. Dunn of Winnipeg was typical. On 11 March he arrived at East Fortune Air Station on the south shore of the Firth. Like other new pilots, he practised landing on a simulated ship's deck painted on the runway.† In June he was transferred to Turnhouse, an RAF station closer to Rosyth that was the main supply depot for fighters as well as a pilot pool. From this base Dunn completed his final test of flying a fighter off the deck of *Pegasus* five times.‡ He then joined *Birkenhead* of the 3rd Light Cruiser Squadron as her turret pilot.[7]

---

under the orders of the Admiral Commanding 2nd Battle Squadron. R.F.J. Dixon and R.M. Walkey, both of Toronto, were aeroplane pilots who served with the Grand Fleet in the last few months before the Armistice. Later arrivals among seaplane pilots were N.J. Laughlin of Belfountain, Ont., and H.R.F. Richardson of Ottawa in *Pegasus*, and G.H. Simpson of Toronto, a veteran carrier pilot, in *Nairana*.

* The first official use of the generic term 'aircraft carrier' appears to have been made by Scarlett in a minute for transmission to the Air Ministry on 4 May 1918. The Admiralty confirmed it by Interim Order to the fleet at the end of the month, substituting the designation 'Aircraft Carriers' for 'Seaplane Carriers' because the latter 'now carry both Seaplanes and Aeroplanes.' The Admiralty's instructions have been omitted from Roskill's discussion of the subject. Scarlett to DSD, 4 May 1918, Air 1/277/15/226/126 pt I; Confidential Admiralty Interim Order 2592, 31 May 1918, confirmed by Confidential Monthly Order 2592, July 1918; S.W. Roskill, ed., *Documents relating to the Naval Air Service*, I: *1908–1918* (London 1969), 668

† M.C. Dubuc of Montreal, an experienced Canadian carrier pilot, served at East Fortune in 1918, apparently as an instructor. Two Canadians died there: F.A. Cash as the result of a 'spinning dive' on 25 July 1918 and E.F. Kerruish on 13 July 1918. Both were from Hamilton, Ont.

‡ It was Dunn who flew the first Sopwith 2F1 Camel off *Pegasus*. Unlike the land-based Camel, this fighter had a detachable rear fuselage for close stowage. Designed to engage zeppelins over the North Sea, it mounted a single Lewis gun over the wing centre section and a fixed synchronized Vickers above the fuselage.

By mid-summer the Grand Fleet had a substantial fighter force of thirty-four aircraft. The fleet's fighter pilots, among whom were a number of Canadians, were supposed to operate in pairs of flights during action. At first, tactics were rudimentary and group leadership in the air was determined by ship seniority.* Thus, Second Lieutenant W.S. Lockhart of Moncton became the flight commander over four or five pilots in the 4th Cruiser Squadron because *Sydney* was flagship, his responsibility being to lead them in 'loose formation' back to shore base when the fleet returned from exercise or operations. Later, the effort was made at Turn-house to weld the Camels into useful tactical groups. Each air unit practised getting off together from its ship squadron and assembling overhead in two formations of eight aircraft.[8]

The care and handling of their aircraft on shipboard was a responsibility the young Canadian pilots had to accept. Too often, they found, over-enthusiastic mariners were inclined to treat their machines as stoutly-built picket boats. One pilot complained that 'a large petty officer was allowed to walk right through the top plane ... when trying to unhook the purchase and was only extracted with much difficulty.'[9] The pilot had to work closely with the turret officer and his gun crew, since once the Camel was on the platform they became the 'flight deck party.'

Taking off from a gun turret platform was a tricky affair. The procedure involved the ship's commander, other officers on the bridge, someone to take the wind pressure, and the aircraft's mechanic as well as the pilot. W.S. Lockhart had a vivid and precise recollection of the routine. When the aircraft, attached to the deck by cables ending in a quick release shackle, was in flying position the pilot and mechanic got the engine turning over. It was important to warm up the engine thoroughly despite the frequent impatience of the captain; otherwise the pilot might find himself moving down his twelve-foot runway with an engine barely ticking over. Once the engine was warm and the rpms and oil pressure in order, it was necessary to be dead into the wind, with at least twenty knots of wind pressure. 'I always figured if 20 knots would take you off,' Lockhart recalled, '24 knots ... would take you off better.' He went on:

The Snotty [midshipman] reports to the Commander an 18 knot wind pressure. The Commander says to me, '18 knots.' I answer, 'The ship will have to steam ahead 6 knots more.' He says 'How do you want your platform trained?' I say, '3 points green' ... The bridge is right behind me and up about 8 feet, but I can't talk to the bridge. The Commander tells the bridge to steam ahead 6 knots faster and train the platform 3 points green. You feel the ship going ahead and the platform moves to starboard. Then the Snotty reports to the Commander '24 knots.' I nod O.K. to the Commander, I try my ailerons, I try my rudder, my oil

---

* Serving aboard turret ships at various times during 1918 were H.E. Cooper of New Westminster, BC, in the light cruiser *Comus*; W.D.E. Donaldson of Ottawa in *Comus* and the battleships *Barham* and *Marlborough*; V.S. Grigg of Toronto in the battlecruiser *New Zealand*; N.J. Laughlin of Belfountain, Ont., in the battleships *Emperor of India* and *Orion*; W.S. Lockhart of Moncton, NB, in the Australian light cruiser *Sydney*; C.B. Rutherford of Toronto in the battlecruiser *Indomitable*. In addition, a Canadian observer officer, A.W. Green of Fort Saskatchewan, Alta, flew from the heavy cruisers *Courageous* and *Glorious*, as well as the battleship *Bellerophon*.

pressure is all right, my RPM is all right, I set my stick a little forward. I want to nose down a little to start with. I hold everything as is. I raise my left hand high. The Commander raises his white flag and my mechanic is watching him under the fuselage. I drop my hand back into the cockpit. The Commander lowers his flag. Birch [his mechanic] sees the signal and he pulls the trip cord. For the next two seconds you don't know what has happened but you soon discover you are out there flying an aeroplane.[10]

Even at nearly full revolutions the aircraft sank perceptibly after leaving the platform. That was the signal for the pilot to pull back on the stick and begin the long climb to join his companions from the squadron.

Getting off from a gun turret was hazardous enough, but the recovery proce-dure after landing in the sea was full of risk as well. *Furious* was supposed to cut through this problem, but she turned out to be a disappointment.* The effects of the disturbed air conditions over her new after-landing deck, caused by funnel fumes and the mass of midships superstructure, were too much for her pilots. Of sixteen experimental landings, thirteen ended in crashes. Clearly the exponents of a flush-deck carrier were right. Pilots were given the option of either landing on deck or returning to the procedure of ditching near a destroyer. No one seems to have chosen the former.[11]

Much of the airmen's time at sea in 1918 was taken up with tactical exercises in fleet action. Ordinarily the battle fleet's advanced anti-submarine escort was provided by coastal airships from east-coast stations.† Otherwise a single Sopwith 1½ Strutter ranged ahead of the light cruiser line, in communication directly with the flagship on the Admiralty's new continuous wave wireless set. Kite-balloon observers from the light cruisers also passed early warnings to the Commander-in-Chief.‡ The rest of the scenario called for the turret-launched fighters to be ready on their platforms in case scouting zeppelins were spotted, while five 1½ Strutters were to be in the air reporting the movements of the German battle line should a fleet action occur.[12]

In late April they got their chance. The first indication that the High Seas Fleet was stirring came from two flying-boats of Great Yarmouth, which had been sent out on the 20th to investigate the Heligoland Bight because of heavy wireless traffic from Wilhelmshaven to its minesweepers. At 1045 hrs the flying-boats, both under the operational command of Captain Robert Leckie, sighted four destroyers and four minesweepers near the Terschelling Light Vessel. Within another quarter of an hour they spotted two battlecruisers, 'probably *Derfflinger* and *Moltke* ... in

---

* The first Canadian in 1918 to be part of the flying complement of *Furious* was H.E. Cooper of New Westminster, BC. He was followed by B.E. Barnum of Kingston, Ont., G.H. Boyce of Ottawa, R.W. Frost of Hamilton, O.P. Gosling of Brandon, Man., R.F. McRae of Niagara Falls, Ont., D.J. Munro of Montreal, and R.M. Walkey of Toronto.
† There were four coastal airship bases, and a Canadian served at each: J.P. Haworth, address unknown, an airship technical officer at East Fortune; J.O. Hoddart of Port Glasgow, NS, at Longside; J. Sproston of Montreal at Howden; R.F.E. Wickham, address unknown, at Pulham.
‡ The four Canadians on Grand Fleet Kite Balloon duty in 1918 spent most of their time in battle-ships. L.B. Calnan of Picton, Ont., in *Ajax*; G.B. Carr in *King George V* and *Resolution*; L.G. Gallwey in *Erin* of the 2nd Battle Squadron; A.B. Hopper in *Erin* and *St Vincent* of the 4th Battle Squadron.

company with two four-funnelled ... cruisers, probably *Stralsund*-class ... two small three-funnelled ... cruisers, probably *Pillau* and *Gradenz*, eight destroyers ...course east, destroyers zig-zagging at 20–25 knots.' As he turned for base, Leckie brought his machine down to 4500 feet in order to circle the first party of destroyers while his observer took photographs and passed derogatory signals to the enemy on the Aldis lamp. Although sighting reports were immediately signalled back to shore, the home station failed to pick them up, and it was not until the F2As returned to Great Yarmouth at 1410 hrs that the information was passed to Harwich Force.[13]

Throughout 1918 aircraft and fleet units co-operated in the closing off of the Heligoland Bight. To that end 129 new minefields, comprising 21,000 mines, were sown, and air patrols kept the minefields under observation.* These patrols provided regular reports of ship movements in the Bight; unfortunately, air and sea elements did not always co-operate effectively in making the best use of the information which was obtained with such difficulty.[14]

The patrolling of the Bight and the adjacent waters of the North Sea was initially the business of flying boats. Under Scheme 'A' of the standing orders issued in February, F2As were transported on lighters supported by naval forces to the chosen area if it was outside a radius of 150 miles from Great Yarmouth.† Inside that range they flew directly from east-coast bases, as laid down in Scheme 'B.' By May aeroplanes from *Furious* were covering the northern and eastern sections of the minefield, while flying boats from Yarmouth and others launched from lighters were patrolling the area near Terschelling and the western Bight, respectively.[15]

German efforts to combat British excursions into the Bight were helped by an outstanding new seaplane, the Brandenburg W 29, first put into service at Zeebrugge in April and now flying out of these bases. Fast and manoeuvrable, this fighter was designed by Heinkel as a monoplane version of the Brandenburg W 12 with a similar 150-hp engine and gun armament. Because the W 29 had a short range, its pilots adopted the tactics of alighting on the sea to await enemy sightings reported by aircraft with longer ranges.[16]

The first reconnaissance mission under Scheme 'A' took place on 12 March and the three flying-boats involved were under the command of Flight Lieutenant

* This was not simply an exercise in bluff to convince the Germans that information on sweeper movements came from aircraft, when actually it came from the naval intelligence division. (Cf H.A. Jones, *The War in the Air: being the Story of the Part played in the Great War by the Royal Air Force*, VI (London 1937), 351.) Beatty had been much shaken by Room 40's inability to forewarn him of the German sortie in April: '... we must reconsider the outlook which permits apparently considerable Forces indeed *the High Seas Fleet* to get out without our knowledge – otherwise we might meet with a disaster of some magnitude over this cursed convoy supporting Force.' As Marder makes clear, never again did Beatty feel he could rely fully upon naval intelligence. Beatty to Wemyss, 26 April 1918, in A.J. Marder, *From the Dreadnought to Scapa Flow: the Royal Navy in the Fisher era, 1904–1919*, V: *Victory and Aftermath, January 1918-June 1919* (London 1970), 155

† These lighters were designed for an Anglo-American bombing offensive against German naval bases in 1918. The vulnerability of Large Americas and their supporting ships and the technical progress made with long-range bombing aeroplanes caused this scheme to be scrapped. 'Memo on Seaplane Offensive against German North Sea Bases' [3 Dec. 1917], Air 1/465/15/312/151; Nicholson to Sims and enclosed staff memorandum, 18 Dec. 1917, DAD memorandum [Aug. 1918], Air 1/652/17/122/519; DAD memorandum, 20 June 1918, Air 1/283/15/226/135 pt II

N.A. Magor of Westmount, Que. The F2As were launched south of the Haaks Lightship; once airborne, Magor led them around Terschelling into the Bight. As they were photographing minesweepers at work, two of the Borkum fighters rose to the attack. Magor's second pilot quickly sent one seaplane down in flames while another Canadian, Flight Lieutenant C.J. Clayton of Victoria, forced the other to return to its base. But the enemy had scored some hits. For an hour Magor had to fly on one engine as his engineer climbed out on the wing to repair a water-pipe pierced by gunfire. After five-and-a-half hours in the air, Magor brought his formation safely to Felixstowe at 1230 hrs. Nineteen days later a similar enterprise took place, the flying-boats led this time by Flight Lieutenant J.O. Galpin of Ottawa. Though shadowed for a while by two seaplanes, there was no air action, and Galpin's pilots eventually used up their ammunition raking the decks of a flotilla of minesweepers.[17] As a direct result of these patrols British minelayers re-sowed the area in which the Germans had been seen at work.

In early May the aerial contest over the waters of the Bight spread to the zeppelins. On 10 May L 56 from Wittmundhaven and L 62 from Nordholz set out on a routine patrol, the first to the west, and the second to the northern area. In Whitehall the Admiralty began to pick up their signals, and at 1008 hrs it was clear that one airship was heading westward. At 1320 hrs an F2A from Killingholme, commanded by Captain T.C. Pattinson and with Captain A.H. Munday of Toronto* as second pilot, took off to intercept. At 1630 hrs, fifty miles north-northwest of Borkum Reef, they sighted a zeppelin some 2000 feet higher than their own altitude of 6000 feet. As Pattinson opened full throttle to climb, the airship jettisoned bombs and fuel tanks and shot upward, while Munday and the engineer kept up a brisk fire. After a chase of over an hour, Pattinson broke off the action seventy miles northwest of Heligoland because of shortage of fuel and engine trouble. The F2A alighted briefly, though half-a-dozen German destroyers were converging upon it, to allow the engineer to repair a broken pipe. The crew last sighted the zeppelin 'headed for Holstein ... emitting much smoke.'[18]

Pattinson and Munday were credited with the destruction of L 62, which German records show to have been lost at sea on 10 May. However, we now know that the zeppelin pursued by the Killingholme crew was L 56. The airship's report was that the F2A was never within range, and that the only effect of the attack was to cut short the patrol because of loss of fuel. L 62 was seen by surface craft, patrolling northwest of Heligoland, to enter a cumulo-nimbus cloud at 1005 hrs. She shortly afterwards blew up, and her burning halves fell into the water almost

---

* Albert Henry Munday, born in Melbourne, Australia, the son of an English Lawyer, was a reporter for the Toronto *Telegram* at the time he joined the RNAS in 1916. His educational background included Eton College, St Boniface College, Manitoba, and Queen's University at Kingston. (After the war he took a doctorate at Columbia University.) While on active service, Munday published *The Eyes of the Army and Navy: Practical Aviation* (New York and London 1917), an informative and reliable guide to every aspect of airmanship, including contemporary tactics. A prolific writer in a number of fields after the war and one of the founders of the Toronto Flying Club, Munday published an updated and expanded version of his 1917 guide at the beginning of the Second World War (*Practical Flying in War and Peace*, Toronto 1940). His brothers W.A. and E.R. Munday (KIA 5 Aug. 1918), also from Toronto, served in the RAF as well.

hitting the trawler *Bergedorf*, which picked up five bodies. Strasser thought that lightning was the most likely cause of the disaster.[19]

On 30 May a flying-boat from Yarmouth was forced down with engine trouble in the Bight and was destroyed by five German seaplanes from Borkum. Leckie, accompanied by another Canadian, Lieutenant W.H. Comstock of Brockville, Ont., who was acting as his gunlayer, conducted a fruitless search for the missing aircraft. This was the first long night flight by a flying boat over the North Sea. On his return Leckie landed at Yarmouth's foreshore with the aid of flares. Less than a week later he led another foray into the Bight that precipitated the largest seaplane action of the First World War.[20]

The ostensible object of this enterprise was to investigate heavy wireless-telegraphy traffic apparently emanating from airships off the Texel, but suspected to be a ruse to lure flying boats on routine patrols into a trap. On Leckie's suggestion a strong force of two F2As from Yarmouth, and two F2As and an H12 from Felixstowe, set out on 4 June to 'deal with the situation in the appropriate manner.' At 1520 hrs, when off Terschelling, an F2A was forced to alight with a burst feed pipe. The rest were left to contend with five seaplanes of the 'dear old Borkum crowd,' one of which went back for help. At 1630 hrs 'a compact swarm of black specks [appeared] ... on the western horizon, which ... proved to be about 15 or 16 seaplanes flying low.'[21]

The two forces met head on. According to the testimony of other pilots, Leckie, leading his formation straight through, carried away 'the wireless aerial of his boat on the top plane of the leading enemy machine.' The RAF formation then wheeled to port in line ahead to cut off the German right wing of three seaplanes. In the ensuing melee 'the air was thick with the smoke from tracer bullets' and the pilots of the lumbering flying-boats had a hard time following Leckie, 'who was in and out all over the place.' When the Germans finally retired to Borkum at least one and possibly two of their number had been shot down, while the British had lost the F2A that had gone down off Terschelling and the H12. Both crews were interned by the Dutch. Leckie's leadership and tactical skill had extricated three of five aircraft from the trap so astutely laid for the patrol. But as he pointed out to his CO, three of five boats had suffered from engine failures: '... it is obvious that our greatest foes are not the enemy but our own petrol pipes.'[22]

Pilots flying from turret-platforms also took part in the struggle for air supremacy over the Bight. Aircraft from Harwich Force and from Grand Fleet units, as well as from *Furious*, were frequently so engaged. The most spectacular of these strikes was an attack on the Tondern Airship Station by Camels each carrying two Cooper 60-lb bombs specially made for the raid. After bad weather had halted two earlier attempts, on 19 July *Furious* launched her Camels from a position eighty miles northwest of the zeppelin base. The Germans at Tondern were defenceless; their protective force of five Albatros D-IIIs had been taken away on 6 March. L 54 and L 60 went up in smoke from direct hits upon the huge 'Toska' hangar. A second wave of three Camels arrived over the target ten minutes later. Their bombs, dropped from a hundred feet, destroyed the base's captive balloon. Of the six pilots to reach the target, one was lost in the sea on the way back, three landed in Denmark, and two rejoined the fleet.[23]

The Tondern raid was an important event in the history of naval aviation. From it stemmed the evolution of the aircraft-carrier technique used so successfully, for example, by the United States Navy against Japan during the Second World War. Its effects were immediate. Senior British naval officers began at once to plan for a second raid, using DH9s with extra tanks and detachable wings, the target to be Ahlhorn. For their part, the Germans relegated Tondern to an emergency landing ground and cleared the pine forests around Nordholz to prevent them from being set on fire. Only Ahlhorn, because of its distance from the sea, was now considered to be reasonably safe.[24]

The German Naval Airship Division made a direct and aggressive response when on 1 August L 70, the first of a new type of extended airship, unloaded ten 220-lb bombs in the vicinity of Harwich Force. The British took up this challenge the next day by sending six flying-boats into the Terschelling area.* The F2As caught sight of L 64 through the rain at 0819 hrs and 'chased ... for 24 mins. when it gained height of 5000 feet above us and then turned towards its own territory.'[25]

This brush was prelude to a more novel and successful attempt to meet the challenge of the zeppelins. Experiments had been going on for some time in the use of flying-boat lighters to fly off fighter aircraft. On 30 May C.R. Samson, now commanding No 4 Group, RAF, had nearly drowned while testing a Camel fitted with skids that ran in wooden troughs on the lighter. On the advice of a young pilot on his staff with recent deck landing experience, Lieutenant S.D. Culley of Montreal, Samson decided that an ordinary wheeled fighter should be used for the next trial. On 31 July, as the destroyer *Redoubt* towed the lighter at 36 knots, Culley ordered the release of his Camel and became airborne almost at once.

The new technique was put to use on 10 August, when Rear-Admiral Tyrwhitt brought the entire Harwich Force, comprising four cruisers and thirteen destroyers, into the contested zone. The cruisers were carrying six coastal motor boats (CMBs) between them, while *Redoubt* and other destroyers were towing lighters carrying Culley's fighter and three flying-boats. Soon after 0600 hrs on 11 August the force hove to off Terschelling. The cruisers lowered the CMBs and in line ahead they raced away towards the mouth of the Ems in search of German surface craft. Though surface conditions prevented the F2As from taking off, three Yarmouth flying-boats under Leckie arrived at 0710 hrs. Leckie's formation spotted L 53 cruising westward at 15,000 feet, and so reported to the flagship.

To draw the airship westward, Harwich Force came round 180 degrees, making a heavy smoke screen. At 0841 hrs Culley took off from *Redoubt*'s lighter after a five-foot run. By about 0930 hrs he had reached 18,000 feet and found L 53 coming right at him on a reciprocal course slightly above him.

Very soon the huge bulk of the Zeppelin loomed ahead of me. I could see the control car and the engine gondolas with their propellers turning ... and as she passed over me I pulled the little Camel back into what was almost a stalled position, and pressed the trigger ... One

---

* Three Canadians were on this special patrol: Captain Gordon in the lead F2A, No 4284, with Second Lieutenant J.A.Y. LaForest of Hull, Que., acting as gunner and Second Lieutenant C.W. Gracey of Weston, Ont., second pilot in No 4300.

gun fired its complete pan without a break, but the other one jammed after firing only about half a dozen rounds.

... when my guns ceased firing, the Camel fell into a stall and dropped some 2000 feet, completely out of control. This gave me no chance to watch the airship until after I had got back on an even keel ... suddenly, at three widely separated points, bursts of pure flames shot out from the envelope; and within a minute the whole airship except the tail section was a mass of flames ... The burnt-out frame, still with a flag flying from the tail section, then dropped in one piece ... The time was 9:41, exactly an hour after I had taken off from the lighter.[26]

Harwich Force had a grandstand view of the great fire, explosion, and falling debris that marked the end of L 53. Wary of German seaplanes, Culley flew on to the Dutch coast before making a rendezvous with the force at Terschelling Bank. When he came down near *Redoubt* at 1124 hrs he had a pint of fuel left. The sailors paid their personal tribute when Tyrwhitt in *Curacoa* led the entire force in line ahead, cheering ships' companies lining the rails, past Culley standing alone on *Redoubt*'s after-gun platform.[27]

The force then turned to search for the overdue CMBs, rejoined by Leckie's Yarmouth patrol. In fact, however, the CMB flotilla had ceased to exist several hours before, all the boats having been sunk or run ashore by the scourging of Brandenburg monoplanes from Borkum. It was the first example of what can happen when warships are caught without cover by overwhelming air forces, and it had been predicted at the planning stage of the operation by pilots at Felixstowe and Yarmouth, who argued for Camel cover.[28]

This was the last major operation in the Bight. Experience had demonstrated that the Grand Fleet was well in advance of the High Seas Fleet in heavier-than-air resources and in operating techniques. British reconnaissance aircraft had denied the German navy complete freedom in the waters adjacent to its home ports and had played a useful part in this aspect of the anti-submarine campaign.

The Dover Patrol's part in the anti-submarine campaign was to seal off the southern exit from the North Sea and harass the Flanders submarine and destroyer flotillas and their bases. It remained, in addition, the left flank of the Western Front and the defender of the lines of communication across the Straits. To carry out these tasks Vice-Admiral Keyes had more than three hundred ships, but was much under strength in air power. His air force, now No 5 Group under command of Lieutenant-Colonel F.C. Halahan at Dover, was reduced to a single wing, No 61, at Dunkirk. No 202 (reconnaissance) Squadron and 217 (anti-submarine) Squadron both flew DH4s, and there were three Camel squadrons, 201, 210, and 213.* The navy had relinquished control of its former bombing squadrons on the promise of RAF tactical support; they and other units of the former RNAS organization became 64 and 65 Wings and remained in the area as VII Brigade RAF, commanded by Lambe, now a brigadier-general. With the German spring offen-

---

* Under the RAF system former naval wings had 60 added to their previous designation. Thus 1 Wing RNAS became 61 Wing RAF. Squadrons were renumbered from 200 upwards. Thus 1 Squadron RNAS became 201 RAF.

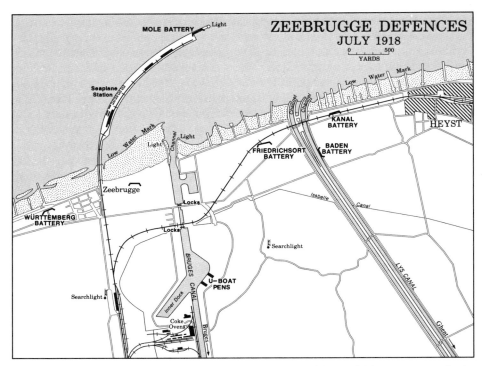

sive, many of Lambe's squadrons, along with Nos. 201 and 210, went to assist in stemming the enemy advance further south.[29] Thus on the day the RAF came into being, there were only eleven Canadian airmen left under naval command.*

The first major operation mounted by the Dover Patrol after the creation of the RAF was the Zeebrugge-Ostend raid. British strengthening of the mine defences had been so successful that after February none of the larger U-type submarines attempted passage of the Strait of Dover. The smaller UB and UC boats of the Flanders flotillas, however, were able to slip past despite some losses, and thence to account for a high proportion[†] of merchantmen sunk. Keyes was therefore given a free hand by the Admiralty to deal with this problem in his own way.

His plan called for the sinking of ships loaded with cement at the entrances to Zeebrugge and Ostend, thereby closing the canals running to Bruges and making it impossible for U-boats and destroyers to use the two ports. The air arm was to divert the attention of the German gun and searchlight crews by bombing the batteries around Zeebrugge and Ostend beginning two-and-a-half hours before the

---

* They were J.F. Chisholm of Westmount, Que. (POW 26 Sept. 1918), J.W. Kennedy of Montreal and B.S. Wemp (Officer Commanding) of Toronto in 202 Squadron; P.E. Beasley of Victoria, BC, J.E. Green of Winnipeg (KIA 14 Oct. 1918), and G.C. Mackay of Toronto in 213; R.M. Berthe of Montreal, H.H. Gonyon of Wallaceburg, Ont., and C.E.S. Lusk of Toronto in 217; G.E. Hervey of Calgary in Dover Aeroplanes; A.C. Reid of Winnipeg in Dover Seaplanes.

† The figures for tonnage sunk per submarine per day at sea between January and September 1918 indicate that the Flanders boats surpassed those of the High Seas Fleet, averaging 258 tons per day as against 192 tons for the HSF boats. Marder, *Dreadnought to Scapa Flow*, V, 46n

naval zero hour. At that point they were to switch to incendiary bombing and the dropping of parachute flares to light up the assault areas. Detailed plans and training models of the area and its approaches had already been prepared as a result of a complete photographic survey carried out by 202 Squadron.[30]

The first attempt, on 11 April, was called off because a sudden change in the wind direction to offshore made it impossible to lay a smoke screen to conceal the approaching ships. Handley Pages of VII Brigade, despite rain and poor visibility, had already been carrying out their part: 'We could clearly see the searchlights turned upwards ... the "flaming onions" soaring skywards ... hear the booming of the enemy's anti-aircraft guns and our bombs exploding.' One bomber crashed off Ostend, the crew all being rescued by a CMB except for the veteran Canadian pilot, Captain J.R. Allan, of whom there was no trace.[31]

The Germans now knew what was afoot. Nevertheless, Keyes persuaded the Admiralty to allow him to try again. In the interval, his air support had been much depleted.* In bright moonlight the naval armada set out again for Zeebrugge and Ostend on the evening of 22 April. Half way across rain began falling and visibility dropped to a mile. The Dunkirk bomber force was grounded and the attackers, in a 'forlorn hope' that brought them four VCs, scrambled on to the Zeebrugge Mole without the benefit of a distracting aerial bombardment. When they withdrew, they had sunk blockships off the entrance and had blown a gap in the railway viaduct linking the Mole to shore, at a cost of more than two hundred killed and four hundred wounded. The raid on Ostend, however, had been a complete failure, thanks to the wind veering and blowing the concealing smoke back on the ships.

When the DH4s of 202 Squadron were making their first reconnaissance over the damaged Mole on 23 April, the Admiralty had already discovered that the canal had not been blocked from an intercepted German signal. After his first dismay at seeing the blockships lying athwart the narrow harbour mouth, Admiral L. von Schröder, the German flag officer at Bruges, quickly found that he could pass his smaller torpedo boats by them. Only the larger destroyers and U-boats had to use Ostend temporarily. By 14 May dredgers restored complete freedom of movement in and out of Zeebrugge.[32]

Strategically the raid had been a failure. Psychologically, in those black days of April, its offensive daring greatly heartened the allied forces and civilian populations. Keyes, however, tried to keep up the pressure by a sustained aerial offensive against the large group of submarines and destroyers lying in the basin at Bruges. When he had taken over from Bacon he had lifted his predecessor's restrictions on bombing; he gave Lambe 'full liberty to attack the many military objects within

---

* On 13 April, in the face of German advances on the line of the Lys, Trenchard approved Salmond's evacuation plans for the Dunkirk area. Two bomber squadrons, 207 and 215, left for England at once, though the rest of the plans never went into effect. In return, Keyes got back a Camel Squadron, 204, on 18 April. With it came seven Canadians with RNAS experience: B.E. Barnum of Kingston, Ont., A.C. Burt of Brantford, Ont., G.S. Harrower of Montreal, C.R.R. Hickey of Parksville, BC, R. McN. Keirstead of Toronto, W.F. Robinson of Davidson, Sask., and A.M. Shook of Red Deer, Alta; and a newcomer, W.J.P. Jenner of Blenheim, Ont. Trenchard to Salmond, 13 April 1918, CGS Army to RAF, 18 April 1918, Air 1/913/204/5/852

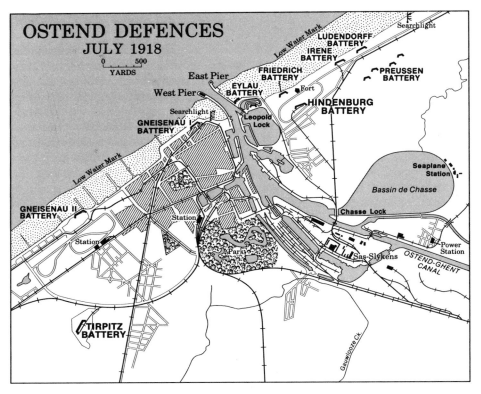

OSTEND DEFENCES
JULY 1918

0 ... 500
YARDS

Searchlight

LUDENDORFF
BATTERY

IRENE
BATTERY

PREUSSEN
BATTERY

East Pier

FRIEDRICH
BATTERY

West Pier

EYLAU
BATTERY

Fort

Searchlight

HINDENBURG
BATTERY

GNEISENAU I
BATTERY

Leopold
Lock

Seaplane
Station

Bassin de Chasse

GNEISENAU II
BATTERY

Chasse Lock

Station

Power
Station

Station

Park

Sas-Slykens

OSTEND-GHENT
CANAL

TIRPITZ
BATTERY

Gauwlooze Ck.

reach, by day and night ... and assured him that the more offensive he was the better I would be pleased.'[33]

But the navy no longer controlled the bombers. VII Brigade had dwindled to one night-bombing and two day-bombing squadrons, with two fighter squadrons under training. Moreover, General Lambe had been ordered by the Chief of the Air Staff to cease dealing directly with the navy's No 5 Group as of 1 May: 'Any local arrangements that have to be made with this Group, will be made between the G.O.C., R.A.F., in the Field, and the O.C. No. 5 Group.' Lambe was incensed beyond measure, and his prime service loyalty asserted itself. 'If the anti-submarine campaign is to be continued,' he wrote Keyes, 'Bombing Squadrons must be placed under the direct command of the Vice Admiral, Dover.'[34] In a private letter he went further:

I have received orders to evacuate all the stores in the Dunkerque area, and that arrangements will be made for the supply of the Naval Squadrons through the Army. This is most unsatisfactory and is the thin edge of the wedge to take over the complete control.

In my own private opinion, the present R.A.F. – which was previously the R.F.C. – have more than enough to do to run their own show without interfering with the Navy, and at present they have so complicated affairs that the whole is absolute confusion.[35]

Keyes immediately protested to the Admiralty. The weakness of the new Air Ministry was demonstrated when it yielded to almost all of Keyes' demands. Lambe was given command of all Dover Patrol air units. R.H. Mulock, now a lieutenant-colonel on the Dunkirk headquarters' staff, was given the job of phasing out VII Brigade. No 65 Wing was to come directly under RAF HQ in France; all other units were to be attached to No 5 Group, which Lambe took over officially on 16 May. The navy's demand for additional bombing squadrons was met by the Air Council only in part, 'in view of the extreme urgency of demands ... elsewhere.' No 218 Squadron of DH9s, then forming at Dover, was allocated to No 5 Group, and 214 Squadron was made available on a temporary basis. Instead of meeting Keyes' request to return 201 and 210 fighter squadrons to naval control, the Air Ministry agreed instead to strengthen the six flights of 204* and 213 by two pilots and two Camels each.[36]

The navy was still dissatisfied. After a second expedition to block Ostend on 9 May had proved no more successful than the first, the Admiralty once more demanded additional bombers, pointing out to the Air Ministry that 'it is of the *greatest importance* that this opportunity of destroying enemy craft in their harbours should be taken every advantage of.' No less a personage than Foch backed them up. Hearing of congestion in the Flemish ports from French naval air authorities, he asked Haig to concentrate bombing squadrons to 'conclude the work so happily begun by the British Navy.' Haig concurred, and Salmond thereupon transferred 98 Squadron of DH9s to No 5 Group, while the Air Ministry sent over 38 Squadron, a home defence unit of FE2bs. Keyes again protested. FE2bs were poor substitutes for heavy bombers, he pointed out. The Handley Page squadron, 214, had only been made available on a temporary basis, and he did not have full control over it. Finally, Haig's GHQ met the Admiral half way and on 4 June agreed to give him 214 Squadron for a month (it was, in fact, to remain under naval control until October); in exchange No 98† was returned to the GOC RAF on 6 June.[37]

During May, while controversy continued over its strength, the Dunkirk air force dropped nearly seventy tons of bombs on the Bruges and Zeebrugge targets. No 98 Squadron, during its brief stay from 27 May to 3 June, made eleven daylight raids on Ostend and Bruges.‡ On 28 May Captain C.H. Darley of Montreal, an

---

* One of the twelve extra pilots was Second Lieutenant W.B. Craig of Smiths Falls, Ont., who joined 204 Squadron.

† Prior to the departure of 98 Squadron, there were fifty-one Canadians serving in the Dover/Dunkirk Command. No 38 included L.M. Goodfellow, address unknown, D. Humphrey of Montreal, W. Marginson of Winnipeg, and W.W. Waterson, address unknown. In 98 were G.D. Dardis of Morrisburg, Ont., R. McK. Hall of Ingersoll, Ont. (KIA 28 May 1918), G.D. Horton, address unknown (KIA 31 May 1918), F.A. Laughlin of Thorold, Ont., E.R. Macdonald of Matheson, Ont. (POW 9 Aug. 1918), N.C. Macdonald of Bluevale, Ont., F.F.H. Reilly of Welland, Ont. (KIA 28 May 1918), C.D. Taylor of Edmonton. With 214 were J.R. Belton of Ottawa, C.H. Darley of Montreal, C.G. Lee of Winnipeg, H.A. McCormick of Pembroke, Ont., E.F. McIlraith of Lanark, Ont., J.M. Nichol of Vancouver, and J.D. Vance of Toronto. No 218 included A.M. Anderson of Toronto, M.G. Baskerville of Dominion City, Man., J.F. Chisholm of Westmount, Que. (POW 26 Sept. 1918), W.F. Cleghorn of Toronto (KIA 2 Oct. 1918), J.W. Kennedy of Montreal, W.F. Purvis of Toronto, R.W. Robinson of Komoka, Ont. (KIA 10 June 1918), B.H. Stata of Morrisburg, Ont. (KIA 28 Sept. 1918), and B.S. Wemp of Toronto.

‡ Four DH9s were lost during these raids, and among the aircrew casualties were the Canadians R. McK. Hall (KIA 28 May 1918), G.D. Horton (KIA 31 May 1918), and F.F.H. Reilly (KIA 28 May 1918). GOC No 5 Group to GOC RAF in the Field, 6 June 1918, Air 1/913/204/5/852

experienced Handley Page pilot, was chosen to carry out the destruction of the lock gates at the northern end of the Bruges-Zeebrugge Canal at low water. Had the plan succeeded all vessels would have been stranded in the system. Darley glided in from seaward at 200 feet, and released three 520-lb bombs, two of which fell in the water, while the third detonated close to the northern gate. Neither this attack, nor another a few minutes later by a DH4 (shot down by anti-aircraft fire), was successful.[38]

The offensive strategy Keyes and Lambe were able to push with their augmented air strength soon brought a powerful German response. On the nights of 4, 5, and 6 June the Gotha wings in Flanders made a series of strikes against the RAF aerodromes at Bergues, Coudekerque, Petite Synthe, Capelle, and Teteghem. Hangars were wrecked and forty-two aircraft were rendered unserviceable. Coudekerque had to be abandoned except as a landing ground and the Handley Pages of No 214 moved to St Inglevert, southeast of Calais.[39]

To combat British bombing, the Germans also revised their fighter organization. The commander of the marine air forces at Bruges had three squadrons, with the main base at Varssenaere. In the spring of 1918 these squadrons were combined with two others to form a naval fighter wing (*Marine Jagdgeschwader*), commanded by *Oberleutnant zur See* G. Sachsenberg. With the commencement of the British bomber offensive, Admiral Schröder ordered that control over the commitment of fighter squadrons against bomber attack was to be given directly to Sachsenberg, rather than remain at the corps level. The Germans could now react more quickly to attack, but when Sachsenberg discovered that RAF bombers stayed at high altitudes until his fighters used up their fuel, he decided to go over to the offensive. 'We attacked the opponent in his airports with successive waves of squadrons,' he later wrote, 'and ... moved above enemy territory at great heights, waiting for the returning ... formations and forcing them to fight.'[40] The *Jagdgeschwader*'s effectiveness was further enhanced with the first deliveries of the Fokker D-VII, an aircraft much superior in performance to the Fokker Triplane, Albatros, and Pfalz fighters it was then using.

With both sides now dedicated to an offensive policy, the stage was set for a struggle for aerial supremacy as relentless as that waged over the Western Front. On the night of 29–30 June Gotha bombers destroyed twelve Camels, damaged twenty-six other aircraft, and gutted two hangars at Bergues. Within hours there occurred the first of a series of large-scale air battles in the Flemish skies. No 204 Squadron, with fifteen Camels, was escorting No 218 on a raid against Zeebrugge when the British force was attacked by thirty German fighters. Similar odds were encountered by No 218 five days later on a raid against Bruges, when the Canadian pilots Cleghorn and Baskerville shot down two enemy fighters. At Keyes' urging the Admiralty, citing the 'large increase' of enemy aircraft on the coast, demanded the return of its lost fighter squadron. Haig yielded, and on 8 July 210 Squadron, a unit then almost 50 per cent Canadian in composition, was transferred back to naval control.* Despite stiffening German opposition, No 5 Group dropped 134

---

* No 210's Canadian pilots were E.H. Bullen of Petrolia, Ont. (POW 22 July 1918), H.J. Emery of Edmonton, E.N. Gregory of Lindsay, Ont., W.W. Gyles of Virden, Man., A. St G. Highstone of Sault Ste Marie, Ont., W.S. Jenkins of Montreal, G.A. Welsh of Sunderland, Ont., H.H. Whitlock of Charlottetown (POW 14 Oct. 1918), and G.B. Wootten of Andover, NB.

tons of bombs on naval targets in June* (Dunkirk's high point for the war); the
total declined to 83 tons in July, with bad weather as much to blame as enemy
fighters. These totals were supplemented by those recorded by 211 Squadron from
the RAF's 65 Wing, and later by 108 Squadron of the same wing,† which made its
first raid for the navy on 12 August.[41]

For the bombing campaign against naval targets to have any chance of success,
ascendancy had to be gained over German fighter forces. On 13 August a major
operation was launched against the main German base at Varssenaere. Fifty
Camels of 204, 210, and 213 Squadrons – and of 17th US Aero Squadron, attached
to the RAF – headed up the coast and turned inland over Ostend at the leader's
signal. Out of the dawn they swept in low over the airfield, shooting up everything
in sight and dropping HE and incendiary bombs. No 211 Squadron rounded out
the attack by bombing the aerodrome as the fighters sped away. On the ground
there was chaos, the Germans having been caught with flights of Fokkers lined up
for take-off: 'Like startled birds airmen and mechanics were rushing out of their
lodgings, only to have to throw themselves immediately flat on the ground while
British fighters flying a mere 5–10 metres above ground were spraying them with
machine-gun fire ... we lost more than a dozen aircraft and had to see our *Schloss*
and a number of hangars going up in flames.' Yet, though Varssenaere took some
time to recover from this onslaught, German resistance in the air was not perceptibly diminished. On 15 August a patrol of 204 Squadron engaged thirteen Fokker
and Pfalz fighters east·of Ypres and claimed four shot down, two of them credited
to Lieutenant W.B. Craig of Smiths Falls, Ont. On the evening of the same day
another patrol from 204 fought a fifteen-minute engagement with a large enemy
formation; Captain C.R.R. Hickey of Parksville, BC, sent one down in flames and

* Since June No 5 Group's night bombers had been under the command of Lt-Col R.H. Mulock,
  the senior Canadian pilot at Dunkirk. Nos 38, 214, and 218 Squadrons had been formed into 82
  Wing, based at Capelle. Shortly after the wing had been organized the Air Ministry requested
  Mulock's services for another appointment, but were put off when Keyes stated that 'it would be
  disastrous to move him at this period.' Mulock finally relinquished command of 82 Wing and
  ended his long association with Dunkirk on 28 July, when he left to take command of No 27
  Group. Keyes to Admiralty, 9 June 1918, Air 1/77/15/9/186; Scarlett memorandum, 18 June 1918,
  Air 1/308/15/226/193; No 5 Group, fortnightly summary, 16–31 July 1918, Air 1/39/AH/15/9/6.
  Canadians joining 82 Wing after its formation in June included B.L. De Salaberry, address
  unknown, in 38 Squadron; and W.F. Bates of Aylmer, Que., H.P. Brumell of Buckingham, Que.
  (POW 28 Sept. 1918), G. Carmichael, address unknown, M.J. Carroll of Toronto, J.A. Eyres of
  Eyremore, Alta, F.J. Gallant of Rogersville, NB, H.R. Murray of Toronto, S.W. Orr of Hamilton,
  N.M. Scott of Ottawa, and T.M. Steele of Stratford, Ont. (WIA and POW 28 Sept. 1918) in 218
  Squadron.
† Between April and September 1918 thirteen Canadians served in 211 Squadron. They were H.
  Axford of Winnipeg, P.E. Beasley of Victoria, BC, C.O. Carson of Morrisburg, Ont., L.K.
  Davidson, address unknown (POW 8 Aug. 1918), C.H. Dickens of Edmonton, J.S. Forgie and
  H.M. Ireland, both of Toronto, J.H. McLellan of Vancouver, J. Munro, address unknown, H.H.
  Palmer of Richmond Hill, Ont., V.G.H. Phillips of Shelburne, Ont., G.T. Scott, address
  unknown, and A.G. White of Victoria, BC (KIA 29 Sept. 1918). During the period that 108
  Squadron flew bombing raids for the navy, H.D. Buchanan of Lévis, Que., C.P. Crites of
  Simcoe, Ont. (POW 4 Sept. 1918), G.R. Harrison of Dartmouth, NS, A.M. Matheson of Meadow-
  ville, NS (POW 1 Oct. 1918), J.J. McDonald of Sydney, NS (POW 15 Sept. 1918), H.L. McLellan
  of Tatamagouche, NS (KIA 21 Sept. 1918), G.C. Page of Calgary, and D.A. Shanks of Hawick,
  Que., were with the squadron.

shared in the destruction of a second. Again, on 21 August 210 Squadron had a brush with enemy fighters during which Second Lieutenant W.S. Jenkins of Montreal shot down an Albatros; the enemy scout crashed near a kite balloon west of Warneton.[42]

Ultimately the fighter struggle in this sector became a thing in itself. Thus, while the bombing of naval targets from Dunkirk began to taper off in September, the tempo of air fighting actually increased. In air actions during the closing weeks of the war for which there is sound evidence that enemy fighters were destroyed, Canadian pilots in 204, 210, and 213 Squadrons took a part at least commensurate with their numbers. On 5 September Greene and Mackay of 213 both shot down Fokkers that crashed close to one another; the same day Mackay shared with another pilot the destruction of a Rumpler that was 'seen to crash.' On 16 September nineteen Camels from 204 duelled with fourteen Fokkers, four seaplanes, and three LVGs between Ostend and Blankenberghe. Hickey and Craig each shot down a Fokker in flames, while G.E.C. Howard of Toronto saw his LVG opponent hurtle into the sea (he himself was shot down and taken prisoner on 26 September). No 204* seems to have been in almost constant action during these days. On 20 September F.R. Brown of Winnipeg and H.G. Clappison of Hamilton, Ont., both destroyed Fokkers; Craig won another victory on 24 September (he was killed over Dunkirk two days later) and Hickey added another on the 25th.[43] For 210 Squadron, W.S. Jenkins had shot down two Fokker biplanes on 17 September south of Ostend, one of which crashed by the canal bank, and another on 24 September following a raid upon Ghistelles aerodrome.†

Alongside the bombing campaign, and the spectacular outburst of fighter activity that outlasted it, the daily work of other units of No 5 Group continued unabated. Thus 202 Squadron‡ ranged constantly over its sector of the Flemish coast to provide photographic intelligence for the bomber force and to spot for naval siege guns and the monitors. The Camels of 213 Squadron were responsible

---

* No 204 Squadron was about half Canadian in the period July–October 1918. Its pilots included H.A. Argles of Toronto, S.C.J. Askin of Windsor, Ont. (POW 12 Aug. 1918), B.E. Barnum of Kingston, Ont., W.E. Baxter of Vancouver, L.S. Breadner of Ottawa, F.R. Brown of Winnipeg, A.C. Burt of Brantford, Ont., H.G. Clappison of Hamilton, Ont., W.B. Craig of Smiths Falls, Ont. (KIA 26 Sept. 1918), H.W.M. Cumming of Toronto, A.C. Evans of Windsor, Ont., C.R.R. Hickey of Parksville, BC, G.E.C. Howard of Toronto (WIA 3 Sept. 1917, POW 26 Sept. 1918), W.J.P. Jenner of Blenheim, Ont., R.M. Keirstead of Toronto, P.A.H. King of Victoria, BC, H.G. Murray (KIA 27 Oct. 1918), and R.C. Pattulo (KIA 15 Sept. 1918), both of Toronto, W.A. Pomeroy of Esquimalt, BC, J.R. Robertson of Blenheim, Ont., W.F. Robinson of Davidson, Sask., E.G. Rolph of Toronto (POW 20 Sept. 1918), A.J.F. Ross of Calgary, W.G. Sibary of Renfrew, Ont., and L.P. Worthington of Westerdale, Alta.

† Canadians in 210 in the period Aug.–Oct. 1918 were A.G. Baker of Toronto, E.M. Faris of Bradford, Ont., E.N. Gregory of Lindsay, Ont., W.W. Gyles of Virden, Man., A. St G. Highstone of Sault Ste Marie, Ont., R.W. Hopper of Toronto (POW 8 Oct. 1918), W.S. Jenkins of Montreal, D.D. McQuat of Brownsburg, Que., J.E. Pugh of Stony Plain, Alta, G.A. Welsh of Sunderland, Ont., and H.H. Witlock of Charlottetown, PEI.

‡ New arrivals at 202 in June 1918 were C.R. Moore of Toronto (POW 28 Sept. 1918) and A.M. Stephens of Moose Jaw, Sask. Another was J. Robinson of Toronto, an RNAS veteran of the East African campaign in 1916 and later special pilot to the King of the Belgians who had served with No 2 (N) from May to November 1917 until wounded.

for seaward fleet defence, while the DH4s of 217 Squadron complemented the land bombing by frequent attacks upon the submarines and surface vessels operating out of Ostend and Zeebrugge.* This squadron began to encounter the fine mono-plane fighter, the Brandenburg W 29, in July. On 29 July Lieutenant A. McM. Phillips of Toronto and another DH4 pilot were given joint credit for shooting down a Brandenburg, which 'was completely destroyed on impact with the water.'† Phillips, who shot down two other aircraft during his time with the squadron, was respon-sible for half the total claimed by the unit. In addition to the work of all these squadrons, the seaplanes and aeroplanes at Dover‡ continued their duties of anti-submarine patrols and the escort of coastal convoys.[44]

As the allied armies moved forward to the last great assault upon the German lines, No 5 Group was switched, on 28 September, to support of the Belgian army in the Flanders offensive. On 17 October a pilot of 210 Squadron touched down in Ostend's market place, while Keyes, offshore in *Termagant*, watched the pilots of 202, 204, and 210 'looping the loop' over the town. By 20 October the left flank of the allied front ran to the Dutch border. The day before the Armistice three Cana-dians, Lieutenant G.C. Mackay and Second Lieutenants A.B. Rosevear and H.H. Gilbert, shared with another pilot of 213 Squadron in destroying the group's last victim, an LVG two-seater that crashed after a low-level dogfight over Ghent.[45]

From the creation of the RAF in April 1918 113 Canadians had flown out of Dunkirk and another eight from Dover. Forty-four of them had become casual-ties, 16 per cent of the total at Dunkirk.§ Of the 169 German aircraft claimed by No 5 Group, Canadians were credited with thirty-eight and shared ten more with other pilots. The most successful fighter pilot in the group was C.R.R. Hickey, who apparently shot down eight aircraft and shared in the destruction of two more before his death in a mid-air collision on 3 October. J.E. Greene of No 213 was

---

* New Canadian members of 217 during 1918 were W.F. Anderson of Toronto, K.G. Boyd of Amberley, Ont., D.W. Davies of Victoria, BC, A.W. Farquhar of Toronto, C.J. Moir of Killarney, Man. (KIA 30 June 1918), C. St C. Parsons (POW 22 April 1918), and A. McM. Phillips, both of Toronto, and H.S. Stidson of Winnipeg.

† RAF reports claim that two monoplanes were destroyed in the action, but the war diary of *Seeflugstation Flanders I* shows only one aircraft lost. See No 5 Group fortnightly summaries, 16–31 July 1918, Air 1/39/AH/15/9/6; 'The Hornets of Zeebrugge,' *Cross & Cockade Journal*, XI, spring 1970, 27.

‡ From July 1918 there were two flights of aeroplanes and one of seaplanes under Halahan at Dover. The aeroplane flights were used by Lambe to rest pilots from front line duties; the first two Canadians to benefit were Lieutenants J.E. Greene and G.C. Mackay. Captain A.C. Reid flew seaplanes out of Dover until the end of the war; before the Dover organization was formed into 233 Squadron in October he was joined by Captain H.H. Gonyon and Second Lieutenant R.M. Mulvihill of Arnprior, Ont.

§ Dunkirk returns show that many of the casualties occurred after the arrival of the Fokker D-VII, and that DH9 crews were especially vulnerable. Pilot wastage from accidents, however, was 'most appalling' in Lambe's view. Though new pilots were arriving with double the hours of their predecessors in 1917, and were given intensive advanced training in the pilots' pool at Adembert, established in May under the command of the much-decorated Canadian fighter pilot, Captain A.M. Shook, Lambe considered that there was still poor aerodrome discipline and that young pilots were taking too many careless and unnecessary risks. Lambe to OC's 61 and 82 Wings, 23 Aug. 1918, Air 1/73/15/9/150; Lambe to Halahan, 30 May 1918, Air 1/57/15/9/55

credited with five victories and two shared before he was killed in the Belgian offensive, while in No 210 W.S. Jenkins was the leading Canadian, being credited with five aircraft shot down.[46]

The work of these Canadians and their fellow flyers had been shaped by the offensive strategy of Keyes and Lambe, centred upon the bombing of the Bruges basin. The bombing attack had been far more concentrated than previous Dunkirk bombing campaigns; a third of the 510-ton total dropped during the six-month period was directed at the area of the Bruges docks. The total effect of the bombing upon German naval bases and ships is difficult to establish, partly because, when they departed, the Germans carried out extensive demolition of key installations. It is known that Handley Pages from 214 Squadron put UB 59 out of the war with a hit on 16 May, and that in the same month aircraft sank the destroyer V74 at Zeebrugge. Four other derelict destroyers, V47, V67, V77, and S61, which were blown up at the time of the German evacuation, may also have received their original damage from air attacks.* Nevertheless, the RAF committee of investigation which assessed the bombing after the Armistice concluded that 'the results ... were not decisive either in the whole area or in any single part of it.'[47]

Part of the explanation for the relative failure of the bombing campaign was technological. Inaccurate bomb-sights and unreliable bomb-release gear were important factors. Many of the bombs dropped were far too light for effective use against heavy installations, especially those reinforced with ferro-concrete. The SN 1660-lb bombs had the needed penetrating power, but for the Handley Pages to carry them the weather conditions had to be ideal. From August onwards only one Handley Page was kept armed with this bomb and ready, weather permitting, to attack the Bruges docks. In giving that order, Lambe noted that none of the SNs released to that date had fallen 'within miles of their objectives.'[†48]

It might also be argued that neither the Air Ministry nor the army had been sufficiently generous in allotting the Dover Patrol the numbers of heavy night bombers it needed, failing to recognize the vital importance of striking at German-held ports. This is another way of saying that bombers might more usefully have been allocated to the navy than turned over to the Independent Force for its offensive against Germany. But given the purposes which led to the creation of the RAF, the composition of the Air Ministry, and the political and public pressures working upon it, it would seem more realistic to conclude that the Admiralty did well to extract from the ministry and the army any squadrons at all. Though the importance of destroying the target gave Keyes and Lambe a good case, their demands, at least in part, constituted an attempt to challenge the consequences of the formation of a third service. Unquestionably, however, the Air Ministry in its

---

* For example, on 10 August a DH4 of 217 Squadron, in which the Canadian pilot A. McM. Phillips was flying as observer, damaged the stern of a destroyer with a bomb hit that produced 'a very big explosion accompanied by dense clouds of smoke.' No 5 Group fortnightly summary, 1–15 Aug. 1918, Air 1/39/AH/15/9/6

† The first 1660-lb bomb was dropped on the night of 24–25 July. The shaken inhabitants of Middelkerke immediately doused all lights and the anti-aircraft guns in the vicinity fell silent. Later photographs showed that the bomb had made a huge crater in a field half-a-mile out of town.

disposition of available bombers was unduly affected by political considerations, including inter-service politics. Both the nature of its origins and production short-ages meant that the RAF lacked the flexibility that air mobility was supposed to permit and therefore was unable to concentrate a bomber force in Flanders at a time when it might have accomplished something. It should not be overlooked, however, that of the total tonnage dropped upon German naval targets during this period, more than a quarter was contributed by the RAF's 65 Wing.

The Dover Patrol's prime function was to shut off the Strait of Dover to the U-boats. In this task it was largely successful. After May 1918 few submarines risked the hazards of the air-sea patrol and the deep minefields; the last to try got through on 14 August. Of the forty-four boats in the Flanders Flotillas in 1918, thirty-three were sunk or interned, three were rendered unserviceable through damage, and one was retired from service. At the time, aeroplanes were credited with destroying two submarines, and on both occasions Canadian pilots took a leading part. On 3 April Captain H.H. Gonyon of Chatham, Ont., made the first of several promising bombing runs on a U-boat seen to dive off Dunkirk. On 12 August Captain K.G. Boyd of Toronto appeared to score a hit on the conning tower of a submarine steering towards Ostend. He reported that it 'rolled slowly over to starboard and lay bottom up for five minutes sinking slowly.'[49] Despite such persuasive detail, German records show that no submarines were lost in the area on either date.

The naval task in the Mediterranean in 1918 was the protection of maritime routes against surface and underwater attack, in support of the Italian, Macedo-nian, and Palestinian military theatres. Most of the fleet had to be deployed on various anti-submarine duties to counteract the Austro-German flotillas based in the Adriatic. Capital ships were still required to counter the Austrian Fleet as well as *Goeben* at Constantinople. It had been decided at the allied Naval Council meet-ing in Rome on 8–9 February that the principal thrust of the year would be an offensive in the Strait of Otranto and against U-boat bases, rather than in the strengthening of the convoy organization. Air tasks to meet naval priorities were carried out by the Adriatic, Aegean, Egypt, Gibraltar, and Malta Groups, each under the orders of the local senior naval officer.[50]

Air support for the Otranto Barrage was provided by the Adriatic Group* under command of General Longmore, with headquarters at Taranto. For airmen the

---

* Canadians with the Adriatic Group, all members of the former RNAS organization in the area, were A.R. Layard of Saanich, BC, a technical officer, A.L. Huether of Guelph, Ont., H.G. Raney of Ottawa, and E.C.R. Stoneman and F. Wood, both of Toronto. E.C. Bredin, address unknown, was on Kite-Balloon operations out of Brindisi. By the late summer a number of other Canadians had joined the group, including two technical officers, A.P. Beal of Lindsay, Ont., and F.W. Mansell of Lethbridge, Alta; two observers, C.K. Chase, address unknown, and J.P. Corkery of Almonte, Ont. (killed in a raid on Cattaro on 23 Aug. 1918); three seaplane pilots, W.R.S. Henderson of London, Ont., G.K. Lucas of Markdale, Ont., and H.L. Nunn, address unknown; and seven aeroplane pilots, E.I. Bussell of Toronto, D.M.B. Galbraith of Carleton Place, Ont., M. Hellwell of Toronto, B.W. Hopkins of Hamilton, Ont., A.B. Shearer of Neepawa, Man., G.W. Stubbs of Victoria, BC, and A.L. Taylor, address unknown. Later arrivals were two pilots, H.W. Pope of Moose Jaw, Sask., and J.T. Rose of Toronto, and three observers, J.A. Simmers and K.P. Kirkwood, both of Toronto, and G.E.S. McLeod of Saint John, NB.

daily patrolling of the barrage was extremely monotonous. It was relieved by periodic bombing raids against u-boat bases in the Adriatic. The raiding of bases in the upper Adriatic was an Italian responsibility; the RAF directed its attacks against Cattaro in Austria and Durazzo in Albania. The Austrian Naval Air Service, with less than a hundred aircraft available for war service, never offered significant opposition. The Adriatic Group itself was well below the planned complement both in personnel and aircraft, and so, at least until the end of July, its raids were on a small scale. In August it was possible to mount more ambitious attacks, though they were not without their hazards. The round trip to Cattaro was over four hundred miles, most of it over water; Captain A.B. Shearer of Neepawa, Man. (a future RCAF Air Vice-Marshal), came to grief on his first crossing of the Adriatic. Bucking headwinds, he took four-and-a-half hours to reach Cattaro and, with insufficient fuel to get back, had to cross enemy lines and land on the Italian-held beach at Valona in Albania.[51]

On two occasions the Adriatic Group provided support to army operations. Between 6 and 10 July aircraft from Otranto assisted the advance of the Italian XVI Corps up the Adriatic coast from Valona. On 2 October the group provided bombers, fighters, and reconnaissance aircraft for a naval attack upon Durazzo undertaken by Italian and British vessels. E.C.R. Stoneman of Toronto was one of the pilots in the first wave of bombers over the target at 0615 hours. As this wave landed at Andrano airfield a second formation, in which Captain C.K. Chase and Second Lieutenant G.W. Stubbs, of Victoria, BC, were flying as observers, took off, and carried out their bombing runs while the allied fleet was manoeuvring off Durazzo prior to its bombardment. Second Lieutenant B.W. Hopkins of Hamilton, Ont., flew a DH9 of the third wave that bombed during the naval bombardment itself, while Stoneman returned with the last formation of seven aircraft that hit the town at 1130 hrs, by which time the fleet had ceased firing and hauled off.[52] As military operations drew to a close, aircraft of the group joined in the harrying of the Austrian army as it retreated on the Albanian front. By the end of October the German submarines had abandoned their bases, and the bombing of Cattaro and Durazzo ceased.

In its assessment of the bombing operations the Admiralty was enthusiastic, describing the attacks as being of 'the greatest possible value'; it considered that 'besides the damage probably caused to submarines themselves and certainly to their depots and shops, the moral effect must be considerable.' These opinions, as in so many other cases, appear to have little foundation in fact. There is no evidence that u-boats were either damaged or destroyed in harbour, and Durazzo by August had already become of little importance as a base.[53]

The Eastern Mediterranean was the preserve of the Aegean Squadron, with headquarters at Mudros on the island of Lemnos. Its job was to blockade the Dardanelles and to combat u-boats operating in its sector. The Aegean Group's tasks, therefore, were to carry out reconnaissance of the Strait and the Sea of Marmara to alert the navy of enemy fleet movements, and to maintain routine anti-submarine patrols. In addition, the RAF was also responsible for giving air support to the army operations on the Salonika front, and for carrying out 'independent' bombing of Turkish rail communications, air bases, and Constantinople itself. To carry out these commitments, the group had slightly more than its authorized establishment of seventy-two aeroplanes and twenty-four seaplanes. Two bomber and two fighter squadrons were allocated to 62 Wing, while all seaplanes were attached to 63 Wing. The force included adequate numbers of Camels and Short seaplanes, but there was also the usual collection of vintage aircraft such as BE2cs, Henri Farmans, and Sopwith Pups. These aircraft were distributed in small detachments at bases on the Greek mainland and the Aegean Islands.[54]

At least twelve of the eighteen Canadians serving with the Aegean Group at the beginning of April were flying with 62 Wing.* At Stavros, on the mainland, Captain D.M. Ballantyne of Montreal and Lieutenant W.R. Glenny of Little Britain, Ont., were involved in military reconnaissance, offensive patrols, and the bombing of Drama aerodrome and other targets in the lower Struma River area. In May the group provided additional assistance on the Macedonian front when DH4s and Camels from Imbros co-operated with 17 and 47 Squadrons in attacks on Drama and the Ruppel Pass. Ordinarily the Imbros Camel pilots, who included Captain D.F. Murray of Victoria and Lieutenants A.S. Girling and F.M. McLellan of Springhill, NS, carried out the important daily reconnaissance of the Strait, the Gallipoli peninsula, and enemy airfields at Galata and Chanak. Camels went up in relays of two from 0300 hrs until 1100 hrs, when the intense heat of mid-day over the Dardanelles forced a break until the late afternoon. Longer-range reconnaissance flights over Constantinople to check on the battlecruiser *Goeben* were carried out by DH9s fitted with extra fuel tanks. Lieutenant T.H. Blair, flying out of Lemnos, took part in a successful flight of two DH9s which photographed the *Goeben* lying in Stenia Bay after two earlier attempts had ended in loss of aircraft.[55]

Both the bombers from Imbros and seaplanes carried out frequent raids on the enemy airfield at Galata. On 24 August Lieutenant S.A. Grant of Montreal, flying a seaplane from Talikna, fired an 18-inch torpedo on the hangars 'with good results.' On another night-bombing attack on Galata, Grant and his observer, Lieutenant F.R. Bicknell of Dunnville, Ont., had their radiator punctured by machine-gun fire. The engine rapidly overheated as they limped back across the Gallipoli peninsula. 'We crashed in flames in the Gulf of Xeros,' Bicknell recalled, and 'remained afloat by hanging to the small tail float which we had managed to hack off with pocket knife before the plane sank about one hour after landing at mid-nite.' After twelve hours in the water they were picked up by the Greek destroyer *Leon*.[†56]

---

* D.M. Ballantyne of Montreal, T.H. Blair of Toronto, H.J. Elliott of Edwards, Ont. (KIA 29 June 1918), A.S. Girling, address unknown, W.R. Glenny of Little Britain, Ont., F.M. McLellan of Springhill, NS, D.F. Murray of Victoria, BC, G.M. Scott of Westmount, Que. (KIA 13 June 1918), W.J. Sussan and H.A. Urquhart, both of Ottawa, A.Y. Wilks of Montreal, and H.J. Wiser of Prescott, Ont.

† In addition to Grant and Bicknell, there were C.A. Beattie of Ingersoll, Ont., and F.J. Mackie of Winnipeg at Talikna; and G.S. Abbott of Ottawa (WIA 30 Nov. 1916), R.E. Spear of Winnipeg, and F.P.L. Washington of Hamilton, Ont., at Suda Bay on Crete. Later reinforcements were W.H. August of Winnipeg, R.H. Cross and H.M. Keith, both of Toronto, R.G.K. Morrison of Chesterville, Ont., H.G. Thompson of Belmont, Ont., and G.K. Waterhouse, of Kingston, Ont. B.N. Harrop of Indian Head, Sask., flew seaplanes from *Vindex*.

The Air Ministry had plans for the Aegean Group that had nothing to do with anti-submarine operations. It wished to use the group to bomb Constantinople, and in June transferred two squadrons from the Middle East Brigade to the Aegean. When the transfer was held up, the group was left to carry out the job from its own resources, a policy the air adviser to the Commander-in-Chief Mediterranean thought ill-judged. 'This will be done but in a very spasmodic way with the present strength allowed,' wrote General A.V. Vyvyan, 'and I very much doubt if it is worth doing unless doing well.' Two flights of bombers, assembled at Romanos aerodrome on Lemnos, made a total of nine raids on the Turkish capital between July and September with no discernible effects. Yet the Air Ministry, still pursuing the will-o'-the-wisp of 'decision through strategic bombing,' continued to reinforce the Aegean Group until the close of hostilities. No 144 Squadron reached Mudros in mid-October, and No 226 was transferred to the Aegean from the Adriatic Group. Large drafts of pilots and observers were also sent in,* so that by November the group was well over establishment and had been reinforced more heavily than any of its Mediterranean counterparts. On 18 October twelve bombers struck at Constantinople for the last time. The airmen of the group do not appear to have attached any high degree of seriousness to that raid, or to the whole bombing enterprise against Turkey. As the lead aircraft, its engines throttled back, touched down at Lemnos after its five-hour flight, a visiting senior officer noted that its pilot, the officer commanding 226 Squadron, and his observer, the 'light hearted' Canadian C.K. Chase, were serenading the spectators with mouth organ and drum.[57]

The other three groups in the Mediterranean could have used some of the reinforcements granted the Aegean. The Royal Navy and its supporting RAF units in the central and western Mediterranean had been denuded of strength to supply the Otranto Barrage organization in the spring, while playing a crucial role in the anti-submarine warfare for the whole theatre. The Malta, Gibraltar, and Egypt groups were all much under strength during 1918 and the number of Canadians serving in them was correspondingly small.† At Malta, Shorts and F3s were flown out of Kalafrana. The Malta seaplane station was supposed to have fifty officers; the aver-

---

* At least thirteen Canadians were among the reinforcements for 62 Wing. They were N.M. Craig of Fergus, Ont., H.E. Dobson of Toronto, H.F. Farncomb of Trenton, Ont., H.G. Fraser of Norwood, Ont., W.S. Haney of Sarnia, Ont., B.W. Hopkins and C.I. Lancefield, both of Hamilton, Ont., K.G. MacDonald of Victoria, BC, J.W. McArthur of Quebec City, V.J. O'Neill of Ottawa, F.M. Ramsay of Inglewood, Ont., A.H.K. Russell of Toronto, A.P. Stock of Peterborough, Ont., and J.S. Wood of Oakville, Man. With 144 Squadron were W.F. Willis of Winnipeg and S.E. Young, address unknown.

† Canadians at Kalafrana were B.N. Harrop of Indian Head, Sask., D.H. Hartness of Nanaimo, BC, K.P. Kirkwood of Toronto, C.W. Lott of Brussels, Ont. (KIA July 1918), J.A. Munn of Hensall, Ont., and F.J. Vincent, address unknown, in *Riviera*; and L.E. Nicholson of Winnipeg in *Manxman*. Both these carriers were attached to Malta Group for a time. E.C. Potter of Winnipeg, in *Engadine*, is the only Canadian known to have served with Gibraltar Group. Three Canadians were with the Egypt Group: H.W. Eades of Nelson, BC, an observer, and two pilots, L.E. Best of Victoria, BC, and W.T. Ward of Vancouver. There were four Canadian KB officers at Malta: T.D. Fitzgerald of Hamilton, Ont., G.O. Lightbourn of Toronto, R.W.R. Waage-Mott of Victoria, BC, and A.H. Walker of Toronto; while Alexander Ross of Toronto served in a similar capacity at Gibraltar.

age through the year was about twenty. Gibraltar never got its planned squadron of F3s; seaplane patrols there were provided first from *Empress* and later from *Engadine*. The Egypt Group (administered by RAF Middle East Brigade but under naval authority for operations) worked from Port Said and Alexandria; it too was short of personnel. In addition to these units the RAF also created a network of kite balloon stations under the groups to protect Mediterranean convoys.[58]

As an increasing proportion of Mediterranean shipping came to be in organized convoys or under escort for part of a journey, seaplane patrols began to be superseded by air escort work. Convoy escort provided the best form of protection for merchant shipping, and the best opportunities for attacking submarines. Figures for aircraft in the Egypt Group illustrate the general trend:

EGYPT GROUP PATROLS, APRIL–OCTOBER 1918

MONTH	S/M & OTHER PATROLS	CONVOY PATROLS	TOTAL
April	24	61	85
May	40	52	92
June	14	54	68
July	18	93	111
August	15	107	122
September	15	111	126
October	28	101	129
	154	579	733

From the increasing emphasis given to convoy patrol it would appear that the offensive potential of the convoy system had been recognized in the Mediterranean. Unfortunately, there was a general shortage of airmen and aircraft in the Mediterranean anti-submarine groups. The pilots in the Egypt Group flew more hours a day, on the average, than the pilots in any other RAF command engaging in anti-submarine work. The average number of pilots available for patrols never exceeded thirteen for any month and the average number of serviceable seaplanes at Alexandria and Port Said combined was never more than twelve.[59]

The Mediterranean convoy system was a dramatic success, although at the time the naval command credited the victory over submarines to the Otranto Barrage.* In March 1918 U-boats were sinking a major vessel (one of 500 tons or more) every day; in June only thirteen such ships were lost. Overall, only 1.43 per cent of the 627 vessels on 'through' convoys were sunk and only 1.17 per cent of the

---

* Considerable resources were expended to little effect on the Otranto Barrage. Despite constant air activity and the assembling of a surface fleet virtually as large as the Dover Patrol, submarines actually penetrated the barrage more frequently than in the period prior to its strengthening. It was technically impossible, in the three to five hundred fathoms of the Strait of Otranto, to sow deep mines (which had brought about most of the U-boat sinkings in the Strait of Dover), and surface and air forces were incapable of sealing off the Adriatic by themselves. Marder, *Dreadnought to Scapa Flow*, v, 35

10,882 vessels on local convoys. Despite the preoccupation of the naval command with Otranto, and the bombing priorities of the Air Ministry, the slow-moving, weak convoy escorts backed up by the bluff of kite balloons and a handful of out-of-date seaplanes defeated the U-boat threat.[60]

But for the Royal Navy the Mediterranean anti-submarine campaign was of little significance compared to the struggle being waged in the approaches to the British Isles. As the German unrestricted attack upon shipping entered its second year, allied hopes for victory were far from being realized, despite the measures taken during 1917. During the first year the Entente lost 6.2 million tons of shipping, the British share being 3.75 million tons, or 20 per cent of the ship tonnage on hand twelve months earlier. At the end of the year the U-boats were still sinking shipping faster than it could be replaced by new construction.

In March 1918, for the first time, the Entente rate of production of new ships surpassed sinkings from all causes, a significant change chiefly attributable to American shipyards. In June British output of merchant shipping rose beyond the tonnage destroyed by direct war causes, and by September it exceeded the total of war and marine risk losses. By that time U-boats were sinking, on average, about 275 tons of shipping a day, in contrast with the 700 a day sunk during the early months of the unrestricted campaign. This was not because critical losses had been inflicted upon the German submarine fleet. Although an average of 6.8 submarines per month destroyed was maintained during 1918 – the highest rate of the war – the Germans managed to commission new submarines at the rate of eight a month. In January Germany had 167 submarines on strength; by the Armistice there were 180. Nevertheless, the war against the submarine had virtually been won by June, a victory that passed almost without recognition. How had it come about?[61]

There were two main reasons, one well known and the other less familiar. The first was the adoption of a complete convoy system instead of the ocean convoy system. In January 1918 50 per cent of the United Kingdom's overseas trade was in convoy; by November the proportion had risen to 90 per cent. The second reason was the use of the aircraft to round out the protection afforded to merchantmen by the convoy organization.

The major advantage of general convoy was that it imposed limits upon the previously wide-ranging activities of the U-boats. When ocean convoy began in 1917 German submarines were forced to move closer to the waters of the British Isles and to find most of their victims among the small, independently-routed ships moving up and down the heavily patrolled northeast and southwest coastal waters. In March 1918 a regular Irish Sea convoy began to run out from Liverpool; at the same time the revitalized Dover Barrage was cutting down on the number of submarines passing through to the western English Channel. When the Flanders flotillas were deflected to the northeast, where only part of the shipping was in convoy, losses rose steeply. From June, however, virtually all trade from the River Humber northward was in convoy. This development, coupled with a general extension of the inshore convoy network elsewhere, forced the U-boats once more to the deep waters of the Atlantic, out of range of aircraft, although they continued to pick off ships in those coastal areas still not part of the convoy system.

The British sea and air escort forces defeated the submarine despite an Admiralty attitude that, at best, was ambivalent towards convoying. Most senior naval officers took the view that it was 'a deterrent, and not a reliable safe-guard.' As Commander D.W. Waters has explained: 'the Naval Staff was untrained in the work, and by training was antipathetic to the whole concept of mercantile convoy which, to the end of the war, it regarded as a palliative and not as a system of war.' What the staff favoured was the 'offensive' strategy exemplified by such large mined areas as the Dover, Otranto, and Northern barrages. Naval Headquarters was torn between those who favoured hunting patrols and those who favoured convoy escorts, with the result that the whole convoy organization suffered in the competition for equipment. Hunting patrols were created for the Irish Sea and North West Approaches, and in the spring the Admiralty further stripped the escort force to create another patrol that covered the Fair Isle passage between the Orkney and Shetland islands. The convoy system was left with slow older vessels, unequipped with hydrophones because it was thought that the underwater noise of many propellers rendered the listening device ineffective, while newer destroyers better suited to the work were fruitlessly chasing about elsewhere.[62]

The employment of aerial resources in anti-submarine work was similarly affected. In January 1918 291 seaplanes (a sixth of them flying-boats) and twenty-three aeroplanes were being used for patrols around the British Isles. Convoy escort was left to fifty-four non-rigid airships and kite balloons. At that time the Admiralty, which had originally hoped to strengthen its patrols with fifty Handley Pages, looked forward to receiving a squadron of Blackburn Kangaroos and perhaps some DH4s and DH9s. Most pressing was the need for short-range aircraft to operate over the inshore shipping routes, particularly as the U-boats began to concentrate along the northeast coast and the waters off Devon and Cornwall. The outcome was a makeshift plan to establish 'protected lanes' for shipping up to ten miles from the coast, a plan very similar to the discredited scheme of anti-submarine ship patrols that had operated in 1917. The intention was 'not so much to destroy the submarines ... but to frighten them off' by sending an aircraft along the protected lane every twenty minutes. Ready to hand, and in plentiful supply, was an outdated trainer, the DH6. Available to fly it were a miscellaneous assortment of airmen who, for one reason or another, had been rejected by the Training Division for full operational flying, and who could be 'stiffened by ... 10% admixture of effective pilots.'[63] As it happens, a good many Canadians found themselves involved in this *ad hoc* enterprise, though it is now impossible to determine what proportion of them were considered a part of the 'effective' 10 per cent.

The Air Ministry agreed to allocate twenty-nine flights of six aircraft each to carry out the protected lane plan, the DH6 to be used as a 'temporary expedient' for four months. The flights began to form in April, and were located in accordance with naval priorities. They were incorporated into the RAF's United Kingdom organization, which comprised five areas each containing a number of groups. The process of consolidating the DH6 flights, and other maritime units, into squadrons and wings was spread out over most of 1918.[64]

As far as Canadians were concerned, it was the area coming under the Vice-Admiral East Coast of England that drew the majority of them. From its headquarters at Habrough, Lincolnshire, No 18 Group controlled the non-rigid airship base at Howden, three squadrons of DH6s, a flight of Blackburn Kangaroos* at Seaton Carew, seaplanes from the latter station and from Hornsea, and, for a time, seaplanes at Killingholme and South Shields.† From early summer onwards Killingholme was in process of being taken over by the United States Navy. During the period of transition Captain A.H. Munday, one of the last Canadian pilots to leave the station, attacked a U-boat on 8 June. Another Canadian, Lieutenant R.R. Richardson of Guelph, Ont., stationed at Seaton Carew, was one of the more successful and aggressive pilots in the command.‡ He was in action against a U-boat on 10 May while flying a Sopwith Baby over Robin Hood's Bay. In June Richardson was one of the pilots selected to fly the Blackburn Kangaroo, together with Second Lieutenants W.F. Stephens of Gananoque, Ont., and G.F. Ward of Stratford, Ont.[65]

This useful aircraft gave the Seaton Carew flight the best anti-submarine record of any British unit and demonstrated what could be done with better machines. Between 1 May and 11 November airmen flying the Kangaroos sighted twelve U-boats and attacked eleven of them; they averaged a sighting for every fifty hours compared to 196 hours for flying boats and 2416 hours for coastal aircraft. On 28 August a Kangaroo dropped a 520-lb bomb on a submerged submarine off Runswick Bay that had been attacked by trawlers after torpedoing a merchantman. The aircraft was then joined by the destroyer *Ouse* and between them they destroyed it with depth charges and another bomb. On a rocky bottom in fourteen fathoms of water divers found the remains of UC 70. Before the end of August Richardson had bombed submarines off the coast on at least three occasions. In the swept channel off the Tees on 3 September, Richardson reported: 'I sighted a hostile submarine in position 54° 38′ N, 0° 52′ W ... She was steering slowly N.E. and the top of her conning tower was just visible ... about a mile away on my port bow ... I released my first bomb at 1225 which detonated 15 yards astern of the conning tower ... Oil and some bubbles rose to the surface but no further results were observed.'[66]

The DH6 squadrons on the east coast contained many Canadians, especially No 256, with flights at Seahouses and New Haggerston in Northumberland, which appeared to have been about half Canadian.§ The DH6 airmen operated under

---

* The Blackburn Kangaroo was a heavy bomber and anti-submarine patrol biplane. It was powered by two 250-hp Rolls-Royce Falcon motors. It had a maximum speed of 98 mph and could carry four 230-lb bombs. Only fourteen Kangaroos saw service and these flew anti-submarine patrols on the east coast. Owen Thetford and E.J. Riding, *Aircraft of the 1914–1918 War* (Marlow, England 1954), 7

† Before the expansion of the command there were four Canadians flying seaplanes and flying boats: A.B. Massey, A.H. Munday, and V.H. Ramsden, all of Toronto at Killingholme; and A. Woods of Elmira, Ont., at South Shields, which was not used for operational flights after May. At Howden, J. Sproston of Montreal was flying non-rigids.

‡ Other Canadians in the Command were L.F. Ross of Hamilton, Ont., at Hornsea; and N.E. Lashbrook, address unknown, and H.M. O'Loughlin of St Catharines, Ont.

§ Of the twenty-four officers in 256 Squadron in September, eleven were Canadians: G.E. Douglas of Tecumseh, Ont., T.A. Duval of Quebec City, W.G. Freel, address unknown, A.F. Head of Hagersville, Ont., H. Jamieson, address unknown, C.W. Kerr of Hamilton, Ont., E.D. Macfarlane of Vancouver, W.G.G. Murdoch, address unknown, W.R. Reid of Seaforth, Ont., W.N. Stanley of Lucan, Ont., and W.J. Tansey, address unknown.

conditions of extreme difficulty. Their obsolescent aircraft was powered by an unreliable 90-hp Curtiss OX 5 engine and could not carry both an observer and bombs. The view from the cockpit was poor. The machine was known in the service by such terms of derision as 'the Sky Hook,' 'the Clutching Hand,' 'the Crab,' 'the Flying Coffin,' and 'the Dung Hunter.' Its only saving grace was that it was easy to fly. Aircrews, however, were mostly inexperienced and untrained for the job; many suffered from medical disabilities contracted in other theatres. Pilots were always in short supply, meaning a heavy work load for those available. So were observers, and their ranks were often filled up by trawlermen borrowed from local naval bases. On the ground conditions were no better. Supply and repair facilities were poor, there were never enough armourers, and the bombs, piled in open fields under tarpaulins, often failed to detonate. Living accommodations were primitive, as illustrated by the following signals, cited by the Admiralty when attempts were being made to persuade the Air Ministry that better treatment was needed:

Camp at Tynemouth, flooded out; all men's clothing and bedding wet through and in a disgraceful condition. Some of the tents blown down, others floating about.
  Officer's marquee at Elford collapsed during last night; impossible to re-erect as canvas is rotten. Men's field kitchen has no cover. Cooking only possible in boilers and field urns out in the open.
  All tents at Seahouses flattened, messing being arranged in temporary billet.[67]

It was not the trenches, but it was bad enough.

  Yet had the DH6s not been flying their patrols, shipping losses would have been much greater. In the narrow war channels, hedged to seaward by minefields, U-boats knew exactly where to wait to catch vessels steaming independently. Once aeroplanes began periodically crossing their routes, submarine commanders had to be warier. If all went well, the DH6s usually stayed aloft for more than an hour, but ditchings, caused by engine failure, were frequent. The aircraft's unexpected seaworthiness – it was known to stay afloat for as much as six hours – reduced drownings from these mishaps.

  Moreover, DH6 crews were frequently in contact with submarines. Many Canadians on the east coast had this experience; for example, Lieutenant D. Girardot, address unknown, on 14 July and Second Lieutenant G.E. Douglas of Tecumseh, Ont., on 24 August. Both carried out bombing runs upon submerging U-boats before calling destroyers to their assistance. Two pilots from Seaton Carew, Lieutenant H. MacPherson of Calgary and Second Lieutenant H.C. Cook of Gravenhurst, Ont., were both in contact with what may have been the same submarine off Whitby on 29 September. That same month Second Lieutenant J.A.R. Mason of Stratford, Ont., flying out of Tynemouth,* was one of four pilots recommended to

---

* Other pilots on these DH6 squadrons included E. Anthony of Maitland, NS, E. Langston of Winnipeg, J.B.B. Paterson of Saint John, NB, and H.W. Press, address unknown, with 251 at Atwick and Owthorne, Yorkshire; H.L. Stevenson of Chatham, Ont., with 252 at Redcar; A.D. Geiger of Cobourg, Ont., and F.L. McGuire of Chelmsford, Ont., with 252 at Seaton Carew; and T.G. Blakely of Winnipeg, C.B. Gibson of Welland, Ont., and H.O. Prout, address unknown, with 252 at Tynemouth.

the Admiralty as having 'distinguished themselves in regard to DH anti-submarine work at the commencement of this class of flying.'[68]

The other RAF groups in which DH6s served were Nos 9, 10, 14, and 22, operating off the south, southwest, and west coasts. Though there were fewer Canadians flying DH6s in these groups, they were to be found in virtually all their scattered flights.* Most Canadians in these commands, however, were operating flying-boats or seaplanes to seaward of the protected lanes, either on patrol or on convoy escort, and a few were lighter-than-air pilots.[†] The seaplane stations in the four groups formed an interlocking network of patrol areas, stretching from Newhaven around to Stranraer in the North Channel. One of No 10 Group's units, 243 Squadron, was based at Cherbourg and co-ordinated its efforts with the French Naval Air Service. Calshot in the Solent was the group's principal station and operated the RAF seaplane training school as well. The stations of No 9 Group were responsible for patrolling from Lyme Bay around to the turbulent waters off Land's End. On 8 July Lieutenant F.H. Prime of Toronto was second pilot of a flying-boat that was forced down by engine failure off the Cornish coast. The crew had to be rescued by the hospital ship *Braemar Castle* as their aircraft broke up in the heavy seas. No 14 Group had only one seaplane station, at Fishguard on the Welsh coast, where Shorts co-operated with airship and DH6 patrols in the Irish Sea. Because there were few shipping routes through the western isles, most of No 22 Group's anti-submarine stations were on the Scottish east coast. A number of Canadians had long service in this area. At Dundee Captains A.H. Sandwell, W.R. Kenny, and J.G. Ireland were all veterans, the last two having started their third year in mid-1918. All had brushes with U-boats, those of Kenny being typical. On 3 June, when flying an H16, he carried out a bombing attack on a diving submarine. The next month, when piloting a Short 184, he interrupted a U-boat 'manoeuvring to attack ... [a] large steamship,' and dropped two 100-lb bombs aimed at its periscope from a height of seventy feet. German records indicate that neither attack was successful.[69]

The circle round the British Isles was completed by No 23 Group in the extreme northeast and No 4 Group in the southeast of England. Both groups lent them-

---

* In No 9 Group O.H. Bertrand and T. Derval, addresses unknown, I.W. Dunbar of Brandon, Man., H.M. Fletcher, address unknown, F.E. Fraser of Winnipeg, L.M. Lewis of Montreal, C.A. McConville of Kingston, Ont., and J.A. Shaw of Edmonton, flew with 252 Squadron, Prawle Point; H.E. Bourke of Winnipeg, and W.W. Brown of Montreal were with 236, Mullion; and C.R. Hoare, address unknown, was at 250, Padstow. With No 10 Group were J.W. Reid, and R.T. Steward, addresses unknown (KIA 13 Sept. 1918), and S.B. Wright of Perth, Ont., in 242 at Newhaven. L.G. Arcand of Montreal, R.S.S. Chaffe of Waterdown, Ont., and H.L. Tamplin, address unknown, flew with 255, Pembroke, part of No 14 Group. G.A. Coulter of Toronto and M. Furtney, address unknown, were in 258, Luce Bay, a No 22 Group squadron. With 253 Squadron at Newhaven were A.A. Forhan, J.A. Glen, and H. Gordon, all of Toronto, H.C. Hagaman of Oakfield, Ont., and H.A. Peck of Montreal, all of whom flew DH6s. On the same station were two Canadian observers, A.R. Beveridge, address unknown, and H.S. Quigley of Toronto.
† R.H. Berryman, address unknown, G. Moore of Montreal, A.R. Purchase, address unknown, and F. Van Praagh of Vancouver were pilots at Pembroke Airship Station; while J.G.G. Layton of Dundalk, Ont., was a pilot at Luce Bay Airship Station.

selves to 'offensive' operations, and were demonstrably favoured by the Admiralty in material allocations.

No 23 Group's job was to provide air patrols for the Northern Barrage. This great minefield, stretching between the Orkneys and the approaches to Hardanger Fjord in Norway, had been started in early March. It had been sown by the RN and the USN, with the Americans laying most of the mines. Its surface patrols, equipped with hydrophones, had been milked from the convoy organization. Since these patrols could not cover the whole of the barrage, the rest was placed under aerial surveillance from towed kite balloons and flying-boat patrols. Most of the twelve Canadians with this force flew from Houton Bay Station in the Orkneys; two were at Catfirth Station in the Shetlands.* The Admiralty gave the northern air patrol 'first priority' for aircraft, but got little co-operation from the Air Ministry. 'A great naval effort is being made during the summer months to attack enemy submarines passing Northabout, and it had been hoped to obtain considerable assistance from air patrols,' the Admiralty complained in July. 'Their Lordships have been much disappointed in this respect.' Ultimately the Air Ministry proved compliant, but its efforts came too late. The inshore convoy network was already forcing the U-boats into the Atlantic deeps west of Ireland. Moreover, as with the Otranto Barrage, U-boats do not appear to have had much difficulty in sneaking through the mine fields, whether by way of Norwegian territorial waters or through the Fair Isle passage.[70]

No 4 Group, embracing the former RNAS bases from East Anglia round to the Thames Estuary, was the largest and operationally the most active in Britain. Lieutenant-Colonel C.R. Samson commanded six squadrons of flying-boats (the largest such concentration in the service) at Felixstowe, as well as seaplanes, flying-boats, and aeroplanes at Westgate, Manston, Yarmouth, and Burgh Castle, the airship station at Pulham and the KB Section at Lowestoft. More Canadians were borne on the books of this command in 1918 than on those of any other group. Nearly half of them were pilots at Felixstowe, flying Large Americas.

Because submarines seldom ventured into the shoal waters off East Anglia, the convoy network was not extended below the Humber. No 4 Group's only involvement with convoys was to provide escort for the Anglo-Dutch 'beef trade.' Most of the aircrew of Samson's command were occupied in a constant routine of dawn-to-dusk patrolling. As we have already seen, much of the work of 228 Squadron, commanded by Leckie at Yarmouth,† and the flying-boat organization at Felixstowe, including 232 Squadron commanded by Major J.L. Gordon of St Lambert, PQ, was in contact with long-range special reconnaissance and offensive operations

---

* At Houton Bay were H.V. Acland, G.S. Black, T.G. Gordon, and J.D. Guild, addresses unknown, C. MacLaurin of Lachine, Que., A.B. Massey of Toronto, J.P. Pile, address unknown, W.B. Powell of Hamilton, and P.H. Take, address unknown. G.R. Hodgson of Montreal, and H.A. Wilson of Westmount, Que., served at Catfirth.

† Other Canadians who served in 228 Squadron included A.P. Bell of Belleville, Ont., W.H. Comstock of Brockville, Ont., F. Eppinger of Vancouver, V.S. Green, address unknown, L.W. Kidd of Listowel, Ont., G.E. Lewtas of Conston, BC, A.L. Rice of Edmundston, NB, E.D. Warren of Winnipeg (killed 5 Dec. 1918), and L.W. Wilson of Lakeville, NS.

in the Heligoland Bight.* Other seaplane units operated inshore, performing 'all the routine dirty work' including escorting single merchantmen, patrolling over the War Channel and minefields, responding to submarine alarms, and flying anti-zeppelin patrols.† The aeroplane pilots‡ in the command were part of the home defence organization, and were also used for such duties as anti-submarine patrols.[71]

The main anti-submarine work, however, remained with Groups 9, 10, 14, 18, and 22. After a few months' experience it was plain that the projected lane patrols were as ineffectual in safeguarding merchantmen as were the long-standing sea-plane patrols. Instead, most heavier-than-air craft, by July, had been incorporated in the steadily growing coastal convoy system, and provided constant air escort within the limitations of weather and light conditions. Over the last six months of the war a daily average anti-submarine strength of 189 aeroplanes, 300 seaplanes and flying boats, and 75 airships was maintained at Home Stations, and on average 310 of these were operational.§ During the year over seven thousand escort sorties were flown, nearly five thousand of them by heavier-than-air craft, and as well there were 131 kite balloon-escorted passages. Despite a steady increase in the number of vessels using the system, the already small loss rate in convoys was

---

* From available records it is difficult in most cases to determine whether a Canadian was flying on operations or was at Felixstowe for flying-boat training only. Squadrons are shown where known: G.B. Anderson of Ottawa, C.W. Bailey of Winnipeg, H.J. Bath of Oakville, Ont., L. Bennett of North Vancouver (230), W.G. Boyd of Hamilton, Ont., C.H. Browne of Toronto, C.J. Clayton (230) of Victoria, BC, W.H. Comstock of Brockville, Ont., A.R. Cotton, address unknown, S.D. Culley of Montreal, R.D. Delamere (231) and A.S. Downey, both of Toronto, J.O. Dufort of Ottawa, N.G. Fraser and J. Freeman, both of Toronto (POW 9 Nov. 1918), J.O. Galpin of Ottawa, J.L. Gordon (232) of St Lambert, Que., C.W. Gracey of Weston, Ont., F.E. Griffis of Toronto, J.D. Guild of Kenney, Man., T.D. Hallman of Toronto, H.H. Harvey of Avonport, NS, D.H. Hartness of Nanaimo, BC, G.R. Hodgson of Montreal, L.W. Kidd of Listowel, Ont., J.A.Y. La Forest of Hull, Que., J.W. Locke, address unknown, C. MacLaurin of Lachine, Que., E.L. Macleod of Atchelitz, BC, L.W. Marwick of Hamilton, Ont., C. McNicoll of Montreal, E. McC. Moir of Halifax, A.H. Munday of Toronto, A. Partridge (Tech), address unknown, A. Rankine of Montreal, P.H. Take, address unknown, J.C. Watson of Victoria, BC, L.E. Wells of Belleville, Ont., H.A. Wilson of Westmount, Que., W.E. White of Oshawa, Ont., and A. Woods of Elmira, Ont.

† Canadians in these units included Sydney Anderson and R.O. Cutler, both of Vancouver, G.R. Halliday of Victoria, M.J.P. Hennessy of Haileybury, Ont., and T.B. Simpson of London, Ont., at Yarmouth; and O.J. Dean of Regina, Sask., A.G. Hodgson of Nelson, BC, A.H. Pearce, address unknown, and R.S. Percival of Ottawa, at Westgate.

‡ In No 273 at Burgh Castle were J.N. Bicknell of Toronto, W.J. Carroll of Kingston, Ont., J.L. Killoran of Peterborough, Ont., and W.R. Waterman of Ottawa. At Yarmouth there were R.E. Cameron and S.D. Culley, both of Montreal, G.D. Kirkpatrick, E.R. Munday, and W.K. Prendergast, all of Toronto, and G.T. Scott, F.J. Vincent, and F.R. Walpole, addresses unknown, all in 212 Squadron. At Manston in 219 Squadron were R.O. Ellis of Toronto, D.M.B. Galbraith of Carleton Place, Ont., L.M. Lewis of Montreal, H.H. Reade of Ottawa, G.H.G. Smythe of Toronto, R.E. Sproule of Ottawa, J. Tomkins of Kingston, Ont., W.J. Windrum of Parry Sound, Ont., and L.E. Wood of Winnipeg.

§ By comparison, during the most critical periods of the Battle of the Atlantic, in February 1943, Coastal Command RAF mustered 118 flying-boats and 293 A/S aircraft based in the UK, Northern Ireland, Iceland, and Gibraltar, of which total 210 were operational. There is no comparison, of course, between the capabilities of aircraft in the two periods.

reduced by two-thirds in the period of aircraft participation. In the course of the six attacks on convoys with air escort in 1918, U-boats succeeded in sinking only three ships, two of them during the same attack. Merchantmen sailing alone continued to bear the brunt of the submarine onslaught.[72]

Air tactics in coastal convoy were simple. Airships accompanied convoys for all or most of their passage; heavier-than-air craft worked in relays as convoys passed along the coast. Normally airships worked close in to the convoy, while aeroplanes and seaplanes patrolled at its head, or, 'where two were available ... the second Seaplane should patrol on ... the most dangerous side ... and where three were present ... there should be one ahead and one on each beam.' The effect of these dispositions on U-boats was twofold. They were deprived of the advantage of surprise by the distant air escort ahead and forced to dive, thus curtailing their ability to manoeuvre for attack. Secondly, they gave away their exact position to the close escort as soon as a torpedo was fired. The contact records show how shy submarines were becoming of aircraft: in 1917 U-boats were spotted on 169 occasions and engaged 106 times; in 1918, with a flying effort three times as great, there were 192 sightings and 131 attacks.[73]

Air surveillance forced the U-boats to change tactics. Nearly two-thirds of attacks in the last stage of the war were made by lone surface boats at night, when air coverage was reduced to slow airships or kite balloons and submarines could best take advantage of their high speed and low silhouette. In addition, submarine commanders became highly skilled in taking avoiding action when under aerial attack. Their boats were later fitted with altiscopes that permitted them to scan the skies before surfacing. The U-boats also redirected their attention to ocean convoys outside the one- to two-hundred-mile range of aircraft based in the British Isles, while others moved across the Atlantic to the American and Canadian eastern seaboards.[74]

Many technical counter-measures were under investigation in Britain before the end of the war, but few had reached the operational stage. For example, seaplanes equipped with hydrophones had carried out trials in early 1917 in the smooth waters of the Aegean, and these trials were followed up the next year at Grain Experimental Depot.* A few hydrophones were fitted to operational aircraft but little use was made of them. Nevertheless, SSZ [Sea Scout Zero] airships at Mullion were regularly using, in late 1918, what might be described as the father of 'dunking sonar,' towed hydrophones, and the Admiralty had on order an improved set known as the 'Rubber Eel.' Aircraft needed an explosive suitably fused for dropping on submarines. Most bombs employed were much too light, while depth charges dropped from aeroplanes burst upon hitting the water. To illuminate surfaced submarines attacking at night, Scarlett proposed that aircraft carry a searchlight, along the lines of the Leigh Light used so successfully in conjunction with radar twenty-five years later. Various experiments were also carried

* At Grain, the Canadians serving were H.B. Brenton of Vancouver, L.L. Lindsay of Calgary, K.D. MacLeod of Ste-Anne-de-Bellevue, Que., A.B. Massey of Toronto, L.S.S. Punnett of Victoria, BC, and K.M. Smith of Toronto, all senior pilots; and H.O. Merriman of Hamilton, Ont., a technical and wireless expert.

out to develop mines that could be dropped from the air, but the technical difficulties proved too great.[75]

The role of aircraft in defeating the U-boat campaign in 1918 has frequently been overlooked. While it is true that, with one notable exception, aircraft failed to destroy submarines, they exercised, when employed as close and distant escorts to convoys, a most decisive effect – they rendered convoys virtually immune from successful attack. The effectiveness of air cover for convoys was not perceived at the time, because shipping losses remained fairly high to the last weeks of the war. On analysis, however, it becomes clear that these losses occurred mainly among single vessels steaming towards a convoy assembly port, heading away from a convoy dispersal point, or among stragglers from convoy. Even so, there were those who saw the value of air cover. The Rear-Admiral Commanding at Falmouth assigned the success of the French coal trade convoys, which lost fifty-three ships out of 39,352 or a loss rate of 0.14 per cent, to the air escort which rendered them safe from attack by day. The Vice-Admiral Commanding East Coast of England reported that attacks on convoys with aerial escort 'were becoming increasingly rare no matter how favourable ... the circumstances were. An attack on a convoy protected by a kite balloon never took place.'[76]

The success of the anti-submarine campaign was partly the result of the harnessing of aircraft to the convoy system. It was in no way attributable to the development of any high degree of collaboration between the Admiralty and the Air Ministry. The early promise of amicable relations had faded in little more than a month after the birth of the RAF. In May Geddes, the First Lord, told the Air Ministry that the Admiralty had accepted the extinction of the RNAS under protest, and that its fears 'are being confirmed as time goes on. The use of aircraft with the Navy is not developing as it should.' Quarrels between the two services punctuated the remainder of the year. Most of them centred upon the allocation of aircraft.[77]

One of the most acute clashes was over torpedo-carrying aircraft. Beatty had been promised a hundred Sopwith Cuckoos by the end of July and a supply of trained pilots to fly them a month later. Only three of the new aircraft had appeared at East Fortune by the beginning of August. Beatty, who wanted the Cuckoos to launch an attack upon the High Seas Fleet, exploded in anger to Wemyss. The latter agreed that 'the Air business is the very devil, and we are having a regular rumpus with the Air Ministry.' A few days later the Air Ministry sliced the navy's allocation for 1919 from 130 squadrons to ninety-five and, on the basis of a paper from Sykes, increased the quota of bombers at the expense of anti-submarine aircraft. Here was something much more serious than material shortages. Was it true that bombing was more important than the anti-submarine campaign? And was the Air Ministry the appropriate and competent body to decide such a question? Geddes declared that 'the responsibility for anti-submarine strategy must always rest with the Admiralty, and the Board could not accept reduction of its demands for aircraft on the grounds of disagreement or criticism by the Air Council in any detail of its submarine strategy.' In reply, Sykes simply asserted that the Air Council had every right 'to examine requirements and to advise on how aircraft should be employed.' Much more conciliatory, Weir managed to find a formula for adjusting the 1919 allocations that was satisfactory to both parties. But the questions raised by this clash had not been resolved, nor were they during much of the Second World War.[78]

Some of the navy's problems, however, could be laid at the door of the Admiralty itself. The delay in receiving torpedo-carrying aircraft had less to do with the Air Ministry's inefficiency than with the navy's own downgrading of the need for such aircraft. The Sopwith Cuckoos did not find a home until the carrier *Argus*, a flush-decked 'super-haystack' gaudily painted in blue and white, joined the fleet on 14 September 1918. Pilots for her had been under training at East Fortune, and on 1 October 185 Squadron of twenty Cuckoos was formed for service with her.* The crude arrester gear, consisting of wooden ramps and fore-and aft wires, gave some trouble initially. 'During my whole service afloat I never saw so many people in the sea as I did while I was in command of the *Argus*,' wrote H.H. Smith; 'but although many ... went overboard, not a single pilot was injured in any way.'[79]

Events almost gave the new squadron an opportunity against the High Seas Fleet. On 20 October all U-boats were called in, since one of the stipulations for negotiating an armistice was that no further attacks upon merchantmen take place. They were now available to act as an advanced scouting force for the High Seas Fleet. On 29 October, with Scheer's approval, Von Hipper issued orders for the entire fleet to raise steam for a sweep into the North Sea. This order brought disorder throughout the German fleet. The ships did not put to sea, and by 4 November all German naval ports were in the hands of mutineers.[80]

The first Canadians on maritime duties to see tangible results of the Armistice agreement were R.D. Delamere and Robert Leckie of No 4 Group, as they flew over a contingent of U-boats surrendering to the Harwich Force on 20 November. The next day the Grand Fleet, reinforced by ships from the French and American navies, steamed to meet the High Seas Fleet. Lindley B. Calnan, a young kite-balloon specialist from Picton, Ont., viewed the scene from *Ajax*: 'I was fortunate enough to be in the foretop ... and so was one of the first to see through the mist a balloon ... carried by our own light cruiser *Cardiff*. Following her the Huns were in "single line ahead." This conquered line steamed between our lines so that three miles on either hand they saw an escort more powerful than themselves ... we escorted them to a point off Inchkeith, where they anchored and were searched by us.'[81] At sunset the High Seas Fleet hauled down its colours for the last time.

The Royal Navy had achieved the ultimate objects of Admiralty policy. Its distant blockade had weakened the will of the enemy populace to resist, and the navy and its airmen had overcome all interference with allied use of the oceans. Faulty judgment and plain conservatism had affected adversely the naval use of air earlier in the war, but in 1918 senior officers had attained a more mature appreciation of the importance of air power. In September (at the request of the Air Ministry) the Admiralty had sent out a questionnaire to Commanders-in-Chief and Flag Officers Commanding, asking for their 1920 aircraft requirements. The replies were illumi-

---

* W.H. Mackenzie of Victoria, BC, was a senior instructor at East Fortune. Serving with No 185 were pilots H.J. Armstrong of Toronto, A.M. Avery of Delhi, Ont., G.H. Boyce of Ottawa, and I.M. Martin of Kingston, Ont.

nating: they included requests for long-range shore-based air escorts for convoys, merchant aircraft carriers, and escort convoys. They indicate that the navy had finally grasped that the most valuable work done by naval airmen in 1918 was in anti-submarine operations. This task, involving at least 215 Canadians, was anything but dramatic in nature, nor did it result in a heavy toll being taken of submarines. Yet the defeat of the submarines owed much to aircraft, and that defeat meant that enough merchantmen were able to deliver their cargoes.

The measures recommended in 1919 were all eventually adopted during the Second World War; the 1918 questionnaire itself, however, was never acted upon and faded quickly from official memory. The myth that anti-submarine aircraft were involved hardly at all in the battle against German U-boats was created by their rapid and complete disappearance from air force lists soon after the Armistice. When RAF Coastal Command later came into existence, its roles were defined as co-operation with Bomber Command in the main strategic offensive and co-operation with naval forces, in that order. At the same time, naval planners downgraded convoy to the status of a 'defensive' measure in the postwar era. No complete British record of anti-submarine air and sea operations in the First World War was written. The official air history had many gaps, while that of the navy could well be an account of an earlier 'Great' war for all the mention it makes of aviation. Most of the lessons in anti-submarine warfare would have to be re-learnt the hard way over the wastes of the North Atlantic two decades later.[82]

PART THREE
Strategic Airpower

This crater in a London street was the result of an early zeppelin raid. (LC 56)

The wreckage of L 31, at Potter's Bar, London, on 2 Oct. 1916 (AH 466)

On her first raid L 48 fell to the guns of Torontonian L.P. Watkins on 17 June 1917. Among the fourteen victims was *Korvettenkapitän* Viktor Scheutze, the chief of the German Naval Airship Division. (Q 58467)

Lt Wulstan J. Tempest, of Perdue, Sask., who shot down the L 31. Tempest won the DSO for his night's work and he later won an MC on bomber operations. (RE 21004)

2/Lt L.P. Watkins of Toronto who shot down L 48. Three of the crew of 17 survived. Watkins, who was awarded an MC for his feat, died of wounds received on the Western Front in July 1918. (AH 604)

The Gotha G-V had an additional pair of wheels under the nose, to ease the stress of landing, and a 'tunnel' through the fuselage which permitted the rear gunner to fire downwards as well as laterally and upwards. (PMR 72-526)

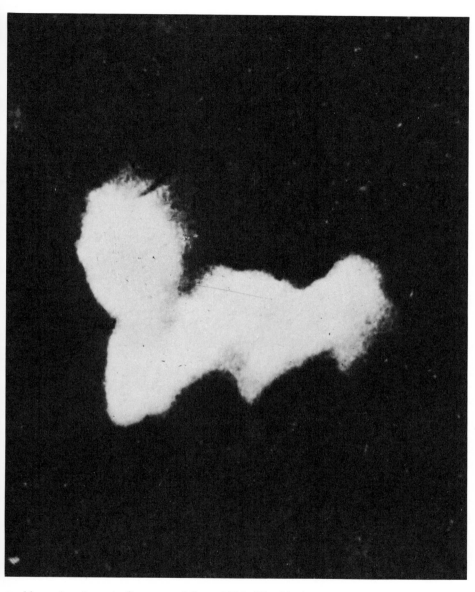

SL 11 coming down in flames on 2 Sept. 1916. 'The blazing mass radiated a red-yellow light and illuminated the area over a wide radius and fell slowly,' reported the commander of another zeppelin who watched the incident. There were no survivors. (Q 68200)

Gotha G-IVs of *Kagohl 3*, later known as the *Englandgeschwader*, lined up on one of the squadron's three airfields near Ghent in Belgium, in the spring of 1917. (Q 108845)

An awed crowd of German officers and men inspect one of *Kagohl 3*'s new Gotha bombers, 1917. (Q 108838)

Hauptmann Ernst Brandenburg, the 35-year-old commander of the *England-geschwader*. At his throat hangs the eight-pointed blue and gold cross of the Pour le Mérite, Germany's highest decoration for valour, awarded him after the first Gotha raid on London, 13 June 1917. (Q 108840)

Officers of the *Englandgeschwader* (and their lady friends) on the terrace of the Chateau-Drory in the spring of 1917 (Q 109948)

The wreckage of a Gotha bomber shot down over Manston, Kent, in August 1917
(PMR 70-104(e))

A London bus which was damaged in the vicinity of Liverpool St railway station. It was
probably a victim of the first raid by the Gothas of the *Englandgeschwader*, on 13 June
1917. (Q 70238)

London firemen hose down a bombed building after a German bomber raid. (HO 77)

A German air gunner in the forward cockpit of a Gotha bomber, holding an oxygen tube in his mouth. (Q 73550)

Airmen and groundcrew pose in front of a Gotha bomber.

A balloon apron used for the defence of London, 1917–18. At least two of the 'R' bombers ran into similar aprons but on each occasion the bomber was damaged but not brought down. (Q 61156)

Canadian nurses picking up souvenirs from the German Gotha which was brought down in flames over the Pas de Calais at Mingoval, 1 June 1918. (CO 2741)

A Fokker *Eindekker* single-seat fighter parked under the wing of a Staaken R-VI. Only six 'R' machines were ever used against England and no more than two ever bombed English targets on one night. (*Archiv für Fluggeschichte*)

One way to keep fighter aircraft at height in readiness to attempt interceptions of enemy bombers was to suspend them from airships. In a 1918 experiment this Sopwith Camel was slung beneath the R33. (AH 198)

Soldiers search through the debris of the Royal Hospital, Chelsea, hit by the first 1000-kg (2200-lb) bomb to be dropped on Britain, on the night of 16/17 Feb. 1918. (CO 3922)

The largest operational aircraft of the First World War, the Staaken R-VI, could deliver a 1000-kg bomb against English targets.

The zeppelin shed at Tondern burning after the July 1918 attack by six Sopwith Camels – one flown by F/L Stephen Dawson of St John, NB – from HMS *Furious* which destroyed L 54 and L 60. Dawson was one of the four pilots who landed in Denmark after the raid; he was killed in action on 10 August. (Q 47941)

L 70 was destroyed by Maj. Egbert Cadbury and Capt. Robert Leckie on the night of 5 Aug. 1918. (Q 58479)

A Sopwith Camel modified for night-fighting. Pilots using standard Camels found that the muzzle-flashes from the twin Vickers guns mounted over the engine cowling, directly in front of the pilot, 'blinded' them. (RE 64-1186)

Pilots of 44 (Home Defence) Squadron which pioneered the use of single-seat night fighters, pictured in front of one of the squadron's Sopwith Camels in the winter of 1917/18. Squatting, second from right in the front row, is Capt. A.E. Godfrey, MC, of Vancouver. (RE 21010-1)

The Sopwith 1½ Strutters of 3 (Naval) Wing, RNAS – single-seat bomber and two-seat fighter variants – lined up at Ochey, ready for a raid. (PMR 73-531)

Officers of 3 (Naval) Wing at Luxeuil-les-Bains in late 1916. Seated in the centre are Wing Capt. W.L. Elder and Wing Commander R. Bell-Davies, VC. All of the officers around them are Canadians, with three exceptions. (RE 19562)

This picture of the instrument panel of the Sopwith 1½ Strutter flown by F/S/L R.F. Redpath of Montreal on the Oberndorff raid of October 1916 shows how limited were his aids to night navigation. The only relevant instruments are a compass, clock, and altimeter. (RE 20962)

Ottawan F/S/L Charles Butterworth's Sopwith 1½ Strutter bomber in German hands on Freiburg airfield after the Oberndorff raid of 12 Oct. 1916. (RE 64-1498)

'Here enemy airmen can see you – transport should not halt here' (Q 65529)

Two members of 3 (Naval) Wing at Luxeuil-les-Bains, 1916. On the left F/S/L Lord Tiverton, who would become a devoted advocate of 'terror bombing' as an Air Staff officer in 1918. (PMR 73-518)

Bomb damage inflicted on a hangar and a German aircraft near Ghent 1917 (Q 109949)

Maj.-Gen. Hugh Trenchard in 1918
(PMR 80-270)

Handley Page 0/100 bombers at one of the Dunkirk airfields, 20 April 1918 (AH 553)

FE 2b night bombers of 149 Squadron newly arrived in France, 1 June 1918 (Q 11552)

Air mechanics working on a Handley Page 0/400 bomber (Q 23610)

Bombing up an FE2b of 149 Squadron in preparation for a night raid. This picture was taken on 1 July 1918 when at least six Canadians were flying with the squadron. (AH 436)

Officers of 207 Sqdn RAF, a unit of Trenchard's Independent Force, photographed August 1918. This group illustrates the great variety of RNAS, RFC, and RAF uniforms in vogue at the time. Seated, hatless in flying boots, is Captain Gordon Flavelle of Lindsay, Ont. (Q 12103)

A Handley Page 0/400 bomber of the Independent Force at Ligescourt, France, 29 Aug. 1918. The device below the Lewis gun in the nose is a bomb-sight: held by a safety strap the observer leaned out from his cockpit to use it. (AH 437)

On the night of 28/29 Sept. 1918 bombers of the RAF's Independent Force dropped seventeen tons of bombs on Thourout railway junction. Some buildings (on the right) were still burning when this picture was taken. (Q 60301)

A prototype V1500 Handley Page bomber photographed in November 1918 (PMR 71-401)

Another view of a Handley Page V1500 bomber (AH 502)

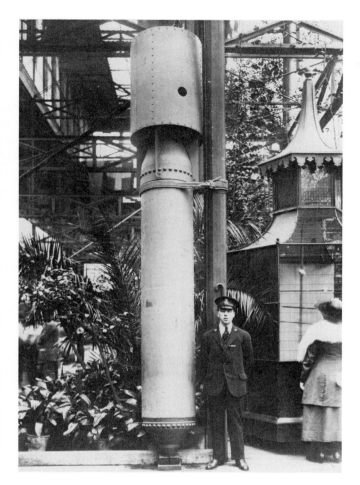

This 3300-lb 'blockbuster' was designed to be carried by the Handley Page v1500. The war ended before the v1500s became operational and the bomb was never used. (AH 455)

The officers and men of the Independent Force's No 27 Group, under the command of Col. R.H. Mulock of Winnipeg (inset), line up in front of a Handley Page v1500 bomber at Birchall Newton. (RE 204-31)

Corporal R.H. Mulock of Winnipeg, seen here serving with the Canadian Field Artillery on Salisbury Plain in late 1914, would become Canada's top-ranking operational airman and the RAF's leading bomber commander in 1918. (PMR 71-389)

Col. R.H. Mulock of Winnipeg (sitting) with Maj. J.W.K. Allsop, his British chief of staff in No 27 Group, photographed at the end of the war when they were training to raid Berlin with Handley Page v1500s. (PMR 71-406)

Introduction

The idea of 'victory through airpower,' usually attributed to such interwar theo-rists as the Italian general Giulio Douhet, was in fact born during the 1914–18 struggle. Indeed, at the very inception of the air age the notion of using flying machines as platforms from which to bomb an enemy nation-state into submission had quickly taken hold. In the hands of a brilliant fantasist like H.G. Wells the idea had been developed so tellingly that it affected the social psychology of the era, but the gulf between Wells' imaginary armadas of the air and the actual state of avia-tion technology was enormous. It was hardly surprising that no military staff gave serious attention to the subject before 1914. From the first days of manned flight the idea of strategic bombing had been discussed, luridly by some, apprehensively by others, and professionally by a few. All, however, wrote about it as an inevitable consequence of the harnessing of the flying machine to war. So rapidly did the air weapon evolve that by late 1914 the first long-distance raids had taken place. By the end of the war the use of aircraft to achieve strategic goals had become settled policy for all major belligerents. Within eighteen months of the outbreak of war the British, French, and Germans had all espoused forms of strategic bombing; and before the war was over some strategic thinkers, horrified by the catastrophic battles of attrition on the Western Front, went so far as to propose strategic bomb-ing as an alternative war-winning strategy.

The term 'strategic bombing' was used no more precisely during the First World War than it has been subsequently. Often, any bombing at some distance from the fighting fronts was called 'strategic,' as if distance alone was the determining char-acteristic. Conversely, some theorists of airpower wished to confine the use of the term to that form of bombing intended, by itself, to bring victory. Although this view has the virtue of clarity, it is a considerable over-simplification, as the authors of the British official history of strategic bombing in the Second World War have pointed out. In their analysis, one that depends heavily upon the much more extensive experience of bombing operations upon which they were able to draw, there are three ways in which the term may appropriately be used.

The first use is that directly connected with the operations of land and sea forces. Almost from the beginning of the First World War air bombing was used tactically to strike at ammunition dumps, troop concentrations, lines of communication, and shipping. But when aircraft came to be used to attack not ammunition dumps but ammunition factories, not ships but shipyards, they were then being employed strategically – that is, they were contributing to the strategic objectives of the armies and navies of which they were an extension. The air battle, however, can be thought of as distinct from the land and sea battles, as the separate struggle of air forces with its own distinct tactical and strategic levels. A second form of strategic bombing, therefore, is that concerned with attacks on the resources upon which enemy air strength is based. Strategic bombing in this sense was unknown during the First World War.

The third and ultimate dimension of strategic airpower is that in which bombing is conceived as the primary means of achieving victory. The advocates of strategic bombing in this sense have always rested their case upon the speed, range, and flexibility of the air weapon, its allegedly relative invulnerability to defensive measures, and the accuracy and destructive power with which high explosive and incendiary bombs could be dropped upon their targets. In more recent times the introduction of nuclear bombs has notably strengthened their case. By devastating blows at vital political centres, key industries, and, above all, the will of the enemy nation, the independent bombing force – or so its supporters have contended – can smash or fatally weaken an enemy's capacity to continue the fight.

The belief was strong among many proponents of the air weapon during the First World War that this last kind of bombing was the proper role of air forces. It was a belief without much relationship to technological reality. From early 1915 the Germans waged a strategic air offensive against the British homeland, first by night-raiding zeppelins of the German army and the Naval Airship Division and then, in 1917–18, with multi-engined aeroplanes. Enthusiastic German airmen hoped to achieve spectacular and even decisive results, but their high command never sought or expected more than the diversion of some British air and ground strength to the task of defence. The use of the air weapon in this manner had the strategic aim of assisting the ground forces in the main battle, and within that limit certainly enjoyed some success.

The British involvement in strategic bombing was pioneered by the Royal Naval Air Service, as has been shown in Part Two, 'Admiralty and the Air.' It was natural for the navy to think strategically about airpower and how it might be deployed with maximum flexibility; such modes of thought were almost conventional in a service historically charged with world-embracing duties. The RNAS, however, did not always subordinate bombing to the strategic aims of the navy. The attacks against German industry conducted from French bases in 1916–17 by 3 Wing RNAS, though ostensibly designed to damage industries producing material for the war at sea, were often launched against targets based upon French command priorities that had little or no relation to the war at sea.

The production of aircraft and engines for bombing purposes by the RNAS and the mounting of bombing offensives against Germany from Luxeuil and Dunkirk caused a series of ruptures between the naval air service and the Royal Flying Corps. This inter-service friction, combined with public demands for retaliation for the German raids upon England and the vision held out by airpower proponents of victory through bombing rather than the attrition-battle on the Western Front, brought about the amalgamation of the RFC and the RNAS into the Royal

Air Force and the creation of a special formation of the RAF called the Independent Air Force. The impossible task assigned to the IAF was to bomb Germany into submission by obliterating its war industries and by breaking the enemy's will to fight.

To a remarkable degree Canadians were linked with the beginnings of the strategic use of airpower during the First World War. Though relatively few in numbers, they contributed more than their share of victories to the battle against German zeppelins, a battle which saw the evolution of the first systematic defence against bombing attack. There were many Canadians with the RNAS at Dunkirk; 3 Wing at Luxeuil was mainly Canadian in composition; and in the sustained bombing offensive against Germany carried out by the Independent Air Force in 1918 Canadians served in significant numbers.

9

The Air Defence of Britain

The history of German air raids on England and Scotland during the First World War is a classic example of the achievement of significant military results through the use of relatively insignificant forces. The raids caused neither heavy civilian casualties nor important damage, yet so powerful was the public demand for stronger air defences that the politicians yielded, and substantial air and ground forces were withheld from the fighting fronts. But the German raids had other less calculable consequences. Adverse public criticism of the flying services, not all of it ill-informed, led to technological and tactical improvements in defensive methods of long-term importance. Moreover, the demand by public and politicians alike for retaliation against German raiding was a direct cause of the creation of the Royal Air Force, conceived as an instrument for independent strategic bombing.

The rigid airship, pioneered by Count Ferdinand von Zeppelin, was the chief weapon employed against Britain until mid-1917. Before the war the airship's potential as a bombing vehicle was hardly considered. Both naval and army airships were regarded as scouting weapons; the German Naval Airship Division, which was to carry out most of the raids against Britain, received no bombs until October 1914.[1] Yet the popular press held out to the German people exaggerated hopes for the destruction of England from the air, and senior military authorities were not exempt from such illusions. In late August 1914 *Konteradmiral* Paul Behncke, Deputy Chief of the Naval Staff, proposed airship raids on the London docks and the Admiralty; he believed that the resultant panic would possibly 'render it doubtful that the war can be continued.' The Army Chief of Staff, *General* von Falkenhayn, also requested permission to use military airships against Britain. The 'very serious scruples' of the Kaiser against bombing gave way on 10 January 1915, when he approved the bombing of docks and military establishments along the English coast and on the lower Thames.[2] Following the first raid of 19–20 January, greeted enthusiastically in the German press, the imperial scruples were further diminished. On 12 February 1915 an imperial order was issued:

1. His Majesty the Kaiser has expressed great hopes that the air war against England will be carried out with the greatest energy.

2. His Majesty has designated as attack targets: war material of every kind, military establishments, barracks, and also oil and petroleum tanks and the London docks. No attack is to
be made on the residential areas of London, or above all on royal palaces.[3]

Such precise targetting instructions reflected the unbounded optimism then existing in German military circles, for almost unfailing inaccuracy was the chief characteristic of all high-level bombing during the First World War.

The terms of reference for the German Naval Airship Division, which remained
in force for the rest of the war, were laid down by the Commander of the High
Seas Fleet in June 1915. Fleet co-operation and reconnaissance were the division's
main functions, but 'operations of the airships against enemy territory from the
North Sea airship bases'* were also included. Though the establishment of the
division was fixed at eighteen airships, there were only seven fit for service in early
1915. The largest, L 9,[†] had a trial speed of slightly more than 50 mph and a useful
lift of about 25,000 pounds.[‡] In May L 10, the first of a new series, was delivered
to Nordholz. A larger and faster type, she had a volume of 1,126,400 cubic feet, a
useful lift of 35,000 pounds, a trial speed of almost 58 mph, and an overall length
of 536 feet. L 10 could operate up to a ceiling of 11,000 feet.[4]

It should be borne in mind that performance figures for airships, especially
those for ceiling and lift, vary considerably with air temperature and barometric
pressure. The static lift from the hydrogen-filled gas cells was higher in cool air and
in periods of high pressure because of the greater weight of the air displaced.
Airship raids, therefore, normally took place during the colder months of the year.

In the course of the twenty airship raids during 1915, 208 persons were killed
and 532 injured. The total damage was estimated to be over £800,000, much of it
the work of L 13, commanded by *Kapitänleutnant* Heinrich Mathy, on the night of
8–9 September, when incendiaries had started fires in the warehouse district of
London. The air defences had been unable to down a single airship; in fact, during
the whole year only two pilots had intercepted zeppelins in the course of a raid.
Night-landing accidents had taken the lives of three pilots and fifteen aircraft had
been wrecked or damaged.[5]

Home defence was a responsibility neither flying service wanted. By September
1915 the Admiralty had secured from the War Office agreement in principle for
the transfer of this unwelcome burden from the RNAS to the RFC. Kitchener was
deeply reluctant to accept this task for the RFC when 'the army had no aircraft to

---

* The main naval airship bases were at Tondern, near the Danish border, Fuhlsbüttel, Nordholz,
  Wittmundhaven, Hage, and Ahlhorn, near Oldenburg. All except the last named were on or
  near the North Sea coast.
† German rigid airships came from both the Zeppelin and Schütte-Lanz works, the Shchütte-Lanz
  airship using plywood rather than aluminum in its interior structure. Naval zeppelins were designated L (*Luftschiff*) and were numbered consecutively in order of receipt from the builder. Army
  zeppelins were designated LZ (*Luftschiff Zeppelin*); they were numbered by adding '30' to the
  builder's number. Schütte-Lanz airships were designated SL plus the builder's number by both
  services.
‡ Useful lift meant the load (crew, stores, ballast, fuel, armament, and bombs) that could be
  carried in addition to such fixed weights as the structure, engines, and gondolas.

spare, while more calls were being made for aircraft in France,' and when anti-aircraft guns were in limited supply.[6] The responsibility for this unwanted child finally passed to the RFC as a result of a decision of the Cabinet War Committee in February 1916. The two services were to co-operate thus:

(a) The Navy to undertake to deal with all hostile aircraft attempting to reach this country, whilst the Army undertake to deal with all such aircraft which reach these shores.

(b) All defence arrangements on land to be undertaken by the Army which will also provide the aeroplanes required to work with the Home Defence troops and to protect garrisons and vulnerable areas, and the Flying Stations required to enable their aircraft to undertake these duties.

(c) The Navy to provide the aircraft required to co-operate with and assist their Fleets and Coast Patrol Flotillas and to watch the Coast, and to organise and maintain such Flying Stations as are required to enable their aircraft to undertake these duties.[7]

This arrangement was not to change, but the artificial 'high water mark' between the responsibilities of the RNAS and those of the RFC could only work well if the two services, and their parent organizations, collaborated closely on such matters as air intelligence and interception tactics. Frequently that was not the case.

The RNAS and the RFC were in disagreement, for example, on the fundamental matter of the place of the aeroplane in defence against airships. The RNAS agreed with a September 1915 report of the Board of Invention and Research which had concluded that night-flying against airships was not only 'ineffective' but costly and dangerous; this judgment reinforced the Admiralty's assessment of the Paris defence system, to the effect that guns, searchlights, and ground observers were the key elements. Sir David Henderson, at a home defence conference with Admiralty representatives on 10 November, was told that 'so far experience had shown that aeroplanes were not at the present time of much use for the defence of a city like London, and therefore no elaborate scheme had been drawn up on the subject.' After the transfer of home defence responsibilities in early 1916, the RNAS curtailed night-flying operations and posted a number of experienced night pilots overseas, a course unanimously recommended by east-coast station commanders.[8] At that time Rear-Admiral Vaughan-Lee, the Director of the Air Service, summed up the position of the RNAS in an internal memorandum: 'Not much importance is attached to flying at night against Zeppelins. It is considered that everything that can possibly be done to meet the Zeppelin should be carried out so long as undue risks to personnel and materiel are not incurred. Moreover, as the Military are undertaking this work on a large scale, it is considered that for public opinion alone the Navy should do a certain amount.'[9] In the light of this succinctly expressed position, it is not surprising that the War Office had already concluded that 'we must be self-supporting.'[10]

The RFC had drawn quite different conclusions from the report of the Board of Invention and Research and from its own experience. The board had recommended that the effectiveness of night-flying aeroplanes should be increased: 'it must be assumed that night flying for war purposes is necessary,' not only because of zeppelins but because 'in the present state of development of aeronautical engineering, the raiding of England by large aeroplanes at night is possible, and it would be imprudent to ignore the fact that it is likely to become a reality within a few months.' RFC planning, tested experimentally during the raid of 13–14 October 1915, was based upon the assumption that defence against the airship called for the co-ordinated use of searchlights, guns, ground observer cordons, and information about zeppelin movements derived from directional wireless equipment, and that the aeroplane was an essential part of this system. Aeroplanes, it was considered, should be stationed in the immediate vicinity of vulnerable areas.[11]

A considerable gap existed between planning and available means in early 1916. Twenty BE2cs, dispersed at ten airfields around London, were the RFC's immediate answer to the German airships. These aircraft were armed with four small bombs and Ranken darts.* These weapons could only be used by getting above an attacking airship; therefore two-hour standing patrols, at heights up to 10,000 feet, were laid on. At first no RFC airfield sent more than a single aircraft aloft at any one time to carry out these patrols.

Before the RFC had an opportunity to augment its home defence force the German airships began their 1916 campaign. On 18 January *Vizeadmiral* Reinhold Scheer, the new commander of the High Seas Fleet, had approved a plan for diversified raids on the United Kingdom drawn up by *Fregattenkapitän* Peter Strasser, the chief of the Naval Airship Division. Strasser specified three attack zones: England North, from the Tyne to Edinburgh; England Middle, from the Humber to the Tyne; and England South, in which London was the prime target. On 31 January nine airships raided the Midlands. The few aeroplanes that were sent up saw nothing and several crash-landed. Difficulty with the new Maybach 240-hp engines probably caused the loss of L 19, which came down in the North Sea. Much controversy resulted from the action of a fishing trawler, the *King Stephen*, whose captain left the L 19's crew to drown because he feared that if they were taken aboard he and his men would be overpowered. The Bishop of London condoned this action because the Germans had bombed innocent civilians; to the *Frankfurter Zeitung* the bishop was a 'jingoistic hatemonger.'[12]

The bishop's statement was representative of the anger and consternation aroused by the raid – and by the inadequacy of the defences. A week after the raid the Midlands was still 'suffering from shock'; men were refusing to work night shifts and munitions production had dropped. Demands for reprisals on German cities, voiced in Parliament by such members as William Joynson-Hicks, gripped the public mind, though the Convocation of Canterbury denounced retaliation as immoral and barbarous. The Bishop of Bangor, the convocation's only dissenter, believing that all citizens were now combatants, argued that if a hundred aeroplanes 'dropped bombs all over the rich business part of Frankfurt,' zeppelin raids would cease immediately. C.G. Grey, the fire-eating editor of *The Aeroplane*, congratulated the bishop on 'his intellectual honesty and freedom from cant.'[13]

---

* Two 16-lb incendiaries and two 20-lb Hales high-explosive bombs were provided. The Ranken dart was equipped with tail vanes designed to spread on release, so that the dart, when it penetrated the envelope of an airship, would be held long enough for the charge in the head to detonate inside. The darts were carried in containers of twenty-four.

The most powerful advocates for a policy of retaliation were to be found within the Admiralty. Towards the end of the first raiding period of 1916, Vaughan-Lee submitted a memorandum in which he argued that the best response was 'an organised and systematic attack on the German at home,' which, somehow, would reduce zeppelin activities and at the same time have 'an immense moral effect on Germany itself.' He proposed that 'a definite policy of Retaliation be laid down and carried into effect without any further delay,' that French bases for long-range operations be obtained with the co-operation of that government, and that pilots, '*if necessary ... taken from the defence stations on the Coast,*' be trained for this work.[14] Vaughan-Lee's memorandum set in train a bombing offensive of 3 Naval Wing from Luxeuil and Ochey, an offensive that, in part at least, derived from the unhappy experience of the RNAS with home defence and the belief that the best reply to the airship was to employ the aeroplane as an offensive weapon.

Meanwhile, the defences had claimed a victim, though not before a raid on 5–6 March had set off rioting in Hull and caused the mobbing of an RFC officer in nearby Beverley. On 31 March six airships crossed the English coast at or close to the naval airfields at Felixstowe and Great Yarmouth. Not an aeroplane stirred because of a communication breakdown. Though London was the target, five of the airship commanders decided that the air temperature was too high to allow the bombing of the capital from a sufficiently safe altitude. Only L 15 pressed on, to be caught by the searchlights, attacked by an RFC pilot who dropped his Ranken darts with no apparent effect, and finally to come down off the mouth of the Thames as a result of anti-aircraft fire.[15]

London's defences were becoming more formidable, but progress elsewhere was slow. On the night of 1 April L 11 worked its way down the east coast without opposition, bombing Sunderland and Middlesbrough. Flight Sub-Lieutenant Grant Gooderham of Toronto, flying from Whitley Bay, was one of those sent out to intercept the zeppelin. Having no specific information on L 11's flight path or height, Gooderham flew down the coast at 8000 feet, just a few minutes, had he known it, behind the zeppelin, but he saw nothing. Similar frustration attended the work of pilots during further raids on northern England and Scotland on 2 and 24 April and 2 May.[16] Most naval air stations, however, generally attempted to combine normal scouting activities with anti-zeppelin patrols, as a report from RNAS Scarborough illustrates: 'During fine weather, machines are carrying out special flights to Flambro Hd [sic] leaving at dusk and returning after dark. Seven flights have been made, machines arriving over the Hd at heights from 3000 ft. to 5000 ft. Nothing has been seen of hostile aircraft, but from reports received, one machine missed a Zeppelin by 10 Mins. If these patrols can be kept up it is quite possible one may be caught, but more machines and Pilots are urgently required.'[17] Chance encounters were always possible, but patrols by the clock, flown at low altitudes, ending at an hour when zeppelin activity normally was beginning and bearing no relation to intelligence reports of airship movements, showed that little had been done to co-ordinate the work of the two air services in home defence.

During this first raiding period of 1916 most Canadians concerned with home defence were to be found on RNAS stations. Many of them were at Dover and Felixstowe; others were scattered from Dundee to the south coast. Most of their

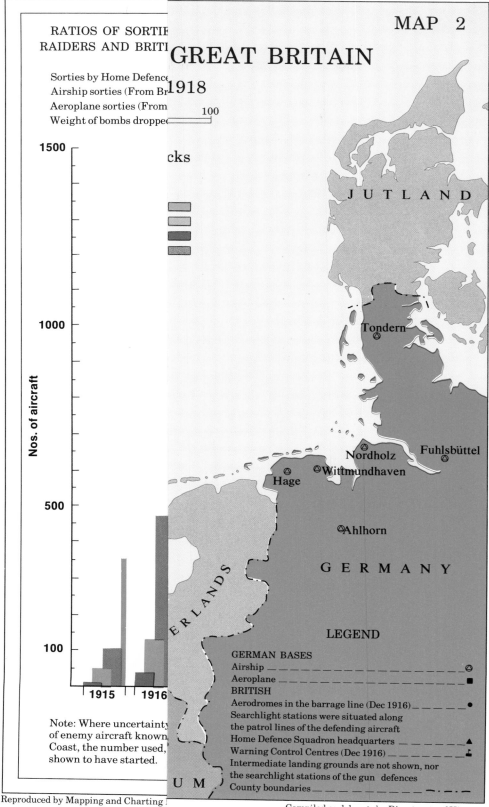

RATIOS OF SORTIE[...]
RAIDERS AND BRIT[...]

Sorties by Home Defence[...]
Airship sorties (From Br[...]
Aeroplane sorties (From [...]
Weight of bombs dropped[...]

100

1500

Nos. of aircraft

1000

500

100

1915   1916

Note: Where uncertainty[...]
of enemy aircraft known[...]
Coast, the number used, [...]
shown to have started.

MAP 2

GREAT BRITAIN

1918

JUTLAND

Tondern

Nordholz   Fuhlsbüttel
Wittmundhaven
Hage

Ahlhorn

GERMANY

ERLANDS

U M

LEGEND

GERMAN BASES
Airship _
Aeroplane _ _ _ _ _ _ _ _ _ _ _ _ _ _ _ _ _ _
BRITISH
Aerodromes in the barrage line (Dec 1916) _ _ _ _ _ •
Searchlight stations were situated along
the patrol lines of the defending aircraft
Home Defence Squadron headquarters _ _ _ _ _ ▲
Warning Control Centres (Dec 1916) _ _ _ _ _ _
Intermediate landing grounds are not shown, nor
the searchlight stations of the gun defences
County boundaries _ _ _ _ _ _ _ _ _ _

flying time was taken up with other duties and it was only rarely that they joined in the hunt for zeppelins. Six Canadians, all with 33 Squadron, were on the RFC's home defence establishment in the same period.*

In May and June the Air Board's review of recent home defence operations enumerated a number of continuing weaknesses making clear the fact that neither air service had given a high priority to the function. The RFC, which had earlier estimated that it needed 138 machines for home defence, could muster only seventy-five and lacked the pilots to fly those; and the squadrons allocated to home defence were still seen as part of the corps' training organization. General Henderson, once a believer in the value of aeroplanes against zeppelins, now thought their usefulness at night was 'somewhat problematical,' and preferred to regard home defence aircraft as a reserve to be transferred to France on short notice if required. Lord Curzon offered the judgment that 'home Aerial Defence rested more on guns than on Aeroplanes' and concurred in General Henderson's view 'on the understanding, however, that the transfer proposed should only be made in case of emergency.'[18]

Significant improvements in the strength, organization, and methods of the RFC were nevertheless made, partly through the initiative of Brigadier-General W. Sefton Brancker, the Director of Air Organization. Brancker had already taken issue with Henderson's views before the Air Board; he now took the lead in organizing a War Office conference to revise the RFC's strategic approach to home defence in the light of recent experience. The new defence system evolved after this conference discarded the principle of static protection of likely targets, although these continued to be shielded by belts of anti-aircraft guns. Instead of stationing squadrons close to target areas (some of them in the west of England), a 'barrage line' of aeroplanes and searchlights was to be built up along the east and southeast coast to intercept raiders on their arrival and upon their outbound flight as well. Although the line was never quite completed, it remained a fundamental principle of defence for the remainder of the war. As of 14 July home defence squadrons were detached from the training organization and reconstituted as an operational wing under the command of Lieutenant-Colonel F.V. Holt, with headquarters in Adastral House, London. By the end of the year eleven squadrons had been formed, each with two or three flights dispersed to cover the squadron's patrol responsibilities along the barrage line, and guns, lights, and aeroplanes were tied in with the communications network the RFC had slowly built up since February. England and Scotland were divided into warning control areas, each subdivided into warning districts thirty to thirty-five miles square. Since a zeppelin took about thirty minutes to cross a district, it became possible to institute a graduated series of alerts, instead of the blanket warnings issued previously, which had considerably disrupted munitions production.[19]

Important as these innovations were, the most significant development was the adoption by the RFC in June and July of new types of ammunition designed

---

* J.S. Beatty of Toronto, J.B. Brophy of Ottawa (WIA 8 Aug. 1916), C.J. Creery of Vancouver (KIA 20 Oct. 1916), the brothers E.J. and L.P. Watkins of Toronto (the latter KIA 1 July 1918), and F.H. Whiteman of Kitchener, Ont.

specifically for use against airships and balloons and forbidden for use against any other targets. The Buckingham bullet was a combination of tracer and incendiary; the Brock and Pomeroy types combined explosive and incendiary qualities. The three were usually mixed with standard ammunition and fired by means of a Bowden cable from a Lewis gun mounted on the top plane. The useless armament of bombs and darts could now be discarded; airships could be attacked from below. A technological turning-point had been reached in the struggle against the night raiders.[20]

Meanwhile the German Naval Airship Division and its army counterpart were preparing for a resumption of the offensive in a spirit of confidence. Strasser, ever optimistic, wrote to *Admiral* Scheer on 10 August:

The performance of the big airships has reinforced my conviction that England can be overcome by means of airships, inasmuch as the country will be deprived of the means of existence through increasingly extensive destruction of cities, factory complexes, dockyards, harbour works with war and merchant ships lying therein, railroads, etc. ...

I am well aware of the generally prevailing personnel problems, but believe that the personnel must be made available, if necessary through reduction in other areas, since the airships offer a certain means of victoriously ending the war.[21]

Strasser's new airships were those of the L 30 type, received at Nordholz in May. These giants had a gas volume of nearly 2,000,000 cubic feet; their six engines drove them at 62 mph. With a useful lift of over 60,000 pounds, they could carry five tons of bombs. Yet the new type did not add greatly to the problems of the defence, since the L 30 was little faster than earlier types and its operational ceiling was about the same.[22]

In a series of raids in late July and early August the airships probed the region between the Thames and The Wash and then on 8–9 August shifted their attention to northern England. Once more, there was strong public criticism of the flying services.* It redoubled when Heinrich Mathy, commanding L 31, penetrated the London defences on 24–25 August, causing substantial damage. Now Strasser determined to make a major effort. On 2–3 September he launched the largest airship raid of the war. Sixteen raiders took part, including four from the army. The target was London, but the only airship to reach the city was SL 11 commanded by *Hauptmann* Schramm. Subsequently his course intersected with that of a BE2c flown by a young British pilot, Second Lieutenant William Leefe Robinson, who had been guided by searchlights which had picked up the airship. Attacking

---

* Major J.L. Baird, MP, the Air Board's spokesman in the House of Commons, told RNAS representatives at a meeting of the board that 'justifiable ground for complaint' existed. Subsequent staff conferences within the Admiralty showed, among other things, that the RNAS had rejected the new ammunition, still regarded night flying in 'high performance' aircraft as dangerous for pilots, and was not properly tied in to the home defence intelligence network. Though Admiralty representatives disputed the claim of station commanders that War Office intelligence of zeppelin movements was not being passed to them 'sufficiently rapidly' by the Admiralty, the raid record would seem to bear the latter out. LZ 97, for example, bombed the environs of Felixstowe on 23 August before any response could be made from the air station. Minutes of 21st meeting of Air Board, 14 Aug. 1916, Air 6/2; minutes of Admiralty meetings, 11 and 18 Aug. 1916, Air 1/667/7/122/739

from below, Robinson fired three drums of 'alternate New Brock and Pomeroy' before he saw a glow. The enormous flame of the stricken airship 'lit up bright as day the L 16,' which was nearly ten miles to the north. Robinson, the first airman to demonstrate the vulnerability of airships to air attack, was awarded a Victoria Cross for his efforts. That the destruction of SL 11 was not a fluke was proved on 23–24 September, when L 33 was shot down by gunfire and L 32, already damaged by the London guns, was brought down by a pilot from 39 Squadron 'with a mixture of Brock, Pomeroy and Tracer ammunition.'[23]

The tide had turned. Strasser henceforth permitted only the newer airships to attack the London area, and army airships never attempted to raid England again. Morale dropped among the crews of the Naval Airship Division, one officer recording that 'If anyone should say that he is not haunted by visions of burning airships, then he would be a braggart.'[24] Nevertheless, another raid was ordered for 1 October. While five naval airships meandered aimlessly over the eastern Midlands, the able Heinrich Mathy in L 31 struck straight for London. As he came into the searchlight zone he veered to the northwest and, hoping to elude the gun defences, cut his engines and drifted with the wind to the south and east. At about 1130 hrs he opened up his engines, was picked up by the lights, and immediately came under fire from the guns.

At this point L 31 was sighted by a pilot from Canada, Second Lieutenant W.J. Tempest.* Tempest later reported:

About 11:45 p.m. I found myself over S.W. London at an altitude of 14,500 feet. There was a heavy ground fog on and it was bitterly cold, otherwise the night was beautiful and star lit at the altitude at which I was flying.

I was gazing over towards the N.E. of London, where the fog was not quite so heavy, when I noticed all the searchlights in that quarter concentrated in an enormous 'pyramid.' Following them up to the apex I saw a small cigar shaped object, which I at once recognized as a Zeppelin about 15 miles away ...

At first I drew near to my objective very rapidly (as I was on one side of London and it was on the other and both heading for the centre of the town) all the time I was having an extremely unpleasant time, as to get to the Zepp I had to pass through a very inferno of bursting shells for the A.A. guns below.[25]

To make matters worse, Tempest's fuel pressure pump failed and he had to resort to the exhausting exercise of maintaining pressure with a hand pump. As he approached L 31, at a slightly higher altitude than the airship, he discovered that she was gaining height at a rate that his BE2c could not match:

I therefore decided to dive at her, for though I held a slight advantage in speed, she was climbing like a rocket and leaving me standing. I accordingly gave a tremendous pump at

---

* Tempest, though Yorkshire-born, had been homesteading and horse-breeding along with his brother Edmund (also a notable RFC pilot, see chapter 12) near Perdue, Sask., for some years before 1914. After being wounded with the army in France, he had transferred to the RFC and joined 39 Squadron in July 1916. Though he was later to serve in the RAF during the Second World War, attaining the rank of wing commander, he established permanent residence in Canada after 1918.

my petrol tank, and dived straight at her, firing a burst straight into her as I came. I let her have another burst as I passed under her and then banking my machine over, sat under her tail, and flying along underneath her, pumped lead into her for all I was worth. I could see tracer bullets flying from her in all directions, but I was too close under her for her to concentrate on me.

As I was firing, I noticed her begin to go red inside like an enormous Chinese lantern and then a flame shot out of the front part of her and I realized she was on fire.

She then shot up about 200 feet, paused, and came roaring down straight on to me before I had time to get out of the way. I nose dived for all I was worth, with the Zepp tearing after me, and expected every minute to be engulfed in the flames. I put my machine into a spin and just managed to corkscrew out of the way as she shot past me, roaring like a furnace.

I righted my machine and watched her hit the ground with a shower of sparks. I then proceeded to fire off dozens of green Very's lights in the exuberance of my feelings.

I glanced at my watch and saw it was about ten minutes past twelve.

I then commenced to feel very sick and giddy and exhausted, and had considerable difficulty in finding my way to ground through the fog and landing, in doing which I crashed and cut my head on my machine gun.[26]

Tempest received a Distinguished Service Order for his night's work.

The last raid of 1916 saw nine naval airships attack the east coast of England at various points from Norfolk to Durham, with some penetrating well into the Midlands. All refrained from attacking southern England, but this new caution was to no avail. For the first time the RFC organization outside the London defence region proved effective in meeting enemy raids. The log of 36 (HD) Squadron shows that word of the impending raid reached squadron headquarters at Newcastle at 1945 hrs, almost four hours before L 34 and L 35 crossed the coast between the Tyne and the Tees. With such forewarning a pilot from the Seaton Carew flight of the squadron was able to shoot down L 34. L 21 was finally overtaken on her outward passage and shot down by RNAS aircraft from Great Yarmouth. It seems likely that one of the RFC pilots who first gave chase to L 21 was Lieutenant J.B. Brophy of 33 Squadron, the only Canadian then with the unit. Flying from Kirton-in-Lindsey in a BE12, Brophy was aloft for three hours. About 1000 hrs he spotted the zeppelin well ahead, between 8000 and 9000 feet above him, and pursued it against a headwind for fifty minutes before abandoning the chase 'as it was obvious that I could not catch her up.'*[27]

Despite the disasters of late 1916, Peter Strasser believed that improved zeppelin performance could still overcome the British defences. His solution was to sacrifice speed to gain height and thus to place the airships beyond reach of both guns and aircraft. Fuel supply, defensive armament, and quarters for the crew were all cut back drastically, the number of engines was reduced by one, and structural members were lightened. The result was a new zeppelin type, 'the

---

* Don Brophy, from Ottawa (WIA 8 Aug. 1916) was an outstanding all-round athlete who had played football for his city in the Big Four, the predecessor of the eastern conference of the Canadian Football League. He was killed in a flying accident at Kirton-in-Lindsey in December 1916 when his BE12 failed to recover from a loop. He left one of the most detailed personal diaries of any Canadian flyer during the war, now held at DHist.

height climber,' that could operate at ceilings from 16,000 to 20,000 feet. The new heights meant new problems. Intense cold and lack of oxygen affected the performance of both engines and crew. An oxygen supply system became necessary for flight personnel. Navigation was more difficult since weather at the new heights was unpredictable. Since the airships now flew above all normal cloud levels except cirrus, they became more dependent than before upon wireless bearings. All these factors help explain the generally ineffective record of zeppelins for the rest of the war. During the whole of 1917 there were only seven raids by airships on England, as compared with twenty-two in 1916 and twenty in 1915, and the great heights from which bombing was carried out further reduced the Naval Air Division's significance as an offensive weapon.[28]

Of the seven zeppelins lost over England in 1917, only one was shot down by home defence forces, and that by a Canadian, Lieutenant Loudon Pierce Watkins of Toronto. Watkins, who with his brother Edward had been commissioned in the RFC in late 1915 after learning to fly at the Toronto Curtiss School, had joined 37 Squadron in December 1916 after a few months of service on the Western Front.* He had gained some limited experience of the nature of anti-zeppelin operations during the raid of 16–17 March, and probably during that of 23–24 May as well, but like other airmen was unable to come to grips with the height climbers. Then, on the night of 16 June, Strasser sent four of the new airships to attack London. Only two, L 42 (*Kapitänleutnant* Martin Dietrich) and L 48 (*Korvettenkapitän* Viktor Schütze, Strasser's deputy), were able to reach England.

Why this raid was launched, at a time of year when the airships would have only a few hours of midsummer darkness over England, is inexplicable. Though attracting the attention of the defences, Dietrich managed to bomb Ramsgate from a great height and get safely back to his base, having been nineteen hours in the air and for eleven hours at heights over 16,500 feet. From about 18,000 feet L 48 attempted to bomb the naval base at Harwich, but her bombs fell in fields some miles away. Schütze, however, was now having navigational difficulties. His liquid compass had frozen, and to free it he seems to have decided to descend into warmer air. Meanwhile, Watkins had taken off from Goldhanger airfield with instructions to seek a zeppelin near Harwich.

When at 11,000 feet over Harwich I saw the A.A. guns firing and several searchlights pointing towards the same spot. A minute later I observed the Zeppelin about 2,000 feet above me. After climbing about 500 feet I fired one drum into its tail but it took no effect. I then climbed to 12,000 feet and fired another drum into its tail without any effect. I then decided to wait until I was at close range before firing another drum. I then climbed steadily until I reached 13,200 and was then about 500 feet under the Zeppelin. I fired three short bursts of about 7 rounds and then the remainder of the drum; the Zepp burst into flames at the tail, the fire running along both sides, the whole Zepp caught fire and fell burning.[29]

---

* Other Canadians who flew with 37 Squadron during 1917 included W.A. Bishop of Owen Sound, Ont., W.R.S. Humphreys and C.J.L. Lawrence of Parry Sound, Ont., D.R. Smith of Sherbrooke, Que., and A.R. Stevenson of Peterborough, Ont. (WIA 5 June 1917).

Captain Robert Saundby, who had ascended from the experimental station at Orfordness in a DH2, also fired at L 48, but Watkins had delivered the decisive blow, and was rewarded with a Military Cross.

One other 1917 raid is worthy of note: the 'silent raid' of 19–20 October. The great heights at which the eleven raiding airships operated rendered the defence forces all but powerless, but at the same time proved disastrous to the attackers. As the zeppelins rose to altitudes of 16,000 feet or more on approaching the English coast, the light winds they had encountered were replaced by gale-force winds from the northeast, which heralded the onset of a deep depression. The peculiar atmospheric conditions deadened the sound of their engines and thus baffled the home defence organization, but hostile guns and aircraft were the least of the airship commanders' worries. Freezing cold, engine breakdown, height sickness, and, above all, navigational confusion caused by failure to recognize soon enough the change in wind conditions combined to bring disaster. Five zeppelins were lost: one crashed in southern Germany after having drifted over the trench lines of the Western Front, another was shot down over the front, and L 50 was lost somewhere over the Mediterranean. A fourth came down, virtually intact, in France. L 45, according to a member of its crew, made a European tour from Denmark to the Riviera, via London and Paris, in twenty hours. The zeppelin was blown south from the Midlands over London, and dropped bombs as it crossed the city. London was the commander's first positive navigational fix in some hours and he promptly turned eastward, on a homeward course bucking the strong winds. L 45 would probably have made it home had she not been pursued by a BE2c flown by Second Lieutenant T.B. Pritchard of 39 Squadron. Pritchard, some 3000 feet below where the winds were lighter, followed the airship out to sea and fired on it. L 45 immediately altered course to the south, gained height and outran her attacker, but in so doing was irrevocably committed to a track that brought her down in France. Pritchard, meanwhile, succeeded in making the English coast and crashed while attempting to make a forced landing in the blackness. He was one of six defence pilots to do so that night.*[30]

By the time Watkins had shot down L 48, the British Cabinet, the public, and the RFC's higher command had shifted their attention to a new menace: daylight raids by German aeroplanes. As long ago as the autumn of 1914 Germany had organized a squadron (its cover name was 'the carrier pigeon squadron') at Ghistelles, near Ostend, under the command of *Major* Wilhelm Siegert, with the objective of bombing England. Because of the short range of existing aircraft it was vital to this plan that Calais be seized; the failure of the Germans to do so resulted in the dropping of the plan and the transfer of the squadron to Metz. Nevertheless, development work continued on longer-range aircraft, and by the end of 1915 Germany had a few machines of the G series (*Grosskampfflugzeug*) in action on the Western Front. When *General* Erich von Hoeppner became commander of the reorganized German air force in 1916 he proposed to the High Command that

---

* Pritchard, address unknown, transferred from the Canadian Expeditionary Force to the RFC in April 1917. Awarded the MC for this attack, he died in hospital of pneumonia on 5 December 1917.

because of the failure of the zeppelin campaign and the potential of G-type aircraft, attacks on England must be launched 'as soon as practicable.'[31]

It was the G-IV, the 'Gotha,' that made such raids possible. A large, ungainly biplane, it was powered by two 260-hp Mercedes pusher engines and could carry a bomb load of 300 to 500 kg. With a maximum speed of 87.5 mph, a ceiling of 21,000 feet (though usually it operated at 15,000 feet or slightly higher), and an endurance of about four hours (longer with auxiliary tanks), the Gotha was a formidable aircraft. Her crew of three had two or three machine-guns as defensive armament, including the famous 'sting in the tail' which could be fired through a tunnel in the belly, eliminating the blind spot to the rear.[32]

To carry out Hoeppner's plan for raiding England (code named *Türkenkreuz*), elements of Siegert's original squadron were formed into *Kampfgeschwader 1 (Kagohl 1)*, universally known as the *Englandgeschwader*. After a period of flying training over the North Sea, the unit was moved to Belgium, two *Staffeln* being based at each of three airfields, St Denis Westrem, Gontrode, and Mariakerke.* The objectives of the *Englandgeschwader*, as laid down by the German High Command, were to disrupt British industry, communications, and transport, and to strike at the morale of the British people. According to *General* von Hoeppner, the bombing offensive was also designed 'to split up the numerically superior forces of the Allies in the air.'[33]

The possibility of German aeroplane raids against southeastern England had not been entirely overlooked by the home defence organization. Hit-and-run raids, usually by single aircraft, had become a regular occurrence along the Channel coast. At a meeting of the Air Board in December 1916 the means of combating an aeroplane raid in strength had been discussed, although the possibility of adequate resistance without unduly weakening the front line seemed unlikely. But the defeat of the zeppelins, the need for more guns to protect shipping against U-boats, and the rising demand from the Western Front for more pilots and aircraft led to reductions in both gun and air defences in early 1917. In March thirty-six pilots were sent from home defence squadrons to the Western Front; as Sir David Henderson said, 'the diminished risk from Zeppelins amply justifies this temporary reduction.' It was also decided that gun defences outside the coastal areas need not be manned by day, and the experienced gunners thus relieved were transferred for duty elsewhere. At the same time, the home defence staff continued to plan against the possibility of German daylight raiding and attempted to concert a new system of patrols with the RNAS. Although the Admiralty agreed to co-operate, it proposed to withdraw its fighting aircraft from Grain and Detling, two coastal stations, as soon as the RFC was in a position to accept its full responsibilities for home defence. Field Marshal Lord French, Commander-in-Chief of the Home Forces, expressed deep concern on 20 March that the Home Defence Wing had been reduced 'to a dangerously low point,' but the opinion of the War Office was that the home defence shortage was not disproportionate to that existing in RFC establishments overseas.[34]

---

* Each *Staffel* consisted of six Gothas and their crews. The squadron's designation became *Kagohl 3* early in 1917.

Late in the afternoon of 25 May German aircraft appeared high over the south coast of England. Heat haze, cloud, and the silvery-white colouring of the aircraft prevented any accurate estimate of their numbers (there were in fact twenty-one); some observers thought there were zeppelins with them. Encountering high cloud over the Thames estuary, the Gothas abandoned London as a target and swung about to bomb Shorncliffe (where thirteen Canadian soldiers were killed and seventy-six more wounded) and Folkestone. Only the coastal guns fired while, according to the intelligence summary issued by GHQ Home Forces, the pilots reported 'unanimously on the impossibility of their rising to the same height as the enemy, attaining the same speed, or engaging him with sufficient reserve of power with the engines at their disposal ... They could not do anything.' Two Canadian lieutenants with 37 Squadron had typical experiences. L.P. Watkins sighted the Gothas, but his BE12 was too slow 'so could not engage'; W.R.S. Humphreys, a prewar English immigrant to Canada who had joined the CEF at Valcartier in 1914, 'chased hostile aircraft 20 miles out to sea. Owing to their superior speed could not engage.'[35] Although fighters from RNAS Dunkirk shot down one of the raiders off Ostend, the first German test of the daylight defence of England had proved most successful.

This was confirmed by a second raid on 5 June when, with almost no advance warning for the defences, twenty-two Gothas swept in over the Essex coast, bombed Shoeburyness and the naval installations at Sheerness in Kent (including four bombs on 'the Rear Admiral's tennis ground'), and were homeward bound before much defensive reaction occurred. One raider was shot down in the sea by a coastal battery, but none of the sixty-six aircraft which attempted to thwart the raiders was able to come to grips with them. RFC aircraft were unable to get above 15,000 feet; their pilots estimated that the enemy formation was at least 2000 feet higher.[36]

The confused and angry public reaction to the Gotha raids was dealt with by the editor of *The Aeroplane* in his usual trenchant fashion:

Of course, we shall have the usual outcry about the Hunnishness of bombing women and children, but we should clear our minds of cant in this matter. Women and children should not remain in the war zone. If the enemy is so efficient as to increase the depth of the war zone, either by long-range guns or by improved aeroplanes, and if he is allowed to operate those improved weapons, that is his good fortune and our misfortune. Our authorities are to blame for casualties, not the enemy. We must either stop the raids or evacuate the civilian population from the raidable area.

We can draw a map of England showing the area over which raiders can operate, within the known limits of their petrol supply, or we can draw a map of Flanders showing the area within which concentrations of enemy raiding machines are not to be permitted. The choice lies entirely with us ...[37]

The War Cabinet chose not to reply to what a minister termed German 'frightfulness' because bombing aircraft could not be spared from the Western Front. Instead, English air defences were patched up. On 25 May there had been only twenty-two home defence aircraft in that part of southeastern England (including

London) within the Gothas' calculated radius of 125 miles. Pilots were also in short supply. Since February seventy-seven experienced pilots had been posted out of home defence squadrons which had just over half their total establishment of 198 pilots. A War Office conference on 31 May adopted a makeshift solution. Home defence duties were assigned to the experimental stations at Orfordness and Martlesham Heath, to staff pilots at aircraft acceptance parks, and to instructors in a number of training squadrons which were shifted to the southeast for the purpose. The conclusion of the conference that 'under the arrangements proposed there was no likelihood that the enemy aeroplanes would be able to avoid an engagement with our own fighting machines' seemed unwarranted to Lord French. As Commander-in-Chief Home Forces he bore the ultimate responsibility for home defence, and he concluded that 'the means placed at my disposal are now inadequate and ... a continuance of the present policy may have disastrous results.'[38]

On 13 June *Hauptmann* Ernst Brandenburg, the commander of *Kagohl 3*, was advised by the army's meteorological service that conditions were right for a strike at London itself. His aircraft were able to fly above the clouds until the Thames estuary was reached; from Southend to London no cloud cover existed, but though anti-aircraft guns opened fire, the defences had been caught napping. According to Brandenburg's report, only one defence aircraft attacked his formation 'with vigour.' He claimed to have bombed a railway station (it was in fact Liverpool Street Station), Tower Bridge, and docks and warehouses in the City. Casualties from the raid were the worst of the war; 161 people were killed and 429 injured.[39]

Numerically, at least, the air defences had responded well: there were fifty-three aircraft aloft against the Gothas and, within eight minutes of the first warning, thirty had been in the air, most of them from home defence squadrons. But very few of these aircraft could be described as first-line fighters. No 37 Squadron, for instance, put twelve aircraft up from its three airfields. Its night pilots, including L.P. Watkins, were flying the inadequate BE12; others were in Sopwith 1½ Strutters (the two-seater variety), or BE2ds and 2es. One pilot flew an RE7. With aircraft of every type coming from a wide variety of squadrons and other formations, lacking common direction and having had no firm instructions on tactics to be employed, it was natural that for the few pilots who actually saw the enemy the fight was one of individual tactics. Not a single German aircraft was lost. The Air Board later noted that neither guns nor aeroplanes had been able to break up the Gotha formation. It was also clear that the expedient of 31 May had failed. The training squadrons and aircraft acceptance parks had reacted slowly to the raid alert. No concentration of effort had been achieved.[40]

For the War Cabinet and the public alike, what was wanted was a bomber-proof defence system. In General Trenchard's memorandum of 15 June 1917, 'Methods suggested for the preventing of air raids in the United Kingdom,' there was little comfort. Some public men had suggested round-the-clock patrols. Trenchard dismissed the ideas as totally beyond the capabilities of the RFC. The only real solutions were either to capture Brandenburg's airfields during the Flanders offensive, or to destroy them through sabotage. Trenchard did not reject the popular remedy, reprisal, but 'to outlast the enemy' (a necessary corollary to it) a bomber force would first have to be built up. For the time being the War Cabinet was obliged to accept that it was neither technically possible to construct an invulnerable defence system, nor militarily feasible to mount a bombing offensive. In the War Cabinet discussions, however, the effect of Brandenburg's London raid had been to associate directly the need for a defence against the bomber with the idea of attacking Germany.[41]

Two raids at the beginning of July showed that, even with somewhat strengthened defences, the problem of the bombers was far from being solved. On 4 July sixteen Gothas attacked Felixstowe air station and Harwich. They were not seen until 0555 hrs, just five minutes before they commenced bombing; by 0720 hrs the formation, still intact, was on its way back to its Belgian bases. Although neither casualties nor damage was heavy (a Large America seaplane was destroyed on the slipways at Felixstowe), the suddenness of the raid revealed serious deficiencies in the British intelligence and communications system. In all, 103 aircraft of many types were airborne, but the order to patrol was not given until the Germans had already turned for home. Of the three home defence squadrons taking part, 37 Squadron got its orders at 0729 hrs on two of its airfields, and at 0735 hrs on the third, while 50 Squadron was ordered up at 0727 hrs and 39 Squadron a minute later. As a result of a War Cabinet decision of 20 June, two fighter squadrons, 56 and 66, had been transferred temporarily to the home defence organization on 21 June. No 56 Squadron, stationed at Bekesbourne near Canterbury, had its SE5s into the air within four minutes of receiving patrol orders at 0727 hrs, but sighted no Gothas.* No 66 Squadron, based at Calais, found the returning bombers and then lost them in cloud. Nevertheless, a furious fight developed when a flight of Sopwiths of 4 Squadron sent up from Dunkirk intercepted the enemy formation. 'Two machines were brought down in flames and a third machine was seen to have only one engine running ... Several other machines were attacked with indecisive results.'[42]

On 7 July, a hazy but fine Saturday morning, occurred the most spectacular aeroplane raid of the war, a raid that shook the British government, set off anti-alien riots in several parts of London, and brought profound changes in air policy. All this was accomplished by a mere twenty-two Gothas, twenty-one of which reached London. First reported off the Kentish coast at 0914 hrs, the German formation, described by observers as diamond-shaped, began its attack on London at 1020 hrs. The last bomb fell twenty minutes later. The raid was witnessed by millions of people, and the impotence of the home defence forces was never more graphically exposed. The warning time given the defenders had been adequate: all air units were given patrol orders between 0924 hrs and 0933 hrs, and ninety-five aircraft, all but sixteen of them from the RFC, rose to meet the bombers. Four of the home defence squadrons contributed forty-six aircraft, the balance coming from experimental and training establishments. Yet the defenders seemed virtually powerless. Captain J.B. McCudden, an outstanding British fighter pilot, was

---

* V.P. Cronyn of London, Ont., and R.T.C. Hoidge and R.G. Jardine of Toronto (the latter KIA 20 July 1917) took part in this fruitless exercise.

stationed at this time at Joyce Green as an instructor with 63 (Training) Squadron. He repeatedly attacked the German formation at a height of 17,000 feet, and after using all his ammunition, flew in close to it, 'endeavouring to draw Hostile Fire to enable several Sopwith Scouts and Camels, which were following Hostile Formation, to close and get in a good burst while Hostile Gunners were engaging me. Either our machines did not appreciate my intention, or did not want to, I do not know, but they had a splendid opportunity if they had availed themselves of it.'[43]

The reports of two Canadians involved did not show any reluctance to engage the enemy and their reports were typical of those submitted, at least from home defence pilots. L.P. Watkins chased the enemy five miles out to sea, finally overtaking the formation in his slow BE12, fired one drum of ammunition, and then had to return with engine trouble. Lieutenant G.A. Thompson of Vaudreuil Station, Que., from 37 Squadron, had engine trouble with his Sopwith Scout almost from the moment of take-off. He nevertheless clawed his way up over London to engage Gothas from below, only to become an easy target for the German tunnel-gunners. Thompson breezily reported that his aircraft had been sprayed with bullets, 'one in the seat, others just round about.' Two British pilots were killed while attacking the bombers; one Gotha, lagging behind the main body, was shot down in the sea by an Armstrong-Whitworth from 50 Squadron.* It was not resolution that was wanting, but co-ordinated fighter tactics and more first-line aircraft. Only fifteen of the aircraft sent up from home defence squadrons were of the latest type. Other units contributed, in ones and twos, twenty-one additional aircraft, few of them first-class machines. Yet when accounting for the lack of success in its defensive effort the RFC home defence staff gave prominence to 'the apparent invulnerability' of the Gotha.[44]

In an atmosphere of tension the War Cabinet met a few hours after the raid had ended. The Chief of the Imperial General Staff, General Sir William Robertson, wrote to Sir Douglas Haig that 'One would have thought that the world was coming to an end. I could not get in a word edgeways.'† Although the War Cabinet was once again forced to accept the opinion of its military advisers that the resources to attack German cities were not available, in its next meeting it proceeded to set up a sub-committee to examine the home defence system and 'the air organization

---

* RNAS pilots from Manston also claimed to have shot down three bombers, but *Kagohl 3*'s additional losses were incurred in crashes of four aircraft on landing after the raid.

† There was considerable agitation when it was discovered that 56 and 66 Squadrons had been returned to France two days before the raid, despite a protest from Lord French. His memorandum, written on 2 July but side-tracked by administrative muddling before it reached the Cabinet, declared that without these fighter squadrons his forces would be inadequate to defend London. Robertson had some sympathy for French's position. 'There is no doubt that French has not got a very good force. It is mainly made up of oddments, and of course oddments will not do.' The War Cabinet, while unravelling this tangle, decided to have two more fighter squadrons sent over to England. When Haig protested on 7 July that the 'fight for air supremacy preparatory to forthcoming operations was definitely commenced by us this morning,' and that the loss of two squadrons would 'certainly delay favourable decision in the air,' the War Cabinet reduced its demand to one. See Sir William Robertson, *Soldiers and Statesmen, 1914–1918* (London 1926), II, 17; Chief to Chief, London, 7 July 1917, Air 1/522/16/12/5; minutes of 178th, 179th, 180th War Cabinet meetings, 7, 9, 10 July 1917, Cab 23/3.

generally and the direction of aerial operations.' General Jan Christian Smuts of South Africa was, in effect, the sub-committee. His chief recommendation was that the 'nerve centre' of the British Empire demanded 'exceptional measures' for its defence and that therefore the whole of the London air defence organization should be placed in the hands of 'a senior officer of first-rate ability and practical air experience.' He also recommended that gun defences be strengthened, that three more squadrons be added to home defence, that formation tactics be adopted, and that an air reserve be constituted to counter the possibility of a diversionary attack followed by a major assault.[45]

Brigadier-General E.B. Ashmore was the officer selected to take over the responsibility for the defence of the capital, exchanging, as he later wrote, 'the comparative safety of the Front for the probability of being hanged in the streets of London.' Not only was he given command of the London Anti-Aircraft Defence Area but also of Zone 'x,' which included the whole area of southeastern England considered vulnerable to aeroplane attack. Ashmore's appointment took effect on 8 August. By the end of the month he had received more guns and three new squadrons to add to the existing six, not to speak of naval fighters at Manston and Walmer and the usual mixed collection of aircraft from training squadrons, depots, and experimental stations. The nine home defence squadrons became the Home Defence Group, under Colonel T.C.R. Higgins. Large white arrows, visible (in clear weather) from 17,000 feet, were placed about southeastern England to direct aircraft towards hostile formations.[46]

Scarcely had Ashmore taken over his new command when the Gothas returned. This time they did not have things all their own way. The German formation was sighted by a patrol of five aircraft from 3 (Naval) Squadron at Dunkirk, out on a fleet protection sweep. The patrol, which included Captain G.S. Harrower of Montreal and Lieutenant R.F.P. Abbott of Carleton Place, Ont., pursued the Gothas at 15,000 feet almost to Harwich. Harrower put all his ammunition into the hindmost machine without result, and then the naval pilots had to land at English airfields to refuel. As the Gothas approached the English coast, one of their number veered away from the formation, dropped its bomb-load on Margate, and turned back across the sea. It was pursued by a patrol of Sopwith Pups from the RNAS Home Defence Flight at Walmer, including Flight Lieutenant H.S. Kerby of Calgary and Flight Sub-Lieutenant M.R. Kingsford of Toronto. Kingsford had to turn back, but the others pursued the raider almost to Zeebrugge before losing it. The Gotha in fact crash-landed on the beach.

Meanwhile, the German formation had continued towards its objective, the naval base at Chatham. Wrongly deciding that the enemy's target was London, Ashmore held back his defence aircraft, either keeping them in reserve on the ground or ordering them to fly patrols inland, guarding the capital.* Contrary winds and the ascent of fighters from 61 Squadron at Rockford, over whose airfield the Gothas had passed, prompted the German commander to bomb his secondary

---

* Their number included eighteen Sopwith Pups from 46 Squadron, based at Sutton's Farm. This was the squadron the Cabinet had requested from France after the 7 July raid; its pilots included R.L.M. Ferrie of Hamilton (KIA 31 Jan. 1918) and L.M. Shadwell of Belmont, Man.

target of Southend and turn for home. Kerby, returning from his North Sea flight, flew towards anti-aircraft bursts he saw over Southend and met the Gothas in an engagement that won him a DSC.

The hostile aircraft [he recalled] were about 2,000 ft above me when I got under them. I followed climbing to 18,000 ft and attacked without result. I then observed one Gotha 4,000 ft below the formation, but with it. I attacked from the front and drove him down to water, where I observed him to turn over.

One of the occupants I saw hanging on the tail of Gotha, I threw him my lifebelt and did two or three circuits round him and then returned to England.

On my way back I observed four destroyers when at 6,000 ft going towards Dunkirk. I fired three Red Very's Lights to try and get them to follow me back to the machine in the water, but they continued on their course.[47]

Despite this rough handling (in addition to Kerby's victim, five had crash-landed), the temporary commander of *Kagohl 3* launched another attack on 22 August upon Southend, Chatham, and Dover. As the German formation approached the English coast it became apparent to the crews that a hornet's nest awaited them. Anti-aircraft fire was more intense than they had encountered before. Fighter aircraft from the RNAS stations at Manston, Eastchurch, Walmer, and Dover were already at their height. A confused mêlée ensued and three Gothas were shot down. A number of Canadians were prominent in this action, including Kingsford and Kerby from Walmer and Flight Commander G.E. Hervey of Calgary from Dover. Hervey and Kerby got to close quarters with the bombers and both claimed to have shot one down in the sea. It is possible that both engaged the same aircraft. In any case, two Gothas were credited to the anti-aircraft gunners and a third to a naval pilot from Manston.* Although only a few RFC aircraft were in contact with the enemy, a total of 120 went up on patrol, the largest number of home defence machines to take to the air during the war.[†48]

After this raid the Germans decided that daylight operations were no longer feasible because of 'better organized air defence.'[49] For the German crews the chief difficulty in the decision to switch to night attacks was navigational, but for the defence the German resort to night operations meant that the elaborate system built up to counter day raids had to be discarded. When, on 3 September, the first night raid occurred, only sixteen RFC aircraft went up. None of the pilots saw the

---

* Hervey was awarded a DSC for his part in this encounter.

† Just a day before this raid there had been an informal meeting of pilots from both RFC and RNAS units in the London Anti-Aircraft Defence Area. The subject of discussion was the apparent invulnerability of the Gotha to .303 machine-gun fire; doubtless information was exchanged about tactics as well. Among other things the pilots discussed the possibility of using a heavier calibre than the .303 or of using Brock and Pomeroy ammunition against Gothas. Although the use of this ammunition had been permitted against zeppelins, it was against regulations to employ it against aeroplanes. The outcome of the meeting was a request from the Admiralty to the Air Board for permission to use such explosive bullets against the raiders. The matter finally went to the War Cabinet, approval being given on 28 September 1917. Minutes of meeting, 21 Aug. 1917, Vyvyan memorandum, 28 Sept. 1918, Air 2/02156/1917

enemy. The warning system broke down as well; a drill hall at Chatham full of sleeping naval ratings was bombed, 130 men being killed and eighty-eight injured.

The methods used against night-flying zeppelins were of little avail against Gothas. Scant warning was possible and the bombers were much more elusive targets than the airships. Although the chance of night raids had preoccupied the defence staff (indeed, on 3 September a rehearsal for such an eventuality was in progress), no one believed that serious opposition could be given, especially in view of recent night-bombing experience on the Western Front. Both flying services were convinced that first-line, single-seater fighters like the Camel and the SE5 were too unstable to fly at night. Out of the 191 BE2s, BE12s, RE7s, FE2s, and Armstrong Whitworths available to the defence, only twelve FE2ds fitted with 250-hp Rolls-Royce engines were capable of coping with the Gothas. On 3 September the RFC staff estimated that there were fewer than three 'efficient' aircraft in each flight of the home defence squadrons. The one bright spot for the defence was 44 Squadron's use of three Camels during the raid. The proof that this first-class fighter could function at night without undue difficulty paved the way for a significant strengthening of the defence forces.[50]

Meanwhile, the Germans struck at London on 4 September, and were virtually unopposed. The War Cabinet, advised that 'no local means of keeping off such attacks had yet been discovered,' turned again to General Smuts for advice on home defence and also for suggestions on 'carrying the air war into Germany at the earliest possible moment.' Smuts judged that home defence aircraft, unable to locate the enemy even at a range of a few hundred yards, 'might just as well have remained on the ground.' More powerful searchlights and the balloon barrage that General Ashmore was experimenting with were only palliative methods. He concluded that 'we can only defend this island effectively against air attacks by offensive measures, by attacking the enemy in his air bases on the Continent and in that way destroying his power of attacking us over the Channel.'[51]

General Ashmore was certainly not prepared to concede that the defence was powerless. Banking on acquiring more Camels and other first-class fighters, he cleared the guns from the area between London's outer defences and the city itself, filled this zone with searchlights, and used the surplus guns to extend the barrier about the city, which eventually encircled it at a distance of some ten miles from the populated area. The balloon barrage was designed to prevent hostile aircraft from flying below a certain height, thus limiting the zone to be searched by defending aircraft to that between the balloon 'apron' and the operational ceiling of the Gothas. As well, a number of top fighter pilots were posted into the home defence squadrons. For example, Captain A.E. Godfrey from Vancouver, an accomplished pilot serving with 40 Squadron in France, was transferred to 44 Squadron towards the end of September. Godfrey, whose operational experience was largely on Nieuports, had never flown a Camel, and found it 'so much more active – it would do everything faster and climb just like a rocket.' He and others like him were put through intensive training in night landing and night navigation over their patrol areas and in the handling of guns and the clearing of gun stoppages in the dark. Though cockpit illumination of instruments was soon provided, for the most part the pilot was very much on his own. There were other hazards during an actual raid. 'We were depending on picking up the Hun from the flame of his exhaust,' Godfrey recalled, 'and the anti-aircraft [bursts] were supposed to be around them. But we found that mostly the anti-aircraft were around patrolling aircraft.'[52]

Before there was any real opportunity to train pilots in the new system, and before adequate numbers of good fighter aircraft could be obtained, the Germans launched a series of strikes, known as the 'Harvest Moon' raids, between 24 September and 1 October. London was bombed during five of the six attacks. Not a single raider was shot down by patrolling fighters although the guns accounted for four, chiefly through bearings from sound-ranging equipment. Five home defence aircraft crashed on landing, including one lost during a zeppelin raid which followed the Gotha attack of 24 September.* The defence never succeeded in putting more than thirty-three aircraft up during a raid. Towards the end of the raiding period seven or eight Camels from 44 Squadron were taking part. Most squadrons, however, made do with obsolete types. For example, 39 Squadron based at Biggin Hill and North Weald opposed the raid of 29–30 September with three BE12s, six BE2es, and two BE2cs, one of the latter being flown by the flight commander, Major J.A. Dennistoun of Winnipeg. During the six Harvest Moon raids, 151 flights were made, yet only five pilots even 'thought' they saw hostile aircraft, and only two pilots opened fire.[53]

These raids were the last straw for the War Cabinet. Absenteeism in munitions factories, running as high as 73 per cent, and outbreaks of panic as hundreds of thousands of Londoners thronged nightly to the Underground for shelter seemed to dictate a new policy. On 1 October Field Marshal Haig was ordered to launch bombing raids on Germany; when he objected, General Robertson replied that 'the War Cabinet have decided, in view of the air attacks on London, that it is necessary to undertake a continuous offensive, by air, against such suitable objectives in Germany as can be reached by our aeroplanes.' Haig was told to make immediate arrangements with the French for the accommodation of RFC bombing squadrons behind their lines. The result was the formation of 41 Wing at Ochey, the precursor of the Independent Air Force.[54]

As the British intelligence later discovered, during the Harvest Moon raids the R-plane (*Riesenflugzeug*) had been used for the first time. This giant aircraft, a multi-engined type much larger than the Gotha, had initially been employed on the Eastern Front. A squadron of the Giants, *Riesenflugzeug Abteilung* (*Rfla 501*), had been transferred to a Belgian airfield, Scheldewindeke, in August 1917. The airfield had a specially constructed concrete apron to handle the six aircraft that composed the squadron, commanded by *Hauptmann* von Bentivegni.[†]

---

* J.A. Menzies of Ottawa, an observer with 33 Squadron at Gainsborough, was killed in this crash.

† The R-plane, never mass-produced, was made in a number of types by several German factories. Those employed against England were made by the Staaken works, but since each was, in effect, hand-made, it is not possible to make specific statements about performance of the aircraft as a type. The Staaken R-VI had a wing-span of nearly 140 feet, and carried four 245-hp Maybach engines mounted in pairs, back to back. Most of the seven- to nine-man crew were housed in an enclosed plywood fuselage; only the flight mechanics, who serviced the engines in flight and doubled as gunners, were exposed to the elements in their airy cockpits in the engine nacelles.

Further raids by *Kagohl 3* and *Rfla 501* took place at the end of October and again on 6 December. In the latter raid some defence squadrons had been partially re-equipped with more efficient aircraft. Two Bristol Fighters, for example, accompanied the BE12s of 39 Squadron from North Weald; Lieutenant V.A. Lanos of Kingston, Ont., flew in one of them as an observer. It was the gunners, however, who achieved great success during this raid. Six Gothas were destroyed as a result of gun-fire: two over England, three crippled machines which crash-landed in Belgium, and one which failed to return to base.[55]

Kagohl 3 was also used in Western Front operations. During the raid on the British rear areas near Ypres on 12 December 1917 the squadron lost its commander, who was in the crew of the first Gotha to be shot down over France. Captain William Wendell Rogers of Alberton, PEI, leading a patrol of five Nieuports from 1 Squadron, was responsible: 'Just after climbing through the clouds I saw two formations (9 and 8) of Gothas coming West about 7,500 feet. I climbed up with the patrol and observed one E.A. turn back East, so attacked it, firing ¾ drum at 30 to 20 yards range. E.A. burst into flames, fell to pieces and crashed North of FRELINGHIEN [sic] ...'[56] Rogers' achievement was followed by the first success of a home defence aircraft at night, when a 44 Squadron pilot shot down a Gotha during the raid of 18 December 1917. Despite this victory, the defence had little to crow about. In the last three raids of 1917 131 defence aircraft went up, fifty-eight of them first-class fighters, yet the enemy was sighted only eight times and only three combats took place, for a total of one Gotha shot down. As Ashmore put it, 'a large number of pilots were risking their necks for a pitifully small result.'[57]

Raiding resumed on the night of 28–29 January. Although a Gotha was shot down by defence aircraft, the most notable occurrence was the loss of life and devastation caused by a 1000-kg bomb from a Giant aircraft which fell on a London printing establishment being used as an air-raid shelter. The following night three Giants returned: one was compelled by the guns to turn away from London and the other two were unsuccessfully engaged by aircraft. Two more raids on London occurred on 16 and 17–18 February, five R-planes flying in the first and one in the second. It is an indication of the slowness with which the RFC home defence squadrons were being re-equipped that of the 129 flights made during these two raids, forty-three were by Sopwith Camels, Bristol Fighters, and

Many of the mechanics who served with *Rfla 501* had come from zeppelin service where they had been familiar with the Maybach engine. The Giant tended to be somewhat temperamental from the maintenance point of view, but once committed to a raid was much more reliable than the Gotha. None of the Giants was shot down and only two were lost through accident. Although its bomb-load varied with individual aircraft, it carried more than three times the load of the Gotha, including large 1000-kg bombs. Nor was the aircraft slow. Its cruising speed was over 80 mph, and it had a range of some 300 miles. The best account of the R-plane is in G.W. Haddow and Peter M. Grosz, *The German Giants: the Story of the R-planes, 1914–1919* (London 1962). See also Raymond H. Fredette, *The Sky on Fire: the First Battle of Britain, 1917–1918, and the Birth of the Royal Air Force* (New York 1966), 132–6; and Arthur Schoeller, 'Mit dem Riesenflugzeug R27 über England!' in Walter von Eberhardt, ed., *Unsere Luftstreitkräfte, 1914–1918* (Berlin 1930), 441–4, DHist SGR 1 196, Set 81. Schoeller gives a ratio of forty ground-crew per aircraft for *Rfla 501*; the figure in Haddow and Grosz, p. 38, is 125.

SE5s, the remainder being the usual collection of BE2s, BE12s, and Armstrong Whitworths. About the same proportion of first-class fighters took part in an unavailing search for five Giants by forty-two machines during the raid of 7–8 March. Two new squadrons, 141 and 143, authorized in December 1917, came into action for the first time on this night. Captain A.E. Godfrey, now transferred from 44 Squadron to command a flight with 78 Squadron, reported that despite the blackout 'the visibility of London was perfect. The glow of the lights of London could be seen thirty miles away at a height of 12,000 ft. The river Thames could be traced by the lights on boats.' Despite the good visibility, however, the typical report was that of Lieutenant Charles Osenton of Armstrong, BC, flying with 143 Squadron from the former RNAS airfield at Detling: 'No H.A. seen.' The Giants, as always, had everything their own way; one of them dropped a 1000-kg bomb on a London residential street, wrecking most of it and causing heavy casualties.[58]

No further aeroplane raids took place until May. Instead, three nocturnal visitations from zeppelins, absent since October, occurred in March and April. The Naval Airship Division had not attacked during the winter because of the heavy losses suffered in its last raid and because of a fire which swept the Ahlhorn sheds in January, when five airships were lost. Moreover, the lesson of the 'silent raid' had been learned: more powerful engines were needed to cope with the high winds and rarified air encountered at great heights. By early 1918 a new power plant, the Maybach MB-IVa, with oversize cylinders and a higher compression ratio, was being installed to replace the Maybach HSLu engines, in service since 1915. At the same time two wireless stations were set up in Germany to transmit directional signals at regular intervals. Now, instead of having to break wireless silence by a request for a bearing, the airship could determine its bearing from each station by using its receiver and a trailing antenna. This innovation deprived the defence of its most valuable source of early intelligence of airship movements.[*][59]

The raid of 12–13 March was not a fair test either of the improved zeppelins or of defensive readiness, since it took place in weather so bad that few fighters took to the air. The zeppelin commanders had no clear idea of their whereabouts. On 13–14 March two of the three airships sent to raid northern England were recalled, but *Kapitänleutnant* Dietrich in L 42 persisted, bombing the dock areas of West Hartlepool from 18,000 feet. The defence was caught by surprise; Dietrich reported that the town's lights were still on when he began bombing. According to the intelligence officer of the Tees Garrison, 'the civilian population of West Hartlepool shows considerable feeling and resentment at the fact that the attack took place before T.A.R.A. [Take Air Raid Action] was given.' A month later, on 12–13 April, five naval airships attacked the Midlands at heights well beyond the reach of the defence. Among those vainly attempting to reach the zeppelins were pilots from the former RNAS station at Great Yarmouth. Like

* The frequency of zeppelin raids on England for the remainder of the war was fundamentally determined by a high policy decision taken in August 1917. In order to conserve rubber and aluminum for the production of German army aeroplanes, it was decided to hold the total establishment of the naval airship division to twenty-five airships, and to reduce the replacement rate to one zeppelin every two months. Douglas H. Robinson, *The Zeppelin in Combat: a History of the German Naval Airship Division 1912–1918* (London 1966), 262–3

other home defence units outside the London Anti-Aircraft Defence Area, Great Yarmouth had to make do with obsolete aircraft. Lieutenant G.R. Halliday of Victoria was up more than two hours in a BE2c, but did not come within several thousand feet of the height at which the attack was delivered. The same held for the F2a flown by Captain Robert Leckie of Toronto; its service ceiling was less than 10,000 feet.[60]

The last aeroplane raid on England, that of 19–20 May 1918, was also the largest. Brandenburg's squadron had been increasingly employed on Western Front duties but for this attack he managed to assemble forty-three bombers, including two Giants, to raid London. The bombers, spaced at five-minute intervals, came over England from 2242 hrs until well after midnight. Against them, the defence mustered eighty-four aircraft including thirty-one Camels, twenty-eight SE5s, and fourteen Bristol Fighters. Although nearly half the bombers may have reached London, the resistance offered was strong and effective. Seven enemy aircraft were lost to the fighters and guns of home defence. Though no Canadians were successful in shooting down enemy aircraft, several took part in the night's action, including three pilots experiencing their first night-fighter operation, Lieutenants W.M. Partridge of Winnipeg from 50 Squadron, F.B. Baragar of Elm Creek, Man., from 112 Squadron, and S.H. Love of Toronto from 39 Squadron. Love was forced to crash-land his Bristol Fighter near his home field of Hainault Farm.[61]

German bombers did not attack England again during the First World War, not because of their losses, heavy though they were, but because the need to support the German armies in the field was more important to the High Command than the continuation of strategic bombing against England. The RAF had to assume that further attacks would be forthcoming, and so continued to strengthen the home defence organization until war's end. The single most important development was the installation of wireless receiving sets in aircraft in September, making possible the manoeuvring of defence forces in the air while a raid was actually in progress. Information about hostile aircraft movements reaching a central control in London was plotted on a large table-map, over which sat General Ashmore and the Director of Fighter Operations, Brigadier-General Higgins, the commander of what was now VI Brigade. 'In effect,' Ashmore later wrote, 'I could follow the course of all aircraft flying over the country as the counters crept across the map.' Higgins had direct command lines to his squadrons and to a long-range transmitter at Biggin Hill. 'This transmitter was used for giving orders to leaders of defending formations in the air, during day time ... For night work, until the individual pilots should be thoroughly trained in wireless receiving, we confined ourselves to a simple system. Each squadron commander, as he received information of the enemy through the central control, was able, with a short range wireless transmitter, to concentrate his machines in the air at any part of their patrol line, and at any named height.'[62]

These methods were not far removed from those to be employed against the Germans during the Second World War. Ashmore did not consider that the problem of the bomber had been solved; indeed, in the complex inter-relationship between offence and defence, there could never be, in his view, anything like 'complete immunity' from bombing. It seems doubtful that the various defensive measures taken during the war accomplished anything more than forcing the enemy to change his form of attack. Ashmore was convinced, nevertheless, of the deterrent value of the British air defence system. The fact is that the German decision to abandon further aeroplane raiding had nothing to do with the substantial improvement in British air defences. Yet the mere threat of a resumption of bombing was sufficient to maintain in being an elaborate defensive organization. At the end of the war the operational units of VI Brigade, with its headquarters in London, comprised eleven squadrons of aircraft and three balloon squadrons in the Southern Group (London Anti-Aircraft Defence Area) and five more home defence squadrons in the Northern Group. The number of men required to operate the ground defences, including headquarters staff, searchlight and sound-ranging crews, gunners and support staff, was 15,115.[63]

In July 1917, in response to Chancellor Bethmann-Hollweg's denunciation of German raids on England as 'irritating the chauvinistic and fanatical instincts of the English nation without cause,' *Feldmarschall* von Hindenburg had replied: 'We must ... prosecute the war with all our resources and the greatest intensity. Your Excellency deprecates the aerial attacks on London. I do not think the English nature is such that anything can be done with them by conciliation or revealing a desire to spare them. The military advantages are great. They keep a large amount of war material away from the French front and destroy important enemy establishments of various kinds. It is regrettable, but inevitable, that they cause the loss of innocent lives as well.'[64]

Although it is true that casualties and property damage caused by German raiding were not great when measured against the immense loss of life and property in the battle zones of the armies, the German objective of tying down a significant part of the British aerial forces at relatively small cost was certainly achieved. Even leaving out of the calculation the production losses caused by absenteeism in war factories, and taking into account that a portion of the manpower needed to support the defence organization was not fit for military service overseas, it remains true that more than two hundred first-class fighter aircraft and the crews to man them were unavailable to the British forces on the Western Front for the greater part of 1918. Weighed against this consideration, and in a sense supporting the position of Bethmann-Hollweg, is the fact that German air raiding had a direct bearing on the formation of the RAF, the creation of the Independent Air Force, and the launching of a strategic bombing campaign against Germany, though that, too, could be regarded as a diversion of effort from the main battle zone.

With the exception of the numerous Canadians on RNAS home stations, the number taking part in the defence against German raids was never large, although it rose steadily throughout the war, and sharply in 1918. At the end of 1916 there were only eight Canadians flying with the eleven home defence squadrons then operational. By December 1917 there were thirty-one. From 1 September 1917 to the Armistice a total of 145 Canadians were posted to home defence. Of these, thirty had previous operational experience as pilots and five more as observers. A majority of this group probably passed through the operational night training provided by the home defence squadrons before being posted to other operational units, or to another home defence squadron. It is no longer possible to determine accurately the precise status of those listed on squadron strength returns from this period. Even so, it is evident that by the closing months of the war Canadians were serving in VI Brigade in numbers far exceeding those reached at any earlier period. The jump in their numbers was probably related to the output of the RAF's training programme in Canada.[65]

Despite their relatively small numbers, Canadians gave an excellent account of themselves, especially against the zeppelin. Of the twelve shot down by British aircraft in the course of the war, six were accounted for by Canadians, single-handedly or as part of a team. And a Canadian was to figure prominently in the dramatic climax to zeppelin raiding on England.[66]

In July 1918 an enormous airship of a new type made her maiden flight at Friedrichshafen. L 70 was nearly 700 feet long and her huge envelope had a gas capacity of 2,195,800 cubic feet. Driven by seven of the new Maybach MB-IVa engines, she was the fastest airship yet produced, with a maximum trial speed of 81 mph, a dynamic ceiling of 23,000 feet, and the capacity to carry at least four tons of bombs.[67] Peter Strasser did not allow his new weapon to rust. On the afternoon of 5 August five airships left their North Sea bases. L 70 was among them and accompanying her commander, *Kapitänleutnant* von Lossnitzer, was Strasser. But the weather was scarcely suitable for a zeppelin attack. Air temperatures over England were high and the barometer level low, sharply reducing the potential ceiling of the airships. Moreover, an anticipated westerly wind faded and the airships closed on the English coast sooner than had been estimated. Their presence was reported by a lightship while they were still off the Norfolk coast and the alert spread throughout the northern home defence network.

At Great Yarmouth air station most of the flying personnel, including the station commander, had gone off to town for the evening. On receiving the warning, the acting commanding officer, Captain Robert Leckie, proceeded to round up the missing airmen and at the same time to ready sufficient aircraft for them. Captain C.B. Sproatt, like Leckie from Toronto, was walking on the seaside boardwalk when he looked up and saw a zeppelin – 'there it was in the evening sky as plain as anything could be.' He flagged down a motorcycle, hopped into the sidecar, and sped off to the station. Sproatt had been flying a DH4 with a Rolls-Royce 375-hp Eagle VIII engine and was intent on getting it into the air. He was forestalled by Major Egbert Cadbury. Cadbury had been attending a concert party when he got the word. 'Knowing that there was only one machine available that had the necessary speed and climb,' Cadbury recalled, 'I roared down to the station in an ever-ready Ford ... and semi-clothed ... sprinted as hard as ever Nature would let me, and took a running jump into the pilot's seat.' According to Cadbury, he defeated Sproatt by a fifth of a second. No observer having appeared, Cadbury shouted to Leckie (who was not supposed to be flying) to jump into the rear seat, and the DH4 took off. Joining them were thirteen other aircraft from Great Yarmouth and its subsidiary fields, including two other DH4s, five DH9s, a Large America flying-boat, and five Camels. In addition to Leckie and Sproatt, three other Torontonians, Captain George Dennison Kirkpatrick and Lieutenants W.K. Prendergast and E.R. Munday, joined in the frenzied scramble into the air.[68]

Immediately after take-off Cadbury sighted three zeppelins in a 'v' formation about forty miles out to sea. Leckie could scarcely credit the sight. As he wrote a few days after: 'I am still astounded at the audacity of the German Commanders in bringing their ships so close to the Coast of England in broad daylight. I can only conclude that their navigation must have been seriously adrift.' After an hour's chase the DH4 closed up to L 70 and about six hundred feet below her. In Cadbury's words, 'my Observer trained his gun on the bow of the Airship and the fire was seen to concentrate on a spot under the Zeppelin ¾ way aft.' The Pomeroy bullets tore a great hole in the fabric and the fire ran the whole length of the stricken monster. L 70 'raised her bows as if in effort to escape, then plunged seaward a flaming mass.' Leckie reported later that the shooting from the zeppelin 'was as usual very bad,' which he put down to poor training in deflection firing and to the fact that the DH4 'must have been practically invisible against the dark clouds beneath us.' Though his gun had no sight, his tracer enabled him to bring his fire to bear after he had missed his huge target with the first five rounds.[69]

As Cadbury turned to pursue the two remaining zeppelins, he experienced temporary engine trouble. When the engine recovered the powerful DH4 moved in on one of them. An attack was made 'bow on,' and when Leckie opened fire a blaze of light was seen briefly in the amidships gondola. (The blaze of light, which the two had thought was a fire aboard the airship, resulted from a crewman inadvertently releasing a black-out curtain. It was immediately extinguished.) At this point Leckie's gun jammed. While he tried to clear the stoppage with frozen fingers (in the rush to take off, he had brought no gloves), L 65 made her escape. In this fashion, and with the death of its commander in L 70, the German Naval Airship Division ended the raiding of England. In a letter to his father, Egbert Cadbury wrote: '... another Zeppelin has gone to destruction, sent there by a perfectly peaceful "live-and-let-live" citizen, who has no lust for blood or fearful war spirit in his veins. It all happened very quickly and very terribly.'[70] Doubtless Cadbury's ambivalence stemmed from his Quaker upbringing. All zeppelin fighters, however, whether British or Canadian, were similarly affected by the peculiar horror of an airship in its death throes.

10

The RNAS and the Birth of a Bombing Strategy

The first British long-distance bombing force, 3 (Naval) Wing (sometimes known as the Luxeuil Wing), had the highest Canadian participation of any air formation in the war, because it was formed just as the first sizeable group of Canadians finished their training. The Luxeuil Wing has received cursory treatment in general histories.[1] There are good reasons for this. Its limited resources, and the short-comings of the air weapon itself, meant limited results. The force had no clearly stated objective and its operations have been overshadowed by those of its successor, the Independent Force. Yet the wing and its work did have considerable significance. It was created partly as a result of the influence of public opinion upon policy; it operated independently of other fighting arms; it directly co-operated with an allied force, the French Air Service; and it specialized in one thing: strategic bombing.

Because strategic bombing was rarely anything but indiscriminate, and because very often its targets were those another age (one which died during the First World War) would have termed non-military, there has been no rush of candidates to claim credit for having originated the idea. A favourite slander, echoed even by the British official history, attributed the practice of bombing non-military targets to German 'frightfulness.'[2] But Germany had no monopoly upon that commodity. A differing national style and political system dictated that Britain would engage in more soul-searching debate than did Germany, but in the end the British became whole-hearted advocates of 'strategic bombing,' for many of the same reasons that the Germans did.

Although the wing is very much part of Canadian air history, as with virtually every other instance of Canadian participation in the war in the air the airmen involved were masters of their fate only at the tactical level. The policy that placed them at Luxeuil, and indeed the entire debate about strategic bombing, was British, and it deeply divided opinion, whether public, political, or military-professional. At the level of policy, men were torn between moral scruples and the belief that German air raids upon England demanded retaliation from a proud people. Among the military, some took the view that bombing was a weapon of high potential that should be exploited to the maximum extent, possibly as a way to circumvent the stalemate on the Western Front, while others were dubious about the weapon and believed, in any event, that tactical needs and Haig's often desperate shortage of aircraft should be given primacy.

The debate was full of confusion and misconceptions as well, mostly on the side of the bombing enthusiasts whose hopes invariably outran the true capabilities of the air weapon. The belief that Germany could be defeated by bombing, held by some in high places and at least abetted by high-ranking military professionals, was illusory and fantastic, a product of the horror of the trenches and a wishful readiness to accept extreme claims for a solution to military stagnation. Even those who had a more limited view of the potentialities of bombing and who simply believed that air attack upon key German industries could make a substantial contribution to victory were victims of illusion. It was but a short step to argue for attacks upon the industrial labour force and to broaden the definition of a military target from the war industry to the people manning it.* Whatever the merits of their arguments, it is a fact that the advocates of strategic bombing triumphed over their opponents: an independent bombing force and its corollary, a separate air force, were created, partly at the expense of Haig's air strength on the Western Front.

The origins of this development are to be found in the activities of the RNAS. Spurred on by Winston Churchill, an enthusiastic believer in hitting zeppelins at their bases, the RNAS had undertaken the first long-distance raids in 1914. It was Churchill, too, who had authorized the design and construction of the Handley Page heavy bomber in December 1914 and who had urged the Admiralty Air Department to develop the capability to carry large amounts of explosives deep into enemy territory. Both at Dunkirk and the Dardanelles bombing became a chief task of the RNAS units. Even when Churchill and Fisher left the Admiralty, and air development in important respects languished, Rear-Admiral Vaughan-Lee continued to push the expansion of the aeroplane for long-distance bombing. By the end of 1915 the nucleus of a bombing squadron was under training at Detling, commanded by the British pilot who had successfully bombed airship sheds in Düsseldorf in September 1914. All the other airmen at Detling as of 18 December 1915 were Canadian. Meanwhile, the RFC subordinated bombing to artillery observation and reconnaissance and confined it to the tactical level. In October 1915, anticipating the acquisition of Sopwith 1½ Strutters, Trenchard considered the possibility of reprisals for the German zeppelin raids, an idea that got short shrift from Haig's staff: 'Reprisals are rarely effective in stopping the enemy permanently from taking any particular course,' one of them minuted.[3]

In France units specializing in bombing had an early start. The French had formed their first *Groupe de Bombardement* on 23 November 1914. Initially consisting of three squadrons of six Voisins each, by June 1915 the force had swollen to four groups, twenty-one squadrons, and 126 aircraft. Strategic objectives were at least part of its mission, since as well as attacking enemy lines of communication it was also directed against enemy industry with the special aim of demoralizing German workers. Concentrated at Malzéville, near Nancy, the force carried out long-distance raids on industrial targets in the Saar, Moselle, and Rhine valleys. Demands from the front put a stop to this precocious development. After September 1915 the force was broken up, and many of its aircraft were converted

---

* The Germans always claimed that their raids were upon specific military objectives, but of course they, like the British, necessarily engaged in indiscriminate bombing of built-up areas and frequently released their bombs through intervening cloud layers.

to gun-buses (*avions-canon*) armed with 37-mm Hotchkiss guns for strafing trains and troop columns. Only two squadrons remained to continue the bombing of industrial targets from their base at Belfort.[4]

As we saw in the last chapter, German air raids set off a rising demand in England for reprisals. In the House of Commons W. Joynson-Hicks had suggested in February 1916 that a few bombers with the range to attack Essen, Cologne, and the Rhine bridges 'would go a long way towards ending the war.' After the raid of 3 April on London, N. Pemberton Billing protested 'this affront to our national dignity, and this blow at our national life.'[5] On 17 May, in the course of an attack upon the Admiralty's 'navalization' of the RNAS, Winston Churchill lent his eloquence to the cause of strategic bombing. 'The air is free and open,' he pointed out: 'There are no entrenchments there. It is equal for the attack and for the defence. It is equal for all comers. The resources of the whole world are at our disposal and command. Nothing stands in the way of our obtaining the aerial supremacy in the War but yourselves. There is no reason, and there can be no excuse, for failure to obtain that air supremacy, which is, perhaps, the most obvious and most practical step towards a victorious issue from the increasing dangers of the War.'[6] He gave much the same advice to the Air Board, telling its members that the RNAS was 'being run on the little "Navyite" principle.'[7]

In terms of bombing the RNAS was certainly abreast of parliamentary opinion. The naval initiative to bomb industrial targets from Dunkirk in February had brought RFC protests and was a factor in the creation of Lord Derby's Joint War Air Committee. When the committee examined the RFC charges of RNAS poaching and found that while the Admiralty had surplus material, the War Office did not, it reached an important conclusion: 'Although co-operation between the two Services in long-range operations is ultimately desirable, the Naval programme for aircraft suitable for such raids should not be delayed until the Royal Flying Corps is ready to co-operate.' Having in mind Haig's shortage of seven squadrons, the committee nevertheless declared that support of the army and the fleet should be the first supply priority. Only after their requirements were met should long-range offensive operations be favoured. Home defence was given the next priority.[8]

Although the committee had thus backed in general terms the idea of a bombing offensive, it also considered arguments which were distinctly sceptical about the merits of this type of attack:

Opinion has been misled by the air raids against towns, munitions factories, aerodromes, etc., which are really secondary operations as were the raids of German ships across the North Sea for somewhat similar purposes. Those raids tended to weaken the German main fleet and were thus unsound in principle. The false ideal engendered by basing policy on the secondary operation instead of on the primary tends not only to mistaken strategy but to the production of ships and air machines unsound in principle. The force produced in view of the primary operations will probably cover the needs of the secondary ones.[9]

This view was challenged by Vaughan-Lee, who argued that an organized and systematic attack on Germany from bases in France was the right response to zeppelin raids and would have the strategic effect of drawing German air strength from the front. He suggested an approach to the French government for co-operation and requested from the Admiralty terms of reference which, 'speaking sensibly,' would amount to 'a free hand all round.' On the day that Derby handed in his resignation, the naval members of the committee underlined their rejection of his work by calling for full prosecution of long-distance bombing.[10]

The Admiralty adopted Vaughan-Lee's proposals and an invitation was procured from France to co-operate in bombing operations. On 1 May the Admiralty, which had worked through the French naval attaché in London without reference either to the War Office or the War Cabinet, sent Wing Captain W.L. Elder to Paris to discuss the proposal. On 5 May the personnel and aircraft of the new bombing force moved from Detling to Manston, becoming 3 (Naval) Wing (the original 3 Wing having been disbanded after withdrawal from Gallipoli).* On 16 May the first advance party went to Luxeuil-les-Bains in order to prepare the necessary facilities. By using the French base it would be possible to bomb German targets without flying over neutral territory – this was why the wing did not operate from southeast England, which would have meant flying over Holland.[11]

Conflicting requirements in France delayed Elder's preparations. At Dunkirk Wing Captain C.L. Lambe, strongly supported by Vice-Admiral Bacon, requested and received immediate reinforcements to counter growing enemy air strength in Flanders. In preparation for the Somme offensive the Admiralty had already agreed to divert sixty aircraft to the RFC. Thus it was not until late July that Elder was able to gather sufficient personnel and equipment for limited operations in conjunction with the French, and not until October that his wing was fully able to commence operations on its own.[12]

Elder's terms of reference were drawn up on 27 July, although they may not have been received by him until after the first raid, in which two Sopwith 1½ Strutters joined with French forces in attacking the benzine stores at Mülheim on 30 July. The instructions allowed Elder the 'free hand all round' which Vaughan-Lee had sought. The Admiralty was to play little part in target selection, which was left to the French, but wished merely to be kept informed of 'the general lines of your proposed operations.' Elder was told that he was always to obtain the consent of the 'General Officer Commanding the French Armies' for any planned operation. Naturally the Director of Air Services and the Sea Lords also wished to know of any disagreements with the French. The wing's situation, after all, was dependent upon French sufferance and co-operation. Thus, in September, when Squadron Commander H.A. Williamson tried to persuade the Admiralty to attack Friedrichshafen he was told: 'The French are not particularly anxious for us to carry out the, raid and, due to other matters of much greater import, we do not wish to press them in any way for the present at any rate ...'[13] If Vaughan-Lee's 'systematic' attack upon German cities was to be carried out, it would not be as the result of Admiralty planning and control.

Two paragraphs of Elder's instructions were of special interest:

* Canadians in the wing when it was reactivated were F.C. Armstrong of Toronto (KIA 25 March 1918); P.E. Beasley of Victoria; A.O. Brissenden of Halifax; S.T. Edwards of Carleton Place, Ont.; G.R.S. Flemming of Toronto (shot down and died of wounds on 14 April 1917); E.C. Potter and F.E. Fraser of Winnipeg; J.A. Glen of Enderby, BC; A.B. Shearer of Neepawa, Man.; L.E. Smith of Mystic, Que. (KIA 25 Feb. 1917); D.H. Whittier of Victoria (killed in a flying accident in July 1916); and G.K. Williams of Toronto (killed in a flying accident in June 1916).

4. It should be laid down that, as a general rule, the objectives should be of military value and promiscuous bombing of unfortified towns should on no account be permitted.

5. It should be borne in mind that it is a bad policy to attack an important objective, until you have sufficient force at your command to make the attack effective. To attack important objectives with small forces only serves to put the enemy on his guard.[14]

The first paragraph has a touch of the Nelsonian blind eye, though it may well be that no one at the Admiralty appreciated that the bombing of cities was of necessity 'promiscuous.'* The second was wise counsel, yet it must be said that the force required to render bombing truly effective was vastly larger than the Admiralty imagined, or Elder was to command.

Aircraft of the naval wing carried out all their raids between 30 July 1916 and 14 April 1917. For much of the time Nancy or Ochey, rather than Luxeuil, served as the base – a development that played an important part in target selection. From Luxeuil aircraft could easily fly to the Belfort Gap, which opens up between the Jura and Vosges mountains. Beyond lay the Black Forest, and only on the other side of that inhospitable terrain were the factory towns of the German homeland. From Ochey and Nancy, in contrast, situated as they are in the heart of Lorraine, it was easily possible to reach any number of targets in the highly industrialized valleys of the Saar and Moselle rivers. The targets to be attacked from Luxeuil in the ensuing months – Mülheim, Oberndorf, and Freiburg – were farther away, more difficult to reach and of lesser industrial significance. The raids from Luxeuil were carried out at ranges between sixty and a hundred miles; those from the more northerly airfields were carried out at ranges between thirty and seventy miles.

The first major operation, which falls into a special category, was the raid of 12 October. On 3 September the commander of the French aviation service, *Lieutenant-Colonel* Barés, ordered *Capitaine* Happe, commanding the French bombing squadrons now at Luxeuil, to bomb the Mauser rifle factories at Oberndorf. Wing Captain Elder agreed to participate with all the aircraft and pilots then available. The French squadrons were not ready to undertake so ambitious a project until 11 October, however, so 3 Wing was able to accumulate more strength while it waited for the French and to engage in intensive training for the operation.[15]

The 220 miles of cross-country flying was a particular challenge for the pilots. They were given a route direct to Oberndorf, returning by way of Schlettstadt and Corcieux (a French aerodrome).[16] The wing had been organized into Red and Blue Squadrons, each broken up into two flights of bombers with escorting fighters. Two pilots who had flown to Mülheim in July, the Canadians J.A. Glen

---

* Current sighting equipment (the CFS bomb-sight) and technique required a bomber to approach the target directly up- or down-wind while the bomb aimer used a stopwatch to measure his speed by two sights of one object on the ground and then set the movable foresight on a timing-scale to correspond with the observed time interval between the two measured sights. C.B. Sproatt of Toronto, who was a flight sub-lieutenant at Dunkirk towards the end of 1916, has recorded that '... the bombsights were so bad ... that an experienced pilot could do better bombing without a sight than he could with one.' W.A.B. Douglas, taped interview with Sproatt, 22 Dec. 1968, transcript, 28, DHist 74/43

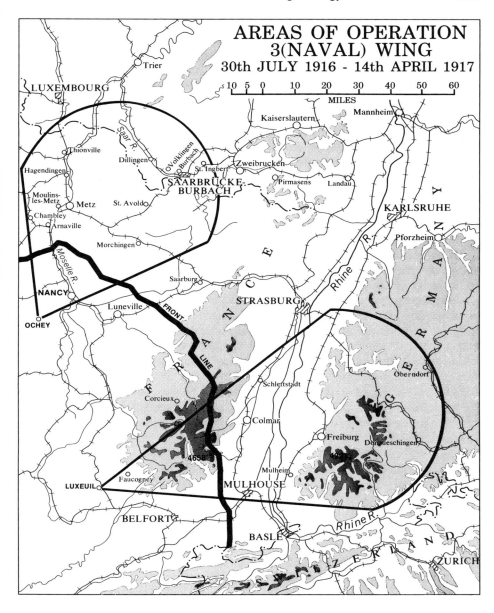

AREAS OF OPERATION
3(NAVAL) WING
30th JULY 1916 - 14th APRIL 1917

and E.C. Potter, were the only members of the wing who had first-hand knowledge of some of the terrain. Both flew bombers in 'A' flight of the Red Squadron.
Red Squadron consisted of Sopwith 1½ Strutters; Blue Squadron had one flight of
1½ Strutters and one of Bréguet Vs.* Both French and British aeroplanes took off
in their flights at fixed intervals, circling to rendezvous above the aerodrome
before setting course for the target.

The mixture of obsolescent Bréguet Vs and the relatively up-to-date Sopwith
1½ Strutters in the wing created a number of problems. The Sopwith was an
impressive machine for its day, even though the two-seater fighter versions on the
Somme had finally met their match in September. The synchronized Vickers gun
on the engine cowling and the ring-mounted Lewis gun in the observer's seat
provided an unusually strong armament. The single-seat bomber version, fitted
with internal tandem carriers designed to carry two 112-lb bombs but also capable
of carrying four 65-lb bombs when the vanes were cut down, had a slower rate of
climb than the fighter (over twenty-four minutes to 10,000 feet compared to
seventeen minutes, fifty seconds) but could maintain slightly better speed. The
Bréguet V was so radically different from either version of the Sopwith that it was
clear to Wing Commander R. Bell Davies he could not hope to mount a co-
ordinated bombing strike without exceptional allowances. The outdated Bréguet
took twice as long as the Sopwith to reach altitude (forty-nine minutes to 10,000
feet) and was about 15 mph slower than the British machine. It was unstable fore
and aft, slow on turns, and almost impossible to fly on instruments. This lumbering machine did have one virtue, however – a good arc of fire from the forward
nacelle. Perhaps remembering the performance of FE2bs in combat, Bell Davies
thought that if the squadron could meet an attack without breaking formation
some measure of safety could be achieved. He was prepared to test the theory in
action, provided fighters escorted each Bréguet flight.[17]

What kinds of formation could best protect bombers against enemy fighters,
faster, more manoeuvrable, and perhaps better armed than they? The solution
adopted was the first British attempt to come to grips with this fundamental problem of bombing operations. In a formation of six, including a single fighter
escort, the Sopwiths were staggered in height, increasing by 150 feet towards the
rear, with the fighter about 750 feet above the leader in the opening of the 'v'
behind the formation. The Bréguets, in flights of six, formed a triangle with the
machines staggered downwards in height so that they could cover each other. The
formation gave these slow aircraft the maximum amount of mutual protection,
buttressed by two or more fighters stationed behind and above them.

Much effort had gone into practising the rendezvous and formation, which were
essential to success. For the two flights of the Red Squadron the process was
completed without incident. They proceeded to the target according to plan but on
the return journey one of the bombers was attacked by an enemy machine. Flight
Sub-Lieutenant Raymond Collishaw recorded how 'When at 12000 [feet] 10 miles
across the Rhine, dived at a Hun with full engine, firing machine gun, to protect
Butterworth from attack. When closing the enemy my motor cut out completely,

* The Bréguets had been acquired when it was clear that Short Bombers would not be available.

veered away and got my motor again at 900 revs, recrossed the lines at 6000 ft. and returned to Luxeuil. Shot down one Fokker Scout over Rhine.'[18] A subsequent inspection of his engine by the ground crew revealed that the distributor was damaged and that the lead to one plug had broken. As for Flight Sub-Lieutenant C.H.S. Butterworth, of Ottawa, his bomber was hit in the engine by the Fokker D-II that attacked him, but he was able to glide to a landing on a German airfield at Freiburg. By the time the Blue Squadron took off, heavy banks of clouds had moved in. The Sopwiths failed to rendezvous. One crashed at Faucogney twenty-five minutes after take off; the other three eventually returned independently to the landing field. Flight Sub-Lieutenant L.E. Smith of Mystic, Que., part of the Bréguet's escort for this flight, joined Wing Commander Bell Davies and Flight Sub-Lieutenant R.F. Redpath of Montreal, who were awaiting the Bréguets above the clouds. After an anxious delay, Davies 'saw a disturbance in the white layer below and the top plane of a Bréguet appeared. The machines came out one by one looking like a string of hippos emerging from a pool.'[19]

The raid was an instructive experience. German air defences were perhaps more effective than anticipated. The first allied flights reached Oberndorf without being intercepted, but later French flights were attacked by German aircraft, including slow reconnaissance machines.* The Bréguets, which bombed Donaueschingen, thinking that it was Oberndorf, lost two of their number to German air attacks over Alsace. Had it not been for the watchfulness of their fighter escorts, all of them might have had to land in Switzerland, where their crews would have been interned. Bell Davies thought they were drifting over the Swiss border as they flew home and Flight Sub-Lieutenant Redpath apparently recognized the terrain. He flew out in front of the formation and made a sharp turn, leading the bombers back to a safe course. The four surviving Bréguets had to land in pitch darkness, but they all reached friendly territory.[20]

The Board of Admiralty derived much satisfaction from the initial reports. '... I trust a good start has been made,' wrote the Third Sea Lord:

These raids should have the result of withdrawing large numbers of enemy's machines from the front as well as men and munitions just as the Zeppelin raids have accomplished against us; & this quite in addition to actual damage which may be caused to important works.

Incidentally, the lighting of German Towns is now being restricted & special prayers in the Churches, so there is immense moral effect as well.[21]

The First Sea Lord, Admiral Sir Henry Jackson, pointed out that such raids, having 'a strategical value & also a moral one,' should be kept up as long as weather permitted and opportunities arose. The First Lord, A.J. Balfour, noted these comments with apparent approval.[22]

French reaction was quite different. For them, the raid had been a disaster. Two out of twelve Farman XL-IIs and four out of seven Bréguet Michelin IVs had

---

* One squadron of Fokkers was based at Freiburg for air defence; other squadrons were based near Colmar for reconnaissance and artillery co-operation over the lines.

been shot down; a Bréguet V borrowed from the RNAS had met with a similar fate. The famous *Escadrille Lafayette* had provided a measure of protection, but the limited endurance of their Nieuports had prevented them from remaining with the bombers for very long. Consequently, even a humble German AGO C-I aircraft was able to shoot down one of the Bréguet IVs. 'It is permissible to state,' ran the French report, 'that raids of a very great distance can be carried out with very few losses if the [Farman and Bréguet] Squadrons ... could be transformed into Sopwith Squadrons and could work with the English.'[23] Whatever the results at Oberndorf (these proved to have been disappointing), and whatever the weather, so long as French aircraft did not improve further opportunities for raids like this one were not going to arise. It was this realization that led directly to the next phase of 3 (Naval) Wing's operations.

It was partly because the French decided not to attempt any more daylight raids for the time being, and partly because weather made Luxeuil-based operations almost impossible, that both French and British bombing forces shifted to the advanced base at Nancy. From there they hoped to deliver successive day and night attacks on industrial targets. The first took place on 22 and 23 October against the Essingden steel works at Hagendingen, about forty miles north of Nancy in the Moselle Valley. Following a night attack by the *4e Groupe de Bombardement*, two flights of Sopwith bombers escorted by six fighters set out. One bomber crashed taking off. The remainder found the target and reported dropping at least thirty 65-lb bombs on the factories and blast furnaces at the objective. The Germans put up heavy anti-aircraft fire, but not many aircraft rose to challenge the intruders. Those that did failed to press home their attacks.[24]

Wind and rain grounded all aircraft for the next two weeks. During this period the RNAS aircraft moved to Ochey, about twelve miles southwest of Nancy, a transfer that was not, in every case, as simple and uneventful as might be expected. As Raymond Collishaw recorded, he

... was detailed to ferry a new machine from Luxeuil to the new base and took off without a gunner in the rear cockpit. Enroute I was jumped on by enemy fighters and a bullet passed through my goggles, temporarily blinding me. Diving into German territory, I shook off my pursuers momentarily, but they caught up with me and I flew deeper into Germany in an effort to shake them off. Finally I did so, and after flying back towards French territory prepared to land at an aerodrome I saw below. I put down and taxied in among the aircraft parked on the ground, and then it dawned on me that they bore the German Iron Cross marking! I jammed the throttle forward and managed to take off, although I clipped off the tops of two trees close to the field.[25]

The new airfield was less cluttered and probably in no worse condition than the one they were leaving. The only damage suffered on the raid of 23 October had been caused by one bad take-off and three rough landings resulting from the appalling state of the ground at Nancy. Wing Captain Elder, realizing that the move to an advanced base would be more or less permanent, ordered the setting up of huts and workshops at Ochey. When the weather cleared up on the night of 9 November there were three flights of bombers and about eight fighters ready for operations. They were called upon to launch daylight raids, following night raids by the French, for the next three days. The targets were the steel works at Völklingen and St Ingbert in the Saar Basin, sixty to seventy miles distant. On 10 November nine bombers escorted by eight fighters dropped thirty-five 65-lb bombs on Völklingen; on 11 November fourteen bombers escorted by seven fighters dropped more than fifty bombs on the same target in weather conditions that were rapidly deteriorating. Stiffer air defence was now being encountered and some of the Sopwith pilots were lucky to escape unharmed.* On 12 November nine bombers escorted by seven fighters, hampered by the ever thickening haze, attacked the steel works at St Ingbert. All aircraft returned.[26]

Bad weather, and the fact that the 130-hp Clerget engines built in England were wearing badly and developing excessive tolerances, prevented further attacks until 24 November. By that date nine bombers with seven fighters were able to bomb the blast furnaces and iron works at Dillingen. As before, there were no casualties. Wing Captain Elder announced the intention of continuing raids on this target until it was destroyed, but not for another month did the weather again permit effective bombing. The chief problem was low visibility which made recognition of the target from 7000 feet impossible, while a combination of anti-aircraft fire and balloon barrages made bombing from lower heights impracticable. Compounding this difficulty was the condition of the ground at Ochey. '... unless it is frozen,' reported Wing Captain Elder, 'it is almost impossible for machines to get off owing to the depth of the mud: accidents to propellers are frequent.' His remarks were borne out on 27 December, when eleven bombers and five fighters set out to raid Dillingen. One of the fighters trying to take off broke a propeller on the field. Although nine bombers reached the target, haze and clouds hampered observation. Nevertheless, the effort to reach the target aroused sufficient admiration to make the wing's commanding officer gloss over such dubious results. '... as the target is a large one,' Elder wrote blithely, 'it is probable that many bombs reached the Objective.'[27]

In January only one raid took place, against Saarbrücke-Burbach. It was in this raid that the first serious RNAS casualties occurred. Flight Sub-Lieutenant M.H. Stephens of Toronto landed without realizing a bomb was hung up in the rack. It exploded while mechanics were handling the aircraft. Three of them were killed and Stephens lost a leg. In the freezing weather only sixteen of twenty-four aircraft had reached the objective and five severe cases of frostbite were reported after the raid. Even more significant was the difficulty of running aircraft engines in low temperatures. Early in February, when the temperature appears to have fallen well below freezing, it was found impossible even to start the engines.[28]

It was not until 25 February that the wing again launched a raid, this time with twenty aircraft against the iron works and blast furnaces at Saarbrücke-Burbach. German air defence was apparently becoming increasingly effective, and L.E.

---

*   It was on the raid of 11 November that Flight Sub-Lieutenant G.S. Harrower of Montreal (WIA 23 Sept. 1917) became separated and, unsure of his position, flew in a westerly direction until he could be certain that he was clear of the enemy lines. When he landed he found that he had succeeded so well in his aim that he was at Dijon, more than 100 miles southwest of Ochey.

Smith and his gunlayer were shot down and killed on this raid; Winnipegger E.C. Potter was lucky to glide to a forced landing behind French rather than German lines. On 4 March two squadrons of seven bombers and three fighters each tried again but the raid was not one of 3 Wing's more successful ones. Five of the bombers returned with engine defects and one bombed the railway station at St Avold instead of the designated target. Ten German aircraft in formation attacked the Sopwiths, prompting Wing Commander C.E. Rathbone (who had taken over from Bell Davies) to conclude that 'the enemy appears to be collecting machines for the protection of the Saar Valley.' A third attack by seven bombers and four fighters was attempted on 16 March. Flight Sub-Lieutenant J.E. Sharman of Oak Lake, Man., leading the raid, decided to divert to the alternative target of Morchingen aerodrome because the wind was too strong to reach the Saar Valley. Only one more raid of this nature was carried out by the Sopwiths, on 22 March, again against the blast furnaces at Saarbrücke-Burbach. On this occasion six bombers and three fighters took part.[29]

By this time several important developments had begun to exert their influence on the Luxeuil Wing. Aircraft production was not maintaining pace with RFC requirements on the Western Front, and the RNAS was being called upon to place fully equipped and manned fighter squadrons at the disposal of RFC headquarters. This was a crisis that not only prevented the expansion of the wing to its planned size, but actually forced the Admiralty to reduce the existing establishment. At the end of January 3 Wing pilots began transferring to Dunkirk for duty on the Western Front. The first group of nine left at the end of January, and a second group of nineteen in March.* After their departure nineteen Canadians still remained with the Luxeuil Wing. Sixteen of them were Sopwith pilots; the others, two observers and a pilot, were attached to the wing's Handley Page 0/100s.

The Handley Page became the most important British bombing aircraft in the war, but not before it had suffered extraordinary growing pains. The RNAS had begun trials with the aircraft on 17 December 1915. Flight Lieutenant J.T. Babington, with an engineer who was to be intimately concerned with the Handley Page development, Lieutenant-Commander E.W. Stedman,† carried out the first flights for the RNAS, formed the first Handley Page squadron, and also flew the aeroplane into battle for the first time more than a year later. The designers had to overcome defects in the dynamic stability of the aircraft and it was not until October 1916 that the first production model reached an operational unit. To airmen accustomed to Sopwiths it seemed like 'a grotesque giant ... as though a fifty-

---

* Canadians in the first group were F.C. Armstrong of Toronto (KIA 25 March 1918), R. Collishaw of Nanaimo, BC, J.S.T. Fall of Hillbank, BC, P.G. McNeil of Toronto (KIA 3 June 1917), J.J. Malone of Regina (KIA 30 April 1917), and A.T. Whealey of Toronto. In the second group were G.B. Anderson of Ottawa, P.E. Beasley of Victoria, A.W. Carter of Calgary (WIA June 1918), W.H. Chisam of Edmonton (WIA 8 April 1918), S.T. Edwards of Carleton Place, Ont., N.D. Hall of Victoria (POW 3 Sept. 1917), M.R. Kingsford and G.D. Kirkpatrick, both of Toronto, G.G. MacLennan of Owen Sound, Ont., D.H. Masson of Ottawa, Q.S. Shirriff of Toronto, and H.D.M. Wallace of Blind River, Ont.

† Stedman came to Canada after the First World War and joined the Canadian Air Force in 1922. In 1924 he became Assistant Director, Supply and Research, RCAF. He rose to become Director-General Air Research as an Air Vice-Marshal in 1942.

story skyscraper ... had suddenly been erected in London.' The first Handley Page went to 3 Wing* where Elder formed a poor opinion of its capabilities. Magneto trouble caused delays in flying as did distorted propellers 'through either inefficient design or bad material, as far as one can judge, from the former.' A second aircraft arrived in February, and by this time the Handley Pages may well have been serviceable. It was not, however, until 16 March that the weather was judged good enough to attempt the first raid. The aircraft selected was No 1460, which had joined the wing in October. The crew consisted of Babington; Stedman, acting as observer; Flight Sub-Lieutenant C.L. Hains of Salmon Arm, BC, who served as after gunlayer; and *Adjutant* Chasard of the French air service who accompanied them as forward gunlayer and guide.[30]

The great advantage of the big bombing aircraft was its capacity and what we would now call cost-effectiveness. The Rolls-Royce Eagle engines, each developing 250 hp, gave the 0/100 an endurance of nine-and-a-half hours with an all-up weight of five-and-a-half tons, including 380 gallons of fuel and ten 112-lb bombs. For shorter raids, carrying 250 gallons of fuel in wing tanks and seventy gallons in the fuselage, the aircraft could carry fourteen 112-lb bombs. If the fuel in the fuselage was removed the load could be increased to sixteen bombs. There were sixteen cells in bomb bays under the fuselage in which bombs were hung by their nose. The bombs, when released, forced open the spring-loaded doors that covered the bomb bays. There was a bomb release handle in the cockpit beside the floor sighting opening which the observer operated by crawling under the pilot's seat. The real weaknesses of the 0/100 were its lack of speed and the inaccuracy of its bomb-dropping. From the first it was considered a night bomber, with its bombing altitude of 6000 feet and cruising speed of 60–75 mph. Its bombs were to be aimed so as to straddle a target. 'The general design and operation of these machines,' stated the official training notes, 'resemble airships more than aeroplanes.'[31]

The first raid was to be fairly simple. Hagendingen was reckoned to be within the radius for which no more than two-hours endurance was required, allowing for a 30-mph headwind and a return speed of 75 mph. Babington did not take a full load of bombs because it had been found difficult to obtain correct balance both with the full load and after dropping the bombs. Consequently only the foremost bays were used, and twelve 100-lb bombs were carried. At 6000 feet a headwind of 36 mph was encountered and heavy cumulo-nimbus clouds rapidly began to form. Mist obscured the valleys so the target was changed to the railway station of Moulins-les-Metz. The aircraft reached the objective and the bombs were released, but they stuck in the bomb bay doors. Stedman had to put all his weight on the bombs to push them through, two of which were seen to explode 'close to

---

* Not, as claimed by some authorities, to Dunkirk. It may have staged through Dunkirk, but the destination was Luxeuil. The second went to Dunkirk and then joined 3 Wing later in 1917. The third Handley Page left England on 1 January 1917 and landed by mistake twelve miles behind the German lines. The fourth seems to have gone to Dunkirk on the same date and stayed there. Air 1/2387/228/11/38; Stedman and Waller biographical files, DHist; 'Raids Carried out by Handley Page Machines nos. 1459 and 1460,' Air 1/2266/209/70/18. Cf Bruce Robertson, *British Military Aircraft Serials, 1912–1966* (London 1966), 271; Owen Thetford, *British Naval Aircraft Since 1912* (London 1962), 212.

the objective.'[32] The Englishman Paul Bewsher, who served as an observer in Handley Pages, witnessed the take-off and landing for this historic raid from the ground. He heard the engines of the returning aircraft, then they switched off and No 1460 suddenly appeared '... a few hundred feet in the air, brilliantly lit up by two blindingly white lights which burned fiercely below both wing-tips, and from which dropped little gouts of luminous liquid. The powerful illumination lighted up every face, every dress, every shed and pile of stones in clear detail with its quivering glare.'[33] It was a moment of exhilaration. Even though the bombs had dropped harmlessly, Wing Captain Elder reported himself satisfied with the aeroplane and the suitability of the area for its operations. 'The machine itself ...' he was persuaded, 'exceeded all expectations.'[34]

Three more Handley Page raids took place from Ochey in April, although on 25 March Elder had received his instructions for disbanding the wing in the near future. On the night of 5 April both Handley Pages, one of which was flown by Flight Sub-Lieutenant E.B. Waller of Toronto, flew on a raid against the railway junction at Arnaville. The other aircraft had to return with engine trouble, but Waller and his observer, Flight Sub-Lieutenant D.R.C. Wright of Toronto, dropped all their bombs at the objective. On 14 April two separate raids were carried out. One machine attacked the blast furnaces at Hagendingen; Waller and Wright bombed the depot and aerodrome at Chambley.[35] In only four flights the Handley Pages of 3 Wing had dropped almost as much explosive as twenty-one 1½ Strutters had been able to drop in two separate raids with ten fighter escorts.*

Where all this explosive was actually landing, however, was another matter. The CFS bombsight was still in use. As the machine approached the target the bomb aimer conveyed his course corrections to the pilot by a tug on the appropriate flying boot from where he lay beneath the pilot's seat, peering down between the sliding range bars fixed at right angles to a direction bar that comprised the sighting mechanism. Nor was the mechanical bomb release gear entirely reliable. In an attack on the blast furnaces at Metz – a highly visible target at night – one flyer '... pressed over my lever and heard a clatter behind. I pressed it over again and looked back. Many of the bombs had disappeared – a few remained scattered in different parts of the bomb-rack. I looked down again, and pressed over my lever twice more ... I looked back and saw by the light of my torch that one bomb was still in the machine. I walked back to the bomb-rack ... put my foot on the top of it and stood up. It slipped suddenly through the bottom and disappeared.'[36]

Possible reduction of the Luxeuil Wing had been foreseen in the Admiralty as early as 12 December 1916. At that time it was only stated that 'the development of No. 3 Wing will be retarded,' but the writing was on the wall. The irrepressible C.G. Gray expressed the trend accurately on 3 January 1917 when he took to task '... the addle-pated incompetents who have thrown away good men and man-

* That is, the raids of 25 February (3380 lbs) and 16 March (1560 lbs), for a total of 4940, compared to 4800 lbs dropped by the four Handley Pages. After the first raid the spring doors were removed. Brown paper fairings in their place permitted the bombs to burst through so that the crews were subjected to a fearful draft during the flights home until the doors were modified and replaced. E.W. Stedman, *From Boxkite to Jet: the Memoirs of an Aeronautical Engineer* (Mercury Series, Canadian War Museum, Paper No 1; Ottawa 1972), 25

power on useless work, both in the air and in aeroplane factories.' The operations of 3 Wing were included in his indictment.[37] In February Commodore D.G. Paine, now Fifth Sea Lord and Director of Air Services, visited Haig in France. As Paine had foreseen, it would be necessary for the RNAS to draw in its horns in order to keep up the strength of squadrons on loan to the RFC on the Western Front. Paine was willing to withdraw the Luxeuil Wing, even though the French were sorry to lose the help of day bombers.

Behind Paine's co-operation in this matter lay one of the most bitter inter-service squabbles of the war. The chief protagonists were Lord Curzon, President of the Air Board, and Arthur Balfour, First Lord of the Admiralty. It was impossible for Balfour to get around the fact that the Admiralty had consistently by-passed the War Office and the Air Board in determining naval air policy. When, amidst the euphoria surrounding the aftermath of the Oberndorf raid, Colonel Barés of the French air service had visited London late in October 1916, the Admiralty's methods had finally forced the matter into the open. The French commander had been invited without consulting either the War Office or General Haig in France. Barés, it is true, did attend a meeting of the Air Board, but he had first attended a special meeting in the Admiralty which considered ways and means of conducting a strategic bombing campaign independent of other arms. This meant procuring large numbers of engines for the RNAS at a time when the RFC was desperately short. Haig was very angry and wrote, probably with the help of Trenchard and his staff, one of the seminal documents in the history of air warfare. Barés' arguments, Haig insisted, were 'based more on enthusiasm for his own particular service than on sound military judgement.'

In my opinion our military policy in aerial, as in other respects, must be based on the principle that a successful end of the war can be brought about only by decisive victory over the enemy's forces in the field.

For this, in aerial matters, the first requirement is an adequate supply of efficient artillery, photographic and contact patrol machines, with sufficient fighting machines, of the best types that can be procured to protect them.

The next most urgent requirement is reconnaissance behind the enemy's lines, and bombing of such railways, headquarters, bivouacs, etc., as may affect the issue of a battle by upsetting the enemy's organization and command, and interfering with his tactical and strategical movements.

Long distance bombing as a means of defeating the enemy is entirely secondary to the above requirements. Its success is far more doubtful, and, even when successful, both theory and practice go to show that usually its results are comparatively unimportant.

I have no reason to suppose that the bombing of open towns merely for the purpose of terrorizing the civil population is a method of warfare which would be approved by His Majesty's Government, nor would I recommend its adoption.

Colonel Barés contends that the bombing of German towns has caused the Germans to withdraw a number of their machines from the front. I do not agree with this, as there are no signs on the western front that the Germans have done this ...

In short, I am of opinion that the views attributed to Colonel Barés, as stated, are unsound in theory and should not be accepted in practice.[38]

Curzon expanded upon Haig's theme and put forward the principle (echoing the words of the Derby Committee in April) that long-range bombing must be related to the army's plans.[39]

By the end of March the end was near for 3 Wing, but on 1 April Elder received orders to postpone disbandment until a reprisal raid had been carried out against Freiburg. The use of the wing for this purpose had been discussed in October during the meetings with Barès, at a time when British opinion was especially agitated by alleged German atrocities. In August the British government had cited a number of incidents to the International Red Cross, including the execution of Edith Cavell, the neglect of allied prisoners of war suffering from typhoid fever, the sinking of the passenger ships *Lusitania* and *Sussex*, and the execution of Captain Charles Fryatt. Fryatt, a merchant marine captain, had attempted to ram a U-boat and was executed on the grounds that he had contravened the rules of war. When Captain James Blaikie of the SS *Caledonia* seemed in danger of a similar fate, there was agitation in Britain that his death be paid for by the execution of a high-ranking German prisoner of war. Instead, the British government determined to use 3 Wing in an attack on Freiburg, an open town. The wing remained under orders to prepare for this mission until 19 December, when the planned raid was abandoned after the German Foreign Office indicated that no action would be taken against Blaikie. It was revived when the hospital ship *Asturias* was torpedoed on 20 March 1917; an infuriated English public demanded revenge both for this and what were deemed a whole series of German atrocities.[40]

The Freiburg raid of 14 April was the wing's last and it did not go smoothly. Two flights took off at about 1100 hrs, but one, 'B' flight, failed to rendezvous properly and returned to base. Wing Commander Rathbone, however, remained aloft to join 'A' flight as a fighter escort, replacing Flight Sub-Lieutenant E.V. Reid, who had engine trouble. Led by J.E. Sharman, this flight flew directly to Freiburg and bombed the town centre. Not until the flight swung round the Kaiserstuhl hill, north of town, did Sharman sight the first opposition. Three biplanes, identified as Fokkers, took off from Colmar and attacked the escorts, flown by Rathbone, Flight Lieutenant G.R.S. Fleming, and Flight Sub-Lieutenants W.E. Flett and W.M. Alexander, both of Toronto. A brief and costly combat ensued. Flett sent one of the German aircraft down out of control, but both Rathbone and Fleming were shot down. The tail of Fleming's machine was blown off and he died of injuries sustained in the crash; Rathbone became a prisoner of war. Flett had to fight his way back after becoming separated, his aircraft damaged and his gunlayer being twice wounded. Although it is possible that Sharman had not sighted all the German aircraft, there is nothing to indicate that more than one German flight took off to defend Freiburg. The loss of two of the wing's most experienced pilots to such meagre opposition was a severe blow.[41]

After the return of the first group, Sharman undertook to lead 'B' flight for an afternoon raid* leaving at 1530 hrs. Once again, an uneventful flight except for anti-aircraft fire marked the outward journey. In the morning Sharman had avoided enemy airfields on the return by swinging northwest to Corcieux. In the afternoon

---

* Sharman was awarded the DSC for this day's work.

he led 'B' flight to the northern end of the Belfort Gap, crossing the lines near Luneville before returning to Luxeuil. Enemy aircraft were not encountered until 'B' flight neared the lines. Flight Sub-Lieutenants Harold Edwards of New Aberdeen, NS, and C.E. Pattison of Winona, Ont., succeeded in bringing down one of the Germans, but Edwards was then attacked and brought down himself, so that he became a prisoner of war. The bomber of Flight Sub-Lieutenant A.C. Dissette of Vancouver was hit by anti-aircraft fire, but he crashed two kilometres inside the French lines and managed to escape unhurt.[42]

French machines, consisting of six Sopwith bombers, five Sopwith fighters, three Nieuports, and one Spad, bombed Freiburg immediately after 'B' flight and returned without any losses. Wing Captain Elder in his report to the Admiralty pointed out that the heavy French fighter escort had thus shown its worth: '... Sopwith fighters ... are now quite outclassed by the German type of machines, and no longer form adequate protection to the bombing machines. It is only through the self sacrifice of the three missing Fighter Pilots and their Gunlayers that all our bombing machines returned safely.'[43] Altogether the allied aircraft had dropped nearly 5500 lbs of bombs, and the pilots reported extensive fires when they returned from the afternoon raid. They had also dropped leaflets on which was printed 'Als Vergeltung fur [sic] den Untergang des HOSPITAL-SCHIFF "ASTURIAS" welche am 20–21 Marz 1917 stattfand.'*

The Admiralty seems to have taken little interest in the results of this final raid. Not so the French. In an information bulletin based on German newspaper reports, dated 18 April and issued at Belfort, it was stated that the Karlsruhe-Leopoldville line had been blocked, the Freiburg station damaged, and about twenty soldiers killed or wounded. It was also claimed that six bombs had fallen on a theatre and an ophthalmological clinic had been hit, resulting in about thirty casualties, mostly soldiers. Months later an English professor of bacteriology, abstracting intelligence from German medical journals, learned from the *Münchener Medicinische Wochen-Schrift* that the entire comparative anatomy collection at the University of Freiburg, with its teaching materials, pictures, models, and microscopes, had been destroyed. The anthropological collection had also been pulverized. It cannot be said, then, that much satisfaction was to be taken from the reprisal. In the British Parliament Mr Bonar Law stated that the government did not wish to compete with the enemy over reprisals except when 'inevitable.' But as the French bulletin had stated, probably quoting German sources, 'L'attaque de FRIBURG forme une triste pendant au meurtre d'enfants de CARLSRUHE, le 22 juin de l'année dernière.'†[44]

The Luxeuil Wing thus brought its operations to a close. Most of the Sopwith bombers were turned over to the French; the naval airmen were dispersed, most of them to Dunkirk for service with the RNAS squadrons on loan to the RFC. Their task, as it turned out, had been a thankless one. Their commander met not praise but recriminations. Why had there been so few raids? Why were the

---

* 'As a reprisal for the sinking of the hospital ship *Asturias*, which took place on the 20–21 March 1917.'
† This referred to a French air raid in which a bomb had fallen on a circus on 21 June 1916.

material results so meagre? Elder could only reply that the operational period had been during the worst time of year, though the RNAS had flown even when the French thought the weather unsuitable. He had never been given the promised number of aircraft; most of those he had were becoming obsolete. Yet his airmen had never shirked their duty and many had far exceeded it.*

In 1937 the British official historian came to Elder's defence: 'With our fuller knowledge it is clear that the effect produced by the naval bombing wing was disproportionate to the number of raids.' He claimed that German morale in industrial centres had been shaken and that bombing had 'compelled the Germans to divert aeroplanes, labour, and material to the beginnings of widespread schemes of home defence.' The only evidence offered about the disruption of German industry is a telegram to the High Command of 18 November 1916 warning of the 'serious dislocation of work' in Düsseldorf steel plants. The same telegram is cited in the German official history for the period, published in 1938. That history attributes improvements in German home defence not to a reaction to bombing but to experience derived from the Battles of Verdun and the Somme.[45] Without further authentic German evidence, it is impossible to estimate the degree and duration of work stoppages in industry.

Did the work of 3 Wing cause a diversion of German air strength to the home front? The evidence does not appear to support such a conclusion. For example, air headquarters of the French Seventh Army reported that only seven German aircraft were available for the defence of Freiburg. All seven were committed during the raid; two were shot down and four damaged.[46] Yet they had destroyed three British aircraft, while a fourth was shot down by anti-aircraft fire. It is true that in the course of the wing's operations there had been an increasing number of air combats, but they were not because the Germans had concentrated larger numbers of aircraft on the home front, as Rathbone had suggested in March, but because improved warning systems and better machines had enabled the defenders to reach their opponents and bring them to battle.

The breakup of 3 Wing meant the loss of many pilots experienced in long-distance bombing to quite different tasks at the front. Nor was any advantage taken by the Admiralty of the knowledge acquired by the officers who had led the wing. Rathbone, of course, was a prisoner of war; Bell Davies had been transferred to flying operations with the Grand Fleet; Elder reverted to general service in an obscure sea command. Only the Handley Pages and their crews were to continue in the long-range bombing role.

Though this appears a cavalier disregard of hard-won skill, there was plenty of expertise at Dunkirk where, in fact, bombing operations had been more extensive

---

* Five pilots, the Canadians W.H. Chisam of Edmonton (WIA 8 April 1918), W.E. Flett of Toronto (WIA April 1917), C.A. Magwood and E.C. Potter, both of Winnipeg, and the Englishman Fitz-Gibbon, underwent some Admiralty harassment for failure to complete the raid on Saarbrücke-Burbach on 4 March. All except Potter received official censure, but Magwood did not cease to protest this decision and in June the Admiralty 'decided to accept his ... explanation and withdraw the censure.' Rathbone to Elder, 22 March 1917, Air 1/648/17/122/397; further correspondence in ibid. of 17 April 1917, May 1917, and 23 June 1917

than at Luxeuil. The Luxeuil Wing had flown eighteen raids; during the same period 4 and 5 Wings had flown fifty-two missions at comparable ranges. Though many of these were tactical in nature, against aerodromes, ammunition dumps, and lines of communication, and were intended to support military operations on the Somme, most of the Dunkirk raids after November 1916 were upon Ostend, Zeebrugge, and Bruges. These raids, since they were intended to destroy shipping and dockyard facilities, may be described as having a quasi-strategic dimension.[47]

As for the RFC, its bombing policy continued to reflect Trenchard's firm adherence to conventional military wisdom. It is true that Martinsydes of 27 Squadron had been flying long-distance raids for some time. In May 1917 they were joined by the DH4s of 55 Squadron. Throughout the summer and fall they raided deep into enemy-held territory, concentrating upon the area surrounding Ghent.* Since both squadrons were in Headquarters Wing, however, they came immediately under Trenchard's eye and he subordinated their work to the requirements of the army.

The meetings of the Air Board also reflected the consistency of view held by Haig and the RFC towards strategic bombing. Initially *laissez-faire* in its attitude towards the Luxeuil Wing, the RFC soon became actively disapproving, Rear-Admirals Tudor and Vaughan-Lee having to face stiff questioning from General Henderson about the deployment of naval aircraft. As always, the Admiralty was accused of staffing RNAS requirements on the basis of the engines it could get rather than on sound tactical and strategic grounds, and of being evasive about decisions it had taken. On 1 November 1916 Henderson observed that if Haig controlled the Luxeuil bombers, 'he thought that General Trenchard would bring them to the Somme, take the engines out of them and put them into fighting machines and would confine himself to bombing behind the enemy's lines as at present.' At the time the Luxeuil Wing's operations were coming to an end, Trenchard himself, in policy notes prepared in early April 1917, restated his position that bombing had to be integrated with other aerial tactics in support of ground operations – that it was by offensive fighter patrols and by bombing in the rear of the lines that German air strength was diverted from the front. As late as

---

* Canadians who served in 27 Squadron up to October 1917 included T.D. Campbell, E.P. Charles, and G.C. St G. de Dombasle, addresses unknown, C.M. De Rochie of Cornwall, Ont. (MIA 14 July 1917), E.D. Hicks (WIA 8 Sept. 1916) and C.N.F. Jeffery, both of Winnipeg, Man., E.W. Kirby and W. Mason, addresses unknown, A.E. McVittie of Sudbury, Ont., G.H. Morton, address unknown, W.E.G. Murray of Vancouver, P.C. Sherren from PEI, H.S. Spanner of Huntsville, Ont. (MIA 28 Dec. 1916), F.L. Stevens, address unknown (POW 4 June 1917), E. Waterlow of Regina, H.O.D. Wilkins of Norwood, Ont. (POW 28 July 1917), F.V. Woodman of Winnipeg, and P.A. Wright of Fort Frances, Ont. (wounded 3 Sept. 1916). Canadians who served in 55 Squadron during this period included S.H. Allen of Toronto, C.A.S. Bean, address unknown (POW 9 Aug. 1917), W.R. Cooke of Orillia, Ont. (WIA 13 Aug. 1917), J.B. Fox, address unknown, J.C. Hanson of Fredericton, NB (KIA 14 July 1917), J.H. Hedding and R.A. Logan (POW 8 April 1917), addresses unknown, J.C. McKeever of Listowel, Ont., P.B. McNally of Fredericton, NB (KIA 13 Aug. 1917), N.R. Murphy of Montreal, S. Nixon of Toronto, Daniel Owen from NS (POW 21 Oct. 1917), G.E.S. Rogers of Barrie, Ont. (KIA 10 Aug. 1916), A. Sattin, address unknown, and A.H. Waterman of Vancouver.

November 1917 Trenchard still held to these principles, stating that long-range bombing raids 'cannot be isolated from other work in the air, and are inseparable from the operations of the Army as a whole.'[48]

It has been suggested that Trenchard professed such views out of loyalty to Haig and that once released from his command and the obligations it carried to his chief, he became free to voice other views. Hence his association both with the Independent Force and with the gospel of strategic bombing in the postwar years.[49] It is quite possible that had he at any time possessed bombing aircraft surplus to requirements of the front, Trenchard would not then have been averse to a long-range bombing offensive. Certainly he said as much. But up to mid-1917, at least, that situation had never existed. At this point events began to move swiftly to force upon Trenchard the strategic bombing role, whether it corresponded with his secret views or not.

More than to any other single factor, this change was due to the German bombing campaign against England. These raids, however, brought to a head tendencies already well advanced, both in the public mind and at official levels. Ever since the Cowdray Air Board had begun to function in January 1917, the idea of building a long-range bombing force had never been far from the surface. Most of its work had been focused upon the immediate problem of aircraft and engine production, and by 21 April it had devised a production programme that successfully related RNAS and RFC requirements to industrial capacity. Public opinion was already moving toward future bombing operations, however. On 26 April, during a parliamentary debate on the Air Board, Joynson-Hicks and Lord Hugh Cecil discussed the possibility of 'an independent striking force' and of 'sending a vast number of machines over German territory.' The Air Board was already moving toward the creation of what Cowdray was to call a surplus air fleet.* He was able to report to the Cabinet on 9 June that a considerable long-distance bombing force was a possibility for the 1918 campaign. Early that month the board decided to order a thousand DH4s, of which seven hundred were to be modified for long-range bombing to 'provide material for an interim bombing programme pending the production of a specially designed long-distance bomber.' Thus even before the German raids had had their shock effect, the process was underway.[50]

By early June the first two Gotha raids on England had taken place. The War Cabinet had considered, and postponed decision on, 'frightfulness' as an appropriate response, despite the suggestion of the Consul-General at Rotterdam that Frankfurt, as 'a centre of finance and of socialism,' would be a target from which 'good psychological results' might be harvested. But the Cabinet was driven to act by the emotion generated over the raid of 13 June with the heaviest casualties of

---

* Cowdray first used the phrase 'Surplus Aircraft Fleet' in a letter to Smuts of 28 July 1917. He seems to have been an early convert to the views of Sir William Weir. A Scottish engineer and industrialist, Weir had become an official of the Ministry of Munitions in 1915. In December 1916 he was given a seat on the Air Board. In February 1918 he became Director-General Aircraft Production. Following the resignation of Lord Rothermere he became Secretary of State for Air on 27 April 1918. See W.J. Reader, *Architect of Air Power: the Life of the First Viscount Weir of Eastwood, 1877–1959* (London 1968); Cowdray to Smuts, 28 July 1917, Air 1/33/15/1/199.

the war, including sixty-six school children killed. Under mounting public pressure the War Cabinet made a remarkable series of decisions. Aircraft manufacturing was to be given priority over all other forms of weapon production; there was to be a spectacular increase in the number of RFC squadrons, from 108 to 200, and a comparable increase for the RNAS; the output of engines was to be stepped up from the current 1200 to 4500 a month; forty of the new squadrons were to be set aside to undertake the reprisal bombing of German cities. None of these decisions had any immediate effect. Despite its evident belief that Germans were more susceptible to the terrors of bombing than were the English, the War Cabinet accepted the report of a committee, composed of Generals Henderson and Trenchard and Commodore Paine, that it was useless to strike at Germany before enough aircraft were available to mount a continuous offensive and that this was unlikely before the spring of 1918 unless Haig were to be deprived of badly needed air strength.[51]

Then came the dramatic raid of 7 July, during which the utter helplessness of defence forces was demonstrated to millions of Londoners. That same afternoon the Cabinet requested Haig to undertake a reprisal raid against Mannheim, unless 'this would completely dislocate his plans.' When Haig and Trenchard demurred on the grounds of limited resources and scepticism about the utility of reprisals, the project was dropped. Nevertheless, Trenchard began preparations for such a raid, should it be ordered, including the provision of a train for shuttling squadrons from the British sector to Nancy and the investigation of aerodrome facilities and fuel supplies.[52]

On 11 July, as was noted in the last chapter, the Cabinet took a more significant action. It named Lieutenant-General J.C. Smuts as a committee of one (nominally joined by the Prime Minister) to report on aerial home defence and upon air organization and the future direction of air operations. Smuts' chief adviser was Sir David Henderson, a fateful choice. From his years of experience in dealing with the politics of a divided air service, Henderson had become an advocate of unification. In a long memorandum for Smuts, he rehearsed the many problems that had arisen between the RFC and the RNAS and concluded that 'logically the desirability of a separate unified Air Force is almost beyond dispute.' He therefore supported the creation of an air ministry with control over air policy, provided such a step could be taken without serious damage to the war effort.[53]

When Smuts submitted his own report on 17 August, the influence of Henderson was plain. Much of its first section was a recapitulation of Henderson's evidence. Its chief recommendations, that an air ministry be instituted 'as soon as possible' and that the RNAS and the RFC be amalgamated, were in accord with Henderson's views. But there was another dimension. Unlike other army corps such as the artillery, Smuts argued, an air service 'can be used as an independent means of war operations,' as the German raid of 7 July had proved. He went on: 'Unlike artillery an air fleet can conduct extensive operations far from, and independently of, both Army and Navy. As far as can at present be foreseen there is absolutely no limit to the scale of its future independent war use. And the day may not be far off when aerial operations with their devastation of enemy lands and destruction of industrial and populous centres on a vast scale may become the

principle operations of war, to which the older forms of military and naval operations may become secondary and subordinate.'[54] How far Henderson accepted the
apocalyptic strain in Smuts' report is impossible to say. Presumably, however, it
was a price he was willing to pay for the creation of an independent air force.

On 24 August, seized by the vision that the war might be won by means more
economical, at least in manpower, than the ghastly slaughter of the trenches, the
War Cabinet approved in principle the recommendation that a separate air service
be formed. A committee headed by Smuts and including Henderson, Paine, and
Lord Hugh Cecil was set up to work out the procedures for amalgamation of the
air services and to draft the necessary legislation.[55]

Reproof was not long in coming from the soldiers. Writing to Haig's chief of
staff, Trenchard vehemently and even contemptuously attacked the Smuts report.
'The contention,' he wrote, 'on which the whole argument for a separate Air
Service is based is that the War can be won in the air as against on the ground.
Nothing but bare assertion is urged in support of this contention. It is, in fact,
merely an opinion ...' Glossed over was the hard challenge of bombing Germany,
when the whole route would have to be flown over hostile territory. Why should it
be imagined that the bombing of German cities would bring strategic results when
German raids upon England 'have had no effect whatever on the course of the
war'? Turning to the proposal for a separate air ministry, he argued that such an
organization, with a civilian head and without the saving check of professional
military and naval control, would inevitably be exposed to 'popular and factional
clamour' and hence 'be drawn towards the spectacular, such as bombing reprisals
and home defence, at the expense of providing the essential means of co-operation
with our Naval and Military Forces.'[56]

Haig waited two weeks before passing on the substance of Trenchard's argument, in somewhat more diplomatic form, to Sir William Robertson. Under certain circumstances, he conceded, a case was to be made for long-range bombing:
'Long distance bombing designed to cripple the enemy's naval and military
resources and hamper his movements may certainly give valuable results. The
bombing of populous centres may also be justifiable, and may prove effective, in
order to punish the enemy for similar acts previously committed by him, and to
prevent their recurrence. Once such a contest is commenced, however, we must
be prepared morally and materially to outdo the enemy if we are to hope to attain
our ends.'[57] From Haig's viewpoint, however, the Smuts report gave a weight to
bombing that officers having 'wide *practical knowledge*' could not accept. Bombing
might well have profound significance for wars of the future but the experience of
the present war showed only its limitations. In their different ways, Haig and
Trenchard were both apprehensive that the expansion of squadrons in pursuit of
what they could only regard as a visionary objective would be at the expense of
aircraft for the army. Neither had much confidence in Weir's optimistic production
forecasts; both were aware that the original RFC expansion programme of 1916
was still far from being met; and both knew, and feared the Cabinet did not, that
there was an inevitable lag between increased production levels and the appearance of trained crews ready for actual operations.

No longer, however, could Haig and Trenchard count upon staunch support at home. Not only had Henderson shifted his ground, but even Robertson had done so, albeit temporarily, after the raid of 7 July. Perhaps the most significant changes of view had been taking place within the Admiralty. In the Air Department itself, of course, bombing had always been regarded more sympathetically than at the War Office and the recent turn of events was much to its liking. Squadron Commander Williamson, in the course of a paper discussing the possible bombing of German chemical works, recommended formulation of a clearly defined bombing policy and warned that the navy must not lay itself open 'to the charge that there has been a lack of official foresight and imagination.' There was little danger of that.[58]

Now the Air Department found new allies on the Air Board. Instead of the two services being at daggers drawn over the value of bombing, they debated such matters as the relative merits of day and night bombing. Henderson upheld the performance of the DH4 and the superior accuracy of day bombing, while Paine, with Weir's backing, spoke for the Handley Page because it carried six times the load of the DH4 and had three times the endurance. Moreover, no Handley Page had been lost to enemy action during night raids and there had been no exceptional difficulty about finding targets. Seven hundred DH4s were earmarked for bombing, but development work continued on the improved DH9, and the Air Board also decided at the end of July to go ahead with the production of a hundred Handley Page bombers. By 6 September orders had increased to over 2700 DH4s and 9s, and 300 Handley Pages. So complete was the ascendancy of the bomber school at this point that on 24 September the Air Board noted that it could use 'every bombing machine we could get,' foresaw a production rate of three hundred DH9s per month by the end of January, and approved an increase in Handley Page 0/400 production, already at around a hundred per month, to two hundred per month by June 1918. At the same time, at the highest level of the Admiralty, there had been a radical change of heart since the debates between Balfour and Curzon. At the time the Smuts report on air organization was discussed by the Cabinet the new First Lord, Sir Eric Geddes, stated that 'His Department recognized ... that there were strong reasons in favour of a definite development of Air Policy, and they accepted without question the views of those who had investigated it ...' Although he wanted to preserve the RNAS and keep air operations at sea under naval command, Geddes was ready to turn over to a new service duties not 'of a purely Naval character.'[59]

There were still those in the Cabinet who doubted both the bombing strategy and the idea of a separate air force, two policies now inextricably joined. The Germans supplied the final push with their switch to night raids. For three nights, beginning on 2 September, raids were launched, with London the main target on the 4th. The next day the War Cabinet agreed that 'we must carry the aerial war into Germany, not merely on the ground of reprisal,' and got assurances from Weir and Henderson that the necessary aircraft and trained airmen would be available.[60] The Cabinet then marked time until the night raids were resumed on a larger scale on 14 September and, with the exception of 26 and 27 September, were continued until the end of the month. The Cabinet's reaction was summed up in a cipher telegram sent to Haig by the CIGS on 1 October: 'Continuous Aircraft raids on ENGLAND are causing interruption in munitions work and having some effect on general public. Cabinet desire immediate action against those German objectives which can be reached from neighbourhood of NANCY. Send Trenchard over at once to me to discuss scale on which you can undertake these operations and necessary arrangements for them. Cabinet wish for at least one squadron to be employed with least possible delay.'[61] For the last time Haig and Trenchard registered their objections, but the Cabinet was in no mood to entertain them. No faith was left in the successful outcome of the Flanders battle, now mired at Passchendaele; a public outcry had to be stilled and bombing, politically and perhaps militarily, seemed the answer. When Trenchard returned to France he took with him orders to Haig to detach a day- and a night-bombing squadron from Headquarters Wing, and as soon as possible 'to undertake a continuous offensive, by air, against such suitable objectives in Germany as can be reached by our aeroplanes.' Eight Handley Pages with crews were detailed to join this force from the Admiralty, and Trenchard was further ordered to consult the Vice-Admiral Dover about using Dunkirk Handley Pages for the bombing of the Rhine towns in the Cologne area. Thus was 41 Wing established, under the command of Lieutenant-Colonel C.L.N. Newall of Headquarters Wing, with its base at Ochey.[62] An 'independent' bombing force had come into being, and its corollary, an independent air force, was shortly to follow.

A last flurry of debate ensued before the final step was taken, for there were lingering doubts in the mind of the Prime Minister and misgivings about the efficacy of a bombing offensive held by some of his colleagues. During October the air power enthusiasts vigorously pushed for a final decision. Prominent among them was Rear-Admiral Mark Kerr, now a member of the Air Board,* who attacked, in simplistic fashion, criticism of the Smuts report. Kerr argued that 'whichever side first gets its great bombing squadrons to work, automatically establishes superiority in every branch of offensive weapons by reduction of the enemy's output and victory naturally follows.' On 10 October he was told by Lord Cowdray that it was almost certain that an independent bombing force to attack Germany would *not* be formed, an opinion that probably reflected Lloyd George's wavering on the subject during the previous day's Cabinet meeting, and perhaps also a belated plea by the CIGS at that meeting for a reconsideration of Haig's needs at the front. Kerr promptly prepared a memorandum which Cowdray delivered to Lloyd George and Smuts. Citing Italian and other intelligence, Kerr alleged that the Germans were building four thousand large bombers, many of

---

* Kerr had little practical experience to back his role as an adviser on air power. He had qualified as a pilot in 1914, but at the outbreak of the war he was on loan to the Greek government, and served as Commander-in-Chief of the Royal Greek Navy. Subsequently he commanded the British Adriatic Squadron until August 1917, by which time he was scarcely in touch with significant wartime developments in military aviation. In September the Admiralty saw fit to recall him to London to serve as an adviser on aviation. After the birth of the RAF, Kerr became its Deputy Chief of Staff. See his *Land, Sea and Air: Reminiscences of Mark Kerr* (London 1927), 284–94.

which were huge six-engined machines capable of carrying up to five tons of explosives. 'Woolwich, Chatham, and all the factories in the London district will be laid flat,' he predicted, 'part of London wiped out, and workshops in the south-east of England will be destroyed, and consequently our offensive on land, sea, and air will come to an end.'* He urged 'the building of 2000 big bombing machines as a minimum,' and warned once more that 'the country who first strikes with its big bombing squadrons of hundreds of machines at the enemy's vital spots will win the war.'[63]

This absurd document, or 'bombshell,' as its author termed it, was duly considered by Cabinet. It was an example, though an extreme one, of the kind of emotional support the idea of strategic bombing, and hence a separate air service, was now receiving, and it seems to have made some impression upon the Prime Minister. In 1934 Trenchard recalled that 'At a Cabinet meeting Lloyd George said to me "The Germans are going to bomb London with 4,000 aeroplanes." I said to him, "Nonsense, 40." We had a row. He said, "Why do you talk like that?" I replied that even if the Germans had 4,000 aeroplanes to bomb London with, which I did not believe, it would take them months to organize aerodromes and the whole paraphernalia of preparation. I gave him practice not theory.'[64]

Surprisingly enough, in view of his early and aggressive backing of long-distance bombing, it was Winston Churchill, the Minister of Munitions, who was the chief spokesman for the views of Haig and Trenchard. He debunked the notion that an air offensive, by itself, could bring victory. British morale had not really been fundamentally shaken by German raids and 'nothing that we have learned of the capacity of the German population to endure suffering justifies us in assuming that they could be cowed into submission by such methods, or, indeed, that they would not be rendered more desperately resolved by them.' Churchill believed that a bombing offensive ought to be co-ordinated with the operations of land and sea forces and should strike at enemy bases and communications 'upon whose structure the fighting power of his armies and his fleets of the sea and of the air depends.'[65]

But the time had passed when such arguments could sway the Cabinet. On 6 November it approved the Air Force bill. Duly passed by Parliament, it received royal assent on 29 November. The way was now clear for a strategic bombing offensive against Germany, conducted by an independent air force to come into being in early 1918. These great decisions were to affect the employment of Canadians in air operations, and, in the long run, were to have a fundamental influence upon Canadian defence policy.

---

* It seems scarcely credible that such a memorandum should have been written by a responsible staff officer, and even less credible that its contents apparently went unchallenged. Obviously he was referring to the German giant bombers, and possibly to the Staaken R-VI which had a disposable load of two tons. This aircraft was virtually hand-constructed; four thousand of the type was utterly beyond German capacity. During the entire war only 117 R planes were built, and only thirty-seven of them were delivered during the final two years of the war. See G.W. Haddow and P.M. Grosz, *The German Giants: the Story of the R-planes, 1914–1919* (London 1962).

11
The Strategic Air Offensive against Germany

From October 1917 to the end of the war the claims for the strategic effectiveness of the air weapon which had formed so important a part of the decision to create the Royal Air Force were put to the test. Admittedly, the test was hardly a fair one. Neither the Independent Force nor its forerunner, 41 Wing, received aircraft and aircrew in numbers even remotely approximating those promised. At the same time, however, there was a curious disjunction between the aims and aspirations of the new Air Staff in London, dreaming its dreams of victory through airpower, and the actual nature of the operations carried out by the strategic bombing force upon which so many hopes were pinned. The air commanders in the field did not set out deliberately to frustrate the plans of the Air Staff, for those plans were essentially unrealizable. But in the end it was Trenchard and not the Air Staff who called the tune.

Such a split was clearly probable from the outset. Controversy surrounded the first appointments to the Air Ministry, including that of the first Air Minister, Lord Rothermere. An Air Council under his presidency was established on 3 January 1918; its vice-president was Sir David Henderson. Trenchard was prevailed upon to become Chief of the Air Staff and was given Rear-Admiral Mark Kerr as his deputy. Within a few weeks of the official birth of the Royal Air Force, on 1 April 1918, not one of these men remained at his original post. Kerr had disagreed with Trenchard, and Brigadier-General R.M. Groves had been appointed in his place. Rothermere had given way to Sir William Weir; Trenchard had resigned, to be replaced by his old rival Major-General Frederick Sykes; Henderson had left, finding it impossible to work with Sykes.

These events had much to do with personal antagonisms and old service rivalries, but policy was also at stake. Trenchard did not get on with Rothermere, but just as important, the Minister did not regard him as his only source of professional advice. As Trenchard wrote to Haig, the Minister had 'introduced a lot of people to the Air Ministry without consulting anybody'; moreover, Rothermere 'preferred any advice to that of his professional advisers.'[1] In frustration, Trenchard bypassed his Minister and wrote to Lloyd George. He pointed out that Air Staff planning was proceeding on the assumption that by the end of May there would be twenty-five bombing squadrons at Nancy, and that by the beginning of July there would be forty. Yet so far as he could see, there could not possibly be more than nine by the latter date. Therefore, he argued, 'It is far better to know what can really be done so as to be able to count on it than to indulge in more generous estimates which cannot be realised.' His own prescription was to use this small force to attack the 'big industrial centres on the Rhine' when weather permitted, and, when long-distance raiding was ruled out, to strike at the steel centres closer at hand. He also suggested using Dunkirk's two Handley Page squadrons to attack the submarine facilities at Bruges and Zeebrugge, and employing army bombing squadrons to raid the bases near Ghent from which the Gothas were launching their attacks upon England. Targets of immediate concern to the army, such as lines of communications, headquarters, ammunition dumps, railway stations, and aerodromes could be tackled by short-range squadrons working directly under GHQ control.[2]

These proposals, though they conformed closely to the realities of industrial production, were unwelcome to Rothermere. They may be contrasted with the advice offered the Minister by Sir Henry Norman, an MP who was an additional member of the Air Council. Norman was deeply concerned by the failure of bomber production to meet expectations. On 25 March he wrote to Rothermere that 'we shall not be in a position to carry out bombing operations in Germany upon a large scale likely to have an appreciable influence upon the course of the war before next autumn, if even then.' Unlike Trenchard, however, his solution was not to adjust bombing operations to the resources likely to be available. For Norman, bomber production had to be given the highest priority, for 'The future of our race and Empire may depend upon whether or not we rise now – though it be at the eleventh hour – to this conception.'[3]

The conception (provided the bombers were available) was the total obliteration of six German cities: Essen, Cologne, Frankfurt, Düsseldorf, Stuttgart, and Mannheim. He hypothesized that this could be done by a force of 250 bombers, which would attack a given city in flights of twenty-five aircraft at hourly intervals. A ten-hour raid would deliver two hundred tons of bombs, a weight sufficient to swamp the city's fire fighting services and air defence forces. The German cities would be 'practically wiped out, so far as their collective existence and productivity were concerned ... My own opinion is that if such attacks were pursued for a month, our victory in the war would be in sight.'[4] It is clear that Norman grossly underestimated the amount of force required to cause the kind of damage he had in mind. Moreover, his ideas had so little relationship to reality that he was actually proposing to drop a greater weight of bombs in a ten-hour period than the existing bomber force, 41 Wing, managed to drop in five months of operations.

The new team of Weir and Sykes was as dedicated to strategic bombing as Rothermere and his associates had been, though their aspirations lacked the grandiose character of the Norman proposals. Shortly after taking over as Chief of the Air Staff Sykes established a 'Strategic Council' consisting of himself, the Director of Flying Operations, and the Controller of the Technical Department to 'consider questions of policy in their strategic aspect and the best utilization of aerial resources.' On 22 April this body met for the first time to evaluate a working paper which accurately reflected the hopes held out for the bombing offensive by the staff.

The object of the bombing offensive, as outlined in this document, was not to wipe out whole cities but, if possible, key German industries. This was much closer to Trenchard's position than to Norman's. At this early stage, however, staff planning was based upon a much rosier view of the aircraft supply situation than that taken by Trenchard. It was argued that conceivably as much as 80 per cent of the German chemical industry could be destroyed in twelve raids, and that perhaps 95 per cent of the magneto industry could be similarly destroyed in three raids. These tentative projections were based upon the calculation that a thousand DH4 sorties in a single raid would obliterate a chemical works and that a typical magneto factory would be destroyed by five hundred sorties.[5] In other words, to achieve these objectives some 13,500 sorties would have to be flown. As it happens, the Independent Air Force, during the whole period of its operational existence, was able to fly only about one-fifth this number of sorties. A raid of one thousand sorties was totally beyond the realm of possibility. During June 1918, an active flying month, the Independent Force never managed to mount more than forty-five sorties in a single twenty-four-hour period. The 'obliteration theory' was simply unworkable.

Nevertheless, it was upon the assumption that the obliteration of key German industries could be accomplished that plans were made for the establishment of a strategic bombing force, to be called the Independent Air Force. General Trenchard, in deciding to accept the command of this force on 8 May, seems to have been influenced by erroneous accusations that he had resigned as Chief of the Air Staff 'at the height of a battle,' when in fact his resignation had been tendered prior to the beginning of the German offensive in France. Yet the appointment was a strange one. Despite Trenchard's experience and high qualities of leadership, he was on bad terms with Sykes and suspicious of Weir. Even more important, he had been the most vigorous opponent of strategic bombing and of the concept of an independent force.[6]

The cornerstone upon which Trenchard's new command was to be built was 41 Wing. The wing had arrived in the Nancy area on 11 October 1917, and its commander, Lieutenant-Colonel C.L.N. Newall, had established his headquarters at Bainville-sur-Madon. His day-bombing squadron, No 55, was also based there, while the two night-bombing squadrons, No 100 and 'A' Naval,* were based at Ochey.

No 55 Squadron had been engaged in day-bombing operations with 9 (Headquarters) Wing since March 1917.† It was equipped with the DH4 and its airmen were thoroughly familiar with the characteristics of this excellent aircraft. When powered by a 375-hp Rolls-Royce Eagle VIII engine the DH4 was capable of a speed of 133.5 mph at 10,000 feet, could climb to 15,000 feet in a little over sixteen minutes, and had a service ceiling of 22,000 feet. With a bomb-load of two 230-lb or four 112-lb bombs, its endurance was nearly four hours. This could be

---

* 'A' Squadron was redesignated as 16 (Naval) Squadron on 8 Jan 1918. Upon the birth of the RAF it became 216 Squadron RAF.
† At the time of its attachment to 41 Wing, five of No 55's airmen were Canadians. They were J.B. Fox and N.R. Murphy, both of Montreal, Daniel Owen of Annapolis Royal, NS (POW 21 Oct. 1917), and A. Sattin and J.H. Hedding, addresses unknown.

stretched to five-and-a-half hours by reducing bomb-load and adding extra fuel tanks. The DH4 was faster than the Gotha IV and had a higher service ceiling; the Gotha carried a heavier bomb-load of 660 lbs. It was undoubtedly the best day bomber the Independent Force was to have. As flown by 55 Squadron, the DH4s were deployed in triangular formations of six with the second two machines fifty feet above and the three rearward aircraft below the formation leader. As long as close formation was kept, enemy aircraft found the DH4s a formidable and unrewarding target.[7]

No 100 Squadron, however, was poorly equipped. On its arrival in France in March it had received FE2bs, obsolescent aircraft which had first flown operationally in 1915. Their 120-hp Beardmore engines brought them struggling to their 9000 foot service ceiling in thirty-four minutes. They could carry a bomb-load of three 112-lb bombs; their endurance with that load was about three hours. These characteristics made them suitable only for short-range night operations.* Many of the airmen with 'A' Naval had learned their business with 7 (Naval) at Dunkirk, while others had begun training at Manston only in June and July.† It was equipped with ten Handley Page 0/100s, six of them from 7(N) and the other four from Redcar, where they had been used in September on anti-submarine patrols. The Handley Pages were not markedly faster than the FE2bs, but, as we have seen, in other respects were vastly superior. Their bomb-load was at least three times as great and their remarkable endurance of eight hours made them eminently suitable for long-distance night operations.[8]

The operational base of 41 Wing was behind that portion of the French line held by the *Groupe des Armées de l'Est* commanded by *Général* de Castelnau. At the time of the wing's arrival the GAE was commencing a strategic bombing offensive of its own, the main objective of which was to 'blockade'‡ the coal and iron resources and steel plants of Lorraine and Luxembourg. The French night-bombing units, equipped with Voisin 8s, were to attack mines and steel works at Thionville, Bettembourg, Luxembourg, Maizieres-les-Metz, and Longeville, and were given Treves and Saarbrücken as 'reprisal' targets should the need arise. Their Sopwith 1½ Strutter day bombers were to attack railyards, industrial plants, aerodromes, and thirteen designated 'reprisal' towns.

---

* When 100 Squadron arrived at Ochey it was at least half Canadian. The pilots were L.M. Archibald of Toronto (POW 24 Oct. 1917), J.J.L. Drummond of Spencerville, Ont., W.H. Jones of Winnipeg (POW 25 Oct. 1917), W.K. MacNaughton of St Jean, Que., V.E. Schweitzer of Portage la Prairie, W.J. Tempest of Perdue, Sask., and G.M. Turbull of Manville, Alta. The observers were S.M. Duncan of Ottawa, J.W. Edwards of Cataraqui, Ont., J.S. Godard of Ottawa (POW 24 Oct. 1917), R.C. Pitman of Saskatoon (POW 17 Sept. 1918), J.W. Price of Moncton, and A.H. Thompson of Penetanguishene, Ont. (KIA 26 Sept. 1918).

† When the squadron arrived at Ochey, only three Canadians were on its strength. They were H.M. Costain of Brantford, Ont., G.A. Flavelle of Lindsay, Ont., and A. Macdonald of Toronto. All were pilots. Before the end of the year two more Ontarians, L.R. Shoebottom of London and A.H. Thompson of Penetanguishene (KIA 26 Sept. 1918), joined the squadron as pilots.

‡ The word is taken from a British translation of de Castelnau's operation order of 18 Oct. 1917, and seems to imply an attempt to isolate Germany from the iron and coal resources of Luxembourg and Lorraine. 'Plan of Bombardment Operations during Winter of 1917–1918,' 18 Oct. 1917, Air 1/970/204/5/1108

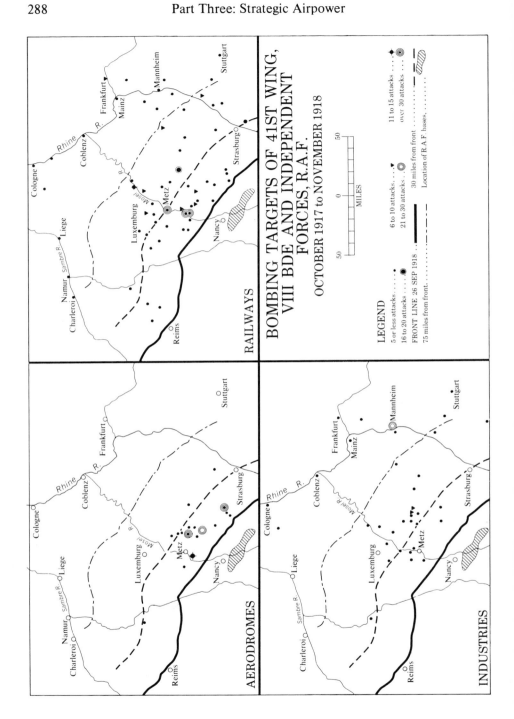

BOMBING TARGETS OF 41ST WING, VIII BDE AND INDEPENDENT FORCES, R.A.F.
OCTOBER 1917 to NOVEMBER 1918

These targets overlapped considerably with those contemplated by 41 Wing, although the DH4s and Handley Pages had a much greater range than the French aircraft. Haig's orders were that 41 Wing was to confine itself to the Saarbrücken area until the pilots had learned the country. Only then did he authorize co-operation with the French 'whenever the weather is not settled enough for long-distance raids into Germany.' In fact, the French and British bombing forces were mounting parallel offensives from the same bases, but there was little genuine co-ordination of activities until the German offensive in March. Nevertheless, on 21 October *Général* Pétain, Commander-in-Chief of the French armies, wrote to Haig enclosing a copy of de Castelnau's plan of bombing operations. He drew Haig's attention to the fact that French bombing forces had been ordered to avoid provoking unnecessary reprisals on French towns through 'promiscuous bombing by isolated aeroplanes' and urged Haig to adopt a similar policy for 41 Wing. Newall was cautioned to restrict daylight raids to legitimate objectives, to employ no fewer than six aircraft per raid, and to keep night raids as concentrated as possible.[9]

Meanwhile, on 17 October the wing had launched its first raid. The target was the large steel works at Saarbrücken-Burbach. Eleven DH4s, of which three returned with engine trouble, took part. According to German records, the raid inflicted 17,500 marks' worth of damage upon the works and houses in the area. Five people were killed and nine injured. On 21 October 55 Squadron attacked the factories and railyards at Bous with twelve DH4s. The target, on the Moselle north of Hagendingen, was about sixty miles from Ochey. Only one aircraft was forced to return with engine trouble; the rest bombed the town. As they completed their bombing runs they were pounced upon by a formation of ten Albatros D-I fighters. In a short, sharp encounter the squadron claimed four Albatros shot down, at the cost of one DH4. It was piloted by one of the flight leaders, Captain Daniel Owen of Annapolis Royal, NS. During the battle Owen had his left eye shot out, but despite this most painful wound was able to force-land his aircraft ten miles inside enemy territory.*[10]

On the night of 24 October, one of fog, wind, and rain, the night bombers got their baptism. 'A' Squadron despatched nine Handley Pages against the Burbach works, while 100 Squadron sent sixteen FE2bs against the railyards between Falkenburg and Saarbrücken. The Handley Pages do not appear to have found their assigned target, for the Burbach works, where a complete record of bomb damage was kept, listed nothing for that date.[11] Nevertheless, two of the Handley Pages failed to return and for Flight Sub-Lieutenant Alec MacDonald of Toronto it was the beginning of thirteen months in a German POW camp. Flight Sub-Lieutenant Gordon A. Flavelle of Lindsay, Ont., making his first operational flight,† recorded his experience in his logbook: 'Dropped bombs on target but

---

* At the time of his capture Captain Owen had just been sent a letter from his brother, also with the RFC and a Bulgarian prisoner, envying his freedom. Owen was repatriated in August 1918 as unfit for further military service.

† It is instructive to note that at this point Flavelle had a grand total of fifty-three hours' flying time, of which eleven were on Handley Pages. This limited experience was typical of most of the pilots in the Independent Force.

could not see results for clouds. Lost ourselves on way back. Crashed machine near St. Dizier. Nothing left but tail and part of fuselage. 1 blade of starboard prop dug into Halley's back but did not cut. Self thrown clear. Hit on head and left shoulder cutting head slightly.'[12] No 100 Squadron seems to have had somewhat more success, reporting several direct hits on the railyards, as well as one by a 230-lb bomb on a train caught by the raid. Two aircraft, both flown by Canadians – Lieutenants L.M. Archibald of Toronto and W.H. Jones of Winnipeg – were lost. Both these pilots and Archibald's observer, Lieutenant J.S. Godard of Ottawa, were taken prisoner.[13]

As October drew to a close a few more raids were launched. One of them, an attack by nine FE2bs on the Völklingen steel works, caused a moderate amount of damage according to German reports. Overall, the wing had dropped over eleven tons of bombs in eight raids during its first month of operations, but the force was not really in a position to mount a strong offensive. Wing Captain Lambe, who visited Ochey to find out why his naval pilots had been sent on no further raids after 24 October, reported angrily to Vice-Admiral Bacon that Newall had thrown the Handley Pages into battle indiscriminately. The squadron had no skilled workers on strength, such as acetylene welders, fabric workers, painters, or vulcanizers. Of the ten machines sent to Ochey, two were missing, one was wrecked, two were damaged and could not be repaired until stores arrived from England, and two complete crews were lost. The Fifth Sea Lord, who saw Lambe's report a week later, commented that '... these machines were collected and dispatched with the utmost speed by order of War Cabinet & were necessarily a scratch lot & the only H. Page machines available. If the Officer in Command will use the machines for extended raids directly they arrive & in unsuitable weather numerous casualties must be expected.'[14]

The onset of bad weather confined 41 Wing's operations to one raid in November and four in December, all against industrial targets. The Germans chose to retaliate by attacking 41 Wing itself. Two bombing attacks were made upon the Ochey aerodromes in November, and two more in December. In the raid of 4–5 December sixteen of the wing's aircraft were damaged, while at a neighbouring French aerodrome two sheds were burnt, destroying ten aircraft and damaging fifteen more. There was some disgruntlement with their allies among the British airmen, because 'The French either cleared off the moment the attack started or else went into dug-outs leaving our men to put out the fires that had started in the French sheds.'[15]

During the late winter months 41 Wing's operational activities were limited by weather. Otherwise it was a hive of industry, since it was the nucleus for the planned new departure in air warfare. In February the wing was placed under a new headquarters, VIII Brigade, and Newall was promoted to brigadier-general to command it. Work was pushed on to provide room for seventeen additional day-bombing squadrons at Azelot, Frôlois, and Bettoncourt. For eight projected night-bombing squadrons, fields were being prepared at Xaffévillers and Roville. At Vezelise the existing park and railhead were being expanded, while an additional park was under construction at Rambervillers. When requesting space for these new squadrons (and sweetening the pill by promising bombing support whenever possible to the French army), Major-General Salmond informed the Commandant of the American Aviation Service that between 1 April and 31 July VIII Brigade was to be built up to forty squadrons.*[16]

Meanwhile, Newall seized every opportunity to send out his bombers, though the targets attacked were almost invariably within close range. The exposed observer's seat right in the nose of the FE2b was an unenviable position during these winter raids, as Lieutenants G.E. Lucas of Sarnia and W.H. Curry of Toronto found when 100 Squadron raided the blast furnaces of Maizières, just north of Metz, on 4–5 January 1918. Curry was out again the next night when six FE2bs attacked the railway station and sidings at Conflans, a few miles to the west of Metz, along with another Canadian observer, Lieutenant J.W. Price. On both occasions the weather was so poor that no estimate of results could be made. On 14–15 January the steel works at Thionville (Diedenhofen) was the squadron's objective, but S.M. Duncan of Ottawa claimed to have dropped his bombs in the 'centre of town' along with the other observers. Twice during the winter period the squadron was stretched to the limit to make the two-hundred-mile round trip to Treves (Trier) and its barracks and railway installations. Lieutenant J.W. Edwards of Cataraqui, Ont., made the first trip, while Duncan and Price took part in the second. This latter raid, of 18–19 February, was a severe one according to German accounts. The Chancery Court building was destroyed, as were a number of railway buildings. One aircraft 'flew very low, just missing the tops of the houses'; the town's anti-aircraft guns were depressed so far that they had to cease firing to avoid hitting houses. This aircraft was flown by a British pilot; Duncan, his observer, managed to plant two bombs near the station during his wild ride.[17]

The day bombers of 55 Squadron were also quite active during the winter period. The fortunes of Captain J.B. Fox of Montreal, an experienced pilot who was one of the squadron's flight leaders, illustrate the nature of its operations, and some of its difficulties. Shortly after noon on 12 February two formations of six DH4s each, the second led by Fox, departed to bomb Karlsruhe. Diverted by poor weather to Offenburg, they bombed its railway yards from 13,500 feet, though incendiaries were seen to fall upon houses in the town. The first formation returned to base uneventfully, but low cloud which had moved in swiftly forced Fox to steer a compass course for home. A radical shift in wind drove his formation off course and his six aircraft made emergency landings at widely scattered points south of Nancy. On 19 February he led twelve DH4s to bomb Mannheim, but finding the Rhine Valley shrouded in mist, he decided instead to attack Treves. His formation bombed from 15,000 feet, its incendiaries starting fires, later confirmed by photographs, in two residential areas. On the way home the formation was attacked by five Albatros scouts, an observer being wounded, and one DH4 was shot down by anti-aircraft fire.

Fox and the squadron were back at work the next day, as he led ten machines against either Mannheim or Kaiserslautern. Shortly after an 0846 hrs departure

* At the bottom of the draft, in Salmond's handwriting, there is a note indicating that the Independent Force would eventually have fifty-five squadrons, including thirty-eight of DH9s and seventeen of Handley Pages.

one bomber spun (retaining its bomb-load) from 5000 feet to 1000 feet and the shaken crew chose to return to base. Heavy cloud conditions caused a second machine to lose touch with the formation, and it too returned. Having led his remnant across the lines at 14,000 feet, Fox discovered that a strong headwind was reducing ground speed so drastically that both original targets were beyond his reach. Over Pirmasens, with a thick blanket of ground mist obscuring any possible targets north of that town, he decided to bomb the most convenient target. Thus ill-defended Pirmasens, maker of army boots, received the explosives and incendiaries of eight DH4s. 'A very quiet journey,' Fox reported, 'no trouble being experienced with either A.A. or E.A.' He experienced a less pleasant and more exciting time on 10 March when, at 4000 feet, he accidentally knocked the compensator open and the exhaust ignited the gasoline vapour in the pilot's compartment. Though his clothes were on fire and he himself was slightly burnt, he managed to crash-land on the allied side of the line. He and his observer escaped from the wreckage.[18]

With the beginning of March the pace of VIII Brigade's operations picked up, but once the great German ground offensive of that month began,* its priorities were radically changed. As early as December Trenchard had heard rumours of an impending offensive and when the storm broke he wrote directly to Newall authorizing a withdrawal to Tours, on the Loire, should the need arise. Since the main German thrust did not affect the Nancy sector, VIII Brigade stayed where it was, although 100 Squadron was redeployed from Ochey to Villeseneux, closer to the front, from 29 March to 10 May. Between 23 March and 16 May the brigade flew more than two hundred bombing sorties, almost all of them in support of the ground armies, particularly against railways. This reversed previous priorities when the bulk of bombing had been directed against industrial targets.† It was during this period that 100 Squadron carried out one of its more spectacular raids. On the night of 24–25 March it sent 14 FE2bs against the Metz-Sablon rail triangle, Lieutenants L.A. Naylor of Winnipeg and G.E. Lucas of Sarnia manning two of them as observers.[19] The squadron dropped sixty-nine bombs on or near its objective. The German report stated: 'Several bombs fell on the main No. 6 track in the station. 15 trucks caught fire and seven munition wagons amongst them exploded, tracks No. 6 and 16 were very extensively damaged, and others also suffered (20 in all). The whole train exploded, blew up and burnt itself out. Seven houses were very seriously damaged. The Northerly gasometer in the triangle was struck and damaged. The force of the explosion was so great that the building South of the

---

* See chapter 16.
† Railway bombings might be considered dual purpose raids, since they served the strategic aim of inhibiting the flow of coal and steel from Lorraine to the German interior as well as the operational purpose of interfering with the movement of troops and material to the front. However, during the period of the Ludendorff offensives the pattern of rail bombing, directed as it was against rail centres close at hand, such as Juniville, Beltenville, and Amagne-Lucquy, strongly suggests that the prime consideration was the interdiction of the flow of men and material to the front. Another prime target of a purely military nature was the German HQ at Spa, which 55 Squadron tried unsuccessfully to destroy in three raids. H.A. Jones, *The War in the Air: being the Story of the Part played in the Great War by the Royal Air Force, Appendices* (London 1937), app. XIII, 42 ff

gasometer had its roof blown off and exploding shells damaged the machinery ...
Only 6 men killed and 2 wounded.'[20] All the raiding machines returned safely.

Once the crisis of the offensive was over, VIII Brigade returned to its prime
mission. On 16 May 55 Squadron resumed the attack upon German industry by
raiding Saarbrücken. A number of Canadians took part in this raid, including two
who had no previous experience of industrial attacks, Second Lieutenant W.I.
Parke of Vancouver, a probationary observer who had come to the squadron less
than a month before, and Second Lieutenant W.J. Pace of Edmonton, a pilot who
had taken some part in raids during the Ludendorff offensives. On their way to the
objective the DH4 crews could see enemy scouts rising towards their height of
13,000 feet. As they bombed their target, causing sixty casualties and damage to
workshops, trains, and signal apparatus, the German fighters closed in. A DH4 fell
in flames over the city, and as the formation turned awkwardly for home, three
more observers were wounded, including Parke. Pace's observer reported that he
had counted more than twenty Albatros at one point during the running fight back
to the lines. After the machines had landed it was found that several had been so
shredded by machine-gun fire that they were unserviceable.[21]

The rise in enemy air activity experienced by 55 Squadron was an omen of
things to come. Night raiders were meeting no such resistance. Thus on the night
of 21–22 May 100 Squadron sent fourteen aircraft against Saarbrücken and
Thionville. Though three force-landed within the lines, the remainder, whose
crews included Second Lieutenant F.R. Johnson, a pilot from Westmount, Que.,
and three Canadian observers, Lucas, Naylor, and R.C. Pitman of Saskatoon,
Sask., obtained direct hits on railway installations at Saarbrücken, causing some
dislocation of traffic and twenty-four casualties in the barracks there.[22]

On 21 May VIII Brigade's original squadrons were joined for the first time by 99
Squadron, which attacked Metz-Sablon. Formed as a day-bombing unit at Yates-
bury, Wiltshire, in August 1917, the squadron arrived in VIII Brigade's area from
England on 3 May and since that date had been completing its training and familiarization.* Not only was this a totally inexperienced unit (though of course its
senior members had had service with other squadrons), but it was the first
assigned to the brigade to be equipped with the new DH9 bomber. This aircraft was
the outcome of the Cabinet's decision on 2 July 1917 to enlarge greatly the
bomber strength of the RFC and to produce a bomber with greater range than the
DH4. De Havilland was responsible for the redesign of the airframe, but every-

---

* When it arrived in France the squadron contained ten Canadians (roughly one-quarter of the aircrew establishment); seventeen more joined it during the ensuing months. Nine of the originals
were pilots: S. McB. Black of Springfield, Ont. (POW 31 July 1918), C.C. Conover of Leamington,
Ont., E.L. Doidge of Vancouver (KIA 31 July 1918), N.S. Harper of Kamloops, BC (KIA 25 June
1918), D.A. Macdonald of Saint John, NB, K.D. Marshall of Tara, Ont., W.G. Stevenson of
Toronto, C.A. Vick of Montreal, and H.D. West of Toronto. The lone observer was D.G.
Benson of Aylmer West, Ont. (KIA 25 June 1918). Subsequent members during the squadron's
operational life were E.C. Clark of Regina (KIA 13 Aug. 1918), N.W. Davidson of Westmount,
Que., M.A. Dunn of Bobcaygeon, Ont. (POW 7 Sept. 1918), J.H. Hall of Toronto, H.H.R.
Hanford of Fort William, Ont., J.L. Hunter of Walkerville, Ont., G.W. Irving of Gretna, Man.,
W.H.R. Jarvis of Fort William, Ont., W.C. Jeffries and W.T. Jones of Toronto, C. Lambe of
Saskatoon, Sask., H.C. Peat of Winnipeg, and M.J. Poulton of Toronto.

thing depended upon the success of the Beardmore-Halford-Pullinger (BHP) engine contracted for by the Air Board. If this produced less than the desired 300 hp, then it would be inferior to the 275-hp Rolls-Royce engine of the DH4. As early as August 1917 Trenchard began to express grave doubts about this aircraft, already suspecting that its performance would not be up to that of the DH4.[23]

He was right. The BHP engines yielded only 230 hp and the aircraft with bomb-load could barely struggle to 15,000 feet, 7000 feet below the service ceiling of the DH4. Its bomb-load was no greater and its endurance was only marginally better than that of the DH4. Moreover, the new engine was failure-prone. During its service with the Independent Force, of a total of 848 attempted sorties by individual aircraft no fewer than 123 had to return with engine trouble, a 14 per cent failure rate.[24]

Despite its inexperience and its questionable engines, 99 Squadron, having received its baptism of fire, was given no special treatment by Newall. On 24 May the Thyssen blast furnaces at Hagendingen were its target. Six of the fourteen DH9s that took off were flown by Canadians – Macdonald, Doidge, Black, Stevenson, Marshall, and West. Only eight reached the target area, where they were attacked by the same number of Albatros scouts. Doidge's observer, along with one of his colleagues in another DH9, jointly claimed an Albatros shot down. In the scuffle over the target two other observers were wounded, and in the confusion of it all the green crews neglected to make estimates of bombing results.[25]

Three days later the first aircraft to be lost to enemy action by 99 Squadron was flown by a Canadian, Lieutenant Donald A. Macdonald of Saint John,[26] whose diary tersely sums up his experience: 'Left ground at 10 a.m. for raid on Bensdorf. Met 5 Huns. Only 4 in our formation & I was out of luck for a position. Got out of formation after dropping bombs & had my tail plane shot off on left side. Loop & spin ... Landed one mile from lines. Oh! What a feeling. For duration now.'[27] For Macdonald and his British observer a long confinement at Stralsund POW camp lay ahead.

As these early raids show, the DH9 engines were already proving a headache. On 29 May twelve aircraft set out for Metz-Sablon, with Doidge, West, Marshall, Stevenson, and Black among the pilots. Half their number, including the machines flown by West and Black, had to return prematurely with engine trouble. Despite hot and hard work in the target area, Doidge and two other pilots were able to provide some estimate of results, an indication that the squadron was gaining competence.[28]

On 21 May another DH9 squadron, No 104, had arrived. Formed in England in November 1917, the squadron's service was marked by bad luck and heavy casualties. These began immediately. Arriving late at night at Azelot, having flown for hours in darkness over unfamiliar terrain, two of the squadron's machines crashed on landing. On 27 May Lieutenant William Bruce of Plenty, Sask., and his British observer went missing while ferrying another DH9 from England.* The squadron

---

* There were ten Canadians with 104 Squadron when it joined VIII Brigade: P.E. Appleby of North Sydney, NS, J.E. Belford of Toronto, George Beveridge of Westmount, Que., J.B. Home-Hay of Wadena, Sask. (POW 22 Aug. 1918), H.A.B. Jackson of Victoria (POW 25 June 1918), E.A. McKay of Toronto (POW 22 Aug. 1918), A. Moore of Treherne, Man., C.G. Pickard of Exeter,

did not fly its first mission until 8 June, by which time VIII Brigade had become the Independent Air Force under General Trenchard's command.[29]

In its 231 days as an independent formation, 41 Wing and its successor, VIII Brigade, carried out 110 bombing raids in steadily mounting activity.* About two-thirds of all missions flown were in daylight, yet the night losses were proportionally heavier, a factor that came to be reversed in the months ahead. In this early period German defences were not yet of high quality and the major risks were the usual hazards of night flying.

Faulty navigation, especially at night, was an important cause of casualties. Navigational training in the RFC largely consisted of map reading, adequate for the needs of reconnaissance, fighter, and tactical bomber pilots but insufficient preparation for round-trip flights of more than two hundred miles. Even following the advent of longer-range two-seater aircraft, navigational training was not significantly increased. Separate schools for observers were not introduced until 1918, and then the chief emphasis was still placed upon gunnery, photography, and radio telegraphy. It is true that airmen who survived long enough often became accomplished map readers, but even for them the difficulties of using the large maps needed for longer raids in the cramped conditions of open windswept cockpits were formidable. A protracted period of flying in or over cloud almost invariably resulted in the crew becoming seriously lost. In such circumstances, simple dead reckoning was used, based upon the wind prediction given to crews by meteorologists before the flight began, adjusted later by whatever estimates of wind direction and velocity the crew was able to make in the air.[30]

Since many day-bomber crews went astray using map reading and dead reckoning, it might be expected that those who flew at night over blacked-out towns and the persistent European night mists would be worse off. Yet night crews achieved remarkable standards of navigation. Captain W.A. Leslie of Toronto recalled that 'it was not nearly as difficult as you might think,' at least in FE2bs, since these aircraft, with bomb-load, flew at heights below 5000 feet and normally bombed from 1000 feet or less. At such heights roads, villages, and waterways were discernible to the experienced night flyer, especially since an airspeed of 70 mph gave ample time to pick up landmarks. Moreover, Leslie pointed out, many of the targets, such as Metz-Sablon, Thionville, Boulay, and Frescaty, were raided repeatedly. The aircrews became thoroughly familiar with the night landscape along the way. Night flyers relied heavily, as well, upon the allied system of 'lighthouses,' beacons which flashed identifying letters in morse code. Leslie con-

Ont. (KIA 22 Aug. 1918), T.M. Steele of Stratford, Ont. (POW 28 Sept. 1918), and James Valentine, address unknown (POW 22 Aug. 1918). Others who later served on operations with the squadron included H.D. Arnott of Toronto (KIA 29 Oct. 1918), W.E. Bottrill of Hamilton, E.C. Clarke of Regina (KIA 13 Aug. 1918), E.A. Forbes of Westmount, Que., W.H. Goodale of Wadena, Sask. (KIA 1 Aug. 1918), W.B. Henderson of Toronto, J.L. Hunter of Walkerville, Ont., W.T. Jones and O.L. Malcolm of Toronto (KIA 26 Sept. 1918), B.F. Ross of Grimsby, Ont., and J.C. Uhlman of Carleton, NS.

* The official British history states that only fifty-seven raids occurred during this period. This calculation was based upon a target count. Since on many occasions the same target was attacked by different squadrons on the same day, often several hours apart, the present calculation has been made upon a squadron basis.

sidered them 'a great help,' since in good weather they could be seen up to fifty miles away. Once one was identified, a 'fix' could be obtained, since the bearing and distance of each beacon from the home station was known. The Germans had a rather better system, and one which came to be used by RAF crews because the code was not often changed. Batteries in known locations fired colour-coded flares which could be seen even in relatively poor weather, whenever an aircraft was heard overhead.[31]

Immediately prior to Trenchard's assumption of the command of the Independent Force in June there were sixty-two Canadian officers in the five squadrons of VIII Brigade, representing about 30 per cent of its aircrew strength. In all, seventy-three Canadians had taken part in bombing operations and of these only one had been killed, two wounded, and seven made prisoners of war since the inception of 41 Wing, but German resistance during the period was only in process of stiffening. Initially there had been few home defence aircraft to oppose the British bombers. *Kampfgeschwader 2* at Saarbrücken, along with *Kampfstaffel 31* at Trier and *Kampfstaffel 32* at Freiburg in Breisgau, had been assigned to the task of bombing the British aerodromes in the Nancy area. Fighter defence had been left to a single unit based near Mannheim.[32]

As British raiding proceeded, however, so did a progressive reform of the German home defence system. A telephone-linked reporting grid monitored the approach of British aircraft and made rational planning for counter-measures possible. An undetermined number of home defence squadrons (*Kampfeinsitzerstaffeln* or *Kests*) was added, though their effectiveness was limited until mid-1918. The bulk of the defence rested with flak gunners and searchlight crews. Around important sites the guns and lights were supplemented by balloon barrages, trailing heavy steel cable nets to discourage bombers from gliding in at low levels. Such obstacles were often effective, but it was only during the period of Independent Force operations that German defence measures began to take a heavy toll.[33]

Trenchard did not take formal command of the Independent Force until 6 June, by which time he had already been in France for three weeks. Some of that period was spent working out with Salmond the way in which their commands were to relate to one another.* The terms of reference laid down by General Sykes for the Independent Force gave it a role remote from that of the RAF's main force. The general objective (and Sykes insisted that there must be absolutely no divergence from this aim) was nothing less than 'the demobilization of the German Armies-in-the-Field, by attacking the root industries which supply them with munitions.' Trenchard was not to turn his force to strategic reconnaissance or to attacks upon enemy airfields, railway centres, or transport. These tasks belonged to Salmond's force. Were Trenchard's squadrons to take them up, 'with the very limited force available for independent operations no real progress will be made in the destruction of key industries.' The Independent Force was ordered, in Sykes' phrase, 'to

---

* Trenchard later described his relations with RAF Headquarters as 'very strained.' 'I found myself writing to Haig for things I wanted and I got peevish letters from RAF HQ saying they were worried by great battles on the Western Front and could not be bothered with my petty requests for bakeries, etc. I do not blame them one little bit, I understood Salmond's point of view exactly.' Trenchard interview with H.A. Jones, 11 April 1934, Air 8/167

obliterate' the German chemical industry, 80 per cent of which could be attacked from Trenchard's bases. Since it was the chemical industry which supplied 'the necessary material for explosives, propellants and poison gas,' Sykes ordered that no other targets should be attacked until the chemical plants were 'completely crippled.' Only if weather were unsuitable was Trenchard permitted to attack, as secondary targets, the steel factories of the Lorraine Basin.[34] The new Chief of Staff had little sympathy with those extremists among his officers who believed that the new force, if given the chance, could win the war on its own, but he certainly shared their conviction that essential German industries could be obliterated. From a memorandum he prepared for the War Cabinet in June it is apparent that he did not expect decisive results from bombing until June 1919. Nevertheless, he was adamant that a start be made immediately, even though the Independent Force was badly under strength.[35]

Apart from establishing an accord with Salmond in the light of these orders, Trenchard had also to face the problem of his relationship to the Allied High Command. At that level the very concept of an 'independent force' was viewed, at best, with wry amusement. *Général* Duval, Deputy Chief of the French General Staff, is said to have asked: 'Independent of what? Of God?' As Trenchard wrote to Sir William Weir: 'It is very difficult to explain on paper the various difficulties which crop up if it is not clearly laid down what I am.' The co-operation of French authorities, from the highest level down to station-masters and municipal officials, was vital because Trenchard was confronted with an immense administrative problem. His concerns about status were not finally laid to rest until October; in the meantime, he found a friend in *Général* de Castelnau, in whose theatre the Independent Force was based.[36]

When Trenchard began he had five squadrons under command. The three day-bombing squadrons (55, 99, and 104) remained in 41 Wing, while 100 and 216 (Night) Squadrons were transferred to the newly formed 83 Wing. On 3 May he was allotted seven new squadrons, five of DH9s and two of Handley Pages. All were to be fully equipped by 1 June and to arrive by 15 July. Between the latter date and 24 October Trenchard was told to expect another twenty-seven squadrons (twenty DH9s, one DH10, and six Handley Pages). He was ultimately forced to make planning, administrative, and other provision for some thirty-four squadrons. Yet the fact is that by the end of the war he had received only four squadrons in addition to the original five.*[37]

In June, though suspicious of staff projections, Trenchard had no way of knowing that this astonishing short-fall was to occur. When more French squadrons were moved during June to the Nancy area to meet the needs of the armies at the front, Trenchard pointed out to Castelnau that this buildup was taking up available land in the area allotted to the Independent Force. The problem became more

---

* With characteristic bluntness and realism Trenchard recalled in 1934 the situation in which he had been placed: 'When I took farewell of the Independent Force just after the war ... I told them that this high-sounding name was all moonshine. What the Independent Force was, was nothing more than the 8th Brigade which had been under my command long before. What I commanded was a few squadrons which represented a tiny part of my original command. In other words I was not anybody much.' Trenchard interview with H.A. Jones, 11 April 1934, Air 8/167

acute in July and August, when American air units were based in the same general region in preparation for the fall offensive. Through adamant insistence upon his own requirements, Trenchard was ultimately able to expand the Independent Force's territorial boundaries.[38]

The ground support organization required to keep an air force flying was – and has remained – very large, and the Independent Force was no exception to this rule. To service and fly the five squadrons in the force in June, there was an establishment of 1342 all ranks. Since the force was independent, and a substantial expansion was expected, there was in addition a huge headquarters and supporting group. A strength return of 25 May showed 9181 all ranks in these categories.* Among this group were the medical service staff of No 8 Canadian Stationary Hospital (183 all ranks), as well as a labour force of 2838 East Indian troops and 2869 prisoners of war, which was required primarily for the construction of air fields and necessary installations. As Trenchard pressed vigorously on with his expansion programme three Canadian Forestry Companies, Nos 9, 10, and 11, were added in August, numbering about 510 all ranks.† To keep his force supplied, Trenchard had to organize transport to move an average of 165 carloads of stores weekly over the already heavily burdened French rail system. Whatever its shortcomings as an operational formation, the Independent Force was a solid administrative success.[39]

No attempt will be made here to offer a detailed narrative of Independent Force raids during the period of Trenchard's command. Inevitably raids tended to be repetitive in character, though for the men who flew them no single one was routine. Squadron and wing records were concise documents, in which the minimum of information about objective, aircraft, weight of bombs dropped, estimate of results, and presence of hostile aircraft was recorded in the space provided on printed forms. Squadron commanders only infrequently enlarged upon such details. Nor was there a substantial flow of correspondence between the Independent Force staff and the Air Staff in London. Instead, Trenchard chose to report directly to Weir on a monthly basis. Sykes' staff chafed over this situation, but the Chief of Air Staff did not elect to assert his authority. As a result, the Air Staff got its information about the manner in which the Independent Force was carrying out its orders chiefly from Trenchard's summaries to Weir, from Independent Force *communiqués*, and from periodic 'approximate results' reports. Not infrequently there were discrepancies in these documents.

Trenchard, then, was left largely to run his own show; his force was independent in more than one respect. Staff memoranda complaining of this situation, and pointing out not only inconsistencies but also, and more important, radical departures from orders, seem never to have got farther than General Sykes. The historian is confronted by the same problem which confused the Air Staff. For example, Trenchard's monthly totals of bomb tonnage dropped do not appear to

* This figure excludes Trenchard's personal staff of twenty-six.
† The foresters were sent to Nancy without tractors. Instead, they were provided with three hundred horses 'which are blind or otherwise unfit for ordinary work.' War Office to Secretary Canadian Forces in Britain, 16 Aug. 1918, War Office to C-in-C BEF, 24 Aug. 1918, Air 1/521/16/12/4

tally with totals obtained by adding those of individual squadrons. Similarly, there are occasional clashes between Trenchard's monthly reports of squadron objectives and those which appear in daily squadron returns. Finally, it is difficult to determine precisely what both the Independent Force and the Air Staff meant by a raid. 'Raids' seem to have been defined by the target actually bombed, or thought to have been bombed, rather than in terms of operations conducted by formations against predetermined objectives. Thus, if squadron aircraft were forced, for whatever reason, to bomb targets other than the stated objective itself, each of these forays seems to have been recorded as a raid. For all these reasons, statistical analysis of the operations of the Independent Force can only be approximate, resting as it must upon figures of an arbitrary nature.

From the beginning, it is clear, General Trenchard did not follow closely the orders he received. On the basis of a subsequent analysis by the Air Staff it appears that seventy-seven raids took place in June, during which almost sixty tons of bombs were dropped, a substantial increase over the May tonnage. Only 14 per cent of these raids were directed against the German chemical industry, the primary objective laid down by Sykes. A further 13 per cent were flown against the secondary objective, the iron and steel industry. The remainder were against targets Trenchard had been specifically told to ignore. More than half of all raids, forty-three in all, were against the enemy railway network and most of these targets were within seventy-five miles flying distance of Nancy. Another 13 per cent were against enemy aerodromes and the rest against such targets as motor transport parks and barracks. In sum, Trenchard had devoted almost three-quarters of the Independent Force's first month of operations to targets of a non-strategic nature.[40]

In a brief covering letter to his first month's report, Trenchard explained his course of action to Lord Weir. He had planned, he wrote, to inaugurate the air offensive by attacks upon a large number of scattered objectives in order to disperse German defence forces and to follow this initial phase by concentrated assaults upon a single target. Adverse weather had frustrated his intentions, but even had it not, the task of training new squadrons and inexperienced pilots dictated the selection of 'easy objectives.' Another inhibiting factor was 'the large number of failures in the BHP Engine' of the DH9s; moreover, 'the range of these machines, even with a 5 mph wind, was not sufficient to reach objectives such as COLOGNE, FRANKFORT, or even COBLENZ or MANNHEIM with any degree of regularity.'[41]

A review of squadron operations bears out the explanation he offered to Weir. Thus the inexperienced 99 Squadron occupied itself from 6 to 8 June with raids upon a target close at hand, the Thionville rail complex. The BHP engines gave repeated trouble. On 6 June six of eleven DH9s returned to base with engine failures of various kinds. 'The next day's work,' the squadron history noted, 'was even more depressing.' Only four of twelve aircraft completed the assigned mission; the rest returned with engine problems or because green pilots 'failed to get together owing to misunderstanding as to formation places.' On 8 June four aircraft returned with their bomb-loads, two having suffered ignition trouble, another with a magneto failure, while the fourth 'would not give satisfactory results at a height.' Only on 9 June was the squadron allowed to attack its 'first target in Germany proper,' the steel works and blast furnaces at Dillingen in the Saar Valley; it was confidently asserted that 'excellent results were obtained.' On the other hand, the far more experienced night bombers of 100 Squadron attacked blast furnaces at Maizères on the night of 6–7 June, a raid in which Second Lieutenant J.A. Chambers of Winnipeg and Lieutenant G.E. Lucas of Sarnia, Ont., an observer, participated. On 13 June, however, the spell of fine weather broke. Not until the last week of the month was Trenchard again able to mount a series of raids.[42]

Attacks resumed on 23–24 June with 100 Squadron's raid on the Metz-Sablon railway triangle. Judging by the wide assortment of targets attacked, Trenchard's aim in this period seems chiefly to have been the maintenance of offensive pressure so far as weather and material permitted. Thus the three day squadrons launched attacks on 24 June, and after a break because of rain during the night, new raids were made at dawn the next day. No 55 squadron attacked the factories and railyards of Saarbrücken and was itself attacked over the objective by nine German aircraft. Second Lieutenant G.A. Sweet of Hamilton, Ont., together with his observer, was killed during this combat. The two DH9 squadrons were also in action. Though bedevilled as usual by engine failures, 99 Squadron sought to bomb Offenburg station and railway sidings, some forty-five miles over the lines, but just as its aircraft were releasing their bombs they were jumped by seven enemy scouts. Their bombs scattered ineffectually, and Lieutenant N.S. Harper of Kamloops, BC, and his observer, Second Lieutenant D.G. Benson of Aylmer West, Ont., 'last seen going down under control in the Rhine Valley,' were killed. No 104 Squadron, bound for Karlsruhe, seventy-five miles over the lines, had five of twelve aircraft return with engine trouble. The remainder, led by the seasoned pilot Captain J.B. Home-Hay, a former farmer from Wadena, Sask., successfully bombed the munitions factory at Karlsruhe causing, according to later intelligence, some three hundred casualties. Home-Hay shepherded his formation back to base despite the hounding tactics of enemy scouts, but at the cost of a second DH9 shot down and two pilots and an observer wounded.[43]

That same night the Handley Pages of 216 Squadron attacked Metz-Sablon, claiming 'good shooting.' Meanwhile, 100 Squadron carried on a private war it had begun some time before with the German bombing force based at Boulay aerodrome. The raid was typical of the many assaults the squadron had made, and was to make, upon Boulay. Fifteen FE2bs left the ground just after midnight. Among the pilots were Chambers and Lieutenant D.L. Hobson of Mount Elgin, Ont.; the observers included Lucas and Naylor. Because of cloud conditions four aircraft went astray, but the rest found the target after the leader managed to illuminate it by dropping two 40-lb phosphorous bombs from 1200 feet.[44] According to the squadron's report: 'A number of hangars seem to have received direct hits, the remaining bombs bursting close to and wide of the hangars. Two phosphorous bombs caused a large fire to the north of road not far from the hangars, which was still burning when the last pilot left. The buildings to the West of the hangars received direct hits with 25-lb bombs. Nearly 3,000 rounds were fired into the hangars and into the buildings on the West side. No activity and no machines were observed on the aerodrome.'[45] Evidence from German sources bears this out. Unfortunately, burning hangars do not necessarily mean burning aircraft; while four hangars containing stores were burnt out and had to be rebuilt, no aircraft were destroyed.* Altogether, the squadron dropped 18.5 tons of bombs on Boulay, and by the end of August photographs showed that twelve of its twenty-two hangars had sustained 'appreciable damage.'[46] The concentrated use of one of his squadrons in this fashion is a measure of the threat Trenchard believed that German bombing forces posed to his own activities, as well as to the armies. He therefore persisted in ordering such attacks, both on Boulay and many other aerodromes, though little concrete evidence was forthcoming to show either that significant damage was being inflicted or that the German bombing effort was being usefully impeded.

German fighters and flying accidents hurt the Independent Force more than the enemy bombers ever did. In June the force claimed to have shot down ten enemy scouts and to have 'driven down' ten more. It lost nine of its own aircraft to enemy action and a further twenty-four wrecked in various accidents.[47] Of the sixty-one Canadian airmen who served with the Force during June, six, all with day squadrons, were casualties, five of them in DH9s.

In July, despite less favourable weather than the previous month, the Independent Force stepped up its tonnage dropped to eighty-eight tons in 116 raids. What was most significant about the month's operations was that the pattern established in June remained the same. Only 18.5 per cent of all raids were against the chemical and steel industries to which Sykes had attached such high importance; all the rest, including 46 per cent against the railways and 28 per cent against aerodromes, were against objectives either outside Trenchard's terms of reference or given a low priority by the Air Staff. In his report to Lord Weir, Trenchard made no effort to excuse his breach of orders. Instead, he set down plainly the extent to which his operations had been dovetailed to the needs of ground forces. For instance, at the request of the French GHQ, he had ordered the railway station at Lumes attacked on two nights. Similarly, night reconnaissance was being carried out 'systematically over the Railway System in the LORRAINE area ... at the special request of the General Officer Commanding the Group of Armies of the East.'[48]

As German home defences improved, daylight raiding was becoming more and more costly to the Independent Force. Sixteen machines were lost to enemy action, as well as forty-one from other causes, and the bulk of the losses were DH9s. Increasing numbers of Pfalz and Albatros fighters, and even the occasional Fokker (probably from front-line squadrons since so many of Trenchard's raids took place relatively close to the lines) were being encountered by the day squadrons. The month got off to a bad start with a raid by nine DH9s of 104 Squadron on the railway station and sidings at Karthaus. The formation leader, Captain E.A.

---

* Trenchard's report identifies the target as 'Bolchen' aerodrome, Air 1/2000/204/273/275; cf 'Operations of 100 Sqn,' 23–24 June 1918, Air 1/721/48/2. This is one of the rare occasions on which bombing reports can be checked against German information. Although the Independent Force attempted to secure photographic evidence of the results of bombing, it did not do so in the systematic manner of the Second World War, nor was assessment of photographs made with consistent rigour. Aircrew reports tended to be accepted uncritically, yet, when evidence exists to check them, they prove to have been, on the whole, over-optimistic.

McKay of Toronto, lost three of his aircraft immediately, one crashing on take-off, another force-landing with engine trouble, and a third limping back to base from the same cause. Shortly after McKay led his formation across the lines at Verdun, a DH9 lost power, dropped out of the formation, and was last seen gliding down towards the ground. McKay pressed on, but when yet another machine was forced down by two enemy scouts, he decided to turn aside from the objective and attack the railway triangle at Metz-Sablon instead. Constantly harassed by enemy scouts, the four DH9s fought their way to the new target, only to encounter an additional twelve German aircraft over it, one of which was shot down by the Canadian observer Second Lieutenant P.E. Appleby of North Sydney, NS. The four survivors then recrossed the lines without further mishap. On 7 July 99 Squadron had better luck. Returning from a raid on Kaiserslautern, six of its DH9s were attacked by eight to ten enemy scouts. In the running fight which ensued, Lieutenant William G. Stevenson of Toronto assumed command following the loss of the flight leader and distinguished himself for his steady handling of the situation, bringing the remainder of the squadron safely back.*[49]

By comparison, the night squadrons were relatively unscathed during the month. One of their most successful operations was that undertaken by 100 Squadron on the night of 16–17 July, the Canadians Naylor and Second Lieutenant F.R. Johnson of Montreal taking part. The Hagendingen steel works were hit hard. Photographs taken the next day showed that the central blowing station had received a direct hit and that a workshop next to the rolling mills had been destroyed. German reports confirmed this, giving casualties to workers at the plant as eight killed and fourteen wounded.[50]

The month ended as it had begun, with a disastrous raid. This time it was 99 Squadron's turn. By now the squadron had become much more proficient at formation keeping, but German tactics were developing rapidly. Six or more fast Albatros or Fokker fighters would manoeuvre above the bomber formation, while 'two or three machines concentrated on a single DH9 from below at very close range.' On this occasion the formation leader decided that it was hopeless, in face of such odds, to try to reach Mainz, and so diverted his aircraft to Saarbrücken. Before the new objective could be reached, four DH9s had been shot down. Three more were lost in the running fight on the homeward leg. In all, the squadron lost fourteen airmen. Among them were Lieutenant E.L. Doidge of Vancouver, commanding 'A' flight at the time, who was killed, and Lieutenant S. McB. Black of Springfield, Ont., who was taken prisoner. These heavy losses crippled 99 Squad-

---

* For his leadership, skill, and gallantry, this veteran of twenty-six raids received the DFC. Stevenson had had an interesting history. Born in North Bay, he moved with his family to Toronto, where his father became a police constable. After attending the city's public schools, young Stevenson took a job at the Toronto filtration plant. He managed to put together the money to buy himself thirty-three minutes of flying time at the Toronto Curtiss School, but when he applied in Ottawa to join the RNAS, Admiral Kingsmill judged that he lacked the education to become a probationary flight sub-lieutenant. He and another Canadian in similar case were sent overseas as chief petty officers, 3rd grade, and were rejected by the Admiralty, which was no longer accepting 'men' as pilots. Returned to Canada in March 1916, Stevenson was not taken on strength by the RFC until December 1917.

ron for some time, until new pilots and observers could be trained in formation flying. It is small wonder that the squadron's history noted a 'feeling of despondence' among the survivors. The DH9 was an extremely vulnerable machine.*[51]

The reinforcements for the Independent Force which arrived in August were therefore doubly welcome, since both 97 Squadron and 215 Squadron were equipped with Handley Page 0/400s. Of the fourteen Canadians who served with 97 Squadron during its period of operations (it had had no previous operational experience), six were already with it when the squadron joined the Independent Force on 9 August.[†] Nine Canadians were with 215 Squadron during its service under Trenchard; the squadron, as part of 5 (Naval) Wing, had taken part in night bombing operations as early as April in the attempt to block Zeebrugge.[‡][52]

The appearance of these two squadrons shifted the balance of the force towards night operations and the addition of the Handley Page 0/400 was itself a notable improvement in the capacity of the force. The 0/400 was superior to the 0/100 (which 216 Squadron continued to fly) in a number of respects. It had an improved fuel system, better engines (the twin Eagle VIIIs made it slightly faster), and a higher service ceiling of 8500 feet. Its new bombracks permitted it to carry varied bomb-loads, from sixteen 112-lb bombs to a single 1650-lb bomb.[53]

The advent of these two squadrons was partly responsible for the general increase in the activities of the Independent Force. Over a hundred tons of bombs were dropped in August, a proportion upon long-range targets such as Düren, Frankfurt, Darmstadt, Coblenz, Karlsruhe, and Mannheim by day, and Cologne and Frankfurt at night. The number of actual raids, however, dropped to eighty-eight. Of these, only 15 per cent were upon the chemical and steel industries, the least attention the Independent Force had given thus far to what were, after all, its major objectives. Of the remaining raids, almost 50 per cent were against

---

* In his report to Weir, Trenchard drew attention particularly to difficulties experienced with broken inlet valve springs on its BHP engine. Consequently, 'Formations of these machines, not infrequently, were reduced owing to this trouble to three or even two machines before the Lines were crossed.' Another major source of trouble was cracked cylinder heads; indeed, one machine had been forced back because of this malfunction on the fateful raid of 31 July. The design requirement which placed the radiator under the fuselage increased the size of the target vulnerable to attackers from behind and below by at least one-third. Beyond everything else was the fact that the engine simply did not develop enough power to enable the DH9s to fly high enough, fast enough, or far enough either to evade at least a proportion of the enemy's fighters or to render them efficient for the purposes of long-range bombing. Report on Independent Force operations during July 1918, 1 Aug. 1918, Air 1/2000/204/273/275

† The six were C.F. David of Killarney, Man., L.R. McKenna of Ottawa, G.T. Reid of Toronto, J.A. Stewart of Montreal, P.D. Taylor and G.L. Warner, both of Vancouver. Later reinforcements were H.S. Boocock and J.J. Campbell, addresses unknown, F.M. Dunlop of Richmond Hill, Ont., R.A. Gunther of London, Ont., G.L. MacPherson of Toronto, D.B. McColl of Walkerville, Ont., P.B.O.L.B. Morency of Quebec City, and F.R. Orris of Springfield, Ont.

‡ They were W.E. Crombie, address unknown (KIA 31 Aug. 1918), Frank R. Johnson of Westmount, Que., W.B. Lawson of Barrie, Ont., J. Lorimer, address unknown, H.B. Monaghan of Picton, Ont. (POW 17 Sept. 1918), and M.C. Purvis of Toronto (all of whom were with the squadron when it came to the Independent Force); J.S. Ferguson, address unknown, S.J. Goodfellow of Toronto (POW 30 Oct. 1918), and A. Tapping of Revelstoke, BC (POW 15 Sept. 1918), who joined it later.

airfields* and another 31 per cent on various railway targets. What prompted this extraordinary concentration upon the German bomber bases? Although Trenchard told Weir that 'Up to date the attacks made by the enemy against our aerodromes have been insignificant,' he seemed to be haunted by fear of the damage that German squadrons might do to his own bases. 'It is certain,' he wrote, 'that desperate efforts will be made by the enemy to defeat our object by the destruction of our aerodromes, and a hard-fought bombing battle must be anticipated.' No such bombing duel ever materialized.[54]

Nevertheless, the enemy's battle with the Independent Force continued in the air with mounting intensity. During the month Trenchard estimated that the enemy had increased its home defence force by four squadrons, noting that 'Our formations invariably meet with heavy opposition, and have on several occasions been attacked by 20, 30 and as many as 40 hostile machines.'[55] It was during one such encounter that 104 Squadron met disaster on 22 August. Just after 0500 hrs on that morning thirteen DH9s left to bomb the *Badische Aniline und Soda Fabrik* (BASF) chemical works at Mannheim. The first formation of seven machines (including one spare) was led by Home-Hay. The second formation of six machines was led by another Canadian veteran, Captain E.A. McKay of Toronto.† Initially all went well and the reserve machine turned for home at 0740 hrs, just before the remainder of the squadron crossed the lines at Raon l'Etape.[56]

Then their troubles started. On crossing the lines both formations encountered heavy anti-aircraft fire which destroyed one machine. As soon as the firing let up the crews sighted a formation of eight enemy scouts. A few shots were exchanged at long range, serving to keep the scouts at bay, though they continued to hover at the flanks and rear of the British formation, waiting for stragglers. They did not have long to wait before another Canadian, Lieutenant J. Valentine, firing a green signal flare to indicate that his temperamental BHP engine had failed him, began to lose altitude. The enemy scouts pounced on him but despite their harassment during the long and harrowing descent, Valentine managed to land his machine under control. Both he and his observer were taken prisoner. Valentine's mishap had drawn off the enemy formation and for the moment at least the squadron flew on unmolested. Over the Forest of Waldeck in the Vosges Mountains, however, Captain McKay developed engine trouble and was forced to land in enemy terri-

---

* Few crews were presented with the kind of opportunity given to Lieutenant Frederick R. Johnson of Montreal and his British observer, Captain H.B. Wilson. Returning from a raid by 100 Squadron upon Bühl, Boulay, and Friesdorf aerodromes on the night of 15–16 August, and with Friesdorf just slipping behind them, they saw twin exhaust flames sinking below them and realized that a German bomber was dropping towards the flares of Friesdorf. Johnson dove on the aircraft as Wilson opened fire. 'After a burst of about 45 rounds,' they reported, 'the machine crashed alongside the flare path, the searchlight on the ground immediately put its beam on to this machine which was observed to be a total wreck.' No 100 Squadron operations summary, 15–16 Aug. 1918, Air 1/176/15/199/1

† These were two of the most experienced pilots in the squadron, both having been flying operationally since 1916. J.B. Home-Hay (POW 22 Aug. 1918) had already won an MC flying with 53 Squadron as an artillery observer, while E.A. McKay (POW on the same day) had an MC from flying photo reconnaissance missions under fire with 42 Squadron. Both won their DFCs for conspicuous gallantry and outstanding leadership in bombing raids with 104 Squadron.

tory. He and his observer were captured before they could destroy their crippled machine.

Under the leadership of Home-Hay the remainder of the squadron made its approach to Mannheim at 11,500 feet, arriving over the city at 0800 hrs. At the outskirts of the city the hapless DH9s were met by a formation of fifteen Fokker and Pfalz scouts mixed with Halberstadt two-seaters. This time the enemy was more aggressive and during the bombing run itself a fierce battle took place. Despite this sixteen bombs were released (eight 230-lb and eight 112-lb) from which 'seven bursts were observed on the factory' causing four fires. 'A direct hit was also obtained on a large new building immediately south of the BADISCHE ANILINE UND SODA FABRIK works. In addition a fire was caused in a factory on the east side of the river.' What happened next is best told in the words of one of the observers, Lieutenant W.E. Bottrill of Hamilton:

Shortly after the bombs were dropped, I broke the top extractor of my Lewis Gun. The Observer flying with Capt. Home-Hay also had a stoppage or jamb, I noticed him working on his Lewis Gun, while both our guns were out of action an enemy scout (Phalz [sic]) dived at Capt. J.B. Home-Hay's machine. His Observer was still working on his gun. When I had my gun again in working order I immediately opened fire on the Phalz that was attacking Capt. Home-Hay (Leader). The E.A. had hit the leaders [sic] machine which emitted smoke and steam [from the vulnerable exposed radiator] and went down in a wide spiral. As a result of my fire the enemy Phalz caught fire, and his machine lost flying speed and stalled and finally went down vertically, still burning.[57]

In the meantime, the remainder of the squadron had followed Home-Hay's machine down to 6000 feet and in so doing the formation broke up. This was the opportunity which the enemy had hoped to create and the scouts dived in on the scattered machines from all sides. The fight was short but furious, lasting only about ten minutes. In the process another DH9 went into a spin carrying Second Lieutenant C.G. Pickard of Exeter, Ont., and his pilot to their deaths. Home-Hay managed to execute a forced landing with his battered machine behind enemy lines.

Lieutenant Bottrill and his pilot tried to gather the scattered and leaderless formation. Eventually Bottrill was able to signal his pilot's intention by tying a handkerchief to the Scarff mounting of his machine-gun. The survivors quickly rallied around their new leader and turned for home. Order having been restored, the enemy scouts broke off the engagement. The survivors and their five machines landed without further incident at 0930 hrs.* In a little over four hours 104 Squadron had lost seven out of twelve machines and most of its knowledge-

---

* The reader will note that 104 Squadron took almost three hours to reach its objective and only ninety minutes to return to base. The elapsed time for outward trips was always longer than for the homeward trips, since bombing aircraft had to climb to height (in this case 12,000 feet) and assemble in formation before crossing the lines. No 104's flight to Mannheim was probably lengthened by the running battle with German fighters and the survivors may have been assisted during their return by a following wind. The airline distance from their field at Azelot to Mannheim is 103 miles.

able aviators.[58] Temporarily it was destroyed as a fighting unit, but in less than a month it was back to full-scale activity.

In striking contrast was 215 Squadron's first night attack on the Badische Works. On 25 August two Handley Pages set out, flown by Captain W.B. Lawson of Barrie, Ont., and Lieutenant M.C. Purvis of Toronto, with two other Canadians in their crews, Lieutenants H.B. Monaghan (a pilot who volunteered to act as gun-layer in Lawson's machine) and W.E. Crombie. A low-level night attack was planned, and the movements of the two aircraft in the target area were carefully co-ordinated in advance. Lawson was to approach Mannheim at 5000 feet, draw enemy fire, and when Purvis arrived, was to 'veer off four miles, shut off our engines, turn and silently glide toward the target ...' It was calculated that a four-mile glide would bring the Handley Page over Mannheim at 1000 feet, the mini-mum height from which bombing was supposed to take place because of blast effect. The two aircraft made contact over Mannheim according to plan, but Lawson seems to have commenced his glide more than four miles from the target. As Monaghan later recalled, 'the silence was startling with only the whistle of the flying wires and the soft sound of the wind to break the quiet ... I stood on a wooden lattice support with my arms resting on the fuselage gazing at the country-side below, wondering what was in store ahead.' When the Handley Page reached the 1000 foot level, 'to our dismay the huge factory, now in view, was about a half mile further on.' Lawson, Monaghan continued:

... flew steadily ahead, and as we swept over the huge works at 200 feet the full load of bombs crashed dead centre and exploded with a roar. The plane lurched and reared but held together and with full power on and dropping the nose to pick up speed we tore ahead. At this time a most fortunate occurrence took place. Alerted by the noise of our engines the searchlight swung down in our direction lighting up the area like day and outlining two high smokestacks and a church steeple directly in our path which Lawson just missed. Mean-while I was throwing the Coopers [20-lb bombs] overboard and I remember looking down a long street and seeing, with astonishment, a house topple into the roadway.[59]

Lawson reported that he 'circled round for seven minutes sweeping the various works and searchlights with M.G. fire.' As he left the target area Purvis glided in to 400 feet, again claiming direct hits and 'Enormous damage done.' He then swept the town with 1100 rounds of machine-gun fire. Though German reports show the damage caused to have been somewhat less than that claimed, some of the bombs failing to explode, it was nonetheless true that a division of the works was put out of action for two weeks.[60]

These two raids emphasized what Trenchard already knew only too well: that day bombing was becoming prohibitively expensive in lives and machines and that the balance was swinging in favour of night raiding. As early as July 1917 he had warned that a quarter of future bombing forces would have to be trained and equipped as long-range escorts, and the Air Board itself had predicted in Novem-ber that stiffening German air defences would probably force a shift to night bombing by the summer of 1918. Accurate though they were, these appreciations had produced neither the required numbers of night bombers nor aircraft suitable for long-range escort. On 4 August 1918 Trenchard consulted Sykes directly on the escort issue, a step that testified to the importance he attached to the problem.[61] One of Sykes' staff officers, Major Lord Tiverton (serving as FO 3 under the Director of Flying Operations,) argued for larger formations of bombers: 'If the enemy attaches such high importance to the results of our bombardments that he is willing to divert such personnel and material to cover his vulnerable points, and if we increase the strength of our formations in such a way as to enable the bombers not only to hold, but to defeat the hostile fighters, it follows that a constant supply of these enemy machines must flow into the area. As it will not be necessary in these circumstances to divert any of our own fighting machines, the advantage to us is obvious.'[62] But Trenchard lacked the men and machines for mass attacks. Moreover, the problem of station-keeping in large formations, not to speak of control over them in flight, was insuperable, given the mechanical unreliability of aircraft, the primitive means of intercommunication, and the widely varying flying competence of the pilots.

There was scant sympathy for Trenchard and his problems within the Air Staff by this time. Too many hopes had been disappointed by his obvious lack of enthusiasm for the mission of strategic bombing. The imbalance between raids devoted to the industrial targets favoured by the Air Staff and those upon targets of lesser significance had become so blatant that Brigadier-General P.R.C. Groves, Director of Flying Operations and one of the chief proponents of the obliteration approach, was moved to protest to Sykes. 'I would submit that the policy pursued at present amounts to the diversion of maximum effort against targets of subsidiary importance. Such a dissipation of Air Force is at variance with the policy laid down by the Air Council ... and with the views put forward by you in the declared policy of the Air Staff submitted to the War Cabinet in a printed paper on June 27th.* Moreover, I consider that if the G.O.C., I.F., continues to pursue his present policy it will be difficult to justify the allocation of Air Forces as between the Army, Navy and the Independent Force, in which the War Cabinet has recently concurred.'[63] Behind Groves' blunt statement lay feelings of deep frustration on the part of members of the Air Staff. Such feelings were disclosed in a memorandum to Groves by Lord Tiverton, a self-confessed extremist on the subject of strategic bombing.†

The person who will offend no one offends everyone and accomplishes nothing. The fate of the new staff will be that of all invertebrates. They will have to give in to a reactionary staff who at least believe in a policy with sufficient zeal to see it carried through. Nor is it very difficult to foresee how this will be brought about. There is an evil report already abroad that

---

* This document, 'Review of the Air Situation and Strategy for the Information of the Imperial War Cabinet,' is printed in full in General Sykes' *From Many Angles: an Autobiography* (London 1942), 544–58.

† In June Tiverton had volunteered his services as an 'observer-bomber' with the Independent Force, arguing to Groves that 'it would not be a bad thing to have an older man who was a fanatic on the subject.' Memorandum to DFO, 21 June 1918, Air 1/461/15/312/107

the new staff are incapable of giving a virile decision. ... those who disagree with the long distance bombing policy will not be averse to seeing eye to eye with those who look askance at the new staff. This atmosphere will be studiously cultivated ... It may be advisable up to a point to sacrifice personnel, material, policy and personal good name in order to obtain the good will of one officer, but it must be remembered that the good will of many others will be alienated in the process and it therefore logically follows that the success of such policy may be too dearly bought.[64]

Only Weir had the authority to bring Trenchard back to the true path, but his early zeal for the strategic bombing offensive, based as it was upon his own overly-optimistic forecasts to aircraft production, had been much diminished. Trenchard's monthly reports for the period June-October were sometimes addressed to Weir personally and at other times to him through the Secretary of the Air Ministry. These reports were, of course, much more informative and candid than the Independent Force *communiqués* issued for public consumption, and Weir had no reply to Trenchard's repeated references to the inferior quality and inadequate number of aircraft he was receiving.

The Air Staff had little more success in advancing the cause of strategic bombing and of British primacy in it in another conflict of the same period. In May Sykes had drafted a proposal to give Trenchard command of an inter-allied independent bombing force to include French and American as well as British units. Presented to the Supreme War Council in June, the proposal met from Foch almost precisely the same arguments previously employed by Haig and Trenchard when they had attacked the idea of independent air operations. Not until 24 September was agreement reached to establish an Inter-Allied Independent Air Force. Even then the Supreme War Council laid down that the IAIAF was to engage in independent operations only after 'the requirements of battle' had been met; during periods of 'active operations' of the armies its prime function was to supply bombing support for the ground battle. Trenchard was not finally confirmed as its commander until 29 October 1918.[65]

The striking power of the Independent Force reached its maximum in September, when Trenchard received his last reinforcements. No 110 Squadron was equipped with the new DH9As, and since they had been donated by His Serene Highness the Nizam of Hyderabad, the unit became known as the Hyderabad Squadron.*[66] The DH9A was the long-awaited replacement for the DH9, but unfortunately it too had many defects. It used the 12-cylinder American Liberty engine, whose 400 hp made it the most powerful in operational use, but in terms of rated performance the 9A was still not up to the older DH4.

---

*   When 110 Squadron was taken on strength on 31 August, only four Canadians were with it. They were H.V. Brisbin, address unknown (POW 30 Oct. 1918), J.D. Thomson of Winnipeg, N. Wardlaw of Brampton, Ont., and K.B. Wilkinson of Toronto. Later arrivals were D.B. Aitchison of Hamilton, A.P. Cannon of Winnipeg, J.C. Gilchrist, address unknown, S.C. Henderson of Winona, Ont., A.S. Robertson of Pownal, PEI, and W.E. Windover of Petrolia, Ont. (POW 7 Nov. 1918).

BOMBER PERFORMANCE CHARACTERISTICS (NO BOMB-LOAD)[67]

	DH4	DH9	DH9A
speed at 10,000 feet	133.5 mph	114 mph	120 mph
service ceiling	22,000 feet	18,000 feet	19,000 feet
endurance	6¾ hrs	4½ hrs	5¾ hrs

The operational record of the DH9A with the Independent Force was most disappointing and its loss rate exceeded that of both the DH4 and the DH9. Undoubtedly the heavy rate of loss was owing in part to the inexperience of 110 Squadron, which had seventeen of its aircraft shot down and another twenty-eight wrecked during its two months of operations. But the DH9A was not a successful machine.*

The other new squadron was No 115. Though it too was untested, having been formed at Netheravon in April, it was equipped with the far more reliable Handley Pages. The squadron did not have a strong Canadian representation – there were six on strength when it arrived on 31 August, and only three more joined it subsequently – but of this small number one was wounded, two injured, and two taken prisoner within the squadron's first three weeks of operational duty.† On its first raid, against the Metz-Sablon rail complex on the night of 16–17 September, the squadron claimed that six of its aircraft reached the target area and that 'The Station was well plastered with bombs, several fires were started, and a searchlight got a direct hit.' Anti-aircraft fire over the target was heavy and a machine piloted by Lieutenant E.G. Gallagher of Leamington, Ont., was crippled and forced down. Both Gallagher and his observer, Second Lieutenant R.S. Lipsett of Holland, Man., became prisoners of war.[68]

The night-bombing squadrons now outnumbered the day squadrons five to four, and with their superior load-carrying capacity they became the predominant arm of the Independent Force. The force was reorganized into three wings. While 41 Wing consisted of the day-bombing squadrons excluding the DH9As of 110 Squadron, 83 Wing comprised all five of the Handley Page squadrons. With the arrival of 45 Squadron from Italy in September a third wing, No 88, was formed to

---

* No 110 Squadron was the only IF Squadron to be fully equipped with the DH9A. No 99 Squadron began to replace its DH9s with the DH9A on 4 September, but this programme remained incomplete at the Armistice. It was considered impractical to fly mixed types of aircraft in formation, and therefore 99 Squadron used its new machines operationally on only a few occasions. L.A. Pattinson, *History of 99 Squadron, Independent Force, Royal Air Force, March 1918–November 1918* (Cambridge 1920), 43, 55

† The original Canadians on the squadron were G.A. Firby of Toronto (WIA 21 Sept. 1918), E.G. Gallagher of Leamington, Ont. (POW 17 Sept. 1918), T.E. Greer of Toronto, R.S. Lipsett of Holland, Man. (POW 16 Sept. 1918), J.W. Taylor of Guelph, and R.J. Whitaker of Kenora, Ont. J.A. Bell of Edmonton, J.M. Catto of York Mills, and W. Dougall joined later. Whitaker and Greer were the first members of the squadron to undertake a night flight, on 13 September, but were injured in what the squadron history described as a 'bad crash.' 'History of No. 115 Squadron, Royal Air Force,' nd, Air 1/176/15/206/1

include this unit and 110 Squadron.* The posting of 45 Squadron to the force was a belated and rather inept attempt to solve the escort problem. The Sopwith Camel did not have the endurance to escort bombers. This distinguished squadron took no part in the operations of the Independent Force, though administered by it, and was confined instead to patrols of the front-line area.[69]

During September the Independent Force reached its peak of bombing activity, dropping over 178 tons. The overall pattern of the force's operations during the first ten days of the month remained as before, with the day squadrons encountering heavy resistance. For example, ten DH9s from 104 Squadron attacked the BASF works at Mannheim on 7 September, together with eleven more from 99 Squadron. On both the outward and homeward flights the two squadrons met strong formations of enemy scouts. Second Lieutenant P.E. Appleby, of North Sydney, NS, was credited with having shot down two fighters during this taxing operation, but his squadron lost three, and 99 Squadron another, before the mission was concluded.[70]

On 12 September the operations of the Independent Force were suddenly shifted to the support of an offensive of the American First Army, launched on the Meuse with the intention of pinching off the German salient at St Mihiel. To this offensive 1481 allied aircraft were committed, 'the largest aggregation of air forces that had ever been engaged in one operation on the western front at any time during the entire progress of the war.' All aircraft except the squadrons of the Independent Force were placed directly under American command.[71]

Trenchard seems to have played little part in planning this operation, and indeed received only two hours' warning on 12 September that it was about to commence. Nevertheless, during the period from 12 September to the night of 16–17 September the force dropped over sixty-one tons of bombs in support of the Americans. Its principal targets were the railway junctions at Metz-Sablon and Courcelles, as well as a number of enemy aerodromes near the front. On 13 September, beginning at 1210 hrs when Appleby took off with his British pilot, 104 Squadron sent out all its machines against Metz-Sablon in a series of attacks lasting until nearly 1800 hrs. Other Canadians joining in this operation were the observer W.E. Bottrill of Hamilton, Ont., and pilots E.A. Forbes of Westmount, Que., O.L. Malcolm of Toronto, and B.F. Ross of Grimsby, Ont. Again on 14 September both 99 Squadron and 104 Squadron raided Metz-Sablon, Bottrill receiving credit for destroying an enemy fighter. The next day these squadrons once more attacked this familiar objective, while 110 Squadron raided the aerodrome at Bühl. Extremely heavy German resistance was met, and though three enemy scouts were claimed shot down (one by Appleby), 104 Squadron lost three DH9s.[72]

The involvement of the Independent Force in the highly successful St Mihiel offensive had been at the express desire of Marshal Foch. He then ordered the

---

* No 45 Squadron, largely Canadian while in Italy, still had six on its strength when it came to the Independent Force. These pilots were J.R. Black of Orillia, Ont., H.H. Crowe of Victoria, A.V. Green of Vancouver, M.R. James of Watford, Ont., G. McIntyre of Montreal, and J.C. McKeever of Listowel, Ont. L.F. Hawley of St Catharines, Ont., and J.C. Williams of Westchester, NS, flew with them before the war ended.

Franco-American forces to launch a further attack in the Verdun-River Suippes sector to cut off enemy troops retreating northward. On 23 September Trenchard was informed that this new offensive would start in three days. Despite the advance warning, the force was unable to play much of a part in these operations because of deteriorating weather conditions. On 26 September, the first day of the offensive, both day and night attacks were carried out against Mezières, Metz-Sablon, Thionville, Ars, Audun-le-Roman, and Frescaty aerodrome. On one of these raids, that by 99 Squadron against Thionville, severe losses were sustained. Ten machines took off for the raid. Engine trouble brought two back early, and another subsequently returned, having lost the formation. The remaining seven pushed on for the objective, but over Metz were attacked by large enemy formations estimated at between thirty and forty aircraft. In order to manoeuvre more freely the DH9s dropped their bombs on Metz. Either over Metz, or on the return flight, five of the seven were shot down. A sixth was destroyed upon landing. Only Lieutenant H.D. West of Toronto, bearing home his dead observer, survived. For the next three days weather grounded Trenchard's squadrons, and operations in support of the Franco-American offensive were not resumed until the end of the month.[73]

Army operational support did not preclude long-distance bombing. The night of 16–17 September saw the commitment of all night squadrons against Cologne, Frankfurt, Coblenz, and Treves, as well as targets closer at hand. The Handley Pages were hard hit, seven being lost to enemy action and three more crashing on the allied side of the lines. The aircraft piloted by Lieutenant F.R. Johnson of Montreal had just released its bomb-load when one of its two engines quit. Johnson coaxed it another ten miles before being forced to land in a field near Darmstadt. The aircraft's three crew members, including rear gunner Lieutenant R.C. Pitman of Saskatoon, then set off on foot for the Swiss border, only to be captured two days later, hungry, footsore, and exhausted. Lieutenant H.B. Monaghan of Picton, Ont., and his crew were approaching Treves 'when, without warning, there were two deafening explosions on our port side and the port engine ground to a stop.' Monaghan lost control of the aircraft during descent, but their crash-landing was cushioned by telegraph wires. After setting fire to the Handley Page the three set off for neutral Luxembourg, carrying their stores of two tins of sardines and a few chocolate bars, but they were picked up the next day by soldiers with police dogs.[74]

More fortunate were Lieutenant J.A. Stewart of Montreal and his observer, Captain G.T. Reid of Toronto. Their Handley Page was the only one sent out that night by 97 Squadron to reach Frankfurt. Over the target heavy anti-aircraft fire was experienced, but Stewart dove through fire and searchlight beams to 500 feet, at which height Reid released his load of nine 112-lb bombs and four cases of incendiaries. Escaping unscathed, Stewart and Reid reported that many direct hits had been obtained on the railways and adjacent buildings.[75] A few days later a letter was taken from a German prisoner which told a fuller story: 'G.F. arrived yesterday from Frankfurt and was therefore an eye-witness of the English raid on Sunday. The Opera House and a great part of the splendid street "*Die Zeil*" are a heap of ruins, and 120 were killed.'[76] If the report was true, then this attack had caused the heaviest casualties to have been inflicted by the Independent Force during its entire bombing campaign. Both Stewart and Reid were awarded the DFC.*

The matter did not end there, however. On 21 September the *Daily Mail* published an interview with Trenchard in which he used the captured letter to demonstrate the effectiveness of the bombing campaign upon German civilian morale. Within the Air Staff this story aroused a protest on the ground that Trenchard had declared publicly that 'the morale damage is of far greater importance than the material,' and that he was substituting psychological effect for the Air Ministry's policy of physical destruction of German war industry.[77]

The author of this objection was Lieutenant-Colonel J.A.H. Gammell, who had recently joined Lord Tiverton in the Directorate of Flying Operations. Gammell's protest was at least curious. Whatever its public professions, the Air Ministry contained many men who were as anxious to destroy German morale as they were to damage German industry. Such views began at the top. Weir had suggested to Trenchard, according to the latter's biographer, that 'I would like very much if you could start up a really big fire in one of the German towns.' Elaborating, he told Trenchard that 'If I were you, I would not be too exacting as regards accuracy in bombing railway stations in the middle of towns. The German is susceptible to bloodiness, and I would not mind a few accidents due to inaccuracy.'[78]

For his part, General Sykes had no doubt about the psychological value of bombing. In his June memorandum to the War Cabinet he had proposed 'numerous attacks by small forces on all the larger cities of Germany with the object of obtaining the most widespread dislocation of municipal and industrial organization.' He went on to explain that '... the aim of such attacks would be to sow alarm broadcast, set up nervous tension, check output, and generally tend to bring military, financial, and industrial interests into opposition ... The wholesale bombing of densely populated industrial centres would go far to destroy the *moral* of the operatives.'[79] Gammell, indeed, had to look no further than his own office. In June Tiverton had pointed out to Groves that the 'Baby Incendiary' was ineffective against industrial plants but could be used for 'burning down a town of residential houses.' With characteristic zeal he suggested that they should be used during the daytime, 'when the people are out at work, and perhaps only children left to look after the house.' A special target list of towns containing large concentration of workers' dwellings, 'such dwellings therefore forming a reasonable target,' had been compiled within the directorate, and Gammell had given it his approval.[80] There can be little doubt that like its German counterpart, the Independent Force was indulging in terror bombing, and that this was both known and approved of by all concerned.

In October the pace of activity for the Independent Force slackened considerably, just over ninety-seven tons of bombs being dropped because of 'extremely

---

* Neither citation specifically mentioned the Frankfurt raid, but 97 Squadron's historical report states that the decorations were awarded for it, although the report mistakenly identifies Cologne as the target: 'The theatre at the time was crowded and the raid had a great moral effect on the people of Cologne. For this both officers were awarded the DFC.' 'The History of No. 97 Squadron, Royal Air Force,' 14 Jan. 1919, Air 1/176/15/196/1

unfavourable weather conditions' with 'prolonged periods of mist, fog and low cloud.' On nineteen days and twenty-two nights of the month even short-distance raids could not be made. Most of the force's operations continued to be in support of the Franco-American offensive in the Rheims-Verdun sector, with over seventy tons of bombs being dropped on railways at Mezières, Thionville, and Metz-Sablon and upon German aerodromes. In the strategic aspect of its operations the Independent Force achieved some spectacular results with the 1650-lb bomb now being routinely used by the Handley Page squadrons. On the night of 9–10 October, for instance, such a bomb dropped by 216 Squadron struck a powder magazine in the Metz Weise island, causing 1,000,000 marks damage and a fire that burned for four days. On the night of 21–22 October a 1650-lb bomb dropped by 97 Squadron completely demolished a munitions factory at Kaiserslautern, with damage estimated at 500,000 marks. Weisbaden was the recipient of the large bomb two nights later when a Handley Page of 97 Squadron dropped one in the 'middle of town' despite bad visibility, causing forty-nine casualties.[81]

Though operations were reduced in October, casualties remained fairly high. During the month the force lost fourteen machines in action and fifty-nine in accidents. Particularly hard hit was 110 Squadron. On 5 October twelve of its DH9As had set out for Cologne, but poor weather and continuous attacks by German fighters forced a diversion to Kaiserslautern and Pirmasens. One of its two formations, led by Captain E. Windover of Petrolia, Ont., lost two machines to enemy action and another in a crash short of its base. The second formation also lost two aircraft.[82] Even more disastrous was the fate that overtook the squadron on 21 October. Its two formations were led against 'railways and factories near Frankfurt' by Windover and the squadron commander, Major L.G.S. Reynolds. What happened to this inexperienced squadron was graphically set down in the bomb raid report:

Twelve machines left in good formation. Crossed lines at 16,000 ft. Course followed at first about 15° afterwards erratic. Evidently crossed Rhine and ... appeared to have mistaken it for Moselle. Wind must have increased from the West ... After crossing River big bank of cloud encountered, formation then at 17,000 and cloud going much higher. Leader fired Red Light. Formation closed up, Leader went down and all machines followed. Machines got broken up in cloud, Leader appears to have turned, apparently to try and get a gap, other machines over shot him. Two machines climbed and went s.w. until they came out of cloud. 1 machine followed Leader till out of cloud at about 11,000, Leader waved 'Wash out' at about 9,000 ft but continued descending. Two machines which went up again bombed Railways and a Factory and returned to Aerodrome ... Three others including deputy leader of No. 1 Formation came back climbing again. A few E.A. Scouts were met but easily driven off or outdistanced. 1 machine landed at 1730 [hrs] near Toul by the light of a burning dump of American Ammunition which almost immediately commenced to go off. 1 machine landed 1730 [hrs] near Mamey in amongst barbed wire close to lines. Third machine landed near Pierrefitte at 1730 [hrs]. The remaining 7 machines are missing.[83]

Among the aircrew who returned from this raid were two Toronto pilots, Lieutenants D.B. Aitchison and K.B. Wilkinson. Neither Reynolds nor Windover were

as fortunate, both becoming prisoners of war. According to the squadron's historical report, Windover failed in a desperate attempt to avoid capture when he '... had
his petrol tank pierced when close to Coblenz. He landed, and his Observer Lt.
Simson kept the Huns off with his gun whilst Capt. Windover attempted to plug
the leak in the tank. He was unable to do this and had to take off again and flew
until his petrol ran out, when he was compelled to land on the German side.'[84] As
an operational unit the Hyderabad Squadron was finished, and was grounded for
the remainder of hostilities.

It could be spared. With the end of the war in sight, the Independent Force
wound down its activities and only a few raids were conducted in November. At
the same time, however, frantic efforts were made to bomb Berlin before the war
ended. It is not clear who was responsible for this push, nor what such a gesture
was meant to signify. But on 7 November Major W.R. Read, commander of 216
Squadron, was ordered by Trenchard to take a flight of six Handley Pages to
Bohemia, find a suitable landing ground north of Prague, and bomb the German
capital. Read used the next three days to select crews and assemble stores. Then,
on 10 November, he got new orders. A single machine was to be prepared for what
he interpreted as a raid on Berlin direct from France, with a subsequent landing at
Prague. Though he had grave doubts that the loaded Handley Page could make
such a flight, Read volunteered for it as pilot. The order, however, was cancelled
the next morning.[85]

The wish to bomb Berlin originated at Cabinet level, and the idea of a strike
against the German capital was entertained until very close to the end of the war.
The chosen instrument for this purpose, however, was not one of Trenchard's
squadrons in France but another unit under his command and based in England.
No 27 Group, with headquarters at Bircham Newton near King's Lynn in Norfolk,
had been formed with considerable secrecy at the end of August. Its commander
was a Canadian, Colonel R.H. Mulock, whose leadership qualities and organizational skill had long impressed his superiors. Mulock later stated that 'we were
known as the 27th Group of the Midland area; however, we never took instructions or had anything to do with Midland area, England, but were an Active
Service Unit reporting directly to Trenchard, only hidden and camouflaged in various ways in England.'[86]

No 27 Group was to be equipped with the Handley Page v1500, the British
answer to the German giants. In July 1917 both Handley Page and Vickers had
been awarded contracts to develop heavy bombers with sufficient range to attack
Germany from bases in England. By April 1918 the Handley Page prototype was
close enough to the testing stage for the Air Staff to begin planning for its operational use. One of the first decisions taken was that these 'super-bombers' should
raid Germany from an airfield in Norfolk. Mulock's recollection was that an
English base was decided upon because 'these machines were so large that they
could not be operated from France as the railway clearances were not large enough
to take spares over.' Though this may have been a factor, the reasons offered by
the staff were purely strategic. Mulock did not take any part in planning until after
the middle of July, but Lord Weir's authority for the Bircham Newton base was
given no later than the beginning of that month. Well before then the staff had
founded its planning upon the selection of a Norfolk base. In a paper probably

written in late April Brigadier-General P.R.C. Groves, the Director of Flying Operations, saw a Norfolk base as offering three advantages. It would be 'on the flank of the German position in Flanders,' and aircraft would therefore not have to cross trench lines; it would be 'within easy striking distance' of the German industrial heartland in the Cologne area; and it had 'very salient advantages for an attack on Hamburg, Berlin and Central Germany.'[87]

Target selection for the new British giant preoccupied the staff for some months. Although they were informed, optimistically, that the v1500 would have an endurance of fourteen hours at a cruising speed of 100 mph, with a bomb load of perhaps two tons, the staff made their calculations on the basis of a 1000-mile round trip. A common concern of planners was that neutral Holland lay inconveniently across the direct track to the German heartland. Just over the Dutch frontier were such great industrial cities as Essen (with its Krupp works), Düsseldorf, Krefeld, and Cologne. A number of staff papers were predicated upon the infringement of the neutrality of Holland, either with Dutch collusion or unilaterally, because such an overflight would be both shorter and safer than alternative routes.

Production estimates were that eight aircraft would be available by the beginning of October, thirteen by early November, and forty-two by the end of the year. The weight attached to these figures in operational planning varied with the gullibility of the planner. Those who took a rosy view argued for the 'material' approach to the use of the v1500, and for a concentration upon industrial targets. If as many as twelve Handley Pages were available by early October, and since each giant 'carries roughly the same amount of bombs as would be carried by a squadron of 18 DH9s,' then there were real prospects of causing heavy damage.* If the Norfolk force concentrated upon the Düsseldorf group of industrial towns while Independent Force struck at the Frankfurt group even greater results might be achieved: 'It is ... most attractive to use this independent force in conjunction with the force under General Trenchard's command, for the purpose of obliterating, as soon as possible, root industries. The strength of General Trenchard's command, during this year, if unaided will not be sufficient to accomplish much but if it were aided by this strength the effect would be very marked indeed ...'[88] This appreciation combined a good deal of wishful thinking mixed with some uncharacteristic realism about the potential of the Independent Force.

Most planners were much less optimistic about the prospects of obtaining v1500s in sufficient quantities to inflict significant material damage before the end of the year, and they therefore argued for the 'moral' use of the new weapon.

---

* A sample target analysis based on previous bombing results was completed by the staff in June. It indicated that only 23.5 per cent of bombs dropped could be expected to be effective in the selected target area, a finding most discouraging to those who believed in obliteration. Only the inimitable Tiverton was undismayed. 'Putting aside all error curves and coming down to simple arithmetic,' he argued, 'it is a considerable underestimate to suggest that a 230 lb. bomb will obliterate everything within 10 yards of it. Assuming this, however, one could divide an area into squares of 20 yards × 20 yards, with a bomb in the middle of each. Krupp's works and workmen's dwellings would contain 7,744 such squares. It is proposed to drop in one effort 20,000 such bombs ... If Krupp's works are not obliterated by such an attack, then there is something very peculiar about them.' FO 3 to DFO, 21 and 22 June 1918, Air 1/461/15/312/107

Judging by the material results of our bomb attacks in France and by the results obtained by the enemy's raids on London no very effective *material* results could be obtained in a short time by 12 'v' type Handley Page machines. So far as I am able to ascertain 12 of these machines could drop approximately 12 tons in a single attack. At this rate and taking into account that in the present system of high flying attack 75% of effort is wasted, a long series of raids would be necessary to bomb to 'cessation' or 'obliteration' any one of the 'root' industrial groups. On the other hand the moral and political results ... by even six 'v' Type Handley Page machines would be considerable. These results would be of a 'disintegrating' character i.e. they would tend to set the capitalist and the masses against the military power.[89]

This officer therefore gave primacy to Berlin and Hamburg as political targets of the first magnitude and it was this view that gradually became dominant within the Air Staff. The 'material' approach was never lost sight of – as late as 17 August Mulock was given a staff briefing paper on the obliteration of the Westphalian industrial complex – but the slow development of the v1500 meant the gradual abandonment of the staff vision of a master weapon striking crippling blows at German industry. Its best use – and that of all other bombers – was as a weapon of terror. As Colonel Gammell admitted, 'we are in fact attempting to frighten the German people out of the war.'*[90]

As the Air Staff began to wrestle with the problem of the best use of the v1500s, Mulock, quite unaware of what was in store for him, was going about his duties as a lieutenant-colonel on the staff of No 5 Group at Dunkirk. At the end of May he was given command of 82 Wing, the group's bomber force. Almost at once orders were received from the Air Ministry that he was to report for other duties. Brigadier-General Lambe, commanding No 5 Group, pressed Vice-Admiral Keyes to block this transfer, because 'it is essential to retain this officer's services.' Mulock, 'an officer of very high ability,' wanted to stay with the group and Lambe thought it 'would be disastrous to move him at this period.' All that Keyes could get was a postponement. He warned Lambe that it was probable that Mulock would have to go 'at an early date' to a more senior appointment.[91]

*   Scenarios in which the Handley Page v1500 figured as vengeance-dealer and destruction-bringer proved irresistible to the Air Staff. As late as 30 September 1918 a staff paper outlined the virtues of the combined use of incendiary bombs and high explosive on population concentrations. It was estimated that the v1500 could carry 16,000 Baby Incendiaries, and lay down a belt of fire sixty yards wide and 2500 yards long. 'If the target is large the operation may be described as simply a plastering of the locality with a predetermined density of fire nuclei.' Night attacks with incendiaries would produce 'a magnificent spectacle' that would 'engender a spirit of enthusiasm in the attacking personnel.' 'To obtain the maximum strategic, moral and material effect from an attack upon a suitable target such as a town or large works the effect of depositing high explosives closely followed by B.I. Bombs could hardly be improved upon. The results might safely be described as terrific, and no ordinary populace could contemplate with equanimity the possibility of further similar attacks.' Such use of the v1500s would 'bring home to the Hun populace ... a due reward for the approval shown by them of the barbarous acts perpetrated by their Armies on the Western and other fronts.' Before this paper was circulated, the Cabinet had already laid down that the destruction of German towns with incendiaries was to be undertaken only 'as a defensive act of retaliation.' 'Incendiary Operations as a Means of Aerial Warfare,' 30 Sept. 1918, Air 1/461/15/312/111; FO3 to DFO, 18 Sept. 1918, Air 1/461/15/312/107

The Air Ministry had in fact already settled upon Mulock as the commander of the Norfolk striking force, and the Admiralty's intervention served to confirm the estimate that had been made of him. His appointment was deferred only because calamity had befallen the V1500 programme. In May the prototype had made its first flight. Over the next few weeks further test flights took place during which problems were experienced with the control surfaces. Then, in June, the prototype crashed, killing all but one of the six occupants. There was no duplicate prototype. Production of the V1500, which had already begun, was continued, but the first production model would not be available for further testing until the autumn.[92]

The V1500 had virtually been ordered off the drawing board, and the first, ill-fated machine had been produced in the remarkably short time of six months. It was not quite so large as the Staaken VI, the German giant, its wing span of 126 feet being twelve feet shorter and its weight 700 lbs lighter. Its engines – four Rolls-Royce Eagle VIIIs of 375 hp – were much more powerful and gave it a maximum load of 7500 lbs against the Staaken's 4400, but over extended ranges this advantage disappeared. Though in its final form the V1500 was undoubtedly much better engineered than its German equivalent, the British, as it turned out, had entered the super-bomber competition too late.[93]

This Mulock could not know. On 18 July he was ordered to report to the Air Ministry and plunged immediately into a series of briefing sessions with the operational planning staff, discussions with senior officers such as Sykes and Groves, and visits to General Trenchard in France. By early August he had won acceptance of his organizational plans for the group, including a promotion policy, normal in operational units, that conflicted with headquarters practice. Though the Deputy Chief of Air Staff would have preferred to exert headquarters control over promotions, he thought it best to accept all Mulock's recommendations, 'in view of the important political effect of the operations of the British Independent Force.'[94]

Nor did Trenchard delay long in imposing his views about the structure and role of the new formation upon the Air Staff. In a forceful letter to Sykes he recommended, in terms that left no room for discussion, that the new group should be an integral part of the Independent Force and that, except for matters of administration (which were to be handled by the Air Ministry), Mulock should deal directly with him. Therefore he had 'delegated to him [Colonel Mulock] a large amount of responsibility on lines which I have laid down ...' Above all, he asserted that 'this organization is based upon my plan of operations, and operation orders will be issued by me.' He went on:

There is, however, one point connected with operations which it is necessary to lay down and lay down very clearly and definitely. That is, it would be a great mistake in policy to use these machines for active operations until such time as I consider we shall get the utmost efficiency out of the machines and have the confidence of the Pilots who carry out the operations.

I fully realize the necessity of starting operations early, and therefore I would press that the organization ... is provided at the earliest moment. If this is done, I hope it will be possible to start work with these machines by October. It may be earlier, but it is useless to be too optimistic.[95]

All was carried out in accordance with Trenchard's wishes. On 29 August authority was given for the formation of No 27 Group, Independent Force, with two wings, Nos 86 and 87, to be based at Bircham Newton. Mulock now took up his new command.[96]

Shuttling between Norfolk and London, Mulock soon found himself immersed in administrative details. As he wrote his parents, 'some of my friends have given me a new name, "The Wanderer." It fits my duties and mode of life very well. I wonder what the end will be, as usual I am tackling something so large that at times it seems almost impossible but I never suffered much from a weak heart and we are driving away at it.' To Lieutenant-Colonel E.B. Gordon, Trenchard's senior staff officer, he was more explicit. 'We are all "full out" up here,' he told him, 'and are just in the throes of trying to get to the bottom of this Home Administration. After Active Service, it is rather a shock to see what one has to go through with over here in order that we may go out to kill Huns.'[97]

By judicious use of his direct access to Trenchard, Mulock was able to cut through most of the bureaucratic snares laid in his path. Pilots and observers experienced in bombing operations, many of them with distinguished records, were obtained from the Independent Force and from General Salmond's command. Training courses for them, and for the navigators, wireless operators, engineers, and gunners who would make up each crew of six, were set in motion. A meteorological staff was assembled at Bircham Newton whose duty it was to make 'accurate weather forecasts for a period of sixteen hours from the time machines started,' using information 'covering a distance of 1,600 miles in a circle from our base.'[98] Wireless operators and navigators were given special training in the use of the directional wireless equipment being fitted to the v1500. As Mulock later explained: 'To control the operation of these machines, it was necessary to have exceptional Wireless equipment and Meteorological forecasts. The Wireless control was accomplished by cutting-in the Wireless Marconi Station at Chelmsford, which had been shut down by order of the Admiralty at the outbreak of the War – [the] Eiffel Tower in Paris and the large Wireless Station at Lyons. This was the main Wireless control from which code messages were sent to the machines, and by taking back bearings on these stations, the machines with their Directional Radio, could locate themselves without giving their positions away.'[99] These and a host of other matters were taken care of with Mulock's usual down-to-earth efficiency.

Mulock's chief concern, however, was with the v1500s and the infinite difficulties being encountered in their development. On this crucial subject he communicated with Trenchard every three or four days, as well as seeing him occasionally in London, and he worked closely with Frederick Handley Page and Brigadier-General J.G. Weir (the Air Minister's younger brother), who was the RAF's chief technical officer. On 28 August the first production v1500 had left the Handley Page works and been flown for testing to Martlesham Heath. Problems with the rudder and ailerons, engine placement and radiators plagued the aircraft, so much so that on 20 September Mulock was forced to report that the first machine was unsatisfactory and would have to undergo extensive changes. Meanwhile the second machine, by this time ready for testing, would be 'tied up.' The best estimate he could get was that four V1500s would be ready for service by the end of October.[100]

By early October modification and flight testing on the two completed aircraft began to progress more favourably. On the 15th the impatient Trenchard wired: 'Understand V1500 been tested last few days. Send full report of trials.' One of Mulock's crack pilots, Major F.T. Digby, a much-decorated British veteran of 216 Squadron, had been flying the new bomber, and Mulock reported that he found it 'as nice as 0/400 to fly.'[101] On receiving this favourable news Trenchard posed the big question to Mulock: 'Urgent your definite views as to whether the V1500 as result of your experience can do the long trip and if so the earliest it can be used. Wire me again when you are going to be at Air Ministry. Important that I talk to you on telephone ...'[102] Mulock's reply was simple: 'Yes, it is possible under favourable weather, with the figures we have at present.' In fact, he had already discussed 'the long trip' with Sykes and Lord Weir on 15 October. Both 'were very anxious that a long-distance trip be made at the earliest possible moment on account of the general conditions prevailing both at the Front and internally in Germany.' When Mulock told them that two V1500s would be ready in two weeks, Weir asked that they 'be put in action at the earliest possible moment,' instead of being used for training purposes. Mulock had therefore selected crews for the two aircraft and ordered the Meteorological Section to begin making forecasts 'for the whole area concerned i.e. NORFOLK and 'X' and NANCY.' What was 'X'? There seems no doubt that it was Berlin. In his letter to Trenchard Mulock argued for a 'Northern route.' A map in Mulock's papers shows the intended track: 240 miles from Bircham Newton to Borkum, thus avoiding an infringement of Dutch territory; an alteration to starboard and a 300-mile flight to Berlin; a last leg of 420 miles to one of the Independent Force fields in the Nancy area.[103]

Mulock had only one other question to raise. 'You have definitely laid down in your original letter to me that no operations are to be carried out except under your instructions,' he wrote Trenchard. 'In view of the above, would you kindly give me the orders required for this emergency operation.' In his reply Trenchard expressed his full agreement with the steps Mulock had taken, and then gave him a free hand: 'I give you freedom to carry out this operation on the lines you propose when you consider you are ready, as you are in a better position to judge for an emergency operation than I am.' So to Mulock was given responsibility for what would have been, politically, the most significant British air operation of the war. But Berlin was not to know the roar of hostile bombers for another generation. Early on 11 November Mulock received a signal from Trenchard: 'Hostilities cease today at 11.00. You will not carry out operations without orders from this HQ but preparations are to proceed.'* The strategic bombing campaign was over

* In a short historical account of No 27 Group in his personal papers Mulock stated that because the Air Staff was fearful that 'we might push off and take a chance' on bombing Berlin, he was 'withdrawn from my Unit and kept in London the last ten days of the war,' returning to Bircham Newton only on the afternoon of 10 November. 'They thought it was too big a temptation to leave in the hands of anybody.' Nonetheless, No 27 Group had a last fling of sorts. On Armistice Day one of the V1500s flew over London 'with forty-one on board – ten girls and thirty-one men.' After the Armistice, Mulock recalled, 'our Unit was kept on duty and the Germans were

before the machine, which more than any other embodied the hopes of the Air Staff, could be used. Except for a single aircraft which bombed Kabul in early 1919 during the Afghan War, the Handley Page v1500 was never to be employed in operations.[104]

In assessing the work of the Independent Force as an autonomous 'strategic' weapon, that is as a war-winning weapon separate from other armed forces, it is important to emphasize once again that in Trenchard's hands it was never used primarily for that purpose. Despite Sykes' instructions, only 16 per cent of Independent Force raids from 5 June to 30 September were directed against German chemical and steel plants.* By October the force was committed so heavily in support of ground forces that Trenchard no longer had a genuine free-dom of choice with respect to targets. In his final despatch to Lord Weir he defended his decision to give low priority to industrial targets:

(i) It was not possible with the forces at my disposal to do sufficient material damage so as to completely destroy the industrial centres in question.
(ii) It must be remembered that, even had the Force been still larger, it would not have been practical to carry this out unless the War had lasted for at least another four or five years, owing to the limitations imposed on long range bombing by the weather.†[105]

Nor was it weather alone which limited the effectiveness of the British bombing force. As we have seen, the Independent Force was a long way from having solved its technological problems. It is also questionable whether, measured against its limited effectiveness, the force could have been sustained indefinitely in view of its heavy losses. There surely can be no quarrel with Trenchard's rejection of the Air Staff's 'obliteration' approach as utterly impracticable. For it, however, he had substituted another strategic aim: the crippling of the German will through the psychological effects of bombing. As he told Weir, he had spread the raids of his bombers over as many targets as possible in order to maximize these effects, for 'at present the moral effect of bombing stands undoubtedly to the material effect in a proportion of twenty to one.'[106]

---

told that if they hesitated or played any tricks, these long distance bombers would go over and pay a visit to Berlin. The Unit was kept armed and on duty for about two weeks.' Mulock Papers, 121, R.H. Mulock biographical file, DHist. Confirmation of part of the last statement is to be found in the minutes of the Air Council of 29 November 1918, in which it is noted that two v1500s 'must remain available fully equipped for carrying out special demonstrations [over Berlin] if needed.' The phrase 'over Berlin' is stroked out in the draft copy of the minutes. Minutes of 64th Air Council meeting, 29 Nov. 1918, Air 6/13

* During the 396 days of the strategic bombing campaign from bases in the Nancy area, 508 raids and 51 individual bombing sorties were carried out, during which 14,911 high explosive bombs and 816,019 incendiaries of a total weight of over 665 tons were dropped. Bombing records show that in the June–September period there were 416 raids, of which 34 were against chemical works and 34 against steel plants, while there were 185 raids against rail targets and 139 against aero-dromes. Miscellaneous targets of purely military value accounted for the remaining 24 raids. Air 1/415/15/312/20; Alan Morris, *First of the Many: The Story of the Independent Force, R.A.F.* (London 1969), 172–3

† Trenchard's final despatch was published as a supplement to the *London Gazette* on 1 January 1919 and was subsequently reprinted in the 9 January issue of *Flight* (52–55) under the title 'The Work of the I.A.F.'

Trenchard's doubts about the importance of the material damage wrought by his squadrons were confirmed by a British investigating commission which surveyed some of the force's chief targets immediately after the Armistice. The commission found that the physical results of bombing had been minor. Little impact had been made on the steel industry: 'With perhaps few exceptions, damage of Works cannot be said to have been great. Very complete records have been kept of the position in which every bomb has fallen that was anywhere near the Works, together with reports stating what damage each bomb caused. The damage has, except on rare occasions, been confined to masonry, roofs, gas pipes, windows, blowing engines, coke ovens and machinery shops. It is very noteworthy how surprisingly little serious damage has been throughout 4 years of war, and on no occasion has a Works been forced to close down for more than a week as the direct result of bombing.'[107] The commission's findings were similar with respect to the chemical plants it visited: 'Generally speaking the damage caused has never been of such a formidable nature that repair has been impossible. Such damage as was caused was annoying and entailed extra labor, but did not affect the output of the factory in any way. The total output from a military point of view was never once diminished.'[108] In monetary terms the damage inflicted upon German industry by allied bombing in 1918 amounted to 15,380,000 Reichsmarks – a sum that is less than a tenth of 1 per cent of German war expenditures.* Trenchard's judgment had been convincingly vindicated.

How successful had the bombing campaign been in sapping the morale of the German people, and hence in adding to the political pressures to end the war? Both Trenchard and the Air Staff had been encouraged to believe that civilian morale was breaking down in the face of the bombing by an intelligence survey based upon agents' reports and a number of letters taken from German prisoners of war. Typical of such letters was the following, written from Mannheim in late March 1918: 'Today at noon they were here again. The noise of the bombs and crashings was terrible. How will all this end? Others will be so affected that they will be ill all their lives, and still no peace.'[109] Unquestionably, in the case of this individual, the bombing campaign had already been spectacularly successful. But how general were such feelings, and what was their duration? The survey men-

---

* It is impossible to determine with any reasonable degree of accuracy what proportion of the damage was done by British bombers alone. The nine centres surveyed by the commission had received 59 British and 110 French attacks. On the other hand, a detailed examination of operation summaries for October (the only month in which the IF provided French tonnages) shows that the British, at that point, were accounting for two-thirds of the tonnage.

   Gen Hugo Grimme, *Der Luftschutz im Weltkrieg* (Berlin 1941), 109, 136, DHist SGR 1 196, Set 87, is a guide to German property damage from air raids. Though property owners had a natural tendency to exaggerate damage, their estimates were thoroughly investigated by German officials and the figures they finally accepted probably reflected fair market value. The significance of monetary estimates of damage is affected by the wartime depreciation of the mark – it fell by 50 per cent in terms of the United States dollar between 1914 and 1918 – but it by no means invalidates them, since hyperinflation did not hit Germany until 1922. See Gustave Stopler, Karl Hauser, and Knut Borchardt, *The German Economy, 1870 to the Present* (New York 1967), 57, 84. Because of the decentralized nature of the German federal system, it is impossible to give a precise figure for German war expenditures. Grimme estimated an expenditure of 147,000,000,000 RM, while Stopler *et al* give the figure 164,300,000,000.

tioned made use of several such letters; there seems to have been no follow-up. Since wartime intelligence is of necessity built up from such shreds of evidence, it is understandable that some weight – perhaps undue weight – was given to this tiny sampling by those most concerned with the bombing offensive.

The British commission of investigation seems to have expected to encounter all the signs of a widespread collapse of civilian morale caused by the bombing. Certainly they were extremely sceptical of any evidence to the contrary. When a director of the Rombas steel works stated that the time spent by workers in air raid shelters was 'largely devoted to dancing and other amusements,' the commissioners were notably unimpressed. 'Although the Directors of one or two of the Works visited affected to make light of the moral effect produced by air raids, there can be no doubt whatever that it has been very considerable in many cases,' they reported, 'and, if we regard the results as a whole, relatively greater than the material damage achieved.'[110]

Nevertheless, the commissioners were impelled to record evidence in conflict with their views: 'The management of the Works visited did not appear to have experienced much difficulty in retaining their employees, even during 1918 when the moral effect of bombing was beginning to make itself seriously felt. In the case of the men this is not surprising as, in the event of their refusing to remain, they would doubtless have been sent to the trenches or other unhealthy spots. But equally little trouble seems to have been experienced with regard to the women.'[111] At the Oppau Chemical Works in Ludwigshafen the commissioners were told that absenteeism had been high during the spring and summer of 1918, but had dropped sharply in the autumn. They attributed the absenteeism to bombing and the influenza epidemic and the recovery from it to higher wages which had been given to workers in the fall.[112] Yet the influenza epidemic reached its height in Germany during the autumn months; the earlier outbreak had been comparatively mild. Even leaving influenza out of account, how serious was the malaise from bombing if it could be dispelled by higher wages? It is worth noting that Ludwigshafen, unlike some other industrial centres, continued to receive raids until 24 October. The likeliest explanation seems to be that, as in Britain, there was considerable early unease among industrial workers because of bombing, but that ultimately most workers were able to build up mental defences against it.

The commission, one of whose members was Brigadier-General Newall, concluded that 'had the war continued a few months longer, a more or less total breakdown of labour at several of the Works might have been confidently expected.' On its own evidence, this claim was unconvincing. No more persuasive was Sykes' judgment that 'Had these attacks been carried out earlier and with adequate forces, say, five hundred bombers devoted solely to this purpose, there can be no reasonable doubt that the Germans must have collapsed during the summer of 1918, owing to the disorganization of their munition factories and industrial resources.'[113] The myth that the Independent Force had made major inroads upon the German psyche was given further credence by the treatment accorded the question on the part of the British Official historian. Although *War in the Air* did refer to the 'unevenness' of the effects of bombing upon morale, the evidence there presented accords with the commission's findings. The further claim is made that 'There were German authorities who believed that a stage had been reached in the autumn of 1918 when intensification of the bombing attacks must have caused a break-down of labour in those steel works which had suffered most.' This judgment appears to be based upon a speculative statement made by a certain Major Grosskreutz, writing in *Die Luftwacht* in October 1928: 'The direct destructive effect of the enemy air raids did not correspond with the resources expended for this purpose. On the other hand, the indirect effect, namely, *falling off in production of war industries*, and also the *breaking down of the moral resistance of the nation*, cannot be too seriously estimated.'[114]

It is undeniably true that bombing affected morale. As the directors of some of the firms surveyed pointed out, even an air raid warning could cause workers to down tools for an hour or so, a break that could spell the most serious consequences for a steel plant.[115] A case in point, mentioned in *War in the Air*, was that of *Roechlingsche E & S Werke* of Völklingen. According to the management of this large steel works the production loss during the last year of the war amounted to 15,563 tons. Impressive at first glance, this figure in fact represents only 4.6 per cent of the factory's 1913 production of over 340,000 tons.* Even if extended to the whole of that fraction of the German war economy touched by Independent Force raids, losses such as these are well within tolerable limits. They scarcely testify to a morale problem so acute as to threaten the capacity of the state to wage war. To put the matter in proportion (having in mind the limited incidence of the 1918 raids), it was not until the end of 1944 that significant deterioration occurred in German war production as a result, in part, of the allied bombing offensive in the Second World War. By then the Anglo-American bomber fleet had reached a delivery rate of over 90,000 tons of bombs monthly, the product of a staggering 18,000 sorties per month.† This deterioration was the result principally of *material*, not *moral* damage, through pinpoint raids on the oil industry and other key industries.

Absenteeism induced by bombing may have caused a slight drop in German war production. Raids and raid alarms may also have added to the general war-weariness of the population, at least in the affected zone. There was sufficient dispirit in early 1918 for a Cologne deputy to propose 'a cessation of bomb raids other than on battle fronts.' The public voicing of such sentiments is surely of some significance, even though the Cologne press repudiated them. The government position, as stated in the Reichstag, was that the deputy 'had lost sight of the plight of French cities which had endured more than three years of war with great steadfastness, and that up to the present we have received no proposals from hostile governments and that no definite measures could be taken unless certain advances were made by the enemy.'[116] Perhaps had Berlin been bombed the

---

* Although the 1918 production of this works in not known, the 1913 figure was available to the British official historian. The 1918 production is unlikely to have been lower and was conceivably considerably higher than the prewar output. Minute to FO3, 5 July 1918, Air 1/460/15/312/97

† For the allied bombing effort see Appendices 40 and 44 of Sir Charles Webster and Noble Frankland, *The Strategic Air Offensive Against Germany, 1939–1945*, IV: *Annexes and Appendices* (London 1961); Appendix 49, 'Indices of German Finished Munitions Output,' gives monthly figures for eight classes of war goods.

Cabinet and the High Command might have had a different reaction, but under the circumstances, and given the nature of Imperial Germany's political system, it would be difficult to contend that the psychological effects of the bombing of the German southwest had much to do with the decision of the government to seek an armistice.

Despite the claims of the Air Staff, therefore, and despite the report of the commission, it cannot really be said that the work of the Independent Force was a success strategically, either in terms of the damage it caused or the psychological havoc it wrought. What is surprising about Trenchard's assertion (not to speak of the uncritical acceptance it has received) is that it should have been made at all, given the disproportionate attention he gave to targets of a non-industrial character.* It is here that the real criticism of the force is to be made. Nearly half of all raids were directed against railways, yet it is hard to see that these targets merited the lives and material expended upon them. Trenchard himself told Weir: 'I ... had to decide, when it was impossible to reach their objectives well in the interior of Germany, what alternative objective should be attacked, and which attacks would have the greatest effect in hastening the end of hostilities. I decided that railways were first in order of importance ... The reason of my decision was that the Germans were extremely short of rolling stock, and also some of the main railways feeding the German Army in the West passed close to our front, and it was hoped that these communications could be seriously interfered with, and the rolling stock and trains carrying reinforcements or reliefs or munitions destroyed.'[117]

Trenchard's decision was a rational one. It was based firmly on his previous experience and was perfectly consistent with the principle for which he had fought so tenaciously before the formation of the RAF and the creation of a strategic bombing force – that is, that the prime use of the air weapon was as an auxiliary to the armies in the field. The bomber, however, was not yet a lethal weapon against rail traffic. The most heavily attacked target of the whole campaign was the Metz-Sablon railway triangle, a scant twelve miles behind German lines and of purely local military significance. Though occasionally spectacular results were obtained, such as when 100 Squadron blew up a munitions train in Metz station, for the most part the lines there were never completely closed to traffic, and in all cases normal service was restored within a short time. As the official British historian has said, in characteristic style, 'the results of the bombing operations against railway stations and rail communications generally may be summed up as, on the whole, disappointing.'[118]

---

* In his diary Trenchard was much more cautious about the material and moral effects of bombing than he was in his public pronouncements. On 18 August 1918 he wrote: 'I wonder whether when the war is over what truth we shall get out of the enemy with regard to the actual damage done by this bombing. I am certain the damage done both to buildings and personnel is very small compared to any other form of war and the energy expended. The moral effect is great – very great – but it gets less as the little material effect is seen.' And then he added a sentence which allows quite another construction of his famous dictum: 'The chief moral effect is apparently to give the newspapers copy to say how wonderful we are, though it really does not affect the enemy as much as it affects our own people.' Quoted in H.M. Hyde, *British Air Policy Between the Wars, 1918–1939* (London 1976), 44

Of all the aspects of the Independent Force's work, the bombing of enemy aerodromes was the most dubious. No less than 40 per cent of the entire tonnage of bombs dropped between 6 June and 10 November was aimed at aerodromes. According to the force's commander, such a concentration of effort was necessary to 'prevent enemy's bombing machines attacking our aerodromes and in order to destroy large numbers of the enemy's scouts on their aerodromes, as it was impracticable to deal with them on equal terms in the air.' There are, unfortunately, no trustworthy German accounts of aircraft losses resulting from bombing, but verifiable fragmentary returns show that on six raids a total of twelve aircraft were destroyed and twenty-one damaged. Nor in postwar German accounts of the air battle do losses from aerodrome bombing figure as a problem.[119]

What is important to stress is that the forces opposed to Trenchard were not large, being neither so formidable as he thought nor as postwar British commentators believed them to be. Only one bombing wing, No 8, a Bavarian unit composed of eighteen Class B aircraft, was directly opposite the Nancy bases. Its base at Boulay was attacked forty-nine times from June until September, including twenty-two raids in August alone. This amounted to a third of all aerodrome attacks by the Independent Force. Yet even in August this wing managed to retaliate against Xaffévillers five times and Azelot four, with a signal lack of success.[120]

The inroads made by German fighters upon the day bombers were probably good cause for counter-attacks upon their home fields. Yet there were never more than six home defence squadrons defending the area attacked by the Independent Force. Moreover, *Kest* airfields at Saarbrücken and Mainz, two areas where heavy bomber losses were sustained, were never attacked, nor were the two *Kest* bases at Freiburg. The success of the German interceptors (though they were probably aided by front-line squadrons) led to a natural exaggeration of their magnitude by Trenchard and by later commentators. Sykes, for example, stated that Independent Force bombing had caused twenty squadrons to be withdrawn from the front for home defence, while E.J. Kingston-McCloughry, using Air Ministry estimates, wrote in 1935 that the Independent Force was opposed by sixteen home defence flights and five pursuit squadrons, a total of 330 aircraft. Had the true strength of German forces been established, perhaps a sounder estimate of the challenge of fighter forces to unescorted bombers would have obtained prior to 1939.[121]

The losses of the Independent Force were indeed high. As the direct result of enemy action 104 day bombers were lost, against sixty-four German machines claimed to have been shot down. In night operations thirty-four bombers were lost, most of them probably to anti-aircraft fire or because of navigational error or mechanical failure. To these figures must be added the enormous total (in First World War terms) of 320 bombers which crashed behind allied lines. Casualties reached their height in September, when thirty-seven machines were lost over enemy territory and fifty-four crashed within the lines; in a single month the force lost 75 per cent of its establishment of 122 aircraft. A concerned Air Staff noted that during the same period No 5 Group, flying long-distance raids out of Dunkirk, had lost a single DH9 out of fifty-eight and one Handley Page of sixteen.[122]

Though invited to do so, Trenchard never offered an explanation of his losses. He might legitimately have given many reasons, but his own approach to the air battle was not a negligible factor, and certainly stood in contrast to that of No 5 Group, a formation infused with RNAS thinking. Thus when Trenchard appointed Major Read to command 216 Squadron, a former naval unit, he did so in order to purge it of 'RNAS ideas.' According to Read, Trenchard took exception to the reluctance of naval airmen to fly in poor weather, or to fly more than one raid a night. He objected to their general conservatism and lack of 'ginger.' No 216 Squadron, having lost only two aircraft in its previous ten months of operations, obviously required shaking up. Read was an aggressive commander, but even he was not prepared to push his squadron quite as hard as Trenchard would have wished.[123]

Trenchard's own aggressiveness and apparent readiness to accept high casualties were inseparable from his idea of war. His central belief was in the relentless pursuit of battle, in the seeking out of combat, in the incessant struggle in which the weaker side ultimately gave way. His ruthless application of this approach to the RFC had caused Sir William Robertson qualms as early as September 1916 and had brought serious morale problems to the front-line squadrons in 1917. Like most of his fellow army officers, Trenchard accepted the idea of victory through attrition. Such a cast of mind, wedded to the weapons then in use, had led to four years of profitless slaughter on the Western Front. Neither the RNAS nor the German air force seem to have taken the view that the technological factors which had created the stalemate on the front, and seemed to dictate the war of attrition, necessarily applied to the air. Trenchard was of another opinion.*[124]

Though the Independent Force was successful neither as a strategic weapon nor as an auxiliary to the allied armies, the achievement of its airmen was extraordinary. Some of the young men who found their way to its squadrons were unable to meet the harsh demands of the bombing campaign. But under adverse circumstances most of the force's airmen carried out their missions with high courage and tenacity. Some were outstanding, among them the twelve Canadians who received the DFC. For all Canadians, as for all their crewmates from Britain and other parts of the empire, the bombing war was a test of steadfastness and teamwork in the face of multiple hazards. Of the more than 150 Canadians who served with the force, a third became casualties on actual operations.

Given the central place that strategic bombing occupied in the operations of the Second World War, it seems appropriate to consider whether the Canadians who took part in the work of the Independent Force had any influence upon the RCAF prior to 1939. This does not seem to have been the case. Most of the Canadians who survived the bombing campaign went back into civilian life, some, of course, to civil aviation. None who joined the RCAF rose to high rank in that service. Not

---

* Trenchard's private valedictory was filled with bitterness. 'A more gigantic waste of effort and personnel there has never been in any war,' he wrote in his diary on 11 November. Though his airmen had 'done splendidly,' they would have done as well had an independent force never been created. 'It has certainly taught me what I really knew before – an impossible organization was set up by the politicians simply in order that they could say, "I am bombing Germany."' Trenchard Diary, 11 Nov. 1918, quoted in Hyde, British Air Policy, 44–5

even R.H. Mulock, most advantageously placed of all the Canadians to form an assessment of the worth of strategic bombing, seems to have become a convert. He imparted his thoughts on air power to a meeting of the Canadian Club in Winnipeg on 18 September 1919. His remarks made clear his strong belief in the future of military aviation, but in an auxiliary role only. He mentioned bombing only in passing, and then apparently because pressed to do so.

Mulock did attempt to explain why Canadians should have taken, numerically, so large a part in the war in the air: 'The men of the air service would take any risk, do anything. And the wonderful thing we found towards the end was that, no matter how much our losses were – and they were terrific – there was never any lack of volunteers. And the colonial chaps came forward in greater numbers than anyone else. There is perhaps a reason for that. Perhaps it is due to the freedom in which the colonial chap is brought up.'[125] Mulock here was touching on an explanation offered by many Canadians of his time, who thought of themselves as tough, individualistic northerners schooled by a rugged environment and therefore possessing the kind of qualities the air war pre-eminently demanded. Yet those who flew with the Independent Force were scarcely frontiersmen or 'wild colonial boys.' Of the eighty-nine whose occupations are known, 40 per cent came from the professions or from business and another 31 per cent were university students. Most of the students and fifteen of the twenty-seven professionals were, like Mulock, engineers. Two-thirds of the 120 men whose place of residence upon enlistment is known were from urban centres.[126] In other words, the typical Canadian member of the Independent Force was a well-educated, technically-oriented, middle-class city dweller, at a considerable remove from the picture of the airmen held in popular mythology. Yet this conventional background seems to have instilled the quiet courage to endure patiently the numbing cold and unpredictable hazards of black night flights, and the discipline to hold to tight formation when every normal instinct urged otherwise.

PART FOUR
Airpower in the Land Battle

M.M. Bell-Irving and A.D. Bell-Irving, Loretto, Jan. 1915 (RE 19933)

Lt-Col. F.A. Wanklyn of Montreal was the first Canadian to join the British flying services. This photograph was taken at the time he flew his tests for his RAeC pilot's certificate no 284, dated 3 Sept. 1912. (AH 585)

The Vickers FB5 'Gun Bus' – the first aircraft designed for air-to-air combat – reached the Western Front in the spring of 1915. (AH 177)

Stanley Winther Caws, who enlisted in
Edmonton, was probably the first
Canadian airman to be killed in action.
(AH 596)

One of the first Canadians to fly in France was Capt. K.E. Kennedy of Sherbrooke, Que.
He was an observer with 4 Squadron from mid-April to mid-August 1915. This BE2c
was unusually well armed. (DND 65-188)

Grant A. Gooderham of Toronto in a BE2c at Chingford, Aug.–Sept. 1915. Note the Union Jack on the rudder, an identification marking that was soon dropped in favour of a tricolour roundel on the fuselage. (PMR 71-24)

'BEWARE OF THE HUN IN THE SUN'

This poster, illustrating one of the best remembered catchphrases of a First World War pilot, was used to drive home to airmen the need to keep a careful look-out. (AH 559)

Lt W.A. Bishop of Toronto (right) serving with the 8th Canadian Mounted Rifles at London, Ont., in February 1915. He subsequently went overseas with the CEF, then transferred to the RFC in December 1915. (RE 22064)

A German observation balloon on the Western Front (AH 490)

A captured Fokker E-III at Candas, France, 20 April 1916 (PMR 73-500)

The RNAS airfield at Furnes in July 1916. The Sopwith Triplane at left is probably the first prototype, N500, which was sent to Furnes in June to undergo operational trials. (PMR 71-40)

A 1916 aerial photograph, clearly showing first, second, and third line German trenches, and, in the top right-hand corner, the communications trenches which linked them with the ruins of Beaumont Hamel. (Q 61479)

Morane-Saulnier Type L 'Parasols' of 3 Squadron, RFC, at La Houssaye in September 1916. When this picture was taken at least four Canadians – Lts K.A. Creery of Vancouver, W.W. Lang of Toronto, G.A.H. Trudeau of Longueuil, Que., and 2/Lt F.H. Whiteman of Kitchener, Ont. – were serving with the squadron. (AH 578)

An observer in the basket of an artillery observation balloon on the Somme in September 1916 tests his telephone before ascending. (PA 2057)

Oswald Boelke, one of the greatest of the German fighter pilots, was a tactical innovator and born leader who played a major role in the early development of fighter team tactics until his death on 28 Oct. 1916. (AH 508)

'B' Flight, 3(N) Squadron, RNAS, photographed at Bertangles in March 1917. The pilots are seated in the front row – A.W. Carter of Calgary, second from left, and L.S. Breadner of Ottawa (hatless), second from right – and the ground crew are behind them. At this time the squadron was commanded by another Canadian, R.H. Mulock of Winnipeg. (RE 17683)

A bulldog and three flying officers of 7 Squadron outside their quarters at Bailleul in December 1916. The officer on the right, wearing gloves and sheepskin flying boots, is Capt. E.J. Watkins of Toronto who served with the squadron from May 1916 to May 1917 – an unusually long and successful career for a corps squadron pilot of the time. (RE 64-487)

A 1917 German reconnaissance photo of the RNAS airfield at Bray Dunes, on the French coast near Dunkirk (Q 69454)

A photographic officer points out to the
pilot of a BE12 the areas to be photographed. The map is resting on the aerial
camera. (Q 12288)

A chaplain used the forward cockpit of an FE2b night bomber as a pulpit while preach-
ing his sermon during a service at an RFC airfield in France. (AH 438)

Ground crew stand by their machines as HM Queen Mary, with Maj.-Gen. Hugh Trenchard, GOC RFC in France, inspects aircraft and ground crew at St Omer on 5 July 1917. (Q 11848)

HM King George V inspecting pilots of 'B' Flight, 3(N) Squadron, 5 July 1917. They are (l to r): F/S/Ls Gordon S. Harrower, Montreal, two British officers, James A. Glen, Enderby, BC, Joseph S.T. Fall, Hillbank, BC, Fred C. Armstrong, Brockville, Ont., and F/L Harold S. Kerby, Calgary (shaking hands with the king). At extreme right is F/C Lloyd S. Breadner of Ottawa. (AH 476)

An RFC mobile photographic dark room and a section of photographers at work at an airfield in France. (AH 460)

The Officers' Mess at 'Naval Ten' in the summer of 1917, when all three flight commanders and half the flying personnel were Canadians. The Albatros rudder hanging from the roof came from a machine shot down by F/L A.W. Carter of Calgary. (RE 196-25)

Capt. W.A. 'Billy' Bishop checking the mechanism of the Lewis gun mounted on the top plane of his Nieuport Scout. The picture was taken on 6 Aug. 1917, and 'up to this date he had brought down 37 German aeroplanes.' (AH 470A)

RFC mechanics examine a captured Albatros D-V. (DND 65-184)

Capt. A.E. Godfrey of Vancouver (left) served in 40 Squadron in the autumn of 1917 and was credited with his first seven victories while flying a Nieuport 17. His was the first British single-seat machine to mount twin machine-guns. (RE 21011-3)

The Sopwith Triplane in which Raymond Collishaw of Nanaimo, BC, scored many of his victories during 1917, when he led the famous 'Black Flight' of 'Naval Ten.' (RE 19255)

Nieuport Scouts of 1 Squadron, RFC, at Bailleul, 27 Dec. 1917. The officer in the fore-ground is Capt. Guy B. Moore of Vancouver, KIA 7 April 1918, a month before his MC was gazetted.

Lt A.G. Goulding of Holland, Man. (right), together with a British pilot and the crew of an Austrian aircraft brought down by the British pilots. (RE 20644)

An Austrian DFW, one of the thirteen machines out of 'thirty or forty' that were shot down or force-landed in the British area during the Boxing Day 1917 raid on Istrana airfield. Lt T.F. Williams, of Woodstock, Ont., recalled that 'We were pretty near all day picking up prisoners.' (AH 513)

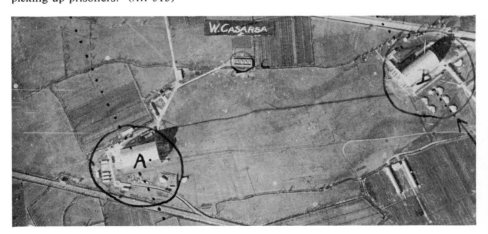

On 19 Feb. 1918 eleven Sopwith Camels of 28 and 66 Squadron, RFC, each carrying four 25-lb bombs, attacked the Austrian airfield at Casarsa and set fire to one of the former airship sheds ('A' and 'B' on this marked reconnaissance photograph) being used as hangars. (RE 15537)

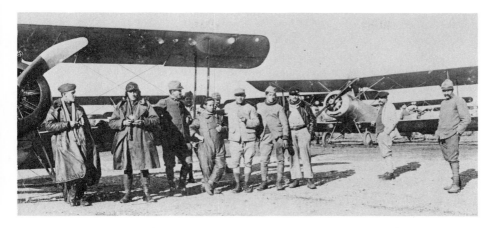

Lt C.M. McEwen of Radisson, Sask. (second from left, in flying helmet), poses beside his Sopwith Camel while serving with 28 Squadron in Italy in 1918. McEwen's flight commander was Capt. W.G. Barker of Dauphin, Man., in an 'all-Canadian' flight which included H.B. Hudson of Victoria, BC, and D.C. Wright of Toronto. (RE 15544)

An oblique reconnaissance photograph of the Val d'Assa. Austrian trench lines can be distinguished in the right foreground.

British airmen – probably of 34 Squadron RAF – at San Luca, north of Istrana, in the summer of 1918. Twenty-two Canadians flew with the squadron during the year. (RE 15551)

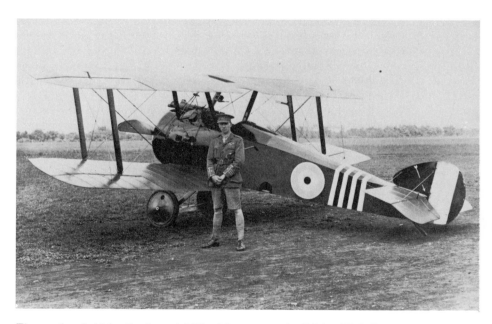

The caption held by the Imperial War Museum reads: 'Major W.G. Barker, Commander of 28 Squadron, beside his Sopwith Camel.' Barker did not command 28 Squadron, however, and he was not promoted to major – as he appears in this photo – until he took over 139 Squadron. (AH 517)

Sopwith Camels of 45 Squadron, RFC, on the Italian front during 1918. More than forty Canadians served with this squadron, which flew two-seater Sopwith 1½ Strutters in France before being equipped with single-seater Camels. It was moved to the Italian Front in December 1917. (AH 514)

An RFC aircraft repair park. The machine in the foreground, with an instrument mechanic sitting in the pilot's cockpit, seems to be a DH9. Other aircraft include Sopwith Camels, an SE5a, and a DH4. (AH 433)

Photographic plates being handed to the observer of a DH4 reconnaissance machine of 27 Squadron at Serny on 18 Feb. 1918. The crown of the pilot's head can just be seen, bent over his instruments. At least twelve Canadians were flying with the squadron at this time. (AH 543)

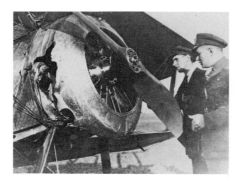

Damage to the engine cowling of a Sopwith Camel of 'Naval Three,' January 1918. The officer on the right is F/C Lloyd Breadner of Ottawa. (RE 64-3010)

Laying-out a photo-mosaic of pictures taken over enemy lines, near Arras, 22 Feb. 1918. (AH 479)

Capt. W.S. Stephenson of Winnipeg, Man., transferred to the RFC and went to France in February 1918 as a Sopwith Camel pilot in 73 Squadron. He was credited with 7½ enemy aircraft and considerable damage to enemy ground forces, winning an MC and DFC before being shot down in error by a French pilot while over enemy lines on 28 July. Ending the First World War in a German prison camp, he distinguished himself in the Second as 'a man called Intrepid.' (RE 19641-1)

Manfred, Freiherr von Richthofen, the famed 'Red Baron,' who had been credited with eighty victories when he was killed in action on 21 April 1918. Here he stands between four of his pilots. The dog's name was 'Moritz.' (AH 489)

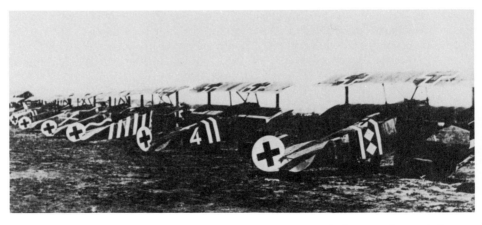

Fokker triplanes of *Jagdgeschwader 1* – Manfred von Richthofen's 'circus' was distinguished by its vivid paint schemes and dramatic markings – lined up in readiness for a patrol. The 'Red Baron' was flying a 'pure red triplane' when he was killed. (AH 491)

The crew of an RE8 of 15 Squadron, stationed at Lechelle, near Amiens, report at the squadron 'office' after returning from a patrol. This picture was taken on 25 March 1918, at the height of the great German attack on the Third and Fifth Army fronts: 15 Squadron was part of III Brigade's 12 (Corps) Wing and therefore part of Third Army. (AH 544)

Maj. Raymond Collishaw, DSO and Bar, DSC, DFC, of Victoria, BC, credited with 60 victories and therefore the second-ranking Canadian 'ace.' (PMR 71-788)

Lt A.A. McLeod of Stonewall, Man., Canada's second VC of the air war. (PL 35319)

RE8s of 15 Squadron, III Brigade, lined up along a roadside near Albert on 25 March 1918. The untidy condition of the grass behind them was probably due to the pace of operations at the time, when Ludendorff's March offensive had driven deeply into the British front and the RFC was working flat out to stem the German advance. (AH 545)

Manfred von Richthofen's death on
21 April 1918 was then attributed to
Capt. A. Roy Brown of Carleton Place,
Ont. Subsequent research has made it
difficult to accept that Brown shot down
the 'Red Baron.' (RE 18431-24)

Von Richthofen's triplane after souvenir hunters had been at work. (AH 494)

RAF air mechanics pose beside an RE8 at Acq, 20 May 1918. Note the canvas hangar and the sandbag blast wall along the side. (AH 480)

Capt. A.A. Leitch, a Canadian of unknown address who lived at High River, Alta, after the war, standing beside the fuselage of an Albatros he shot down near Senlis on 25 May 1918. (DND 65-8)

Aircrew of 22 Squadron at Serney, 17 June 1918. Nearly fifty Canadians flew with this squadron during the last two years of the war. (AH 439)

Officers of 85 Squadron and their pets at St Omer on 21 June 1918, with their SE5a fighters and groundcrews lined up in the background. A third of the squadron's pilots were Canadian at this time. (AH 558)

Bombing up an FE2b in preparation for a night strike against the enemy, 18 July 1918 (AH 436)

RAF armourers check their bomb supplies. This load of 112-lb bombs was dropped during a single night by FE2bs of 149 Squadron. (AH 435)

The nose of a Handley Page bomber. The drum on top of the Lewis gun is the magazine and the pouch below it, on the gunner's right, collected used casings and stopped them flying back in the pilot's face. (AH 530)

Capt. F.R.G. McCall of Calgary examines an aerial photograph. The 'Canada' badge on his shoulder has been scratched out by a censor. (AH 478)

Capt. A.T. Whealy of Toronto watches armourers 'bombing up' one of 203 (formerly 'Naval Three') Squadron's Sopwith Camels at Izel-les-Hameau on 10 July 1918. (AH 472)

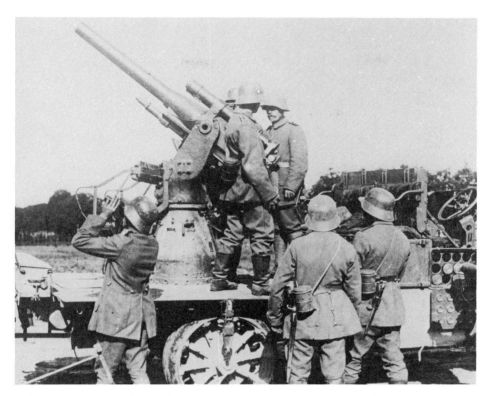

A German 77-mm anti-aircraft gun mounted on the back of a truck (AH 487)

Bombing up a DH4 for a day strike against the enemy. At the right is a Nieuport fighter ready to fly as escort for the bomber. (AH 432)

Part of a letter written by Maj. W.G. 'Billy' Barker of Dauphin, Man., while in the military hospital at Rouen recuperating from the wounds he received in the epic air battle that won him the VC on 27 Oct. 1918. (C 92620)

Maj. W.G. Barker, VC, DSO and Bar, MC and two Bars, Croix de Guerre, Valore Militaire, standing beside the engine and fuselage of the Sopwith Snipe in which he won his VC, at the Canadian War Memorials Exhibition in London in February 1919. Barker (here still convalescing from the wounds to his left arm) was eventually killed in an air crash at Ottawa on 12 March 1930: the Snipe is on permanent display at the Canadian War Museum in Ottawa. (M 804-C)

A postwar photograph of Capt. D.R. MacLaren, DSO, MC and Bar, DFC, Croix de Guerre, in a Sopwith Snipe. In eight incredible months MacLaren claimed 54 victories (48 aircraft and 6 balloons) to become the fourth-ranked Canadian ace of the war. (RE 20555)

A Fokker D-VII. This is one of the trophy machines turned over to Canada after the war's end. (PMR 72-489)

An SE5a – the most sophisticated allied fighter of the war – of the RCAF photographed at Camp Borden during the postwar era (RE 15536)

Introduction

The most important developments in aviation during the First World War were those bearing on the relationship with the ground battle. In the popular conception, of course, First World War flying was about the exploits of the fighter 'aces,' a conception which omits the larger design of which fighter forces were only a part. The chapters in this section are concerned exclusively with the evolution of the air weapon on the Western Front, in Macedonia, and in Italy. In all these theatres the air arm was subordinated to the ground forces.

Canadians who flew on active service from 1914 to 1918 should have had no misconceptions about the relationship between aviation and the war on land. Most of them flew with units that were serving the needs of armies, for from the beginning of its existence, and especially after the outbreak of the war, the Royal Flying Corps was an auxiliary of armies in the field. Except for its home defence organization, the RFC was shaped, in every important particular, by its relationship to the army.

On the Western Front the size and organization of the RFC was a function of the size and organization of the British Expeditionary Force. Early in the war it was determined that the RFC's basic formation, the squadron, should serve an army corps; hence, as the BEF expanded, so necessarily did the corps squadrons of the RFC. Along with expansion went specialization. The first RFC squadrons in France performed the whole range of tasks then demanded of them, but from an early stage distinct duties, and therefore specialized aircraft, equipment, and training, were imposed on each squadron. At the corps level the prime requirements to be met were co-operation with the artillery and the provision of tactical and photographic reconnaissance. At the 'army' level were squadrons whose duties were also connected with ground operations, but in a less direct way: their tasks were bombing and air fighting. The prime duty of the fighter squadron was to provide protection so that all other formations could carry out their work. As the RFC reached organizational maturity by 1916, corps and army wings were grouped together, so that each of the British armies on the Western Front was served by an RFC brigade.

Just as RFC operations within each army were directed by a brigadier attached to army headquarters, so at the BEF's headquarters there was a general officer commanding the whole of the RFC in the field. In addition to his command over the brigades, the GOC had directly under his hand a strategic reconnaissance element and a number of units which could be shifted rapidly to points along the front where their services were most needed. These forces, first known collectively as 9 Wing, ultimately grew to brigade strength; as IX Brigade the formation, chiefly composed of fighter squadrons, was an easily disposable force which gave its commander a high degree of operational flexibility.

The organization of the RFC reached its fullest development on the Western Front, and was preserved intact when in 1918 the RFC became part of the Royal Air Force. In other theatres of war, where the ground forces committed were smaller, RFC organization did not reach the same degree of complexity. Nevertheless, within their limitations the RFC formations in Italy, Macedonia, and the Middle East conformed to the principles established on the Western Front: specialization of function, direct linking at every level to the army staff, and absolute subordination of roles to the requirements of the army.

Although all functions of the RFC in the field were dictated by the army, the air service, for the most part, decided how these functions were to be carried out. Here there was some room for variations from squadron to squadron. Corps squadrons, for example, acquired an exact knowledge of every feature of their section of the front, and developed the closest possible working relationship with artillery units, intelligence staffs, and so on. For this reason it was unusual for corps squadrons to be moved about and even more unusual for them to be detached from ground formations with which they had worked for some time. Inevitably much of the practical training of new pilots and observers lay in the acquisition of this local lore, just as in the fighter squadrons new pilots sought to survive, and to become effective in combat, through the lessons passed on to them by veterans.

But the RFC's norm was uniformity, not diversity. Its patterns were set mainly from the top; it was the GOC and his staff who laid down procedures, tactics, and operational objectives. More than anyone else General Hugh Trenchard, who commanded the RFC in the field for most of the war, put his stamp on the service. In his soldierly view the RFC existed to assist the army. Coupled with this was his intense and unswerving belief in the value of the offensive. These principles, enunciated by a commander of powerful personality, dominated the RFC's approach to the air battle. Trenchard adhered to them consistently even in the dark periods of heavy casualties when the German air force possessed a clear margin of technological superiority.

It was a service given form and spirit by Trenchard that most Canadians joined. A few were present during the opening phases of the war on the Western Front, but they began to appear in appreciable numbers only towards the end of 1915. By the time of the Somme campaign in 1916 Canadians were to be found in nearly every operational squadron. The heaviest Canadian involvement, however, was in 1917–18, when the air war reached its peak and their numbers alone became an important element in the eventual success of the British air arm. This was the period of large-scale fighter engagements, a form of war in which many Canadians won distinction. But, as these chapters show, many others were engaged in the tasks which in Trenchard's view were essential to victory on the ground: artillery observation, reconnaissance, co-operation with the tanks, low-level strafing of German troops in close support of allied infantry. It was here, as well as in the more familiar and dramatic fighter role, that Canadians both on the Western Front and in other theatres made major contributions.

12

Experiments on the Western Front, 1914–15

In 1914 the brunt of the land campaign in the west was borne by the French and the Germans. The British had only a minor part to play and no Canadian forces at all were caught up in the vast military movements with which the European war began. All the great powers had their plans; all failed. The German plan, however, came closest to success, and determined the subsequent line of battle in the west. It had been conceived in the first place by *Graf* Alfred von Schlieffen, Chief of the General Staff between 1891 and 1905, and was his solution to the problem of a two-front war.

To win a quick victory over France, Schlieffen proposed to avoid a frontal assault along the short and heavily fortified Franco-German frontier. Instead he would launch a great flanking movement on the right. The German armies, swinging through Belgium, would sweep down the Channel coast west of Paris, and then turn eastward, to take the main French forces in the rear and isolate the French capital. While five of the seven German armies were to join in this enormous encircling movement, pivoting on Metz, the two on the left would deliberately fall back in the face of the anticipated French attacks in Alsace and Lorraine, thus drawing French forces further into the trap. If the British chose to fight beside the French, Schlieffen believed that they could be shut up, along with the remnants of the Belgian army, in Antwerp where the British soldiers would be 'securely billeted ... much better than on their island.' But *General* Helmuth von Moltke, Schlieffen's successor, seeing the problem in slightly different terms, chose to modify Schlieffen's vision. While keeping the right strong, he considerably strengthened his left as well when additional troops became available. Whether he was right to ignore Schlieffen's injunction to put every possible ounce of weight into the right wing is still open to discussion.[1]

With the outbreak of the war the German western deployment included twenty-eight corps (plus one infantry and one cavalry division) on the right wing and eight corps on the left wing. The French forces of approximately thirty-one equivalent corps were distributed in four armies between Epinal and Reims, with one army in reserve behind Verdun. The small British Expeditionary Force of two corps and a cavalry division was to take up position on the French left and act in concert with the French. The German air arm consisted of five airships, twenty-nine field aviation sections of six aircraft, and four fortress flights of four aircraft. The French had thirteen airships and twenty-one squadrons of six aircraft each, and the British were to send to France an air contingent of four squadrons, each having twelve aeroplanes. Air strengths in the west were approximately equal, but the Germans had a superiority of about 10 per cent in ground forces.[2]

As early as 1912 the British war plan had called for eight squadrons to accompany the British Expeditionary Force to France. Such an air arm would have required more than one hundred aeroplanes and pilots, with another hundred trained pilots and serviceable aeroplanes in the United Kingdom for replacement and training. In July 1914, however, the Royal Flying Corps was under strength and poorly equipped. Between 25 July and 9 August Brigadier-General David Henderson and Lieutenant-Colonel Sefton Brancker gathered up all the privately owned aeroplanes in the United Kingdom and most of the civilian pilots, all of whom were required to sign a declaration that they would not loop-the-loop or perform any aerobatics while serving with the RFC. Out of four weak squadrons and this makeshift increment, four full squadrons were mobilized, the Central Flying School was maintained on a low establishment, and a reserve squadron for training was created at Farnborough.[3]

General Henderson was appointed to command the RFC in France; Brancker was left in charge of the Military Aeronautics Directorate in the War Office; and Lieutenant-Colonel H.M. Trenchard, who had been second-in-command at the Central Flying School, was made commander of the Military Wing. Nos 2 and 4 Squadrons were equipped with BE2s, 3 Squadron had a mixture of Bleriots and Henri Farmans, and 5 Squadron had Farmans, Avro 504s, and BE8s. The mechanical transport was equally variegate. Most of the vehicles were requisitioned from civilian sources and included two Maple furniture vans, a truck that had originally carried liquid refuse, and a huge red van with the gold letters 'Lazenby's Sauce (The World's Appetiser)' on its side, which went to 5 Squadron.[4]

An advance party was sent to France on 11 August to co-ordinate arrangements with the French authorities at Amiens. By then 2, 3, and 4 Squadrons had been mobilized and the next day they assembled at Dover aerodrome. On 13 August these three squadrons flew across the Channel to Amiens, except for one Maurice Farman flight of 4 Squadron that was left behind at Dover to protect the coast of Kent. No 5 Squadron, whose mobilization had been delayed, assembled at Southampton on the 13th and flew across to Boulogne the following morning, joining the rest of the RFC at Amiens on 15 August.[5]

Meanwhile, the British Expeditionary Force was beginning to concentrate in the area south of Maubeuge, on the left flank of the French armies. Commanded by Field Marshal Sir John French, the BEF consisted of I Corps, under Lieutenant-General Sir Douglas Haig, and II Corps, under Lieutenant-General Sir Horace Smith-Dorrien. On 16 August the aircraft and motor vehicles of the Royal Flying Corps left Amiens for Maubeuge, where all four squadrons, with a total strength of 105 officers, 755 other ranks, and sixty-three aircraft, concentrated in the vicinity of the BEF's General Headquarters (GHQ). The aircraft park remained at Amiens. The first two RFC reconnaissance missions of the war were flown on 19 August but both pilots got lost and returned without having discovered either the enemy or the Belgian army, whose respective whereabouts they had been asked to

SEARCHING FOR THE BRITISH ARMY
AERIAL RECONNAISSANCE TASKS ORDERED BY GERMAN
FIRST ARMY HEADQUARTERS, 22 AUGUST, 1914

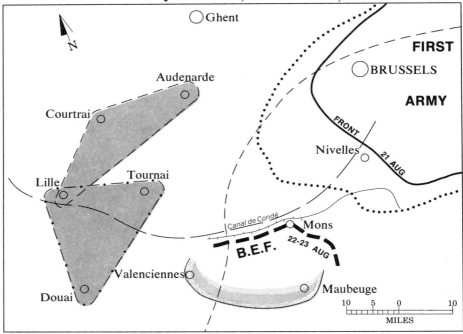

PLANNED RECONNAISSANCE BY NO. 7 FELDFLIEGER ABTEILUNG

PLANNED RECONNAISSANCE BY NO. 30 FELDFLIEGER ABTEILUNG

RECONNAISSANCE AHEAD OF ARMY ADVANCE BY
NO. 11 FELDFLIEGER ABTEILUNG

LIMIT OF RECONNAISSANCE BY NO. 12 FELDFLIEGER ABTEILUNG

report. On the 20th air reconnaissance discovered large columns of enemy troops near Tervueren and Wavre. On the 21st, although it was too misty to do any flying until the afternoon, further German concentrations were sighted near Nivelles and Charleroi.

That morning the British Expeditionary Force had begun its advance to contact, marching north towards Mons. During the afternoon aerial reconnaissance reported at least two German corps attacking the French on the Sambre and late reconnaissance that evening brought back word that the French were now five to ten miles south of the Sambre River. By late afternoon of the 22nd the BEF was in position about Mons, with II Corps holding the line of the Mons-Condé Canal and I Corps almost at right angles to it, facing eastward between Mons and the Sambre River. Only cavalry skirmishes had so far occurred on the British Front.[6]

Here the Royal Flying Corps made its first vital contribution to the allied cause. Twelve reconnaissance missions were flown on 22 August* and one of them brought back word that a German corps had been observed marching westward

---

* At least two British aircraft were fired on from the ground (one was brought down) during the course of this day and one observer was wounded, thus gaining the distinction of becoming the RFC's first battle casualty.

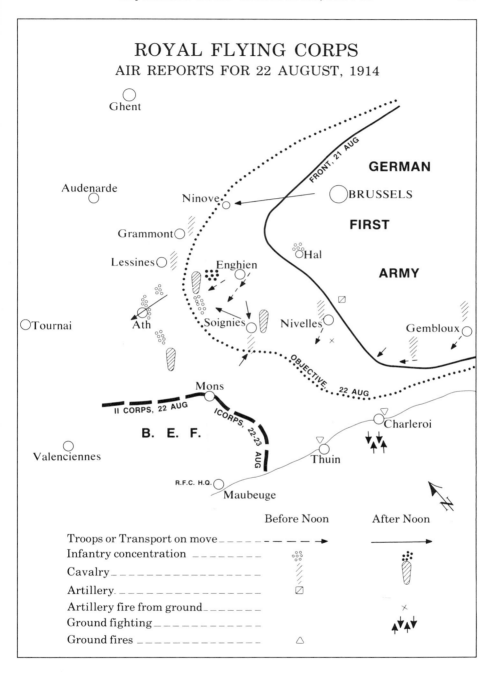

ROYAL FLYING CORPS
AIR REPORTS FOR 22 AUGUST, 1914

Ghent

Audenarde

Ninove

FRONT, 21 AUG

GERMAN

BRUSSELS

FIRST

Grammont

Lessines

Enghien

Hal

ARMY

Tournai

Ath   Soignies   Nivelles

Gembloux

OBJECTIVE, 22 AUG

Mons

II CORPS, 22 AUG   I CORPS, 22-23 AUG

Charleroi

B. E. F.

Valenciennes

Thuin

R.F.C. H.Q.
Maubeuge

N

	Before Noon	After Noon
Troops or Transport on move _ _ _ _ _ _ _ _ →		
Infantry concentration _ _ _ _ _ _ _ _		
Cavalry _ _ _ _ _ _ _ _ _ _ _ _ _ _ _ _		
Artillery _ _ _ _ _ _ _ _ _ _ _ _ _ _ _ _		
Artillery fire from ground _ _ _ _ _ _ _		
Ground fighting _ _ _ _ _ _ _ _ _ _ _ _		
Ground fires _ _ _ _ _ _ _ _ _ _ _ _ _		

along the Brussels-Ninove road, then turning southwards towards Grammont. General Henderson at once recognized the significance of this information and lost no time in bringing it to the attention of the Commander-in-Chief, for this was the first positive information that the German right was certain to outflank the British left. Until this time GHQ, in common with the French High Command, had believed that the Germans were advancing in column of route through Belgium, turning inwards as they reached the Sambre. According to French intelligence estimates, a movement further north could not have been in serious strength nor have presented any grave threat.[7]

Now, however, an entirely different and much more ominous picture began to form. The German armies marching through Belgium were swinging down far to the west of the French and, it seemed certain, west of the BEF as well. That evening Sir John French cancelled the offensive which had been scheduled for the 23rd and decided to remain where he was for the time being. The following morning six divisions of the German First Army, commanded by *General* Alexander von Kluck, made contact one after the other with Smith-Dorrien's II Corps along the Mons-Condé Canal. The German attacks were launched with dash and pressed with determination for about six hours but were everywhere beaten back with heavy losses by British rifle and field artillery fire. The French Fifth Army was also heavily engaged, and its commander, *Général* Lanrezac, decided to retreat just before dawn on the morning of the 24th.

In order to keep in touch with the French and because he was naturally apprehensive about his exposed left flank, Sir John French ordered a withdrawal in a southerly direction towards the line La Boisserette-Bavai-La Longueville. No sooner had the British begun to move than another air reconnaissance reported a German column five to ten miles long marching south towards Peruwelz – that is, well to the west of the British left. The retreat from Mons had begun only just in time.

The RFC moved from Maubeuge to Le Cateau on the 23rd and remained there during the first day of the retreat. Thereafter RFC Headquarters and the squadrons moved almost daily. During the next twelve days, as the whole allied line swung backwards, pivoting on Verdun to escape the groping claw of the German right, the RFC had both to keep pace with the retreat and act as the eyes of the army. Flying at 50 to 60 mph (provided there was no headwind), in machines cobbled together from wood, wire, fabric, and glue, its pilots scoured the Flanders countryside. A few hundred feet above the ground, monitoring the beat of their uncertain engines, calculating their endurance in terms of fuel margins, and always facing the threat of ground fire from either side, almost the only thing that airmen did not have to worry about was attack by enemy aircraft. Although pilots were armed with a pistol for self-defence in the event of a forced landing, the day of air-to-air combat had not yet dawned and the concept of aircraft recognition had not been thought of by other than a few specialists.

The pilots who took off each day could never be sure whether their 'aerodrome' would still be there when they returned from patrol. If they found that their base had moved, standing orders were that they should fly approximately twenty miles to the south and look for the remainder of the machines and their transport on the ground. Fortunately, the heterogenous transport of the RFC was relatively easy to spot from the air and 5 Squadron's gaudy scarlet van, which had been pressed into service to carry bombs and ammunition, proved a useful marker.[8]

Haig's I Corps broke clean at Mons but Smith-Dorrien's II Corps had to fight several sharp actions as Kluck continued to attack from the west and northwest. On the 24th and 25th II Corps suffered almost twice as many casualties as at Mons itself. The Forest of Mormal lay athwart the path of the BEF's retreat and the British Commander-in-Chief ordered I Corps to fall back to the east of this wooded area and II Corps to the west of it, leaving the British force dangerously separated. Smith-Dorrien decided that it would be necessary for him to make a stand at Le Cateau. With the 4th Division added to his corps that morning,* his strength increased substantially, but the decision to stand and fight was nevertheless a choice between desperate alternatives. The Battle of Le Cateau began early on the morning of 26 August.

During the day several air reconnaissances were made from GHQ but for some reason the results were not sent to Smith-Dorrien. It is an astonishing fact that all through the 26th there was no direct communication between I and II Corps, although both were in touch with GHQ. In the early morning GHQ had sent one aircraft to Smith-Dorrien who promptly used it to reconnoitre both his flanks and then returned it. By 1340 hrs Smith-Dorrien felt his troops under such pressure that he ordered a further withdrawal, although this meant breaking off an engagement in broad daylight while being attacked by superior forces. II Corps suffered severely. Of the 40,000 men engaged some 7800 became casualties and almost forty guns were lost.[9]

It appeared that the Schlieffen Plan was unfolding almost exactly as its originator had hoped. The slight checks that had been delivered to the advancing Germans by the British at Le Cateau and by the French on the 29th at Guise had done little to secure the situation. These were days of great danger for the allied cause, for if the retreat became disjointed, if a portion of the swinging line was pinned by battle, or if a serious gap developed between the various armies, utter and irretrievable disaster would almost certainly ensue. The RFC kept pace with the BEF on the outer arc of the swing, working every day to obtain the overall strategic picture and to bring back tactical reports of the immediate British front. The airmen also began to observe enemy artillery in action and report its position to the British gunners.

The vast bulk of the RFC's work revolved about the reconnaissance function but some bombing experiments were carried out in an effort to hamper the German advance. Each day 'the usual orders on the retreat were dawn reconnaissances [and] dropping hand grenades and petrol bombs on the enemy.'[10] There was no sighting or bomb-dropping gear; grenades were usually carried in the airman's pockets and the home-made bombs were either placed inside the observer's cockpit or slung on cords along the sides of the fuselage.

On 31 August the French government abandoned Paris and fled to Bordeaux,

---

* On 30 August III British Corps, consisting of the 4th Division and the 19th Brigade, was formed under Lieutenant-General W.P. Pulteney.

but the next day Joffre, the French Commander-in-Chief, allotted his Sixth Army to *Général* Galliéni, and it became part of a new 'Army of Paris' under the operational command of *Général* Maunoury. On 3 September the Germans took Reims and on this day RFC reported to Sir John French (who at once told Joffre) that Kluck had turned southeast and that some of his columns were now marching due east. Early on the morning of 4 September RFC reconnaissance reported sighting German bivouacs northeast of Paris. In fact, the German Supreme Command had now completely abandoned the Schlieffen Plan. Instead of marching all the way around Paris, Kluck, who believed that he was dealing with a defeated enemy, had shortened his wheel by turning east and southeast in the hope of driving in on the flank of the retreating Allies and cutting them off from the French capital. This manoeuvre meant that the German First Army was marching across the front of the Paris defences, presenting its flank to a counter-stroke. Joffre's opportunity had come. Now at last the long retreat came to an end as the French Commander-in-Chief ordered a major counter-attack for 6 September.

On the 5th the British retreat continued, but on the following morning the BEF was on a line Brie-Tournan-Rozoy and also preparing to counter-attack. The general plan for what was to be the Battle of the Marne envisaged the Army of Paris driving east and northeast to get around the flank of the Germans; the BEF was to attack in the centre across the Grand Morin and Petit Morin rivers; the Fifth French Army was to launch a converging assault almost due north; and the Ninth Army under *Général* Foch was to hold the exits of the marshes of St Gond.

Joffre had visited Sir John French at Melun on the 5th and outlined his plan for the coming counter-attack. The French Commander-in-Chief paid generous tribute to the work of the RFC, saying that 'The British Flying Corps had played a prominent, in fact a vital part, in watching and following this all-important movement on which so much depended. Thanks to [the British] aviators he had been kept accurately and constantly informed of Kluck's movements. To them he owed the certainty which had enabled him to make his plans in good time.'[11]

This tribute was well deserved. Indeed, it is difficult to escape the impression that of all the mighty armies that were deploying across the countryside of Europe that summer, from East Prussia to the Carpathians and from the Channel coast to the Swiss frontier, only the tiny British Expeditionary Force was adequately served by its aerial arm. In the east both the Austrians and the Russians blundered blindly into tremendous battles, and the Germans, who did not, owed little of their success to aerial reconnaissance.[12] Only the BEF knew from day to day with any reasonable degree of accuracy what enemy forces were facing it, what their strengths were, and in what direction they were advancing. This information came almost entirely from the RFC. Moreover, it was, as Joffre had admitted, on the strength of RFC reports, and not initially by any other means, that the French general staff at long last was able to form a correct impression of the strategic situation.

However, German aerial reconnaissance on 2 and 3 September had warned Kluck of his danger from the area of Paris, and accordingly on the 6th he turned west and made sharp contact with Maunoury's Sixth Army. As he did so he pulled away from von Bülow's Second Army. If this gap could be widened, and if the French Sixth Army could overlap it from the north, then Kluck's First Army might be destroyed. Unfortunately the allied counter-stroke lacked precision. Foch's Ninth Army was repulsed by von Bülow, *Général* D'Esperey's Fifth Army was diverted from its advance into the gap by this development, and Sir John French did not push the BEF forward with sufficient vigour. Throughout the day the RFC flew reconnaissance missions from Melun, providing a continuous, accurate, and detailed picture of German movements and dispositions on the BEF's front. Many of the flights were used to determine the location of the British columns and to investigate the flanks.[13]

Moltke, on the other hand, was ignorant of the location and exact position of his armies. On 8 September he sent one of his staff, *Oberstleutnant* Hentsch, to investigate the situation, giving him full power to co-ordinate a retreat, if such proved necessary. Hentsch spent the night at Second Army Headquarters, while the BEF, which crossed the Petit Morin on the 8th and reconnoitred to the Marne, seized a bridge over the latter. At 0900 hrs the following morning a German air report informed Bülow that five British columns were near or across the Marne, and his troops therefore began to retire north. Hentsch had earlier proceeded to First Army Headquarters where he had ordered Kluck to conform to Second Army's movements. It was a momentous and probably unavoidable decision: now the entire German right wing of five great armies reversed direction and began to pull back towards the Aisne.

Both sides thereupon began that progressive extension of the battle line known as the 'Race to the Sea.' The coast was eventually reached, but getting there was not, in fact, the object of the operation. Rather, the aim was the outflanking of the opposing line. Both the Allies and the Germans moved north-westward in bounds, feeling for an exposed flank, but they did so cautiously because the troops were tired and the weather was bad. This last factor seriously restricted aerial reconnaissance during the period. In any case, neither side was successful in developing a turning manœuvre. Thus the result of these operations was the mere prolongation of the battle lines past Ypres to the Channel coast. By mid-October there was a continuous front, partially entrenched, from the Swiss border to the English Channel and the first phase of the war was over.

The Battle of the Marne was a strategic but not a tactical victory for the Allies. Nevertheless, those who spoke of 'the miracle of the Marne' were certainly right, for it was here that Germany lost the war. Opposed on both the east and the west by forces that were potentially much stronger than she could herself muster, Germany's only hope of victory had lain in a quick decision. Failure to achieve this flowed from faults of organization, administration, command and control, the willfulness of some army commanders, and the weakness of Moltke. On the allied side we must count the fighting quality of the troops, the imperturbable resilience of Joffre, and the self-sacrificing pressure of the Russians in the east. There must be added to this list – and in a prominent place – the reconnaissances of the Royal Flying Corps that provided in time the essential information that enabled the German dispositions to be understood and without which the counter-stroke of the Marne could not have been conceived.

No Canadian airman had been involved in the flying operations that were such a vital part of the so-called mobile war. Fewer than two dozen flew in the fledgling RFC on the Western Front during the 1914–15 period, and only one actually saw war service in 1914. He was Captain Frederick A. Wanklyn of Montreal, a 1909 RMC graduate serving in the British Army. Wanklyn was a gunner by trade and in 1910 had visited Port Arthur, in Manchuria, a city whose siege and capture had been a key event in the Russo-Japanese war of 1904–5. There he had walked over 203 Metre Hill, which the Japanese had taken at a cost of 14,000 casualties while the Russian defenders lost 6000 (he was told 30,000 and 25,000 respectively), primarily in order to establish an observation point for their artillery. It had occurred to Wanklyn shortly afterwards that 'in days to come, a man lifting kite, a balloon, or possibly an aeroplane could do this job.'[14] Two years later he applied to learn to fly; he earned pilot's certificate No 284 and was seconded to the RFC in November 1912. When war broke out he was an assistant instructor at the Central Flying School and joined 4 Squadron at St Omer on 26 November with the appointment of flight commander. Wanklyn flew several reconnaissance missions over the lines of Ypres, when operating out of St Omer and Bailleul after the front had begun to congeal, and he was gazetted for the Military Cross in June 1915, probably for these early reconnaissance flights although it has not been possible to find a citation for the award.*

The RFC, in its embryonic form, had withstood the first shock of mobile battle well, perhaps as much by good luck as good judgment, by individual improvisation and initiative more than staff foresight and planning. Now, however, as entrenchments deepened across the front and field fortifications multiplied, the war underwent a fundamental change. Static, siege warfare was setting in and the deadlock would not be broken for nearly four years. Air doctrine had to adapt itself to the new conditions and to the new demands placed upon it by the army. By the end of 1915, when Canadians in significant numbers began to take their places in squadrons flying on the Western Front, the RFC had undergone important organizational changes, and the roles and tactics of the air arm had evolved remarkably from the simplicity of the early days of the war.

Changes in organization stemmed from the growth of the BEF and from the consequent necessity to decentralize flying operations. By mid-September 1914 there were three corps of two divisions each plus the Cavalry Division under Sir John French's command; then in December the BEF was reorganized into two armies totalling eleven infantry divisions and five cavalry divisions. On 30 October Henderson (already a major-general) had submitted a plan to reorganize his squadrons into wings and to attach one wing to each army, should the BEF be divided into separate armies. Sir John French approved these proposals on 1 November and that month 1 Wing, commanded by Lieutenant-Colonel Trenchard, was formed from 2 and 3 Squadrons, and 2 Wing, under Lieutenant-Colonel C.J. Burke, was made up of 5 and 6 Squadrons. The reorganization was approved by the Army Council in mid-December and when, on 25 December, the BEF corps were converted into armies, 1 Wing was assigned to First Army and 2 Wing to Second Army.

---

* Wanklyn was posted to the Aircraft Repair Park in January 1915, to 5 Squadron in May, and to the newly-arrived 15 Squadron at the end of the year. He was promoted and appointed OC the Experimental Station at Orfordness in July 1916. He commanded training establishments in Canada from mid-1917 until the end of the war when he returned to the Royal Artillery, retiring from the service in 1928.

No 3 Wing was formed in March 1915; it consisted of 1 and 4 Squadrons and was commanded by Lieutenant-Colonel H.R.M. Brooke-Popham. On 8 December 1914 the wireless unit had become 9 Squadron although it continued to supply wireless aeroplanes on detachment as required by the corps. These aircraft served as nuclei for flights which were transferred to 2 and 6 Squadrons in February 1915 when it was realized that each wing needed its own wireless flight. Later 16 Squadron was added to 1 Wing and by the end of March the strength of the RFC in France was seven squadrons and one flight (of 9 Squadron), totalling eighty-five aeroplanes in the line and eighteen in reserve. Six months later it had grown to twelve squadrons totalling 161 machines in the line and forty in reserve, plus four Kite Balloon Sections.[15]

The rapid expansion of the RFC was accompanied by startling technological advances. Once the opposing armies had adopted fixed positions and dug in, so that lines of trenches scarred the landscape from the Swiss border to the Channel shore, aerial observation entered a new phase. Strategically, railheads, aerodromes, camps, and dumps had to be located and mapped; tactically, the minute changes in enemy dispositions and installations that, taken together, might indicate a forthcoming attempt to break the deadlock, had to be identified and assessed; positions of enemy artillery batteries needed to be identified for counter-battery work and the whole enemy trench network uncovered.

Strategic air reconnaissance was equally important to both sides, for there was no way that light cavalry, the traditional reconnaissance arm, could operate once the lines of wire and trenches ran uninterruptedly from the Alps to the sea. But while tactical air reconnaissance was useful to the Germans, it was vital to the western Allies. Because they had driven deep into Belgium and northern France during the mobile phase of the war, when the lines began to solidify the Germans had a freedom of operations denied to their opponents. For political and psychological reasons the Allies could never afford to surrender another inch of ground. Their enemy, in contrast, need not hesitate to exchange territory for tactical advantage. Consequently, the Germans had withdrawn a little in places where it suited them and dug their front lines high on the forward slopes of the gentle, low ridges about Ypres, Armentières, Arras, and Albert, where they could see far over the British or French lines. Their own reserve dispositions, lines of communications, and gun positions were hidden behind the crests of the ridges, only visible to airborne observers. In fact, as early as mid-November Sir John French had asked the War Office to ensure that all artillery officers in England receive instruction in directing fire by aeroplane observation.[16]

The location of hostile batteries was particularly important, as the British guns were often outranged and outnumbered, and observation by wireless aircraft quickly proved to be faster, more accurate, and economical of ammunition. The first aeroplanes used for this purpose were BE2as from 4 Squadron, equipped with transmitters but lacking receivers which were still too weighty and cumbersome to be fitted into the machines. Indeed, even the carriage of a transmitter meant that the pilot had to fly alone and observe and transmit as well as fly the aircraft. The primitive sets then in use weighed about seventy-five pounds and had a range of no more than three or four miles. Very lights and battery-operated signalling lamps were also used until well into 1915, while messages from the ground were either received in Morse code flashed by signalling lamps or by codes employing white cloth panels (known as Popham panels) laid out on the ground.[17]

Initially the gunners were not always prepared to use this new form of direction. Trenchard, commanding 1 Wing, complained in December 1914 that the batteries 'crept up' to the targets instead of making the bold corrections requested by the pilots. Furthermore, only a few artillery commanders trusted the observers sufficiently to allow them to engage targets discovered on their own. Trenchard concluded that 'The co-operation with the artillery is fairly good, and will undoubtedly get rapidly better as soon as the gunners realize that our observers in the air are to be trusted in marking shots.'[18] Observers were soon beset by a variety of other problems, including the virtually smokeless burst of TNT which made registration most difficult in anything less than perfect weather, wireless 'jamming' by enemy transmitters, interference due to improper allocation of wireless frequencies, improvement of enemy camouflage techniques, and the use of faked gun flashes to frustrate counter-battery work.

Improvement was also needed in the system of describing the position of targets on a map if more accuracy were to be achieved. At first, the target was indicated by such imprecise map-based directions as 'under the Y in VIMY.' A Royal Engineer officer in 4 Squadron soon devised a gridded reference system using letters and numbers, so that a target could be pinpointed to within a few yards. Major W.G.H. Salmond, a staff officer at RFC Headquarters and a gunner by training, quickly saw the value of this and had a number of maps overprinted with the grid system. They were first used for artillery co-operation by I Corps during October 1914 and were soon taken into use on the whole of the Western Front. Shortly afterwards the infantry 'clock code' method was adopted for reporting the fall of shot, and air/artillery co-operation became an established and accepted part of military doctrine.[19]

Still another technique, of great significance for the field of military intelligence, was developed very closely with, if not exclusively for, artillery co-operation. Early air photographs were usually oblique exposures, taken from a fairly low angle. Vertical shots, made from greater heights, could include larger areas and gave less distortion. Pieced together in a mosaic, they provided an accurate and up-to-date map of the area photographed. The first successful British aerial camera, referred to as the 'A Camera,' was a conical box with a five-by-four-inch slide and envelope, and a lens set at a fixed distance from the plate. By the summer of 1915 the camera had been secured to the side of the aeroplane for greater vertical stability and a semi-automatic plate-changing device had been introduced. Until these developments took place the observer had to lean over the cockpit, holding on to the camera's brass handles or straps. He was required to go through ten distinct operations for each exposure (eleven for the first), while fighting against the wind and the cold and all the other aggravations of operational open-cockpit flying. Before the end of February a complete mosaic of the Neuve Chapelle area – where, in the battle that began on 10 March 1915, Sir John French made his first great attempt to break the trench deadlock – had been compiled by 2 and 3 Squadrons. No Canadians were involved, however, because Wanklyn, who was still with 4 Squadron where he served for a time as squadron commander, remained the only Canadian airman in France.[20]

Only three days before the Battle of Neuve Chapelle began a second Canadian arrived at the front, the first of what would soon become a trickle, then a stream, and finally a torrent. The newcomer was more representative of those who would follow, for he was the first of the war volunteers. Lieutenant Malcolm McBean Bell-Irving, the son of a Vancouver civil engineer and pioneer salmon canner, H.O. Bell-Irving,* had left home only three days after the BEF had clashed with Kluck's army at Mons and paid his own way to England, determined to get into the air war. The relentless determination to fly that he displayed in London, combined with an instinctive and almost irresistible charm, led to his acceptance for flying duties without the customary formalities and enabled him to jump the queue for instruction. On 9 October 1914, after only nine days' training, he was awarded the Royal Aero Club's pilot certificate No 928. Within twelve days he had been gazetted a second lieutenant in the RFC and posted to 1 Squadron.

Bell-Irving crossed over to France with his squadron on 7 March 1915 and was soon engaged in the whole gamut of duties then expected of every airman: reconnaissance, photo-reconnaissance, artillery co-operation, and that embryonic form of air combat then known as patrolling. Two more Canadians arrived at the front a month later, Lieutenant Edmund Tempest, of Perdue, Sask., and Lieutenant William Ewart Gladstone Murray of Vancouver. Murray, a Rhodes scholar at Oxford when the war began,† had joined a British infantry regiment, been wounded and awarded a Military Cross for his bravery before transferring to the RFC and qualifying as an observer. Both Murray and Tempest flew to France with 7 Squadron on 8 April 1915.

It is unlikely that any of the four Canadians at the front in mid-May, except possibly Bell-Irving (the sole Canadian in 1 Wing at the time), played any part in the battle of Festubert from 15–22 May. But Wanklyn, temporarily attached to 16 Squadron, and Lieutenant William Reid of Port Arthur, Ont., a pilot who arrived in 2 Squadron on 4 June, both flew artillery registration missions during the First Army action at Givenchy on 15 June. Lieutenant T.D. Leeson of Vancouver, an observer posted to 16 Squadron on 9 May, may also have flown there. Lieutenant K.E. Kennedy of Sherbrooke, Que., arrived at the front with Leeson but was sent to a detached flight of 4 Squadron, with 2 Wing. The experiences of these Canadians, and of the others who were to follow them over the next several months, were typical of those of the RFC as a whole. Most of them found themselves flying in two-seaters and working near the lines. Though by July distant reconnaissance missions were normally flown by aircraft armed with machine-guns, those flying closer to home still relied largely on rifles and revolvers to defend themselves.

A refinement of the reconnaissance role arose out of the nature of trench warfare itself. Once attacks were launched, many commanders soon found themselves isolated from their troops by a curtain of enemy artillery fire that cut most of their communications with the front. This communication problem was never fully solved during the war, but the aeroplane, flying over the advancing lines, offered one means of bridging the gap. Such missions were later called contact patrols.

---

* Bell-Irving's five brothers and two of his four sisters all served in the war, two of them, Alan Duncan and Richard, in the RFC.
† In 1936 he became the first general manager of the Canadian Broadcasting Corporation.

One of the first uses of aircraft in this role occurred at St Julien on 25 April 1915. Unfortunately, although the resulting report stated that there was a continuous and intact line, it was discovered later that some Germans had been mistaken for British troops and the situation was not nearly as favourable as the report had suggested.[21] Such misfortunes did nothing to develop staff confidence in airmen as reporters of the ground battle.

Another attempt to solve the problem of keeping track of the forward infantry was made two weeks later at Aubers Ridge. Three Maurice Farmans of 16 Squadron were ordered to patrol continuously over the troops and report the progress of their advance. The infantry upon reaching a certain line were to spread out strips of white sheets each measuring seven by two feet, and their positions were then to be relayed from the Farmans by wireless to any one of four ground wireless stations set aside for this purpose. Forty-two messages were sent down during the battle, but the information received was neither sufficiently detailed nor reliable enough to impress the staff. Observers had had difficulty distinguishing friend from foe, much more training was obviously required, and simpler signalling procedures had to be devised.[22] Nevertheless, contact patrols were to be persevered with until a system was developed for obtaining a reasonably accurate picture from the air of what was happening in the heat of battle on the ground.

Whatever the problems that beset attempts at contact patrols, the proven value of information collected by aerial reconnaissance and artillery co-operation aircraft led directly to efforts to intercept and bring them down, and then, consequently, to protect them with armed escorts. Yet despite experiments in the arming of aircraft carried out before the war, aerial fighting only slowly became one of the characteristic aspects of air warfare over the Western Front. Rifles and revolvers remained the general armament in most RFC aircraft well into the summer of 1915. There are very few first-hand accounts of early air combats, since it was not until 20 April 1915 that squadrons were ordered to forward combat reports to wing headquarters for record and intelligence purposes and, even then, it took some time to convince squadrons that such reports were of value. Malcolm Bell-Irving, showing the aggressive spirit that had served him so well in training, tried to shoot down a German machine on some unspecified date during these early days. His younger brother, Alan Duncan, many years later recalled the event in words which suggest that the story may have gained something in the telling: 'Finally he came up to a Hun from behind, a German single seater, which, as you know can be done without being seen or heard. He attempted to shoot the German but his revolver jammed so he threw it at him and hit him on the back of the head, which upset him but otherwise no known damage.'[23]

The earliest official reports involving Canadians show that inconclusive aerial fighting was an almost inevitable consequence of the simple weapon technology of the time. However, squadron commanders were beginning to complain about the lack of light machine-guns in the RFC. In a memorandum of 29 April Bell-Irving's Commanding Officer used the Canadian's experiences of the previous day to illustrate the need, commenting that 'It was impossible to arm Lt. Bell-Irving with a machine gun, since all three machine guns [held by the squadron] were out ...' His squadron was 'responsible for the protection of the batteries belonging to the

2nd Corps,' a difficult assignment under the best of circumstances since 'the Ypres Salient has now become so contracted that it has become possible for hostile aeroplanes over their own country on the north side to observe artillery fire directed on our batteries stationed on the East and South East side.' Bell-Irving, in a Martinsyde Scout and armed only with two automatic pistols, had been ordered to 'patrol' the salient on the afternoon of the 28th. He had an exciting time:

First Engagement. Three Machines. At about 4.30 p.m. two machines were observed approaching from Handzaeme and another from Thourout. Of these, two (apparently L.V.Gs.) were slightly slower, and the other (apparently an Aviatic [sic]) faster than Lt. Bell-Irving's machine, which was at 5,500 ft. at the time. Lt. Bell-Irving attacked these with an automatic revolver, and when all his ammunition was expended did his best to turn them by nose-diving. One of the machines did not observe Lt. Bell-Irving when he was nose-diving, and a collision was only narrowly avoided. After this incident it took the pilot 10 minutes to gain sufficient height before he could attack the other machines, and while doing so he pursued one of the slower machines which dived towards Nachtigaal [sic] Forest, where an anti-aircraft gun opened fire. Lt. Bell-Irving pursued the faster machine, but could not succeed in forcing him down. He gave up the chase after he had succeeded in driving him six miles beyond our lines. Lt. Bell-Irving reports that had he had a machine gun he ought to have accounted for one of the slower machines, and also for the faster machines, but adds that at 5,500 ft. the Martinsyde without machine gun has to be flown at 65 m.p.h., in order to fly level, and with a machine gun his speed would be reduced below this. Consequently, unless the hostile faster machine failed to observe his approach (as in fact he did for a considerable time) a machine gun on a Martinsyde would be of no great assistance when attacking an aeroplane of superior speed.

Second Engagement. Two Machines. About 20 minutes later an 'Aviatic' came from the same direction in which the fast machine had disappeared, and when dived upon descended about 500 ft. and opened fire with a machine gun. Shortly afterwards an L.V.G. was engaged in a similar manner and chased over Nachtigaal Forest.

Third Engagement. Three Machines. The Martinsyde was now at 3,800 ft. and it took 20 minutes to ascend to 5,800 ft., by which time three machines were observed over Merckem, two of which were probably L.V.Gs., and a third either an Aviatic or an Albatross, but more like the latter. All these machines were at much the same height, and owing to the time taken in regaining height after diving and forcing one of them to descend, Lt. Bell-Irving reports that it was quite impossible to interfere with the two remaining machines which could do exactly as they pleased until he was in a position to engage them. Actually he engaged them all.

Fourth Engagement. One Machine. Hardly had the last of these three machines gone down, when another machine came from the direction of Dixmude, but dived on being approached. Lt. Bell-Irving's general impression was that there were only 3 or 4 machines really, and that they were playing with the slow-climbing Martinsyde.[24]

On the same day Murray reported that a German machine, apparently co-operating with enemy anti-aircraft batteries near the Forêt d'Houthuilst, climbed into his vicinity. He engaged it with his service rifle and the eleven rounds he fired drove the German away. Another Bell-Irving report recorded a combat on 7 May over

Gheluvelt, against a 'big pusher, with long-span "Voisin" undercarriage, wide tail and tubular fuselages running to [the] tail carrying two rudders.'* The enemy opened up with very rapid but inaccurate machine-gun fire, to which Bell-Irving replied with forty-five rounds from his revolver, fired at a range of seventy to a hundred yards. The enemy aircraft was last seen gliding towards Menin at 4000 feet, his engine shut off, and 'if he was not hit he was badly frightened.'[25]

In early February 1915 a set of notes on aerial fighting had been distributed by Lieutenant-Colonel Brooke-Popham to each RFC flight commander in France. Their elementary nature was an accurate reflection of the current state of the art. 'The moral effect of a fast machine, however skillfully manoeuvred, will be very small if no weapon of offense is carried,' he ventured. Suggested forms of fighting hostile machines included dropping steel darts, bombs, and even 'charging the enemy' if need be. This last resort was hardly likely to prove acceptable to pilots who were not even equipped with parachutes. In any case, Brooke-Popham recognized the use of firearms as the most effective method of air-to-air fighting and he pointed out that their effect depended upon the volume and accuracy of the fire that could be brought to bear. An increase in the relative volume could be obtained by more efficient weapons, proper manoeuvre, and concentrating the fire of two or more aeroplanes. Accuracy could be improved by training gunners properly. He recommended an automatic pistol for single-seaters and a carbine or rifle in most two-seater machines, since the weight of a machine-gun was likely to reduce the rate of climb far too much. Nevertheless, a Lewis gun expert was assigned to tour 2 Wing squadrons during April to impart a more systematic approach to 'aiming-off,' based on established theories of fire deflection. Short burst and the idea of traversing fire were also emphasized.[26]

Less than two months later aerial fighting became part of the reorganized duties of RFC squadrons. On 29 March 1915 16 Squadron, recently formed from flights of 2, 6, and 5 Squadrons and part of 1 Wing, was ordered to 'patrol between 9 a.m. and 12 noon the line Aire-Lille-Béthune-Estaires to attack any hostile aircraft,'† in addition to reconnaissance work and photographic missions. The order was repeated with slight variations on 1, 7, and 12 April, and on 7 May all squadrons in the wing were assigned various patrol hours for the next day. This procedure was formalized on 24 June 1915, when the squadrons of 1 Wing were instructed to prepare fighting patrols to prevent observation by hostile aircraft beyond a specific line in the dawn and early evening hours.[27]

---

* Probably one of the rare, double-fuselage, twin-engined Aviatik biplanes. These were actually tractor aircraft but the protruding crew compartment behind and in the centre of the wings may well have deceived Bell-Irving into identifying it as a pusher.

† The rise of air fighting meant that the identification of friend and foe became a vital consideration. Tricolour roundels (or *cocardes*) painted on the wings and on the sides of the fuselage were the most common form of marking national identity. France, Italy, Belgium, Austria-Hungary, Russia, and later the United States all adopted the roundel, using their respective national colours, and striped the rudder in similar colours. Germany (and shortly after the outbreak of war, Austria-Hungary, whose aircraft were being confused with Italian machines) adopted the Maltese cross from the symbol of the old order of Teutonic knights. The British initially decided to use the Union Jack, but this proved to be a liability because it was indistinguishable from the German cross at medium distances in the air. The RFC therefore adopted the roundel, reversing the order of the colours used by the French.

Since the first duty of the RFC was still reconnaissance and, on occasion, bombing and artillery-spotting, its few single-seaters were essentially high-speed scouting machines, not fighters. As of 10 March 1915 the RFC's Order of Battle consisted of twelve different types, yet there was only one genuine fighter aircraft among them, a solitary, pusher type, two-seater Vickers FB5 in 16 Squadron. The observer sat in front, where he had an unobstructed field of vision and could swing a machine-gun through a 60-degree arc. The FB5's presence was entirely due to the foresight of Vickers Ltd, who had begun constructing a batch of fifty before the outbreak of war without a government contract. But not until the end of July 1915 would the first full squadron of FB5s reach the front.[28]

At the same time as the RFC was moving to improve its fighting efficiency, the German air arm was taking steps that would give it dominance for the balance of 1915. The first was the reorganization of the German air corps, which was removed from the sphere of the Inspectorate of Military Transport and henceforth commanded by a *Feldflugchef*, appointed to advise the High Command and initiate measures for making the air force more effective. This post was given to *Major* Hermann von der Leith-Thomsen. In quick order additional field units were organized, the replacement units in the homeland increased to meet the growing demands of the front, and a chaotic supply situation rectified.[29]

What was most urgently required, however, were specialized aircraft to replace the obsolescent all-purpose machines. Towards this end the hitherto haphazard production of aircraft was streamlined. The industry was organized in accordance with official directives, and operational experience made available to the design staffs of manufacturers. The first result of this was an improved reconnaissance machine, the 150–60-hp C-plane, a tractor-type aircraft of improved flight characteristics, increased speed, and greater climbing capacity. It was equipped with an air-cooled light machine-gun on a mount, operated by the observer from a rear cockpit. Machines of this type were usually fast and manoeuvrable enough to escape from any contemporary allied aeroplane when attacked, but what was even more badly needed was an aircraft that could deny the advantages of aerial reconnaissance to the Allies, for whom, as we have already noted, it was vital.

Suddenly good fortune, helped along by engineering skill, solved the problem. Lieutenant Roland Garros, a French airman, had the misfortune to be forced to land near Ingelmunster behind the German lines when his Morane-Saulnier was hit by a rifle bullet. Of more serious consequence than the capture of Garros – an innovator and experimenter as well as an excellent and aggressive airman – was the discovery of the apparently magical device which had permitted him to fire through his revolving airscrew. The Morane's armament was a single Hotchkiss machine-gun mounted centrally in front of the pilot, and the new device consisted of two hard steel deflectors mounted on the inside of the propeller at the level at which its rotation coincided with the bullets' trajectory. Some bullets ricochetted off the steel plates but those that missed the propeller travelled forward along the line of flight. Garros could aim his machine-gun simply by aiming his whole aeroplane at the target. The first true fighter aircraft had been created.

A hasty attempt to copy the Morane-Saulnier armoured airscrew was a dismal failure, but the Dutch designer, Anthony Fokker, was loaned the French propeller and a Parabellum machine-gun in the hope that he might discover something equally workable and less hazardous. The solution was a device which allowed shots to be fired through the propeller arc by automatically interrupting the flow of bullets whenever the blade passed before the gun muzzle. Fokker has been generally credited with inventing this synchronizing mechanism. In fact, the invention was not his, although it was on a Fokker M5K flown by him that the first demonstration of firing a synchronized gun was successfully carried out in the air. After making some refinements on both, Fokker married his synchronized machine-gun to his new single-seater monoplane, the Fokker E (for *Eindekker*) I, and demonstrated it to German pilots in the Verdun and Arras areas. When he left Douai on 12 July 1915 eleven pilots were already flying the E-I in that vicinity.[30]

Among the German pilots of *Fliegerabteilung 62* at Douai were Oswald Boelcke and Max Immelmann. Together these two German 'aces'* established new tactical standards for air fighting and it was to be some time before allied airmen could catch up with the concepts they introduced. The use of height and the sun, combined with aerobatic excellence and good marksmanship, characterized their tactics, summed up by RFC pilots in the pithy maxim, 'Beware of the Hun in the sun.' Immelmann's use of the roll off the half loop, a manoeuvre that enabled him to change quickly from attacked to attacker or to resume an interrupted attack with a sudden height advantage, was not invented by him, but the 'Immelmann turn' became part of the standard repertoire of German pilots, and of those allied airmen lucky enough both to see and survive it. As for Boelcke, he was not only an outstanding pilot with a flair for leadership, but a thoughtful student and innovator of group tactics in which one machine provided the offensive striking force while one or two more were solely responsible for guarding his tail.[31]

In July 1915 the Canadians began to experience the growing strength and efficiency of the German air force. On 26 July Bell-Irving was unsuccessfully attacked by an LVG armed with a machine-gun, near Roulers. Three days later Kennedy, observing in a Vickers FB5 (fondly termed the 'Gun Bus' by its aircrews), opened fire on a Fokker near Cambrai; the German aircraft, faster and more manoeuvrable, made a steep spiral descent which brought it underneath the Vickers, from where it fired and hit the lower plane, cutting two bracing wires and breaking a rib. Kennedy and his pilot, well over the German lines, flew home very cautiously.[32]

Air fighting imposed new psychological strains on airmen and turnover was rapid. New arrivals had to learn quickly the lessons acquired in combat by those who had gone before, or suffer the consequences. In July and August Murray, Wanklyn, and Kennedy were replaced by Lieutenant J.H. Scandrett of London, Ont., F.F. Minchin, an ex-PPCLI 'original' of British descent, who went to 1 Squadron, and Captain R.W. Bruce of Winnipeg and Lieutenants S.W. Caws of Edmonton, Alta, and J.L. Williams of Toronto, all of whom went to 10 Squadron. Caws and Williams were pilots, the others observers. Scandrett's tour with 5 Squadron was abruptly halted on 1 August when he was shot down and shortly after posted to

---

* The use of the term 'ace' originated with the French, who bestowed the title upon any pilot who had scored five or more confirmed victories. The idea was soon adopted by other countries, although at first a German pilot had to be credited with ten victories to achieve the corresponding title of *Aberkanone*. The British never formally accepted the system.

England. No 2 Squadron's William Reid of Port Arthur, Ont., was wounded and taken prisoner the same day.[33]

A number of significant changes in RFC organization and personnel occurred during the summer, as preparations went ahead for the forthcoming Battle of Loos (25 September–10 October 1915), Sir John French's third and last attempt to break the trench deadlock with a frontal assault.* Trenchard was appointed General Officer Commanding the RFC in the field, *vice* Sir David Henderson who returned to the War Office to administer the growing Military Aeronautics Directorate. The RFC's Order of Battle, which had consisted of three wings since 1 March 1915, had increased by three more squadrons – Nos 10, 11, and 12 – and all three wings got new commanders. Lieutenant-Colonel E.B. Ashmore, an expert on artillery co-operation, was given command of 1 Wing; Major John Salmond, who had proven himself a most successful squadron commander, was promoted to command No 2; and 3 Wing was given to Sefton Brancker, who had helped Henderson recruit those first wartime flyers and had since been serving in the position that Henderson now took up.[34]

Trenchard, whose character and outlook have already been mentioned in earlier sections of this book, had no doubt at this stage in his career that the prime duty of the air arm was to support the army. He also saw clearly that it would not be able to do so effectively unless it could establish and secure aerial superiority. His strategy may have been questionable – indeed, it will subsequently be questioned in the course of this narrative – but his aim was certainly correct. How effective his attempts to achieve that aim could be in 1915 is another matter.

A production crisis in Britain had left the BEF seriously short of ammunition for its heavy guns. In planning for the forthcoming attack at Loos, therefore, it was vital that every available shell be used to best advantage. The artillery found it necessary to choose carefully the targets most likely to threaten the success of the offensive, judgments which required extensive and repetitive aerial photography, and to rely heavily on visual inspection and direction during and after their bombardments in order to programme their fire for maximum benefit. The brunt of the work at Loos fell on the four squadrons of 1 Wing (supporting First Army). The front was divided into four zones, one for each army corps and its supporting squadron; of the twelve flights, ten were earmarked for artillery co-operation, with an emphasis on counter-battery work.

By the time that the battle began the new Sterling wireless set, a transmitter with a range of eight to ten miles, had been issued to most of the squadrons and fitted in the artillery co-operation aeroplanes. Its antenna consisted of a stranded copper wire 120 feet long, weighted by a three-pound lead plumb dangling through an insulated aperture. Wound on a drum in the observer's cockpit, it was allowed to run out by releasing a hand brake and had to be rewound by hand following a shoot.

Prearranged signals were devised for informing contact patrols of the infantry's situation. In addition to displaying white strips of cloth to indicate the position of

---

* Blamed for the failure at Loos, French was relieved of his command and succeeded by Sir Douglas Haig on 17 December 1915.

the line, certain designated soldiers were to light yellow smoke candles and all were to wave their helmets on the points of their bayonets. A system of cloth bars and arrows was also devised for use by battalion HQs to indicate the direction and distance of obstacles holding up their advance. Arrows would point to the obstacle and bars placed across the stem would indicate the distance, each bar denoting two hundred yards. Contact patrol aircraft were sent up by 3 Squadron, but no one had been appointed to replace casualties among the individuals responsible for displaying signal sheets or lighting flares, and the system broke down.[35]

Before the Battle of Loos began, Lieutenants Alan Duncan Bell-Irving (the younger brother of Malcolm McBean) and John Beverley Robinson, a Torontonian, the former an observer and the latter a pilot, had arrived in France. Three more Canadians arrived by the end of the month; Lieutenants R.C. Morgan of Farrans Point, Ont., a 1909 RMC graduate, went to 6 Squadron and J.S.B. Macpherson of Ottawa, a 1914 RMC graduate (who would return to Britain in December to qualify as a pilot) to 1 Squadron. Second Lieutenant K.A. Creery of Vancouver was posted to fill an observer's slot in 1 Squadron. Morgan's arrival in 6 Squadron on 21 September coincided with Caws' death.

Stanley Winther Caws was the first Canadian airman to be killed in action.* Caws was Canadian by choice, having been born on the Isle of Wight and, at thirty-six, was unusually old to be flying in the RFC. He had served in the Boer War as a trooper in Paget's Horse, and afterwards emigrated to Canada, where he had been 'on an important and remunerative expedition in North-West Canada when the war began.' Returning to Edmonton, he enlisted in the 19th Alberta Dragoons and went overseas with the First Contingent. In February 1915 he transferred to the RFC. Another RFC candidate remembered him thus:

Barely had we been shown to our rooms, when a strikingly good-looking man made his appearance, grinning, and asked us if we were the two 'new guys.' In an obviously Canadian accent he ... welcomed us to Brooklands ... when we first met him [he] was the doyen of the learners at Brooklands. A grand character, the life and soul of our little party ... he was always with us to give advice where it was needed ...

Caws always sat at the head of the table in our little mess-room in the Blue Anchor, and I can hear him now, saying grace when the maid had served dinner, on the night of our arrival. It was a solemn little utterance that went like this: 'For what we are about to receive, may the Lord make us truly thankful, and see to it that we have the strength to keep the god-damned stuff down!'

He had the disconcerting habit, while we were waiting for the next course to be brought in, of suddenly snatching up any table-knives within reach, and slamming them, one after the other, across the room, into the woodwork of the door.[36]

---

* Second Lieutenant John Parker was the first airman from Canada to be killed. He was observing from a Voisin machine on 21 July 1915 when it was forced down over the German lines. His pilot was unwounded but Parker died in hospital as a result of four wounds he had received. Parker was a British student (his father was a warrant officer in the British Army) who had completed a first-year programme at the University of Alberta in the spring of 1914. He returned to England to enlist and there is no evidence that he ever thought of himself as Canadian or intended to stay when he had completed his education.

Manners were more stereotyped in 1915 and a man like Stan Caws must have impressed the sheltered eighteen- or twenty-year-olds with whom he was thrown into such close contact. Perhaps his peculiar social graces help to explain how Canadians in the RFC got their reputation for unorthodoxy and mild rowdyism in a service where unorthodoxy and mild rowdyism were a way of life.

Caws graduated as a pilot in May 1915 and was posted to 10 Squadron, where he flew BE2cs. With a British observer he was flying a reconnaissance mission on 21 September when their machine was attacked by several German fighters and, after 'a great fight, lasting fifteen minutes, in which they expended all their ammunition ... Caws was shot dead when they were 11,000 feet up, the bullet afterwards hitting [the observer] Mr. Wilson in the leg.' The aircraft must have glided down, or Wilson managed to control it, for he came down in enemy territory and survived to write an account of the combat from a German prison camp.[37]

The day before Caws' death Alan Duncan Bell-Irving, who had been posted to 7 Squadron, was observing from a BE2c when he opened fire with rifle and Lewis gun on a nearby Albatros two-seater. The enemy observer, 'with ample room to use his machine gun, which was mounted on a swivel and turn table,' fired back from two hundred yards and one of his shots hit the BE's engine, putting it out of action and compelling Bell-Irving's pilot to start a glide towards his own lines. The Canadian removed his Lewis gun from its simple peg mount in an attempt to get the enemy in his sights, but the German machine 'crossed and recrossed our front so that we were unable to return his fire except for a few seconds on his turns.' His pilot managed to land the disabled machine near Poperinghe, luckily behind the allied lines. Two days later Bell-Irving was observing for another pilot in a RE5 near Menin when they were overtaken by an Albatros similarly armed. A round from the enemy's machine-gun hit Bell-Irving's own gun, causing it to jam, but they completed their reconnaissance even though two other German aeroplanes rose to meet them. On 26 September Bell-Irving was attacked once more, this time by a Fokker monoplane armed with a machine-gun and allegedly (there was no two-seater monoplane in service at this time) carrying an observer, but the encounter was again inconclusive. The next day Leeson's pilot was taken in by a trick used fairly often. While on a reconnaissance over Courrière the BE2c encountered an Albatros. Leeson fired a whole drum of ammunition at it without success, when the Albatros went down 'almost vertically' to a height of 1800 feet, followed by the BE2c. The enemy then fired a white flare and heavy rifle and machine-gun fire from the ground focussed on the British machine, forcing it to give up the chase.[38]

Whatever the technical difficulties of air fighting or battle reconnaissance, they paled into insignificance beside those that beset the development of air bombing. The first organized attempt had come at Neuve Chapelle when 2 and 3 Wings had been instructed to carry out tactical bombing raids in support of the attack, using 20- and 100-lb bombs against targets that included Courtrai, Menin, Lille, Douai, and Don railway stations. Raids took place on 10, 11, 12, and 13 March; a few direct hits were scored on junctions, on a stationary troop train, and a suspected divisional headquarters. But as Trenchard's biographer noted, 'piecemeal blows falling almost at random could not influence the main land battle, since even their nuisance value was small.' The first bombing raid ever carried out in darkness by the RFC was a total failure, as all four machines assigned to attack the rail junction at Lille crashed before reaching the target.[39] Again, on 9 May the battle of Aubers Ridge had been opened by an aerial bombardment preceding the usual artillery bombardment. The bombing, planned to interrupt rail communications and harass back areas and army headquarters, was another failure. None of the bombs were observed to hit their targets.

The French were doing no better and, to try to solve this intransigent technological problem, a conference was called on 7 August between representatives of the French air service, the RFC, and the Royal Naval Air Service to review these picayune results. It was reported that in a total of 483 bombing operations carried out by the three services between 1 April and 18 June, 4062 bombs had been dropped with little material result. Attempts to hinder enemy movements by bombing railway junctions and stations had been made on 141 occasions during which 991 bombs were dropped. Of these attempts only three had been successful. Nevertheless, the potential was there if only the technological problems could be mastered and the RFC persevered in its efforts to turn bombing into a practical proposition.[40]

Only two makeshift bomb-sights had been in general use until mid-1915, the 'nail-sight' and the 'lever-sight.' The former was simply a piece of board with a spirit level attached and two nails set at an angle, only useful for dropping bombs from a fixed height and speed. The lever-sight incorporated changes which allowed for several heights and speeds according to a pre-established angle sighting table. In mid-1915 the CFS (Central Flying School) bomb-sight came into use; it had a vertically moveable foresight which, when used in conjunction with a stop-watch and timing scale, permitted bombing at varying heights and ground speeds, although it was still necessary to bomb directly up or down wind. A modification was subsequently introduced which did away with the watch and the scale and consisted of a horizontally sliding backsight which was appropriately nicknamed 'the trombone.' Like playing a musical instrument, bomb aiming in 1915 was much more an art than a science.*[41]

The CFS sight brought better results. Over five-and-a-half tons of bombs were dropped in support of the Loos attack at the cost of two aircraft lost and two wounded pilots. The railway line was damaged in fifteen places, three trains were partly wrecked, two ammunition trains were blown up, a signal cabin was destroyed, and locomotive sheds were set on fire, despite extremely adverse weather conditions which forced the bombing machines to fly under heavy fire at very low altitudes. On 4 October, even before the end of the battle, Sir John French cited the RFC's contribution in a special order of the day. Yet the delays to German troop

---

* The CFS sight held the field until replaced during 1917 by the 'drift' sights, devised by H.E. Wimperis and produced in several versions, which could be used for both low and high altitudes and allowed flying in from any direction regardless of wind; drift sights were to remain in standard use until the end of the war. Other types of bomb-sights used were the 'low height bomb-sight,' developed by the RNAS, the 'equal distance sight,' invented by W.O. Scarff in 1916, the 'negative lens sight,' and later on, the 'RAF periscope bombsight,' used on heavy bombers. None of them were much good.

transports were only temporary and, according to the German official historians, all reinforcements to the front arrived in good time.[42]

In the realm of air fighting, however, the technological keys to effective combat were already firmly in German hands. The Fokker E-III was appearing at the front: stronger and faster than the original *Eindekker*, by December there would be forty of them. Allied aircraft could be attacked from above or behind without awkward jockeying to bring fire to bear and, even in a dogfight, the difficulties of double deflection shooting were eliminated through the use of the Fokkers' fixed, synchronized machine-gun. The consequences for both German and allied morale were considerable as the idea of the 'Fokker scourge' spread. No consistent statistics of sorties flown were kept at this time. Indeed, no one had yet defined exactly what constituted a sortie. Although the ratio of combat losses to sorties flown was certainly increasing, however, it was probably not excessive in view of the numerical expansion of the RFC that was taking place at the same time. RFC losses jumped towards the year's end, owing in large part to the steadily rising curve of British aerial activity. The number of aircraft on squadron strength had doubled – from eighty-five to 161 – between 10 March and 25 September and the rate of increase was speeding up all the time. The fortnightly casualty lists sent home by RFC Headquarters in France make possible a compilation of those missing or killed in action (no distinction was made between airmen wounded in action and those hospitalized for other causes) and the total for June 1915 was six. In July, when the first *Eindekker* with a synchronized gun appeared, the total was fifteen, in August, ten, September, fourteen, and in October, twelve. In November and December, because poor weather was probably reducing the number of sorties flown, the numerical expansion of the RFC was of less significance, although the casualty figures were sixteen and seventeen, respectively. In January 1916 the total would rise to thirty. The scourge was then reaching its heights. The psychological impact was, in fact, more significant than the actual losses. In the later months of 1915 RFC Headquarters became increasingly concerned at the frequency with which its pilots broke off combat. On 20 October Trenchard minuted four such combat reports, and although he suggested that the pilots concerned 'are not good at describing their combats,' his questions make it plain that he was disturbed about what was happening.[43]

In these anxious days Canadians acquitted themselves as well as any airmen in the RFC. On 10 October Leeson had fallen victim to Immelmann while on a photographic reconnaissance mission near Lille; his pilot, with six bullet holes in him, died soon after their forced landing and Leeson, with a slight leg wound, was taken prisoner. Somewhat luckier, Williams, with 10 Squadron, photographing German defences in a BE2c near Lille on the same day, managed to escape with a damaged propeller and a few hits on part of the fuselage and in the petrol tank after being surprised by an Albatros. On 26 October he was attacked by a Fokker. His observer was hit in the left hand and Williams, attempting to manœuvre out of a precarious position, was wounded in the arm and shoulder and lost consciousness. His BE2c began to spin down out of control, but the observer climbed over between the two back struts and attempted to regain control of the machine. He was able to crash-land behind the French reserve trenches, where the machine turned over and Williams was thrown out. Both men survived the crash but Williams was subsequently evacuated to England.[44]

Winnipegger R.W. Bruce was observing in a BE2c of 10 Squadron near Valenciennes on 14 October when he and his British pilot were attacked by an Aviatik. Bruce's Lewis gun jammed and they were pursued as far as Douai by the Germans. On 28 November the same pair were attacked by another Aviatik near La Bassée while on reconnaissance duty. This was a very brief encounter but the enemy machine was driven off. Bruce and his pilot also showed the required offensive spirit two weeks later, while flying as escort to a reconnaissance machine, another BE2c of 10 Squadron. They drove off both an Albatros and a large two-engined enemy machine allegedly equipped with fore-and-aft-firing machine-guns. During the fight one of the enemy machines 'threw out a white light' and the BE returned to its escort duty under heavy anti-aircraft fire.[45]

Four more Canadians arrived on the Western Front by Christmas 1915, Lieutenants E.S. Wilkinson from Montreal and J.R. Dennistoun of Winnipeg, as observers to 1 and 7 Squadrons, respectively, and Lieutenants F.D. Pemberton of Victoria and C.V.G. Field as pilots, Pemberton to 5 and Field to 2 Squadron. All four of them were destined to be killed in action. Field and Wilkinson went down together on 12 January 1916, and Dennistoun, mentioned in despatches for his work in April, was killed while observing for Macpherson on 4 May 1916. Pemberton lasted until 21 August 1917, but life was getting nastier, more brutal, and shorter for airmen on the Western Front.

A.D. Bell-Irving was wounded on 14 December and evacuated to England. His irrepressible elder brother, Malcolm McBean (who had been promoted captain on 9 July), was also wounded on 19 December when, in a single-seater Morane Scout, he took off after an unidentified enemy aircraft which quickly disappeared. Over Perenchies he found and attacked another German machine which made off toward Lille without fighting. He then attacked a third opponent over Quesnoy and sent it down in a steep dive emitting large puffs of smoke, before the pilot seemed to regain control and disappeared in a heavy mist. The Canadian climbed to 12,000 feet, spotted two more enemy aircraft, and dove on the larger. As he followed it down three more enemy machines joined the fight and Bell-Irving wisely withdrew. Then he sighted yet another enemy aircraft over Polygon Wood, but while he was manœuvring for position he was hit in the hand by a splinter from a British anti-aircraft shell, compelling him to abandon the chase and return to his aerodrome. For his conspicuous and consistent gallantry and skill during the past nine months, but notably for his efforts on this last occasion, he was awarded the Distinguished Service Order, the first Canadian airman to be so decorated.

By Christmas 1915 the nature of aerial warfare on the Western Front had changed as dramatically as the ground fighting. Initially the excitement (and danger) had been almost exclusively in the act of flying itself. In 1914 enemy aircraft had posed no threat to the pioneers who, in their reporting of the movements of great armies, had been able to accomplish, virtually unimpeded, a revolution in the art of warfare. Now the air itself had become a battlefield: aircraft had become far handier to fly and far more reliable, but as their machines became safer the lives of the men who flew in them became daily more hazardous.

The BEF had increased in size to three armies of ten corps, totalling nearly sixty divisions, and the RFC had grown proportionately. Other air forces had also expanded. At the end of the year the Germans could muster about eight hundred aeroplanes for their eastern and western fronts, and France deployed that number on the western front alone. The Flanders sector, where the BEF held most of the allied line, was the vital one in the west and the Germans concentrated a high proportion of their best machines and airmen there. Even so, and despite the enemy's technological edge, the RFC had been able to increase its monthly flying time from some 2100 hours in July 1915 to over 4700 hours in September, during the battle of Loos. At year's end, ten of the twenty-one Canadian pilots and observers who had joined operational squadrons were still at the front, one had been killed, and three others were prisoners. Of the six returned to England, two would later fly in the Middle East and three would come back to fly again over France, next time in the company of many more of their countrymen.

The Birth of Airpower, 1916

The fighting on the Western Front in 1916 occupies a special place in the history of the First World War. Its two biggest battles, Verdun and the Somme, were not different in kind from what had gone before, but they were so huge in scale and so grievous in losses that they opened a new and critical phase of the war.

At the outset of the season for active operations each of the high commands had its particular vision of what was to be gained through a massive offensive. In July 1915, at Chantilly, the Allies had agreed on a joint Anglo-French offensive in 1916. To *Général* Joffre, the aim, aside from involving the British more fully, was to wear out the enemy. To General Sir Henry Rawlinson, commander of the Fourth British Army, the objective was simply to push the enemy back, step by step, after thorough bombardment. But to General Sir Douglas Haig, who had taken command of the British forces on 19 December 1915, the aim was nothing less than a massive rupturing of the enemy's front. By passing cavalry through the break, he hoped to ensure that the victory so won was chiefly accomplished by 'the Forces of the British Empire.' Though Haig's ideas were greeted with derision by his critics in the War Cabinet, he remained firm in his resolve, despite his recognition that the bulk of the troops he proposed to employ were new to combat. 'I have not got an Army in France really,' he confided to his diary in March, 'but a collection of divisions untrained for the Field. The actual fighting army will be evolved from them.' Since fire and movement tactics were thought too advanced for inexperienced troops, the British soldiers, following thorough artillery preparation, would simply walk to their objectives, inserting themselves through breaches in the German wire blasted by the guns. It was a recipe for disaster.[1]

The attack on the Somme was planned for midsummer. Long before then, however, the German High Command had unexpectedly taken the initiative. On 21 February it opened an offensive against the fortress of Verdun and the terrible battle of attrition that ensued altered the complexion of the war. The Germans had determined to break the French will to fight. In the words of *General* Erich von Falkenhayn, First Quartermaster-General of the High Command and therefore in effect the Commander of the German forces in the field, 'If we succeed in opening the eyes of her people to the fact that in a military sense they have nothing more to hope for, that breaking point would be reached and England's best sword knocked out of her hand.'[2] The immediate effect of Verdun was an extension of the BEF's share of the front, as French forces were drawn into the cauldron. Moreover, as the character of the German offensive became clear, and losses reached staggering levels, Joffre urgently demanded as early a start as possible to the allied offensive. In May he and Haig agreed to mount an assault on 1 July 'athwart the Somme.'

Long before the starting date of the offensive had been fixed the British had been preparing for it by building up, behind their lines, the communications and logistical support the 'big push' demanded. Masses of materiel were accumulated close to the trenches, including nearly three million rounds of artillery ammunition. War on this scale was a major industrial undertaking.* Military aviation, of necessity, made a proportionate leap as well. The RFC had to expand to meet the demands of the new mass armies, and during the first six months of 1916 Trenchard, with Haig's strong support, strove to create an air weapon that could meet the challenge of the offensive. Beginning in January the RFC had been reorganized into brigades, one to each army, a process completed on 1 April when IV Brigade was formed to support the Fourth Army. Each brigade consisted of a headquarters, an aircraft park, a balloon wing, an army wing of two to four squadrons, and a corps wing of three to five squadrons (one squadron for each corps). At RFC Headquarters there was an additional wing to provide reconnaissance for GHQ, and, as time went on, to carry out additional fighting and bombing duties.[3]

Artillery observation was now the chief function of the RFC, with subsidiary efforts concentrated on close reconnaissance and photography. By early March the corps squadrons carrying out these tasks could no longer be spared for other roles; henceforth they remained specialized units tied to a particular sector of front. No 10 Squadron of I Brigade, for instance, flew in support of XI Corps, First Army. Between March and July the majority of its sorties were concerned with artillery co-operation, more than half of them for target registration. The workhorse of the corps squadrons was the BE2, though two of the fourteen squadrons still used the Morane Parasol. In the army squadrons the FE2b was replacing the Vickers FB5; it was used for fighting, reconnaissance, and bombing, and remained operational throughout the course of the war. The army squadrons also flew Martinsyde Scouts and DH2s.[4] The establishment for all these squadrons was eighteen aircraft, but in early 1916 none had more than twelve. An increase to establishment took place slowly over the next months, with priority being given to those squadrons allocated to the coming offensive.

The RFC learned much from the rapid development of French aviation during the Verdun campaign. At the opening of the battle Germany had a decided advantage in the air. Although France had an equivalent number of aircraft at the front, she had fewer first-class aircraft (Nieuports and a few Spad-Bechereaus) than did Germany, whose best were the E-type Fokker and C-type Albatros. At Verdun itself the French had only one fighter and three reconnaissance squadrons when the Germans attacked.[5]

Prior to the offensive German air reconnaissance had provided the High Command with an accurate and detailed picture of the unchanging French dispositions around Verdun. During the first few days German aviation carried out

---

* At Loos in 1915 the ammunition supply had been 35,000 rounds for the heavy artillery, and about 500,000 for the field batteries. *Military Operations: France and Belgium, 1915*, II, 163n, 174–7

highly successful artillery co-operation and bombing operations. French aerial reconnaissance had been, by comparison, dangerously lax and German preparations had gone undetected until shortly before the attack was launched. The situation was rectified by deliberately weakening other sectors of the front. The French concentrated six fighter squadrons, mostly Nieuports, eight reconnaissance squadrons, and two heavy artillery aviation sections at Verdun. On 29 February orders were issued that gave official recognition to the use of formation tactics as opposed to the often individualistic methods that had marked earlier fighter operations. Offensive air patrols were to be carried out *in formation* by groups of at least three or four aircraft in order to seek out and destroy the enemy.[6]

These tactics were the key to French aerial success at Verdun, but there were other factors. The German response to French formation patrols was to bring up their Fokkers closer to the front and to group them into three fighter commands. Initially they achieved some success, but they ultimately proved incapable of dealing with the larger French formations. The results were extremely important for the ground battle; the supremacy of the French fighters permitted their artillery aircraft to function effectively, while their German counterparts were harried from the air. The German solution was to carry out 'barrage' patrols; that is, their aircraft constantly flew up and down their own lines, hoping to deny that air space to the French and thus free their artillery and infantry from the consequences of French aerial observation. In fact, the tactic merely dissipated German strength without preventing French penetration in force.[7]

Trenchard learned of these developments partly as a result of the friendship he had formed in 1915 with *Commandant* du Peuty, who had then been the Air Commander in the French Tenth Army. When du Peuty moved to the Verdun sector he and Trenchard exchanged liaison officers, and thus du Peuty's April report of air operations was made immediately available to Trenchard. Du Peuty drew three lessons from French achievements: first, the necessity for overall direction of fighter forces working in offensive formations; second, the primary importance of intelligence gathered by reconnaissance and photographic work, which 'in this particular battle far exceed in importance, urgency and results, all artillery work'; third, the need for adaptable air units able to perform a variety of tasks.[8] Captain R.A. Cooper, Trenchard's liaison officer with du Peuty, supported those conclusions. 'Above all,' Cooper wrote: 'It appears that in a big offensive it is of the utmost importance to have great numerical superiority in fighting machines. It is thought that the Germans have readily learned this lesson at Verdun, and that if there is an offensive in the North they will oppose an even greater force in fighting machines than that which they have already concentrated at Verdun and that probably all their energy will be concentrated on fighting machines such as the Fokker single-seater.'[9] Numerical superiority, according to du Peuty, should be used to mount continuous fighter patrols, in formation, over the enemy lines, thus creating a zone where no hostile aircraft could venture unescorted. As he pointed out, the method was a costly one since 'our machines fight in the enemy country,' resulting in losses of pilots and aircraft forced to land behind enemy lines. Moreover, the constant offensive was 'a wearing out method for pilots and observers.' Yet he concluded: 'However heavy our losses may have been, those of the

Germans have been heavier.' He also warned that there was no such thing as total air superiority. The weaker side could always gain momentary dominance by concentrating strength at a given point, single machines could always find opportunities to carry out bombing and reconnaissance missions, and low-level operations might often evade the surveillance of the offensive fighter formations. When forwarding du Peuty's report to Brancker at the War Office, Trenchard found it necessary to make only one qualification, with respect to the low priority assigned to artillery co-operation. 'For an offensive battle,' Trenchard noted, 'he considers that the relative importance of the various nature of the work would be different, artillery work being of primary importance, especially during the preliminary stages of the battle.' In making this observation he was clearly thinking of the task confronting the RFC for the Somme offensive. For the rest, du Peuty's findings anticipated to a remarkable degree the offensive tactics Trenchard was to pursue relentlessly for the remainder of the war.[10]

Early in the year air operations over British sections of the front were, by comparison with Verdun, desultory. Between January and the end of April brigade records show a total of 148 combats in the air. Only twenty-six aircraft were lost as a result of enemy action; aircraft accidents claimed eighty. Nine Canadians took part in these combats, and five of them became casualties. Lieutenant C.V.G. Field and Lieutenant E.S. Wilkinson, pilot and observer, respectively, were killed while carrying out a reconnaissance mission for 1 Squadron when their Morane was shot down. Both had been engineering students at McGill University when the war broke out. On 29 March Second Lieutenant F.G. Pinder of Victoria was wounded and became a prisoner of war. Max Immelmann's twelfth victim, Pinder was flying an FE2b with 23 Squadron, which had arrived in France only two weeks before. On 16 April Second Lieutenant W.S. Erle, also of Victoria, was engaged in artillery co-operation work with 9 Squadron when he was shot down in flames over enemy lines by Rudolph Berthold. On 26 April Second Lieutenant James Mitchell of Montreal, an observer with 18 Squadron, was killed during a fight with four enemy aircraft near Arras. Most combats in this period were between enemy scouts and reconnaissance and artillery aircraft. Combats between opposing fighters were infrequent and, it appears, rarely deliberately sought in the early months of the year.[11]

Nevertheless, even before the lessons of Verdun had been received, the RFC was beginning to change its methods. In part this was made possible by the appearance of two aircraft which were better than anything the Germans could bring against them. Both the FE2b and the DH2 were pusher aircraft, thus sidestepping the British failure to produce an interrupter gear. The FE2b was a versatile two-seater in which both the pilot and the observer occupied cockpits forward of the wings. Though the aircraft, in its first version, had a maximum speed of only 73 mph, it was sturdy and manoeuvrable. The FE2b was also heavily armed; most squadrons mounted two Lewis guns in it, giving the crew an exceptionally wide arc of fire. No 20 Squadron first brought it to the front in January, when Lieutenants W.K. Campbell of Mitchell, Ont., and T. Jones of Toronto were the only Canadians with the unit. The DH2, a single-seater, was faster than the FE2b, having a top speed of 86 mph, and was esteemed for its excellence in aerobatics. It was first flown at the front in early February by 24 Squadron, a unit which soon became one of the RFC's best fighter squadrons.

As early as mid-January Trenchard had encouraged his squadrons to develop formation tactics for air fighting. His views were reflected in a letter to the Prime Minister, signed by Haig, that the answer to the 'Fokker scourge' was not to refrain from flying. 'We must continue to reconnoitre,' he wrote. 'The remedy is not to stop sending machines out for this purpose but to send them out in groups rather than singly.' Trenchard's ideas took hold only slowly with his fighter squadrons, but well before the French example was available for imitation a number of squadrons were experimenting with formation tactics. On 30 April 25 Squadron's Captain William Milne of Chamadaska, BC, led a 'finger-four' formation of four FE2bs, including one flown by Second Lieutenant Charles Elias Rogers of Toronto, with a Bristol Scout trailing behind and somewhat above them. The formation flew deep behind enemy lines, in order to be up-sun and to cut off escape to the east. No decisive results were obtained on this occasion, but 25 Squadron, and other RFC fighter units which were pursuing similar approaches, were shortly to reap the benefit. French experience, then, served to confirm the line the RFC was already taking. By mid-June RFC fighter aircraft had established a clear superiority over German aviation on the Somme front, thanks to their new tactics, to their better aircraft, and to the fact that more than half the aircraft the RFC had concentrated on this front were fighters.[12]

The winning of air superiority through aggressive fighter operations was only a means to an end. The whole point of these operations was to permit freedom of action to artillery, reconnaissance, and other ground support aircraft and to deny such freedom to the enemy. Even if air superiority were achieved, it was worthless unless ground forces could use the product of the aerial work done on their behalf, and that depended both upon the quality of the product and the ability of army staffs to make use of it. Cases in point are the Canadian operations at St Eloi and Mount Sorrel in the Ypres Salient.

On 27 March the British 3rd Division, part of V Corps, in an endeavour to pinch out a small German salient at St Eloi, exploded several mines beneath 'The Mound,' a slight elevation overlooking ground that was otherwise flat and water-soaked. Desperate fighting for this scrap of deeply-cratered terrain took place over the next few days, until the British were so exhausted that relief was mandatory. On 4 April, therefore, the Canadian Corps relieved V Corps and 2nd Canadian Division found itself in possession of the morass created by the British operation.[13]

The next afternoon the Germans counter-attacked strongly and succeeded in retaking all the ground they had lost to the British. In the course of local Canadian counter-attacks the situation quickly became confused, partly because of contradictory reports from units and battalion scouts. One correct report, stating that the Germans had recaptured all the mine craters (numbered 2, 3, 4, and 5), was not believed at Brigade Headquarters, because it was understood that craters 4 and 5 had been recovered. In fact, however, Canadian troops had occupied two old craters, numbered 6 and 7. On 8 April an air photograph showed a newly-dug trench around craters 4 and 5, but the 'ineffectual ditches which had been attempted around 6 and 7 were overlooked. We congratulated ourselves on the splendid work that we thought had been done by our crater garrisons.' Not until 16 April did the weather permit another air photograph to be made and the situation (which had evidently already been suspected at various levels of command) was conclusively revealed. Yet the evidence was already present in the air photographs of 8 April. The craters occupied then by the Canadians, and mistaken for 4 and 5, were half full of water; the real 4 and 5 craters, however, had no water in them.[14]

The St Eloi fiasco brought changes in the command of the Canadian Corps. 'General Plumer commanding 2nd Army wishes to remove General Turner ... and Brig. Gen. Ketchen,' wrote Haig in his diary. But Turner and Ketchen were Canadians and political considerations were uppermost in the decision to sacrifice instead the British corps commander, Lieutenant-General E.A. Alderson. Lieutenant-General Sir Julian Byng replaced Alderson on 29 May, just in time for the next large encounter with the enemy at Hooge and Mount Sorrel.[15]

The battle of Mount Sorrel was the first major engagement involving the entire Canadian Corps. In two well-rehearsed attacks on 2 and 6 June, each preceded by a storm of artillery fire, the Germans seized commanding ground around Mount Sorrel, Observatory Ridge, Hill 61, and Hill 62, as well as the spur at the ruined village of Hooge. The air assistance received by the Canadians prior to and during this first phase of the battle was not great. Five squadrons had a part in the engagement: 6 Squadron served the Canadian Corps, and had done so since early in the year; 5 Squadron supported v British Corps on the Canadian left; 16 and 20 Squadrons, escorted by scouts from 29 Squadron, carried out reconnaissance duties in the corps area.* RFC reconnaissance in May had alerted Corps Headquarters to German offensive preparations and indeed had discovered, well behind the German lines on the Menin road, practice trenches which closely resembled the Canadian positions on Hill 62. Bad weather, however, had prevented systematic observation of enemy rear areas.[16]

Provision already existed, under emergency conditions at army level, for the issuance of the call 'General Artillery Action,' at which time all routine air operations were to cease and all squadron aircraft concentrate upon artillery co-operation and tactical reconnaissance. On 21 May, as a result of a meeting between squadron commanders and artillery officers of the Second Army, these orders were changed to permit each corps to issue the emergency call to their own corps squadron and to summon help from neighbouring corps if required. At 1025 hrs on 2 June, after the terrible violence of the enemy's preliminary bombardment had first shaken the Canadians, 6 Squadron's record book shows the entry 'General Action.' But only one aircraft went up. Lieutenant R.A. Logan, a Canadian with 16 Squadron, flew over the battlefield on an early morning patrol; he seems to have had no particular instructions, but simply hoped to find an

---

* Canadians flying with these squadrons at the time of the Mount Sorrel battle included J.S. Beatty of Toronto and J.S. Scott of Roberval, Que., with 5 Squadron; D.L. Macauley of Montreal, R.H. Martin of Viking, Alta, A.L. Wilson of Vegreville, Alta, and J.A. York of Vancouver with 6 Squadron; C.G. Davidson of Montreal, G.E. Hewson of Amherst, NS, R.A. Logan of Toronto, and G.A. Thompson of Vaudreuil Station, Que., with 16 Squadron; Kenneth Mathewson of Montreal, R.W. White and W.J.T. Wright, both of Toronto, with 20 Squadron; J.H.N. Drope of Grimsby, Ont., G.M. Murray of Toronto, and William Stobart of Winnipeg with 29 Squadron.

enemy scout in the area. The next day the squadron was much more active, six aircraft flying between 0300 and 0900 hrs to spot flashes from German batteries.[17]

Given the importance of the ground that had been lost, it was inevitable that General Plumer should seek to recover at least some of it. His battle plan drew upon the tactics employed by the Germans at St Eloi, making artillery the key. 'One of the greatest arrays of guns yet employed on so narrow a front' preceded the Canadian counter-attack on 13 June with a devastating bombardment. The success of this assault owed a good deal to the RFC. On 7 June excellent aerial photographs had revealed the new German trenches at Mount Sorrel and in Sanctuary Wood. Based upon these photographs, the Canadian artillery began a systematic bombardment of German positions. Between 9 and 12 June four false bombardments were carried out to deceive the Germans as to the timing of the forthcoming assault. On the 12th a massive ten-hour shelling preceded a final forty-five-minute barrage just before the infantry left their trenches. So effective was the target registration that the preliminary bombardment prior to the Canadian infantry attack virtually destroyed the German ability to resist. The Germans themselves cited allied artillery and air superiority as the prime causes of the Canadian success.[18]

This was the formula that the Allies hoped would bring victory in the Somme battle. In preparation they concentrated at least four hundred aircraft, and among the two hundred machines the RFC committed to the offensive were seventy-six of the new fighters. These forces were considerably in excess of German strength. At the Somme on 1 July the Germans had fifty-two reconnaissance aircraft, thirty-six bomber-fighters, and sixteen single-seater fighters, for a total of 104 machines. Not only were the Germans at a numerical disadvantage, but morale was low within the air arm. By comparison with the allied air forces, the German air force suffered from inadequate co-operation with ground formations and an overly rigid organization. Initially, their answer to the offensive air tactics of the Allies remained the wasteful method of barrage patrol which had already proved wanting at Verdun; moreover, during the early phase of the Somme campaign, the Germans chose not to reinforce their air units because the High Command was unwilling to abandon the offensive operations in progress at Verdun for the sake of stemming the allied relief operation on the Somme.[19]

In order to build up the level of strength Haig's plans demanded, Trenchard had to dilute his squadrons with many airmen who had little or no combat experience. He could only insist that pilots possess basic flying skills and trust that most of them would survive the stern test of actual combat. It was the same for observers. In the spring Trenchard had increased the establishment of observers in two-seater squadrons from seven to twelve, most of the new intake coming from army units already in France, including the CEF. A new observer got little formal training. Beyond what was imparted at the squadron, he might, if it were thought necessary, be sent for a short period to an artillery battery or to a front-line infantry unit to develop an appreciation of the needs of the ground forces with which he must work. All observers had to learn morse code and how to operate a wireless set and a camera. They had to acquire, as rapidly as possible, a detailed familiarity with

MAP 3

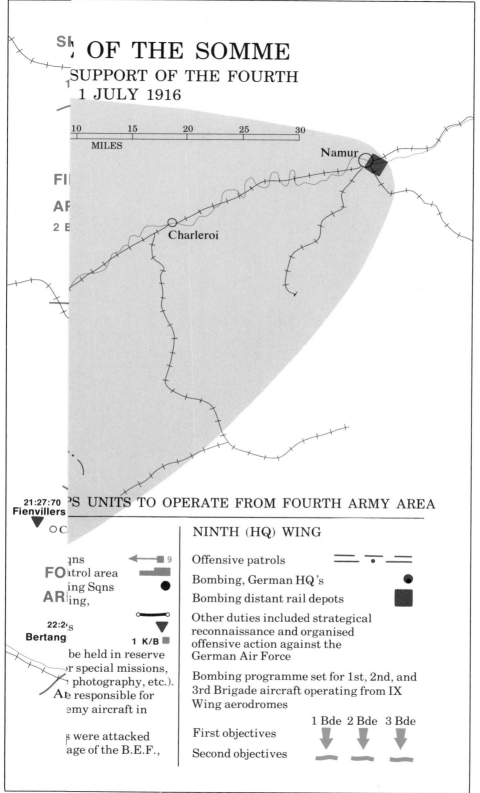

Compiled and drawn by Directorate of History

their squadron's 'beat' at the front; they had to master the handling of machine-guns. They picked up what they could by word of mouth, but there was no substitute for practical experience.[20]

At the time when the preparatory phase of the Somme offensive began, there were about eighty Canadians at the front with the RFC, half of them with the headquarters, army, and corps wings slated for employment over the Somme battlefield. They formed approximately 10 per cent of RFC flying personnel at the front; this proportion was to remain fairly constant over the next six months, as Canadian inflow kept pace with RFC expansion. Most of the Canadians had transferred from the CEF. Trooper W.G. Barker followed a typical path. He had enlisted in the 1st Canadian Mounted Rifles in Winnipeg in December 1914 and after taking a machine-gun course in England he went with his unit to France in September 1915, when the CMR relinquished their horses and went into the trenches. From there he subsequently applied for transfer to the RFC. In March 1916 he was sent, as an observer under training, to 9 Squadron, then commanded by Major F.A. Wanklyn of Montreal. While on probation with this reconnaissance squadron he made nine patrols during March, was struck off the strength of the CEF and commissioned as an observer in early April, and then posted to 4 Squadron at Baizieux. (It was normal practice for observer-trainees to be posted elsewhere on being commissioned.) After 7 July he flew with 15 Squadron based at Marieux for the rest of the year. By the end of the Somme campaign he had won the Military Cross and had been recommended for pilot training.

This was how many other Canadians came into the RFC during the same period. Officers commanding CEF units were not eager to lose good men; nevertheless, neither the Canadian Corps in the field nor the authorities responsible for Canadian troops under training in England placed any official barrier upon such transfers until early October 1916, two weeks after the Canadian Corps had incurred its first severe losses on the Somme, at the Battle of Flers-Courcelette. At that time the Canadian Training Division in England was authorized to place a freeze on all transfers to the flying services until the reinforcement needs of the CEF had been met.[21]

The plan for the Somme offensive was simple. Along the entire front of Fourth British Army and, on its left, VIII Corps of Third British Army, a seven-day preliminary bombardment was to take place, intended to destroy German wire and machine-gun posts. It was to be so powerful that, in the confident words of General Rawlinson, 'nothing could exist at the conclusion of the bombardment in the area covered by it.' The job of the infantry, advancing in lines with soldiers three paces apart behind a lifting barrage, was simply to walk the mile or mile-and-a-half to the devastated zone and take possession of it.

The plan for RFC employment in support of the offensive was the most elaborate yet devised by the British, reflecting both the importance Haig attached to the air arm and the lessons Trenchard had learned from du Peuty. As at Verdun, formations of fighters were to escort reconnaissance aircraft and also to patrol aggressively over the German lines. The fighters were drawn from 22 and 24 Squadrons of IV Brigade and from 27, 60, and 70 Squadrons of 9 (Headquarters)

Wing.* Most of Trenchard's fighters at the Somme were FE2bs, DH2s, and Martinsydes, but there were also Morane Scouts and biplanes (now entering the last stages of their operational use) and a few Bristol Scouts and Sopwith 1½ Strutters. All the roles assigned to the fighters were important, but the most vital was to ensure that the corps squadrons were able to carry out artillery co-operation and other observation work with as little interference from hostile aircraft as possible. 'The provision of the means for this observation,' it was laid down in a GHQ paper, 'must be regarded as of primary importance ... so far as the Flying Corps is concerned efforts should be devoted to provide observation requirements in the first instance.'[22]

For the five corps of Fourth Army and the one corps of Third Army taking part in the initial attack, 3, 4, 8, 9, and 15 Squadrons provided about eighty aircraft to carry out artillery work, contact patrols, and trench flights.† Since the British attack was to take place over a frontage of 25,000 yards, each corps squadron was responsible for a frontal zone of little more than three miles (the zones overlapped so that squadrons could assist one another). During the weeks preceding the attack, pilots and observers came to know their areas thoroughly. The usual attempts were made to standardize contact patrol procedures to ensure the rapid transmission of reliable information. Some infantrymen wore reflecting metal discs on their backs, others carried large fabric ground panels, and some were to set off flares upon reaching their objectives. On identifying and locating a unit, pilots were either to drop written messages or to land at specially prepared advanced landing grounds to pass on their information to the army command. Contact patrol aircraft were also expected to provide barrage information for corps headquarters and the artillery. Those airmen assigned to trench flights were to carry out close reconnaissance of enemy trenches and to bring down artillery fire upon them where required. In addition, the corps squadrons were to conduct a co-ordinated attack on kite balloons along the whole front.[23]

Another feature of the RFC plan for the opening phase of the Somme battle was a programme of bombing designed to strike at enemy communications and headquarters. Trenchard assigned the slow-moving RE7s of 9 Wing's 21 Squadron to

---

* When the Somme battle opened, Canadians with these fighter squadrons included C.M. Clement of Vancouver, A.B. Coupal of Sedley, Sask., W.R.C. Dacosta and J.H. Firstbrook, both of Toronto, W.L. Scandrett of London, Ont., A.M. Thomas of Toronto, W.O.T. Tudor-Hart and J.S. Williams, both of Vancouver, with 22 Squadron; Henry C. Evans of Macleod, Alta, A.G. Knight of Toronto, A.E. McKay of London, Ont., and H.A. Wood of Toronto, with 24 Squadron: A.D. Bell-Irving of Vancouver, J.A.N. Ormsby of Danville, Que., and J.H. Simpson of Saskatoon, Sask., with 60 Squadron; P.C. Garratt and J.A.G. Gilray, both of Toronto, with 70 Squadron. When the battle began there were no Canadians with 27 Squadron; on 25 July H. Spanner of Huntsville, Ont., became the first to join it.
† Canadian pilots and observers with these corps squadrons at the beginning of the battle included K.A. Creery of Vancouver and W.W. Lang of Toronto, with 3 Squadron; W.G. Barker of Winnipeg, T.L. Brennan of North Sydney, NS, R.S. Carroll of London, Ont., R.H. Jarvis and J.W. Langmuir of Toronto, J.H. Ross of Montreal and G.E.F. Sutton of Saskatoon, Sask., with 4 Squadron; R.W. Young of Toronto was the lone Canadian with 8 Squadron; C.P. Creighton of New Westminster, BC, I.C. Macdonell of Winnipeg and H.E. Paquin of Montreal were with 9 Squadron; F.G.H. Manville of Leask, Sask., and A.L. Taylor of Prince Albert, Sask., were with 15 Squadron.

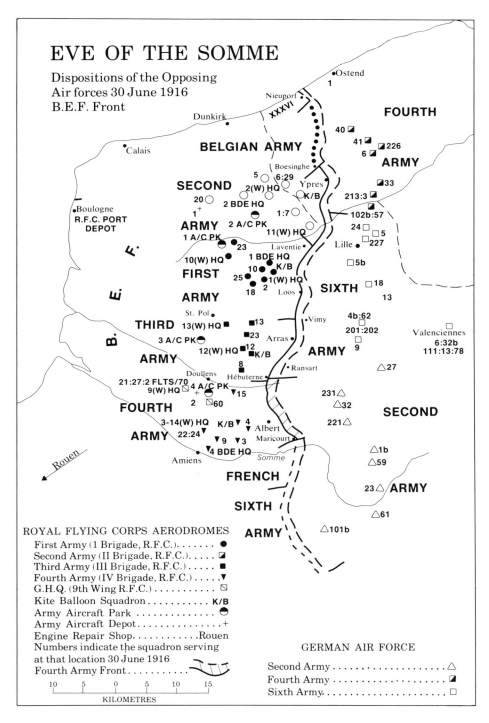

EVE OF THE SOMME

Dispositions of the Opposing
Air forces 30 June 1916
B.E.F. Front

•Ostend
1

Nieuport

Dunkirk •

XXXVI

FOURTH

40

41   226
6

ARMY

•Calais

BELGIAN ARMY

Boesinghe •

33

SECOND   5   6:29
2(W) HQ   Ypres
20   K/B   213:3

•Boulogne   1   2 BDE HQ   1:7   102b:57

R.F.C. PORT   ARMY   2 A/C PK   11(W) HQ   24   5
DEPOT   1 A/C PK   Laventie •   Lille •   227

23   1 BDE HQ   5b
10(W) HQ   10   K/B
FIRST   25   1(W) HQ
18   2   Loos   SIXTH   18

ARMY   13

St. Pol •   •Vimy   4b:62
THIRD   13(W) HQ   13   201:202
3 A/C PK   23   Arras •   9   Valenciennes
12(W) HQ   12   6:32b
ARMY   K/B   ARMY   111:13:78
8
Doullens •   Hébuterne •   • Ransart   27

21:27:2 FLTS/70   4 A/C PK   231
9(W) HQ   15   32
2   60
FOURTH   SECOND
3-14(W) HQ   K/B   4   221
ARMY   22:24   • Albert
9   3   Maricourt •
Rouen   4 BDE HQ   Somme   1b
Amiens   59
FRENCH

SIXTH   23   ARMY
61
ARMY

ROYAL FLYING CORPS AERODROMES   101b

First Army (1 Brigade, R.F.C.). . . . . . . ●
Second Army (II Brigade, R.F.C.). . . . . ◪
Third Army (III Brigade, R.F.C.). . . . . ■
Fourth Army (IV Brigade, R.F.C.). . . . . ▼
G.H.Q. (9th Wing R.F.C.). . . . . ◺
Kite Balloon Squadron. . . . . K/B
Army Aircraft Park . . . . ◑
Army Aircraft Depot. . . . .+
Engine Repair Shop. . . . . .Rouen
Numbers indicate the squadron serving
at that location 30 June 1916
Fourth Army Front. . . . .

10   5   0   5   10   15
KILOMETRES

GERMAN AIR FORCE

Second Army. . . . . △
Fourth Army . . . . ◪
Sixth Army. . . . . □

the more distant targets. These bombers carried a single 336-lb fragmentation bomb.* For the tactical bombing of railways, railway cuttings, bridges, trains, and stations he drew upon BE2s from 2 and 10 Squadrons of I Brigade, 7 and 16 Squadrons of II Brigade, and 12 and 13 Squadrons of III Brigade.† The BE2s were to fly down each day to airfields in the IV Brigade area, leaving their home fields in early morning and returning to their bases at the end of the day's operations.[24]

On 24 June the bombardment preceding the 'big push' began. The sheer weight of shells, combined with accurate registration of targets, was supposed not only to destroy the German wire, but to obliterate trenches and trench-support systems, fortified villages, and other strong points and artillery and machine-gun positions. The fire of the heavy batteries was directed by aeroplanes and balloons. On the first day of the bombardment low cloud restricted observation and the corps machines were unable to register many targets, but on the 25th improving weather and German retaliatory fire helped them to spot 102 hostile batteries. The next day destructive fire on registered targets began and air photographs taken in the afternoon appeared to show good results. Bad weather interfered with air work on the 27th and 28th, but on the 29th fifty-seven German batteries were spotted. The next day ninety-five targets were brought under fire through aerial observation. All seemed ready for the great attack: the bombardment had been heavy and thorough and excellent air photographs showed much damage to German positions. That the entrenched Germans could have endured this storm of fire without serious losses and lowered morale seemed unimaginable. Unfortunately for the attacking forces, however, much German wire remained uncut and the bulk of German troops had been sheltered from the effects of the bombardment in deep dugouts.[25]

At 0630 hrs on 1 July, an hour before British troops were to go over the top, the bombardment reached its crescendo. Ground mist prevented air observation for a time, but aircraft were aloft. A British pilot of 9 Squadron described the scene: 'On the dawn patrol it was difficult to see what was happening on the ground. It was like looking at a bank of low cloud, but one could see ripples on the cloud from the terrific bombardment that was taking place below. It looked like a large lake of mist, with thousands of stones being thrown into it.'[26] At zero hour the whole

---

* Their crews had no high regard for the RE7, a cumbersome aircraft much given to engine failure. In his diary, J.B. Brophy of Ottawa recorded that when a new RE7 was demolished shortly after being delivered to the squadron. 'A cheer went up from all down the sheds ... The good will in which the RE7 is held by the Boys was plainly shown by the vicious kicks and heavy rocks directed against what was left of it. Everyone hates them ...' Diary, 11 June 1916, J.B. Brophy biographical file, DHist

† Canadians with the bombing squadrons at this time included H.H. Whitehead of Winnipeg, with 2 Squadron; D. Carruthers of Kingston, Ont., W.H. Hubbard of Toronto, Eric McIver of Oakville, Ont., J.G. Robertson of Vermilion, Alta, and E.J. Watkins of Toronto, with 7 Squadron: W.J. Clifford of Mount Hamilton, Ont., T.G. Gordon of Merritt, BC, A.E. Godfrey of Vancouver, and J.B.R. Langley of Edmonton, with 10 Squadron; G.P. Alexander of Toronto, E.W. Farrow of Ottawa, and C.I. Van Nostrand of Toronto, with 12 Squadron; R.A. Delhaye of Brandon, Man., and P.R. Meredith of Toronto, with 13 Squadron; J.B. Brophy of Ottawa, C.J. Creery of Vancouver, E.S. Duggan and A.M. Goulding, both of Toronto, C.V. Hewson of Gore Bay, Ont., L.M. McCoy of Quebec City, and L.P. Watkins of Toronto, all of 21 Squadron.

spectacle was visible to the airmen as the British troops rose and in endless lines moved against the waiting Germans. Nothing of this incredible panorama, nor of the terrible casualties suffered by many of the attacking units long before the German front lines were reached, entered the running reports from the air. On the right wing, where the Fourth Army won its chief success of the day, 9 Squadron co-operated with XIII Corps to useful effect. When unable to call down artillery fire, some of the aircraft attacked enemy targets with bombs and machine-guns. Not a single enemy aircraft interfered with their work because of the fighters above; only three German machines were sighted, at a distance and altitude that precluded engagement.

The contact patrol aircraft accurately reported the most advanced positions of attacking troops, while the squadron's trench flight aircraft provided additional details on their return to confirm the reports. One of the trench patrol aircraft, flown by Lieutenant Ian C. Macdonell of Winnipeg, dropped bombs on a quarry full of German infantry and then successfully ranged the 15th Siege Battery on to this target.* By 1700 hrs 9 Squadron aircraft reported Marlboro Wood, Caterpillar Wood, Bernafay Wood, and Trônes Alley all abandoned by the enemy. XIII Corps, at the cost of more than six thousand casualties, had captured its objectives and had been well supported by the RFC. Had the corps been prepared to take advantage of the reliable reports by 9 Squadron about limited German resistance on its front, a much more significant penetration might have been achieved. But the corps and divisional commanders adhered to their instructions and made no serious attempt to exploit beyond their immediate objectives.[27]

Elsewhere on the front the corps squadrons coped as best they could with a battlefield on which all had gone awry. There had been tragic failure in nearly every sector and communications between attacking troops and higher formations had completely broken down. The aircraft serving XV Corps were unable to deliver an accurate picture of what was happening. The corps' objective was to capture Mametz and then to advance beyond that village to the German third line on its right; on its left it was to capture Fricourt and press on to Quadrangle Wood. By noon only some of the first objectives had been taken. However, aerial reports received just before noon described enemy guns being withdrawn to the rear of the German lines and identified British infantry in the communication trenches between Fricourt and Contalmaison. The commander of XV Corps, Lieutenant-General H.S. Horne, apparently misled by these reports and encouraged by the good news from XIII Corps on his right, ordered an attack upon Fricourt at 1430 hrs.[28]

Horne had also been deceived by over-optimistic reports about the progress of III Corps on his left. This formation, served by the same RFC contact aircraft as XV Corps, was supposed to take Contalmaison and Pozières, fortified villages which lay behind an intricate network of defences. The night before a German listening-

---

* Macdonell, the son of Brigadier-General A.C. Macdonell, GOC 5th Canadian Infantry Brigade (and later Major-General commanding the 1st Canadian Division), was killed the following day. Another Canadian contribution of note in this sector was made by H.E. Paquin of Montreal, an observer in 9 Squadron who provided target information for the French artillery in support of XIII Corps' right flank.

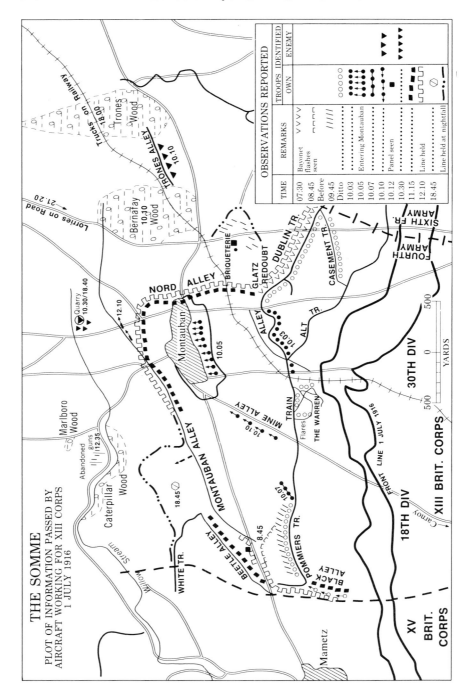

THE SOMME
PLOT OF INFORMATION PASSED BY
AIRCRAFT WORKING FOR XIII CORPS
1 JULY 1916

post in the sector had overheard enough of General Rawlinson's final order that the defenders were thoroughly prepared; 'the extended lines of British infantry broke against the German defence like waves against a cliff, only to be beaten back.' Yet to the air observers, remote from 'the moans and groans of the wounded, the cries for help and the last screams of death,' it appeared that the first advance had taken the front line at 0845 hrs. Later reports qualified this by noting that the advance was held up at two points, Ovillers and La Boisselle, but on the right airmen saw infantry penetrating as far as Peake Wood, towards Contalmaison. However, the main body of troops had advanced only half that distance, many units having been shattered or disoriented under heavy enfilading machine-gun fire. Horne's attack on Fricourt therefore received no help from his left, and in any event the wire and deep dugouts at that strongpoint were virtually intact. Though RFC observers had managed to bring down effective counter-battery fire upon German artillery positions in xv and iii Corps sectors, there was no way to neutralize the German machine-guns. Mainly because of them, xv Corps suffered over eight thousand casualties and iii Corps over eleven thousand during the day.[29]

The most dismaying failure took place on the northern half of the battlefield. Thiepval and the Thiepval spur dominated this point, but it was thought that the position could be turned if St Pierre-Divion and Grandcourt, both on the Ancre, could be captured. But German artillery, laying down supporting fire in front of both hamlets, remained active all day in spite of counter-battery work directed from the air, and the German garrisons held firm. Thus Lieutenant J.W. Langmuir of Toronto and his British observer, flying a BE2c of 4 Squadron, tried to range the 72nd Siege Battery upon a German battery. Although thirty shots were fired upon it Langmuir reported that 'The pits were not damaged, and the hostile battery was active throughout the shoot.' Moreover, the three corps squadrons had difficulties with mist and swirling smoke apparently not encountered farther south.

No 4 Squadron brought in the most crucial information, but unfortunately what its contact patrols were able to see – the advance by the 36th Division against the Schwaben Redoubt – was misleadingly encouraging. By 1400 hrs British troops were in possession of the redoubt and German batteries were reported to be withdrawing from the Grandcourt-Courcelette Ridge. But this was an isolated penetration and, unhappily, the RFC could supply little accurate information about the position on the rest of the corps front. Before noon air reports identified British troops in Thiepval, a report not corrected until late in the afternoon. Meanwhile, supports had been pushed forward, taking heavy casualties. Even with respect to the troops in Schwaben Redoubt air intelligence was not uniformly good. Information that German counter-attacks against this point were weak may conceivably have influenced the failure to reinforce the troops holding it. By 1000 hrs the British infantry had been forced to withdraw, their ranks sorely depleted and their supplies of water and ammunition exhausted. At the end of the day x Corps held only part of the German first line north of Thiepval and the Leipzig Salient to the south, at the cost of over nine thousand casualties.[30]

North of the Ancre, VIII Corps fared even worse, suffering more than fourteen thousand casualties. At first, success seemed imminent. On the left, aircraft observed troops entering Pendant Copse, though smoke and dust made observation difficult. To obtain this intelligence, pilots had 'displayed amazing daring, flying along the front sometimes only fifty feet above the troops under heavy small-arm fire.' What they could not see was that the troops which had succeeded in penetrating the German lines were rapidly enveloped and overcome. As on X Corps' front, counter-battery work failed to silence German artillery, nor could anything be done to stop the murderous fire from German machine-gun positions.[31]

The full dimensions of the disaster that had overtaken the British Army on the first day of the Somme took some time to sink in. The RFC, however, was confident that it had done a good job, particularly in its vital task of keeping enemy aircraft away from the machines of the corps squadrons. 'The general impression of the day's work,' wrote the commanding officer of 9 Wing, 'has been that the Germans started with the intention of attacking any of our machines which might cross their lines. As the day wore on they were gradually driven from the sky, and after 1.0 pm scarcely a German machine was seen in the air, and those which were seen manifested no aggressive tendencies.' German sources tell the same tale. Only nine aeroplanes of IV Brigade reported combats in the air. RFC losses were light; fourteen casualties occurred over the entire front, four of them Canadians. Two FE2bs were lost over the Somme. In one of them Lieutenant J.H. Firstbrook of Toronto was flying over the enemy lines at five thousand feet when he was shot in the back by an enemy aircraft he failed to see. Though he had no recollection of doing so, he managed to land his aircraft behind enemy lines. Lieutenant W.O.T. Tudor-Hart of Vancouver was an observer on a similar mission; his pilot was killed but he survived the crash. Both Canadians became prisoners of war.*[32]

The RFC's performance in battlefield reconnaissance, despite the courage and daring of its airmen, had been weak. In part this was undoubtedly because of the large number of relatively inexperienced pilots and observers. At the same time, however, the demand placed upon the air arm was without precedent. No previous experience even remotely approached the scale and complexity of the Somme battle. It is hardly surprising that airmen were not always accurate in reporting the details of confusing battles in the vast warren of the German trench system. By the end of the Somme campaign the RFC's performance in this respect would be much better.

The RFC, and the British official air historian, believed that the bombing operations on 1 July were successful, the latter citing evidence to show that the bombs dropped on St Quentin station by 12 and 13 Squadrons disrupted the dispatch of reinforcements. On the other hand, the British Army's historian took the view

---

* Lieutenant C.I. Van Nostrand of Toronto (the first of the Toronto Curtiss School graduates to have been accepted by the RFC) was taken prisoner after his 12 Squadron RE7 was forced down behind enemy lines. The fourth Canadian casualty was 32 Squadron's G.C. Simpson of Guelph, Ont., who was killed when his DH2 was shot down after he launched a single-handed attack on ten German bombers near Festubert. H.A. Jones, *The War in the Air: being the Story of the Part played in the Great War by the Royal Air Force*, II (London 1928), 332

that 'air activity against material objects ... in no way affected the fate of the battle.' What is certain is that unescorted bombing missions needlessly lost aeroplanes, while army squadrons searched vainly over the lines for enemy fighters because of the assumption that such fighting patrols were the only effective method of preventing enemy air activity. When, two days later, more BE2cs were lost for the same reason, 13 Squadron's commander pointed out that 'Experience has shown that hostile machines avoid Allied machines flying in formation and attack isolated machines. This increases the likelihood of being attacked when the patrol is not at hand.' Trenchard's decision was to withdraw the BE2cs and return them to their parent brigades; 9 Wing assumed responsibility for bombing and distant reconnaissance in the Somme region.[33]

Whatever criticisms have been made of RFC dispositions and performance on 1 July, two conclusions are evident. The first is that the RFC had seized and maintained air supremacy over the battlefield; the second is that even had RFC airmen been able to provide intelligence of the situation on the ground with flawless accuracy, it would have made virtually no difference to the outcome of an attack doomed to failure through faulty conception. However, had the quality of RFC work been better, or at least more consistent, there might well have been significantly fewer casualties.

In the pause that followed that terrible day's fighting some regrouping was carried out in the BEF. Lieutenant-General Hubert Gough took over X and VIII Corps on 2 July and the next day his command was designated the Reserve Army (ultimately to become the Fifth Army). The RFC conformed; 4 and 15 Squadrons were combined to form 15 Wing, the nucleus of the future V Brigade.* On 7 July Haig began to bring down reinforcements from quieter sections of the front, but bad weather was hampering air operations and he resolved not to resume the main attack until the weather permitted the RFC to bring its superiority once more to bear. Nevertheless, the RFC continued to accumulate information about enemy dispositions. The work of 4 Squadron was typical. During the week following 1 July two Canadians, Second Lieutenant J.H. Ross of Montreal and his observer, Lieutenant G.E.F. Sutton of Saskatoon, Sask., carried out several important special reconnaissances until Ross was wounded on 7 July. Both received the Military Cross for their work; Ross' citation read in part: 'On two occasions he carried out reconnaissances at a very low altitude to determine the general situation. His machine was repeatedly hit by rifle fire, and he was severely wounded in the arm. His reports were most valuable.'[34]

Less spectacular but equally important were the artillery patrols carried out during this period by Second Lieutenant R.S. Carroll, a Curtiss School graduate born in London, Ont., and his British observer. Their reports, couched in the technical

---

* On 21 July 32 Squadron (DH2s) was transferred from I Brigade to the Somme front and on 27 August was grouped with 15 Wing to form V Brigade. When, on 5 September, 23 Squadron (FE2bs) came from III Brigade it joined 32 Squadron to form 22 (Army) Wing. When 32 Squadron came to the Somme there were only two Canadians with it: C.L. Bath of Toronto and G.H. Bonnell of Halifax. In mid-September the Canadians with 23 Squadron included V.C. Gordon, J.H. Kelly, and A.P. Maclean, all of Toronto; they were later joined by W.B. Kellogg of the same city and K.C. MacCallum of Vancouver.

language and studded with the abbreviations and coded map references now standard in corps squadron work, were packed with detail. Thus on 3 July, while on a three-hour patrol in the early evening, they discovered an enemy battery firing. They reported its location by message bag to the artillery. As a result 17th Siege Battery was 'turned on to the target,' the enemy battery was silenced, and seven ammunition wagons were blown up. Later in the patrol they noted a 'train with steam up at Achiet-Le-Grand'; then, when over Le Sars, were attacked by a hostile aircraft whose fire damaged their propeller, before it was chased off by a British fighter. They finished off their patrol by sighting a column of German motor transport of twenty vehicles, noting laconically, 'H.A.G. [Heavy Artillery Group] informed but no shots fired.' On the 6th, in the course of another three-hour patrol, they examined from 3000 feet the whole of the German second line opposite their corps front, recording the location of new trenches and saps, the information that at two points 'the second line trench and wire appear to have been slightly damaged ... but on the whole of the remainder of the line there is very little damage done,' and the location of eleven enemy batteries whose flashes they spotted. On three of them they brought down artillery fire until 'batteries temporarily silenced ... Shoot discontinued owing to want of petrol, when batteries recommenced firing.'[35]

Work of this kind, routine in nature, was vital to the fortunes of the armies below. The airmen who carried it out were almost never in the limelight, but a study of corps squadron records during the Somme battle shows a steadily rising proficiency on the part of aircrews in the little-heralded corps squadrons that was as impressive as any of the other work performed by the RFC. Perched directly over the battlefield in their slow two-seaters, flying their unchanging beats, despite enemy fighters, ground fire, and the threat of being struck in the air by shells fired by the artillery of either side, they were developing a meticulous expertise in their hazardous and crucial task, a task largely unappreciated except by the gunners and intelligence officers who worked directly with them. And there were other hazards. On 9 July Carroll and his observer were on a shoot with 20th Siege Battery, from which six shots had been fired, 'when Morane aeroplane carried away aerial. Returned for new aerial but battery could not receive signals.' Grit, constant watchfulness, and, above all, patience were the hallmarks of good corps squadron airmen.[36]

After 9 July, when the weather improved, heavy slogging by the infantry edged the allied front ahead. Contalmaison fell to III Corps on 10 July, Mametz Wood to XV Corps on the 12th. During these lesser operations the RFC kept up its air offensive and Trenchard reported with evident satisfaction that German machines were not getting across the lines. Though on several occasions aircraft from IV Brigade attacked columns of troops on the march with machine-gun fire, no German aircraft responded in kind, nor were allied troop movements even observed from the air, a great advantage in preparing for the second major push of 14 July. German infantry of this period are supposed to have scrawled on their dug-out walls the imprecation 'May God punish England, our artillery and our airmen.'[37] Yet when challenged by bombing raids behind the front, the German air force could respond fiercely. On 9 July 21 Squadron flew an early-morning raid against Marcoing station. J.B. Brophy described in his diary the action over the target: 'We turned south just beside Cambrai, and found our mark, Marcoing station. I let my bomb go and had to turn off quickly to dodge a bomb from another youth who was above me. I saw his bomb go down. Several lit on the tracks in the station yards, and probably ruined them. As soon as our bombs were dropped we turned and lit out for home, divil [sic] take the hindmost. He did, as poor old Hewson was picked off by a bunch of huns, who attacked us from behind, and fired at us and went away. We haven't heard what happened to him, and hope he landed safely.'*[38]

On 14 July the British Army attacked once more on a two-corps front, this time without the collaboration of the French, whose staff refused to join in 'an attack organized for amateurs by amateurs.' In fact, the assault was a distinct improvement on the performance of 1 July. Large numbers of air photographs taken in the preceding days had outlined the second German trench system plainly. A creeping barrage, timed to the movement of the infantry, was employed and air co-operation with ground formations was highly successful. In spite of low clouds and a strong west wind, 3 and 9 Squadrons flew continually from dawn until dusk. The infantry, as the result of a devastating but brief preliminary bombardment, a jump-off at first light, and the well-timed creeping barrage, were able to take most of their objectives. Contact patrol aircraft, some of them equipped with a Klaxon horn to remind infantry to indicate their position, brought in accurate reports. Despite such work, the great chance of the day was missed. Infantry of XIII Corps had broken through all opposition by 1000 hrs and found the way clear to High Wood. Further infantry advance by reserves close at hand was forbidden by higher authority, however, since this part of the operation was to be entrusted to the cavalry. As late as 1500 hrs an air report showed that the approaches to High Wood were still clear of the enemy, but not until 1900 hrs did cavalry units begin their advance. When a German machine-gun post on their right opened up on them, it was silenced by fire from a low-flying aircraft. But when darkness made further operations impossible, the cavalry had reached only the wood's outskirts; two months of bitter fighting were to pass before High Wood was completely in British hands.[39]

After 14 July the Somme campaign, begun, at least on Haig's part, with visions of a clear-cut breakthrough, was transformed into a battle of attrition. The British remained upon the offensive and in the end won their way across the gentle ridges which had so dominated their positions on 1 July. These limited gains were made at enormous cost, for not only did armament and terrain favour the defence but the Germans had been ordered to defend every inch of ground to the death. So unyieldingly did German troops adhere to this order that by the close of fighting their casualties, at least according to some estimates (themselves the subject of much controversy), equalled or even exceeded those of the Allies. Many of the engagements fought before the offensive concluded in November have been accorded distinctive names, such as the Battle of Flers-Courcelette in which the Canadian Corps figures prominently and tanks were used for the first time, but

* C.V. Hewson of Gore Bay, Ont., was reported killed in action as the result of this encounter.

they were all of a piece: desperate struggles for stretches of churned-up soil, unrecognizeable villages, and segments of devastated trench line. From the sweeping advances it had first hoped for, the British staff was reduced to a preoccupation with the minor tactics of trench warfare, in which the gaining of a few hundred yards could be hailed as a victory. The Somme battle did achieve one of its desired results, however; ten days after it began Falkenhayn brought the offensive at Verdun to an end.[40]

Until late in the Somme battles the RFC retained the upper hand. In part, this was because the Germans kept much of their air strength at Verdun until the end of August. It was also because of Trenchard's driving insistence upon the doctrine that 'Protection of artillery, photographic and similar machines is best secured by an active aerial offensive, carried out by offensive patrols and bombing raids.' This principle, towards which Trenchard had been moving for some time, was enunciated explicitly during the Somme campaign. It was to govern British flying operations on the Western Front for the rest of the war. As Trenchard later stated, offensive fighter patrols were to 'seek for, fight, destroy and drive down the enemy's machines'; bombing raids were to induce enemy commanders to demand air protection for communications, depots, and headquarters, 'which will result in the withdrawal of aeroplanes and anti-aircraft artillery from the battle area.'[*41]

Since bombing raids were launched not solely to damage enemy targets but to draw off enemy air strength as well, Trenchard maintained direct responsibility for the bombing programme at RFC Headquarters. Tactical bombing was carried out by the corps squadrons in front of their respective armies. Since the corps squadrons of the Fourth and Reserve Armies were fully occupied in reconnaissance and artillery work, 8, 12, and 13 Squadrons of the Third Army's III Brigade carried out the major share of tactical bombing on the Somme front. Martinsydes of 9 (HQ) Wing's 27 Squadron and RE7s (later BE12s) of 21 Squadron were used on occasion against more distant targets in the zone of operations, including the railway facilities at Mons, Maubeuge, Quievrechain, Valenciennes, and Aulnoy, and also undertook the major responsibility for bombing targets south of the Ancre.[42] The Brophy diary describes one such raid, on 11 July:

The chief kicks about our bomb-raids ha[ve] been the poor formation, leaving us in danger of being separated, and 'done in' by huns. The Colonel[†] decided he'd lead us to show us how. He was to lead and Capt. Carr and I were next, and four others in pairs behind, and nine scouts. At 6,000 we met thick clouds, and when I came through I couldn't see anyone anywhere, so I just flew around and finally sighted 3 machines. I went over and found Carr and the Colonel, and two scouts, so I got into place and the Colonel went over to the lines, and kept circling to get higher for half an hour, right over the lines. I thought this was a foolish stunt, as I knew the huns could see us, and would be waiting for us. I was very surprised that they didn't shell us, but there was a battle on, and they were probably too

* It was a policy that was to be questioned from the beginning, however. In England Sefton Brancker and Sir David Henderson 'discovered without surprise, that Sykes was damning it in private at a time when the unfinished Air Enquiry provided an easy platform for the disgruntled and misinformed.' Andrew Boyle, *Trenchard* (London 1962), 185
† Presumably Lieutenant-Colonel H.C.T. Dowding, the officer commanding 9 Wing.

busy. We were right over Albert, as I recognized two huge mine craters that had been sprung July 1st. When we did cross over with only two scouts, we hadn't been over more than a couple of minutes before I saw 3 Fokkers coming towards us, and a couple of L.V.G.'s climbing up to us. Another Fokker was up above me, and behind, between our two scouts. I knew he was going to dive at one of us, but expected the scouts to see him and attack him, so I didn't bother about him, but began to get the stop-watch time of my bomb-sight to set it for dropping. While I was doing this I suddenly heard the pop-pop-pop's of machine guns, and knew the huns had arrived. I looked and saw them diving in amongst us, and firing. There were seven L.V.G.'s and 3 Fokkers as far as I could make out, but they went so fast I could hardly watch them. Our scouts went for them, and I saw the Colonel turn about. My gun being behind me I couldn't get in a shot, and turned around after Carr and the Colonel. They fired some more as we went back but didn't hit me. The Colonel was hit and so the show was over. He had about a dozen bullets in his machine, and was hit in the hand. His gun was shot through, and his observer hit in the face. He probably won't try to lead us again.[43]

This somewhat breezy account reveals that the RFC's air dominance was by no means all-pervasive, and that in their own rear areas the Germans could react vigorously to bombing attacks, especially to those in which close formation had been lost.

Trenchard tended to spread his targets very widely along the whole front, but certainly not indiscriminately. Between mid-July and early August he favoured the triangle formed by Douai (an important railway junction), Oppy (billets and supply dumps), and Corons, whose dumps on the Douai-Arras rail line were attacked by the night bombers. Naturally most of the bombing in this period was directed against targets immediately behind the German third line of defence at the Somme; Bapaume, Irles, Le Transloy, Thilloy, Beugny, Rocquigny, Sailly-Saillisel, Epehy, Marcoing, Cambrai, and Aubigny-au-Bac all were attacked at least twice. In August, too, the largest number of raids were behind the Somme front, but such raids were co-ordinated with attacks elsewhere, including some by the RNAS at Dunkirk. Trenchard also directed corps squadrons north of the Ancre to carry out daily raids against German troops, using groups of about five aircraft; target selection was left to corps staff to approve and attacks on towns and villages took place only at the request of army and corps commanders.[44]

In September the growing German strength in the air led the RFC to begin systematic bombing of enemy aerodromes as well. None of these raids caused heavy damage, though they stirred up a certain amount of enemy air activity. Flight Sub-Lieutenant Charles Sproatt of Toronto, flying a Caudron with 5 (Naval) Wing, recorded that only three or four aircraft out of a formation of fourteen, fighting a heavy rainstorm, managed to find St Denis Westrem, although they were attacked by enemy aircraft. Lieutenant P.C. Sherren of Crapaud, PEI, with 27 Squadron, dropped six 20-lb bombs from 10,000 feet on Beaucamps aerodrome (he claimed that two hit it, surely with little effect) before he was attacked by a Nieuport with French markings![45]

Few attacks were made at such high altitudes. Usually when raiding dumps and billets, aircraft flew at around 6000–8000 feet, and came much lower when attacking railways. Much of the railway bombing continued to be done by 27 Squadron. Three Canadians, P.C. Sherren, H.S. Spanner of Huntsville, Ont., and E.D. Hicks of Winnipeg took part in most of them. On 15 September Sherren came down to 500 feet to drop two 112-lb bombs on Gouzeaucourt station; he claimed to have destroyed an engine and an ammunition train. Nine days later Hicks bombed a train at Aulnoye from 400 feet, destroying the engine and damaging some coaches, according to his report. On 16 November Sherren, by this time a captain and shortly to be gazetted for the Military Cross, led a formation of six Martin-sydes from the squadron's airfield at Fienvillers to attack the important railway junction at Hirson, ninety miles distant. From a thousand feet their bombs blew six coaches off the track, destroyed other rolling stock on sidings, and caused the collapse of two station buildings. All six returned after a four-and-a-half-hour flight, very close to the limit of the Martinsyde's endurance.[46]

Most bombing raids were merely of nuisance value, their chief importance being to divert and hold German air units from the immediate battle zone. But the brunt of Trenchard's offensive policy fell upon the fighter squadrons. When the Somme battle began many of the German fighter units were still equipped with the Fokker *Eindekker*. This machine, a terror in its time, was no longer a match for later British types and in fact had become an easy victim. On 18 June the great Immelmann, flying an E-III, met his death at the hands of an FE2b crew from 25 Squadron. On 29 July Lieutenant A.M. Thomas of Toronto and his British observer, flying a 22 Squadron FE2b, encountered eight enemy aircraft, including several *Eindekkers*, over the Bapaume-Peronne road. They immediately attacked one of them, Thomas firing a drum of ammunition and his observer two more from eighty yards range. 'The machine spun and was nose-diving to earth when last seen,' Thomas reported. 'At this moment we were attacked by other Type E which retired when we opened fire ...'[47] Another example comes from a report by Second Lieutenant C.S. Duffus of Halifax, also with 22 Squadron, of a patrol over the Fourth Army front on 23 August: '... we saw an F.E.2b doing photography N[orth] of LE SARS. We followed this machine going E[ast] of it, when we saw 5 H[ostile] A[ircraft], type E, coming from BAPAUME, evidently with the intent to attack the photographic machine. We dived at the H.A., opening fire at about 500 yards. The H.A. immediately split up their formation, diving and making off in all directions. We closed with one machine firing two drums into it and actually set it on fire but after a few seconds the flame went out. The H.A. then dived rapidly for ground.'[48]

These were probably E-IIIs or E-IVs, the last versions of the series produced by Fokker. In mid-1916 German squadrons had begun re-equipping with a new generation of Fokkers, the D-I and D-II biplanes. The Fokker D-I had an in-line engine, was clumsy in manoeuvre, and had a slow rate of climb; the D-II, with a lighter rotary engine, was more manoeuvrable but no faster. Both were re-engined (as the D-III and D-IV) without much improvement in performance, but neither aircraft had a long operational life. When superior types became available later in the summer, the Fokkers were sent to the Eastern Front or used as trainers.*

---

* The Fokker D-V, a much improved version of the rotary D-III, came into service in September 1916. It had a top speed of 106 mph.

Much superior to them were the Halberstadts and Rolands. The first Halberstadt fighter had appeared in 1915; in 1916 it was re-engined like the Fokkers and it turned out to be a better aircraft. With a top speed of only 90 mph the Halberstadt D-II was nevertheless an exceedingly agile and strongly-built little machine, a formidable opponent for British airmen. Another good fighter which came into service in July was the LFG Roland D-I, an aircraft with clean lines and a large streamlined spinner. Though not so handy as the Halberstadt, it was much faster; more important, it was armed with twin Spandaus firing forward, making it the most heavily-armed single-seater on the Western Front.[49] All these aircraft were faster than anything the RFC had, but the British still had numerical superiority and a strong offensive spirit.

Canadian casualties from mid-July to mid-September illustrate the shift in the balance of the air war. In late July there were no casualties whatever among Canadians in fighter squadrons, but in August seven were killed, and in the first part of September three were killed and one wounded. Corps squadron casualties among Canadians were much lighter: two in July (one wounded, one captured), five in August (one killed, two wounded, and two captured), and three in the first half of September (two killed, one wounded). As it happened, two-thirds of the Canadians in fighter squadrons were with units involved in the fighting over the Somme front. An analysis of squadron records and RFC communiqués shows, not surprisingly, that most combats in the air involved 9 Wing and IV Brigade squadrons. Of these, 24 Squadron took part in more combats than any other unit.[50]

This squadron, under the leadership of Major Lanoe Hawker, had pioneered in the development of RFC formation fighting tactics.* Hawker was an outstanding pilot who had first come to France in October 1914 with 6 Squadron. In 1915 he had won the Victoria Cross – the first pilot to do so – and in September of that year had been given command of the newly formed 24 Squadron. He personally instructed most of the pilots who joined the squadron from the Central Flying School. When the unit went to France in February 1916 only one Canadian, Second Lieutenant R.H.B. Ker of Victoria, was among its pilots. Ker left in mid-July to become a flight commander with 41 Squadron. When the squadron expanded from twelve to eighteen pilots in May, however, four other Canadians joined it. They were Second Lieutenants H.A. Wood, a civil engineer from Toronto; A.G. Knight, who had joined the RFC in Canada on leaving the University of Toronto; H.C. Evans, thirty-seven years old, an Alberta rancher, and a veteran of the Boer War who had transferred to the RFC from the Alberta Dragoons in 1915; and A.E. McKay of London, Ont., who had learned to fly at the Wright School in Augusta, Georgia. All these pilots had outstanding careers.

---

* After Major R.R. Smith-Barry took over 60 Squadron in August, he also advocated formation tactics. Some airmen opposed this trend, notably the officer commanding 11 Squadron, which had been the first homogeneous fighting squadron on the Western Front. Trenchard had no patience with such views and suppressed them without ceremony. His pencilled comments on a communication from this officer were scornful: 'What does he mean ... bunkum ... no ... vague ... rot.' To the suggestion that 'Enemy A.A. fire is becoming so good that possibly in a year's time no flying in daylight over hostile areas will be undertaken except on special missions' he commented: 'This really shows this officer wants a rest.' See 'Notes on Aerial Fighting,' 15 Aug. 1916, Air 1/920/204/5/885.

Before he was killed on 3 September 1916 Evans won the Distinguished Service Order and a Mention in Dispatches; Knight received the DSO and Military Cross before meeting his death at the hands of Manfred von Richthofen in December; Wood gained the MC in 1917 and was considered an 'ace' at the end of the war; and McKay, although he received no decorations, was mentioned in communiqués frequently, being credited with two enemy aircraft destroyed and five or six out of control before he was killed on 28 December 1917.[51]

Pilots of 24 Squadron flew out of an airfield at Bertangles and most of their combats took place over German lines in the triangle formed by the Bapaume-Albert road, the Bapaume-Peronne road, and the German trenches between Pozières and Bouchavesnes. Some or all of the four Canadians on the squadron were involved in more than twenty combats between 14 July and 15 September.[52] Their DH2s flew in formations of four to six, usually at 10,000 feet at the beginning of an offensive patrol. The point drummed into them all was to attack first: 'In addition to the moral ascendancy gained by offensive tactics, the material advantage in aerial fighting is with the attacker. Every machine has its blind side ... All the machines should concentrate on the leader's opponent. This has a great moral effect and prevents our formation from splitting up.'[53]

On 20 July 24 Squadron was heavily embroiled with German fighter forces and its Canadians took part in four air battles during this day. The last of them, fought out between 2020 and 2045 hrs over High Wood opposite the right flank of the Fourth Army, involved McKay, Evans, and two British pilots. Their patrol encountered five LVGs (presumably the C-II, the German air force's equivalent of the BE2c as maid of all work) escorted by three Roland D-IIs and three Fokker E-IIIs. The highly manoeuvrable DH2s were at their best in the confused *mêlée* that ensued: '... Lieutenant Evans closed with a Roland and fired half a drum at a range of only 25 yards. The Roland went straight down apparently out of control, and Lt. Evans was attacked from behind by two Fokkers, but these nearly collided and Lt. Evans escaped them and attacked an LVG firing the remaining half of his drum.' Meanwhile, McKay was having his problems: 'A Roland dived at him from in front, but Lt. McKay outmanoeuvred it and attacked, firing the remainder of his drum. The Roland ceased fire and fell in a spinning nose dive. Lt. McKay was now attacked by a Fokker which he could not outmanoeuvre owing to his engine being shot, so to escape its fire, he descended in a steep spiral. Lt. Chapman observing this, dived to the rescue and attacked the Fokker at 1000 feet over HIGH WOOD. The Fokker fell into a spinning nose dive, hit the ground ... and burst into flames ... Meanwhile Lt. Evans attacked and drove off an LVG and a Fokker. All H.A. had now been driven off ...'[54]

On the basis of reports from British anti-aircraft batteries McKay and Evans were credited with a Roland apiece. Two weeks later Evans attacked an LFG Roland C-II (the fast two-seater which had inspired the Roland D-II) over the Bapaume-Peronne road: 'The observer was either hit or else his gun jammed as he waved his arm at me. I put on another drum and waved to him to turn West but he kept on diving E. I fired a burst at him and the machine went down vertically turning over and over.'[55] The Roland, having refused quarter, crashed east of Bois des Vaux. Again, on 14 September, when five DH2s were escorting a 22 Squadron bombing attack on Bapaume, Knight and a British sergeant pilot combined to attack a German single-seater: 'Sgt Cockerell at once opened fire and Lt. Knight at once followed up, getting on to the H.A.'s tail and firing about 15 rounds at very close range. The Pilot fell forward, and flames came out of the cock-pit which gradually enveloped the whole machine. After falling 1500 ft., the wings came off and the remains hit the ground near MANANCOURT. The other H.A. turned East and disappeared.'[56] The same pair, along with Wood, employed similar tactics over Bapaume to account for another German fighter on the following day.[57]

At the end of August and the beginning of September a sudden surge in enemy air activity led Trenchard to conclude, correctly, that the air battle was entering a new and even more testing phase. But nothing could shake his total commitment to an offensive doctrine. As he emphatically restated it: 'The sound policy would seem to be that if the enemy changes his tactics and pursues a more vigorous offensive, to increase our offensive, to go further afield, and to force the enemy to do what he would gladly have us do now. If, on the other hand, we were to adopt a purely defensive policy, we should be doing what the French have learnt by experience to be a failure, and what the rank and file of the enemy, by their own accounts, point to as being one of the main causes of their recent reverses.'[58]

Offensive spirit alone was hardly enough. Trenchard cast his eyes longingly upon the Sopwith 1½ Strutters of the RNAS as the means to tide the RFC over its crisis in aircraft supply. General Henderson and the Admiralty had been talking since July, in very general terms, about the possibility of drawing upon naval resources in case of a breakthrough at the Somme and Henderson had found an ally in Lord Sydenham of the Air Board.* Now Trenchard suggested to Haig, in the course of reporting the advent of a formidable new German fighter, the Albatros, that the Admiralty be asked to replace the RFC's 18 Squadron which was being withdrawn from the front to undertake co-operation with the cavalry.[59]

Meanwhile Trenchard had to turn his attention to the major attack scheduled for 15 September. In briefing the airmen of 9 Wing he was full of aggressive fire: 'No German machines could be allowed near enough to the lines for any observation. We must shoot all Hun machines at sight and give them no rest. Our bombers should make life a burden on the enemy lines of communication. Infantry and transport were to be worried, whenever possible, by machine-gun fire from above. Machines would be detailed for contact work with our infantry. Reconnaissance jobs were to be completed at all costs, if there seemed the slightest chance of bringing back useful information.'[60]

When it came to the actual attack at Flers-Courcelette the RFC emphasized even more than usual the necessity of silencing the enemy artillery. Corps

---

* RFC airmen, immersed in the tense day-to-day struggle on the Western Front, tended to take a jaundiced view of the RNAS and its 'easier' life. Don Brophy, while on leave in London from his work with 21 Squadron, set down in his diary impressions which were not untypical of RFC thinking. The RNAS, he wrote, was known in the RFC as the Hot Air Service; its pilots 'receive military crosses if they fly in winter weather ... They have an enormous mess in the [Crystal] Palace, and sit down when they drink the King's Health ... The place was alive with Naval youths, whom I scorned and classed with the Army Service Corps ... They sure have a nice place at the Crystal Palace, but it is not war.' Diary, 21 Aug. 1916, J.B. Brophy biographical file, DHist

machines took part in more than a hundred counter-battery shoots and success-fully directed the guns to numerous other targets. For the first time field as well as heavy artillery was included in 'zone' or area calls, a method by which aircraft could bring down concentrated fire upon important targets. Area calls were used repeatedly to direct fire against hostile batteries and targets of opportunity. For example, Second Lieutenant Norman Goudie of Kamloops, BC, flying one of 34 Squadron's artillery patrols with his British pilot, sent four area calls during a flight of over three hours: one against a hostile battery, two against enemy transport, and one against 'guns moving off towards LE SARS.' Goudie reported 'good shooting,' and, as all observers on this day were careful to do, the specific location of a 'tank with red flag' seen near Martinpuich. There were very few reports by artillery aircraft of failure to make and hold contact with the guns, nor do interruptions from hostile machines appear to have been frequent. Despite this, German artillery fire remained heavy throughout the day, a testimony to German skill in siting and masking their batteries.[61]

For the whole of the RFC 15 September was a day of maximum effort. Never since the war had begun had so many operational hours been flown and so many combats taken place on a single day. Never had so much emphasis been placed upon aerial reporting of the course of the battle. At the time of the initial assault corps squadrons provided two contact patrols and continued such patrols through-out the day, while Army and GHQ staffs were directly served by special patrols. Even before the attack was launched Lieutenant A.M. Thomas of Toronto, with his observer, was flying a dawn patrol for 22 Squadron and reported 'intense artillery activity' and 'big explosions' at Martinpuich and Courcelette. In addition to Thomas' early patrol, the FE2bs carried out a photo reconnaissance between 0930 and 1130 hrs. One of the photographic machines was flown by Captain W.R.C. Da Costa of Toronto, while Captains C.M. Clement of Vancouver and W.L. Scandrett of London, Ont., flew two of the three escorting aircraft. Clement's proba-tionary observer was J.K. Campbell of Scotsburn, NS, a corporal in a divisional signals unit. While this reconnaissance was in progress, another observer on proba-tion, Private J.S. Williams of the Canadian Army Service Corps, was flying a line patrol with a British pilot. Williams reported that he dropped four bombs on Le Sars. Then, as his pilot let down, he 'fired on small parties of men from 2000 ft. over Le Sars and East Thiepval.' Major C.S. Duffus concluded what was, for this period of the war, a remarkable degree of participation by Canadians in the work of a single squadron by carrying out a mid-afternoon patrol and reporting slight enemy air activity.[62]

Such work, repeated all along the line, ensured that commanders and staffs were more abundantly and accurately informed than ever before. Contact patrols had been particularly successful. The infantry used flares much more intelligently (though it was reported that some isolated advanced parties had done so too freely) and Klaxon horns were now in general use. Observers could identify troops at distances up to 700 feet and in good light could ascertain trench occupation at heights up to 2000 feet. Aircraft were plainly making some headway in dispelling the fog of battle; the 2nd Canadian Division, for example, reported flatly that the position of its most advanced troops during the attack had been established only through intelligence from contact patrol aircraft.[63]

German regimental histories confirm that the RFC held sway over the battle-field, not only on 15 September but during the preparatory phase prior to the attack and for a period following it. The 211th Reserve Regiment, which went into the line opposite the Canadians in the Pozières sector on 7 September, dis-covered that on the first morning in their new position 'swarms of planes are passing over our trenches.' The infantry reacted with small arms fire, but this brought 'heavy artillery fire on our lines.' From earlier experience on the Somme the regiment had become almost fatalistically resigned to enemy air dominance: '... even when later on our own planes take to the air to free us from our disagree-able tormentors, the British reconnaissance planes do not allow themselves to be disturbed, but strong enemy defensive formations pounce on our airmen who cannot dare to become seriously embroiled with such superior forces. This we had to endure all summer; from early to late enemy planes continuously overhead, watching every movement; work on the trenches as well as all arrivals and depar-tures. Disgusting! Nerve-shattering!'[64]

Another German unit on the Canadian front, the 209th Reserve Regiment, found that on 13 September enemy artillery fire on Thiepval was extremely heavy, but that the German guns were 'firing blindfolded' in reply because ranging from the air was impossible. 'Our own airmen must remain satisfied with keeping the enemy long-distance planes in check.' On 14 and 15 September 'droves' of RFC machines attacked the regiment's trenches and dug-out entrances with machine-gun fire. Misconstruing the work of trench patrol aircraft, the regimental history conjectured that 'apparently they are directing the artillery fire too, for from time to time they are giving signals with the [Klaxon] hooter.'[65]

Yet the period of RFC ascendancy was even then coming to an end. The begin-nings of German resurgence in the air can be traced to the appearance of such good German fighters as the Roland and the Halberstadt. These aircraft had started to take a toll of the weaker RFC squadrons not long after the Somme battle had begun. For example, 60 Squadron, equipped with obsolete Morane Parasols and biplanes, had lost its squadron commander, two flight commanders, three pilots, and two observers, as well as several others wounded between 1 July and 3 August.* Lieutenant-Colonel Hugh Dowding, who commanded the wing that included this squadron, and who was one of the few officers of his rank who still flew on operations, asked that the unit be temporarily withdrawn into reserve. Trenchard took the unusual step for him of resting the squadron, observing that 'They have a very difficult machine to fly, and I think a rest from work is abso-lutely necessary.' But Dowding's approach left him uneasy and in a letter to Sefton Brancker he stigmatized Dowding as a 'dismal Jimmy' whom he proposed to replace as soon as that could be conveniently arranged.† When 60 Squadron returned to action it had been partly re-equipped with a very good single-seater, the French-designed Nieuport 17. This fast scout, with a top speed of 107 mph, mounted a single machine-gun firing forward over the top plane.[66]

---

* Among the casualties was Lieutenant J.A.N. Ormsby of Danville, Que., who died of his wounds after being shot down on 2 August.
† Dowding was posted to the Home Establishment six weeks later. In 1940 he was to lead Fighter Command in the Battle of Britain, before being unceremoniously dumped once again.

The Nieuport had a useful life as a first-line fighter, especially in the hands of pilots like W.A. Bishop. Other things being equal, however, it was outclassed by the Albatros D-I, which first reached the front in early September. The Albatros was an important, almost revolutionary, advance in aircraft design; the fuselage was of semi-monocoque construction, being formed of plywood bent into place around the longerons, and except for its awkward, box-like radiators, from the tip of its large spinner to its rounded tail surfaces the Albatros was sleekly tapered and streamlined. It was also the most powerful fighter in existence, its engine (either the 150-hp Benz or the 160-hp Mercedes) giving it a top speed of 109 mph. This power plant made it possible for the Albatros to mount twin Spandaus firing forward through the propeller arc. Previously only the Roland had successfully carried such armament; attempts to mount twin machine-guns on the Halberstadt and Fokker D-IIIs and IVs had failed.[67]

The Albatros, through its successive modifications, remained the standard German fighter for the rest of the war, though it was later eclipsed by the Fokker D-VII. The Albatros D-I, however, did not immediately sweep the skies clear of DH2s and FE2ds. Though in most respects far superior to these aircraft, its weight, power plant, and armament combined to give it a wing loading of 8 pounds per square foot as against 5.5 for the DH2 and 5.7 for the FE2b.* Consequently, it could not turn nearly as sharply, and their superior agility, larger numbers, and aggressive tactics meant that RFC fighter pilots could still often hold their own in dogfights.

Indeed, more than new aircraft was needed to correct the imbalance in the air. The High Command, according to the German official history, had recognized that a chief characteristic of the Somme battle was 'the extraordinary increase in importance of the air force to the battle on the ground ... Control of the air over the battlefield had now become imperative for success.' Even before the team of Hindenburg and Ludendorff replaced Falkenhayn at the end of August, steps to reorganize the air arm had already been taken. The shake-up thus begun ultimately culminated, on 8 October, in the establishment of the German air force, with Ernst von Hoeppner as its Commanding General.[68]

The single most significant innovation was the decision to distinguish air fighting units from 'working aeroplanes' carrying out artillery co-operation, reconnaissance, and other duties. This development had, of course, long been anticipated by the British and French flying services. The new fighter units, called *Jagdstaffeln (Jastas)*, were slightly smaller than an RFC squadron, having an establishment of fourteen aircraft. Seven had been formed in late August and early September, the first, *Jasta 2*, under the command of the redoubtable Oswald Boelcke.

Before the Somme campaign dragged to its close in November, German technological superiority, revised organization, and better tactics had put an end to the superiority of the RFC and had given the German air force a lead it did not relinquish until the arrival of the Sopwith Camel and the SE5a, well into 1917. The German resurgence in the air, however, made itself felt only gradually, not only

* The Albatros D-II had a larger wing area and weighed slightly less than the D-I, reducing the wing loading factor to 7.4.

because the RFC still had the advantage of numbers as well as skilful and determined airmen, but also because faulty German air dispositions took time to correct and because the new Albatros types were not available in quantity until late autumn. Although transfer of air units from the Verdun front had begun in early September, by the end of that month there were still only three *Jastas* in the Somme area to assist twenty-three reconnaissance and artillery flights and sixteen bomber-fighter squadrons. By the middle of October, however, almost six hundred machines had been concentrated on the Somme front. Most were still C types, but nearly a hundred Albatros D-Is and D-IIs were now in service.[69]

The steady rise in German air strength can be traced in the casualties of RFC corps squadrons during the last two months of the Somme battle. In the week following the limited gains of 15 September, as the Fourth and Reserve Armies struggled, without much success, to advance the line, the RFC continued its work according to the pattern established on the first day of the battle. But losses in the air were the heaviest since the first week in July, and included five Canadians.*[70]

Desperate ground fighting continued throughout October and the last convulsions of the Somme battle came between 13 and 19 November, when the Fifth Army captured Beaumont-Hamel and Beaucourt. During this period corps squadron work was spotty, partly because of the deteriorating weather, partly because corps aircraft were having to fight to get their job done. On 9 October, for example, Lieutenant R.H. Jarvis of Toronto, flying an artillery patrol near Loupart Wood for 4 Squadron, was attacked from above by an enemy aircraft. Jarvis turned to fight, 'but at that moment the BE2c was hit by an A.A. shell which severed the aileron control wire and made several holes in machine.' His British observer was stunned when hit on the head by a piece of shell, but the two managed to return safely. On 17 October Jarvis was once more attacked by 'two Rolands with wings coloured brown with green blotches and with blue crosses.' Though he succeeded in repelling the attack, his shoot was disrupted; he noted in his report that 'None of our machines were in the vicinity at the time.' Similarly, on 20 October, Lieutenant F.W. Carter of Orillia, Ont., flying a photographic mission in the Miraumont sector for 15 Squadron, was attacked by six biplanes, one 'faster than the rest.'[71]

On the same day, in precisely the same area, Second Lieutenant W.M.V. Cotton, until very recently a driver in the Canadian Army Service Corps, and his British pilot from 7 Squadron, were attacked by five Rolands while engaged on a counter-battery shoot. The two defended themselves stoutly. Cotton described the action: 'The five H.A. ... turned and dived upon us, 2 of the machines opening fire at about 500 yards. I did not reply until they were within 150 yards, and opened fire on the leading machine who immediately turned North on a steep bank. Then I emptied about 25 rounds into him and immediately emptied the remainder of the

---

* These were D. Cushing of Montreal from 2 Squadron (POW 16 Sept.); W.M. Kent of Bathurst, NB (WIA 24 Sept.) from 7 Squadron; 11 Squadron's H. Thompson of Port Arthur, Ont., who died of his wounds on 18 September; E.S. Duggan of Toronto (WIA 17 Sept.) from 21 Squadron; and W.J. Gray of Weyburn, Sask., captured while flying with 22 Squadron on 21 September.

drum into the second machine which had turned South. The first machine made a steep nose-dive for about 1000′ and then glided down apparently under control to the ground at about G7a. I could not see whether the enemy machine was damaged on landing.'[72] From these and similar incidents it is evident that RFC fighter squadrons were no longer able to provide the same measure of security to corps aircraft that they had done earlier in the year.

The ground forces were quick to notice the change in the air environment. During October the strafing of troops by low-flying German aircraft had become more and more frequent. On 7 October a Canadian battalion commander who only three weeks before had extolled the virtues of the RFC observed that 'Our aircraft were not as bold or efficient as usual.' During the Fourth Army attack of 23 October, despite dense fog and low clouds, German aircraft flew low over XIV Corps with no rejoinder from the RFC. On 9 November Trenchard attempted to take the pressure off by the bombing of enemy rear areas.[73] The device was not a success, as the RFC communiqué made clear: 'A bombing raid of the 3rd Brigade consisting of 16 bombing machines and an escort of 14 was attacked on its way to Vraucourt by at least 30 Germans, chiefly fast scouts. The enemy attacked from the front, and our scouts dived and got to close quarters with them. As the fight progressed the escort got gradually below the bombing machines. Meanwhile the enemy was reinforced and the bombers were attacked from both sides. Numerous individual fights ensued.'[74] Two BE2cs and two DH2s failed to return and three other escorting aircraft were damaged and members of their crew killed or wounded.

As the record of air fighting from mid-September to the end of the year demonstrates, the German *Jastas* only gradually established their superiority, and, at least in 1916, never obtained the degree of dominance the RFC had enjoyed earlier in the Somme battle. German tactics were less aggressive than those of the RFC, and the Germans never established the kind of numerical superiority that would have enabled them to blanket the efforts of a stubborn opponent. The combat reports of RFC pilots, however, make clear that not only had the air war entered a new phase, but that the pilots themselves were fully conscious that technically they had become the underdogs. On 17 September Boelcke blooded *Jasta 2* in spectacular fashion; before their guns 11 Squadron alone lost four FE2bs and 12 Squadron two BE2cs. Also suffering were 23, 27, and 70 Squadrons. A patrol of five DH2s from 24 Squadron, including the Canadians A.G. Knight and H.A. Wood of Toronto, had a tantalizing encounter with fast enemy scouts over the Bapaume-Peronne road. They repeatedly attempted to close with the Germans, but were 'unable to get to close range' except in the case of a single aircraft surprised by Wood and another pilot, which then 'completely outclimbed and outpaced' the de Havillands.[75]

After a day of poor weather Boelcke was in the air again on the 19th. FE2bs of 11 Squadron, escorted by 60 Squadron's Nieuports, were unable to complete a reconnaissance to Quéant, turning back after a running fight of some duration. Two FE2bs of 18 Squadron photographing the lines were repeatedly attacked; one was shot down near Flers. Their escorts, four DH2s from 24 Squadron whose pilots included Knight and Wood, fought for three hours, Wood having to make a forced landing. The tempo of this day's fighting was caught by a German anti-aircraft officer at Achiet-le-Petit. He saw seven German biplanes in formation join battle with a large formation over Irles. The British machines seemed to be 'attempting to form squadrons and chains and to seek greater heights ... in curves, the red-blue streamers of their leading airplanes clearly visible.' The German aircraft outclimbed their opponents and then dove into their midst, while other pilots, attracted by the *mêlée*, hastened to take part. 'To the observer,' he wrote, 'it looks like a sensational moving picture being run off too fast. Here and there aircraft coming down in flames, others, rendered rudderless ... slithering down awkwardly.' Trenchard's personal directive to RFC airmen, issued this same day, was expostulatory but from the point of view of the combat pilot not particularly helpful: '... driving hostile machines away from our line is not sufficient. The pursuit and destruction of hostile machines must be carried out with the greatest vigour.'[76]

That is exactly what Lieutenant C.L. Bath of Toronto and Second Lieutenant G.H. Bonnell of Halifax attempted to do on the 22nd, when flying as part of a 32 Squadron offensive patrol in the Flers-Le Transloy-Le Sars area. Bath spent the better part of two hours trying to catch up with three patrolling German fighters, but could neither overtake them nor reach their altitude. Bonnell, on the other hand, may well have shot down one of three German scouts he encountered attacking an FE2b, but a later attempt to pursue two German fighters returning to base ended in failure: 'They were very fast, and got away.'[77] The next day Trenchard conceded that the new German aircraft were faster than anything the RFC had. For the 24th, therefore, turning to quantity in the absence of quality, he ordered sixty aircraft to attempt the destruction of the new types in the Cambrai area, where they had been particularly active. The luck of some of the Canadians on this sweep was typical of the day's results: C.J. Creery of 21 Squadron got off a few rounds at a pair of German fighters and some LVGs, without result; H. Spanner of 27 Squadron had a brush with another fighter at 13,500 feet, again without result; Second Lieutenant J.S. Williams of Vancouver, an observer with 22 Squadron, was credited, together with his pilot, with the destruction of a Fokker *Eindekker*. Aside from this museum piece, and vague claims of other victories, the RFC had little to show for the operation; moreover, they lost two outclassed BE12s and suffered other casualties. If this was an attempt to recapture the initiative, it was a distinct failure.[78]

There were still victories to be had. On 20 October Lieutenant F.S. Rankin, a 1914 RMC graduate from Woodstock, NB, who had joined 18 Squadron in May, was flying an FE2b patrol near Le Sars with his British pilot when their aircraft was attacked by 'White biplanes. Very fast. Looked like Rolands.' They engaged at least four enemy aircraft in a fight that spiralled from 10,000 feet to 2,000 feet; after Rankin had emptied a drum at one enemy machine 'it was observed to descend steeply and crash in a shell hole ...'[79] Most days, however, were more like 22 October. On a dawn patrol Second Lieutenant C.M. Clement of Vancouver and his British observer, together with another 22 Squadron FE2b over Sailly Saillisel, easily drove off four Fokker E-IIIs, but then were attacked by 'two small brown machines which dived on us in front and endeavoured to get on our tail.' Despite the assistance of some DH2s the enemy fighters proved a handful. As Clement reported, one of them 'began manœuvring very quickly and by a good stall succeeded in getting above us. The engagement then became very close, the H.A. attempting to get on our tail and we endeavouring to prevent it ... It did some very good shooting and was so quick that it succeeded in keeping behind and to the sides of us most of the time.' By this time Clement was down to 800 feet over Le Transloy and running for home; he finally landed at 9 Squadron's airfield instead because 'the machine was considerably shot about.' Later the same day Haligonian G.H. Bonnell and four companions from 32 Squadron were on offensive patrol when their DH2s were attacked by overwhelming numbers of Rolands, Albatroses, and 'German Nieuports.'*[80]

During the afternoon Rankin and his British pilot, F.L. Barnard, were embroiled in a series of fights while escorting a photo reconnaissance mission. Barnard reported:

When escorting a camera machine over BAPAUME we attacked one of several H.A. which were in the neighbourhood of camera machine ... Shortly after two more appeared above us ... When these had been driven off we turned for home ... but found three more H.A. on our tail ... The observer put one drum into one which was passing straight over our heads at very close range, and this machine immediately became out of control, the tail and back of fuselage being on fire. It went down in a spin. The remaining two H.A. were now firing from behind and the observer stood up to get a shot at them ... one more H.A. was seen to go down in a nose dive with smoke from its engine ... The observer was still firing when he was hit in the head and fell sideways over the side of the nacelle. I managed to catch his coat as he was falling, and by getting in the front seat pulled him back. I then got back in the pilot's seat. The engine and most of the controls had been shot but I managed to get the machine over our lines and landed 200 yards behind our front line ...[81]

Rankin had been wounded before, on 1 September; this time his wound proved fatal. The same day three Sopwith 1½ Strutters of 45 Squadron failed to return from their first offensive patrol; among them was Second Lieutenant W.H.F. Fullerton of Edmonton.[82]

The factors which brought the eclipse of the RFC's fighter superiority can be summarized in the combat experience of a single pilot, Alan Duncan Bell-Irving. In 1915, as we have seen, he had spent three months as an observer with 7 Squadron; after being wounded he had trained as a pilot in England and joined 60 Squadron in April 1916. By August he was a thoroughly experienced and combat-wise pilot, certainly one of the ablest on his squadron, but no battle skills could turn the Morane scout into an aircraft capable of dealing with the newer enemy types. On 28 August (his birthday) Bell-Irving flew his last mission in a Morane, a dispiriting one in which he was unable to come to grips with three German aircraft he encountered. By 14 September he was flying a Nieuport 17, a great improve-

---

* The German Siemens-Schuckert D-1 was a direct copy of the Nieuport 17, and was often called the German Nieuport by the RFC.

ment over the Morane but still not capable of meeting the best enemy machines on equal terms.[83]

Bell-Irving was one of the first pilots to employ the new 'compass stations' designed to direct patrolling fighters upon enemy aircraft from the ground. While flying near Grandcourt on 22 September he 'observed BEAUMETZ arrow in position ... I followed it and observed a hostile machine ...' Diving on the machine, which he identified as a Roland, he found it to be faster than the Nieuport. The next day, however, while escorting a bombing formation, he managed to close to within twenty yards of a Roland and after opening fire was able to see it crash to the ground. His squadron commander, Major Smith-Barry, confirmed another Roland which Bell-Irving shot down on 30 September. By this time he had had several frustrating experiences with Albatros D-Is or IIs; 'with their noses only slightly down they were faster' than his Nieuport, he reported.[84]

By late October Bell-Irving, like his fellow fighter-pilots, was finding the strain great. An encounter with Roland scouts on 21 October must have added to the stress. While escorting FE2bs and BE2cs south of Arras, he turned to engage the enemy fighters:

After firing about 8 rounds my gun stopped ... and I was temporarily unable to rectify it. I turned west, and climbed, trying to put the gun right and reach another Nieuport which was higher & further west. The H.A. turned and out climbed me so I put my nose down to get over the lines. A bullet then hit my tank and I stopped up one of the holes with my hand, having to leave the gun. The H.A. shot away a flying wire and damaged my planes on the right side so that my machine became uncontrollable. After falling for some distance I regained partial control with my engine off and full rudder and aileron. I glided across the lines without directional control at about 100 feet, landing between front and support lines. I jumped clear as the machine ran into a trench and turned over.[85]

On 9 November he was shot down once again, this time while endeavouring to fend off a swarm of Halberstadt fighters bent on attacking a bombing formation of BE2cs. During the fierce engagement bullets from a German aircraft set his Very light cartridges afire; he spun his Nieuport to 200 feet over Le Transloy to extinguish the blaze and landed just behind the trenches. 'Sometime during the fighting,' Smith-Barry reported, 'Lieut. Bell-Irving was wounded in both legs.' It was the end of his combat flying.[86]

The loss to the RFC of such experienced and able pilots as Bell-Irving was now a frequent occurrence. A short time before, however, the German air force had received a heavier blow. On 28 October Knight and McKay were on an afternoon patrol between Pozières and Bapaume when they were attacked by six Halberstadts. As the fight developed six Albatros D-Is and IIs of *Jasta 2* joined in. The two Canadians found themselves in desperate straits, and they had to make the most of the DH2's agility:

The H.A. dived in turn on to the de H's tail, but the de H. promptly turned sharply under the H.A., which usually switched on and climbed again. The de H's were very careful to avoid diving straight at any H.A. that presented tempting targets, but fired short bursts as

H.A. came into their sights. It was after about 5 minutes of strenuous fighting that two H.A. collided. One dived at Lt. Knight, who turned left handed. The H.A. zoomed right handed, and its left wing collided with the right wing of another H.A. which had started to dive on Lt. Knight. Bits were seen to fall off; only one H.A. was seen to go down, and it glided away east apparently under control, but was very shortly lost to sight as the de H's were too heavily engaged to watch it.[87]

Surprisingly, the German fighters broke off the engagement and McKay and Knight were able to return to base. The damaged Albatros had been flown by Oswald Boelcke; it crashed behind German lines. Boelcke's death was an accident of war, coming at a moment when German aerial superiority could hardly have been more convincingly demonstrated.

By this time the Germans had also gone some way towards correcting the numerical imbalance which had existed for most of the Somme campaign, while the RFC was suffering from an apparent inability to concentrate its forces effectively. RFC strength on the Somme in October (including III Brigade) was 328 serviceable aeroplanes, as opposed to 333 with the German First Army. North of the Somme, the RFC on 22 October had 175 aeroplanes with I and II Brigades, and at least ninety more were with the RNAS at Dunkirk. In addition, there were a few Belgian air units north of II Brigade. Facing these allied aircraft were 101 machines with the GAF and a few others with Marine Korps units (under naval command). Similar disparities may be noted on the French front. With the German Second Army, facing the French Sixth Army, there were 207 aircraft and there were 244 more between this sector and the Swiss border. Opposed to them there were purportedly over 1400 French machines, although most were obsolescent. Despite being out-numbered by nearly three to one, the Germans enjoyed unchallenged air supremacy over a good part of the French-held front by late September. The RFC could look for no help from the French.[88]

From early September General Haig and RFC Headquarters had begun to press the home authorities for reinforcements. In turn, the War Office applied pressure to the Admiralty despite the fact that fifty-six fighters had already been turned over by the RNAS to the RFC. On 18 September the Admiralty drew the line: '... having regard to the heavy demands which have been made on the Royal Naval Air Service for supplying machines to Russia and to the British Expeditionary Force in France, they regret that it is not possible at the present time to supply the machines asked for.' What the Admiralty neglected to mention was the fact that 3 (Naval) Wing at Luxeuil, already possessing fifty aircraft, was to be expanded to two hundred by the spring of 1917. Moreover, the War Office was not only aware of, but also objected to, the direct negotiations between the Admiralty and French military authorities which had created the Luxeuil establishment.[89] The RFC's reinforcement crisis, and the navy's intransigence, had already caused Sir David Henderson to write with unwonted bitterness to Haig: 'I have put forward the request to the Admiralty very reluctantly, for throughout the whole war we have never got much value out of any attempt at securing their co-operation, and sometimes the attempts have had only unpleasant and useless results. If the Admiralty comply with this request I fear you may be sorry afterwards. You had some experience of the Naval Air Service at the beginning of the war, and take it all round, I do not think it has improved much since then.'[90] At an earlier stage Trenchard as well as Henderson had been reluctant to accept RNAS squadrons, fearing that he might not have proper control of them and that their provision might prevent the acquisition of new RFC squadrons. Naturally, Admiralty concerns paralleled those of Trenchard: they feared loss of control over their units, a possible threat to their long-range bombing plans, and, more particularly, the hampering of Vice-Admiral Bacon's operations at Dunkirk.[91]

That good machines were available from Dunkirk was known to the Air Board, possibly through Commodore Sueter. Haig took up the cause with the Chief of the Imperial General Staff, Sir William Robertson, warning that unless a dramatic expansion in RFC strength took place shortly the aerial situation might be completely out of hand by the spring. Thereafter matters moved quickly. Trenchard shortly heard directly from Wing Captain Lambe, commanding RNAS forces at Dunkirk, that he and Rear-Admiral Vaughan-Lee were planning the transfer of a complete unit to the RFC. The loan of a squadron from Dunkirk 'as a temporary measure' was approved by the War Committee on 18 October; three days later the War Office informed Haig that 8 (Naval) Squadron was to be sent to Trenchard. By a process of compromise and persistence airmen in both flying services had contrived to overcome service shibboleths and to make possible the concentration of previously unavailable forces. One outcome of their efforts was the Admiralty's authorization for Lambe to co-operate directly with Trenchard.[92]

Naval Eight came into existence on 26 October and on 3 November began operations from Vert Galand, attached to V Brigade. The pilots in this squadron were selected for their experience in fighter aircraft and six were Canadians. One of them, Flight Sub-Lieutenant D.M.B. Galbraith, was the first in the squadron to be credited with a victory, which took place on 10 November. Of the six, four had attended the Curtiss School in Toronto. Galbraith was one of that remarkable group to come out of Carleton Place, the small Ontario town that sent so many of its sons to fly in the European war. He had already won the Distinguished Service Cross and was to win further decorations before his combat career was over. At the end of the war he was credited with fourteen victories. Flight Sub-Lieutenant E.R. Grange of Toronto was also to win the DSC before being wounded in January 1917 and Flight Sub-Lieutenant G.E. Harvey of Edmonton gained the same decoration the following year. Other Canadian members of Naval Eight were Flight Sub-Lieutenants A.H.S. Lawson of Little Current, Ont., G. Thom of Merritt, BC, and S.V. Trapp of New Westminster, BC. Between 9 November and 26 December these Canadians were involved in about twenty combats. All but two of them were carried out in Sopwith Pups, a fine fighter with an operational ceiling of close to 18,000 feet and a low wing loading that made it highly manoeuvrable even at great heights.*[93]

---

*   The Pup got its name when General Brancker first saw it alongside the large 1½ Strutter. 'That they had come from the same stable was obvious. "Good God!" said Brancker, "Your 1½ Strutter has had a pup!" And Pup it was ever after, capturing the affection of all who flew it with flying qualities of such exceptional standard that fighter pilots ... recollected it as "The perfect flying machine" ...' But the Pups had some teething problems, the most serious of which was

The RFC had also acquired two other fighter squadrons in late October, 45 Squadron with Sopwith 1½ Strutters and 41 Squadron with FE8s. But GHQ continued to demand further reinforcement. As Haig wrote on 16 November, '... in order to get information and to allow artillery machines to carry on their work, it is becoming more and more necessary for the fighting squadrons to be in strength in the air the whole day.' When in June Haig had forecast RFC requirements, he had asked for twenty-three corps squadrons, twenty-four fighter squadrons (four with each army and four with GHQ), and nine reconnaissance squadrons (one for each army and four with GHQ). In November there were nineteen corps squadrons, thirteen army squadrons, and four GHQ squadrons in the order of battle, a shortfall of twenty. Now Haig asked for yet another twenty fighter squadrons.[94]

Fighter operations had become the crucial role of air forces, for without the local air superiority granted by successful fighter actions the essential work of the corps squadrons could not be carried out. The Somme had taught this lesson both to the RFC and the GAF; moreover, both high commands had come to realize the vital importance of the air weapon to the ground battle. The immense casualties to both sides that were suffered in the ground battle overshadowed the air operations. Yet miniscule though they were in comparison to the vast losses of the armies, the wastage rate of the RFC was at least as great as that of the ground forces.

Corps squadrons suffered less than army and headquarters squadrons, another way of saying that despite mounting German opposition RFC fighter squadrons were doing their job. Most RFC casualties from June to December occurred over the Somme battlefront. There were 583 casualties in all; of these sixty-five are known to have been Canadian (32 killed, 21 wounded, and 12 captured). Only a third of the Canadian casualties were members of corps squadron. Of the forty-four Canadian casualties in army and headquarters squadrons, 75 per cent occurred over the Somme battlefield. For Canadians, the worst single week was that of 20 to 27 October, when six Canadians (only one with a corps squadron) were killed.[95]

Between June and December at least 240 Canadians flew at the front, though at the end of the year there were probably no more than 130 remaining in front-line squadrons. In the coming year their ranks were greatly to be swelled, both from the RNAS and by new products from the RFC training schools, especially RFC Canada. The situation facing these fresh arrivals was to be very different from the predominance the RFC obtained in the opening weeks of the Somme offensive. Not until the last stages of the war were the British again to establish a comparable ascendancy; 1917 was to be a year of bitter struggle in the air waged by greatly expanding air forces in which the Germans yielded only slowly and grudgingly the margin of superiority they had so convincingly seized by the end of 1916.

described by E.R. Grange. When closing upon an adversary it was necessary to throttle down to prevent over-shooting, but this slowed down the rate of fire. The solution eventually arrived at was to place a double cam on the gun, making it fire twice for every rotation of the propellor. Harald Penrose, *British Aviation: the Great War and Armistice 1915–1919* (London 1969), 112; 'Notes by Sub Lieutenant Grange,' Air 1/73/15/9/158

14

Stalemate on the Western Front, 1917

In allied planning for the renewal of the offensive on the Western Front in 1917 *Général* Robert Nivelle was the key figure. His effective use of artillery to achieve deep penetration in counter-attacks at Verdun had vaulted him into the command formerly held by Joffre. In his spring offensive Nivelle proposed to make his main thrust on the Aisne River using all available French resources and spoke of breaking the enemy front within forty-eight hours. This blow was to be preceded by a diversionary attack astride the Scarpe River by the British Third Army, which would link up later with the French in the region of Cambrai. North of the Scarpe the Canadian Corps, part of the British First Army, was to seize Vimy Ridge.

There were, however, conflicting portents. Before the attack began on 9 April revolution in Russia and the declared belligerency of the United States had altered the strategic balance in as yet incalculable ways. More immediately, Nivelle declined to heed warnings by Major-General Trenchard, and probably du Peuty as well, that he could not count on air superiority as had been provided at the Somme. Nevertheless, despite requests that he delay his plans or at least limit his objectives, Nivelle's confidence, which had mesmerized the politicians, remained unshaken; the offensive would destroy the German armies and bring an early end to the war.[1]

Nivelle's plan was based on concentrating artillery in overwhelming force. The French were in the process of doubling their ordnance production. In the British Expeditionary Force the number of heavy guns and howitzers, generally those above 4.5-inch calibre, had grown from 761 in July 1916 to 1157 in November and was expected to double again by the end of March.[2] With these means at his disposal Nivelle's tactical approach set the allied offensive pattern for operations during the first half of 1917, including the forthcoming battles of Arras and Vimy, the Second Battle of the Aisne and Messines. It laid a great responsibility on the air arm; as the Somme had shown, the effective use of heavy artillery concentrations was largely dependent upon airborne target spotting and fire control. Successful artillery co-operation required command of the air.

Control of the air was equally important to the Germans. Retaining the superiority which they had established by the end of the Somme campaign in order to curtail the effectiveness of observation aircraft was a major factor in the enemy's plan for countering allied artillery. In addition, the Germans abandoned the policy of desperately defending every foot of ground. Rather, front-line positions were thinned out and the defence was based on strong reserve forces ready to counter-attack when allied formations had outdistanced the support provided by the main body of their artillery.[3]

The new system of defence was implemented as part of a larger plan which provided for withdrawal in March 1917 to the heavily defended Hindenburg Line, some twenty miles east of the old Somme front. The shortened line eliminated two large salients, one between Arras and Bapaume, the other between Peronne and Soissons. The position was hinged on Vimy Ridge, the great bastion north of Arras which linked the Hindenburg Line to the defences in Belgium and barred the approach of the Allies to the industrial centres of Lens and Lille. The withdrawal inevitably had an adverse effect upon German morale, but militarily it undercut the strategic justification for Nivelle's offensive at one stroke.

Allied air operations during Operation *Alberich*, the German withdrawal to the Hindenburg Line, were not notably effective either in providing useful intelligence or in disrupting the enemy's plans. In October 1916 reconnaissance aircraft of the Royal Flying Corps had reported that new trenches were being dug far behind the front lines but bad weather which prevailed throughout much of the winter hampered efforts to obtain more certain intelligence. Not until late February was the shape of the new line apparent. Even then, however, the Allies found it difficult to accept that the Germans would voluntarily abandon any of their hard-won territory. On 4 March, when the withdrawal was well under way, Lieutenant-Colonel C.L.N. Newall, commanding 9 (HQ) Wing, was ordered to reconnoitre the new German line and obtain air photos 'if possible.' That same day 18 Squadron, from V Brigade,* successfully photographed suspected lines in German rear areas and two days later six Sopwiths of 9 Wing's 70 Squadron[†] also obtained photographs. Other flights followed, although casualties were heavy. On 14 March the full German intentions were revealed when their detailed plans for the withdrawal and rearguard defences were found in a captured dug-out. Four days later a general advance began and six allied armies closed up to the shrinking German front.[4]

Throughout this period British commanders gave only part of their attention to the German withdrawal; their prime concern was their own offensive, scheduled to begin on 9 April. The concentration of the air arm for the assault, in fact, took place while the Germans were withdrawing, and it presented certain difficulties. By early 1917 the Germans had formed 37 *Jagdstaffeln*, equipped with Albatros D-Is and IIs, Rolands and Halberstadts which had proven so effective in late 1916, and also with Albatros D-IIIs. The latter preserved the best characteristics of the earlier designs and, in addition, borrowing deliberately from the Nieuport 17, had a new wing and strut configuration which much improved visibility from the cockpit.

---

* Canadians with 18 Squadron at this time included J.T. Anglin of Toronto (WIA 28 April 1917), J.F. Ferguson of Regina (WIA 26 Feb. 1917), V.H. Huston and W.F. Lees, both of Vancouver, W.F. MacDonald of Crooked River, Sask. (KIA 23 May 1917), E.G. Rowley of Guelph, Ont. (KIA 6 July 1917), J.R. Smith, address unknown (WIA 29 April 1917), and M.T. Trotter of Montreal (WIA 1 June 1917).

† Although more than one hundred Canadians served with 70 Squadron in the course of the war, only one, Captain G.C. Easton of Galt, Ont., was with the squadron at this time.

These 'veestrutters,' as British pilots termed them, now appeared in increasing numbers and were to take a heavy toll of allied aircraft during the first part of the year. Many of Richthofen's victories during this period were won while flying his red Albatros D-III.[5]

At the turn of the year the RFC had thirty-nine squadrons available for operations on the Western Front, but only twelve were classed as suitable for escort work, offensive patrols, and general air combat. Only five of these, equipped with Nieuport 17s and Sopwith Pups, were capable of meeting the German *Jastas* on anything like even terms. Trenchard had been promised eleven additional fighter squadrons by March, but as of 10 February none had arrived. On learning from Sir David Henderson that he could expect no more than two by the scheduled date, he wrote to General L.E. Kiggell, Haig's Chief of Staff, explaining once more the gravity of the situation: 'There is no possibility of improving matters before operations are likely to commence, and, in view of the hostile aerial activity now being disclosed, our fighting machines will almost certainly be inferior in number and quite certainly in performance to those of the enemy. The success of our aerial offensive will consequently be very seriously jeopardized, and we cannot therefore hope that our Corps machines will be able to accomplish their work as successfully or with as few casualties as during the battle of the SOMME.'[6]

The one bright spot in the supply problem was the assistance provided by the Royal Naval Air Service. By the end of 1916 the Board of Admiralty had formally approved Trenchard's request for four additional naval squadrons on the Western Front. He already had 8 (Naval) at his disposal, and the others arrived at intervals between February and May. Three of the squadrons, Nos 1, 8, and 10, were equipped with Sopwith Triplanes. The triplane structure gave the pilot a wide field of vision, an exceptional rate of climb, and an extremely manœuvrable aircraft, capable of attaining a speed of 117 mph. Unfortunately for the RFC the Triplane was flown operationally only by the RNAS.*[7]

It was through the naval squadrons that Canadians made some of their most significant contributions in the spring offensive. Pride of service made the naval authorities anxious for their squadrons 'to put up a good show with the RFC.' One outstanding example was 3 (Naval), commanded by Squadron Commander R.H. Mulock of Winnipeg and equipped with Sopwith Pups. During the heavy fighting in March and April it was one of the few allied squadrons which gave out more punishment than it received. Its success was attributable in large measure to Mulock's ability as a leader and organizer and his extensive knowledge of aeroplanes and engines.

To a greater degree than most squadron commanders Mulock made each of his flight commanders responsible for keeping his flight in fighting trim. His administrative methods were directly related to operational requirements because the flight of five or six aircraft remained the tactical air unit, each patrol being carried out by a flight or section of a flight. One naval officer, attached to the RFC in

---

* The Fokker Dr-1 was the German response to the Sopwith Triplane. It was powered by a French-designed Le Rhône rotary engine, obtained from a Swedish firm which had built them under license. An extremely agile aircraft, the Dr-1 did not appear on the Western Front until August; its most famous pilots were Richthofen and Werner Voss. It remained in service until mid-1918.

France to monitor the performance of the naval squadrons, reported to his head-quarters at Dunkirk that Mulock's 'is the best organized and the best run of any Squadron I have seen down here (including R.F.C. Squadrons).'[8] On his sugges-tion a study was made of Mulock's methods, and when the squadron returned to the RNAS in June 1917 after four-and-one-half months of service with the RFC, he commended Mulock on its good record: 'Your men have done invaluable work, overcoming all difficulties, and have maintained Machines, Engines, Guns and Transport in a very high state of efficiency, and it is largely due to their self sacrifice and hard work that the pilots have been able to gain their undoubted supremacy in the air.'[9] Trenchard, too, expressed his appreciation:

They [Naval Three] joined us at the beginning of February at a time when aerial activity was becoming great and were forced to work at full pressure right up to June 14th. when they left us.

Eighty enemy aircraft were accounted for* which, with only a loss of nine machines missing, alone shews the efficiency of the Squadron as a fighting unit.

The escorts provided by the squadron to the photographic reconnaissance and bomb raids enabled our machines to carry out these tasks unmolested.

The supremacy in the air which they undoubtedly gained, is largely due to the manner in which the machines, engines, guns and transport have been looked after by the Flight Commander[s], Flying Officers and Mechanics.

The work of Squadron Commander Mulock is worthy of the highest praise; his knowl-edge of machines and engines and the way in which he handled his officers and men is very largely responsible for the great success and durability of the Squadron.[10]

On 1 February, when Naval Three joined 22 (Army) Wing of V Brigade, half of its twelve pilots were Canadians and three more arrived later that month. Besides Mulock the six originals included Flight Sub-Lieutenants R. Collishaw of Nanaimo, BC, P.G. McNeil and A.T. Whealy, both of Toronto, J.P. White of Winnipeg, and Flight Lieutenant H.R. Wambolt of Dartmouth, NS. Collishaw was the most experienced fighter pilot of this group. The three who followed them, Flight Sub-Lieutenants F.C. Armstrong of Toronto, J.S.T. Fall of Hillbank, BC, and Flight Lieutenant J.J. Malone of Regina, were all decorated for service with the squadron during the following months. Fall and Armstrong received the DSC and Malone, who was killed in April, was posthumously gazetted a DSO. Another notable group arrived in March, including Flight Sub-Lieutenant L.S. Breadner of Carleton Place,[†] who succeeded to command of one of the three flights a month later.[11]

---

* The claim of eighty enemy aircraft being accounted for by the Squadron may be taken as an instance of the general tendency to exaggerate enemy losses. Naval Three was credited with twenty aircraft destroyed and twenty-four damaged in RFC communiqués during the period under review, but even these figures are questionable in the light of admitted German losses.

† Subsequently Air Chief Marshal and Chief of Staff of the RCAF in 1940–3. In addition to those mentioned above, Canadians known to have flown with 3 (Naval) Squadron in the February to June period include R.F.P. Abbott of Carleton Place, Ont. (WIA 17 Aug. 1917), M. Allan, address unknown (KIA 6 July 1917), G.B. Anderson of Ottawa, A.R. Brown of Carleton Place, Ont., A.W. Carter of Calgary (WIA 17 June 1918), J.B. Daniell of Prince George, BC (POW 12

More Canadians came in with the other RNAS and RFC squadron reinforcements to supplement those already at the front. Twenty were flying with the seven
squadrons of 9 (HQ) Wing at the beginning of April, and three times that number
served during the month with III Brigade, half of them with corps and half with
army squadrons. In I Brigade, on the left of the Vimy-Arras front, many Canadians flew with 2 and 16 Squadrons, both equipped with BE2s and the only corps
units directly involved in the Vimy area.* In the fighter squadrons of I Brigade,
Naval Eight had several Canadians and so did 40 Squadron flying Nieuport 17s.†
The other army units, 25 and 43 Squadrons, flying FE2bs and Sopwith 1½

May 1917), J.A. Glen of Enderby, BC, (WIA 18 April 1918), N.D. Hall of Victoria (POW 3 Sept.
1917), G.S. Harrower of Montreal (WIA 23 Sept. 1917), H.M. Ireland of Toronto, H.S. Kerby
(WIA 20 Nov. 1915) and L.L. Lindsay, both of Calgary, H.S. Murton of Toronto (POW 5 May
1917), W.E. Orchard of St Lambert, Que. (KIA 2 June 1917), A.M. Shook of Tioga, Ont. (WIA
16 May 1916, 21 Oct. 1917), and W.R. Walker of West Kildonan, Man. (POW 11 Dec. 1917). No
6 (Naval) Squadron, which arrived six weeks after No 3 (Naval), was also heavily Canadian. Its
members in this period included C.L. Bailing of Toronto, P.E. Beasley of Victoria, R.E. Carroll,
W.A. Curtis, and G.C.W. Dingwall, all of Toronto, S.T. Edwards of Carleton Place, Ont., J.H.
Forman of Kirkfield, Ont. (WIA 28 July 1917, POW 4 Sept. 1918), O.J. Gagnier of Montreal (WIA
11 May 1917), G.A. Gooderham, M.R. Kingsford, and G.D. Kirkpatrick, all of Toronto, D.H.
Masson of Ottawa (KIA 20 April 1917), G.G. McLennan of Eugenia, Ont. (KIA 20 July 1917),
R.F. Redpath of Montreal, R.K. Slater of Ottawa (POW 5 April 1917), G.L.E. Stevens of Peterborough, Ont., and A. McB. Walton of Toronto.
* Because of the heavy casualties in this period a large number of Canadians passed through
several of these squadrons. This was especially the case with 16 Squadron. Canadians who served
in it during the January-June period included Major E.O. McMurtry of Montreal, a 1914 RMC
graduate who won his rank in the 24th Battalion, CEF, transferred to the RFC on 1 January 1917,
and was killed in action on 28 April 1917. Others were E. Alder, address unknown (WIA 12 May
1917), F.H. Baguley of Toronto, F.L. Baker of Vancouver (WIA 2 July 1917), J.S. Black of
Regina (KIA 28 April 1917), J.W. Boyd of Toronto (KIA 5 Feb. 1917), G.J.O. Brichta of North
Battleford, Sask. (KIA 6 March 1917), W.A. Campbell of Vancouver (KIA 26 April 1917), K.P.
Ewart, address unknown (KIA 4 Jan. 1918), A.E. Hahn of Tavistock, Ont., O.R. Knight, address
unknown (KIA 6 April 1917), R.H. Lloyd of Wingham, Ont. (WIA 28 March 1917), H.D. Mason
of Canton, Ont. (KIA 28 April 1917), D.A. McDougall and W.E. McKissock (KIA 1 June 1917),
both of Toronto, D.J. McRae of Ste Anne de Prescott, Ont. (KIA 1 Feb. 1917), C.N. Milligan of
Victoria (WIA 21 April 1917), F.E. Neily of Esquimalt, BC (KIA 27 Dec. 1917), J.F. Proctor of
Calgary, R. Ritchie of Maisonneuve, Que., G.R. Rogers of Kingston, Ont. (KIA 21 April 1917),
U.H. Seguin of Ottawa (KIA 6 April 1917), A.E. Watts of Fort Frances, Ont. (KIA 6 March
1917), H.W. Wheatley of Montreal, and A. Willans of Ottawa (WIA 6 Oct. 1917). No 2 Squadron
included H.J. Bennett of Pembroke, Ont. (POW 24 Sept. 1918), F.E. Brown of Quebec City, G.B.
Davies of Medicine Hat, Alta, W.P. Eastwood of Peterborough, Ont., F.C. Higgins of Sher-
brooke, Que., R.H. Kelly of Toronto, F.A. Looseley of Hamilton, Ont., M.W. Richardson of
Durham, Ont., A.S.H. Ryding of Toronto (WIA 7 April 1918), F.B. Scullard of Chatham, Ont.,
N.E. Wallace (WIA 19 Sept. 1917), and R.V. Waters, addresses unknown.
† No 40 Squadron included C.L. Bath of Toronto (WIA 3 November 1917), J. Gagne of Ottawa
(KIA 24 May 1917), A.E. Godfrey of Vancouver, H.A. Kennedy of Hamilton, Ont. (KIA 22 Aug.
1917), H.S. Pell of Toronto (KIA 6 April 1917), A.B. Raymond of Nanaimo, BC (POW 13 May
1917), F.W. Rook of Toronto (KIA 21 July 1917), and G.C.O. Usborne of Arnprior, Ont. Cana-
dians with 8 (Naval) from 28 March, the date it arrived on the Western Front, to the end of
June included A.E. Cuzner of Ottawa (KIA 29 April 1917), C.B. de T. Drummond of Montreal,
A.R. Knight of Collingwood, Ont., J.N. McAllister of St Andrews, Man., S.H. McCrudden of
Toronto (WIA 5 Sept. 1917), Roderick McDonald of James River Station, NS (KIA 8 May 1918),
E.D. Roach of Toronto (KIA 1 May 1917), J.A. Shaw of Edmonton, and D.M. Shields of Mount
Albert, Ont. (WIA 1 May 1917, June 1917).

Strutters, respectively, were responsible for long-distance reconnaissance, bombing, and line patrols.*[12]

The air plan for the spring attack was based, as always, on the offensive doctrine which Trenchard had adopted from the moment that he first took command, and to which he adamantly adhered throughout his three-year tenure as commander of the RFC in the field. Air superiority was to be obtained by carrying the fight to the Germans over their own territory. This offensive pressure, it was assumed, would enable 'our Corps machines to cooperate with the artillery and infantry during the ground operations with as little interference as possible from the enemy.' Trenchard expected his fighter pilots to penetrate well behind the lines 'seeking out and fighting the enemy over his own aerodromes.'[13] 'The aim of our offensive,' he stressed to his brigades, 'will therefore be to force the enemy to fight well behind, and not on, the lines. This aim will only be successfully achieved if offensive patrols are pushed well out to the limits of Army reconnaissance areas, and the G.O.C. looks to Brigadiers to carry out this policy and not to give way to requests for the close protection of corps machines except in special cases when such machines are proceeding on work at an abnormal distance over the lines. The aerial ascendancy which was gained by our pilots and observers on the SOMME last year was a direct result of the policy outlined above, and with the considerable addition to our strength provided by the new type fighting squadrons now available the G.O.C. feels confident that a similar ascendancy will be gained this year.'[14]

Within these general directives, on 4 April, five days before the Canadian Corps went into action at Vimy Ridge and the Third British Army began its drive along the Scarpe River, the RFC launched an all-out air offensive, attacking enemy observation balloons, bombing rail centres and aerodromes, and carrying the fighting deep into enemy territory. In order to seal off the battle area and allow the artillery aircraft to operate with as much freedom as possible, a large quadrilateral-shaped intercept zone extending about fifteen miles into enemy territory was

---

* The squadron commander of 25 Squadron during this period was Major C.S. Duffus of Halifax. Other Canadians with it during the first half of the year included D.L. Burgess of Ottawa, H. Cotton of Paris, Ont. (POW 28 May 1917), H. St G.S. de Carteret of Halifax, J. Gagne of Ottawa (KIA 24 May 1917), D.E. Holmes of Wingham, Ont., V. McL. Howard and S.A. Hustwitt, both of Toronto, J.H. Kirk of Sussex, NB, N.L. Knight, address unknown (KIA 28 March 1917), R.R. Laing of Westmount, Que., C.T. Lally of Wainwright, Alta (WIA 18 Dec. 1917), D. Leishman of Westmount, Que. (WIA 7 May 1917), R.G. Malcolm of Grimsby, Ont., W.D. Matheson of New Glasgow, NS (WIA 16 March 1917), A.H.K. McCallum of Victoria (POW 8 April 1917), P.L. McGavin of Toronto (KIA 14 Aug. 1917), W.M. Munro, address unknown, L.F. Williams of Fort Frances, Ont., and C.M. Wilson of Vancouver (KIA 14 Oct. 1918). Also with the squadron was J.F.W. Blackall of St John's, Nfld (POW 21 May 1917). With 43 Squadron were W.G. Bell of Toronto, H. Burnett, address unknown, F.S. Coghill of Stratford, Ont. (POW 25 July 1918), H. St G.S. de Carteret of Halifax, J.L. Dickson of Burgessville, Ont. (WIA 7 May 1917), G.C. Dixon of Vancouver (WIA 16 Sept. 1918), J. Gagne of Ottawa (KIA 24 May 1917), F.C. Gorringe of Prince Albert, Sask., L.H. Gould of Winnipeg (KIA 15 Oct. 1917), J.B.B. Harvey of London, Ont. (POW 9 May 1917), R.T.C. Hoidge and E.H. Jones (WIA 24 May 1917), both of Toronto, H.S. Lewis of Orangeville, Ont. (WIA 6 April 1918, POW 10 April 1918), M.J. Morris of Ottawa (KIA 3 May 1917), S.J. Pepler of Toronto (KIA 6 March 1917), A.E. Pickering of Grandview, Man., W.H. Schoenberger of Toronto, D.R. Smith of Sherbrooke, Que., J.D. Stuart of Vancouver (WIA and POW 6 March 1917), and C.P. Thornton of Moose Jaw, Sask. (POW 4 April 1917).

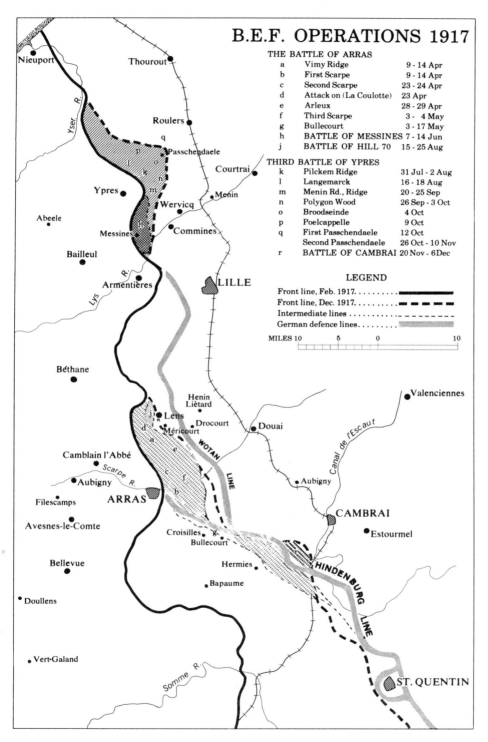

B.E.F. OPERATIONS 1917

THE BATTLE OF ARRAS

a	Vimy Ridge	9 - 14 Apr
b	First Scarpe	9 - 14 Apr
c	Second Scarpe	23 - 24 Apr
d	Attack on (La Coulotte)	23 Apr
e	Arleux	28 - 29 Apr
f	Third Scarpe	3 - 4 May
g	Bullecourt	3 - 17 May
h	BATTLE OF MESSINES	7 - 14 Jun
j	BATTLE OF HILL 70	15 - 25 Aug

THIRD BATTLE OF YPRES

k	Pilckem Ridge	31 Jul - 2 Aug
l	Langemarck	16 - 18 Aug
m	Menin Rd., Ridge	20 - 25 Sep
n	Polygon Wood	26 Sep - 3 Oct
o	Broodseinde	4 Oct
p	Poelcappelle	9 Oct
q	First Passchendaele	12 Oct
	Second Passchendaele	26 Oct - 10 Nov
r	BATTLE OF CAMBRAI	20 Nov - 6 Dec

LEGEND

Front line, Feb. 1917.........	▬▬▬
Front line, Dec. 1917.........	▬ ▬ ▬
Intermediate lines	– – – – –
German defence lines........	▒▒▒▒

MILES 10   5   0   10

established. It was bounded on the west by a line running from Lens to Bullecourt, approximately twenty miles, and on the east from Henin-Liètard to Sains. At times there were as many as fifty single-seater fighters patrolling this area seeking to bring the enemy to combat, while half as many two-seaters, principally 1½ Strutters and FE2bs, patrolled defensively closer to the battle line to protect the artillery aircraft.*[15]

The Germans, however, found it relatively easy to penetrate the air screen. Although they also stressed the offensive, they were selective in their application of it. The chief task of the German fighters was to destroy allied artillery and reconnaissance aircraft and bombers which crossed the lines. As a rule they attacked allied fighter patrols only when the situation was particularly favourable and seldom did they carry the fight across the line. Taking advantage of cloud cover and aided by ground observation centres which determined the best time to bring the fighters into action, small enemy formations, usually two or three fighters, slipped past the allied patrols and attacked the vulnerable artillery aircraft. So while allied offensive patrols could count on a scrap only when they were escorting bombers and reconnaissance machines, the corps two-seaters felt the full weight of the German fighters. On the Vimy front in April, of thirty-eight aircraft known to be missing, wrecked on landing after combat, or returned with wounded airmen, thirty-five were two-seaters while only three were single-seater fighters.[16]

A factor which contributed to the heavy losses suffered by RFC corps aircraft during 'Bloody April' was the coming into service of a new machine, the RE8, designed to replace the BE2s. As early as the end of 1915 it had been recognized that the BE2c was obsolete (although seventeen squadrons were still equipped with the machine in January 1917), and RFC Headquarters had asked for a new reconnaissance and artillery aircraft that could defend itself. The RE8 was the Royal Aircraft Factory's answer. During tests in 1916 the aircraft acquired an evil reputation which never quite deserted it. The gas tanks were directly behind the engine; if a crash occurred, fuel from the tanks burst into flame on contact with the hot engine. The fuselage had a peculiar upward tilt, intended to increase the angle of attack of the wings on landing. The consequent braking effect made the aircraft at home in small fields. Many pilots, however, failed to adapt to the air-craft's strange attitude, and crashes from overshooting were frequent. Finally, the RE8 was far too stable (a characteristic of Royal Aircraft Factory designs) and it proved an easy target for the fast German fighters. By the beginning of April three corps squadrons had been furnished with the RE8. On 13 April one of them, 59 Squadron, lost six of these unwieldy aircraft and ten pilots and observers killed in a few minutes to a patrol led by Richthofen.†[17]

---

* The map in H.A. Jones, *The War in the Air: being the Story of the Part played in the Great War by the Royal Air Force*, III (London 1931), facing 330, shows the offensive patrol area as being further east than it actually was, but this may represent the patrol area before the land offensive began.

† Only one of the casualties was a Canadian, Lieutenant W.J. Chalk, address unknown, a recent transfer from the CEF. Other Canadians with 59 Squadron during the early months of 1917 included J.W.G. Clark and R.M. Grant (WIA 8 April 1917), both of Toronto, B. Harvey, address unknown, E.O. Houghton of Ingersoll, Ont., J.F. MacKinnon of Victoria (WIA 24 Sept. 1916,

Of the ground operations fought on the British front in April and known collectively as the Battles of Arras, the Canadian Corps' attack on Vimy Ridge was the only one entirely successful. The ridge, rising gently to a height of over two hundred feet above the Douai plain, had been one of the dominating features of the northern sector of the Western Front for more than two years. The Germans had taken possession of it in October 1914 and since then had worked continuously at fortifying it. On the forward slope a system of trenches with interconnecting tunnels and deep dug-outs barred the way. On the other side of the crest, visible in most places only from the air, a second network of trenches had been constructed. Fortunately for the Canadians, however, plans to introduce the principle of defence in depth were not carried out. The bulk of the defending troops were in the front trench system with orders to hold their ground at all costs. The immediate purpose of the assault on the ridge was to form a defensive flank for the advance of the Third Army along the Scarpe and to deprive the enemy of observation into the valleys running southwest. A secondary purpose, arising from plans for a northern offensive to be undertaken later in the year, was to secure a commanding view of the plains to the north and east and thus threaten the German hold on the Belgian coast.[18]

The Vimy offensive was marked by careful planning, meticulous preparation, and effective air-artillery co-operation. The artillery plan was carried out in two phases – a preliminary bombardment which began on a limited scale twenty days before the attack and gradually increased in weight, with an intense barrage supporting the assault itself. Prior to this much aerial photography had been completed, information obtained, and damage done to trench systems and hostile batteries. By early March air photos of the entire German defence system formed the basis of a new map which was continually brought up to date as enemy dispositions changed. Of 212 hostile batteries deployed on Vimy Ridge and beyond, over 180 were accurately located and plotted by aerial photography and other means.[19]

The most effective work of 16 Squadron, supporting the Canadian Corps, was accomplished during the preparatory period, bad weather restricting flying during the actual assault. Based at Bruay about six miles behind the front and making use of a forward landing field close by the Corps Headquarters at Camblain l'Abbé, the squadron was organized in three flights of eight aircraft each.* Two flights were assigned to counter-battery work and one to trench bombardment.[20]

Each flight of BE2s worked with a particular artillery group and also carried out photographic reconnaissance of its own area up to four thousand yards beyond the front-line trenches, where the FE2bs of 25 Squadron took over. Neutralizing fire, intended to silence enemy guns temporarily, was conducted through RFC wireless

MIA 28 Nov. 1917), G. Maddock, address unknown, T.W. McConkey of Bradford, Ont. (WIA 11 May 1917), F.D. Pemberton of Victoria (WIA 11 May 1917, KIA 21 Aug. 1917), J.M. Souter of Hamilton, Ont. (KIA 11 April 1917), R.S. Stone, address unknown (WIA 24 April 1917), L.A. Wheatly of Winnipeg (KIA 2 July 1917), and B.A. Wilson of Fernie, BC (WIA 7 May 1917).
* An increase in establishment from eighteen to twenty-four aircraft in corps squadrons had been sanctioned by the War Office, but because of shortages the only squadrons with twenty-four aircraft were No 16 of I Brigade, and Nos 8, 12, and 13 of III Brigade. All reverted to eighteen aircraft by June. Jones, *War in the Air*, III, 313–14; IV (London 1934), 111n

stations at battery positions, and through an advanced central wireless station which monitored and assisted calls for fire and provided communication between the aircraft and the Canadian Counter Battery Office. Tasks were prepared, targets identified, batteries assigned, and observation schedules issued by Canadian Corps Heavy Artillery. Before and after each shoot aerial photos were taken from which damage assessments could be made and plans adjusted accordingly. A proficient observer was expected to control two shoots simultaneously and complete four during a regular two-hour flight.[21]

The air battle of Vimy Ridge started long before the ground fighting began. Left relatively unprotected by the application of Trenchardian doctrine, 16 Squadron's BE2s were no match for the marauding German fighters. Four Canadians were killed and one wounded during February and March. On 1 February Lieutenant D.J. McRae of St Anne de Prescott was operating a camera when he and his pilot were surprised by Richthofen, who had made Vimy Ridge one of his favourite hunting areas. Twin Spandaus poured a hail of bullets into the aircraft, sending it down into the German trenches near Thélus within view of the troops of the 3rd Canadian Division. The pilot and observer both died from their wounds. Lieutenant P.B. Boyd of Toronto, who was wounded on 4 February and died the next day, and Second Lieutenant A.E. Watts of Fort Frances, Ont., and Lieutenant J.G.O. Brichta of North Battleford, Sask., both killed on 6 March, were the other Canadian fatalities. Lieutenant R.H. Lloyd of Wingham, Ont., was wounded on 28 March. In return, Second Lieutenant F.H. Baguley of Toronto had the satisfaction of sending a Halberstadt down out of control on 6 March; five days later the observer of Lieutenant F.L. Baker damaged and drove off another machine of the same type.[22]

The pressure on 16 Squadron became so great that on 19 March III and V Brigades were ordered to help I Brigade by maintaining offensive patrols in the neighbourhood of Douai, the home of *Jasta 11* and the source of much of 16 Squadron's grief. This added measure of protection may have brought some relief because in the first week of April only two of their machines were lost.* The enemy remained active, however. After a lull from 17 to 20 April caused by bad weather, air fighting was again severe until the end of the month. The Germans concentrated so effectively on the corps machines that, despite Trenchard's explicit instructions, offensive patrols were forced in closer to the lines to provide direct protection for the artillery aircraft. Nevertheless, the BEs continued to fall. On I Brigade front between 20 and 30 April eight were reported missing, five of them from 16 Squadron, four were wrecked on landing after being damaged in combat, two returned with wounded observers, and in another the pilot was fatally wounded. In all, six Canadians were missing and one wounded in this climactic ending to 'Bloody April.'[23]

Much of the air fighting took place within full view of the front-line troops and the war diaries of various units of the Canadian Corps contain a number of eye-

---

* One of them was flown by Second Lieutenant O.R. Knight, address unknown, formerly with the CEF, with Second Lieutenant U.H. Seguin of Ottawa as observer. I Brigade work summary, April 1917, Air 1/768/204/4/252

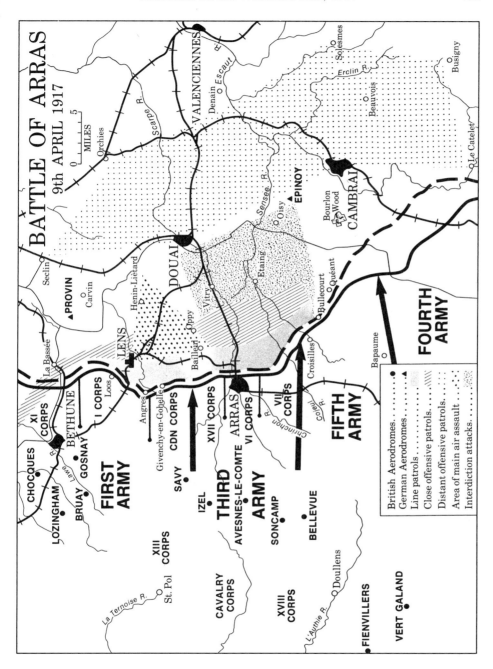

BATTLE OF ARRAS
9th APRIL 1917

MILES
0 5

Legend:
British Aerodromes. . . . . ●
German Aerodromes. . . . . . . ▲
Line patrols. . . . .
Close offensive patrols. . . . . .
Distant offensive patrols. . . . .
Area of main air assault . . . . .
Interdiction attacks. . . . .

FIRST ARMY

THIRD ARMY

FIFTH ARMY

FOURTH ARMY

XI CORPS
I CORPS
XIII CORPS
CDN CORPS
XVII CORPS
VI CORPS
VII CORPS
CAVALRY CORPS
XVIII CORPS

CHOCQUES
LOZINGHAM
BRUAY
GOSNAY
BETHUNE
SAVY
IZEL
AVESNES-LE-COMTE
SONCAMP
BELLEVUE
St. Pol
FIENVILLERS
VERT GALAND
Doullens

La Ternoise R.
La Lawe
L'Authie R.

La Bassée
Seclin
PROVIN
Carvin
Hénin-Liétard
LENS
Loos
Angres
Givenchy-en-Gohelle
Baillleul
Oppy
Vitry
DOUAI
VALENCIENNES
Orchies
Denain
Escaut R.
Scarpe R.
ARRAS
Crinchon R.
Cojeul R.
Croisilles
Bullecourt
Quéant
Étaing
Oisy
EPINOY
Sensée R.
Bourlon Wood
CAMBRAI
Bapaume
Beauvois
Erclin R.
Solesmes
Busigny
Le Catelet

witness accounts. Understandably, artillery units were most interested in the air battle: 'Situation very quiet with the exception of air activity, several air fights took place, one enemy and one British plane came down,' the diary of a field artillery formation recorded on 7 March 1917. On 12 March another entry noted that 'Two of our planes brought down and one hostile plane.'[24] The diarist of the 2nd Canadian Divisional Artillery commented that 'enemy machines seem considerably superior to our own': 'For the past three weeks enemy planes have had the best of every encounter on our front, & there have been many. The German fast red plane can make circles round our slow F.E. patrol & artillery machines, many of which have been shot down. Our new Sopwith triplanes seem to be useful.'[25] Two observation aircraft came down in flames in front of the 3rd Canadian Siege Battery on 6 April, provoking the comment: 'A great many of our observing planes have been lost during the past few weeks and it is a wonder to us that some steps are not taken to give them proper protection.' Still, the enemy did not always dominate the action. An entry for 3 April in the diary of the 2nd Brigade, Canadian Field Artillery, located near Neuville St Waast, recorded that during the day 'Our aeroplanes were very active as many as 35 being counted at one time, while enemy planes were not in evidence.'[26]

The danger of being hit by artillery shells was another hazard that the corps squadron crews faced. Major E.O. McMurtry of Montreal and his observer, Lieutenant H.D. Mason of Canton, Ont., were both killed when their BE2 was apparently struck by an artillery shell.[27] Fighter pilots, especially on low-flying missions, also ran the risk of being blown out of the air in this way. In his 1918 book, *Winged Warfare*, W.A. Bishop related: 'Over and over again one felt a sudden jerk under a wing-tip, and the machine would heave quickly. This meant a shell had passed within a few feet of you. As the battle went on the work grew more terrifying, because reports came in that several of our machines had been hit by shells in flight and brought down ... Yet the risk was one we could not avoid; we had to endure it with the best spirit possible.'[28]

The high toll among two-seaters brought into question the efficacy of Trenchard's offensive policy. Corps and divisional commanders, the primary users of the vulnerable corps aircraft, began to press for protective fighter escorts. Their requests, however, were quashed with the support of General Kiggell, Haig's Chief of Staff, who circulated a statement of air policy stressing once more the importance of keeping the offensive patrols well beyond the enemy lines and pointing out the folly of weakening the fighter force by using it in a defensive role. Kiggell's directive, expressing Trenchard's views, claimed that 'since our aerial offensive commenced early this month, the losses among fighting machines has been more than five times as many as among Corps machines, and the work of the latter has been very little interfered with.'[29] While this statement may have been true for the RFC as a whole, it did not fit the situation in I Brigade. The brigade's loss ratio in April was about one army to two corps aircraft. Eight Canadians were reported killed or missing in corps aircraft as compared with three in fighter and fighter-reconnaissance planes.

South of Vimy in the valley of the Scarpe where the objective of the Third British Army was to drive through to Cambrai and link up with the French forces, more decisive clashes between the rival fighter arms took place. Here the ratio of casualties between co-operation and fighter aircraft was closer to that claimed by General Kiggell. Of the sixty Canadians flying with III Brigade in support of the Third Army, nine were killed, five wounded, and one captured during April. Five of those killed, the prisoner of war, and two of the wounded were members of fighter squadrons.[30]

Three of the Canadian casualties were members of 60 Squadron, whose record exemplifies the struggle of the fighter squadrons in 'Bloody April.' Its pilots patrolled an area east of Arras, from the slopes of Vimy to Fampoux. This sector was also frequented by Richthofen and clashes between Nieuport and Albatros were frequent. The squadron had its first serious setback on 7 April when three Nieuports were shot down in an encounter with *Jagdstaffel 11*. One of those killed was Second Lieutenant C.S. Hall, address unknown, who had been with the squadron since 6 January. Major J.A. Milot of Joliette, Que., was killed the next day and on the weekend of 14–16 April the squadron lost ten Nieuports out of an establishment of eighteen, including that of Lieutenant J.McC. Elliott of Winnipeg who was wounded on 16 April.*[31]

It was during this dark period, one of the most critical that the RFC was to undergo during the war, that W.A. 'Billy' Bishop emerged as 60 Squadron's foremost fighter pilot, beginning a career that was to make him one of the most famous airmen of his generation. Of that extraordinary group of Canadian fighter pilots of the First World War – Collishaw, Bishop, MacLaren, Barker, McKeever, Claxton, to name the most prominent – it was Bishop more than any other who caught the public eye. More has been written of him than of any other airman in Canada's history. A decidedly erratic RMC cadet, he left the college to join the Mississauga Horse when war broke out and went overseas in 1915 with the 7th Canadian Mounted Rifles. In September of that year, when his unit crossed to France, Bishop was left behind; he had transferred to the RFC, where he was training with 21 Squadron as an observer. After a brief period on the Western Front with that squadron in early 1916 he underwent pilot training in England. In March 1917 he reported to 60 Squadron at Izel-le-Hameau. By that time, according to his logbook, he had a total of seventy-five hours, and experience on BE2s, BE12s, Avro 504s, and Sopwith Pups.[32]

No 60 Squadron, however, flew Nieuports, and Bishop, a better fighter than he was a pilot, had trouble adjusting to this sensitive aircraft. On 11 March he began practice flying; over the next two weeks he and the groundcrew endured burst tires, strained airframes, and at least one crash-landing. A less discerning squadron commander might well have returned Bishop to the pilot's pool before he had had an opportunity to show what he could do. But Major A.J.L. Scott, one of the RFC's most perceptive leaders, recognized that the ham-fisted young Canadian flew with

---

* Canadians flying with 60 Squadron in the first half of 1917, in addition to those mentioned above, included W.A. Bishop of Owen Sound, Ont., G.D. Hunter of St Mary's, Ont. (POW 6 May 1917), C.W. McKissock of Toronto (POW 6 May 1917), R.U. Phalen of Lockeport, NS (KIA 28 May 1917), W.J. Rutherford of Westmount, Que., F.O. Soden, born in New Brunswick, E.J.D. Townesend of Cowichan, BC (POW 31 March 1917), and G.C.O. Usborne of Arnprior, Ont.

the calculating aggressiveness that marked the great fighter pilots. After five hours of practice flying in France, he flew his first operational patrol on 17 March. On 25 March he shot down his first enemy aircraft, an Albatros, while flying as rear man in a formation of four Nieuports. The combat began at 9000 feet near Arras and demonstrated that, whatever Bishop's weaknesses as a pilot, he was a first-class shot with the true killer instinct:

While on D[efensive] P[atrol] 3 Albatros Scouts approached us. One, separating from the rest, lost height and attempted to come up behind our second to the rear machine. I dived and fired about 12 to 15 rounds. Tracers went all around his machine. He dived steeply for about 600 ft. and flattened out. I followed him and opened fire from 40 to 50 yards range. A group of tracers went into the fuselage and centre section, one being seen to enter immediately behind the pilot's seat and one seemed to hit the pilot himself. The machine then fell out of control in a spinning nose dive. I dived after him, firing. I reached 1500 or 2000 ft. My engine had oiled up and I glided just over the line ... The Albatros Scout when last seen by me was going vertically downwards at a height of 500 to 600 ft. ...[33]

On 30 March Scott demonstrated his prescience by sending the still inexperienced Bishop out as the leader of a five-man offensive patrol. Within a month of his first operational flight Bishop had become the squadron's 'ace,' and Scott was permitting him to fly roving missions by himself in addition to his normal patrol duties.

Like all the great air fighters, Bishop was an expert deflection shot, a skill he maintained by constant practice. His tactics, a subject to which he gave much thought, were built around surprise, which he regarded as the essence of air fighting. In part, his methods were forced upon him because the Nieuport was much slower than the best German fighters; even so, his combat reports from this period show that, once surprise was lost, he was usually willing to break off combat. When that was not possible, his heavy-handedness became a positive advantage in the rough-and-tumble of air combat. He threw the little Nieuport about with complete abandon and a rare tactical sense. As his letters home reveal, he was also driven by an intense urge to win recognition. His personal and family correspondence contains many accounts of his victories, as well as references to his 'score,' his decorations, and the number of victories registered by RFC and French rivals. Joined to his skill and drive was a relentless courage that impelled him constantly to seek combat. On 30 April, for example, in a space of two hours before noon, he reported eight distinct combats against a total of nineteen aircraft. As Scott noted at the bottom of his report: 'Comment, I think, is unnecessary.'[34]

Naval Three also acquitted itself exceptionally during the April battles, its Pups usually getting the better of the Halberstadt and Albatros scouts. It was employed principally on escort duty providing protection for BE2s used as bombers. The nature of this work was almost bound to bring on an encounter with the German air force, yet only three of the Pups were lost during the month of April. The squadron had one of its busiest days on 11 April while escorting a formation of BE2s on a bombing raid on Cambrai. L.S. Breadner destroyed one Albatros in the air, forced another out of the fight, and sent an unidentified enemy machine down in flames. J.S.T. Fall scored three remarkable victories for which he was awarded the DSC. He attacked and destroyed one enemy aircraft; he was driven down toward the ground by hostile scouts, but manoeuvred onto one of them from behind and saw his tracers go into the pilot's head; later he brought down another enemy who attacked him. He returned with his own aircraft riddled with bullet holes.[35]

Two weeks later Breadner, described by one of his acquaintances as a 'fire-eater,'[36] brought down an enemy aircraft not far from his own aerodrome at Marieux and within an hour or so was back in his room telling about the adventure in a letter to Canada: 'I was going down to the aerodrome when I heard the anti-aircraft guns going. On looking up I saw a Hun directly over-head at about 10,000 ft. So I scrambled into my "bus" & after him. He was at 12,000 ft. when I got up to him (a great big double-engined pusher type machine) so I sat right behind his tail where he couldn't shoot at me. I fired 190 rounds at him & shot both his engines.'*[37]

The German aircraft crashed on the allied side of the lines and Breadner landed in a field close by. He was unable to converse with the occupants of the downed machine, a pilot and two observers who were captured by some 'Tommies,' since they spoke no English. Their aircraft was still burning, but before it was destroyed Breadner cut away the cross insignia, boasting that 'We have it in the mess now.' The letter ended with a hurried notation: 'I'll have to close now as we are going out on a "Big Stunt" in a few minutes & I have to put my kit on yet.' Breadner then led his flight of five Pups in escorting a formation of six FE2bs en route to bomb Epinoy aerodrome. Soon after crossing the line they were met by two formations of enemy fighters. After making sure that the bombers were back over the British lines the escort turned on their pursuers. J.J. Malone attacked one enemy plane, shooting the pilot, drove down a second, and went after a third. Flight Sub-Lieutenant G.B. Anderson of Ottawa sent another German down out of control. The skirmish attracted other machines from both sides and a free-wheeling battle developed and spread over a large area. During the engagement Malone ran out of ammunition, flew to a nearby aerodrome, reloaded, returned to the fight, and drove down another hostile aircraft. Malone was reported missing the following week. At that time he was credited with seven downed enemy aircraft and was posthumously gazetted for the DSO for his victories.[38]

In April, reflecting the intensity of the fighting, casualties reached an all time high in the RFC. In the four-week period ending 27 April 238 personnel were reported missing or killed and 105 wounded. Known Canadian casualties for the month totalled twenty-six killed, thirteen wounded, and six missing. German losses from 31 March to 11 May were thirty-three killed, sixteen missing, and nineteen wounded. Thirty German aircraft were destroyed in the same period, compared with 122 RFC machines, but the RFC was continually operating over enemy territory and its pilots were much more vulnerable than their German adversaries, who were seldom far from the safety of their own aerodromes.[39]

A classic illustration of this is provided by a letter written by Lieutenant T.W. McConkey of Bradford, Ont., the observer in an RE8 of 59 Squadron engaged on routine corps reconnaissance duties on 11 May. It describes how he won the MC

---

* Presumably the enemy machine was either a Friedrichshafen G-III or a Gotha G-IV or V. All of these bombers were in service at that time.

'... while photographing about 9000 yards into Hunland. We were attacked by five Albatross scouts which broke up our formation. Between us we shot down two of the enemy and drove another down, apparently out of control. My pilot, Captain Pemberton from B.C., manoeuvred the machine in a most excellent fashion, evading the fire of Huns as much as possible and giving me every opportunity to bring my Lewis gun into play. He received a spent bullet in the back, necessitating his spending a week in the casualty clearing station. I came off less fortunately, with four bullet wounds in the right thigh, one in shoulder and one in face ...'[40]

The bloody operations about Arras, which had originally been intended as diversionary attacks to draw off German reserves from Nivelle's offensive on the Aisne, were prolonged into May because of the collapse of the French assault after the first few days. The French debacle was compounded by widespread mutiny among the troops. Nivelle was replaced by *Général* Henri Pétain, and the new commander-in-chief was compelled to adopt a defensive stance for the rest of the year, while the morale of his shattered forces was rebuilt. As a result, the major responsibility for offensive action on the Western Front passed to the British, with predictable consequences for the focus of the air war.

Plans for an assault on the Messines-Wytschaete Ridge, which commanded the British position on the right flank of the Ypres Salient, had been included in the original offensive plans for 1917. Its seizure was necessary for a successful offensive in Flanders to free the Belgian coastal region, a course urged by the Lords of the Admiralty who wanted the ports of Ostend and Zeebrugge. But it was to be undertaken only on the condition that Nivelle's master plan failed to achieve a decisive breakthrough. The British, Nivelle had agreed, would then be free to break off the fighting east of Arras and attack in Belgium with the Second British Army supported by the Belgian army and the French forces at Nieuport. Consequently, with the French halted on the Aisne and Pétain asking for time to restore the confidence of his demoralized troops, Haig decided to implement the plans for a British offensive in the north. The first move was to be against the Messines Ridge, 'whose capture would deprive the Germans of valuable observation points and form a solid right flank for the advance into the coastal region.

The offensive was mounted by the Second British Army and its air arm, II Brigade, which was significantly reinforced for the operation. Two corps squadrons of RE8s and BE2es were added along with two army squadrons, 1 and 10 (Naval) with their Sopwith Triplanes. In addition, 23 (Spad) and 40 (Nieuport) Squadrons of I Brigade were detailed to extend their offensive patrols to cover the II Brigade area, while the fighter, bomber, and reconnaissance squadrons of 9 (HQ) Wing were moved north at the end of May to the Second Army zone.* By the beginning of June Trenchard had concentrated twenty squadrons (half of them equipped

---

* Canadians serving in 23 Squadron in the first half of 1917 included W.R. Brookes of Jerseyville, Ont., Lloyd Elsley of Ridgeway, Ont. (KIA 5 April 1917), V.C. Gordon of Toronto, T.G. Holley of Winnipeg (POW 2 Feb. 1917), E.G. Joy of Toronto, K.C. McCallum of Vancouver (WIA 22 April 1917), G.I.D. Marks of Toronto, W.W. Stratton of Peterborough, Ont., and R.W. Young of Toronto. No 46 Squadron included F.B. Baragar of Elm Creek, Man. (WIA 3 Sept. 1917), N.S. Caudwell of Brantford, Ont. (WIA 25 May 1917), R.L.M. Ferrie of Hamilton (KIA 21 Jan. 1918), A.L. Fleming of Toronto, and A.R. Fortin of Winnipeg.

with single-seater fighters) mustering well over three hundred serviceable aircraft. German reinforcements for the entire Fourth Army front, from Messines to the sea, fell short of this number, and in the battle area further reinforcements did not arrive in time for the fight. Although a detailed German air order of battle has not been found, it seems likely that enemy aircraft on the Flanders Front were outnumbered two to one, and along the Messines Ridge by a much higher margin.[41]

Using its numerical advantage the RFC tried to seal off the battle area by a system of barrage patrols flown by the army squadrons along a line that corresponded approximately with the enemy's line of observation balloons, tethered about a mile behind his front line. This system had brought the Germans little success at Verdun in 1916, but the margin of numerical superiority held by the RFC enabled it to police the barrage line from dawn to dusk, with patrols maintained at two or more levels, and still form an outer screen of distant offensive patrols. The main task of the fighters on the barrage line was to protect the corps aircraft. They were also expected to prevent the enemy from using his own artillery co-operation machines and force him to haul down his observation balloons. Orders were issued that no German planes were to be permitted to cross the barrage line. Some of course did. But it is remarkable, in view of what had happened in April, and a measure of the air superiority established in the battle area, that between 31 May, when the main bombardment began, and 6 June only one corps machine was lost. This was an RE8 of 42 Squadron carrying Second Lieutenant C.J. Baylis of Victoria as observer. He was killed.*[42]

The fighter patrols were supplemented by the compass stations installed in each army area late in 1916. These were located at widely separated points, and by obtaining cross-bearings on the wireless transmissions of an enemy artillery-ranging aircraft they could trace its movements with a fair degree of accuracy. By the spring of 1917 the system was in full operation with all the compass stations linked in a single network. When an enemy aircraft was located in this way its position was relayed to the appropriate army wing headquarters and from there by telephone to a squadron or flight on standby for such emergencies.[43] The response bears close resemblance to the fighter 'scrambles' of the Second World War. The procedure followed in 60 Squadron was probably typical of the RFC as a whole: '... in order efficiently to answer the compass calls, as they were termed, three or four pilots always had to be standing by to leap into their machines and be off the ground, in formation, inside of two minutes. Nevertheless, they became extraordinarily smart at this manoeuvre, and answered to the [Klaxon] hunting horn – doubled blasts of which were the signal at that time – as keenly as a fashionable pack of foxhounds.'[44] In the first week of June the army wing headquarters of II Brigade received forty-seven calls from the wireless interception centre at Messines. The net result was one enemy aircraft destroyed, seven estimated to be damaged, and twenty-two enemy artillery shoots abruptly terminated.[45]

---

* Jones, *War in the Air*, IV, 119, states that until 7 June no artillery planes were shot down. Since the RE8 in which Baylis was flying was reported missing on the evening of 6 June, after the day's entry had been made in the Squadron Record Book, the casualty was counted as occurring on 7 June.

The Battle of Messines, like that at Vimy, was based on limited objectives, to be achieved by concentrating an overwhelming weight of artillery fire on a narrow front. The artillery bombardment and counter-battery programme began on 21 May and increased in intensity as the day of the attack, 7 June, approached. Within the security screen provided by the fighters and assisted by good weather the artillery flights were able to direct the British guns on to enemy positions on the far side of the ridge with devastating effect. When the ground attack went in almost a quarter of the German field artillery, and nearly half of their heavy artillery, had been knocked out. The assault itself was preceded by the detonation of nineteen mines, with over 450 tons of explosives, which had been placed under the German front lines more than six months before. Immediately after the mines were blown, at 0310 hrs, the whole of the artillery of the Second Army began to fire at the maximum rate. From the air the ground appeared to be 'bouncing up like the surface of water in a heavy storm.' Although there was stiff resistance in places, the infantry assault was successful, most of the assigned objectives being taken that same day.[46]

Strong air support was one of the key factors in the victory. The fighter screen was so effective that Maurice Baring, Trenchard's personal aide and secretary, was moved to comment that 7 June was 'the finest day in the air we have ever had. Our people entirely prevented the Boche Flying Corps from working, and our artillery work in co-operation with aircraft went without a hitch.' Twenty-nine corps aircraft worked along the front of the three attacking corps, a distance of about 17,000 yards, almost doubling the highest density employed previously. No 6 Squadron attached to X Corps was the only corps unit to lose aircraft.* Two of its RE8s went missing and in other combats four members of the squadron were wounded. In 42 Squadron on the II Anzac Corps' front Lieutenant W.F. Anderson of Toronto, flying an RE8, was attacked by three fighters while on a photo mission, but his observer sent one of the attackers down in flames and damaged another.[†] Their aircraft 'was very badly shot about but neither was injured.' Apart from these incidents, the corps squadrons carried on without any interference, adjusting artillery fire on to 157 enemy batteries. Nos 1 and 41 Squadrons,[‡] flying Nieuports

---

* Canadians with 6 Squadron during the first half of 1917 included C.A.S. Bean, address unknown (POW 9 Aug. 1917), C.N. Bennett of Halifax (KIA 25 June 1918), W.B. Ferguson of Amelias-burg, Ont. (KIA 7 July 1918), S.H. Glendinning of Sunderland, Ont. (KIA 17 July 1918), P.L. Goudie of Toronto (WIA 11 April 1917), M.O. Haskell of Lachine, Que., E.A. McKay of Toronto (POW 22 Aug. 1918), J. O'Rorke of Winnipeg, W.D. Thomson of Saskatoon, Sask. (KIA 5 Jan. 1917), R.J. Warner of Toronto, and A.L. Wilson of Vegreville, Alta.

† Canadians in addition to Anderson flying with 42 Squadron from January to June included C.J. Baylis of Victoria (KIA 6 June 1917), L.R. Brereton of Winnipeg (WIA 22 July 1918), G.T. Dracup of Yorkton, Sask. (KIA 28 July 1917), E. Hamilton of Princeton, BC (KIA 15 Feb. 1917), F.A.N. Haultain of Port Hope, Ont., H.L. Kennedy of Talbotville Royal, Ont., W.A. Landry of Dorchester, NB (WIA 15 Feb. 1917), H.A. Laws of Winnipeg, E.A. McKay of Toronto (POW 22 Aug. 1918), W.E.G. Murray of Vancouver (WIA four times: 7 June 1915, 26 Sept. 1916, July 1917, June 1918), B.H. Smith of Halifax (KIA 22 July 1917), and A.W. Waddy of Vancouver.

‡ Major G.C.St P. de Dombasle, formerly of the Royal Canadian Regiment, had been Officer Commanding 1 Squadron since late in 1916. Other Canadians with the unit in the first half of 1917 included G.H. Armstrong and G.C. Atkins (POW 19 June 1917), both of Toronto, E.S.T. Cole, address unknown, R.H. Cronyn of London, Ont., L. Drummond of Toronto (POW 18 May

and FE8s, respectively, were specifically assigned to provide close ground support over the battlefield while other fighter squadrons were given ground attack as a secondary role. Aerodromes and ground transport were the main targets, but they had a roving commission to strike at anything they saw 'in order to harass the enemy as much as possible and spoil the morale of his troops.'[47]

During June ninety Canadians served with the squadrons of the reinforced II Brigade operating in support of the Messines attack, of whom ten were killed, six wounded, and three reported missing.*[48] The most distinctively Canadian unit was 10 (Naval) in which thirteen of the squadron's fifteen pilots were Canadian when the unit joined II Brigade in mid-May.†

Naval Ten was formed at St Pol (Dunkirk) on 12 February and was shortly thereafter equipped with Sopwith Triplanes. Its original pilots were considered unready for action, however, so in the spring it was restaffed with seasoned veterans, almost all of whom were Canadians. Eight were posted in from Naval Three with the others coming from various sources. Collishaw, for instance, had recently

1917), S. McKercher of Wroxeter, Ont. (WIA 23 April 1917), F.M. McLaren, address unknown (KIA 12 Aug. 1917), and W.W. Rogers of Alberton, PEI. In 41 Squadron during the same period Canadians included W.I. Bailey of St Mary's, Ont. (WIA 8 June 1917), A.W. Hogg of Winnipeg (WIA 9 June 1917), R.H.B. Ker of Victoria, and H.E. Paquin of Montreal.

* Canadians in 20 Squadron from January to June included J.L. Boles of Ingersoll, Ont. (KIA 13 June 1918), F.H. Bronskill of Ottawa (POW 1 Feb. 1917), G.T.W. Burkett, address unknown, C.M. Carbert of Campbellville, Ont. (KIA 1 Feb. 1917), W.M.E. Chester of Toronto (WIA 13 July 1917), E.B. Cogswell of Ottawa (WIA 24 May 1917), W. Durrand of Edmonton, H.E. Hartney of Pakenham, Ont. (WIA 14 Feb. 1917), A.N. Jenks of Coaticook, Que., H.W. Joslyn of Sintaluta, Sask. (MIA 17 Aug. 1917), W.T. Jourdan of Vancouver (WIA 14 Feb. 1917), A.C. Lee of Stoney Creek, Ont. (POW 20 May 1917), W.R. Macaskill of Baddeck, NS (POW 19 June 1917), I.M. MacLean of North Sydney, NS (WIA 15 Aug. 1917), R. MacK. Madill of Beaverton, Ont. (KIA 21 July 1917), R.G. Masson of Ottawa (KIA 24 May 1917), H.R. Nicholson of Hamilton (KIA 24 April 1917), W.P. Scott of Toronto (WIA 28 May 1917), A.G. Stewart and S.F. Trotter (KIA 6 July 1917), addresses unknown, M.W. Waddington, R.W. White (POW 25 Jan. 1917), E.A. Wickson (KIA 16 June 1917), and H. Reid Wilkinson (POW 10 Sept. 1917), all of Toronto, and F.W. Wright of Tottenham, Ont. In 45 Squadron there were R.S. Bennie of Leamington, Ont. (MIA 5 June 1917), W. Birkett of Moose Jaw, Sask. (WIA 17 June 1917), G.W. Blaiklock of Montreal, C. St G. Campbell of Cobalt, Ont. (KIA 6 April 1917), E.F. Crossland of Toronto, J.B. Fotheringham of Ottawa (KIA 7 July 1917), F.G. Garratt of Montreal, J.E. MacKay of Toronto, T.A. Metheral of Moose Jaw, Sask. (KIA 5 June 1917), J.F. Scott, address unknown, W.W. Shaver of Woodstock, Ont., F.C.H. Snyder of Kitchener, Ont. (MIA 7 July 1917), T.R. Sorton of Toronto, C.T.R. Ward of Lennoxville, Que., R.S. Watt of Langton, Ont. (KIA 12 June 1917), and W.T. Wood of Sackville, NB. No 70 Squadron included D.J. Allan of Killarney, Man. (WIA 15 June 1918), C.A.S. Bean, address unknown, A.S. Bourinot of Toronto (POW 3 June 1917), W.R. Cooke of Orillia, Ont. (WIA 13 Aug. 1917), J.G. Crang of Toronto, G.C. Easton of Galt, Ont., S.W. Graham of Toronto (WIA 6 June 1918), L.A. Kelwig, address unknown, L.H. Kennedy of Montreal, L.A. Kiburz of Vancouver, H.D. Layfield of Vancouver (WIA 21 Sept. 1917), S.L. Shannon of Prince Albert, Sask., J.A. Sully of Ottawa, and F. Tapping of Toronto. This squadron was commanded by Major A.W. Tedder, subsequently Marshal of the Royal Air Force.

† Aside from Collishaw, the other Canadians were W.M. Alexander and K.G. Boyd, both of Toronto, A.C. Dissette of Vancouver (KIA 2 June 1917), J.H. Keens (WIA 7 June 1917), P.G. McNeil (KIA 3 June 1917), E.V. Reid (KIA 28 July 1917), and Q.S. Shirriff, all of Toronto, G.E. Nash of Stoney Creek, Ont. (POW 25 June 1917), J.A. Page of Brockville, Ont. (KIA 22 July 1917), L.H. Parker of Leeds Village, Que. (KIA 14 June 1917), C.E. Pattison of Winona, Ont. (WIA 20 May 1917), and J.E. Sharman of Oak Lake, Man. (KIA 22 July 1917).

returned from convalescent leave and was available for a new posting. As one of the most experienced pilots he assumed command of 'B' Flight* and took a leading part in preparing the unit for action. Collishaw remained with the squadron until the end of July and received a DSC and DSO for his service on the Ypres front.[49]

The Canadian pilots soon established the squadron as one of the leading fighter units in II Brigade. In June its aircraft destroyed fifteen of the forty-six enemy machines claimed by II Brigade and twenty-seven of eighty-three others damaged or driven down out of control. Naval Ten's biggest day was 6 June when it claimed five destroyed and five others forced down. Collishaw, whose logbook records sixty missions that month, destroyed or sent down out of control thirteen enemy aircraft.[50] His combat report for 17 June describes one of these encounters:

Near Armentieres [sic] our patrol [six aircraft] met five Spads,[†] who accompanied us. Over Roulers, we saw and dived on eight enemy Scouts, followed by Spads. After diving on three different Scouts and missing them with my fire, I climbed away each time. I then saw an E.A. attacking one of the Spad machines and dived on him firing about 50 rounds, when the E.A. stalled and fell out of control.

I attacked another enemy Scout, which was attacking a Spad, but after 30 rounds my gun jambed and I could not clear it.

I saw Flt. Sub-Lt. Reid close one ... and fire into it. I was able to see the E.A. go down in a series of stalls and spins, and I am certain he was out of control beyond recovery.

I also saw another machine go down out of control after attack from a Spad.[51]

Notwithstanding the fact that they were rated as generally superior in performance to the Albatros and Halberstadt scouts, the Sopwith Triplanes by no means had it all their own way. Between 15 May and 30 June the squadron lost six of its Canadian members, three killed and three wounded or missing. In addition, at least two other members of the squadron were lost, one being killed and the other taken prisoner.[52]

Although Messines was the main centre of air action in the latter part of May and early June, the most publicized event in the air war was the strafing of a German airfield on the Arras front by W.A. Bishop on 2 June. His action brought him a Victoria Cross, the tenth to be won by an airman and the first by a Canadian flyer. The attack had its origin in Bishop's brief association with Captain Albert Ball, recognized at the time as the most outstanding airman in the RFC. During a visit to 60 Squadron on 5 May Ball had invited Bishop to join him in a surprise raid on a German aerodrome with the object of destroying aircraft on the ground. There were obvious hazards, but the aggressive young Briton felt that surprise, in

---

* 'B' Flight was nick-named 'Black' Flight because the engine cowlings and top and side fuselage panels were painted black to enable the flight mechanics to recognize their own aircraft and go immediately to their assistance as they returned from patrol. 'A' and 'C' Flights used red and blue colour schemes respectively to identify their aircraft. Raymond Collishaw with R.V. Dodds, *Air Command: a Fighter Pilot's Story* (London 1973), 81

† There were no Spad squadrons in II Brigade and the five that joined Collishaw's patrol must have been from 23 Squadron of I Brigade or from a French squadron.

as much as a low-level attack on an aerodrome had never been attempted and would not be expected, would enable them to turn the trick. A few days later, before anything definite had been organized, Ball was killed in action. But the idea kept churning in Bishop's mind.

By the end of May, with the Arras front relatively quiet, 60 Squadron was mainly occupied with answering compass calls. Bishop disliked this exhausting and unrewarding type of work: there were frequent chases but few combats. Moreover, he found the sound of that 'damned Klaxon horn' used to alert the pilots was becoming 'hard on the nerves – and the legs.' It was in this mood that he determined to carry out the proposal which he and Ball had briefly discussed. He chose a free day, 2 June, for his self-assigned mission and took off before dawn in his Nieuport. At the aerodrome he attacked the Germans as they were getting ready for the day's work.[53] Always a key factor in his tactics, surprise worked for Bishop here as it did on so many other occasions. His combat report tells what happened during the few minutes he was over the enemy airfield:

I fired on 7 machines on the aerodrome, some of which had their engines running. One of them took off and I fired 15 rounds at him from close range 60 ft. up and he crashed. A second one taking off, I opened fire and fired 30 rounds at 150 yards range, he crashed into a tree. Two more were then taking off together. I climbed and engaged one at 1,000 ft., finishing my drum, and he crashed 300 yards from the aerodrome. I changed drums and climbed E [ast] a fourth H.A. came after me and I fired one whole drum into him. He flew away and I then flew 1,000 ft. under 4 scouts at 5,000 ft. for one mile and turned W. climbing. The aerodrome was armed with one or more machine guns. Machines on the ground were 6 scouts (Albatros Type I or II) and one two-seater.[54]

A note appended to the combat report by the squadron commander observed that Bishop 'was several times at a height of 50 ft. over this enemy aerodrome* at least 17 miles East of the lines. His machine is full of holes caused by machine gun fire from the ground.' A fellow pilot remembered 'clearly seeing a group of about five bullet holes in the rear half of his tailplane, the elevator, within a circle of not more than six inches diameter at the most. Whatever machine was on his tail must have been very close indeed to achieve that group.'[55]

Although an isolated event and really an episode in the private war which Bishop, like many another fighter pilot, carried on against the German air force, the action did have a wider significance. As the most daring and successful low-level attack yet carried out, it provided an example which was repeated during the Battle of Messines and later. Thus, the orders issued to 9 (HQ) Wing for 7 June included specific reference to low-flying attacks on aerodromes of a kind which had not been attempted before Bishop's exploit.[56] On the announcement of

---

* The location of the airfield Bishop attacked has never been definitively established. Arthur Bishop identified Estourmel as the airfield attacked, on the basis of his father's recollections and a study of the ground. William Arthur Bishop, *The Courage of the Early Morning: a Son's Biography of a Famous Father* (Toronto 1965), 100. The combat report gives the location as 'either Esnes Aerodrome or Awoignt,' but by Bishop's own admission he didn't know where he was. All three airfields were clustered within a few miles of each other southeast of Cambrai.

Bishop's having been awarded the Victoria Cross, more than two months later,* General Trenchard removed him from operational flying. He was not to return to the Western Front until 1918, when he came back as a squadron commander. Until he left for England in August, however, Bishop continued to take a prominent part in the air war, which now centred upon a major British offensive in Flanders.

Sir Douglas Haig had been favourable to the idea of a Flanders offensive since January 1916. It had been his alternative to operations on the Somme and now, with the clean, if very limited, success of Messines behind him, and the French incapable of mounting a significant attack, he was in a strong position to push for it as a better choice than the Italian offensive backed by the 'Easterners' on Lloyd George's newly-formed War Policy Committee. Strategic justification for the Flanders offensive was given to the committee in a week-long series of conferences attended by Haig starting 19 June. The demoralized French armies needed time to recover from the mutinies of the previous month; Admiral Sir John Jellicoe considered that unless the German submarine warfare campaign could be restricted by the capture of the Channel ports, Britain would have to end the war in 1918 because of shipping losses; any breakthrough in Flanders would threaten the main communication of the German armies there, which ran through bottlenecks north and south of the Ardennes; and if the enemy could be driven from the Belgian coast it would compel his heavy bombers to cross the BEF lines to carry out raids against London.[57]

The War Policy Committee reluctantly accepted Haig's arguments although it still doubted the ability of the BEF to achieve such ambitious goals. Finally, on 16 July, a clear decision was reached 'to allow Haig to begin his offensive, but not to allow it to degenerate into a drawn out, indecisive battle of the "Somme" type.' The first phase of the ground offensive was to drive a wedge into the German defences around the Ypes Salient. From the expanded salient the British would then advance northeastwards, with their right on the high ground of the Passchendaele Ridge, to gain the Thourout-Couckelaere line on their way to Bruges.[58]

Prior to the infantry assault, scheduled for 15 July, General Gough's Fifth Army would lay down a massive sixteen-day artillery bombardment. Since the main German defences lay along the crest and reverse slope of the low ridge which dominated the Ypres Salient, the British artillery – especially the heavy guns engaged in counter-battery work – were, as usual, heavily dependent on aerial observation for accurate ranging. This, together with the army's demands for photo-reconnaissance and protection against enemy air observation, required that the RFC establish and maintain aerial superiority for a considerable period. Thus the Third Battle of Ypres really began on 11 July with the opening of an RFC offensive designed to secure an aerial corridor over the front and to prevent the intrusion of enemy reconnaissance aircraft.[59]

---

* 'This must surely be a very unusual case of a Victoria Cross or any high honour being awarded on the word of the recipient only as to his exploit and without any witnesses or participants. Our CO knew Bishop so well as to believe in him implicitly, as did the whole squadron and higher authority.' William Frye, *Air of Battle* (London 1974), 136

The artillery preparation ruled out the possibility of strategic surprise and the air build-up on both sides had become obvious several weeks earlier still. Between the middle of June and the end of July the Allies and the Germans had concentrated every available aircraft into the thirty-mile corridor between the Lys and the sea – the entire Belgian air force, forty strong, some two hundred French and over five hundred British machines (totalling 60 per cent of the RFC in France and half of them single-seater fighters), facing about six hundred Germans. Many famous squadrons were gathered there, including the French 'Les Cigognes,' the American 'Lafayette Escadrille,' the RFC's 56 and 60 Squadrons,* and the RNAS' Naval Ten.†60

The German force included *Jagdgeschwader* I – *Jastas 4, 6, 10,* and *11* under the overall command of Germany's top-scoring pilot, Manfred von Richthofen, who had already been credited with fifty-six victories when his 'Circus' was formed on 23 June. But the Allies had a clear-cut numerical advantage and they added to it an advantage in morale on 6 July when, in a dogfight between the 'Circus' and six FE2ds of 20 Squadron‡ and four Sopwith Triplanes of Naval Ten, Richthofen was shot down by an FE observer, temporarily blinded and paralyzed by a bullet which creased his skull. The enemy's premier fighter ace was thus removed from the battle for six weeks.

By the opening of the offensive the technological superiority so decidedly in the Germans' favour earlier in the year had evaporated. Three new British aircraft were responsible. The first was the Bristol F2A, or Bristol Fighter, a large, powerful, and fast two-seater, designed as a fighter-reconnaissance machine and commonly called the 'Brisfit.' Its first employment on operations, by 48 Squadron on 5 April,§

---

* No 56 Squadron spent fourteen days in England during this period, as a home defence squadron against German day bombers. It returned to France on 5 July, two days before the second Gotha daylight raid on London. Jones, *War in the Air*, IV, 134–5, 152; V, 36. Canadian airmen serving in 56 Squadron in summer 1917 included V.P. Cronyn of London, Ont., C.B. Fisher of Lindsay, Ont., R.T.C. Hoidge and R.G. Jardine (KIA 20 July 1917), both of Toronto, I.C. MacGregor of New Glasgow, NS (WIA 9 Aug. 1917, 21 Sept. 1917), and L.J. Williams of Vancouver. No 60 Squadron had three Canadian flight commanders: Bishop, W.J. Rutherford of Westmount, Que., and F.O. Soden, born in New Brunswick.

† Seven of those who had been with Naval Ten when it joined II Brigade in mid-May – Collishaw, Alexander, Boyd, Reid, Shirriff, Page, and Sharman – were still with it. Canadians who had joined it since then included A.W. Carter of Calgary (WIA 7 June 1918), C.B. de T. Drummond of Montreal, H.J. Emery of Edmonton, T.L. Glasgow of Toronto (KIA 19 Aug. 1917), N.D. Hall of Victoria (POW 3 Sept. 1917), T.B. Holmes and T.C. May (KIA 24 July 1917), both of Toronto, H.B. Mound of Winnipeg (WIA 28 May 1918), G.L. Trapp of New Westminster, BC (KIA 12 Nov. 1917), and C.H. Weir of Medicine Hat, Alta (KIA 21 Aug. 1917).

‡ Canadians flying with 20 Squadron in July 1917 included J.L. Boles of Ingersoll, Ont. (KIA 13 June 1918), C.H. Cameron of Victoria, W.M.E. Chester of Toronto (WIA 13 July 1917), W. Durrand of Edmonton, A.N. Jenks of Coaticook, Que., H.W. Joslyn of Sintaluta, Sask. (MIA 17 Aug. 1917), I.M. MacLean of North Sydney, NS (WIA 15 Aug. 1917), R. MacK. Madill of Beaverton, Ont. (KIA 21 July 1917), S.F. Trotter, address unknown (killed in this fight), M.W. Waddington of Toronto, and F.W. Wright of Tottenham, Ont.

§ Canadians flying with 48 Squadron when it acquired Bristol F2As included W.G. Bell of Toronto, W.J. Clifford of Hamilton (KIA 25 April 1917), H.St G.S. de Carteret of Halifax, Robert Dodds of Hamilton, J. MacL. Hutcheson, address unknown, H.P. Lale of Calgary, F.M. Magenais of Lachine, Que. (WIA 11 May 1917), N.C. Millman and L.E. Porter (WIA 23 April 1917), both of Toronto, W.L. Rutledge of Fort William, Ont., A.C. Simpson of Montreal, and J.W. Warren, address unknown.

was an unqualified disaster, four of a flight of six being shot down by Richthofen and his companions. Richthofen judged the machine as 'quick and rather handy, with a powerful motor,' but considered the Albatros D-III 'undoubtedly superior.' Yet within a few weeks the Brisfit had emerged as a most formidable and versatile aircraft. Its most notable pilot was Lieutenant A.E. McKeever of Listowel, Ont., who demonstrated that the best use of the machine was to fly it as if it were a single-seat fighter, instead of using it in the standard two-seater fashion as a firing platform for the observer. McKeever was thus able to exploit fully the Bristol's flying qualities and the firepower of its fixed, forward-firing Vickers, while his observer was left to cover the tail with a Lewis gun on a flexible ring mounting.[61]

The second new aircraft, beset with engine problems, also had an inauspicious debut in April. The SE5 and its subsequent modification, the splendid SE5a with a 200-hp Hispano-Suiza engine, were among the fastest fighters manufactured during the war, showing top speeds in the 120–130 mph range during 1917 tests. The aircraft was the first British two-gun single-seater fighter, having a Lewis gun mounted on the top plane and a Vickers synchronized to fire through the airscrew.*[62]

Finally, in July, some RFC and RNAS squadrons began to re-equip with the Sopwith Camel, a stubby little machine that was to become the most famous of all British fighters. The Camel did not have the speed of the SE5a, but the concentration of weight in the forward section of its short fuselage and the pronounced torque of its engine, which made it unstable and somewhat hazardous to fly, also meant that in the right hands it had a quite startling agility. The Camel mounted a pair of belt-fed Vickers firing through the propeller arc, giving it even greater firepower than the SE5. In 1917 the Germans had no real answer to these aircraft, the Albatros D-V and D-Va, introduced in mid-summer, not being appreciably better than the D-III.[63]

Tactically, however, the Germans continued to hold the edge. Their *Geschwadern* – Richthofen's Circus was the first of them – were self-contained fighter wings which could be deployed on any part of the front to establish local air superiority, then moved again as the tactical situation demanded. This concept was well ahead of current British tactics. While the RFC was only now enlarging its basic tactical formation from three- to five-machine flights and was endeavouring to maintain such a continuous offensive strategy that 'along the whole stretch of the British Front there were seldom more than 25 fighting aircraft in the air together,' the Germans usually chose to mass one or more fighter wings at times and places of their own choosing and then make sudden sweeps over the line. Casualties were

---

*   As well as engine problems, the SE5 had initial difficulties with the synchronizing gear. In a letter home on 22 July W.A. Bishop wrote: 'Yesterday we did our first jobs on S.E. 5s and my gun was the only one that fired. It shot holes through my propellor.' Nevertheless, the strength, speed, and firepower of the aircraft was ideally suited to Bishop's heavy-handed flying and his tactical approach; he himself soon termed the SE5 'the best machine in the world.' In a period from 28 July to 16 August, when he was taken off operations, Bishop and his SE5 were credited with bringing down eleven aircraft, nine of them Albatros fighters. This brought his score to forty-seven. See Bishop biographical file, DHist.

heavy in the sparse and outnumbered British fighter patrols and even heavier among the relatively unprotected artillery and reconnaissance machines. 'If not before, Webb-Bowen [commanding v Brigade, RFC] ought to have changed his policy of withholding escorts at the beginning of July 1917,' recalled one former British pilot, 'when the new *Jagdgeschwader* moved north ... and British squadrons ... faced a much greater concentration of German fighters than before.'[64]

On 7 July, for example, a formation of six Sopwith 1½ Strutters of 45 Squadron, returning from a photo-reconnaissance mission to Wervicq, was attacked by eighteen or more Albatros scouts from the *Richthofengeschwader*. Two of the Sopwiths fell in flames, carrying with them their pilots and two Canadian observers, Lieutenants J.B. Fotheringham of Ottawa and F.C.H. Snyder of Kitchener, Ont. On this occasion Lieutenant C.T.R. Ward of Lennoxville, Que., flying as observer in the formation commander's machine, was able to bring back twenty-one exposed plates, but fifteen days later another formation of eight aircraft from the same squadron, sent to photograph Menin, was much less successful. Attacked by the Circus before it reached the objective, the formation was quickly broken up, three of its aircraft shot down, and the remainder driven back without any photographs. It was small consolation that a Canadian crew, piloted by Lieutenant E.F. Crossland of Toronto with G.W. Blaiklock of Montreal as observer, claimed one enemy machine driven down out of control.*[65]

Meanwhile, the fighter squadrons which might have been protecting these obsolescent fighter-reconnaissance machines or defending their ground forces against enemy bombing raids† were dissipating their strength flying distant offensive patrols far over the enemy lines. Arthur Gould Lee, then a junior pilot of 46 Squadron,‡ later an RAF air vice-marshal, has eloquently recorded the fighter pilot's disillusion with this interpretation of the offensive spirit:

The futility of such wasteful losses was the deeper because if a D[istant] O[ffensive] P[atrol] were weak in numbers ... it could easily be overwhelmed, but if the patrol were strong, the Germans could, and frequently did, ignore it, leaving us with a debit of forced-landed aeroplanes, wasted engine hours and wasted petrol.

Had there been a specific object in our deep penetrations, such as covering a bombing raid or a photographic reconnaissance, we would have thought nothing of it, but we could see no rational purpose in our coat-trailing D.O.P.s ... Was it to lower the morale of the

---

* Other Canadians flying with 45 Squadron in July included A.V. Campbell of Toronto, C.R. Hall of Sweetsburg, Que. (POW 13 June 1918), and A.E. Peel of Vancouver (WIA 10 Aug. 1917). No 45 Squadron's 1½ Strutters were replaced by Camels in July and August 1917. Jones, *War in the Air*, IV, 199

† 'Enemy planes visited us that week ... We looked up to see not one visitor but a fleet of them, great bombers riding the skies in battle formation. There were twenty-four of them, flying in perfect order and making straight for us ... Then there was a soft whirring noise and the first bomb fell with a thud and crash of flame. Then came the deluge – CRASH! CRASH! CRASH! – down they came, thick and fast.' Aubrey Wade, *Gunner on the Western Front* (London 1959), 85

‡ No 46 Squadron's Canadians during July included F.B. Baragar of Elm Creek, Man. (WIA 3 Sept. 1917), A.L. Fleming of Toronto, A.R. Fortin of Winnipeg, R.L.M. Ferrie of Hamilton (KIA 3 Jan. 1918), and H. Townson of Burnaby, BC. The squadron was withdrawn to the United Kingdom for home defence duties from 10 July to 30 August 1917. Jones, *War in the Air*, IV, 153

German Air Forces? This notion we found laughable, for ours was the morale that suffered.

Then did we find more fights or shoot down more Huns ...? On the contrary, combats were fewer, for the really intensive fighting was always near the Lines, within reach of the artillery-spotting and other patrolling two-seaters.

Unfortunately High Command held to the illusion that D.O.P.s not only produced bigger and better combats but were an important instrument of offensive policy, which was a meaningless slogan, for an offensive spirit in the air meant attacking the enemy with resolution, not showing the flag over Tournai. The consequence was that fighter pilots built up a deep resentment ... These insubordinate notions did not all come unbidden in the air but later on the ground, when there was time and mood to reflect.[66]

Despite being frequently outnumbered things did not always go so badly for the fighter pilots of the RFC. McKeever in 11 Squadron started his remarkable record of success by claiming his first victim on 26 June. He and his observers – 'gunners' might have been a more appropriate term – were credited with their eighth victory only eighteen days later.* On 21 July Raymond Collishaw and four other Canadians from Naval Ten – Flight Commander J.E. Sharman of Oak Lake, Man., Flight Lieutenant W.M. Alexander of Toronto and Flight Sub-Lieutenants E.V. Reid of Toronto and G.L. Trapp of New Westminster, BC – dived on about twenty enemy scouts over Passchendaele. Collishaw claimed three out of control in the course of a long general combat.[67] This struggle for air superiority imposed a considerable physical strain on the pilots, as 'Mel' Alexander recalled in tranquillity many years later. At nineteen years of age he was an experienced pilot in perhaps the most successful of all British air formations, the famed 'Black Flight' of Naval Ten.† 'Butterflies in your stomach is what you call it – nervous tension. You're almost panicky ...' he remembered, and after most patrols his jaws ached from the prolonged muscular tension.

On 24 July the staff of V Brigade could confidently report that 'the number of decisive combats had considerably decreased during the last few days which is a sure sign that the German morale is breaking down,' but the truth of the matter

---

* Before 1917 was out McKeever was awarded the MC and Bar and promoted captain. No 11 Squadron had many other Canadians on its rolls during July and August 1917. They included D.G. Davidson of Westmount, Que. (KIA 23 Aug. 1917), F.J. Foster of Clinton, Ont. (KIA 23 Aug. 1917), H.G. Kent of Toronto, J.A. LeRoyer of Quebec City (WIA 5 July 1917), W.B. MacKay of Ingersoll, Ont. (POW 27 July 1917), P.D. McIntosh of Toronto (WIA 17 July 1917), H.C. McKinney of Shannonville, Ont., T.W. Morse of Toronto (POW 20 Nov. 1917), E.D. Perney of Hamilton (KIA 23 Nov. 1917), J.A. Revill of Edmonton (KIA 11 Nov. 1917), C.E. Robertson of Walkerton, Ont. (KIA 12 July 1917), N.J. Taylor of Regina (POW 19 Sept. 1917), W.H. Walker of Saskatchewan Landing, Sask. (KIA 18 Aug. 1917), and J.L. Williamson of Toronto.

† The commander of this all-Canadian flight, Raymond Collishaw, with twenty-seven victories to his credit by 5 July, added ten more to his score and was shot down himself twice in three days before going on two months well-earned leave in early August. 'Pilots soon wear out as such,' recorded General Trenchard on 30 August 1917 when offering GHQ some points concerning the formation of a separate air service. 'There are not enough ground billets for all worn out pilots. Arrangements should be made for them to be received into the Army or the Navy if they desire such employment.' Air 1/521/16/12/3

was that the enemy, subject to similar strains, was holding up about equally well. This brief lull in the air battle had more to do with re-deployments in the air arm of the Fourth German Army and the difficulties of finding sufficient airfields on the watery Flanders plain than it had with German morale. In an air battle over Polygon Wood two days later a German force of about fifty fighters engaged almost as many British scouts, while down below four German two-seaters successfully reconnoitred the British line in front of Ypres. That neither side was able to shoot down a single opponent in such a large dogfight suggests that they were very well-matched, rather than that the German morale was breaking down. Throughout this period, too, enemy reconnaissance machines were able to keep a satisfactory watch on the two-and-a-half mile wide main zone of traffic which ran parallel to the front some three miles behind. A single reconnaissance machine, flying at high speed, could cover the whole corridor of the British front in less than an hour. The observed volume and regularity of ground traffic contributed greatly to the enemy's understanding of the British build-up.[68]

On the other hand, the German scouts were even less able to prevent the RFC's reconnaissance and artillery observation aircraft from fulfilling their functions. The weekly intelligence summary of the Fourth German Army recorded on 18 July that 'the number of [enemy] reconnaissance formations has doubled,' although 'these mainly confined themselves to close reconnaissance; the line Courtrai-Tourcoing was reached only once.' Reconnaissance on this scale meant that the Germans could keep few secrets, and it could only have been a slight consolation to them that forty-five British machines were claimed to have been shot down in the week under review, twenty-two of them falling within the German lines. By the end of the month 9 Squadron,* attached to the Fifth Army's XIV Corps in the tip of the salient, was flying fifteen counter-battery and twenty or more trench shoots a day despite all attempts to stop them.[69]

After several postponements the ground attack was finally scheduled for the morning of 31 July. As had happened earlier at Vimy, however, the most effective air operations had been conducted prior to the ground assault. The weather deteriorated so badly on the 29th that the air war virtually ceased until dawn on the 31st. In late afternoon the weather again closed in and flying had to be postponed. In the interval overcast skies and drizzling rain severely limited air operations. The artillery machines were unable to conduct a single shoot, contact patrolling was ineffective, and neither bombing nor close ground support missions could claim much success. For their marginal efforts the RFC paid dearly; thirty machines were rendered unserviceable (mostly by ground fire) during the day.[70]

It continued to rain intermittently for ninety-six hours while the poor British infantry carried the line forward to a maximum depth of 3000 yards at the cost of some 31,000 casualties. Every small British advance was met by a determined German counter-attack, in which the German *Schlachtstaffeln*, unlike their British

---

* Canadians with 9 Squadron during the period of the offensive included J.P. Cunninghame of Red Deer, Alta, F.W. Curtis of Toronto (KIA 14 Aug. 1917), F.B. Doran of Iroquois, Ont. (KIA 14 Aug. 1917), G.D. Gillie of Cornwall, Ont., C. Knowles (WIA 24 July 1917), A.G. Peace, and H.S. Quigley, all of Toronto. G.S.B. Fuller of Sherbrooke, Que, joined the squadron in September 1917.

opponents, used large formations of close support aircraft to aid their ground forces in tactical arrangements which had been carefully worked out and rehearsed beforehand.[71] With only half of the planned territorial gains actually in British hands, Haig temporarily called off the ground attack, explaining to the British government that 'The low-lying, clayey soil, torn by shells and sodden with rain, turned to a succession of vast muddy pools. The valleys of the choked and overflowing streams were speedily transformed into long stretches of bog ... In these conditions operations of any magnitude became impossible, and the resumption of our offensive was necessarily postponed until a period of fine weather should allow the ground to recover.'[72]

The aerial battle could not so easily be stopped and restarted. Airpower's battlefield mobility, born of its speed and ability to manoeuvre in a third dimension, means that it cannot be turned on or off as simply as ground power. Armies can fight hard for days or weeks or months, and then relapse into a semi-comatose state operationally, without losing the ability to hold their ground – indeed, that was the essence of trench warfare on the Western Front. But, as Trenchard clearly saw, airpower is offensive by definition. It must hold at least a local superiority or it holds nothing: superiority cannot be maintained by 'holding ground.' Air forces, like navies, can ensure superiority only by an offensive strategy. It was therefore impossible for the RFC to adopt a static, defensive posture. But even after the rain stopped, on the 5th, the development of the British air offensive was seriously impeded by heavy cloud cover. Artillery co-operation was particularly hampered, being made 'most difficult, if not impracticable.' When the skies did clear a little the corps pilots might have to contend alone with German fighters. On 6 August, for example, an RE8 of 4 Squadron, on artillery observation duties over Zillebeke Lake and piloted by Captain W.H. Gilroy of Mount Forest, Ont., with Lieutenant H.K. Thompson of Erindale, Ont., as observer,* was attacked by an enemy scout which shot away the rudder controls. Using the ailerons, Gilroy turned and dived at once towards Ypres while his observer held the enemy off with his Lewis gun. They made a successful crash-landing inside the British lines.[73] Neither was hurt but the British artillery on II Corps front was temporarily blinded.

Three days later another RE8, of 16 Squadron, flown by Second Lieutenant J.A. Hutchison of Fordwich, Ont., with Lieutenant A. Willans of Ottawa as his observer, encountered two Albatros scouts.† They shot down the first and drove off the second. Few corps squadron aircrews were as successful in combat as those of No 16, supporting the Canadian Corps. It usually had a very high proportion of Canadians and enjoyed a widespread reputation for skill, courage, and tenacity. 'On every flight over the lines we met their ugly two-seaters dodging Archie ...'

---

* Other Canadians serving as aircrew in 4 Squadron on 6 August 1917 included A.H. Bailey of Saskatchewan, C.E.B. Corbould of New Westminster, BC, T.F. Flanagan of Waterville, NS (who had just returned to the squadron after being wounded on 12 June 1917), R.G. McMullen of Woodstock, Ont., F.L. Steben of Brockville, Ont. (WIA 16 Sept. 1917), T. Weir of Toronto, and W.H. Weller of St Peter's, NS (WIA 16 Sept. 1917).

† Other Canadians in 16 Squadron at this time included E. Alder, address unknown (WIA 12 May 1917), F.H. Baguley of Toronto, A.E. Hahn of Tavistock, Ont., F.E. Neily of Esquimalt, BC (KIA 27 Dec. 1917), J.J. O'Loughlin of Toronto, E.H. Read of Ottawa (KIA 26 Dec. 1917), and R.J.S. White of Regina.

wrote an admiring British fighter pilot, '... they never "gave-way" to the German fighters unless they were hopelessly outnumbered, but, staying to fight, succeeded occasionally in bringing down enemy fighters.' Perhaps their performance was influenced by a new commanding officer who had joined the squadron in early July. Major C.F.A. Portal would win a Bar to his DSO before he was posted back to England in June 1918. Twenty years later another Englishman who had served with him in 16 Squadron guessed that 'by now [he] must be a big noise in the Royal Air Force; his officers then deeply respected his coolness and gift of leadership.'*[74]

After an unsuccessful attempt to storm the Gheluvelt plateau on 10 August, GHQ resolved to renew the offensive. Twenty-four hours before the assault in Flanders was renewed, however, a diversionary attack was launched by the Canadian Corps in the south against a feature known as Hill 70 on the outskirts of Lens. This attack went in on 15 August and, for obvious reasons, little attempt was made to achieve surprise. On 9 August a simultaneous low-level attack by six Nieuport 17s of 40 Squadron, including two flown by Lieutenant H.A. Kennedy of Hamilton, Ont., and Second Lieutenant W.L. Harrison of Toronto,† brought down all six enemy observation balloons on that sector of the front. This certainly hampered enemy observation but it also gave a preliminary indication that something unusual was happening. Then for two days and nights prior to the assault bombers of 10 (Armstrong-Whitworth), 25 (DH4), and 27 (Martinsyde) Squadrons‡ attacked railway junctions, aerodromes, and rest billets behind the German line. A prolonged and very thorough artillery bombardment preceded the assault; but, despite all these clear warnings, the Canadian staff work achieved its now customary standard of excellence and the troops fought so well that within an hour and thirty-five minutes all the key objectives had been taken and the summit of Hill 70 was firmly in Canadian hands.

No 16 Squadron furnished contact and artillery observation patrols for the ground attack and 8 (Naval) Squadron's Sopwith Camels§ endeavoured to keep

---

* As Chief of the Air Staff, 1940–5, Air Chief Marshal Sir Charles Portal (later Marshal of the Royal Air Force Viscount Portal of Hungerford) was to play a dominant role in the setting of allied air policy and the direction of the Commonwealth air forces during the Second World War. See Denis Richards, *Portal of Hungerford* (London 1977).

† Canadians serving in 40 Squadron during August 1917 included Kennedy (KIA 22 Aug. 1917), Harrison (WIA 12 April 1918), C.L. Bath of Toronto (WIA 3 Nov. 1917), and A.E. Godfrey of Vancouver. L.A. Edens of St John's, Nfld (KIA 18 March 1918) was also with the squadron.

‡ Canadian aircrew serving in 10 Squadron this month included W. Crowther of Welland, Ont. (KIA 31 Oct. 1917), W.E. Dexter, address unknown (WIA 3 Dec. 1917), R.C. Farrow of Vancouver, T.G. Gordon, address unknown, C.N. Milligan of Victoria (WIA 21 April 1917), G.M. Morrison of Amherst, NS, and W.G. Stuart of Cardston, Alta (WIA 13 Dec. 1917). Among those in 25 Squadron were D.L. Burgess of Ottawa, J.H. Kirk of Sussex, NB, C.T. Lally of Wainwright, Alta (WIA 8 Dec. 1917), P.L. McGavin of Toronto (KIA 14 Aug. 1917), E.A. Plamondon of St Hyacinthe, Que., F.A. Watson, address unknown, L.F. Williams of Fort Frances, Ont., G.S. Wood, address unknown, and A.J. Wright of Barrie, Ont. In 27 Squadron were C.N.F. Jeffrey of Winnipeg and A.E. McVittie of Sudbury, Ont.

§ Canadians serving in 8 (Naval) Squadron during August 1917 included H.H.S. Fowler of Bowmanville, Ont., A.R. Knight of Collingwood, Ont., S.H. McCrudden of Toronto, R. McDonald of James River Station, NS (KIA 8 May 1918), and H. McK. Reid of Belleville, Ont. (KIA 23 Feb. 1918).

the upper air clear of enemy fighters. However, it was two new tactical procedures intended to dislocate the inevitable German counter-attacks that particularly distinguished the air plan for the assault on Hill 70. Fighter aircraft patrolling at high altitudes (where they had to be if they were to meet the enemy fighters on equal terms) had always found it extremely difficult to spot low-flying enemy machines whose upper surfaces had been skilfully camouflaged to blend into the battle-scarred earth below. In the past German artillery observation and ground support aircraft had often been able to operate unchallenged at low levels even when the British had an immediate air superiority.

This problem was met by having six Nieuports of 40 Squadron stationed on an advanced landing ground at Mazingarbe and a ground observation station set up on the high ground west of Loos overlooking the battlefield. Whenever a low-flying enemy machine was seen over the front a message was wirelessed to Mazingarbe where a waiting Nieuport could take off immediately and be at the specified point within a few minutes. Then a system was developed that, by means of a letter code laid out on the ground in white canvas, permitted a machine already in the air and circling the landing ground to be directed to a particular target area. During the day sorties from this advanced landing ground resulted in two enemy aircraft destroyed, three shot down out of control, and a number of others driven off, as well as the frequent 'blinding' of the German artillery. Against this only one British machine was lost. The accuracy of the wireless messages was especially remarked upon, pilots reporting that in the majority of cases enemy aeroplanes were found at the height and locality indicated.*[75] Indeed, Second Lieutenant A.E. Godfrey of Vancouver, one of the pilots detailed for duty at Mazingarbe, was credited with three victories in three days, starting on 15 August.†

The second new tactic also involved the use of an advanced landing ground, although in this case the purpose was to allow the machine concerned more time over the battlefield rather than to get it there quickly. No 43 Squadron, flying its obsolescent Sopwith 1½ Strutters out of Mazingarbe about five miles back, was employed all day in flights of three aircraft at a time, closely watching a zone about 7000 yards wide and 1500 yards deep behind the German lines where any counter-attacks must necessarily form up. In addition to reporting back to the British artillery liaison officers at the airfield, the crews were ordered to attack with their machine-guns any concentrations of infantry or artillery they might observe. The Sopwiths, although slow, were exceptionally strong. Despite being 'frequently hit' from ground fire which left four of them unserviceable by the end of the day, only two machines were lost and three airmen wounded, while one German aircraft was destroyed and several others driven away.

---

* But it would seem that not all enemy aircraft were being reported. The 5th Canadian Infantry Battalion's War Diary for 14–18 August 1917 records that on the 16th '... German aeroplanes were very active flying at an extremely low altitude, and firing on parties of our men, spotting our new positions, and registering their batteries on them. Our planes flew much higher and part of the time did not appear to interfere with the Hun Machines, nor make any attempt to hinder their operations.' DHist 112.3H1.009 (D259), vol. II

† Godfrey's successes may have been due in part to his having fitted his Nieuport with a twin Lewis Gun mounting of his own design which enabled him to double his rate of fire. Godfrey biographical file, DHist

More important, many potential counter-attacks were broken up by pilots like Second Lieutenant S. McC. Peterkin of Toronto, who attacked 'a great number of troops' gathering in the Drocourt trenches from a height of 200 feet. A 1½ Strutter in which Lieutenant W.G. Bell of Toronto was flying as observer attacked a German transport column near Fouquières and then machine-gunned troops near Annay and in the Bois de Quatorze. Another Sopwith observed a body of German infantry estimated to be 1600 strong forming up behind the Bois de Dixhuit, about 3000 yards north of Lens. After a low-level machine-gun attack the aircraft returned to Mazingarbe, where a liaison officer telephoned the map reference of the enemy concentration to the Canadian Corps heavy artillery. In the cryptic words of I Brigade's official report, 'The counter-attack did not materialize.' No 16 Squadron, too, was busy spotting for the Canadian artillery; in the afternoon four waves of German infantry, marching across the open 'through fountains of earth sent up by the heavy shells' and then 'through a hail of shrapnel and machine-gun bullets' delivered by the BEs of 16 Squadron, were all but annihilated.[76]

The resumption of the Flanders offensive was preceded by a week of intense air fighting, marked on the British side by 60 Squadron's 'Billy' Bishop being credited with his 43rd and 44th victories on 13 August.* With these successes Bishop surpassed the late Albert Ball's claims and was recognized as the top-scoring RFC pilot. Other aces, such as McCudden and Rhys-Davids and the Canadians McKeever, Godfrey, and 56 Squadron's Lieutenant R.T.C. Hoidge of Toronto (who was credited with sixteen victories by the end of July) continued to add to their personal scores, but the Allies were still far from having their own way in the air. On the German side, Werner Voss had returned from leave to take command of *Jasta 10* and his score was mounting steadily into the forties. By 31 July Richthofen, recovered from his wound, was flying again. On 16 August he shot down his 58th victim, and the next day presided over a celebration marking *Jasta 11*'s one hundredth victory. In this stern battle of attrition the toll of British casualties rose by over 100 during August, from 209 in the four weeks ending 27 July to 328 in the four weeks ending 31 August. On 13 August a letter from Sir Douglas Haig to the Chief of the General Staff, reflecting Trenchard's views, asked that the Admiralty be informed that the shortage of pilots in the RNAS squadrons attached to the RFC raised the possibility of a deterioration of their morale.[77]

If the assault on Hill 70 had been a demonstration of how a set-piece attack should be carried out, the Battle of Langemarck, which began the next day in front of Ypres, provided an excellent illustration of how it should *not* be done. The British air plan was hampered by a misty morning and cloud patches which made observation uncertain but the principles which had been so effectively applied at Lens were in any case diluted and much of their potential lost at Langemarck. There was still a grave lack of consistency in RFC staff work. One RE8 was to patrol each corps front to report counter-attacks, but this arrangement was by no means foolproof. Thus the 8th British Division, which had suffered over 3000 casualties on Pilckem Ridge only two weeks earlier, was struck by a powerful German

---

* Other Canadians serving in 60 Squadron during August 1917 included J.B. Crompton of Toronto, W.J. Rutherford of Westmount, Que., and F.O. Soden, a New Brunswick-born pilot whose family was living in England.

counter-attack. Prior to it the division had received only one indefinite air report of enemy infantry forming up. Two DH5s were allotted to each divisional front for close ground support duties during the assault on the final objective, but the weather and the confused nature of the ground fighting prevented the pilots from properly fulfilling their role. Two patrols, of four Nieuports each, whose orders were to fly the whole Fifth Army front and help break up counter-attacks, tried to make up for the DH5's failures by engaging some of the enemy strong points holding up British attacks, but this inevitably distracted them somewhat from their other duties. They were also instructed, together with two other fighters, to drive off all low-flying enemy machines along the whole army front. Such wide-ranging and disparate orders demonstrated the failure of some RFC brigade staffs to appreciate the problems and pressures of combat flying.[78]

Ever since Bishop's spectacular low-level, single-handed fighter attack on a German aerodrome the possibility of destroying enemy machines on the ground by a series of individual assaults seems to have been much in the minds of British planners. Thus the air operation orders for the Battle of Langemarck instructed one fighter, armed with four 20-lb bombs, to attack each enemy airfield in the vicinity shortly after first light, with further attacks throughout the day as opportunity offered. None of these attacks appears to have done any significant damage.[79] The experience of 70 Squadron's Lieutenant J.G. Crang of Toronto* was, largely by chance, one of the more successful. He was ordered to attack Bisseghem.

I crossed the lines over ARMENTIERS [sic] and proceeded south of COMMINES and arrived over BISSEGHEM aerodrome. I found it exactly in accordance with the photograph. All the hangars were closed; there were no machines on the ground and no people about.

I came up from the S.E. over two Bessonaux Hangars, and I dropped a bomb from about 500 feet over these hangars, but it fell on the road behind and a little to the right. I went straight across the aerodrome, diving down all the time, on two groups of R.E. Hangars on either side of some trees. I dropped all my bombs and observed one fall in the trees between the two groups of hangars.

I then circled round at about 100 feet and fired into the two Bessonaux hangars with both guns, but could see no effect. The aerodrome still presented a deserted appearance, the hangars all remaining closed, and nobody appearing on the scene ...

I then turned south and [about 2½ miles S.W. of Coutrai] ... I observed another aerodrome: there were at least five hangars ... I fired both guns into one R.E. Hangar from about 20 feet above, and as I crossed the aerodrome, I saw a 2-seater machine on the ground with nobody about.

I immediately turned back and fired both guns into it. As I did so I turned and observed the R.E. hangar, into which I had previously fired, in flames. The canvas had already burnt off, and I could see a 2-seater machine burning inside.[80]

Another notable effort on the 16th was that of Second Lieutenant R.D. Starley, a prewar English immigrant to Canada. He was flying a machine of 4 Squadron

---

* Canadians serving in 70 Squadron during August also included R.S. Ashby of Greenwood, BC (WIA 15 Sept. 1917), J.W. Gillespie of Toronto (POW 19 Aug. 1917), J.C. Huggard of Winnipeg (POW 5 Sept. 1917), H.D. Layfield of Vancouver (WIA 21 Sept. 1917), A.A. Lessard of Haileybury, Ont., and A.J.S. Sisley of Toronto (KIA 10 Sept. 1917).

detailed for counter-attack patrols and had just located 'a large force of the enemy infantry who were about to attack' when his machine was hit by a passing shell. Two longerons, a main spar, a centre section strut, two fuselage struts, and the aileron balance wire of his machine were cut through, while his radio transmitter was also destroyed and his observer wounded. Starley flew his wrecked RE8 first to the divisional HQ, where he dropped a written message which led to nine artillery batteries being switched on to the German concentration, and then back to his base at Abeele. He was awarded an MC for his efforts. Many others were not so fortunate. No 9 Squadron, attached to XIV Corps, lost twelve aircrew killed when their machines were hit in the air by shells from the British barrage.[81]

But generally speaking, in the air as on the ground, the courage and skill of the fighting man were not sufficient to overcome the poor staff work and over-optimism of the higher commanders. The inefficient use of resources, vagueness of assignment, and dispersion of effort ensured that no aspect of the low-level plan proved quite adequate. The German artillery concentration behind the Gheluvelt plateau continued to punish the attackers on the ground both during and after the assault. Prompt counter-attacks drove the British back from many of their gains. Although the remnants of Langemarck village had been taken and held by night-fall, and the salient deepened by more than a mile at one spot, nothing of conse-quence had been gained. The enemy was basing his defence on the bastions of Gheluvelt plateau and the Forêt d'Houthuilst; as long as they were secure a British advance in between them was of little consequence.[82]

During all this time bombing continued to absorb a large percentage of resources. Whenever the weather permitted the high-level day bombers of the RFC plugged away at enemy aerodromes and communication and transportation centres with-out any very noticeable effect, while the night bombers attempted similar raids from much lower heights with similar results. The combination of difficulties imposed by First World War navigation techniques and bomb-sight technology, added to the comparative paucity of bombers and their limited weight-carrying capacities in relation to their objectives, made bombing a questionable proposi-tion. Its main effect may have been to harm enemy morale, to judge from the effect of German night bombing on British troops. In mid-August, for example, one British battalion bound for the Ypres Salient and encamped behind the town, found its twelve nights there 'almost nightmares. We had very little sleep, for instead of one visit from the enemy bombers, they came over in relays and some-times we had four doses in one night.'[83]

While the great Flanders offensive petered out in the mud and degenerated into limited, expensive, but largely vain attempts to gain minor tactical advan-tage, the struggle for air superiority went on unabated. On 21 August an RE8 of 7 Squadron flown by Second Lieutenant M.A O'Callaghan of New Westminster, BC,* was attacked by four Albatros scouts while taking photographs near St Julien. O'Callaghan's observer opened fire on the nearest and sent down in

---

* O'Callaghan was wounded in action on 8 October 1918. Among other Canadians serving in 7 Squadron during August 1917 were G.W. Butchart of Owen Sound, Ont., L.V. Gray of Vancouver (KIA 16 Aug. 1917), R.H. Jarvis of Toronto, B.W. Ryan of Calgary (KIA 20 Sept. 1917), and G.F. Turberville, address unknown.

flames *Oberleutnant* Eduard Dostler, the CO of *Jasta 6* with twenty victories to his credit. The next day a patrol of Naval Ten, led by 'Mel' Alexander, intercepted a number of Albatros scouts which were attacking a formation of DH4s. In the dogfight that followed Flight Sub-Lieutenant J.G. Manuel of Edmonton, who had joined the squadron on his first operational posting only nine days earlier, destroyed one enemy machine and drove another down out of control, while Alexander and Flight Sub-Lieutenant G.L. Trapp were each credited with one out of control. This marked Alexander's third victory in five days, a feat which won him the DSC.[84]

By the end of August the Flanders offensive had cost the British some 68,000 casualties for very little gain in ground, but it had ensured that the French front would remain free from major attack for another month. The navy's anti-submarine campaign and convoy system was also proving successful. It might seem, therefore, that the Cabinet and War Policy Committee could now have cancelled the offensive. Lloyd George personally wished to do so, but on 4 September Haig once again convinced the politicians in London that the offensive must be maintained and the Germans prevented from taking the initiative.[85]

The Commander-in-Chief had already decided that, in view of the casualties of the Fifth Army, the principal role in any further operations must be transferred to the Second Army. Haig had enlarged General Plumer's command to include much of the Fifth Army and ordered him to prepare an attack between the Ypres-Comines canal and the Ypres-Roulers railway, with his axis of advance on the Menin Road and his main objective the Gheluvelt plateau. Plumer asked for and received three weeks for his preparations.[86] This lull in the ground fighting was distinguished by the best weather of the whole campaign.

With clearer skies air fighting increased and formations grew significantly in size, as the tactics of aerial combat changed and the air battle of attrition approached its climax. The Germans were now attacking British corps machines in formations of two layers, the upper echelon being intended to keep any British fighters busy while the lower one 'went in and did fearful execution among the FE's.' The British answer was to develop an additional layer for their own fighter patrols, so that squadron formations were now seen over the front. The enemy promptly retorted with three-layered formations, in which the first two engaged the two echelons of British fighters while the third, biding its time, waited until the others were engaged and then attacked the corps machines. The RFC response was the predictable one of also introducing a third layer, so that as many as sixty machines might be involved in one engagement. The nature of the actual combat was changing as well. One pilot reported that 'large formations don't mix it like small ones. Instead of short close-up dog-fights, with in-fighting and duels and quick results, we're having long-drawn-out skirmishings between massed groups taking nibbles at each other.'[87]

But such massive engagements did not occur every day. On a smaller, more frequent scale, corps machines continued to be shot down for lack of close protection by fighter escorts; British offensive patrols of four, five, or six machines, flying deep over enemy territory, continued to be whittled down by enemy anti-aircraft fire and engine failure, as well as the inherent disadvantages of fighting on the enemy's terms. There were 276 RFC casualties on the Western Front during the four weeks ending on 28 September, at least forty-five of them Canadians. The rate of casualties per hundred sorties rose from 7.97 in August to 8.06 per cent, a figure only surpassed when the RFC had been so disastrously outclassed technologically in the spring of the year.[88] There was, however, no alteration in General Trenchard's relentless policy of total offensive. The merit of an offensive strategy combined with defensive tactics which might have saved both men and machines was apparently never seriously considered at RFC Headquarters. Indeed, although Trenchard made frequent visits to his front-line units, it is not at all clear whether he appreciated fully the morale problem developing in his squadrons.

Those outstanding pilots whose actions and opinions have since been most frequently recorded and dramatically presented seem – perhaps naturally, since they were the most successful – to have felt these pressures less than most aircrew. Very little has been written about the morale problems which developed among ordinary flyers during the summer and early fall of 1917, but one undistinguished participant has recorded how

Our casualties mounted alarmingly. There was hardly an evening when the same people gathered in the mess. It was here that a certain amount of frank and free comment on our casualty rate could be heard ... our commanding officer discouraged it; but it continued ... We did not believe that the losses we were suffering were helping the allies in their war effort.

This feeling, although officially looked on as defeatist, was prevalent among operational pilots ... Officers of the higher command, from Major-General Hugh Trenchard as he was then, down to the commanders of wings, according to the critics, were throwing away aircraft and lives for no distinguishable purpose. At any rate they did not convince their pilots that there was a purpose. The aim seemed to be to contrive the greatest number of confrontations of British and German aircraft and to have the greatest number of battles in the air. To us junior officers there was no discernible military objective.[89]

In the trenches infantry subalterns were saying the same kind of things about Haig and his generals.

Squadron commanders sometimes privately shared the feelings of their pilots. While admiring Trenchard's integrity and 'the magnificent influence that he exerted in France,' Major W. Sholto Douglas, commanding 84 Squadron,* makes it clear in his memoirs that he, too, questioned the inflexibility of Trenchard's policy.[90] His doubts, and Haig's and Trenchard's own tentatively expressed fears of a crisis in morale amongst their airmen, were to be disagreeably vindicated before the end of the month.

In the meantime General Plumer was assembling the resources of both the Fifth and Second Armies for the Battle of the Menin Road. The weight of the

* Douglas ended his career as Marshal of the Royal Air Force, Lord Douglas of Kirtleside. Included on the strength of 84 Squadron when he took it to France in September were W.H. Brown of Victoria, W.R. Kingsland of Ottawa (POW 18 Nov. 1917), T.V. Lord of Fenelon Falls, Ont. (POW 15 Oct. 1917), P.J. Moloney of Peterborough, Ont. (WIA 22 Nov. 1917), and F.L. Yeomans of Belleville, Ont. (POW 21 Oct. 1917).

attack would be on the Second Army front and the initial operations order for II Brigade, RFC, showed an improved understanding of the need to provide support for corps machines by establishing a two-layer system of protective fighter patrols over the battle zone, with the upper layer operating at a height of about 10,000 feet and the lower patrols being ordered to 'go right down' if necessary to protect corps aeroplanes. But there were still unreasonable demands included in the operation orders. It was carefully stipulated that 'no formation of more than six Scouts is permitted.' In addition, three pairs of ultra low-level (less than 500 feet) 'rover' scouts were detailed primarily to 'attack parties of enemy infantry, artillery and transport' along the entire army front. They were to give 'special attention ... to the discovery and attack of the enemy's Counter Attack troops.' The 'rovers' were also to report 'any information' which might be useful to the Army Report Centre established at Locre. In other words, while flying their machines at a dangerously low level, attacking any ground targets noticed, and keeping a weather eye open for developing counter-attacks, these aerial paragons were to fight any enemy contact patrols or scout aircraft which they might encounter and write, on 'cards conveniently fixed in the nacelle,' particulars of anything happening on the ground which they felt might interest Army Headquarters. These cards then had to be dropped in message bags on a spot nearly nine miles from the battleground.[91]

Another planning weakness lay in the noticeable absence of arrangements to have any fighter element on stand-by at an advanced landing ground in the manner which had proven so successful at Hill 70. Here the II Brigade staff was in a difficult position. By mid-August British field commanders had realized that fighter aircraft were useful for more than air fighting and had subsequently suggested to higher authorities that they should be allowed to make fuller use of them in ground support roles. GHQ took up the idea with alacrity, but on 19 September General Trenchard laid down that 'the number of fast fighting machines at present available does not admit of such a large proportion being allotted for these operations.' Trenchard's concern was the maintenance of his offensive patrols and, with this sort of disagreement occurring at the highest levels, the predicament of RFC brigadiers endeavouring to please two masters was not enviable.[92]

Not surprisingly, when the battle was joined on 20 September, the enemy was able to make good use of his ground support and trench patrol aircraft.* The Australians, advancing to their final objective on the Second Army's left flank, were machine-gunned by a formation of eight aircraft which also strafed the field artillery batteries behind them. The 9th (Scottish) Division found that 'while the consolidation was in progress a hostile aeroplane, flying up and down our line, roughly indicated the position to the German gunners.' The next day 'the German artillery, assisted by aeroplanes, persistently shelled our battery areas,' reported

---

* By the fall of 1917 the Germans were using specialized machines for both these roles. The Junkers J-1 *Infanterieflieger* was framed in metal and the wings covered with corrugated sheet duralumin; the only non-metallic elements were the ash tail skid and the fabric that covered the fuselage behind the 5mm armour that housed engine, pilot observer, and fuel tank. The two-seater Halberstadt CL-II was the first aircraft specially designed for ground attack. It also had an armoured shell for engine, crew, and fuel tank, but was otherwise built of wood and fabric. Being much lighter, it was faster and more manoeuvrable than the J-1 *möbelwagen*.

the 23rd Division historian; two days later, 'hostile artillery and aircraft were very active.'[93]

In other respects, however, the RFC did much better. During the 20th there were a total of 108 air combats recorded along the battlefront but only ten of them involved corps machines, indicating that the policy of layered protective patrols was working well. Consequently, once the morning mist had cleared the corps machines had a most successful day, 394 zone calls being sent down to the artillery, about one-third of them bringing immediate fire responses. There were also at least eight instances of imminent counter-attacks being broken up by artillery fire which, by the Germans' own accounts, 'tore great gaps in the advancing companies and caused complete disorganization.'[94]

At first light the usual attacks were made on all the German aerodromes in the vicinity. This time, instead of single-seater fighters, Martinsyde bombers of 27 Squadron* hit all four fields of the Richthofen Circus simultaneously and inflicted serious damage in at least one case. Richthofen's own *Jasta 11*, at Marcke near Courtrai, sustained the heaviest attack, three machines being destroyed, four damaged, and four ground crew killed with a number of others wounded,[95] and this success may have played a part in the German failure to challenge successfully the British high-altitude offensive patrols on the 20th.

The aircraft allocated to ground support also provided very useful assistance on occasion, 70 Squadron's Second Lieutenants F.G. Quigley of Toronto and H.D. Layfield of Vancouver† being singled out for their work in suppressing fire from enemy machine-gun emplacements. Second Lieutenant J. MacHaffie of Oakville, Ont., serving with 29 Squadron‡ and destined to be killed the following day, 'swooped down on a party of about 70 enemy troops on the POELCAPPELLE-WESTROOSBEKE [sic] road and scattered them,' while 23 Squadron's Lieutenant G.A.H. Trudeau of Longueuil, Que.,§ 'attacked enemy infantry ... from 500 feet and scattered them.' He then returned to strafe the villages of Passchendaele and Westroosebeke 'from a low altitude, scattering several bodies of troops. He also dispersed troops on the roads north-west of ZANDVOORDE.'[96]

No 1 (Naval) Squadron made a very strong impression on the enemy with what the squadron diarist chose to describe as 'crawling patrols.' Among the most

---

* Canadians serving with 27 Squadron in September 1917 included A.E. McVittie of Sudbury, Ont., and E. Waterlow of Regina (KIA 16 July 1918).

† Layfield was wounded in action the next day. Other Canadians in 70 Squadron in September included R.S. Ashby of Greenwood, BC (WIA 15 Sept. 1917), R.O. Babbitt of St Thomas, Ont., E.B. Booth of Toronto (WIA 11 Nov. 1917), H. Cook, address unknown (KIA 17 Oct. 1917), T.B. Fennwick of Cranbrook, BC (POW 26 Sept. 1917), W.H.R. Gould of Uxbridge, Ont. (KIA 26 Sept. 1917), J.C. Huggard of Winnipeg (POW 5 Sept. 1917), E.D. Neal of Toronto (WIA 30 Sept. 1917), C.W. Primeau of Toronto (KIA 27 Oct. 1917), C.D. Scott of Vancouver (KIA 30 Sept. 1917), and A.J.S. Sisley of Toronto (KIA 10 Sept. 1917).

‡ Canadians in 29 Squadron included S.L. Crowther of Toronto (KIA 20 Sept. 1917), D.A.F. Hilton of St Catharines, Ont., E.S. Meek of Sandford, Ont., F.M. Nash of Charlottetown, PEI (POW 3 Oct. 1917), and G.B. Wigle of Ruthven, Ont. (WIA 10 Oct. 1917).

§ In 23 Squadron Canadians in addition to Trudeau included G.I.D. Marks and N. McLeod (KIA 14 Oct. 1917), both of Toronto, R.M. Smith of Ottawa (POW 31 Oct. 1917), and E. Taylor of Vancouver (WIA 14 Sept. 1917, POW 26 Sept. 1917).

notable attacks recorded, Flight Sub-Lieutenant S.W. Rosevear of Port Arthur, Ont., poured four hundred rounds into a column of troops he found on the road northeast of Becelaere and 'caused general panic. Pilot saw a number of dead on the road as he was leaving and others ran into the ditches.' On a second sortie Rosevear 'used all his ammunition up on small scattered bodies of troops near the YPRES-ROULERS railway and E. of POLYGONE [sic] WOOD.'* Flight Sub-Lieutenant A.G.A. Spence of Toronto, on his second sortie of the day, strafed a force of enemy troops in the vicinity of a large dug-out, driving them into it and pinning them there for some time before causing some casualties on a nearby road. Meanwhile his fellow Torontonian, Flight Sub-Lieutenant W.M. Clapperton, fired 250 rounds at a group of enemy infantry near Becelaere (they 'scattered wildly in all directions') and got his Sopwith Triplane 'riddled from machine gun and rifle fire' in return.[97]

Although these operations may have influenced the progress of the battle, fully effective ground attack techniques still had to be developed by the RFC. It was claimed that more than 28,000 rounds were expended against ground targets during the day, yet a study of all available ground support reports suggests that comparatively few pilots were willing to expend more than one drum of Lewis ammunition per sortie against their ground targets. This reluctance may have been a result of burdening them with too many different tasks, thus making them hesitant to over-emphasize any one. Not until the Battle of Cambrai in late November would there be any real attempt to implement a training programme for units allocated specifically to ground attack roles. This was particularly unfortunate since German infantrymen were already being trained in the use of machine-guns against enemy aircraft and, as Rosevear commented in a letter to his parents in Port Arthur, 'we paid for it in the pilots missing.'[98]

By the end of the day the British armies were firmly astride the plateau and the following days were marked by a series of local attacks and counter-attacks as both sides attempted to improve their positions. On 26 September the British attacked again with the objective of occupying the rest of Polygon Wood, the summit of Hill 40 north of Zonnebeke station and the southern part of Zonnebeke village. For a change, reasonable flying weather prevailed and very effective air-artillery co-operation in breaking up German counter-attack formations limited the still high rate of British ground casualties. German casualties were so heavy that their High Command felt compelled to make major changes in their defensive

---

* After winning the DSC and Bar and being credited with twenty-three victories, Rosevear was killed in action on 25 April 1918. Other Canadians with 1 (Naval) Squadron during its February to November tour with the RFC included E. Anthony of Maitland, NS, W.J. Beattie of Stratford, Ont. (KIA 30 Sept. 1917), C.G. Brock of Winnipeg (WIA 21 Aug. 1918), C.W.L. Calvert of Toronto (WIA 26 Sept. 1917), W.H. Chisam of Edmonton (WIA 8 April 1918), W.M. Clapperton of Toronto (WIA 27 Oct. 1917), E.D.G.W. Desbarats of Montreal (POW 20 Sept. 1917), J.H. Forman of Kirkfield, Ont. (WIA 28 July 1917, POW 4 Sept. 1918), A.P. Haywood of Toronto (WIA 30 April 1917), J.E.C. Hough of Winnipeg (MIA 24 Oct. 1917), H.M. Ireland of Toronto, P.W. Jenckes of Sherbrooke, Que., R.E. McMillan of Jacquet River, NB (POW 19 Sept. 1917), G.B.G. Scott of Guelph, Ont. (KIA 3 Sept. 1917), W.N. Smith of Sudbury, Ont., A.G.A. Spence of Toronto (WIA 8 Nov. 1917), H.D.M. Wallace of Blind River, Ont. (KIA 7 June 1917), H. leR. Wallace of Lethbridge, Alta, and J.R. Wilford of Lindsay, Ont. (POW 13 Sept. 1917).

tactics. Their main line of defence was strengthened and the concept of immediate counter-attacks was abandoned in favour of a policy of pre-planned, systematic strikes delivered the following day, when the German artillery might be more effectively ranged. However, this delay also permitted the British troops to consolidate their gains.[99]

For the bombing squadrons of both sides the last week of September was a lucky one. A German attack on the RNAS depot at St Pol, near Dunkirk, on the evening of 24 September destroyed the engine repair shop, sawmill, machine shop, spare engine shop, engine packing shed, and the drawing and record offices. One hundred and forty aero engines were lost, including 93 Clergets which powered the new Sopwith Camels. The raid was repeated each night for a week, culminating on 1 October when twenty-two Gothas and two smaller bombers dropped about one hundred bombs weighing approximately ten tons on the same target. Twenty-three more machines and nine more engines had to be written off, while thirty other aircraft suffered minor damage that night.[100]

The British bombing success was more ephemeral but nevertheless established a new yardstick for this type of operation. Thus far all the RFC's bombing of bases, aerodromes, bridges, railways, and depots had met with little success, but on the night of 27–28 September 100 Squadron launched another in its long series of raids against Ledeghem station, halfway between Menin and Roulers and a key point on the lateral rail line which distributed reinforcements and supplies to the German battlefront. Eight 230-lb, six 112-lb, and forty-two 25-lb bombs were dropped, 'practically all of which hit the Station or Buildings in vicinity of same.' The damage 'threw out of joint part of the German railway system for two days.' Canadians taking part in the raid included two pilots, Second Lieutenants G.M. Turnbull of Mannville, Alta, and L.M. Archibald of Toronto, and three observers, Lieutenants S.M. Duncan of Ottawa, R.C. Pitman of Saskatoon, Sask., and A.H. Thompson of Penetanguishene, Ont.*[101]

The corps work of the RFC was spectacularly successful during the month of September, not only because of the courage and skill of the aircrew but also because of careful standardization of the methods of ranging artillery and of communication between observers and the batteries. Ground support was becoming sufficiently important to warrant its own section in brigade war diaries, even though the organization and training now lavished on artillery observation had not yet been extended to this newer function. Many Canadian pilots were singled out for mention in this particularly dangerous and unpleasant work during the month.[102]

Above the corps machines and the ground support details, the harsh, inexorable battle for air superiority went on throughout the month. Both sides were adhering to their established tactical concepts; on each side of the line new pilots joined their squadrons, began operational flying, and were shot down. The lucky few who

---

* Archibald became a POW on 24 October 1917 and Pitman on 17 September 1918. Other Canadians serving with 100 Squadron at this time included J.J.L. Drummond of Spencerville, Ont., J.W. Edwards of Cataraqui, Ont., J.S. Godard of Ottawa (POW 24 Oct. 1917), W.K. MacNaughton of St Johns, Que., J.J. O'Loughlin of Toronto, J.W. Price of Moncton, NB, and V.E. Schweitzer of Portage la Prairie, Man.

survived their first two months at the front to become experienced hands concentrated primarily on survival, while the even fewer aces steadily increased their victory scores. The famous Richthofen *Geschwader* (whose leader was on leave for the whole of the month) was piling up an impressive record of 'kills.' On the British side 56 Squadron, which had come to the Front in April flying the first of the new, two-gun SE5s and had been the first to re-equip with the more powerful SE5as, chalked up its two hundredth victory on 30 September.[103] Elite squadrons, as well as individual aces, were now recognizable on both sides of the lines.*

Among the Canadians, two days earlier 11 Squadron's A.E. McKeever had downed two enemy fighters over Bugnicourt, marking the sixteenth and seventeenth victories credited to him and his various observers. Earl Godfrey had been awarded an MC and posted to home defence during the month after being credited with his twelfth victory. R.T.C. Hoidge of 56 Squadron had added six victims to his total during September, the penultimate one coming on the 23rd in the course of a patrol in which his colleague, Rhys-Davids, shot down the great Werner Voss. Voss, trapped while attacking a straggler from another British formation, chose to fight rather than run and for ten minutes fought single-handedly against seven British machines, putting bullets through each of them before falling to his death behind the British lines. His death was a great blow to German morale. 'His flying was wonderful, his courage magnificent, and in my opinion he is the bravest German airman whom it has been my privilege to see fight,' wrote the top British ace, James McCudden.[104]

The RFC had a morale problem too, but the British crisis was kept secret at the time and one of the most bizarre episodes in First World War aerial operations was successfully buried in the files. On 28 September Lieutenant-Colonel F.V. Holt, who commanded 22 (Army) Wing of the RFC's V Brigade, had ordered a major low-level bombing and strafing attack of Rumbeke aerodrome. The attack was made by Naval Ten,† supported by 23 and 70 Squadrons. The RNAS pilots bombed their target and fired 1420 rounds into ground targets on the field, but they failed to come down below 3000 ft to do so, so that 'the value of the operation had been at least halved.' When Holt complained, however, the newly appointed acting Squadron Commander, Flight Commander R.F. Redpath of Montreal,‡ and the British officer who had actually led the sortie both assured him that the failure

---

* Captain J.T.B. McCudden was the outstanding pilot with 56 Squadron. Canadians who flew with the squadron during the period include V.P. Cronyn of London, Ont., J.N. Cunningham of Moose Jaw, Sask. (POW 18 Oct. 1917), B.W. Harmon of Stanley, NB (WIA 2 Dec. 1917, KIA 10 May 1918), R.T.C. Hoidge of Toronto, R.T. Townsend, address unknown (KIA 30 Nov. 1917), L.J. Williams of Vancouver, and R.W. Young of Toronto.

† Canadians serving with Naval Ten at this time included W.M. Alexander, E.I. Bussell, R.E. Carroll, W.A. Curtis, and W.N. Fox (WIA 21 Oct. 1917), all of Toronto, H.J. Emery of Edmonton, W.C. Johnston of Copper Cliff, Ont. (WIA 24 Sept. 1917), J.G. Manuel of Edmonton (WIA 9 May 1918), K.V. Stratton of Aylmer West, Ont., and G.L. Trapp of New Westminster, BC (KIA 12 Nov. 1917).

‡ Redpath, after making a name for himself on the Western Front and with the Luxeuil Bombing Wing, had only come to Naval Ten three days earlier. He never again held an operational command in wartime but did become, in 1921, the second Director of the newly formed and short-lived Canadian Air Force.

was because of a misunderstanding of the orders and that 'the Squadron would like the chance of doing the operation again.'[105] What happened next can best be described in Holt's own words:

On September 30th, as weather and activity conditions appeared suitable for a repetition of the operation, I called up Flight Commander Redpath about 11.45 am, and told him that I proposed repeating the operation in exactly the same way as on September 28th, but having the rendezvous at 2.0 pm. ... He then asked to put it off for the day to which I objected, as the conditions were very suitable. He then said that 'his pilots weren't for it.' I tried to point out to him what a serious statement he had made and asked if he was quite certain that he was truly representing his Squadron, as I couldn't understand it. He informed me that he was, and I then told him that an original situation had been created which I must report to the G.O.C. Brigade, and in the meantime the operation would be off. About ten minutes afterwards he rang up to say that he had a counter suggestion for another operation to replace the one that I had ordered, and I told him that I was coming over in the afternoon and would hear it then.

I went over in the evening and Flight Commander Redpath's suggestion was that the bombing attack should be carried out with D.H.4.s instead of Scouts. I explained that if an Infantry Battalion, when told to attack, suggested that the operation would be better performed by cavalry, it would be a similar suggestion to his. I again asked him if he was quite sure that he was fairly representing his pilots and asked why they had behaved in such an extraordinary way. He replied that they did not consider that the probable results were worth the risk to machines and pilots. I pointed out that one couldn't run a war on those lines and that the orders were very carefully considered before being issued.[116]

Holt did not again order the operation to be carried out after Redpath's determination had become evident, 'as a refusal would have led to a very serious situation,' nor did he personally interview the pilots concerned. In fact, it would seem that most of the squadron knew nothing about this disagreement between their seniors. Certainly Flight Sub-Lieutenant W.A. Curtis, a future Air Marshal of the RCAF, knew nothing of it, although he did know that the British flight commander concerned no longer cared for operational flying. The problem appears to have been created by the reliance of a very recently appointed acting squadron commander upon the claims and views of one of his senior flight commanders who was his equal in rank and experience but who had, temporarily at least, lost his nerve.[107] It may also have been compounded by a personality clash between the rather fiery Holt and the sometimes stubborn Redpath. But none of this information was available to Holt's superiors (and some of it not to Holt); they were faced with an apparent mutiny of a squadron with a magnificent fighting record at a moment when the pendulum of air superiority, although swinging in the British favour, was still quite delicately balanced.

In this 'original situation' there were really only two courses of action open to General Trenchard. He could risk bringing the whole question of fighter pilot morale on the Western Front to a head by instituting formal proceedings against the responsible officers of Naval Ten, with all the attendant publicity which that must bring, or simply remove the whole squadron from centre-stage for a while, hoping that the incident would then pass unnoticed and that there would be no repercussions among his remaining squadrons and especially among the other RNAS squadrons under his command. In the past Trenchard had always been a notable disciplinarian and it may be a measure of his own uncertainty about the morale of his force at this time that he chose the latter alternative. The squadron was quickly transferred to IV Brigade while the necessary arrangements were made, and on 20 November it was moved out of the RFC sphere entirely, to 4 Wing, RNAS, at Dunkirk.* Even Trenchard's memorandum to GHQ confirming his intention to return Naval Ten to RNAS command did not mention why this was being done, remarking only (in a handwritten addition to a typed letter) that it was 'according to previous correspondence,' which does not seem to have been preserved.[108]

The wisdom of this decision became apparent almost at once. The air war was now 'peaking,' winter was approaching, and aircrew could look forward to a period of comparative placidity that would allow morale to recover to some degree. When major combats did occur they were likely to be as uncompromising as ever,[†] but both total casualties and the percentage of casualties per hundred machines leaving the ground decreased slightly during the next month. Indeed, while the RFC had incurred 434 officer casualties during the fifty days that elapsed between the opening battle of Third Ypres on 31 July and 19 September, in the sixty days between 20 September and the beginning of the Cambrai offensive on 20 November it lost no more than 247, a reduction in the casualty rate of better than 50 per cent.[109] This can only partly be explained by the reduction of daylight flying hours and the deterioration of the weather that accompanied the onset of winter.

At the beginning of October the main axis of the British ground attack was swinging northwards towards the eastern end of the Gheluvelt plateau and the village of Passchendaele, in the hope of gaining the Passchendaele-Staden ridge by the end of October. General Plumer's step-by-step technique had proven itself sufficiently to be continued and Haig still harboured illusions of an eventual cavalry breakthrough. On 4, 9, 12, 22, and 26 October additional small patches of watery mud were wrenched from the Germans at a cost of a hundred thousand casualties.[110] But there was no breakthrough.

There was little attempt to develop further aerial initiatives during the latter stages of the Passchendaele battle. High winds, heavy drizzle, low cloud, and poor visibility greatly reduced the efficacy of the air operation. Although there was still no formal training in ground support work for the British pilots, selected squadrons were now detailed to concentrate on this type of activity. No 84 Squadron,

---

* On 27 March 1918, as the first great Ludendorff offensive once again strained the RFC's resources to their limits, Naval Ten was returned to RFC control under the Commanding Officer who had led it before Redpath took over. He retained command of the squadron until the end of the war.

† *Jasta 7*, for example, shot down two Camels, a Bristol Fighter, and a DH4 in less than two hours on 18 October. William R. Puglisi, 'Jacobs of Jasta 7,' *Cross & Cockade Journal*, VI, winter 1965, 313

commanded by Major W.S. Douglas and newly formed in England, was one of them: 'All through October we fought up and down the Menin-Roulers road to the east of Ypres. It was a hard school for a new and untried squadron; and at first, owing to the inexperience of the pilots (only the flight commanders had been overseas before), we suffered heavy casualties. But bitter experience is a quick teacher.'[111] Two of the five Canadians in the squadron when it arrived in France were among those lost, Lieutenant T.V. Lord of Fenelon Falls, Ont., taken prisoner on the 15th and Second Lieutenant F.L. Yeomans of Belleville, Ont., on the 21st, while Lieutenant G.R. Gray of Victoria, who had joined as a replacement on the 18th, was killed on the 31st.[112]

These low-flying sorties undoubtedly had an effect. One German soldier wrote: 'His [the British] airmen perform magnificent deeds and fire on us in shell-holes from a height of 50-30 yards.' The British machines, however, worked in ones and twos and the pilots, 'with freedom to make our own choice of values,' all too often wasted their ammunition on small parties taking cover in shell holes rather than concentrating their efforts on artillery and supply teams or massed bodies and marching columns of troops where they could do the most damage. In contrast, although the German *Schlachstaffeln* may have flown less often, they tended to fly to more purpose. On 24 October the Princess Patricia's Canadian Light Infantry, moving up for the final attacks on Passchendaele, were 'bombed in broad daylight by squadrons of attacking planes in groups of eleven and thirteen at a time.' Two days later, during the battle, the historian of the 31st Battalion, CEF, reported that 'In broad daylight they would fly in squadrons low over the crowded roads of the rearwards areas, bombing and machine-gunning infantry on the march, artillery and transport ...'[113]

It was recognized that 'complaints about low flying enemy machines are usually well founded.' Fighter aircraft were not normally held on alert at advanced landing fields, as they had been at Hill 70. Ground observation posts were in use, but their personnel were poorly trained and their procedures were slow and inefficient. The reports of the gunners or infantrymen who usually manned these posts were 'frequently inaccurate and always arrive[d] too late to allow action to be taken,' and it was not until late October that Lieutenant-Colonel Holt, on the basis of experiments he had made during the month, was prepared to recommend a properly thought-out system of trained observers in telephone and wireless communication with the various wing headquarters. Ground troops thus had to protect themselves from aerial attack. 'It must be clearly understood that the duty of defending themselves against low flying a/c rests with the Infantry. Our own a/c cannot effectively deal with them but recent experience on this front has conclusively proved that rifle and M.G. fire from the ground is most effective for the purpose,'* proclaimed the staff of the Canadian Corps, which was preparing to move into the salient. A

* The 2nd Canadian Division Order of 31 October 1917 illustrated this statement by pointing out that, on 26 October, '2 of our low flying fast scouts were brought down by hostile rifle and M.G. fire while out of a patrol of 12 scouts, 11 machines were considerably damaged by the same means.' '25th Canadian Infantry Battalion,' 6, DHist 112.3H1.009(D259), vol. II. For instructions to German anti-aircraft gunners see translation of German paper, 'The Employment of Machine Guns in Trench Warfare,' 10 Sept. 1917, DHist SS 707.

line of anti-aircraft Lewis guns was established about 300 yards behind the front and 400 yards apart, with a second line of heavier machine-guns to be set up 1000 yards back and 800 yards apart all along the Corps front.[114]

The gallant crews of the RFC's corps machines did not find it so easy to protect themselves. The acting CO of a fighter squadron, paying his first visit to the trenches, 'saw two, if not three R.E.8's shot down on the front line, and the picture that stuck in one's mind was entirely one of Corps aeroplanes, continually under fire, molested and harassed, chased and shot down.' It was not a true picture but there was enough truth in it to make many airmen question the validity of a policy which kept the bulk of the British fighter force engaged on high-altitude offensive patrols of one kind or another. But not until the last attack of the month – the opening of the so-called Second Battle of Passchendaele – was any significant modification attempted. Then the core of the offensive patrols, from 11 Wing, were ordered to start their activities a little earlier in the day, so that 'our front line will be patrolled at a low alt.[itude] until it is fully light. Patrols will then proceed to a rendezvous well within our lines, gain a sufficient height and continue their normal patrol. The last patrols of the day will gradually descend and close on our front line as light fails.'[115]

The British failures were all ones of defensive policy, however, and offensively the Germans were now receiving as much as or more than they could give. On 20 October, for example, V Brigade's 22 (Army) Wing launched another multiple bombing and machine-gunning attack against Rumbeke aerodrome. Half of 70 Squadron went in at 400–500 feet, closely protected by the other half, and with 23 and 28 Squadrons providing 'top cover.' The field, its machines and personnel were thoroughly bombed and strafed. On the return journey another airfield was briefly attacked and 'various ground targets were engaged by Machine Gun fire, one being a train on the ROULERS-MENIN Railway, whose occupants were seen to rush out and dive into ditches each side of the railway.'[116]

Perhaps more important, seven enemy machines were destroyed in the air during the operation, four by 70 Squadron. One of 70's victims fell to the combined guns of three young Torontonians, Second Lieutenants E.B. Booth, C.W. Primeau, and F.G. Quigley. All three were also mentioned for their strafing activities. Second Lieutenant A. Koch of Edmonton, who had served as an observer in 6 Squadron during 1916, had joined 70 Squadron on his first operational posting as a pilot only two weeks earlier. He was part of the covering force when he was attacked from behind and above by enemy machines: 'He fired about 20 rounds at almost point blank range into the first machine which came near him, causing it to go down out of control. Then he fired 80 rounds into a second E.A. which was attacking another British machine, probably forcing it to land. Towards the end of the engagement 2/Lieut KOCH was pursued by three other scouts which, however, he out-manoeuvred, finally crossing his own lines at 400 feet.'[117] From his earlier experiences Koch knew something about air combat, but this account of a fledgling pilot's success suggests that the general level of competence of German airmen was declining. Support for this suggestion also comes from 28 Squadron which was on its first mission over the lines. Two of its three victims fell to the guns of novices, although the third was shot down by one of their experienced flight commanders, Captain William George Barker, a former observer and pilot with 15 Squadron who hailed from Dauphin, Man.*[118] Barker had time for two more victories over the new Albatros D-Vs before his squadron was posted to Italy at the end of the month, but he was destined to make a spectacular, if brief, reappearance on the Western Front during October of the following year.

Two other demonstrations of inadequate enemy fighter skill were provided by the experiences of Lieutenant T.F. Williams of Woodstock, Ont., a thirty-year-old novice who joined 45 Squadron on 24 September. Exactly one month later he was flying in a five-machine offensive patrol when he was caught out of position by a patrol of seven Albatros scouts which promptly attacked him. 'Williams quickly saw that the leader was well ahead of the other six enemy machines and he made a swift turn and placed his Camel behind the Albatros leader and in front of the six behind him who dared not fire because of the risk of hitting their own leader. Williams fired about 150 rounds into the enemy leader's machine, aiming around the cockpit; it went down in a slow spin and crashed at Coucou ... As soon as his opponent went down Williams quickly nipped back under Frew's formation at full throttle.'[119] Two weeks later he had another narrow escape when isolated by eleven scouts east of Houthuilst. 'According to the record he escaped by spinning down from 12,000 to 2,000 feet and again to 200 feet, when he managed to escape and cross the lines unscathed. Some spin!'[120]

Another Canadian to experience an exciting day on 5 November was Flight Sub-Lieutenant W.A. Curtis of Toronto. His opponents proved to be rather more skilful when, leading a patrol of five Camels over the German side of the lines, he engaged a formation of eight enemy machines.

Bullets went through my main spar on the lower starboard wing and before I knew it I was in a steep dive but upside down, hanging onto the cowling openings beside the guns with both hands and my toes pressed up against the toe straps on my rudder bar for all I was worth. My seat belt had too much elasticity and did not hold me fast.

German machine guns were rat-tat-tatting away as the different pilots took turns shooting at me.

I went from 12,000 to 3,000 feet in this position, swearing at the Huns for shooting at me when I was obviously going to crash in a few minutes. I was panicky. At about 3,000 feet I went into heavy cloud, collected my panicked brains, reached up into the cockpit with one hand, caught the spade grip on the joy stick, pressed the blip switch cutting the engine and slowly pulled back on the stick, coming out of the cloud right side up with no German pilots around.

I was over the German lines, did not want to be a prisoner, did not know whether the wing would stay together if I put the engine on or not but decided it was the only thing to do if I did not want to crash behind the lines and be a prisoner.

I put the engine on slowly, the wing held together and with no one shooting at me from the air I stooged back home, a very thankful and less cocky fighter pilot.[121]

---

* Canadians, besides Barker (WIA 7 Aug. 1917, 27 Oct. 1918), serving in 28 Squadron at this time included J.N. Blacklock of Elora, Ont., H.B. Hudson of Victoria, G.S. McKee of Vancouver, and L.P. Watt of Westmount, Que.

By the end of October the British fighter pilots were generally justified in feeling a little cocky. The air war was still far from won, but the RFC was now clearly establishing a degree of overall superiority in the middle and high altitude fighting which – theoretically, at least – reflected command of the air. Even though British fighter formations were often smaller than German ones, their pilots and aircraft were at least as good and their tactical leadership frequently better. The policy which packed the Richthofen Circus with the best fighter pilots, and made it such a notable propaganda success, had a serious weakness. Though the Circus might enjoy momentary superiority whenever it operated, other German fighter formations had been drained of their fighting leaders to create this élite unit, and were therefore relatively weak. On the other hand, although the RFC (and RNAS) had their élite squadrons too, they arose more or less spontaneously and other squadrons were not deprived of their own leaders to maintain the formers' reputations.

Consequently, the British were gaining an edge over the long haul. The superiority established during the late summer and fall of 1917 was to continue and increase, with only very brief breaks, until the end of the war. It was perhaps unfortunate that better use was not always made of this superiority to give more protection to their own corps and ground support machines, or to monitor the enemy's ground support activities more closely, but for two years the air staff had been completely dedicated to the development of an extreme offensive spirit and it could not be expected to modify that concept just when it had begun to justify itself.

By the time the Canadian Corps was brought up from the south to take Passchendaele, all but nine of the sixty British and dominion divisions on the Western Front had been engaged in the Flanders offensive. The Canadians launched their attack on 26 October in a steady downpour of rain. On the right flank they captured their objectives, but then crept back to hold just short of their assigned line. On the left, where the ground was even muddier and more torn up, the attack stalled halfway to the objective. Nevertheless, by nightfall, the troops were firmly established on drier, higher ground southwest and west of the village, at a cost of 1500 casualties.[122]

The weather, as usual, was not suited to the proper operation of the air arm. Air fighting was virtually impossible and the various kinds of low-level work were very difficult, but the airmen did their best, most of the effort falling on the corps machines whose slower speeds and two-man crews permitted them to get a better idea of what was going on in the murk below. Second Lieutenant J.E. Mott of Waterford, Ont., observing from an RE8 on contact patrol, found that he could get no reply to his repeated signals calling for flares, so his pilot dropped the machine to 200 feet in order to identify the men below. 'Their machine was shot down by rifle fire, but the report was handed in at Divisional Headquarters,' while three other RE8s of 9 Squadron, including one piloted by Lieutenant A.G. Peace of Toronto, with Lieutenant G.D. Gillie of Cornwall, Ont., as his observer and another flown by Captain W.F. Anderson of Toronto, fired a total of 1700 rounds at groups of men and various other targets 'with good effect ... from altitudes varying between 150 and 800 feet.'[123]

On the 27th the weather improved and although there was comparative quiet on the ground there was increased activity in the air. British offensive patrols claimed nine enemy machines destroyed in the course of a great number of combats, including victories by W.G. Barker and Naval Ten's Flight Sub-Lieutenants Curtis and K.V. Stratton of Aylmer, Ont. The corps squadrons had a good day, claiming 116 German batteries engaged along the whole front, and over 6000 rounds were fired at various targets on ground support sorties, the great majority of them by pilots of II Brigade. If they were not always very well placed in terms of target selection, at least they were delivered with *panache*. Two Spads of 19 Squadron, one of them flown by Lieutenant J.D. De Pencier of Vancouver,* seeing troops in the main street of Moorslede, 'flew down it practically between the houses at a height not greater than fifty feet,' firing as they went.[124]

The Canadians renewed their assault on 30 October, in cold windy weather which brought rain in the afternoon. This time they carried their objectives and successfully repelled a series of counter-attacks in the afternoon and all day on the 31st. There was very little fighter activity on the 30th but, during the following day, while a low mist hampered artillery co-operation work, there was a great increase in air combats as the German fighter elements chose to deliver one of their periodic challenges to British superiority. Three hundred and eighty-nine flights were made by RFC fighter aircraft, in the course of which seven enemy machines were claimed destroyed and sixteen driven down out of control. Three of them fell far behind their own lines to the guns of 11 Squadron's Andrew McKeever – who had been awarded a Bar to his MC on 27 October – and his observer.[125] The RFC's offensive patrolling, however, failed to interfere with the German day bombers, accompanied by a close escort of fighters. The 14th Battalion, CEF, encamped outside Ypres, 'witnessed aerial activity on a scale which dwarfed anything in their previous experience ... Over Camp 'A' sailed one magnificent squadron of fighting planes, escorting heavily-laden Gotha bombers, which contemptuously flung down some fifteen bombs and then proceeded towards Ypres.' The RFC also carried out limited day bombing, and reported some success in their night bombing of German rail centres, industrial targets, aerodromes, and rest areas.[126]

The Canadians were now firmly established on the slightly higher ground immediately southwest of Passchendaele and astride the spur which jutted westwards from the main ridge just north of the village.[127] However, the village itself and the remaining high ground to the north were still in enemy hands and Sir Arthur Currie, the Commander of the Canadian Corps, planned to take them in two steps. On 6 November he attacked again with the intention of securing the village.

November weather in northwest Europe is usually wet and windy. The sixth of November 1917 was no exception. During the day only a couple of air combats took place, artillery observation was severely restricted by rain and mist, and air deployment was confined mainly to the work of ground support machines under conditions which made their work of little benefit, despite the expenditure of some 11,000 rounds, nearly half of them by one squadron. Since the pilots were sent out

* De Pencier was wounded on 22 November 1917, and again on 5 December 1917. Other Canadians flying with 19 Squadron on 27 October included A. Des B. Carter of Point de Bute, NB (POW 19 May 1918), G.A. Cockburn of Toronto (KIA 8 Nov. 1917), and G.W. Taylor of Gagetown, NB (WIA 13 March 1918).

on roving missions with neither definite courses nor specific targets, many of them quickly became lost. Some came down well inside the German lines, one patrol from 3 Squadron landing its four Sopwith Camels near Namur, a hundred miles in front of the Canadian infantrymen they were supposed to be supporting. The RFC reported twelve officers missing at the end of the day as a result of these ill-directed activities.[128]

The British efforts contrasted poorly with those of the enemy, whose *Schlacht-staffeln* were employed according to a well-developed tactical doctrine. 'During the day, enemy aeroplanes in groups from 3 to 8 and 9 were continuously overhead and kept up machine-gun fire but our casualties from this were slight as our men kept out of sight,' recorded the 1st Battalion, CEF, on the left flank of the attack. The 31st Battalion, in the centre, were not so lucky: 'enemy air craft, flying low, dropped bombs upon, or machine-gunned, every group of the attacking Canadian forces which they were successful in sighting.' The battalion suffered a number of casualties as a result.[129] However, the poor visibility did save them from a certain amount of shelling and strafing during the consolidation period. 'At Jumping Off point men were permitted to leave their Overcoats and the reserve platoons were to look after these when the situation was cleared up. Low flying a/c spotted these coats and, mistaking them for troops, directed a heavy fire on them during the morning with the result that our men in Passchendaele had less shell fire to contend with whilst consolidating.'[130] At the end of the day the Canadians still held the village but there were 2250 fewer of them than there had been at dawn, exchanged for approximately one thousand square yards of Flanders mud.[131]

The final phase of Third Ypres came on 10 November, when the Canadian Corps attacked the remaining high ground to the north of Passchendaele, which could give them complete observation over the German positions to the north-east. It rained heavily all day and 'very little work was accomplished.' The attack was successful, both the cost and the results being approximately half those incurred four days earlier, in terms of casualties and square yards of ground gained.[132]

British losses in the Ypres Salient between 21 July and 10 November totalled some 260,000, while the enemy had lost about 60,000 fewer men.* Exact figures for aircrew casualties are difficult to calculate on both sides but it seems likely that about seven to eight hundred RFC officers were killed, wounded, or taken prisoner during the battle,[133] while German air force casualties are likely to have been rather lighter, since so much of the air fighting took place over the German lines. But the air war was now part of a vast battle of attrition, and German losses, though probably numerically smaller, were more serious than those of the RFC. In material terms they were far less able to afford the casualties than the British, whose own resources were greater and who knew that the Americans were massing behind them. Psychologically the effect of a successful offensive, however meagre the actual gains, stimulated morale amongst the fighting men more than a successful defence.

---

* See G.W.L. Nicholson, *Canadian Expeditionary Force, 1914-1919* (Official History of the Canadian Army in the First World War; Ottawa 1964), 329, for a critical assessment of the figures produced by various authorities.

When the Third Battle of Ypres petered out on Passchendaele Ridge, preparations were already well under way for the BEF's final offensive of 1917. On 20 October final approval had been granted by GHQ for the launching, at Cambrai on the Third Army front, of the first battle in history to be founded on the internal combustion engine.[134] The tactics were to be based on the employment of tanks *en masse* spearheading a surprise attack, and the major supporting role was allotted to low-flying, ground support aircraft.

For the tanks both time and place were well chosen, the ground being comparatively firm and its surface still largely intact, while the restricted visibility to be expected of the mid-November weather would protect the machines to some extent from anti-tank gun fire. For aircraft, in contrast, the outlook was not so good, since the possibilities of rain, wind, and fog seriously threatened their role. Nevertheless, the air planning was carried out with a care and thoroughness not previously seen in the RFC, at least as far as ground attack was concerned. The designated 3 Brigade was quietly reinforced until it mustered 125 corps machines, 134 single-seater fighters, eighteen Bristol Fighters, and twelve DH4 bombers, and arrangements were made for it to draw additional fighting and bombing squadrons from I Brigade and 9 (HQ) Wing on demand. Against this force the enemy could, at the opening of the battle, count on only seventy-eight machines, of which twelve were fighters. III Brigade alone outnumbered the opposing units of the German air force by about four to one, with a superiority of ten to one in fighters.[135]

Steps were taken to give the pilots allocated to the ground support role some training in their work. No 3 Squadron, for example, put in eleven hours 'mainly [in] low flying work' on 15 November and the next day practised 'low bomb dropping, and low flying formations throughout the day. Everyone worked with a will to become really proficient in as short a time as possible.' A.G. Lee has recounted that 46 Squadron, caught in the middle of exchanging their Sopwith Pups for Camels, fitted the remaining Pups with bomb racks and practised low-level bombing and cross-country flying in the days immediately before the attack although low-level flights were 'normally ... officially frowned on.' After a week of this training, Lieutenant-Colonel G.F. Pretyman, commanding 13 (Army) Wing of III Brigade, forbade his squadron commanders to send any 'insufficiently trained' pilots over the lines during the attack, while stressing that 'we must have as many machines as possible on ground target work.'[136]

The operation order produced by III Brigade was much more detailed and specific about ground support than those issued previously. The SE5s were reserved for offensive patrols and balloon busting and the DH5s and Sopwith Camels were to concentrate on low-flying activities. They were to work in flights if the weather was good enough and if not, then in pairs. The types of targets they were to attack were stipulated as well as the areas of front where they should concentrate at given times. As at Hill 70, an advanced landing ground was set up with four Camels or DH5s 'always ready ... to attack low-flying E.A. ... Arrangements will be made for the A.A. look-out post to give warning of such E.A. direct to the advanced landing-ground by priority telephone.'[137]

Unfortunately, 20 November dawned with a heavy fog blanketing the ground that made all flying difficult and low-flying exceptionally so. Fighter attacks on enemy airfields yielded no significant results. The one German flight on the front was surprised on the ground, preparing to attempt a take-off in the deplorable weather after the CO had been threatened with a court martial if he did not. When three Camels of 3 Squadron suddenly appeared, four of the twelve Germans took off as the Sopwiths bombed and strafed the field without effect. One of the Camels, piloted by Second Lieutenant G.W. Hall of Shelbourne, Ont., was shot down.* The other Sopwiths collided with trees while hugging the land contours on their way back home, all three pilots being killed. Little more was achieved in the other aerodrome raids: two pilots became disoriented and landed behind the German lines and one was shot down by ground fire.[139]

With no preliminary artillery barrage the ground attack began at 0610 hrs. Initially, the thick mist hid the 380 British tanks until they were almost upon the enemy and the German front-line defences quickly crumbled before this mechanized onslaught. By 1030 hrs the infantry and cavalry in immediate support of the breakthrough were advancing towards Marcoing through the open country beyond Ribécourt and only on the northern flank had the tanks been seriously challenged.[139]

The low-flying squadrons had been given as their primary objectives three groups of artillery batteries, two on the southern flank at Lateau and Vaucelles Woods, and one on the northern flank along Flesquières Ridge. The latter was assigned to 64 Squadron[†] and, at 0700 hrs, four DH5s thoroughly bombed and strafed the emplacements there. But the guns, protected by their pits, had not been seriously damaged and, although one of the attacking pilots reported the positions deserted forty-five minutes later, very little harm had been done by the initial attack. Unfortunately, perhaps as a result of the report that the positions were deserted, no further special attention was directed towards the Flesquières area during the day by low-flying aircraft.[140] The Germans, however, had simply pulled the guns from their pits and deployed them in the open along the reverse slope of the ridge. From here they wreaked considerable destruction on the British armour.[‡]

The weather deteriorated still further so that after 0900 hrs flying became 'absolutely impossible' for a while.[141] Towards noon conditions improved very slightly

---

* Hall, together with the only other Canadian known to be serving in 3 Squadron at this time, F.H. Stephens of Uxbridge, Ont., was detailed to attack Carnières aerodrome, but the patrol seems to have lost its way in the fog. Stephens, who was to be killed three days later, made a forced landing at Aizecourt le Bas behind allied lines. No 3 Squadron Record Book and War Diary, Air 1/166/15/142/19

† Canadians flying in 64 Squadron, which had only arrived in France on 14 October (Jones, *War in the Air*, IV, 235n), included J.P. McRae of Ottawa (POW 20 Nov. 1917), H.G. Ross of Montreal, E.R. Tempest of Perdue, Sask., and V.W. Thompson of Ottawa.

‡ It is difficult not to agree with Sir John Slessor that 'It is a little strange to find the [British] Official History saying "even had the fighting pilots known of it and realized its importance, it would be idle to claim that their attacks could have been made powerful enough to wipe out the German resistance" and going on to suggest that artillery in the open is not a particularly suitable target for assault action.' *Air Power and Armies* (London 1936), 109. Nor can one altogether accept the British Air Historian's thesis that 'The guns could be more easily dealt with in their known pits ...' Jones, *War in the Air*, IV, 236

again, so that the ground support squadrons could continue to harass the enemy. Both Captain Edmund Tempest and Lieutenant J.P. McRae of Ottawa were prominent amongst the pilots of 64 Squadron engaged in this work. '*Capt. E.R. Tempest* ... obtained direct hits on one or two Gun emplacements near MARQUION. He then circled about for 20 minutes until he had expended his ammunition at the Gun teams and on dug-outs. He returned to his Aerodrome and filled up again with ammunition and bombs, one of which he dropped 2 yards from a house outside which troops were halted. He also engaged troops and transport on the road ... *Lieut. J.P. McRae* ... dropped bombs on and engaged hostile batteries from 100 feet.'[142]

By nightfall the Third Army had punched a hole six miles wide and three to four miles deep in the German defences and inflicted heavy losses upon the enemy, while incurring only light casualties, although a large number of tanks had been destroyed. However, the attack had gradually lost momentum throughout the day,* and it was becoming apparent that there was little hope of achieving Haig's aim of clearing the whole great quadrilateral bounded by the old enemy front line, the St Quentin canal, the Sensée River, and the Canal du Nord.[143] Yet despite the losses of tanks and aircraft it was decided to resume the assault on the following morning, because Bourlon Ridge, just north of Flesquières, was still held by the enemy and the higher ground there dominated all the Third Army's new-won gains.

The weather was no better on the 21st. The mist was possibly a little thinner but rain and low clouds persisted and visibility was 'very poor.' III Brigade could muster 229 serviceable machines in both wings but, in any case, there was little that aircraft could do. Nine successful reconnaissances were flown, and four successful contact patrols. One solitary hostile battery was reported by an artillery observation machine. No enemy air activity at all was recorded by the brigade, although British ground forces complained that German low-flying machines were giving them 'considerable trouble' at Bourlon, and the German fighter commander found that 'as aerial combat was still impossible, we carried out the tasks normally done by infantry pilots; our own front lines were reported constantly, and ground targets – especially tanks – were fired upon.' At the end of the second day Bourlon Ridge still held out and German reinforcements were now arriving on the scene. The limits of the British advance were untenable in the long run unless the ridge could be taken. The alternative was to relinquish some territory at the point of greatest advance and await the almost inevitable German counter-attack on favourable ground. Sir Douglas Haig decided to continue the attack.[144]

The British troops were rested on 22 November, when the only significant ground action consisted of a limited enemy counter-attack which recovered Fontaine-Notre-Dame and strengthened their position in Bourlon Wood. In the

* '... the original plan for a large scale raid ... had been changed to a major offensive with far-reaching aims; and virtually no reserves had been assembled to exploit the success achieved by the initial surprise.' Stephen Roskill, *Hankey: Man of Secrets,* I: *1877–1918* (London 1970), 461. For a more detailed analysis see B.H. Liddell Hart, *The Tanks: the History of the Royal Tank Regiment and its Predecessors, Heavy Branch Machine-Gun Corps, Tanks Corps and Royal Tank Corps, 1914–1945,* I: *1914–1939* (London 1959), 129–34.

air the prolonged poor weather still hampered the development of any worthwhile air support, although twenty-seven combats were reported with two enemy machines destroyed and one forced down inside the British lines. III Brigade, however, lost nine single-seater pilots killed, wounded or missing.

During the low-level operations it is not clear how many of these officers were shot down by ground fire, flew their machines into trees or hillsides, or were the victims of German fighter patrols, but the increase in the number of air combats reported is significant. The Richthofen *Geschwader* was moved hurriedly south from Ypres and, although their leader did not get his first victim on the Cambrai front until 23 November, some of his pilots may well have been in the air by the afternoon of the 22nd. One Canadian, at least, came to realize very clearly that there were certainly rather more German fighters in the vicinity. When 84 Squadron's Second Lieutenant P.J. Moloney of Peterborough, Ont., became separated from his patrol, he found himself attacked by six enemy machines. His flying wires, right-hand aileron wires, radiator, and engine were all shot through in a ten-minute fight and he was wounded in the hip, but he managed to drive one of his attackers into a spin, apparently out of control. When the German machines finally made off, Moloney found that his compass had also been hit but he succeeded in making a forced landing inside the British lines.[145]

On the 23rd when the attack on Bourlon Wood was resumed, the British tanks could no longer rely on surprise. The enemy had brought up anti-aircraft guns mounted on trucks and used them most effectively in an anti-tank role. Apparently the British pilots failed to locate them. Since the weather was noticeably better, although visibility was still limited, one hundred and twenty 25-lb bombs were dropped and 14,600 rounds fired by the army wing against various ground targets. Tempest was again singled out for mention, together with Lieutenant V.W. Thompson of Ottawa and 46 Squadron's Second Lieutenant R.L.M. Ferrie of Hamilton, Ont.* However, III Brigade had sixteen aircrew wounded or missing during the day, and were only able to claim three enemy machines 'brought down' and one 'out of control.' One of those destroyed fell to the guns of an SE5a from 56 Squadron flown by Lieutenant B.W. Harmon of Stanley, NB.[146]

By the end of this third day of fighting, III Brigade had lost, from one cause or another, 30 per cent of the aircraft initially available, 'but the verbal testimony of the tank personnel and of the infantry was that the aeroplane pilots often made advance possible when the attacking troops would otherwise have been pinned to their ground.'[147] That was all very well when the troops were not getting pinned, but it was not a casualty rate acceptable now that the Third Army seemed unable to make any further significant advances. For the next few days the bitter struggle continued, as Bourlon and Fontaine-Notre-Dame were taken and lost again to determined German counter-attacks.

---

* Ferrie was killed on 3 January 1918. Other Canadians serving in 46 Squadron on 23 November included A.L. Clark of Toronto (POW 13 Dec. 1917) and R.K. McConnell of Victoria. T.L. Atkinson of Renfrew, Ont., had been taken prisoner the previous day, and on the 23rd E.G. McLeod of Hunter's River, PEI, died of wounds received the day before. In three days' time a Canadian novice destined to become one of the last and greatest of the First World War aces would join the squadron: D.R. MacLaren of Vancouver.

During this time the close support squadrons were retained on expensive and now mostly futile attacks against the enemy front-line positions. Meanwhile, German reserves were pouring into the area, reconnaissance aircraft reporting 'a congestion of trains in Douai station – much movement south from that rail-head – columns of troops and transport marching on Cambrai from Douai – other columns moving south on the Lens-Douai road.' These concentrations were largely unhindered from the air. The high-level day bombers detailed to attack the targets had difficulty in finding them, and their bombing was ineffective.[148] Better results probably could have been obtained by diverting close support squadrons to these vital targets.

The British position was becoming more and more dangerous. However, GHQ, apparently quite confident that any counter-attacks would be only local ones, stopped the special bombing operations associated with the Cambrai offensive. On 26 November the squadrons of I Brigade, which had been working in the Cambrai sector, were ordered to revert to their previous operational programmes. On 28 and 29 November 9 Wing's two day-bombing squadrons reverted to general stra-tegic targets, and were therefore attacking Courtrai and Roulers stations as Third Army observers were reporting 'much railway movements towards Cambrai from the north-west (Douai) and north-east (Denain), towards Busigny from the north-east (le Cateau), and further south beyond Villiers Outreaux.'[149]

Air reconnaissance was still greatly hampered by bad weather, but both GHQ and Third Army felt that any counter-attack which did develop would be launched against the northern flank, around Bourlon. However, on 30 November the Germans focussed the weight of a major assault against the southern flank, between Masnières and Vendhuille, catching the British badly off balance.* *General* von der Marwitz, the German commander, intended to pinch off the salient by a dual attack, his right wing operating from Bourlon southwards and his left from Honnecourt westwards. The northern attack was stopped in its tracks. In the south, however, the German infantry, strongly supported by specially trained and equipped ground-support squadrons flying in tight formations, quickly burst through the front.[150]

The day was fine, with low clouds but 'fair' visibility, and there was soon more aerial activity developing than had been seen since the British Third Army had crossed its start lines ten days earlier. III Brigade could muster only 230 serviceable aircraft now, ninety-nine of them corps machines, but around Bourlon Wood the sky was 'black with German and British machines.' Fighter patrols of both sides were busy as sixty-one combats were reported, twenty-three of them being claimed as 'decisive.' The most spectacular of them involved a Bristol Fighter of 11 Squadron, flown by Andrew McKeever. He and his observer were on a solo reconnaissance flight over Cambrai when they encountered an enemy patrol of two two-seaters and seven fighters which appeared suddenly out of the mist on their right. McKeever unhesitatingly attacked and shot down one of the enemy

---

* 'The three tank brigades ... move to winter quarters ... had already begun, and neither officers nor men suspected that they would be called upon to fight again before the spring.' *Military Opera-tions: France and Belgium, 1917*, III, 170

with ten rounds at a range he estimated to be only fifteen yards. In the dogfight that followed his observer accounted for two more. A fourth enemy aircraft, closing on them from the rear, made the mistake of overshooting them and was promptly knocked down by McKeever. At this stage his observer's gun jammed so the Canadian put his Brisfit into a dive to within twenty feet of the ground. The remaining two enemy machines thereupon abandoned the chase and McKeever tore back over the lines at ground level. The action brought the total number of victories claimed by McKeever and his observers to thirty in his first half year at the front and won him a DSO to add to the MC and Bar already awarded.[151]

Not every corps pilot was lucky enough to be flying a Bristol, however. Lieutenant A.M. Kinnear of Quebec City, flying an RE8 of 8 Squadron, found himself in real trouble when 'seven [enemy machines] got after me, wounded my observer and shot my [elevator] controls away. How I got away I do not know, but I was lucky – the machine had over 60 holes in it.' The next day was no better, but this time the danger came from ground fire: 'I had 110 holes in the bus and one in my head ... I had to come down low to ascertain certain things and ''umpteen'' machine guns started to shoot the bus to pieces. I was hit on the head and faded away, and when I came to my observer was pushing a flask down my throat and the bus was diving for the earth. I had enough sense to pull her up and managed to steer west. When I crossed our lines the engine died, so I planted her in a field and once more passed away.'[152] Apparently Kinnear's head was only grazed by the bullet, for 'in a couple of days I buzzed back to the squadron. So far I have had five machines shot to pieces – but what of it – the Government pays for them.' Kinnear's nerveless flying was rewarded with an MC and before the end of the war he had one of the new Air Force Crosses as well.[153]

Kinnear's was one of the few combats on 1 December, for the weather closed in again and 'little flying was done' as the Germans pressed their advantage on the ground. III Brigade managed to drop only forty-eight 25-lb bombs and fire over 2500 rounds against ground targets as compared with 111 bombs and 15,000 rounds expended the previous day, and reported only five combats. On 2 and 3 December conditions gradually improved, but low-level work was of a rather perfunctory nature on both sides.[154] The German ground attack was now petering out as the British carried out a fighting withdrawal from the salient.

Part of this withdrawal was conducted in a snow-storm and the final onset of winter brought both ground and air campaigns to a stop on the Western Front. Sporadic artillery duels continued, with the guns ranged by corps machines when the weather permitted,* and on occasion the British bombers and reconnaissance

---

* Personnel turnovers, squadron and regimental transfers, and all the depersonalization inevitable as the scale of battle continued to increase, had brought a great need for more standardization in artillery-air co-operation. From 11 July to 11 November 1917, for example, there were 691 shoots ranged successfully from the air in Fourth Army's area, and 256 failures of which 100 were classed as 'avoidable.' Paper on standardization of aeroplane-artillery cooperation, 16 Aug. 1917, paper on aeroplane-artillery cooperation in Fourth Army, [November 1917], Air 1/918/204/5/879. Steps were now being taken to correct this, however, as a result of a study prepared during August (see Jones, War in the Air, IV, 214–19), and the winter lull provided the necessary training opportunity.

machines flew their missions far over the enemy lines. Above them all the high altitude fighting patrols still struggled desultorily for that intangible will-o'-the-wisp, 'command of the air.' But winter was a quiet interlude during which new pilots had a reasonable chance to learn their trade, relieved only by the exploits of a few pugnacious individuals like eighteen-year-old Second Lieutenant Alan Arnett McLeod of Stonewall, Man., who had joined 2 Squadron* on 29 November.

On 18 December McLeod was flying an old Armstrong-Whitworth FK8 on artillery observation duty near Hulluch when a nearby Albatros Scout mistakenly dived to strafe the British line. 'We in turn dived on E.A. and drove it off by the fire of pilot and observer's guns,' recorded McLeod in his combat report. The next day, while engaged on the same mission at almost the same time and place, eight Albatrosses were there to attack them and the observer could fire only three rounds before his gun jammed. McLeod, however, dived on one of the enemy machines beneath him, fired into it, and watched it spin out of sight before fighting his way back over the British lines.[155]

With not enough photographic or artillery co-operation flights to keep them busy, some of the corps squadrons were turned to night bombing. A British observer with 16 Squadron has recorded the circumstances of his first operation of that kind, flown on a 'dark and misty night' at the turn of the year.

A hair on the head is little, a hair in the soup is much; the hairs breadth by which our starboard wing-tip missed the dimly-seen squadron offices as we left the ground with engine all out was a great deal. Peering down the narrow funnel of relative visibility directly beneath us which was all that the mist-banks allowed us to see, we dumped our bombs when we thought we recognized an enemy land mark and turned with quaking hearts for home and a dreaded landing. Fumbling through the fog, we at last hit on the flares and Compton throttled down to land ... I thought we were going to overshoot the aerodrome, which we could scarcely see, and hit that squadron office ... so wrong was I that just then we hit the ground and overturned ...[156]

Thus General Trenchard ensured that the air weapon did not rust in his hand.

In London Colonel Maurice Hankey, the secretary of the Imperial War Cabinet and also of that same War Policy Committee which, in July, had vowed to stop Haig's offensive if it degenerated into a drawn-out, indecisive battle, was pessimistically writing in his private diary that now 'the whole position is very different. Russia practically out of the war; Italy very much under the weather after [her] defeat [at Caporetto]; France unreliable; the U.S.A. not nearly ready; our own man-power much exhausted by the senseless hammerings of the last three years.' Hankey might have gone on to note that, because of the heavy casualties which it had incurred, the RFC had been unable to increase its overall fighting strength on

---

* Other Canadians serving in 2 Squadron during December 1917 included C.A. Burpee of Edmonton, J.B.L. Heney of Ottawa (KIA 9 March 1918), F.C. Higgins of Sherbrooke, Que., W.H. Kilby of Vancouver, H.I. Pole of Winnipeg (WIA 9 May 1918), H.L. Polson of Toronto, L.C. Spence of Ottawa (POW 25 May 1918), D.S. Thompson of Canfield, Ont., and W.H.M. Wardrope of Hamilton (WIA 27 March 1918).

the Western Front by more than one squadron – from 51 to 52 – over the past six months. The Canadians, for example, forming a major source of aircrew manpower,* with about 240 flyers on the Western Front in July, had been unable to do more than maintain their strength. They suffered some 220 casualties in six months, close to 100 per cent turnover, to end the year with approximately the same total that they had mustered at the end of June.[157]

The German air force had undoubtedly been effective in 1917. Its large proportion of good single-seater aircraft, its tactical innovations, and the skill of its experienced pilots made it seem larger than it actually was. Yet it was unable to maintain the superiority it had enjoyed at the beginning of the year. Despite the disproportionate losses inflicted by their smaller forces, the Germans lacked the resources to contain the RFC and limit the effect of the numerical and technological advantages it had begun to establish. In Britain and Canada training schools were full and large numbers of better aircraft, especially fighters, were coming into service. The Germans could not keep pace.[†158]

---

* R.W. MacLennon of Toronto (KIA 23 Dec. 1917), who joined 60 Squadron on 25 November, wrote home three days later to assure his parents that 'There are about twenty-four officers in the squadron, and more than half of these are Canadians, so I feel quite at home.' Quoted in A.J.L. Scott, *Sixty Squadron R.A.F.: a History of the Squadron from Its Formation* (London 1920), 81. Canadians known to have been on the strength of 60 Squadron at that time included J.L. Armstrong of Keremeos, BC, A. Carter of Calgary (KIA 25 June 1918), J.B. Crompton and W.J.A. Duncan, both of Toronto, W.J. Rutherford of Westmount, Que., and O. Thamer of Kitchener, Ont.

† With its much smaller intake the RNAS found it difficult to replace its battle casualties. It could only maintain its fighter commitment on the Western Front by disbanding 3 (Naval) Wing, using its thirty-five airmen as replacements, and by reducing squadron establishments from twenty to an eventual fifteen.

15

Italy and Macedonia, 1917–18

Units of the RFC or RAF were found wherever the British Army went into action during the First World War. Inevitably, therefore, Canadians flew in every theatre. Macedonia and Italy were two of the most important allied 'sideshows.'* Only about twenty Canadians flew with the RFC and the RAF during the Macedonian campaign (several more serving with the RNAS during its periodic involvements there), but in Italy more Canadian airmen participated than on any battlefront save France. In many ways the two groups had similar experiences. In both Macedonia and Italy the air arm was serving relatively small British forces, yet was itself under strength. As a result airmen were called upon to perform a wide range of duties and could not specialize to the same degree as in France. For much of the time the armies they worked with remained static, but the airmen always had to be offensive-minded in order to carry out their duties. In both theatres the air service had to come to grips with the many problems inherent in operating over mountainous terrain.

There were strong contrasts as well. From the start the air contingent in Italy was equipped with excellent aircraft and could count upon resupply and reinforcement from France and England. Its units all had experienced the air war on the Western Front, coming directly to Italy from there. Of the two squadrons initially sent to Macedonia, on the other hand, one had seen limited action in the Middle East theatre against the Senussi, the Sultan of Darfur, and for some weeks against the Turks, while the other had been a training unit in England. The aircraft of both squadrons were obsolescent, including at least two types that had been rejected for service in France. Supply was handled by the RFC's Middle East Brigade, and the Macedonian front was low on its pecking order; not until the last year of the war were first-class aircraft made available. Whereas in Italy 14 Wing took command of the air almost from the start against its Austrian opponents, 16 Wing in Macedonia had a hard struggle against a small but first-rate German air service.

Allied intervention in Macedonia grew out of the impact of the war upon the tangled web of Balkan politics. The immediate cause of the world struggle had been the collision between Serbian nationalism and Hapsburg imperialism, but the Sarajevo assassination had a regional as well as a profoundly international signi-

---

* See also Appendix B.

ficance. There had been two Balkan wars immediately before 1914, and the outbreak of the First World War, in Balkan terms, was an opportunity for the vanquished to become victors, for the unsatisfied to realize territorial ambitions.

Serbia, a beneficiary of these earlier wars, was initially the *Entente*'s only ally in the area; Turkey, a loser by them, declared for the Central Powers in November 1914. In a supreme national effort the Serbians threw out an invading Austrian force when defeat seemed certain, and then held their own. But Germany, intent upon a direct and uninterrupted rail link with Constantinople, persuaded the Bulgars, another of the losers in 1913, to enter the war in exchange for Macedonia and the Vardar corridor to the Aegean. On 22 September 1915 Tsar Ferdinand of Bulgaria ordered general mobilization, and on 6 October the Serbs were assailed by German, Austrian, and Bulgar forces. Serbia appealed to Greece, bound to her by a convention of mutual assistance in case of Bulgarian attack, and to the French and British governments. Greece, divided between a king tied by blood and marriage to the Hohenzollerns and a premier inclined toward the *Entente*, remained neutral. Premier Venizelos was unable to do more than authorize the passage through Salonika of a French and a British division, both evacuated from the Suvla positions at Gallipoli, before he was dismissed from office by King Constantine. On 5 October the first contingent of what ultimately became 90,000 French and 60,000 British troops began to disembark, to entrench themselves around Salonika and in due course to take up positions along the Greek frontier. The Bulgars, meanwhile, occupied the high ground and mountain passes along the Serbian and their own southern borders facing the Allies and the still-neutral Greeks.

By the summer of 1916 the allied 'Army of the Orient,' commanded by *Général* Maurice Sarrail, totalled 300,000 men and included not only the French and British but also the remains of the Serbian army and contingents from Russia and Italy. The Allies had scant respect for Greek neutrality, but a great deal for the wall of mountains that harboured the Bulgarians, so that the Germans referred to the Salonika theatre as 'the greatest Allied internment camp.' The Serbs occupied the Monastir sector on the left, the French held the centre, and the British were consigned to the right, where their ninety-mile front began at the sea, ran north up the Struma Valley, then west along the southern shore of Lake Doiran to the Vardar River. On these lines the British were fated to remain until the last days of the war, despite a number of bloody but unavailing attempts to crack the Bulgar defences.[1]

Initially the British forces were supported in the air by the French and by RNAS units from the Aegean. In July 1916 17 Squadron was sent from Suez and in September was joined by 47 Squadron from England. Both these units were corps squadrons, 47 working with XII Corps on the Doiran front and 17 with XVI Corps on the Struma front, but their BE2s, BE12s, and Armstrong-Whitworths had to serve as fighters as well. As time passed the squadrons acquired a few Vickers Bullets, DH2s, and Bristol Scouts, but none of these aircraft was a match for German Halberstadt fighters. As Sir David Henderson observed at an October meeting of the Air Board, the RFC in Macedonia was 'quite inadequate to cope with the normal requirements of the Army there.'[2]

Nevertheless, the RFC's airmen did the best they could. Artillery observation work was hazardous and frustrating, not just because of the Halberstadts but also because of the peculiarities of the terrain. The Bulgars had located most of their batteries in deep ravines in the plentiful natural camouflage of the rocks and low bushes which covered the mountain slopes. On the heights, however, they posted anti-aircraft guns and machine-gun nests. On the Doiran front, dominated by the massive hills known as the Grand Couronné, the Petit Couronné, and 'P' Ridge, it was not unusual for observation machines to come under ground fire from above. The gusty winds and treacherous air currents over the mountains made flying difficult, the winter cold was as extreme as the summer's heat, and the sector was malarial. The Bulgars, however, perched in their lofty defences, could survey every detail of the British lines and had no need of aerial observation.[3]

Because activity on the ground was infrequent, air operations tended to settle into the routine of reconnaissance and artillery observation on a daily basis, broken occasionally by bombing raids and brief individual combats. During these early months Lieutenant L.R. Andrews of Toronto and Captain George M. Croil* carried out all these tasks for 47 Squadron, while Lieutenant J.S.B. MacPherson of Ottawa served briefly as an observer with 17 Squadron. There was nothing routine, however, about the assignment of Flight Sub-Lieutenant H.V. Reid, formerly of the Royal Newfoundland Regiment, and Flight Sub-Lieutenant F.S. Mills of Toronto. In late August Romania had made its ill-timed declaration of war against the Central Powers; in October, as things began to go badly for King Ferdinand's army, an RNAS detachment that included Reid and Mills flew to Bucharest to lend assistance. There is no record of Reid's adventures – perhaps he was with Mills – but both of them escaped from Bucharest on 3 December, just three days before the Romanian capital fell to a combined attack by the German generals von Mackensen and von Falkenhayn. Mills, we know, accompanied the dispirited remnants of Ferdinand's army in their headlong retreat towards the Russian border. Then he was stricken with appendicitis, fortunately not acute, and was evacuated to England via Russia and Scandinavia. Both Canadians were back on operations in the spring of 1917 and Mills was subsequently awarded a DSC for his 'zeal and devotion to duty during the period from July 1st to December 31st, 1917,' when he was stationed at Eastbourne.

The initial six months of the RFC's Macedonian campaign were distinguished by the relatively little air-to-air fighting that took place. The greatest danger facing airmen of both sides was that associated with flying fragile and unreliable machines among the wind-laced peaks of the battlefield.

The first Canadian casualty on the Macedonian front was Lieutenant J.C.F. Owen of Annapolis Royal, NS, a pilot with 17 Squadron. On 18 February 1917 he was shot down by *Oberleutnant* Rudolf von Eschwege, the leading German fighter pilot in the theatre. Making a forced landing near the German airfield at Drama, Owen set fire to his BE12. When the Bulgars inexplicably proposed to court-martial him for destroying his aircraft, von Eschwege successfully interceded on his behalf.[4]

---

* Born in Milwaukee, Wisc., Croil moved to Montreal with his family at the age of eleven. His later education was in Scotland. He worked as a civil engineer in Scotland and as the manager of a tea and rubber plantation in Ceylon before returning to Britain to join the Gordon Highlanders. In 1916 he was seconded to the RFC. He later served as Canada's first Chief of the Air Staff, 1938–40.

There were almost mediaeval elements of chivalry to that incident, but it marked the end of an era. Only a week later, on the morning of 26 February 1917, 'like a bolt from the blue,' twenty German aircraft 'in superb formation' swept down the Vardar and bombed the French airfield at Gorgop, destroying or damaging twelve of its machines. In the afternoon they were back to bomb 47 Squadron's base at Yanesh, killing and wounding twenty-eight. This was *Kampfgeschwader 1*, just moved from the Romanian front where the victorious German campaign had ended. It was a self-contained bombing unit with a number of twin-engined aircraft, indiscriminately called 'Gothas' by the British soldiers but including AEGs, Rumplers, and Friedrichshafens as well as a single Gotha, with its own fighter protection flight and a railway train which carried its administrative services and supplies. After its effective attacks on the two airfields, *Kampfgeschwader 1* returned the next day to bomb the British military camp outside Salonika, causing 376 casualties. Croil was one of those who tried ineffectually to drive off the Germans. His slow BE12 was no match for the aircraft he had singled out; 'owing to the speed of the enemy machine,' he reported, 'I was unable to climb to its height and at the same time keep pace with it.'[5]

Lieutenant-General G.F. Milne, commanding British troops in Macedonia, had only sixteen anti-aircraft guns for the whole of his front. He therefore appealed to Vice-Admiral C.F. Thursby, commanding the Eastern Mediterranean Squadron, to provide help for the hard pressed RFC. Thursby immediately sent a few Sopwith 1½ Strutters, and these were combined with RFC BE12s and DH2s to form a makeshift fighting unit. Effective German bombing continued, however, until the RNAS supplied a unit selected from 2 Wing, and known as F Squadron, to mount a counter-bombing offensive. From 29 April to 25 May this squadron, in which at least nine Canadians* were flying, raided dumps and enemy bases, as well as Hudova aerodrome. On 10 May its members observed that *Kampfgeschwader 1* had decamped, along with its special train, subsequently to reappear in Belgium. It seems likely that the German decision to shift its crack bombing unit was related to Western Front priorities and to the projected air offensive against England, but F Squadron had undoubtedly made life difficult for it. Flight Sub-Lieutenant D.D. Findlay of Carleton Place later recalled that once the naval pilots had mastered the then unfamiliar tactics of formation flying, they 'literally ruled the skies' over Macedonia.[†6]

After the German bombers had gone, F Squadron made only intermittent visits to Macedonia following its month-long stay. The two corps squadrons got on with their work as best they could, with some of their members doubling as fighter

---

* H.R. Aird of Toronto (POW 30 Sept. 1917), H.H. Arundel of Winnipeg, D.M. Ballantyne of Montreal, E.S. Boynton of Toronto, D.D. Findlay of Carleton Place, Ont., F.J. Mackie and D.P. Rowland, both of Winnipeg, J.L.A. Sinclair of Toronto, and A.Y. Wilks of Montreal.

† Findlay, later a group captain in the RCAF, recalled that 'We bombed enemy shipping, bridges, railway centres, troop concentrations and, I am ashamed to say, burned the ripe grain crops in Bulgarian Macedonia with petrol bombs.' The raids on crops took place from 6 to 17 June 1917. Findlay to Halliday, 23 June 1962, D.D. Findlay biographical file, DHist; H.A. Jones, *The War in the Air: being the Story of the Part played in the Great War by the Royal Air Force*, V (London 1935), 401

pilots. One of these was Lieutenant A.G. Goulding of Holland, Man. He had joined 17 Squadron in February and would serve there for more than a year, longer than any other Canadian. During the summer Goulding, who earned the MC, DFC, and *Croix de Guerre* for his work, usually flew as one of the escorts for the regular bombing missions conducted by a combined flight from the two squadrons, as well as doing a certain amount of low-level bombing himself. On 21 May, to take an example, he attacked a column of twenty-six horse-drawn wagons going through the Rupel Pass and claimed to have destroyed seven of them and caused a stampede. But even in the hands of pilots as expert as Goulding the BE12 was grossly unsuitable for fighter operations against much superior German aircraft. Goulding and the other escorts attempted to cope with several attacking Albatros D-IIIs during a 17 Squadron bombing raid on Drama airfield on 28 June. That they were able to protect the bombers, though their inadequate machines were riddled, was testimony both to their skill and courage.[7]

During the latter part of 1917 bombing operations continued at a relatively low level of intensity. This was just as well. Whenever the Germans chose to react to British raids, their fighters found the RFC's antiquated machines easy prey. In September General Milne urged the War Office to enlarge and improve the air service in Macedonia: 'I am responsible for a wide extent of front, which entails heavy demands on the Flying Corps for reconnaissance, photography and artillery observation. In addition to this, offensive bombing raids are undertaken as often as possible, and there is constant fighting in the air with an enemy whose machines are more up to date than our own. I am anxious to widen the scope of the offensive measures undertaken by the Flying Corps, the more so as the size of my force precludes any other method of making our presence really felt in this country.'[8] Given the positions of the enemy, which seemed impregnable, the air arm was the only means Milne could see of bringing the war home to the Bulgarian people.

A number of Canadians arrived as reinforcements in the autumn, including Lieutenant E.J. Cronin of Saint John, NB, who went to 17 Squadron, and Second Lieutenants A.S. Clark, address unknown, D.L. Graham of Griswold, Man., and W.D. Robertson of Victoria, who joined 47 Squadron. An observer who had recently transferred from the CEF, Clark had an experience on 5 October which was typical of the position in which the RFC found itself at this time. While returning from a bombing raid on Cestovo, the Armstrong Whitworth in which he and his pilot were flying was attacked by three Halberstadts and an Albatros two-seater. The Germans split into pairs and attacked from either side, Clark switching his fire from side to side to meet each pass. By the time they had reached the northern shore of Lake Doiran the AW's engine had been knocked out and the pilot was wounded; only the appearance of three more RFC machines saved the pair. The pilot glided to a landing on the British side of the lines, although he 'ran into a barbed wire barricade sustaining considerable damage.'[9]

By the end of 1917 both the *Entente*'s situation in Macedonia and the RFC's position had improved. In June a *coup d'état* had been engineered as a result of which King Constantine abdicated in favour of his more compliant second son, Alexander. Venizelos returned to power, Greece entered the war, and Greek troops took over most of the Struma front. For the RFC the most important development was the appearance of a number of SE5as to replace the BE2s. The acquisition of this fine fighter enabled the RFC to win air superiority in 1918.

Meanwhile a new theatre of operations was opening for the RFC in Italy. When that country declared war on Austria-Hungary on 23 May 1915, the Italian land forces were organized in four armies. The First and Fourth Armies were deployed on the Trentino sector from the Swiss boundary to the Upper Piave; two Alpine groups occupied the Carnia sector in the centre; the Second and Third Armies covered the right flank along the Isonzo River; and another seven divisions were held in reserve. The *Aeronautica del Regio Esercito* (Royal Army Air Service), consisting of four dozen aeroplanes and three dirigibles, was organized into twelve *squadriglie*.[10]

The Austrians opposed the Italians on the same three sectors with only ten divisions and eight in reserve, that is, at about half the strength of the Italians. The *K.u.K. Luftfahrttruppen* (Imperial and Royal Air Service Troops) had thirty-six aeroplanes, one dirigible, and ten balloons in July 1914 and had not appreciably increased by May 1915. Little bombing was done and there appears to have been a tacit agreement between the Italian and Austrian air forces that the Italians would not interfere too much as long as their cities were spared from aerial bombardment.[11]

The battlefront stretched for 375 miles along the lower Alps from Switzerland to the Adriatic. The Italians had the advantage of interior lines of communications but the Austrian salient in the Trentino was a continual threat to Italy's own salient in the Isonzo sector. Between late June 1915 and mid-September 1917 the Italians fought no fewer than eleven battles on the Isonzo, with Trieste as their main objective. They were not conspicuously successful in any of these offensives, and in May 1916 the Austrians attempted a diversion in the Trentino sector. Although they achieved some success, the Italians regained most of the lost ground in subsequent operations.

In January 1917 an inter-allied conference was held in Rome where a 'frank discussion of the whole military and political situation' took place, including a review of the Italian campaign. An Anglo-Italian convention was signed on 7 May 1917 and contingency plans were made for British assistance. Shortly afterwards sixteen howitzer batteries were sent from England to bolster the Italian artillery. Allied reinforcements were followed by German ones, after the near collapse of the Austrians during the Eleventh Battle of the Isonzo in September 1917. Seven German divisions under the command of *General* Otto von Below reinforced the Austrians. The Julian Alps, with summits around 6500 feet, provided an excellent screen for massing reserves and artillery and the head of the British Mission in Italy reported that 'a considerable reinforcement of German aeroplanes has been received by the Austrians.'*

Meanwhile the Allies decided to withdraw twenty-three of the twenty-eight batteries they had loaned the Italians because the latter had switched from the

---

* A report by Lieutenant-Colonel T. Carthew dated 15 April 1918 indicates that the following types of German and Austrian aeroplanes were flying on the Italian front: Albatros D-III and D-V, Berg, KD, Phönix, two-seater Brandenburg, two-seater DFW, and three-seater AEG bombers. Carthew report, 15 April 1918, Air 1/463/15/312/137

offensive to the defensive and because the batteries were required elsewhere. By 17 October the guns had left Italy for France, Egypt, or Mesopotamia. By then, the Austro-German Order of Battle contained some forty-five divisions, but the Italian armies had also more than doubled in strength. Their air force, re-equipped with newer aeroplanes, now consisted of thirteen fighter squadrons, fourteen bomber squadrons, and thirty corps squadrons.*[12]

The Twelfth Battle of the Isonzo, which resulted in the Caporetto *débâcle*, began on 24 October 1917. Following a bombardment by some 300 Austrian and German guns the Italian Second Army's left wing melted away. Von Below captured 275,000 prisoners, the Italians lost twice that number through casualties and desertions, and Italy urgently sought help from her allies. The British ordered two divisions, organized as XIV Corps, to be sent from France; the French despatched four French divisions. One fighter and one corps squadron were detailed to accompany XIV Corps, 28 (Camel) Squadron and 34 (RE8) Squadron,[†] forming 51 Wing, RFC. As the extent of the Italian disaster came to be more clearly realized, additional assistance was despatched. Another British formation, XI Corps, was ordered to Italy together with 42 (RE8), 45, and 66 (Camel) Squadrons, 14 Wing Headquarters, a balloon wing of two companies, an aircraft park, and a supply depot. On 18 November 1917 Brigadier-General T.I. Webb-Bowen, the commander of the RFC in Italy, opened VII Brigade Headquarters in Mantua.[‡] When the British divisions were moved closer to the front than had originally been anticipated in order to help in the revival of Italian morale, RFC formations moved in concert with them. By early December 28 and 66 Squadrons were based at Grossa, northwest of Padua, with wing headquarters close by at Villalta, and 34, 42, and 45 Squadrons at Istrana aerodrome, west of Treviso.[13]

---

* The Italian army occupied roughly the same front as before with sixty-eight infantry and four cavalry divisions. Eight fighter squadrons were now equipped with Hanriot HD1s, four with Spad 13s, and one with Nieuport 17s; all the bomber squadrons were equipped with Italian-built Caproni three-engined bombers.

† No 28 Squadron had been assigned to V Brigade (RFC) in France on 8 October 1917. No 34 Squadron had carried out corps duties with IV Brigade (RFC) since mid-July 1916. Canadians with 28 Squadron at the time of its move to Italy included W.G. Barker of Dauphin, Man., H.B. Hudson of Victoria, C.M. McEwen of Radisson, Sask., C.W. Middleton of Toronto, L.P. Watt of Westmount, Que., and D.C. Wright of Toronto (KIA 20 Feb. 1918). With 34 Squadron were C.G. Andrews of Regina, G.E. Creighton of Dartmouth, NS, A.S. Dunn of Campbellford, Ont., C.L. King of Sault Ste Marie, Ont., H.J.W. McConnell of Owen Sound, Ont., and J.G. Sharp of Toronto.

‡ Nos 42 and 45 Squadrons were withdrawn from II Brigade (RFC) on the Western Front on 16 November 1917, concentrated at Fienvillers, and entrained at Candas beginning 25 November. No 66 Squadron, employed on special missions and especially low-level work since March 1917 with 9 (HQ) Wing, left France on 17 November. The only known Canadian with 42 Squadron at the time of its transfer to Italy was H.A. McEwen of Regina. With 45 Squadron were J.R. Black of Orillia, Ont., R.J. Dawes of Montreal, E.M. Hand of Sault Ste Marie, Ont. (POW 1 June 1918), D.W.R. Ross of Vancouver (KIA 11 Jan. 1918), H.J. Watts of Winnipeg (WIA 24 May 1918), and T.F. Williams of Woodstock, Ont. Those with 66 Squadron included H.B. Bell of Toronto, W.C. Hilborn of Alexandria, BC (WIA 16 Aug. 1918, POW 26 Aug. 1918), A.B. Reade of Toronto (KIA 21 Feb. 1918), J.A.M. Robertson of Westmount, Que. (POW 8 Dec. 1917), M.A. Rowat of Sudbury, Ont. (KIA 12 Feb. 1918), R.W. Ryan of Goderich, Ont., and S. Stranger and T.R. Whitehead, both of Montreal.

Well before allied assistance could make itself felt, the Italians had reconstituted the front along the line of the River Piave and the despondency engendered by the Caporetto disaster had been swept away by a remarkable upsurge in the national will to resist. The British relief of Italian formations only began on 30 November, elements of the XIV Corps taking position on the line of the upper Piave in a region known as the Montello, with the French on their left. Behind the British was the Montello plateau; to their front, across eight hundred yards of the many-channelled Piave and exposed to view, were the Austrian lines. The rear areas of the enemy, however, were considerably higher than the British position, affording him excellent observation while hiding his own dispositions. The uneven ground, similar to that in Macedonia, permitted easy concealment of artillery. Consequently both artillery co-operation and general reconnaissance became vital tasks for the RFC, whose airmen had to adapt themselves quickly to a terrain utterly different from the Western Front and to provide intelligence for army staffs seeking to do the same.

Even before British units came into the line, therefore, the RFC undertook its first operational flight. On 29 November 1917 an RE8 from 34 Squadron, escorted by four of 28 Squadron's Camels, flew a photographic reconnaissance mission over the Montello front. The escort was led by Captain W.G. Barker, who had been slightly wounded in the head while flying with 15 Squadron on the Western Front in August. Posted to England as a flying instructor with four victories to his credit, he had wangled his way to 28 Squadron instead and now found himself in Italy. He and his companions discovered immediately that the Austrian air force was ready to contest vigorously any intrusion on their air space.*

Barker estimated that the Camels were attacked by about twelve Albatros D-IVs. 'I dived on one & fired about 50 rounds and he went down in a vertical dive.' he reported. 'I followed & as he flattened out at 5000 feet I got a burst of about 80 rounds at close range. His top right wing folded back to the fuselage and later the lower wing came off.' But the Camel pilots had no easy task. As Barker observed, 'During all the ... fighting we were outclassed in speed & climb'; it was not until the contending fighters had spiralled down to 5000 feet that 'the Camel was a match for the D.4.'[14]

Barker was to become by far the most successful allied fighter pilot on the Italian front. Air Chief Marshal Sir Philip Joubert de la Ferté, who as a lieutenant-colonel commanded 14 Wing in Italy, once said of him 'that of all the fliers of two world wars none was greater than Billy Barker.' Despite such praise, and his position as fourth-ranking Canadian ace, Barker's reputation has been overshadowed by others, probably because he won most of his laurels in Italy. He is chiefly known for his spectacular solo fight against overwhelming numbers when he was with 201 Squadron on the Western Front in October 1918. This exploit, which

---

* By late 1917 the *K.u.K. Luftfahrttruppen*, under the command of *Generalmajor* Emil Uzelacs, had grown considerably. Nearly all its available aircraft had been transferred to the Italian front from Russia, though small detachments flew in the Balkans. It was supported by a domestic aircraft industry and no longer had to rely upon German aircraft, though many of its machines were German types produced under licence. Its basic flying unit was the *Fliegerkompagnie (FK)* of up to eight aircraft; in early 1918 there were at least 63 *FKs* on the Italian front, a high proportion being *Jagdfliegerkompagnien*, with as many as twenty fighters each.

won him the Victoria Cross, has caused him to be remembered as a lone wolf and something of a gambler. The testimony of those who were associated with him, however, shows Barker to have been a very different kind of man. As both flight leader and squadron commander he concerned himself with the careful indoctrination and shepherding of inexperienced pilots. Though among the most decorated of all RAF airmen – in addition to his VC he was awarded the DSO and Bar, the MC and two Bars, the *Croix de Guerre*, and the Italian Silver Medal for Military Valour – he was not regarded by his companions as a trophy-hunter but rather as one generous in sharing his triumphs and in assigning victories to others that he might well have claimed for himself. Barker excelled in individual fighting tactics, especially the head-on attack, but the record shows him to have been also a highly effective formation leader.[15]

Some of his qualities as leader and fighter pilot emerge from his account of an offensive patrol undertaken on 3 December:

After ... escorting RE8's, Lt. Cooper, Lt. Woltho and I crossed the river Piave at a low altitude and attacked a hostile balloon N.E. of CONEGLIANO. I fired about 40 rounds into it at a height of 1,000 feet and it began to descend. I then observed an Albatros Scout about to attack Lt. Woltho. I immediately engaged the E.A., drove him down to 300 feet, and then succeeded in getting a burst of fire into him. He dived vertically, crashed, and the wreckage burst into flames. I then reattacked the balloon, and after firing at very close range, saw it in flames on the ground. I broke up a party of enemy who were at the balloon winch. A large covered car proceeding E. from CONEGLIANO turned over into a ditch when I attacked it. Later I attacked small parties of enemy and dispersed them.[16]

This report also brings out Barker's taste for low-level attacks, a pursuit he seems genuinely to have enjoyed, unlike most of his fellow fighter pilots.

In the period before the arrival of RFC units the Austrians and their German allies had dominated the air over the Italian front and their observers had succeeded in photographing most of the Venetian plain. The challenge to enemy air superiority first offered by 28 Squadron was soon taken up by 66 Squadron as well. From 6 December the squadron began to fly regular offensive patrols, mostly between Pieve di Soligo and Santa Lucia di Piave on XIV Corps front, but also on the Italian front between Asiago and Valstagna, thirty miles to the west of the British sector. After an initial brush with eight enemy fighters, 66 Squadron had some difficulty in bringing their opponents to battle, though during the next two weeks Second Lieutenants T.R. Whitehead of Montreal and M.A. Rowat of Sudbury, Ont., were each credited with victories and Second Lieutenant S. Stanger of Montreal with an aircraft driven down out of control. Losses also occurred, such as on 8 December when Second Lieutenant J.A.M. Robertson of Westmount, Que., was 'last seen going down N.E. in steady glide with 3 E.A. following him.' Robertson became a prisoner of war. The same day 28 Squadron was over Asiago and Second Lieutenant C.W. Middleton of Toronto shared in the shooting down of an Aviatik two-seater.[17]

In the course of their offensive patrols both squadrons had reported enemy airfields at a number of locations, including Godega and San Felice. On 15 and 16 December 42 Squadron carried the fight to the enemy and bombed the latter field, but not until the RFC extended its attacks to a second airfield was the enemy driven to retaliate. According to T.F. Williams of Woodstock, Ont., then a second lieutenant with 45 Squadron, Barker and Lieutenant H.B. Hudson of Victoria 'went over to some Austrian airfield on Christmas Day with a placard saying "Merry Christmas" and they proceeded to shoot up the place good and plenty.'[18] On Boxing Day, a member of 34 Squadron has recalled, he was walking to the aerodrome at Istrana when he noticed that the British anti-aircraft guns had gone into action: 'This was a most unusual occurrence, and when I looked to see what the target was, I could hardly believe my eyes. About five miles away, flying at all heights between 500 and 3,000 feet, was the most heterogeneous collection of aircraft I have ever seen. Making no attempt to keep together, but on the contrary, widely scattered, thirty or forty Austrian machines were slowly approaching us ... Every few hundred yards one would drop its bombs, and make for home. Finally, about twenty reached the aerodrome and bombed it. After bombing the aero-drome they did not go straight back, but becoming more dispersed they wandered all over the country at about 1,000 feet.'[19] This untidy raid, it seems, was the aftermath of an over-long Christmas celebration and the idea, born sometime in the small hours, was to exact reprisal for the raids of the RFC. Six enemy machines came down at scattered points in the neighbourhood of Istrana; as Williams remembered it, 'We were pretty near all day picking up prisoners.'[20]

As the year turned, fighting on both the Italian and Macedonian fronts was mainly confined to the air and, ultimately, the allied air forces established a measure of aerial superiority in both theatres. In Macedonia the relatively small numbers of aircraft involved gave the air war the appearance of a series of indivi-dual combats, in which A.G. Goulding, flying a Nieuport 17 obtained from the French rather than one of the SE5as now coming into use, took a leading role. On 5 January 1918, while on an offensive patrol at 12,000 feet over Seres, he was 'coming out of the sun' when he encountered an Albatros D-III. He fired only one round when his gun jammed but fortunately his enemy spun out and fled. Later in the month while on another patrol he met a DFW Aviatik attempting to recon-noitre the XVI Corps front. Again attacking from the sun, Goulding fired two magazines of 150 rounds before his gun jammed once more. The Aviatik, how-ever, was forced down by an SE5a and then bombed where it lay. Goulding shared credit for the victory and was subsequently awarded the MC for this action and 'great determination and gallantry [shown] on many occasions.' In March Gould-ing, now flying an SE5a and with the help of another machine, forced down another Aviatik intact after its observer had waved a white handkerchief as a sign of surrender; the two fighter pilots then landed beside the enemy aircraft in an open field and took the crew prisoner.[21]

Other Canadians arrived in Macedonia over the winter, although few stayed long. Among them were Captain G.M. Brawley of Toronto, Lieutenants H.M. Jennings of Hagersville, Ont., C.D.B. Green of Oakville, Ont., J.P. Cavers of Toronto, A.M. Pearson from Manitoba, and three who were awarded DFCs before the fighting finished – Captain G.G. Bell of Ottawa and Lieutenants Walter Ridley from British Columbia and the piquantly-named Arthur Eyquem de Montaigne Jarvis (known more usually as 'Jock') of Toronto. They, along with Goulding, became members of the new 150 Squadron, RAF, formed on 1 April 1918 from the 'A' Flights of 17 and 47 Squadrons. No 150 was given a fighter role while the old squadrons, relieved of this responsibility, performed corps duties as well as long-distance reconnaissance and bombing. The new squadron saw considerable action. In April and May the pilots regularly broke up enemy patrols and recorded a number of enemy machines probably destroyed. On 28 May Goulding shared his seventh victory when he attacked a DFW at twenty yards range, firing two hundred rounds from both guns until they jammed and he had to break off the engagement. The German was finished off by another pilot.[22] On 1 June two enemy aircraft fell victim to the guns of Bell and Green, who managed to defend themselves against a dozen attackers. Bell reported: 'When escorting bomb raid on CESTOVO, Captain Bell and Lieutenant Green on S.E.5a's, were attacked by twelve hostile machines over CASANDULE. A lengthy combat ensued. An E.A. (Siemens Schuckert) Immelmanned in front of my machine. I fired at point blank range. He burst into flames. Two E.A. then dived on my tail, I turned sharply to my right and observed Lieutenant Green diving on one of them which turned over on his back and went down out of control. We were attacked continuously but managed to keep E.A. off until bombers regained our lines. My engine then cut out and as Vickers gun was jammed we fought a defensive fight towards our lines.'[23]

On 12 June Green and three others were attacked by four enemy aircraft while escorting a bombing raid. Green put a short burst into one which crashed in a field on the west side of the Vardar. He then attacked a second which dived away with engine trouble and was seen burning on the ground. Three days later, when Green was on an offensive patrol with Goulding, Bell, and a fourth pilot, they were attacked by eight Albatros D-Vs, one of which Green sent down out of control near Smokvica, Goulding meanwhile claiming his eighth victory with Bell's assistance. Green sent another machine down in flames near Palmis on 20 June 1918, and with Brawley's help Bell shot down still another near Kalateppe on 23 June. Five days later, while escorting a photographic reconnaissance over Paljorka and Furka, Green fired at an enemy aircraft, followed it down from 9000 to 1000 feet, and saw it crash southwest of Furka. In all, thirteen of the enemy were destroyed or driven down out of control for the loss of only one British aeroplane. The casualty was Lieutenant D.L. Graham whose machine was hit by anti-aircraft fire and came down in flames. Graham along with Jennings had remained in 47 Squadron in the essential if perhaps less glamorous tasks of reconnaissance, bombing, and artillery spotting. Jennings transferred to 150 Squadron in August.*[24]

Escorted by the superior fighting machines of 150 Squadron the two corps squadrons went about their business of reconnaissance and bombing virtually unmolested. Their bombing effectiveness was greatly enhanced in August and September when each squadron received a flight of DH9s, a year after General Milne had requested aircraft of this type. Meanwhile their protectors steadily increased their claims of enemy aircraft destroyed or forced down, through offensive patrolling as well as escort duties. On 26 July, Jock Jarvis claimed two victories within three hours. While returning from escort duty over Kalinovo at about 1000 hours he attacked a machine which had been engaging one of his wing

---

* R.P.A. Crisp of Hamilton, Ont., and B.M. Murray of Foxwarren, Man., arrived during the summer of 1918. The former went to 47 Squadron, the latter to 17 Squadron.

men. The enemy promptly broke away but Jarvis 'had another burst at him' and the German machine went into a steep dive and crashed southeast of Cerniste. That afternoon Jennings went patrolling over Orlyak and opened fire at very close range on a DFW two-seater. The enemy aircraft went into a flat spin as the fabric peeled off the top port plane, and the machine hit the ground south of Elisan. The pilot and observer were taken prisoner.[25]

On 3 September, while escorting a reconnaissance machine on photographic duties near Lake Doiran, Cavers was attacked by six hostile planes. He crash-landed in the lake and, while swimming from the wreckage to the shore, was shot to death by the pilots who had brought him down. Ridley and the rest of his flight had witnessed the final stages of Cavers' combat while returning home in their SE5as from bomber escort duty. Joined by two nearby Camels, they went after his killers, and four of them were destroyed, one by Ridley, in a general fight which started at 13,000 feet and came down to a few dozen feet above the ground.[26]

In Italy the pattern of air operations was generally similar, if on a larger scale. Early in January 1918 VII Brigade Headquarters issued new offensive patrolling instructions to 14 Wing. The squadrons were ordered to provide four patrols daily of four to six aircraft each in three sectors, designated as Western, Central, and Eastern. The Western Patrol covered the area from Asiago to Mount Grappa during the hours of greatest activity; the Central Patrol, opposite the British front, covered from Valdobbiadene to Pieve di Soligo and from Farra di Soligo to Conegliano; and the Eastern Patrol flew between Conegliano and Ceggia, well down towards the mouth of the Piave. In addition, one flight of six machines was detailed for escort duties as the need arose. The instructions stipulated that henceforth artillery, photographic, and reconnaissance machines in corps areas would not normally be accorded close protection and the fighter squadrons would not be permanently detailed for specific patrols but rather would be rotated regularly according to roster, the normal patrol lasting two hours.[27] In sum, by these dispositions the RFC accepted a share of responsibility for fighter patrols over a major portion of the Italian front from Asiago to the Adriatic, in addition to its normal support duties for British ground formations. The RFC in Italy, imbued with Trenchard's offensive doctrine, was seeking to impose its will upon the enemy air forces.

One way to force the enemy to commit himself was to bomb his airfields and static installations, and a series of raids were mounted as the RFC pressed for air superiority. On New Year's Day, for example, ten RE8s from 42 Squadron, escorted by two flights each of five Camels from 28 and 66 Squadrons, bombed the German Fourteenth Army Headquarters at Vittorio. This raid provided Barker with the opportunity to drive down one enemy aircraft and shoot down another that crashed on a mountain side northwest of Vittorio, when 'the wreckage burst into flames and was seen rolling down in the Valley.'* On 5 January a bombing raid

---

* Barker's flight consisted of H.B. Hudson, C.M. McEwen, D.C. Wright, and one non-Canadian. In his combat report Barker states his flight was attacked by twelve enemy aircraft, later reinforced by six more. The eighteen enemy aircraft were in fact attacking ten RE8s and ten Camels. Two Canadians were in the other flight, H.B. Bell and A.B. Reade; their flight commander failed to return and the lateral controls on Reade's aircraft were shot away by an enemy observer.

was carried out on the Cordenons aerodrome three miles northeast of Pordenone by ten RE8s of 34 Squadron escorted by fifteen Camels. The aircraft were detailed to rendezvous at Castelfranco at 0930 hrs but, according to 66 Squadron's report, the RE8s went by at such a speed that the Camels could not overtake them! Nevertheless, the fighter group encountered enemy aircraft over Sacile at 14,000 feet where Barker's flight drove down two of the enemy.[28]

Fog and rain restricted flying operations for the remainder of the month but did not halt them altogether. In one action on 11 January Lieutenant D.W.R. Ross of Bobcaygeon, Ont., was killed. His section leader at the time, Williams, who had now been promoted captain, recalled the occasion fifty years later:

I was leading the show where Ross was killed. We were escorting reconnaissance machines which photographed quite a large number of aerodromes that afternoon. We had six Camels – two threes – Captain John Firth was leading one section on one side and I was leading the three on the other. Ross was one of my wing men. When we got almost to the last aerodrome a cloud of Huns were collecting above us. They hadn't attacked up to that point and then they started coming down in two and threes at a time. Ross signalled that he was being attacked but he was much too high. I signalled to him to come down a little closer but that was the last I ever saw of him. We were tangled up in continuous fights. I remember having three head-on actions with this one man. I could have turned over but to do so I would have had to have left the RE8. So I had to watch him until he turned and then come back at him and keep over the RE8 all the time because I felt responsible for getting this RE8 back. On the last part of the show, when there were only three of us left, one Hun came down in a highspeed dive. I got that machine, I am sure. I had to use fifty per cent more deflection on account of his speed. My shots happened to hit him and he went down so I got a credit on that show.[29]

Losses were inevitable at any stage of the air war, but there is every indication that the RFC was gaining the upper hand over its antagonists during the late winter of 1917–18. In Williams' view this came about because the RFC had better fighter aircraft, more experienced fighter pilots, and more skill in formation flying than its opponents. In his opinion the Italians had suffered from the lack of any established patrolling procedure and because their leading fighter, the Hanriot, carried only a single gun and lacked the performance of the Albatros. The Austrians were no mean opponents, but the Camel had already proved itself against the Albatros on the Western Front, and did so again over Italy. Speed was the Austrians' chief advantage; by crossing the lines at points where the Italian air force had prime responsibility, they would sweep around from the rear, sometimes catching the RFC's patrols on their way home. To the experienced airmen in the RFC squadrons there was a great contrast between the strain and intensity of the virtually incessant air battle in France and the hide-and-seek tactics of the Austrians. As Williams saw it, 'Flying in Italy was a holiday by comparison with that in France. It was a different type of warfare entirely. It was more of a gentleman's war. The scout pilots we encountered in Italy didn't seem to have the same viciousness that we met up with on the Western Front where it was a blood for blood affair. They were not so aggressive in Italy.'[30]

It is probable that Austrian airmen held a different opinion. During January 1918 the RFC claimed to have destroyed twenty-nine enemy aircraft and two kite balloons at the cost of four of their own machines. Barker and his wing-man, Hudson, accounted for the balloons. On 24 January the two were ostensibly engaged in 'Practice Fighting, and Machine Gun Test': 'While testing guns over the lines we sighted two balloons in a field which we attacked and destroyed in flames,' Barker reported. 'A horse transport column of about 25 vehicles which was passing these balloons was also attacked and stampeded.'[*][31]

Though the weather deteriorated in February, the RFC continued to take advantage of the opportunities it was offered and Canadians took a particularly prominent part.[†] On 2 February all the fighter squadrons were out in force. At 1050 hrs Barker was leading Hudson, Lieutenant C.M. McEwen[‡] of Griswold, Man., and Second Lieutenant Woltho, a British pilot who frequently flew with him, on a regular offensive patrol when they intercepted a group of five Aviatiks escorted by three Albatros D-Vs. In a few brief minutes McEwen had shot down two of the Aviatiks; Barker despatched another, an Albatros as well, and 'seeing a crowd around the E.A. ... attacked it and set the wreckage on fire.'[32] An hour later, in the same sector, four Camels from 45 Squadron overtook an Albatros two-seater and its escorting fighter: 'The formation dived down from the sun and 2/Lt G.H. Bush fired a good burst into the Scout at close range. It dived down for about 5,000 feet and then started a wide spiral but 2/Lt T.F. Williams headed it off from the Enemy side of the Lines and on the formation closing round, the enemy pilot put his hands above his head and glided down and landed at Road 2, on Montello.'[33]

On the 4th Second Lieutenant H.B. Bell of 66 Squadron shot down an Albatros D-III in flames near the Austrian airfield at San Giacomo di Veglia, and each member of a four-Camel formation from 45 Squadron, escorting RE8s, accounted for an Albatros. This fight was a 'hard' one, lasting for thirty minutes, 'enemy pilots being aggressive and skillful but being completely outmanoeuvred by Camels.' Second Lieutenant D.G. McLean, a newcomer to the squadron, 'drove down 1 E.A. in spin and spinning down on top of it shot E.A. down near SUSEGANA as it pulled out of spin,' reported his fellow pilots. But McLean himself was killed when his aircraft crashed and burnt near San Croce. The next day

---

* Lt-Col Joubert, commanding 14 Wing, demanded, 'in writing,' Barker's explanation of why, 'contrary to orders,' he made this attack. Barker's reply was singularly lame. When he and Hudson spotted the balloons, he wrote, 'I regret very much that for the moment I forgot the order against low flying.' Correspondence of 25–26 Jan. 1918, W.G. Barker biographical file, DHist

† Canadian arrivals during the first two months of 1918 included J.E. Hallonquist of Mission City, BC (WIA and POW 29 Oct. 1918), C.L. Amy of Prince Albert, Sask., J.B. Guthrie of Oakville, Ont. (KIA 10 May 1918), G.D. McLeod of Westmount, Que. (POW 8 June 1918), and D.W. Pratt of Toronto, to 28 Squadron; R.C. Cain of Ottawa and H.L. Holland of Toronto, to 34 Squadron; A.D. MacDonald of Cobalt, Ont., to 42 Squadron; M.R. James of Watford, Ont., J.C. McKeever of Listowel, Ont., and D.G. McLean of Bridgeburg, Ont. (KIA 4 Feb. 1918), to 45 Squadron; and A.L. Mercer of New Aberdeen, NS, to 66 Squadron.

‡ As an Air Vice Marshal, McEwen commanded 6 (RCAF) Bomber Group of the RAF's Bomber Command during the Second World War.

Barker and Hudson went up to look for an enemy two-seater reported to be working over the Italian lines and at 17,000 feet just north of Odense they encountered an Aviatik escorted by two Albatros D-Vs. Barker shot the left wing off an Albatros, which broke up in the air; he then chased down the Aviatik, which landed in a field and turned over. Meanwhile Hudson fought the other Albatros down to two hundred feet before it crashed near Portobuffole.[34]

On 12 February Barker and Hudson once more converted a gun test into a destructive operation, Colonel Joubert raising no objection on this occasion:

On approaching the PIAVE preparatory to testing guns, Capt. Barker observed that thick ground mist made conditions ideal for attacking balloons. He and Lt. Hudson crossed the PIAVE at NERVESA and flew to CONEGLIANO, then turned E. to FOSSAMERLO ... where 2 large observation balloons and 3 small ones were closely parked a few feet in the air, the small ones being between the large ones. Capt. Barker and Lt. Hudson attacked the large balloons which caught fire and all five were destroyed. There was no interference from the ground, except desultory and very badly aimed firing from 2 heavy tracer batteries near the balloons. The haze formed a good screen for the machines.[35]

All these activities demonstrated the ascendancy the RFC fighter squadrons had obtained. It was rare that Austrian aircraft had the opportunity to observe allied movements, or to work with artillery, while British corps machines were almost unimpeded in their tasks. It had not been so at the beginning. On 29 November 1917, when 34 Squadron first began operations, Lieutenant R.H. Luxton from Saskatchewan, in making his observer's report, noted that 'Formations of E.A. very active. Patrol and escort were repeatedly attacked from W. and E. sides of the River Piave at 9,000 feet, which eventually rendered further photos impossible.' It was the same on the following day. Luxton reported that 'although well escorted, photo machine was continually harassed,' while Lieutenant H.J.W. McConnell of Owen Sound, Ont., piloting another RE8, and his observer, had to fight off enemy attacks and so took no photographs whatever. Crews also found it wise, in these early days, to skirt carefully round the Italian lines, for their allies made no distinction between them and the Austrians.[36]

The corps squadrons naturally took some time to acquaint themselves with the terrain, and to establish a good working arrangement with the British, French, and Italian artillery. Of six RE8s working with the guns on 7 December, five reported unsuccessful shoots. This was partly because of poor visibility, as Luxton and a Toronto pilot, Lieutenant W.M. Davidson, reported, but there were indications that airmen and gunners were not communicating well with each other. For example, Lieutenant A.S. Dunn, an observer from Campbellford, Ont., alleged that 247th Siege Battery had failed to put out ground strips at the place agreed on, and therefore no shoot could take place. By mid-month, however, co-operation between aircraft and artillery was improving and enemy interference had begun to diminish. On 17 December twelve machines from 34 Squadron were able to carry out a variety of missions without distraction. Lieutenant C.L. King of Sault Ste Marie, Ont., with his observer, engaged in a successful shoot with a British battery; though they were up for two hours, they saw only two enemy aircraft, which approached the Piave and then turned tail. Lieutenant C.G. Andrews of Regina and his observer, Lieutenant J.G. Sharp of Toronto, found the 'line very quiet-no movement observed' until their carburettor was damaged by anti-aircraft fire and they were forced to return to base.[37]

By the turn of the year the corps squadron airmen had become thoroughly conversant with the front and were developing a close working relationship with their batteries, although on 4 January Andrews could not persuade 247th Siege Battery to alter the direction of its fire, even though most of its rounds had been off target. Most of the time, however, the shoots went well and the Austrians began to take great pains to conceal the location of their batteries. As Lieutenant G.E. Creighton of Dartmouth, NS, discovered, 'the quantity of scrub and soft ground' around battery positions made observation very difficult, because bursts were small or hidden altogether. By early March, nevertheless, 14 Wing's corps squadrons were carrying on shoots as competently as their counterparts on the Western Front. In a typical shoot on 13 March Lieutenant H.L. Holland of Toronto and his observer, working with 176th Siege Battery, ranged over two hundred rounds on a number of Austrian gun positions, destroyed one gun pit and damaged two others, and though they were in the air for over three-and-a-half hours they saw no enemy aircraft whatever.[38]

The mastery the RFC had obtained over a broad sector of the front had no crucial effect on ground operations, since neither side contemplated offensive action during the winter months. At most, it made life a little easier for British and allied troops, and correspondingly worse for the Austrians. This inactivity, and mounting evidence that Germany intended a major offensive on the Western Front, induced the British and French governments, without consulting their Italian partner, to withdraw some of their troops from Italy. During March and early April the British transferred the 41st and 5th Divisions to the Western Front, and the RFC withdrew several units, including 42 Squadron. The remaining corps squadron and the three fighter squadrons were grouped in 14 Wing, under the command of Lieutenant-Colonel Joubert de la Ferté,[39] and figured in the order of battle as part of 'General Headquarters Troops.'

Prior to the decision to reduce their forces in Italy the French and British had been planning a spring offensive, not across the Piave into the Venetian plain but rather against the Trentino sector. Only after the threat of the Austrians debouching from the Trentino had been eliminated could a Piave offensive be confidently undertaken. It had therefore been agreed that the British and French should be transferred to the Asiago plateau, to launch, under Italian command, an attack in the direction of Trento. In mid-March the British XIV and the French XII Corps began the shift to their new positions and the RFC moved in conformation. No 66 Squadron moved to Casa Piazza, 45 Squadron joined No 28 at Grossa, 34 Squadron went to Villaverla, and 14 Wing HQ went to Sarcedo in the XIV Corps rear area. All were stationed within ten miles of Vicenza and within easy range of both the new and the old fronts.[40]

To compensate for the loss of 42 Squadron, 14 Wing received a flight of six two-seater Bristol F2bs in mid-March. This superb all-round aircraft was exactly what was needed for the mountain operations now facing the RFC. 'Bristol Flight' was first attached to 28 Squadron, but on 30 March it became part of 34 Squadron as 'Z' Flight. A third of its complement was Canadian, Lieutenants Amy, Guthrie, and Pratt joining it from 28 Squadron, Sharp coming from 34 Squadron.[41]

The Asiago sector was a key part of the Italian mountain front. About twelve miles behind the British front-line trenches lay the Lombardy plain, the object of any Austrian attack from the Trentino. From the plain the ground rose to a range of foothills close to 5000 feet high, along the summits of which the British reserve line was placed. To the front of the reserve line the ground fell away abruptly to the Asiago valley, the front line running along the foot of this rugged and thickly wooded slope. Nowhere were the Austrian trenches closer than half a mile; behind them rose a second series of 5000 foot peaks. Defence in depth, according to the best Western Front precepts, was out of the question; if the British and French were compelled to fall back upon their reserve lines, it would be impossible for their guns to support them. Even as it was, the artillery from its positions along the reserve line had to accustom itself to large angles of depression in order to carry out its work. Precision firing under such circumstances was unlikely, and for artillery co-operation aircraft the situation was further complicated by the many difficulties in observing fall of shot in mountainous terrain.

For the corps machines to function effectively it was necessary, as always, for the fighter units to establish air superiority in this new sector. The accepted method of bringing the enemy to battle was to attack his observation and ground co-operation machines, and this the RFC proceeded to do. Thus on 10 March Second Lieutenant R.J. Dawes of Montreal was given credit for shooting down a DFW, on 18 March Lieutenant G.A. Birks, also of Montreal and a new arrival to 66 Squadron, claimed a Rumpler, and on the 24th Birks' destruction of an Aviatik was confirmed by Stanger, his wing-man. The Austrians reacted vigorously at first and combats became frequent, with Barker, Birks, McEwen, and Stanger playing prominent roles. On 18 March Stanger and another pilot were attacked by four red Albatros D-Vs while on Eastern Patrol,* and Stanger was credited with shooting one down. On 27 March T.F. Williams registered 45 Squadron's two-hundredth victory.[42]

On 10 April Barker moved to 66 Squadron as a flight commander; his new surroundings had no perceptible effect upon his extraordinary career. On 17 April he shot down an Albatros D-III, verified by his companions, Stanger and W.C. Hilborn of Alexandria, BC. Stanger claimed another. On this day alone the RAF – as it had now become – claimed to have shot down eleven enemy aircraft and it was becoming clear that the tide of battle had turned decisively.† In May the air struggle became even more one-sided, the RAF claiming to have shot down sixty-four machines at little cost to itself. Of these, 28 Squadron records

---

* It is possible that these were part of *Hauptmann* Godwin Brumowski's *Fliegerabteilung*; its aircraft were painted red in imitation of Richthofen's 'Circus.' Brumowski, Austria's leading fighter pilot, was credited with forty victories by the end of the war.

† New Canadian arrivals in April included J.M. Kelly of Montreal (POW 22 Oct. 1918) and J.T.J. McA'Nulty of Ottawa, who were attached to Wing HQ until October, when they went to 66 Squadron; L.A.A. Bernard of Montreal (WIA 9 May 1918), R.E. LaDouceur, an Ontarian whose address is unknown, and R.H. Lefebvre of Montreal (K 13 April 1918), all of whom went to 66 Squadron; A.E. Ryan of Brantford, Ont. (WIA 29 July 1918), to 34 Squadron and N.H. Hamley of Red Deer, Alta (WIA 20 Aug. and 1 Nov. 1918), to 28 Squadron.

credit McEwen with six, Stanger with four, Hudson with three, and one each for
Hallonquist, Dawes, and McLeod. In 66 Squadron Barker received credit for eight,
Birks for seven, Hilborn for three, and Bell and MacDonald with one apiece.[43]
Though pilots' scores were invariably inflated during the latter stages of the First
World War,* there seems little doubt that on the Asiago front the Austrians and
their German allies were badly over-matched. On 24 May, for example, Barker, in
company with Birks and a British pilot, Lieutenant G.F.M. Apps, caught up to a
pair of Albatros D-Vs and a Berg scout 'just over the valley at the southern foot of
M. COPPOLO':

> Capt. Barker attacked the rear E.A., which spun down. Lt. Birks attacked the Berg and after
> a very short fight E.A. went down with wings off. This was observed by Capt. Barker. At this
> time Capt. Barker observed three D.V.'s diving from the S. towards Lts. Birks and Apps,
> who were engaging the remaining two E.A. in the valley. Capt. Barker got under the tail of
> one of these E.A. unobserved and after firing about 40 rounds E.A. went down out of
> control and crashed on some hutments in the valley and burst into flames. This was seen by
> Lts. Apps and Birks. Lt. Apps engaged one of the two remaining E.A. of the first formation,
> who was on Lt. Birks' tail. Lt. Apps fired a long burst when E.A. was doing a climbing turn
> and E.A. went down out of control and crashed in the valley. E.A. was observed to go down
> out of control by Capt. Barker and to crash by Lt. Birks. The remaining D.V. of the first
> three E.A. was an exceptionally skilful pilot and Lt. Birks fought him for a long time then Lt.
> Apps joined in the attack. Neither pilot could get E.A. down so Capt. Barker joined in the
> fight and got on tail of E.A. Capt. Barker fired a short burst at E.A. who went down out of
> control and dived vertically into the same hutments where Capt. Barker's first E.A. burst
> into flames. This was observed by Lts. Apps and Birks.[44]

The three RAF pilots saw only one out of six machines escape from this fight, one
which 'went away very low down in the direction of FELTRE.' The whole affair
lasted just fifteen minutes.

The Camels also undertook a good many bombing missions, usually against
enemy airfields. Since they could carry only four 20-lb or 25-lb bombs, such raids
were only of nuisance value. One occasion merits mention, however. On 14
March Stanger and a British colleague were sent to bomb enemy shipping in the
Adriatic. It seems likely that they followed the Piave to its mouth, then flew along
the coast until they caught sight of two vessels off Miramare, a port just north of
Trieste. They claimed direct hits on the second 'tramp,' since 'black smoke and
debris blew into the air,' and machine-gunned both vessels. The round trip from
their airfield must have been close to two hundred miles.†[45]

Corps squadrons on the Western Front undoubtedly would have envied the
degree of protection enjoyed by 34 Squadron. Even lengthy reconnaissance missions often took place unhindered. On 2 May Lieutenant J.B. Guthrie of Oakville,
Ont., and his observer, flying a Bristol Fighter at 14,500 feet, made a round trip of
enemy installations to the rear of the Asiago front without challenge from an
enemy machine, though visibility was 'perfect.' They were able to report in con-

---

* See 572–4.
† During the Italian campaign Stanger was awarded both the MC and the DFC

siderable detail upon enemy activity in the Val d'Assa, a deep gorge on the British left, at Folgaria, where there was a large camp, and at Mattarello in the Adige valley. They described the situation at the enemy base at Trento, reported the number of aircraft on the ground at Pergine airfield east of Trento, and noted dumps, airfields, and train and troop movements at various points in the Val Sugana, through which ran the River Brenta, a rail line, and the main road to Bassano. Along the way they took forty photographs. The cumulative worth of such intelligence, built upon as weather permitted, gave the British command a clear picture of the enemy's situation.[46]

Artillery co-operation work in the Asiago sector did not proceed so smoothly, despite the absence of enemy aircraft. Shoots could be disrupted, and often were, for many reasons – from a careless hand upon the Morse buzzer to a defective wireless receiver. But the mountain front had special problems. For example, on 7 June Lieutenant R.C. Cain, an English immigrant to Canada in prewar days and a former federal civil servant, who had enlisted in the RCHA in 1914 and was now serving as a pilot in 34 Squadron, located an anti-aircraft gun firing from the Val d'Assa. He sent the call 'NF' ('Guns firing at ...') and the correct map co-ordinates to his battery but 'the rounds in response fell about 250 yards over.' Such inaccuracy resulted because the enemy battery was 'just behind the crest and not down in the valley'; a near-miss in these circumstances was as good as an eighth of a mile. Very often the airmen simply could not find their targets, though their location was known, because the Austrians had used natural cover so well. On 17 April Holland spent forty-five minutes circling in the area of the target before he gave up and flew a patrol instead. Until adequate maps from aerial photographs were prepared, the airmen were often led astray. Only persistence enabled Cain to find his target on 23 April, because his map 'only gave an approximate idea of the roads at this spot.'[47]

Time and time again crews reported their inability to send corrections to batteries because they were unable to locate the fall of shot. On 3 May Cain, on a destructive shoot with 302nd Siege Battery, recorded the twenty rounds fired as 'WS' (washouts). 'Target very difficult to observe on. Most bursts never showed, and others, when the smoke appeared above the trees, were impossible to locate with any exactitude. The smoke was so slow in mounting that it dispersed considerable [sic] and necessitated a wait between rounds.' Not only tree cover but haze, deep shade, and the shadows cast by passing clouds complicated the task of observation of fire. On 10 May King and his observer failed to see many rounds which disappeared into the impenetrable darkness of a gorge. 'Enemy battery position was located near a cliff, which on the North side dropped sheer away,' he reported; 'consequently any shells falling plus were unobserved causing a great number of washouts ...' Just a month later, after a similar experience, Cain summed up the problem: 'This shoot should be done at a considerable height, otherwise the bottom of the valley can only be seen when almost directly over it. The haze in the bottom of the valley ... made bursts difficult to spot and easy to imagine.'[48]

In spite of everything, 34 Squadron conducted many successful shoots. On 10 May Andrews found the shooting during a bombardment of the Austrian trenches 'very good'; the majority of rounds he observed were direct hits. On 1 June

Holland carried out an excellent shoot for an alert battery. Spotting ten vehicles in convoy, he sent a 'GF' call (used for fleeting targets). The response was immediate: '9 M.T. were set on fire and completely burned. They were evidently filled with ammunition as they were exploding every 2 or 3 seconds.' On 10 June Lieutenant K.B. Forster of Red Deer, Alta, and 197th Siege Battery formed a potent combination; several direct hits were obtained within the first few rounds fired against a hostile battery and this exemplary shoot continued through two-and-a-half hours and 150 rounds. At its close, air-ground teamwork had in all likelihood destroyed the enemy battery.[49]

All this air work had been predicated upon an allied offensive. By late May, however, the signs had multiplied that the Austrians were themselves about to attack and the Italian Supreme Command dropped all offensive plans. This last effort by the Austro-Hungarian Empire to achieve victory in Italy was made possible by the release of their divisions from the Eastern Front, and prompted also by Ludendorff's urgings as the German assaults on the Western Front waned at the end of April. Though the Austrians knew that they were inferior in manpower, guns, and aircraft, they hoped to collapse the allied front by simultaneous attacks upon the British and French in the Asiago-Mount Grappa sector and upon the Italians along the Piave, concentrating especially upon Papadopoli Island. In early June the enemy renewed his attempts at aerial observation of the Asiago front. This was countered by instituting a close patrol between Forni and Gallio, along an eight-mile stretch of the front, pilots being ordered not to leave this line except to attack a hostile aircraft in the immediate vicinity, and a 'long offensive patrol' five miles deeper in enemy territory between Casotto and Cismon. These patrols effectively prevented enemy attempts at reconnaissance.[50]

At 0300 hrs on 15 June the Austrian bombardment opened all along the front from the Adriatic to the Asiago plateau. On the allied right, a thick fog combined with artificial smoke and tear-gas soon filled the valley of the Piave, enabling the Austrian infantry to cross the river by boats and pontoons at a number of places. On the left, British veterans of the Western Front found the bombardment less severe than those that they had known in France and Flanders. Much of it was unregistered, in part an indication of the success of the RAF in preventing aerial artillery observation. At 0700 hrs Austrian troops began to penetrate the British wire and during the morning they achieved limited gains at several points. RAF assistance was much reduced because of mist and low clouds; nevertheless, the fighters were out by 0435 hrs when Lieutenant R.G. Reid of St John's, Nfld (a cousin of the RNAS' H.V. Reid who had participated in the ill-fated Romanian venture), took off as part of a 66 Squadron patrol. A few minutes later Lieutenants W.M. MacDonald of Vancouver and H.D. McDiarmid of Victoria let down through the clouds to drop bombs on marching troops north of Asiago; having returned for more, they bombed 'a mass of troops' in Val d'Assa and optimistically claimed 'great havoc caused.' Barker, Birks, and Bell also found targets in Val d'Assa some time later, but by 0900 hrs visibility was too poor to continue.[51]

Given the weather, some crews from 34 Squadron did surprisingly effective work. Second Lieutenant H.W. Minish of Gilbert Plains, Man., directed fire on three hostile batteries in the Val d'Assa. Lieutenant C.L. King and his observer,

Lieutenant K.O. Bracken of Toronto, were out at 0520 hrs. They sent down three 'GF' calls on enemy transport, 'NF' calls on twenty-one active enemy batteries, and dropped two 20-lb bombs on a touring car. A direct hit on the car was obtained, King reported, 'and car was seen to leave road.' Lieutenant R.C. Cain and his observer were quite as enterprising, being in the air from 0825 hrs until noon. They machine-gunned enemy infantry, horse lines, and transport; shortly after 1100 hrs they found field guns firing in the open from a slope. Finding that machine-gun fire stopped the batteries only momentarily, they called down artillery fire. The batteries ceased firing; 'several shell holes were just by the guns and must have done considerable execution among the personnel.'[52]

Meanwhile the RAF had been shifted to the Piave front. All units joined in low-level operations which T.F. Williams recalled clearly:

Every Camel was loaded up with four 20-lb Cooper bombs and we were sent out to bomb and strafe the troops and the pontoon bridges. I can well remember the masses of troops up on the east side of the Montello, shooting into the Austrians making the crossing. We were down low enough to see the expressions on their faces. We bombed the pontoon bridges and I then took my flight entirely on ground strafing. I flew about four patrols that day on low-level work. We were going from dawn to dusk, dropping bombs and strafing. We bombed so low that the blast of the bombs just lifted our aeroplanes.[53]

Just after noon nine Camels from Williams' 45 Squadron attacked the enemy crossing in the Montello sector; by 1600 hrs more than thirty Camels from all the fighter squadrons were involved, as well as some of the Bristols and RE8s of 34 Squadron. Barker led a strong attack by 66 Squadron against the bridges in the Montello sector. He later stated:

The Montello, owing to its height, dominated the Venetian plain and under its cover [the Austrians] had thrown two pontoon bridges across the river. The leader selected the bridge farthest upstream and individual bombing commenced from about 50 feet. This bridge was quickly broken in two places and the pontoons, caught by the fast current, were immediately dashed against the lower bridge, carrying it away also. When this attack commenced these bridges were crowded with troops which were attacked with machine-gun fire. Many were seen to be in the water. This done, troops on small islands and in row boats were machine-gunned.[54]

Successful attacks were also made on Austrian bridges lower down on the Piave, and on troop concentrations on Papadopoli Island. During the night the Austrians succeeded in repairing some bridges and building new ones, but the RAF again knocked several of them down. Renewed air attacks on the 16th were again highly successful. Cain, of 34 Squadron, flying solo with two 112-lb bombs, attacked two bridges in the Montello sector, where the Austrians had established their most dangerous bridgehead: 'First burst was on the bridge at H95.25 which hit about 10 yards N.E. of eastern end of bridge among a considerable quantity of transport some of which galloped over the bridge and jambed, while others went straight into the river. The second bomb was an OK on the western end of the other bridge ... This bridge was evidently under repair from previous raids ... There are a considerable number of pontoons stranded at different points down the river.'[55] Five Camels from 66 Squadron, led by Barker, destroyed another bridge below the Montello, shooting up troops in the bridgehead. Nevertheless, in the early afternoon Andrews of 34 Squadron reported that seven bridges on the lower Piave were still intact.[56]

But what the RAF had begun, the river itself completed. On the 17th heavy rain fell, preventing further bombing, but during the night the Piave rose and its torrents ripped away almost all the bridges which remained. On the 18th special air reconnaissances covered the whole of the Piave front from Vidor above the Montello to the Adriatic. Cain and his observer brought intelligence about the stretch of river from Vidor to S. Dona di Piave, finding only two bridges intact near the latter point. They reported bridges from the Austrian-held shore across the Papadopoli Island but none from it to the Italian side. King and Bracken, who flew the line later in the day, confirmed these findings: all the bridges, including those to Papadopoli, had now been washed away. But from S. Dona to the sea they found eleven bridges intact.[57]

Faced with this interdiction of their supply lines by both men and nature, and therefore unable to expand their several bridgeheads over the river into a continuous line, the Austrian command decided to withdraw and did so successfully on the night of 22–23 June. Rarely did aircraft play so significant a part in a major military operation during the First World War.[58]

The RAF casualties during and immediately following these operations were remarkably light, given the amount of low-level work. Only three Canadians were lost during the period: Lieutenant J.G. Russell of St Thomas, Ont., and Second Lieutenant C.P. Urich of Winkler, Man., were among 28 Squadron's fatal casualties, while Lieutenant E.M. Brown of Princeton, Nfld, a member of the Bristol Fighter flight of 34 Squadron, became a prisoner of war.*

According to Barker's personal records, it was sometime during June that he, Birks, and McEwen dropped the following note at Godega airfield:

Major W.G. Barker, D.S.O., M.C., and the Officers under his Command present their compliments to Captain Bronmoski, 41 Recon. Portobouffole, Ritter von Fiala, 51 Pursuit, Gajarine, Captain Navratil, 3rd Company and the Pilots under their command and request the pleasure and honour of meeting in the air. In order to save Captain Bronmoski, Ritter von Fiala, and Captain Navratil, and gentlemen of his party the inconvenience of searching for them, Major Barker and his Officers will bomb GODIGO [sic] aerodrome at 10-0 a.m. daily, weather permitting, for the ensuing two weeks.

Hauptmann Godwin Brumowski was Austria's leading ace; *Oberleutnant* Benno Ritter von Fiala Fernbrugg and *Oberleutnant* Friedrich Nav atil were also well-

---

* Russell (KIA 15 June 1918) had arrived on 28 May and Urich (KIA 24 June 1918) on 22 June, two days before his death. During the month R.G. McLaren of Ormstown, Que., joined 28 Squadron and D.J. Teepoorten of Vancouver went to 66 Squadron. Arriving at 34 Squadron's Bristol Flight were A.A. Harcourt-Vernon of Toronto (POW 4 Nov. 1918), A.G. Lincoln of Calgary, W.W. McBain from Atwood, Ont., and A.L. McLaren of Montreal.

known and distinguished fighter pilots. There is no record that they responded to Barker's absurd and vainglorious challenge.[59]

After the failure of the Austrian offensive, the Italian Supreme Command was urged by *Général* Foch to undertake offensive operations of its own. To the Allied Supreme Commander it was important that pressure be maintained upon the Austro-Hungarian army, not only to take advantage of the rebuff just administered to it, but also to co-ordinate operations in Italy with those planned against the Germans on the Western Front for mid-July. Moreover, it seemed obvious that the Hapsburg Empire had reached a state of incipient disintegration and that the deep national schisms within it were having disruptive effects upon the army, a good part of which was non-Austrian. *Generale* Armando Diaz, the Italian CGS, was able to resist these and later arguments for offensive action, however, at least in part because Italian politicians were not prepared to risk again the heavy casualties the country had sustained earlier in the war. Not until 1 October, after the spectacular allied successes on the Western Front in September, did Italy decide to take the offensive.[60]

In the long pause from late June to 24 October the Italian front remained static, though there were the usual trench raids and artillery 'hates.' Unlike the other arms, however, the RAF, faithful to its offensive doctrine, continued to patrol aggressively, if only to ensure that the routine work of daily reconnaissance and artillery co-operation was carried on without hindrance. On 3 July a new Bristol Fighter squadron, No 139, was formed, made up of 'z' Flight from 34 Squadron and drafts of aircrew from England and the Western Front. The seven Canadians already in 'z' Flight were joined by Captain G.W. Curtis of Montreal and Second Lieutenant W.B. Ramsay of Lumsden, Sask.* On 14 July Barker was promoted major and given command of the new squadron. He took his Camel with him from 66 Squadron and continued to add to his victories until posted to 201 Squadron in France at the end of September.[61]

The addition of 139 Squadron was balanced by the departure of 45 Squadron to France on 20 September. Its departure was linked to a general reorganization and reduction of the British contingent in Italy. Infantry brigades were reduced from four to three battalions (this had been done on the Western Front in early 1918) and the nine battalion surplus went to France. The British 48th Division and a French division remained on the Asiago front while, in October, the other two British divisions, together with an Italian corps, were formed into Tenth Army under a British commander, Lord Cavan, and placed on the Piave front to spearhead the coming attack.[62]

Prior to the opening of the offensive the RAF dealt two punishing blows to the Austrian air force by striking at the chief sources for pilot reinforcements on each of the battle fronts. On 4 October every available Camel from 28 and 66 Squadrons, armed with phosphorus and high-explosive bombs, attacked the Campoformido advanced training school southwest of Udine. The attack was a complete

---

* Canadians arriving in Italy during the June-October period included D.B. And R.H. Foss, brothers from Sherbrooke, Que., to 28 Squadron; W.N. Hanna of Sarnia, Ont., A.E. Popham of Victoria, L.J. Shepard of Port Stanley, Ont., and Harold Shone of Toronto, to 34 Squadron; A.V. Green of Vancouver to 45 Squadron; W.J. Courtenay of St Thomas, Ont. (KIA 7 Oct. 1918), A.G. Kettles of Bruce Mines, Ont., and Robert Menzies, address unknown, to 66 Squadron.

surprise, and many aircraft and several hangars were destroyed. The attackers were escorted by Stanger and McEwen and the two Canadians were credited with shooting down three Albatros D-IIIs over the mouth of the Tagliamento River. So successful was this raid that the next day the flying school at Egna, northeast of Trento, was bombed.* Twenty-two pilots took part, among them Ontarians W.J. Courtenay and A.G. Kettles, R. Menzies, address unknown, R.H. Foss of Sherbrooke, Que., and the Newfoundlander, R.G. Reid. According to the report sent the Air Ministry by Colonel Joubert, at least three hangars and several parked aircraft were set ablaze and mechanics who rushed out to save the burning machines and buildings were driven off by machine-gun fire. Joubert noted particularly the action of Foss, who sent an LVG plunging into a nearby canal before dropping his bombs.[63]

Before the end of the Italian campaign RAF squadrons were to be surfeited with such low-level work. The crux of *Generale* Diaz's plan was to force a crossing of the Piave while containing the Austrian Sixth Army on the Trentino front. The key sector was that between the Montello and Papadopoli Island. Lord Cavan's Tenth Army was to cross at Papadopoli, with the Italian Eighth Army on its left. Together the two armies were to strike north and northwest for Vittorio Veneto and Sacile, aiming to cut the communications between the Austrian forces in the mountains and those on the Venetian plain.[64]

The air plan was simplicity itself: 'to obtain the mastery of the air and to maintain it throughout the action.' The roles assigned the RAF's 14 Wing placed emphasis upon 'free scouting and cruising expeditions' for the fighters, in addition to bomber escort duties. Ground attack at low levels was to be 'an integral part of the bombing raids' and was to be conducted by all types of machines. In keeping with the tight security which was a notable feature of this offensive, RAF squadrons did not leave their concentration in the rear of the Asiago sector until the eve of the battle. On 22 October 14 Wing HQ moved to Dosson, three miles south of Treviso and near Lord Cavan's headquarters at Villa Marcello. On the same day 28 Squadron moved to Limbrage and 34 Squadron to San Luca, both airfields being in the Treviso area. No 66 Squadron remained at Casa Piazza, ready if need be to support the British 48th Division on the Asiago.[65]

The exception was 139 Squadron, which moved to Grossa on 9 October to be in a better position to carry out strategic reconnaissance in the period preceding the attack. The Bristol Fighters, operating in formations of three to five machines, carried out extensive photographic work, including low-level flights over Papadopoli Island on 17 and 20 October. Their photographs showed sixteen bridges intact between Papadopoli and the Austrian-held bank. On 22 October five Bristol Fighters reconnoitred the Tenth Army's proposed line of advance as far as Sacile

---

* Jones, *War in the Air*, VI (London 1937), 288, and map opposite 273, locates Egna immediately south of Bolzano and southeast of Udine, in the Venetian plain. In his report Colonel Joubert identifies it as 'N.E. of Trento, 50 kilometres over the lines,' and describes it as 'a finishing school for pilots destined for the TRENTINO front.' In his combat report Second Lieutenant R.H. Foss says that he pursued an LVG 'down the ADIGE valley away from aerodrome.' See Joubert to Air Ministry, 10 Oct. 1918, Air 1/1985/204/273/97; Foss combat report, 5 Oct. 1918, Air 1/1854/204/213/15.

and Pordenone, taking numerous photographs and reporting enemy activity in detail. A final photographic mission was flown on the 23rd to gather intelligence of the Livenza, the next river barrier beyond the Piave. This invaluable work took place without any serious challenge from enemy aircraft.[66]

The Tenth Army's crossing of the Piave was to take place in two phases: first the capture of Papadopoli, a low, sandy island about four miles long, covered with trees and scrub and entrenched by the enemy, and then the passage of the several shallow channels which separated the island from the east bank. The photographs obtained by 139 Squadron, of which five thousand copies were made for distribution to formations, made plain the problems involved and helped determine Lord Cavan upon a night crossing to make an initial lodgment on the island. On the night of 23–24 October a territorial battalion of the Honourable Artillery Company (despite its title, an infantry unit) was ferried in flat-bottomed boats across the several hundred yards of the main channel, surprising the Hungarian garrison and securing the western half of Papadopoli. By the 27th the whole of the island had been taken and the Tenth Army and its flanking neighbours were ready for the main assault. Just before 0700 hrs the 7th and 23rd British Divisions moved off to attack the Austrian works on the left bank, and at 0705 hrs R.C. Cain, now a captain with a DFC, took off to work with the British guns against enemy batteries. In half an hour he was back; his observer, Second Lieutenant M. Nicol of Edmonton, had been wounded by machine-gun fire from the ground. Picking up Second Lieutenant L.J. Shepard of Port Stanley, Ont., Cain was in the air again by 0810 hrs. The pair sent down several 'NF' calls against Austrian batteries firing upon the advancing groups, but at 0955 hrs were attacked by a pair of Albatros D-IIIs. Cain, wounded in the foot, managed to return to base. For the first time in some weeks enemy aircraft were both numerous and aggressive over the front. Two other Canadians, King and his observer, Bracken, had taken off very early, at 0620 hrs, but had not been heard from since that time.*[67]

Early intelligence of the development of the attack was brought in by a number of 34 Squadron's artillery and contact patrol machines. At 0840 hrs Lieutenant K.B. Forster of Red Deer, Alta, and Second Lieutenant A.E. Popham of Victoria reported to Corps Headquarters that the Austrians were holding trench systems behind the Piave in strength, but half an hour later they passed word that 'Our troops appeared to be holding the N. bank of the PIAVE in considerable force.' Later in the morning two more Canadians, Lieutenant P.M. Hodder and Second Lieutenant H.W. Minish, found that British troops were close to their final objectives for the day. Some anxiety was caused at the command level by the initial failure of the Italians to move up on the flanks, but at 1240 hrs Popham, in a message dropped at Corps Headquarters, reported that large numbers of Italian troops had crossed the river on the British right. Less than an hour later he added that on the left a line of trenches was 'heavily held by Italian Infantry and the cavalry on N. bank of PIAVE.' At this point the RE8 was attacked by two Albatros D-IIIs and returned home 'badly shot about.' At 1300 hrs units of the 23rd Divi-

---

* King brought his damaged RE8 down in enemy territory. The two apparently evaded capture and
   rejoined their unit on 4 November.

sion, having reached their final objectives at Borgo Malanotte, were counter-attacked, and having run short of ammunition had to give ground. Two RE8s, one flown by Hodder and Minish, were sent out at 1540 hrs to drop ammunition to them and the position was quickly retaken. So good was the collaboration, through ground signals, between advancing units and corps aircraft, and so specific were the reports of air observers that after the first suspenseful hour commanders had at their disposal throughout the day a clear account of the constantly changing course of battle.[68]

While 34 Squadron airmen went about their duties, the fighter pilots, as ordered, were scouring the battlefield at low level. They sought their targets chiefly in the area immediately behind the battle line. At 0730 hrs a 28 Squadron flight, including Hallonquist and R.H. Foss, took to the air, spending two hours attacking troops and batteries close to the front. Later in the morning Hamley and R.G. McLaren went down to a hundred feet to bomb a kite balloon; after it burst into flames they attacked retiring transport.* Several patrols from 66 Squadron found more targets than they could handle. H.D. McDiarmid was one of several pilots to bomb and stampede a mass of enemy transport fleeing from the front, while A.G. Kettles claimed yet another kite balloon. In the afternoon Hamley and a companion bombed a bridge across the Monticano River from fifty feet. Becoming separated from his wing-man, Hamley climbed to 3000 feet and single-handedly attacked five Albatros D-Vs. After shooting one down within sight of some British infantry, he himself was brought down when his engine was hit and a bullet lodged in his finger. He crash-landed on Papadopoli; though the Camel was further damaged, Hamley returned safely to his squadron. The work of the fighters was not so important to the course of the battle as that of 34 Squadron, but for the Austrians it was an omen.[69]

On the 28th Tenth Army did not resume the attack until noon. It was able, however, to enlarge the bridgehead by up to two miles, with some elements reaching the line of the River Monticano, where the Austrian defensive works were known as the *Königstellung*. No 34 Squadron continued its careful and detailed reporting of the allied advance, while 28 squadron spent the day driving enemy aircraft from the battle zone, though Hallonquist and Foss attacked troops and transport on the army's left, close to the front of the Italian XVIII Corps. Low-level work was left to 66 Squadron, whose pilots ranged over the whole arc of the bridgehead. McDiarmid's early morning patrol attacked targets around Oderzo on the Monticano, directly to the front of the Italian XI Corps, the army's right wing. At the same hour Menzies and Kettles were part of a patrol that shot up troops in Codogne, marching south towards the British 7th Division while Lieutenant D.J. Teepoorten of Vancouver attacked a supply column moving towards Vazzola, one of the division's objectives for the day. Shortly after the ground assault began a

---

* Both pilots and groundcrew of 28 Squadron were laid low by influenza on the eve of the offensive. 'A' Flight had only a flight sergeant, two corporals and two air mechanics to maintain six Camels and the wing commander's Pup, and the other two flights were in worse state. To keep aircraft flying, the groundcrew available worked eighteen hours and more a day during the offensive; 'the poor old "busses" [sic] didn't get cleaned up for days,' Flight Sergeant Frank Brook later wrote. Brook to Williams, 5 Dec. 1918, T.F. Williams biographical file, DHist

patrol which included Lieutenant J.T.J. McA'Nulty of Ottawa saw troops retreating north from Codogne and infantry milling about at the Visna crossroads. Both groups were attacked at low level, and 'many casualties' claimed. Two patrols, whose members included Teepoorten, Menzies, and Kettles, discovered troops concentrated in a wood west of S. Stino di Livenza, with their equipment 'laid out in rows' in an adjoining field. These troops, who were in a position to move against the right flank of the advance, were heavily attacked with bombs and machine-guns by the fighters and Teepoorten finished off the exercise by destroying a kite balloon.[70]

The 29th was the climactic day of the campaign. The Austrians meant to make a stand on the Monticano-Conegliano line and had brought up reinforcements to do so. The river itself was contained within twenty-foot dikes which commanded the flat vineyard country to the south. But as early as 0930 hrs British infantry had crossed the river and punched a hole in the *Königstellung*. According to Austrian accounts this first break-in occurred when a Czech regiment panicked and fled when machine-gunned from the air, never having been exposed before to this form of attack. So numerous were such attacks that it is impossible to identify the patrol involved. Though British troops did not advance far beyond the Monticano on the 29th, the breach they had made split the Austrian Sixth and Isonzo Armies; by the afternoon airmen were reporting that the roads leading away from the front were clogged with retreating troops and transport, upon which they inflicted serious damage. Three RAF aircraft were lost on this day, two of them flown by Canadians. Shortly after noon Captain Hallonquist's machine was hit by 'vigorous machine-gun fire from the ground' after he had released four bombs on a transport column going north into Veneto. He was seriously injured when his aircraft landed atop a truck.* Lieutenant W.W. McBain of Atwood, Ont., was shot down near Pordenone, a town through which elements of the Isonzo Army were streaming. He survived the landing unscathed, though the Camel was a total wreck, but was then fired upon by understandably hostile infantry. He bolted for a farm house and there he hid, in civilian clothes provided by his sympathetic hosts, until the Allies swept through.[71]

On the 30th the Tenth Army approached the Livenza, a river wide, swift, and deep. Under other circumstances it would have constituted a major obstacle. By this time, however, a large part of the Austrian army was in full retreat, the Austro-Hungarian Empire itself in dissolution, and resistance minimal. A bridgehead was secured at Sacile, and the River Tagliamento reached on 3 November; British troops had crossed it when the armistice accorded the defeated Austrians took effect on the 4th.

In these last days RAF fighter pilots saw spread before them the spectacle of an army in collapse. Roads leading back to the Tagliamento and to Austria were clogged with masses of troops, some maintaining marching order, others mere

---

* Hallonquist was well cared for in Sacile hospital until released by British troops 'to the great joy of all in No. 28 Squadron.' On 2 November he was awarded the bronze medal of the *Valore Militare* and later the DFC for his 'display of the highest skill and courage' and for 'setting a fine example to other pilots.'

crowds. Mingled with them were staff cars, horse transport, horse- and tractor-drawn artillery, and all the impedimenta of a huge army. By the roadsides were trails of discarded uniforms, stores, baggage, and weapons. Many of the troops were no longer armed; even those who were, however, had no real defence against the cruel punishment now meted out to them. Flying down the roads at tree-top level, the Camels attacked relentlessly until the end. The devastation wrought by RAF strafing during Allenby's Palestine offensive is usually regarded as one of the great air achievements of the First World War, yet British air attacks in the final phase of the Italian campaign were equally devastating, though almost unknown.

The chaos created by the fighters fills many pages of squadron record books. A few instances drawn from 66 Squadron will suffice. On the 30th Teepoorten's patrol found the road leading to Pordenone 'full up with motor and horse transport, facing east, mostly stationary, the road being blocked up. Attacked a battalion of infantry ... the infantry being mixed up with the stationary transport, going in no particular direction.' The next day ten Camels, including machines flown by McDiarmid, Menzies, Kettles, and Teepoorten, swept down the main road between Sacile and Pordenone, Menzies' patrol reporting 'great damage done on this road with our bombing, causing huge blockages.' On 1 November the Camels caught endless columns of the fleeing enemy at the congested approaches to the crossings of the Tagliamento, where converging roads caused enormous jams. McA'Nulty and Teepoorten bombed 'a large amount of transport and troops, stationary and facing east ... the majority were direct hits.' At S. Vito al Tagliamento McDiarmid and Kettles, with two others, came upon and attacked thousands of infantry who could not move because of a block created by several howitzers drawn by steam-tractors. The next day, in the same sector, Menzies and McA'Nulty machine-gunned a battalion of troops they found 'engaged in destroying bridges and roads, also burning villages behind them.'[72]

In the wake of the Camels came marching British infantry. What they found was described in the history of the 23rd Division:

Along the Pordenone road, which ran wide and straight through open country, there was terrible evidence of the loss in power of a river to save a routed army. Before war was carried into the air a defeated army, by placing a river between itself and pursuit, might hope to gain some respite to restore its shattered morale, but the deepest and widest river is of no avail against aircraft. The sights on the Pordenone road moved the victorious British troops to horror and to pity; to the weary half-starved enemy, whose disorganised masses had blackened the broad high-road during the past few days, the vision of the fate which might at any moment visit them must have brought a terror which eclipsed even the bitterness of defeat. For mile after mile the road was flanked with wreckage of troops and transport, shattered guns and waggons, the mangled remains of drivers intermingled with those of the horses, corpses of infantrymen riddled by machine-gun fire.[73]

Major-General J.F. Gathorne-Hardy, who had been Brigadier-General, General Staff, of the British XIV Corps, also gave an account of the campaign after the war. He noted that on 29 and 30 October the RAF expended thirty thousand rounds of ammunition and three-and-a-half tons of bombs upon targets on the Conegliano-

Pordenone road. 'Subsequent examination of the road almost forced the observer to the conclusion that this form of warfare should be forbidden in future.'[74] The tactics which produced scenes like these would be all too familiar to another generation, but they rapidly disappeared from the memory, and the repertoire, of the post-1918 RAF.

In Macedonia the war reached its climax a month earlier than in Italy. The final offensive had been planned by *Général* Franchet d'Espérey, who had succeeded to the overall command in June 1918. He gave the leading role to the Serbs and assigned to those hardy mountaineers the breaching of the Moglena range. So lofty and forbidding were these heights that the Bulgarians had neglected to fortify them heavily, yet if they could be passed an invader could lay his hands upon the main line of communications and collapse the whole of the front. The French were to attack on either side of the Serbian armies, while the Italians on the left and the Greeks on the far right had as their chief task the holding of the enemy in order to prevent reinforcement of the centre. The British were to attack between the Vardar and Lake Doiran.[75]

The Serbian attack began in the early hours of 15 September, and within two days a blunt wedge twenty-five miles wide and six miles deep had been driven into the enemy front. The British, attacking the sector RAF pilots deemed the strongest on the whole front, took heavy losses for slight gains. During this attack, on the 18th and 19th, the corps squadrons carried out contact patrols and low-level strafing, while the fighter pilots took part in a final dogfight with their German opponents, 'the last encounter of its kind on the British Macedonian front.' While leading his flight of SE5as Captain Gordon Bell caught sight of twelve Fokkers over Cestovo. 'The leader of hostile formation was attacked by Capt. Bell head on at close range,' Bell's report states. 'E.A. did an Immelmann turn in front of S.E. D3495. After short burst E.A. centre section burst into flames.' A pilot from 47 Squadron saw the crash of the last enemy aircraft to be destroyed on this front.[76]

Meanwhile, west of the Vardar, the Serbs and French were rapidly exploiting their breakthrough. On the morning of 21 September RAF machines brought back word that the enemy had begun to retreat all along the line, including the British sector. Not a German plane could be found in the sky, the hangars at Hudova airfield had disappeared, and the rear areas were dotted with burning dumps of material. It was a situation precisely similar to that on the Piave front little more than a month later, though not quite on the same scale. And as they were to do in Italy, RAF machines took full advantage of the opportunity to harry the retreating enemy. According to the historical report submitted by 16 Wing shortly after the end of operations, 'the retreating troops and transport were followed up from the time the retirement started.'

The roads running north from Rabrovo, Kosturino [sic], Strumica and Jenikoj were seen to be black with traffic, and were bombed continuously by our machines. As soon as the machines had dropped their load of bombs and expended their ammunition they returned immediately to the aerodrome two and three times for fresh supplies, everyone showing the greatest keenness, and the fullest advantage was taken of these exceptional targets. During this period our machines came down to as low as 50 and 20 feet, and fired into convoys and bodies of troops. Exceptional targets presented themselves in the closely packed transport, and independent evidence, testifying to the enormous casualties and damage inflicted, is contained in telegram received by Advanced G.H.Q. from Advanced 16th Corps.[77]

The telegram referred to attributed the 'indescribable confusion' that marked the Bulgar retreat directly to the activities of the RAF. In the narrow defiles through which the mountain roads passed, congestion was unavoidable, and after a few hours of bombing and strafing a brave and resolute enemy, retreating undefeated from a front against which the British had hurled themselves unavailingly for years, had been reduced to a panic-stricken mob. It was a harsh conclusion to the Macedonian campaign. On 30 September hostilities ceased on this front.

16
The Ludendorff Offensives, 1918

Germany's last great effort to win the war, and her last real opportunity, came in the spring of 1918. That such was the case was as evident to the Allies as it was to the German High Command. By the winter of 1917–18 Russia, torn by revolution and internal dissension, was all but out of the war. Germany was in a position to deploy in the West divisions that could be released from the Eastern Front, an access of strength that would give her an advantage over the Allies. This advantage, however, could only be temporary; once the full weight of American deployment was brought to bear, the German opportunity would be gone. During the winter, therefore, the German High Command made preparations for a supreme effort on the Western Front in the spring, while at the same time the Allies addressed themselves to the problems of defence against an onslaught they knew to be inevitable.

It was the concept of defence-in-depth to which British GHQ turned. The chief architect of this form of defence during the First World War was Colonel von Lossberg, Chief of Staff of the German First Army. He had been appalled by the casualties suffered when holding linear defences against the British attacks of 1916, and had in consequence devised a defence system in which the bulk of German forces were held back beyond the initial range of enemy artillery. Allied assault formations thus had to contend not only with interlocking machine-gun fire from carefully sited forward strong points and with a heavy defensive barrage, but once through the advance positions, they had to attack trench systems virtually untouched by shell fire or gas. Should they penetrate these lines, they would then have to withstand immediate counter-attacks from German forces held yet further back. Von Lossberg's ideas were taken up with enthusiasm by Ludendorff when the latter moved to the Western Front, and became accepted doctrine for the German army.

The British had learned the effectiveness and economy of these German measures at Passchendaele. This costly experience, in addition to the unwillingness of Whitehall to authorize further increases in the strength of the British Expeditionary Force, the need to reinforce the Italians after the rout at Caporetto, and the acceptance of another twenty-eight miles of French front by the BEF, would have dictated a resort to defence in depth even had a major German offensive not been so obviously in the offing.[1] To convert the BEF to the defensive after three years of offensive warfare was not an easy task, however. The existing front line marked, for the most part, the ultimate limit of past advances and not necessarily the best tactical positions. Behind the front line protective belts of barbed wire were not extensive, switch lines were virtually non-existent, and reserve trench systems had fallen into decay. In many places the French peasantry 'had actually begun to fill in and clear away some of the back lines in order to restore the land to cultivation.'[2]

It was a question of men and methods as well as of material. The new defensive techniques, calling for mental flexibility and a considerable measure of confidence and self-reliance on the part of small groups under attack, placed heavy demands upon a BEF trained in the principles of static warfare and in the formal, well-rehearsed frontal attack. Too little practice had lowered the quality of musketry among the infantry, and too much close supervision by higher levels of command had sapped the tactical flexibility and initiative of regimental officers. Staff officers had been selected for their adeptness in the meticulous preparation of series of set-piece attacks, which seemed without end, an exercise which ill-fitted them to adjust to the balanced stance and quick counter-attack capability which were the nub of the new tactics. Commanders, who all too often owed their rank to the mental toughness which enabled them to go on committing men to a succession of hopeless assaults, also found the transition to the subtler principles of defence-in-depth difficult to make.[3]

Yet Sir Douglas Haig had no choice. He would have to face a German attack of unparalleled ferocity, and he must prepare for it. In mid-December he issued a 'memorandum on Defensive Measures' which emphasized the need for economy of effort and organization in depth. Two translated German documents, 'The Principles of Command in the Defensive Battle in Position Warfare' and 'General Principles of the Construction of Field Positions' were recommended to commanders as 'thoroughly sound' and worthy of careful study.[4]

No such fundamental change was contemplated for the RFC. A memorandum, 'The Employment of the Royal Flying Corps in Defence,' issued in January 1918, laid down that the first duty of the RFC was to detect through reconnaissance the initial stages of logistical build-up, and then to hamper it through sustained bombing attacks. Once an enemy offensive had begun the principal duty of the RFC was 'to render our artillery fire effective.' Beyond that, the corps was (in order of importance) to attack enemy reinforcements a mile or two behind the assault line, to attack de-training points, road transport, artillery positions, and reserves, and finally to send 'low-flying machines, on account of their moral effect, to cooperate with the infantry in attacking the enemy's most advanced troops.' All these defensive roles were dependent upon maintaining ascendancy in the air. This memorandum was probably prepared by Trenchard before he left to take up his appointment in England as Chief of Air Staff on 27 December 1917. It presented a perceptive assessment of what the RFC could do against a German offensive, though it failed to recognize the importance of the physical as well as the moral effects of forward ground support operations in open warfare. The RFC's new commander, Major-General J.M. Salmond, fully supported his predecessor's philosophy: 'This can only be done by attacking and defeating the enemy's air forces. The action of the Royal Flying Corps must, therefore, always remain essentially offensive ...'[5]

Whenever the German offensive came the RFC would be better prepared than ever before to fulfil its responsibilities. During the winter the corps had expanded rapidly, and so had the number of Canadians in it. In the period from 1 September 1917 to 1 March 1918 the total number of Canadian airmen grew from 223 to 319. On 1 January 1918 there were fifty-seven squadrons on active service with the BEF and under RFC command, with an average of slightly less than four-and-a-half Canadians per squadron.* By 1 March the average number of Canadians per squadron had risen to rather more than five; in other words, nearly one-quarter of the airmen with the BEF at this time were Canadians.†

After the closing down of active operations at Cambrai in December, air activities had settled into a winter routine. Corps squadrons maintained the monotonous grind of line patrol, reconnaissance and artillery observation whenever weather permitted, while above and beyond them, often many miles to the rear of German lines, fighter patrols from the army squadrons endeavoured to keep the skies clear of enemy scouts.‡ George Owen Johnson, an RFC lieutenant (and later an RCAF air marshal) flying SE5as on the Fifth Army front at the time, recalled nearly half a century later that: 'Throughout the winter of 1917–18 we were located in front of St. Quentin, employed primarily on high altitude (18 to 20 thousand feet without oxygen) offensive patrols 15 to 20 miles behind the German lines. It was a tiresome job as many of the patrols did not encounter any enemy aircraft ...'[6] He might have added that to fly at those heights in an open cockpit, at temperatures far below freezing, taxed endurance and resolution to the limit.

Corps squadrons, which operated at much lower levels, did not face weather conditions quite so rugged but did have to endure the harassment of ground fire. The work of 16 Squadron, attached to the Canadian Corps, was typical. In January the squadron was able to fly on only twelve days, but on those days eighty operational sorties were made, even though visibility was often so poor that only the general position of targets could be distinguished. During the month the squadron made fifty-six artillery registration flights, forty-one of which were termed 'successful.' Lieutenant F.A. Nicholson of St Stephen, NB, and his observer, Lieutenant R.H. Carter of Truro, NS, ranging a hostile battery for the artillery on the 13th, defined their shoot as 'unsuccessful' because in three hours no more than twenty-five rounds were ranged.§ Only four hits were registered within twenty-five

---

* Two RNAS squadrons, 8 and 16, were under RFC command. In all there were twenty-three single-seater fighter squadrons, eighteen corps squadrons, eleven day- and night-bomber squadrons, and five fighter-reconnaissance squadrons.

† This estimate is based upon an establishment of twenty-four pilots for Sopwith Camel squadrons, eighteen for other single-seater fighter squadrons, and thirty pilots and observers for all other squadrons.

‡ A Canadian, 70 Squadron's F.C. Gorringe of Prince Albert, Sask., was credited with the first combat victory of 1918 when he claimed one of two enemy aircraft which his patrol encountered on New Year's morning. Another member of his patrol was G.R. Howsam of Port Perry, Ont. (WIA 24 March 1918). Other Canadians in the squadron on 1 January 1918 included F.W. Dogherty of Montreal (POW 22 Jan. 1918), A. Koch of Edmonton (WIA 27 March 1918), F.G. Quigley of Toronto (WIA 27 March 1918), and W.E. Wood of Vancouver.

§ As of New Year's Day other Canadians with 16 Squadron included B.E. Gilbert of Paris, Ont., A.C. Gilmour of Saint John, NB (KIA 6 March 1918), J.A. Hutchison of Fordwich, Ont., R.O. McMurtry of Montreal, and D.J. Nickle of Kingston, Ont. (WIA 23 April 1918).

yards of a gun pit, while in the subsequent 'fire for effect' no direct hits were observed. Visibility was so poor that at one point firing had to be interrupted for twenty minutes. But if the ranging and shooting and weather were all something less than satisfactory, Nicholson and Carter were still able to return with useful information about rail movements behind the enemy front. On the 25th Nicholson ranged for 9 Canadian Siege Battery. Visibility was better and registration more precise, so that 'fire for effect' included at least three direct hits. Again the crew was able to return with a tabulation of enemy train and aircraft activity in the vicinity.[7]

During January 16 Squadron's single casualty was an observer wounded by ground fire. Though the airmen often reported enemy aircraft in their neighbourhood, German scouts only interrupted their work twice. The fact that corps squadrons like No 16, flying their unwieldy and underpowered RE8s, could operate so freely over enemy lines is a measure of the air superiority held by the British fighter squadrons at this stage of the war.* Their methods are brought out in a letter written by the commanding officer of a Fourth Army anti-aircraft section, complimenting the Camel pilots of 11 (Army) Wing's 65 Squadron. He noted that 4 January had been 'a very clear day and they were apparently on patrol the whole time,' and continued: 'Though at times the enemy opened very heavy Anti-Aircraft fire on them they continued their patrol, all the time roughly over the German front line at about 8,000 ft and practically prevented every enemy machine, except those flying at about 20,000 ft, from crossing the line at all. They ... harassed the enemy's patrolling machines considerably. On several occasions I observed enemy fighting patrols of 5 to 9 machines approaching our lines, but almost every time they were turned by the Sopwith Camels before they came within the range of my guns.'[8]

The price of supremacy was still blood, however; 65 Squadron lost two of its pilots that day while so successfully keeping the skies clear over their own lines. About mid-morning a flight of four Camels dived on a formation of 'about 12' German aircraft and claimed to have shot down six of them in the ensuing dogfight. Second Lieutenant R.E. Robb of St Thomas, Ont., who had joined the squadron only two days earlier and was flying on his first operational sortie, was shot down behind the German lines and severely wounded, dying of his wounds the next day. Lieutenant E.C. Eaton of Montreal, another member of the patrol, downed two of the six Germans claimed by the squadron. Later that same morning the squadron lost a second pilot, not to combat but, as so often occurred, during a simple training exercise. Captain George Baxby Syddall of Toronto, who had been with the squadron since mid-November, was practising formation flying when a wing of his machine collapsed. He died in the crash. The day's occurrences and the squadron's achievements and misfortunes were quite typical of those of fighter squadrons along the length of the Western Front in the winter of 1918.[†9]

---

* No 84 Squadron's SE5a pilots, at the other end of the front, were complaining that enemy machines 'refused to engage.' No 84 SRB, Jan. 1918, Air 1/1795/204/155/2

† Other Canadians with the squadron at this time were A.A. Leitch of High River, Alta, E.F.W. Peacock of Montreal, and H.L. Symons of Toronto.

By the end of January aerial reconnaissance had located many new airfields, supply dumps, railway sidings, and hospital sites behind the German lines opposite the British Third and Fifth Armies. Sir Hubert Gough, whose Fifth Army was destined to bear the brunt of the assault, had learned meanwhile that *General* von Hutier, the victor of Riga, had taken command of the German Eighteenth Army which opposed him. Shortly afterwards *General* Otto von Below, described by British GHQ as 'probably the best Army Commander in the German Army,' was reported in command of a new Second Army, inserted into the German front between the Seventeenth and Eighteenth Armies. This evidence convinced both Gough and Salmond that the German attack would be launched along the Somme. In March Salmond ordered his IX (HQ) Brigade's reconnaissance and fighter squadrons to concentrate on the area opposite the southern wing of the British front. He expanded the Fifth Army's own reconnaissance squadron by eight machines; subsequently, reports were brought in almost every day of heavy train movements opposite the fronts of the Third and Fifth Armies.[10]

On 6 March 1918 headquarters squadrons had been regrouped to form IX Brigade made up of 9 (Day) Wing and 54 (Night) Wing. The former included 25, 27, 62, 73, 79, and 80 Squadrons, the latter 58, 83, 101, and 102 Squadrons. Until 26 March, however, 9 Wing continued to operate under the direct orders of RFC headquarters. Meanwhile, Salmond was concentrating the operations of IX Brigade's bombing squadrons in this area. Bombing operations were designed to inhibit the German build-up and to depress the morale of German assault troops now moving into rear-area billets. It was not a particularly successful programme, physically or morally. Night bombing especially was still at an elementary stage. Results were uncertain at the best of times, the number of aircraft and their bomb-delivery potential were Lilliputian in proportion to the scale of the enormous German build-up, and in any event the night-bombing squadrons were allocated too many targets for their resources. No 102 Squadron,* for example, was able to bomb on only five nights between 5 and 21 March, dropping a total of 1404 bombs of twenty-five pounds each on airfields and billets opposite the Third Army front. The Germans made little response to these pin-pricks, since it was their policy to restrain their own air elements during the period of build-up and conserve their men and machines for the decisive moment.[11]

The lull in German fighter activities was to be broken a few days before the great offensive began. The growing reputation of Canadians as combat flyers was enhanced, even during the lull, by the activities of a number of previously unheralded pilots.† Lieutenant F.R. McCall of Calgary, with 13 Squadron, drew

---

* As of 1 January 1918 Canadians with 102 Squadron included J.P. Alexander of Toronto, H. Fall of Montreal, F.I. Livingstone of Winnipeg, A.B. Whiteside of Inverness, Que., and G.L. Zeigler of Hamilton, Ont.

† During this period W.G. Barker was in Italy and W.A. Bishop in England on the staff of the School of Aerial Gunnery. Raymond Collishaw, appointed to the command of I Brigade's 3 (Naval) Squadron on 11 February 1918, was too busy to do much flying. Canadian flyers with 3(N) Squadron when he took over included O.P. Adam of Westport, Ont. (KIA 1 April 1918), F.C. Armstrong of Toronto (KIA 25 March 1918), L.D. and D.L. Bawlf (KIA 21 April 1918) of Winnipeg, W.H. Chisam of Edmonton, J.A. Glen of Enderby, BC (WIA 8 April 1918), D.A. Haig

attention to himself when credited with four victories while flying the inoffensive
RE8.* Frank Quigley of 70 Squadron also claimed four victories in January. The
period encompassed most of the meteoric career of 56 Squadron's Lieutenant
K.W. Junor of Toronto.† Junor joined the squadron on 15 December 1917, and
was credited with his first successes on 20 January when his patrol engaged a
formation of Albatros 'V' Strutters northwest of Wambaix. He sent one of them
down in flames and another out of control. On 17 February he claimed an Albatros
down in flames near Mœuvres and nine days later was credited with an LVG at
Awoingt and another Albatros out of control near Sains-les-Marquion. Four more
victories followed before he was promoted captain on 22 April and awarded an MC.
A day later he was posted missing in action.

Another Canadian 'ace' began his career rather differently during this same
spring. Donald Roderick MacLaren had not left his father's fur trading post in
Alberta's Peace River country until the spring of 1917 and it was only in November that he joined 46 Squadron in France.‡ Another month went by in squadron
practice before he was allowed to fly operationally, and for nearly three months,
from 15 December until 5 March 1918, the only things to distinguish Second
Lieutenant MacLaren from most of the other Sopwith Camel pilots of the Western
Front were his age – he was then twenty-five, old for a fighter pilot – and the fact
that he had not yet either shot down an enemy plane or been shot down himself.

MacLaren had obviously learned a great deal, however, and on 6 March he
began his spectacular transformation into one of the war's most skilled and
dangerous combat pilots. On that day he was credited with shooting down out of
control a 'double tailplane scout – W of Douai.' Four days later he claimed an
Albatros, the second success of a career that eventually saw him credited with
forty-eight victories in eight months, won him the DSO, MC and Bar, and DFC,

of Agincourt, Ont., H.M. Ireland of Toronto, K.D. MacLeod of St Anne de Bellevue, Que.,
W.A. Moyle of Paris, Ont. (KIA 22 March 1918), L.A. Sands of Moncton, NB (KIA 22 March
1918), and A.T. Whealy of Toronto. No 11 Squadron's A.E. McKeever, the top-scoring two-
seater ace with thirty victories credited to him, went back to England as an instructor in late
January. When he left 11 Squadron on 26 January those Canadians remaining with it included
A.R. Browne of Collingwood, Ont. (WIA 30 Sept. 1917), F.H. Cantlon of Toronto (KIA 18 March
1918), E.C. Gilroy of Sarnia, Ont., H.E. Hall, address unknown, H.R. Kincaid of Ottawa (WIA 17
May 1918), A.P. Maclean of Toronto (KIA 18 March 1918), E.A. Magee of Kennay, Man. (POW
5 June 1918), G.H.L. Ray of Vancouver, and A. Reeve of Toronto (KIA 27 March 1918).
* Other Canadians in 13 Squadron included F. Belway of Richmond, Ont., R.F. Browne of Toronto
(WIA 8 Oct. 1918), A.G. De Young of Dartmouth, NS (KIA 12 Jan. 1918), S. Grossberg of
Hamilton, Ont. (WIA Jan. 1918), R.R. Millar of Winnipeg, and K.W. Murray of Vancouver (KIA
1 July 1918).
† Among Canadians with 56 Squadron in this period were H.J. Burden of Toronto, L.R. Charron
of Ottawa, A.M. Clermont of Toronto, W.E. Gilbert of Cardinal, Ont. (WIA 2 May 1918), W.R.
Irwin of Ripley, Ont. (WIA 15 Sept. 1918), B. MacPherson of Montreal, C.E. Morgan of Aults-
ville, Ont., J.G. Moore of Toronto, W. Porter of Port Dover, Ont. (KIA 24 March 1918), R.J.G.
Stewart of Hayfield, Man. (WIA and POW 3 Jan. 1918), and L.J. Williams of Vancouver.
‡ During the first three months of 1918 Canadians in the squadron besides MacLaren included
H.F. Dougall of Winnipeg (POW 26 Feb. 1918), G.D. Falkenberg of Quebec City (whose brother
was serving with 84 Squadron and who was shot down and taken prisoner on 12 March 1918),
R.K. McConnell of Victoria, J.K. Shook of Tioga, Ont. (POW 2 Oct. 1918), J.H. Smith of Camp-
bellford, Ont., and W.A. Watson of Verona, Ont.

THE AIR CONCENTRATION FOR THE LUDENDORFF OFFENSIVE
21 MARCH 1918
MAP 4

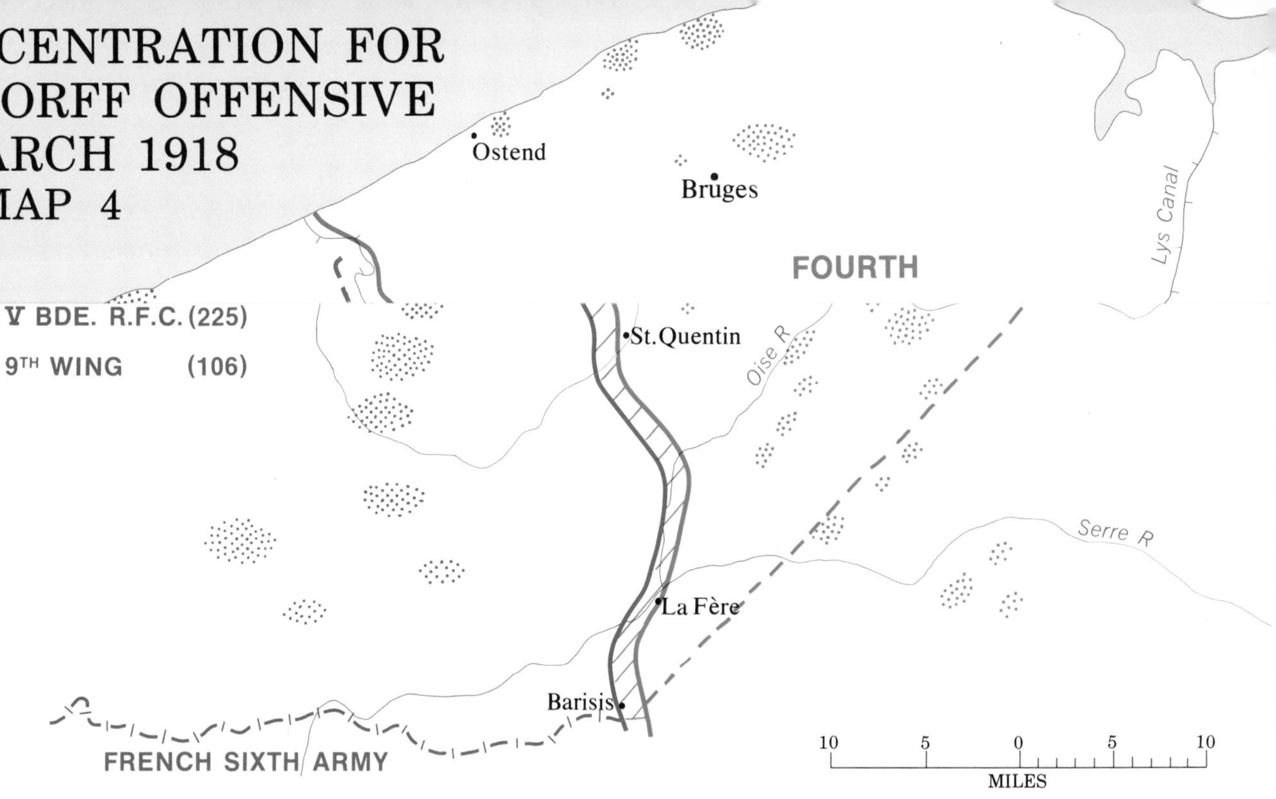

V BDE. R.F.C. (225)

9TH WING (106)

FOURTH

Ostend

Bruges

•St. Quentin

•La Fère

Barisis•

Lys Canal

Oise R

Serre R

FRENCH SIXTH ARMY

Front of attack, 21 March

One dot represents one aeroplane Groups of dots are placed in geographical relationship to the aerodrome from which the aircraft operated.

Arabic numerals (108) indicate the number of serviceable operational aircraft in each Army area.

Figures based upon H.A. Jones *War in the Air*, Vol. IV. Appendices XV and XVI and disposition map

Notes

The figures for the following squadrons are not included on this map.
No. 17 Naval Squadron
No. 12 Naval Training Squadron
No. 15 Naval Squadron (Forming)

Nos. 6 and 42 Squadrons (H.Q.R.F.C.) which were posted to 1 Bde. 22 March 1918

Total of British on Battle Front	579
Total of German on Battle Front	730
Total of aircraft shown on B.E.F. Front	1179
Total of German aircraft opposing	1020

The figures for German aircraft are approximate and are from Air Ministry

```
10        5        0        5        10
         MILES
```

File extract 557339/24. The actual strength of a German air unit is calculated as being 2/3 of its nominal strength.

South of the Somme 471 German aircraft were deployed against a build-up of French machines, which by 1 April 1918 had reached approximately 2063.

gave him command of the squadron he had joined as a second lieutenant, and left him the third-ranking Canadian 'ace' of the war. Among his fellow Canadians only Bishop and Collishaw, both of whom had been flying operationally before MacLaren had even made his first flight, were credited with greater scores.[12]

MacLaren's talents in deflection shooting and as a fighter-leader were perfectly adapted to the form that aerial combat was now assuming. Air fighting, which had begun merely as a clash between individual pilots and then evolved into formation combats between flights numbering from three to six machines, was becoming an affair of squadron actions by the winter of 1917–18. Occasionally even whole wings would become involved in battles that took up cubic miles of air space when, on each side, individual squadron-sized sweeps became sucked into *mêlées*. In January 1918 an additional aeroplane had been added to the strength of each RFC fighter squadron in order that units might be led into battle by their commanding officers, whose functions up until that time had been primarily administrative; early in February the establishment of Camel squadrons was raised by another six machines in order to meet the need for stronger combat formations.[13]

In the early spring of 1918 squadron-strength patrols were becoming commonplace and the RFC was experimenting with multi-squadron formations. At first three squadrons were sent out together, the squadron formations being in a triangular relationship both laterally and vertically – for example, Sopwith Camels flying at 15,000 feet, front and centre, SE5as at 16,000–17,000 feet to the right rear, and Bristol Fighters 18,000–19,000 feet, behind the SEs and to the left of the Camels. But it was soon found that the enemy, faced with such a formidable force, was reluctant to accept battle. As soon as these large formations crossed the lines the German fighting patrols drew off east and continued to fly in that direction as long as they were followed. Then, when the British turned west again, the Germans would turn too and hover around the flanks of the formation, firing at long range and trying to pick off stragglers.

A second plan was therefore tried. Three squadrons, some or all of them carrying bombs, were instructed to fly by widely divergent routes to a specified enemy airfield, ten to fifteen miles east of the lines. At that point they would drop their bombs and then adopt the 'stepped triangle' formation and make a wide return sweep from east to west in an attempt to trap any enemy machines between them and the lines.

The first of these massive sweeps took place on 9 March 1918, when a total of fifty-three machines participated in an attack on enemy airfields at Busigny, Bertry, and Escautfort, three closely grouped aerodromes opposite the Fifth Army front. But the eighty-eight bombs they dropped did little harm, and the Germans chose not to react; nothing was caught in the return sweep, so that many of the pilots ended up 'contour-chasing' as they machine-gunned ground targets on the way home.[14]

The Germans, however, were beginning to concentrate single-seater scouts in the locality, ready for the offensive scheduled to start on the 21st. For reasons both of concealment and morale they did not want a large number of British machines overflying the area with impunity. The tactical restrictions previously imposed on their own aircraft as part of their offensive preparations were relaxed and the next few sweeps brought German fighters out in force. No 62 Squadron, which had brought its Bristol Fighters to France in a 'fighter reconnaissance' role only two months earlier, was one of the squadrons used to provide top cover between 11 and 14 March. Reporting on the work Lieutenant Percy R. Hampton of Toronto* wrote that 'this squadron has done the hardest day's fighting ever known to any squadron' – a claim that might well have been questioned by airmen who had been at the front longer. He continued:

the first day we got six Huns, the second day six, the third day five and the fourth day eight ... and all the fighting takes place from fifteen to twenty miles over Hunland. The day we got five Huns I accounted for two of them in this way. I was leading our top formation of three machines, and it was my business to prevent Huns getting above our fellows fighting below and then diving on them; two of them did get above and dived, so I dived after them with my engine on and opened fire. I fired two hundred [rounds] in the first one before he went down and a hundred into the second one; I shot both down within a minute of each other, but of course it was a very easy target. Diving on another machine which is also diving is much the same as shooting at a stationary target. It is a great sight to watch one's tracers go into the other machine. The Hun pilots can see them too. I saw both pilots look round at me a couple of times, as we were quite close together.[15]

Hampton's version of his squadron's score is clearly exaggerated when contrasted with the enemy's admitted losses. On 11 March the Germans lost two aircraft over the British front; on the 12th, nine, on the 13th, six, and on the 14th none at all, according to their official history.[16]

On St Patrick's Day a sweep which was baited with a flight of DH4 day-bombers from 5 (N) Squadron† saw Captain F.E. Brown of Quebec City, leading a flight of 84 Squadron's SE5as which included G.O. Johnson, claim two enemy planes shot down out of control and another, which was actually seen to crash in the village of Becquigny, was credited to a third member of his formation. A second flight of the squadron also claimed two enemy machines destroyed – one by J.V. Sorsoleil of Toronto‡ – and two down out of control, although German records show only two aircraft lost on this front during the day.[17]

On the following day, the 18th, both sides were in the air in force and spoiling for a fight. Nine of the DH4s were directed to attack a single target – the airfield at

* There were five other Canadians besides Hampton known to be flying with 62 Squadron in March 1918: H.B.P. Boyce of North Battleford, Sask. (POW 12 March 1918), J.A.A. Ferguson of Unionville, Ont. (POW 12 March 1918), K.B. Forster of Red Deer, Alta., E.T. Morrow of Toronto (WIA 22 Aug. 1918), and W.K. Swayze of Lindsay, Ont. (POW 4 Sept. 1918).
† Only one Canadian, C.B. de T. Drummond of Montreal, is known to have been serving in the squadron at this time.
‡ No 84's pilots also included N.G. Bray of Oshawa, Ont., W.H. Brown and L. de S. Duke (WIA 23 April 1918) both of Victoria, C.F. Falkenberg of Quebec City (WIA 10 May 1918), and R. Manzer of Oshawa, Ont. (POW 8 Aug. 1918). Together with F.E. Brown (WIA 3 May 1918), Johnson, and Sorsoleil they earned eight decorations for gallantry among them by the end of the war, several of them won during the coming March offensive.

Busigny – while 54 and 84 Squadrons provided direct cover and 62 Squadron's Bristol Fighters from 9(HQ) Wing were also ordered to patrol the area. They were met over Busigny by a stronger force of more than fifty German single-seaters, including the whole of von Richthofen's *Jagdgeschwader 1* thirty strong, led by the *Rittmeister* in person. The result was the biggest air *mêlée* yet seen, large enough, confused enough, and profound enough in its implications to have been subsequently entitled the Air Battle of Le Cateau. Richthofen described it thus: 'The outcome was a tremendous turning-combat. It was no longer possible to think of maintaining wing formations. Everyone pounced on the nearest opponent. The result was a pell-mell of individual dogfights. Frequently it was impossible to tell friend from foe. The air was criss-crossed by the white ribbons of tracer-ammunition, in between one could see burning or disabled aircraft plunging towards the ground.'[18]

Most of the aircraft 'plunging towards the ground' were British. Not only were numbers against them but they were fighting the *élite* of the German air force. No 54 Squadron lost five of its Camels, including one flown by Lieutenant E.B. Lee of Kearney, Ont.,* who made a forced landing on the wrong side of the lines and was taken prisoner. The other three squadrons lost two machines each, making a total of eleven British aircraft lost, while the Germans only lost four. Further experimentation was brought to a stop for the time being, first by a deterioration in the weather and then by the opening of the German offensive.

Throughout February and the first half of March British GHQ had apparently remained unconvinced that the major attack would come on the Somme, partly because the Germans had constructed dummy aerodromes, dumps, and sidings on other fronts and partly because they had masked their intentions by diversionary attacks against the French and by stepping up the tempo of trench warfare on the Second Army front. GHQ, moreover, was obsessed with the threat of a major assault in the north, where, with the vital Channel ports only thirty or forty miles to the rear, the BEF would have dangerously little room for manœuvre. The evidence for an attack on the British right, obtained from air reconnaissance, prisoner interrogation, and analysis of wireless traffic, was piling up as March began. GHQ, however, remained all but impervious to it; on 2 March its appreciation was that the Germans in that sector were planning nothing more than the pinching off of the Cambrai salient.[19]

A week later GHQ claimed that there were no indications of an attack south of St Quentin. Only on 19 March did Haig's intelligence chief concede that the weight of the impending offensive was to fall upon the Third and Fifth Armies. On the eve of the offensive, therefore, the main strength of the British Army was still held in the north. In the south Gough's Fifth Army, holding a front of forty-two miles, disposed of twelve infantry and three cavalry divisions with 1566 artillery pieces, the cavalry and one infantry division being his only reserve, while Sir Julian Byng's Third Army held twenty-eight miles of front with fourteen divisions and 1120 guns. Opposite them, in and behind the German line, were massed seventy-four divisions with enough artillery to place ninety guns to the mile.[20]

---

* Two other Canadians, C.S. Bowen (WIA 22 April 1918) and N.M. Drysdale (WIA 22 March 1918), both from Vancouver, were also flying with 54 Squadron on this day.

Because of the RFC's numerical superiority over the whole British front – 1255 aeroplanes against 1020 – and their comparative ease and speed of deployment since no machine was more than an hour-and-a-half's flying time from any part of the line, the situation in the air over the Third and Fifth Army areas was not perhaps quite as serious as that which prevailed on the ground. There were thirty-one squadrons available in the area south of Arras with a total of 579 serviceable aircraft among them, 261 being single-seater fighters. Against them were ranged 730 German planes of which 326 were single-seater scouts and 108 belonged to the *Schlachtstaffeln* – fast, well-armed two-seaters, some of them armoured and carrying grenades and bombs, which specialized in close ground support operations.* North of Arras, where the Germans were not going to attack, 489 British aircraft were facing 172 Germans, and on the French front a total of up to 2590 French aircraft were confronted by no more than 471 German. Although from the Channel to the Swiss border the Allies outnumbered the opposing forces by nearly three to one, at the point of decision the enemy possessed a local superiority of nearly 30 per cent.[21]

Though the Royal Flying Corps reconnaissances and line patrols had successfully reported the long-range German preparations for the great offensive in the west and quite accurately predicted the location of attack, the RFC was less effective in providing precise information as to the imminence of the assault. On the 19th and most of the 20th poor weather made aerial reconnaissance impossible all along the Fifth Army front, but by the early evening of 20 March 8 and 82 Squadrons were able to fly over the line. 'No unusual movement' was reported, and it was left to the front-line ground troops to secure specific information concerning the timing of the attack from German deserters and prisoners taken by patrols.[22]

The failure of air reconnaissance to find any significant activity behind the German front on the evening of the 20th pays tribute to the calibre of German planning, discipline, and organization. At 0440 hrs on 21 March nearly 6500 artillery pieces opened *Die Grosse Schlacht in Frankreich* by deluging the Third and Fifth Army fronts, between Chérisy and La Fère, with gas and high explosive shells. 'A tremendous, roaring cataract of noise made the solid dug-out shake ... The air screamed as if in pain, or on the point of reaching some wild transport of sound beyond human comprehension ...' recalled one survivor. 'Fierce red glares, springing from the ground near at hand, told of shells bursting dangerously close, but their explosions were lost in the gigantic clamour. A thousand railway engines

---

* A German account states that 'From the total of all formations in being, by 21 March one third of all Field Flights, all ground support squadrons and more than half of the fighter and bomber forces had been marshalled with the three Armies of attack. An aerial force of 49 Field Flights, 27 bomber squadrons, 35 fighter squadrons and four bomber wings (with a total of 12 bomber squadrons) was to accompany the attack of the ground forces ...' In this author's opinion the German air commitment might have been decisive 'if instead of one third of all Field Flights, and one half of all fighter and bomber forces, right from the start three quarters of all Field Flights, and all fighter and bomber squadrons, had been marshalled for the decisive battle.' [H.] von Bülow, *Geschichte der Luftwaffe*, 2d ed. (Diesterweg 1937), 103, 110, DHist SGR I 196, Set 89

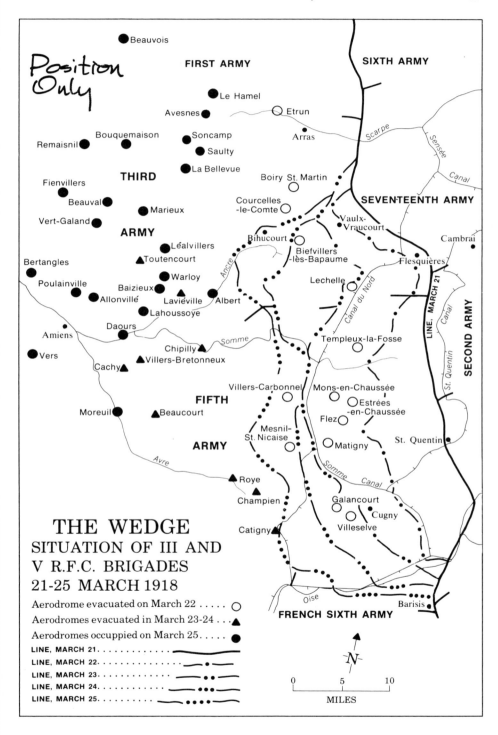

Position Only

Beauvois

FIRST ARMY

SIXTH ARMY

Le Hamel

Avesnes

Etrun

Scarpe

Sensée

Arras

Bouquemaison

Soncamp

Remaisnil

Saulty

La Bellevue

Boiry St. Martin

SEVENTEENTH ARMY

Canal

THIRD

Courcelles -le-Comte

Fienvillers

Beauval

Marieux

Vaulx- Vraucourt

Cambrai

Vert-Galand

ARMY

Bihucourt

Léalvillers

Biefvillers -lès-Bapaume

Flesquières

Bertangles

Toutencourt

Lechelle

Warloy

Ancre

Canal du Nord

Poulainville

Baizieux

Allonville

Lavièville

Albert

LINE, MARCH 21

Canal

SECOND ARMY

Lahoussoye

Daours

Amiens

Somme

Templeux-la-Fosse

St. Quentin

Vers

Chipilly

Cachy

Villers-Bretonneux

Villers-Carbonnel

Mons-en-Chaussée

FIFTH

Estrées -en-Chaussée

Moreuil

Beaucourt

Flez

Mesnil- St. Nicaise

St. Quentin

ARMY

Matigny

Avre

Somme

Canal

Roye

Galancourt

Champien

Cugny

Catigny

Villeselve

THE WEDGE

SITUATION OF III AND
V R.F.C. BRIGADES
21-25 MARCH 1918

Aerodrome evacuated on March 22 . . . . . ○

Aerodromes evacuated in March 23-24 . . . ▲

Aerodromes occuppied on March 25 . . . . . ●

LINE, MARCH 21 . . . .

LINE, MARCH 22 . . . .

LINE, MARCH 23 . . . .

LINE, MARCH 24 . . . .

LINE, MARCH 25 . . . .

Oise

Barisis

FRENCH SIXTH ARMY

N

0   5   10

MILES

roaring and screaming over a thousand girder bridges might have equalled the noise – or passed unnoticed.'[23] Against the dazed and shell-shocked recipients of this unparalleled barrage the specially trained German assault troops soon began to seep forward, through a thick ground mist that stretched all along the battlefield from the Oise to the Sensée rivers.

The mist – in many places it was thick enough to be described as fog – complicated the battle on the ground for both sides. The British found that it largely neutralized the complex patterns of interlocking machine-gun fire on which their forward defence zone depended. The Germans, on the other hand, soon realized that it made even more difficult the intricate problems of command and control associated with their new 'fluid' offensive tactics in an era when communications still depended primarily upon aural and visual means. The fog, moreover, diminished the advantage that the Germans' carefully arranged local air superiority had given them. Their ground support squadrons, which had 'important tactical tasks' to carry out, could not immediately be deployed. The new offensive tactics expected the first thin line of assault troops to probe for weak spots in the British line and keep advancing, while the second line would both feed the first with replacements and, with close air support from the battle flights, clean up any strong points or isolated pockets of resistance which were left. But the fog kept the *Schlachtstaffeln* on the ground all morning. What they might have done, had they been flying from first light, can only be guessed at. In writing of events later in the day German historians have attributed much of their army's success in taking such stubbornly defended strong-points as the village of Roupy, in front of St Quentin, to an initial 'softening-up' carried out by the *Schlachtstaffeln*. The British have also recorded that as soon as flying was possible the German 'low flying contact patrols, aiding the attack, found our new fronts too swiftly; and their use of signal flares came from careful practice.' The Royal Munster Fusiliers, for instance, found that 'heavy infantry attacks on the front and low flying aeroplanes enabled the enemy to envelope and capture Malassise Farm.'[24]

During the morning the fog became patchy and thinned somewhat towards the north of the battlefront, in the Third Army area. But the British were not significantly more successful in halting the initial onslaught. Visibility in the Lagnicourt area had improved sufficiently by 0630 hrs for an early reconnaissance of 59 Squadron to follow the German bombardment along the whole front of IV Corps. That particular flight was cut short quite suddenly by a shell which whipped through the fuselage of the RE8, cutting loose some of its control wires, but later patrols from the same squadron, including machines piloted by Lieutenants L.R. Brereton of Winnipeg and C.L. Hilborn of Alexandria, BC,* were able to add further information concerning the development of the attack during the morning. Both Canadians drove off attacks by enemy aircraft, Hilborn and his observer managing to take some sixty photographs of the main battlefield before noon.[25]

The initial German penetration, spectacularly successful by the offensive standards of the previous two years, was another measure not only of the weight and

* Other 59 Squadron Canadians flying on this day included J.E. Hanning of Fredericton, NB, W.B. Powell of St Catharines, Ont., and I.D Smith of Toronto. M. Sworder of Edmonds, BC, had been killed on 18 March 1918.

precision of the attack but also of British confusion that occasionally verged on panic. By noon on the 21st four more aircraft of 59 Squadron had overflown the battlefield on their corps front and sent down a number of zone calls for counter-battery fire, all of which had been ignored. From a sky infested with enemy scout planes Lieutenant J.E. Hanning of Fredericton, NB, vainly called for neutralizing fire on different enemy batteries eight times in twenty minutes. Shortly after noon he even sent an 'LL' call – '... only to be used in case of really important targets' and demanding '... as powerful a concentration of fire as the situation permits' – against a mass of infantry, estimated to be two battalions strong, on the Pronville-Quéant road, but that also was ignored. Hanning and his pilot were able only to fire two hundred rounds into the enemy mass from 900 feet, release their six 25-lb bombs, and return to base by way of IV Corps Headquarters, where they dropped a message bag reporting the location of the German concentrations. Later, however, another flight of 59 Squadron did get an effective response to their 'LL' call on 'a large number of the enemy advancing in the open' west of Lagnicourt.[26]

On the Fifth Army front the fog was so thick that no flying was possible before 1000 hrs and the five corps squadrons – 8, 35, 52, 53, and 82 – were not able to carry out more than three artillery co-operation patrols each by 1600 hrs. Since their airfields were closer to the original line than those of the army squadrons, several of them were ordered to move back during the morning, and the administrative problems of organizing the evacuation of aerodromes now in the combat zone over roads already jammed with retreating troops interfered with their operational efficiency. No 8 Squadron pilots, based only four miles behind the old front line and so ordered back to Chipilly, twelve miles west of Peronne, at 1100 hrs, found that, while they simultaneously moved and flew operational sorties, 'the battle was obviously getting very much closer, batteries were firing from the edge of the aerodrome, tanks were rallying back from the fight, just beside us, shells were exploding close ...'[27]

On the southern flank of the Fifth Army, 82 Squadron's Armstrong-Whitworth machines were unable to get into the air until 1300 hrs, when Captain G.I. Paterson of Regina (pilot) and Lieutenant T.I. Findley of Toronto (observer)* found the sunken roads south and west of Urvillers 'packed with enemy troops' and German artillery in action in the open, alongside the roads. Other guns were limbered up on nearby roads and they could see 'batteries all over this region of country,' but their repeated calls for fire on specific targets went unanswered. A second patrol, flying some forty-five minutes later, had much the same experience, although British guns certainly were in action because the airmen could see heavy fire coming from field batteries behind the St Quentin canal. But in one case at least 'our own artillery fired short, smashing our already weakened defences.' Two later flights resorted to dropping message bags at the appropriate spots. This reversion to pre-electronic air-to-ground communications may well have affected the ground battle. Enemy infantry, reforming on the high ground just west of

---

* Paterson and Findley were flying together on 2 April 1918 when Paterson was killed and Findley badly wounded. Findley was awarded the MC for his work during the March offensive and was invalided out of the service in October.

Moy, reported that, shortly after a lone British aeroplane had overflown them, 'already the hitherto planless British artillery fire is being concentrated on this height.' As a result of this concentration the Germans retreated quickly, if not very far or for very long.[28]

However, it remained true that much of the long-range destructive potential of artillery against troops in the open was not put to use by the British artillery during the first few days of the German offensive. The commanding officer of 8 Squadron doubted if many of the zone calls sent down were ever answered and certainly his own squadron found that very few were successful. Consequently, on the morning of the 22nd he dispatched his squadron wireless officer, together with all the spare radio equipment he could transport, in an attempt to locate IV Corps' batteries and re-establish air-to-ground communication. Not one of the batteries his specialist could find even had an antenna up. 'As soon as the retreat had started all idea of cooperating with aeroplanes seemed to have been abandoned. Many batteries had simply thrown their wireless equipment away, others had retained the instruments only ... Under these circumstances little use was made of the zone calls which were sent down ...'[29]

If the artillery thus played a rather lesser role than it might have done in slowing or stopping the German advance, the air arm did its best to make up the deficiency. Earlier RFC planning for the allocation of fighter resources in the event of an attack had called for the Camel squadrons to engage in a substantial amount of low-level strafing and ground support work while the SE5as had been scheduled to concentrate on providing fighter cover for the other air activities. It quickly became clear, however, that the ground forces were going to need all the support they could get. Almost immediately the SE5as were ordered to provide additional ground support whenever and wherever possible.[30]

Consequently, although V Brigade reported thirty-eight combats during the day, their losses were limited to one Armstrong-Whitworth of 8 Squadron and five pilots wounded, four of them by ground fire. III Brigade engaged in thirty-two combats with one Camel lost and two RE8 pilots wounded, while IX Brigade had no casualties at all and I Brigade reported four enemy aircraft destroyed on the Third Army front without loss to themselves. The German air force along the same length of front lost a total of eight machines from either ground fire or aerial combat. Four of them may have fallen to Canadian airmen: 56 Squadron's Lieutenant H.J. Burden of Toronto – Bishop's brother-in-law – was credited with his first victim on this day, while Lieutenant V.W. Thompson of 64 Squadron claimed a second and Donald MacLaren of 46 two more as well as a balloon.*[31]

Low-level bombing and strafing by aircraft had not proved, in the past, to be of much practical value against entrenched troops. Now, however, the enemy was

---

* Both British and Germans consistently claimed and credited in 1918 far more victories than were actually scored. On the 21st, in fact, the British claimed a total of twenty-five enemy aircraft either crashed or 'completely' out of control. The Germans, on the other hand, claimed nineteen British downed along the same stretch of front. The true figures appear to have been eight and two. Brigade work summaries, 21–22 March 1918, Air 1/838/204/5/285; Deutschland, Oberkommandos des Heeres, *Der Weltkrieg 1914 bis 1918*, Band XIV *Beilagen: Die Kriegführung an der Westfront in Jahre 1918* (Berlin 1944), Beilage 40

mostly in the open, and the fast and nimble British scouts, unhampered by the need to defend themselves against aerial attack, could often achieve tactical surprise. They were especially successful against artillery and supply columns whose horsedrawn equipment left them peculiarly susceptible to surprise attack from the air. One unit complained that 'everywhere grievous losses occurred ... at the limbers, too ... there were palpable losses of men and horses.' British strafing was to make this a common German refrain over the next few days. 'Troops would scatter into the fields, leaving men lying prostrate in the road; wagons and horses would be thrown into confusion and overturned,' recalled Sholto Douglas, whose 84 Squadron flew SE5as, and whose pilots at that time included eight Canadians. 'Pilots for the first time in their experience ... were presented with perfect ground targets – troops marching in fours along the roads, batteries and ammunition wagons moving across the open ...' The only effective defence against these low-flying fighters was a concentration of entrenched machine-guns. Time and circumstance usually prevented the Germans from assembling such defences during their big push, so that 'the fire directed at one from the ground was sporadic and innocuous. Tragic as was the great retreat to other arms, to the air force it was something of a picnic.'[32]

Perhaps the *Jagdflieger* approach to the question of aerial combat, which had permitted the British to operate unhindered, was conditioned to some extent by the attitudes of their General Staff. German theories on the employment of air power had been significantly influenced by the success of their ground-support operations in the Cambrai counter offensive of 30 November. In February a memorandum on the 'Employment of Battle Flights' had stipulated that 'the systematic participation in the battle of massed flying formations [battle-flights] against ground targets is of extreme importance.' Their fighter squadrons, too, 'as far as fighting in the air will allow ... must also participate in the battle, diving steeply and firing both their machine-guns at the enemy on the ground.' Such imprecise instructions may have encouraged many fighter pilots to develop reservations about wholeheartedly adopting either role. Certainly German fighter forces did not play a part commensurate with their strength on the first day of the offensive. *Jasta 23* was flying 'at least four sorties a day' and it is likely that the other German fighter squadrons were doing much the same, but the principal emphasis seems to have been on ground attack. Although 'large formations' of enemy scouts were reported patrolling at heights between 3000 and 7000 feet and 'great numbers' of aircraft were all over the front by mid-afternoon, air combats were comparatively few. The entire British force was generally engaged in close ground support, but the German fighters seemed reluctant to pick a quarrel unless the direct support of their own battle-flights demanded it. Squadron record books and brigade work summaries suggest that only 23 Squadron's Spads were seriously troubled by enemy aircraft while strafing German troops and transport along the Vendhuile-Marcoing line that bracketed the boundary between the Third and Fifth Armies.* Richthofen's adjutant, Karl Bodenschatz, remembered that, in the

---

* This was in the area for which Richthofen's *Jagdgeschwader I* was responsible for fighter cover.
  G.P. Neumann, ed., *In der Luft unbesiegt* (München 1923), 228, DHist SGR I 196, Set 72

Circus's area, 'The British airmen were notably reserved. Commitment of individual German squadrons sufficed to protect the reconnaissance elements over the battle-field ...'[33]

At a higher tactical level, however, the RFC responded less successfully to the initial emergency. As early as 0930 hrs RFC Headquarters had ordered 9 Wing of IX Brigade, which included at least forty Canadians, to attack the vital railway junctions at Le Cateau, Wassigny, and Busigny. During the afternoon and early evening all three points were bombed, Wassigny by nine DH4s of 25 Squadron, under the command of Halifax-born Major C.S. Duffus,* and Le Cateau and Busigny by seven DH4s of 27 Squadron.[†] Between them they dropped nearly 4000 pounds of high explosive bombs in the vicinity of the junctions, but since they bombed in each case from heights of 14–15,000 feet (in accordance with an HQ instruction of August 1917 designed to limit losses of the valuable DH4s) little damage was done. The same problem beset 5(N) Squadron of V Brigade's 22 (Army) Wing, which spent the afternoon trying to hit key bridges over the St Quentin canal around Honnecourt, Vendhiule, and Le Catelet. A total of 176 25-lb and six 112-lb bombs were dropped but none of the bridges was broken. With the primitive bomb-sights of 1918 such targets could only be hit from 15,000 feet by sheer chance, and the exigencies of the situation on 21 March clearly demanded low-level attacks, even at the cost of heavy losses. But no one at Headquarters had thought to rescind the seven-month-old instruction that inhibited effective bombing, and apparently no one at the tactical level was prepared to ignore it.[34]

At dusk on the 21st the enemy had made gains averaging more than a mile-and-a-half all along their front of attack. In the vicinity of Essigny, just south of St Quentin, they had penetrated nearly four miles into the British defences. Their advance continued throughout the night while bombers from IX Brigade's 54 (Night) Wing attacked an aerodrome and a railway junction well to the north of the battlefront. Flying on their first operational mission six FE2bs of 83 Squadron, which included at least six Canadians on its flying roster,[‡] bombed the junction at Don and shot up transport on the Lille-La Bassée road, beyond their First Army front. The 'old hands' of 58 Squadron, meanwhile, with four Torontonians on strength in the persons of Lieutenants J.F. White, M.C. Healey, and the brothers H.T. and W.A. Leslie,[§] struck the German airfield at Ramegnies Chin, eleven miles west of Lille. Nevertheless, by dawn of the 22nd the Germans had driven another four miles into the British line opposite St Quentin.[35]

---

* No 25 Squadron's flying personnel at this time also included M.L. Doyle of River Louison, NB, E.W. Gordon of Ottawa (KIA 31 July 1918), J.E. Pugh of Stoney Plain, Alta, E. Waterlow of Regina (KIA 16 July 1918), and A.J. Wright of Barrie, Ont.
† Flying personnel included B.I. Johnstone of Tara, Ont. (WIA 24 March 1918), J.A. McGinnis of Battleford, Sask., A.F. Millar of Rapid City, Sask. (KIA 14 Aug. 1918), and G.E. Wait of Ottawa.
‡ G.G. Bell of Ottawa, G.W. Higgs of Kemptville, Ont. (WIA 20 April 1918), N.S. Jones of Toronto, L.B. Palmer of Ottawa, G.E. Race of Montreal, and C.S. Stonehouse of Wallaceburg, Ont.
§ W.A. Leslie (WIA 5 Oct. 1918) was one of the few pilots who had flown at least seventy-five operational bombing and reconnaissance missions when he was awarded the DFC in October 1918.

On the second day of the offensive heavy mist again blanketed the battlefield until midday and kept both sides out of the air. Fighting was intense on the Third Army front but there the British were now giving ground in comparatively good order, so that when flying did become practicable III Brigade was able to use its squadrons in their proper and pre-determined roles. By 1330 hrs the corps squadrons were busy with line patrols, artillery registration, and photography despite the dislocation caused by the need to withdraw to reserve airfields. As for the fighter squadrons, No 46's Sopwith Camels were the only single-seaters used exclusively for low-flying ground attacks on the 22nd. While 70 Squadron (Camels), as well as Nos 56 and 64 (SE5as), concentrated on offensive patrols with occasional support from I Brigade's 3(N) Squadron, there was a noticeable increase in the tempo of air combat. Lieutenant Hank Burden 'sat up at 18,000 feet for over an hour and didn't get a shot at a Hun. Came down with a rip-roaring headache.'[36] Some of his colleagues, however, had a very different experience in the vicinity of Havrincourt.

On the German side the Havrincourt area was within the responsibility of Richthofen's fighter wing, *Jagdgeschwader 1*. When twelve Camels of 70 Squadron, led by Captain F.G. Quigley of Toronto, along with a flight of SE5as from 56 Squadron, met about forty-five Fokker triplanes and Albatros D-Vs over Havrincourt Wood a major *mêlée* developed. It resulted in Quigley being credited with two victories and Lieutenant W. Porter of Port Dover, Ont., and Second Lieutenant A. Koch of Edmonton with one each. III Brigade* lost two aircraft, one corps machine for 12 Squadron and a Camel of 45 Squadron, while recording twenty-five 'decisive' victories that day. Donald MacLaren was also credited with two of III Brigade's claimed victories. Both were gained against LVGs, reflecting the low-level ground support role allotted 46 Squadron. His squadron carried out only three patrols during the day, however, and none of the flights involved more than six aircraft.[37]

German machines were considerably more numerous and much more prominent, as far as the British ground forces were concerned. A South African officer serving with the 1st Royal Scots Fusiliers, then holding the line in the Wancourt region on the centre of the Third Army front during the 22nd and 23rd, recalled: 'During the two days that we held the line the enemy had the mastery of the air, in our quarter at any rate, and they were extraordinarily active, swooping over us at a low altitude in flights of fifteen to twenty machines at a time, machine-gunning as they came, and hovering over British batteries in the rear, dropping flares to guide their artillery.'[38] On the Fifth Army front, where much of the army was now in full retreat, things were even worse. The German operations here were mainly directed towards securing bridgeheads across the Crozat Canal, rather than gaining any available ground, but in the early afternoon the observers of 82 Squadron were noting 'many abandoned British field gun positions ... Much movement of transport at the trot Westwards.' They found that roads and communication

---

* The Germans lost possibly as few as three and certainly no more than six machines on the Third Army front, two of them downed in the British lines by anti-aircraft fire. *Der Weltkrieg 1914 bis 1918*, XIV *Beilagen*, Beilage 40; RFC war diary, 22 March 1918, Air 1/1186/204/5/2595

trenches around Urvillers were packed with German troops moving forward. Isolated British parties were apparently still holding out 'in very good spirits,' but by 1630 hrs an Armstrong-Whitworth piloted by Second Lieutenant H.S. Morton of Victoria was bombing German infantry at Dury, a mile west of the westernmost point of the Crozat Canal. An hour-and-a-half later 52 Squadron's Lieutenant T.E. Logan of New Glasgow, NS,* flew his RE8 over Contescourt, east of St Quentin, finding the village plugged with German transport. He dropped eight bombs from 350 feet 'with excellent effect' and returned westwards along the Contescourt-St Simon road, flying at a hundred feet and finding it, too, 'blocked with transport and infantry' moving forward. His observer had pumped some 250 rounds into them before Logan was wounded three times by ground fire,† but despite his wounds he succeeded in landing behind the British front. His observer was able to report to a passing staff officer the progress of the German advance.[39]

By the evening of the 22nd every component of V Brigade, including the brigade headquarters, had had to move back. The inevitable administrative dislocation critically hampered air operations. One commanding officer recalled that several squadrons were seriously handicapped by the lack of fuel, oil, and bombs on 22 and 23 March: '... we had to supply the nearest squadron to us, which would not have been able to carry on otherwise.' Because of their proximity to the original front the corps squadrons suffered most severely and V Brigade's 15 (Corps) Wing could only report two-thirds of their eighty available pilots actually flying during the day, although they had eighty-six serviceable aircraft in hand.[40]

No 22 (Army) Wing was in better shape, with all but four of its 106 pilots‡ flying during the day. But the situation on the ground was so critical that every squadron was concentrated on close support duties again, and although 'many combats took place in the air' these were almost incidental. The work of 23 Squadron's Spads was typical, with the whole squadron, including two machines flown by Lieutenant M.S. MacLean of Winnipeg and Second Lieutenant R.J. Smith of Kingston, Ont.,§ putting its primary effort into bombing and strafing the Clastres-St Simon-Grand Seraucourt triangle, on the south-central sector of the Fifth Army front. They dropped more than sixty 20-lb bombs on infantry, artillery, railways, and road transport in the area and followed up the bombing with machine-gun attacks from heights as low as 150 feet. Their one successful air combat of the day came when two aircraft, returning from one of these sorties, attacked and shot down an enemy reconnaissance plane behind the British front.[41]

---

* Other Canadians flying with 52 Squadron on 22 March 1918 included P.E. Biggar (WIA 1 Oct. 1916) and A.D. Pope (POW 28 March 1918), both of Ottawa, and T.J. Wilson of Edmonton. H.P. Illsley of Westmount, Que., joined two days later.

† The 22nd was a particularly bad day for the Canadians, four of them becoming casualties: N.M. Drysdale of Vancouver (WIA), G.B. Knight, address unknown (WIA, and died 7 April 1918 as a result of these wounds), T.E. Logan of New Glasgow, NS (WIA), and W.A. Moyle of Paris, Ont. (KIA).

‡ Including at least twenty-five Canadians.

§ B.S. Johnston of Courtright, Ont., E.G.S. Mortimer of Ottawa (KIA 3 April 1918), and V.R. Pauline of Victoria (KIA 8 May 1918) were among other Canadian pilots serving with 23 Squadron on 22 March. Smith was wounded on 28 March 1918.

Although most of the Third Army front was holding up reasonably well, the Fifth Army defences were bulging ominously by nightfall on the 22nd. The army's left wing was being forced back at a steadily increasing rate south of the Fles-quières Salient, which was now in the process of being 'pinched out' by the Germans. Over 30,000 lbs of high explosive were dropped that night and many thousands of machine-gun rounds fired at billets and railways behind the German front by the four night-bombing squadrons of IX Brigade,* but the effect was negligible.[42] On the 23rd the Germans resumed their advance, to make their biggest gains yet on the Fifth Army front and the southern flank of the Third Army, where a British stretcher bearer noted in his diary:

... as we left the cross-country track, and hit the roadway at Ytres, we became submerged in a medley of troops all moving towards the rear ... There was disorder everywhere, men of many different units were hopelessly intermixed – some were without equipment or rifle ...

On every face was a kind of hopeless look, nowhere did I discern a smile, and to my eyes, at the time, it looked certainly like a rout. It seemed everyone's aim to get as far away from the battle as possible, and it was surprising how, soon after being amongst the crowd, we appeared to be obsessed with the same idea ...[43]

That description was probably applicable to most of the Fifth Army as well. The remainder of the Third Army, however, was more or less holding its own and its overall balance enabled III Brigade, desperately endeavouring to strengthen the southern flank by developing a real air supremacy, to concentrate its machines on the threatened wing and deploy them in their scheduled roles. As the fighter squadrons returned to their proper duties 117 air combats were recorded, nearly triple the number of the previous day, with thirty-seven of them being marked down as 'decisive' victories. Twenty-one German aircraft were reported as 'crashed.' Donald MacLaren was credited with one of them as well as two out of control, while Second Lieutenants J.H. Smith, from Campbellford, Ont., and R.K. MacConnell, from Victoria, claimed one each. No 64 Squadron's Captain E.R. Tempest of Perdue, Sask.,[†] had a Pfalz D-III confirmed by other pilots; Frank Quigley and Alfred Koch of No 70 were also credited with one enemy aircraft each. Dumps and detraining points behind the German front were bombed by the DH4 day-bombers of 49 Squadron.[‡] Altogether the army wing of III Brigade dropped 149 25-lb bombs during the day and fired nearly 7000 rounds from their machine-guns at ground targets while the corps wing flew five photographic missions, eleven artillery co-operation flights, and five contact patrols; four hostile batteries were 'engaged for destruction' and seventeen neutralized.[44]

---

* For operational purposes 101 and 102 Squadrons were attached to V and III Brigades, respectively.

† Tempest was now a flight commander with 64 Squadron, which also numbered W.C. Daniel of Toronto (WIA 18 May 1918), H.G. Ross of Montreal, and V.W. Thompson of Ottawa among its Canadian pilots on 23 March 1918.

‡ No 49 Squadron's crews included G.A. Leckie of Vancouver, E.B.G. Morton of Barrie, Ont., A.V. Price of Toronto, H.L. Rough of Victoria, and E.H. Tredcroft of Kamloops, BC.

In the brigade as a whole 228 pilots were used out of the 232 available, at least seventy-five of them being Canadians. During the day the brigade was reinforced by the arrival of 22 (Bristol Fighter),* 43 (Sopwith Camel),† and 60 (SE5a)‡ Squadrons from the north. No 40 Squadron (SE5a),§ although remaining under I Brigade's command, also began to operate exclusively on the Third Army front during the 23rd. Even I Brigade's corps squadrons were pulled into the battle. An English observer with the Canadian Corps' squadron has recorded his experience:

> Sixteen Squadron was sent into the air to a man and a machine. For the first time I saw something like war as the picture books show it. Instead of the lifeless lunar landscape of the trenches, masses of Germans moving forward in the open. The air was so packed with aeroplanes that sardines in comparison seemed to be lolling in luxury. The cloud ceiling was low, about 2,000 feet and in that narrow space hundreds of machines swooped and zoomed, spitting fire at each other and at the troops below.
>
> Nickle, my Toronto pilot [Lieutenant D.J. Nickle was actually from Kingston, Ont.] dived on German troops marching along a road, machine-gunning them furiously through the airscrew, and as he turned to regain height I continued with my gun. Black anti-aircraft shells burst on all sides; and the flaming onions, green incendiary projectiles that rose as if tied together on a string, came groping towards us. Aeroplanes flashed by on all sides, friend and foe almost impossible to distinguish.
>
> We dropped our bombs on a German battery ...[45]

On the Fifth Army front the situation was becoming chaotic. V Brigade, its operational efficiency as much impaired as that of most other elements of the army by the speed and weight of the German advance, worked desperately hard to stem the tide. In the brigade work summary the columns for tabulating offensive and line patrols for army and corps squadrons respectively were typed over with the blunt words 'Counter Attack' to characterize 136 of the 195 operational missions flown during the day, the balance being made up by artillery co-operation, contact, and reconnaissance missions. The RFC, clearly, was emphasizing those aspects of

---

* Canadians serving with 22 Squadron at this time included B.C. Budd and W.G. Bulmer of Toronto, H.F. Davison of Forfar, Ont. (WIA 13 April 1918), O. St C. Harris of Toronto, W.S. Hill-Tout of Abbotsford, BC (WIA 12 March 1918), D.M. McGoun of Westmount, Que., H.F. Moore of Winnipeg, G. Thomson of Celista, BC, G.N. Traunweiser of Grand Forks, BC (KIA 15 April 1918), and F.M. Ward of Victoria (KIA 22 April 1918).

† No 43 Squadron's Canadian pilots at this time included A.C. Dean of Chatham, Ont. (POW 12 April 1918), J.A. Grenier of Quebec City, H.S. Lewis of Orangeville, Ont. (POW 6 April 1918, died of wounds 16 April 1918), M.F. Peiler of Montreal (POW 6 April 1918), W.J. Prier of Brantford, Ont. (POW 28 March 1918), and C.S. Sheldon of Winnipeg (KIA 27 June 1917).

‡ Canadians in 60 Squadron included J.N. Bartlett of Winnipeg, K.P. Campbell of Brandon, Man. (WIA 27 June 1918), W.J.A. Duncan and H.A.S. Molyneux of Toronto, J.W. Trusler of Camlachie, Ont., and R.K. Whitney of Abbotsford, Que. (WIA 11 Aug. 1918).

§ Only two Canadians are known to have been serving in 40 Squadron at this time: H. Carnegie of Port Perry, Ont. (WIA 10 April 1918) and W.L. Harrison of Toronto (WIA 12 April 1918). When he was wounded Harrison had been with the squadron less than nine months and he was quoted as saying that, in that time, the squadron personnel had changed completely three times. Only he and the equipment officer remained of those who had been there when he joined. Canadian Associated Press release, nd, W.L. Harrison biographical file, DHist

the air battle which most effectively supplemented the efforts of the ground forces to stop the onslaught. 'During this period there were sometimes a dozen or more German aeroplanes over our aerodromes at a height of 10–12,000 ft but we did not attack them as they were doing no harm there and all our aeroplanes were required to help meet the emergency that had arisen on the ground,' recalled the commandant of the postwar RAF Staff College.[46]

Although 'many combats took place in the air' – the same phrase had been used on the previous day – this time only three 'decisive' fights were recorded. The SE5as, which were intended to provide high-level cover, were working nearly at ground level and finding targets for themselves. 'For several days,' wrote the historian of 24 Squadron, 'the Squadron practically operated on its own, carrying out low bombing attacks all day and concentrating mostly on the bridges across the Somme, at Pargny and Béthencourt.' He went on to recall that 'during part of this period [the March offensive] all communications were cut ... We were dependent entirely on our own reconnaissance for ascertaining the position of the enemy ...'[47]

Three pilots of 24 Squadron, including Lieutenant G.B. Foster of Montreal who had joined it on his first operational posting only two weeks earlier, caught a column of German troops at lunch on the road just outside Croix Moligneaux. Although hampered by enemy aircraft, they scattered the column with machine-gun fire, keeping it 'under cover for a considerable period.' A formation of 84 Squadron which included the Canadians Sorsoleil, Falkenberg, W.H. Brown, and Duke fired off 4000 rounds on their morning patrol alone, inflicting 'severe losses' on three large columns of enemy infantry in the vicinity of Matigny, where the squadron had been based only two days before. 'They attacked them for about twenty minutes and kept them at a standstill ... Hostile field guns were taking shots at them all the time' as the SE5as strafed from as low as one hundred feet.[48]

Since the British fighters were concentrating on delaying the German ground advance rather than shooting down enemy aircraft, the German pilots were having good hunting: 'On the third day of the battle,' *General* von Hoeppner has recorded, 'the German ground attack squadrons found excellent targets in the retreating British columns of route. Thus their attack in the afternoon on the straight as a line Roman Road (from Roupy to Ham) caused traffic congestions lasting for hours. Teams of horses went wild, every one was seeking cover in the trenches to the left or right, or panic-like raced from the road into the open fields.'[49] On the evening of the 22nd the artillery of the 9th (Scottish) Division found 'throngs of hostile aeroplanes flitting above them which sprayed the teams with bullets and engaged our infantry.' Their fate, even so, was perhaps happier than that of the Lowland Brigade of the same division, which found itself 'greatly harassed by bombs and machine gun fire from aeroplanes flying low and bearing British colours' on the morning of the 24th.[50] There were bound to be mistakes with such a fluid front, a badly strained command organization, and so many pilots unfamiliar with both the topography of the area and the techniques of close ground support.

Later that evening fog kept the night bombers of Fifth Army on the ground and protected targets opposite their front, but to the north the bombers of Third Army and IX Brigade's 54 (Night) Wing were back at work. No 102 Squadron dropped 663 bombs and fired nearly 14,000 rounds into billets behind the front of the

German Seventeenth Army,* while twelve machines of 58 Squadron attacked dumps at Iseghem and Bisseghem and started fires which were visible from Clair-marais aerodrome, about forty miles away. No 83 Squadron spent half the night trying to hit the long-range gun which the Germans had mounted on railway tracks at Meurchin, opposite the Canadian Corps' front, and then bombed an ammunition dump on the Carvin-Carnin road and set it on fire. The bombers were out every night, making every effort to disrupt German logistics, but the nature and circumstances of their work made them comparatively ineffective.[51]

Dawn on the 24th brought no easing of the German pressure. As the Third Army more or less held its ground in the Flesquières Salient while the Fifth was pushed further and further back, a line of weakness developed along their common boundary which Ludendorff was quick to exploit. The Third Army's flank was being left 'in the air' and the enemy began to push into the gap between the two armies, driving the one southwest and rolling the other back towards the northwest, so that a wedge aimed towards Albert appeared in the British front with a deep bulge opposite St Quentin to the south of it.

To counter the grave danger posed by this wedge, Salmond ordered III Brigade's squadrons and as many planes as could be spared from further north to this point. 'We managed to concentrate 100 machines on the threatened line,' he told Trenchard. 'They had orders to fly low and take every risk;[†] nothing was to count in carrying out their duties. I had news from the 1st Bde.[‡] that our machines were so thick over this point that there was every danger of collision in the air ...'[52]

If Salmond's was an apt description of air activities on the 24th from a command standpoint, then the war diary of 3 Squadron,[§] flying its Sopwith Camels out

---

* The effectiveness of this form of attack is hard to assess. Obviously the physical damage would be minimal and not worth the effort expended, but the effect on troop morale may have been significant. On this same night German bombers were busy over the British lines and artillery-man Arthur Behrend found that 'German planes were humming overhead all night long, and bombs were dropping north, south, east and west. It was the worst and noisiest night yet ...' Arthur Behrend, *As From Kemmel Hill* (London 1963), 89

† Some of the pilots obeyed orders to the letter. H.A. Jones, *The War in the Air: being the story of the Part played in the Great War by the Royal Air Force*, IV (London 1934), 316, cites a bugler of the 8th Grenadier Regiment, caught in the open by British fighters. 'My company commander, Lieutenant Nocke, had to fling himself flat on the ground, but for all that he was struck on the back by the wheels of one machine ... Not far from me an aeroplane appeared at about one metre above the ground, making straight for me and for the moment I did not know in what direction to throw myself: the pilot appeared determined to run over me. At the last moment I was able to spring clear as the machine whizzed past me and through the firing-line.' However, the real value of Salmond's orders should be assessed against Raymond Collishaw's criticism that 'Orders for fighter squadrons to participate by attacking German troops were issued in the vaguest terms and it was extraordinarily difficult for fighter pilots to discern who was who on the ground ... Fighter pilots ... were sent more than a 100 miles to intervene ... where they could scarcely identify friend from foe.' *Cross & Cockade Journal*, VIII, summer 1967, 148–9

‡ Salmond was 'temporarily out of touch' with III, V, and IX (HQ) Brigades at this time. See Salmond to Trenchard, 25 March 1918, Air 1/475/15/312/201.

§ At this time something of an Ontario preserve as far as Canadians were concerned, with six of them on the squadron strength: W.H. Boyd of Campbellford, R.F. Browne of Toronto (WIA 8 Oct. 1918), V.H. McElroy of Richmond (KIA 2 Sept. 1918), L.H. McIntyre of Peterborough (KIA 21 Aug. 1918), T.F. Rigby of North Bay (KIA 27 March 1918), and H.E. Stewart of Seaforth (WIA 27 March 1918).

of Warloy, a few miles east of Albert, exemplified the battle at the 'sharp end': '9.30 am. Low Work. 10 machines. Enemy troops and transport bombed and machine gunned ... 1.40 pm. Low Work. 11 machines. Great havoc worked by all pilots on close masses of enemy during the attack on VRAU[LX] VAUCOURT. Very successful bombing and machine gunning ... 5.0 pm. Low Work. 6 machines. Good work done again on close masses of enemy.'[53] As for the recipients of this onslaught, they recorded that 'like swarms of angry hornets British aircraft are circling around the German troops moving from the height of Biefvillers towards Bihucourt,' while a little farther south '... low-flying enemy planes were delaying the advance with bombs and machine gun fire, especially at the road Le Transloy-Lesboeufs. Anyone trying to get across the road was shot down.'[54]

This was all aimed against the wedge driving towards Albert. Further south, where the Fifth Army line was sagging back towards Amiens,* every effort was being made by V Brigade, with more than forty Canadians on its flying strength, to prevent the Germans crossing the Somme canal. No 23 Squadron's M.S. MacLean of Winnipeg was one of several to bomb and machine-gun enemy troops on either side of the canal at Béthencourt. Kingstonian R.J. Smith 'dropped 4 bombs on bridge at Béthencourt. One seen to burst just off end of bridge, others not observed,' while another Spad of the same patrol claimed a direct hit 'amongst infantry crossing' the bridge. Later in the afternoon Smith was back, bombing the village again and strafing artillery and infantry in the vicinity, while MacLean was scoring a direct hit on the canal bridge at Pargny, a mile or so to the north. All along the battlefront other squadrons were busy at the same kind of work, so that even in the extreme south, where French reinforcements were now intermingled with the British as the Germans fought their way past Cugny, the latter reported 'enemy planes constantly buzzing around them.' All these, of course, are subjective descriptions of the fighting, and although they indicate its nature, they do little to explain the degree to which the ground support battle was intensifying.[55]

A few figures may help here. On 21 March some 28,000 rounds were fired at ground targets by the RFC and fifteen-and-a-half tons of bombs were dropped during the day and night. The next day 41,000 rounds were fired and twenty-one tons of bombs dropped; on the 23rd, 44,000 rounds and thirty-three tons of bombs were expended. But on the 24th the expenditure of ammunition rose to 82,000 rounds, although the tonnage of bombs dropped only increased by three-and-a-half tons.[†56]

This marked increase in the intensity of ground support operations by the British brought about a parallel intensification of the air fighting when the German army staffs reacted to the increasing number and effectiveness of British aircraft intervening in the ground battle. Their assault troops were now complaining about British strafing, von Below's Second Army Headquarters telling the commanders of its fighter wings that their troops were being 'incessantly harassed by enemy

---

* '5th Army has practically broken down ... The worst show since the beginning of the war. Troops and transport of all kinds have been streaming past the aerodrome all day,' recorded Burden of 56 Squadron. 'A copy of the 1918 Diary of Captain Henry John Burden, DSO, DFC,' Burden biographical file, DHist

† These figures applied to the whole of the Western Front but by far the greater part of the action was occurring south of Arras.

aircraft' and demanding that this be stopped. The *Jagdgeschwadern* promptly abandoned their high-level patrolling and came down to seek combat.[57]

'Owing to the low altitude at which fighting was carried out, there was little time for enemy machines to manœuvre, and consequently more than the usual proportion were crashed,' noted III Brigade's daily work summary in the course of claiming twenty-one enemy aircraft destroyed during the day. V Brigade reported thirteen victories and IX Brigade eleven, while I Brigade's operations on the Third Army front added two more, for a total claim of forty-seven machines. The RFC admitted losing fifteen of their own aircraft but most of them were probably brought down by ground fire. Canadians shot down included 53 Squadron's Captain R.H. Martin of Viking, Alta, and Second Lieutenant Wilson Porter of Port Dover, Ont., from 56 Squadron, both of whom were killed, while Lieutenant C.W. Cook of Guysboro, NS, Martin's observer, was taken prisoner.* Three other Canadians were credited with destroying enemy machines, Lieutenant W.L. Harrison of 40 Squadron and Second Lieutenant W.S. Stephenson of 73 Squadron† and F.H. Taylor of 41 Squadron‡ each claiming one victory. Lieutenant H.F. Moore of Toronto, an observer in a Bristol Fighter of 22 Squadron, was credited with participating in the destruction of a fourth.[58]

Not only did the Germans fail in their attempt to limit or prevent the massive deployment of RFC resources on ground-support operations, but their air effort was also being undermined by serious logistical and command problems. As their armies advanced German air units needed new airfields as close as possible to the moving front, but good locations were few on the trench-furrowed and shell-pitted Somme battlefields. Because the German air force had adopted an essentially defensive posture on the Western Front their designers had paid more attention to aircraft performance than endurance. The standard German fighters in the spring of 1918 (Albatros D-V and Pfalz D-III) could stay aloft for only one-and-a-half hours as against two-and-a-half hours for the equivalent British machines (SE5a and Sopwith Camel). Consequently aircraft had to be over-concentrated on the useable forward fields, which were then subjected to intensive attack by the RFC, and the more remote air formations came to be from their command headquarters, the more difficult communications became. 'Fighter groups and Wings which quite correctly had moved forward quickly, for days on end received no directives from Army Headquarters located far to the rear. Therefore they ... lacked the possibility of co-ordinating their activities as to time and place with the events on the ground. Thus it happened that frequently at the decisive point and at the critical time the troops failed to receive fighter support.'[59]

---

* Other Canadian flying personnel in 53 Squadron on 24 March 1918 included W.M. Emery of Ottawa, W.R. McCoo of Montreal (WIA 11 April 1918), E.L. O'Leary of Richibucto, NB, J.J. Quinn and W.D. Stroud, both of Ottawa.

† Stephenson hailed from Winnipeg. Other Canadians serving in 73 Squadron included W.H. Collins of Chatham, Ont., J.H. Drewry of Victoria, E.J. Lussier of Medicine Hat, Alta, and J.J. McDonald of Sydney, NS (WIA April 1918, POW 15 Sept. 1918).

‡ Taylor was a Torontonian. His compatriots serving in 41 Squadron on 24 March 1918 included E.F.H. Davis of Oxbow, Sask., W.J. Gillespie of Daysland, Alta, A. Goby of Avonlea, Sask., and S.A. Puffer of Lacombe, Alta.

The British, too, had often found themslves in these critical days without adequate air support. But for troops fighting on the defensive, usually from cover and sometimes from prepared positions, the absence of air cover was not so serious as for troops who must keep attacking incessantly. To attackers, moving in the open, it was vital that their aircraft keep the enemy from the skies overhead and compel defending forces to keep their heads down. The Germans, however, were losing the air battle: 'on 24 and 25 March the ... situation of our pilots in the battle zone was worsening constantly ... Numerically the enemy had already reached superiority again.'[60] This loss of air superiority was to have a material effect upon the ground battle.

Nevertheless, the German advance flowed on. When, on the 24th, the drive towards Albert came virtually to a standstill, pressure was shifted southwards. On the 25th the Germans began to align their main effort along the St Quentin-Amiens axis, pushing hard against the junction between the Fifth Army and elements of the French Third Army now taking over the southern end of the Fifth Army's front. By nightfall on the 25th, after five days of fighting, the Germans had gained more than four hundred square miles of territory and their advance, probing constantly for weak points in the British line and shifting direction and weight as circumstances suggested, showed no signs of flagging.

In the air, however, they had now lost their initial advantage. On the Fifth Army front, after five hectic days, the tempo of German air activity was reported as 'normal' on the 25th; in confirmation of this claim, 15 (Corps) Wing of V Brigade was able to carry out a total of forty-two reconnaissance flights during the day without losing a machine. Only two decisive combats were recorded in the whole brigade, both Germans being sent down in flames by 84 Squadron's W.H. Brown, a former bank clerk from British Columbia, who gained a Military Cross in recognition of his day's work. III Brigade found 'hostile activity strong but nothing like the same intensity as on the previous day of the battle,' with eleven out of thirty-two combats claimed as 'decisive.' As for I Brigade, it reported that 'E.A. activity was slight ... a very few machines seen on Third Army front.'[61]

All the low-flying offensive patrols took full advantage of the opportunity presented them by the slackening of German activity. Twenty-six of 22 (Army) Wing's 108 aircraft were unserviceable after their herculean efforts of the previous four days, but every machine that could still fly was pressed into service. One hundred and thirty-one sorties were flown and because they were less threatened from the air, RFC pilots were able to wreak even more destruction on the ground. No 84 Squadron's early patrol, including Sorsoleil and Duke, found a 'massed formation of Huns' on the Peronne-Albert road and fired two thousand rounds into them from a hundred feet 'with good results.'[62] Duke's diary reported the attack from a more personal perspective which adds colour to the bald prose of the official record: 'I went down low to look at some troops marching along the Peronne-Albert road. I got down low and saw they were Boche. They turned machine guns galore on me, and shot my lower left longeron clear through, besides the rear spar in the r[igh]t hand plane and several other holes, machine is a "write off" so I'll get a new one.' Things went better for him on the afternoon patrol, however. 'Went out at 5 o'clock on a low-strafing patrol with Shutley,

Brown and Falkenburg. I dropped bombs and shot up Boche troops on the Nestle-Curchy road. It was good sport and they all scattered to the side of the road.'[63]

To the north I and III Brigades, operating on the Third Army front, were enjoying equally satisfactory conditions. Setting an example were two Canadians from 70 Squadron, Frank Quigley, who already had an MC and Bar, and Alfred Koch, both of whom were to find references to this day's work in their citations for the DSO and MC, respectively. Quigley started his day by strafing German transport near Le Sars and then, on his second sortie, 'dropped 2 bombs on transport from 500 ft. He then fired on it [the transport] disorganizing it. Afterwards he fired from 500 ft on enemy [infantry] advancing in open order.' Koch had an even better time, 'thoroughly' dispersing an entire battalion of infantry which he found marching in close column on the road to Irles, bombing another column marching west between Bapaume and Avesnes-lès-Bapaume and strafing a third column 'which scattered and did not reform.'[64]

Since every available pilot in I, III, and IX Brigades was doing his best to emulate Quigley and Koch and was operating under nearly optimum conditions, the cumulative effects (92,000 rounds were fired at ground targets) were significant despite the immensity of the war machine that Ludendorff's staff had deployed along the Somme. Indeed, German historians have recorded the increasing effectiveness of the RFC role in stemming the offensive. At the tactical level the 14th Bavarian Infantry Regiment, pushing towards Sapignies, found their advance 'rendered more difficult by the presence overhead of several British air formations.' The German official history, describing the air situation on 25 March, records that 'low-flying enemy planes attacked time and again,' while the German infantry 'urgently requested protection against enemy aircraft' on their Second Army front.[65] Even the high-level day bombers made their presence felt at an immediate tactical level. During the morning, as the 100th Leibgrenadier Regiment was moving into assembly positions at Athies:

... suddenly at the greatest height enemy aircraft appeared. They had been noticed too late, and already groups of bombs were crashing into the midst of the units, inflicting heavy casualties. Within a few seconds, 8 officers and 125 men were incapacitated, and in addition also 28 horses ...

As a result of the heavy loss of horses, some vehicles had to be left behind at Ennemain. The MG Coy had only five vehicles left for the continuation of the advance.[66]

During the afternoon the 52nd Reserve Infantry Regiment, near Thiepval, despondently recorded that '... enemy aircraft abound. We count 30 of them above our heads at one and the same time. But when the long hoped-for German planes appear ... they disappear in no time. Only a few accept combat, and they are shot down.'[67]

On the 26th the importance of the air in slowing down the Germans became even more pronounced as the RFC command and logistics organizations re-stabilized. The number of machine-gun rounds fired at ground targets more than doubled to 228,000. Moreover, they were probably fired to better purpose because British airmen had now formulated a special technique for this kind of work. The Camels and Bristol Fighters came in low and stayed low, strafing key roads and bridges and the small bodies of enemy troops which formed the spearheads of the attacking forces. The commander of 22 (Army) Wing told his pilots to 'first identify one's front line then fly up and down it at 50 feet to encourage the troops. Then ... turn east and fly up and down the Hun line at 50 feet and shoot them up, to encourage *them*.' The SE5as, fulfilling the double function of providing air cover and engaging in ground attack, specialized in transport, artillery, and the larger troop formations found slightly farther back behind the line.[68] Sholto Douglas described their technique:

The method of attack that we evolved against these ground targets was first of all to fly over the enemy, always in formation, at a height of between eight and ten thousand feet. At that height we presented to the enemy guns fast-moving targets that were difficult to hit, and we were too high for their machine-guns to be effective. On the other hand we could scan wide stretches of country in search of suitable ground targets. Having selected his target, the leader would dive at it, but not too steeply: more flying down to it from a distance with engine full on. When we were within range we opened up with our machine-guns; and at about two hundred feet away from the target we dropped our bombs.

Immediately after our attacks we zoomed up as hard as we could go, usually turning at the same time. In the dive we would be doing between one hundred and fifty and one hundred and eighty miles an hour, and in the zoom that followed we rocketed up to about a thousand feet. We would go on repeating this performance until we were out of bombs and ammunition; and so much practice did we have against those live targets that we were able to plant our bombs with an accuracy that, being fighter pilots and not bombers, surprised even us.[69]

The corps squadrons and the northern brigades were also doing their bit. German infantry found that 'enemy air reconnaissance was extremely lively and obnoxious' on the 26th: '... they accompanied our troops flying brazenly low and dropping bombs on the marching column. That they were in touch also with their artillery we were to feel shortly, for we had hardly reached our assembly position in an old British billet and had installed ourselves more or less comfortably, when a hail of shells and shrapnel bombs hit us like a thunderstorm.'[70] I Brigade's 10 (Army) Wing, with at least thirty-five Canadian airmen on strength, and aided by thirty machines from II Brigade (1, 19, and 20 Squadrons with another twenty or so Canadians) was still attacking ground targets around Bapaume: 'Troops and transport were scattered and many casualties caused. Excellent targets were obtained. Bombs were dropped on troops in close formation ... from a low height. Direct hits were obtained and troops scattered in all directions.'[71]

Cataloguing all the individual sorties would soon become monotonous, but one example may be selected to show the variety of work carried out. In the course of one mission Second Lieutenant Roy Kirkwood McConnell* of Victoria, who had enlisted as a nineteen-year-old schoolboy in February of the previous year and had been flying Sopwith Camels with 46 Squadron since receiving his first operational

---

* McConnell won a DFC for his five credited victories by the end of the war.

posting in mid-November, dropped two 20-lb bombs on a 'group of officers having a conference.' He then fired twenty rounds at them, apparently killing two and wounding another with his bombs and bullets and scattering their horses. Finding a German observation balloon in action he fired another twenty rounds at it, 'causing the observer to jump out.' He then returned home, strafing and dropping his remaining two bombs on troops in Ervillers on the way.[72]

The evening of the 26th saw the Chief of the French General Staff, *Général* Ferdinand Foch, appointed by mutual agreement to 'coordinate the actions of all Allied armies on the Western Front.' This was a much needed and long overdue reform of the allied command structure, made especially necessary by the German drive against the junction of the French Third and British Fifth Armies. Although it nominally increased French air participation in the battle, the effect on the RFC and on the air war was not significant, for the French, despite their nominal air strength, were a relatively negligible force in the spring of 1918. Between 26 March and 5 April 1918, inclusive, the Germans only lost five aircraft along the whole length of the French front.[73]

One of Foch's first instructions as supreme commander concerned the strategic conduct of the air war. The essential principle laid down in his order was the much needed one of proper concentration. Until Foch took over the British alone had been dealing with nearly fifty specific bombing targets. Now both air forces were allotted a total of eight, Foch pointing out that 'the essential condition of success is the concentration ... on such few of the most important of the enemy's railway junctions as it may be possible to put out of action with certainty, and to keep out of action.'* The principle was sound, even if the technology of the time made the objective virtually impossible to attain.[74]

Général Foch's instructions about air fighting and the tactical handling of aircraft during the current emergency were just as specific and no less correct. He directed that 'the first duty of fighting aeroplanes is to assist the troops on the ground by incessant attacking with bombs and machine guns on columns, concentrations or bivouacs. Air fighting is not to be sought except as far as it is necessary for the fulfillment of this duty.' In this case the RFC had nothing to learn, for that same evening Major-General Salmond reported to Trenchard in London that his squadrons had done 'really magnificent work.' He went on to say: 'When I was in GHQ tonight I heard a telephone message ... saying that without a doubt the concentration of aircraft in the south had frozen up the attack there temporarily. Similarly, Cox (Intelligence) told Davidson† that he considered the concentration of aircraft west of Bapaume had had the same effect.'[75]

These contemporary assessments of the situation have since been supported by the German official history, which, although primarily a narrative of ground opera-

---

* This instruction was dated 1 April 1918 and directed to *Général* Fayolle. James E. Edmonds, *Military Operations: France and Belgium, 1918*, II (London 1937), app. V, 506–8. However, ibid., 117, reports that it was forwarded to British GHQ with Foch's 'General Directive No. 2' of 26 March 1918.

† Brigadier-General E.W. Cox, Haig's Chief of Intelligence, and Major-General J.H. Davidson, his Chief of Operations.

tions, admits that on the 26th: 'Quite particularly and probably most strongly felt was the shift in the strength ratio in the air ... Enemy air formations of up to 60 aircraft – as recorded by Seventh Army on that day – pounced on the infantry with great élan and attacked them with bombs and machine gun fire. Against this enemy numerical superiority the German airmen had a hard time ... it was ... impossible to meet the demands of the troops for continuous air protection.'[76]

On 27 March, as the Germans drove to within fifteen miles of Amiens, the RFC continued to press its assault against their ground forces. This day saw the culmination of the British effort at close ground support. III, V, and IX Brigades were reinforced by ninety-seven machines of I Brigade and 30 of II Brigade and, along the length of the British front, the RFC discharged 313,000 rounds of machine-gun fire and fifty tons of bombs at the enemy. Using pilots of locally-based squadrons as patrol leaders because of their knowledge of the front, even I and II Brigade's fighters made an average of four flights each and some machines of Raymond Collishaw's 3(N) Squadron made as many as six sorties during the day.[77]

That the cumulative effect of the RFC operations was beginning to tell is revealed by the pilots' comments that targets were 'not quite so good as yesterday as the main roads were not being used to the same extent.' Nevertheless, 'heavy casualties' were claimed and British air supremacy was becoming more pronounced as patrols were 'splitting up' and proceeding 'individually to attack enemy troops and transport.' The Germans on their Second Army front found that '... already in the early hours of the morning enemy aircraft caused a considerable number of casualties in the most forward lines.' Infantry in the south, near Lassigny, reported 'Much fire from French artillery, but above all the Corps was seriously troubled by enemy aircraft now obviously having superiority in the air.'[78]

The RFC was suffering – besides actual losses of men and machines, a fifth of the machines of III and V Brigade's army wings were now unserviceable – but the German air force was suffering more. Although V Brigade, directly facing the main weight of the German assault once again, described enemy activity as 'above normal,' I and III Brigades found it only 'slight.'[79] The RFC by delivering such a quantity of ammunition and bombs against the enemy, in weather conditions that were something less than satisfactory, demonstrated that the German air force had been outnumbered and was now being outfought.

The spirit which Trenchard had inculcated and which had enabled the RFC to attain this air supremacy was once again superbly demonstrated on 27 March by Second Lieutenant Alan Arnett McLeod (one of whose initial exploits has already been recorded in an earlier chapter),* and his observer, Lieutenant Arthur Hammond. With six other Armstrong-Whitworth FK8s of 2 Squadron, McLeod and Hammond took off that morning to bomb and strafe German troop concentrations around Bray-sur-Somme, near Albert, but limited visibility soon left them separated from their colleagues and unable to locate their targets. Hampered by low cloud, they eventually landed on 43 Squadron's field. After repairing damage to the machine's tail skid which had resulted on landing the

---

* See 447 above.

heavily-laden machine, McLeod and Hammond took off again, determined to reach their target. Despite the poor weather, they finally located it and were about to bomb an artillery battery when they spotted a Fokker triplane below them.

The FK8 was not designed as a fighter but it was a strong machine and easy to fly. Flying with another observer, McLeod had already used one to shoot down a German scout in January and now he turned on the triplane. Hammond promptly shot it down but, almost immediately, seven more fighters belonging to the Richthofen *Geschwader* dived on them. One was sent down in flames but then the British machine was raked by a burst from one of the Fokkers which came up from below and behind. Both McLeod and Hammond were hit and the gas tank punctured, setting the machine on fire. They were then at about 2000 feet and, as McLeod put the machine into a dive to try to reach the ground, the floor fell out of the rear cockpit and forced Hammond to climb out onto the cockpit coaming, where he continued firing as best he could. Flames then enveloped the pilot's cockpit and McLeod climbed out onto the lower left wing and worked the controls from there, putting the machine into a side-slip to draw the flames away from himself and Hammond, who had by now been wounded several times. As McLeod struggled to maintain control they were followed down by a third enemy machine which continued to fire at them and wounded both McLeod and Hammond again. Somehow McLeod kept control, flattening out his dive just before hitting the ground in 'No Man's Land.'[80]

The FK8, still bearing eight bombs and a thousand rounds of ammunition, was now blazing fiercely. Hammond had received six wounds and was badly burnt; he was virtually helpless but McLeod, despite his own five wounds, managed to drag him from the wreckage, receiving one more wound from an exploding bomb. Under heavy enemy machine-gun fire he then dragged Hammond towards the British line and, after again being wounded, collapsed only a short distance from the forward trenches. They were rescued by South African troops and sixty years later one of them recollected: 'We attended their wounds but could not safely get them away until dusk. Both were burnt and in a bad way. Captain Ward and I cheered them as best we could until dark enough for our bearers to carry them back to a dressing station. In trying to cheer McLeod I said "You will be in Blighty [England] in a few days." He said, "That's just the trouble, I would like to have a crack at that so-and-so that brought me down." The observer was too bad to talk; both smelt terribly of burnt flesh.'[81] Subsequently Hammond received a Bar to his MC and McLeod was awarded the Victoria Cross, the second Canadian airman to win it.*[82]

The Germans continued to advance on the 28th along the eighteen miles of front between the Somme and Montdidier, where they moved forward some six miles during the day. They were to gain a maximum of six more miles, just south of Amiens, before the offensive was finally halted on 5 April, bringing them at that point within eight miles of the city centre. Before then it was already becoming

---

* McLeod returned to Canada in September 1918. In late October he contracted influenza and died in Winnipeg in November. Hammond, like the observer who had flown with McLeod before him, Reg Keys, emigrated to Canada after the war.

clear that they could not break cleanly through the allied line or even take Amiens. 'The enemy's line was now becoming denser, and in places they were even attacking themselves,' wrote Ludendorff, 'while our armies were no longer strong enough ... the ammunition was not sufficient, and supply became difficult. All troops, especially mounted troops, had suffered heavily from bombing by hostile airmen.' Ludendorff's account is buttressed by the German official history which records that, on the 28th, *General* von Kuhl, the Chief of Staff of Crown Prince Rupprecht's Group of Armies, had reported the Second Army's supply difficulties, the considerable number of casualties suffered in the attack on Albert, and 'the very disagreeable enemy air activity, *which had caused about one half of all casualties suffered.*'*[83]

Whether the RFC was, in fact, responsible for anything like such a high proportion of the German casualties is questionable. As Napoleon was fond of pointing out, however, in war the moral is to the physical as three is to one, and the important thing is what von Kuhl believed to be the case. It led the German General Staff, perhaps, to over-emphasize the importance of British air supremacy, an opinion which was becoming increasingly shared by the troops under their command. From 28 March on unit battle reports indicate that they found the sky above them more and more the exclusive domain of the RFC. 'From 39 Reserve Corps, located close by [the Richthofen *Geschwader*] there were continuously reports on low-flying British aircraft severely harassing our infantry.' On the 30th the 243rd Division, spearheading the German attack, found its 'dense marching columns attracted numerous enemy air units which attacked with bombs and machine guns' in the Moreuil area. 'With improved weather and good visibility numerous enemy planes were constantly and without hindrance circling above our positions ...' while 'some British aircraft were passing so closely over the woods that one could think that they would graze the tree tops ... the enemy planes were attacking ever more boldly.'[84]

Conversely, British battle reports and reminiscences make fewer references to German air activity each day, until, by 3 April, the attack south of Arras had ground to a complete halt, both on the ground and in the air. Enemy planes were still over the battlefield in substantial numbers on occasion, but they had largely reverted to their practice of the first days of the battle, flying in massed formations at high altitudes, where they caused little inconvenience to British aircraft which were intervening in the ground operations. Rarely did the enemy choose to seek combat, and when he did – on 3 April, for example, some thirty came down to engage twenty-seven Camels and SE5as of 65 and 84 Squadrons – he was badly mauled. An entry in the record book of 84 Squadron[†] for the 3rd summed up the general situation at the end of the battle. It reported an engagement at about 1500 feet over the German advanced landing ground at Rosières, which was more than twenty-five miles west of the old front line which had been broken two weeks

---

* Author's emphasis.
† Its Canadian contingent was now reinforced by the addition of Roy Manzer of Oshawa, Ont. who had joined the squadron on 19 March 1918 and won a DFC before being taken prisoner on 8 August 1918.

before. No 84's pilots claimed five enemy aircraft shot down without loss in the course of 'fighting continuously for an hour. In the end our patrol and a patrol of 65 Squadron were left in possession of the sky.'[85]

The predominant impression left by the March offensive, in so far as the air was concerned, is that the Germans did not employ their air arm with the skill which they displayed on the ground. The further from the ground combat situation their air operations were, the less well they were handled. The *Schlachtstaffeln* and the reconnaissance and artillery observation flights did excellent work directly over the front, but they did not take much advantage of the opportunities for intensive tactical bombing offered by long, straight, narrow French roads jammed with retreating British columns.[86]

The RFC, on the tactical level, showed an exceptional degree of flexibility and versatility, with the corps squadrons focussing on their accustomed roles of reconnaissance and artillery observation and, in addition, doing some work as 'battle-flights,' while the army wings, which were rightly concentrated upon a ground support role to which they were largely unaccustomed, not only accomplished it brilliantly but also managed to assert and subsequently maintain a combat superiority.* Moreover, the concentration of RFC machines at decisive points was competently handled, despite the communications problems of the first days. Thus, on 26 March, thirty-seven out of the sixty-nine squadrons on the Western Front were involved in the Bapaume area alone. But, like the Germans, the RFC's command and control efficiency deteriorated badly in those aspects of the air battle more remote from the ground fighting. Neither day- nor night-bombing operations seem to have been adequately thought out at this stage. On the 25th, for example, the DH4s of 27 Squadron were employed on 'Bombing (Roving Commissions)' and on the 26th and 27th they bombed and machine-gunned troops and transport around Bapaume and Albert. They should surely have been dropping heavier bombs on key rail junctions and bridges. They were now, however, bombing from heights as low as one thousand feet.[87]

Ludendorff decided to cut his losses south of Arras and launch his Sixth Army against the junction of the British First and Second Armies, striking towards the vital Channel ports. Such an attack had been proposed by Crown Prince Rupprecht's staff when the 1918 strategy had first been considered, but had been rejected in favour of an attack upon the weakest part of the British front. Now German morale had been weakened and efficiency impaired – particularly in the air – by the strategic failure of the southern attack, while the British, though they had suffered severely,

---

* Air fighting was a very specialized skill, demanding outstanding physical and mental attributes on the part of successful practitioners. To be a good pilot and shot was not enough; even good pilots needed the confidence and tactical skills that only much combat experience could give to become superior air fighters. Experienced and talented leaders were therefore essential operationally, both to achieve results and to coach and encourage novices. But the chancy nature of anti-aircraft fire and the frequent inability of either skill or judgment to affect the outcome of close ground support operations, as far as the individual aircraft was concerned, tended to eliminate the experienced leader and the neophyte without distinction and was thus potentially capable of destroying, in a matter of days, the fighting value of a force carefully built up over a period of years.

had learned the hard way to meet the new German tactics. Moreover, Haig had toughly resisted the temptation to weaken his key positions in the north unduly, although it had been necessary to reinforce the Somme front.

The Battle of the Lys was, on a smaller scale, virtually a replica of the March offensive. Even the weather conformed; as the Germans launched their initial assault against the northern flank of the First Army on 9 April they moved forward through a thick fog which blanketed the battlefield and reduced visibility to forty yards. The Portuguese division which held a part of XI Corps' front broke almost immediately and disappeared from the battlefield. The Germans quickly began to exploit this gap, swinging north on the flank of the British 40th Division towards the Lys at Bac St Maur. By evening German troops were across both the Lys and the La Lawe rivers and in the suburbs of Estaires, having penetrated more than four miles into the British line on a front of ten miles.[88]

As a result of the chaos brought about by the speed and momentum of the German advance, 208 Squadron at La Gorgue, on the banks of the Lys some three-and-a-half miles behind the original front, quickly lost touch with all higher authority.* The arrival of the Germans on the airfield was erroneously reported to be imminent and the squadron's Camels were earthbound by the fog, so seventeen machines were burnt in one enormous bonfire and the squadron moved back to Serny on its ground transport. It is a measure of the capacities of the Royal Air Force, as it now was, that within forty-eight hours the unit was fully re-equipped and shooting down enemy aircraft.[89]

The fog did not lift until 1400 hrs, but as soon as it did the RAF made its presence felt, using the same techniques which had worked so well in the Somme battle. Twenty Camels of Collishaw's 203 Squadron, five from 40 Squadron and fifteen from 210 Squadron,† began to bomb and machine-gun German infantry in the neighbourhood of Bac St Maur, Estaires, and Festubert with persistence and accuracy. The historian of the enemy's 51st Reserve Regiment, assembling just north of Estaires, stated:

With great punctuality the strong formations reappeared every ¾ hours above the stretched out columns and covered everything richly and plentifully with high explosive bombs. The bomber attacks continued with regularity until evening ...

There was no counter-action; our flak was still far to the rear, the fighter squadrons presumably busy elsewhere; in our area they appeared only in the evening when the British pilots tired from continuous flying had called it a day.[90]

---

* Among the pilots of 208 Squadron were W.E. Cowan of Hamilton, Ont. (POW 16 May 1918), H.H.S. Fowler of Bowmanville, Ont., D.C. Hopewell of Ottawa (POW 7 April 1918), M.C. Howell, address unknown, A.R. Knight of Collingwood, Ont., R. McDonald of James River Station, NS, and E. Taylor of Regina.

† RNAS squadrons had 200 added to their old RNAS squadron number when the RFC and RNAS were amalgamated into the RAF on 1 April 1918. Thus Naval Ten became 210 Squadron: Canadians in the unit included W.M. Alexander of Toronto, W.A. Carter of Calgary (POW 1 June 1918), H.J. Emery of Edmonton, F.C. Gorringe of Prince Albert, Sask., E.N. Gregory of Lindsay, Ont., J.G. Manuel of Edmonton (KIA 10 June 1918), and M.T. McKelvey of Holmfield, Man. (POW 11 April 1918).

RAF airmen found that German fighters were not numerous, but they claimed to have shot down five two-seaters for the loss of one of their own machines. Indeed, in contrast with the skill and determination of German ground forces, the German air force was now showing the effects of the battle of attrition that the British air arm had been pressing upon them for the past three years.* On the Somme the British had won in the air despite losing two aircraft to each of the enemy's one; on the Lys, the proportions were reversed and the result even more decisive.[91]

On 10 April, when the Germans widened their attacking front to include part of the British Second Army's sector, the weather was again foggy in the morning and the ceiling remained at a thousand feet for the rest of the day. Under these conditions the army wings of both First and Second Armies were used exclusively for close ground support. Even the DH4s of 18 Squadron were bombing from four to six hundred feet along the Estaires-La Bassée and Estaires-Merville roads.† On the 11th the Germans took Merville in the north and Nieppe in the centre, pushing the First Army back into Messines on the southern flank, but their gains were far short of those on the first day. The British retirement was orderly, unlike the confused retreat of the Fifth Army three weeks earlier. With clear weather in the afternoon, the squadrons of I Brigade were able to drop four hundred 25-lb bombs and fire fifty thousand rounds at ground targets. More significantly, they were reinforced during the day by 22 (Bristol Fighter) and 41, 46, and 64 (single-seater fighter) Squadrons.[92]

The 12th was the critical day, when Haig, apparently made nervous by the proximity of the Channel coast, issued his famous 'backs to the wall' order. Fortunately for the British, the day was fine so that full advantage could be taken of their air superiority. Air reconnaissance reports made German movements and intentions utterly clear, and artillery aircraft signalling important targets of opportunity found a ready response from British batteries. Thirty-seven enemy artillery batteries were engaged for destruction with air observation and thirty-six of them were neutralized, the work of an Armstrong-Whitworth of 2 Squadron piloted by Second Lieutenant H.I. Pole, a prewar English immigrant who had enlisted in Winnipeg, being particularly noticeable. During a flight of four-and-a-quarter hours Pole and his observer registered twenty-three of thirty-nine ranging rounds of howitzer fire within fifty yards of a hostile battery and during the subsequent 'fire for effect' watched 160 further rounds put down either directly on or very close to the target. 'Position well covered,' they recorded. 'Northern pit hit during ranging. Two explosions caused during ranging. One huge explosion during fire for effect. Fire caused early in ranging, and was still burning when machine left line.'[93]

---

* The German Fourth and Sixth Armies had available for this attack two bomber wings, twenty-eight field flights, seventeen ground support squadrons, and twenty-five fighter squadrons, a total of 492 aircraft. By 25 April and the attack on Mount Kemmel, the culminating point of the offensive, their strength had been lessened by fourteen field flights, one ground support squadron, and eight fighter squadrons, and the total number of aircraft available had been reduced by 174 machines to 318. *Der Weltkrieg 1914 bis 1918*, XIV, 270, 294

† On 10 April 18 Squadron had at least three Canadian airmen on strength. They were A.C. Atkey and R.C. Bennett (WIA and POW 27 Sept. 1918), both of Toronto, and J.G. Gillanders of Highgate, Ont. D.W. Gordon of Toronto had been wounded the previous day.

On this day the RAF flew more hours, dropped more bombs, and took more photographs than on any day since the war had begun. A subsequent RAF *communiqué* summarized accurately the scale and nature of the air operations:

During the whole of the day, pilots of the 1st and 2nd Brigades were employed bombing and machine-gunning, from a low height, the enemy's attacking groups between Wytschaete and La Bassée Canal. Pilots flew from anything between 2,000 and 50 ft. At the same time, machines of the 9th Brigade flew at a height to fight hostile machines. Machines of the 1st Brigade dropped about 800 bombs and fired 15,000 rounds. Very low reconnaissances were also carried out by the machines of these Brigades, very useful information being brought in as to the position of our own and the enemy's troops. Especially useful reports as to the location in which hostile troops were massing were brought in, enabling our guns to engage them and our low-flying machines to go out and attack them with their machine-guns and drop bombs on them.[94]

Canadians of the RAF were deeply involved in all these activities. The Sopwith Camels of 73 Squadron, twelve strong and led by Captain W.H. Hubbard of Toronto, found 'all villages between Merville, Estaires, and Locon on fire.'[*] Lieutenant E.T. Morrow of Toronto, flying a Bristol Fighter of 62 Squadron,[†] reported 'large masses of Huns and transport on La Bassée-Estaires road.' Setting an example closely followed by many of the other squadrons involved, the sixteen available pilots of 201 Squadron, at least five of them Canadians,[‡] logged a total of eighty-nine hours of operational flying during the course of 'a very hot day's work.' The phrase was S.W. Rosevear's, the Port Arthur man who was one of the Squadron's three Canadian flight commanders. He reported catching German infantry 'on the march along a road and swept them three times leaving many of them lying on the road. The others jumped into ditches and I gave them some more.' Another Camel squadron with a sizeable Canadian complement, Collishaw's No 203, dropped 196 bombs and fired 23,000 rounds during the day.[95]

Enemy aircraft were still in the air;[§] Burden of 56 Squadron, flying high above the battlefield in his SE5a, found that 'The whole country NW of Arras to St. Omer

[*] Six of the twelve were Canadians. Aside from Hubbard (WIA 26 Dec. 1916), they were A.N. Baker of Rodney, Ont. (KIA 25 April 1918), W.H. Collins, J.H. Drewry, E.J. Lussier, and Winnipeger W.S. Stephenson. In seven months at the front Stephenson was credited with eight-and-a-half enemy aircraft, not the twenty often attributed to him: the citations for his MC (10 April) and DFC (11 Aug.) emphasized his work against ground targets rather than air combat. On 28 July 1918 he was shot down in error by a French pilot and taken prisoner by the Germans. His postwar career was in business and (1940–5) espionage, under the code name 'Intrepid.' In 1946 he was knighted for his Second World War services. W.S. Stephenson biographical file, DHist

[†] Other Canadians in 62 Squadron included A.W. Blowes of Mitchell, Ont., L. Campbell of King, Ont. (KIA 9 Oct. 1918), E.G. Grant of Edmonton (WIA 3 May 1918), P.R. Hampton (POW 3 May 1918), and A.V. Sutton, both of Toronto, W.K. Swayze of Lindsay, Ont. (POW 4 Sept. 1918), and L.M. Thompson of Balgonie, Sask. (WIA 21 April 1918).

[‡] They were J.H. Forman of Kirkfield, Ont. (WIA 28 July 1917, POW 4 Sept. 1918), G.A. Magor of Montreal (KIA 22 April 1918), S.W. Rosevear of Port Arthur, Ont. (KIA 25 April 1918), A.G.A. Spence of Toronto (WIA 8 Nov. 1917), and H. le R. Wallace of Lethbridge, Alta.

[§] The RAF claimed fifty-one enemy aircraft 'brought down' and twenty-five more 'driven down out of control.' RAF communiqué no 2, DHist 75/414. The Germans actually lost sixteen. *Der Weltkrieg 1914 bis 1918*, XIV *Beilagen*, Beilage 40

is in flames. Worse than the first days of the Somme show 3 weeks ago ... but didn't see a Hun in the sky.'[96] R.G. Lye of Toronto, who had joined 19 Squadron on 17 March, 'didn't see a Hun in the sky' either, as he flew an early morning offensive patrol on 19 April, the day he was wounded in action. His experience graphically illustrates several of the problems which confronted a fighter pilot of the First World War and helps to explain why the life expectancy of a novice pilot was so short: '... I noticed an Allied Camel in the sun. I took no particular notice of this machine and kept up with my formation. Less than a minute after this, there was a loud explosion in my cockpit, this was the first indication I had of being fired at. I felt paralysed all over my body and could not turn round to look for the Camel or even to make sure whether or not it was the Camel which had fired at me.'[97] Lye, with a bullet wound in his neck, finished his 33rd and last day as an operational fighter pilot in a casualty clearing station after being dragged from his wrecked machine by ground troops.

There is no doubt that the Germans were becoming more and more hesitant about their air commitment on the Lys. According to the adjutant of the Richthofen *Jagdgeschwader*, left on the Somme front but expecting to be sent north: '... orders and counter-orders were arriving in quick succession; now we were leaving, now we were staying; this went on for several days ... and on 15th April the Wing was ready and standing beside the machines for the flight to the north. Richthofen was just putting on his fur-lined boots when a despatch rider arrived: – everything was cancelled.'[98]

Indeed, after 12 April, though the German Fourth Army continued to make some progress on the northern flank of the Lys front, the impetus of the offensive began to slacken. From the 12th to the 15th the weather was wet and misty, but it would seem that more than the weather bore on the decision not to move Richthofen's unit. Bailleul fell on the 15th, but on 17 April the Germans failed to storm Kemmel Hill. By this time the German High Command no longer had any illusions about a breakthrough in the north, although the hill was taken on the 25th. At that point the second of the Ludendorff offensives ground to a halt.

Four days earlier the German air force had suffered an irreparable loss, psychologically even more than physically, with the death in action of Manfred von Richthofen. By that time the 'Red Baron' had eighty victories marked against his name and had established himself as the greatest air fighter of the war on either side. Since the end of 1916 when, with fifteen enemy aircraft credited to him, he had taken command of the *élite* Boelcke *Jagdstaffel*, his record of success had gone far to neutralize single-handedly the psychological advantage given to the British flyers through the aggressive fighting spirit so painstakingly enforced by General Trenchard. Now he was dead, apparently killed in aerial combat by a Canadian flight commander of 209 Squadron, Captain A. Roy Brown of Carleton Place, Ont.*

---

* Other Canadian pilots in 209 Squadron on 21 April 1918 included A.W. Aird of Victoria (KIA 23 May 1918), C.G. Brock of Winnipeg (WIA 5 Sept. 1918), S.T. Edwards of Carleton Place, Ont., J.S.T. Fall of Hillbank, BC, W.J. Mackenzie of Port Robinson, Ont. (WIA 21 April 1918), W.R. May of Carberry, Man. (WIA 8 Aug. 1918), and M.S. Taylor of Regina (KIA 7 July 1918).

'Apparently killed,' because this notable success was also claimed by Australian anti-aircraft machine-gunners firing from the ground. Von Richthofen had been flying very low over the front lines in hot pursuit of Lieutenant W.R. May of Edmonton, a novice pilot in Brown's flight, and a number of guns had fired virtually simultaneously on the same 'pure red triplane' which Brown recorded shooting down in his logbook entry for that day. A week later the Canadian reported, in a letter to his father recounting the fight, that 'We shot down three of their triplanes ... Among them was the Baron whom I shot down on our side of the lines.' Awarded a Bar to his Distinguished Service Cross for this victory, Brown was morally certain that he had accounted for the 'Red Baron'; the fledgling RAF, well aware of the propaganda value of having the great German ace shot down by one of their fighter pilots, was quick to report 'Captain M von Richthofen ... shot down and killed behind our lines near Corbie by Capt. A.R. Brown.' Popular histories crudely but vigorously supported the RAF claim after the war and it was subsequently given scholarly recognition in the British official history. Australian official historians, understandably, have taken a different view and more recent research and analysis has confirmed beyond a reasonable doubt that one or other of the machine-gunners on the ground fired the actual bullet that killed Richthofen.*[99]

The capture of Kemmel Hill by the Germans brought a general slackening of the tempo of operations on that portion of the Western Front held primarily by the British armies and the RAF. Ludendorff regrouped once again and then launched a series of major attacks against the French, along the Aisne, the Matz, and the Marne during May, June, and July, respectively. Each of them in turn was brought to a stop without achieving any significant strategic advantage, and, like the two earlier offensives, they cost the Germans dearly in first-line troops.

In the air over Flanders both protagonists took advantage of the lull to recuperate and to train their novice pilots and observers in the harsh realities of the air war. Those realities, for British airmen, still included facing up to the possibility that they would one day have to choose between burning to death in a falling torch constructed largely of wood and 'doped' fabric or jumping without a parachute. Lieutenant C.A. Crysler of Welland, Ont., who had joined 23 Squadron[†] on 30 March, found himself separated from his flight in the course of an engagement just north of Villers-Bretonneux on 20 May. Attacked by three triplanes he shot one down and then – his own Sopwith Dolphin being on fire – rammed a second one,

---

* Specific studies of the circumstances of von Richthofen's death often lean heavily towards a romantic and imaginative interpretation of the peripheral events. In each case, however, they appear to have been well researched on the essential points. It is now difficult to argue that Roy Brown killed Richthofen. See P.J. Carisella and J.W. Ryan, *Who Killed the Red Baron? The Final Answer* (Wakefield, Mass. 1969); Dale M. Titler, *The Day the Red Baron Died* (New York 1970); F.R. McGuire, 'Who killed von Richthofen?' *Cross & Cockade Journal*, IV, summer 1963, 158–67; DHist files on von Richthofen's death.

† No 23 Squadron had turned in its Spads and had been re-equipped with the new Sopwith Dolphin by April. Besides Crysler, H.N. Compton of Westholme, BC, A.B. Fairclough of Toronto, and K.D. MacPherson of St Thomas, Ont. (WIA 5 July 1918) had joined the squadron since March.

so that both triplane and Dolphin fell blazing to the ground. Torontonian Percy Hampton, in 62 Squadron, was luckier when his 'Brisfit' caught fire two weeks earlier, and he lived to write about it from a German hospital:

I was flying south from Ypres-Menin Road, and about Armentières I dived from 15,000 feet to about 12,000 feet to attack some enemy aircraft. I was almost within range when an Archie shell burst under me, hitting my front petrol tank and wounding my observer in the thigh. The petrol then caught fire, and I unfastened my belt and got almost out to jump from the flames, but got back [in] again and put the machine into a violent side-slip. I couldn't breath and my leather coat, boots and gloves started to burn, and then my own ammunition, about eleven hundred rounds, started exploding. Five enemy machines followed me, shooting all the time. They hit my bus alright but didn't hit me. They hit my instrument board in front of me and I became unconscious several thousand feet from the ground, but my observer prevented a very bad crash. When we hit, my bus went on its nose and I was thrown out, also my observer.[100]

A week later another letter reported that 'I have now recovered from the shock but the burns are not healed yet. My nose, which was knocked almost flat between my eyes and a little to one side, is now back to its normal position ... My burns are not real serious; my right big toe and left ankle lightly burned, and also my right thumb and arm, but nothing to worry about.'

Meanwhile, the balance of air power continued to swing even further in favour of the RAF as the German airmen began to suffer from the serious logistical problems which were now affecting the entire German economy. The naval blockade had long prevented any significant seaborne importation of oil into Germany, and the dislocation in their Balkan supply brought about by Romania's entry into the war against the Central Powers in 1916 and her subsequent defeat in 1917 was now making itself felt directly. An armistice had been concluded with Romania on 9 December 1917, but, 'since Rumania's geographical situation made it impossible to extend German rule over her directly,' and 'the Rumanians resisted the ... heavy economic demands of Germany and her allies most obstinately,' a peace treaty which gave Germany a dominating influence over the production and development of Romanian oil was not signed until the first week in May 1918. Stock-piles were running low and the reorganization of the Romanian industry so as to provide an adequate flow of oil once more would take time.[101]

As early as March 1918 some sort of informal rationing scheme may have been introduced and 'At the beginning of June the monthly fuel quantity (of the German air force) was reduced to 7,000 tons. At the same time the High Command gave orders to avoid all unnecessary flights, above all to curtail photo reconnaissance; in the home area to use only Benzol ['ersatz' fuel] ... inspection tests were reduced to random checks.'[102] Fighter squadrons were rationed to 14,000 litres (3080 gallons) per month. The new Fokker D-VII fighters, which were issued to front-line squadrons from May onwards, had a consumption rate in excess of ten gallons per hour, and an airborne endurance limit of one-and-three-quarters hours, so that, from June on, the fighter squadrons were virtually limited to less than ten individual flights per day.* Skilled ground crew were being taken from the squadrons for service with other arms and the aircraft production stream was drying up, so that some German squadrons found that they must wait as long as three weeks for their replacements because additional aircraft of the requisite types were not available. All these logistical difficulties had their effect on German morale, which was only given a temporary boost by the introduction of the Fokker D-VII.[103]

This machine, which had been adopted as the standard German production fighter for 1918 after an open competition held in January in which most of the top German aces had participated, has often been described as the outstanding fighter aircraft of the First World War. The Allies thought it so good that the Armistice terms specifically ordered the surrender of all D-VIIs. Three versions were produced, but most effective was the 185-hp BMW-engined version. This aircraft had a better rate of climb and higher operational ceiling than either the Sopwith Camel, the SE5a, or the Sopwith 5F1 Dolphin which was just beginning to come into service with the RAF. It was not quite so fast as the British machines but exceptionally manoeuvrable above ten thousand feet and gave its pilots a significant edge in high-level combat, other things being equal.† But other things were rarely equal. Numbers and morale more than compensated for the technical superiority of the Fokker. As each RAF squadron came up against the D-VIIs, there were only a few bad days before the RAF pilots reasserted their psychological dominance and restored the *status quo*. The historian of 64 Squadron, flying SE5as out of Le Hameau,‡ recalled that 'During June and the first half of July we expended much petrol looking for Huns but they had disappeared from our front – apparently they were recalled to learn to fly Fokker biplanes. These appeared during the latter half of July and some fierce fighting took place. One Flight was practically wiped out in a week, 3 missing (2 dead), 1 died of wounds, 1 wounded; they got plenty of Fokkers but it left a gap.'[104]

This was the pattern of the early summer as Haig arranged his forces for the hammer blow at Amiens which he hoped would have the effect on the Germans that Ludendorff had intended his spring offensives to have on the Allies.

---

* In practice, according to W.R. Puglisi, the ration was not averaged out among all the pilots of a squadron, but was distributed mainly amongst those individual fliers who had proved most successful. Puglisi to Collishaw, 27 Oct. 1966, Raymond Collishaw Papers, DHist 78/132, 2-A, folder 14b. This suggests that most replacement pilots would have got very little operational flying experience even after reaching the front.

† For a detailed performance comparison see W.M. Lamberton, *Fighter Aircraft of the 1914–1918 War* (Letchworth, Herts. 1960).

‡ Canadian pilots flying with 64 Squadron at this time included W.J. Cockburn and W.C. Daniel (WIA 18 May 1918), both of Toronto, F.L. Gall of Montreal, B.N. Garrett of Toronto (POW 14 July 1918), G.W. Graham of Shuswap, BC (KIA 1 Nov. 1918), W.R. Henderson of St Catharines, Ont. (POW 25 July 1918), M.L. Howard of Cranbrook, BC (KIA 25 July 1918), H.G. Ross of Montreal (KIA 25 July 1918), and E.R. Tempest of Perdue, Sask. (KIA 25 July 1918).

17

Amiens

Amiens was important not solely because it inaugurated what became the allied victory campaign, but also because the battle itself was tactically innovative and set the pattern for the remainder of the war. However, despite its initial success, achieved by stressing the effective combination of infantry, cavalry, armour, and aircraft, at the operational level Amiens was still a flawed battle. Surprise permitted allied assault troops to break into the German defences and quickly seize assigned objectives, forcing enemy infantry and artillery to abandon their prepared positions. On the first day the attackers advanced some six to eight miles on a wide front; the disorganized Germans streamed eastwards, easy targets for the swarms of low-flying RAF aircraft that were in close support of the ground forces. Then, after a particularly successful first day, the attack ground to a halt, partly because allied commanders were confused about the extent and purpose of the operation. It was a symptom of this weakness that in the middle of the battle the role of the RAF squadrons was changed and they were unable to seal off the battlefield from German reinforcements.

When the Germans had been stopped at the Second Battle of the Marne it was apparent that Ludendorff had failed to achieve the decisive victory he had been seeking. Equally significant, there remained few replacements for the million casualties inflicted on his battered armies. In early August the enemy was able to muster 201 infantry divisions on the Western Front, 106 of which were considered by British Intelligence as unfit for battle. In comparison, the 206 allied divisions in the field were still being reinforced at the rate of 250,000 men every month as fresh American troops arrived to join the million in France. With German morale crumbling, the time was ripe for the Allies to take the offensive. French counterattacks in the Compiègne area began the process and early in July Sir Douglas Haig had issued instructions to his army commanders to prepare offensive plans in the north.

On 17 July Sir Henry Rawlinson, Commander of the British Fourth Army, submitted a proposal for a limited attack to push the Germans from the salient they had gained in the spring offensive, and from which their artillery threatened Amiens and the vital railway line connecting that city with Paris. His plan was developed from the initially successful Cambrai assault in the previous year and a smaller operation earlier in July, when Australians cleared the village of Hamel directly east of Amiens. In both, surprise had been obtained by replacing the customary prolonged preparatory bombardment with the striking power of massed tanks.

The Fourth Army's objective was the line of the old outer defences of Amiens, between Méricourt and Hangest, which was to be occupied and prepared as a new defence line. To enhance security Rawlinson wished to keep the attack solely a British operation, but Haig decided to enlarge its scope. He met with Foch on 24 July, and proposed a combined Anglo-French operation which would include the French First Army on Rawlinson's right. Foch agreed and *Général* Debeney's First Army was placed under Haig's command for the offensive. Although the aim of the attack – to disengage Amiens and its rail link with Paris – remained the same, the objective was now set some seven or eight miles to the east and south-east of the old Amiens defence line, towards Chaulnes and Roye. On 29 July Haig issued his operation order to Rawlinson and Debeney, directing that the line should be quickly seized and made secure. As soon as this was accomplished the French First Army, its right on the Avre, would press towards Roye, while the Fourth Army with its left on the Somme would continue the attack towards Chaulnes, the Roye-Amiens road forming the boundary between the two armies.

Haig met with Foch again on 3 August to discuss plans for the offensive and the latter, convinced that German morale was breaking, urged that the coming attack be exploited as fully as possible, suggesting that the final objective be set south and east of Chaulnes. Haig replied that he had named Ham, fifteen miles beyond Chaulnes and across the Somme, as his final objective. Two days later Haig met with Rawlinson and Debeney to confirm plans and emphasize the extended nature of the operation. Haig recorded that

I thought that the Fourth Army orders aimed too much at getting a *final* objective on the old Amiens defence line, and stopping counter-attacks on it. This is not far enough, in my opinion, if we succeed at the start in surprising the enemy. So I told Rawlinson (it had already been in my orders) to arrange to *advance as rapidly as possible* and capture the old Amiens line of defence ... and to put it into a state of defence; *but not to delay*; at once reserves must be pushed on to capture the line Chaulnes-Roye. The general direction of the advance is to be on Ham ... I said that the cavalry must keep in touch with the battle and *be prepared to pass through anywhere between the River Somme and the Roye-Amiens road*. Also that a cavalry brigade with a battery R.H.A. and some whippet tanks are to be placed under General Monash's orders ... for pursuit and to reap the fruits if we succeed ...[1]

Three additional British divisions were placed in reserve close behind the front to exploit any early success.

Despite Haig's personal intervention, it does not seem that his principal commanders fully understood the manner in which the forthcoming operation had been both modified and extended. The years of trench warfare had not prepared commanders and staffs for a quick change to mobile operations and the fact that changes were introduced very late in the planning process no doubt fostered some confusion. Moreover, the ultimate purpose of the offensive was stated in such general terms that commanders could easily place differing emphasis on either the set-piece battle at the beginning, or the exploitation which was expected to follow. Although in his meeting with Foch, Haig had specified that Ham was the final objective, his orders to Rawlinson and Debeney were considerably less precise, simply stating that after taking the Amiens defence line, 'The next object is to push forward in the general direction of the line Roye-Chaulnes *with the least possible delay*, thrusting the enemy back with determination in the general direction of Ham, and so facilitating the operations of the French from the front Noyon-Montdidier.' Nevertheless, Haig's emphasis was on the forward aspects of the plan; he considered that now 'it is probable that in the event of an initial success the battle will develop into one of considerable magnitude.'[2]

The primary emphasis in Rawlinson's Fourth Army Headquarters, however, was not on the exploitation phase but on the initial battle. Although Fourth Army Headquarters repeated Haig's orders, the successive enlargements which these incorporated were considered merely as 'minor modifications'* to Rawlinson's original plan. At least one of his corps commanders had a similar view. 'The objective of the Battle of Amiens,' in the mind of General Currie, commanding the Canadian Corps, 'was the old Amiens outer defence line, a position eight miles within the German lines on the morning of August 8.'[3] These differing views on the nature of the battle to be fought were to have an important effect upon its development.

For the attack General Rawlinson deployed the Canadian Corps on the right between the Roye-Amiens road and the Villers-Chaulnes rail line, the Australian Corps in the centre between the railway and the Somme, and III British Corps on the left between the Somme and the Ancre. Three Canadian, two Australian, and three British divisions were to mount the assault, supported by the massive firepower of almost 1400 field guns, 684 heavy artillery pieces, 324 heavy tanks, and ninety-six Whippets. There were another Canadian and two more Australian divisions in reserve. Four heavy tank battalions were allotted to each of the Canadian and Australian Corps, one to III Corps, and one was held in reserve. In addition, the Cavalry Corps, supported by two Whippet tank battalions, was placed under Rawlinson's command to assist the infantry assault and then drive forward to cut the German communications.[4]

The Allies were able to count on a local margin of superiority of about three to two over the Germans. The enemy, however, had more than twenty-five additional divisions in reserve in the north, some of which could be shifted quickly to the battlefront if needed. Forestalling the movement of the German reserves,

---

* This was the description of Major-General Sir Archibald Montgomery, Rawlinson's chief of staff, in *Story of the Fourth Army in the Battles of the Hundred Days, August 8th to November 11th 1918* (London 1918), 7, 11. Using Montgomery as his principal source, the British official historian, Sir James Edmonds, echoes this view, describing the final plans as differing 'only slightly from that suggested to Sir Douglas Haig by General Sir H. Rawlinson on the 5th July,' *Military Operations: France and Belgium, 1918*, IV (London 1947), 3. On the other hand, it was the view of the then Wing Commander J.C. Slessor in *Air Power and Armies* (London 1936), 150, that the changes promised 'the most far-reaching results and aiming at a penetration little inferior in depth and importance to the great German break-through on the Fifth Army front, in the previous March.'

therefore, was most important to the success of the offensive. Security was vital, and in the preparatory stages the allied logistical buildup had to be carefully concealed. It was no easy matter to mask the movement of almost three hundred special trains which were required in addition to normal supply runs. The movement of the Canadian Corps from its location on the British First Army front to its assault positions with Fourth Army was particularly difficult, Rawlinson's headquarters taking great pains to stage an elaborate deception to maintain security.[5]

On 1 August General Salmond submitted proposals to Haig for the employment of the air force. In the preparatory phase the RAF's principal task was to help maintain security for the forthcoming operation. This meant preventing German reconnaissance of the allied positions, as well as patrolling behind the Fourth Army front in order to report on any abnormal movement which might also be visible to the enemy. Bad flying weather during the first week of August, however, greatly restricted German air reconnaissance and even when they were able to fly, German pilots and observers saw little to arouse their suspicions. They reported active traffic behind Fourth Army lines on 1 August but considered it normal. When the weather cleared during the late afternoon of 7 August German reconnaissance aircraft took to the air but RAF interference was so effective that the enemy observed nothing of significance. German airmen reported heavy flying activity at the Bertangles and Bovelles airfields on the 7th, 'But any positive indication that a large scale attack against the front of the German Second Army was being prepared or was immediately at hand, did not come to hand.'[6]

Eight hundred British aircraft were made available to support the ground attack. Assembling such a force required considerable redeployment and Salmond instituted his own deception plan, stepping up patrols elsewhere along the First and Fifth Army fronts while preventing any undue air or communications activity in the area of the Fourth Army. The formation most immediately involved, V Brigade, was placed at the disposal of Fourth Army, and substantially reinforced for the attack. No 5 Squadron,* which had worked previously with the Canadian Corps, was moved with it from the First Army to join the five other corps squadrons in V Brigade's 15 Wing. Three additional Camel squadrons were transferred to 22 (Army) Wing of V Brigade to join the five fighter, one fighter reconnaissance, one day- and one night-bomber squadrons already there. Under the direct command of RAF headquarters and supporting the attack were sixteen squadrons of IX Brigade, seven of III Brigade, and one each from I and X Brigades. IX Brigade, which formed the GHQ reserve, was moved from the Reims front

---

* The squadron contained fourteen Canadian pilots: G.I. Carr, address unknown, E.P. Eveleigh of Sussex, NB, L.H. Eyres of Brandon, Man. (WIA 27 Sept. 1918, POW 29 Oct. 1918), W.T. Fothergill, address unknown (KIA 20 Aug. 1918), C.F. Galbraith from Manitoba (WIA 15 Sept. 1918, POW 16 Sept. 1918), N. Goudie of Kamloops, BC, C.F. Grant of Bella Coola, BC (KIA 10 Aug. 1918). R.W. Jackson of Ilderton, Ont., W.C. Lynch of Port Robinson, Ont., L. Oertling, address unknown (KIA 8 Aug. 1918), G.W.H. Parlee of Stewiacke, NS (KIA 20 Aug. 1918), A.C. Pollard of Victoria, E. Shamper of Kingston, Ont., and W.H. Webber, address unknown (MIA 10 Aug. 1918).

where it had been flying in support of the French. For security purposes squadron moves were delayed until just before the attack and unit markings were switched to prevent accurate identification.

By the eve of the battle the available air support comprised:[7]

V BRIGADE		SQUADRON	AIRCRAFT
15 (Corps) Wing	Corps Squadron	No 3 AFC	RE8
		No 5	RE8
		No 6	RE8
		No 8	AW
		No 9	RE8
		No 35	AW
22 (Army) Wing	Fighter Squadron	No 23	Dolphin
		No 24	SE5a
		No 41	SE5a
		No 65	Camel
		No 80	Camel
		No 84	SE5a
		No 201	Camel
		No 209	Camel
	Fighter-Reconnaissance	No 48	Bristol Fighter
	Day Bomber	No 205	DH4
	Night Bomber	No 101	FE2b
IX (HQ) BRIGADE	Fighter Squadron	No 1	SE5a
		No 32	SE5a
		No 43	Camel
		No 54	Camel
		No 73	Camel
		No 151	Camel (night fighter)
	Day Bomber	No 27	DH9
		No 49	DH9
		No 98	DH9
		No 107	DH9
	Night Bomber	No 58	FE2b
		No 83	FE2b
		No 207	Handley Page
		No 215	Handley Page
	Fighter-Reconnaissance	No 25	DH4
		No 62	Bristol Fighter

III BRIGADE		SQUADRON	AIRCRAFT
	Fighter Squadron	No 3	Camel
		No 56	SE5a
		No 60	SE5a
		No 87	Dolphin
	Fighter-Reconnaissance	No 11	Bristol Fighter
	Day Bomber	No 57	DH4
	Night Bomber	No 102	FE2b
I BRIGADE	Day Bomber	No 18	DH4
X BRIGADE	Day Bomber	No 103	DH9

The French also reinforced their air arm for the offensive. The *Division aérienne*, which had a general reserve function similar to that of IX Brigade, was placed under the command of *Général* Debeney and its machines increased French air strength to about 1025 aircraft.*[8] The allied total of more than 1800 fighting aircraft vastly out-numbered those available to the Germans. The British official history states that there were 365 aircraft, of which only 140 were fighters, with German armies on the front opposing the allied forces. German accounts of their air strength indicate an even smaller total. On the eve of the battle there were only 106 serviceable aircraft available, the others having been withdrawn for rest after uninterrupted combat duty since March. The apparent result was overwhelming allied air superiority. The Allies had already concentrated their squadrons, however, while the bulk of the German air force was still located in the Champagne area. There, with the German Sixth and Seventh Armies, were about 850 aircraft, including 430 single-seater fighters, which could easily and quickly be shifted to the Amiens battlefield.[9]

The RAF's overriding concern, once the battle had begun, was to assist the ground attack. More than in any previous battle of the war, Amiens was to feature planned co-operation of the closest kind between the air and ground forces. Besides hindering German air reconnaissance, the RAF was required to fly contact patrols with infantry, cavalry, and tanks, co-ordinate artillery shoots, provide an unprecedented degree of close ground support for the assault troops, neutralize enemy aircraft, and interdict the battlefield.

General Salmond believed that bombing the German airfields would greatly diminish the effectiveness of the enemy's air force. The first targets for his bombers, therefore, were the enemy aerodromes at St Christ, Ennemain, Bray

---

* H.A. Jones, *The War in the Air: being the Story of the Part played in the Great War by the Royal Air Force*, VI (London 1937), 435, gives a figure of 1104.

station, and Moislains, which would be attacked at daybreak at low level. Only in the evening, if surprise had been achieved, would enemy ground reserves begin to join the battle. Then the bombers were to switch their efforts to the outlying centres through which German reserves might be expected to flow. The main targets were the railway stations at Peronne, Chaulnes, Marchelepot, Villers-Carbonnel, and Etricourt. After dark the night bombers would take over, continuing the attacks on the rail centres, as well as on billets and road and rail movement. The Amiens-St Quentin road was to receive particular attention between Foucaucourt and Mons-en-Chausée and Peronne and Cambrai. Meanwhile the fighter squadrons of IX and III Brigades were ordered to 'hold the ring' by flying high offensive patrols to protect the low-flying aircraft of V Brigade which would be working in direct support of the ground troops.[10]

The brigade commander, Brigadier-General L.E.O. Charlton, allotted his six corps squadrons to the attacking Canadian, Australian, III British, Cavalry, and Tank Corps and one was assigned to resupply ammunition to machine-gun detachments of the Australian and III British Corps. The squadrons were responsible for their usual duties of ground co-operation and artillery co-ordination and, in addition, 5 and 9 Squadrons were to lay smoke screens at selected points on the Australian and Canadian fronts. Special markings for the corps machines were devised to facilitate identification and a scheme of signals was arranged between aircraft and tanks. V Brigade's fighter squadrons in 22 Wing, similarly assigned to specific attacking formations, provided additional ground support. For control purposes the front was divided into Northern, Central, and Southern Sectors corresponding with the corps boundaries. Nos 80 and 48 Squadrons were assigned the Northern Sector, 201, 84, and 41 Squadrons the Central and 209, 23 and 24 Squadrons the Southern Sector. No 65 Squadron was allocated to the Cavalry and one flight of 48 Squadron was detailed to provide low-altitude reconnaissance of the front. V Brigade's day bomber squadron, No 205, was assigned the German aerodrome at Bouvincourt as its target for a dawn attack.[11]

The command arrangements for the air battle were not the most effective. Both Salmond and Charlton were directly involved, the latter under command of the Fourth Army, the former responsible for the operational direction of IX Brigade, as well as the additional supporting squadrons made available from I, III, and X Brigades. Salmond was also given authority by GHQ to deal directly with General Rawlinson on matters pertaining to the battle. Unfortunately, it is not possible to trace how and where the lines of command crossed, or to describe precisely how they functioned in practice, because most of the staff work was conducted verbally. By this time staff officers apparently believed they had mastered procedures to an extent that made written orders largely unnecessary. The appointment of an overall air commander for the battle might have produced a clearer conception of the RAF's role. As it was, a primary operational objective for the air arm was never clearly defined on paper and confusion resulted. Like General Currie, Charlton assumed that the attack was a limited one and he designed his plan accordingly, for a one-day battle only.[12]

Charlton defined the strategic objective of the attack simply: to disengage Amiens and its rail network, this to be achieved by seizing the Amiens defence line. As he saw it, the task of his squadrons was 'not only to help the infantry directly to their blue line objective, [the old Amiens defence line] but to help every other arm as well, Cavalry, Artillery, and Tanks, to help the infantry.' Ironically, at the same time that Charlton was limiting the scope of the attack, Haig was pressing his ground commanders to prepare for a vigorous pursuit beyond the initial objective, a task which the air forces were admirably equipped to support. Charlton was either not informed of the changes made to the original plan or, like others in Fourth Army, remained unaware of their significance. Equally important, only passing reference to air operations was made in army orders and these lacked any clear definition of the specific objectives which the RAF was expected to attain. Consequently, while his squadrons were assigned tasks for 8 August, their employment on subsequent days, when a sustained mobile battle might have been expected, was not made clear.[13]

Low clouds and driving rain made flying extremely hazardous during the night of 7–8 August. Nevertheless, two pilots in 207 Squadron, Captains G.A. Flavelle of Lindsay, Ont., and W.J. Peace of Hamilton,* managed after several attempts to get their Handley Page bombers off the ground. Flying through the black night on compass heading at dangerously low levels they reached the lines where they flew an exhausting three-hour patrol to drown out the noise of British tanks being assembled for the attack, an effort which won them both Distinguished Flying Crosses.[14] By 0330 hrs other aircraft were in the air. Fifty minutes later a deafening artillery barrage opened up and the Fourth Army's assaulting infantry and tanks moved across their start line. The Germans were taken completely by surprise.

The effect of this surprise assault was enhanced in the early stages by the inevitable heavy ground mist which masked the forward movement of tanks and infantry. The same mist, however, diminished the effectiveness of the air support, just as it had done for the Germans in March. The fourteen bombers of 27 Squadron escorted by Bristol Fighters of 62 Squadron were unable to find their primary target, the enemy aerodrome at St Christ. Instead they dropped their 25-lb bombs in the area of Peronne. No 98 Squadron, escorted by twelve Camels of 43 Squadron, was switched to St Christ when its original target at Ennemain was discovered to be unoccupied. It managed to find the aerodrome, but by then the Germans had dispersed their machines and the squadron dropped its bombs with little effect on the hangars and landing field.[15]

Neither 98 nor 43 Squadron met any opposition, but in its attack on the aerodrome at Moislains 57 Squadron did come under attack. Second Lieutenant H.S. Musgrove of Canmore, Alta, and Lieutenant J.F.D. Tanqueray from British Columbia each claimed an enemy aircraft driven down as the objective was successfully bombed from low altitude, but Lieutenant L.L. Brown, from Westmorland Point, NB, was shot down and later reported a prisoner of war.† Other

---

* Other Canadians with 207 Squadron included R.K. Brydon of Toronto and J.H. Johnson of Kenora, Ont.

† Other Canadians with 57 Squadron included E.M. Coles of Vancouver, J.B. Cunningham of Ottawa (KIA 22 Aug. 1918), L.K. Devitt of Brougham, Ont., W.H. Kilbourne of Winnipeg (POW 16 Aug. 1918), J.A. Mackay of Oakville, Ont., F.G. Pym from Alberta, J.L. Standish of Lacombe, Alta, and O.M.I. Turnbull of Galt, Ont. (KIA 21 Sept. 1918).

squadrons had mixed results. No 49 Squadron dropped almost one hundred bombs on Bray station; 107 Squadron caused some damage among the houses and dumps in Harbonnières village and silenced some anti-aircraft guns which fired at them; 205 Squadron found targets at Bouvincourt aerodrome and the station at Chaulnes. The morning mist over many targets not only limited the effectiveness of their bombing, but also prevented accurate assessment of bombing damage.[16]

Until the mist lifted, at around 0900 hrs, the corps machines were unable to observe neutralizing fire, nor could they effectively establish their contact patrols. However, once visibility improved the artillery patrol aircraft performed valuable service. The infantry and tanks, pressing the initial assault with great speed, quickly went beyond the range of their supporting artillery. The guns had to leap-frog forward to maintain continuous support, but a scheme had been devised which enabled the air patrols to keep in direct touch with the guns during the advance. Information written on strips of white canvas placed on the ground, identifying the battery, the number of guns in action, and the amount of available ammunition, was relayed by message-dropping patrol aircraft to the artillery commanders farther back, who were then in a position to co-ordinate the fire and movement of the guns. This supplemented the use of wireless to range and correct shoots on previously selected targets and effective support was maintained throughout. When the assault troops overran the enemy front line they also forced the Germans to abandon their prepared artillery positions for new ones, often visible only from the air. Neutralizing fire calls from the patrol aircraft proved the best means of engaging these new, unregistered gun positions. In addition, air photographs, developed quickly and then passed to artillery commanders, enabled counter-bombardment staffs to plot new tasks for the guns.[17]

Despite the fog, 5 Squadron, working with the Canadian Corps, sent up four of their RE8s at 0400 hrs. The pilots, by flying at very low altitudes, were able to locate some of the enemy whom they bombed and machine-gunned. Ground fire was heavy and, by the time the early patrols were relieved at about 0730 hrs, the battle had become extremely confused. Both allied and German troops were on the move in the open and hundreds of aircraft filled the air. Contact patrols had much difficulty in locating the front positions of their own men because of the fluid nature of the fighting. The troops were reluctant to use Very flares to mark their positions because that marked them for the enemy as well.* Thus, contact patrol aircraft often found allied troops by a process of elimination, first being fired upon from German-held positions and then circling back until they could identify their own forces. To quicken their response time 5, 6, and 9 Squadrons worked out of an advanced landing field at the old Amiens drill ground where the aircraft picked up ammunition, bombs, and fuel. The advanced field was later shifted forward to Caix as the front moved east.[18]

---

* Allied aircraft also found it easy to locate enemy positions when German units used flares to identify themselves to GAF machines. HQ RAF, 'Notes on Corps Squadrons Work on the First and Third Army Fronts during Recent Operations,' 14 Sept. 1918, Air 1/725/97/2; 'No. 5 Squadron Work under Command of Major C.H. Gardner from July 18 to November 11th 1918,' Air 1/1313/204/13/96

Besides their primary tasks of co-ordinating artillery fire and contact patrolling, the corps squadrons also were called upon to lay smoke screens and attack targets of opportunity with their 25-lb bombs and machine-guns. Captain N. Goudie of Kamloops, BC, and his observer, flying an RE8 of 5 Squadron, forced about one hundred German troops, massed in a sunken road and holding up the advance, to surrender by keeping them under continuous machine-gun fire. They then kept the Germans under observation until infantry could collect them. Goudie was awarded the Distinguished Flying Cross. So was another Canadian in the squadron, Captain C.F. Galbraith from Manitoba, for outstanding work in attacking the enemy, reporting important information, and taking low-level photographs.[19]

No 8 Squadron* was responsible for developing aircraft-tank co-operation for the battle at Amiens. Commanded by Major T.L. Leigh-Mallory, the squadron had been attached to the Tank Corps on 1 July and immediately began a period of intensive training. Flights were assigned to specific tank units and tank officers were taken up in the air for familiarization flights, while pilots and observers were introduced to the close confines of the tanks. During the battle for Hamel in July, 'C' Flight had operated with the tanks and both units gained valuable battle experience. Although they had held trials with wireless, it was not possible to provide direct radio communication with the tanks before 8 August. Instead, reliance was placed upon a system of directional signals involving variously shaped discs swung out from the fuselage on iron rods. Theoretically they were visible to about four thousand feet, but in the smoke and heat of battle tank crews were not always able to see them. It was extraordinarily difficult to see anything at all from the interior of a First World War tank, much less an aeroplane which would only be in the field of vision for a few seconds at the most and whose sound was completely drowned out by the noise of the tank engine. The aircraft were able to send wireless information to the tank unit headquarters and assist the tanks' forward movement by bombing and machine-gunning enemy strong points.[20]

Pilots and observers, however, had great difficulty in locating German anti-tank guns, and, as allied tank casualties on 8 August showed, protection from these guns was vitally important. By the morning of the 9th only 145 tanks (of 415) remained fit for action. Brigadier-General Charlton subsequently stated on 14 August that it was 'not too much to say that without the Anti-Tank gun the advance of our line would be irresistible.'[21] Charlton ordered that offensive action against enemy anti-tank gunners be given the highest priority by both corps and fighter aircraft. Smoke screens seem to have been the most effective means of controlling the anti-tank guns, as the Germans themselves commented: 'British low-flying planes rendered valuable service to their own tank units by laying smoke screens between advancing tank units and strongly defended German points of resistance.'[22]

---

* Canadians with 8 Squadron included J.E. Cave from British Columbia (KIA 14 Aug. 1918), A. Grundy of Merritt, BC, J.R.R.G. McCallum of Toronto (KIA 23 Aug. 1918), C.W. Prynne of Calgary, W.F.R. Robinson of Davidson, Sask. (MIA 24 Sept. 1918), and F.A. Whittall of Montreal.

Inadequate equipment along with low clouds and German opposition made liaison extremely difficult in such fluid conditions. The battle was a valuable testing-ground for air-ground co-operation. Flares and panels were helpful, but the most important factor remained the skill and initiative of individual pilots. During the confusion of the ground battle they had to talk to the ground troops as best they could by dropping messages, landing in open fields, and in various other ways. Lieutenant W.C. Lambert, an American who had joined the RFC in Toronto, was flying close support missions with 24 Squadron on the morning of 8 August when he spotted a column of British motor transport, accompanied by a light tank, moving forward. As Lambert recalled the scene:

At 200 feet, I fly over the road to see what might be down there ... I catch a reflection from some sort of metallic object. What is it? Everything seems too quiet. Back on my stick and up to 300 feet. I make a fast 180 degree turn, head back to our convoy and approach them at 50 feet. I rock my wings and kick my rudders to attract their attention. The wind almost tears my left arm off as I try to wave them to a stop but they continue to roll forward. I must stop that convoy until I can find out what is in front of them! Then a thought strikes me ...

I head straight across the bows of the leader with my wheels almost on the ground and fire a short burst about 50 feet ahead of him. This does the trick and they come to a dead stop ... Now to find out what is in that hedge. My head is out to the left with my eyes peering into the hedge. Within seconds I see the strangest gun. A contraption like a very large rifle ... I had heard of their 'Anti-tank' gun. This must be one of them and in good place to ambush our convoy ... pulling ... up to about 300 feet, I turn and come in on the gun, pressing the button for both guns. One of the men has disappeared and the other is preparing to leave, when my burst changes his mind. My bullets strike all over their gun. I go around for another look. No activity. The remaining body is sprawled, head down, in a sort of a hole behind the gun.[23]

Scouts were based at advanced flying fields from which they could reach the front quickly. When a patrolling corps machine spotted a likely target it would fly to the advanced field and lead the fighters to the enemy position. Nos 6 and 9 Squadrons employed this technique on two occasions, on one of which cavalry was able to capture Le Quesnel Wood after it had been held up for a time by strong German resistance. Having scouts on call at advanced fields also enabled them to be directed to enemy strong points indicated by artillery fire requests from the corps machines.[24]

The principal danger to the six corps squadrons during the battle was from ground fire, most of the thirty-one casualties they suffered between 8 and 11 August coming from that source. Air attacks could not be discounted, however. Late in the morning of the 8th Lieutenant J.R.R.G. McCallum of Toronto, with 8 Squadron, was attacked by five enemy scouts during a tank contact patrol. His observer was badly wounded, and McCallum made a forced landing, striking a shell hole, completely wrecking his aircraft. Australian infantry found them and brought both back to safety. Three Canadians with 5 Squadron were killed: Lieutenant L. Oertling, address unknown, on 8 August and Second Lieutenants C.F. Grant of Bella Coola, BC, and W.H. Webber, address unknown, on 10 August.*[25]

The fighter squadrons of 22 Wing had the major responsibility for providing close ground support for the attack. As soon as the morning fog cleared their fighters were sent out in pairs at half-hour intervals to attack enemy targets with their machine-guns and 25-lb bombs. In the confusion caused by the surprise and ferocity of the initial assault and with an open mandate to hit any target which presented itself, the fighters attacked enemy infantry, guns, transport, ammunition dumps, and trains from near ground level. 'Our planes seemed like things possessed ...' a member of the Canadian Corps commented. 'The air was thick with them, and never an enemy plane to be seen.' In the air continuously, except for refuelling and rearming stops at advanced aerodromes, the fighter squadrons were able to exert tremendous pressure on the Germans and there was 'no question but that the action of the low-flying fighters was a factor of immense importance in the overwhelming success of the initial attack ...'[26]

The efforts of 24 Squadron, flying SE5as in support of the Canadian Corps, were perhaps typical. On 8 August Lieutenant W.C. Sterling, address unknown, dropped four 25-lb bombs on a locomotive which was leaving the village of Rosières. He then attacked horse transport in the area with machine-gun fire, 'piling up the leaders and halting the whole lot.' Lieutenant C.M. Farrell of Regina dropped his bombs on an ammunition dump at Foucaucourt and later attacked a train and other targets in the area of Marcelcave. Farrell's fourth sortie of the day was with a patrol of five aircraft, including Lieutenant E.P. Crossen of Sunderland, Ont. They were attacked by nine Fokker biplanes near Lihons. In the resulting *mêlée* Crossen 'was driven down and had a good deal of indecisive fighting' and Farrell was shot down. Farrell was able to return to flying operations on 10 August and was subsequently awarded the DFC for his work on the 8th. Second Lieutenant F.E. Beauchamp of Meyronne, Sask., was not so lucky; forced down that day, he was taken prisoner.[27]

Pilots in other squadrons had similar experiences. Lieutenant J.L.M. White of Halifax was leading a formation of 65 Squadron which was attacked by eight Fokkers. The Camels turned west and climbed, but on meeting another flight of 65 Squadron, White led the combined force back against the enemy. He promptly shot one Fokker down and then began to chase another west. The whole formation got on the tail of the enemy machine and forced it to land behind British lines.[28] Partly for their efforts during the day White was awarded a Bar to his DFC and Captain A.A. Leitch of High River, Alta, and Lieutenant J. MacLennan of Whitehorse received DFCs.†

Meanwhile, the action over the Australian sector was equally hectic. The pilots of 41 Squadron, twelve of whom were Canadian, were in continuous action. At

---

* The three were the only Canadian fatalities with the corps squadrons during the battle. RAF war diary, 8–11 Aug. 1918, Air 1/1187/204/5/2595
† Leitch had already received the MC. MacLennan is believed to be the only recipient of a First World War DFC to fly on active operations with the RCAF in the Second World War.

noon Captain F.O. Soden, from New Brunswick,* shot down in flames a bright yellow biplane which had just forced down a British machine. The other SE5a squadron in the area, No 84, attacked enemy kite balloons, bombed troops and transport, and provided other close support. Captain R. Manzer bombed enemy troops northeast of Proyart and then began to strafe them until he was hit by ground fire and forced to land near the German trenches. He was taken prisoner. Lieutenants C.F. Falkenberg of Quebec City and A.C. Lobley of Winnipeg each carried out three missions bombing and strafing the enemy trenches and transport.[†] Despite such a high rate of activity in this very dangerous low-level work, 41 and 65 Squadrons lost only three pilots on the 8th.[29]

There were seven Canadians flying Camels with 201 Squadron in the Australian sector. Lieutenant N.O.M. Foggo of Vernon, BC, was forced down over enemy territory and made a prisoner on the 8th. Lieutenant M.S. Misener of Toronto[‡] successfully attacked an inviting target – three trains south of Harbonnières, one of which might have carried the long-range railway gun which had been used by the Germans to bombard Amiens. Later, Misener drove off a group of enemy troops attacking a downed aircraft which had landed in no-man's land. His own aircraft was so badly riddled with shrapnel that it was written off after he landed. Misener was killed in action the next day. On the 9th Lieutenant J.M. Mackay of Vancouver was attacked from behind while hotly pursuing a Fokker and, with his aircraft badly damaged, was forced to land in the midst of the battle. As he made a dash for safety he met a British tank into which he climbed. When he realized that the tank was about to go into action, however, he wisely withdrew and made his own way back under heavy machine-gun fire.[30]

The surprise and ferocity of the allied assault on 8 August cracked the crust of the enemy defences. Within a few hours seven German divisions had been badly battered. The first British objective, the Demuin-Marcelcave-Cerisy-Morlancourt line, was quickly reached and while the leading troops paused, the immediate reserves with cavalry and tanks passed through to press the advance. By dusk an advance of six to eight miles had been achieved and the Amiens defences had been taken except for Le Quesnel in the south, which was captured before dawn the next day. The initial attack had been a classic example of inter-arms co-operation, and in it the air arm had played a significant part.

The Allies' very success also presented the possibility of opening up a wider battlefield where German disorder could be exploited to the full. From about noon on the 8th the enemy situation seemed precarious. The Allies dominated the air,

---

* Other Canadians with the squadron included W.G. Claxton (POW 17 Aug. 1918), and F.W. Douglas (KIA 12 Aug. 1918), both of Toronto, W.J. Gillespie of Daysland, Alta, A. Goby of Avonlea, Sask., J.A. Gordon of Wallaceburg, Ont. (KIA 12 Aug. 1918), W.E. Huxtable of Victoria, F.W.H. Martin of Regina (KIA 9 Aug. 1918), F.R. McCall of Calgary, W.E. Shields of Lipton, Sask., F.B.K. Sleightholm of Toronto, and H.C. Telfer of Westmount, Que. (POW 28 Sept. 1918).

† Other Canadians with 84 Squadron included H.C. Anderson of Winnipeg, D. Carruthers of Kingston, Ont., J.A. Jackson of Dunnville, Ont., and R. Manzer of Oshawa, Ont.

‡ The other Canadians in 201 Squadron were W.A.W. Carter of Fredericton, C.E. Hill of Collingwood, Ont., W.A. Johnston of Barrie, Ont. (POW 14 Sept. 1918), and F.T.S. Sehl of Victoria.

and the bulk of the German defenders had been forced either to surrender or fall back in headlong retreat towards safety over the Somme. It seemed that if the momentum of the assault could be maintained, and if the escape routes across the Somme could be blocked, the whole of the German force west of the river might be destroyed. The break-in had been an unqualified success; the break-out was at hand.

The Australian official historian has summed up the problem at the end of the first day: 'everyone's thoughts turned to what had been done rather than to the next step.'[31] Once the first day's objectives had been seized, the confusion within the allied command about the scope and ultimate purpose of the operation caused the attack to slow down and then grind to a halt. Sir Arthur Currie, commanding the Canadian Corps, later recalled that no one really expected that the old Amiens Line would be taken on the first day and, when it was, there was no clear idea of what to do next: 'I also know that senior staff officers hurried up from GHQ to see me and to ask what I thought should be done. They indicated quite plainly that the success had gone far beyond expectations and that no one seemed to know just what to do. I replied in the Canadian vernacular: "The going seems good: let's go on!!"'[32] When the attacks finally were resumed along the front they were inadequately co-ordinated and lacked the vigour and momentum of the initial assault.

The British estimate of a ten-to-twelve-hour delay before the enemy would be able to reinforce his front-line troops proved to be too optimistic. Ludendorff claimed that 'By the early hours of the forenoon of August 8th I had already gained a complete impression of the situation.' He immediately ordered reinforcements forward. Remnants of the seven battered divisions which had borne the brunt of the morning's attack, along with the four others still in relatively good shape, began to receive help from the neighbouring Eighteenth and Ninth Armies as well as from Crown Prince Rupprecht's Army Group in the north. Elements of five fresh divisions joined the battle during the day and on the 9th parts of six more began to arrive.[33]

The air commanders of all the German armies had previously made arrangements to reinforce immediately any sector which came under attack and by noon on the first day of battle there were fifty-seven machines employed on army co-operation duty; eighty-six fighter, nineteen ground attack, and sixteen bomber aircraft had been made available to the Second Army from nearby fronts. During the afternoon entire wings and groups began to arrive, including the Richthofen *Jagdgeschwader*, now commanded by *Hauptmann* Herman Goering, who was away at the time, leaving the unit in charge of *Leutnant* Lothar von Richthofen, the younger brother of Manfred. Goering's wing, made up of four fighter *Staffeln*, moved into the aerodromes at Ennemain and St Christ and was operational by 1630 hrs. In all, by the evening of 8 August, 294 additional machines, including thirty-four night bombers, had been assigned to support the German Second Army.[34] Of this total, thirty-six fighters were not transferred to the Second Army, but operated over the battlefield from their bases in neighbouring army areas.

The key to sealing off the battlefield appeared to be the obstacle of the Somme and the interdiction of its numerous crossings. In the sector which contained the fighting eleven different road and rail bridges provided access to or from the battle.

From Amiens the Somme twisted eastwards and was bridged at Bray, Cappy, Eclusier, and Feuillères before swinging south through Peronne, Brie, St Christ, Falvy, Bethencourt, Voyennes, and Offey. An extremely tempting target thus presented itself to allied commanders. If the RAF could destroy the bridges the enemy would be trapped in a pocket enclosed on two sides by the river and a local retreat might be transformed into a full-scale disaster for the shaken Germans. The possibility was discussed by allied commanders in a number of telephone conversations on the 8th and, around noon, General Salmond cancelled all existing bombing plans and ordered that every effort be directed against the Somme bridges. The bombers and fighters of IX Brigade, supported by other available bomber squadrons, were to attack 'until the bridges are destroyed.'[35]

The airfields where the bulk of the German air strength was concentrated – Moislains, Ennemain, and Foreste – were all within five miles of the southern Somme bridges which were the principal targets of 9 Wing. During the afternoon of the 8th the protection of the bridges became the principal object of the German air arm. The result was an exceptionally intensive air battle and RAF casualties began to mount.[36]

The first attack on the bridge at Brie, which carried the main Amiens-St Quentin road, was made during the early afternoon of the 8th in the middle of a driving rainstorm. Eight DH9s of 107 Squadron and eleven Camels of 54 Squadron attempted to drop their bombs on the bridge. No direct hits were recorded and each unit lost one aircraft while returning. Later that afternoon Captain W.H. Dore of Arichat, NS,* led another attack on Brie by the same squadrons; this time they reported that they had inflicted some damage near the middle of the bridge. A third bombing attack was made on Brie in the evening by eight day bombers of 205 Squadron. Sixteen 112-lb bombs were dropped from 12,000–14,000 feet and, although a direct hit was claimed, clouds prevented close observation so that no confirmation was possible. Another flight attacked the bridge at St Christ through a gap in the clouds but, again, no hits were recorded. Seven German scouts attacked this formation as it was returning; when one was shot down in flames, however, the others left. A final raid on St Christ was carried out by four Camels of 54 Squadron. They dropped twenty 25-lb bombs from 7000 feet. German fighters had intercepted all the raids and shot down four Camels and one DH9.[37]

DH9 bombers of 98 Squadron, accompanied by the Camel and SE5a fighters of 1 and 43 Squadrons, mounted three raids against the road and rail bridges at Peronne. Sergeant E.R. MacDonald of Matheson, Ont., and his pilot claimed a direct hit on the northern end of the railway bridge on the second attack but no

---

* Dore was a flight commander in 107 Squadron. Other Canadians with the squadron included A.W.H. Arundell of Winnipeg, F.M. Carter of Orillia, Ont., S.L. Dunlop of Ottawa, J.H. Grahame of Stony Mountain, Man., A.B. Holden of Victoria, F.C. King of Ottawa, F. Player of Moose Jaw, Sask. (KIA 4 Sept. 1918), J.V. Turner of Brockville, Ont., and P. Willis of Calgary (MIA 9 Aug. 1918). Canadians in 54 Squadron were H.R. Abey of Kaslo, BC (POW 2 Nov. 1918), A.H. Belliveau of Fredericton (POW 27 Aug. 1918), A.S. Compton of Toronto, J.V. Dallin of Peterborough, Ont., H.B. Lockwood of Long Branch, Ont., E.J. Salter of Mimico, Ont., G.M. Saunders of Toronto, and R.E. Taylor, address unknown (POW 8 Aug. 1918). In 205 Squadron were W.B. Elliot of St Catharines, Ont., and F.O. MacDonald of Penticton, BC.

additional hits were reported by the bombers on the other raids. The attackers met opposition on all three occasions. On one, McDonald fired a short burst at a Pfalz scout before his gun jammed. He fired a Very light flare at the German to keep him at bay while clearing his weapon, and then shot him down. Another observer, Second Lieutenant N.C. McDonald of Bluevale, Ont., was credited with a Halberstadt two-seater, while a third, Captain G.H. Gillis of Halifax, claimed a Fokker triplane. Captain F.G. Powell of Toronto was lost.*[38]

The bridges in the southern sector, at Bethencourt and Voyennes, were allotted to 9 Wing. Bethencourt was attacked twice in the afternoon by 49 and 32 Squadrons. In the first attack ten DH9s and twelve SE5as took off shortly after 1400 hrs, but the formations were separated by enemy fighters so that six of the bombers, prevented from reaching their objective, dropped their bombs on various other targets in the area. Two DH9s were shot down. During a second attempt seven bombers were attacked by ten Fokker biplanes as they were diving on the bridge from a thousand feet. Another DH9 was lost. As dusk fell the bridge at Bethencourt still stood, and the enemy was reported to be building a footbridge one kilometer to the north.[39]

The DH9s of 27 Squadron and the Camels of 73 Squadron were ordered to destroy the bridge at Voyennes. In their first raid six bombers attacked the bridge from under five hundred feet, claiming one direct hit. Six others attacked the railway bridges at Pithon and Offoy from a similar height; one bomber was shot down. At the same time ten of the fighters, including six flown by Canadian pilots, were attacked by eight enemy machines and two Camels were lost, one of them being that of Lieutenant G.W. Gorman of Edmonton. Another attempt on the Voyennes bridge was made late in the afternoon, but the DH9s were attacked by enemy fighters on the way in, and the formation split up. The bomber pilots were prevented from coming in low over the target, one being chased back to the lines while another was shot down, and the ten 112-lb bombs that the squadron dropped were not seen to do any damage. Eight Camels of 73 Squadron, five flown by Canadians, met little opposition over the target but one enemy two-seater was claimed near Nesle by Lieutenant E.J. Lussier of Medicine Hat, Alta,† and two other pilots. Their light bombs also failed to hit the bridge.[40]

During the same afternoon the original night operation order for 8–9 August was cancelled. The new order confirmed Salmond's telephoned instruction that it was 'of the first importance that the bridges over the river Somme should be destroyed behind the retreating enemy.' In accordance with this directive fifty

---

* Other Canadians with 98 Squadron included J.M. Brown of Vancouver, H.J. Fox of Toronto, and I.V. Lawrence of Kingston, Ont.

† Lussier was credited with seven enemy aircraft during the operation, three of them in one day, and was awarded the DFC. Other Canadians with 73 Squadron included E. Barker of Newboro', Ont., W.A. Brett of Dugald, Man. (KIA 21 Sept. 1918), G.C.L. Carr-Harris of Kingston, Ont., S.A. Dawson of Saint John, NB (KIA 10 Aug. 1918), J.H. Drewry of Victoria, H.V. Fellowes of Grimsby Beach, Ont. (POW 1 Oct. 1918), W.H. Hubbard of Toronto, O.T. Moran of Winnipeg, D.B. Sinclair of London, Ont. (POW 2 Sept. 1918). With 27 Squadron were H.M. Broun of Hamilton, A.V. Cosgrove of Winnipeg (KIA 25 Sept. 1918), F.C. Crummy of Toronto, W.J. Dalziel of Wapilla, Sask., M.L. Doyle of River Louison, NB, H.W. Hewson of Clarenceville, Que., E.J. Jacques of Battleford, Sask., and A.F. Millar of Rapid City, Man. (KIA 14 Aug. 1918).

FE2bs and Camels of 83, 101, 102, and 151 Squadrons attacked with nearly six tons of bombs in the late evening, but the bridges remained intact and German reinforcements continued to cross. The RAF lost forty-five machines during the day and another fifty-two had to be struck off strength as a result of the day's fighting – a wastage rate of more than 13 per cent. About thirty of those lost were destroyed in attacks on the bridges and it seems probable that about the same proportion of those that were struck off strength would have been damaged on sorties against the bridges, too.[41]

When the attacks were resumed the next morning the heavy casualties taken on the first day, when the bombers had been left without fighter protection because the fighter squadrons themselves were attacking with their loads of 25-lb bombs, brought a tactical change. The operation order for the 9th noted that, on the previous day, 'E.A. scouts molested our bombers by diving on them from the clouds and preventing them carrying out their mission effectively.' The squadrons were now told to 'detail scouts for close protection of bombers to ensure that the latter are not interfered with by E.A. while trying to destroy bridges. This is the sole duty of these scouts who will not, therefore, carry bombs.'*[42]

The bomber squadrons of IX Brigade divided their operations between southern sector bridges at Falvy, Bethencourt, and Voyennes and the northern bridges between Cappy and Brie. The southern attack did not go well when fighter escorts from 73 Squadron, assigned to 27 Squadron, failed to appear for the morning raid. The DH9s were scattered by enemy fighters and only a few of them attacked Voyennes, the others dropping their 112-lb bombs on a variety of targets. The escorting Camels also apparently failed to meet 49 Squadron and only a few bombers were able to reach the bridge at Falvy. None of the DH9s was lost, although at times they were involved with formations of up to twenty German fighters. The bombers claimed to have shot down several enemy aircraft, one crew from 49 Squadron claiming five.[43]

Attacks on the northern bridges did bring more casualties. When six DH9s of 98 Squadron, escorted by five Camels of 43 Squadron, bombed Feuillères bridge from 3000 feet, they were attacked over the objective by a formation of Fokker and Pfalz scouts, and E.R. Macdonald and his pilot were among those lost. The most disastrous losses occurred early in the morning over the bridge at Brie when 107 Squadron lost five machines. The first flight of four DH9s, led by Captain F.M. Carter of Orillia, Ont., was attacked by twelve enemy aircraft about two miles west of the objective. Carter fired off a red Very light and a Camel from the escorting squadron, No 54, came to their assistance as Carter turned on a Fokker with his front guns and brought it down in flames. The flight lost one of its DH9s. The second flight of four was also attacked on its way to Brie, and when its flight commander, W.H. Dore, 'in a wonderful piece of pluck and daring,' turned on a formation of twelve Fokkers, he was shot down himself. The third flight of five DH9s had four Camels as escorts, but three of the bombers were lost over enemy

---

* However, the fighter squadrons did, with the exception of aircraft so detailed, continue to carry out bombing attacks on the bridges. IX Brigade Summary, 8–9, 9–10 Aug. 1918, Air 1/977/204/5/1135

lines and another crashed on the British side while the escort also lost two aircraft.[44]

Lieutenant S.L. Dunlop of Ottawa, a Canadian observer, won an immediate DFC on this occasion. His citation recorded that he and his pilot, Lieutenant G. Beveridge of Westmount, Que., were attacked by seven or eight enemy aircraft almost as soon as they crossed the German lines. The formation was broken up but they held to their course. One German dived on their tail and Dunlop shot it down in flames; while over the objective another enemy scout flew in front of the DH9 and Beveridge sent it down out of control; they were then attacked again from all sides by a large number of enemy machines, one of which Dunlop managed to shoot down. Beveridge, however, was wounded, fainted from loss of blood, and slumped onto the controls. The aircraft went into a steep dive until Dunlop reached over, pulled Beveridge back, and managed to get control of the machine. Still holding Beveridge, he connected the controls in his own cockpit and flew the aircraft west, somehow continuing to fire on attacking enemy aircraft. Beveridge revived over the British lines and together they safely crash-landed the machine.[45]

At 0700 hrs two flights of 205 Squadron, V Brigade's day bombers, went after the bridges at Brie and St Christ. Again, clouds and bad visibility obscured the results. At the same time two flights of III Brigade's 57 Squadron took off to bomb the bridges at Peronne but their escorting flight of five Bristol Fighters from 11 Squadron got into a fight with eight Fokkers between Bray and Peronne and lost contact with the DH4s. The leader of the bombers decided that it would be inadvisable to attempt a low-level attack on the bridges, so they dropped their bombs from 12,000 feet over the railway sidings while still under attack from the enemy fighters. One DH4, with Second Lieutenant H.S. Musgrove of Canmore, Alta, as observer, went missing (Musgrove was made prisoner), while four other bombers had to land away from their base.[46]

No 205 Squadron appears to have been the only day-bomber squadron which carried out a raid in the early afternoon of the 9th, two flights, each of seven machines, once more attacking the bridges at Brie and St Christ. On the flight to St Christ the DH4s encountered ten German aircraft over Rosières but the enemy kept his distance; DH4s which held a tight formation were not easy pickings. The bombers, several of which were damaged by heavy ground fire, subsequently claimed a direct hit on the western end of the Brie bridge. At 1800 hrs the squadron bombed both bridges from 12,000 feet, and once again enemy fighters were seen but did not attack. Two direct hits were claimed at St Christ but could not be confirmed, and for the most part damage was confined to the area around the bridges. The skill and endurance of the eighteen crews of 205 Squadron, including Captain W.B. Elliott of St Catharines, Ont., and Lieutenant F.O. MacDonald of Penticton, BC, is noteworthy; they spent over five hours each in the air on the 9th and dropped five-and-a-half tons of bombs on the bridges without, unfortunately, inflicting any serious damage.[47]

A further directive issued during the early afternoon on the 9th ordered a major, concentrated attack for the early evening. All available IX Brigade bombers were ordered to be over their assigned targets precisely at 1700 hrs. As the morning's escort arrangements had been ineffective, more elaborate measures were planned, the fighters being detailed to escort the bombers at the same altitude and to remain in the immediate vicinity until the mission was completed. In addition, 62 Squadron's Bristol Fighters were ordered to patrol the Peronne-Bethencourt line when they finished their regular patrols and four of I Brigade's squadrons, Nos 19, 22, 40, and 64, were assigned to patrol parallel lines on either side of the objectives, creating a corridor for the bombers and their close escorts to fly through. In all, thirty bombers with fifty close escorts and an additional seventy-four fighters guarding the flanks were involved in the attack. There was little opposition in the north, but in the south the bombers were attacked by enemy scouts flying in the cloud cover below the flank guards. They forced the bombers to abort the raid and in neither sector was any effective damage inflicted on the bridges. Nor were the efforts of the five night-flying squadrons, 106 aeroplanes in all, on the night of 9–10 August any more successful. Photographs taken the following day showed that all the bridges between Cappy and Bethencourt were intact, and the Peronne rail bridge, while damaged, remained open for traffic, despite the delivery of another eighteen tons of bombs.[48]

With German reinforcements moving across the bridges, and the Allies still dazed by their own initial success, the ground attack stalled. The Canadian Corps was able to advance two to three thousand yards on the 9th but was unable to reach as far as the line Chaulnes-Roye. The attacks that day were weaker and they were mounted piecemeal, unco-ordinated by Fourth Army Headquarters. Moreover, the Allies were encroaching on the old 1916 Somme battlefield which was studded with obstacles. As the offensive slowed and the German defences strengthened, the battle degenerated into one of local attacks and counter-attacks across the front. These continued on the 10th and 11th until, at the behest of Rawlinson, Haig ordered a halt on the Somme and began to look elsewhere for weak spots in the German defences.[49]

While the battlefield stabilized, V Brigade fighter squadrons were kept busy. On the 9th they had been in the air even before the ground attack began but, because of the confusion, their efforts were not well synchronized with the infantry. They were also harassed by growing numbers of enemy aircraft whose pilots resumed their low altitude attacks. Rather than flying, as they had done at first, in large formation of up to thirty aircraft at heights of 12,000–15,000 feet, the Germans now flew in small formations of eight to ten machines at low levels over the forward area. Here they offered effective opposition to both the RAF squadrons flying close-support missions, compelling Salmond to divert some fighters to protective duties and reducing the number of aircraft committed to low-flying work. Nos 23 and 48 Squadrons, and one flight from each of the other fighter squadrons, were ordered to patrol around 4000 feet to protect the lower-flying aircraft.[50]

A battle of attrition in the air ensued, individual and formation combats going on continuously over the battlefield. No 41 Squadron claimed five victims on the 9th, for the loss of one pilot, Lieutenant F.W.H. Martin of Regina. Lieutenant W.G. Claxton of Toronto and Captain F.R. McCall of Calgary were especially effective. In the morning Claxton destroyed a balloon near Bray and in the afternoon was credited with shooting down two Fokker biplanes. McCall, on an offensive patrol over Bray, got into a dogfight and shot down two more enemy machines, one from only ten yards range.[51]

Over the next few days each pilot reported a startling series of successes. Claxton claimed a Fokker biplane on the 10th, and another on the 11th. On the 12th both Claxton and McCall claimed victories. On 17 August Claxton was wounded and crashed behind enemy lines when, with McCall, he attacked a German force estimated at forty aircraft. In three months' fighting Claxton was credited with thirty-seven enemy aircraft, including four on one eventful flight.*[52]

No 65 Squadron, which had lost four pilots in the first day's fighting, lost another four on the 9th, including Lieutenant H.E. Dempsey of Souris, Man. On the 12th the squadron was withdrawn from the line for rest, but before then the unit had been awarded six DFCs.† The squadron's leading pilot, Captain J.L.M. White, a former machine-gun officer with the CEF, was credited with thirteen victories by the war's end. On the 9th he was chased off the line at Meharicourt by fourteen Germans but was able to climb above them. He then dived on the enemy machines while they were attacking a formation of Sopwith Dolphins from 23 Squadron and sent one down in flames and forced another to spin away before he had to break off, 'there being too many E.A. attacking me.'[53]

Other Canadians had similar experiences. In 24 Squadron Farrell and Lieutenant G.F. Foster of Montreal each claimed an enemy aircraft on 10 August. Lieutenant C.F. Falkenberg of Quebec City won a DFC leading a patrol from 84 Squadron against a formation of twelve enemy aircraft. From 14,000 feet the SE5as dove out of the sun upon the unsuspecting Fokker biplanes 5000 feet below them. Falkenberg selected his victim and followed it despite a series of vertical banks by the Fokker. The enemy pilot, finding his tactics unsuccessful, dropped into a steep dive but Falkenberg managed one final burst from both guns. He reported that the enemy machine's 'right hand top plane collapsed and fell back flush with the fuselage.' Falkenberg then seized a position on the tail of another aircraft and fired a drum of Lewis gun ammunition into it. It disappeared into cloud in a series of spins and stalls. Captain D. Carruthers of Kingston, Ont., also on this patrol, fired a long burst into an enemy machine on the initial dive; the German aircraft rolled on its back and fell to the ground.[54]

The fighter squadrons of III Brigade were busy as well. Three Canadians in 3 Squadron, Captain H.L. Wallace of Lethbridge, Alta, and Lieutenants L.H. McIntyre of Peterborough, Ont., and W.H. Boyd of Campbellford, Ont.,‡ were each

---

* Claxton received a DSO and DFC and Bar. McCall's claims also totalled thirty-seven by the end of the war. He was awarded a DSO, MC and Bar, and DFC.

† Including those awarded to A.A. Leitch from Ontario, J.M. McLennan of Whitehorse (POW 28 Sept. 1918), and J.L.M. White of Halifax (who would get a Bar to his before the war ended). Other Canadians with the squadron included W.J. Brooks of Toronto (POW 28 Sept. 1918), R.O. Campbell of Kincardine, Ont. (KIA 27 Sept. 1918), M.L. Fitzgerald of Hamilton, J.C. Malcolmson of Toronto (POW 28 Sept. 1918), R.C. Mitten of Punnichy, Sask. (POW 28 Sept. 1918), E.F.W. Peacock of Montreal, R.L. Scharff (POW 1 Sept. 1918), and P.L. Teasdale, addresses unknown, W.R. Thornton of Dresden, Ont. (POW 26 Sept. 1918), and G.D. Tod, address unknown.

‡ Other Canadians in 3 Squadron were C.G. Brock of Winnipeg, V.H. McElroy of Richmond, Ont., and V.B. McIntosh of Toronto.

credited with a kill on 10 August. In all, the four fighter squadrons of III Brigade claimed twenty-eight enemy crashed or out of control between 1600 hrs on the 9th and 1600 hrs on the 10th, ten of them claimed by Canadians. They lost only six pilots, including two Canadians.[55] It is certain, however, that the brigade was mistaken in its victory estimate, and that the relationship between victories and losses was much less lopsided than its figures indicate.

The exploits of Torontonian H.J. Burden highlighted the work of 56 Squadron. At 0900 hrs Burden left the ground leading a patrol that included Lieutenants C.B. Stenning and H.A.S. Molyneux, both also from Toronto.* An hour later, west of Bray, they sighted six Germans heading east. When the patrol closed with the enemy Burden forced down two and the other four spun down to ground level before making their getaway. After climbing west to 12,000 feet Burden's patrol attacked another formation of twenty enemy machines, diving on them out of the sun. Burden got on the tail of the top enemy fighter and, holding his fire until he approached to within fifty yards, fired a long burst which broke up the enemy machine. During the evening patrol, encountering a flight of enemy scouts, Burden forced one to spin and crash. Climbing above his antagonists he met yet another in a head-on duel. The German lost, crashing into a field to become the fifth victim claimed by Burden for the day.[56]

Near Marchelepot another Canadian flight commander in 56 Squadron, Captain W.R. Irwin of Ripley, Ont., spotted a formation of fifteen enemy aircraft below. He led his three aircraft and those of two other RAF patrols into an attack. Irwin finally got behind an enemy machine and fired a hundred rounds at point-blank range. The German 'went over on his back and went down like a falling leaf, slipping from side to side, obviously out of control.' A second enemy machine, after he had fired about 150 rounds into it, burst into flames and fell burning and smoking into the clouds. Irwin, who was awarded a DFC, was then attacked himself but spun to safety in a cloud, where he reloaded his Lewis gun and climbed again, only to find the fight over.[57]

Bombing policy was again changed for operations on 10 and 11 August. Most of the day bombers were ordered to attack the railway stations at Peronne and Equancourt, the targets they had originally been assigned.† Peronne was the principal target on the 10th and late that morning two formations of six bombers each from 27 and 49 Squadrons were escorted to the city by forty fighters from 32 and 62 Squadrons. The ratio of fighters to bombers gives some idea of the ferocity of the fighting as the Germans sought desperately to preserve their supply and reinforcement routes. The flight from 27 Squadron, led by Captain M.L. Doyle of River Louison, NB, and including Lieutenants E.J. Jacques of Battleford, Sask., and H.W. Hewson of Clarenceville, Que., was attacked five minutes before reaching Peronne by eight Fokkers and a general *mêlée* developed in which seven SE5as

---

* Other Canadians with 56 Squadron were W.O. Boger of Winnipeg, A.M. Clermont of Toronto, G.A. Elmslie of Montreal, T.D. Hazen of Sarnia, Ont., V.H. Hervey of Calgary, and F.A. Sedore of Sutton West, Ont.

† The Somme bridges were left for the DH4s of 205 Squadron which made morning and afternoon raids against Brie and St Christ. A direct hit on each bridge was claimed, but the bridges, in fact, were unscathed.

from 56 Squadron joined. The bomber crews claimed one victim and one of the escorting fighter pilots, Captain J.H.L. Flynn of Waterloo, Ont., was credited with another out of control. One DH9 and four fighters fell behind enemy lines, however, including 32 Squadron's Lieutenant W.E. Jackson of Peterborough, Ont. Despite the opposition, the bombers managed to drop their twenty 112-lb bombs on the railway sidings and the town, but low clouds obscured the results, as they did with some of the raids by 107 and 98 Squadrons, which attacked Equancourt's railway station.[58]

Because of its importance as a rail centre, Peronne was attacked repeatedly. In the early evening it was the turn of 103 Squadron of X Brigade and 18 Squadron of I Brigade to mount a raid. During their attack Second Lieutenant I.B. Corey of Barnston, Que.,* claimed one of No 103's four victories over the defending fighters. Later, 83 and 207 Squadrons dropped over two hundred 112-lb bombs and ninety 25-lb bombs on the target from heights of 1000 to 6000 feet. The next day the DH4s of 205 Squadron made three raids on Peronne. The two formations of eight and six aircraft in the first raid were attacked as they approached their target. Between them they claimed five enemy fighters, including one that was hit by a falling bomb which broke off its left wing. The afternoon raid of fourteen DH4s shot down one German scout which ventured into the middle of the formation. The enemy machines which attacked the bombers in the evening raid were driven off by the escorting Bristol Fighters, although the DH4s claimed one forced down. The raids on railway centres were pressed through 11 August but it was too late to make much difference to the battle. On that day, despite Foch's urging that the attack be continued, Haig called a halt on the Somme, turning instead to the British Third Army to continue the offensive in the north.[59]

In four days' fighting the allied front had been advanced by ten to twelve miles at some points and the Amiens rail link had been secured from German shelling. At a cost of about twenty thousand casualties the Australian, British, and Canadian troops inflicted almost four times as many casualties on the enemy, more than eighteen thousand of them prisoners, and captured 240 guns. Most of the gains had come on the first day of the battle.[60]

The principal contributions of the air arm, too, were made at the outset, during the logistical build-up preceding the attack and in the initial assault on 8 August. After the undoubted success of the first hours of the attack, however, the effectiveness of RAF operations certainly diminished. Indeed, one authority has observed: '... it is impossible to assert with any confidence that the result of the battle after about 14:00 hours on the 8th would have been materially different, or that the ultimate line reached and held by our forward troops on the 11th would have been materially short of where in fact it was, if not a bomb had been dropped or a round fired by aircraft against ground objectives.'[61] In assessing the reasons for the relative ineffectiveness of air operations after a brilliant early showing, the confusion among allied commanders about the ultimate purpose of the offensive

---

* Other Canadians with 103 Squadron included A.A. Adams of Moose Jaw, Sask., D.M. Darroch of Montreal, C.H. Heebner of Toronto (POW 24 Sept. 1918), J.B. Russell of Ottawa, P.S. Tennant of Vernon, BC (POW 2 Nov. 1918) and J.H. Whitham of Fort William, Ont.

seems to have been important. Unfortunately those directing the operation were unclear in their own minds whether their objective was the line of the old Amiens defences or Ham, or somewhere in between. They also failed to lay down the objective of the RAF in unequivocal terms. Like many others intimately involved in planning the battle, Brigadier-General Charlton clearly had the impression that the attack was a limited one. Moreover, the operation raised serious questions about the efficiency of the RAF chain of command. Both the appointment of an overall commander of the air forces in the offensive, and a clearly stated objective for the RAF, were required and would have allowed a more efficient use of air power. As it was, Charlton's stated purpose of assisting the ground troops to achieve their objective made no provision for a continuing battle. Also, while Salmond's strategic objective included sealing off the battlefield from enemy interference by attacking aerodromes and railway centres through which reinforcements might be expected to reach the battle, he miscalculated the speed of the German reaction and, in the event, abandoned both targets for the chimera of the Somme bridges.

The decision to switch the bulk of available air resources to the Somme bridges in mid-battle was a questionable one. Despite 700 sorties, and fifty-seven tons of bombs, the bridges were not seriously damaged and German reinforcements continued to reach the battle area by rail and road.[62] No written record was kept to indicate how and exactly why the decision was taken, but bridges were among the most difficult of bombing targets. A miss of inches and the bomb exploded harmlessly in mud or water while if a lucky hit was made, the damage could usually be repaired quickly; effective demolition was almost impossible.

General Salmond subsequently maintained that had the bombers of Trenchard's Independent Force been available to him, he could have made the rout complete. Even at the time, however, there was clearly a difference of opinion about the efficacy of bridge bombing. On 29 July 1918 a memorandum on target selection for bombers prepared by the Inter-Allied Transportation Council was forwarded to Major-General F.H. Sykes, the Chief of the Air Staff, for his comments. The memorandum gave bridges a high priority as targets, since 'The partial destruction of bridges will cause more prolonged interruption of [train] traffic than the breaking of tracks at any other points.'[63] In his reply, Sykes, while agreeing, pointed out that 'Experience has shown that a bridge offers so small a target that even from a low altitude it is exceedingly difficult to hit, even direct hits will not as a rule cause any very prolonged interruption of traffic. To destroy a bridge an attack in considerable strength and carried out from a low height is necessary. Such an operation must inevitably be costly as all important bridges are very strongly defended against aircraft attack. Systematic raids on bridges would, under existing condition, entail a policy too expensive to be maintained.'[64] Sykes' comments, dated 13 August, were made at virtually the same time that the accuracy of his assessment was being proven in battle.

The cost of the air battle was extremely high. On the first day of the battle the RAF suffered eighty-six casualties, sixty-two of them killed, missing, or prisoners. Fifteen of these were Canadian. On the 9th there were forty-eight casualties, thirty-four of whom were killed or missing and there were eight Canadians in the latter group. Canadian casualties alone, in the four-day air battle from 8 to 11

August, were thirty-one, twenty-six of whom were killed or became prisoners of war. German losses were much smaller, forty-eight aircrew and thirty aircraft. On the surface it would appear that the Germans won the engagement, but this verdict has to be qualified. The German air force was far less able to absorb heavy casualties than was the RAF. 'Compared with the German air casualties,' the German history of the battle noted, 'those of the enemy had to be called very high. Of course, on the German side, the loss of aircraft was more serious in view of the dwindling flow of materiel.'[65]

Normally, the GAF wisely chose to fight on its own terms; at Amiens circumstances compelled it to fight on allied terms. The attack on the Somme bridges had posed the most serious possible threat to the seventy thousand German Second Army men and their equipment still west of the river. A threat to the bridges was a threat to the survival of almost every one of them. The destruction of the bridges, as we have seen, was beyond the capacity of the bomber weapon of 1918. Protection by ground fire alone would probably have sufficed to keep these bridges in use but they were so important that the Germans did not dare take the risk and every effort had to be made to keep them intact, either for reinforcement or evacuation. In fact, by 11 August eighteen reserve divisions had been moved up to join the remnants of the Second Army's original six. It seems unlikely that anything else that the RAF might have done would have brought the German airmen to battle in such numbers and kept them fighting at such a pitch. In the process, as the British official historian has pointed out, 'the German air-service was so roughly handled that it was never able fully to recover.'[66]

Actual German losses in the air battle are not the true measure of the punishment that their air force had taken. Their casualties take no account of machines flown back to bases (their aerodromes were so close to the bridges that they could often glide down to them right out of the battle) so badly damaged that they could not fly again without major repairs or replacement. The forty-eight airmen that they lost* contained an inordinate proportion of the pilots from the élite *Jagdgeschwadern* that had borne the brunt of the battle. When the Richthofen wing moved to Bernes on 11 August, it had been reduced to a quarter of the strength with which it had entered the battle three days earlier; and, unlike its opponents, it was virtually impossible for the GAF to make good its losses in men or *matériel*.

---

* The figure would have been higher had it not been for the use of parachutes by the German fighter pilots. On 29 June *Leutnant* Ernst Udet of the Richthofen *Jagdgeschwader* had made a successful operational jump when he 'bailed out' under fire from a height of 500 metres, and was back in the air that same afternoon. Just the day before another of the pilots in Udet's squadron had also jumped successfully from a burning aircraft. 'Suddenly there came a day when no pilot would take off without one,' recalled a German air liaison officer some years later. Two more pilots of the wing jumped in July, one successfully and one unsuccessfully. On 10 August the wing recovered one out of two jumpers – in a span of six weeks four out of six parachutists had made successful jumps. Karl Bodenschatz, *Jagd in Flanderns Himmel* (München 1942), 110, 115–16, 125, and Hans Schroeder, *An Airman Remembers* (London nd), 273. No doubt other fighter wings had a similar record and the number of parachute escapes from burning or disabled aircraft continued to mount. British airmen, however, were never issued parachutes during the First World War.

18

Perfecting the Air Weapon

Despite the imperfect planning and staff work that had prevented the Amiens battle from becoming anything more than a limited success, both Foch and Haig were quick to appreciate the possibilities which now opened up. The Allies had found an effective tactical doctrine that would break the deadlock of trench warfare without incurring the casualty levels which had marked their earlier attempts. Tanks, artillery, and aircraft, properly co-ordinated so that they provided support for each other as well as for the infantry, could smash the wire and machine-gun defence systems which had dominated the Western Front for nearly four years. Most of the major logistical and production problems which had plagued the Entente for so long had been overcome. The promise of an end to the battles of attrition signalled by Amiens had done as much to improve allied morale as it had done to impair the German. Late on the evening of 21 August 1918 Foch had told Haig that 'any timidity on their [British Third Army's] part would hardly be justified in view of the enemy's situation and the moral ascendancy you have gained over him.' Haig, writing to his army commanders the next day, proclaimed that 'Risks which a month ago would have been criminal to incur ought now to be incurred as a duty ... The situation is most favourable. Let each one of us energetically and, without hesitation, push forward to our objective.'[1]

These exhortations were aimed most immediately at Rawlinson's Fourth Army, the victors of Amiens, and Sir Julian Byng's Third Army, which had just struck between Ayette and the River Ancre in an operation designed to secure the line of the Albert-Arras railway. This was scheduled to become the starting line for a much greater assault by both armies along the thirty-three miles of front from Neuville, just south of Arras, to Lihons, the point of junction with the French. Their attack was launched on 23 August and, during the next eight days, the German position which hinged on Roye was turned from the north. Ludendorff's forces were pushed back behind the east bank of the Somme, with a loss of some 34,000 prisoners and 270 guns.

Before these operations began one significant alteration in RAF dispositions had been made. No 73 Squadron (Sopwith Camels), with at least nine Canadians among its twenty-four pilots,* was attached to the Tank Corps in order to reinforce

---

* E. Barker of Newboro', Ont., W.A. Brett of Dugald, Man. (KIA 27 Sept. 1918), G.C.C. Carr-Harris of Kingston, Ont., J.H. Drewry of Victoria, H.V. Fellowes of Grimsby Beach, Ont. (POW

8 Squadron's* specialized tank-support role. At Amiens the tanks had clearly demonstrated their ability to dominate most aspects of the battlefield. Impervious to small arms fire, they had plunged through wire and over trenches, grinding enemy strong-points beneath their huge tracks. They had also shown themselves, with their slow speeds and limited vision, to be easy targets for the German anti-tank guns just coming into use (the 7.7 cm anti-aircraft 'flak' gun was sometimes pressed into service as an anti-tank gun, the precursor of the dreaded dual purpose '88' of the Second World War) and for field artillery hastily adapted to an anti-tank role. On 10 August, for example, 'some 67 tanks in all were engaged, and of these 30 received direct hits. On one occasion, a single, well-sited gun had disabled eight tanks in succession.'[2]

The response to 'LL'[†] calls sent down by artillery observation aircraft working with the Tank Corps was too slow to be very useful against concealed anti-tank guns, which might not open fire until the tanks were within a few hundred yards. The proximity of friendly armour and infantry then made it hazardous to employ artillery fire to suppress or destroy these guns; it was considered that the most feasible way to neutralize them was to attack directly with low-flying aeroplanes. However, the one flight which 8 Squadron was normally able to spare from contact patrol and artillery observation duties was numerically too weak to be effective in this counter anti-tank role, nor were their Armstrong-Whitworth FK8s really fast or nimble enough for this ultra low-level close support work. The addition of twenty-four Camels to the Tank Corps' air arm, however, permitted the deployment of at least one machine well-suited to the role over each two thousand yards of front during tank assaults. By carefully studying the ground on layered maps and air photographs, the Camel pilots were able to make up charts which plotted likely German gun positions.[‡] These locations were then examined frequently during the course of the tank assault and any sign of activity brought a thorough strafing of the spot.[3]

The reconnaissance of these anti-tank gun positions was not left as an exclusive responsibility of the fighters and one flight of 8 Squadron. After Amiens all corps aircraft in the battle zone were instructed that '... it will be seldom that the duty in which machines are at the moment engaged will not yield in importance to offensive action at once against the anti-tank gun.' Corps squadron aircrews were therefore to keep a special eye open for anti-tank guns and to facilitate the rapid bringing down of fire on these vital targets. A Wireless Central Information Bureau (known as the CIB) was set up to co-ordinate artillery and low-level air support and monitor enemy activity. Corps patrols observing either enemy air

1 Sept. 1918), W.H. Hubbard of Toronto (WIA 26 Dec. 1916), E.J. Lussier of Medicine Hat, Alta, O.T. Moran of Winnipeg, and D.B. Sinclair of London, Ont. (POW 2 Sept. 1918)
* Canadian flying personnel included J.R. Desy, address unknown (KIA 27 Oct. 1918), A. Grundy of Merritt, BC, V.R. Homersham of Winnipeg, J.R.R.G. MacCallum of Toronto (KIA 23 Aug. 1918), W.F.R. Robinson of Round Hill, NS (MIA 24 Sept. 1918), W. Spriggs of Port Williams, NS, R.F. Talbot of Montreal (KIA 2 Sept. 1918), S.B. Trites of Salisbury, NB, and F.A. Whittall of Westmount, Que.
† 'All available batteries to open fire (sudden attack on very favourable target).'
‡ This process of potential gun-site identification was made significantly easier after 2 September, when a document was captured setting forth German principles for the deployment of anti-tank guns in the defence. J.F.C. Fuller, *Tanks in the Great War, 1914–1918* (London 1920), 247–8

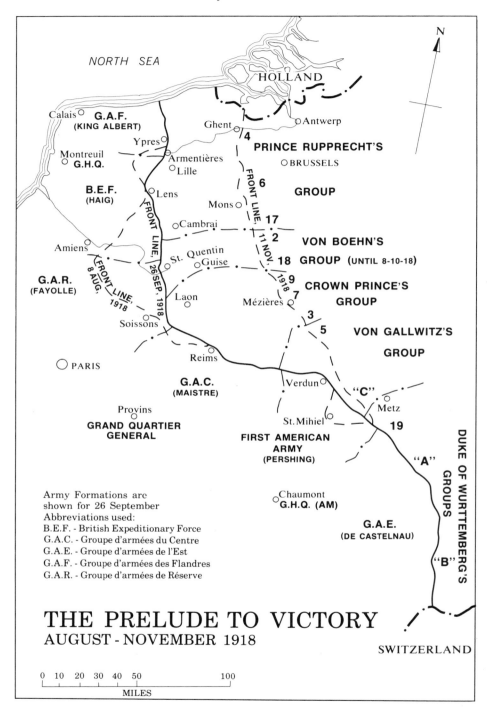

NORTH SEA

HOLLAND

N

Calais○ **G.A.F.**
(KING ALBERT)

Ghent○ /4

○Antwerp

Ypres○

PRINCE RUPPRECHT'S

Montreuil
○ **G.H.Q.**

Armentières
○Lille

○BRUSSELS

B.E.F.
(HAIG)

○Lens

Mons○

6

GROUP

○Cambrai

17

2

VON BOEHN'S

Amiens○

St. Quentin○
○Guise

18

GROUP (UNTIL 8-10-18)

G.A.R.
(FAYOLLE)

Laon○

9

CROWN PRINCE'S

Mézières○

7

GROUP

Soissons○

3

5

VON GALLWITZ'S

Reims○

GROUP

○ PARIS

G.A.C.
(MAISTRE)

Verdun○

"C"○

Provins
○

Metz○

**GRAND QUARTIER
GENERAL**

St.Mihiel○

19

**FIRST AMERICAN
ARMY**
(PERSHING)

"A"

Army Formations are
shown for 26 September
Abbreviations used:
B.E.F. - British Expeditionary Force
G.A.C. - Groupe d'armées du Centre
G.A.E. - Groupe d'armées de l'Est
G.A.F. - Groupe d'armées des Flandres
G.A.R. - Groupe d'armées de Réserve

Chaumont
○ **G.H.Q.** (AM)

G.A.E.
(DE CASTELNAU)

"B"

DUKE OF WURTTEMBERG'S GROUPS

THE PRELUDE TO VICTORY
AUGUST - NOVEMBER 1918

SWITZERLAND

0 10 20 30 40 50   100

MILES

activity or vital ground targets were to transmit their target locations by wireless telegraphy (Morse) to the CIB, which would immediately re-transmit the information by wireless telephone (voice transmission) to the appropriate artillery battery or fighter squadron headquarters. The original observer of the target was also to fire a red Very flare in order to attract any other British aircraft which might be already in the vicinity. A constant flow of information was ensured by instructing all artillery and contact patrols to make a routine call to the CIB every half hour. If a call was not made on schedule it could be assumed that the machine was for some reason no longer operational and a replacement was to be promptly dispatched.[4]

A direct wireless link between tanks and aircraft had for some time been recognized as the best solution to communications problems. As the events of July and August had shown, however, contemporary wireless telephony equipment was impractical for such an operational task. Although tests proved that it was possible for tanks to receive messages clearly in Morse from aircraft at 2500 feet altitude and 9000 yards away, the supply of wireless telegraphy sets for the allied armies had already been allotted to the end of the year. None were available for this new requirement. Consequently, communication between tanks and aircraft remained tenuous and irregular and was largely restricted to written messages dropped at tank brigade and battalion level and at pre-selected rallying points.[5]

The essence of the new approach was the co-ordination of the various arms in a series of attacks based on the operational and tactical concepts of fluidity and of reinforcing success rather than failure. This form of warfare embodied all the fundamental principles, materials, and technology of the 'blitzkrieg' which so astonished the world in 1939 and 1940, first in Poland and then in France. From the experience of Amiens the allied commanders had now devised ways – not a moment too soon – to pull all arms together. The new techniques were not to be fairly tested upon their first application, however. The dawn attack on 21 August was launched, as so often on the Western Front, through a thick fog. The entire RAF flew only twenty-five reconnaissances and forty-five contact and counter-attack patrols during the day; on the Third Army front no flying was possible until 1100 hrs, when the first contact patrol of 8 Squadron, piloted by Lieutenant A. Grundy of Merritt, BC, reported that the attack was developing successfully. On a counter-anti-tank gun sortie flown by 8 Squadron, Lieutenant F.A. Whittall of Westmount, Que., was also able to silence two enemy guns that were firing on British tanks. Driving off an enemy aircraft which was attacking another of the Armstrong-Whitworths, Whittall and his observer then engaged and silenced a third gun which was firing on two Whippet tanks. However, the bulk of the counter-anti-tank gun patrols were flown by the newcomers of 73 Squadron, out to prove their worth.[6]

The tank attack was restricted to the area between Bucquoy and Moyenneville, since the ground south of this frontage was unsuitable for tank action. No 73's first patrol, five strong and led by Captain W.H. Hubbard of Toronto,* attacked gun

---

* Hubbard's wingman was R.N. Chandler, a young Londoner who was to be awarded a DFC for his work in the last three months of the war. Chandler emigrated to Canada in the early postwar years and joined the RCAF in 1940. He retired in 1946 with the rank of wing commander.

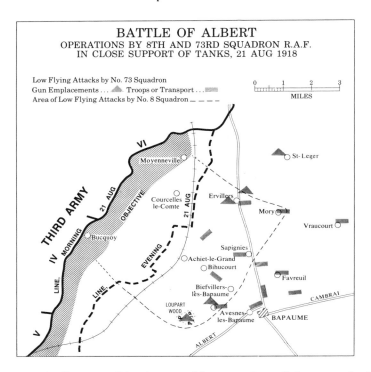

BATTLE OF ALBERT
OPERATIONS BY 8TH AND 73RD SQUADRON R.A.F.
IN CLOSE SUPPORT OF TANKS, 21 AUG 1918

emplacements in Loupart Wood, near Mory, and strafed troops in Favreuil, Grevillers, and Mory. A second flight of six machines, including Second Lieutenants E. Barker of Newboro', Ont., and W.A. Brett of Dugald, Man., took off before the initial flight had landed, dropped all their bombs on Mory, and then heavily machine-gunned columns on the Ervillers-Bapaume road, which ran laterally behind the German front. During the early afternoon a third patrol, which included Lieutenant E.J. Lussier of Medicine Hat, Alta, hit the gun emplacements in Loupart Wood again with twenty 25-lb bombs, dropped four more on Ervillers, and shot up motor transport and troops in the vicinity of Achiet-le-Grand and Sapignies. Each of the three flights (with Second Lieutenant G.C.C. Carr-Harris of Kingston, Ont., substituting for Brett) then carried out second strikes in the same general area, so that the tank battlefront was under virtually continuous surveillance and attack by this one squadron from noon until 1900 hrs.[7]

Close air support was so successful in this operation that only thirty-seven of the 190 tanks employed in the assault received direct hits. This unprecedentedly small casualty figure might have been even lower if the morning fog had not lifted gradually from the west, thus giving the anti-tank gunners a golden opportunity to engage their targets for the few minutes that they themselves remained invisible to the British close support machines.[8]

The three fighting squadrons – Nos 3, 56, and 60 – which had been allocated to additional ground-attack roles sent their machines off in pairs at half-hourly intervals during the time that flying was possible. 'A series of low bombing and ground attacks were carried out ... in and around Bapaume. In the evening Sailly dump on the Bapaume-Peronne road was bombed and machine-gunned, and [enemy gun] pits were attacked, resulting in twenty-three of the latter suffering destruction by Burden and Holleran,' wrote 56 Squadron's historian.* Burden's diary added that 'on my last trip in the afternoon I got a railway station complete also a team of horses, a wagon and a billet with 4 bombs and shot up all manner of Huns from 100 feet with Armour Piercing Ammunition.'[9]

No 3 Squadron's Camels also attacked the Sailly-Saillisel supply dump that evening and Lieutenant V.H. McElroy of Richmond, Ont., reported dropping two bombs 'which caused large explosions in the dump.' Earlier in the day he had strafed troops in Favreuil with bombs and machine-gun fire from 'a very low altitude' and shot up a kite balloon south of Tilloy. His machine had been hit a number of times but he was back in the air for the attack on Sailly dump within a few hours. Lieutenant C.G. Brock of Winnipeg was not quite so lucky. In a low-level attack on a transport column that caused 'many casualties' he was hit in the knee – his second wound – but managed to get his machine back to base. Unluckier still was Lieutenant L.H. McIntyre of Peterborough, Ont.,[†] who was 'last seen diving steeply on an enemy balloon.'[10]

No 60 Squadron's SE5as, flying in pairs, were working the same area of the front and flew fourteen patrols during the day. Only one patrol, which included Lieutenant A.R. Oliver of Galt, Ont., was 'prevented from going far over the line, as every time they attempted to do so they were chased by 6 Fokker biplanes and a two-seater.' Second Lieutenant A.N. Westergaard of Macoun, Sask., on his second sortie of the day, was again reduced to 'bombing buildings' instead of more specific targets, until he discovered that a fault in the fuel system was starving his engine of gasoline. Limping homewards at 1000 feet he had the misfortune to be attacked by a German two-seater which shot away most of his control wires and the leading edges of both top and bottom left-hand planes, before he was able to edge across the lines and land the badly damaged machine at the nearest aerodrome.[‡][11]

At the same time, squadrons from IX (HQ) Brigade were striking deeper into enemy territory. Eleven de Havilland bombers attacked the road and rail bridges at Aubigny-au-Bac, some twenty miles behind the front. The formation, led by Captain M.L. Doyle of River Louison, NB,[§] met heavy and accurate anti-aircraft fire over the target but, although five Fokker triplanes were seen, enemy aircraft

---

* Other Canadian pilots with 56 Squadron at this time included G.F. Bayne of Montreal, A.M. Clermont of Toronto, G.A. Elmslie of Montreal, T.D. Hazen of Sarnia, Ont. (KIA 19 Aug. 1918), V.H. Hervey of Calgary (WIA 13 Aug. 1918), W.R. Irwin of Ripley, Ont. (WIA 15 Sept. 1918), G.O. MacKenzie of Embro, Ont. (KIA 27 Sept. 1918), H.A.S. Molyneux of Toronto, and F.A. Sedore of Sutton, Ont. (WIA 24 Sept. 1918).

† Other Canadians serving in 3 Squadron on 21 August included W.H. Boyd of Campbellford, Ont., and P.R. Davis of Simcoe, Ont.

‡ Canadian pilots with 60 Squadron on 21 August also included J.N. Bartlett of Winnipeg, C.S. Hall of Seaforth, Ont., B.S. Johnston of Courtright, Ont., and S.A. Thomson of Vancouver, who joined the squadron this day and was to be killed in action on 5 September 1918.

§ Other machines participating in this raid were flown by F.C. Crummy of Toronto, W.J. Dalziel of Wapella, Sask., H.W. Hewson of Clarenceville, Que., and J.B. Hutcheson of Kerrobert, Sask. Other Canadians with the squadron on 21 August included A.V. Cosgrove of Winnipeg (MIA 25 Sept. 1918), P.V. Holder of Lunenburg, NS, and E.J. Jacques of Battleford, Sask. A.F. Millar of Rapid City, Man., had been killed in action a week earlier.

made no attempt to interfere. That evening a flight of six DH9s from 107 Squadron, each carrying two 112-lb bombs and with the leader's machine equipped with the new high-altitude drift sight, bombed Roisel station from 13,000 feet. This mission, led by Captain F.M. Carter of Orillia, Ont., with Lieutenant A.W.H. Arundell of Montreal as his observer,* was attacked by eight triplanes but the enemy was driven off without loss.[12]

Such high-level interdiction bombing remained a regular feature of RAF operations during the last two-and-a-half months of campaigning on the Western Front, but little damage appears to have been done and that which did occur was easily repaired. Selection of targets by the staff had improved; it was generally much more relevant to the development of current ground operations than had previously been the case, but there was still too much dispersion of effort and an inability to appreciate the technical difficulties of hitting small targets such as bridges. Even if good fortune brought a direct hit, the damage inflicted by a single bomb was easy to repair. High-level day bombing, at least in the tactical and operational zones, continued to absorb a proportion of RAF resources in men and machines which could have been better employed in low-bombing, reconnaissance, and artillery observation missions.

Low-level tactical night bombing and strafing was much more successful, and it became progressively more important as overwhelming British air superiority compelled the Germans to move by night. A fine example is provided by the work of 102 Squadron's FE2bs on the night of 21–22 August when a total of thirty-eight sorties were flown against troops, trains, and transport facilities opposite the Third Army front. A machine flown by Lieutenant J. Farley of Toronto dropped six 25-lb bombs on a column of horse transport on the Albert-Bapaume road, scoring at least one direct hit and scattering the remainder. It probably took hours to reorganize the column; panicked horses, overturned wagons, and demoralized drivers were not easily reformed in the dark and the supplies they carried are unlikely to have reached their destination before first light. Even more successful was a machine in which Second Lieutenant E.J. Clark of Montreal† was flying as observer. On their first trip Clark and his pilot bombed and badly damaged a column of motor transport and in the course of a second sortie they caught about twenty horse-drawn wagons just after first light:

Bombs burst in the midst of this transport and knocked out 6 or 8 teams. Some of the rear teams took refuge in the sunken road just west of the CANAL DU NORD. There were also two large lorries in here. We were at 200 feet and dived right down on the sunken road with altimeter registering Nil, and secured a direct hit among the teams and lorries [with] one 25-lb bomb. Waggons and dead horses could be seen scattered all over the road and also several men. 250 rounds of S[mall]. A[rms]. A[mmunition]. were fired into the wreckage. 4 Teams escaped, 2 along road to BAPAUME and 2 towards CAMBRAI.[13]

---

* Flying in Carter's formation were J.H. Grahame of Stony Mountain, Man., and J.V. Turner of Brockville, Ont. Other Canadians serving with the squadron included S.L. Dunlop and F.C. King of Ottawa and F. Player of Moose Jaw, Sask. (KIA 4 Sept. 1918).

† Other Canadians flying on this night included J.A. Le Royer of Quebec City (WIA 5 July 1917), G.L. Shephard of Kingston, Ont. (WIA 4 Oct. 1918), and C.S. Stayner of Noel, NS (WIA 24 Aug. 1918). Canadian aircrew in 102 Squadron included F. Collins of Toronto and H. Fall of Montreal.

The rest of the squadron also found satisfactory targets and during the night a total of seven 112-lb bombs, 250 25-lb bombs, and nearly 5000 rounds of machine-gun ammunition were expended. During the last two-and-a-half months of the war this type of action was employed most successfully on all but the darkest nights.

On 22 August, as the ground forces resumed their attacks just after dawn, four Sopwith Camels of 54 Squadron, led by Captain E.J. Salter of Mimico, Ont., and including Lieutenants A.H. Belliveau of Fredericton and A.S. Compton of Toronto,* met a patrol of four enemy aircraft coming west from Bapaume. The German machines were obviously flown by inexperienced pilots. Despite having the sun in their eyes, Salter's flight apparently saw their enemy first and were able to manoeuvre themselves into a position above and behind the Germans. They then dived in line-ahead formation on the highest of the enemy machines, a two-seater Albatros, and each of them gave it a short burst in turn. The Albatros went into a nose-dive and was seen to crash near Grevillers.[14]

Another Canadian, Captain E.T. Morrow of Toronto, won a DFC when a flight of IX Brigade's 62 (Bristol Fighter) Squadron was assigned to escort eleven day bombers of 27 Squadron, commanded by his fellow-Torontonian, Lieutenant F.C. Crummy, in a raid on Cambrai. The Brisfits, led by Morrow with Second Lieutenant L.M. Thompson of Balgonie, Sask.,† as his observer, engaged 'a large number of hostile scouts' and Morrow and Thompson claimed two destroyed before Morrow was badly wounded in the leg and their machine set on fire. Morrow lost consciousness and the aircraft went into a spin but after a few moments he recovered and managed to regain control, while Thompson battled the flames with a fire extinguisher. They crashed inside the British lines where Thompson carried his pilot clear of the burning plane.[15]

On 23 August 56 Squadron, 'in all kinds of machines,' was out again, strafing the enemy in front of the Third Army. 'Since the push started our machines have been shot up and shot down and we only have about 10 serviceable,' complained Burden in his diary. The next day Burden noted that 'This low stuff isn't nearly good enough on SE's. Machines come home written off or else get shot down.' The SE5a was not as manoeuvrable at low altitude as the Sopwith Camel, but Burden might have been more cheerful if he had realized how badly the other side was hurting. That same day Karl Bodenschatz, the adjutant of the Richthofen *Jagdgeschwader*, recorded in his diary that 'the German Luftwaffe is choking to death under the weight of enemy strength in the air. There is little left that can be done.' That morning the Fourth Army had joined the ground attack, stretching the battlefront from Neuville to Lihons, south of the Somme. On the Fourth Army front the bulk of the low strafing work fell to 203 Squadron, still com-

---

* Other Canadians flying with 54 Squadron on 22 August included H.R. Abey of Kaslo, BC (WIA and POW 2 Nov. 1918), J.V. Dallin of Peterborough, Ont., M.A. Genest of Trois Rivières, Que., H.B.T. Lockwood of Long Branch, Ont., G.M. Saunders of Toronto, and J.M. Stevenson of Charlottetown.

† Canadians serving with 62 Squadron on this day included A.W. Blowes of Mitchell, Ont., L. Campbell of Hamilton (KIA 9 Oct. 1918), W.E. Hall of Foxwarren, Man. (POW 4 Sept. 1918), P.S. Manley of Thorold, Ont. (POW 27 Sept. 1918), C.H. Moss of Moose Jaw, Sask. (WIA 16 Sept. 1918), G.K. Runciman, address unknown (WIA 29 June 1918), J.R. Stewart of Hamilton (WIA 1 Sept. 1918), and W.K. Swayze of Lindsay, Ont. (POW 4 Sept. 1918).

manded by Raymond Collishaw, who now had fifty-four victories to his credit. His skills in air combat honed to a fine edge, Collishaw disliked the chancy nature of close ground-support work, recognizing that a stray bullet was as likely to bring down a veteran ace as the rawest novice. His skill and experience counted for little when he flew against ground targets at fifty feet. Nevertheless, he was leading his squadron when one of his flight commanders, Lieutenant J.P. Hales of Guelph, Ont.,* was shot down near Villers-Bretonneux. Collishaw reported that he had seen the body lifted from the crashed Camel: from the ground the view was very different and an enemy war diarist plaintively reported 'Low flying enemy aircraft overhead. No German planes in sight, no "flak" guns firing.'[16]

Poor weather on the morning of the 24th brought air operations almost to a stop, a circumstance that significantly hindered the British advance. However, there was flying during the afternoon despite continued bad visibility; 60 Squadron, for example, managed to fly eight two-plane strafing missions. With the clouds still low and offering good cover and escape routes, the German air force was more evident that afternoon than it had been during the earlier phases of the battle. But shortages of fuel, parts, and mechanics, meant that many of the German airmen were not getting enough training time in the air to enable them to match the RAF's skills. One pair of pilots from 60 Squadron were 'attacked by 8 Fokker biplanes' – but they both escaped undamaged, although one of the SE5as developed engine trouble and had to make a forced landing just southwest of Achiet-le-Grand. Lieutenant Allan R. Oliver and his flight leader had a similar experience. Oliver, who had only two weeks of operational flying experience at this time, reported being 'chased by 4 Fokker biplanes – must have been very dud pilots as they were on my tail and above me, but I only got two holes in my machine.'[17]

The weather cleared towards nightfall and the FE2bs of 102 Squadron were in the air until 0230 hrs on the 25th, when a rising ground mist made further flying impossible. Especially successful were two of the squadron's Canadians. Between midnight and 0130 hrs Farley's machine strafed a column of horse transport and bombed a train in Velu station from 1000 feet, claiming at least four direct hits, while Captain J.A. Le Royer of Quebec City dropped fourteen 25-lb bombs on a 'column of infantry over ¼ mile long at Beugny' on the Bapaume-Cambrai road and totally disorganized it. A German infantryman wrote this night of '... consecutive waves of enemy aircraft which attacked the low ground of the Ancre valley and the roads ... against which no German planes took to the air and no "flak" gave fire, [and] even during the hours of moonlight dropped their bombs without hindrance.' Indeed, No 102's only casualty was Lieutenant C.S. Stayner of Noel, NS, who was badly burnt by the ignition of a magnesium flare inside his cockpit.[18]

These night intruder sorties, as a later generation would describe this type of operation, were a game that two could play successfully in a pre-radar age, when

---

* Other Canadian pilots serving with 203 Squadron on 23 August included F.G. Black of Orillia, Ont. (WIA 21 Sept. 1918), H.J.L. Botterell of Ottawa, P.B. Calder of Edmonton, Alta, M.G. Cruise of Port Dover, Ont. (KIA 20 Sept. 1918), D.A. Haig of Agincourt, Ont., and A.T. Whealy of Toronto.

level attacks. These aircraft came from Nos 54, 208, and 209 (Sopwith Camels) and 64 (SE5as),* which had at least thirty Canadians flying with them during the last two-and-a-half months of the war. All four were, at this time, put under the operational command of Major B.E. Smythies, the Commanding Officer of 64 Squadron, as a specialist formation for the purpose of close ground support. This was the first time that one officer had been given a free hand to direct all close-support attacks on a given front. The only pre-condition 'was that the attacks were to be from as low a height as possible, and never from above 1,000 ft.'[23]

Smythies' four squadrons dropped more than 550 25-lb bombs and fired 26,000 rounds against ground targets along a front of some 8000 yards, extending about 1000 yards deep during their first day under his command. On the 27th they and 73 Squadron – the unit dedicated to knocking out anti-tank guns – in spite of low clouds and rain, dropped 646 bombs and fired 47,570 rounds. Their impact was substantial. On targets in each thousand-yard square of front they had expended an average of 150 bombs and nearly 10,000 rounds of small arms ammunition in the course of two days. General Salmond proudly explained to a visitor to his headquarters that 'The enemy could scarcely make a movement without some slow old observation plane of ours calling up the fighting planes, which were on to the enemy in a flash.' Prisoners, he added, were reporting that against these low-flying aeroplanes 'it was almost impossible to re-form beaten troops.'[24]

Under this impressive umbrella of air support more Germans were qualifying as beaten troops every day. On the 27th the Canadians took Monchy-le-Preux and, by the evening of the 28th, they were established on the western edges of Boiry-Notre Dame and Rémy, right against the Hindenburg Line. That night the Australians stormed Mont St Quentin, to the south, a move which threatened the Somme crossings and compelled the enemy to abandon Bapaume. Ludendorff was forced to sanction a general withdrawal of his Second, Eighteenth, and Ninth Armies towards the prepared defences of the Hindenburg position. Just southeast of Arras, where the northern end of the Hindenburg Line was intersected by the southern end of another prepared defensive position known as the Wotan Line, lay the Drocourt-Quéant switch, a complex of wire, trenches, and strong-points which, if it could be broken, offered the possibility of rolling up both defence lines from the north and south, respectively. At 0500 hrs on 2 September 1918 the Canadian Corps of the First Army and XVII Corps of the Third Army attacked the switch line, supported by strong elements of the Tank Corps.

The evolving specialization of air roles meant that many of the same airmen and machines were again to the fore. Nos 5 and 52 Squadrons were still working

---

* Canadians serving with 208 Squadron included H.J. Botterell of Ottawa, R.E. Goodfellow of Toronto, E.A. Kenny of Orillia, Ont., C.H. Living of Ottawa (POW 2 Sept. 1918), H.J. Philp of Nestleton, Ont., C.G. Swannell of Nelson, BC, and G.A. Wightman of Westmount, Que. No 209 Squadron had W.R. May of Edmonton (WIA 8 Aug. 1918) as one of its flight commanders and R.L. Scharff (POW 1 Sept. 1918) and J.E. Walker (WIA 17 June 1918, MIA 17 Sept. 1918), addresses unknown, among its pilots. Only one Canadian has been identified as serving in 64 Squadron, H.T. McKinnie of Del Bonita, Alta (WIA 4 Sept. 1918).

with the Canadian Corps, and No 13* with XVII Corps. No 8 Squadron was co-operating with the tanks, No 73 was concentrating on neutralizing the enemy's anti-tank defences, and the same four fighter squadrons were allocated to the ground-support role again. Fighter cover immediately over the battlefield was the responsibility of 40 Squadron's SE5as[†] and the Bristol Fighters of 22 Squadron,[‡] while the fighters of II and X Brigades were assigned to provide more distant, high-level cover.[25]

There had been little time for adequate ground reconnaissance but air photographs had plainly revealed the enemy's position. The attack went in smoothly enough on the ground. During the morning the close-support squadrons dropped 573 bombs and fired nearly 50,000 rounds at ground targets, claiming 'A large number of direct hits ... on troops, transport and batteries in action,' while 73 Squadron 'effectively engaged anti-Tank guns with bombs and machine gun fire,' despite low cloud and poor visibility. A representative patrol was that of 8 Squadron's Lieutenant A. Grundy and his British observer, who started an early morning counter-attack patrol by dropping six 25-lb bombs on several anti-tank guns and their crews. 'Did not see flash of guns again and men were dispersed,' their terse report read. Half-an-hour later they were machine-gunning more anti-tank guns and enemy infantry formations before coming back to report the latest positions of a number of British tanks. By noon the ground troops had broken through the German defences, but the cost, both on the ground and in the air, had been high. Clouds provided good cover for aircraft and the German fighter elements were out in force. In heavy fighting the RAF lost thirty-six aircraft during the day from I and III Brigades alone.[26]

The bulk of the damage was done by a formation of *Jagdgeschwader 3*, thirty strong, which claimed twenty-six victories during the morning in the course of two confused and prolonged engagements which began near Marquion about 0930 hrs. Despite their many and increasing logistical problems, the Germans adhered to their fundamental doctrine, keeping their machines well dispersed on the ground but concentrated in the air when they chose to fight. Their basic tactical formation, by this time, was the fighter wing, while the British still predicated their fighter tactics on the flight or squadron grouping. Thus, throughout this fight, and, indeed, on most other occasions when their fighters chose to accept combat in the last weeks of the war, the enemy enjoyed a numerical superiority. An increasing proportion of the German airmen were veteran combat pilots, only the best being sent into action as their air force shrank in terms of men and material. On the

---

* Canadians flying with 13 Squadron included F. Belway of Richmond, Ont., L.S. Bowker of Granby, Que., C.A. Brown of Montreal, R.F. Browne of Toronto (WIA 8 Oct. 1918), W.G. Campbell of Saint John, NB, J.W.G. Clark of Toronto, R.G. Michaelson of Virden, Man., J.P. McClelland of Arthur, Ont., J.F. Robb of Portage la Prairie, Man., F.P.J. Travis of Saint John, NB (WIA 2 Sept. 1918), W.W. Van Blaricom of Neepawa, Man. (WIA 15 Jan. 1917), and H.W. Wynn of Vancouver (KIA Oct. 1918).

† Canadian pilots serving with 40 Squadron on 1 September included G.C. Dixon of Vancouver (WIA 16 Sept. 1918) and A.R. Whitten of Toronto.

‡ No 22 Squadron's flying personnel included T.J. Birmingham of Jameson, Sask., B.C. Budd of Toronto, L.N. Caple of Vancouver, and G.S. Routhier of Walkerton, Ont.

nine enemy machines. Only one or two aircraft were actually lost by the Germans. Later that day 70 (Sopwith Camel) Squadron, temporarily detached from II Brigade, met an estimated thirty Fokkers over the First Army front and lost eight aircraft, three of them being flown by Canadians, Captain J.H. Forman of Kirkfield, Ont., and Lieutenants J.L. Gower of Toronto and R. McPhee of South Vancouver,* each of whom became a POW.[32]

Aircrew morale seems to have remained high but momentum could not be kept up uninterruptedly at the level of the past month, either on the ground or in the air. On 5 September 1918 the activities of the fighter squadrons were curtailed by an important HQ memorandum:

1 Orders have been issued to Armies to press the enemy with advanced guards with the object of driving in his outposts and rearguards and ascertaining his dispositions, but to undertake no deliberate operations on a large scale for the present. Troops are to be rested as far as possible and our resources conserved.

2 The G.O.C. wishes brigadiers to adopt a similar policy in the case of the RAF which has now been working at high pressure for many months. Should the enemy adopt an aggressive policy in the air,† it will, of course, be necessary to continue a vigorous offensive but, provided he keeps well back at a distance behind his lines, the policy of seeking out and destroying his machines will be less actively pursued and offensive patrol work will be restricted to keeping back his artillery and reconnaissance machines and enabling ours to do their work.

3 To carry out the above policy the GOC wishes brigadiers to reduce the number of fighting squadrons working over the lines to a minimum each day, and to take individual squadrons definitely off this work for a day or more at a time, during which they will carry out training only.[33]

There was still plenty to do for the bombing and fighter-reconnaissance aircraft, as well as the corps machines. The work of II Brigade's 20 (Bristol Fighters) Squadron over the next three days is a case in point. On the day that the above memorandum was issued a high-level offensive patrol led by Captain H.P. Lale, an Englishman who had enlisted in Calgary, with Second Lieutenant H.L. Edwards of Smiths Falls, Ont., as his observer, was surprised by eleven Fokker biplanes which dived out of a cloud a thousand feet above them. Lale turned to meet the enemy and his observer engaged the leading machine with his Lewis guns. At the third burst his target 'broke up in the air, pieces falling from it as it went down.' In the meantime the remainder of the Brisfits were being attacked from the rear and, in the ensuing dogfight, one other Fokker was definitely driven down 'with smoke issuing from it' and a third, fired at by the observer in a machine flown by Second

---

* Other Canadians serving with 70 Squadron included E.A. Copp of Sackville, NB, K.B. Watson of Malton, Ont., and J.S. Wilson of Edmonton (POW 29 Sept. 1918).

† An unlikely possibility, bearing in mind the logistical situation of the German air force. The German ace Friedrich Noltenius wrote in his diary for the same day that 'Because of the petrol shortage we now flew only once a day, in the evening.' 'War Diary of Friedrich Noltenius,' *Cross & Cockade Journal*, VII, winter 1966, 329

Lieutenant A.B.D. Campbell of Macleod, Alta, went into 'a vertical dive which developed into a spin. It could not be watched to the ground.'[34]

The next day Lale was leading nine aircraft which, after bombing Roisel, continued north until they got into a fight with seven Fokkers just southeast of Cambrai. Shooting down one enemy machine for certain, with the possibility of a second, the Brisfits then swung south again and saw formations of DH4s, Sopwith Dolphins, and SE5as going towards St Quentin, about two thousand feet below. Following them, the Brisfits caught up just as thirty to forty Fokkers dived on the Dolphins. One German passed less than thirty yards in front of Captain Lale's machine and he 'put about 50 rounds into it and sent it down in flames.' Meanwhile, Edwards, in the rear cockpit, was firing his twin Lewis guns at another enemy aircraft about forty yards away on the left. 'This E.A. first spun, then appeared to gain control, but a few seconds later burst into flames.' Three other German aircraft were credited to the guns of 20 Squadron and Second Lieutenant D.M. Calderwood of Minto, Man., flying as Campbell's observer, was credited with one 'out of control.'* On the 7th, for the third day in succession, Lale and Edwards got at least one victory. Patrolling north of St Quentin they surprised seven Fokkers four thousand feet below them and Lale dived on them, 'getting a good burst' into one which subsequently crashed and opening fire on a second before the ammunition belt of the Vickers broke and allowed the enemy to escape. The other enemy machines 'made off East before the rest of the formation could get to them.' The Bristol Fighters seemed to have less trouble handling the Fokker D-VII than any of the British single-seater fighters and 20 Squadron in particular enjoyed considerable success during September.[35]

Both British and German air forces reduced their activities through the middle of September, with indifferent weather conditions and the American attack in the south, at St Mihiel, taking much of the pressure off the British front for a while. Only the three top-scoring British fighter pilots still flying on the Western Front – the South African Beauchamp-Proctor of 84 Squadron, Raymond Collishaw, commanding No 203, and Donald MacLaren, now leading a flight of No 46[†] – were able to record any number of victories during the last half of the month. Collishaw claimed two Fokker D-VIIs over Bourlon Wood on the 24th and two more over Lieu St Amand on the 26th, while MacLaren was credited with his second D-VII on the 15th, a share of two more on the 16th, another on the 26th, and his penultimate victim on 29 September, for a total of forty-seven credited victories in 201 days of service in an operational squadron.[36]

In the attacks south of Lens the British Third and Fourth Armies had now taken over 53,000 prisoners and 470 guns. After ten days of comparative rest a further attack was launched between Gauzeaucourt and Holnon, designed to bring the

---

* Campbell became a prisoner on 15 September 1918. Other Canadians flying with 20 Squadron included H.E. Johnston of Winnipeg, S.A. Mowat of Vancouver, and W.M. Thomson of Toronto.

† Other Canadian pilots flying with 46 Squadron included G.E. Dowler of Calgary (KIA 10 Nov. 1918), R.K. McConnell of Victoria, R.F. McRae of Niagara Falls, Ont., H.C. Saunders of Kingston, Ont. (KIA 18 Sept. 1918), L.L. Saunders of Brantford, Ont. (KIA 4 Oct. 1918), J.K. Shook of Tioga, Ont. (POW 2 Oct. 1918), and E.R. Watt of Edmonton.

southern wing of the victorious British armies up against the main defences of the Hindenburg Line. Visibility was poor and little flying could be done as the assault began on 18 September. Nevertheless, it went in successfully and another 11,750 prisoners and 100 guns were taken on the 18th and 19th.[37]

In the air the Germans reappeared in strength on the 20th and there was a furious encounter on the Fourth Army front between twenty D-VIIs on the one side and seven Brisfits of 20 Squadron and eleven SE5as of 84 Squadron on the other. The fight lasted for half-an-hour and reached from 14,000 down to 1500 feet. Eight enemy aircraft were claimed, for the loss of two machines. Only one Canadian, D.M. Calderwood, was flying with the Brisfits on this occasion and he was one of those killed, but one flight of the SE5as was led by Captain C.F. Falkenberg of Quebec City, who claimed two Fokkers.* At one point in the fight, Falkenberg reported, a number of enemy aircraft which had a distinct height advantage 'were afraid to come down,' which suggests that the German side of such battles was more than ever being carried by the hard core of veterans among the German pilots, while replacements were held out of the fighting as long as possible.[38]

As a result of this and earlier combats instructions were issued to III Brigade on 22 September that 'offensive patrols will normally consist of two or more fighting squadrons ... the patrol should be comprised of an SE5 or "Dolphin"† squadron above, with one or more Camel squadrons below it.' This was an advance in British tactical doctrine which was now long overdue. Nevertheless, the rising total of British losses had done nothing to affect seriously the overall British supremacy in the air. The vast majority of reconnaissance, artillery spotting, and bombing patrols went about their duties without any interference other than that caused by ground fire. As an example, 13 Squadron's Lieutenants J.P. McClelland (pilot) of Arthur, Ont., and J.W.G. Clark (observer)‡ of Toronto, who had begun to establish a high reputation as experts in their unspectacular business, were able to conduct a very elaborate artillery shoot lasting some four hours on 20 September. The guns they ranged 'thoroughly smashed' two enemy batteries and a number of other gun positions were knocked about without any interruption by enemy aircraft, while the next day another four-hour shoot ranged by them brought a report that 'Enemy Air activity [was] slight.'[39]

Artillery co-operation, which had developed almost wholly in response to the conditions of static warfare and the procedure for which had been standardized most recently in December 1917, underwent significant changes during the more fluid fighting of 1918. For much of this period the counter-battery staff officer of the Canadian Corps was Lieutenant-Colonel A.G.L. McNaughton. His work,

---

* Other Canadian pilots flying with 84 Squadron on 20 September 1918 included D. Carruthers of Kingston, Ont., and J.A. Jackson of Toronto.

† The Sopwith Dolphin 5F1, first issued to Western Front squadrons in January 1918, was the successor to the Camel. Slightly faster than the Camel, it was still no match – in speed, rate of climb, or ceiling – for the Fokker D-VII.

‡ Clark, who was to win the DFC in October, was on his second tour of operations. In the Second World War he was to be Director of Public Relations for the RCAF. McClelland, in contrast, was a novice on the Western Front. No 13 Squadron was his first operational posting and he had only joined the squadron on 12 August.

followed up by his successor, Lieutenant-Colonel H.D.G. Crerar, was decidedly innovative in character and attests to the importance of the role of the RAF. A postwar report, prepared over Crerar's signature, recorded the procedures of the Counter Battery Office and outlined the importance of airpower in mobile operations. According to the report, the Counter Battery Office, handling the vital calls – 'N' ('guns in position at ...'), 'NF' ('guns firing in position at ...'), 'WPNF' ('many batteries active at ...'), and 'GF' ('fleeting target at ...') – transmitted from the reconnaissance and spotting aircraft through the Central Wireless Station nearby, was of 'increasing importance' as an intelligence centre once open warfare replaced the positional deadlock of the past three years.* Air photographs, written reports dropped from contact patrol machines, wireless messages from their own artillery aircraft and intercepts from the enemy's, sound-ranging and ground observers' reports were all funnelled through the Counter Battery Office, so that 'During a battle it has been found necessary to maintain constantly on duty at the Counter Battery Office one officer whose sole responsibility is the reception of Intelligence and, whenever required, its further transmission to the Headquarters of formations which it may affect.'[40] It is clear from Crerar's account that among the varied sources of information reaching the Counter Battery Office and formation headquarters the data provided by the corps squadrons was the most valuable and usually the most reliable in conditions of open warfare.

In the last months of the war the Canadians had also worked out a procedure for using the tactical day-bombing squadrons of the appropriate army wing under the direction of the Counter Battery Office: 'Important Targets, such as large bodies of enemy infantry, artillery on the move, convoys of motor transport which were either beyond the effective range of the Artillery, or which, by reason of their extreme importance required a very intense bombardment, were engaged by the Army Bombing Squadrons in response to "LL" ["all available batteries to open fire (sudden attack or very favourable target)"] or "GF" calls sent from the Counter Battery Office and outlined the importance of airpower in mobile operathe Counter Battery Office during a battle is considered to be of the very greatest importance.'[41]

No such procedure was possible for the night bombers, but their reports show them to have been doing good work as well. On the night of 20/21 September eight FE2bs of 83 Squadron bombed Bazuel aerodrome, dropping six 230-lb, eight 112-lb, two 40-lb, and fifty-three 25-lb bombs from 4000 feet. Visibility was poor and little damage was done but the only opposition encountered came from anti-aircraft fire over Cambrai and Le Cateau. Two other machines of the squadron were flying reconnaissance missions that night and one, flown by Major D.A. McRae of Aylesbury, Sask., was brought down by a shot from the ground which went through the fuel tank. The second, piloted by Captain G.E. Race of Montreal,† saw no movement of troops or transport and came back from a three-hour

---

* 'The "NF" call ... is very often the only reliable source of information and the effective neutralizing of hostile artillery fire at critical moments may depend upon the work of the Corps Squadrons,' wrote Lt-Col. H.D.G. Crerar in his postwar report on the 'Organization and Procedure of Counter Battery Office, Canadian Corps Artillery,' 25 Jan. 1919, DHist 72/13.
† Other Canadian flying officers with the squadron on 21 September included K. de W. Cleveland of Kingston, NS, N.S. Jones of Toronto, and C.S. Stonehouse of Wallaceburg, Ont.

patrol having done nothing more violent than firing some three hundred rounds of small arms ammunition at searchlights and machine-gunners on the ground.[42]

On the following night an FE2b of 102 Squadron, flown by Lieutenant G.L. Shephard of Kingston, Ont., checked roads and railways in the vicinity of Cambrai for enemy troop or transport movement and found only one train, on the line east of Sancourt, going towards Cambrai. Two 112-lb and six 25-lb bombs were dropped but 'Searchlights prevented observation of result.' A second machine, with Second Lieutenant E.J. Clark of Montreal as observer, patrolled between Gauzeaucourt and Cambrai and reported 'all roads closely watched and appeared quite clear,' although when flying over Rumilly they were fired on by ground machine-guns and 'hit in several places.'[43]

Massed German fighter sweeps, already infrequent, were becoming more rare as the British went about their multitudinous duties in support of their ground forces. 'I returned to France in September,' testified Captain R.T.C. Hoidge, who was posted to IX Brigade's 1 Squadron,* on 25 September; '... there weren't very many Huns in the sky, they were pretty well thinned out.' Hoidge, a Torontonian, had spent ten months with 56 Squadron during the desperate days of 1917 and was well qualified to make the comparison. His judgment is confirmed by the experience of Josef Raesch, a pilot of *Jasta 43*, who was shot down on 25 July and parachuted to safety within the German lines. After two weeks' leave Raesch returned to his squadron, but there was no machine available for him until 3 September and, on the 5th, the squadron's fuel ration was cut to two thousand litres of benzine per month. 'It is getting worse all the time,' he wrote. 'The British are superior to us, not only in numbers but in their tactics and organization.'[44]

With Ludendorff pressed back against his prepared defensive lines all along the front, the British began an assault on the Wotan and Hindenburg Lines simultaneously on 27 September. The Second Army, in co-operation with the Belgians, attacked from St Eloi north to Dixmude; the First, Third, and Fourth Armies moved on the St Quentin-Cambrai front. The southern attack covered a wider frontage and faced more serious obstacles, but it also offered more decisive possibilities since an advance of some twenty miles at one point would bring the British to the western edge of the Ardennes and thus virtually split the German armies on the Western Front in two. It was here, on the Canal du Nord sector of the Hindenburg Line, that the attack was therefore most strongly pressed and most stubbornly resisted.

Long stretches of the Canal du Nord, which had been under construction at the outbreak of war, were still dry. It was, in fact, more in the nature of a gigantic ditch than a canal. It varied from thirty-six to fifty feet wide at the bottom and was twelve feet deep; and the Germans had strengthened its defensive potential by cutting back the eastern bank into a vertical wall of some nine feet at the places where an attack seemed likeliest. Both banks were studded with concrete strongpoints and deep dug-outs and the whole structure formed the core of a defensive line about five miles thick. To assault it the RAF provided the three Armies

---

* Other Canadians in 1 Squadron when he arrived included L.H. Phinney of Winnipeg and F.M. Squires of Toronto.

involved with more than a thousand aircraft in the squadrons of I, III, V, and IX Brigades.[45]

The battle opened along a thirteen-mile front between Sauchy Lestrée and Gauzeaucourt, with the Canadian Corps again assigned to spearhead the attack. No 8 Squadron, still being used for tank support, contact patrols, and artillery observation, was working with the Canadians. A machine flown by Lieutenant S.B. Trites of Salisbury, NB, was in the air by 0600 hrs and back again by 0640 hrs with a bullet hole in its fuel tank. The tank was changed and Trites was airborne again in half-an-hour, charged with bombing enemy trenches, noting those areas where they were *not* fired at from the ground, and recording the intensity of the rolling artillery barrage that preceded the infantry assault. While 'Prisoners were noticed coming back along the road going S[outh]. W[est],' he reported 'No sign of E[nemy]. A[ircraft].' Before Trites returned Lieutenant W. Spriggs of Port Williams, NS, was over the front, bombing and machine-gunning enemy troops and transport and reporting tank locations, casualties, and the presence of British infantry in Bourlon Wood by 1100 hrs.[46]

No 73 Squadron, led by Captain W.H. Hubbard of Toronto, who won a Bar to his DFC for the day's work, showed how thoroughly the counter anti-tank gun role had been mastered. In November 1917, during the First Battle of Cambrai, the tanks had 'suffered heavy casualties' from anti-tank guns sited behind Flesquières Ridge. Ten months later the tanks were attacking again over the same ground with Sopwith Camels keeping the ridge under close observation all the time. The losses were minimal. Hubbard alone, coming in at heights as low as two hundred feet, 'engaged and silenced many anti-tank guns,' and 'Countless instances could be recounted of German gunners being chased away from their guns and then prevented from working them until captured by the tanks.' It was a measure of their success that, of the sixteen Mark IV tanks working with the Canadian Corps, fifteen successfully crossed the Canal du Nord near Moeuvres and only three were subsequently put out of action during the day, one by a mine and two by artillery.[47]

On the First Army front there were now five squadrons allocated exclusively to the ground support function under Major Smythies, 40 Squadron having been added to the old hands of 54, 64, and 209 Squadrons, and No 203 having replaced 208. Their main objectives were the crossings over the Sensée and L'Escaut canals and 'in many cases large numbers of troops, mechanical and horse transport, were seen on the bridges and heavily engaged with machine gun fire and 25-lb bombs. Many direct hits were made and numerous casualties observed.' Seven hundred bombs were dropped and 26,000 rounds fired by the five squadrons during the day.[48]

Further south, only 201 squadron was allocated exclusively to a ground support role in III Brigade. Its pilots were not given particular tactical objectives but told to choose targets of opportunity when not responding to specific wireless calls from the Central Information Bureau. Lieutenant W.A.W. Carter of Fredericton*

---

* Other Canadians flying with 201 Squadron on 27 September 1918 included J.M. MacKay of Vancouver, C.M.K. Morrison of Wapella, Sask., E.F. Nicholson of Morganston, Ont., and F.T.S. Sehl of Victoria.

found that '... smoke from barrage caused thick mist over [ground] objectives, so returned and followed up our advancing infantry and tanks, helping infantry at points where held up by firing bursts into machine-gun emplacements and trenches from very low altitude. Dropped bombs on machine-gun emplacements offering particularly strong resistance to our advance; and then saw our infantry capture the point. Fired remainder of ammunition into trenches in front of our tanks.'[49] Lieutenant Carter was frequently under intense machine-gun and small arms fire from the ground and finally his fuel pipe was ruptured by a bullet. He crashed right in the middle of the British artillery barrage but escaped uninjured from the wreck of his Camel; he began to run westwards until he stumbled across a wounded British infantryman. Carrying him, Carter kept on until he met two unescorted German prisoners whom he requisitioned to carry the wounded man back into the British lines.[50]

The weather closed in during the night, although the night-bombing squadrons had been in action early on. Before dawn, rain and low cloud made flying impossible, and it was not until the afternoon of the following day that the RAF could get into the air again. The low-flying attacks on the First Army front were confined to the three Sopwith Camel squadrons – Nos 54, 203, and 209 – on the afternoon of the 28th, the SE5a squadrons being diverted to offensive patrols with orders to pay special attention to enemy observation balloons. Since the German air arm remained quiescent these patrols were made uneventful. The Camels, in contrast, had an exciting time attacking troops and transport in the neighbourhood of the canal crossings, including a 'large column' that the pilots of 209 Squadron found on the Cambrai-Le Cateau road. 'The pilots concentrated on their attacks upon the column from a low height, dropping thirty-six bombs and firing some thousands of rounds of machine-gun ammunition, as a result of which the column was thrown into confusion.'[51]

The weather was again bad for flying on the 29th – indeed, it continued to be poor until 1 October – but air support was hardly necessary any more. Crown Prince Rupprecht recorded, on 28 September, that 'the [German] troops will no longer stand up to a serious attack' and the Reichstag party leaders were told that the war was lost and 'that every twenty-four hours can only make the situation worse.' Ludendorff sent a message that a peace offer must be made at once. Even as the Kaiser's Chief of Staff was admitting defeat, the 61st Infantry Regiment, in line just north of Cambrai, found that 'there was little cover. It was important to burrow into the ground quickly and to be seen as little as possible because numerous enemy aircraft soon fired on any unit that was incautious.' The 176th Infantry Regiment, moving up to Eswars for a local counter-attack, recorded that 'on the way enemy bombing cause the loss of 25 men from the small remnants of the regiment.' The next day the 119th Reserve Regiment, fighting to hold Tilloy, observed bitterly that 'during the entire day enemy aircraft were cavorting above the positions without any hindrance.'[52]

Victory was a monotonous affair, were reliance to be placed solely on the summaries of work produced daily by RAF brigades. In the confined vocabulary of military reporting these summaries repeated, day after day, the same story as RAF machines bombed and strafed the enemy ground forces, knocking out transport, immobilizing artillery, scattering infantry, and reporting the remorseless advance of their front line. But to individual airmen the experience of victory was enormously exhilarating. On 1 October Carl Falkenburg, leading a patrol of 84 Squadron over the Fourth Army front, saw 'our infantry and tanks advancing towards Estrées and several hundred of the enemy running in front of them; he thereupon dived on the enemy with his flight as they crossed the open, inflicting heavy casualties.' The measured phrases of the official RAF *communiqué* reporting Falkenburg's work contrast with the disorganization and chaos into which the German ground forces were now falling.[53]

By 5 October 1918 the British line in the south had advanced to the outskirts of Montbrehain and Ponchaux, the Third Army was in Crevecoeur and Proville, and the First Army through Tilloy, so that Cambrai was now threatened from both flanks. The RAF reported that 'all enemy airfields west of the railway St Quentin-Bohain-Busigny-Le Cateau were evacuated and that the great ammunition dumps at Fresnoy le Grand and Brancourt-le-Grand were empty.'[54] In the north, where the Second Army's attack in front of Ypres had met with less resolute resistance, the British had taken Dadizeele, were through the Gheluwe switch line, and in Comines and Armentières by 3 October. The Germans, who had already pulled back from the Lys salient, won at such cost in April, were now left with the beginnings of a new and far larger salient between Ledeghem and Aubencheul, more than forty miles across and deepening every day.

They were also threatened on a strategic scale west of Verdun, where the French Fourth and American First Armies were pushing slowly northwards on each side of the Argonne Forest and were now poised to strike at the key railway which ran along the southwestern flank of the Ardennes from Metz and Thionville to Mezières. Since the middle of July the German armies on the Western Front had lost nearly 4000 artillery pieces, 25,000 machine-guns, and over a quarter of a million men as prisoners, in addition to their killed and wounded. On 8 October the three southern British armies resumed their offensive, pushing through Cambrai on the 9th and reaching Busigny on the 10th and Le Cateau on the 11th.[55]

In the air tactical and technological evolution went on apace, if rather informally, unhindered by any aerial opposition. The SE5as of 84 Squadron took up ultra-low-level reconnaissance duties during one spell of poor weather during the middle of the month.

The line had been advancing very rapidly, communications from the front were bad and General Rawlinson was often uncertain as to the position of his advanced troops. At this time No 84 Squadron was carrying out a series of low-flying attacks on the retreating enemy so that the pilots became very familiar with the lie of the land over which our troops were advancing ... About the middle of October there came a week of foggy weather, when ... reconnaissance became almost impossible. It then occurred to someone to ask No 84 Squadron to try and discover the position of our own and the enemy's advanced troops ... The method employed was as follows ... From Le Cateau half a dozen roads radiated eastwards, and led through the enemy's front line. Making Le Cateau one's base one flew out along each road in turn at twenty to thirty feet until either one saw enemy troops or was fired on. One then turned, and flew back to Le Cateau, marked on the map the point where the enemy's troops were encountered, and set off eastward again along another road. Each road was thus prospected in turn, and by this means half-a-dozen points were obtained which if joined gave roughly the enemy's front line.[56]

According to a German historian, the close-support Camel squadrons devised new weapons with which to harass the retreating Germans: '... the enemy pilots were contriving new ways of harassment. Bombs and machine-guns seemed no longer to inflict sufficient devastation, and they invented a new instrument of destruction by joining together 20-30 hand-grenades which fell on the troops and caused terrible devastation. I was a witness when an enemy air formation carried out an attack on a firing battery. The battery commander recognized the danger immediately and tried to save the battery by moving off the guns, but it was too late. The entire crew and all horses were wiped out ...'[57]

Even the corps squadrons were becoming rather venturesome, with artillery patrols, finding their normal duties impossible because of mist and cloud at five hundred feet, beginning to indulge themselves in ground strafing roles. After a while they ceased to need even the excuse of poor visibility and, on 22 October, a slow old RE8 of 16 Squadron, piloted by Captain H.L. Tracy of Toronto and with Captain J.E. Purslow, address unknown, as observer, noticed a forty-coach passenger train passing through Callenelle while flying an artillery patrol. Despite heavy ground fire, they strafed it from 1500 feet, 'after which the train stopped.' They then went on to 'engage a body of hostile troops on road with their M[achine] G[uns] and succeeded in inflicting some casualties while the remaining hostile infantry rushed for cover.' Their actions were out of the ordinary, but not, perhaps, quite as unusual as those of 4 Squadron's Lieutenant R.H. Schroeder of New Westminster, BC, on 22 October, who, when 'flying at low height well in advance of infantry was forced to land at Wasquelles [sic], which had only been vacated by the enemy two hours previously. He was the first British officer to enter Roubaix.'[58]

The enemy was falling back not only in the areas under direct attack, but also from the huge salient which had developed in the centre, evacuating an area nearly forty miles square during the second half of the month. German infantry in the Catillon area, facing the Fourth Army some four miles southeast of Cambrai, noted despondently that 'During these days enemy aircraft participated with special intensity in the enemy infantry attacks. Flying along the front at extremely low levels, they fired on the German troops in their positions and shell-holes, dropped bombs and even hand-grenades, which was particularly depressing because no German planes could be seen and help or support from them was no longer to be expected.'[59] The author, a regimental runner with the 413th Infantry Regiment, found himself under personal attack by a British machine shortly afterwards as he carried orders from the regimental headquarters to the battalions: 'At first I believed that the hits around me were coincidental, but as the enemy aircraft turned around and fired on me from the front, I realised that the ammunition waste was meant for me ... this game lasted for quite some time. What a superabundance of men and materiel the enemy must have had that he could permit himself to hunt a single man from the air.'[60]

The British 'superabundance' of men and materiel was now well established, but in the Fokker D-VII the Germans had retained a technological supremacy which had gone some way to make up for their logistical difficulties and increasing shortage of adequately trained pilots. British airmen often gave better than they got in combat, a fine example being 46 Squadron's action on 26 September, when two flights of Camels, led by Donald MacLaren and including A.M. Allan of Toronto and R.F. McRae of Niagara Falls, Ont., met 22 Fokkers near Havrincourt. MacLaren, with the lower flight, immediately attacked the lower level of Fokkers and brought down one enemy machine. Outnumbered and with some novices in their ranks (Allan had been flying operationally only since 5 September 1918), No 46 still had the better of this exchange.[61] Usually, however, the Germans had the best of it, and it was not the Fokker D-VII alone which gave them the upper hand. Normally they chose to fight in large formations, and since their appearances were irregular they were able to achieve both surprise and a strong, if brief, local superiority. In August the RAF had lost 215 machines, the highest monthly total of the war to date. In September the figure rose again, to 235, and although it dropped substantially to 164 in October, their combat/loss ratio was probably at least as high as in September since the enemy was accepting battle less and less often.[62]

When he did choose to fight neither technological nor numerical superiority was of much avail against the finely pitched tactical skills of the RAF pilots. On one occasion a pair of Camels from 65 Squadron, led by Captain J.L.M. White of Halifax who had won a DFC earlier in the summer, dived on a formation of fourteen enemy scouts and White shot down two of them before making off unharmed with his wing-man. White led twelve offensive patrols during the month: on the 14th one of the flights encountered eleven D-VIIs over Courtrai:

He got a burst at one E.A. from 20 feet range and the machine went down in a spin but came out of it and went gliding East. He then attacked another which was on the tail of a Camel and fired about 100 rounds into it as he approached, observing his tracers to be hitting the nose of the E.A. The enemy machine went down vertically, black smoke coming out of the fuselage and was last seen diving vertically and was burning. He then attacked another Fokker biplane from behind and, after having fired three bursts into it, the machine turned over on its back and a piece of the tailplane folded over. The E.A. righted itself and Capt. White put another burst into it, after which it went down completely out of control.[63]

In November White was awarded a Bar to his DFC and in December a Croix de Guerre was added to his decorations.

What was still needed, however, was a British aircraft to match the capabilities of the Fokker D-VII. During October such a machine began to appear on the Western Front. The Sopwith Snipe was a lineal descendant of the Sopwith Camel and the Dolphin. Although it could not challenge the operational ceiling or the rate of climb of the D-VII and was fractionally slower in level flight, it was as well armed (with twin Vickers firing through the airscrew), it provided just as stable a gun-platform, and it could turn more tightly than the D-VII, an immense advantage in the tangled, twisting dogfights which characterized air combats of the era. Nos 43, 208, and 4 (Australian Flying Corps) were the first squadrons to be equipped with the Snipe. On 17 October 1918, however, one more Snipe arrived in France, flown by a man who was worth a squadron in himself.

Major William George Barker of Dauphin, Man., was now twenty-three years old, with two aerial victories officially credited to him for every year of his life. The threads of his career to this point have already been woven into earlier chapters of this book. After serving as an observer and pilot with the RFC for a year-and-a-half on the Western Front in 1916 and 1917, he had commanded 28 Squadron in Italy for almost a year before being posted to the UK to take command of an air-fighting school at Hounslow. But recognizing that the air war in France had become tactically very different from that which he had known earlier on the Western Front and had been experiencing more recently in Italy, Barker applied for a refresher course before taking up his new appointment. He was promptly attached to 201 Squadron (Sopwith Camels) at La Targette for ten days.

Barker saw no enemy aircraft during his stay with 201, however, and when he took off on 27 October he was *en route* to the UK and his non-operational posting. One last look at the front seemed in order. He climbed to 21,000 feet over the Forêt de Mormal. There he spotted a Rumpler two-seater reconnoitring the lines, attacked it, and set off an air fight against sixty Fokkers which won him the Victoria Cross, the third and last Canadian airman to be so decorated in the First World War.

Barker's fire broke up the Rumpler in the air. He then found his own machine peppered by a Fokker biplane, climbing in a near stall, almost a thousand feet below him. Wounded in the right thigh, Barker threw his Snipe into a spin and spiralled down two thousand feet, only to find himself in the midst of fifteen more D-VIIs. He fired at two which disappeared and then got a burst into a third from ten yards' range and set it on fire. The other Fokkers were now milling around him, firing from all angles; wounded again in the other thigh, he fainted and the Snipe went into another spin, dropping to 15,000 feet before he recovered consciousness in the middle of a lower echelon of the enemy formation. The Canadian got behind one of them and opened fire, while another Fokker got on his tail. The machine in front soon burst into flames, but the one behind was riddling the Snipe with bullets and Barker was hit once more and his left elbow shattered. Again he fainted and again the Snipe went into a spin and lost its immediate pursuer. At 12,000 feet Barker came to, this time to find himself in the midst of a third echelon of enemy fighters whirling in to the attack from all directions. With the Snipe's airframe punctured by innumerable bullet holes and its engine smoking, Barker picked out one more D-VII and flew straight for it, firing as he went. The Fokker disintegrated and the Snipe suffered further damage as Barker hurtled through, fragments of the German machine tearing the punctured remnants of its fabric. Yet the Snipe kept flying and Barker, momentarily in the clear, dived westwards and raced for the British lines, dodging a fourth enemy formation as he did so. He crossed the lines at tree-top height and finally crashed into the barbed-wire entanglements which protected a British balloon site, with four more aircraft added to his roll of victories. One of the many witnesses to this spectacular episode – he termed it a 'stimulating incident' – was A.G.L. McNaughton, now the commander of the Canadian Corps Heavy Artillery, who watched from his advanced headquarters between Bellevue and Valenciennes. The encounter took place in full view of many thousands of British and Canadian soldiers in the trenches. 'The hoarse shout, or rather the prolonged roar, which greeted the triumph of the British fighter, and which echoed across the battle front, was never matched ... on any other occasion,' McNaughton later wrote. 'By Jove, I was a foolish boy, but anyhow I taught them a lesson,' Barker exulted from a hospital bed in Rouen, ten days later. 'The only thing that bucks me up is to look back and see them going down in flames.'[64]

As Barker lay in hospital recovering from his wounds, the war was drawing to a close. Yet there was much bitter fighting remaining; on 30 October the British admitted losing forty-one aircraft while claiming a record number of sixty-seven Germans shot down. The heavy fighting was precipitated by the attempts of the RAF day-bomber squadrons to interdict the railway system which supplied the northern group of German armies and constituted the primary means by which they might be withdrawn from northern France and Belgium. The DH9as of 205 Squadron were given Namur as their objective.* On 28, 29, and 30 October they reached their target and bombed without loss. The DH9 squadrons, however, were not quite so fast and their operational ceiling was only 13,000 feet. They were scheduled to attack slightly closer junctions at La Louvière, Charleroi, and Mariembourg. On the 28th and 29th they were driven back by enemy fighter concentrations; on the 30th only ten of thirteen machines from 107 Squadron were able to reach Mariembourg.[65]

The bomber leader on that occasion, Captain F.M. Carter of Orillia, Ont., with Lieutenant A.W.H. Arundell of Montreal as his observer, reported two direct hits on Mariembourg junction with his 112-lb bombs and claimed an enemy fighter shot down on the return trip. His deputy, flying with Second Lieutenant F.C. King of Ottawa as his observer, also claimed two direct hits; a third machine, with Second Lieutenant H. Wittup of Calgary as observer, reported success as well. One of the aircraft which failed to reach the assigned target, flown by Second Lieutenant J.H. Grahame of Stony Mountain, Man., developed engine trouble on the way out but dropped its bombs on Landrecies railway junction instead. The bombers of 107 Squadron were escorted over the lines by Sopwith Snipes of 43 Squadron; its pilots claimed five victories during the operation, including one by Lieutenant G.R. Howsam of Port Perry, Ont.† On the same day the DH9s of I Brigade's 98 Squadron, on a short-range mission against Mons, were intercepted by 'a large formation of E.A. Scouts, chiefly Fokker Biplanes,' their escort of Sopwith Dolphins from 19 Squadron having to fight desperately hard to protect them. Five Dolphins and four DH9s were lost and nine German fighters were claimed destroyed and two others driven down out of control. Lieutenant W.F.

---

* Canadians flying in 205 Squadron at this time included W.B. Esplen of Pense, Sask., F.O. McDonald of Penticton, BC, and K.G. Nairn of Winnipeg.
† Other Canadians in 107 Squadron included L. Ashton of Mairkirk, Ont., I.H. Christie of Toronto, S.L. Dunlop of Calgary, and A.B. Holden of Victoria. In 43 Squadron the Canadians included J.P. Bernigand of Montreal, G.F. Geiger of Brockville, Ont., W.G. Holden of Indian Head, Sask., R.L. Houlding of Brantford, Ont., L.N. Mitchell of Liverpool, NS, J.K. Pickard of Ridgeway, Ont., and W.H. Temple of Toronto.

Hendershot of Kingsville, Ont., claimed one shot down and one out of control, while Lieutenant C.M. Moore* reported shooting down a D-VII in flames.[66]

The strong German reaction to these raids prompted another heavy attack by the RAF. At last Trenchard's war of attrition was paying substantial dividends even if the benefits were accruing under his successor, Salmond, and this was no time to be easing the pressure. During the morning a reconnaissance by pilots of the Australian squadrons in X Brigade had revealed that many of the enemy fighters were operating out of Rebaix, just north of Ath. All the squadrons of the brigade were therefore detailed to make a low-level attack on the aerodrome during the early afternoon. Sixty-two British aircraft, bombing from heights as low as twenty feet, completely destroyed two hangars and their contents, wrecked two machines parked in the open, and systematically shot up miscellaneous ground targets on or near the airfield. 'Horses were stampeded in all directions, M[otor] T[ransport] attacked with machine gun fire, trains and motor cars damaged and casualties caused to personnel,' as the result of bombing and machine-gunning by 2(AFC), 54 and 103 Squadrons, while 4(AFC) and 88 Squadrons supplied top cover.[67]

The whole attacking force had to fight its way to and from Rebaix. During the course of the flight two DH9s and a Snipe were lost while nine enemy aircraft were claimed destroyed, one of them by 88 Squadron's Lieutenant K.B. Conn of Almonte, Ont., as well as two out of control, one of which was credited to Lieutenant J. Deslauriers of Montreal.[†] Taken as a whole, 30 October was the most intensive day of air fighting during the war, and although the bombing attacks which set it off had little effect, the damage done to the German fighter force during the ensuing combats was irreparable. There were to be further brief flurries of fighting, but deteriorating weather and the progressive collapse of German resistance on the ground[‡] brought a general reduction in air fighting.

On 1 November the Canadian Corps attacked Valenciennes in their last major assault of the war. When the infantry moved forward early that morning without any preliminary bombardment the German artillery was quick to open a heavy fire on them, 'but its fire rapidly dwindled under the accurate counter-bombardment of the Canadian guns.' On this occasion the Canadians' Counter Battery Office also had operational direction of the day bombers from I Brigade's 10 (Army) Wing 'in engaging suitable targets on which it is impossible to develop a sufficient volume of artillery fire.' These were the DH9s of 98 Squadron commanded by Major Percy

---

* Moore was born in Quebec City, but was living in Bermuda before the outbreak of war. Other Canadians serving in 19 Squadron on 30 October included W.H. Barlow of Montreal (WIA 29 May 1918), F.H. Hall of Saint John, NB, J.S. Hewson of Amherst, NS, L.H. Ray of Toronto, W.C. Seymour of Niagara Falls, Ont., and N.A. Weir of Elbow, Sask.

† Canadians in 54 Squadron included H.R. Abey of Kaslo, BC (WIA and POW 2 Nov. 1918), J.V. Dallin of Peterborough, Ont., M.A. Genest of Trois Rivières, Que., H.T.B. Lockwood of Long Branch, Ont., G.M. Saunders of Toronto, J.M. Stevenson of Charlottetown, and S.B. Taylor of Chester, NS With 88 Squadron were C.E. Lacoste of Montreal, F.A. Lewis of Toronto, J.L. Marshall of Vancouver, C.E. Mitchell of Victoria, and J. Thibaudeau of Montreal.

‡ 'The enemy's main line ... in some cases retired 10,000 yards in a single night, and ... had in many cases retired so far as to be beyond the range of our guns.' G. Knight, 'Canadian Corps War Records; No. 5 Squadron's Work under Command of Major C.H. Gardner, from July 1918 to November 11th 1918,' 12 Jan. 1919, PAC RG 9 III, vol. 4611, folder 11, file 5

Clark Sherran* of Crapaud, PEI, which bombed the key railway junction southwest of Mons during the day. The fighter squadrons of I Brigade also found 'very good targets.' On the Valenciennes-Mons road 64 Squadron strafed transport columns, though Second Lieutenant G.W. Graham† of Shuswap, BC, lost his life during the action. Meanwhile 209 Squadron‡ punished troops and transport just north of Jenlain where a body of German troops 'who were apparently releasing gas' were scattered.[68]

In the last ten days of the war such scenes became numerous as the RAF strafed the fleeing enemy undisturbed by hostile aircraft. The diarist of 8 Squadron recorded: 'The German retreat now became general and was so rapid that tanks were unable to keep in touch with the enemy's rearguards. The squadron therefore became purely a harassing patrol unit. By low flying along highways and diving on transport, infantry columns and artillery on the march they caused great disorder in the enemy line of communications and inflicted enormous casualties.'[69] No 5 Squadron found that 'this was the easiest period we had. Our scouts appeared to hold the mastery of the air, the hostile anti-aircraft guns were rarely in action, and no defence appeared to have been organized against our aircraft.' Lieutenant N. Butt of Vancouver, observing the German retreat from an RE8 of 5 Squadron as the Canadians swept towards Mons on 9 November, reported that 'There was no shelling observed on [the] Front ... No enemy troops seen west of Mons. Civilians and Belgian flags seen in all towns as far east as Jemappes ...'[70]

The triumph of the Allies, and the collapse of their own air force, spelled horror for the retreating Germans. An American who had flown with 46 Squadron recalled, forty-three years later, his unit's last operation on 10 November:

We went out on a squadron sweep of trench strafing, and I might say that trench strafing was about the bloodiest work we had to do. We found a long straight road filled with retreating German supply trains. We saw horse drawn artillery, motor trucks, infantry and other military equipment of one kind or another. We formed a big circle and dropped our 25-lb bombs. When we got through with that road it was one unbelievable scene of chaos, with dead horses, lorries and dead soldiers all over the road. As I went down the last time to use up what was left of my ammunition and bombs, the two planes in front of me collided. In one of them was a chap by the name of Dowler, who had been a school teacher in Calgary. We had joined up the same day in Canada, but he came to the squadron later than I did. He was a damned good pilot.[71]

---

* Sherran had joined the RFC on 30 July 1916, had been awarded the MC and a Bar to it in June 1917, and had taken command of the squadron on 28 August. After the war he remained in the RAF and rose to the rank of wing commander, losing his life in the King's Cup Air Race of 1937. Other Canadians serving in 98 Squadron on 1 November 1918 included G.H. Gillis of Halifax (WIA 23 Oct. 1918) and N.C. MacDonald of Tugaske, Sask.

† Graham's real name was Hoffman, but he had enlisted under his mother's maiden name to disguise his German parentage. Other Canadians in 64 Squadron at this time included J.W. Bell of Charlottetown (WIA 11 March 1918) and B.J. Forester of Vernon, BC.

‡ In 209 Squadron were E.W. Mills of Hamilton, G.T. Porter of Montreal, J.B. Saer of Toronto, and J. Shaw of St Catharines, Ont.

Second Lieutenant George Emerson Dowler and the pilot of the machine which collided with him on 10 November appear to be the last RAF flyers to have been killed in action during the First World War. On the same day 84 Squadron's Lieutenant F.H. Taylor of Toronto was credited with bringing down an enemy machine, scoring the last victory of the war to be recorded in the RAF *communiqués*.* At 1100 hrs the next morning, as the ground forces ceased firing, history's first air war also came to an end.[72]

In his penultimate despatch, dated 21 December 1918, Sir Douglas Haig paid formal tribute to 'the work of our airmen in close co-operation with all fighting branches of the Army' during the last year of the war:

> Some idea of the magnitude of the operations carried out can be gathered from the fact that from the beginning of January, 1918, to the end of November, nearly 5,500 tons of bombs were dropped by us, 2,953 hostile aeroplanes were destroyed, in addition to 1,178 others driven down out of control, 241 German observation balloons were shot down in flames, and an area of over 4,000 square miles of country has been photographed, not once but many times.
>
> The assistance given to the infantry by our low-flying aeroplanes during the battles of March and April was repeated during the German offensives on the Aisne and Marne ... During our own attacks, hostile troops and transport have been constantly and heavily attacked with most excellent results.
>
> Both by day and night our bombing squadrons have continually attacked the enemy's railway junctions and centres of activity, reconnaissance machines have supplied valuable information from both far and near, while artillery machines have been indefatigable in their watch over German batteries and in accurate observation for our own guns.[73]

Haig's appreciation was the just and necessary official recognition of the gallant work of the air arm, but was, despite its statistics, hardly an evaluation of the capabilities of the air arm in war. The men who performed so many roles in the air were doubtless equally brave and dedicated, but some elements of the RAF were distinctly more important than others, both in the war effort and for the future of military aviation. There was much to be learnt from the record of the RFC, RNAS, and RAF in the First World War which had to be learnt again, at great cost, in the Second.

By the end of the war on the Western Front every capability of air power had been investigated and employed in actual operations – namely, reconnaissance,

---

* Canadians were credited with four of the last sixteen air victories recorded in the RAF *communiqué*. The others were credited to 29 Squadron's H.B. Oldham of Yarker, Ont., and two to 210 Squadron's W.S. Jenkins of Montreal (WIA 29 July 1918). Yet another, not recorded in RAF *communiqué* no 32, was the LVG shot down on 10 November by four Camel pilots of 213 Squadron, flying out of Bergues, near Dunkirk. Three of them were Canadians: H.H. Gilbert of London, Ont., G.C. Mackay of Mimico, Ont. (WIA 15 Sept. 1918), and A.B. Rosevear, address unknown. See H.H. Gilbert, 'Memories of the War,' *Cross & Cockade Journal*, XVIII, summer 1977, 132–41.

artillery observation, the use of fighters to achieve air superiority, ground support, tactical and strategic bombing, and intruder operations. The varying capabilities of the aircraft in these roles, however, had not always been properly appreciated. From the beginning it had been clear that the aeroplane had no equal as an instrument of reconnaissance. In this static war, with no prospect of outflanking the enemy in the vital theatre, massive frontal assaults requiring enormous logistical build-ups were highly susceptible to air reconnaissance. Air photography made it possible to study the enemy's defence systems and his back areas in detail and at leisure. Two or three fast machines, flying high over enemy lines and echeloned over his rear areas, could bring back a mosaic of photographs that, subjected to expert analysis, would reveal nearly everything there was to know about the enemy's preparations and immediate resources within a matter of hours.

The value of the aircraft as an observation and ranging adjunct of the artillery also won early recognition. By 1917 90 per cent of counter-battery fire, crucial to this war of sieges, was being directed from the air. Artillery was the dominant arm of the war and aircraft had become an essential part of the artillery system. In the case both of reconnaissance and of artillery observation the technical proficiency of the aircrews in carrying out their tasks had reached a high level by 1917. The postwar RAF, however, had only one squadron assigned to army liaison duties – reconnaissance and artillery co-operation – by 1923.*

As the air arm's roles increased in number and importance, air superiority became an essential element in the planning and carrying out of ground operations, a factor first fully recognized in 1916. As a result, the fighter-interceptor aircraft assumed a significance it had not previously had, and which it has not yet lost. Indeed, that significance and the aura of glamour which, for reasons of public relations, came to surround the 'aces' of the air war tended to obscure the equally dangerous and important work performed by the crews of reconnaissance and artillery aircraft.

To a considerable degree both the Germans and the British exaggerated the effectiveness of their fighter forces. The graph on page 573 compares the number of aircraft *claimed* to have been shot down by the British and German air services on the Western Front in 1918 with the number each side actually lost. The figures of claimed victories do not include aircraft alleged to have been driven down out of control but only aircraft considered to have been destroyed in the air.

Because the German official history, *Der Weltkrieg*, lists German victories and losses under each army, and because German army boundaries did not correspond precisely with those of the BEF, it has not been possible to establish an exact relationship between British and German claims and losses. Nevertheless, the representation in the graph is, it is believed, the most accurate possible reconstruction and not far removed from the reality of losses in 1918. The figures incorporated in the graph are derived ultimately from victories credited to individuals; a brief study of claims against losses will show that many an alleged 'ace' could not

---

* In 1939 the air component of the British Expeditionary Force that went to France included four squadrons of obsolescent Westland Lysanders assigned to army co-operation duties.

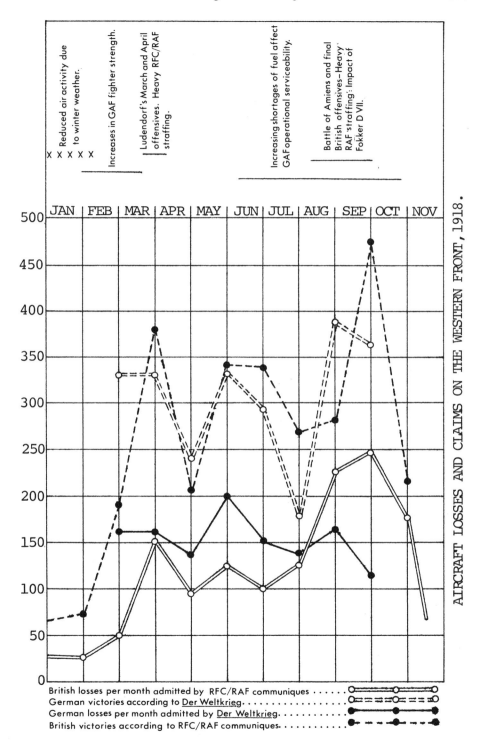

AIRCRAFT LOSSES AND CLAIMS ON THE WESTERN FRONT, 1918.

British losses per month admitted by RFC/RAF communiques · · · · · ·

German victories according to Der Weltkrieg · · · · · · · · · · · · · · · · ·

German losses per month admitted by Der Weltkrieg · · · · · · · · · · · ·

British victories according to RFC/RAF communiques · · · · · · · · · · · ·

have merited the title and, among those who could justly claim it, few can have been entitled to the full number of victories with which they were credited.*

The exaggerated claims of 1917 and 1918 were brought about not by deliberate misrepresentation but by the ever more rigorous exigencies of combat flying. Early in the war, when the air environment was one of relatively low intensity, when aircraft were slower and less manoeuvrable, tactics rudimentary, and the cubic area of combat significantly less due to low operational ceilings, claims were likely to be much more reliable. At that time a victorious pilot could often afford to follow a solitary enemy down, to deliver another burst of fire or two to make sure of his victim and to report the co-ordinates of the point at which he saw the enemy machine crash. By 1918 fighters had an operational ceiling of at least three-and-a-half miles, speeds of well over 150 mph could be reached in a dive, airframes were stronger, fire power was more than doubled, and a cubic mile of air space might contain a hundred weaving, diving, circling aircraft between two cloud layers. The pilot who kept his eyes fixed on a single enemy aircraft for more than a few seconds was likely to be shot down himself.

An increasing divergence between what the airman thought had happened and what really happened was thus inevitable. In the later stages of the war, it is also necessary to observe, both sides exploited the propaganda value of successes in the air battle. It was probably not entirely coincidental that air staffs gradually relaxed the criteria they employed to determine when a combat victory had been won. Nevertheless, as the graph clearly shows, the degree of exaggeration maintained a curiously stable relationship to reality, the most notable exception being the month of September, when the lines of German claims and British losses were briefly on converging paths.

Despite their inflated claims and credits, the 'aces' of the air war – the Vosses, von Richthofens, Bishops, Barkers, and Collishaws – were anything but fakes. They earned and held the respect of their peers as well as that of the public by their flying, shooting, and tactical skills rather than by self-advertisement or the assiduous labours of public relations staffs. But the compilation of lists of scores and the many rankings of allied and German pilots so plentiful in the romantic and sensational literature which has been built up since the First World War often rest upon assumptions which will not bear critical scrutiny. At least as far as 1918 is concerned, claims of air victories by either side should be reduced by at least one-third.

With this qualification in mind, however, there can be no doubt that the fighter aircraft was the crucial instrument in the securing of air superiority. Many ele-

---

* This was even more true of the French and Americans. The British and Germans divided credits so that each individual who participated in a victory received an appropriate proportion of the credit. The French and Americans, however, gave a full credit to each person involved. If two fighter pilots contributed to bringing down one enemy machine, then each was credited with a victory. If either pilot or observer in a two-seater shot down an enemy machine, each received one credit, and when several pilot/observer teams were involved the results could be absurd. 'In two cases sixteen men (eight pilots and eight observers) were each given credit for the E.A. they all helped to bring down.' USAF Historical Study No 131, *US Air Service Victory Credits, World War I* (Air University 1969)

ments entered into the contest between the German air force and the British flying services for the upper hand in the air. At different stages of the war, technological advantages, as in the appearance of the Fokker E-I or the DH2, were the most important factor. In the long run, superior productive capacity favoured the Allies: they could afford to produce more aircraft and could draw upon larger supplies of pilots, not to speak of fuel, than could the Germans. On the whole, however, despite some fumbling in 1916, the Germans proved more inventive in the development of fighter tactics. It was they who pioneered flight, squadron, and wing formations, and the British who followed behind. The Germans also had a better understanding of the significance of tactical air superiority. As they demonstrated repeatedly, even in the last months of the war, the application of powerful forces at the right place and time was superior to the expensive and inefficient Trenchard doctrine of attempting to be everywhere at the same time.

The expenditure of effort by the RAF on bombing was also scarcely commensurate with the results. Whether tactical or strategic, bombing was limited by technology; bomb-sights were inadequate and bomb-loads were too small. Tactical bombing, especially at low levels, frequently achieved good results, but even here there was a tendency to exaggerate its effects. Strategic bombing was vastly overrated; there was an enormous gap between the state of the art and the objectives sought. Nevertheless, the concept was seized upon by politicians as a cheap method of winning the war, and by senior air officers because it gave airpower an independent role. The illusion that airpower can win wars was created during the First World War but, except for the use of nuclear weapons against Japan in 1945, the results of strategic air assault have consistently failed to live up to expectations. Nevertheless, because the concept of strategic bombing as a decisive weapon justified the continued existence and development of a totally independent air force, and because 'tactical' bombing seemed to offer a cheap, cost-effective (and indiscriminate) way to police areas of the empire,* bombing became the *raison d'être* of the postwar RAF.

A very different fate lay in store for the close ground-support role that had come to play such an important and effective part in the ground battle during the last eighteen months of the war. It disappeared quickly and completely from the corpus of doctrine upon which RAF procurement and training was based, so that in May 1940 the British military theorist, Basil Liddell Hart, found it necessary to comment in his diary that 'we have no suitable machines for low-flying attack, and the Air Staff object to the idea of air counter-attack against troops moving up.'[74] The Germans, like the British, had discovered the value of ground support almost by accident when pilots of low-flying aircraft assigned to other duties found themselves unable to resist the opportunity to swoop down unexpectedly upon an enemy position or column, strafe it, and then zoom up and away leaving chaos on

---

* Air Commodore L.E.O. Charlton, who had ended the war commanding V Brigade on the Western Front, resigned his post as Chief Staff Officer, Iraq Command, in 1924 over the moral issue involved in this kind of bombing. He was put on half-pay and finally retired from the RAF in 1928. See Andrew Boyle, *Trenchard* (London 1962), 511, and Charlton's autobiography, written in the third person and entitled simply *Charlton* (London 1931).

the ground behind them. The practice became increasingly common on both sides by late 1916, especially when the enemy could be caught off-balance in the open, in course of either attack or retreat. Gradually airmen were assigned to such work, on the British side in conjunction with various other duties. RFC fighter pilots, most of whom disliked the assignment heartily, proved again and again how effective it could be. But it was the Germans who first institutionalized the ground-attack function, establishing specially trained units, the *Schlachtstaffeln*, developing doctrines for their tactical use *en masse*, and designing aircraft for this one particular purpose.*

The British, on the other hand, were late in regarding ground attack as a specialized function, never trained pilots exclusively for it, and were only experimenting with a distinctive aircraft type, the armoured Sopwith Salamander, when the war came to an end. Nor did the RAF ever accept the doctrine of ground attack by massed formations which the Germans used with great effect between July 1917 and July 1918. Although as many as five RAF fighter squadrons were, in effect, brigaded together under the operational control of one individual during the last three months of the war, British machines were still used singly or in pairs. Only in the realm of tank-aircraft co-operation did the RAF lead the way, a leadership that was inevitable by virtue of the fact that the Germans had only a nominal tank arm even by the end of the war.† But the welding of infantry, artillery, tanks, and aircraft into a closely-knit combat team – something the British had experimented with at Cambrai in 1917 and pushed much farther in 1918 – was left to the post-war *Wehrmacht*, which unveiled its mastery of the technique in the whirlwind Polish campaign of 1939.

Although the First World War never saw an exclusively Canadian squadron in action and no Canadian rose to a command above Group level, thousands of Canadians passed through the flying ranks of the RFC, the RNAS, and the RAF during the four years of war. A few of them returned, not to civilian life like most of their brethren, but to join a new Canadian air force. In the very different circumstances of peacetime aviation the principles and prejudices that had been instilled in them during the war had limited relevance, but when Canada began to prepare for war again, less than twenty years later, their background was to be strongly reflected in the expanding, battle-conscious RCAF. It was inescapable that the basic premises and doctrine of the Royal Canadian Air Force during the Second World War should stem directly from Canadian experience in the British flying services during the First World War.

---

*   In restrospect, this specialization of design may have been a mistake. The Ilyushin II-2, a specialized design, served the Russians well during the Second World War, but the most effective ground-attack machines were probably modifications of heavy fighter designs, the Hawker Typhoon, Curtiss P-40 (Kittyhawk), Focke-Wulf 190, and MIG-3.
†   Sixteen tanks of their own design and a small number of salvaged British tanks.

Conclusion

Maj.-Gen. S.C. Mewburn (Minister of Militia), Sir Robert Borden (Prime Minister), and Sir A.E. Kemp (Minister of the Overseas Forces of Canada) in London to attend the Imperial War Conference, July 1918 (PA 5725)

Sir George Perley, Canada's High Commissioner to the UK (and Overseas Minister from November 1916 to November 1917) on a London street (PA 7722)

F/C J.A. Barron, of Stratford, Ont., was one of the four known Canadians who flew with the RNAS airship branch. He was subsequently appointed to the Board which set up the RCNAS in the fall of 1918.

Col. Redford H. Mulock of Winnipeg was a prime mover in the formation of the CAF and could have commanded it. Instead he chose to return to civilian life after the war and became an important figure in Canadian civil aviation. (PMR 71-404)

Brig.-Gen. Alfred Critchley, in 1918 the highest ranking Canadian in the RAF, who supported enthusiastically the concept of a Canadian Air Force. 'We owe it to Canada that the magnificent work of the Canadian Airmen in France is not lost to our country,' he wrote, in April 1918. Critchley, from Calgary, went overseas with the CEF in 1914; in Feb. 1918 he was seconded to the RFC and placed in charge of cadet training in Britain, a brigadier-general at twenty-eight. He settled in England after the war. (AH 443)

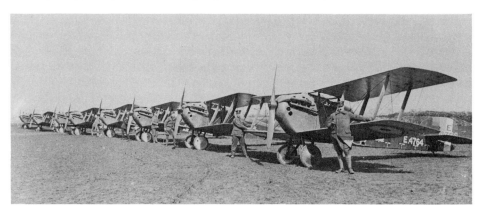

Sopwith Dolphins of 1 (Fighter) Squadron, CAF, at Upper Heyford, their UK base, in early 1919. The squadron marking on the side of the fuselage (obscured in this photograph by the lower left plane of each aircraft) was a black '1' inside a white maple leaf. (M 816-R)

The officers of 1 Squadron CAF. Standing (l to r): Lt W.L. Rutledge, AFC, MM; Lt P.F. Townley; Lt G.R. Howsam, MC; Lt E.A. Kenny; Lt F.V. Heakes; Lt C.M. McEwen, MC, CFC; Lt H.A. Marshall; Lt J. Whitford; Lt R.W. Ryan. Seated (l to r): Capt. D.R. MacLaren, DSO, MC, DFC; Capt. G.O. Johnson, MC; Maj. A.E. McKeever, DSO, MC (CO of Squadron, killed in car accident in 1919); Lt J.F. Verner; Capt. C.F. Falkenberg, DFC. Four of them – Howsam, Heakes, McEwen, and Johnson – subsequently achieved Air rank. (RE 17474)

Maj. A.D. Carter, subsequently the commanding officer of 2 Squadron, CAF, with fellow POWs in the summer of 1918. Carter, with 31 victories to his credit when he was taken prisoner in May 1918, was killed when 'stunting' with a Fokker D-VIII which fell apart in the air shortly after taking command. (RE 24067)

Groundcrew of 1 and 2 Squadron, CAF, awaiting inspection in a hangar at Upper Heyford. Late in 1918 tradesmen for the CAF were recruited from Canadians in the RAF and from members of the CEF with the appropriate civilian experience. (PA 6037)

19

Towards the Establishment of a
Canadian Air Force

In 1917–18, for the first time in her national history, Canada was in the vanguard of world events, and the accomplishments of her soldiers, as well as their heavy casualties, inspired a more assertive and powerful national feeling. The work of Canadian airmen helped to stimulate the rise of Canadian nationalism, but for the most part it was Vimy Ridge and the other great hammer blows dealt by the Canadian Expeditionary Force which reverberated in the public consciousness. The existence of a distinct army corps, commanded by a Canadian, gave a focus for national sentiment that aviation could not provide. The exploits of individual Canadians, notably W.A. Bishop, were well known and a source of pride, but there were no formations in the British flying services that could be associated with the maple leaf.

By 1917 the public had become more conscious that Canadians were playing an important, if unsung, role in the air war but there was certainly no important movement calling for the creation of a Canadian air service. The Aero Club of Canada requested the government 'to give serious consideration to the matter of eventually establishing a Canadian section of the Royal Flying Corps or a Canadian Flying Service,' but it was scarcely a representative body. Most Canadian newspapers carried feature stories about the war in the air, but these accounts had little Canadian content and were usually sensationalized and ill-informed. Some Toronto newspapers gave consistent support to the idea that Canada should have an air service of its own, the arguments they most commonly employed having to do with national identity and numbers. Why should Canadians not have 'a chance for laurels as distinctively Canadian flyers' when the Australians had? Newspaper estimates of the numbers of Canadian airmen varied from 'thousands' to the Toronto *Star*'s gross exaggeration of '35 to 50 percent of the total.'[1] Press handling of aviation in 1917 probably reflected a more general public feeling that a great many Canadians were serving in the air without having received proper credit, and that it was time they were given due recognition.

Canadian airmen shared such feelings, and so did many in the army. Distinguished pilots like Bishop and Mulock were reflecting the views of their countrymen in the flying services when they advocated the formation of a Canadian air force. Their opinions were echoed by such highly-placed officers as Sir Arthur Currie and Sir R.E.W. Turner, who were both nationally-minded and thoroughly conversant with the importance of air support in army operations. Sentiment in Canada, pressure from within the services, and the very scale of Canadian participation in the air war eventually impelled the government to accept the necessity of an air service. Consequently, in mid-1918 the government decided to bring its aviation policy into line with its established concerns about identity and status in the military and constitutional spheres by the creation of a Canadian air force, but this decision was taken so late and in such a manner that the new service was virtually stillborn.

At the end of 1916, it will be recalled, the government had set its face against a separate air service. Aviation in Canada had been left to the Royal Flying Corps and the Imperial Munitions Board, and overseas to the War Office and the Admiralty. Most of the developments which led to a retreat from this position, a retreat which took many months, occurred in London. When Sir Sam Hughes resigned in late 1916 Sir Robert Borden seized the opportunity to reorganize Canadian military affairs in England. The Prime Minister appointed Sir A.E. Kemp to succeed Hughes as Minister of Militia and Defence, but at the same time removed from the new Minister's control an area of responsibility much prized by his predecessor. Hughes, when distant from the watchful eyes of his officials in Ottawa, had taken a free hand in England. To remedy this, Borden established an Overseas Ministry in London, with Sir George Perley, the Canadian High Commissioner, as its head. To rectify the divided and inefficient administration of Canadian troops in England and of support services for the CEF in France, a headquarters of the Overseas Military Forces of Canada (OMFC) was formed in London, commanded by General Turner. In most ways, this wartime expedient was successful. Perley proved a careful and solid administrator; Turner, thwarted in his hope to succeed to the command of the Canadian Corps, was an effective staff officer.

As the new administration took hold in London, and as its reputation for efficiency spread not only among Canadian formations but also with the various British ministries and agencies having dealings with it, it became a centre and clearing house for information and problems having to do with Canadians in the forces. Perley, Turner, and their aides soon discovered that matters concerning aviation were continually coming their way. One of the first questions with which Perley came to grips in his new ministry was one left over from the Hughes period. In January 1917 Grant Morden asked for an interview with Perley in order to discuss proposals relating to aviation. After cautiously asking to inspect a copy of the order-in-council appointing Morden personal staff officer to Hughes, Sir George agreed to discuss a Canadian air service with him.[2] Had Perley chosen to act in conformity with the Cabinet's rejection of the idea, he could have given Morden short shrift. Perhaps Morden's political connections influenced him, but it is just as likely that he was swayed by the case Morden had put together, one that was much superior to his earlier submissions.

In late October 1916, on the authority of Hughes, Morden and another Canadian, Captain K.E. Kennedy of Sherbrooke, Que., had visited the RFC on the Western Front. Since that time Morden had been in consultation with Brigadier-General W.S. Brancker, Director of Air Organization, and his staff and had recognized that the new state of affairs in Canada had made irrelevant the scheme he had proposed to the RFC in August. Yet, as he wrote to Perley, a major question remained: 'whether we are going to have distinct Canadian Squadrons in the field working as part of the Royal Flying Corps, or whether we are going to continue the policy of training and equipping Canadian officers' for the RFC, in which 'they simply become members ... without retaining any Canadian individuality.' Were the army run on the same basis, there would be no Canadian divisions at the front; Canadian troops would have been parcelled out among British battalions.[3]

Morden did not emphasize 'this possibly somewhat sentimental and political standpoint,' but argued that the war presented a chance for Canada to get in on the ground floor in aviation. It was not enough that a great many Canadians were accumulating experience as pilots and observers. What Canada was missing was the challenge to put together and actually operate a flying organization, so that invaluable executive and administrative experience would be acquired, to be used in the future both for military and civil aviation at home. During his tour of the front, he had found '15% to 20% of the Squadron Officers Canadians, and in most cases they are the pick of the Squadrons.' Only if the hard-won knowledge of these individual airmen were pooled could Canada take full advantage of their service. Four Canadian service squadrons should be formed, recruited both from the veterans already in the RFC and RNAS and from RFC Canada direct entries. 'Even if nothing further is done as regards the formation of distinct Canadian Squadrons,' he told Perley, the Canadian government had to begin to accept some responsibility for the welfare of its citizens in the British flying services. Claiming that 'for a long time past' Canadian officers had been appealing to him for help in their various difficulties with the RFC, he argued for the appointment of a Canadian liaison officer attached to RFC Headquarters. In this he undoubtedly had a strong point.

Perley thought enough of these arguments to talk them over with Sir David Henderson, whom he visited on 15 February in company with his Deputy Minister, Walter Gow, and Morden. The next week Borden arrived in London and Perley became caught up in the Prime Minister's heavy schedule of meetings. It has been suggested that the two discussed the aviation question, though no evidence to that effect has survived, Borden merely recording that during his visit he dealt with 'almost every question connected with the prosecution of the War,' and examined 'an enormous mass of reports and documents.' At any rate, Gow suggested to Morden at a time when the Prime Minister's visit was in its early stages 'that something concrete had better be prepared so that when the subject [of aviation] came up for discussion there would be a proper understanding of what was proposed.'[4]

The document Morden then produced, entitled 'Recommendation for the establishment of Canadian Flying Corps,' owed much to the advice he had received from Brancker. It provided for two administrative headquarters, one in England headed by a director (Morden himself) to handle pay and records and to deal with transfers to the new service from the CEF, the RFC, and the RNAS, and another in Canada under an assistant director with responsibilities for records and recruiting in collaboration with RFC Canada. Morden recommended the creation of four squadrons, perhaps because together they would constitute a wing, the largest organization he could hope to command in his present rank as lieutenant-colonel, or perhaps because, in the view of the British Air Staff, the creation of more would seriously weaken the RFC by draining too many experienced Canadian personnel from its roster. Most of the flying officers of the four squadrons would come from RFC Canada, and flight and squadron commanders would presumably be obtained from among the experienced pilots with the RFC and RNAS, though Morden was not entirely clear on this point. All officers, however obtained, would be paid by Canada at RFC rates. The British government would be responsible for equipping the squadrons and the RFC would have the right to approve all personnel for the Canadian squadrons and to appoint non-Canadians to command them if no suitable Canadian was available. The RFC command would employ the Canadian squadrons as it thought best.[5]

It was on the basis of this memorandum that Brancker proposed a conference for 9 March, to include both the Canadians and the Australians, who still had a number of details to work out with respect to their squadrons. He made his request to the new Headquarters, Overseas Military Forces of Canada, whose staff, at this stage, knew nothing of the aviation question – their understanding was to be much improved before the year was out – but ultimately Brancker's invitation found its way to Perley. It was refused on the grounds that although the formation of Canadian squadrons was under consideration, 'it is not understood that any proposals regarding the same have as yet been submitted by the Canadian authorities.' With characteristic tenacity Brancker proposed instead a 'really necessary' informal meeting to explore air policy problems, on the understanding that any agreement reached 'would be in no way binding on the Canadian Government.'[6]

Under these ground rules Perley agreed to participate, and a meeting was held at the Air Board office on 29 March. There the minister took a non-committal stand. He refused to be specific about the number of squadrons Canada might conceivably offer, scaled down Morden's elaborate administrative arrangements to a single officer to be attached to HQ OMFC, and opposed outright the recommendation that non-Canadian officers might command Canadian squadrons together with that providing for RFC control over officer selection. The Morden document was merely a talking-point, however, and there was no follow-up to it or to the conference. From the Canadian point of view the chief significance of the episode lies in what it reveals about Perley's position, since he was to play an important part in later debates upon the aviation issue. Perley had been willing enough to consider the aviation issue upon its merits, despite its sponsorship by Morden, whose association with Sir Sam Hughes was no longer a political asset. But there is no evidence that he thought aviation important enough to give it priority among the press of other business. As he wrote in mid-April, in response to a letter from Henderson, meetings of the Imperial War Cabinet were engrossing his time, 'but I will take up the Flying Corps question just as soon as I can and arrive at some decision.'[7]

For Perley the issue was shelved, at least for the time being; for Morden, the failure to enlist the High Commissioner's active support meant the end of his aviation ambitions. Over a period of some weeks a number of his friends urged his appointment as director of a Canadian air service, or to some other important job, in letters to Perley, Borden, and Hazen. Even Henderson complained that 'a good deal of pressure is being brought on me' to recommend Morden. Perley finally cabled Borden to ask what course he should take: 'Opinion regarding him appears much divided he has ability and some warm friends who consider him capable and straightforward. On other hand general feeling seems against him and understand this is specially so in Canada.' Since Morden's appointment could scarcely be divorced from the issue of a Canadian flying corps, it is noteworthy that Borden submitted the matter to Cabinet. His reply, that 'Majority of Council consider that Morden's appointment would not be well received in Canada,' closed what may be termed the entrepreneurial phase in the pre-history of the Royal Canadian Air Force.[8]

With the end of the Morden episode the question of a Canadian flying corps seemed to be at rest, at least for the immediate future. Perley was up to his neck in his responsibilities, and in any case was giving the matter no priority. The British authorities had been helpful and co-operative, but had no reason to push the question of Canadian squadrons. At home, Borden and his colleagues were embarked upon 'the exceedingly stormy political sea' whipped up by the Prime Minister's decision in favour of compulsory military service. The matter of a Canadian flying service might have slumbered indefinitely, had it not been for an extraordinary reversal of opinion by Sir Robert himself. Both in England and upon his return to Canada he had received a number of complaints from Canadian officers serving in the RFC. They were of such a nature as to cause the Prime Minister to explode with anger in a cable to Perley:

Since returning to Canada representations have been placed before me which indicate that Canadians in Flying Service are not receiving reasonably fair play or adequate recognition. There seems to have been a disposition from the first to assign them to subordinate positions and to sink their identity. They were forbidden to wear any distinguishing badge to indicate that they were Canadians. They have been discriminated against in promotion. One of the clearest evidences of this is the fact that the officer sent out to command the British Flying School in Canada was taught by a Canadian pilot now at the front and that the officer under whom the pilot served is still a subordinate officer after two years active service at the front. This is a typical illustration. I am afraid this is only another indication of a certain tendency which I took pains to correct in other matters during my recent visit to England. The question of establishing a Canadian Flying Corps demands immediate and attentive consideration. I am determined that Canadians shall not continue in any such position of unmerited subordination. Please give that subject immediate and attentive consideration and make such thorough inquiries through the best independent means available to verify the truth of what has been represented to me. I am inclined to believe that the time for organizing an independent Canadian Air Service has come and that we must ask the Imperial authorities to release all Canadians now in the British Flying Service.[9]

Borden's anger had led him to propose measures far more sweeping than any of those put forward previously. It is of interest that what aroused his feelings were not generalized arguments based upon nationalism or upon the importance of aviation, but circumstantial detail about injustices suffered by Canadians as a result of their subordinate status within an imperial force.*

The effect of Borden's intervention was to reopen, at Cabinet level, the whole question of Canadian policy with respect to a separate flying service. The investigation of that issue, much more searching than ever before, was to take up the next several months. Of more immediate concern to Perley was the task of assessing the validity of complaints that Canadians had been discriminated against in the RFC. Borden had told him to do this through 'the best independent means available,' but there was no such means. Had Canadian headquarters in London taken the view, from the inception of the war, that the fortunes of Canadian aviators were part of its concern, then some documentation might have been available. But it had not; nor, given government policy, was there any reason why it should. Morden's charge, that once Canadians entered the British flying services they lost their identity as Canadians, was substantially correct. So, although both Perley and General Turner 'quietly made enquiries' where they could, the only real source of information was the RFC itself, and it was to General Henderson that they turned.

When confronted with Borden's charges, Henderson's first response was that 'there is no real ground' for them. He immediately seized upon the specific case cited by Borden to demonstrate this. While it was true that Frederick A. Wanklyn, a Canadian, had been C.G. Hoare's instructor at the Central Flying School in 1913, and that Wanklyn in 1917 was a major while Hoare was a lieutenant-colonel, no real discrimination was involved. In 1913 Hoare had been a captain with twelve years of British and Indian Army service behind him, while Wanklyn was a subaltern who had graduated from the Royal Military College of Canada only in 1909. As Henderson pointed out, there was no relationship whatever between serving as a flying instructor and rapid promotion; the man who had taught Henderson himself to fly in 1911 was still only a flight commander. When Henderson had had the task of building the RFC from nothing in the prewar period, he had sought, not superlative pilots, but experienced regular officers like Hoare, and 'those of them who have justified expectations have been promoted in the Corps much more rapidly than the young and inexperienced gentlemen who were merely gallant soldiers and good fliers.'† Canadians, he assured Perley, were in exactly the same position as their young British counterparts: 'The statement that there is a prejudice against Canadians in the Corps, because of their nationality, I believe to be absolutely unfounded ... When a boy is a failure, it is very natural for him to try to

---

* It is very likely that one of the complainants was Capt Kennedy. Borden's language is close to that employed by Kennedy in a letter to Hazen of 1 June, and in interviews with the Chief of the General Staff and with the secretary to the Minister of Militia, in which Kennedy raised the same grievances of which Borden complained and cited 'various injustices' and the lack of 'equitable treatment.' Kennedy to Hazen, 1 June 1917, P–5–94, PAC RG 25, vol. 267; Bristol to Gwatkin, 15 June 1917, Gwatkin to Bristol, 18 June 1917, OS 10–9–27, PAC RG 9 III, vol. 80

† Wanklyn himself assured Perley that he harboured no resentment over the fact that Hoare outranked him. 'With regard to alleged unfairness in promotion of Canadian officers, I have never heard of a single case, nor cause for complaint in this matter, and, as a Canadian officer, I have no hesitation in stating that this is of no foundation.' Wanklyn to Perley, 29 May 1917, P–5–94, PAC RG 25, vol. 267

excuse it by alleging an unwarranted prejudice of some kind on the part of his superiors.'[10] With respect to distinctive badges that would identify Canadians within the Corps, Henderson was not disposed to be accommodating. Canadians commissioned in the RFC (as distinct from those seconded from Canadian units, who still were entitled to wear their own uniform with an RFC badge) had to wear the RFC uniform 'without any distinctive badge to show their nationality, just as they would if they joined the British Artillery or the North Stafford Regiment.' While he agreed to put the question of a distinctive badge before the Army Council, he doubted if 'such permission would be welcomed by the Canadian Officers of the Royal Flying Corps.'[11]

Henderson followed up his initial reaction with a statistical table, compiled by Colonel W.W. Warner of his staff, which showed that for the 525 Canadians upon whom the RFC possessed reliable information there was no significant difference in the amount of time they had to wait for promotion in comparison to the average for the whole of the RFC's officer corps. While this table demonstrated that the RFC lacked even a rough estimate of the actual number of Canadians in the Corps, so, for that matter, did Perley. Nor could he challenge Henderson's statement that 'nearly all the Canadian officers joined the Royal Flying Corps with very little, if any, military experience, and they had to be turned into soldiers as well as fliers. A considerable proportion of those who joined from the United Kingdom were regular officers of experience, and naturally these filled a considerable proportion of the appointments of Squadron and Wing Commanders, which, to my mind, is just as it should be.'[12] How, indeed, could it be otherwise? So long as Canadians remained members of a corps of the British Army, subject to the conditions upon which promotion within that service was based, they had little legitimate reason to anticipate senior appointments within it. As Henderson's table showed, the root of the Canadian complaints was psychological, not statistical, and Perley had no option but to report to Borden that while he and Turner had encountered some general feeling 'that our men have not been given fair play in promotions,' he was compelled to conclude that there was 'no serious foundation' for such a belief.*[13] But the last words upon RFC promotion policy and upon the identification of Canadians in the RFC had not been spoken.

* Canadians had a genuine problem in securing promotion in the RFC that neither Perley nor Henderson referred to, possibly because it was one over which the RFC had no control. Officers seconded to the RFC from the CEF remained on the establishment and rolls of their units, but in order that replacements for them could be demanded, they were considered as having been struck off strength. Nevertheless, they could only be promoted on their own unit's establishment. This awkward situation gave rise to frequent complaints. The RFC solution was to give them temporary rank while they waited for a vacancy to occur in their original unit. In mid-1917 definite procedures governing seconded officers were finally established, but confusion and complaints continued. The new procedures remained in effect until the end of the war, although their fairness to both seconded and unit officers was improved somewhat by a provision of 20 March 1918 laying down that seconded officers were to be promoted on their regimental list and not on the list of their field unit. Bristol to CGS, 15 June 1917, OS 10-2-27, PAC RG 9 III, vol. 80; letter to Turner, 20 Feb. 1917, Montague to HQ Canadian Corps, 21 March 1918, OS 10-12-24, ibid., vol. 91; AG to War Office, 27 Dec. 1916, War Office to [AG], 20 Jan. 1917, AG to Shoreham, 8 May 1917, HQ OMFC 0-130-33, ibid., vol. 2890; letters to Hughes, 17 May and 28 Sept. 1916, Spry to Carson, 29 May 1916, OS 2-2-38, ibid., vol. 4

Following the Prime Minister's directive of 22 May, both the Minister of Militia and Defence and the Overseas Minister embarked on enquiries to determine whether the time had come to establish a Canadian flying corps. Kemp had no option but to rely upon the advice of Gwatkin, and the Chief of the General Staff, in an interim report, once more made clear that he was 'strongly opposed to the formation, while war lasts, of a Canadian Flying Corps in Canada.' The last two words were an important modification of his earlier views. Gwatkin was convinced that any Canadian formation employed on operations must have a training and reinforcement pool at home, but this would needlessly duplicate what the RFC was doing in Canada, would involve heavy outlays for site and equipment, would 'set up friction' with the Army Council in Britain because experienced Canadian officers would have to be recalled, and might produce no worthwhile results before the war ended. RFC Canada had therefore become a new weapon in his armoury of arguments against a Canadian flying corps.[14]

Gwatkin was at pains to point out that he believed that a Canadian flying corps ought to be formed, but only as part of Canada's postwar defence arrangements. At that time the country could build upon its experienced airmen and upon the facilities the RFC had established in Ontario. With some prescience Gwatkin argued that the kind of air force Canada needed had to be something more than a unit of the militia. To some extent it would have to be 'commercialized' and have to work 'with the Topographical Surveys, Geographer's and Forestry Branches of the Department of the Interior, perhaps with the Post Office Department, certainly with the Department of the Naval Service.' He implied, therefore, that a war-born force might be irretrievably biased against the special needs of the country.

Having said all this, Gwatkin then made a proposal which went well beyond his previous position and a long way towards meeting the feelings of Canadians for some form of recognition: 'Meanwhile, there being so many Canadians in both Wings of the R.F.C., I think the time has come when the Canadian Government might reasonably propose the organization of units exclusively Canadian; and that such units, if organized, should be allotted to the Canadian Corps now serving in France, or to the Army of which the Canadian Corps forms part ... I see no reason why the units in question, if formed and allotted as proposed, should cease to belong to the R.F.C. If they were transferred to the C.E.F., the cost of maintenance would fall, of course, on the Canadian Government.'[15] The only qualification he placed upon this important suggestion was that, 'should the proposal embarrass the Army Council, I hope it will not be pressed.'

Gwatkin's suggestion was soon watered down as the result of consultation with Colonel Hoare of RFC Canada. There would be no difficulty, Hoare agreed, in forming squadrons with an officer complement that was exclusively Canadian, but the situation was by no means simple with respect to other ranks. Both the Director General of National Service and the Imperial Munitions Board had objected to the idea of sending mechanics out of Canada. As far as RFC Canada was concerned, 'we have had sufficient difficulty in getting men for our training scheme here, and only few of them would pass medically fit for overseas.' He was also dubious about the idea of attaching Canadian squadrons to the CEF. 'Squadrons, especially the Artillery Squadrons, are kept for long periods, years in some cases, on the same portion of the line,' he wrote, 'and I doubt whether for the sake of putting Canadian Squadrons in their place, it would be considered worth moving them.' Though this observation had some validity, Hoare's objection was by no means insuperable, whether with respect to corps squadrons or fighter squadrons, but Gwatkin had no means of assessing the argument. Nevertheless, Hoare agreed that 'if men were available I might be able to train Canadian Squadrons over here in the same way that I am training American Squadrons,' a statement that unwittingly summarized the consequences of the government's timid air policy. Hoare added that if the government were seriously contemplating forming Canadian squadrons, it ought to be aware that the cost of maintaining a single front-line squadron was about \$2.5 million for six months.[16]

Hoare's observations weighed heavily with Kemp when, on 11 August, the militia minister submitted his recommendations (drafted by Gwatkin) to the Prime Minister. It would be 'folly,' he thought, to start a Canadian flying corps in Canada, and the questions of cost and the unavailability of groundcrew turned him against overseas squadrons that were exclusively Canadian. Instead, he thought that 'it might be suggested to the War Office that a certain number should be officered exclusively by Canadians, and so far as the exigencies of war permit, employed in conjunction with the Canadian Divisions.'[17]

Sir George Perley, however, was not prepared to go even this far. In making up his mind he had gone over the question with many knowledgeable people within the air services and outside. His most notable Canadian advisers were Lieutenant-General R.E.W. Turner, Chief of the General Staff of OMFC, and Wing Commander R.H. Mulock of the Royal Naval Air Service.

Turner had become an enthusiast for the idea of a Canadian air service. As early as December 1916, on returning from France to take over his new appointment, he had declared to the press that he intended to take up vigorously the question of a Canadian flying corps. On the Western Front he had become aware of the large number of Canadians 'merged' into the RFC. As a result, little was heard of their work.[18] Early in 1917 he had set his staff to work compiling a list of Canadian aviators. By mid-1917 they had already found substantially more than Henderson's estimate and had acquired evidence to show that there were at least 1200 in the RFC and RNAS combined. On 13 July Turner passed his list of Canadians to Perley.

I consider that as Canada is supplying such a proportion of the personnel, that we should proceed with the organization of a Canadian Flying Corps. This would enable the Canadians to take their rightful place in the Imperial Forces, to receive the full credit for the work being done by them, and to provide an organization of experienced personnel to carry on the flying service after the war.

I would propose the Canadian squadrons be organized as rapidly as conditions would allow with the ultimate object of having, if possible, a Canadian Brigade in the Field, together with the necessary reserve formations in this country and in Canada.[19]

He was confident that groundcrew could be obtained by remustering other ranks from Canadians stationed in England, and giving them trades training in British schools. His suggestion that the objective should be a flying corps of brigade strength arose from his knowledge that only at that level would all branches of military aviation be covered, and Canadian officers be given an opportunity for staff experience.[20]

Turner's proposal for a Canadian brigade reflected his familiarity with the evolution of the RFC. In a subsequent letter to Perley, after explaining the growth of the RFC in terms of its increasingly vital role in ground operations, he raised a second point with which, as a former divisional commander, he was well acquainted. This was the fact that a great many of the Canadians in the RFC had arrived there not through enrolment in Canada but by transfer from the CEF. This fact, at that point unappreciated in Canada, meant a constant drain of able soldiers from the Canadian forces. In view of this, Turner was led to appeal to Perley in the strongest fashion:

There continues to be a large and insistent demand for Canadian personnel, and we are sending a large number of our best young men to fill these demands. The distinguished service which these young men are rendering the Empire reflects only indirect credit on Canada, as there is no official organization which protects their interests and ensures their proper promotion. We are supplying a large part of the personnel of the Flying Services, and we have to content ourselves with the junior positions and no control over the policy or administration of the Canadian personnel.

I feel very strongly that we should at once proceed with the organization of a Canadian Flying Corps ... I feel that it is humiliating that a nation taking such a share in the war as is Canada, should not have an organization in this arm of the Service when she is supplying such an important proportion of the manpower in the Imperial Services.[21]

This renewed plea was too late. Perley had already made his submission to the Prime Minister, and it was the converse of Turner's position.

In making his recommendations Perley had been influenced chiefly by information obtained from Mulock, whom he had been strongly advised to consult. With the co-operation of Commodore Payne at the Admiralty, Mulock came over from Dunkirk in July for interviews with Perley, Turner, and the OMFC staff. Having been instructed by his commanding officer to put nothing in writing, Mulock made no report, but assured Perley that Turner and Colonel H.F. McDonald knew his mind and his sympathies. 'Anything I can do in connection with this matter,' he told Perley, 'I will consider a favour both to our Country and to all the Canadians serving both in the Royal Naval Air Service and the Royal Flying Corps.'[22]

The memorandum, prepared by McDonald, which summarized Mulock's views reveals his intelligence and his ready grasp of the problems inherent in the formation of a Canadian flying service. His was by far the most considered statement yet made on the question, being based on technical knowledge, operational experience, and sound judgment. He began by assuming that 'it was desired to obtain for the proposed Canadian organization as wide experience of the duties and activities of the Flying Services as possible, with the view to such experience being available for future use in Canada.' He carefully outlined the composition of the basic flying units, using as his model the organization of the Royal Flying Corps, rather than that of his own service, the RNAS. With force and clarity he emphasized that the key to an understanding of that organization was the principle of specialization of function. The distinct tasks of fighting, reconnaissance, photography, artillery co-operation, bombing, close support of ground forces, and balloon observation required distinct units, distinct tactics and training, and specialized aircraft. By these functions squadrons were grouped into army and corps wings; a brigade, consisting of two such wings, had 'in no way fixed Establishments,' being elastic enough to meet the requirements of any situation.[23]

If, Mulock argued, his assumption about the desirable nature of a Canadian flying corps were correct, then what was required was not the four squadrons which apparently Perley had mentioned to him, but the creation of a full brigade of at least eight squadrons together with air staff, supply and equipment detachments, and kite balloon establishment that together made up the range of functions carried out by an RFC brigade. Such a formation, he thought, should be built up squadron by squadron as opportunity and the exigencies of the service dictated; as the Canadian organization neared wing and brigade strength, senior officers and staff could be prepared for their duties by attachment for experience to comparable RFC formations.

Thus Mulock's opinions were in accord with General Turner's. There was one issue, however, to which he attached prime importance, and which had not to this time received serious attention. That was aircraft supply. His view, which was to influence Perley decisively, reflected his understanding of the crucial interrelationship of technological improvement, operational effectiveness, and political control:

The efficiency ... in the Field of any Flying Organization depends almost entirely upon the machines with which it is equipped. There is a constant and rapid improvement in such machines, and those in use become out-of-date very quickly. The supply of machines is absolutely controlled by the Air Board, and any Canadian organization would be absolutely subject to it in regard to the supply required. The Canadian Authorities, however, would be held responsible to the people at home for any mis-adventure which might occur to the personnel on account of inferior equipment, and yet the only control which they would have over such equipment would be by means of such representations as the Overseas Minister might make to the War Office.[24]

With the authority of direct experience, Mulock stated that the interval between the introduction of a new aircraft and its operational obsolescence might be as little as three months and that when the latter stage was reached, a squadron so equipped was 'at the mercy of the enemy.'* Through McDonald, Mulock therefore summed up his conclusions as follows:

* Corroborative if less polished testimony was given to Perley by Capt G.C.O. Usborne, a Canadian originally from Arnprior, Ont., who had been with the RFC since 1915 and in 1917 was a flight commander with 40 Squadron. He had been recommended by Henderson as an officer who could 'help you with the Canadian F.C.' Like Mulock, he favoured the creation of a Canadian force covering all aspects of aerial operations: 'unless we do the whole thing complete we are under Sir David Henderson's thumb and would get most of the dirty work without the

From the point of view of securing to Canada the Canadian Officers and other ranks concerned, it would be extremely desirable to have an organization which would be Canadian in name and fact, and there would be no great difficulty in securing sufficient personnel to man such an organization.

It would further be of value to Canada in the development of a permanent Flying Service after the war.

On the other hand, it would be a matter of great difficulty to ensure that such Canadian Flying Units as might be organized and placed on active service, would receive their just proportion of the most up-to-date and efficient equipment which is placed in service.[25]

To Sir George Perley the last paragraph of Mulock's conclusions and his earlier remarks about political accountability for inferior equipment were warning flags and their sober implications determined the advice he furnished to the Prime Minister. 'National pride,' he told Borden, was his first consideration; it was 'a perfectly natural feeling with which I thoroughly sympathize, if there are no practical arguments against it.' It had been a revelation to him 'that 35% of the Royal Flying Corps are Canadians.'* Moreover, he believed that Canadians, because of 'temperament and training,' had an instinctive bent for flying, though the conclusion he drew from this belief was somewhat odd. Since Canadians made such superior pilots, they naturally wished for 'fast scout machines' rather than 'comparatively slow machines for observation work.' They would probably resist service upon such aircraft in a Canadian flying corps. It is plain that Sir George's information about the work of Canadians in the flying services was not yet complete, but this was a minor objection. A major one was his view that although a Canadian air service during the war was essential to the development of postwar civil and military aviation in Canada, he saw no reason why Canada could not draw upon the knowledge being acquired by the RFC and RNAS. He believed, optimistically, that Canadians were bound to occupy senior positions in those services before the war ended.[26]

Nevertheless, he foresaw no real difficulty in raising a Canadian service and would so recommend, were it not for the problem of aircraft supply. Though Henderson had assured him that Canada would get its 'fair share' of the best machines, Perley was not prepared to take the risk. 'I should be in favour of doing it, except for the difficulty of obtaining the latest type of machines but I consider that vital and am therefore of opinion that we had better continue as we are doing, without establishing squadrons of our own, and help to supply both the British Air

---

  other side.' As a fighter pilot he knew that a supply of first-rate aircraft was essential: 'It isn't a case of pluck and clever flying, it's simply a case of a man who can climb the fastest and dive the fastest.' Henderson to Perley, 14 April 1917, Usborne memorandum, May 1917, P-5-94, PAC RG 25, vol. 267

* 'I have not asked for the figures,' Perley told Borden; even if he had, it is certain that the RFC would have been unable to supply them. The figure of 35 per cent gained currency at about this time, and Perley was merely repeating the general belief to that effect. Even if it were applied only to pilots, observers, and air gunners the figure is probably much too high, although it is true that in particular squadrons at certain stages in their operational life the proportion of Canadians was frequently as high as 35 per cent and occasionally substantially more than 50 per cent.

Services with suitable Canadians as they may require them.'[27] He conceded that this left the situation precisely where it had been – one in which 'the Dominion does not get sufficient credit for the splendid work which is being done by the Canadians in both the Air Services' – and he therefore suggested that some good might come from the appointment of a Canadian liaison officer to the staff of the RFC.

During the period in which Kemp and Perley were assembling advice to place before the Prime Minister, Borden himself remained favourably disposed to the idea of a Canadian air service. 'Is anything being done with a view to establishing a Canadian Flying Corps?' he asked Kemp in July. 'It seems unfortunate that when so much splendid work is being done by Canadians that they should have no distinctive part in the service.'[28] When Kemp and Perley submitted their reports in early August they were reviewed for him in an unsigned memorandum entitled 'Notes on Proposals for a Canadian Flying Corps,' the author of which may well have been Loring Christie, the External Affairs official who was one of Borden's closest advisers on imperial questions. To its author Perley had put 'his finger on the vital spot of this whole question,' the matter of aircraft supply; 'any other details in the proposals are insignificant in comparison with this.' How could Canada expect a square deal when it was notorious that the Air Board had been unable to satisfy its two warring clients, the RNAS and the RFC? Yet the case, on national grounds, for a Canadian flying corps was powerful. What arguments could justify taking a different stand on aviation from that taken towards command and control of the CEF? The solution offered in the memorandum was both novel and interesting. Arguing that neither national pride nor postwar aviation needs were arguments relevant 'to the question of efficiency in the present War,' and that neither consideration should 'be pushed to the point of imperilling that efficiency,' the memorandum author claimed:

It is submitted therefore that any change made for the sake of these objects should be limited to the least drastic reorganization which will satisfy them in some reasonable measure. Because of this consideration, and also because of the very nature of the Air Service, it would seem that one should work from the analogy of the Naval co-operation between Canada and Great Britain rather than from that of their Military co-operation. Military land forces, from the nature of their operations, are much more readily susceptible to a considerable measure of separation in respect of their control. The very different kind of operation performed by the Air Service demands a different sort of co-operation.[29]

The conclusion drawn was that a Canadian flying service should be deferred, but that the War Office should be approached to discover whether, 'by a redisposition of the personnel of the Royal Flying Corps,' a number of squadrons, and eventually one or more brigades, might not be 'manned and officered by Canadians and be named as Canadian Squadrons and Brigades.' At the same time, Canadians might be given staff posts at the War Office.

Borden appears to have accepted a version of this solution as the most expedient course to be followed. On 22 August Kemp wrote to Perley, asking him to find out whether the Army Council would be willing to distribute Canadians in the RFC in such a manner that a number of squadrons, or perhaps a wing, could be created that would be officered exclusively by Canadians. If this could be done, it would be gratifying if the Canadian units were employed in conjunction with the Canadian Corps. Perley seems to have done nothing. Kemp's letter had hardly been peremptory; the High Commissioner was to act only 'if the suggestion appeals to you.' Sir George did not reply until 2 October and then merely referred to the advice he had tendered on 10 August, stating that he awaited the opinion of Cabinet upon it.[30] Shortly thereafter Borden formed his coalition government, Kemp replaced Perley as Overseas Minister, and Perley himself, no longer a member of the Cabinet, reverted to his position as High Commissioner.

The only subject upon which Perley approached the War Office was the matter of a Canadian liaison officer, to which RFC authorities proved agreeable. Upon their suggestion Major Malcolm McBean Bell-Irving, then stationed with RFC Canada at Camp Borden after having been wounded on operations, was named to this post with responsibility for 'all matters affecting Canadians in the R.F.C., whether they had enlisted directly into it or had been seconded from our Overseas Forces.' He was told to report to Perley, Kemp, and General Turner. Serving three masters could not have been an easy or congenial task, but in any case Bell-Irving viewed his posting simply as a stepping stone to get back on active operations. In little more than a month, having been passed medically fit for flying, he requested an operational assignment.* Perley acceded, but remained convinced that a liaison officer was needed. Turner had a more ambitious idea; he wanted Canadian representation on the Air Board as more 'in keeping with Canada's position.' Kemp, however, asked Perley to defer any replacement; he hoped 'before long to be able to consider the whole question of our relations with the R.F.C. & R.N.A.S. & whether we should have Canadian Squadrons.' The new Overseas Minister, in other words, was about to follow up the results of the policy discussion of the previous summer, which had gone so strangely awry in Perley's hands.[31]

Before approaching the British authorities once again, Kemp initiated the most thorough examination of the number and status of Canadians in the British air services that had yet been undertaken. The problem of numbers was, of course, impossible of solution. Even if British and Canadian officials had been able to agree upon what a 'Canadian' was, the state of personnel records was such that no precise figure could ever be established. Nevertheless, Perley had already laid the groundwork for a reasonable estimate to be made. At the time that it was

---

* Bell-Irving's wound in June 1916 – a piece of shrapnel in the brain which had temporarily affected both his sight and memory – had kept him out of action for eighteen months. Now he went to the School of Special Flying at Gosport (currently commanded by his brother, Alan Duncan Bell-Irving) for a refresher course. Impatient to get back to France, he soon charmed his way into soloing in a Sopwith Camel, spun it into the ground from a left-hand turn – the Camel's stubby fuselage and the torque of its powerful rotary engine made this particular mishap very easy – and suffered further injuries to his head and the loss of his left leg above the knee. The American brain surgeon who had advised on his earlier head wound saw him in a London hospital on 23 May 1918 and reported that 'he only vaguely recalled me – suffering the tortures of hell from neuromats in the stump of his amputated leg ... Still the same charming person, however, despite his thoroughly drugged condition.' Harvey Cushing, *From a Surgeon's Journal, 1915–1918* (Toronto 1936), 358

announced that Bell-Irving had been awarded both the DSO and the MC, Perley had protested to Sir David Henderson that 'it would have been a wise and proper thing' to make some mention of the fact that the recipient happened to be a Canadian. The RFC therefore agreed that in future notification of such awards would be passed to Canadian authorities and that a list of all Canadians in the services would be compiled, even though 'we have so many Canadians in the Royal Flying Corps that there is, of course, a chance of some of them being missed.' RFC staff officers did not greet the paper work entailed in the monthly compilation of a Canadian list with enthusiasm; one of them, at RFC Headquarters in France, complained 'that the Canadians give more trouble than the rest of the Army as regards the returns, lists etc. which they ask for.' 'Them's my sentiments,' echoed his opposite number at the War Office, 'we have supplied voluminous returns to the Canadian Headquarters, Canadian Pay and Record Office, Sir George Perley, etc. etc.' By the time this staff duty filtered down to squadron level, adjutants met the requirement by simply adding to the form officers completed when joining a squadron the question 'Whether of Canadian birth?'[32]

Analysis of these returns, together with the limited records possessed by HQ OMFC, was carried out by officers of General Turner's staff, a process in which Turner himself took a considerable personal interest. When OMFC records were combined with data obtained from the RAF and from other sources, a memorandum of 26 April calculated that as of 1 April 1918, the date of the establishment of the Royal Air Force, a total of 13,345 Canadians had served with the RFC and the RNAS; by deleting casualties and other forms of wastage it was estimated that 10,990 Canadians remained in the force.[33]

For the first time Canadian authorities were in possession of solid evidence, or what appeared to be solid evidence, of the size of the contribution their compatriots had been making to the air war. It is necessary to reiterate, however, that it was not possible then, nor is it now, to arrive at a total figure for Canadian participation that can be defended with any high degree of confidence. There are a number of reasons for this, beyond those already touched on. It is impossible, for example, to discover from existing records how many Canadians had served with the RFC and the RNAS prior to the beginning of 1917 and the initiation of the compilation of Canadian lists. The lists themselves were far from satisfactory. The question 'Whether of Canadian birth?' excluded men of non-Canadian origins who, nonetheless, had joined the RFC in Canada or, by transfer from Canadian units, had spent a good part of their lives in Canada and had come to think of themselves as Canadians. Such men, or most of those who survived from among them, were to assert this sense of identity by returning to Canada after the war. But RFC records knew them not. Few of the early RFC lists survive, and those that do not only omit such individuals, but also many known to have been of Canadian birth. Such men may have filled out the form incorrectly, but, for whatever reason, they were not returned by their units as Canadians.[34]

On a panel in the Memorial Chamber of the Parliament Buildings in Ottawa it is stated that 22,812 Canadians served in the British air forces during the First World War. This figure was the result of the labours of the Canadian War Records unit at HQ OMFC in 1919, but it is important to note that the officer in charge observed, at the time the list was compiled, that 'no guarantee of its completeness can be given.'* As he had discovered, the inadequacy of the records and the difficulty of defining Canadian status had rendered virtually any statistical assessment of Canadian participation an historical problem of great complexity.[35]

A case in point, worth examining in some detail, is that of the Canadians who transferred from units of the CEF to the flying services during the war. The Memorial Chamber panel gives a total of 3960, but, by collating the many lists compiled in 1918–19 by the Air Ministry and by HQ OMFC, it has been possible to determine that at least 5022 Canadians transferred. The chief reason for the discrepancy appears to lie in the category of other rank transfers.[†36]

Although the loss of upwards of five thousand men might not appear a significant drain upon the CEF, it should be noted that the bulk of those transferred did so from combat units, were of high medical categories, and included large numbers of junior officers and NCOs. From time to time the leakage of men of this quality concerned the GOC Canadian Corps, but it proved difficult to resist appeals for intra- and inter-service co-operation. The process had begun innocently enough in the earliest period of the war. At that time the only barrier to transfer from Canadian units to the RFC and the RNAS seems to have been the requirements, medical, social, and numerical, of those services. Canadian authorities appear to have encouraged this movement, small as it was; indeed, at the end of 1915 officers commanding units were required to explain any case in which they had refused to forward applications. Nevertheless, it is obvious that many unit commanders did what they could to discourage aspiring airmen, especially those considered valuable to the unit, a tendency that grew with time and the greater attractions of the air war. In June 1916, when the RFC became anxious about its recruitment levels, the War Office drew attention to the fact that only one-quarter to one-third of those Canadians whom its interviewing officers had found 'good' prospects for the RFC were recommended for transfer by the CEF, while nearly all those classified as 'fair' were so recommended. Up to this point the numbers were not large. Perhaps two Canadians a month transferred in 1915, while in the earlier part of 1916 the average seems to have been about ten a month.[37]

---

*   Another reason for imprecision is the fact, first discovered in May 1917, that only bulk totals of Canadian other ranks discharged from the CEF to the Imperial Forces had been kept, and that there was no total, much less a name list, for those discharged to the flying services. HQ OMFC attempted to obtain this information from RAF sources in early 1918, but was informed that neither the RFC nor the RNAS had accumulated personnel records in a form that would give an answer. Later, by dint of much research on another issue, the Air Ministry calculated that the total of Canadian other ranks serving in the RAF in October 1918 was only twenty-four, an astonishing under-estimate. It was to tackle problems of this kind that a committee was formed within HQ OMFC in March 1919 in association with the Canadian War Records office. CANRECORDS message, 7 May 1917, HQ OMFC A–67–33, PAC RG 9 III, vol. 2867; Gold to OIC RAF Records, 13 April 1918, HQ OMFC to Gibson, 17 April 1918, OS 10–9–27, vol. 1, ibid., vol. 80; Lott to GSO1, 28 March 1919, HQ OMFC A–6–36, vol. 1, vol. 3068; Air Ministry to HQ OMFC, 30 Oct. 1918, HQ OMFC R–1–49, ibid., vol. 343

†   For a full discussion of the transfer question, together with statistical tables, see Rudi Aksim, 'C.E.F. Transfers to the British Flying Services,' DHist 74/14.

The needs of the expanding RFC became so acute, however, that the rate of transfer tripled by August 1916, and had to be restricted by OMFC a few months later so that reinforcement deficiencies in the CEF could be corrected. In the early months of 1917 the RFC requested and received 140 Canadian officers and men to be trained as observers. In May it asked the Canadian forces in England to supply thirty officers and sixty men a month for aviation training. HQ OMFC agreed, though it defined these figures as an upper limit. No ceiling had yet been placed upon transfers from the CEF in the field, though in July 1917 General Currie called for some limitation. The greatest threat to controlling CEF transfers came in early 1918 with a ruling by GHQ in France that personnel from any branch (including the Canadian forces) could transfer to the RAF regardless of the wishes of their own superiors. Such interference with Canadian control over their own troops was unacceptable; following vigorous Canadian protests the order was amended to provide that transfers from the CEF required the consent of HQ OMFC. Despite this, the drain from the CEF in France continued to be heavy. In July the CEF's artillery commander, Brigadier-General E.W.B. Morrison, complained that too many gunners were going to the RAF, citing the virtual immobilization of one of his batteries when forty men were transferred. A similar complaint was made by Brigadier-General R. Brutinel of the Canadian Machine Gun Corps. Not until August was General Currie given full control over transfers from the Canadian Corps.*[38]

One of the reasons for General Turner's nationalist militancy with respect to Canadians in the RAF was his familiarity with the secondment and transfer process. By the end of April 1918 he believed that as a result of the statistical work of his staff an unanswerable case had been built up for a Canadian air force. That

---

* Transfer procedures differed for officers and other ranks. Officers on transfer were attached to the flying service during training, and seconded upon qualifying as pilots or observers. Other ranks destined for flying training were shown as 'on command' to the RFC during their cadet period. On successful completion of this stage the cadet was discharged from the Canadian forces and became a flight cadet in the RFC. After April 1918 other rank transfers were discharged immediately upon leaving the Canadian forces. The difference was of some importance, since seconded officers continued to be paid by the Canadian government, while discharged ORs, who received British commissions, were paid by the United Kingdom government. In 1915–16 seconded Canadian officers received no flying pay because the Canadian government refused to accept that such pay was part of its obligation, under the reciprocal agreement with Britain governing the pay of officers on loan. Their commissioned compatriots who had been discharged as ORs received, at lieutenant rank, about a dollar a day more. The Canadian government, by PC 2106 of 30 March 1916, awarded flying pay to seconded officers, but their rate of pay was still below that of imperial flying officers. Not until the end of 1916 was rough equivalence established. Even so, grievances about pay differentials, back pay, and other allowances continued until the end of the war. In January 1918 General Turner suggested to Kemp that the reciprocal pay agreement with Britain be scrapped, on the grounds that, because of the heavy flow to the RAF, seconded Canadian officers greatly outnumbered their British counterparts in the Canadian forces. He also argued, equally unsuccessfully, that the British government should reimburse Canada for the monetary contribution and the manpower commitment it was making to the RFC and RNAS. Incidentally, in the case of the RNAS both officers and ORs were discharged from the CEF retroactive to their date of transfer, upon completion of the probationary training period. There were only 152 transfers in all to the RNAS. Aksim, 'C.E.F. Transfers,' 36–43, 48–51, 53–61, 66–7, 84–5

case, he thought, rested only in part upon numbers. It was also based upon the proven fact that 'Canadians can administer their own troops'; his belief that Canadians in the RAF would never receive adequate recognition, especially for promotion, since it was inevitable that regular officers would receive priority consideration; and his conviction that only the creation of a Canadian service could ensure the welfare of Canadians. In summarizing his position to Kemp, he argued that Canadians should have a share in the command of the RAF commensurate with the numbers of their flying personnel, that a Canadian air force should be created immediately, and that as soon as possible thereafter CAF units should be formed.[39] 'Canada is most generously represented in the lower ranks of the flying officers of the Air Force, but she is most inadequately represented in the senior appointments and the administrative positions. So long as this condition exists, the Canadian personnel will feel, as they do, that the Canadian Authorities are lukewarm in their support and careless of their interests and the interests of Canada.'[40]

Kemp was ready to be persuaded. For example, on the key issue of aircraft supply he now thought that a Canadian Air Force could be allocated machines in the same satisfactory manner in which the CEF obtained artillery from the British. However, a CAF could not possibly absorb all the Canadians then serving in the RAF and he feared that, even if it could, the RAF would be irreparably disorganized by their transfer. For Turner, this was not a problem. The creation of a CAF would be a 'paper transaction.' Canadians would be carried on its strength but seconded to the RAF. In this way, 'their Canadian connection would be assured, and the Canadian Authorities would have an accurate and complete record of Canadian personnel.' Canadian units could then be formed gradually, without disrupting the RAF.[41]

Turner buttressed his case with a number of letters solicited from distinguished Canadian officers. In November General Currie had written to him on the subject:

Because you and I have never discussed the formation of a Canadian Flying Corps, I do not know what your views are regarding such a step, but in my opinion such a thing is desirable. In the first place, I think we should aim to make the Canadian Corps as self-contained an institution as possible. While I would not for the world make any reflections on the efficiency of the Flying Corps as a whole, I will go so far as to say that I think we would be better served if the squadron detailed for us were entirely Canadian. Our men have done well in the Flying Corps, and I think it would be an additional incentive to them to know that in battle they were serving Canadian troops. I repeat that, in making such a statement, I do not for a moment disparage the good work which is done for us by the Royal Flying Corps.[42]

A flying corps, Currie thought, would be a necessary part of the postwar Canadian military establishment. He therefore wished to see as its commander someone who from actual experience knew how 'best [to] cooperate with the Infantry and Artillery'; to him an air force was auxiliary to army operations. He concluded by reiterating that 'I am a good enough Canadian to believe, and my experience justifies me in believing, that Canadians are best served by Canadians.'[43]

In a forthright letter Major W.A. Bishop, the premier Canadian fighter pilot, claimed to speak for all his compatriots in the RAF in strongly supporting a Canadian air force. He particularly emphasized morale: 'Under the present circumstances, Canadians in the R.A.F., although doing remarkably well, are certainly not doing as well as if they were in a Canadian Corps for the reasons that (1) They are in a great many cases working under senior Officers who do not understand them. (2) They are also working with Officers who do not understand them nor often appreciate their different point of view. (3) They have not the personal touch with their country which branches of the Canadian Corps have and consequently are not inspired by direct connection with the country they are fighting for and the people at home.'[44] To Bishop, the activities of a Canadian flying corps ought to centre first upon working with Canadian troops on the Western Front; the immediate result would be the implanting of a magnificent *esprit de corps*, as well as a heightened appreciation by the Canadian public for the work of those at present 'lost in the R.A.F.'

Brigadier-General A.C. Critchley,* the highest ranking Canadian in the RAF, and a believer in the closest co-operation with it, nevertheless thought there were powerful national reasons for the immediate formation of a Canadian service: 'Isolated incidents, though we have many, do not count, it is the Canadian Air Force as a whole that must come out of this War with a great reputation and a great spirit. These can only be built up in War. We owe it to Canada that the magnificent work of the Canadian Airmen in France is not lost to our country, and the only way to preserve their individual glories is to hand them down to succeeding generations in the glorious reputation of the Canadian Air Force.'[45] Critchley's letter, together with those from Currie, Bishop, and other Canadian officers were passed to Kemp, presumably to stiffen his resolve. The Minister, however, had already made himself more familiar with the state of military aviation and the Canadian role in it than any of his colleagues in the Cabinet, past or present. In mid-May he decided that the time had come for action.

In a letter to the Secretary of State for Air, Kemp outlined results of his statistical inquiries, on the basis of which he estimated that 25 per cent of all RAF flying personnel, and perhaps 40 per cent of the aviators on the Western Front, were Canadian. In view of these figures, he proposed to Sir William Weir that the Canadians in the RAF should be formed 'into a Canadian section with a distinctive Canadian badge but without segregating squadrons or dislocating in any way your formations in the field,' that Canadians should be given representation at RAF Headquarters and on the staff, and that adequate credit should be given in despatches and reports to Canadians 'for conspicuous services.' He left his most important proposal to the last. He wished the creation of 'a small Canadian flying

---

* Critchley, born near Calgary in 1890, went overseas in 1914 with the Lord Strathcona's Horse, a unit in which his father and a brother were also serving. After being twice wounded in France he organized the Canadian Training School at Bexhill. In 1918 he was seconded to the RAF and given command of the cadet training organization in Britain. After the war he had a notable career in Britain as a sportsman, industrialist, and politician. A.C. Critchley, *Critch! The Memoirs of Brigadier-General A.C. Critchley, C.M.G., C.B.E., D.S.O.* (London 1961)

corps,' to be administered by HQ OMFC, 'except of course in regard to the operations in the field,' and requested Weir to consider the basis upon which this corps could be supplied and provision made for repair services and replacement of equipment. 'My sole desire in making the above proposals,' he assured Weir, 'is to increase, if possible, the efficiency of Canadians in the R.A.F., and to place Canada in a better position to take advantage of the developments in aeroplane construction and flying which will follow after the conclusion of hostilities.'[46]

Since the last occasion when the possibility of forming a Canadian air force had been discussed with the British authorities, the Air Ministry had replaced the Air Board and there were many new faces on the Air Staff. Neither the Secretary of State, nor Major-General F.H. Sykes, the Chief of the Air Staff, had had any previous dealings with the Canadians. To them, and to most members of their staff, the Canadian question was a new one. They tackled it with no apparent preconceptions, and Weir's immediate response was 'that all possible action must be taken to meet the Canadian authorities in the matter.' But neither he nor his staff were ready to go the whole way with Kemp. At a meeting of the Air Council on 23 May it was decided that 'the suggestion that there should be an independent Canadian Flying Corps on the Australian model could not be accepted,' but that it would be 'politic' to fall in with some of Kemp's other suggestions. The Council even toyed briefly with the idea of renaming the RAF the 'Imperial Air Force' to satisfy dominion aspirations, but dropped the notion as likely to have the opposite result.[47]

Sir W.A. Robinson, secretary to the Air Council, had the sticky task of framing a suitable reply to the Canadian Minister. His first attempt passed rapidly from an expression of appreciation for Canadian help and the enumeration of concessions that might be made to the question of the formation of a Canadian flying corps. This, wrote Robinson, was 'a natural development' which must come at some time, but given the war situation the Air Council believed it should be deferred until after the war ended.[48] The Under Secretary of State found this draft reply much too blunt. It failed to take into account the political realities behind the Canadian proposal, which Kemp had already outlined. The Canadian Minister would '... require more arguments regarding disadvantages of starting a Canadian Flying Corps now, in order either to be convinced himself or to convince the Canadian Government. There is no doubt that the strongest possible pressure is being brought to bear on the latter, the line taken being that Canada having created an army of her own it is inadmissable that she, of all the belligerents should be the only one lacking a Flying Corps. I am aware of Gen. Salmond's strong objections to the creation of a Canadian Flying Corps and full weight must be given to these.'[49] Robinson's revised draft took these points into account. Instead of a perfunctory reference to the war situation, he welcomed the prospect of a Canadian flying corps as a normal development. Unfortunately, 'present circumstances are not normal.' General Salmond had declared that the drafting of Canadians into a new corps would inevitably cause confusion and disruption in the RAF, at a moment when 'the utmost possible unity of Command' was vital. Kemp was therefore urged 'to convince your Government that for the moment the position should remain as it is.'[50]

Robinson's task was not yet done. On 27 May Sykes learned that since the interview with Sir Edward Kemp the Under Secretary had 'heard from other and authoritative sources that the creation of, at any rate a nucleus of a Canadian Air Force, is a matter about which very strong feeling prevails not only in Canada but in the Canadian Corps.' It is likely that General Turner was the source. On the same date Major W. Peer Groves of the Air Staff recounted conversations he had had with Turner and Sir George Perley. Turner had expressed, apparently with some vehemence, his dissatisfaction over the absence of Canadian officers on the Air Staff 'to whom Canadians could turn to for advice or assistance,' in Groves' words, 'in their own familiar and intimate way.' Groves had a simple solution. Squadron Commander R.H. Mulock should be named personal assistant to the Chief of Air Staff.[51]

As a Canadian, probably every Canadian pilot in the Service knows him well, many of them not only having passed through his hands but have actually fought beside him in the air. Squadron Commander Mulock is pre-eminently suited to fill a position of this kind. He has the reputation of being a wonderful organiser and is at present thought to be carrying out 'Q' work for General Lambe. In this capacity I venture to think he is wasted. But apart from this he has probably done more for air fighting, at any rate as far as the R.N.A.S. is concerned, than almost anybody else. Among Canadians this is looked upon as an indisput- able fact and is, I think, very generally recognised throughout the Force. At the same time he is an extremely good judge of character and has made a closer study of the psychology of the pilot than almost anyone else.[52]

In Groves' opinion Mulock's appointment 'would go a very long way towards stilling any agitation for a separate Canadian Air Force ...'

The Air Ministry had not yet resolved the issue when Weir, Sykes, and other officials conferred on 28 May with Kemp and Turner. The British record of this meeting indicates merely that the points raised by Kemp were discussed, together with Salmond's counter-arguments. The Canadian minutes, however, record Weir's purported statement that 'there was no objection to forming two or more Squadrons manned and officered by Canadians' and that the details could be worked out by RAF and OMFC staff officers.[53] Weir's position must have been misunderstood, because the next day he signed Robinson's final version of a reply to Kemp which retreated only slightly from earlier drafts. He began with thanks and an oblique reference to Kemp's statistics: 'The Air Council are desirous that I should first of all convey to you a very cordial expression of their appreciation and thanks for the magnificent help which has been given in the past to the R.F.C. and R.N.A.S. by the Dominion of Canada, and which is being continued to the Royal Air Force. Whatever may be the exact figure of officers and men of the Dominion serving in this Force, there is no question as to the very great value of the contri- bution made here and in the Dominion.'[54] On behalf of the Air Ministry Weir then promised that a record of all Canadians in the RAF would be maintained, that Canadians would be permitted to wear Canada badges as a distinguishable mark, and that the RAF would inform Canadian authorities of those Canadians to be listed in the *The London Gazette*, so that publicity might be given at home to their

achievements. Further, he promised that RAF Headquarters in France would com-
pile a monthly record of the work of Canadians at the front, to be furnished for
publicity purposes in Canada. These were useful concessions and were to be welcomed by the Canadians, although Weir had by-passed the request for a Canadian
section in the RAF, which Kemp had probably intended as the equivalent of
Turner's 'paper transaction' for record-keeping purposes. With respect to the proposal for Canadian representation on the Air Staff, Weir temporized, noting
merely that 'it is recognised that Canadian officers serving in the R.A.F. have
precisely the same right as any other officers to serve on the Headquarters and
Staff.'[55]

On the key issue Weir announced the willingness of the RAF to hold staff talks
on the creation of a Canadian air force, but warned that in view of the situation in
France, 'concrete action on these lines, which is bound to produce some dislocation and confusion, should be avoided for the present, and I would suggest to you
that the principle should be to work out a scheme which could be brought into
force, say, next winter.' To Kemp, these words conceded the principle for which
he had contended, and he was not disposed to accept a deferment. 'Something
concrete should be carried into effect as soon as possible, so as to satisfy the wishes
of the Canadian people,' he replied, and requested that action to form Canadian
squadrons should be taken 'as soon as practicable.'[56]

Canadian reluctance to entertain any long delay also appeared at a conference on
5 June between Brigadier-General B.C.H. Drew, the RAF's Director General of
Operations, Lieutenant-Colonel P.R.C. Groves, Director of Flying Operations,
Major T. Gibson, Assistant Deputy Minister of the Overseas Ministry, and
Brigadier-General H.F. McDonald, Turner's senior staff officer. Groves began by
opposing, on grounds of operational efficiency, the formation of a Canadian air
service, but withdrew this objection when the Canadians insisted that Weir's letter
had already admitted the principle. He next argued that the formation of Canadian
squadrons should be delayed 'until the situation in France cleared up,' a formula
so far-reaching that the Canadians rejected it out of hand. In their turn McDonald
and Gibson employed Kemp's statistical data with some apparent effect; their minutes show that 'it was admitted by the Officers representing the Royal Air Force
that quite 35% of the pilots in France are Canadians.' Probably more telling was
their recently-acquired knowledge of the structure and workings of the RAF,
which enabled them to counter effectively arguments based upon military exigency. As they pointed out, new service squadrons for France were constantly
being formed in England, and if two Canadian squadrons were organized in the
normal way, with the usual core of experienced officers drawn from front-line
squadrons, other officers posted from training units, and tradesmen transferred
from the Canadian forces, there need be no disruption whatsoever of the RAF. It
was impossible for Drew and Groves to refute this position. The conference
agreed that 'the formation of two Canadian Air Squadrons shall be proceeded with
forthwith,' that the squadrons should be called 'Nos. 1 and 2 Squadrons, Canadian
Air Force,' and that for the time being no further CAF units should be formed.[57]

With these preliminaries out of the way, the conference got down to details. It
was agreed that the RAF, in conjunction with HQ OMFC, would form the squad-

rons in England and that the Air Council would determine their type and equipment. Their officers would come from among Canadians seconded to the RAF and from officers of the RAF 'who are Canadian citizens'; non-flying personnel would be selected from 'Canadian citizens' in the RAF and from members of the Canadian forces. The Canadian government would be responsible for reinforcements and for pay, allowances, pensions, initial supplies of clothing and personal equipment. The Air Council was to be responsible for the command and administration of the squadrons while in a theatre of war or under training in Britain, for the provision of aircraft and other equipment, and for the training facilities to enable the Canadian government to meet its reinforcement obligations. It was also agreed that all promotions and appointments in the CAF would be made by the Canadian Overseas Minister on the recommendation either of RAF Headquarters in France or of the Air Council. For purposes of discipline and administration, members of the CAF were to come under the Air Force Act.[58]

The meeting of 5 June was pivotal. At a higher-level conference on 27 June General Sykes attempted to reopen the whole question. Observing that the formation of the CAF at that moment was 'a drag rather than a help,' the CAS asked for a postponement until the war ended. 'It was imperative that the natural aspirations of the country should be considered,' General Turner declared in reply, and the Canadians present lined up solidly behind him. The conference thereupon adopted the agreement of 5 June, with some minor amendments. Formal approval was given by an exchange of letters between HQ OMFC and the Air Council.*[59]

Why had the Air Ministry yielded, despite the opposition of its most senior officials? It was partly because the Canadians had done their homework and had a good case. Essentially, however, the decision was a political one, resting upon the belief that not only was Canadian sentiment strongly in favour, but also that Sir Edward Kemp was under heavy pressure from his own government to take action. In fact, Kemp had taken the initiative from the start; as he told Borden, when with a degree of self-satisfaction he summed up his work, he believed that he had been 'anticipating your wishes in the matter.' There had been no real push from the Cabinet. Nevertheless, Kemp must certainly have been aware that aviation had become, in Canada, a hotter issue than at any previous stage of the war. A number of newspapers had begun to campaign actively for a Canadian air force, notably the *Globe* and the *Star* of Toronto. 'We have outgrown the present arrangement,' argued the *Globe* in demanding a separate service consonant with 'a self-reliant

---

* The Air Ministry subsequently tried to renegotiate the financial implications embodied in the understanding of 5 June. Specifically, it sought to make Canada responsible for the cost of equipping the two squadrons and for retroactive payments to meet the cost of training Canadian pilots. The Canadian refusal generated some heat. It was General Brancker who brought the controversy to a halt. In a characteristically sensible minute he declared: 'I can see no solution but to adhere to the terms of the agreement ratified by us ... The situation financially will then be approximately the same as before the agreement; we shall probably get better Canadian personnel as a result of this measure; and Canadian political criticism of Canada's very generous assistance in personnel to the Royal Air Force without a substantial quid pro quo in Canada will be stilled.' His last point referred to the press controversy over the command and control of RAF Canada. McAnally to HQ OMFC, 3 Sept. 1918, McDonald to Air Ministry, 13 Sept. 1918, OS 10–9–27, vol. 1, RG 9 III, vol. 80; RAF staff minutes, 17–26 Sept. 1918, Air 2/109A/1990

Canadianism.' The *Star* drew attention to the inconsistency (which it blamed upon Sir Sam Hughes) between army and aviation policy and observed that 'we have now many more men in the air service overseas than we had all told in the South African War, yet they do not form a Canadian contingent.'[60]

In the House of Commons questions about the status of Canadians in the RAF at home and overseas had been raised by a number of members. On 2 May Sir Sam Hughes had the audacity to ask Borden why steps had not been taken to organize a Canadian air service. To Borden's reply that many difficulties were in the way, Hughes grandly observed that 'I knew all the difficulties and I had them removed.' Borden could only have been grateful to Kemp for having resolved a matter that had bedevilled the Cabinet for years and that was showing signs of becoming more than a political irritant. At any rate, the Cabinet approved with no apparent hesitation an order-in-council confirming the agreement reached by Kemp, authorizing the formation of the Canadian Air Force 'for the purpose of the present war.'* The Minister of Overseas Forces was given authority to form such further units as he might think were required. The CAF itself was defined as a part of Canada's overseas forces and made subject to the Militia Act.[61]

Another factor which may well have influenced the Air Ministry not to block the formation of the CAF was the awareness of its senior officials that yet another Canadian air force, the Royal Canadian Naval Air Service, was in the process of creation while the negotiations with Kemp were in progress. Strangely enough, Kemp and his officials do not seem to have learned of this development for some time. As news of the projected RCNAS filtered through the Air Staff in late May, a number of staff officers expressed unease. One of them, Lieutenant-Colonel R.C.M. Pink, pointed out some of the implications:

> Thirty-five per cent of our total strength in pilots is Canadian. Under the Air Force Act every one of these can walk out of the door to-morrow and return to the Canadian Service unless this service is definitely part of the Royal Air Force.
>
> With the growth of schools, factories, and the size of the service neither the Admiralty nor the Canadian Navy will be able to control the growth of this service and it will become a very good show backed by national enthusiasm.[62]

---

* By this phrase the Cabinet indicated that no decision on a permanent air force had yet been made. On 3 October the Judge Advocate-General, Col O.M. Biggar, raised some important questions about the order-in-council. As he pointed out, although the CAF had been effectively made 'a corps of the active militia,' it was also declared to be a part of the Overseas Military Forces of Canada. In law, he commented devastatingly, 'there is no such thing as the Overseas Military Forces of Canada'; what there was was the Canadian Expeditionary Force. Presumably, therefore, statutory provisions made under the War Measures Act expressly for the CEF did not apply to the CAF. More important for the future of the CAF was his observation that the order-in-council made no provision for the CAF at such time as the Overseas Ministry ceased to exist. The CAF was therefore 'the only unit which will not, automatically, and without any further order-in-council, come upon demobilization under the control of the Minister of Militia and Defence.' This omission, which may or may not have been deliberate, was to have fateful consequences for the infant CAF when the Cabinet, in 1919, took up the question of the postwar military establishment. Biggar to Minister of Militia and Defence, 3 Oct. 1918, HQ 6978–2–131, vol. 9, PAC RG 24, vol. 2043

Moreover, Pink thought, the presence of the RCNAS in Canada would mean that recruiting for RAF Canada 'will practically stop dead.' He warned against lending officers to the new force because the co-existence of competing air forces in the empire would bring 'wastage of man power ... lack of cohesion, lack of cooperation, and jealousy between the various Forces.' Instead, the bold course of immediately establishing Canadian (and Australian) divisions within the RAF should be adopted. Otherwise, the Admiralty would proceed to operate a Canadian naval air service through its local senior officer, the Canadian army might well run its own flying corps, 'and, generally speaking, the position will become so complicated as to be almost inextricable.'[63]

Despite such opposition from within the air staff, the RCNAS was to go ahead, therefore making it most difficult to oppose the CAF. How did Canada come to be blessed in 1918 with a second air force, created almost simultaneously, when for years the Canadian government had consistently refused to consider the formation of any air force whatever? The answer lies in a sudden change in the antisubmarine war which brought Canada's east coast into the war zone. The new circumstances require some explanation.

In July 1915 the Canadian Naval Service had responded to the threat of German attack by forming the St Lawrence Patrol, consisting of seven patrol vessels and twelve chartered motor-boats, to guard the estuary. No German submarines operated in Canadian waters in 1915 and 1916, though U-53 sank five merchantmen off Nantucket on 8 October 1916. It was the appearance of U-53 that prompted the Admiralty to warn Canada and Newfoundland that patrols off their coasts should be strengthened. J.D. Hazen, then Minister of the Naval Service, raised the possibility of employing an anti-submarine air patrol based at Halifax and on the north shore of Cape Breton. His officials favoured the idea and the Admiralty welcomed it when Borden and Hazen broached the matter during their visit to England in February 1917. A party of RNAS officers under Wing Commander J.W. Seddon was sent to Canada to investigate the feasibility of such a patrol. Seddon recommended, after touring the east coast and visiting Canadian Aeroplanes Ltd in Toronto, that a small seaplane force, divided between Halifax and Sydney, be formed, and that the required aircraft be built in Toronto.[64]

The Cabinet (minus Borden and Hazen) discussed Seddon's report at the end of March. They decided to reject it. Sir George Foster cabled their reasons to the Prime Minister: 'Council unanimously of opinion establishment inadvisable. Cost entailed will exceed two and a half millions for first year, abstract skilled men for construction badly needed in other works, utility limited by our seasonal changes. Money better used in providing [more sea] patrols.'[65] Nevertheless, the initiative taken by Hazen, the support he received from his own department, and the general concurrence of the Prime Minister demonstrated that the government was ready to take action should air patrols become necessary along the eastern seaboard.

With the adoption of the convoy system in 1917, Halifax and Sydney became assembly ports for eastward-bound convoys. The very success of the system compelled the Germans to shift the focus of their operations. At about the same time they had developed large ocean-going submarines, capable of staying at sea for three months or more and mounting two 6-inch guns. Suddenly the Canadian coast became a desirable target area. Early in January 1918 the Admiralty warned Ottawa to this effect and the Naval Service immediately set about the further strengthening of its patrol force. No mention of air patrols had been made by the Admiralty, but within its staff the idea was under active consideration. At first the Air Department thought of diverting *Engadine*, *Riviera*, and *Vindex* to Canadian waters, but on 18 February the Operations Committee ruled that these vessels were more usefully employed in the Mediterranean and instead decided that 'the aircraft required for the protection of merchant shipping in Canadian waters could be worked from shore billets.' Where were the aircraft to come from? The Admiralty had no surplus and the only possibility seemed the United States Navy. It was recognized that the Canadian government would have to be consulted first.[66]

Nothing of this was known in Ottawa. When the Admiralty cabled that Flight Commander John Barron (an airship pilot from Stratford, Ontario, then stationed in Washington) could visit Canada 'in the event of your Government contemplating any submarine measures involving the use of airships,' Canadian officials were taken completely by surprise. Scarcely had they declined this puzzling offer when a renewed Admiralty warning of the submarine danger was received, this time coupled with a preliminary plan for an aircraft patrol. The plan was based upon a report to the Operations Committee by Captain F.R. Scarlett. In his opinion the German threat was now so acute that the Canadians ought to be ready to reverse their stand of a year before, and not only create an air service but also the seaplane, airship, and kite balloon factories needed to support it. In the meantime, he recommended that the United States be asked to extend its coastal seaplane organization northwards to protect Nova Scotia and Newfoundland. It was also on the basis of Scarlett's report that the Colonial Secretary urged the Canadian government to arrange for American help, since 'Admiralty fear assistance from this country is not possible.'[67]

Here, indeed, was a crisis, one that placed Canada in a position of singular dependency. Canadian officers were sent to Washington to seek American assistance; within a week an officer of the USN was in Halifax to discuss the possibility of American seaplane patrols across the entrance to the Bay of Fundy. After a month had passed with no further action, Naval Service Headquarters somewhat desperately cabled the Admiralty to 'use influence with Air Ministry to send at once an Officer to take charge and organize.' Meanwhile matters were taken in hand by Admiral Sir W.L. Grant, Commander-in-Chief North America and West Indies, who convened a conference in Washington of British and American naval and air officers, together with Captain Walter Hose, the RCN's Captain of Patrols on the east coast. The conference settled two main points: first of all, that air stations should be established at Halifax and Sydney; secondly, that the United States would supply these stations with pilots, seaplanes, airships, and kite balloons until Canada was ready to take over. On 23 April a second meeting was held at Boston, attended by Rear Admiral Wood, USN, Commandant First Naval District, and Admiral Kingsmill, the Director of the Canadian Naval Service. Here it was agreed that the United States would take responsibility for coastal patrol and anti-submarine work as far east as Lockeport, NS, and that two American torpedo boats and six submarine chasers would be dispatched to Halifax and placed under the operational control of the RCN. These arrangements, approved by the Canadian government, were followed on 7 May 1918 by an Admiralty message that Lieutenant-Colonel J.T. Cull, RAF, had been appointed to overall command of the air patrol.[68]

Cull did not appear in Canada for two months. When the Admiralty asked for three officers to be attached to the Director of Naval Service, Ottawa, for special duty, it was the first time the Air Ministry had heard of the Canadian project. Doubtless wishing to avoid the appearance of meddling, the Admiralty attributed its request to a purported Canadian desire to establish an aerial defence system. Not until Captain Barron, now a member of the RAF and posted to Ottawa, reported on 24 May that the Canadian government wished to organize an air service did the Air Council approve the despatch of Cull and his party.[69]

Up to this point Canadian authorities had been following rather ineffectually in the wake of the Admiralty and the United States Navy. They had no option but to accept the reality of the German threat to the east coast, could not question the Admiralty's view that an air patrol was necessary, and since they had taken no steps to form an air service of their own, were in no position to refuse American help. A step on the road back from impotence was taken on 5 June, when the government formally approved the establishment of two air stations. The Department of the Naval Service, meanwhile, had already begun to plan the organization of an air arm, and had sent a party, including Barron, to Nova Scotia to make a preliminary selection of sites for seaplane and airship bases.*[70]

When Cull arrived from England in July, no real progress had been made in organizing an east-coast system. To get construction started, and to take advantage of the money voted by Parliament in June, Cull approved the Halifax sites selected by Barron's party. The seaplane base was to be at Eastern Passage, while the airship site was also on the Dartmouth side. Keating Cove, Barron's choice at Sydney, he found inaccessible, and so he picked Kelly Beach, on the western side of North Sydney, for the seaplanes and balloons, and a site for airships on the opposite side of the town. He also persuaded the United States Navy Department to act upon the April agreement, despite the lateness of the season and some American reluctance to accept the original financial terms. These provisions were somewhat vague; Canada was to pay for all ground installations and the United States for anything airborne. The Americans stipulated that their airmen must be housed in permanent buildings, erected to their specifications, by 15 October, and that US officers must be in command of the stations, with RAF officers acting only in liaison capacity with the Canadian patrol authorities.[71]

An advance party of USN airmen arrived at Halifax by sea on 5 August. Within two weeks the Baker Point site at Eastern Passage had become a trim American naval establishment, flying the Stars and Stripes under the command of Lieu-

* Kingsmill was rebuffed by General Hoare when he sought RAF Canada's co-operation in giving flying training to the new service's cadets. Hoare thought such training would be useless because the cadets would ultimately have to qualify on USN seaplanes. What he wanted from Kingsmill was the assurance 'that no men from the Royal Air Force will be taken on for this new Service.' Hoare to Kingsmill, 15 May 1918, NS 1034-3-4, vol. 1, PAC RG 24, vol. 3894

tenant Richard E. Byrd, later famous as an aviator and polar explorer. Byrd was also Officer-in-Charge US Naval Air Force in Canada, his appointment document stating that he was 'responsible to the Senior British Naval Officer ... at H.M.S. [sic] Dockyard, Halifax, NS, for prompt response to all demands made upon your forces for cooperation in carrying out the General Mission of the Allied Naval Force in Canada.' With the assistance of Hose, Cull, Lieutenant Donaghue, USN (the commander designate for North Sydney), and Rear-Admiral B.M. Chambers, RN, Byrd worked out a patrol plan for the two stations. Escorts were to be provided for both inward- and outward-bound convoys, with two seaplanes held in reserve at both stations for emergency action against submarines and to allow for maintenance and repair. Baker Point patrols began before the end of August; construction delays prevented the North Sydney HS2Ls from coming into service until the week of 22–28 September. Between this period and the end of the war the flying boats flew regular patrols and carried out coastal searches. From August to October three German submarines cruised off the Atlantic coast between Newfoundland and Cape Hatteras, but only once was one reported in Canadian waters and no aircraft from Canadian stations actually saw a submarine. During the same period kite balloons were flown from HMCS *Acadia*, but equipment shortages prevented the use of the airships.*[72]

None of this work so proficiently carried out by the Americans did much to advance the establishment of a Canadian naval air service. That job had been left to Cull, and he found himself in an almost impossible situation. Not only had he to act as the bridge between the USN, the RN, and RCN, but he was also responsible to the Department of the Naval Service, to his old masters at the Admiralty, and to his new ones at the Air Ministry. Before he left England he had asked the Admiralty what uniform his party should wear. The advice he got was that the RAF uniform should be worn, 'otherwise it seems that some of you will wear R.N.A.S., some R.N., some R.A.F. and some R.N.V.R. uniforms.' When, so attired, he reported to Kingsmill for duty, the Director of the Naval Service was outraged. Since Cull and his party would be working with the USN Kingsmill thought they should hold naval ranks; 'it is most undesirable that they should be in any way under the orders of R.A.F. in Canada as their work is entirely separate.' He therefore proposed that the group should be 'lent to the Government for service in Canadian N.A.S.' Cull's party, however, was really not at the disposal of the Admiralty, since it was in fact on loan from the RAF. Though its orders were to come from the Admiralty, 'for purposes of discipline' the party was under the command of Brigadier-General Hoare in Toronto. Though Hoare wanted as little as possible to do with them, they had perforce to continue to wear RAF uniforms.†

---

* Cull recommended additional sub-stations at Canso, Cape Sable Island, and the Magdalen Islands, and also a station to cover convoys re-routed through the Strait of Belle Isle. None of these had passed the planning stage when the war ended. Cull to Kingsmill, 31 Aug. 1918, draft cable Ballantyne to Admiralty enclosed with Cull to Deputy Minister, 18 Sept. 1918, NS 63–1–1, PAC RG 24, vol. 5666

† After the formation of the RCNAS Cull enlarged on his problems with Hoare in a letter to Ballantyne: '... my position with G.O.C. R.A.F. Toronto, is somewhat anomalous and does not lend itself to correspondence with him on terms of equality. As you may remember, application was originally made for myself and staff to be lent to the Dominion. This was refused and we were told

For all other matters Cull was immediately responsible to Kingsmill, but anything he required in the way of specialized personnel or technical equipment could come only from the Air Ministry. Since that department was cool to his mission, he found that he could get action on his needs only by going through the Admiralty.[73]

It is small wonder that Cull began to find his lot an unhappy one. At the end of July he had received unexpected assistance from the Prime Minister. 'Every effort should be made,' Borden urged, 'to have Air stations in full working order and manned by Canadian personnel by opening of navigation next year.' But Cull soon found himself in the middle of a complex wrangle between the Naval Service and Public Works Departments over the construction of facilities to house the new service. He was momentarily heartened by a government announcement to the press on 8 August that a new naval air service was to be formed, but then affairs came once more to a standstill.[74] Cull's frustration appears in a demi-official report to the Admiralty late that month: 'The Navy Department have their hands quite full, know nothing about the needs of Aviation and, sometimes, one is driven to thinking, care less; anyway the civilian element which curiously forms the chief element are busy over their own little municipal affairs and are apt to think us somewhat of a nuisance. However, we have had one or two fights already, involving threats of resignation and with the assistance of our German Friends on the coast putting the wind thoroughly up seaport mayors and public opinion, have won through to date.'[75] Cull had in fact formally requested to be relieved of his duties, an action which brought quick results. On 30 August the Prime Minister sent for him, and the two discussed the whole situation, including, more than likely, the lack of interest displayed by the Minister of the Naval Service. According to Loring Christie, Sir Robert then advised Ballantyne to 'see Colonel Cull at the earliest moment and take up with him the question of the organization of the Naval Air Service.' On 5 September the new service was officially created. PC 2154 laid down: '1. That the proposed organization shall be regarded as temporary for the purpose of meeting the needs of the war. 2. That it shall be called the Royal Canadian Naval Air Service.' The order-in-council provided for eighty aircraft cadets, twelve airship cadets, and up to one thousand ratings. Officers in the new service were to wear a naval cap and be uniformed in dark blue serge, although with a brown leather Sam Browne belt. RAF rank badges and pilot wings were to be used, with the latter modified to include a green maple leaf and 'RCNAS' in the centre. Men were to be uniformed as 'men not dressed as seamen' in the RCN, and wear appropriate air service badges.[76]

The press did not give the RCNAS much of a welcome. It seemed so much a product of the concerns of Britain and the United States that the *Toronto Star* scoffed that 'one does not observe anything Canadian about this Royal Canadian Air Force [sic] except the name and the solid old sea coast along which it is to operate.' Young Canadians were less opinionated. By mid-September sixty-four

that although we should work separately from the R.A.F. with the Naval Department, we were still to come under R.A.F. Toronto for matters of discipline. As the R.C.N.A.S. is being kept quite distinct from the R.A.F. I think it would be better for the Service if I and my staff had nothing to do with the R.A.F. from the service point of view being either responsible to the Dominion only or to the Air Ministry direct.' The precise status of the RCNAS was never resolved. Cull to Ballantyne, 6 Sept. 1918, NS 1034–3–1, PAC RG 24, vol. 3894

cadets had been recruited in Toronto and Ottawa, and within a few weeks had been sent to the Massachusetts Institute of Technology for ground school. Another contingent was dispatched by 31 October. Twelve airship cadets were also sent to the United Kingdom for training.[77] Once Cull had been given his head, he had put together the RCNAS organization with efficiency and despatch.* But as the end of the war approached, the future of the Canadian naval air arm was back in the hands of the Cabinet.

If public reaction to the creation of the RCNAS was lukewarm at best, that of the staff of HQ OMFC in London was ice-cold. It was not simply that the RCNAS was the senior Canadian flying service (by two weeks), although that rankled. Brigadier-General McDonald and W.A. Bishop (whose secondment to the RAF had ceased in order that he might assist in the organization of the CAF) protested to General Turner over 'the utter futility' of forming two Canadian air forces. Turner passed this complaint, with his strong support, to Kemp; Bishop was impulsive enough to complain directly to General Mewburn, the Minister of Militia, thus by-passing Kemp. Without authorization, Turner then approved a trip to Canada for McDonald and Bishop, in order that they might present a comprehensive plan for the amalgamation of the two new services, thus precipitating an acrimonious clash with the Deputy Minister, Walter Gow. This tempest was quelled by a sharp reproof from Kemp and his statement that the establishment of the RCNAS was the result of 'the very careful consideration of the Prime Minister and certain members of the Government with whom he desired to consult.'[78]

At least some of the anger expressed by these men arose from their frustration with the slow pace at which the CAF was proceeding, after the bright hopes raised by its authorization. On 25 July Brigadier-General Drew had agreed that the two squadrons were to be organized at once. But 'at once' did not mean instantaneously. Not until 5 August did the Air Ministry give notice that two squadrons, first designated as 93 and 123 Squadrons by the RAF, were to be 'manned entirely with CANADIAN personnel.'† The Air Council had decided that 93 was to be a fighter squadron equipped with Sopwith Dolphins, and 123 a day-bomber squadron equipped with DH9s. In order to allow time for the assembling of personnel and necessary training of groundcrew, the mobilization date for the two squadrons was tentatively set as 10 October, at which time preparations would be made for active service on the Western Front.[79]

Prime responsibility for assembling the officers and other ranks belonged to Bishop, who was promoted temporary lieutenant-colonel and attached to HQ OMFC at the head of the CAF Section. He was given general liaison responsibilities with the RAF, and was to act as the minister's adviser for all questions respecting the organization and training of the CAF and for the selection of personnel. Only the most general guidelines for the selection of flying officers had been laid down. All

---

* One of the members of Cull's new organization was Sub-Lieutenant E.L. Janney, RNCVR, formerly Captain Janney of the Canadian Aviation Corps.

† No 93 Squadron was redesignated as 81 Squadron RAF on 19 October. From the outset the squadron was known to the Canadians as 1 Squadron CAF, and 123 as 2 Squadron CAF. 'Notes on the Formation of No. 1 and 2 Squadrons Canadian Air Force,' nd [Aug. 1918], DAO order, 19 Oct. 1918, OS 10–9–27, vol. 1, PAC RG 9 III, vol. 80

were to be Canadian citizens. It was also thought that there should be a mixture of officers with considerable active service and officers who had just completed flying training. When responsibility passed from OMFC officials to the airmen themselves, a tendency began to restrict appointments to active service officers, until, in the final stages of the CAF, the objective clearly became the creation of two élite squadrons. Thus when Bishop took over, he stressed that it was 'preferable to give appointments to people who have served with the C.E.F. in France rather than to those who have enlisted in the Air Force in Canada.' Less than two months later the Air Ministry was told that, in manning 2 Squadron, 'as far as possible it is desired to have Officers who have good records with the Flying Corps in the R.A.F., and have had a certain amount of active service flying in France and other theatres of the war.'[80]

To command 1 Squadron, Bishop's first choice was Major Raymond Collishaw, but when he proved unavailable he secured the services of Captain A.E. McKeever.* For 2 Squadron he recommended Captain Walter B. Lawson.† When, in early October, Bishop decided to relinquish his position and return to Canada, he had put together a list of officers for the fighter squadron which McKeever accepted, but Lawson was left the job of finding suitable bomber pilots. Complete lists were not in the hands of the Air Ministry until 19 November. None of those named were to be offered permanent appointments, partly because McKeever and Lawson wished to leave room for airmen with outstanding operational records. The whole selection process had been slowed by Bishop's departure, by delays in securing the services of McKeever and Lawson from the RAF, and by the uncertainty of whether or not the CAF would survive the end of hostilities.[81]

The RAF had agreed that some of the groundcrew for the two squadrons could be drawn from Canadians in RAF units, while the rest would be chosen from those with appropriate civilian trades in the Canadian forces. The RAF's Director of Manning, ordered to 'comb out' Canadian tradesmen, was able to find only a handful by late September because RAF personnel records did not show the national origins of other ranks. Ultimately the RAF found more than 150 fully-trained Canadian mechanics among its number. Doubtless many more could have been turned up. But long before this the Canadians had selected the 237 other ranks they required from the several Canadian depots in England. Bishop had begun the process at Witley in early August; others were obtained from the camps at Bramshott, Seaford, and Shorncliffe.[82]

Most of these recruits were sent to RAF Halton Park to train as mechanics and riggers, while a smaller number went to Uxbridge for armament training. According to the original plan, at the conclusion of their training they were to be posted to RAF squadrons for a month's experience before being mobilized. This fell through, and the delay in assembling officers for the squadrons, together with indecision about

---

* Andrew Edward McKeever of Listowel, Ont., had been an RFC direct entry in 1916. An outstanding Bristol Fighter pilot, his chief operational service had been with 11 Squadron on the Western Front.

† Walter Brogdin Lawson of Barrie, Ont., was a 1913 RMC graduate who went overseas with the 15th Battalion CEF in the First Contingent. He transferred to the RNAS in 1915. His last operational service was with 215 Squadron of the Independent Force.

whether or not to mobilize the squadrons at all, meant that CAF groundcrew spent much longer in training than had been expected. Many of them began to question the worth of an air force career. When Major J.D. McCrimmon from HQ OMFC arrived at Halton in October to take over the Canadians there, he found 'a pretty bad mixup.' RAF Halton had treated them as RAF recruits, given them new RAF numbers, and managed to lose many of their personal documents. McCrimmon succeeded in restoring morale, but even so these Canadians had more than a month's further wait before they joined their squadrons.*[83]

All this effort would have gone for naught had it not been for the efforts of Major Gibson, the assistant deputy minister. Gibson obtained from General Brancker an assurance that the Air Ministry would uphold its part of the bargain. Brancker told him that the two squadrons 'shall not be broken up as we proposed, but shall be kept as units until such time as you are prepared to move them back to Canada.' With this guarantee, he was able to secure from the Prime Minister, on 17 November, authorization for mobilization to proceed. Borden took under advisement the question of whether the squadrons should be returned to Canada as the nucleus for a future Canadian air force. As a result, 1 and 2 Squadrons CAF were mobilized between 20 and 25 November at their airfield at Upper Heyford, and though somewhat under strength and underequipped, commenced training.[84]

The CAF's position was precarious. No overall command and administrative structure had been established. The CAF itself was nothing more than two squadrons of the RAF which happened to be all-Canadian. No thought had been given to equipping the squadrons for service in Canada rather than for the Western Front, nor had the financial implications of maintaining them for any considerable period after the Armistice been faced. The CAF continued to exist because the RAF was willing to co-operate and because the Canadian government had not made up its mind. But all concerned with it knew that its future was clouded, and they manifested their awareness in a variety of ways. For battle-hardened pilots the transition to peacetime conditions, and to the very different challenges of organization and administration, was difficult enough. The task of formulating a policy that would persuade the government to maintain the CAF was one for which most of them were not equipped.

---

* Another one hundred Canadians were recruited in mid-October as a replacement pool and sent for training at Halton and Uxbridge. All but twenty specially qualified for training as mechanics were returned to their units after 22 November because wartime wastage rates no longer applied. Scarcely happier was the experience of twelve other ranks recruited for training as NCO observers. At the end of August Bishop selected twelve candidates from the Young Soldiers Battalion CEF at Bramshott. They were trained at the Eastchurch School of Aerial Bombing and Gunnery, then at 1 Observers School of Aerial Gunnery at Hythe, and finally at 1 School of Aerial Navigation and Bomb Dropping at Stonehenge. After three months' training they were mobilized with 123 Squadron, but Captain Lawson then decided that they were insufficiently qualified, having only had short courses and 'no Overseas experience.' Further, specialist NCO observers were not wanted for postwar service. Four of the twelve decided to return to their units; the others were employed on ground duties with the CAF. 'Lists of trades and numbers required, [Aug. 1918],' '123 Squadron [2 Canadian] monthly return of other ranks, 30 November 1918,' HQ OMFC R-1–49, PAC RG 9 III, vol. 3432; Lott to McDonald, 22 Nov. 1918, OS 10–9–27, vol 2, ibid., vol. 81; correspondence on NCO observers, 29 Aug. 1918–18 Feb. 1919, HQ OMFC O-1–49, Lawson to GS, 13 Jan. 1919, HQ OMFC P-10–49, ibid., vol. 3431

Continued difficulties with the other ranks were a sign of the disorganized condition of the CAF and betrayed not only the inexperience of its officers but also its indeterminate status and the unsettled feelings of the men in a period when general demobilization was well under way. At Halton Camp, early in January 1919, the Canadians still there refused in a body to obey orders to drill. An investigating officer dispatched by HQ OMFC found that a British RAF officer had 'fallen in the parade on a ground which was in a deplorable condition and began to drill the men before a crowd of young soldiers who obviously took much pleasure in seeing the detail drilling in the mud.' No sooner was this trouble quelled than McKeever reported a 'crisis' with the men at Upper Heyford. This station was under RAF command, and Canadian other ranks had been detailed for fatigue duties by British officers. On 7 January the men refused to move off from morning parade to duty at their flights. As it turned out, they had a number of legitimate complaints. They had had no Christmas leave; because the CAF had no real administrative organization they had been given no trades pay since mobilization; their messing was atrocious; they were anxious to know when the squadrons would be returning to Canada; and some expressed the fear that they would not be permitted to demobilize. Major Marshall, sent from Canadian headquarters to look into the problem, reported that the bearing and discipline of the men was 'anything but good – they being discontented and slovenly.' The senior NCOs, who held their positions because of technical competence, had no experience in handling men, nor had many of the flying officers. Things were straightened out by sending a few men with lengthy crime sheets back to their units, securing regular leave for the rest, setting up an army orderly room, organizing better messing, and posting in a CEF sergeant-major to establish discipline. These incidents (there were others) were trivial in themselves, but they revealed the deficiencies of the CAF.[85]

There was much dissatisfaction among the flying officers as well. The chief cause was the aircraft furnished by the RAF. Neither the Dolphin nor the DH9a was held in any respect by men who knew their operational performance. McKeever wanted Snipes for his squadron, and Lawson Bristol Fighters for his, but junior staff officers at HQ OMFC found no willingness on the part of the Air Ministry to change the original allocations. Lawson had no quarrel with the DH9as as training aircraft. They were safe and reliable enough, though operationally obsolete. In mid-January 2 Squadron established the Hounslow Detached Flight, using their machines to ferry senior officials to and from Paris. The Dolphins were another matter; there had already been one fatal casualty,* and in early February the Air Ministry ordered all service flying on Dolphins to cease until safety modifications could be made. Even when flying resumed, no aerobatics were permitted. At a

---

* On 1 December Lieutenant W.J. Sampson of Vancouver was killed while ferrying a Dolphin to Upper Heyford. There were two other fatal accidents during the CAF's period of existence. On 8 May Captain C.W. Warman was killed while low flying at Chingford. Warman was an American who had gone overseas with the PPCLI in 1914. He was apparently regarded by the CAF as an 'honorary' Canadian. On 22 May Major A.D. Carter of Point de Bute, NB, was killed while flying a Fokker D-VII: 'wing of Fokker folded up and machine descended in nose dive from seven thousand feet.' Staff Captain to GSO1 with attachments, 16 May 1919, Leckie to DAS, [23 May 1919], HQ OMFC A–6–36, vol. 2, PAC RG 9 III, vol. 3068; C.W. Warman biographical file, DHist

conference of squadron commanders and OMFC staff officers those present agreed that the Air Ministry should be pushed hard for better aircraft, on the naïve ground that this was a 'small request' and that 'as the Pilots who are to fly these are the Canadian Pilots with the highest records,' it was 'only fair to give them the Machines which they demand.'[86]

On 28 January McKeever's frustration with the whole position of the CAF boiled over. He called upon the Overseas Ministry to appoint a senior officer to command the CAF, in order that some stability could be given the fledgling organization and also to make some impression upon the Air Ministry. Beyond that, he was as perturbed by the hazy status of the CAF as were the other ranks. 'A definite policy should be arrived at as soon as possible by the Canadian Authorities as to the purpose of the two Canadian Squadrons,' he wrote. 'Is it the intention to use these two Squadrons as the nucleus of the Canadian Royal Air Force?' If it was, then arrangements must be made in Canada for their reception in the form of accommodation, hangars, and other installations, and it was vital to determine what aircraft were most appropriate for a Canada-based force. McKeever's views were received sympathetically at HQ OMFC. 'I cannot help feeling,' wrote Lieutenant-Colonel C.M. Edwards, 'although I hesitate to make the statement, that the Air Ministry take very little interest in our organization and equipment.'[87] In fact, Canadian Headquarters had already been exploring the question of a commander for the CAF.

Their first choice was Colonel R.H. Mulock. However, Mulock did not wish to pursue a career in military aviation, although he was deeply interested in the establishment of a satisfactory Canadian military aviation policy. It was therefore decided to attach Mulock to HQ OMFC, so that he could devote himself to the formulation of a policy proposal, gathering material for the purpose from the Air Ministry, with a view to his eventually laying a policy document before the Cabinet. He took up his duties on 20 February. At the same time Lieutenant-Colonel G.C. St P. de Dombasle, one of the senior Canadians in the RAF, was appointed to command the CAF, initially only working part-time on his new duties until the Air Ministry released him from his previous responsibilities.* One of his first recommendations was that a better airfield be found; he also requested that the Dolphins should be replaced by SE5as so that training could continue. To both requests the Air Ministry agreed, and on 31 March the CAF moved to a new home, Shoreham-by-Sea. By this time de Dombasle's appointment had been changed to Director of the Air Service and he and his administrative staff were housed at HQ OMFC in London. Under his direction, the two Canadian squadrons had been formed into 1 Canadian Wing, CAF. Its commander was the distinguished RNAS pilot, Major Robert Leckie, who was also station commander at Shoreham. In addition, a Technical and Supply Branch was established and its members began the task of acquiring technical data from the RAF for future use in Canada. All these measures were taken by authority of the Overseas Military Council.[88]

---

* Lieutenant-Colonel de Dombasle, of the Royal Canadian Regiment, had transferred from the CEF to the RFC in December 1915. He had had considerable command experience, having been officer commanding 1 Squadron RFC from December 1916, and later commandant of the School of Aeronautics at Reading.

For a brief period the CAF enjoyed relative stability, and as flying training proceeded the organization began to develop its own character and spirit. Part of that spirit, surely understandable in the circumstances, was a certain war-born élitism. McKeever and Lawson had never given up hope of obtaining 'flying officers who will be gradually drifting back from France for Home establishment and who have a good record.' De Dombasle and Leckie were sympathetic; indeed, on 12 April Leckie requested that six of his pilots be posted away. He was actuated, he said, 'simply from a desire to fill their places with more efficient Officers, with longer War Service or special qualifications.' Such officers were available as the result of an Air Ministry notification to all RAF units that applications for transfer to the CAF would be received. To classify the flood of applications, Leckie set up a selection committee. At the same time the Air Ministry was informed that only officers holding two or more decorations could be considered. This provision was cancelled after a protest from HQ OMFC.[89]

The demise of the CAF halted this selection process. Before that occurred the CAF had already departed considerably from the officer mixture that had been planned. Including non-flying staff officers, there were forty-nine officers on the strength of 1 Wing in April-May 1919. Of these forty-one had operational experience, thirty-one had served in France with the CEF before transferring to aviation, and two more had a similar career with the BEF. Only five CAF officers had an RNAS background. Of the forty-two officers on flying duties, twenty-two had been decorated for gallantry and ten had at least two such decorations. The fighter squadron's flight commanders were Captains C.F. Falkenberg, DFC and Bar, G.O. Johnson, MC, and D.R. MacLaren, DSO, MC and Bar, DFC; while those of the bomber squadron were Major A.D. Carter, DSO and Bar, Captain J.O. Leach, MC, AFC, and Captain T.F. Hazell, DSO, MC, DFC. The CAF, in other words, had become an organization weighted towards those with operational experience, outstanding records, and a background of army service on the Western Front. Nevertheless, it was representative of the several ways in which Canadians became aviators during the war; eight of its members, for example, were products of RAF Canada.*[90]

No one connected with the CAF was innocent enough to believe that an all-star cast would guarantee its survival. Both Gibson and Mulock were quite aware that the high cost of military aviation was bound to influence the Canadian government. The crux of the matter was the cost of equipment and of its maintenance and replacement. Ought a future Canadian air force to have equipment identical to that of the RAF, or should its aircraft be adapted to the special features of the Canadian environment? The assumption underlying the first alternative was that

* Not all the wing's officers were Canadian. Two of the flying officers were American graduates of RAF Canada and two others were British. Leckie protested to de Dombasle that 'the Pilots feel very strongly on the subject' and that 'I thoroughly agree with this point of view.' An undated and unsigned memorandum singled out a Major Hazell, appointed by de Dombasle, as an Englishman 'never in Canada,' and also criticized the lack of aviation experience among the officers in de Dombasle's directorate. Leckie to de Dombasle, 20 April 1919, HQ OMFC P-6-49, PAC RG 9 III, vol. 3431; critical memorandum, nd [May-June 1919], HQ OMFC A-6-36, ibid., vol. 3068

the CAF should be primarily a military force, designed to act in concert with the RAF in time of war; the adoption of the second meant a distinctive Canadian force carrying out civil as well as military functions.

Those guiding the CAF chose the first alternative. The decisive consideration seems to have been cost. The RAF had large supplies of aircraft surplus to its requirements, and during his initial discussions at the Air Ministry de Dombasle detected a readiness to make this available to the Canadians. At a meeting with Air Ministry officials on 3 March, therefore, de Dombasle accepted the principle of identical equipment and subsequently requested the allocation to Canada of fifty DH9s, thirty Avro trainers, and twelve Camels, with sufficient spare parts and other equipment to keep them in service for a year. Senior staff officers of the RAF supported the idea, Brigadier-General P.W. Game noting that 'Cols. Mulock and de Dombasle informed me that the chief obstacle to the formation of an Air Force in Canada is likely to be the initial expense.' When opposition from the financial officials to the idea of a free gift arose, Trenchard (Chief of the Air Staff once more) brushed it aside. 'It seems absurd to me,' he wrote to the Under Secretary, '... that we are talking about destroying machines instead of giving them straight-away to Canada.'[91] It was finally agreed that a gift would be made to each of the dominions from RAF surplus aircraft. On 4 June the Colonial Secretary cabled to Ottawa that 'His Majesty's Government have approved of proposal of Air Council that a gift of aeroplanes not exceeding 100 in number should be made to any Dominion requiring machines object of His Majesty's Government being to assist Dominions wishing to establish air forces and thereby develop defence of the Empire by air.'[92]

The Canadian government spent some time in careful examination of this gift horse, and rather more in some picayune bargaining over what aircraft it would be pleased to receive. Eventually Ottawa agreed to accept 62 Avro 504s, 12 DH9as, 12 SE5s, 10 DH4s, two H16 flying-boats, two Bristol Fighters, and a Snipe. In addition, Canada received at least six non-rigid airships, some kite balloons, a large amount of tools, spare engines, and other equipment, and three hundred vehicles of various types. The total value of this gift was approximately $5 million; the only cost to Canada was that of shipment. This, it was later remarked, was 'a sum greater than that which the Canadian government spent on aviation during the four years 1919–20 to 1922–23.'[*][93]

The imperial gift, despite the Colonial Secretary's stipulation that it was intended for dominions willing to establish air forces, was not enough to save the CAF. Its fate had been foreshadowed in the earlier demise of the RCNAS. Only two days after the Armistice Lieutenant-Colonel Cull had been informed by the Deputy Minister that the RCNAS had 'ceased to exist,' and doubtless this followed from a strict interpretation of the order-in-council establishing it. Nevertheless, the Minister of the Naval Service fought a rearguard action to preserve the infant force. On 22 November he cabled Borden that although a majority of the Cabinet

---

* In addition to the imperial gift, Canada also received at least fifteen German aircraft as trophies, as well as engines and spare parts. Finally, a number of aircraft were substituted for the eighteen presented to the British flying services by various individuals and organizations in Canada.

wished to wind up the RCNAS immediately, he personally favoured the maintenance of a small unit at Halifax. Borden did not meet the issue directly, but stated
that in his judgment Canada 'should maintain the nucleus of an air service as that
service is essential to any system of naval or military defence.' He expressed a
preference for a single service uniting both military and naval functions. With no
explicit guidance from the Prime Minister, the Cabinet on 5 December did not
precisely kill the RCNAS, but rather decided not to proceed with it 'on its present
basis.' Instead, they looked forward to its resumption, not with half-trained cadets,
but with Canadian veterans of the RNAS. As Ballantyne explained the decision to
G.J. Desbarats, his deputy, 'the R.C.N.A.S. is not abolished, and the action that is
now being taken is only until such time as the Government decides on the details
and policy of a permanent Air Service.'[94]

The dismantling of the RCNAS was carried through with expedition. The cadets
were speedily released; by early January the last American party had left the
east-coast camps. Cull's final duty was to accompany Desbarats to a meeting in
Washington, called to settle the division of expenses between the two countries.
The Canadian government agreed to purchase all American ground equipment at
the Nova Scotian stations; in exchange, the United States donated to Canada
twelve flying-boats, twenty-six Liberty engines, and four kite balloons. Canada's
first venture into naval aviation had cost a total of $811,168 for bases, equipment,
and personnel. The US donation was valued at about $600,000, and the flying-
boats were to give much valuable service in the years to come.[95] Desbarats
summed up well this early experiment in US-Canadian naval and air co-operation:

> The operation of these two stations has afforded protection to the convoys of British and
> American ships sailing from these ports and has added to the safety of these vessels and
> protected all the troops and supplies which they carried.
> The combined action of the two Governments enabled the stations to be established
> without delay so that they could be operated during the past summer. It would have been
> impossible for Canada to organize a Naval Flying Service on the short notice which was
> given and, on the other hand, the United States needed protection for their shipping along
> the Canadian coast, so that the joint action that was taken seems to have been the best way
> of obtaining this protection.[96]

The last member of the RCNAS, Major C.C. MacLaurin, kept himself busy by
making periodic inspection tours of Baker Point and Kelly Beach, where, doubtless nostalgically, he test flew the aircraft. The end of the RCNAS finally came on
10 December 1919 when the Air Ministry, which was still paying MacLaurin,
refused a Canadian request to extend his tour of duty. Canada's one-man air force
then became a civilian member of the recently constituted Air Board.[97]

The RCNAS had built up no favourable constituency within the government,
and apart from Ballantyne, no one lifted a finger to save it. The CAF, in contrast,
had been preserved by the personal authority of the Prime Minister, had become a
force in being staffed by some of the country's ablest airmen, could look to the
Overseas Minister and his officials for strong support, and could count upon the
sympathy and co-operation of the RAF. When no word of the CAF's future was

received from Ottawa for over two months after its mobilization, Kemp forced the issue by informing the Minister of Militia that the two squadrons would be ready to return to Canada as early as 1 April. He also stated that the Air Ministry was preparing an 'Imperial Flying scheme' and suggested that it might be useful for the government to have a senior flying officer available to help in 'forming your plans for Canadian post bellum Air Force.' Mewburn's reply was a shock. The Cabinet, bearing in mind that the CAF had been formed 'for the purposes of the present war,' had decided that the squadrons would be demobilized on their return to Canada. Nevertheless, Mewburn requested that a senior officer competent to advise the government be sent over.[98]

To Kemp, this decision was quite unacceptable. He wanted, he told Mewburn, swift and positive government action in aviation policy:

Most strongly urge that matters of Canadian post bellum Air Service be considered seriously by Government without delay so that trained Canadian personnel in two Canadian Squadrons and in Royal Air Force may be drawn upon for future Canadian Air Service and aeronautic development before they are demobilized and scattered throughout Canada. Consider most desirable Canadian Air Force should have its natural place in Canadian post bellum military forces as indicated conclusively by experiences of war. In view of great development flying and flying machines in war and in all countries after war, Canada surely should take definite stand now to have Air Force which would enable it to keep pace with rest of world and particularly other Dominions in all matters relative to flying.[99]

At the same time Kemp wrote to the Prime Minister, urging him to 'do everything possible to prevent the total demobilization of the two splendid squadrons which are so capable and so well equipped.' He thought it 'preposterous' that the CAF should disappear, because inevitably the government would have to make up its mind about aviation. 'I understand,' he told Sir Robert, 'we are to have a permanent army of 5,000; surely we should have some sort of Air Service in connection with this force.'[100]

By this time the Prime Minister was in Paris, immersed in the great matters of the peace conference. His preoccupations may account for the singular evasiveness of his reply. He told Kemp that the future of the CAF had been discussed 'somewhat,' but that no definite conclusion had been arrived at; for the rest, he heartily agreed that 'in any permanent organization' an air service 'must have an effective part.' Clearly, Borden could not be counted an ally. Nor could General Mewburn. A propos of Kemp's cable, he told Sir Thomas White that he 'felt it was imperative for me to take some action,' since there was no provision for an air force as part of the military forces of Canada. The action he proposed to Cabinet was the formation of an air board, an idea he owed to Gwatkin, which would advise the government generally upon aviation matters.[101]

The CAF's fate now hung on the strength of the case that could be assembled for it. On 3 March Mulock, Gibson, Edwards, and de Dombasle called on Brigadier-General R.M. Groves, the DCAS. An informal conference followed, attended by other senior members of the Air Staff. At the request of the Canadians the Air Staff agreed to prepare a memorandum which could be used by the CAF 'with a view to pressing for a unified Air Service in Canada.' This paper, drafted initially by Lieutenant-Colonel R.C.M. Pink, Director of Flying Operations, and entitled 'Aerial Expansion With Particular Reference to Canada,' was submitted to detailed examination by the acting CAS, General Game, and by the heads of directorates.[102]

The paper commenced by laying out the general responsibilities of governments with respect to civil aviation. Its argument was centralist; that is, it was contended that no matter what form of political structure existed, a national authority was needed to control the registration of aircraft, the inspection of airfields, the issuance of pilots' certificates and certificates of airworthiness, air traffic, and licenses and franchises to private firms. In the case of Canada, 'with its vast distances and unlimited possibilities for expansion,' the early establishment of a central regulatory agency was particularly important. Neither the Air Staff nor the Canadians had any fault to find with this section, all agreeing that civil aviation in Canada was bound to develop rapidly.

The next section dealt with the manner in which the Canadian government itself might engage in civil aviation as an extension of the current work of government departments. On balance, it was the view of the Air Staff that such activities were 'likely to hold a more prominent place in the immediate future' in Canada than were naval or military aviation. The paper foresaw Canadian (or provincial) government aircraft engaged in such work as forest ranging, police and customs patrols, and photographic surveying for mapping purposes.

The final part of the paper contained the argument for an air force as part of the permanent military organization of Canada. It was couched in the language and reflected the thinking of the strategic bombing advocates, who at that time were well represented among the RAF's senior officers. All agreed that Canada had no need of a large air force. Nevertheless, since 'the wars of the future will be largely wars of the air, and as in consequence the first blow struck will be almost coincident with the declaration of war,' an aerial defence force would clearly be necessary. An air force, it was argued, was no longer simply an adjunct to military and naval forces (although it would still be necessary to retain aircraft for such auxiliary purposes); the bulk of any nation's military aircraft would be employed on operations 'quite unconnected with either the land or sea campaign.' 'A completely new art of aerial strategy, as different in its application from either Naval or Military, as these two now are different from each other,' would have to be developed. In Canada, as in Britain, naval, military, and strategic functions of air power ought to be combined in a single force, for reasons both of economy and for unified control. The original draft of the paper therefore advocated the creation of a single government department on the British model to control both civil and military aviation in Canada, to further imperial standardization, and simplify the conduct of future wars 'on either side of the Atlantic.'

General Game was the only officer who took serious issue with any part of this document. He wondered about the relevance to Canada of arguments based upon the strategic use of airpower; Canada was 'hardly open to aerial attack except from the U.S. and I understand her policy does not contemplate armed resistance to that country.' More generally, he was sceptical of any argument which took for granted the future effectiveness of strategic air power: '... nothing in the late war furnished any convincing proof to that effect. The German bombing of England actually never looked like having any decisive bearing on the war, and the same may be said of the operations of our Independent Force, while admitting that it never approached its full development.'[103] This was too much for the DCAS. Groves conceded that the German bombing of England had been spasmodic, but it had tied down large forces and had greatly interfered with 'the general life of the country.' As for the Independent Force, though it had been rushed into being, it did 'seriously damage the enemy and it is at least possible that much of the enemy's lack of morale towards the end of the war was due to the fear of our aircraft entertained by the civilian populace.' Land-based torpedo aircraft would, he thought, render defenceless enemy fleets even in secure harbours, while air power could also be used as a distinct weapon against, for example, 'a tribe in the interior of Africa ... giving trouble.' None of these were points likely to impress Canadian politicians, as Game dryly pointed out, but he was a minority of one. Trenchard approved the military section of the paper, and subsequently Gibson, who was shown both the original draft and the minutes upon it, approved it as well.[104]

Game had more success in criticizing the recommendation for the creation of a new government department for aviation. If the Canadian air service was to be on the model of the CAF, then a division of an existing government department would be quite sufficient to administer both Canada's air force and her civil aviation until such time as development warranted a larger organization. This point was accepted and the final portion of the paper was so amended. At the same time added emphasis was given to the idea of imperial standardization by noting the continuing ability for 'very close liaison and constant exchange of personnel' between Britain and Canada.[105]

Bearing this document, Mulock left for Canada at the end of April, carrying with him as well the hopes of all associated with the CAF. He had also been furnished with an elaborate document, compiled by de Dombasle, laying out the organization and establishment of the CAF. This paper followed the main lines of the RAF recommendations, except in proposing a separate air department. The CAF was visualized as a cadre organization, making up its full officer complement by secondments from the permanent militia. Other ranks, because of their technical expertise, would have to be kept up to establishment. The total establishment recommended was forty-one officers and 468 other ranks. Though de Dombasle argued that his proposed organization was flexible enough to handle both civil and military aspects of aviation, it was in fact rigid in conception, tied as it was to the concept of a fighter and a bomber squadron, plus a training depot. No estimate of expense was included. Mulock had drafted a far less complex organization in two brief pages, providing at once for dispersal of elements to different parts of Canada and for expansion into a larger force should the times so require. But his sketch was overshadowed by the bulkier document.[106]

Mulock's mission was crucial to the fate of the CAF, because time was now short. The Air Ministry had agreed to underwrite the cost of the Canadian organization only until 30 June, and there was no prospect of an extension. 'A[ir]

M[inistry] funds have borne the cost of keeping up two purely Canadian Squadrons for six months, and the time has come when they should pay for their own Air Force as the Australians do,' a ministry official wrote. 'The Canadians have always been pressing us to take charges which the other Dominions have borne without question, and we think that they should pay the whole cost of *their* Air Force from the 1st July.' On 26 May Gibson heard that Mulock had been before the Cabinet, but that no decision had yet been made. Mewburn, it developed, had come out in favour of bringing home the CAF and making it part of the permanent force for a minimum of two years. On the basis of this favourable sign, Gibson was asked whether the squadrons ought to be sent home, and 'trust to adjustment their status after arrival.' Mulock, with greater prescience, advised against this course. Most CAF officers agreed with him. If nothing had been settled at home before they left England, they preferred to take up the permanent commissions in the RAF which had been offered to them, rather than risk being left high and dry in Ottawa.[107]

On 30 May the Cabinet delivered itself of its judgment on the future of Canadian military aviation: 'for the present, nothing would be done.' 'It is all off,' Gwatkin wrote Mulock; to another he said, 'this is a great disappointment to me.' Kemp instructed Gibson to allow those officers who wished to join the RAF to take their discharges in England. He gave some hint of the factors which had influenced the Cabinet when he added that 'it is hoped that a less elaborate organization and one which would adapt itself to peace conditions in Canada may be worked out.' At the same time, however, he expressed to Borden his 'deepest regret.' 'I am satisfied,' he told the Prime Minister, 'that after we have demobilized our air force it will be apparent to members of Council that a great mistake has been made ...'[108]

Unfortunately the papers Mulock had laid before the Cabinet were not the sort of ammunition Kemp could use effectively in the changed political atmosphere of peacetime Canada. He told Gibson, who had sent him an agitated protest,[109] that his cable of 30 May had set out the position of the government, with which he was not entirely in sympathy.*

It must however be borne in mind that our financial position has to be taken into consideration and other difficulties with which Government is faced in connection with expenditures as Budget recently brought down clearly shows. The two squadrons have been organized on a war basis. In order to have Government reconsider matter I have held out hope that peace conditions in Canada might justify someone who possesses the technical information in submitting a modified plan suitable for peace conditions in Canada and having regard to fact that country is four thousand miles long and that exceedingly small units might be stationed

---

* Kemp was more deeply opposed to the Cabinet's action than he gave Gibson to understand, and hoped to reverse it by encouraging public agitation. His secretary, in giving instructions for the preparation of a paper for circulation to the press, wrote: 'Sir Edward Kemp feels that public opinion has got to be aroused in this country through a press campaign, or in some similar way, to force the Government to take action and not lose the opportunity presented to them just now. IT IS MOST IMPORTANT that Sir Edward Kemp's name be not connected with anything given out ...' Bristol to James, 31 May 1919, Kemp Papers, PAC MG 27 II D 9, vol. 132

at different points, and to put forward a definite proposal as to cost per annum. This is the way business is now done here and what other Dominions are doing will not materially influence situation.[110]

Kemp's statement accurately forecast the air policy of the 1920s. Gibson accepted it as the death-knell for the CAF, and though 'it breaks my heart to see this done,' gave permission for its officers to return to the RAF, 'and practically all are doing so.' The ghost of the CAF lingered for many months, in the form of a packing section at Shoreham, preparing gift aircraft for shipment, which did not close down until late in 1920. Its last vestiges were 'two Aeroplane Engines, part of a Lorry, a Forge and a small quantity of miscellaneous material' reported by the High Commissioner's office still remaining at the Wormwood Scrubs Depot in December 1921; with its disposal the CAF's last employee was released.[111]

In this muted fashion the last institutional link with the great deeds of the Canadian airmen of the First World War was severed. A new air force would grow from modest beginnings in the 1920s, and many of the men who had given Canada so large, if so anonymous, a part in the first war in the air would serve it and provide leadership for it. Future volumes of this history will record the rise and accomplishments of the Royal Canadian Air Force. The foundations for that force, however, were established during the First World War. When the officer in charge of gathering together the records of service of Canadian airmen reported the results of his labours in July 1919, he noted that 'the identity of many Canadians who served with British flying units lies buried.' He respectfully suggested that 'a work of a literary and historical nature which would deal in a broad way with Canada's airmen and their work in the war' should be undertaken.[112] This history has been an attempt to fulfil that task, and to recover for Canadians a chapter of their history that has lain buried for over sixty years.

Appendices

Archangel from the air in 1919 (DND 65-4)

Canadian airmen of the RAF's ELOPE Squadron which flew against the Bolsheviks in North Russia, 1918–19. Lt Dugald MacDougall, DFC, of Lockport, Man. (standing, on right) was subsequently killed in action at Bakaritza on 25 Aug. 1919. (RE 68-1891)

RAF units, including many Canadian airmen, flew in North Russia in 1918–19 against the Bolsheviks. This picture shows the result of a bombing attack on a Red train near Murmansk, 1919. (AH 450)

DH9as of 47 Squadron RAF in South Russia, 1919–20. This unit was commanded by Maj. Raymond Collishaw of Nanaimo, BC, who remained in the RAF after the war. (RE 17203)

Turkish transport destroyed by RAF aircraft on the Nablus-Beisan road in Palestine, 20 Sept. 1918 (AH 444)

Lt H.W. Price of Calgary with his RE8, 63 Squadron, Mosul, Mesopotamia, 22 Dec. 1918 (PMR 75-521)

An armoured car salvaging a British Martinsyde aircraft captured on the German-Turkish airfield in Tekrit, Mesopotamia (AH 510)

Canadian Airmen and the British Intervention in Russia, 1918–20

In March 1917 a left-wing revolution in Russia compelled Tsar Nicholas to abdicate and a provisional 'peoples' government was established. The new régime, dominated by the socialist Minister of War, Alexander Kerensky, pledged itself to continue the war against Germany which had already cost the Russians nine million casualties. But it was obvious, especially after the disastrous Kornilov offensive in July, that Russia's strength was spent. When, as a result of the November Revolution, the Bolsheviks seized power, they responded to the deeply-felt popular desire for peace by opening negotiations with Germany. The Treaty of Brest-Litovsk, signed in March 1918, placed immense areas of European Russia under German and Austro-Hungarian control, made available to Germany the resources of these vast lands, and took Russia formally out of the war.

Long before the advent of the Bolsheviks the Allies had tried to shore up the Russian army and to reconstitute the Eastern Front. Enormous amounts of material were sent to Russia by way of Murmansk and Vladivostok. Military missions were despatched, and even before the Treaty of Brest-Litovsk, at a time when the Allies knew full well that a German offensive was about to be unleashed on the Western Front, military intervention was contemplated, perhaps to support those elements in Russia still prepared to continue the fight but at least to deprive the Germans of some Russian resources and to hold some of their troops in the East. Thus when intervention came, though it was directed against the Central Powers, it inevitably clashed with a Bolshevik government opposed to the renewal of Russian belligerency. By the time of the Armistice on the Western Front the allied powers had become deeply embroiled in civil war in Russia, were backing or working with a variety of separatist and counter-revolutionary movements, and were committed to the overthrow of the Bolshevik régime.*

Britain was the leading allied interventionist power, and Canada, so long as the First World War lasted, tended to follow unquestioningly in her wake.† When Britain was unable to meet its troop commitment to the Supreme War Council for

---

* For a full account of intervention in Russia see Richard H. Ullman, *Anglo-Soviet Relations, 1917–1921* (Princeton, NJ 1961–72), 3 vols.

† For the Canadian part in intervention see Roy MacLaren, *Canadians in Russia, 1918–1919* (Toronto 1976), and J.A. Swettenham, *Allied Intervention in Russia, 1918–1919; and the Part Played by Canada* (Toronto 1967).

intervention in Siberia and asked Canada for help in July 1918, Sir Robert Borden began the leisurely despatch of a Canadian brigade which was still incomplete in December. No air unit accompanied the Canadian Siberian Expeditionary Force to Vladivostok, though the Department of Militia and Defence had requested a squadron from RAF Canada. Since the Canadians took virtually no part in allied operations, no air support was required; in any event the Canadian government lost all interest in the idea after 11 November 1918. Adverse public reaction soon persuaded the government that its forces should be removed from a situation in which Canada appeared to have no direct interest.

Since Canadian airmen were scattered throughout the RAF, their despatch to Russia and their activities while there were subject to British, not Canadian, policy. More than sixty Canadians were with the RAF in Russia, some of them fresh from flying training, others with considerable war experience. Some were volunteers, including a small group that left the Canadian Air Force when it became clear that its days were numbered; others were simply transferred to Russia with their units in the course of duty. Canadians were present in three of the several theatres in which the RAF carried out operations: in North Russia, in the Caucasus, and with General A.I. Denikin's forces in South Russia and the Ukraine. Four Canadians were killed and four wounded in Russia, and another six were injured in flying accidents.

In North Russia intervention began when a party of Royal Marines went ashore at Murmansk on 6 March 1918, the result of a local decision by the commander of the Royal Navy's White Sea Fleet. The first air work was carried out by the seaplanes of *Nairana*; two Canadians, Captain G.H. Simpson of Toronto and Lieutenant Dugald MacDougall of Winnipeg, flew effective co-operation missions at the time of the seizure of Archangel at the end of July. A multinational allied force was rapidly built up, including the RAF's *Elope* Squadron (so named after the codename for the whole operation) commanded by Lieutenant Colonel A.C. Maund, DSO.* Captain F.V. Robinson of Winnipeg commanded the first flight of *Elope* Squadron to reach the theatre and fourteen more Canadians came in the autumn. Most of them had just completed training; they had not volunteered for service in Russia but were posted and sent in the normal line of duty.[†]

The RAF carried out corps squadron duties with the allied forces on the five 'fronts' south of Archangel. Aerial combat with the Red Air Fleet was rare; the real enemy was weather. The water-cooled DH4 was entirely unsuitable for winter operations, and only one air-cooled RE8 survived the winter. Most of the Squad-

---

* Maund was British-born, but had moved to Canada before 1914 and was living at Cando, Sask., when he enlisted in the CEF as a private in February 1915. He served at the front with the CEF, and transferred to the RFC in 1916. As a major he was a member of the RFC mission sent to Russia at the time of the March Revolution, and flew with other members of it in aid of the Kornilov offensive in the summer of 1917. See his 'War experiences' in Air 1/2387/228/11347.

† The Canadians included G.W. Ashbrook of Winnipeg, A.H. Bill of Saskatoon, Sask., F.A. Bradley of Calgary, P.V. Dobby and R.E. Gordon, both of Montreal, J.W. Grant of Lacombe, Alta, B.A. Heeney of Calgary, M.B. Henselwood of Winnipeg, G.W. Jones of Moncton, NB, James McDonnell of Alexandria, Ont., T.F. Naylor of Watrous, Sask., Frank J. Shrive of Hamilton, F.F. Tattam of Winnipeg, and A.E. White of Vancouver.

ron's flying was done on Sopwith 1½ Strutters shared with Russian aviators. In the spring, when it had already been decided to withdraw the demoralized allied force, two fresh brigades were sent out to ensure a safe evacuation; the reinforcements also included new aircraft and aircrew, among them a number of Canadians.* General Edmund Ironside, commander of the force, launched an offensive during the summer of 1919 in order to leave the local Russian governments in a stronger position against their Bolshevik opponents, and during attacks up the Dvina River the RAF saw considerable action. Withdrawal was complete by 21 September.

Subsidiary to the Archangel front was that at Murmansk. With the small force there were six RE8s, the complement of airmen including Lieutenant R.A. Adams of Toronto and Second Lieutenant C.S. Booth of Winnipeg. 'Duck' Flight,[†] made up of seaplanes from *Nairana* and *Argus*, also supported ground and naval attacks,[‡] but the airmen were all evacuated on 27 September 1919, two days ahead of the ground forces.

British intervention took its most significant form in the Caucasus after 11 November 1918, and was justified variously as necessary to protect land communications with India, to sustain the new-born republics of Georgia, Azerbaijan, and Armenia, and to safeguard the rich Baku oil-fields. Two British divisions had been committed to the campaign by the end of 1918; with them came 62 Wing RAF, composed of 221 (DH9) Squadron and 266 (Short 184) Squadron. 'We were asked to volunteer for duty in Russia with extra pay and allowances,' Lieutenant Frank R. Bicknell of Dunnville, Ont., recalled. He, Second Lieutenant H.G. Thompson of Belmont, Ont., and Second Lieutenant R.G.K. Morrison of Chesterville, Ont.,[§] all took a leading part in 266 Squadron's most significant operation during its stay in the Caucasus. On 21 May 1919 the unit bombed a Red flotilla in harbour at Fort Alexandrovsk on the eastern shore of the Caspian Sea, and thirteen vessels were sunk by bombs and naval gunfire. This attack came shortly before the British government decided to withdraw its forces in June 1919.

The Caucasian republics were turned over to General Denikin, a Great Russian who had no sympathy for their autonomist aspirations. With the British Military Mission sent out to Denikin was an RAF training team, commanded by Maund and assigned the task of organizing a Russian air service. Pending that, 47 Squadron, which had served during the war in Macedonia, was sent from Bulgaria to support Denikin's operations; among its pilots was Lieutenant E.J. Cronin of Saint John, NB, who had been with the squadron since 1917. Neither officers nor men

---

* L.A.A. Bernard of Montreal, W.G. Boyd of Hamilton, N.G. Fraser of Toronto, L.W. Kidd of Listowel, Ont., A.A. Leitch of High River, Alta, Claude M. Lemoine of Toronto (killed 20 Aug. 1919), David Neil of Margaree Harbour, NS, L.S.E.S. Punnett of Victoria, A.J. Rankin of Montreal, Earl Scramlin of Weyburn, Sask., and F.O. Soden from New Brunswick.

† Canadians in 'Duck' Flight included L.C. Hooton of Victoria, H.A. Marshall of Vancouver, R.W. Ryan of Goderich, Ont., and F.J. Stevenson of Winnipeg. All four were volunteers from the Canadian Air Force in England.

‡ Including the use of gas-filled bombs against Red forces, the first time that aircraft had been used in conjunction with the gas weapon.

§ Other Canadians in the Caucasus included Second Lieutenant W.S. Haney of Sarnia, Ont., with 221 Squadron, and Second Lieutenants W.H. August of Winnipeg and H.M. Keith of Toronto with 266 Squadron.

had volunteered for this duty; according to Air Vice-Marshal Collishaw's recollections there was a 'severe dragging of heels' at the squadron's base at Ekaterinodar (now Krasnodar) in the assembling of the squadron's DH9s. The squadron went to the Volga front in early June 1919. In order to release officers desiring demobilization Collishaw, then a major, was sent out to command 47 Squadron, and he brought with him a party of volunteers. Cronin elected to stay on, and was joined by two other Canadians, Captains W.F. Anderson of Toronto and J.L. MacLennan of Montreal.

The RAF airmen carried out their duties with Denikin's forces energetically, though their numbers were too few to have any appreciable effect. Anderson and his observer, Lieutenant Mitchell, distinguished themselves on 30 July while carrying out a photographic reconnaissance along the Volga. When Anderson's fuel tank was punctured by fire from the ground, Mitchell climbed out on the port wing and plugged the leaks with his fingers, while Anderson jettisoned his bomb-load on a gunboat in the Volga. Meanwhile, Anderson's escort, a DH9 flown by Captain William Elliott, a future Air Chief Marshal of the RAF, had been shot down by machine-gun fire; Anderson thereupon landed close by. 'Several Squadrons of Cavalry attempted to surround our machine,' he reported, 'but they were kept clear by our machine-gun fire.' Elliott set fire to his aircraft, he and his observer tumbled into the other DH9, and with Mitchell still plugging the holes in the fuel tank with his hand, Anderson flew home. Both Anderson and Mitchell were recommended for the VC by Maund; eventually they received DSOs.

The Red Air Fleet, flying a collection of allied and German aircraft, was more active in this theatre than it had been in North Russia. Collishaw organized a flight of Camels obtained from Mudros to counter the Bolshevik Nieuports. Meanwhile, Russian products of the RAF training team were beginning to fly operationally, using DH9s and RE8s, which the Russians found no easier to fly than had the British when they were first introduced. There appears to have been a good deal of interchange of roles between the instructors with the Mission and the aircrew of 47 Squadron.*

The magnitude of British aid to Denikin was enormous. From March 1919 to March 1920 the Russians received 1200 guns, nearly two million shells, 6100 machine-guns, 200,000 rifles, 500 million rounds of SAA, hundreds of trucks and motorcycles, seventy-four tanks, and 100 aircraft, plus uniforms and many other stores. Only a part of this vast amount of material reached front-line units; the commander of the British Mission, Major-General H.C. Holman, complained in his final report that 'the incompetence and corruption of the administrative services and departments could not be overcome by any scheme.' It was Denikin's successes in an offensive during the summer that persuaded the British government to maintain its support for him, despite his own excesses and rising criticism at home. Even so, domestic political pressure caused the British to withdraw

---

* Canadians who served with the Mission included W.F. Anderson, J.L. Brandon, and H.S. Broughall, all of Toronto, Harold 'Gus' Edwards of New Aberdeen, NS, E.G. Jones, address unknown, H.W. Minish of Gilbert Plains, Man., F.E. Proctor of Thornbury, Ont., Robert Pyper of Stettler, Alta, and N.G. Reynolds of Pembroke, Ont. Anderson, Broughall, and Edwards served with 47 Squadron as well; there may have been others.

47 Squadron from Russia; its members instead were asked to volunteer for the Mission. The squadron was disbanded on 1 October 1919 and in its place appeared 'A' Detachment, RAF Mission, with the same organization, personnel, equipment, and task.

On 13 October Denikin reached his high-water mark upon entering Orel, only 250 miles from Moscow. General Wrangel suggested that the RAF bomb the capital, but the War Office forbade such an attempt, 'as there is no military value in this operation.' Within a few days the bombing of Moscow became physically impossible for on 20 October Denikin was compelled to withdraw from Orel, and a long retreat commenced, ultimately to end in the extinction of his army along the shores of the Black Sea. During the first stages of Denikin's retreat 'A' Detachment flew on the Volga front, around Tsaritsyn. Collishaw joined frequently in fighter patrols, and on 9 October was credited with his 61st air victory, downing an Albatros D-V which crashed beside the Volga. Shortly afterwards he was invalided to the rear suffering from typhus.

When it became obvious to General Holman that Denikin was in grave difficulty, he intervened directly in RAF dispositions and rushed two flights to the Kharkov front and into action on 8 December. Holman flew personally as the convalescent Collishaw's observer on a number of bombing flights, but it soon became evident that irretrievable disaster was overtaking Denikin's forces. Amid scenes of extraordinary confusion, the various elements of the RAF Mission made their separate ways to the Crimea, Rostov, and the Kuban. One air unit remained in the Kuban until evacuated from Novorossisk in March.* Collishaw, with another remnant, carried out bombing and reconnaissance missions for Wrangel's Crimean army in February and March 1920. RAF participation in the Russian Civil War finally ended with the withdrawal of the British Military Mission in the late spring of 1920.

The RAF had no significant influence upon the course of events in Russia. Its employment was piecemeal, and bore no comparison to the massive deployment of air power on the Western Front. Some of its work had a short-term effect upon military operations, particularly the bombing of the Caspian flotilla by 266 Squadron and some notable air co-operation with sea and ground forces in the Archangel theatre. But nowhere could the RAF exert any decisive effect upon the campaigns in which it was employed, nor, it appears, did the service learn much from its experience in operating over the vast Russian lands and in coping with Russian climatic extremes.

The RAF presence in Russia was, in the first instance, an outgrowth of the exigencies of the First World War. With the end of the war the British intervention was transformed into a species of anti-Bolshevik crusade. It is unlikely, however, that many of the Canadians who found themselves flying over the White Sea, the steppeland, or the Caucasus were motivated primarily by ideological considerations. Most of them were relatively inexperienced airmen who were in Russia because of the lottery of service postings. Among the volunteers some were mili-

---

* With 'C' Flight in the Kuban were Anderson, its commander, and Broughall, Edwards, and W.F. Hay of Killarney, Man.

tary adventurers, others already professional airmen, and a few a combination of the two. For young men who had joined the armed forces directly from school or university, and had no trade or profession waiting for them in civilian life, Russian service was a chance to earn a permanent commission in the RAF or in the Canadian air force to come.* For others, it was simply another opportunity to continue their love affair with the aeroplane.

* Some of the Canadians who served in Russia remained in the RAF. Among the more prominent were Maund, who retired as an air vice-marshal in 1937, Collishaw, who retired with the same rank during the Second World War, and Broughall, who as a group captain was Collishaw's senior staff officer in the Western Desert. Harold Edwards went into the peacetime RCAF and headed the RCAF Overseas in 1941 with the rank of air marshal. A.J. Rankin retired as an air commodore, RAF, in 1951. Others went on to distinction as civilian airmen. F.J. Stevenson, for example, became an outstanding bush pilot and winner of the Harman Trophy in 1927; he was killed in a crash at The Pas in 1928.

Canadians in Other Theatres, 1915–18

'Other theatres,' in the context in which the term is used in this appendix, encompassed a vast, elongated, scalene triangle whose baseline stretched some three thousand miles along a north-south axis from Aleppo in Asia Minor, across the equator, to the southern shores of Lake Tanganyika in German East Africa, and whose apex lay eight hundred miles eastwards in the Tigris-Euphrates delta at the head of the Persian Gulf. It embraced nearly every conceivable type of topographical, climatic, and biological unpleasantness, from sandstorm to monsoon, snow-capped mountain to malarial swamp, and tsetse infested savannah to scorpion-haunted desert. Men fell sick – and often only the lucky and hardy recovered – from malaria, sandfly, dengue, and half-a-dozen other less well-known but equally deadly fevers. Their daily companions were dysentery, heatstroke, jaundice, eczema, and an array of insects and reptiles whose respective bites or stings ranged in effect from painful to fatal. For much of the time the German or Turk was only one enemy amongst many, no more and no less dangerous than the others.

Nor was the environment any easier on machines than on men, imposing strains on engines and airframes far in excess of those experienced by more sophisticated equipment in less intemperate regions. Motors laboured mightily to keep primitive Voisin and BE2c aircraft aloft in the rarified air of the central African plateau, where ground level was approximately three thousand feet above sea level; cylinder linings were scored, pistons abraded, and carburettors blocked by sand and dust; propeller glues melted, spars warped, and rubber tubing shrivelled in the torrid heat; fabric stretched and peeled in the humidity; and violent thermals swirled over desert plains when the noon air temperature at ground level sometimes reached 114°F in the shade for as long as a month at a time.

The problem was compounded by the need to transport spare parts, fuel, oil, weapons, and ammunition over immense distances by means which spanned the technological gamut from triple-expansion steam boilers to camel or ox-cart. Even after Brigadier-General W.G.H. Salmond's* newly-formed Middle East Brigade began to administer and co-ordinate air activities in Palestine, Mesopotamia, and

---

* The elder brother of Brigadier-General J.M. Salmond, who had been commanding an RFC brigade in France since February 1916 and who would succeed Trenchard as Commander-in-Chief of the RFC in the Field in January 1918.

East Africa (as well as in Macedonia) from Egypt in July 1916, an engine damaged somewhere up-country from Dar-es-Salaam would still have to travel nearly four thousand miles by land and sea, around the Horn of Africa, to reach the brigade's main workshops at Aboukir, near Alexandria, where major repairs could be carried out. One from Amara, on the Tigris, would face an even longer journey.

Another level of complexity was added by the understandable tendency of higher authority to relegate to these distant theatres a kaleidoscopic variety of aircraft which were obsolete, obsolescent, or, in some technical sense, unsatisfactory in the more sophisticated air environments of the European battlefronts. Each type had a different make or model of engine and only rarely was it possible to interchange motors from one airframe to another. The enemy, whose lines of communication were generally shorter but often even more complex and primitive than those of the *Entente*, simplified his maintenance problems by using few types of aircraft and concentrating upon those which had a common power-plant. The Rumpler C-1 and Aviatik C-III reconnaissance-bombers, for example, used the same basic 160-hp Mercedes engine which powered the Albatros D-III and Fokker D-IV fighters.

In German East Africa *Oberstleutnant* (later *General-Major*) Paul von Lettow-Vorbeck with some three thousand Europeans, eleven thousand *askaris*, and no air support whatsoever waged a campaign of manœuvre that kept, at various times, nearly 300,000 Imperial and Belgian troops and up to three squadrons of aircraft in the field for four years. The aeroplane played no major role in operations after the destruction of the *Königsberg* in the Rufiji delta during July 1915 (see chapter 5). While the British forces were so strong that there could be no question of a major defeat, they were quite unable to pin down Lettow-Vorbeck, and the air function, first to last, was essentially a reconnaissance one. Desultory attempts at artillery co-operation and strafing of enemy columns were made, but the effect seems to have been largely limited to frightening, and thus temporarily disorganizing, the columns of native porters upon which the Germans relied for their very limited logistic support.

Only two Canadians, RNAS Flight Sub-Lieutenants John Robinson of London, Ont., and Rudolf Delamere of Toronto, are known to have served in this campaign, both arriving in March 1916. Robinson spent a year there and Delamere more than two.*

In Palestine and Mesopotamia, where the *Entente* had vital interests at stake, the air arm played a more prominent part, and the equipment and tactical evolution of air warfare generally paralleled, after a significant time lapse, the practices of the Western Front, Italy, and Macedonia. Although the British were nominally opposed by an Ottoman air force only formed in 1915 and supported by squadron-strength elements of the German air force, in fact nearly all the 'Turkish' airmen were actually German. Genuine Turkish representation in air operations,

---

* Robinson subsequently served at Dunkirk (where he was wounded in November 1917) and with 202 Squadron, RAF. On 25 April 1918 he won a DFC for a photo-reconnaissance of Zeebrugge, when his machine was badly damaged by anti-aircraft fire. Delamere also won a DFC 'in recognition of the gallantry and devotion to duty shown by him in carrying out reconnaissance, bombing and photographic flights during the military operations in the Lindi (East Africa) area.'

even at the end of the war, was limited to a few outstanding individuals.* The air war in Asia Minor was only marked by one substantial innovation – and that one of scale rather than of principle – when the besieged and starving garrison of Kut-el-amara was supplied by air with some 19,000 pounds of food prior to its capitulation to the Turks on 29 April 1916.

Seventeen Canadian airmen are known to have participated in the Mesopotamian campaign, the first two being Flight Sub-Lieutenants M.J. Arnold, from the Queen Charlotte Islands, who had won a DSO for his part in the destruction of the *Königsberg*, and W.B. Lawson of Toronto, an RMC graduate who was eventually appointed, in May 1919, to the command of one of the two squadrons that formed the first Canadian Air Force. Lieutenant H.W. Price of Toronto, the longest-serving Canadian airman in the theatre, joined 63 Squadron in June 1917 and served in Mesopotamia until the end of the war. He was wounded on 24 October 1918 but was flying again at Khasvin (Persia) in the early 1919 operations against the Bolsheviks there.

However limited their numbers, aircraft were able to play important roles in Mesopotamia and Palestine. Heat mirages and flat, featureless plains often made artillery observation virtually impossible from the ground, but aircraft enabled both problems to be overcome and thus greatly enhanced the effectiveness of the guns. The comparatively featureless nature of much of the terrain on the fronts also emphasized the importance of airpower in a reconnaissance role, for it proved extremely difficult to camouflage any substantial body of troops or accumulation of supplies in such isomorphous environments. Reconnaissance in depth was carried out by aircraft at a speed and over ranges quite inconceivable in terms of the traditional cavalry reconnaissance capability.† This made it virtually impossible to deny the enemy a comprehensive knowledge of any major tactical preparations or strategic movement. Moreover, in theatres where extant maps were deficient and uncertain in content, photo-survey work by aircraft enabled the Topographical Branch to produce maps adequate to the operational needs of the Army.‡

Airpower particularly distinguished itself in a ground-support role in the course of Sir Edmund Allenby's final Palestinian offensive, when the Turkish army was broken at Megiddo in September 1918. Carefully orchestrated bombing destroyed nearly all the radio and telecommunications which linked the Turkish troops with their headquarters, bringing a total breakdown of the enemy's command and control. Then after ground forces had broken into the Turkish position on 19 September 1918, the fleeing Turks were caught in column between Tul Karm and

---

* The best account in English of German and Turkish air operations in Palestine and Mesopotamia is to be found in B.P. Flanagan's four-part series, 'The History of the Ottoman Air Force in the Great War, the Reports of Major Erich Serno,' in *Cross & Cockade Journal*, II, 1970.

† In November 1916 a machine of the German air force's *Fliegerabteilung 300*, operating from Beersheba, flew over Cairo and took photographs of the pyramids of Gizeh to prove it – a round trip of some eight hundred kilometers. See Flanagan, 'The History of the Ottoman Air Force in the Great War,' *Cross & Cockade Journal*, II, summer 1970, 137.

‡ The planning of operations for the initial campaign in the Sinai had had to be based upon a map series worked up from an 1878 survey done by Lord Kitchener during his service as a subaltern. See A.P. Wavell, 'The Strategy of the Egyptian Expeditionary Force,' in *Army Quarterly*, III, Jan. 1933, 9.

Nablus. Over eleven tons of bombs were dropped and 66,000 rounds fired at ground targets. By nightfall the two Turkish divisions on the Plain of Sharon had been destroyed and some seven thousand Turks had been taken prisoner. Most of the Turkish Eighth Army positions on the left had been abandoned, and Allenby's cavalry, which had overrun Megiddo, reached the German aerodrome at El Affule by 0800 hrs the next morning. On the 20th the RAF dropped another ten tons of bombs and fired forty thousand rounds of machine-gun ammunition into the retreating enemy. The next day an early reconnaissance revealed that a continuous stream of Turkish guns and transport was pouring northeast of Nablus along the Wadi-al-Fara defile, through Ain Shible, and along the road to Tubas. All squadrons participated in the subsequent bombing, which was planned so that pairs of bombing aircraft would fly at three-minute intervals supplemented every half-hour by a formation of six machines. Nine-and-a-half tons of bombs were dropped and 56,000 rounds were fired and, again, an immense amount of destruction was wreaked upon the Turkish remnants.

Only one disciplined body – the German Asia Corps, a few hundred strong – and a thousand or so Turkish stragglers succeeded in breaking out of the trap which Allenby had laid, and for all practical military purposes the Turkish Seventh and Eighth Armies were annihilated. Moreover, the remaining Turkish forces were so demoralized by the fate of their comrades that they were able to offer little opposition to further British advances, which were limited more by problems of logistics than by the efforts of the enemy. Damascus fell on 1 October, Aleppo was taken on 26 October, and five days later an armistice was concluded between the *Entente* powers and Turkey, four years less five days after Turkey had entered the war.

In the Egypt-Palestine theatre at least nineteen Canadians flew on operations, most notably Captains G.M. Croil (see 451–2) who piloted Col. T.E. Lawrence – 'Lawrence of Arabia' – on at least one flight from Aqaba to Jerusalem; F.F. Minchin, born in India but an original member of the PPCLI, who won an MC and a DSO flying in Palestine; R.B. Sutherland of Ingersoll, Ont., who won a DFC in September 1917; and R.C. Steele of Birch Creek, Sask., who was awarded a DFC before being killed in action in March 1918, one of the four Canadian combat fatalities in the theatre.

APPENDIX C

Statistical Analysis of Canadians in the British Flying Services

Because there was no distinctively Canadian air force during the First World War, Canadians enlisted directly into the British flying services or were seconded or attached from other services. The absence of a comprehensive body of personnel records for Canadians has meant that statistical information on the services of Canadians in the British flying services – where, when, and how they enlisted, how they served, and when and how many gave their lives – has been entirely lacking. For this reason a computerized inventory was undertaken to list briefly biographical details for as many Canadians as could be identified. Combining the data presented in these records in various ways would, it was hoped, provide statistical studies offering some insight into the background experience of Canadians in the flying services.

The largest part of the data base was provided from cards for each identified Canadian, at present held by the Directorate of History. Ninety-six hundred individuals were so identified in 1919 by two non-commissioned officers from the Canadian War Records Office working in the lists of the Postings Branch, Royal Air Force, and from British Expeditionary Force ledgers.[1] The cards were sent to Canada, and numbers were lost before they reached the Air Historian in the 1950s. Since that time information has been added to the card file, some reconstruction of the missing parts made, and new names added. Very significant amounts of data on Canadians in the Royal Naval Air Service were drawn from Director of Naval Service personnel files on RNAS candidates, now held by the Canadian Forces Records Centre.[2]

In addition to the information contained on the biographical cards, the data base was supplemented by material from a number of miscellaneous sources of information, such as a two-volume register of Canadian Expeditionary Force officers seconded to the British flying services and the service records of former employees of the Canadian Bank of Commerce.[3]

The computer file contains 13,160 names, of which 6904 were known Canadians, 1736 were known non-Canadians (chiefly Americans who enlisted or trained in Canada), and 4520 were of unknown origin.* There was no evidence to

---

* In cases where it could be determined, a Canadian was considered to be a person born in Canada, a naturalized alien domiciled in Canada, or a British subject domiciled in Canada for three years, in line with the Immigration Act of 1910.

suggest whether the unknown portion would break down the same way as the known group. The file also showed that 5241 joined the Royal Flying Corps, 936 the Royal Naval Air Service, and 6709 the Royal Air Force – that is, enlisted after 1 April 1918. The remaining 174 were in other armed services or of unknown service. Almost all were aircrew, either officers or cadets.

These figures may be compared to the 'official' figure of 22,812 Canadians in the British flying services as inscribed in the Memorial Chamber of the Parliament Buildings.* If the 7453 mechanics recruited in Canada for the flying training scheme are subtracted from this number, the remaining total, 15,359, is still some two thousand individuals greater than the number in the computer file. Indeed, a comparison of figures in each category making up these figures suggests that the computer file is in fact short some three thousand names, and that this shortage is largely among direct enlistments into the RFC/RAF Canada training scheme. The 'official' figures state 3960 joined from the CEF. The computer file has identified 4580. The figures in the Memorial Chamber indicate 10,010 officers and cadets as coming from RFC/RAF Canada. Alan Sullivan's researches unearthed a number only slightly smaller.[4] The computer file has identified only 2250. The 'official' figures show 1389 'other Canadians' joined in England. From the computer file one can isolate 486 names which might come into this category. The computer file contained an additional 5558 names for whom no method of joining was indicated. Some were doubtless direct entries, but it is suspected that most were RFC/RAF Canada entrants for whom there was little information. If the numbers of those joining in England (1389) and the RFC/RAF Canada (10,010) in the 'official' figures are added, the total is 11,399. If the equivalent categories in the computer file are added (489 + 2250 + 5558), the total is 8297. Somewhere in these categories, then, the computer file is short over three thousand names. As the individuals for whom data were scanty or non-existent were generally those who joined near the end of the war, the shortage in the file was reflected in disproportionate figures for the RAF portion of the file. This bias must be kept in mind in any investigation of the following statistical tables.

The information contained in some fields of the individual records was, when considered throughout the file, too sketchy or biased to present any meaningful insights into the characteristics of Canadians who joined the British flying services. For this reason, there are no analyses here of such very interesting questions as joining age of the Canadian airmen, their occupations or experience before enlistment, the length of time they spent training before going overseas, or the awards they won while serving in the flying services. The analyses here have concentrated on the fields of geographic origin, dates and methods of joining the flying services, and casualties.[5]

---

* This figure was based to some extent on approximations and was known even by the end of 1918 to be inaccurate owing to difficulties in the compilation of data. That portion of the figure dealing with Canadians who transferred from the Canadian Expeditionary Force to the flying services has been proven to be considerably low. 'Inscription on Panels, Memorial Chamber, Parliament Buildings,' nd, GAQ 10–20J, PAC, RG 24, vol. 1839; Rudi Aksim, 'C.E.F. transfers to the British flying services,' nd, 1–2, 97, DHist 74/14

TABLE 1

Total Canadians: origin by province

	Number of enlistments	Provincial population (000s)	Rate of enlistments per thousand population
BC	816	392.5	2.08
Alta	423	374.7	1.13
Sask.	396	492.4	.80
Man.	584	455.6	1.28
Ont.	3479	2523.3	1.38
Que.	684	2003.2	.34
NB	172	351.9	.49
NS	298	492.3	.61
PEI	48	93.7	.51
Territories	4	27.0	.15
TOTAL	6904	7206.6	

Total X^2 = 2034.1

Critical χ^2 .001 (9df) = 27.9

The quantity X^2 is a measure of the deviation of the observed value from that expected on the given hypothesis (here that rates are independent of province). It is approximately distributed as χ^2 with degrees of freedom (df) depending on the number of levels in the categories of the table. From the χ^2 distribution one can therefore determine the probability that a value as large as the calculated X^2 could be obtained by chance. (Here for X^2 = 2034 it is less than 1 in a billion.) Alternatively, to a predetermined significance level there corresponds a critical value of χ^2 which would not be exceeded by chance. In the present case with 9 df, there is a chance of less than 1 in a 1000 (.001) that an X^2 value of higher than 27.9 could have resulted by accident. One would therefore reject the hypothesis that the rates are province-independent at the 0.001 significance level.

ORIGIN BY PROVINCE

Table 1 is a breakdown of the 6904 Canadians with known addresses by their province of origin, and shows rates of enlistment per thousand population.* A test for independence of rates by province gave a value of X^2 of 2034.1, significant at well before the .001 level. The joining rates were therefore not independent of province.

The behaviour of Quebec in this table is significantly different from that of any of the other provinces, and this is brought about by the lowest joining rate of any of the provinces, .34 per thousand population. This may be compared to the small Quebec enlistment in the CEF,[6] which historians have linked to inadequate recruiting methods and opposition to taking part in the war.[7] It must also be

---

* Provincial and municipal populations throughout this section were based on the 1911 census figures.

remembered that joining a flying service meant enlistment in a completely non-Canadian, imperial service, where not even the token recognition given to the French language in parts of the CEF would be found.

On the other hand, when the Quebec figures are excluded from the comparison, the British Columbia enlistments, with the highest joining rate in Canada, at 2.08 per thousand, are different from those of any of the remaining provinces. Much of this may be attributed to the proportionately large first-generation British population of the province, who were also quick to volunteer for the CEF.[8]

When the figures for Quebec and British Columbia are excluded from the table, it is not surprising to note that Ontario, which supplied such a large proportion of the enlistments, is different from the remaining provinces. Ontario rates reflected English-Canadian attitudes towards the war and, as well, the substantial British-born population. Many of the important military establishments were in Ontario, which may have been a factor in recruiting for all services. Specifically, many RNAS candidates had to come to the Curtiss Flying School in Toronto at their own expense, clearly an advantage to those living in Ontario.[9] Also, the RFC/RAF Canada training scheme was wholly located within Ontario, encouraging airmindedness within the neighbouring population and providing a convenient stimulus to recruiting.

It is of some interest to compare the rates per thousand of joining the flying services for each province with the rate of joining the CEF.

	BRITISH FLYING SERVICES	CANADIAN EXPEDITIONARY FORCE
BC	2.08	141.59
Alta	1.13	130.48
Sask.	.80	84.66
Man.	1.28	145.39
Ont.	1.38	96.17
Que.	.34	43.95
NB	.49	76.90
NS	.61	72.56
PEI	.51	39.43

It may be seen that the only moderate success of recruiting for the CEF in the Maritimes was quite accurately reflected by the flying services. The considerable British Columbia and Ontario contributions to the CEF were paralleled by high rates of flying services enlistment.

ORIGIN BY CITY

Table 2 shows how the 3660 enlistments were distributed in the fourteen largest cities of Canada. These cities, all those of over 5000 population in the 1911 census, have been arbitrarily classified as the 'urban' portion of the country, although one might well consider centres of considerably under 5000 to have been 'urban' at that time.

TABLE 2
Origin by city

City	Number of enlistments	City population (000s)	Rate of enlistments per thousand population
Montreal	474	538.2	.88
Toronto	1285	384.5	3.35
Winnipeg	377	143.5	2.62
Vancouver	350	100.4	3.50
Ottawa	256	87.1	2.94
Hamilton	157	82.0	1.91
Quebec	35	86.1	.41
Halifax	85	51.7	1.61
London	93	46.3	2.02
Calgary	123	43.7	2.80
Saint John	50	42.5	1.16
Victoria	192	37.6	5.05
Regina	70	30.2	2.33
Edmonton	113	24.9	4.52
TOTAL	3660	1698.7	

Total $X^2 = 1158.6$
Critical χ^2 .001 (13df) $= 34.5$

When the enlistments from Montreal are compared with those of the other cities, it is seen that the low rate of enlistment makes that city different from the others. Similarly, when Montreal is excluded, Quebec is different from the remaining cities in the same way. Much the same reasons for this may be advanced as for the low rate of enlistment in the Province of Quebec as a whole.

If Montreal and Quebec are considered in isolation from the other cities, it is obvious that the number of enlistments from each is not in proportion.

	ENLISTMENTS	REMAINDER	TOTAL
Montreal	474	537,726	538,200
Quebec	35	86,065	86,100
TOTAL	509	623,791	624,300

$$\chi^2 = 20.49*$$

Quebec is significantly under-represented in enlistments. This must be attributed to its greater proportion of francophone population when compared to Montreal.

* This is not, strictly speaking, a χ^2 value, but behaves as one at 1 df.

Returning to Table 2, if the two francophone cities are excluded, the enlistments from Victoria, at the highest rate of all, 5.05 per thousand, are significantly different from those from the remaining cities. Again, if Victoria is also excluded and the enlistments from Vancouver are considered against those of the remaining cities, it is seen that Vancouver's high rate of enlistment also makes it significantly different from the remainder. Again, the high city rate for these two cities is paralleled by the high rate of British Columbia as a whole.

If Vancouver is compared to Victoria in isolation from the other cities, an imbalance in rates of enlistment is seen.

	ENLISTMENTS	REMAINDER	TOTAL
Vancouver	350	100,050	100,400
Victoria	192	37,408	37,600
TOTAL	542	137,458	138,000

$$x^2 = 18.36$$

Victoria is considerably over-represented in the flying services when compared with Vancouver. This may reflect the particularly high concentration of first-generation British settlement in Victoria, and the markedly British character the city has always had. The effect seen in British Columbia as a whole when compared with the rest of Canada is again seen when Victoria is compared with the other major city of the province.

CITY AND RURAL ENLISTMENTS

In Table 3 the numbers and rates of enlistment for the cities in Table 2 are compared with the numbers and rates for the remainder of each province in which the cities are located. Although many urban centres of under 5000 population are included in the remainder of each province, it does give some comparison of city and rural enlistments. On the whole, the city rate of enlistment was somewhat more than three times the rural. It was, apparently, the urban dweller, presumably somewhat familiar with engines and things mechanical, or having the benefits of a better education, or perhaps more easily reached by the recruiting advertising, who was more likely to join one of the flying services than was the rural 'wild colonial boy' sometimes popularly thought to make up the bulk of Canadians in the flying services. It should be noted, however, in Table 3, that the totals joining from the cities and the rural areas were nearly equal.

In Table 3 it was attempted to fit a model in which it was assumed that for given city and rural populations in the provinces the number joining by city or rural areas were province-independent. This would be equivalent to a constant value for city rate divided by rural rate.

The expected values thus determined were used in a goodness of fit test. A value of 25.5 calculated for the statistic distributed as x^2 with seven degrees of freedom. A value as high as this would occur by chance less than once in a thou-

TABLE 3
Comparison of city and rural recruiting: rates by province

Province	City			Rural			Combined
	No joined	Population (000)	Rate per 1000	No joined	Population (000)	Rate per 1000	rate
BC	542	138.0	3.93	274	254.5	1.08	3.65
Alta	236	68.6	3.44	187	306.1	.61	5.63
Sask.	70	30.2	2.32	326	462.2	.71	3.29
Man.	377	143.5	2.63	207	312.1	.66	3.96
Ont.	1791	599.9	2.99	1688	1923.4	.88	3.40
Que.	509	624.3	.82	175	1378.9	.13	6.42
NB	50	42.5	1.18	122	309.4	.39	2.98
NS	85	51.7	1.64	214	440.6	.49	3.39
TOTAL	3660	1698.7	2.15	3240	5387.2	.60	3.58

sand times. Hence the hypothesis that the rate ratio is province-independent is rejected.

It is difficult to assign a significance level to the behaviour of any particular province. However, knowing that the provinces are different, one can look again at those which show a particularly high ratio – that is, at Quebec and Alberta.*

Undoubtedly, it is the high proportion of francophone rural population in Quebec which distorts the rate of that province. The rate of enlistment from Quebec was the lowest of any province, and it is known from individual records that the anglophone community in Montreal made an impressive contribution to the British flying services. These two factors combine to give a very high city-rural rate. Reasons are more difficult to pinpoint in the case of Alberta. Certainly, the province contained a large proportion of first-generation British immigrants. These may have been concentrated in the towns owing to their recent arrival. It may also be that the scarcity of under 5000 population towns and villages in Alberta at that time accentuates the number of enlistments from the two large cities in relation to the remainder of the province.

ENLISTMENTS INTO EACH SERVICE BY PROVINCE

To test whether the enlistments from the provinces were proportionally distributed over the three services, a contingency table was used. The Territories were excluded owing to the small sample and the Maritimes were grouped for convenience.

---

* Alternatively, one can postulate a log linear model expressing the logarithm of the counts in each of the three factors – joining status, province, and area (city or rural) and their two- and three-way interactions. The three-factor interaction is not zero. Individual values for the provinces have been evaluated. Again it appears that for Quebec and Alberta these interactions expressed in terms of their standard deviations are large, 5.7 and 3.8 respectively.

TABLE 4
Numbers of enlistments by province

	BC	Alta	Sask.	Man.	Ont.	Que.	Maritimes	Total
RFC	381	141	160	241	1536	274	203	2936
RNAS	74	30	19	62	510	80	34	809
RAF	354	244	215	278	1402	320	274	3087
TOTALS	809	415	394	581	3448	674	511	6832

TABLE 5
Percentage of enlistments into each service by province

	BC	Alta	Sask.	Man.	Ont.	Que.	Maritimes
RFC	13.0	4.8	5.4	8.2	52.3	9.3	6.9
RNAS	9.1	3.7	2.3	7.7	63.0	9.9	4.2
RAF	11.5	7.9	7.0	9.0	45.4	10.4	8.9

TABLE 6
Percentage of each province's enlistments by service

	BC	Alta	Sask.	Man.	Ont.	Que.	Maritimes
RFC	47.1	34.0	40.6	41.5	44.5	40.7	39.7
RNAS	9.1	7.2	4.8	10.7	14.8	11.9	6.7
RAF	43.8	58.8	54.6	47.8	40.7	47.5	53.6

Total X^2 = 132.8
Critical χ^2 .001 (12df) = 32.9

From the χ^2 values there was evidently no marked preference concerning service of enlistment in various parts of the country. However, the RNAS enlistments from Ontario were considerably over-represented when compared with the other RNAS enlistments and the other services. Certainly enlistment was easier in Ontario, for the applicant could appear directly at Department of the Naval Service offices without great personal travelling expense. The only other locations where RNAS applicants were recruited were Halifax and Esquimalt. Also, for much of the time RNAS candidates were required to hold a civil pilot's certificate, and the only school in Canada was the Curtiss School in Toronto. It may also have been that there was in Ontario a larger proportion of the British background, college-educated young men the RNAS seemed most eager to recruit.*

* That the RNAS was consciously trying to recruit this sort of individual is only an impression gathered from the large number of recruits such as R.H. Mulock, Robert Redpath, A.R. Brown, G.A. Gooderham, or W.H. Peberdy who had this sort of background. This impression was somewhat borne out in the computer programme by the number of students and professionals who

TABLE 7
Enlistments by province by year

	BC	Alta	Sask.	Man.	Ont.	Que.	Maritimes	Foreign	Total
1915	41	8	5	18	159	23	15	22	292
1916	60	32	25	44	381	70	36	77	725
1917	263	106	111	179	1151	183	132	505	2630
1918	321	213	195	244	1314	288	252	711	3538
TOTALS	686	359	336	485	3005	564	435	1315	7185

TABLE 8
Percentages of each year's enlistments by province

	BC	Alta	Sask.	Man.	Ont.	Que.	Maritimes	Foreign
1915	14.7	2.7	1.7	6.2	54.5	7.9	5.1	7.5
1916	8.3	4.4	3.4	6.1	52.6	9.7	5.0	10.6
1917	10.0	4.0	4.2	6.8	43.8	7.0	5.0	19.2
1918	9.1	6.0	5.5	6.9	37.1	8.1	7.1	20.1

TABLE 9
Percentages of each province's enlistments by year

	BC	Alta	Sask.	Man.	Ont.	Que.	Maritimes	Foreign
1915	6.1	2.2	1.5	3.7	5.3	4.1	3.4	1.7
1916	8.7	8.9	7.4	9.1	12.7	12.4	8.3	5.9
1917	38.3	29.5	33.0	36.9	38.3	32.4	30.3	38.4
1918	46.8	59.3	58.0	50.3	43.7	51.1	57.9	54.1

Total X^2 = 161.1
Critical χ^2 .001 (21df) = 46.8

When RNAS enlistments are excluded, a comparison of RAF with RFC enlistments show fewer RAF enlistments from Ontario than one would expect. When Ontario is excluded, the number of RAF enlistments from Alberta is greater than expected. The Ontario enlistments then, being proportionately greater in the RFC and RNAS, were of greater importance earlier in the war. This may be seen in Tables 7–9. Conversely, Alberta's contribution was more important in the last year of the war.

joined the RNAS as compared to the other two services, although incompleteness of the record in this case makes generalization dangerous. Andrew Johnson, 'Canadians in the British flying services: statistical report on the computer programme,' 1973, 11–14, DHist 74/39; Jane Desbarats, 'Statistical study of Canadian participation in the British flying services in World War I,' DMS staff note, no 26/75, Directorate of Mathematics and Statistics paper, 1975, 39–41, DHist 76/123

In Tables 7–9 the enlistments from each province were analyzed by year in the same fashion as they were by service in Tables 4–6. From a χ^2 test it is obvious that the enlistments from Ontario for 1917 were comparatively more important than for other provinces for 1917, or all provinces for the period up until that time. Not only does this figure represent an intensification of the air war in 1917, which made necessary greatly increased direct enlistment of Canadians in 1917, in addition to greatly increased transfers from the CEF overseas, but also it represents the impact of the RFC Canada training scheme. An avenue for direct enlistment in considerable numbers into the British flying services was thus created in early 1917, and the stations of the training scheme were almost wholly located in Ontario. Potential applicants in Ontario were encouraged by recruiting advertising to join through RFC Canada, and they also could see aircraft and airmen, and had places to enlist near their homes.[10]

If the 1917 enlistments from Ontario are excluded, the next most important figure is the foreign enlistments for 1917 compared with the remaining provinces for 1917 and all provinces for 1915 and 1916. Most of the foreign enlistment was American. From April 1917 the United States was also in the war, and the potential applicant could feel that he was fighting his country's enemies through the British services. The US Air Service was still in a position to be extremely selective, but the British, with lower standards after two-and-a-half years of war, were on occasion even seeking out those rejected by the American service.[11] Again, the RFC Canada system gave convenient locations for enlistment particularly during the winter of 1917–18 when many of the units moved to Texas.

METHOD OF ENLISTMENT

Tables 10–12 are a breakdown of enlistments by method of joining the flying services and year of enlistment. Some difficulty was experienced with this because the appropriate field was left blank in individual records both to indicate a direct entry and to indicate that the method was unknown. This blank field was most significant for 1917, when compared with other years and other methods, for the small numbers involved. With 1917 excluded, the large numbers involved through this method for 1918 were a large contributor to χ^2. Comparing this method to others for 1916 to 1915 also resulted in a significant contribution to χ^2 through the small numbers involved. The under-representation of the field in 1916 and 1917 may be explained through the proportionately low number of direct enlistments at a time when many Canadians were joining the flying services through the CEF or the RFC Canada training scheme. On the other hand, the over-representation for 1918 may represent the many individuals about whom so little is known, but most of whom likely joined through RAF Canada, which was under-represented for that year.

When the overseas enlistments (largely from the CEF but also from the British Expeditionary Force and Royal Navy) are compared to the Canadian enlistments, it appears that 1917 was significantly different from other years. Similarly, 1916 was different from 1915. In fact, the overseas enlistments were over-represented for 1916 and 1917, considerably so for the latter year. This may be attributed to the increasing numbers of Canadians in England, and perhaps even more to the

TABLE 10
Enlistments by method by year

	1915	1916	1917	1918	Total
1	141	262	733	4188	5324
2	100	437	1724	2240	4501
3	109	206	710	1354	2379
TOTAL	350	905	3167	7782	12,204

TABLE 11
Percentage of each method's enlistments by year

	1915	1916	1917	1918
1	2.6	4.9	13.8	78.7
2	2.2	9.7	38.3	49.8
3	4.6	8.7	29.8	56.9

TABLE 12
Percentage of each year's enlistments by method

	1915	1916	1917	1918
1	40.3	29.0	23.1	53.8
2	28.6	48.3	54.4	28.8
3	31.1	22.8	22.4	17.4

1 Direct entry or method unknown
2 Overseas enlistments – from CEF, British Army, Royal
  Navy, RNVR
3 Canadian enlistments – from RFC/RAF Canada, Canadian
  and American flying schools, Innes-Ker

Total $X^2 = 1037.5$
Critical $\chi^2 = .001$ (6df) $= 22.5$

increasing numbers experiencing the horrors of the Western Front after the formation of the 3rd and 4th Canadian Divisions. The greater use of the aeroplane in
close co-operation with the ground forces from the time of the Somme offensive
doubtless served to acquaint soldiers with this alternative method of serving. In
addition, lowering of RFC admission standards and official encouragement of
transfers from July 1916 to October 1917 in order to meet the RFC's manpower
needs stimulated joining from the CEF. Overseas transfers were less important in
comparison to other methods in 1918, partly owing to increasing concern by the
Canadian military authorities over manpower losses to the CEF resulting in limitations being put on transfers after October 1917.[12]

TABLE 13
Numbers of enlistments in each service by method

	RFC	RNAS	RAF	Total
1	1219	505	3864	5588
2	2707	216	1728	4651
3	1281	215	1112	2608
TOTAL	5207	936	6704	12,847

TABLE 14
Percentage of each method's enlistments
by service

	RFC	RNAS	RAF
1	21.8	9.0	69.1
2	58.2	4.6	37.2
3	49.1	8.2	42.6

TABLE 15
Percentages of each service's enlistments
entering by method

	RFC	RNAS	RAF
1	23.4	54.0	57.6
2	52.0	23.1	25.8
3	24.6	23.0	16.6

1 Direct entry or method unknown
2 Overseas enlistments – from CEF, British
  Army, Royal Navy, RNVR
3 Canadian enlistments – from RFC/RAF
  Canada, Canadian and American flying
  schools, Innes-Ker

Total $X^2 = 1515.2$
Critical χ^2 .001 (4df) = 18.5

Methods of enlistment were again analyzed in Tables 13–15, this time by the service joined. It is evident that there were considerable deviations from a proportional representation. This may be seen from Table 15, showing the percentage each method represented in a service. In this, the Canadian enlistments came closest to being equally distributed, while the other two methods were out of proportion in opposite directions. Overseas was high (52.0%) in the RFC and low in the other two services, while direct entry/method unknown was the opposite. With high 1918 figures for direct entry/method unknown as mentioned previously, it is not surprising that the RAF should have had the largest percentage (57.6). However, the RNAS, which usually had the fewest unknowns, had 54% by this method, suggesting that the bulk of this figure was probably direct method.

By far the greatest contribution to χ^2 was made by the RFC through the direct entry/method unknown enlistments. The low number of direct entry/method unknown to the RFC doubtless reflects the lack of opportunities to enter that service directly in 1916 and later, and the more complete records in the programme on those individuals who joined the RFC. By contrast, the large proportion of the RAF enlistments in this category, like the same category for 1918, probably is the result of the poorer individual records, as already explained. Similarly, the high proportion of CEF and other overseas entries, when compared to Canadian enlistments, into the RFC was the product of a deliberate policy of encouraging transfers, while, as already explained, such transfers were being controlled in 1918, which accounts partly for the low proportion of this type of enlistment into the RAF.[13]

CAUSES OF FATALITIES

The 1388 fatal casualties (killed or died) were felt to be an almost complete record for Canadians in the British flying services.* Fatalities represented 10.5 per cent of the RFC enlistments, 10.8 per cent of the RNAS, and 10.9 per cent of the RAF.[14] Tables 16–21 analyze the fatalities by cause by year and by service. There are no surprises here. The low figure for died from disease in 1917 makes this category different from other causes and other years. This is not so surprising in the light of the increasing total number of fatal casualties year by year and then the great increase in disease casualties through the influenza epidemic of 1918. Similarly, in Table 21, that 50 per cent of the drownings were of RNAS personnel is not unusual, given the maritime nature of much of the work of that service. In any case, the total number of drownings was only fourteen.

Of some interest was the high rate of accidental deaths, being 32.9 per cent of the total fatalities. As the war progressed, the proportion of those killed accidentally increased, while those killed in action decreased as a proportion of the total fatal casualties.

	1916	1917	1918
Killed in action	46.2	36.7	26.0
Killed accidentally	28.7	29.5	34.8

---

* The Book of Remembrance lists 1563 Canadian flyers dead, but includes all who died up to April 1922. List of Canadians who served in the British flying services, taken from the Book of Remembrance, nd, DHist 75/374

TABLE 16
Fatalities by cause by year
(excluding 1915)

	1	2	3	4	5	6	7	8	Total
1916	8	37	23	3	3	2	1	3	80
1917	66	142	114	17	39	3	2	4	387
1918	148	233	312	85	59	3	49	8	897
TOTAL	222	412	449	105	101	8	52	15	1364

TABLE 17
Percentage of each year's fatalities by cause

	1	2	3	4	5	6	7	8
1916	10.0	46.2	28.7	3.7	3.7	2.5	1.2	3.7
1917	17.1	36.7	29.5	4.4	10.1	.8	.5	1.0
1918	16.5	26.0	34.8	9.5	6.6	.3	5.5	.9

TABLE 18
Percentage of fatalities by cause by year

	1	2	3	4	5	6	7	8
1916	3.6	9.0	5.1	2.9	3.0	25.0	1.9	20.0
1917	29.7	34.5	25.4	16.2	35.6	37.5	3.8	26.7
1918	66.7	56.6	69.5	81.0	58.4	37.5	94.2	53.3

1 Killed, no reason given   5 Died of injuries
2 Killed in action   6 Died as POW
3 Killed accidentally   7 Died of disease
4 Died, no reason given   8 Drowned

Total $X^2 = 69.7$
Critical χ^2 .001 (14df) = 36.1

The enlargement of the flying services, with proportional increases in the training establishment, particularly the RFC/RAF Canada scheme, which was very Canadian dominated, may partly have accounted for this rise in accidental deaths during the latter part of the war. The establishment of new types of operational units, such as home defence squadrons in the United Kingdom, maritime patrol units, and night-bombing squadrons, in which the risk of death from a flying accident was much greater than from enemy action, may have also played a part. Through the enlargement of the flying services, a decreasing intensity in the air war at the individual level may also have been a factor in lowering the proportion of those killed in action.

TABLE 19
Fatalities by cause by service
(excluding 1915)

	1	2	3	4	5	6	7	8	Total
RFC	94	196	169	30	46	4	7	0	546
RNAS	11	33	38	5	5	1	1	7	101
RAF	120	188	244	71	52	3	44	7	729
TOTAL	225	417	451	106	103	8	52	14	1376

TABLE 20
Percentage of each service's fatalities by cause

	1	2	3	4	5	6	7	8
RFC	17.2	35.9	31.0	5.5	8.4	.7	1.3	0
RNAS	10.9	32.7	37.6	5.0	5.0	1.0	1.0	6.9
RAF	16.5	25.8	33.5	9.7	7.1	.4	6.0	1.0

TABLE 21
Percentage of fatalities by cause by service

	1	2	3	4	5	6	7	8
RFC	41.8	47.0	37.5	28.3	44.7	50.0	13.5	0
RNAS	4.9	7.9	8.4	4.7	4.9	12.5	1.9	50.0
RAF	53.3	45.1	54.1	67.0	50.5	37.5	84.6	50.0

1 Killed, no reason given
2 Killed in action
3 Killed accidentally
4 Died, no reason given

5 Died of injuries
6 Died as POW
7 Died of disease
8 Drowned

Total X^2 = 86.5
Critical χ^2 .001 (14df) = 36.1

TOTAL CASUALTIES

Of the 13,160 entries in the programme, 1388 were fatal casualties, another 1130 were wounded or injured, and 377 individuals were listed as prisoners of war or interned before 11 November 1918.* As has been mentioned, it is felt that these figures are very close to a complete record of Canadian service. These casualties are broken down by year in Tables 22–24. Although there was no statistically

* These figures are slightly greater than those in Table 22 because they include those for whom the year of casualty is unknown.

TABLE 22
Fatal and non-fatal casualties by year

	1915	1916	1917	1918	Total
1	8	80	387	897	1372
2	16	75	339	682	1112
3	2	27	113	228	370
TOTAL	26	182	839	1807	2854

TABLE 23
Percentage of each type of casualty by year

	1915	1916	1917	1918
1	.6	5.8	28.2	65.4
2	1.4	6.7	30.5	61.3
3	.5	7.3	30.5	61.6

TABLE 24
Percentage of each year's casualties by type

	1915	1916	1917	1918
1	30.8	44.0	46.1	49.6
2	61.5	41.2	40.4	37.7
3	7.7	14.8	13.5	12.6

1 Killed and missing
2 Wounded and injured
3 POW and interned

Total X^2 = 10.0
Critical χ^2 .001 (6df) = 22.5

significant figure here, these do serve to show the steadily increasing scale of the air war, and the increasing price that Canadians were paying in it.

Table 25 is an analysis of RFC and RAF casualties in the programme as a proportion of the total RFC/RAF casualties.* Even allowing for the incomplete nature of

* It is obvious that the total RFC/RAF casualty figure for prisoners is very low for 1918, and it is suspected that these figures, probably made up in the last days of the war, contain many individuals among the Missing who subsequently turned up as prisoners. A more complete total showed 8136 killed, died, or presumed dead and 7245 wounded and injured. 'Casualties, R.F.C. - R.A.F.; August 1914–Oct., 1918,' nd, Air 1/39/15/7; 'Compiled by Royal Canadian Air Force, Liaison Office, Air Ministry, London, England, and copied from H.Q. 1044–3–5,' 25 July 1935, GAQ 10–20J, PAC, RG 24, vol. 1839

TABLE 25
Casualties in the computer file as a proportion of total RFC/RAF casualties

	1914	1915	1916	1917	1918*	Total
Total RFC/RAF casualties						
Killed & missing	14	129	604	2053	5105	8355
Wounded & injured	15	127	612	2369	3690	6813
POW & interned	8	76	202	544	263	1093
TOTAL	37	332	1418	5416	9058	16,261
RFC/RAF Canadian casualties in computer file						
Killed & missing		5	57	264	659	985
Wounded & injured		13	59	276	645	993
POW & interned		2	22	89	217	330
TOTAL		20	138	629	1521	2308
Computer file casualties as percentage of total casualties						
Killed & missing		3.9	9.4	10.5	12.9	11.8
Wounded & injured		10.2	9.6	11.7	17.5	14.6
POW & interned		2.6	10.9	16.4	82.5	30.2
TOTAL		6.0	9.7	11.6	16.8	14.2

* Figures for November 1918 are not included.

the totals, an increasing degree of Canadianization of the flying services is suggested by the increasing proportion of Canadian casualties, 6.0 per cent in 1915, 9.7 per cent in 1916, 11.6 per cent in 1917, and 16.8 per cent in 1918.

CONCLUSION

The reader must be well aware of the shortcomings of the statistical generalizations made from this computerized inventory. The entries represent neither a total population nor a random sampling, but rather a largely complete listing, with observed shortcomings in certain areas. For this reason, by no means all the data have been presented here, for large numbers of unknowns or clearly biased fields have made numbers of possible analyses valueless. What have been discussed here are results which, given the qualifications which have been stated, are seen as having some utility in statistically describing the nature of Canada's contribution to the First World War through Canadian volunteers to the British flying services.

Notes

CHAPTER 1: MILITARY AVIATION BEFORE THE FIRST WORLD WAR

1 F.T. Miller, *The World in the Air* (New York 1930); C.F. Snowden Gamble, *The Air Weapon* (London 1931), I, 1–73; F.S. Haydon, *Aeronautics in the Union and Confederate Armies, with a Survey of Military Aeronautics prior to 1861* (Baltimore 1941)

2 F.H. Hitchins, 'Pin Points in the Past,' *Roundel*, VIII, June 1956, 24–5; *Royal Engineers Journal*, XV, 1 May 1885, 114; XV, 1 June 1885, 119; XXX, 1 Feb. 1900, 21; XXXI, 1 Nov. 1901, 195; XXXII, 1 April 1902, 51–6

3 M.W. McFarland, *The Papers of Wilbur and Orville Wright* (New York 1953), I, 394–7, II, 886 ff; C.H. Gibbs-Smith, *The Aeroplane: an Historical Survey of its Origins and Development* (London 1960), 224–9

4 H. Gordon Green, *The Silver Dart* (Fredericton 1959), 33–64; J.H. Parkin, *Bell and Baldwin: their Development of Aerodromes and Hydrodromes at Baddeck, Nova Scotia* (Toronto 1964), 40–76

5 The Royal Aero Club of the United Kingdom, *Year Book, 1920–21–22–23* (London nd), 98–103

6 Peter Lewis, *British Aircraft, 1809–1914* (London 1962), 183–201; *Flight*, 3 Sept. 1910, 709–10; Snowden Gamble, *Air Weapon*, I, 74–101

7 David James, *Lord Roberts* (London 1954), 436; Sir Frederick Sykes, *From Many Angles* (London 1942), 90–1; Snowden Gamble, *Air Weapon*, I, 124–5; Sir Walter Raleigh, *The War in the Air: being the Story of the Part played in the Great War by the Royal Air Force*, I (London 1922), 172–4; *Flight*, 30 Sept. 1911, 838, 848

8 *Flight*, 29 May 1909, 308; Raleigh, *War in the Air*, I, 159

9 *Flight*, 8 Oct. 1910, 824; 25 Feb. 1911, 160; 4 March 1911, 179; Snowden Gamble, *Air Weapon*, I, 117–20

10 G.O. Squier, 'The Present Status of Military Aeronautics,' *Flight*, 27 Feb. 1909, 121; 17 Sept. 1910, 759; 24 Sept. 1910, 782; 8 Oct. 1910, 827; 24 Dec. 1910, 1059; 18 Feb. 1911, 148; Arthur Sweetser, *The American Air Service* (New York 1919), 8–10; Erich Ludendorff, *The General Staff and its Problems: the History of the Relations between the High Command and the German Imperial Government as revealed by Official Documents*, F.A. Holt, trans. (London 1920), I, 32–3

11 Great Britain, Parliament, *Memorandum on Naval and Military Aviation* (Papers by Command, Cd 6067; London 1912), 2. See also Raleigh, *War in the Air*, I, 198–9.

12 Raleigh, *War in the Air*, I, 199–201

13 *Memorandum on Naval and Military Aviation*, 8; Great Britain, War Office, *Field Service Regulations, Part 1, Operations, 1909, (reprinted, with amendments, 1914)* (London 1914), 20–1, 126–9; 'Air Power,' *Naval Review*, I, 1911, 57–75

14 Raleigh, *War in the Air*, I, 206–8; *Journal of the Royal United Service Institution*, LVII, Jan. 1913, 130; LVII, Feb. 1913, 270; LIX, Aug.–Nov. 1914, 299–301; *Flight*, 27 April 1912, 379

15 Great Britain, Parliament, *Military Aeroplane Competition, 1912; Report of Judges Committee* (Papers by Command, Cd 6286; London 1912); *Flight*, 25 Feb. 1911, 156–7; 23 Dec. 1911,; Lewis, *British Aircraft*, 198–9; G.R. Duval, *British Flying Boats and Amphibians, 1909–1952* (London 1966), 9–15, 156–7

16 Raleigh, *War in the Air*, I, 224–9; McCurdy to Maunsell, 29 Aug. 1910, HQ 6978–4, PAC, RG 24, vol. 2047; *Flight*, 1 Oct. 1910, 802; 8 Oct. 1910, 824; 11 March 1911, 198–9

17 *Journal of the Royal United Service Institution*, LV, Oct. 1911, 1388; LVI, Feb. 1912, 285; Ludendorff, *General Staff*, I, 47–8; *Field Service Regulations*, 21; *Journal of the Royal Artillery*, XLI, 338–9

18 *Journal of the Royal United Service Institution*, LVI, July 1912, 1062; LVI, Nov. 1912, 1612; LVII, Dec. 1913, 1680–1; *Flight*, 9 Nov. 1912, 1029; 4 Jan. 1913, 19; 11 Jan. 1913, 45; 6 Dec. 1913, 1332–3

19 W.F. Reid, 'The Use of Explosives in Aerial Warfare,' *Journal of the Royal United Service Institution*, LV, June 1911, 735–49; *Flight*, 9 July 1910, 531; 26 Aug. 1911, 748; 11 Nov. 1911, 989; 27 April 1912, 380; 8 June 1912, 518; 9 Nov. 1912, 1035; 23 Nov. 1912, 1091; 7 Dec. 1912, 1137; 25 Jan. 1913, 89

20 Raleigh, *War in the Air*, I, 466–7; *Flight*, 28 Jan. 1911, 67; *Journal of the Royal United Service Institution*, LVI, July 1912, 1059

21 Detailed information on air organization, equipment, and strengths for the European air forces prior to the outbreak of war can be found in Raleigh, *War in the Air*, I, 198–276, 357–8; W.M. Lamberton and E.F. Cheesman, *Reconnaissance and Bomber Aircraft of the 1914–1918 War* (Letchworth, Herts. 1962); J.M. Bruce, *British Aeroplanes, 1914–1918* (London 1957), 350–6, 476–9; *Journal of the Royal United Service Institution*, LV (1911)–LVIII (1914); *Handbook of the German Army, Home and Colonial* (London 1912), 186–8; E. von Hoeppner, *Deutschlands Krieg in der Luft* (Leipzig 1923), 1–6, DHist SGR I 196, Set 3a; Ludendorff, *General Staff*, I, 37–43; D.H. Robinson, *The Zeppelin in Combat: a History of the German Naval Airship Division, 1912–1918* (London 1966), 18–31; G.P. Neumann, *The German Air Force in the Great War* (London 1920), 57–60

22 J.H. Parkin, 'Wallace Rupert Turnbull, 1870–1954: Canadian Pioneer of Scientific Aviation,' *Canadian Aeronautical Journal*, II, Jan. 1956, 2–10; II, Feb. 1956, 39–48; L'Etoile to Minister of Militia and Defence, 27 Sept. 1886, and reply, 7 Oct. 1886, Caron Papers, PAC, MG 27 I D 3, vol. 96, 9752, and vol. 17, 299

23 MGO to Militia Council, 26 April 1909, HQ 6978–2–2, PAC, RG 24, vol. 2034

24 Secretary, Militia Council, to MGO, 5 May 1909, ibid.

25 *Evening Journal* (Ottawa), 29 March 1909, 6, 10; Parkin, *Bell and Baldwin*, 274–311

26 Grey to Crewe, 11 March 1909, HQ 6978–4, PAC, RG 24, vol. 2047; submission to Militia Council, 4 May 1909, HQ 6978–2–2, ibid., vol. 2034
27 *Minutes of the Militia Council, May 4, 1909* (Ottawa 1909); Fiset to Bell, 7 May 1909, Baldwin and McCurdy to Secretary, Militia Council, 14 May 1909, HQ 6978–4, PAC, RG 24, vol. 2047
28 McCurdy to Secretary, Militia Council, 8 June 1909, Maunsell to Bogart, 14 June 1909, HQ 6978–4, PAC, RG 24, vol. 2047
29 Bogart to Director of Engineer Services, 19 June 1909, minute of MGO, 22 June 1909, ibid.; Green, *Silver Dart*, x, 107–9; A.J. Kerry and W.A. McDill, *The History of the Corps of Royal Canadian Engineers* (Ottawa 1962), I, 56
30 *Evening Journal*, 26 July 1909, 1; *News* (Toronto), 26 July 1909, 1; 6 Aug. 1909, 1–2; 7 Aug. 1929, 1
31 Bogart to Director of Engineer Services, 6 Aug. 1909, HQ 6978–4, PAC, RG 24, vol. 2047; *Winnipeg Telegram*, 3 Aug. 1909, 1; *Toronto Star*, 3 Aug. 1909; *Globe* (Toronto), 3 Aug. 1909
32 *Evening Citizen* (Ottawa), 12 Aug. 1909, 1; Maunsell to MGO, 15 Aug. 1909, HQ 6978–4, PAC, RG 24, vol. 2047
33 *Evening Citizen*, 12 Aug. 1909, 1
34 Ibid.
35 *Evening Citizen*, 13 Aug. 1909, 3; Maunsell to MGO, 15 Aug. 1909, HQ 6978–4, PAC, RG 24, vol. 2047
36 *Saturday Evening Citizen* (Ottawa), 14 Aug. 1909, 1
37 McCurdy to Maunsell, 21, 28, 30 Oct. and 2 Nov. 1909, Maunsell to McCurdy, 6 Nov. 1909, HQ 6978–4, PAC, RG 24, vol. 2047
38 Canada, Parliament, House of Commons, *Debates*, 25 Nov. 1909, col. 446
39 Ibid., 13 Dec. 1909, 1369
40 Lohner biographical file, DHist
41 *Evening Journal*, 14 March 1910, 1
42 Lohner biographical file, DHist
43 MGO to McCurdy and Baldwin, 3 March 1910, Baldwin and McCurdy to Secretary, Militia Council, 3 March 1910, Maunsell, 'Notes on Aerodrome Flights,' 17 March 1910, HQ 6978–4, PAC, RG 24, vol. 2047
44 Baldwin and McCurdy to Secretary, Militia Council, 10 March 1910, Maunsell to MGO, 21 March 1910, ibid.
45 'Summary of Report of the Director of Engineer Services on his Visit to the Canadian Aerodrome Company of Baddeck, N.S.,' 29 March 1910, MGO to Secretary, Militia Council, 21 March 1910, ibid.
46 *Minutes of the Militia Council, April 5, 1910*; Minister of Militia and Defence to Governor General, 7 April 1910, HQ 6978–4, PAC, RG 24, vol. 2047
47 Fiset minute, 26 April 1910, MGO to Fiset, 7 May 1910, Fiset minute, 9 May 1910, Minister to Council, 16 May 1910, Maunsell to McCurdy and Baldwin, 10 June 1910, Fiset to McCurdy and Baldwin, 16 June 1910, ibid.; *Minutes of the Militia Council, May 10, 1910*
48 Maunsell to MGO, 29 Aug. 1910, minute of Secretary, Militia Council, 17 Sept. 1910, McCurdy to Maunsell, 29 Aug. 1910, Maunsell to McCurdy, 1 Sept. 1910, HQ 6978–4, PAC, RG 24, vol. 2047

49 Maunsell and Fiset to Minister, 10 Nov. 1911, HQ 6978-2-30, ibid., vol. 2035
50 Maunsell to Fiset, 28 Nov. 1911, Fiset to Governor General, 28 Nov. 1911, War Office to Colonial Office (for transmission to Canada), 2 Feb. 1912, HQ 6978-4, ibid., vol. 2047
51 Maunsell to MGO, 19 Feb. 1912, ibid.
52 MGO to CGS, 22 Feb. 1912, CGS minute, 6 March 1912, MGO to Deputy Minister, 13 March 1912, Deputy Minister minute, 14 March 1912, ibid.
53 Maunsell to MGO, 18 Nov. 1912, HQ 6978-2-37, ibid., vol. 2035
54 CGS to MGO, 23 Nov. 1912, ibid.
55 AG to GOC 6 Division, 2 Aug. 1912, note of Adjutant, RCE, 5 Dec. 1912, Maunsell minute, 3 Dec. 1912, ibid.; Kerry and McDill, *Royal Canadian Engineers*, I, 55

CHAPTER 2: RECRUITING AND TRAINING IN CANADA, 1914–16

1 *Globe* (Toronto), 26 July 1909, 1–2; *Evening Citizen* (Ottawa), 26 July 1909, 1, 7; 10 Aug. 1909, 5; *Le Soleil* (Québec), 26 July 1909, 1; 27 July 1909, 1; *Manitoba Free Press*, 4 July 1914, Women's Section, 3; 'Come Josephine ...' was copyrighted in 1910.
2 See, for example, *Le Soleil*, 29 July 1909, 4; 31 July 1909, 1; C.F. Winter, *Lieutenant-General the Hon. Sir Sam Hughes, K.C.B., M.P.: Canada's War Minister 1911–1916* (Toronto 1931), 104–5.
3 PC 2389, 17 Sept. 1914
4 *Evening Citizen*, 15 Feb. 1915, 1; *Globe*, 15 Feb. 1915, 1; 16 Feb. 1915, 1–2
5 *Daily Mail and Empire* (Toronto), 16 Feb. 1915, 10
6 'List of Aviators who have Volunteered for Service,' [1 Sept. 1914], HQ 6978-2-62, vol. 1, PAC, RG 24, vol. 2031; Maunsell minute, 27 Aug. 1914, HQ 6978-2-41, ibid., vol. 2035; Kennedy to Borden, 14 Oct. 1914, Maunsell minute, 29 Jan. 1915, HQ 6978-2-72, ibid., vol. 2037
7 Maunsell minute, 14 Nov. 1914, Gwatkin minute, 18 Nov. 1914, Maunsell to Kennedy, 19 Nov. 1914 and generally, ibid.
8 Gwatkin minute, 3 Sept. 1914, HQ 6978-2-62, vol. 1, ibid., vol. 2031; F.H. Ellis, *Canada's Flying Heritage* (Toronto 1954), 43
9 War Office to Hughes, cipher, 31 Aug. 1914, HQ 6978-2-62, vol. 1, PAC, RG 24, vol. 2031
10 HQ 6978-2-64, ibid., vol. 2037
11 Quoted in Gwatkin to Under-Secretary of State for External Affairs, 16 Sept. 1914, ibid.
12 'Extracts from Letter Dated September 26th 1914 from the Burgess Company,' enclosure in [Slade] to Sharpe, 29 Sept. 1914, HQ 6978-2-68, ibid.
13 Janney to OC, CEF, Bustard Camp, Salisbury Plain, PAC, RG 9 III, vol. 381; Adjutant-General to Alderson, 20 Nov. 1914, Deputy Minister of Militia to Governor General, 28 Dec. 1914, HQ 593-2-46, PAC, RG 24, vol. 488
14 Stanton to Gwatkin, 23 Feb. 1915, enclosing Colonial Office to War Office, 7 Feb. 1915, HQ 6978-2-92, vol. 1, ibid., vol. 2032
15 F.H. Hitchins, 'Recruiting in Canada for the R.F.C.,' 1–2, Hitchins Papers, DHist 75/514, file D10

16 Gwatkin to Stanton, 27 and 28 Feb. 1915, Gwatkin to Divisions and Districts,
   9 March 1915, enclosure of 13 March 1915 in British Embassy, Washington, to
   Governor General, 17 March 1915, HQ 6978–2–92, vol. 1, PAC, RG 24, vol. 2032
17 McCurdy to Borden, 22 Dec. 1914, 3 Feb. 1915, Borden to McCurdy, 6 Feb. 1915,
   Christie to McCurdy, 18 March 1915, McCurdy Papers, DHist 76/253, files 1 and 2;
   Governor General to Secretary of State for the Colonies, 6 Feb., 3 March 1915,
   Secretary of State for the Colonies to Governor General, 15 March 1915, GAQ
   10–20K, PAC, RG 24, vol. 1839
18 Deputy Minister, DNS, to Deputy Minister of Militia, 16 April 1915, HQ 6978–2–92,
   vol. 1, PAC, RG 24, vol. 2032; Hitchins, 'RNAS Recruiting 1915,' 1, Hitchins Papers,
   DHist 75/514, file D3
19 'Regulations for Special Entry in Canada into the Royal Naval Air Service,' DHist
   112AH.001 (D3)
20 *Daily Mail and Empire*, 11 May 1915, 4; Curtiss School logbook, PAC, MG 28 III 65
21 Hitchins, 'Recruiting ... for the R.F.C.,' 4–6; Logan to RCAF Historical Section,
   17 March 1962, DHist 112AH.001 (D3)
22 Quoted in Hitchins, 'Recruiting ... for the R.F.C.,' 7–8
23 Curtiss logbook, PAC, MG 28 III 65; Hitchins, 'Recruiting ... for the R.F.C.,' 8;
   Ross-Hume to MA 1, 16 Sept. and reply of same date, Air 2/13/058/4047
24 Governor General to Secretary of State for the Colonies, 6 Oct. 1915, Secretary of
   State for the Colonies to Governor General, 10 Nov. 1915, Air 1/656/17/122/552;
   Globe, 14 Sept. 1915, 6; 25 Oct. 1915, 3; 7 Nov. 1915, 8; 16 Nov. 1915, 6; 18 Nov.
   1915, 7; Curtiss logbook, PAC, MG 28 III 65; interview with Air Marshal Robert
   Leckie, May 1964; Henderson to Stanton, 19 Nov. 1915, Air 2/13/058/4047; War
   Office to Governor General, 18 Nov. 1915, HQ 6978–2–92, vol. 3, PAC, RG 24, vol.
   2032
25 Colonial Office to Governor General, 20 Sept. 1915, enclosing War Office to
   Colonial Office, 10 Sept. 1915, HQ 6978–2–92, vol. 2, PAC, RG 24, vol. 2032;
   Henderson to Stanton, 20 Oct. 1915, Air 2/13/058/4047; Hitchins, 'Recruiting ... for
   the RFC,' 10–11
26 Kingsmill to Commanding Officer, HMCS *Niobe*, 22 Nov. 1915, NSS 40–3–2,
   PAC, RG 24, vol. 5636; *Niobe* pay ledgers, PARC; R. Collishaw, 'Canadian
   Volunteers and the Royal Naval Air Service,' DHist 112AH.001 (D3); Secretary,
   DNS, to RNAS candidate, 22 Nov. 1915, ibid.
27 Quoted in Hitchins, 'Recruiting ... for the R.F.C.,' 9
28 Air 2/13/058/4066
29 Burke to Marindin, 19 Dec. 1915, ibid.
30 Goldney to McCurdy, 24 June 1916, McCurdy Papers, DHist 76/253, file 3
31 War Office to Colonial Office, 9 Feb. 1916, Air 2/13/058/4066
32 Stanton to Gwatkin, 26 June 1916, HQ 6978–2–92, vol. 4, PAC, RG 24, vol. 2033;
   Stanton to Gwatkin, 25 March 1916, HQ 6978–2–125, ibid., vol. 2039
33 *Globe*, 13 May 1916, 5; Curtiss logbook, PAC, MG 28 III 65
34 Canada, Department of the Naval Service, *Report ... for the Fiscal Year ending March
   31, 1919* (Sessional Paper no 39; Ottawa 1920); H.A. Jones, *The War in the Air:
   being the Story of the Part played in the Great War by the Royal Air Force*, V (London
   1935), 459; *Navy List, 1916*, II, 965

35 'Regulations for the Special Entry in Canada of Officers and Men for the Royal Flying Corps, Military Wing,' HQ 6978–2–62, vol. 1, PAC, RG 24, vol. 2031; Brancker to Stanton, Aug. 1916 and enclosure, Air 2/9/87/8060

36 Robert Laird Borden, *Robert Laird Borden: His Memoirs*, Henry Borden, ed. (Toronto 1938), II, 603–4; Borden to Foster, 14 July 1916, Perley Papers, PAC, MG 27 II D 12, vol. 5; *Globe*, 20 March 1916, 9

37 Hitchins, 'Recruiting ... for the R.F.C.,' 18–20; Warner to Innis-Ker, 17 Nov. 1916, confirming cable of 15 Nov. 1916, Air 2/9/87/8060

38 Admiralty Monthly Orders, 2027/16, 16 Aug. 1916; DHist 112AH.001 (D3)

39 *Globe*, 11 Aug. 1916, 6; City of Toronto Council minutes, 1918, App. A, 933; City of Toronto, unpublished statement of year-end summaries (receipts and disbursements); PC 1008, 1 May 1915; Curtiss logbook, PAC, MG 28 III 65

40 It is not possible to give a specific reference or references to support these figures. They are based, *inter alia*, on the following sources: Canada, Parliament, House of Commons, *Debates*, 27 May 1919, 2969; HQ 6978–2–92, vols. 1–6, PAC, RG 24, vols. 2032–3; Canada, Overseas Military Forces of Canada, *Report of the Ministry: Overseas Military Forces of Canada, 1918* (London nd), 345–7; Curtiss logbook, PAC, MG 28 III 65; 'RFC-RNAS Recruiting in Canada,' DHist 112AH.001 (D3)

41 *Globe*, 15 May 1915, 23

42 Marindin to Merritt, 18 Feb. 1916, Merritt to Gwatkin, 16 Sept. 1916, HQ 6978–2–125, PAC, RG 24, vol. 2039; *Montreal Herald and Daily Telegraph*, 8 Sept. 1916, 3; Stanton to Brancker, 18 Aug. 1916, Air 2/9/87/8060

43 Secretary, Canadian Aircraft Works, to Department of Militia, 7, 21 Nov. 1914, HQ 6978–2–80, PAC, RG 24, vol. 2037

44 *Toronto World*, 2 April 1915, 1–2; 14 April 1915, 6; 6 May 1915, 1–2; Ellis, *Canada's Flying Heritage*, 113–18

45 R.V. Dodds, 'When the Canadians Took Over U.S. Flying Schools,' *Flight*, LIX, Feb. 1969, 28–32

46 Breadner to his father, [October 1915], Breadner Papers, DHist 74/707, folder A, file 2

47 Carter, 'Difficulties of Enlisting to Serve in Air Services in the Beginnings of Air War in the First World War, 1914–18,' A.W. Carter biographical file, DHist

48 Ibid.; Carter to Dodds, 10 April 1963, Carter Papers, DHist 76/137, file A2

49 'The M.F.P. Tractor Biplane,' *Flight*, VIII, June 1916, 504–7; C.W. Thomas, 'The Polson Iron Works Biplane,' *Aircraft*, XXI, May 1959, 31; K.M. Molson, 'Aircraft Manufacturing in Canada during the First Great War,' *Canadian Aeronautical Journal*, V, Feb. 1959, 54

50 Governor General to Secretary of State for the Colonies, 6 Oct. 1915, Air 1/656/17/122/552; M.R. Riddell, 'The Development and Future of Aviation in Canada,' *Journal of the Engineering Institute of Canada*, II, March 1919, 200–9; K.M. Molson, 'The CURTISS CANADA ... a Canadian First,' *Aircraft*, XXV, May 1963, 16

51 Imperial Munitions Board to Ministry of Munitions, 9, 24 May 1916, Air 2/127/B12062; 'Memorandum on Development of the Royal Flying Corps in Canada,' Air 2/166/RU4527; Hitchins, 'Aircraft Construction in Canada,' 11, Hitchins Papers, DHist 75/514, file D9

52 *Toronto World*, 15 March 1916, 6

CHAPTER 3: SIR SAM HUGHES, THE AVIATION LOBBY, AND CANADIAN AIR POLICY, 1914–16

1 Thacker to Militia Council, 22 Sept. 1914, Gwatkin to Maunsell, 8 Oct. 1914, HQ 6978-2-67, PAC, RG 24, vol. 2037

2 Borden to Perley, 9 Oct. 1914, P-2-29, PAC, RG 25, vol. 253; draft cable of Maunsell, 8 Oct. 1914, Perley to Borden, 21 Oct. 1914, Gwatkin to Slade, 22 Oct. 1914, HQ 6978-2-68, PAC, RG 24, vol. 2037

3 Gwatkin to Bennett, 2 Dec. 1914, Gwatkin Papers, PAC, MG 30 E 51

4 McCurdy to Hughes, 21 Dec. 1914, McCurdy Papers, DHist 76/253, file 1

5 McCurdy to Borden, 22 and 30 Dec. 1914, 3 Feb., 16 April 1915, Borden to McCurdy, 6 Feb. 1915, ibid., files 1 and 2; Governor General to Secretary of State for the Colonies, 6 Feb., 3 March 1915, Secretary of State for the Colonies to Governor General, 15 March 1915, GAQ 10-20K, PAC, RG 24, vol. 1839

6 Brewer, 'Outline of Proposed Canadian Aviation Corps,' Oct. 1914, Cooper to Brancker, 12 Oct. 1914, Brancker minute, 23 Oct. 1914, Air 2/6/87/4069; cf S.F. Wise, 'The Borden Government and the Formation of a Canadian Flying Corps, 1911–1916,' Michael Cross and Robert Bothwell, eds., *Policy by Other Means: Essays in Honour of C.P. Stacey* (Toronto 1972), 126. Brancker's flowing hand led the author of this article to misread 'ten squadrons' for 'this squadron.'

7 F.H. Hitchins, 'Dominion Squadrons, 1915–1918,' 1–2, Hitchins Papers, DHist 75/514, file D1. While serving as a member of the RCAF Historical Section during the Second World War, Dr Hitchins had access to a number of Air Historical Board files which were subsequently destroyed.

8 Under-Secretary of State, Colonial Office, to Secretary, Office of the High Commissioner for Canada, 18 Sept. 1915, enclosing War Office proposal of 10 Sept. 1915, C-9-91, PAC, RG 25, vol. 151

9 Gwatkin to Stanton, 13 and 21 Oct. 1915, Stanton to Gwatkin, 15 Oct. 1915, Gwatkin to Adjutant-General, 21 Oct. 1915, Fiset to Pope, 21 Oct. 1915, HQ 6978-2-92, vol. 2, PAC, RG 24, vol. 2032; Henderson to Stanton, 20 Oct. 1915, Air 2/13/058/4047

10 Merritt to Borden, 20 March 1916, HQ 6978-2-125, PAC, RG 24, vol. 2039; *Montreal Herald and Daily Telegraph*, 8 Sept. 1916, 3

11 Quoted in Merritt to Borden, 20 March 1916, HQ 6978-2-125, PAC, RG 24, vol. 2039

12 Marindin to Merritt, 18 Feb. 1916, ibid.

13 Kemp to Gwatkin, 31 March 1916, ibid.

14 *Toronto World*, 29 March 1916, 6

15 Merritt to Borden, 20 March 1916, HQ 6978-2-125, PAC, RG 24, vol. 2039

16 Gwatkin to Stanton, 7 April 1916, Militia Council minutes, 19 April 1916, Stanton to Gwatkin, 27 April 1916, Borden to Merritt, 28 April 1916, Gwatkin to Adjutant-General, 13 May 1916, ibid; PC 1008, 1 May 1916

17 Canada, Parliament, House of Commons, *Debates*, 14 April 1916, 2895–6, 2898–900

18 *Toronto Star*, 8 April 1916, 10

19 Ibid., 1 Sept. 1916, 8; *Toronto World*, 12 June 1916, 6; 7 Sept. 1916, 6; 26 Sept. 1916, 6; 3 Oct. 1916, 6

20 Merritt to Gwatkin, 27 July, 28 Aug. 1916, Gwatkin to Merritt, 30 July 1916, HQ 6978-2-125, PAC, RG 24, vol. 2039; J.C. Hopkins, *Canadian Annual Review, 1916*

(Toronto 1917), 301; Hearst to Borden, 12 Oct. 1916, Borden Papers, PAC, MG 26 H, vol. 74, 38631–2

21 Merritt to Gwatkin, 16 Sept. 1916, HQ 6978–2–125, PAC, RG 24, vol. 2039
22 Gwatkin to Merritt, 5 Sept. 1916, ibid.
23 Newspaper clipping (unidentified), c March 1916, Dinnick to Harvey, 2 Oct. 1916, Air 2/127/B12062; Hopkins, *Canadian Annual Review, 1916*, 301
24 Dinnick to Air Board, 5 June 1916, Air 2/127/B12062
25 Dinnick to Henderson, 8 May 1916, 'Building Aeroplanes at Cost, Toronto, Canada,' 13 May 1916, ibid.
26 Brand to Perry, 27 April 1916, Perry to Brand, 5 May 1916, ibid.
27 David Carnegie, *History of Munitions Supply in Canada, 1914–1918* (London 1925), 95–100
28 Perry to Brand, 9 May 1916, Air 2/127/B12062
29 Perry to Brand, 27 May 1916, ibid.
30 Brand to Perry, 15 and 23 May 1916, ibid.; Borden to Perley, 19 May 1916, Borden Papers, PAC, MG 26 H, vol. 74, 38566
31 Perry to Brand, 24 May 1916, Air 2/127/B12062
32 Perry to Brand, 25 May 1916, ibid.
33 McCurdy to Kemp, 23 March 1916, McCurdy Papers, DHist 76/253, file 3
34 McCurdy to Desbarats, 12 April 1916, ibid.; Borden to Perley, 11 April 1916, P–5–94, PAC, RG 25, vol. 267
35 Perley to Borden, 4 May 1916, Borden Papers, PAC, MG 26 H, vol. 74, 38567
36 Perley to Borden, 8 May 1916, ibid., 38564–5
37 Gwatkin to Christie, 9 May 1916, Gwatkin Papers, PAC, MG 30 E 51
38 Memorandum [Christie to Borden], 15 May 1916, Borden Papers, PAC, MG 26 H, vol. 74, 38568–70
39 Borden to Perley, 19 May 1916, Perley to Borden, 22 May 1916, ibid., 38566, 38571–3
40 Brand to Curzon, 25 May 1916, Harvey, 'Notes of Meeting with Brand,' 26 May 1916, McCurdy to Curzon, 26 May 1916, Harvey, 'Notes of Interview with McCurdy,' 30 May 1916, Stanley to Baird, 31 May 1916, Air 2/127/B12062
41 Baird to Sydenham, 2 June 1916, McCurdy to Harvey, 6 June 1916, Baird to Sydenham, 6 June 1916, ibid.; Gordon Bruce, 'Canadian Flying Corps; Offer to the Air Board,' *Daily Mail* (London), 3 June 1916, clipping in P–5–94, PAC, RG 25, vol. 267
42 Baird to Sydenham, 2 June 1916, Harvey, 'Canadian School of Aviation and Factory,' June 1916, Air 2/127/B12062
43 Admiralty to Air Board, 16 June 1916, War Office to Treasury, 27 June 1916, Brancker to Harvey, 30 June 1916, Brancker to DFS, 30 June 1916, Treasury to Air Board, 30 June 1916, Treasury to War Office, 4 July 1916, ibid.
44 Air Board minutes, 7 July 1916, ibid.
45 Brand to Harvey, 8 July 1916, Brand to Flavelle, 9 July 1916, Perry to Borden, 18 July 1916, ibid.
46 Harvey to Curzon, 5 Aug. 1916, ibid.; White to Borden, 19 July 1916, Borden Papers, PAC, MG 26 H, vol. 74, 38565A
47 Bonar Law to Governor General, 11 Aug. 1916, ibid., 38587

48 Hazen to Borden, 15 Aug. 1916, [memorandum of meeting with 'Lord Innes-Kerr'], 21 Aug. 1916, ibid., 38590–1, 385600; Innes-Ker to Brancker, 22 Aug. 1916, Air 2/127/B12062

49 Ibid.; [memorandum of meeting], 21 Aug. 1916, Borden Papers, PAC, MG 26 H, vol. 74, 385600

50 Kingsmill to Desbarats, 27 Aug. 1916, Air 2/127/B12062

51 Henderson to Perley, 20 June 1916, Perley to Borden, 22 June 1916, Borden Papers, PAC, MG 26 H, vol. 74, 38574, 38575

52 Kingsmill to Vaughan-Lee, 28 Aug. 1916, Air 2/127/B12062

53 Gordon to Brand and Perry, 29 Aug. 1916, Admiralty to Air Board, 29 Sept. 1916, ibid.

54 Minutes of 22nd meeting of Air Board, 24 Aug. 1916, Air 6/2; Sydenham minutes, 31 Aug. and 29 Sept. 1916, Harvey and Sydenham minutes, 2–5 Oct. 1916, Air 2/127/B12062

55 Canada, Department of National Defence, *Official History of the Canadian Forces in the Great War, 1914–1919*, I: *Chronology, Appendices and Maps* (Ottawa 1938), 162, 229; Morden to Perley, 26 Jan. 1917, P–5–94, PAC, RG 25, vol. 267

56 Murphy to Hughes, 12 April 1916, 8–1–104, PAC, RG 9 III, vol. 35

57 Carson to Hughes, 14 April 1916, A–56–33, vol. 1, PAC, RG 9 III, vol. 2666

58 Carson to Hughes, 20 and 29 April 1916, Hughes to Carson, 20 April 1916, ibid.

59 McCurdy to Borden, 10 July 1916, Morden, 'Draft Proposals for Canadian Air Service,' nd, McCurdy Papers, DHist 76/253, file 3

60 Morden to Hughes, 26 June 1916, ibid.

61 McCurdy to Harvey, 21 June 1916, Harvey, 'Notes to "Draft Proposals for Canadian Air Service,"' nd, Brancker, 'Comments on Draft Proposals,' 24 June 1916, Air Board minutes, 7 July 1916, Harvey to Morden, 10 July 1916, Air 2/127/B12062; Borden to Perry, 23 June 1916, Borden Papers, PAC, MG 26 H, vol. 74, 38578

62 McCurdy to Morden, 11 and 25 July 1916, McCurdy Papers, DHist 76/253, file 3

63 Morden to McCurdy, 3 and 10 Aug. 1916, ibid.

64 *Gazette* (Montreal), 23 Aug. 1916, 16

65 'Minutes of Conversation Held with Representatives of Canada, Australia and South Africa,' 26 Aug. 1916, Hitchins Papers, DHist 75/514, file B1

66 'Seating Plan for Dinner given by Grant Morden,' 29 Aug. 1916, Morden to McCurdy, 4 Sept. 1916, McCurdy Papers, DHist 76/253, file 3

67 Hughes to Borden, 9 Sept. 1916, Army Council to Hughes, 8 Sept. 1916, Borden Papers, PAC, MG 26 H, vol. 74, 38604–9, 38615–17, 38622–63; Army Council to Perley, 20 Nov. 1916, P–5–94, PAC, RG 25, vol. 267; Gwatkin to Kemp, 13 Dec. 1916, 10–9–27, vol. 1, RG 9 III, vol. 80

68 Gordon to Perry, 24 Sept. 1916, Air 2/127/B12062

69 Perry to Gordon, 28 Sept. 1916, ibid.

70 Gordon to Hazen, 4 Oct. 1916, Hazen to Borden, 5 Oct. 1916, Borden Papers, PAC, MG 26 H, vol. 74, 38619–21

71 McCurdy to Hughes, 9 Oct. 1916, McCurdy Papers, DHist 76/253, file 3

72 Borden to McCurdy, 12 Oct. 1916, ibid.; Gordon to Perry, 15 Oct. 1916, Air Board minutes, 27 Oct. 1916, Air 2/127/B12062

73 Harvey and Sydenham minutes, 16 Oct. 1916, Harvey to Brancker, 16 Oct. 1916, Sydenham minute, 24 Oct. 1916, Air 2/127/B12062

74 Air Board minutes, 27 Oct. 1916, ibid.

75 Quoted in Harvey to Sydenham, 1 Nov. 1916, ibid. See also War Office to Treasury, 11 Nov. 1916, ibid.

76 Flavelle to Gordon, 3 Nov. 1916, ibid.

77 Quoted in Gordon to Flavelle, 11 Nov. 1916, ibid.

78 Borden to Hughes, 9 Nov. 1916, in Robert Laird Borden, *Robert Laird Borden; His Memoirs*, Henry Borden, ed. (Toronto 1938), II, 569–70

79 Minutes of conference, 20 Nov. 1916, Air 2/127/B12062

80 Brancker to Harvey, 20 Oct. 1916, ibid.

81 Brancker, 'Memorandum of Conversation with Henderson,' 21 Oct. 1916, ibid.

82 Minutes of conference, 20 Nov. 1916, ibid.

83 Air Board minutes, 22 Nov. 1916, Harvey to Curzon, 14 Dec. 1916, ibid.

84 Army Council to Perley, 23 Dec. 1916, P–5–94, PAC, RG 25, vol. 267

CHAPTER 4: RFC EXPANSION AND THE CANADIAN AIR TRAINING ORGANIZATON

1 Alan Sullivan, *Aviation in Canada, 1917–1918* (Toronto 1919), 16–17; 'Memorandum on Development of the Royal Flying Corps in Canada,' nd, Air 1/721/48/4; Hoare to Charlton, 15 Feb. 1917, Air 1/721/48/5

2 Allen to RCAF Historical Section, 20 Sept. 1962, DHist 76/199

3 Hoare to Allen, 27 Nov. 1962, ibid.

4 Gwatkin to GOC MD 2, 23 Jan. 1917, Gwatkin to Military Districts, 23 Jan. 1917, HQ 6978–2–131, vol. 1, PAC, RG 24, vol. 2040; Hoare to DAO, 28 Jan. 1917, Air 1/721/48/5

5 Air 1/721/48/4; Hoare to DAO, 28 Jan. 1917, Air 1/721/48/5

6 Air 1/721/48/4

7 Hoare to Militia Department, 27 Jan. 1917, Fiset to Under-Secretary of State for External Affairs, 30 Jan. 1917, HQ 6978–2–131, vol. 1, PAC, RG 24, vol. 2040; Long to Governor General, 22 Jan. 1917, Air 1/721/48/5

8 Flavelle to Kemp, 29 Jan. 1917, Kemp to Flavelle, 30 Jan. 1917, HQ 6978–2–131, vol. 1, PAC, RG 24, vol. 2040; Air 1/721/48/4; Hoare to Charlton, 28 Jan., 4 Feb. 1917, Air 1/721/48/5

9 'Memorandum on Development of the Royal Flying Corps in Canada, App. A,' nd, Air 1/721/48/4

10 Hoare to Charlton, 28 Jan. 1917, Air 1/721/48/5; Sullivan, *Aviation in Canada*, 18; David Carnegie, *The History of Munitions Supply in Canada, 1914–1918* (London 1925), 176

11 Carnegie, *History of Munitions Supply*, 174–81; Sullivan, *Aviation in Canada*, 25–43

12 Carnegie, *History of Munitions Supply*, 177; Air 1/721/48/4; Sullivan, *Aviation in Canada*, 21–2

13 Allen to RCAF Historical Section, 20 Sept. 1962, DHist 76/199; H.A. Jones, *The War in the Air: being the Story of the Part played in the Great War by the Royal Air Force*, V (London 1935), 462–3; Hoare to Charlton, 19 March 1917, Air 1/721/48/5

14 Sullivan, *Aviation in Canada*, 261–5; Air 1/721/48/4

15 Sullivan, *Aviation in Canada*, 251–5

16 Ibid., 72, 256–8

17 Ibid., 275–6

18 Ibid., 280–3

19 Air 1/721/48/4

20 K.M. Molson, 'The Canadian JN-4,' *Canadian Aeronautics and Space Journal*, X, March 1964, 57–63

21 Ibid.; Ingoldsby to Fletcher, 10 July 1919, Curtiss Engineering Corporation, re JN4 nomenclature, 14 July 1919, DHist 76/290

22 Caddell to Hoare, 8 Feb. 1917, Hoare to Charlton, 27 March 1917, Air 1/721/48/5; F.H. Hitchins, 'Canadian Aeroplanes Limited,' Hitchins Papers, DHist 75/514, file G21

23 RFC Canada HQ to Hoare, 17 May 1917, Hoare to RFC Canada, 18 May 1917, Air 1/721/48/5; M.R. Riddell, 'The Development and Future of Aviation in Canada,' *Journal of the Engineering Institute of Canada*, II, March 1919, 200–9; Hitchins, 'Canadian Aeroplanes Limited'

24 Air 1/721/48/4

25 Gwatkin to Hoare, 27 Jan. 1917, Hoare to Gwatkin, 30 Jan., 17 Feb. 1917, HQ 6978-2-131, vol. 1, PAC, RG 24, vol. 2040

26 Hoare to DAO, 28 Jan. 1917, Hoare to Brancker, 28 July 1918, Air 1/721/48/5; Sullivan, *Aviation in Canada*, 135, 141; GOC MD 2 to Militia Council, 10 Feb. 1917, HQ 6978-2-131, vol. 1, PAC, RG 24, vol. 2040

27 Hoare to Charlton, 4 Feb. 1917, Air 1/721/48/5; Allen to RCAF Historical Section, 5 Dec. 1962, DHist 76/199

28 Hoare to Charlton, 12 March 1917, Air 1/721/48/5; Hoare to GOC MD 2, 30 Jan. 1917, Adjutant-General to GOC MD 2, 22 Feb. 1917, HQ 6978-2-131, vol. 1, PAC, RG 24, vol. 2040

29 Hoare to Charlton, 15 Feb., 27 March 1917, War Office to Governor General, 21 March 1917, Charlton to Hoare, 31 March 1917, Air 1/721/48/5

30 Hoare to Charlton, 4 May 1917, ibid.; Sullivan, *Aviation in Canada*, 180, 183

31 Hoare to Charlton, 4 May, 15 June 1917, Air 1/721/48/5; Air 1/721/48/4; Sullivan, *Aviation in Canada*, 162

32 Sullivan, *Aviation in Canada*, 156, 159, 162, 165

33 Gwatkin to Hoare, 22 Feb. 1917, HQ 6978-2-131, vol. 1, PAC, RG 24, vol. 2040; Hoare to Charlton, 12 and 27 March 1917, Hoare to DAO, 6 June 1917, Air 1/721/48/5; Air 1/721/48/4; Jones, *War in the Air*, V, 462.

34 Hoare to DAO, 6 June 1917, Hoare to Charlton, 25 April 1917, Air 1/721/48/5; Air 1/721/48/4

35 Hoare to Charlton, 1 and 15 June, 17 July, 25 Aug. 1917, Air 1/721/48/5; Great Britain, War Office, *Army List: September 1917* (London 1917); Pat O'Brien, *Outwitting the Hun: My Escape from a German Prison Camp* (New York 1918), 9; Allen to Director General of Supplies and Transport, 7 June 1917, HQ 6978-2-131, vol. 2, PAC, RG 24, vol. 2040; nominal roll, *Scotian* draft, July 1917, DHist 76/296

36 Hoare to Charlton, 11 May 1917, Air 1/721/48/5; *Globe* (Toronto), 18 Dec. 1916, 12; Hoare to Militia Council, 8 March 1917, Adjutant-General to Hoare, 16 March 1917, HQ 6978-2-131, vol. 1, PAC, RG 24, vol. 2040; Sullivan, *Aviation in Canada*, 147, 148, 312

37 Air 1/721/48/4; Allen to Charlton, 26 May 1917, Air 1/721/48/5; Sullivan, *Aviation in Canada*, 141, 142, 149
38 RFC recruiting material (Newfoundland), 'Flying Corps – General,' PARC box 490010, file M-25; *Daily Mail and Empire* (Toronto), 13 Feb. 1917, 7
39 Hoare to Charlton, 26 Dec. 1916, 20 April, 4 and 11 May 1917, Charlton to Hoare, 11 April 1917, Hoare to Drew, 26 Dec. 1917, Air 1/721/48/5
40 Foreign Office to Army Council, 31 Aug. 1914, CO 616/12
41 Perley Papers, PAC, MG 27 II D 12, vol. 6; Robert Laird Borden, *Robert Laird Borden: His Memoirs*, Henry Borden, ed. (Toronto 1938), II, 601–60; CO 616/12
42 Hoare to Charlton, 1 June 1917, Air 1/721/48/5
43 Hoare to War Office, 30 May 1917, ibid.
44 Hoare to Charlton, 1 June 1917, ibid.
45 Hoare to Charlton, 15 and 30 June, 28 Sept. 1917, ibid.
46 Hoare to Charlton, 30 June 1917, ibid.
47 Charlton to Hoare, 29 June 1917, Hoare to Charlton, 17 July, 26 Sept. 1917, 6 Feb. 1918, ibid.
48 Allen to Charlton, 13 April 1917, Hoare to Charlton, 20 and 25 April 1917, ibid.; Hoare to Allen, 27 Nov. 1962, Allen to RCAF Historical Section, 5 Dec. 1962, DHist 76/199; Hiram Bingham, *An Explorer in the Air Service* (New Haven 1920), 11–22
49 GOC MD 2 to Militia Council, 8 Feb. 1917 HQ 6978-2-131, vol. 1, PAC, RG 24, vol. 2040; Hoare to Charlton, 28 Feb., 12 and 27 March, 25 April, 1 June 1917, Air 1/721/48/5; Air 1/721/48/4
50 Hoare to War Office, 30 May 1917, Hoare to Charlton, 15 June 1917, Air 1/721/48/5; Hoare to War Office, 4 June 1917, War Office to Hoare, 8 June 1917, Air 2/166/RU4867
51 Hoare to War Office, 15 and 27 June 1917, War Office to Hoare, 28 June 1917, ibid.; Hoare to Charlton, 30 June 1917, Air 1/721/48/5
52 Hoare to War Office, 27 June 1917, Air 2/166/RU4867
53 Hoare to Allen, 27 Nov. 1962, DHist 76/199
54 Hoare to Squier, 12 July 1917, Hoare to Charlton, 17 July 1917, Squier to Hoare, 25 July 1917, War Office to Hoare, 23 July 1917, Air 2/166/RU4867; Hoare to Squier, 7 Jan. 1918, Air 2/166/RU4868; Roscoe to Chief Signal Officer, 6 May 1918, Air 2/166/RU4869
55 Roscoe to Chief Signal Officer, 6 May 1918, Air 2/166/RU4869; J. Sterling Halstead, 'A Mission to the Royal Flying Corps,' *U.S. Naval Institute Proceedings*, XCI, Feb. 1965, 78–94; Hoare to Charlton, 17 July, 4 Aug., 12 Sept., 9 Oct. 1917, Air 1/721/48/5; Air 1/721/48/4; Allen to RCAF Historical Section, 22 July, 5 Dec. 1962, DHist 76/199; Williams to DHist, 12 Aug. 1970, 24 Sept. 1972, Walter S. Williams biographical file, DHist; Squier to Hoare, 25 July 1917, Allen to Chief Signal Officer, 31 July 1917, Air 2/166/RU4867; United States, Department of the Army, Historical Division, *Order of Battle of the United States Land Forces in the World War (1917–19); Zone of the Interior* (Washington 1931–49), III, pt 2, 998–1078
56 Hoare to Charlton, 17 July, 4 Aug., 12 and 28 Sept., 9 Oct. 1917, Hoare to Drew, 15 Nov. 1917, Air 1/721/48/5; Air 1/721/48/4; Seymour to RCAF Historical Section, 28 Sept. 1962, Murton Adams Seymour biographical file, DHist; Sullivan, *Aviation in Canada*, 237

57 Hoare to War Office, 22 Oct. 1917, Hoare to Drew, 15 Nov., 26 Dec. 1917, Air 1/721/48/5; Air 1/721/48/4; Mitchell to Militia Council, 1 Feb. 1918, HQ 6978-2-131, vol. 5, PAC, RG 24, vol. 2041

58 Hoare to Drew, 15 Nov., 9 and 26 Dec. 1917, Air 1/721/48/5; Air 1/721/48/4; Roscoe to Chief Signal Officer, 6 May 1918, Air 2/166/RU4869; Hoare to Squier, 7 Jan. 1918, Air 2/166/RU4868

59 Hoare to Drew, 26 Dec. 1917, 14 Jan. 1918, Air 1/721/48/5; Sullivan, *Aviation in Canada*, 180–92, 243–4

60 Hoare to Squier, 5 Oct. 1917, 7 Jan. 1918, E.A. Deeds to Hoare, 25 Jan. 1918, Air 2/166/RU4868; Hoare to Roscoe, 5 April 1918, Roscoe to Chief Signal Officer, 6 May 1918, Air 2/166/RU4869; Hoare to Charlton, 22 Oct. 1917, Hoare to Chief Signal Officer, 5 Nov. 1917, Air 1/721/48/5; Sullivan, *Aviation in Canada*, 248

61 Sullivan, *Aviation in Canada*, 155–61, 288

62 Hoare to Charlton, 26 May 1917, Air 1/721/48/5; Air 1/721/48/4; Jones, *War in the Air*, V, 466n

63 Allen to RCAF Historical Section, 5 Dec. 1962, DHist 76/199; Sullivan, *Aviation in Canada*, 131

64 Sullivan, *Aviation in Canada*, 125–6, 131; Allen to Drew, 2 Feb. 1918, Air 1/721/48/5; K.M. Molson, 'The JN-4 (Can),' pt. I, *American Aviation Historical Society Journal*, XVII, winter 1972, 229–30

65 Air 1/721/48/4; Chief Recruiting Officer, RFC HQ, to MD 5, 30 Aug. 1917, MD 5 17-1-42 a, vol. 3, PAC, RG 24, vol. 4506

66 Chief Recruiting Officer, RFC HQ, to MD 5, 30 Aug. 1917, MD 5 17-1-42 a, vol. 3, PAC, RG 24, vol. 4506

67 Tompkins, 'Report on R.F.C. School of Military Aeronautics No. 4 Toronto, Canada,' (unpublished, Nov. 1917), DHist 112AH.001 (D7)

68 Allen to Drew, 2 Feb. 1918, Hoare to Drew, 6 Feb. 1918, Air 1/721/48/5; 'Minutes of Final Meeting of the Supervisory Board, British Commonwealth Air Training Plan, 16 April 1945,' App. 1, DHist 73/1558, vol. 10

69 'The Training Cycle and Cadet Experience in RFC/RAF Canada,' DHist 76/289; Halstead, 'Mission,' 93; M.C. Kinney, *I Flew A Camel* (Philadelphia 1972), 19

70 Gibbard to RCAF Historical Section, 8 March 1962, DHist 76/288

71 Air 1/721/48/4; Sullivan, *Aviation in Canada*, 20, 54

72 Bill Lambert, *Combat Report* (London 1973), 22

73 Halstead, 'Mission,' 88

74 Ibid.

75 Allen to Bureau of Naval Operations, USNA, RG 72, copy in DHist 112 AH.001 (D6)

76 *Times*, (Orillia), 24 May 1917

77 Ibid, 28 June 1917

78 Gibbard to RCAF Historical Section, 8 March 1962, DHist 76/288

79 Sullivan, *Aviation in Canada*, 76–82, 197–202

80 Ibid., 89; Hoare to Charlton, 9 and 22 Oct. 1917, Air 1/721/48/5

81 Hoare to Charlton, 9 and 22 Oct. 1917, Air 1/721/48/5; Hoare to Drew, 6 Feb., 9 April 1918, Hoare to Brancker, 29 Nov. 1918, ibid.; Hugh Halliday, 'Beamsville Story,' *CAHS Journal*, VII, fall 1969, 75; Sullivan, *Aviation in Canada*, 89–90, 180–94

82 'CFS Fighting Instruction Data No. 8,' Air 1/727/144/2; Smith-Barry, 'General Methods of Teaching Scout Pilots,' Air 1/728/163/3
83 Ibid.
84 Jones, *War in the Air*, V, 431
85 Burton to RCAF Historical Section, 10 May 1962, E.C. Burton biographical file, DHist
86 Jones, *War in the Air*, V, 430–1
87 Ibid., 430
88 Hoare to Drew, 26 March 1918, Air 1/721/48/5
89 Hoare to Air Ministry, 28 May 1918, ibid.; Sullivan, *Aviation in Canada*, 211–23
90 D. Clark, *Wild Blue Yonder: an Air Epic* (Seattle 1972), 42–4, 82; Cyprian Herbert Andrews biographical file, DHist; F.H. Ellis, *Canada's Flying Heritage* (Toronto 1954), 128
91 Ellis, *Canada's Flying Heritage*, 127
92 Halstead, 'Mission,' 88
93 RFC/RAF Canada, 'Reports of Aeroplane Accidents Resulting in Injury or Death,' 1917–18, Air 1/10/15/1/37
94 Sullivan, *Aviation in Canada*, 229
95 Ibid., 231; Department of National Defence, Air Service, 'Final Report of the Chief of the Air Staff to the Members of the Supervisory Board of the British Commonwealth Air Plan, 16 April 1945,' 40–1, DHist 033.013 (D2); Air 1/686/21/13/2252
96 Hoare to Gwatkin, 13 May 1918, HQ 6978-2-131, vol. 6, PAC, RG 24, vol. 2042; Denton to CGS, 14 June 1918, HQ 6978-2-131, vol. 7, ibid.; Minister of Justice to Governor-in-Council, 1 Nov. 1918, HQ 6978-2-131, vol. 9, ibid., vol. 2043; Hoare to Brancker, 28 July 1918, Air 1/721/48/5
97 Hoare to Brancker, 28 July 1918, Air 1/721/48/5
98 Allen to RCAF Historical Section, 5 Dec. 1962, DHist 76/199; Denton to MD 2, 26 June, 3 Aug., 6 Sept., 4 Nov. 1918, 2 MD 34-3-105–22, vol. 1 and vol. 2, PAC, RG 24, vol. 4345
99 PC 1850, 27 July 1918; PC 2584, 23 Oct. 1918; PC 2658, 30 Oct. 1918. See also Militia Orders and instructions from Department of Justice in HQ 6978-2-131, vols. 6–9, PAC, RG 24, vols. 2042, 2043; and Military Service Sub-Committee, Militia Department to Military Service Branch, Department of Justice, 1 Nov. 1918, Denton to CGS, 31 Oct. 1918, HQ 6978-2-131, vol. 9, ibid.
100 Air Ministry to Minister of Militia, 23 Nov. 1918, ibid.
101 Air Council minutes, 40th meeting, 18 July 1918, Air 6/13; Air Ministry, 'Proposals as to Canadian Units and for the Transfer of Training Units in Canada to Canadian Government,' conference minutes, 29 July 1918, Air 2/109/A2271
102 Gibson, 'The Taking Over by Canada of the RAF Organization in Canada,' 2 Oct. 1918, Kemp Papers, PAC, MG 27 II D 9, vol. 143
103 Gibson, 'The Activities of the Royal Air Force in Canada,' 20 July 1918, OSM 10-9-27, vol. 1, PAC, RG 9 III, vol. 80
104 Ross to DAO, 8 Aug. 1918, Drew to Secretary Air Council, 16 Aug. 1918, McAnally to Perley, 31 Aug. 1918, Air 2/109/A2271
105 Allen to RCAF Historical Section, 22 July 1962, DHist 76/199
106 Hoare to Brancker, 28 July, 15 Aug. 1918, Air 1/721/48/5
107 Hearson to Hoare, 27 Sept. 1918, Brancker to Hoare, 30 Sept. 1918, ibid.

108 Mitchell to Secretary, Militia Council, 17 Nov. 1917, 18 Feb., 12 April, 9 Oct. 1918, HQ 6978-2-131, vol. 3, vol. 5, vol. 6, and vol. 9, PAC, RG 24, vol. 2041-3; 'RAF Units in Canada,' *Cadet Wing Review*, I, Dec. 1918, 8

109 'RAF Units in Canada,' *Cadet Wing Review*, I, Dec. 1918, 8

110 Militia HQ Routine Orders, no 257, 2 Feb. 1918, AAG Department of Militia and Defence to all GOCs, 25 Feb. 1918, HQ 6978-2-131, vol. 4, PAC, RG 24, vol. 2041; Gwatkin to Hoare, 3 Oct. 1917, 7 Jan. 1918, HQ 6978-2-131, vol. 5, ibid.; AAG to DOC MD 2, 27 June 1918, HQ 6978-2-131, vol. 7, ibid., vol. 2042; Militia HQ Routine Orders, no 913, 13 Aug. 1918, HQ 6978-2-131, vol. 8, ibid.; F.R.G. Hoare to C.G. Hoare, 18 June 1918, Air 1/721/48/5; Sullivan, *Aviation in Canada*, 148–9

111 Hoare to Gwatkin, 23 Oct. 1917, Hoare to War Office, 23 Oct. 1917, F.R.G. Hoare to C.G. Hoare, 18 June 1918, Hoare to Hearson, 15 Oct. 1918, Air 1/721/48/5; Records and Recruiting Office, RAF HQ to CGS, 18 Jan. 1919, Militia HQ Ottawa to OMFC London, 28 Jan. 1919, HQ 6978-2-131, vol. 9, PAC, RG 24, vol. 2043; 'Sailing List of Canadian Officers in RAF,' nd, PAC, RG 9 III, vol. 4613, folder 16, file 5; Sullivan, *Aviation in Canada*, 146

112 Sullivan, *Aviation in Canada*, 151; 'Strength of RAF in Various Theatres,' 31 Oct. 1918, Air 1/2296/209/77/16; *Globe*, 23 Nov. 1918, 9; 26 Nov. 1918, 8; 9 Dec. 1918, 8; *Toronto World*, 14 Dec. 1918, 4; Seymour to RCAF Historical Section, 28 May 1962, Murton Adams Seymour biographical file, DHist; Hawksford to CGS, 10 June 1919, HQ 6978-2-131, vol. 10, PAC, RG 24, vol. 2043

113 Sullivan, *Aviation in Canada*, 108–24; Air 1/721/48/4; PAC, RG 24, vols. 2041, 2043

114 F.H. Hitchins, 'Canada's Pioneer Air Mail,' *Roundel*, XI, June 1959, 18–22, R.K. Malott, 'Who'll Carry the Mail?' *Sentinel*, IV, June 1968, 44–5; Ellis, *Canada's Flying Heritage*, 136–9; R.K. Malott, 'Toronto-Ottawa Airmail,' *CAHS Journal*, VII, fall 1969, 84; *Gazette* (Montreal), 19 Nov. 1918, 4; 21 Nov. 1918, 5; 22 Nov. 1918, 4; 24 Nov. 1918, 7; 25 Nov. 1918, 9; *Daily Mail and Empire*, 22 June 1918, 22; 24 June 1918, 9; 25 June 1918, 4; Merritt to Borden, 26 Aug. 1918, Borden Papers, PAC, MG 26 H, vol. 74, 38829

115 Molson, 'The JN-4 (Can),' pt I; Carnegie, *History of Munitions Supply*, 189–90; Sullivan, *Aviation in Canada*, 47, 54

116 K.M. Molson, 'Aircraft Manufacturing in Canada During the First Great War,' *Canadian Aeronautical Journal*, V, Feb. 1959, 49; Riddell, *Aviation in Canada*, 200–9; Carnegie, *History of Munitions Supply*, 191–2

117 K.M. Molson, 'The JN-4 (Can),' pt II, *American Aviation Historical Society Journal*, XVIII, summer 1973, 84–7; Lloyd Lott to Gibson, 19 Feb. 1919, OSM 10-9-27, vol. 1, PAC, RG 9 III, vol. 80; *Globe*, 30 Jan. 1919, 1; 31 Jan. 1919, 6

118 DAO to Air Board, biweekly reports of pilots graduating, Dec. 1916–March 1918, Air 1/131/15/40/222; Sullivan, 'RAF Can. Output of Pilots and Observers,' 75

119 Records and Recruiting Office, RAF Canada to CGS, 18 and 25 Jan. 1919, HQ 6978-2-131, vol. 9, PAC, RG 24, vol. 2043; 'Strength of RAF in Various Theatres,' 31 Oct. 1918, Air 1/2296/209/77/16; Sullivan, *Aviation in Canada*, 75; Air 1/686/21/13/2252

120 Chambers to Allen, 28 Feb. 1918, HQ 6978-2-131, vol. 4, PAC, RG 24, vol. 2041

121 Gwatkin to Allen, 4 March 1918, ibid.; Allen to RCAF Historical Section, 5 Dec. 1962, DHist 76/199

122 *Toronto Star*, 16 May 1918, 8

123 Ibid., 25 May 1918, 10

124 Ibid., 12 June 1918, 10
125 Ibid., 3 June 1918, 10

CHAPTER 5: ORIGINS OF NAVAL AIRPOWER

1 Correspondence between Air Department and Director of Transports on Grand
Fleet seaplane carrier acquisition, 6 Sept. to 5 Oct. 1914, Air 1/631/17/122/36;
Great Britain, Parliament, *Parliamentary Papers*, 1919, XXXIII, paper 200, 'Navy
Losses,' 3; Sir Walter Raleigh, *The War in the Air: being the Story of the Part played
in the Great War by the Royal Air Force*, I (London 1922), 367

2 Raleigh, *War in the Air*, I, 368; Churchill to CAS, 21 May 1919, Air 2/166/
MR 17724/7; Great Britain, Admiralty, *History of the Development of Torpedo Aircraft*
(London 1919), 5

3 Great Britain, Admiralty Training and Staff Duties Division, *Naval Staff Monographs (Historical)*, XII: *Home Waters*, Part III ([London] 1925), 133–9, 174. See
also Sir Julian Corbett, *Naval Operations*, II: *From the Battle of the Falklands to the
Entry of Italy into the War in May, 1915* (London 1929), 52–3.

4 Raleigh, *War in the Air*, I, 229, 283–4, 360–1; C.F. Snowden Gamble, *The Story of a
North Sea Air Station: Being some Account of the Early Days of the Royal Flying Corps
(Naval Wing) and of the Part Played Thereafter by the Air Station at Great Yarmouth and Its
Opponents during the War, 1914–1918* (London 1928), 81–3, 87–8, 100, 107; Harald
Penrose, *British Aviation: the Pioneer Years, 1903–1914* (London 1967), 543; Sir
Reginald Bacon, *The Life of Lord Fisher of Kilverstone* (London 1929), II, 161;
Arthur J. Marder, *From the Dreadnought to Scapa Flow: the Royal Navy in the Fisher
Era, 1904–1919*, II: *The War Years: to the Eve of Jutland* (London 1965), 93–7;
John Arbuthnot Fisher, Baron Fisher, *Fear God and Dread Nought: the Correspon-
dence of Admiral of the Fleet Lord Fisher of Kilverstone*, III: *Restoration, Abdication,
and Last Years, 1914-1920*, Arthur J. Marder, ed. (London 1959), 346–8

5 Memoranda to DAD and ADAD, 2 Feb. and 2 March 1915, Air 1/147/15/65;
Christopher Draper, *The Mad Major* (Letchworth, Herts. 1962), chaps. 3, 4; Richard
Bell Davies, *Sailor in the Air: the Memoirs of Vice-Admiral Richard Bell Davies*
(London 1967), chaps. 8–13; Sir Arthur Longmore, *From Sea to Sky, 1910–1945*
(London 1946), chaps. 1–6; H.A. Jones, *The War in the Air: being the Story of the
Part played in the Great War by the Royal Air Force*, II (London 1928), 336–7, 371n;
Charles Rumney Samson, *Fights and Flights* (London 1930), *passim*; 'Naval Air
Service – Reorganization,' *Admiralty Monthly Orders*, 112, (London, 1 March 1915)

6 Winston S. Churchill, *The World Crisis, 1911–1918* (London [1938]), I, 265; Jones,
War in the Air, III (London 1931), 73–6, 78–9

7 Douglas H. Robinson, *The Zeppelin in Combat: a History of the German Naval Airship Division, 1912–1918* (London 1966), 58–64, 69–71

8 RN Air Station Westgate, report on air raid 16–17 May 1915, 18 May 1915, Air
1/295/15/226/143

9 'Air Raid on London on 31st May,' Air 1/569/16/15/140

10 Jones, *War in the Air*, III, 106–7, 153–7

11 Davies, *Sailor in the Air*, 94; Samson, *Fights and Flights*, 3–14; Great Britain,
Admiralty Training and Staff Duties Division, *Naval Staff Monographs (Historical)*,
XI: *Home Waters*, Part II ([London] 1924), 12–13, 153

12 Samson, *Fights and Flights*, 45, 52–3; Sueter memorandum, 1 Sept. 1914, reports of Gerrard and Grey, 23 Sept. and 17 Oct. 1914, Air 1/671/17/128/1; Kenneth Poolman, *Zeppelins over England* (London 1960), app. A, 198–200

13 Samson, *Fights and Flights*, 167–8; reports of attack on Friedrichshafen, 21 and 28 Nov. 1914, Air 1/671/17/128/2

14 Jones, *War in the Air*, II, 350–3; Robinson, *Zeppelin in Combat*, 77; Great Britain, Admiralty Training and Staff Duties Division, *Naval Staff Monographs (Historical)*, XIII: *Home Waters*, Part IV ([London] 1925), 237; Longmore to DAD, 8 June 1915 and enclosures, Air 1/52/15/9/38; memorandum to DAD, ADAD, nd but c June 1915, ibid.

15 Davies, *Sailor in the Air*, 108–10; Samson, *Fights and Flights*, 144, 150–2; Davies telegram, 6 Nov. 1914, Air Department orders, 11 Nov. 1914, Samson to Sueter, 6 Dec. 1914, Air 1/671/17/128/2

16 Samson's Despatch, 27 Nov. 1914, Air 1/671/17/128/2; Samson, *Fights and Flights*, 169–70, 184–5, 188

17 J.M. Bruce, *British Aeroplanes, 1914–1918* (London 1957), 269; Penrose, *British Aviation*, 545–7; Samson *Fights and Flights*, 174–5, 182–3, 188–9; Samson to Admiralty, 6 Feb. 1915, cited in Samson, *Fights and Flights*, 191–4; Air Department orders, 11 Nov. 1914, Dunkirk reports, Nov. 1914, Air 1/671/17/128/2; Davies, *Sailor in the Air*, 113

18 Operations Order AD no 15, 21 June 1915, Air 1/147/15/73; Great Britain, Admiralty Training and Staff Duties Division, *Naval Staff Monographs (Historical)*, VI: *The Dover Command*, I ([London] 1922), 23–5; 'Anti-submarine Campaign,' nd., 27–9, Air 1/675/21/13/1385; Longmore to DAS, 30 Sept. 1915, Air 1/149/15/95/2

19 Lambe to Bacon, 20 Aug., 11 Sept., 16 Nov. 1915, Air 1/69/15/9/112

20 Admiralty to Vice-Admiral, Dover, 13 Dec. 1915, ibid.

21 Robin Higham, *The British Rigid Airship, 1908–1931: a Study in Weapons Policy* (London 1961), 126–7; Churchill, *The World Crisis*, I, 265–6; Churchill memorandum, 18 Jan. 1915, memorandum to DAD, 3 April 1915, *The World Crisis*, IV, app. II, 1411–12. For more on naval aviation at this time see also Jones, *War in the Air*, II, 358–62; Sir Reginald Bacon, *The Dover Patrol, 1915–1917* (New York 1919), I, 73, II, 249–52, 267; Marder, *Dreadnought to Scapa Flow*, II, 46, III: *Jutland and After (May 1916–December 1916)* (London 1966), 43–4, 56–7; Jellicoe to Admiralty, 29 July 1915, Adm 137/1953, copy in Marder Papers, PRO 333, DHist M56; John Rushworth Jellicoe, Viscount Jellicoe of Scapa, *The Grand Fleet, 1914–1916: Its Creation, Development and Work* (New York 1919), 71, 450; John R. Cuneo, *Winged Mars*, II: *The Air Weapon, 1914–1916* (Harrisburg, Penn. 1947), 297, 301; Freiherr Treutsch von Buttlar-Brandenfels, 'Die Aufgaben der Luftschiffe in Dienste der Marine,' in W. von Eberhardt, ed., *Unsere Luftstreitkräfte, 1914–1918* (Berlin 1930), 111–12, DHist SGR I 196, Set 31

22 Beatty to Admiralty, 25 June 1915, Adm 137/2133, copy in Marder Papers, PRO 284, DHist M47; Fisher to Jellicoe, 28 Feb. 1915, in Fisher, *Fear God and Dread Nought*, III, 161

23 Marder, *Dreadnought to Scapa Flow*, II, 297, 301, 413–14; M.P.A. Hankey, 1st Baron Hankey, *The Supreme Command, 1914–1918* (London 1961), I, 335; Sir Percy Scott, *Fifty Years in the Royal Navy* (London 1919), 292; R. MacGregor Dawson, 'The Cabinet Minister and Administration: A.J. Balfour and Sir Edward Carson at the

Admiralty, 1915–17,' *Canadian Journal of Economics and Political Science*, IX, Feb. 1943, 1–38

24 Jones, *War in the Air*, II, 355

25 'R.N. Air Service,' *Admiralty Monthly Orders*, 542 (London, 1 October 1915, but effective 1 August 1915); Samson, *Fights and Flights*, 291; cf Higham, *British Rigid Airship*, 77–8 (his interpretation is based partly on a Sueter interview, 13 July 1959); Jones, *War in the Air*, II, 381

26 Sykes to Admiralty, 9 July 1915, Air 1/669/17/122/788; Jones, *War in the Air*, II, 24, 33–5; Great Britain, Admiralty Gunnery Division, *Report of the Committee Appointed to Investigate the Attacks Delivered on and the Enemy Defences of the Dardanelles Straits, 1919* ([London] 1921), 94, 516

27 *Report of the Committee ... on ... the Dardanelles*, 94, 518, 520; Samson, *Fights and Flights*, 221–4; Sir Ian Hamilton, *Gallipoli Diary* (London 1920), I, 110–11; Hogg to War Office, 9 May 1915, Air 1/2119/207/72/2; Strain interview, 30 May 1923, Air 1/725/101/2; Gerrard, 'Personal Notes,' Air 1/2301/212/7

28 *Report of the Committee ... on ... the Dardanelles*, 30–1, 115–17, 177, 503–10; Hogg to War Office, 9 May, 10, and 25 June 1915, Air 1/2119/207/72/2; Kerby, 'War Experiences,' 19 Aug. 1922, Air 1/2386/228/11/10

29 Kerby, 'War Experiences'; Jones, *War in the Air*, II, 64–5

30 Jones, *War in the Air*, II, 57–8, 62–72; Gerrard, 'Personal Notes,' Air 1/2301/212/7; Kerby, 'War Experiences,' Air 1/2386/228/11/10; *Report of the Committee ... on ... the Dardanelles*, 206–9, 211

31 Jones, *War in the Air*, II, 72–3, 37ln; minute [Vaughan-Lee] to First Lord, 20 Nov. 1915, Sykes to Vice-Admiral Commanding Eastern Mediterranean Squadron, 21 Oct. 1915, Air 1/654/17/122/503; 'R.N.A.S.-Organization of Units,' *Confidential Admiralty Interim Orders*, 715, (London, 9 May 1916)

32 Samson, *Fights and Flights*, 278, 286; Jones, *War in the Air*, II, 72–5

33 Enclosure on aeroplanes, nd, Air 1/649/17/122/422; Jones, *War in the Air*, V (London 1935), 370–1, 389–90

34 Jones, *War in the Air*, III, 1–14; R.V. Dodds, 'The Königsberg Incident,' *Roundel*, XV, Nov. 1963, 12–14; H.J. Arnold biographical file, DHist

35 Jones, *War in the Air*, II, 378–9

36 Davies to DAS, 26 Feb. 1916, Air 1/437/15/294/1

CHAPTER 6: 1916: DIFFUSION AND MISDIRECTION

1 Arthur J. Marder, *From the Dreadnought to Scapa Flow: the Royal Navy in the Fisher Era, 1904–1919*, II: *The War Years: to the Eve of Jutland* (London 1965), 420

2 'Air Attack and London,' *Flight*, 17 Dec. 1915, 979; H.A. Jones, *The War in the Air: being the Story of the Part played in the Great War by the Royal Air Force*, III (London 1931), 135–9, 157

3 Ireland to Director of Air Staff, 20 Dec. 1915, Air 1/659/17/122/615

4 Conclusions of 71st Meeting of War Committee, 15 Feb. 1916, in S.W. Roskill, ed., *Documents relating to the Naval Air Service*, I: *1908–1918* (London 1969), 304

5 Joint War Air Committee, extracts from paper Air 4, 3 March 1916, ibid., 309–10

6 Derby to Asquith, 3 April 1916, Air 1/2312/221/39

7 Balfour, 'A Last Word on the Proposed Air Board,' 8 May 1916, Air 1/2311/221/15
8 Trenchard's notes regarding co-operation with the RNAS at Dunkirk in bombing operations, 25 Feb. 1916, Air 1/921/204/5/888; JWAC conclusions of 28 Feb. 1916, Haig to CIGS, 22 March 1916, Air 1/2265/209/70/1; JWAC conclusions of 6 March 1916, Air 1/270/15/226/115; RNAS return for period 16–31 Dec. 1916, Air 1/629/17/120
9 'Distribution of Airplane and Seaplane Flights,' 20 April 1916, Air 1/146/15/61
10 Ibid.; Tudor minute, 21 March 1916, in Roskill, ed., Documents ... Naval Air Service, I, 333; RNAS return for period 16–31 Dec. 1916, Air 1/629/17/120
11 Breadner to his mother, 2 and 20 Feb. 1916, Breadner Papers, DHist 74/707, files 7 and 9. See generally Breadner letters, February-[July] 1916, ibid., files 12–18.
12 'The Hornets of Zeebrugge: Annotated Extracts from the War Diary of Seeflugstation Flanders I, 1914–1918,' Cross & Cockade Journal, XI, spring 1970, 9
13 Flight Commander, 1 Wing to Senior Officer, RNAS Dover, 27 Jan. 1916, Air 1/630/17/122/31; Sir Reginald Bacon, The Dover Patrol, 1915–1917 (London nd), I, 92; Report of Flight Commander, 1 Wing, 1 Feb. 1916 in Dover Patrol, II, 538–9
14 Owen Thetford, British Naval Aircraft since 1912 (London 1962), 66–7, 272–7
15 CO RN Seaplane Station Dunkirk to SO RNAS Dunkirk, 25 April 1916, Air 1/631/17/122/50; Jones, War in the Air, II (London 1928), 430–1
16 'Hornets of Zeebrugge,' 13–14; 5 Wing general reports, Dover/Dunkirk, late April 1916, Air 1/39/15/9/4; Tooke's report, 2 May 1916, report of operations, 4 May 1916, Air 1/47/15/9/27
17 No 5 Wing, RNAS, raid on Ghistelles Aerodrome, special report, 19 May 1916, Air 1/64/15/9/85; C.F. Snowden Gamble, The Story of a North Sea Air Station: Being some Account of the Early Days of the Royal Flying Corps (Naval Wing) and of the Part Played Thereafter by the Air Station at Great Yarmouth and Its Opponents during the War, 1914–1918 (London 1928), 161
18 No 1 Wing fortnightly report, 14–27 May 1916, Air 1/39/15/9/4; Bacon to Commodore, Dunkirk, 31 May 1916, Air 1/71/15/9/125
19 Jones, The War in the Air, II, 434
20 Quoted in ibid.
21 Deutschland, Marine Archiv, Der Krieg in der Nordsee, Band VI: Der Krieg in der Nordsee von Juni 1916 bis Frühjahr 1917, by Walter Gladisch (Der Krieg zur See 1914–1918; Berlin 1937), 214, DHist SGR I 196, Set 35
22 RNAS return for period 16–31 May 1916, Air 1/629/17/120; Lambe letter, 21 May 1916, Vaughan-Lee minute, nd, Air 1/634/17/122/98
23 Jones, War in the Air, II, 393–4
24 Roskill, ed., Documents ... Naval Air Service, I, 319–21; Sueter minute, 26 Feb. 1916 and passim, Air 1/648/17/122/381
25 Marder, Dreadnought to Scapa Flow, II, 389–91; Jellicoe to Admiralty, 8 May 1916, Air 1/648/17/122/380
26 Charles Rumney Samson, Fights and Flights (London 1930), 298; 'The History of the Ottoman Air Force in the Great War: the Reports of Maj. Erich Sarno,' Cross & Cockade Journal, XI, summer 1970, 128–31
27 Douglas H. Robinson, The Zeppelin in Combat: a History of the German Naval Airship Division, 1912–1918 (London 1966), 130–2; Great Britain, Admiralty Training and

Staff Duties Division, *Naval Staff Monographs (Historical)*, XV: *Home Waters*, Part VI ([London] 1926), 56–9

28 *Naval Staff Monographs*, XV, 160 ff; Marder, *Dreadnought to Scapa Flow*, II, 421

29 John Rushworth Jellicoe, Earl Jellicoe of Scapa, *The Jellicoe Papers: Selections from the Private and Official Correspondence of Admiral of the Fleet Earl Jellicoe of Scapa*, I: *1893–1916*, A. Temple Patterson, ed. (London 1966), 232–7

30 Marder, *Dreadnought to Scapa Flow*, II, 424–5; Robinson, *Zeppelin in Combat*, 141

31 Great Britain, Admiralty Training and Staff Duties Division, *Naval Staff Monographs (Historical)*, XVI: *Lowestoft Raid, 24th–25th April, 1916* ([London] 1926), 28–9; Vaughan-Lee minute, nd, Hyde-Thompson minute, 24 May 1916, Air 1/149/15/104

32 *Naval Staff Monographs*, XV, 196–7; G.E. Livock, *To the Ends of the Air* (London 1973), 33–4; Report of Commanding Officer, *Engadine*, 9 May 1916, Air 1/436/15/279/1; Marder, *Dreadnought to Scapa Flow*, II, 428; Robinson, *Zeppelin in Combat*, 146; Department of Naval Construction, Admiralty, 'Aircraft Carriers, Part I, 1914–1918,' Jan. 1918, Air 1/2103/207/31

33 Great Britain, Admiralty Training and Staff Duties Division, *Grand Fleet Battle Orders*, I: *August 1914 to May 31st, 1916* ([London], July 1919), 246

34 Ibid.

35 Marder, *Dreadnought to Scapa Flow*, II, 445–6; *Campania* and *Engadine* at Jutland, extract from Godfrey Lectures, copy in Marder Papers, DHist M21; *Grand Fleet Battle Orders*, 258

36 Robinson, *Zeppelin in Combat*, 147–9; Livock, *To the Ends of the Air*, 31

37 Jones, *War in the Air*, II, 407–8

38 *Campania* and *Engadine* at Jutland, Marder Papers, DHist M21

39 Arthur J. Marder, *From the Dreadnought to Scapa Flow: the Royal Navy in the Fisher Era, 1904–1919*, III: *Jutland and After (May 1916–December 1916)* (London 1966), 205; *Aeroplane*, 9 Aug. 1916, 220; L. Tomkinson, 'Occasional Return of Flights from Deck of Pilots in *Campania* for the Year 1916 (Period May 29th to Oct. 7th),' Captain, *Campania*, to Vice-Admiral Commanding Second Battle Squadron, 13 June 1916, Air 1/733/187/4

40 Minute of 24 June 1916, Air 1/648/17/122/380

41 Minute of 30 June 1916, ibid.

42 Tudor minute, 6 July 1916, Admiralty to Jellicoe, 14 July 1916, ibid.

43 Robinson, *Zeppelin in Combat*, 157–8; Marder, *Dreadnought to Scapa Flow*, III, 236, 242–3; Jellicoe to Fisher, 23 Aug. 1916, quoted in Marder, *Dreadnought to Scapa Flow*, III, 248; Jones, *War in the Air*, II, 419

44 Vaughan-Lee memorandum, 16 Sept. 1916, Air 1/667/17/122/754; Jellicoe to Admiralty, 14 Oct. 1916, Vaughan-Lee memorandum, 25 November 1916, Air 1/651/17/122/447; Marder, *Dreadnought to Scapa Flow*, III, 248–9

45 Marder, *Dreadnought to Scapa Flow*, II, 335

46 C.V. Usborne, *Blast and Counterblast: a Naval Impression of the War* (London 1935), 96

47 Jones, *War in the Air*, V (London 1935), 370 ff; 'History of the Ottoman Air Force in the Great War ...' *Cross & Cockade Journal*, XI, summer 1970, 143–4

48 RNAS returns for periods 16–31 May and 16–31 Dec. 1916, Air 1/629/17/120

49 James E. Edmonds, *Military Operations: France and Belgium, 1916*, I (London 1932), 32–3

50 Dunkirk Command fortnightly summary, 1–15 July 1916, Air 1/39/15/9/4
51 Sproatt to Commanding Officer, 5 Wing, RNAS Coudekerque, 9 July 1916, C.B. Sproatt biographical file, DHist
52 Ibid.
53 Jones, *War in the Air*, II, 440–1; Dunkirk Command fortnightly summary, 1–15 July 1916, Air 1/39/15/9/4
54 Dunkirk Command fortnightly summary, 1–15 Aug. 1916
55 Ibid., 16–30 Sept. 1916; Trenchard, 'Scheme for Future Bombing Operations,' 7 Aug. 1916, Air 1/921/204/5/888
56 Bacon, *Dover Patrol*, I, 94–5; Dunkirk Command fortnightly summary, 1–15 Sept. 1916, Air 1/39/15/9/4
57 Great Britain, Admiralty, *Report of Committee on the Belgian Coast* (London 1920), 99, 101; *Der Kreig*, VI, 214; Jones, *War in the Air*, II, 445
58 'RNAS Victories 1915–1916,' Air 1/81/15/9/200; Dunkirk Command fortnightly summary, 16–31 Oct. 1916, Air 1/39/15/9/4
59 Marder, *Dreadnought to Scapa Flow*, III, 257–8
60 Thetford, *British Naval Aircraft*, 254–5; Dunkirk Command fortnightly summary, 1–15 Nov. 1916, Air 1/39/15/9/4
61 RNAS bombing statistics, Air 1/271/15/226/118; R. Scheer, *Germany's High Sea Fleet in the World War* (New York 1934), 189
62 Breadner Papers, DHist 74/707, file 30
63 'RNAS Dunkerque Command; HUNS., 1915–1918,' Air 1/81/15/9/200
64 'First Report of the Air Board,' 23 Oct. 1916, Air 1/2311/221/17
65 Ibid.
66 Report of meeting, Director of Air Staff's Room, 22 Oct. 1916, memorandum of Admiralty members of Air Board, 26 Oct. 1916, Air 1/2265/209/70/1; summary of discussions at 140th and 141st Meetings of the War Committee, 27–28 Nov., Roskill, ed., *Documents ... Naval Air Service*, 428–9
67 Marder, *Dreadnought to Scapa Flow*, III, 269–70
68 RNAS returns for periods 16–31 May and 16–31 Dec. 1916, Air 1/629/17/120
69 Ibid., 16–31 Dec. 1916
70 'Anti-Submarine Campaign,' I, 33, Air 1/675/21/13/1385; report of captain, 'C.10,' 9 Sept. 1916, Air 1/423/252/2
71 David Lloyd George, *War Memoirs of David Lloyd George* (London 1933–6), IV, 1854; extracts from minutes of War Cabinet meeting, 22 Dec. 1916, Roskill, ed., *Documents ... Naval Air Service*, 443–4
72 Harvey (Air Board) to Admiralty, 12 Dec. 1916, and reply, 16 Dec. 1916, Air 1/637/17/122/142
73 Director of Air Services to Naval Ottawa, 13 Sept. 1916, Air 1/147/15/68; Director, Air Division, 'Appreciation of British Naval Effort RNAS Aircraft Operations,' Nov. 1918, Air 1/308/15/226/191

CHAPTER 7: ALTERNATIVE ROLES, 1917–18

1 Paine to DAS, 30 Jan. 1917, Air 1/657/117/122/594; W.A.B. Douglas, 'Canadians who Served in the RNAS,' DHist 74/32; H.A. Jones, *The War in the Air: being the*

Story of the Part played in the Great War by the Royal Air Force, III (London 1931), 282–5

2 S.W. Roskill, ed., *Documents relating to the Naval Air Service*, I: *1908–1918* (London 1969), 455–63, 468–73

3 J.K. Waugh, 'War Experiences,' 29 Sept. 1925, Air 1/2388/228/11/67

4 Canadian Bank of Commerce, *Letters from the Front; Being a Record of the Part Played by Officers of the Bank in the Great War, 1914–1919*, C.L. Foster and W.S. Duthie, eds. (Toronto [1920–1]), I, 221–2

5 'Anti-submarine Review, Home Waters,' Air 1/677/21/13/1902; Sir Walter Raleigh, *The War in the Air: being the Story of the Part played in the Great War by the Royal Air Force*, I (London 1922), 465; Owen Thetford, *British Naval Aircraft since 1912* (London 1962), 77, 182–7; H.F. King, *Armament of British Aircraft, 1909–1939* (London 1971), 181–2

6 'Aircraft Carriers,' pt I, Jan. 1919, Air 1/2103/207/31; Jones, *War in the Air*, IV (London 1934), 5–14, 26–44; 'Air requirements of the Grand Fleet: proposed alterations to HMS *Furious*,' Air 1/648/17/122/383; Oxburgh to Nerney, 22 Jan. 1930, Air 1/724/78/2

7 Thetford, *British Naval Aircraft*, 290–1; Murray F. Sueter, *Airmen or Noahs: Fair Play for Our Airmen* (London 1928), 53–4; Arthur J. Marder, *From the Dreadnought to Scapa Flow: the Royal Navy in the Fisher Era, 1904–1919*, IV: *1917; Year of Crisis* (London 1969), 21–2, 236–40; Admiralty to Beatty, 20 Oct. 1917, Air 1/641/17/122/232; 'Letter ... 30 July 1918 ... Beatty to the Admiralty,' Roskill, ed., *Documents ... Naval Air Service*, 684–6; Jones, *War in the Air*, IV, 4–44; Douglas H. Robinson, *The Zeppelin in Combat: a History of the German Naval Airship Division, 1912–1918* (London 1966), 245–6; W. von Gronau, 'German Seaplane Stations, 1917,' app. III, Air 1/677/21/13/1901

8 S.W. Roskill, 'The U-Boat Campaign of 1917 and Third Ypres,' *Journal of the Royal United Service Institution*, CIV, Nov. 1959, 440–2; Marder, *Dreadnought to Scapa Flow*, IV, 205–6

9 Marder, *Dreadnought to Scapa Flow*, IV, 205–6; Roskill, 'The U-Boat Campaign'

10 'Royal Naval Air Service, Home Waters 1917, Part III, Belgian Coast Operations 1917,' Air 1/677/21/13/1930

11 'Fortnightly Summary of Operations,' 1–14 Feb. 1917, Air 1/39/15/9/5; Deutschland, Marine Archiv, *Der Krieg in der Nordsee*, Band VI: *Der Krieg in der Nordsee von Juni 1916 bis Frühjahr 1917*, by Walter Gladisch (Der Krieg zur See, 1914–1918; Berlin 1937), 214, DHist SGR I 196, Set 35

12 Lambe to Wing Commanders, 17 March 1917, Air 1/69/15/9/114; Lambe to Trenchard, enclosing 'Remarks on general policy on employment of aircraft on the Belgian coast during the present situation,' 15 April 1917 and reply, 16 April 1917, Air 1/71/15/9/125

13 'Belgian Coast Operations 1917,' Air 1/677/21/13/1930; 'Notes on Recent [7 Oct. 1916] Visit to Dunkirk,' attached to Edmonds to Williamson, 12 Oct. 1916, Air 1/299/15/226/150 pt I

14 P.S. Fisher, 'Report of Bomb Raid,' 4 April 1917, Air 1/63/15/9/82; 'Belgian Coast Operations 1917,' Air 1/677/21/13/1930; 'The Hornets of Zeebrugge: Annotated Extracts from the War Diary of Seeflugstation Flanders I, 1914–1918,' *Cross &*

Cockade Journal, XI, spring 1970, 9–28; CO Seaplane Station Dunkirk to Lambe, 19 June 1917, Air 1/641/17/122/219; Lambe to Bacon, 10 June 1917, Air 1/71/15/9/124

15 'Daily Report No 7 Squadron, No 5 Wing RNAS,' 23–26 April 1917, Air 1/43/15/9/17; CO 7 Squadron to CO 5 Wing, 10 May 1917, Air 1/63/15/9/82

16 Lambe to Bacon, 8 May 1917, Air 1/660/17/122/622; Lambe to Bacon, 16 May 1917, Air 1/637/17/122/142; Game to RFC Brigades, 22 May 1917, Air 1/913/204/5/851; 4 Wing report of operations, May 1917, Lambe to Bacon, 7 June 1917, Air 1/640/17/122/203; reports of conference, 31 May 1917, Air 1/299/15/226/150 pt I; 5 Squadron, report of bomb raid, 9 June 1917, Air 1/43/15/9/15

17 Bacon to Lambe, 15 July 1917, Air 1/69/15/9/114

18 Jones, *War in the Air*, IV, 146–50

19 Trenchard to Brigades, 23 July 1917, Air 1/69/15/9/114

20 Lambe to Wings, 23 July 1917, ibid.

21 Lambe to Bacon, 12 July 1917, Lambe to Wing Commanders, 19 July 1917, ibid.

22 Ibid.

23 Raymond Collishaw, 'Memories of a Canadian Airman,' *Roundel*, XVI, June 1964, 19

24 W.A.B. Douglas, taped interview with C.B. Sproatt, 22 Dec. 1968, transcript, DHist 74/43

25 'Royal Naval Air Service fortnightly communiqué no. 1,' Air 1/39/15/9/5; Jones, *War in the Air*, IV, 98; F.H. Hitchins, 'Canadian Airmen: World War I,' nd, DHist 73/1551

26 Jones, *War in the Air*, IV, 86; Sir Reginald Bacon, *The Dover Patrol, 1915–1917* (London nd), I, 167–70; 'IV Naval Wing, Report of Operations during Quarter ending September 1917,' Air 1/436/15/291/1

27 Combat reports, 3 Sept. 1917, Air 1/42/15/9/13; CO 5 Wing to Lambe, 3 Sept. 1917, Air 1/63/15/9/84; RNAS communiqué no 5, 2 Sept. 1917, Air 1/39/15/9/5; Sproatt interview, DHist 74/43

28 'Report of Operations Dunkerque Seaplane Station and Seaplane Defence Flight ... 21–22 September 1917,' Air 1/47/15/9/28; 'The Hornets of Zeebrugge,' 23; RNAS communiqué no 6, 22 Sept. 1917, Air 1/39/15/9/5

29 Erich Gröner, *Die deutschen Kriegsschiffe, 1815–1945* (München 1966), I, 364

30 Jones, *War in the Air*, IV, 100; R.H. Mulock Papers, document 68, DHist

31 Haig to Bacon, 4 Oct. 1917, Trenchard to DCGS, 4 Nov. 1917, Air 1/71/15/9/125; 'List of machines which took part in raid 28–29th October 1917,' CO 5 Wing Headquarters, RNAS to Senior Officer 'I' 1917, Air 1/63/15/9/84

32 CO 5 Wing to Lambe, 19 Dec. 1917, combat report, 19 Dec. 1917, Air 1/64/15/9/85

33 Jones, *War in the Air*, IV, 88; Lambe to Wing Commanders, 19 July 1917, Air 1/69/15/9/114; minute, Bacon to the Secretary of the Admiralty, 28 Sept. 1917, appended to Lambe to Bacon, 24 Sept. 1917, Lambe to Bacon, 31 Dec. 1917, Air 1/642/11/122/238; Admiralty to Vice-Admiral Dover Patrol, 4 Jan. 1918, Air 1/71/15/9/124

34 'RNAS Units – Renumbering of,' DAO to Air Council, 9 March 1918, Air 1/913/204/5/851; Lambe to Trenchard, 13 Jan. 1918, Air 1/69/15/9/114; Marder, *Dreadnought to Scapa Flow*, IV, 347–8

35 Sir Rogers Keyes, *The Naval Memoirs of Admiral of the Fleet Sir Roger Keyes*, II: *Scapa Flow to the Dover Straits, 1916–1918* (London 1935); Bacon, *Dover Patrol*, II, 520–77

36 Dunkirk résumé of operations, July–Dec. 1917, Air 1/629/17/117/1–11; Great Britain, Admiralty, Naval Staff, Gunnery Division, *Report of Committee Appointed to Examine the German Defences on the Belgian Coast, 1919* (np, July 1920), 17; Childers and Morris, 'Report of the Aircraft Bombing Committee,' 12 March 1919, Air 1/2115/207/56/1

37 Great Britain, Admiralty Training and Staff Duties Division, *Naval Staff Monographs (Historical)*, XIX: *Home Waters, Part IX, May 1917–July 1917* (London 1939), app. J, 'Auxiliary Patrol Strength, July 1917'

38 'RNAS Anti-Submarine Report,' Dec. 1917, Air 1/2314/223/11/7; Jones, *War in the Air*, IV, 47–9

39 F.W. Walker, 'War and Post War Experiences,' nd, Air 1/2389/228/11/106

40 [F.H. Hitchins], 'Air Vice Marshal Frank S. McGill,' nd, McGill biographical file, DHist

41 Marder, *Dreadnought to Scapa Flow*, IV, 52; Robert M. Grant, *U-Boats Destroyed: the Effect of Anti-Submarine Warfare* (London 1964), 42

42 'Submarine Patrols,' Admiralty to Lambe, 12 Sept. 1917, Air 1/71/15/9/124; South-West Patrol orders, 28 Aug. 1917, Air 1/644/17/122/292

43 Admiralty to Bacon, 9 June 1917, Air 1/73/15/9/159; Jones, *War in the Air*, IV, 48n, 53–4; Walker, 'War and Post War Experiences,' Air 1/2389/228/11/106

44 F.D.L. Smith, 'Canadians in the Air, Major Douglas Hallam,' Sept. 1918, Hallam biographical file, DHist; P.I.X. [T.D. Hallam], *The Spider Web: the Romance of a Flying-Boat War Flight* (London 1919)

45 P.I.X., *Spider Web*, 39–40

46 Ibid., 47

47 Ibid., 48

48 Ibid., 38, 42, 49–51; CO Felixstowe to DAS, 26 April 1917, Air 1/661/17/122/639

49 Jones, *War in the Air*, IV, 54; *Naval Staff Monographs*, XIX, 61–2, 114

50 'RNAS Anti-Submarine Report,' June, July, Aug. 1917, Air 1/2313/223/11/1–3; P.I.X., *Spider Web*, 78–9; Wing Captain, SW Group to C-in-C Plymouth, 23 Aug. 1917, Air 1/644/17/122/295; newspaper clipping, 'Floated Hours after Airplane Sank in Sea, Flight Lt. Walter J. Sussan of War Flying,' nd, Sussan biographical file, DHist

51 Marder, *Dreadnought to Scapa Flow*, IV, 102–65

52 Ibid., 270–81; 'Anti-Submarine Review Home Waters,' Air 1/677/21/13/1902

53 Marder, *Dreadnought to Scapa Flow*, IV, 276–92; 'Comments by Captain Cone, U.S.N. on Memorandum No. 12,' nd, Air 1/273/15/226/124 pt I

54 'RNAS Anti-Submarine Report,' Dec. 1917, Air 1/2314/223/11/7

55 Wing Commander Portsmouth Group to C-in-C Portsmouth, 1 Jan. 1918, Air 1/645/17/122/305; Colin Waugh, 'North Sea Flier, Flt. Sub. Lt. W.A. Davern,' *Cross & Cockade Journal*, XVI, autumn 1975, 195–204; P.I.X., *Spider Web*, 156–61; 'RNAS Anti-Submarine Report,' Oct. 1917, Air 1/2314/223/11/5

56 'RNAS Anti-Submarine Report,' Oct., Nov., Dec. 1917, Feb., March 1918, Air 1/2314/223/11/5–7, 9–10

57 Galpin to CO Great Yarmouth, 14 May 1917, Air 1/660/17/122/623; C.F. Snowden Gamble, *The Story of a North Sea Air Station: Being some Account of the Early Days of the Royal Flying Corps (Naval Wing) and of the Part Played Thereafter by the Air*

Station at Great Yarmouth and Its Opponents during the War, 1914–1918 (London 1928), 237–8

58 Snowden Gamble, *North Sea Air Station*, 242, 245–6; Robinson, *Zeppelin in Combat*, 236–8

59 Hobbs and Dickey to CO Felixstowe, 14 June 1917, Air 1/637/17/122/156

60 Snowden Gamble, *North Sea Air Station*, 246–9; Robinson, *Zeppelin in Combat*, 241

61 Snowden Gamble, *North Sea Air Station*, 254–6

62 'Geschichte der Luftwaffe bis zum Versailler Diktat,' in Hermann Franke, ed., *Handbuch der neuzeitlichen Wehrwissenschaften* (Berlin 1939), III, 177–8, DHist SGR I 196, Set 38; W. von Gronau, 'German Seaplane Stations, 1917,' app. III, Air 1/677/21/13/1901

63 von Gronau, 'German Seaplane Stations'; Peter Gray and Owen Thetford, *German Aircraft of the First World War* (London 1962), 68–71, 117–27

64 'Monthly Report of Home Stations,' July 1917, Air 1/627/17/115/1; Jones, *War in the Air*, IV, 64

65 Nicholl to CO Great Yarmouth, 10 Sept. 1917, Air 1/413/15/243/3; Snowden Gamble, *North Sea Air Station*, 263–71; Robinson, *Zeppelin in Combat*, 241–3

66 Douglas to CO Felixstowe, 2 Oct. 1917, Air 1/641/17/122/221; 'The Hornets of Zeebrugge'

67 'Policy to be Followed as Regards Development and Use of Torpedo-carrying Seaplanes,' 20 Dec. 1916, Roskill, ed., *Documents … Naval Air Service*, 434–43; S.W. Roskill, *Naval Policy between the Wars*, I: *The Period of Anglo-American Antagonism, 1919–1929* (London 1968), 361n

68 'Extracts from Admiralty letter, 3 February 1917, to the C-in-C, Coast of Scotland et al,' Roskill, ed., *Documents … Naval Air Service*, 468; Admiralty to Rear-Admiral Commanding British Adriatic Squadron, 27 Feb. 1917, Sueter to Commodore Commanding British Adriatic Force, 20 Sept. 1917, British C-in-C Mediterranean to Admiralty, 15 Dec. 1917, Air 1/649/17/122/417; George Meager, *My Airship Flights, 1915–1930* (London 1970), 66–9; 'RNAS Anti-Submarine Report,' Dec. 1917, Air 1/2314/223/11/7; A. Lloyd-Taylor, 'Air Communications in World War I,' *The Communicator*, XX, summer 1971

69 Brian P. Flanagan, 'History of the Ottoman Air Force: the Reports of Major Serno; Part 3, The Tide of Battle Turns, 1917,' *Cross & Cockade Journal*, XI, autumn 1970, 224–44; Bruce Robertson, 'Mudros Incident,' *Air Pictorial*, XXXIII, March 1971, 101; Eastern Mediterranean Squadron, 'Resumé of Operations,' July-Nov. 1917, Air 1/627/17/114/1–3; S.J. Wise, 'Most Thrilling Flight,' *Popular Flying*, Aug. 1934, 241–2; Jones, *War in the Air*, V (London 1935), 407–10

70 Wing Commander HQ RNAS, British Aegean Squadron to DAS, 26 Jan. 1918, Air 1/271/15/226/121; Wing Commander HQ RNAS, British Aegean Squadron, to Rear-Admiral Commanding, British Aegean Squadron, 27 Jan. 1918, Air 1/661/17/122/659; Arthur J. Marder, *From the Dreadnought to Scapa Flow: the Royal Navy in the Fisher Era, 1904–1919*, V: *Victory and Aftermath, January 1918–June 1919* (London 1970), 12–20

71 'Appreciation of British Naval Effort,' Nov. 1918, Air 1/308/15/226/191

72 Collishaw, 'Memories,' 21

CHAPTER 8: AVIATION AND THE VICTORY OVER THE SUBMARINE

1 Mark Kerr, *Land, Sea and Air: Reminiscences of Mark Kerr* (London 1927), 294; 'Memorandum on Certain Lines of Policy Regulating the Conduct of the Air Ministry,' 23 May 1918, Air 1/2313/221/48

2 Quoted in Arthur J. Marder, *From the Dreadnought to Scapa Flow: the Royal Navy in the Fisher Era, 1904–1919*, V: *Victory and Aftermath, January 1918–June 1919* (London 1970), 134

3 Ibid., 136

4 H.A. Jones, *The War in the Air: being the Story of the Part played in the Great War by the Royal Air Force*, IV (London 1934), 34

5 Ibid., 38

6 A/S report, March 1918, Air 1/2105/207/41; S.W. Roskill, ed., *Documents relating to the Naval Air Service*, I: *1908–1918* (London 1969), 647–9

7 'Report of Interview with Mr. Garnet Dunn, 16 September 1969,' Dunn biographical file, DHist; W.G. Moore, *Early Bird* (London 1963), 141; 'Flight Operations at Sea: World War One,' W.S. Lockhart biographical file, DHist

8 'Flight Operations at Sea'; W.F. Dickson, 'War Experiences, 1914–1918,' Dec. 1927, Air 1/2389/228/11/110

9 Dickson, 'War Experiences'

10 Interview with W.S. Lockhart, nd, Lockhart biographical file, DHist

11 'Aircraft carriers, part I, 1914–1918,' Air 1/2103/207/31; Moore, *Early Bird*, 122

12 Richard Bell Davies, *Sailor in the Air: the Memoirs of Vice-Admiral Richard Bell Davies* (London 1967), 173; [L.] Tomkinson, 'An Analysis of the Grand Fleet Orders, 1914–1918,' Air 1/733/187/2

13 C.F. Snowden Gamble, *The Story of a North Sea Air Station: Being some Account of the Early Days of the Royal Flying Corps (Naval Wing) and of the Part Played Thereafter by the Air Station at Great Yarmouth and Its Opponents during the War, 1914–1918* (London 1928), 380–2

14 Marder, *Dreadnought to Scapa Flow*, V, 75

15 Jones, *War in the Air*, VI (London 1937), 351

16 Peter Gray and Owen Thetford, *German Aircraft of the First World War* (London 1962), 75–8

17 P.I.X. [T.D. Hallam], *The Spider Web: the Romance of a Flying-Boat War Flight* (London 1919), 220–9

18 Home Waters report, 10 May 1918, Air 1/456/15/312/46; Douglas H. Robinson, *The Zeppelin in Combat: a History of the German Naval Airship Division, 1912–1918* (London 1966), 317

19 Robinson, *Zeppelin in Combat*, 316–18

20 Leckie to CO Great Yarmouth, 31 May 1918, Air 1/416/15/243/5 pt II

21 Snowden Gamble, *North Sea Air Station*, 394–6

22 Ibid., 396; Leckie to CO Great Yarmouth, 4 June 1918, Air 1/458/15/312/70

23 Moore, *Early Bird*, 126–8; 'Bombing Attack on Tondern,' 19 July 1918, Air 1/455/15/312/44; Robinson, *Zeppelin in Combat*, 321

24 Robinson, *Zeppelin in Combat*, 321

25 Patrol reports, Air 1/458/15/312/44

26 Quoted in S.W. Roskill, 'The Destruction of Zeppelin L.53,' *United States Naval Institute Proceedings*, L X X X V I, Aug. 1960, 76

27 Ibid., 76–8

28 Jones, *War in the Air*, V I, 374–5

29 Keyes to Admiralty, 31 March 1918, Air 1/69/15/9/114

30 Fortnightly summary, 1–15 April 1918, Air 1/39/A H/15/9/6; Roger John Brownlow Keyes, 1st Baron Keyes, *The Naval Memoirs of Admiral of the Fleet Sir Roger Keyes*, I I: *Scapa Flow to the Dover Straits, 1916–1918* (London 1935), 226–43

31 Keyes, *Memoirs*, I I, 254–5; fortnightly summary, 1–15 April 1918, Air 1/39/A H/15/9/6

32 Fortnightly summary, 16–30 April 1918, Air 1/39/A H/15/9/6; Marder, *Dreadnought to Scapa Flow*, V, 60–2

33 Keyes, *Memoirs*, I I, 162

34 Sykes to G O C R A F in France, 14 April 1918, Lambe to Keyes, 28 April 1918, Air 1/69/15/9/114

35 Lambe to Keyes, 28 April 1918, ibid.

36 Salmond-Mulock correspondence, 2–10 May 1918, Air Ministry to distribution, 16 May 1918, Air 1/913/204/5/852; Keyes-Admiralty correspondence, 6–20 May 1918, Air 1/308/15/226/193

37 Admiralty to Air Ministry, 22 May 1918, ibid.; Keyes to Admiralty, 28 May 1918, Air 1/69/15/9/114; Air Ministry to G O C R A F in the Field, 4 May 1918, C-in-C B E F to War Office, 14 May 1918, Robinson to Admiralty, 28 May 1918, Cubitt to C-in-C B E F, 3 June 1918, Dill to Vice-Admiral Dover Patrol, 4 June 1918, G O C No 5 Group to G O C R A F in the field, 5 and 6 June 1918, Air 1/913/204/5/852; Jones, *War in the Air*, V I, 393

38 Jones, *War in the Air*, V I, 393; fortnightly summary, 16–31 May 1918, Air 1/39/A H/15/9/6

39 Fortnightly summary, 1–15 June 1918, Air 1/39/A H/15/9/6; G O C No 5 Group to G H Q Army, 29 June 1918, Air 1/58/5/9/62

40 Walter v. Eberhardt, ed., *Unsere Luftstreitkräfte, 1914–1918* (Berlin 1930), 124–6, DHist S G R I 196, Set 66

41 Keyes to Admiralty, 28 June 1918, Air 1/69/15/9/114; fortnightly summary, 1–15 August 1918, Air 1/39/A H/15/9/6

42 Fortnightly summary, 16–31 Aug. 1918, Air 1/39/A H/15/9/6; Eberhardt, ed., *Unsere Luftstreitkräfte*, 126

43 Air combat reports, 5, 16, 24 Sept. 1918, Air 1/59/15/9/65; fortnightly summary, 1–15 Sept. 1918, Air 1/39/A H/15/9/6

44 Fortnightly summaries, summer 1918, Air 1/39/A H/15/9/6; Lambe to O Cs, 13 June 1918, Air 1/58/15/9/65

45 Keyes to G H Q, 21 Sept. 1918, Air 1/913/204/5/852; Keyes, *Memoirs*, I I, 369–70; H.H. Gilbert, 'Memories of the War,' *Cross & Cockade Journal*, X V I I I, summer 1977, 132; fortnightly summaries, Sept.–Oct. 1918, Air 1/39/A H/15/9/6

46 Fortnightly summaries, April–Oct. 1918, Air 1/39/A H/15/9/6

47 Ibid.; R A F committee report, pt I, 12 March 1919, Air 1/2115/207/56/1

48 Lambe to O C 82 Wing, 15 Aug. 1918, Air 1/73/15/9/150

49 No 217 Squadron report on submarine attack, 12 Aug. 1918, Air 1/456/15/312/51

50 Marder, *Dreadnought to Scapa Flow*, V, 30–5

51 Longmore to Air Council, 10 April 1918, Air 1/457/15/312/55; report of Edward, 29 April 1918, Air 1/278/15/226/126 pt II; 'Report on Present Position of Royal Air Force in Mediterranean,' Aug. 1918, Air 1/287/15/226/137 pt II; Scarlett, 'Progress of RAF Units in Adriatic,' memorandum, 27 July 1918, Air 1/286/15/226/137 pt I; 'Enemy aircraft in the Adriatic,' serial no 2, Aug. 1918, Air 1/454/15/312/31; Admiralty to Air Ministry, 1 Nov. 1918, Air 1/291/15/226/140 pt II; A.B. Shearer biographical file, DHist

52 Jones, *War in the Air*, VI, 326–8; report of bombing operations, 2 Oct. 1918, Air 1/456/15/312/53; Arthur M. Longmore, *From Sea to Sky, 1910–1945* (London 1946), 81

53 'Enemy Aircraft in the Adriatic Sea,' Aug. 1918, Air 1/454/15/312/31; extracts from 'Offensive Anti-Submarine Operations,' [Oct. 1918], Air 1/291/15/226/140 pt II

54 Mediterranean District RAF report, 24 May–14 June 1918, Air 1/458/15/312/74; 'Report on Present Position of Royal Air Force in Mediterranean,' Aug. 1918, 1–2, 8–10, Air 1/287/15/226/137 pt II

55 Jones, *War in the Air*, VI, 323–4; R.D. Layman, 'Robert W. Peel, RNAS; an Aegean Airman,' *Cross & Cockade Journal*, IX, winter 1968, 351–65; *Globe and Mail* (Toronto), 21 June 1969, 6; T.H. Blair biographical file, DHist

56 Daily report, 24 Aug. 1918, Air 1/456/15/312/46; Bicknell to Dodds, 23 July 1964, F.R. Bicknell biographical file, DHist

57 Vyvyan to Pink, 1 July 1918, Air 1/463/15/312/131; Mediterranean District RAF report, 24 May–14 June 1918, Air 1/458/15/312/74; Gregson, 'War Experiences,' nd, Air 1/2387/228/11/42; organization and strength, Mediterranean district, Nov. 1918, Air 1/473/15/312/176; Longmore, *From Sea to Sky*, 81

58 'Report on Present Position of Royal Air Force in Mediterranean,' Aug. 1918, Air 1/287/15/226/137 pt II

59 Egypt Group monthly statistical reports, April–Oct. 1918, Air 1/455/15/312/35

60 Marder, *Dreadnought to Scapa Flow*, V, 86–7

61 Ibid., 77–81; Sir Henry Newbolt, *History of the Great War: Naval Operations* (London 1920–31), V, 337

62 Marder, *Dreadnought to Scapa Flow*, V, 86–105

63 Groves, 'In Shore Patrol Work for Aeroplanes,' 18 March 1918, Air 1/6A/AH/4/43

64 Scarlett to distribution, 13 April 1918, Admiralty-Air Council correspondence, April–May 1918, Air 1/465/15/312/153; 'Memorandum on the Organisation of the Royal Air Force in the United Kingdom,' [March 1918], Air 1/450/15/312/5; Air Ministry to distribution, 27 May 1918, Air 1/73/15/9/144

65 Richardson holographic report, 10 May 1918, Air 1/477/15/312/231; CO No 18 Group to VA East Coast of England, 26 Aug. 1918, Air 1/421/15/249/1; report of Naval Staff (Air Division), 8 June 1918, Air 1/465/15/312/149; Admiralty to VA East Coast of England, 30 July 1918, Air 1/285/15/226/136 pt II

66 Jones, *War in the Air*, VI, 340; R.D. Layman, 'Allied Aircraft vs German Sub-marines, 1916–1918,' *Cross & Cockade Journal*, XI, winter 1970, 299; R.M. Grant, *U-boats Destroyed: the Effect of Anti-Submarine Warfare, 1914–1918* (London 1964), 128–9; 'Report of attack on Enemy Submarine,' 3 Sept. 1918, Air 1/456/15/312/51

67 Fisher memorandum, Oct. 1918, Air 1/643/17/122/272

68 Williamson to DAD, 22 Sept. 1918, Air 1/289/15/226/139 pt I; details of attacks, 14 July and 24 Aug. 1918, Air 1/465/15/312/149; 'Report of Attack on Enemy Submarine,' 29 Sept. 1918, Air 1/456/15/312/51

69 Reports of No 10 Group, Sept. 1918, Air 1/411/15/241/4 pt II; reports of No 9 Group, June–Oct. 1918, Air 1/486/15/312/272 and Air 1/486/15/312/274; Brig-Gen No 9 Group to C-in-C Plymouth, 7 July 1918, Air 1/413/15/242/1; attack report, 3 June 1918, Air 1/490/15/312/282; report of attack on 26 and 27 July 1918, Air 1/420/15/246/1

70 Nicholson to Air Ministry, 5 July 1918, Air 1/284/15/226/136 pt I; 'Report of Committee Appointed to Review the Whole Position as regards Aircraft North of 57° North Latitude' [16 August 1918], Air 1/643/17/122/262; Grant, *U-boats Destroyed*, 107

71 Snowden Gamble, *North Sea Air Station*, 367; SO 1 Air to DAD, 30 Sept. 1918, Air 1/291/15/226/140 pt I

72 Great Britain, Admiralty, Historical Section, *The Defeat of the Enemy Attack on Shipping, 1939–1945: a Study of Policy and Operations* (London 1957), IA, 8

73 'Notes on Anti-Submarine Conference held on the 28th August 1918,' Air 1/447/15/303/38; airship tactical diagrams, [June 1918], Air 1/465/15/312/149; *Defeat of the Enemy Attack on Shipping*, IA, 9

74 *Defeat of the Enemy Attack on Shipping*, IA, 9; Marder, *Dreadnought to Scapa Flow*, V, 94–5

75 Scarlett to DOD(M), 16 April 1918, Scarlett memorandum, 22 April 1918, Scarlett minute, 19 May 1918, Air 1/277/15/226/126 pt I; Lambe to Keyes, 13 Jan. 1918, Air 1/72/15/9/141; minutes of CINO and CNO, Dec. 1916 and Jan. 1917, Air 1/656/17/122/555; Great Britain, Admiralty, Historical Section, 'Draft of A/C v U-Boats in WW I in Home Waters, 1917–1918,' nd, and 'Anti-Submarine Measures in World War I,' nd, copies in Marder Papers, DHist M18 and M20

76 *Defeat of the Enemy Attack on Shipping*, IA, 9–10

77 Roskill, ed., *Documents ... Naval Air Service*, 670–1

78 Admiralty to Air Ministry, 18 July 1918, Robinson to War Cabinet, 13 Aug. 1918, Geddes to War Cabinet, 31 Aug. 1918, CAS notes on Admiralty memorandum, [Sept. 1918], extracts from minutes of Air Policy Committee's 7th meeting, 5 Sept. 1918, Air 1/17/15/1/85; Admiralty to Air Ministry, 8 Aug. 1918, Air 1/643/17/122/257; Wemyss to Beatty, 10 Aug. 1918, Wester Wemyss Papers, copy in Marder Papers, DHist M12

79 H.H. Smith, *A Yellow Admiral Remembers* (London 1932), 319–20; Bell Davies, *Sailor in the Air*, 180–2

80 Robert M. Grant, *U-boat Intelligence, 1914–1918* (London 1969), 160–5

81 *The Picton Gazette*, 1 Aug. 1969 (anniversary insert dated July 1969, 14); Delamere to Dodds, 17 May 1965, Delamere biographical file, DHist; Snowden Gamble, *North Sea Air Station*, 427–8

82 Roskill, ed., *Documents ... Naval Air Service*, 715–33

1 Douglas H. Robinson, *The Zeppelin in Combat: a History of the German Naval Airship Division, 1912–1918* (London 1966), 34

2 Ibid., 50, 52–6

3 Quoted in ibid., 67

4 Ibid., 92–3, 378

5 H.A. Jones, *The War in the Air: being the Story of the Part played in the Great War by the Royal Air Force*, III (London 1931), app. III, 'Statistics of German Air Raids on Great Britain, 1914–1916'; Robinson, *Zeppelin in Combat*, 103–9

6 S.W. Roskill, ed., *Documents relating to the Naval Air Service*, I: *1908–1918* (London 1969), 283–4

7 Ibid., 294–5. See also AA defences, transfer to War Office, Dec. 1915 to Feb. 1916, Air 1/2316/223/19/24.

8 Board of Invention and Research, 'Report of Sub-Committee for Aeroplanes on Night Flying of Aeroplanes,' 14 Sept. 1915, Air 1/147/15/72; Jones, *War in the Air*, III, 154–5; Davies to DAS, 26 Feb. 1916, Air 1/437/15/294/1

9 Vaughan-Lee memorandum, 3 March 1916, Air 1/147/15/72

10 Kiggell, minute 20 to report on Zeppelin raid of 13–14 Oct. 1915, 10 Nov. 1915, Air 1/573/16/15/153

11 Board of Invention and Research, 'Report of Sub-Committee for Aeroplanes on Night Flying of Aeroplanes,' 14 Sept. 1915, Air 1/147/15/72; report and minutes on Zeppelin raid, 13–14 Oct. 1915, Air 1/573/16/15/153; 'Instructions Regarding the Aerial Defence of the United Kingdom,' 1 March 1916, Air 1/621/16/15/366

12 Robinson, *Zeppelin in Combat*, 120–8; Jones, *War in the Air*, III, 135–6, 141–2; reports on air raid, 31 Jan.–1 Feb. 1916, Air 1/573/16/15/156

13 Dalton to Secretary of the Admiralty, 7 Feb. 1916, Air 1/573/16/15/156; 'On the Aircraft Debate,' *Aeroplane*, 23 Feb. 1916, 297–320; 'The House of Lords on Aircraft,' *Aeroplane*, 23 Feb. 1916, 324–6

14 Vaughan-Lee memorandum, April 1916, Air 1/300/15/226/151 pt I

15 Reports on air raid on Hull, 5–6 March 1916, Air 1/574/16/15/160; Robinson, *Zeppelin in Combat*, 131–6; Jones, *War in the Air*, III, 188–94; 'Report on Air Raid, March 31, 1916,' Air 1/295/15/226/143 pt I; GHQ HF(1), 'Report on the action taken by the London Anti-Aircraft Defences against Zeppelin Airship (L15) on the night of 31st March, 1916,' Air 1/575/16/15/162 pt II; C.F. Snowden Gamble, *The Story of a North Sea Air Station: Being some Account of the Early Days of the Royal Flying Corps (Naval Wing) and of the Part Played Thereafter by the Air Station at Great Yarmouth and Its Opponents during the War, 1914–1918* (London 1928), 171

16 Maude to DAS, 2 April 1916, Air 1/295/15/226/143 pt I; Philip Joubert de la Ferté, *The Fated Sky* (London 1952), 60–1

17 'Royal Naval Air Service Report,' 3 April 1916, Air 1/212/15/226/29

18 Minutes of 2nd and 12th Air Board meetings, 24 May and 15 June 1916, Air 6/1

19 DAO to GHQ Home Forces, 11 July 1916, Air 1/612/16/15/300A; minutes of 20th Air Board meeting, 8 Aug. 1916, Air 6/2; Jones, *War in the Air*, III, 165–7

20 Jones, *War in the Air*, III, 168, 170

21 Quoted in Robinson, *Zeppelin in Combat*, 165–6

22 Ibid., 153–5

23 Air raid, 31 July–1 Aug. 1916, Air 1/579/16/15/175; air raids, 31 July–1 Aug., 2–3 Aug., 8–9 Aug. 1916, Air 1/295/15/226/143 pt I; RNAS action in air raids, Aug. 1916, Air 2/124/B10908; air raid, 24–25 Aug. 1916, Air 1/581/16/15/180 pt II;

Robinson report, 3 Sept. 1916, Air 1/582/16/15/181 pt III; Robinson, *Zeppelin in Combat*, 172–5; Jones, *War in the Air*, III, 227–30

24 Quoted in Robinson, *Zeppelin in Combat*, 192

25 Tempest's report, 2 Oct. 1916, Air 1/585/16/15/185; Tempest's account, 15 Sept. 1920, Imperial War Museum, copy in Tempest biographical file, DHist

26 Tempest's account, 15 Sept. 1920. See also Murray F. Sueter *Airmen or Noahs: Fair Play for our Airmen* (London 1928), 18–19; Tempest to Dodds, 5 April 1964, W.J. Tempest biographical file, DHist.

27 Jones, *War in the Air*, III, 238–43; Brophy report, 27–28 Nov. 1916, Air 1/586/16/15/188 pt I

28 Robinson, *Zeppelin in Combat*, 204–33

29 Watkins report, 17 June 1917, Air 1/589/16/15/200

30 Pritchard report, 21 Oct. 1917, Air 1/596/16/15/217 pt I; Robinson, *Zeppelin in Combat*, 265–80

31 Raymond H. Fredette, *The Sky on Fire: the First Battle of Britain, 1917–1918, and the Birth of the Royal Air Force* (New York 1966), 34–7

32 Peter Gray and Owen Thetford, *German Aircraft of the First World War* (London 1962), 128–32

33 Ernst von Hoeppner, *Deutschlands Krieg in der Luft* (Leipzig 1921), 112, DHist SGR I 196, Set 3c

34 Minutes of 13th Air Board meeting, 11 Dec. 1916, Air 6/3; Holt to HD Squadron Commanders, 'Day Defence against Hostile Aeroplane Raids,' 18 Jan. 1917, Admiralty to GHQ Home Forces, 18 Feb. 1917, Air 1/647/17/122/361; Jones, *War in the Air*, V (London 1935), 4–8, 11–12

35 RNAS communiqué, 'Air Raid, 25th May, 1917,' Air 1/588/16/15/197

36 DCAS, The Nore, to DAS, 5 June 1917, Air 1/647/17/122/367; air raid, 5 June 1917, Air 1/588/16/15/198

37 'The First Big Aeroplane Raid,' *Aeroplane*, 30 May 1917, 1364

38 Jones, *War in the Air*, V, 22–5; minutes of 154th War Cabinet meeting, 5 June 1917, Cab 23/3; minutes of War Office conference, 31 May 1917, Air 1/614/16/15/318

39 Hoeppner, *Deutschlands Krieg in der Luft*, 111–12

40 Minutes of 100th Air Board meeting, 14 June 1917, Air 6/8; 'Circular No. 131' and air raid, 13 June 1917, police summary 'up to 10 July 1917,' Air 1/589/16/15/199

41 Minutes of 163rd War Cabinet meeting, Cab 23/3; Jones, *War in the Air*, V, app. IV, 479–81

42 RNAS, 'Aeroplane Raid, 4th July 1917,' Air 1/590/16/15/201; Fredette, *Sky on Fire*, 69–71

43 McCudden report, 7 July 1917, Air 1/590/16/15/202

44 Hedges, 'Air Raid July 7th 1917,' 8 July 1917, ibid.; reports of air raid, 7 July 1917, Air 1/646/17/122/360; Fredette, *Sky on Fire*, 75–84

45 Jones, *War in the Air*, V, 38–42; First Report of the Committee on Air Reorganization and Home Defence against Air Raids, nd, Air 1/609/16/17/275; Jones, *War in the Air*, V, app. VI, 487–91

46 Shaw memorandum, 5 Aug. 1917, Air 1/609/16/15/275; E.B. Ashmore, *Air Defence* (London 1929), 36–7, 39, 41–4

47 Kerby report, 13 Aug. 1917, Air 1/640/17/122/197; RNAS supplementary communiqué, air raid, 12 Aug. 1917, Air 1/591/16/15/204; Fredette, *Sky on Fire*, 95–100

48 Fredette, *Sky on Fire*, 107; RNAS supplementary communiqué, air raid, 22 Aug. 1917, Air 1/591/16/15/206; Kingsford, Kerby, and Hervey reports, 22 Aug. 1917, Air 1/296/15/226/143 pt II

49 Hoeppner, *Deutschlands Krieg in der Luft*, 112

50 French to War Office, 3 Sept. 1917, Air 1/129/15/40/201; air raid, 3–4 Sept. 1917, Air 1/592/16/15/208

51 Minutes of 228th War Cabinet meeting, 5 Sept. 1917, Cab 23/4; Smuts memorandum, 6 Sept. 1917, Jones, *War in the Air*, V, app. VII, 491–3

52 Ashmore, *Air Defence*, 54–6; taped interview with A.E. Godfrey, 2 Nov. 1972, transcript, 32–3, Godfrey biographical file, DHist

53 Air raid, 24 Sept. 1917, Air 1/593/16/15/210; Higgins, 'Report on Zeppelin Raid, 24–25th September, 1917,' Air 1/593/16/15/211; air raid, 28–29 Sept. 1917, Air 1/594/16/15/213; 39 HD Squadron report, 29–30 Sept. 1917, Air 1/594/16/15/214; Higgins, 'Report on Action taken by the Royal Flying Corps during Hostile Aeroplane Raid on Sept 30th,' 1 Oct. 1917, Air 1/595/16/15/215; air raid, 1–2 Oct. 1917, Air 1/595/16/15/216; Fredette, *Sky on Fire*, 137–48

54 Jones, *War in the Air*, V, 87–8; minutes of 243rd War Cabinet meeting, 2 Oct. 1917, Cab 23/4. The Haig-Robertson correspondence is in Air 1/522/16/12/5.

55 Air raid, 6 Dec. 1917, Air 1/598/16/15/221

56 Rogers, 'Combats in the Air,' 12 Dec. 1917, Air 1/1828/204/202/19

57 Fredette, *Sky on Fire*, 173–6; Murlis-Green report, 18 Dec. 1917, Air 1/598/16/15/222; Ashmore, *Air Defence*, 74

58 'Report on Bombs Dropped in London during Raids of 28/29th and 29/30th January 1918,' Air 1/562/16/15/65; air raid, 16–17 Feb. 1918, Air 1/600/16/15/226; Higgins' reports on action taken by 6 Brigade RFC during air raids, 16–17 and 17–18 Feb. 1918, Air 1/36/15/1/235; Godfrey report, 7 March 1918, 78 Squadron report, 8 March 1918, Air 1/601/16/15/229

59 Robinson, *Zeppelin in Combat*, 297–8

60 Intelligence officer, Tees Garrison, report, 13 March 1918, Air 1/601/10/15/231; Naval Staff (Ops Div), 'Action taken by Aeroplane Contingents,' 13 April 1918, Air 1/36/15/1/233

61 Higgins, 'Report on Night Hostile Aeroplane Raid, May 19/20th 1918,' 20 May 1918, 50, 12, and 39 Squadrons' reports, 19–20 May 1918, Air 1/603/16/15/233

62 Ashmore, *Air Defence*, 93–4. See also Jones, *War in the Air*, V, app. VIII, 493–504.

63 Ashmore, *Air Defence*, 89, 108–9; Jones, *War in the Air*, V, app. IX, 505–7

64 [E.] Ludendorff, *The General Staff and its Problems: the History of the Relations between the High Command and the German Imperial Government as revealed by Official Documents* (London nd), II, 452, 457

65 Canada, National Defence Headquarters, Directorate of History, Statistical Printout of File by Province, by year of Enlistment, by Service, in Computer Programme of Biographical and Service Information Concerning Canadians in the British Flying Services, Canadian Forces Computer Centre, TCAA-2

66 R.V. Dodds, 'The Zeppelin Hunters from Canada,' *Legionary* (Sept. 1963), 7–10, 15

67 Robinson, *Zeppelin in Combat*, 321–2

68 W.A.B. Douglas, taped interview with C.B. Sproatt, 22 Dec. 1968, transcript, DHist 74/43; Snowden Gamble, *North Sea Air Station*, 408–9

69 Cadbury report, 6 Aug. 1918, Leckie to Lockwood Marsh, 10 Aug. 1918, Air 1/603/16/15/234

70 Snowden Gamble, *North Sea Air Station*, 409–11

CHAPTER 10: THE RNAS AND THE BIRTH OF A BOMBING STRATEGY

1 Chaz Bowyer, '3 Wing, R.N.A.S.: Britain's First Strategic Bombers,' *Aircraft Illustrated*, extra, no 12, nd, 12–17; R.A. Collishaw, '1916 Strategic Bomber Command, No. 3 Wing, Royal Naval Air Service,' *Cross & Cockade Journal*, IV, spring 1963, 88–91; Richard Bell Davies, *Sailor in the Air: the Memoirs of Vice-Admiral Richard Bell Davies* (London 1967), 145–59; Christopher Draper, *The Mad Major* (Letchworth, Herts: 1962), 56–62; H.A. Jones, *The War in the Air: being the Story of the Part played in the Great War by the Royal Air Force*, VI (London 1937), 118–21; Ralph Barker, *Aviator Extraordinary: the Sidney Cotton Story* (London 1969), 30–3; R.V. Dodds, 'Britain's First Strategic Bombing Force: No. 3 (Naval) Wing,' *Roundel*, XV, July–Aug. 1963, 4–10; R.V. Dodds, 'The Oberndorf Raid,' *Legionary*, XLI, Jan. 1967, 16–17, 29–30; H.D. Hastings, 'The Oberndorf Raid,' *Cross & Cockade Journal*, V, winter 1964, 365–84

2 154th War Cabinet meeting, 5 June 1917, Cab 23/3; Sir Walter Raleigh, *The War in the Air: being the Story of the Part played in the Great War by the Royal Air Force*, I (London 1922), 488

3 Trenchard to Kiggell, 22 Oct. 1915, Maurice minute, 1 Nov. 1915, Air 1/2265/209/70/1

4 R. Martel, *L'aviation française de bombardement* (Lille, France 1937), I; Voison, 'Le rendement de l'aviation française de bombardement de jour au course de la guerre de 1914–1918,' *Revue militaire française*, nouvelle série, XI, jan.–mars 1924, 109–28

5 Great Britain, Parliament, House of Commons, *Debates*, 16 Feb. 1916, 92–3, 5 April 1916, 1300

6 Ibid., 17 May 1916, 1582, 1585–9. See also 7 March 1916, 1429.

7 Report of Churchill's evidence to the Air Board, mid-1916, Air 1/298/15/226/149 pt II

8 War Office to JWAC, 13 March 1916, Air 1/270/15/226/115; Interim Report of the JWAC, 20 March 1916, Air 1/2319/223/26; Trenchard to Haig, 20 March 1916, Air 1/2265/209/70/1

9 Private memorandum circulated to the JWAC, 31 March 1916, Air 1/2319/223/26

10 Note of April 1916, Air 1/300/15/226/151 pt I; remarks by naval members of JWAC, 3 April 1916, Air 1/2319/223/27

11 Note on Vaughan-Lee memorandum, 5 April 1916, S.W. Roskill, ed., *Documents relating to the Naval Air Service*, I: *1908–1918* (London 1969), 344; Elder, History of 3 Wing, RNAS, nd, Air 1/648/17/122/397; minutes of 28th Air Board meeting, 1 Nov. 1916, Air 6/3

12 Lambe, Bacon, and Vaughan-Lee correspondence, 21–28 May 1916, Air 1/634/17/122/98; Elder, History of 3 Wing, Air 1/648/17/122/397

13 Admiralty to OC 3 Wing, 27 July 1916, enclosure and papers concerning attack on Friedrichshafen, 29 Sept.–9 Oct. 1916, Air 1/300/15/226/151 pt I

14 Admiralty to OC 3 Wing, 27 July 1916 and enclosure, ibid.

15 Translation of French report regarding expedition of 12 Oct. 1916, nd, Air 1/648/17/122/397

16 Bombing reports, Air 1/111/15/39/1

17 J.M. Bruce, *British Aeroplanes, 1914–18* (London 1957), 541–5; 'Bomb Carrying and Releasing Gear on Aircraft 1914–1918,' Air 1/2301/215/2; Bell Davies to Elder, 4 Sept. 1916, Air 1/115/15/39/51

18 Logbook, 12 Oct. 1916, Raymond Collishaw Papers, DHist 78/132, 1-A, folder 102

19 Ibid.; 'Flight Formation for Sopwiths,' 26 Sept. 1916, 'Flight Formation for Breguets,' 1 Oct. 1916, Air 1/662/17/122/668; Bell Davies, *Sailor in the Air*, 150; bombing reports, Air 1/111/15/39/1; Hastings, 'Oberndorf Raid,' 373

20 Hastings, 'Oberndorf Raid,' 365–84; Bell Davies, *Sailor in the Air*, 150–3

21 Tudor minute, 26 Oct. 1916, Air 1/648/17/122/397

22 Minutes of First Sea Lord and First Lord, 26 and 29 Oct. 1916, ibid.

23 Translation of French report regarding expedition of 12 Oct. 1916, 8, ibid.

24 Davies to Secretary of the Admiralty, 23 Oct. 1916, Air 1/638/17/122/161

25 'Canada's Fighting Airman, A/V/M Raymond Collishaw; Part I, Flying in France and Belgium, 1916–1918; No. 3 (Naval) Wing – The First Independent Air Force in France,' *Cross & Cockade Journal*, VIII, summer 1967, 140–1

26 Ibid.; Elder to Secretary of the Admiralty, 30 Oct. 1916, and to DAS, 13 Nov. 1916, bombing reports, Air 1/648/17/122/397; bombing reports, Air 1/111/15/39/1; summary of 3 Wing bombing operations, Air 1/115/15/39/70

27 Elder to DAS, 21 Nov. 1916, and to Secretary of the Admiralty, 25 Nov. and 28 Dec. 1916, Rathbone to Elder, 4 Dec. 1916, Air 1/648/17/122/397; Ernst von Hoeppner, *Deutschlands Krieg in der Luft* (Leipzig 1921), 136, DHist SGR I 196, Set 3

28 Wolfgang Büdingen, *Entwicklung und Einsatz der deutschen Flakwaffe und des Luftschutzes im Weltkriege* (Berlin 1938), 104; final report on 3 Wing, app. 1, Weston to Elder, 18 May 1917, Air 1/648/17/122/397

29 Rathbone to Secretary of the Admiralty, 4 March 1916, Air 1/648/17/122/397; bombing reports, Air 1/111/15/39/1

30 Harald Penrose, *British Aviation: the Great War and Armistice, 1915–1919* (London 1969), 87f; Paul Bewsher, *'Green balls': the Adventures of a Night Bomber* (Edinburgh 1919), 20–1; Elder to DAS, 13 Nov. 1916, Air 1/648/17/122/397; E.W. Stedman, *From Boxkite to Jet: the Memoirs of an Aeronautical Engineer* (Mercury Series, Canadian War Museum Paper No 1; Ottawa 1972), 18–25

31 'Notes for the Training of Pilots or Observers on Handley Page Machines,' nd, Air 1/1007/204/5/1271; DOD minute, 5 Aug. 1917, Air 1/642/17/122/250; Stedman, *Boxkite to Jet*, 25; Bewsher, *'Green balls,'* passim; Bruce, *British Aeroplanes*, 268–78; Owen Thetford, *British Naval Aircraft since 1912* (London 1962), 212–13; Penrose, *British Aviation*, passim.

32 'Notes for ... Training ... on Handley Page Machines,' Air 1/1007/204/5/1271; 'Raids ... by Handley Page machines nos. 1459 and 1460,' Air 1/2266/209/70/18; bombing report, Air 1/115/15/39/70; Stedman, *Boxkite to Jet*, 25

33 Bewsher, '*Green balls*,' 59–60
34 Elder to Secretary of the Admiralty, 18 March 1917, Air 1/648/17/122/397
35 Bombing report, Air 1/638/17/122/161; 3 Wing historical summary, Air 1/2266/ 209/70/18; Admiralty to War Office, 4 March 1917, Roskill, ed., *Documents ... Naval Air Service*, 411–12; Elder, 'No. 3 Wing, Royal Naval Air Service,' particularly app. II, 'Summary of raids,' Air 1/648/17/122/397
36 Bewsher, '*Green balls*,' 75–7
37 DAS minute, 12 Dec. 1916, note on draft letter to Secretary, Air Board, Dec. 1916, Air 1/637/17/122/142; C.G.G., 'An Appreciation of the Work of the Royal Naval Air Service,' *Aeroplane*, 3 Jan. 1917, 22–34
38 Haig to War Office, 1 Nov. 1916, Air 2/123/B10620
39 Curzon to War Committee, 9 Nov. 1916, ibid.; Roskill, ed., *Documents ... Naval Air Service*, 405–21
40 'No. 3 Wing,' Air 1/648/17/122/397; meeting of 22 Oct. 1916, Air 1/2265/209/70/1; summary of strategic bombing, [mid-1918], Air 1/461/15/312/107; Foreign Office to International Red Cross Committee, 11 Aug. 1916, 'Correspondence with His Majesty's Minister at Berne respecting the question of reprisals against prisoners of war,' Canada, Secretary of State, *Copies of Proclamations, Orders in Council and documents relating to the European war* (Ottawa [1917]), app. CC, 908–9; *The Times History of the War* (London [1914]–1921), X, 53–5, XI, 166
41 Bombing report, Air 1/111/15/39/1; University of Toronto, *University of Toronto Roll of Service, 1914–1918*, G. Oswald Smith, ed. (Toronto 1921)
42 Bombing report, Air 1/111/15/39/1; Elder to Secretary of the Admiralty, 15 April 1917, Air 1/648/17/122/397
43 Elder to Secretary of the Admiralty, 15 April 1917, Air 1/648/17/122/397
44 'Extrait du Bulletin de Renseignement du 18 avril du S.R. de BELFORT; Bombardement sur FRIBURG' and 'Suite de la Communication officielle concernant le Bombardement par avions de FRIBURG en BRISGAU, 17 avril 1917,' DHist microfilm extracts of AHB files; letter of 20 Dec. 1917, Air 2/129/B12149; Great Britain, Parliament, House of Commons, *Debates*, 24 April 1917, 2224–5
45 Jones, *War in the Air*, VI, 118, 122
46 Translation of extract from (French Seventh) Army Aviation Headquarters, report no 139/1, 19 May 1917, DHist microfilm extracts of AHB files
47 Bombing statistics, Air 1/271/15/226/118 and Air 1/111/15/39/1.
48 28th Air Board meeting, 1 Nov. 1916, Air 6/3; RFC HQ, notes on policy, 8 April 1917, paper on long-distance bombing, 26 Nov. 1917, Air 1/477/AH15/312/225
49 Anthony Verrier, *The Bomber Offensive* (London 1968), 9
50 Air Board reports to Cabinet, 21 April, 9 and 16 June 1917, Air 1/2313/221/48; Great Britain, Parliament, House of Commons, *Debates*, 26 April 1917, 2655–8
51 154th and 169th War Cabinet meetings, 5 and 26 June 1917, Cab 23/3; correspondence of 18 June–5 July 1917, Air 2/87/304
52 178th War Cabinet meeting, 7 July 1917, Cab 23/3; Trenchard to G.S. Advanced GHQ, 12 July 1917, Air 1/970/204/5/1108
53 Andrew Boyle, *Trenchard* (London 1962), 226; Jones, *War in the Air, Appendices*, (London 1937), 1–8
54 *War in the Air, Appendices*, 10

55 Ibid., VI, 13

56 Trenchard to Kiggell, 30 Aug. 1917, Air 1/521/16/12/3

57 Haig to CIGS, 14 Sept. 1917, ibid.

58 Williamson to DOD, 3 Aug. 1917, Air 1/305/15/226/153 pt II

59 117th–143rd Air Board meetings, 23 July–24 Sept. 1917, Air 6/9 and Air 6/10; War Cabinet discussion of second report of Air Organization Committee, 24 Aug. 1917, Air 1/22/15/1/115

60 228th War Cabinet meeting, 5 Sept. 1917, Cab 23/4

61 Air 1/970/204/5/1108

62 Haig-CIGS correspondence, 2 Oct. 1917, Haig to C-in-C French Armies of the North and North-East, 3 Oct. 1917, ibid.; 243rd War Cabinet meeting, 2 Oct. 1917, Cab 23/4

63 Kerr, 'Notes on Strategy,' 3 Oct. 1917, Air 1/463/15/312/219; Jones, *War in the Air*, VI, 18; 247th War Cabinet meeting, 9 Oct. 1917, Cab 23/4; Mark Kerr, *Land, Sea, and Air: Reminiscences of Mark Kerr* (London 1927), 289–91

64 Trenchard interview with H.A. Jones, 11 April 1934, Air 8/167

65 *War in the Air, Appendices,* 19

CHAPTER 11: THE STRATEGIC AIR OFFENSIVE AGAINST GERMANY

1 Andrew Boyle, *Trenchard* (London 1962), 261

2 Trenchard to Lloyd George, 13 Jan. 1918, Air 1/522/16/12/5

3 Norman to Rothermere, 25 March 1918, Air 1/2422/305/18/17

4 Ibid.

5 'Proposed minute on the formation of a Strategic Committee dealing with air matters,' 19 April 1918, Air 1/450/15/312/4

6 Boyle, *Trenchard*, 287–8; W.J. Reader, *Architect of Air Power: the Life of the First Viscount Weir of Eastwood, 1877–1959* (London 1968), 73–4

7 J.M. Bruce, *British Aeroplanes, 1914–1918* (London 1957), 166–82; W.B. Farrington, 'War Experiences,' 19 Oct. 1922, Air 1/2386/228/11/6

8 'Dunkirk: Schedule of Operations,' 1–31 Oct. 1917, Air 1/629/17/117/1–11; Lambe to Vice-Admiral Dover Patrol, 31 Oct. 1917, Air 1/640/17/122/210; D. Gates, 'Big bird jockey: Geoffrey Linnell, Handley Page pilot,' *Cross & Cockade Journal*, IV, summer 1963, 180–7

9 Pétain to Haig, 21 Oct. 1917, Trenchard to Newall, 23 Oct. 1917, Air 1/970/204/5/1108; H.A. Jones, *The War in the Air: being the Story of the Part played in the Great War by the Royal Air Force*, VI (London 1937), 125

10 Jones, *War in the Air, Appendices* (London 1937), 42; 55 Squadron combat report, 21 Oct. 1917, Air 1/1058/204/5/1564; 'Burbach Works Damage Survey,' 6 Jan. 1919, Air 1/685/21/13/2240

11 Ibid.

12 Flavelle logbook, 24 Oct. 1917, G.A. Flavelle biographical file, DHist

13 C. Gordon Burge, *The Annals of 100 Squadron* (London 1918), 101

14 No 41 Wing bombing reports, Air 1/1058/204/5/1564; 'Bombing of Germany by British aircraft, 1.10.17–11.11.18,' nd, Air 1/451/15/312/19; Lambe to Bacon, 31 Oct. 1917, Paine minute, 8 Nov. 1917, Air 1/640/17/122/210

15 *War in the Air, Appendices*, 43; HQ RFC to GHQ, 8 Dec. 1917, Air 1/450/15/312/1

16 VIII Brigade progress report, Feb. 1918, Air 1/450/15/312/1; Salmond to Foulois, 13 Feb. 1918, Air 1/970/204/5/1108

17 No 100 Squadron operations summary, 4–5 Jan. 1918, Air 1/176/15/199/1; 100 Squadron operations reports, 18–19 Feb. 1918, Air 1/721/48/2

18 No 55 Squadron bombing reports, 12 and 19 Feb. 1918, and Gray to HQ 41 Wing, 10 March 1918, in Air 1/1750/204/139/8

19 Trenchard to GHQ, 8 Dec. 1917, Air 1/970/204/5/1108; Trenchard to Newall, 29 March 1918, Air 1/978/204/5/1140; Burge, *Annals of 100 Squadron*, 108–9

20 'Results of Air-raids, Metz,' trans. 4 April 1919, Air 1/685/21/13/2240

21 No 55 Squadron combat report, 16 May 1918, Air 1/478/15/312/233; 55 Squadron bombing report, 16 May 1918, Air 1/1750/204/139/8; *War in the Air, Appendices*, 50

22 *War in the Air, Appendices*, 50; 100 Squadron operations summary, 21–22 May 1918, Air 1/176/15/199/1; 100 Squadron operation report, 21–22 May 1918, Air 1/721/48/2

23 R.V. Dodds, 'Notes on Squadron Histories,' 99 Squadron, DHist 73/1552; Harald Penrose, *British Aviation: the Great War and Armistice, 1915–1919* (London 1969), 278–9; Trenchard to DGMA, 16 Nov. 1917, Air 1/970/204/5/1108

24 Bruce, *British Aeroplanes*, 191–9

25 *War in the Air, Appendices*, 51; 99 Squadron bombing and combat reports, 24 May 1918, Air 1/478/AH15/312/233

26 No 99 Squadron bombing and combat reports, 24 May 1918

27 Diary, Donald A. Macdonald biographical file, DHist

28 No 99 Squadron bombing and combat report, 29 May 1918, Air 1/478/AH15/312/233

29 VIII Brigade daily report, 27 May 1918, ibid.

30 Jones, *War in the Air*, III (London 1931), 292–9

31 Transcript of interview with W.A. Leslie, 28 Sept. 1971, Leslie biographical file, DHist. See also Robert H. Reece, *Night Bombing with the Bedouins* (New York 1919), 44–9.

32 Wolfgang Büdingen, *Entwicklung und Einsatz der deutschen Flakwaffe und des Luftschutzes im Weltkriege* (Berlin 1938), 103

33 Ibid., 103–4

34 'Operation order for the guidance of the Independent Force' (draft), nd, Air 1/462/312/16

35 'Review of Air Situation and Strategy for the Information of the Imperial War Cabinet,' 27 June 1918, in Frederick Sykes, *From Many Angles: an Autobiography* (London 1942), app. V, 544–54

36 Boyle, *Trenchard*, 291–2; Trenchard to Weir, 18 June 1918, Air 1/30/15/1/155 1–3

37 'Squadrons Allotted to the Independent Force, Royal Air Force,' 13 May 1918, ibid.

38 Trenchard to de Castelnau, 23 June 1918, Air 1/995/204/273/201

39 'War Establishment, Long Range Bombing Squadron (Independent Force),' 16 July 1918, 'Royal Air Force, Night Bombing Squadron, War Establishment,' 16 July 1918, Air 1/1990/204/273/158; *War in the Air, Appendices*, 162–3; 'Minute of the Quartermaster-General's meeting,' 12 June 1918, Air 1/2000/204/273/273

40 Groves to Sykes, 11 Sept. 1918, Air 1/460/15/312/97; Independent Force statistics, June 1918, Air 1/451/15/312/20

41 Trenchard to Weir, 2 July 1918, Air 1/2000/204/273/275

42 Summary of 99 Squadron operations, 1918, nd, folder 11, file 6, PAC, RG 9 III, vol. 4611; 100 Squadron operation report, 6–7 June 1918, Air 1/721/48/2; 'History of No. 99 Squadron,' 14, Air 1/176/15/198/3

43 'History of No. 99 Squadron,' 18–19; 55 Squadron bombing report, 25 June 1918, Air 1/170/204/139/8; 104 Squadron historical summary, 13 Jan. 1919, Air 1/176/15/202/1

44 Burge, *Annals of 100 Squadron*, 117

45 Report on Independent Force operations during June 1918, 2 July 1918, Air 1/2000/204/273/275

46 No 100 Squadron operation report, 25–26 June 1918, Air 1/721/48/2; 100 Squadron history, nd, 4, Air 1/176/15/199/1

47 Report on Independent Force operations during June 1918, 2 July 1918, Air 1/2000/204/273/275

48 Report on Independent Force operations during July 1918, 1 Aug. 1918, ibid.; 'Appendix to Operations Despatch, Independent Force, R.A.F.,' July 1918, Air 1/451/15/312/20

49 No 104 Squadron operation report, 1 July 1918, Air 1/1750/204/139/9; *War in the Air, Appendices*, 58–60

50 No 100 Squadron history, nd, 4, Air 1/176/15/199/1; 100 Squadron operation report, 16–17 July 1918, Air 1/721/48/2

51 L.A. Pattinson, *History of 99 Squadron, Independent Force, Royal Air Force, March 1918–November 1918* (Cambridge 1920), 29–30

52 Dodds, 'Notes on Squadron Histories,' 97 and 215 Squadrons, DHist 73/1552

53 Bruce, *British Aeroplanes*, 273–8

54 Groves to Sykes, 9 Sept. 1918, Air 1/460/15/312/97; report on Independent Force operations during August 1918, 1 Sept. 1918, Air 1/2000/204/273/275; 'Appendix to Operations Despatch,' Aug. 1918, Air 1/451/15/312/20

55 Report on Independent Force operations during August 1918, 1 Sept. 1918, Air 1/2000/204/273/275

56 No 104 Squadron bombing and air combat reports, 22 Aug. 1918, Air 1/478/15/312/234

57 Air combat report, 22 Aug. 1918, ibid.

58 Ibid.

59 H.B. Monaghan, *The Big Bombers of World War I: a Canadian's Journal* (Burlington, Ont. 1976), 74–5, 77

60 No 215 Squadron bombing report, 25–26 Aug. 1918, Air 1/1985/204/273/100; Independent Force communiqué no 4, 31 Aug. 1918, Air 1/2085/207/5/1; Jones, *War in the Air*, VI, 145–6

61 Trenchard to GHQ, 15 July 1917, Air Board to Haig, 7 Nov. 1917, Air 1/522/16/12/5; Trenchard to Sykes, 4 Aug. 1918, Air 1/460/15/312/100

62 Tiverton to DFO, 'Notes on Defence of Bombing Squadrons Operating with Independent Force,' 8 Aug. 1918, ibid.

63 Groves to Sykes, 11 Sept. 1918, Air 1/460/15/312/97

64 Tiverton to Groves, 4 July 1918, Air 1/461/15/312/107

65 Foch memorandum, 14 Sept. 1918, 'Heads of Agreement as to the Constitution of the Inter-Allied Independent Force,' 3 Oct. 1918, Air 1/30/15/1/155; *War in the Air, Appendices*, app. XI, 41

66 'History of No. 110 Squadron,' 13 Feb. 1919, Air 1/176/15/205/1

67 Bruce, *British Aeroplanes*, 197–8, 203–4

68 Independent Force communiqué no 7, 21 Sept. 1918, Air 1/2085/207/5/1; E.G. Gallagher and R.S. Lipsett biographical files, DHist

69 Bruce, *British Aeroplanes*, 578; Jones, *War in the Air*, VI, 149

70 Report on Independent Force operations during September 1918, 1 Oct. 1918, Air 1/2000/204/273/275; 41 Wing, 'Approximate Results,' 7–8 Sept. 1918, Air 1/2085/207/5/3

71 'Final report of Chief of Air Service, American Expeditionary Forces,' United States, Department of the Army, Historical Division, *United States Army in the World War* (Washington 1948), XV, 230, 249–50

72 No 104 Squadron bombing report, 13 Sept. 1918, Air 1/1750/204/139/9; 41 Wing, 'Approximate Results,' 14–15 Sept. 1918, Air 1/2085/207/5/3; Trenchard to Secretary Air Ministry, 'Operations in September,' 1 Oct. 1918, Air 1/2000/204/273/275

73 'Operations in September,' 1 Oct. 1918; *War in the Air, Appendices*, 75; Alan Morris, *First of the Many: The Story of the Independent Force, R.A.F.* (London 1969), 128

74 Monaghan, *Big Bombers*, 80–2, 84; Morris, *First of the Many*, 126–7; Independent Force, 'Approximate Results,' 16–17 Sept. 1918, Air 1/2085/207/5/2

75 Independent Force, 'Approximate Results'; 97 Squadron History, Air 1/176/15/196/1 (part of this source incorrectly identifies the target as Cologne); Independent Force communiqué no 7, 21 Sept. 1918, Air 1/2085/207/5/1

76 Press clipping, *Daily Mail* (London), 21 Sept. 1918, Air 1/462/15/312/116

77 FO3 to DFO, 21 Sept. 1918, ibid.

78 Boyle, *Trenchard*, 312

79 Sykes, *From Many Angles*, 550–1

80 Tiverton to Groves, 11 June 1918, DFO File, 08/14, quoted in James Howes, 'The Independent Force: an Early Experiment in Strategic Bombing' (unpublished MA thesis, Royal Military College of Canada, 1973), 120; FO3 to AI1b, 26 Aug. and 8 Sept. 1918, AIB and FO3, 4 and 9 Sept. 1918, Air 1/460/15/312/97

81 Trenchard to Secretary Air Ministry, 'Operations in October,' 1 Nov. 1918, Air 1/2000/204/273/275; *War in the Air, Appendices*, 78, 80–1; VIII Brigade bombing reports, 21–22, 23–24 Oct. 1918, Air 1/479/15/312/243

82 No 110 Squadron bombing report, 5 Oct. 1918, ibid.

83 No 110 Squadron bombing report, 21 Oct. 1918, Air 1/478/15/312/235

84 'History of 110 Squadron,' 13 Feb. 1919, Air 1/175/15/205/1; *War in the Air, Appendices*, 78–80 (in which the raid is incorrectly associated with 100 Squadron)

85 W.R. Read Diary, Imperial War Museum, London

86 Mulock's notes on No 27 Group, Independent Force, nd, Mulock Papers, document 121, DHist

87 Ibid.; FO3 to DFO, 4 July 1918, Groves, 'Notes on Potentialities of Norfolk as a Base for the 'V' Type Handley Page Aeroplanes,' [late April or early May 1918], Air 1/461/15/312/107

88 'A base in Norfolk' (draft), 3 May 1918, Air 1/461/15/312/107

89 Undated paper probably written in late May or early June 1918, ibid.

90 Gammell to Groves, 15 Oct. 1918, ibid.

91 Lambe to No 5 Group, 31 May 1918, Lambe to Keyes, 9 June 1918, Keyes to Lambe, 11 June 1918, Mulock Papers, documents 81, 82, 86, DHist

92 Tiverton to DFO, 21 June 1918, Air 1/461/15/312/107; Penrose, *British Aviation*, 402–4; Bruce, *British Aeroplanes*, 283

93 Bruce, *British Aeroplanes*, 285–6; Penrose, *British Aviation*, 404–5; G.W. Haddow and P.M. Grosz, *The German Giants: the Story of the R-planes* (London 1962), 224–40

94 Lambe to Mulock, 18 July 1918, Groves to Sykes, 2 Aug. 1918, Mulock Papers, documents 91, 92, DHist; R.M. Groves Diary I, 30 July and 2 Aug. 1918, Imperial War Museum, London

95 Trenchard to Sykes, 12 Aug. 1918, Air 1/1974/204/273/15

96 DAO order, 29 Aug. 1918, Air 1/1974/204/273/14

97 Mulock to parents, 29 Sept. 1918, Mulock Papers, document 99, DHist; Mulock to Gordon, 20 Sept. 1918, Air 1/1974/204/273/15

98 Mulock-Trenchard correspondence, 30 Aug.–18 Oct. 1918, Air 1/1974/204/273/15; Mulock to FO3, 'Training to Crews of "V" Type Machines,' 29 Aug. 1918, Air 1/461/15/312/103; Walker to Mulock, 14 Sept. 1918, Air 1/1974/204/273/16; Air Ministry and HQ Independent Force correspondence regarding selection and training, 13 Aug.–5 Nov. 1918, Air 1/1974/204/273/20

99 Mulock's notes on No 27 Group, Mulock Papers, document 121, DHist

100 Mulock to HQ Independent Force, progress reports 11 Sept.–8 Oct. 1918, Air 1/1974/204/273/17; Mulock to Trenchard, 29 Aug. and 20 Sept. 1918, Air 1/1974/204/273/15

101 Trenchard to Mulock, 15 Oct. 1918, Mulock to Trenchard, 16 Oct. 1918, Air 1/1974/204/273/15

102 Trenchard to Mulock, 17 Oct. 1918, ibid.

103 Map of bombing routes, nd, Mulock Papers, document 118, DHist; Mulock to Trenchard, 17 and 18 Oct. 1918, Air 1/1974/204/273/18

104 Mulock to Trenchard, 17 Oct. 1918, Trenchard to Mulock, 21 Oct. and 11 Nov. 1918, ibid.; Bruce, *British Aeroplanes*, 284–5

105 Trenchard, 'Final Despatch,' *London Gazette* (Supplement), 1 Jan. 1919

106 Ibid.

107 Survey of damage to steel works, nd, 2, Air 1/1999/204/273/269

108 Survey of damage to chemical and munitions factories, nd, 5, Air 1/1999/204/273/268

109 'Moral and Material Effect of the Operations of the Independent Force, R.A.F., in Germany,' 7 Aug. 1918, Air 1/2104/207/36

110 Survey of damage to steel works, nd, 15, Air 1/1999/204/273/269

111 Ibid., 20

112 Survey of damage to chemical and munitions factories, nd, 17–18, Air 1/1999/204/273/268

113 Survey of damage to steel works, nd, 16, Air 1/1999/204/273/269; Sykes, *From Many Angles*, 231–2

114 Jones, *War in the Air*, VI, 153

115 Survey of damage to steel works, nd, 16, Air 1/1999/204/273/269

116 Ernst von Hoeppner, *Deutschlands Krieg in der Luft* (Leipzig 1921), 108–9, DHist SGR I 196, Set 3

117 Trenchard, 'Final Despatch,' *London Gazette* (Supplement), 1 Jan. 1919

118 'Results of Air-raids, Metz,' trans. 4 April 1919, Air 1/685/21/13/2240; Jones, *War in the Air*, VI, 157

119 Trenchard, 'Final Despatch,' *London Gazette* (Supplement), 1 Jan. 1919; Jones, *War in the Air*, VI, 158–64; Hermann Franke, *Handbuch der neuzeitlichen Wehrwissenschaften* (Berlin 1939), III, Buch 2, 433–4, DHist SGR I 196, Set 53; E.H. Knipfer and Erich Hampe, *Der zivile Luftschutz* (Berlin 1934), 93–103; Hans Ritter, *Der Luftkrieg* (Berlin 1926), 115–16, DHist SGR I 196, Set 6

120 Report on Independent Force operations during August 1918, 1 Sept. 1918, Air 1/2000/204/273/275

121 Robert Endres, 'Dokumente der deutschen luftstreitkräfte 1882–1919' (unpublished research paper prepared for the Military History Research Bureau, Freiburg, 1965), gives a list of German air stations; Sykes, *From Many Angles*, 229; E.J. Kingston-McCloughry, *Winged Warfare* (London 1937), 41

122 FO3 to DFO, 15 Oct. 1918, Air 1/461/15/312/107

123 W.R. Read Diary, 19 and 23 Aug. 1918, 16–17, 24, Imperial War Museum, London

124 Jones, *War in the Air*, II (London 1931), 325; III, 339–41

125 Mulock, 'The War in the Air: Canada's Part,' speech to Canadian Club of Winnipeg, 18 Sept. 1919, Mulock Papers, document 110, DHist

126 Squadron lists, biographical cards and files, DHist

CHAPTER 12: EXPERIMENTS ON THE WESTERN FRONT, 1914–15

1 Gerhard Ritter, *The Schlieffen Plan: Critique of a Myth*, Andrew and Eva Wilson, trans. (London 1958), 58; Martin van Creveld, *Supplying War: Logistics from Wallenstein to Patton* (Cambridge 1977), 109–41

2 John R. Cuneo, *Winged Mars*, II: *The Air Weapon, 1914–1916* (Harrisburg 1947), 16, 384–5

3 Norman MacMillan, *Sir Sefton Brancker* (London 1935), 54, 56, 60

4 Sir Walter Raleigh, *The War in the Air: being the Story of the Part played in the Great War by the Royal Air Force*, I (London 1922), 293, 417; MacMillan, *Brancker*, 61; L.A. Strange, *Recollections of an Airman* (London 1935), 36

5 MacMillan, *Brancker*, 63; Maurice Baring, *Flying Corps Headquarters, 1914–1918* (Edinburgh 1968), 12–14; Raleigh, *War in the Air*, I, 286–7

6 For thorough and detailed studies of the ground campaigns on the Western Front, 1914–18, see the relevant volumes of James E. Edmonds, *Military Operations: France and Belgium* (London 1925–47), and Deutschland, Reichsarchiv and Oberkommando des Heeres, *Der Weltkrieg 1914 bis 1918* (Berlin 1925–44). These are the respective British and German official histories. For a more critical approach in English see B.H. Liddell Hart, *A History of the World War, 1914–18* (London 1934). On the Canadian contribution see G.W.L. Nicholson, *Canadian Expeditionary Force, 1914–1919* (Official History of the Canadian Army in the First World War; Ottawa 1962).

7 'Report of Reconnaissance of Gembloux,' 19 Aug. 1914, reconnaissance report, 22 Aug. 1914, Air 1/749/204/3/76; 4 Squadron war diary, 19 Aug. 1914, Air

1/2162/209/7/2; 5 Squadron war diary, 21 Aug. 1914, Air 1/2163/209/8/2; 3 Squadron war diary, 22 Aug. 1914, Air 1/2162/209/6/2

8 Raleigh, *War in the Air*, I, 287, 304–7

9 No 3 Squadron war diary, 'Note of 26th August by Capt Charlton,' 26 Aug. 1914, Air 1/737/204/2/2

10 Raleigh, *War in the Air*, I, 327

11 Edward Spears, *Liaison 1914: a Narrative of the Great Retreat* (London 1968), 414, map 416–17

12 Ernst von Hoeppner, *Deutschlands Krieg in der Luft* (Leipzig 1921), 12–13, DHist SGR I 196, Set 3

13 No 3 Squadron war diary, 7 Sept. 1914, Air 1/737/204/2/2

14 Wanklyn to Dodds, 4 March 1963, F.S. Wanklyn biographical file, DHist

15 Henderson to French, 30 Oct. 1914, French to War Office, 1 Nov. 1914, minute sheet 87/4234, 9 Dec. 1914, Air 1/503/16/18; H.A. Jones, *War in the Air: being the Story of the Part played in the Great War by the Royal Air Force*, II (London 1928), 79–80, 83–4, app. I, II, and III, 456–7

16 French to War Office, 14 Nov. 1914, Air 1/141/15/40/307

17 Sykes to GHQ, 16 Dec. 1914, Air 1/524/16/12/23

18 Trenchard to Ashmore, 4 Dec. 1914, Air 1/1283/204/11/13

19 'Co-operation of Aeroplanes with Artillery,' Air 1/141/15/40/307

20 Jones, *War in the Air*, II, 87–90

21 Edmonds, *Military Operations: France and Belgium, 1915* (London 1927), 248–9; Air Historical Board, 'Contact Patrol,' nd, Air 1/674/21/6/120

22 'Contact Patrol'; Jones, *War in the Air*, II, 111

23 A.D. Bell-Irving to Dodds, 17 April 1962, M. McB. Bell-Irving biographical file, DHist

24 Salmond to OC 2 Wing, 29 April 1915, Air 1/2151/209/3/241

25 Air Historical Branch to Canadian Joint Staff, 25 Sept. 1962, M. McB. Bell-Irving biographical file, DHist; 7 Squadron, air combat report, 28 April 1915, Air 1/1218/204/5/2634/7

26 Brooke-Popham, 'Fighting Hostile Aeroplanes in the Air,' 1 Feb. 1915, Air 1/746/204/3/22; 2 Wing war diary, 13 April 1915, Air 1/1274/204/10/2; H.E. Chaney, 'Remarks on Diagrams for Assistance during Aerial Combats,' 9 Sept. 1915, Air 1/755/204/4/81

27 No 1 Wing, 'Operation Orders for Tomorrow,' 29 March–12 April, 7 May, and 30 June 1915, Air 1/252/204/8/7; 1 Wing, 'Patrols,' 24 June 1915, Air 1/1254/204/8/31

28 Jones, *War in the Air*, II, app. I, 456–7; J.M. Bruce, *British Aeroplanes 1914–1918* (London 1957), 660–3

29 Helmut Förster, 'Die Entwicklung der Fliegerei im Weltkriege,' in Walter von Eberhardt, ed., *Unsere Luftstreitkräfte, 1914–1918* (Berlin 1930), 43–4, DHist SGR I 196, Set 55; Herman Thomsen, 'Die Luftwaffe vor und im Weltkriege,' in Georg Wentzell, *Die deutsche Wehrmacht, 1914–1939* (Berlin 1939), 501–2

30 A.R. Weyl, *Fokker: the Creative Years*, J.M. Bruce, ed. (London 1965), 95–101; W.M. Lamberton and E.F. Cheesman, *Fighter Aircraft of the 1914–1918 War* (Letchworth, Herts. 1960), 178; Hermann Franke, *Handbuch der neuzeitlichen Wehrwissenschaften* (Berlin 1939), III, Buch 2, 164

31 Jones, *War in the Air*, II, 150, 166; Bruce Robertson, ed., *Air Aces of the 1914–1918 War* (Letchworth, Herts. 1959), 19. See also Franz Immelmann, *Immelmann, 'The Eagle of Lille,'* Claude W. Sykes, trans. (London nd), 139–41.

32 No 4 Squadron air combat report, 29 July 1915, 4 Squadron, 'Hostile Machine Met in the Air,' 29 July 1915, Air 1/1217/204/5/2634/4; RFC communiqué no 2, 31 July 1915, DHist 75/413

33 RFC communiqué no 10, 12 Sept. 1915, DHist 75/413

34 John Laffin, *Swifter than Eagles: the Biography of Marshal of the Royal Air Force, Sir John Maitland Salmond* (Edinburgh & London 1964), 71

35 Air Historical Board, 'The Battle of Loos: Cooperation between Aircraft and Artillery,' Sept. 1925, Air 1/675/21/13/1322

36 A.J. Insall, *Observer: Memoires of the RFC, 1915–1918* (London 1970), 20–1

37 'Naval and Military Aeronautics,' *Aeroplane*, 27 Oct. 1915, 514

38 No 7 Squadron air combat reports, 20, 22, and 26 Sept. 1915, Air 1/1218/204/5/2634/7; RFC communiqué no 12, 27 Sept. 1915, DHist 75/413

39 Andrew Boyle, *Trenchard* (London 1962), 136

40 'Proposals for Bombing ... 7th August 1915,' Air 1/752/204/4/61

41 'General Notes on Bomb Sights' and 'Short Notes on the Evolution and Theory of Bomb Sights,' 6–8, app. I, 8 Feb. 1912, Air 1/674/21/6/77

42 RAF Staff College, 'Air Operations on the Western Front 1914–18: the Development of the Activities of the RFC up to the Battle of the Somme,' nd, Air 1/2385/228/4

43 RAF casualty summary, Western Front 1914–1918, nd, Air 1/8/15/1/12; 'List of Casualties of All Ranks Struck off the Strength of the Royal Flying Corps,' June 1915–January 1916, Air 1/1303/204/11/171; Jones, *War in the Air*, II, 456–9; air combat results summary, 19 Oct. 1915, Trenchard to 2 Wing, 20 Oct. 1915, Air 1/758/204/4/119

44 No 10 Squadron air combat results summary, 26 Oct. 1915, Air 1/758/204/4/119; RFC communiqué nos 14 and 16, 10 and 16 Oct. 1915, DHist 75/413

45 No 10 Squadron air combat reports, 14 Oct., 28 Nov., 14 Dec. 1915, Air 1/1218/204/5/2634/10

46 RFC communiqué no 25, 19 Dec. 1915, DHist 75/413; 1 Squadron air combat report, 19 Dec. 1915, Air 1/1216/204/5/2634/1; A.D. Bell-Irving, 'Flying Reminiscences 1909–1959,' 1 June 1959, biographical summary, A.D. Bell-Irving biographical file, DHist

CHAPTER 13: THE BIRTH OF AIRPOWER, 1916

1 James E. Edmonds, *Military Operations: France and Belgium, 1916*, I (London 1932), vi–viii; Douglas Haig, 1st Earl Haig, *The Private Papers of Douglas Haig, 1914–1919*, Robert Blake, ed. (London 1952), 125, 137; M.P.A. Hankey, 1st Baron Hankey, *The Supreme Command* (London 1961), II, 495

2 Erich von Falkenhayn, *General Headquarters, 1914–1916, and its Critical Decisions* (London 1919), 217

3 Edmonds, *Military Operations: France and Belgium, 1916*, I, 301; War Office to Haig, 10 Dec. 1915, GHQ to Armies, 4 Jan. 1916, GHQ to Armies, 30 Jan. 1916, GHQ to Armies, 30 Nov. 1916, Air 1/529/16/12/72

4 Kiggell to Trenchard, 3 June 1916, Air 1/2265/209/70/1; Trenchard to GHQ, 9 March 1916, Air 1/1001/204/5/1260; 10 SRB, March-June 1916, Air 1/1361/204/22/1–9; 'Organization of the British Royal Flying Corps in the Field,' 10 Feb. 1916, Air 1/1/4/3; H.A. Jones, *The War in the Air: being the Story of the Part played in the Great War by the Royal Air Force*, II (London 1928), 147, 457–9; Henderson to CIGS, 23 Nov. 1915, Air 1/513/16/3/74; 'RFC Establishment for a Service Squadron,' 20 June 1916, Air 1/1266/204/9/63

5 Wilhelm Hoff, 'Die Entwicklung der deutschen Heeresflugzeuge im Kriege,' in *Zeitschrift des Vereins deutscher Ingenieure*, LXIV, 3 July 1920, 493–8, DHist SGR I 196, Set 52; John R. Cuneo, *Winged Mars*, II: *The Air Weapon, 1914–1916* (Harrisburg 1947), 212–13, 225–6

6 Cuneo, *Winged Mars*, II, 220–8

7 Ibid., 212–14

8 'Report by Commandant du Peuty on the Working of the Aviation in the Vaux-Douaumont Sector,' 6 May 1916, 'Notes by Capt. Sewell, RFC Liaison Officer with the French Army,' 28 April 1916, Air 1/1303/204/11/169

9 'Report by Captain R.A. Cooper, RFC Liaison Officer on a Visit to the French Armies at Verdun, March 12th to 19th,' 4 April 1916, Air 1/1585/204/82/41

10 'Report by Commandant Du Peuty,' 6 May 1916, Trenchard to War Office, 15 May 1916, Air 1/1303/204/11/169

11 RFC HQ record of aeroplane wastage, Air 1/2/4/26/8; summary of air combat reports, 5 Jan.–1 May 1916, summary of downed machines, from German sources, 1 Jan.–23 April 1916, Air 1/839/204/5/301

12 Haig, *Private Papers*, 126; order of 14 Jan. 1916, Air 1/1511/204/58/13; 25 Squadron, air combat report, 30 April 1916, Air 1/1382/204/24/16

13 Gunn to A.F. Duguid, 3 Oct. 1938, GAQ 5–81, PAC, RG 24, vol. 1826; 'Notes on a Conversation with Major Styles, DSO,' 18 Aug. 1922, GAQ 5–76, ibid.

14 Ibid.; D.E. MacIntyre, 'The Fight for the Craters,' GAQ 5–67, ibid., vol. 1825; A.W. Currie diary, 11–17 April 1916, Currie Papers, PAC, MG 30 E 100, vol. 43; air photographs, R.E.W. Turner Papers, PAC, MG 30 E 46, vol. 1, file 10

15 Haig, *Private Papers*, 140; G.W.L. Nicholson, *The Canadian Expeditionary Force, 1914–1919* (Official History of the Canadian Army in the First World War; Ottawa 1964), 146–7

16 Nicholson, *Canadian Expeditionary Force*, 147–50; Edmonds, *Military Operations: France and Belgium, 1916*, I, 229–32; 'Report on Operations of Artillery of Canadian Corps – June 2nd to June 14th 1916,' H.E. Burstall Papers, PAC, MG 30 E 6, vol. 2, folder 10

17 Edmonds, *Military Operations: France and Belgium, 1916*, I, 231; Jones, *War in the Air*, II, 192–5; R.A. Logan biographical file, DHist; 6 SRB, Air 1/1316/204/15/7

18 Nicholson, *Canadian Expeditionary Force*, 151–2; Edmonds, *Military Operations: France and Belgium, 1916*, I, 204–45; 'Report on Operations' and 'Reports from German Prisoners,' Burstall Papers, vol. 2, folder 10; air photographs, C.H. Mitchell Papers, PAC, MG 30 E 61, vol. 13

19 A. Morizon, 'L'Aviation Française en 1916,' *Revenue Historique de l'Armée* 22e Année (Aug. 1966), 40–52; France, Ministère de la Guerre, État-Major de

l'Armée, Service Historique, *Les Armées françaises dans la grande Guerre* (Paris 1931), Tome IV, II, 212; [H] von Bülow, *Geschichte der Luftwaffe* (Frankfurt am Main 1937), 74–5 (who calculates the total to have been 114), DHist SGR I 196, Set 20; Deutschland, Reichskriegministerium, *Der Weltkrieg 1914 bis 1918*, Band X: *Die Operationen des Jahres 1916* (Berlin 1936), 341–64, DHist SGR I 196, Set 2; Hans Ritter, *Der Luftkrieg* (Berlin 1926), 68–85, DHist SGR I 196, Set 6; Jones, *War in the Air*, II, 464–70

20 DDMA to GOC VI Brigade, 23 March 1916, Air 1/131/15/40/218; Trenchard to DDMA, 28 March 1916, Air 1/513/16/3/74; E.M. Roberts, *A Flying Fighter* (New York 1918), 97–146

21 W.G. Barker biographical file, DHist; DAO (War Office) to CEF HQ, 18 Oct. 1916, 8-1-121, PAC, RG 9 III, vol. 35

22 Jones, *War in the Air*, II, 198–9, 457–9; Kiggell to Trenchard, 3 June 1916, Air 1/978/204/5/1139

23 Jones, *War in the Air*, II, 198–9, 206–7; 'Distribution of Machines for Action' and IV Brigade instruction no 25, 23 June 1916, Air 1/2248/209/43/12 pt I; 9 SRB, July 1916, Air 1/1233/204/6/13; 'Fourth Army, Tactical Notes,' Edmonds, *Military Operations: France and Belgium, 1916, Appendices* (London 1932), 146–7

24 RFC operation order no 392, 15 June 1916, Air 1/2265/209/70/1; Jones, *War in the Air*, II, 215

25 Edmonds, *Military Operations: France and Belgium, 1916*, I, 299–307, 315, *Appendices*, 148–9; RFC communiqué no 41, 6 July 1916, DHist 75/413

26 Quoted in Martin Middlebrook, *The First Day on the Somme* (London 1971), 116

27 No 9 SRB, 1 July 1916, Air 1/1233/204/6/13; Edmonds, *Military Operations: France and Belgium, 1916*, I, 341–5, *Appendices*, 88–9, 150–1

28 IV Brigade war diary, précis of reports, 1 July 1916, Air 1/2248/209/43/12 pt I; Edmonds, *Military Operations: France and Belgium, 1916*, I, 362

29 Edmonds, *Military Operations: France and Belgium, 1916*, I, 364, 368, 378, 391–3; Jones, *War in the Air*, II, 210–15; IV Brigade précis of reports, 1 July 1916, Air 1/2248/209/43/12 pt I

30 No 4 SRB, Air 1/2198/209/20/2; IV Brigade précis of reports, 1 July 1916, Air 1/2248/209/43/12 pt I; Jones, *War in the Air*, II, 210–12; Edmonds, *Military Operations: France and Belgium, 1916*, I, 402–3, 416–21

31 Edmonds, *Military Operations: France and Belgium*, I, 441, 464–72

32 'Narrative of the Work of the 9th Wing RFC on 1 July 1916,' 5 July 1916, Air 1/759/204/4/137; G.P. Neumann, *Die deutschen Luftstreitkräfte im Weltkriege* (Berlin 1920), 472–7, DHist SGR I 196, Set 4; RFC communiqué no 41, 6 July 1916, DHist 75/413; IV Brigade précis of reports, 1 July 1916, Air 1/2248/209/43/12 pt I

33 Jones, *War in the Air*, II, 216–17, 221–2; 'Report of German Prisoners of War on the Bombing of St. Quentin by RFC,' Air 1/1282/204/10/52; Edmonds, *Military Operations: France and Belgium, 1916*, I, 477–8; OC 13 Squadron to OC 12 Wing, RFC, 3 July 1916, Air 1/1628/204/90/14; Cuneo, *Winged Mars*, II, 246–9

34 IV Brigade précis of reports, July 1916, Air 1/2248/209/43/12 pt I

35 No 4 SRB, Air 1/2198/209/20/2

36 Ibid.

37 Trenchard to GHQ, 9 July 1916, Air 1/841/204/5/358–61; Ernst von Hoeppner, *Deutschlands Krieg in der Luft* (Leipzig 1921), 71–6, DHist SGR I 196, Set 3; IV Brigade précis of reports, July 1916, Air 1/2248/209/43/12 pt I; Maurice Baring, *Flying Corps Headquarters, 1914–1918* (London 1968), 157; Cuneo, *Winged Mars*, II, 251

38 Diary, 9 July 1916, Brophy biographical file, DHist

39 A.H. Farrar-Hockley, *The Somme* (London 1964), 150, 158–63; Jones, *War in the Air*, II, 227–30; Trenchard to GHQ, 14 and 16 July 1916, Air 1/841/204/5/358–61; IV Brigade instruction no 39, 13 July 1916, Air 1/2248/209/43/12 pt. I; Edmonds, *Military Operations: France and Belgium, 1916*, II (London 1938), 62–89

40 Nicholson, *Canadian Expeditionary Force*, 198–9

41 'Employment of Aircraft and Anti-Aircraft,' Air 1/997/204/5/1239; Trenchard to GHQ, 8 April 1917, Air 1/477/AH15/312/225

42 See Trenchard's daily summaries to GHQ, Air 1/841/204/5/358–61.

43 Diary, 11 July 1916, Brophy biographical file, DHist

44 See for example HQ II Brigade to OC 11 Wing, 24 Aug. 1916, Air 1/1282/204/10/52; Trenchard to Lambe, 1,3,5,7,27 Aug. 1916, Air 1/71/15/9/125.

45 Squadron reports on bomb dropping, Air 1/842/204/5/362

46 Ibid.; report of 27 Squadron, 24 Sept. 1916, Air 1/1389/204/25/42; Jones, *War in the Air*, II, 321–2

47 No 22 Squadron air combat report, 29 July 1916, Air 1/2248/209/43/12 pt I

48 Ibid., 23 Aug. 1916

49 Peter Gray and Owen Thetford, *German Aircraft of the First World War* (London 1962), 87–94, 146–9, 162–5

50 RFC communiqué nos 43–54, 19 July–24 Sept. 1916, DHist 75/413; RFC squadron lists, DHist

51 T.M. Hawker, *Hawker, V.C.* (London 1965), 201

52 No 24 Squadron air combat reports, Air 1/1221/204/5/2634/24

53 'Notes on Formation Flying and Fighting in the Air,' Trenchard to DAO, 30 Aug. 1916, Air 1/129/15/40/191

54 IV Brigade air combat report, 20 July 1916, Air 1/2248/209/43/12 pt I; Hawker, *Hawker, V.C.* 195–6

55 No 24 Squadron air combat report, 6 Aug. 1916, Air 1/169/15/160/7

56 No 24 Squadron air combat report, 14 Sept. 1916, 1/2248/209/43/12 pt II

57 Ibid.

58 Trenchard, 'Future Policy in the Air,' Air 1/71/15/9/125

59 Henderson to Trenchard, 24 July, Trenchard to Henderson, 25 July, War Office to Trenchard, 1 Sept., Trenchard to GHQ, 5 Sept., Sydenham to Henderson, 20 Sept. 1916, Air 1/916/204/5/871

60 A.J. Bott, *Cavalry of the Clouds* (New York 1918), 29

61 IV Brigade précis of reports, 15 Sept. 1916, Air 1/2248/209/43/12 pt II; V Brigade précis of reports, 15 Sept. 1916, Air 1/2224/209/40/22; 'Provisional Instructions for Co-operation between Aeroplanes and Artillery during an Advance,' C–203–2, PAC, RG 9 III, vol. 622; 9 SRB, Air 1/1233/204/6/15; V Brigade, 15 Squadron reports, Air 1/1359/204/21/9; 7 SRB, Air 1/1509/16/3/55; RFC HQ précis of squadron reports, 16 Sept. 1916, Air 1/862/204/5/479; Jones, *War in the Air*, II, 276

62 Jones, *War in the Air*, II, 272; Baring, *Flying Corps Headquarters*, 175; IV Brigade précis of reports, 15 Sept. 1916, Air 1/2248/209/43/12 pt II

63 RFC HQ précis of squadron reports, 15 Sept. 1916, Air 1/862/204/5/479

64 '211 Res Regt at the Somme 7–18 Sep 16,' 158, Reproduction no 10, DHist SGR I 196, Set 90

65 '209 Res Regt at the Somme 10–17 Sep 16,' 131–4, Reproduction no 13, ibid.

66 Trenchard to GHQ, 3 Aug. 1916, Air 1/841/204/5/358–61; Andrew Boyle, *Trenchard* (London 1962), 184

67 Gray and Thetford, *German Aircraft*, 42–7

68 Deutschland, Reichskriegministerium, *Der Weltkriege 1914 bis 1918*, Band XI: *Die Kriegführung im Herbst 1916 und im Winter 1916/17* (Berlin 1938), 109–10, DHist SGR I 196, Set 2; Cuneo, *Winged Mars*, II, 276–80

69 Hoeppner, *Deutschlands Krieg in der Luft*, 78; R. Casari, 'The Development of German Army Aircraft, 1914–18,' *Cross & Cockade Journal*, I, autumn 1960, 1–11; Cuneo, *Winged Mars*, II, 264–5

70 'Short Notes on Information Obtained from Units in the Somme Area,' Turner Papers, vol. 2, file 14

71 No 4 Squadron air combat report, 9 and 17 Oct. 1916, Air 1/2224/209/40/23; 15 Squadron air combat report, 20 Oct. 1916, Air 1/1359/204/21/9

72 No 7 Squadron air combat report, 20 Oct. 1916, Air 1/2224/209/40/23

73 Jones, *War in the Air*, II, 300–16; 49th Canadian Battalion War Diary, 15 Sept. and 7 Oct. 1916, PAC, RG 9 III, vol. 4940, folder 440; Trenchard to GHQ, 9 Nov. 1916, Air 1/841/204/5/358–61

74 RFC communiqué no 61, 9 Nov. 1916, DHist 75/413

75 Jones, *War in the Air*, II, 282–3; 24 Squadron air combat report, 17 Sept. 1916, Air 1/2248/209/43/12 pt II

76 Jones, *War in the Air*, II, 284; IV Brigade précis of reports, 19 Sept. 1916, Air 1/2248/209/43/12 pt II; quoted in Hans Jancke, *Flak an der Somme* (Berlin 1939), 109–16, DHist SGR I 196, Set 61; V Brigade operation order no 24, 19 Sept. 1916, Air 1/2224/209/40/22

77 No 32 Squadron air combat report, 22 Sept. 1916, ibid., 27 Squadron air combat report, Air 1/1221/204/5/2634/27

78 Trenchard to GHQ, 23 and 24 Sept. 1916, Air 1/841/204/5/358–61; Haig to War Office, 30 Sept. 1916, Air 1/2265/209/70/1; GHQ précis of combat reports, 24 Sept. 1916, Air 1/862/204/5/479; 21 Squadron air combat report, 24 Sept. 1916, Air 1/2248/209/43/12 pt II; Jones, *War in the Air*, II, 287–8

79 No 18 Squadron air combat report, 20 Oct. 1916, Air 1/2248/209/43/15

80 No 22 Squadron air combat report, 22 Oct. 1916, ibid., 32 Squadron air combat report, 22 Oct. 1916, 1/2224/209/40/23

81 No 18 Squadron air combat report, 22 Oct. 1916, Air 1/2248/209/43/15

82 Jones, *War in the Air*, II, 309

83 No 60 Squadron air combat reports, 28 Aug. and 14 Sept. 1916, Air 1/1225/204/5/2634/60

84 Ibid., 22, 23, 30 Sept. 1916

85 Ibid., 21 Oct. 1916

86 Ibid., 9 November 1916

87 No 24 Squadron air combat report, 28 Oct. 1916, Air 1/911/204/5/835

88 RFC equipment summary, 22 Oct. 1916, Air 1/762/204/4/164–70; Cuneo, *Winged Mars*, II, 260, 288–93; Bruce Robertson, ed., *Air Aces of the 1914–18 War* (Letchworth, Herts 1959), 132–47; *Les Armées françaises*, Tome IV, III, 162–3, Annexes, I, 950, 1368–9

89 Admiralty minute, 17 Sept. 1916, Air 1/2265/209/70/1; Admiralty to Air Board, 18 Sept. 1916, Air 1/513/16/3/71; 'Memorandum for the War Committee,' 9 Nov. 1916, Air 2/123/B10620; War Office to Admiralty, 29 Sept. 1916, Air 1/2265/209/70/1

90 Henderson to Haig, 8 Sept. 1916, ibid.

91 Trenchard to Henderson, 25 July 1916, Air 1/513/16/3/71; Air Board to Admiralty, 26 July 1916, Admiralty to Air Board, 5 and 26 Aug. 1916, Air 1/650/17/122/431

92 Haig to War Office and Haig to Robertson, 30 Sept. 1916, Air 1/2265/209/70/1; Lambe to Trenchard, nd, Trenchard to Lambe and Trenchard to Henderson, 11 Oct. 1916, Air 1/916/204/5/871; Admiralty to War Office, 19 Oct. 1916, Air 1/513/16/3/71; War Office to Haig, 21 Oct. 1916, Air 1/520/16/12/1; Lambe to Bacon, 23 Dec. 1916, Air 1/69/15/9/113

93 Jones, *War in the Air*, II, 447–8; 8(N) Squadron air combat report, Nov.–Dec. 1916, Air 1/1218/204/5/2634/208; Owen Thetford, *British Naval Aircraft since 1912* (London 1971), 298–303

94 Haig to War Office, 16 Nov. 1916, Air 1/520/16/12/1

95 H.A. Jones, *War in the Air*, V (London 1935), 470; order of battle, Air 1/2129/207/83/1

CHAPTER 14: STALEMATE ON THE WESTERN FRONT, 1917

1 Andrew Boyle, *Trenchard* (London 1962), 210–12; France, Ministère de la Guerre, État-Major de l'Armée, Service Historique, *Les Armées françaises dans la grande Guerre* (Paris 1931), Tome V, I, 161–3, 560–7, annex 446

2 *Les Armées françaises*, Tome V, I, 161–3, 560–7, Tome XI, 568, table III; James E. Edmonds, *Military Operations: France and Belgium, 1917*, I (London 1940), 11

3 Edmonds, *Military Operations: France and Belgium, 1917*, I, 87–116; Deutschland, Oberkommando des Heeres, *Der Weltkrieg 1914 bis 1918*, Band XII: *Die Kriegführung im Frühjahr 1917* (Berlin 1939), 31, 36, 49, DHist SGR I 196, Set 2; 'The German Official History – Volume XII,' *Army Quarterly*, XL, April 1940, 144–6

4 H.A. Jones, *The War in the Air: being the Story of the Part played in the Great War by the Royal Air Force*, III (London 1931), 306–7, 324–31; Edmonds, *Military Operations: France and Belgium, 1917*, I, 87–9, 127–70; HQ RFC to 9 Wing, 4 March 1917, Air 1/1001/204/5/1258; V Brigade work summary, 4 March 1917, 9 Wing work summary, 6–25 March 1917, Air 1/767/204/4/251

5 Peter Gray and Owen Thetford, *German Aircraft of the First World War* (London 1962), 48–51

6 Trenchard to Chief of Staff, 11 Feb. 1917, Air 1/522/16/12/5

7 Admiralty to Air Board, 20 Dec. 1916, Air 1/520/16/12/1; J.M. Bruce, *British Aeroplanes, 1914–18* (London 1957), 563–8

8 Collishaw to Grange, 30 Oct. 1965, Raymond Collishaw Papers, DHist 78/132, 1-A, folder 101; Chambers to Hallahan, 10 April 1917, R.H. Mulock Papers, document 43, DHist

9 Chambers to Mulock, 13 June 1917, Mulock Papers, document 53, DHist

10 Trenchard to Senior Officer, RNAS Dunkirk, 27 June 1917, ibid., document 57

11 Collishaw to Grange, 21 May 1965, Collishaw Papers, DHist 78/132, 1-A, folder 101; letters home, 9 March and 11 April 1917, L.S. Breadner Papers, DHist 74/707, files 32 and 34; DHist squadron lists

12 DHist squadron lists; Jones, *War in the Air*, III, map facing 330, app. XII

13 RAF Staff College précis, 'Air Warfare,' nd, 45, Air 1/2385/228/10; HQ RFC to all brigades and 9 Wing, 26 March 1917, Air 1/1008/204/5/1283

14 HQ RFC to all brigades and 9 Wing, 26 March 1917

15 Ibid.; Jones, *War in the Air*, III, 334, 360

16 Jones, *War in the Air*, III, 354–5, 360; RAF Staff College précis, 'Air Warfare,' nd, 44–5, Air 1/2385/228/10; I Brigade work summary, April 1917, Air 1/768/204/4/252

17 Bruce, *British Aeroplanes*, 426–38

18 Edmonds, *Military Operations: France and Belgium, 1917*, I, 300–5; report of Canadian Corps operations, Vimy, folder 52, file 7, PAC, RG 9 III, vol. 3846

19 Report of Canadian Corps operations, Vimy; Edmonds, *Military Operations: France and Belgium, 1917*, I, 311, 314; C.à C. Repington, *The First World War, 1914–1918* (London 1921), I, 530

20 I Brigade to HQ RFC and attached plan, 26 March 1917, Air 1/1008/204/5/1283

21 'Notes on Counter Battery Work in connection with the Capture of Vimy Ridge,' Canadian Corps General Staff, folder 46, file 2, 'Instructions for Co-operation Between Divisional Artillery, Heavy Artillery and R.F.C. during Trench Destruction,' app. E to Artillery Instructions for Vimy Ridge, 28 March 1917, Canadian Corps General Staff, folder 46, file 6, PAC, RG 9 III, vol. 3843; Edmonds, *Military Operations: France and Belgium, 1917*, I, app. 15; Jones, *War in the Air*, III, 311–13, 332, 344–5, app. XII

22 Floyd Gibbons, *The Red Knight of Germany: Baron von Richthofen, Germany's Great War Airman* (London 1930), 126–7; I Brigade work summary, 27–28 March 1917, Air 1/767/204/4/251; 16 Squadron air combat reports, 6 and 11 March 1917, Air 1/1219/204/5/2634/16; RFC communiqué nos 74, 78, DHist 75/413

23 I Brigade work summary, April 1917, Air 1/768/204/4/252; Jones, *War in the Air*, III, 356, 365

24 War diary, I Brigade, Canadian Field Artillery, 7 and 12 March 1917, folder 527, PAC, RG 9 III, vol. 4963

25 War diary, 2nd Canadian Divisional Artillery, 11 March and 5 April 1917, folder 510, ibid., vol. 4959

26 War diary, II Brigade, Canadian Field Artillery, 3 April 1917, folder 529, ibid., vol. 4964; war diary, 3rd Canadian Siege Battery, 6 April 1917, folder 570, ibid., vol. 4976

27 No 16 SRB, 9 April 1917, Air 1/1343/204/19/15; I Brigade work summary, April 1917, Air 1/768/204/4/252

28 W.A. Bishop, *Winged Warfare: Hunting the Huns in the Air* (London 1918), 93–4

29 'Policy in the Air,' attached to Kiggel to distribution, 9 April 1917, Air 1/522/16/12/5

30 Jones, *War in the Air*, III, app. XII; DHist squadron lists

31 A.J.L. Scott, *Sixty Squadron R.A.F.: a History of the Squadron from its Formation* (London 1920), 30, 38, 44–5, app. II

32 W.A. Bishop biographical file, DHist

33 No 60 Squadron air combat report, 25 March 1917, Air 1/1225/204/5/2634/60

34 Ibid., 30 April 1917; Bishop biographical file, DHist

35 RFC war diary, 11 April 1917, Air 1/1185/204/5/2595; J.S.T. Fall biographical file, DHist

36 'Some Notes on Officers who served in R.F.C. and R.A.F. Canada,' app. D, Allen to Dodds, 5 Dec. 1962, D.L. Allen Papers, DHist 76/199

37 Letter home, 23 April 1917, L.S. Breadner Papers, DHist 74/707, file 35

38 Ibid.; RFC war diary, 23 April 1917, Air 1/1185/204/5/2595; J.J. Malone biographical file, DHist

39 'Number of Machines Employed on Each Front and Casualties in France Only,' nd, Air 1/516/16/6/1; DHist squadron lists; 'Functions and Tactics of German Air Service, Spring of 1917, Particularly During Arras Battle April-May, 1917,' [1924], Air 1/9/15/1/22

40 Canadian Bank of Commerce, *Letters from the Front: Being a Record of the Part Played by Officers of the Bank in the Great War, 1914–1919*, C.L. Foster and W.S. Duthie, eds. (Toronto [1920–1921]), I, 210

41 Edmonds, *Military Operations: France and Belgium, 1917*, II (London 1948), 42, 93–4; Trenchard to Advanced GHQ, proposals for organizational changes, 9 May 1917, Air 1/1008/204/5/1283; H.A. Jones, *War in the Air*, IV (London 1934), 111–13, app. III. See also Sir Gordon Taylor, *Sopwith Scout 7309* (London 1968), 103–18.

42 II Brigade work summary, 6–7 June 1917, Air 1/768/204/4/254; Jones, *War in the Air*, IV, 114–15, 118

43 Correspondence and instructions on wireless intelligence of hostile aircraft, 24 Oct. 1916–25 May 1917, Air 1/526/16/12/38

44 Scott, *Sixty Squadron R.A.F.*, 59

45 Ibid., 58–9; Jones, *War in the Air*, IV, 119–20

46 G.W.L. Nicholson, *Canadian Expeditionary Force, 1914–1919* (Official History of the Canadian Army in the First World War; Ottawa 1964), 302; Taylor, *Sopwith Scout*, 111; Edmonds, *Military Operations: France and Belgium, 1917*, II, 41, 43–9, 55

47 Edmonds, *Military Operations: France and Belgium, 1917*, II, 70; 'Resumé of the Wireless Organization of the 2nd Wing, R.F.C. Previous to and During the Offensive Operations of the Second Army in June, 1917,' 11 June 1917, Air 1/1007/204/5/1271; II Brigade work summary, 6–7 June 1917, Air 1/768/204/4/254; 42 Squadron air combat report, 7 June 1917, Air 1/1222/204/5/2634/42; Jones, *War in the Air*, III, 310, IV, 129–30, 132, 410, 413; Maurice Baring, *Flying Corps Headquarters, 1914–1918* (London 1968), 228

48 DHist squadron lists

49 R.V. Dodds, historical sketch of 210 Squadron RAF [10 (Naval)], DHist 73/1552; Raymond Collishaw biographical file, DHist; letter to Vice-Admiral Dover Patrol, 19 April 1917, Lambe to RNAS Dunkirk, 16 May 1917, Lambe to Vice-Admiral Dover Patrol, 23 Aug. 1917, Air 1/637/17/122/142

50 Collishaw's air combats and logbook, Collishaw Papers, DHist 78/132, 1-A, folder 35; RFC communiqué nos 91–4, June 1917, DHist 75/413

51 No 10 (Naval) Squadron air combat report, 17 June 1917, Air 1/1219/204/5/2634/10

52 DHist squadron lists; R. Collishaw, with R.V. Dodds, *Air Command: a Fighter Pilot's Story* (London 1973), 79, 100

53 William Arthur Bishop, *The Courage of the Early Morning: a Son's Biography of a Famous Father* (Toronto 1965), 97–100

54 No 60 Squadron air combat report, 2 June 1917, Air 1/1225/204/5/2634/60

55 Ibid.; William Frye, *Air of Battle* (London 1974), 136

56 Jones, *War in the Air*, IV, 129–30

57 M.P.A. Hankey, 1st Baron Hankey, *The Supreme Command, 1914–1918* (London 1961), II, 677–80

58 Ibid., 683; Edmonds, *Military Operations: France and Belgium, 1917*, II, 124

59 Edmonds, *Military Operations: France and Belgium, 1917*, II, 133–4; V Brigade order, 8 July 1917, Air 1/1592/204/83/17; Jones, *War in the Air*, IV, 145, 148

60 Jones, *War in the Air*, IV, 141, 418; Edmonds, *Military Operations: France and Belgium, 1917*, II, 134

61 Bruce, *British Aeroplanes*, 126–30

62 Ibid., 445–55

63 Ibid., 573–6; Gray and Thetford, *German Aircraft*, xxx, 52–5

64 R. Collishaw's Staff College essay, 23 Sept. 1924, Air 1/2387/228/11/40; Bruce Robertson, ed., *Von Richthofen and the Flying Circus* (Letchworth, Herts. 1959), 64–5; Karl Bodenschatz, *Jagd in Flanderns Himmel* (München 1942), 13–14; Norman Macmillan, *Into the Blue* (London 1969), 125

65 Macmillan, *Into the Blue*, 125–6

66 Arthur Gould Lee, *Open Cockpit: a Pilot of the Royal Flying Corps* (London 1969), 91–2

67 Extracts from III Brigade war diary, June and July 1917, V Brigade war diary, July 1917, Air 1/721/48/2; H.E. Creagan, 'W.M. Alexander of Black Flight, Naval 10,' *CAHS Journal*, III, fall 1965, 64

68 Brigadier-General Commanding V Brigade to 15 and 22 Wings, 24 July 1917, Air 1/1592/204/83/17; Jones, *War in the Air*, IV, 157; Hans Arndt, 'Die Fliegerwaffe,' in F. Seesselberg, *Der Stellungskrieg, 1914–1918* (Berlin 1926), 339–40, 342, DHist SGR I 196, Set 88

69 Translation of 'weekly intelligence summary of the German Fourth Army,' 12–18 July 1917, DHist SS 582; G.S.B. Fuller, 'Reminiscences of Lieut. G.S.B. Fuller, No. 9 Sqdn., R.F.C.,' *Cross & Cockade Journal*, X, spring 1969, 41

70 Jones, *War in the Air*, IV, 161–2; John Charteris, *At G.H.Q.* (London 1931), 238

71 H. von Bülow, *Geschichte der Luftwaffe* (Frankfurt 1937), 95; Arndt, 'Die Fliegerwaffe,' 343–6, sketches 225a and b

72 Douglas Haig, 1st Earl Haig, *Sir Douglas Haig's Despatches*, J.H. Boraston, ed. (London 1919), 116

73 Sir Hubert Gough, *The Fifth Army* (London 1931), 203; extracts from V Brigade war diary, Aug. 1917, Air 1/721/48/2

74 I Brigade work summary, 8–9 Aug. 1917, Air 1/769/204/4/256; Denis Richards, *Portal of Hungerford* (London 1977), 61; Douglas Reed, *Insanity Fair* (London 1938), 37; 'McScotch,' *Fighter Pilot* (London 1936), 55–6

75 'McScotch,' 71–2; Hermann Franke, ed., *Handbuch der neuzeitlichen Wehrwissenschaften* (Berlin 1939), III, Buch 2, 307; Bülow, *Geschichte der Luftwaffe*, 97; A.J. Insall, *Observer: Memoirs of the R.F.C., 1915–1918* (London 1970), 176; I Brigade report attached to Trenchard to GHQ, 17 Aug. 1917, Air 1/971/204/5/1111

76 I Brigade report, 17 Aug. 1917; Jones, *War in the Air*, IV, 170; Edmonds, *Military Operations: France and Belgium, 1917*, II, 226

77 'Number of Machines Employed on Each Front and Casualties in France Only,' nd, Air 1/516/16/6/1; Haig to CIGS, 13 Aug. 1917, Trenchard to SO RNAS, Dunkirk, 21 Aug. 1917, Air 1/913/204/5/851

78 Edmonds, *Military Operations: France and Belgium, 1917*, II, 192n, 193; Jones, *War in the Air*, IV, 173n, 175–7

79 Jones, *War in the Air*, IV, 176–9

80 Report on bomb raid, 16 Aug. 1917, Air 1/917/204/5/875

81 RFC war diary, 16 Aug. 1917, Air 1/1185/204/5/2595; G.S.B. Fuller, 'Reminiscences,' 41

82 Jones, *War in the Air*, IV, 172–6; Edmonds, *Military Operations: France and Belgium, 1917*, II, 184–5, 189–201, sketch 19

83 For example, see 57 Squadron bombing reports of this period, Air 1/840/204/5/340; C. Gordon Burge, *The Annals of 100 Squadron* (London [1919]), 67–138; Frank Dunham, *The Long Carry: the Journal of Stretcher Bearer Frank Dunham, 1916–18*, R.H. Haigh and P.W. Turner, eds. (Oxford 1970), 74.

84 RFC war diary, 21 and 22 Aug. 1917, Air 1/1185/204/5/2595; William R. Puglisi, 'Jacobs of Jasta 7,' *Cross & Cockade Journal*, VI, winter 1965, 309; W.M. Alexander biographical file, DHist

85 Edmonds, *Military Operations: France and Belgium, 1917*, II, 209, 233–4

86 Ibid., 206–7

87 Oliver Stewart, *Words and Music for a Mechanical Man* (London 1967), 130–1; Arthur Gould Lee, *No Parachute: a Fighter Pilot in World War 1* (London 1968), 118

88 'Number of Machines Employed on Each Front and Casualties in France only,' nd, Air 1/516/16/6/1

89 Stewart, *Words and Music*, 132

90 William Sholto Douglas, 1st Baron Douglas of Kirtleside, *Years of Combat: the First Volume of the Autobiography of Sholto Douglas* (London 1963), 179–86

91 II Brigade operations order, 17 Sept. 1917, Air 1/931/204/5/927; Scott, *Sixty Squadron R.A.F.*, 72–3

92 Maxse to Fifth Army, 21 Aug. 1917, XVIII Corps GS70, Maxse Papers, Imperial War Museum, file 39; Kiggell to Army HQs, 12 Aug. 1917, Trenchard to GS, GHQ, 19 Sept. 1917, Air 1/971/204/5/1111

93 John Ewing, *The History of the 9th (Scottish) Division, 1914–1919* (London 1921), 234; H.R. Sandilands, *The 23rd Division, 1914–1919* (Edinburgh 1925), 192–3; Edmonds, *Military Operations: France and Belgium, 1917*, II, 260

94 Edmonds, *Military Operations: France and Belgium, 1917*, II, 276n; Jones, *War in the Air*, IV, 184–6

95 Kelly Wills, 'The Eagle of Lens: Hans Waldhausen,' *Cross & Cockade Journal*, VIII, summer 1967, 107–8

96 Extracts from V Brigade war diary, Sept. 1917, Air 1/721/48/2

97 No 1 (Naval) SRB, 20 Sept. 1917, Air 1/40/15/9/9

98 Jones, *War in the Air*, IV, 183; translation of German paper, 'The Employment of Machine Guns in Trench Warfare.' 10 Sept. 1917, DHist SS 707; Insall, *Observer*, 178; S.W. Rosevear biographical file, DHist

99 Edmonds, *Military Operations: France and Belgium, 1917*, II, 280, 289–95; Jones, *War in the Air*, IV, 192

100 Jones, *War in the Air*, IV, 99–100
101 'Operations of 100 Squadron with Canadians Taking Part,' nd, Air 1/721/48/2; Charteris, *At G.H.Q.*, 263
102 Extracts from brigade war diaries, Sept. 1917, Air 1/721/48/2
103 Jones, *War in the Air*, IV, 198–200
104 R.T.C. Hoidge biographical file, DHist; James Thomas Byford McCudden, *Five Years in the Royal Flying Corps* (London [1918]), 240–3
105 RFC communiqué no 107, 3 Oct. 1917, DHist 75/413; Holt to GOC V Brigade RFC, 1 Oct. 1917, Air 1/913/204/5/851
106 Holt to GOC V Brigade RFC, 1 Oct. 1917
107 Ibid.; Curtis to DHist, 11 Feb. 1973, W.A. Curtis biographical file, DHist
108 Boyle, *Trenchard*, 81–2; Trenchard to GS, Advanced GHQ, 13 Nov. 1917, Air 1/913/204/5/851
109 Great Britain, War Office, *Statistics of the Military Effort of the British Empire During the Great War, 1914–1920* (London 1922), 326–7
110 Ibid., 264
111 W.S. Douglas' Staff College essay, 15 Oct. 1922, Air 1/2386/228/11/13
112 DHist squadron lists
113 'Extract No. 12 from German Documents and Correspondence,' 25 Nov. 1917, DHist SS 712; Macmillan, *Into the Blue*, 167; Ralph Hodder-Williams, *Princess Patricia's Canadian Light Infantry, 1914–1919* (London 1923), 248; H.C. Singer, *History of Thirty-First Battalion, C.E.F.: from its Organization November, 1914 to its Demobilization June, 1919* (np [1939]), 262
114 Holt to V Brigade, 27 Oct. 1917, Air 1/1592/204/83/17; notes on Trenchard's address at a corps commanders conference, 24 Oct. 1917, Canadian Corps Instructions, 23 Oct. 1917, 'Canadian Corps GS,' 112 and 116, DHist 112.3H1.009(D259), vol. I; 2nd Canadian division order, 31 Oct. 1917, '25th Canadian Infantry Battalion,' 5, ibid., vol. II
115 II Brigade to Second Army, 24 Oct. 1917, 'Canadian Corps GS,' 111, ibid., vol. I; G.B.A. Baker's Staff College essay, 10 Aug. 1926, Air 1/2389/228/11/97
116 Annex to V Brigade work summary, 19–20 Oct. 1917, Air 1/770/204/4/258
117 Extracts from V Brigade war diary, Oct. 1917, Air 1/721/48/2
118 Ibid.; annex to V Brigade work summary, 19–20 Oct. 1917, Air 1/770/204/4/258
119 Macmillan, *Into the Blue*, 187–8
120 Ibid., 188
121 Curtis to Dodds, 31 July 1962, W.A. Curtis biographical file, DHist
122 Nicholson, *Canadian Expeditionary Force*, 311, 318–20
123 RFC war diary, 26 Oct. 1917, Air 1/1186/204/5/2595
124 Ibid.; Jones, *War in the Air*, IV, 210; extracts from IV and V Brigades war diaries, Oct. 1917, Air 1/721/48/2
125 '72nd Canadian Infantry Battalion,' 2, DHist 112.3H1.009 (D259), vol. II; RFC war diary, 30 Oct. 1917, Air 1/1186/204/5/2595; III Brigade work summary, 30–31 Oct. 1917, Air 1/770/204/4/258
126 R.C. Fetherstonhaugh, *The Royal Montreal Regiment, 14th Battalion, C.E.F., 1914–1925* (Montreal 1927), 181
127 Nicholson, *Canadian Expeditionary Force*, map 9

128 Jones, *War in the Air*, IV, 211–12; RFC war diary, Air 1/1186/204/5/2595

129 Singer, *History of the Thirty-First Battalion*, 268; '1st Battalion,' 6, DHist 112.3H1.009(D259), vol. II

130 '31st Canadian Infantry Battalion,' 3, DHist 112.3H1.009(D259), vol. II

131 Nicholson, *Canadian Expeditionary Force*, 325, map 9

132 Ibid., 325–6; RFC war diary, 10 Nov. 1917, Air 1/1186/204/5/2595

133 *Statistics of the Military Effort of the British Empire*, 326–7

134 J.F.C. Fuller, *Tanks in the Great War, 1914–1918* (London 1920), 140

135 Jones, *War in the Air*, IV, 230–1

136 No 3 SRB and war diary, Air 1/166/15/142/19; Pretyman to Wing COs, 19 Nov. 1917, Air 1/1431/204/31/31; Lee, *Open Cockpit*, 154

137 Jones, *War in the Air*, IV, app. XI

138 Richard Flashar, 'In der Tankschlacht von Cambrai,' in G.P. Neumann, ed., *In der Luft unbesiegt* (München 1923), 96–8, DHist SGR I 196, Set 71

139 Wilfrid Miles, *Military Operations: France and Belgium, 1917*, III (London 1948), 50–88, 90

140 Jones, *War in the Air*, IV, 235–6, 432

141 No 3 SRB and war diary, Air 1/166/15/142/19

142 III Brigade work summary, 20–21 Nov. 1917, Air 1/770/204/4/259

143 Miles, *Military Operations: France and Belgium, 1917*, III, 17, 90; B.H. Liddell Hart, *The Tanks: the History of the Royal Tank Regiment and its Predecessors, Heavy Branch Machine-Gun Corps, Tank Corps and Royal Tank Corps, 1914–1945*, I: *1914–1939* (London 1959), 130–47

144 III Brigade work summary, 20–21 Nov. 1917, Air 1/770/204/4/259; Jones, *War in the Air*, IV, 241–3; Flashar, 'In der Tankschlacht von Cambrai,' 99, 241 ff; Miles, *Military Operations: France and Belgium, 1917*, III, 115–16

145 No 84 Squadron air combat report, 22 Nov. 1917, Air 1/1797/204/155/8; P.J. Carisella and James W. Ryan, *Who Killed the Red Baron? The Final Answer* (Wakefield, Mass. 1969), 56, 246

146 III Brigade work summary, 22–23 Nov. 1917, Air 1/770/204/4/259; Jones, *War in the Air*, IV, 244–5

147 Jones, *War in the Air*, IV, 247

148 Ibid., 247–8; J.C. Slessor, *Air Power and Armies* (London 1936), 91

149 Miles, *Military Operations: France and Belgium, 1917*, III, 168; Jones, *War in the Air*, IV, 249–50

150 Jones, *War in the Air*, IV, 249–51, 252n; Miles, *Military Operations: France and Belgium, 1917*, III, sketch 14

151 III Brigade work summary, 29–30 Nov. 1917, Air 1/770/204/4/259; 64 Squadron history, Air 1/173/15/182/1; 11 Squadron air combat report, 30 Nov. 1917, Air 1/1219/204/5/2634/11; A.E. McKeever biographical file, DHist

152 Bank of Commerce, *Letters from the Front*, I, 261–2

153 Ibid.

154 RFC war diary, 30 Nov.–3 Dec. 1917, Air 1/1186/204/5/2595

155 No 2 Squadron air combat reports, 18 and 19 Dec. 1917, Air 1/1216/204/5/2634/2

156 Reed, *Insanity Fair*, 39–40

157 Stephen Roskill, *Hankey: Man of Secrets*, I: *1877–1918* (London 1970), 470; Jones, *War in the Air*, IV, app. III and X; DHist squadron lists

158 'Functions and Tactics of German Air Service, Spring of 1917, Particularly during Arras Battle April-May, 1917' [1924], Air 1/9/15/1/22; nominal rolls of Canadians undergoing or graduating from RFC flying training, late 1917, OMFC C–985–33, PAC, RG 9 III, vol. 2741; extracts from Statistical Abstract No 23, Section 1, 'Growth of the Royal Flying Corps,' Air 1/2314/223/10/1. For RNAS reinforcements see Lambe to Vice-Admiral Dover Patrol, 23 Aug. 1917, Air 1/637/17/122/142.

CHAPTER 15: ITALY AND MACEDONIA, 1917–18

1 C.R.M.F. Cruttwell, *A History of the Great War, 1914–1918* (Oxford 1934), 234

2 H.A. Jones, *The War in the Air: being the Story of the Part played in the Great War by the Royal Air Force*, V (London 1935), 358; minutes of 25th Air Board meeting, 4 Oct. 1916, Air 6/3

3 H.A. Jones, *Over the Balkans and South Russia: the History of 47 Squadron RAF* (London 1923), 17, 24

4 Owen biographical file, DHist; F.S. Mills and H.V. Reid biographical cards, DHist; Jones, *War in the Air*, V, 342–3, 378–9

5 Jones, *Over the Balkans*, 38–41; Jones, *War in the Air*, V, 344–65; 16 Wing air combat report, 27 Feb. 1917, Air 1/2353/226/4/105 pt II

6 Jones, *War in the Air*, V, 346–9

7 A.G. Goulding biographical file, DHist; 17 Squadron air combat reports, 13, 22, 25 April and 28 June 1917, Air 1/2353/226/4/105 pt I

8 Jones, *War in the Air*, V, 362

9 No 17 Squadron air combat report, 5 Oct. 1917, Air 1/2353/226/4/105 pt I

10 Bruce Robertson, ed., *Air Aces of the 1914–1918 War* (Letchworth, Herts. 1959), 117

11 Ibid., 198–9; Gunther Rothenburg, 'Military Aviation in Austro-Hungary, 1893–1918,' *Aerospace Historian*, XIX, June 1972, 81

12 France, Ministère de la Guerre, État-Major de l'Armée, Service Historique, *Les Armées françaises dans la grande Guerre* (Paris 1931), Tome V, I, 536–42, and II, 274–87, 296–300; 'The Supreme Military Council, a Summary of its History,' *Army Quarterly*, III, Oct. 1921, 124–7; E.M. Hutchinson, 'The History of the Supreme War Council from its Creation,' *Journal of the Royal Artillery*, XLVIII, 1921–2, 275–391; James E. Edmonds, *Military Operations: Italy, 1915–1919* (London 1949), 43–4, 46, 405–9; V.J. Esposito, *A Concise History of World War I* (New York 1969), 169; Barker's combat report, 29 Nov. 1917, Air 1/1854/204/213/15; Robertson, ed., *Air Aces*, 118–19; W.M. Lamberton, *Reconnaissance and Bomber Aircraft of the 1914–1918 War* (Letchworth, Herts. 1962), 164–7; Delmé-Radcliffe to DMO, 21 Oct. 1917, cited in Edmonds, *Military Operations: Italy, 1915–1919*, 46n

13 Edmonds, *Military Operations: Italy, 1915–1919*, 58; *Les Armées françaises*, Tome V, II, 1141–2; Frederick Rudolph Lambert, 10th Earl of Cavan, 'A Fragment from the Last War,' *Army Quarterly*, XLIII, Nov. 1942, 46–7

14 No 28 Squadron air combat report, 29 Nov. 1917, Air 1/1854/204/213/15; RFC operation order no 1, 28 Nov. 1917, Air 1/1665/204/98/1; Jones, *War in the Air*, VI (London 1937), 276; Rothenburg, 'Military Aviation,' 79–80; 'Summary of overall growth of the Austrian Military Air Force,' *Cross & Cockade Journal*, VII, summer 1976, 126–7

15 Sir Philip Joubert, 'How Billy Barker won his V.C.,' *Weekend Magazine*, 25 May
    1963, 43; Row to Dodds, 5 Nov. 1962, W.G. Barker biographical file, DHist

16 No 28 Squadron air combat report, 3 Dec. 1917, copy extract from AH 204/213/15,
    ibid.

17 Jones, *War in the Air*, VI, 273–4, 277; G.D. Neumann, *The German Air Force in the
    Great War* (London 1920), 235–9; 66 SRB, 6, 7, 8, 13, 14, 15, 16, 18, and 26 Dec.
    1917, Air 1/1575/204/80/76; 28 Squadron air combat report, 8 Dec. 1917, Air
    1/1854/204/213/15

18 No 66 SRB, 15–16 Dec. 1917, Air 1/1575/204/80/76; Jones, *War in the Air*, VI, 277;
    T.F. Williams biographical file, DHist

19 Jones, *War in the Air*, VI, 277

20 Taped interview with T.F. Williams, 1 Feb. 1971, Williams biographical file, DHist

21 *London Gazette*, 15 March 1918, 30583; *Flight*, 28 March 1918, 332; 17 Squadron
    patrol report, 24 March 1918, Air 1/2353/226/4/105 pt I

22 Jones, *War in the Air*, V, 366; 150 Squadron air combat report, 28 May 1918, Air
    1/2353/225/4/105 pt I

23 150 Squadron air combat report, 1 June 1918, Air 1/2353/225/4/105 pt I

24 Ibid., 1, 12, 15, 18, 20, 23, and 28 June 1918; Edmonds, *Military Operations:
    Macedonia*, II (London 1935), 99–100; Jones, *Over the Balkans*, 107

25 No 150 Squadron air combat report, 26 July 1918, Air 1/2353/226/4/105 pt I; W.J.
    Wheeler, 'A.E. de M. Jarvis, A Biographical Sketch,' *CAHS Journal*, VIII, summer
    1970, 40–50; Jones, *War in the Air*, VI, 293–4

26 Jones, *War in the Air*, VI, 300–1; 150 Squadron air combat reports, 1, 2, and 3 Sept.
    1918, Air 1/2353/226/4/105 pt I

27 VII Brigade instruction, 2 Jan. 1918, and VII Brigade letter G 9/8, 4 Jan. 1918, Air
    1/1665/204/98/43

28 VII Brigade operation orders no 6 and 7, 31 Dec. 1917 and 9 Jan. 1918, ibid.; 28
    Squadron air combat report, 1 Jan. 1918, Air 1/1854/204/213/15; 28 SRB, 5 Jan.
    1918, Air 1/1561/204/80/26; 66 SRB, 1, 5 Jan. 1918, Air 1/1575/204/80/76

29 Interview, Williams biographical file, DHist

30 Ibid.

31 No 28 Squadron air combat report, 24 Jan. 1918, Air 1/1854/204/213/15

32 Ibid., 2 Feb. 1918

33 No 45 Squadron air combat report, 2 Feb. 1918, Air 1/1786/204/151/1; list of EA
    shot down and out of control, Air 1/1665/204/98/40

34 No 66 SRB, 4 and 6 Feb. 1918, Air 1/1575/204/80/76; list of EA shot down, 4 Feb.
    1918, Air 1/1665/204/98/40; University of Toronto, *University of Toronto Roll of
    Service, 1914–1918*, G. Oswald Smith, ed. (Toronto 1921), 94, 190; 28 Squadron air
    combat report, 5 Feb. 1918, Air 1/1854/204/213/15

35 No 28 Squadron air combat report, 12 Feb. 1918, Air 1/1854/204/213/15; *London
    Gazette* (Supplement), 18 Feb. 1918, 2157

36 No 34 SRB, Nov. 1917, Air 1/1392/204/26/14

37 Ibid., Dec. 1917

38 No 34 SRB, 4 Jan. and 13 March 1918, Air 1/1393/204/26/15

39 Edmonds, *Military Operations: Italy, 1915–1919*, 146–57; Jones, *War in the Air*, VI,
    280

40 Edmonds, *Military Operations: Italy, 1915–1919*, 158–66; Jones, *War in the Air*, VI, 280–1

41 Lamberton, *Reconnaissance and Bomber Aircraft*, 62, 214–15; J.M. Bruce, *British Aeroplanes, 1914–1918* (London 1957), 135, 434, 578; VII Brigade instruction, 17 March 1918, Air 1/1665/204/98/43

42 List of EA shot down, 10, 18, and 24 March 1918, Air 1/1665/204/98/40; 66 SRB, 18 and 24 March 1918, Air 1/1575/204/80/76; Williams biographical file, DHist

43 Williams biographical file; *London Gazette*, 16 Sept. and 2 Nov. 1918, 11035, 12978; 66 Squadron air combat report, 17 April 1918, Air 1/1788/204/151/6; 34 SRB, 17 April 1918, Air 1/1394/204/26/16; 28 Squadron air combat reports, 2, 3, 4, 9, 13, 19, 21, 23, 26, 30, and 31 May 1918, Air 1/1854/204/213/15; 66 SRB, 17 April, and 1, 2, 3, 4, 5, 6, 8, 13, 19, 20, 21, 23, 24, 30, and 31 May 1918, Air 1/1575/204/80/77; 66 Squadron air combat reports, 8 and 11 May 1918, copy extracts from AH 204/80/63, Barker biographical file, DHist

44 No 66 Squadron air combat reports, 24 May 1918, AH 204/80/63

45 No 66 SRB, 14 March 1918, Air 1/1575/204/80/76

46 'G.H.Q. Reconnaissance by 34 Squadron R.A.F. 2nd May 1918,' Air 1/1394/204/26/16

47 No 34 SRB, 23 April and 7 June, ibid.

48 Ibid., 3 and 10 May and 10 June 1918

49 Ibid., 10 May, 1 and 10 June 1918

50 Edmonds, *Military Operations: Italy, 1915–1919*, 187–93; Jones, *War in the Air*, VI, 282

51 No 66 SRB, 15 June 1918, Air 1/1575/204/80/77

52 No 34 SRB, 15 June 1918, Air 1/1394/204/26/16; C.E. Carrington, 'The Defence of the Censua re-entrant (etc),' *Army Quarterly*, XIV, July 1927, 306–18; Edmonds, *Military Operations: Italy, 1915–1919*, 194–226

53 Interview, Williams biographical file, DHist

54 Jones, *War in the Air*, VI, 284

55 No 34 SRB, 16 June 1918, Air 1/1394/204/26/16

56 No 66 air combat report, 16 June 1918, extract from AH 204/80/44, Barker biographical file, DHist; 34 SRB, 16 June 1918, Air 1/1394/204/26/16

57 Ibid., 18 June 1918

58 Edmonds, *Military Operations: Italy, 1915–1919*, 222–37

59 Barker biographical file, DHist; *Toronto Telegram*, 17 April 1920, 22; Bob Ross, 'Austro-Hungarian Aces,' *Cross & Cockade Journal*, XIV, summer 1973, 124–30

60 Edmonds, *Military Operations: Italy, 1915–1919*, 242–7

61 Jones, *War in the Air*, VI, 280

62 Edmonds, *Military Operations: Italy, 1915–1919*, 260–3

63 Joubert to Secretary, Air Ministry, report of bomb raids, 4–8 Oct. 1918, Air 1/1985/204/273/97; 28 Squadron air combat reports, 4 and 5 Oct. 1918, Air 1/1854/204/213/15; 66 SRB, 4–5 Oct. 1918, Air 1/1575/204/80/77; *London Gazette*, 3 Dec. 1918, 14316, 31046; Jones, *War in the Air*, VI, 288

64 Jones, *War in the Air*, VI, 289–90; Edmonds, *Military Operations: Italy, 1915–1919*, 266–7

65 Jones, *War in the Air*, VI, 289–90; Edmonds, *Military Operations: Italy, 1915–1919*, 269; operation order, 'The Flying Services in the Future Battle,' 21 Oct. 1918, Air 1/1577/204/80/99

66 Jones, *War in the Air*, VI, 290–1; 14 Wing branch intelligence reports of 139 Squadron from 14 Oct. 1918, Air 1/1576/204/80/81

67 Edmonds, *Military Operations: Italy, 1915–1919*, 270–7; 34 SRB, 27 Oct. 1918, Air 1/1396/204/26/18

68 No 34 SRB, 27 Oct. 1918, Air 1/1396/204/26/18; Edmonds, *Military Operations: Italy, 1915–1919*, 292–4

69 No 28 SRB, 27 Oct. 1918, Air 1/1853/204/213/4; 66 SRB, 27 Oct. 1918, Air 1/1575/204/80/77; 28 Squadron air combat report, 27 Oct. 1918, Air 1/1854/204/213/15; *London Gazette*, 8 Feb. 1919, 31170; Brook to Williams, 5 Dec. 1918, Williams biographical file, DHist

70 Edmonds, *Military Operations: Italy, 1915–1919*, 298–303; Jones, *War in the Air*, VI, 292; 28 SRB, 28 Oct. 1918, Air 1/1853/204/213/4; 66 SRB, 28 Oct. 1918, Air 1/1575/204/80/77

71 No 28 SRB, 29 Oct. 1918, Air 1/1853/204/213/4; *London Gazette*, 2 Nov. 1918 and 8 Feb. 1919, 12978, 31170

72 No 66 SRB, 30 Oct.–2 Nov. 1918, Air 1/1779/204/148/28

73 H.R. Sandilands, *The 23rd Division, 1914–1919* (Edinburgh 1925), 330

74 J.F. Gathorne-Hardy, 'A Summary of the Campaign in Italy and an Account of the Battle of Vittorio Veneto,' *Army Quarterly*, III, Oct. 1921, 34

75 Edmonds, *Military Operations: Macedonia*, II, 127–46

76 No 150 Squadron air combat report, 18 Sept. 1918, Air 1/2353/226/4/105 pt I; Jones, *War in the Air*, VI, 305

77 Todd to HQ RAF Middle East, 3 March 1919, 'History of 16th Wing,' Air 1/153/15/122/1

CHAPTER 16: THE LUDENDORFF OFFENSIVES, 1918

1 Douglas Haig, 1st Earl Haig, *The Private Papers of Douglas Haig, 1914–1919*, Robert Blake, ed. (London 1952), 46–7, 280, *passim*.

2 James E. Edmonds, *Military Operations: France and Belgium, 1918*, I (London 1935), 39

3 Rowland Fielding, *War Letters to a Wife: France and Flanders, 1915–1919* (London 1929), 262

4 Edmonds, *Military Operations: France and Belgium, 1918, Appendices* (London 1935), app. VI, 22–9

5 H.A. Jones, *The War in the Air: being the Story of the Part played in the Great War by the Royal Air Force*, IV (London 1934), app. XIV, 444–6; GHQ correspondence on draft paper, 22–28 December 1917, Air 1/526/16/12/36

6 Johnson to CAS, 28 Dec. 1962, G.O. Johnson biographical file, DHist

7 No 16 SRB, Jan. 1918, Air 1/1347/204/19/37

8 Sitwell to Wurtele, 6 Jan. 1918, Air 1/175/15/183/3

9 No 65 SRB, 4 Jan. 1918, ibid.

10 No 9 Wing orders, 14–21 March 1918, Air 1/882/204/5/604; RAF squadron histories, DHist 73/1552; Jones, *War in the Air*, IV, 265–6, 268, 271–2

11 Jones, *War in the Air*, IV, 279; Deutschland, Oberkommandos des Heeres, *Der Weltkrieg 1914 bis 1918*, Band XIV: *Die Kriegführung an der Westfront im Jahre 1918* (Berlin 1944), 47, DHist SGR I 196, Set 2

12 MacLaren logbook, D.R. MacLaren biographical file, DHist

13 Jones, *War in the Air*, IV, 287–8, app. XVII, 453–6

14 Ibid., 284–5

15 Canadian Bank of Commerce, *Letters from the Front: Being a Record of the Part Played by Officers of the Bank in the Great War, 1914–1919*, C.L. Foster and W.S. Duthie, eds. (Toronto [1920–1]), I, 256

16 'Flugzeugverluste an der Westfront März bis September 1918,' in Deutschland, Oberkommandos des Heeres, *Der Weltkrieg 1914 bis 1918*, Band XIV *Beilagen: Die Kriegführung an der Westfront im Jahre 1918* (Berlin 1944), Beilage 40

17 Ibid.; 84 Squadron air combat reports, 17 March 1918, Air 1/1227/204/5/2634/84; 84 Squadron operational record, 17 March 1918, Air 1/1795/204/155/2

18 K. Bodenschatz, 'Das Jagdgeschwader Frhr.v.Richthofen Nr 1,' quoted in G.P. Neumann, ed., *In der Luft unbesiegt* (München 1923), 227, DHist SGR I 196, Set 72

19 [E.] Ludendorff, *My War Memories, 1914–1918* (London nd), II, 589, 596; Edmonds, *Military Operations: France and Belgium, 1918*, I, 109, 154–5; Jones, *War in the Air*, IV, 268

20 Jones, *War in the Air*, IV, 268; Edmonds, *Military Operations: France and Belgium, 1918*, I, 109, 152–4

21 Jones, *War in the Air*, IV, app. XVI, table 'A'; France, Ministère de la Guerre, État-Major de l'Armée, Service Historique, *Les Armées françaises dans la grande Guerre* (Paris 1931), Tome VI, I, 168–9n

22 V Brigade work summary, 21 March 1918, Air 1/838/204/5/285; Ludendorff, *War Memories*, II, 596; Edmonds, *Military Operations: France and Belgium, 1918*, I, 161

23 Herbert Hill, *Retreat From Death* (London nd), 86, 87

24 Ludendorff, *War Memories*, II, 577; Ernst von Hoeppner, *Deutschlands Krieg in der Luft* (Leipzig 1921), 155, DHist SGR I 196, Set 73; W. Shaw Sparrow, *The Fifth Army in March 1918* (London 1921), 74; S. McCance, *History of the Royal Munster Fusiliers* (Aldershot 1927), II, 150; Edmonds, *Military Operations: France and Belgium, 1918*, I, 157

25 Edmonds, *Military Operations: France and Belgium, 1918*, I, 224; 59 SRB, 21 March 1918, Air 1/1781/204/150/14

26 'Quex' [G.H.F. Nichols], *Pushed and the Return Push* (Edinburgh and London 1919); Herbert Read, *In Retreat* (London 1925); Frank Dunham, *The Long Carry: the Journal of Stretcher Bearer Frank Dunham, 1916–18*, R.H. Haigh and P.W. Turner, eds. (Oxford 1970); Great Britain, Army General Staff, 'Cooperation of Aircraft with Artillery,' December 1917, 32, Air 1/918/204/5/880; 59 SRB 21 March 1918, Air 1/1781/204/150/14

27 T. Leigh-Mallory, 'Experiences on Active Service, 1914–1918,' 28 Sept. 1925, Air 1/2388/228/11/80

28 No 82 SRB, 21 March 1918, Air 1/1436/204/34/12; Read, *In Retreat*, 16; Gustav Goes, *Unter dem Stahlhelm*, Band VII: *Der Tag X: die grosse Schlacht in Frankreich, 21. Marz–5. April 1918* (Berlin 1933), 64, DHist SGR I 196, Set 78

29 T. Leigh-Mallory, 'Experiences on Active Service, 1914–1918,' 28 Sept. 1925, Air 1/2388/228/11/80

30 William Sholto Douglas, 1st Baron Douglas of Kirtleside, *Years of Combat: the First Volume of the Autobiography of Sholto Douglas* (London 1963), 262

31 I. III. V, and IX Brigade work summaries, 20–22 March 1918, Air 1/838/204/5/285; 'A Copy of the 1918 Diary of Captain Henry John Burden, DSO. DFC,' Burden biographical file, DHist

32 G.M. Lawson, 'Reminiscences and Experiences, 1914–1918,' 30 Oct. 1922, Air 1/2386/228/11/11; Herman Pantlen, *Die Württembergischen Regiment im Weltkrieg 1914–1918*, Band XLIII: *Das Württembergische Feldartillerie Regiment Konig-Karl (1. Württ.) No. 13 im Weltkrieg 1914–1918* (Stuttgart 1928), 166, DHist SGR I 196, Set 75; 'A Record of Experiences during the War, 1914–1918,' 15 Oct. 1922, Air 1/2386/228/11/13

33 Theodor Rumpel, 'Musings of a Jagdflieger,' *Cross & Cockade Journal*, X, fall 1969, 213–17; G.P. Neumann, ed., *In der Luft unbesiegt* (München 1923), 228, DHist SGR I 196, Set 72; Jones, *War in the Air*, IV, 252, app. XII, 433, 434

34 Jones, *War in the Air*, IV, 296–7; V Brigade work summary, 21–22 March 1918, Air 1/838/204/5/285

35 IX Brigade work summary, 21–22 March 1918, Air 1/838/204/5/285

36 III Brigade work summary, 21–22 March 1918, ibid.; Salmond to Trenchard, 22 March 1918, Air 1/475/15/312/201; 13 SRB, 22 March 1918, Air 1/1629/204/90/19; 'Diary,' Burden biographical file, DHist

37 III Brigade work summary, 22 March 1918, Air 1/838/204/5/285; Jones, *War in the Air*, IV, 302

38 Deneys Reitz, *Trekking On* (London 1933), 212

39 Edmonds, *Military Operations: France and Belgium, 1918*, I, 264; 82 SRB, 22 March 1918, Air 1/1436/204/34/12; annex 'A' to V Brigade work summary, 23 March 1918, Air 1/838/204/5/285

40 Annex 'A' to V Brigade, 22 March 1918; T. Leigh-Mallory, 'Experiences on Active Service, 1914–1918,' 28 Sept. 1925, Air 1/2388/228/11/80

41 V Brigade work summary and annex 'A,' 22 March 1918, Air 1/838/204/5/285

42 III. V, and IX Brigade work summaries, 22–23 March 1918, ibid.

43 Dunham, *The Long Carry*, 151

44 III Brigade work summary, 23 March 1918, Air 1/838/204/5/285; Deutschland, Bayrischeskriegsarchiv, *Erinnerungsblätter deutscher Regimenter*, Band LXXVI: *Das K.B. 14. Infanterie Regiment Hartmann* (München 1931), 280, DHist SGR I 196, Set 80

45 Douglas Reed, *Insanity Fair* (London 1938), 40–1

46 Commandant's lecture, RAF Staff College, nd, Air 1/2385/228/10

47 'No. 24 Squadron History,' nd, Air 1/168/15/160/1

48 Annex 'A' to V Brigade work summary, 23 March 1918, Air 1/838/204/5/285

49 Hoeppner, *Deutschlands Krieg in der Luft*, 156

50 John Ewing, *The History of the 9th (Scottish) Division, 1914–1919* (London 1921), 268, 277

51 IX Brigade work summary, 23 March 1918, Air 1/838/204/5/285

52 Salmond to Trenchard, 25 March 1918, Air 1/475/15/312/201

53 No 3 Squadron war diary, 24 March 1918, Air 1/166/15/142/19

54 Goes, *Unter dem Stahlhelm*, 119; Herbert Ulrich, *Res.-Inf.-Regt 52 im Weltkriege* (Cottbus nd), 470, DHist SGR I 196, Set 96

55 Annex 'A' to V Brigade work summaries, 24 and 25 March 1918, Air 1/838/204/ 5/285; Edmonds, *Military Operations: France and Belgium, 1918*, I, 367; Goes, *Unter dem Stahlhelm*, 119

56 'Air Warfare,' nd, 50, Air 1/2385/228/10

57 Hoeppner, *Deutschlands Krieg in der Luft*, 156; P.J. Carisella and James W. Ryan, *Who Killed the Red Baron? The Final Answer* (Wakefield, Mass. 1969), 63

58 I, III, V, and IX Brigade work summaries, 23–24 March 1918, Air 1/838/204/5/285

59 Hoeppner, *Deutschlands Krieg in der Luft*, 156

60 Ibid.

61 I, III, and V Brigade work summaries, 24–25 March 1918, Air 1/838/204/5/285

62 V Brigade work summary, 24–25 March 1918, ibid.; 84 SRB, 25 March 1918, Air 1/1795/204/155/2

63 L. de S. Duke diary, Duke biographical file, DHist

64 III Brigade weekly summary, 21–28 March 1918, Air 1/838/204/5/285

65 *Das K.B. 14. Infanterie Regiment Hartmann*, 282; 'Air Warfare,' nd, 50, Air 1/2385/ 228/10; *Der Weltkrieg 1914 bis 1918*, XIV, 184–5, DHist SGR I 196, Set 74

66 Heinrich Hermann, *Geschichte des Königlich Sachsischen Leibgrenadier Regts Nr. 100* (Zittau nd), 158, DHist SGR I 196, Set 96

67 Ulrich, *Res.-Inf.-Regt 52*, 474

68 'Air Warfare,' nd, 50, Air 1/2385/228/10; G.M. Knocker, 'Six Months with Sixty-Five,' *Cross & Cockade Journal*, XII, winter 1971, 302

69 Douglas, *Years of Combat*, 280

70 *Das K.B. 14. Infanterie Regiment Hartmann*, 282

71 I Brigade work summary, 26 March 1918, Air 1/838/204/5/285

72 III Brigade weekly summary, 22–28 March 1918, ibid.

73 Edmonds, *Military Operations: France and Belgium, 1918*, I, 542; *Der Weltkreig 1914 bis 1918*, XIV *Beilagen*, Beilage 40

74 Hoeppner, *Deutschlands Krieg in der Luft*, 153, DHist SGR I 196, Set 85; Foch to Fayolle, 1 April 1918, Edmonds, *Military Operations: France and Belgium, 1918*, II (London 1937), app. V, 506–8; J.C. Slessor, *Air Power and Armies* (London 1936), 128

75 Salmond to Trenchard, 26 March 1918, Air 1/475/15/312/201

76 *Der Weltkrieg 1914 bis 1918*, XIV, 196–7, DHist SGR I 196, Set 74

77 'Air Warfare,' nd, 50, Air 1/2385/228/10; brigade work summaries, 27 March 1918, Air 1/838/204/5/285

78 *Der Weltkrieg 1914 bis 1918*, XIV, 210, 212, DHist SGR I 196, Set 74

79 I, III, and V Brigade work summaries, 26–27 March 1918, Air 1/838/204/5/285

80 A.A. McLeod biographical file, DHist

81 G.G.H. Lawrence, 'Echoes of War, 1915–1918 (Pt. 4),' *Militaria*, 8/4, 1978, 62

82 *London Gazette*, 1 May 1918, 30663

83 Ludendorff, *War Memories*, II, 599–601; Edmonds, *Military Operations: France and Belgium, 1918*, II, 152–3; *Der Weltkrieg 1914 bis 1918*, XIV, 221, DHist SGR I 196, Set 2

84 Bodenschatz, 'Das Jagdgeschwader Frhr. v. Richthofen Nr 1,' 229; *History of 101 Regt of 23 Div*, 137, 140, and *History of 122 Fus Regt of 243 Div*, 240, DHist SGR I 196, photo items 48 and 49, Set 75

85 No 84 SRB, 1 April 1918, Air 1/1795/204/155/2; Jones, *War in the Air*, IV, 363–4
86 Ibid.
87 Ibid., 362; 27 SRB, 25–27 March 1918, Air 1/145/15/41/4
88 Edmonds, *Military Operations: France and Belgium, 1918*, II, 164
89 Jones, *War in the Air*, IV, 375; RAF communiqué no 2, 18 April 1918, DHist 75/414
90 *Regimental History of 51 Res Regt of 12 Res Div.*, 229–30, DHist SGR I 196, photo item 47, Set 75
91 *Der Weltkrieg 1914 bis 1918*, XIV *Beilagen*, Beilage 40; Jones, *War in the Air*, IV, 376
92 Jones, *War in the Air*, IV, 376
93 Ibid., 383; 2 SRB, 12 April 1918, Air 1/1460/204/36/71; RAF communiqué no 2, 18 April 1918, DHist 75/414
94 RAF communiqué no 2, 18 April 1918, DHist 75/414
95 Nos 62 and 73 SRB, 12 April 1918, Air 1/145/15/41/4; correspondence, S.W. Rosevear biographical file, DHist; Jones, *War in the Air*, IV, 381, 382n, 383n
96 'Diary,' Burden biographical file, DHist
97 Statement by Lye quoted in OC 22 Casualty Clearing Station to OC 19 Squadron, 19 April 1918, 19 SRB, Air 1/1486/204/37/71
98 Bodenschatz, 'Das Jagdgeschwader Frhr. v. Richthofen Nr 1,' 230
99 Logbook and Brown to his father, 27 April 1918, A.R. Brown biographical file, DHist; RAF communiqué No 3, 15–21 April 1918, DHist 75/414; Jones, *War in the Air*, IV, 393; C.E.W. Bean, *The Official History of Australia in the War of 1914–1918*, V: *The Australian Imperial Force in France during the Main German Offensive, 1918* (Sydney 1937), 693–701; F.M. Cutlack, *The Australian Flying Corps in the Western and Eastern Theatres of War, 1914–1918* (Sydney 1923), 249–52.
100 Bank of Commerce, *Letters from the Front*, I, 267
101 Fritz Fischer, *Germany's Aims in the First World War* (New York 1967), 515–23
102 Hoeppner, *Deutschlands Krieg in der Luft*, 162, DHist SGR I 196, Set 84. See also Hans Arndt, 'Die Fliegerwaffe,' in *Ehrendenkmal der Deutschen Wehrmacht*, von Eisenhart Rothe, ed. (Berlin & München 1942), 114, ibid.
103 Arndt, 'Die Fliegerwaffe'; Puglisi to Collishaw, 4 May and 27 Oct. 1966, R. Collishaw Papers, DHist 78/132, 1-D, folder 13, and 2-A, folder 14-b; W.M. Lamberton, *Fighter Aircraft of the 1914–1918 War* (Letchworth, Herts. 1960), 126; H.J. Nowarra and K.S. Brown, *Von Richthofen and the Flying Circus* (Letchworth, Herts. 1958), 180. See also Hoeppner, *Deutschlands Krieg in der Luft*, 162.
104 'History of 64 Squadron, R.F.C.,' 21 Oct. 1919, Air 1/173/15/182/1

CHAPTER 17: AMIENS

1 John Terraine, *Douglas Haig: the Educated Soldier* (London 1963), 452
2 James E. Edmonds, *Military Operations: France and Belgium, 1918*, IV (London 1947), 573–4
3 Ibid., 574–5; H.M. Urquhart, *Arthur Currie: the Biography of a Great Canadian* (Toronto 1950), 237

4 Sir Archibald Montgomery, *The Story of the Fourth Army in the Battle of the Hundred Days, August 8th to November 11th 1918* (London 1918), 21–4; G.W.L. Nicholson, *Canadian Expeditionary Force, 1914–1919* (Official History of the Canadian Army in the First World War; Ottawa 1964), 393

5 Nicholson, *Canadian Expeditionary Force*, 388–91, 393; Edmonds, *Military Operations: France and Belgium, 1918*, IV, 8

6 H.A. Jones, *The War in the Air, being the Story of the Part played in the Great War by the Royal Air Force*, VI (London 1937), 433–4; Air Historical Board narrative, France May–November 1918, 96, Air 1/677/21/13/1887; Deutschland, Kriegswissen-schaftlichen Abteilung der Luftwaffe, *Die Luftstreitkräfte in der Abwehrschlacht zwischen Somme und Oise vom 8. bis 12. August 1918 und Ruckblicke auf ihre voran-gegangene Entwicklung* (Berlin 1942), 146, DHist SGR I 196, Set 70c

7 Air Historical Board narrative, 104–14, Air 1/677/21/13/1887; Jones, *War in the Air*, *Appendices* (London 1937), 116–23, 130–41, and VI, 434–5

8 France, Ministère de la Guerre, État-Major de l'Armée, Service Historique, *Les Armées françaises dans la grande Guerre* (Paris 1923), Tome VII, 1, 170

9 Jones, *War in the Air*, VI, 436; *Die Luftstreitkräfte*, 155–7, DHist SGR I 196, Set 70d

10 Air Historical Board narrative, 97–9, Air 1/677/21/13/1887

11 Ibid., 104–9

12 Sir J.C. Slessor, *Air Power and Armies* (London 1936), 166

13 Charlton to V Brigade, 5 Aug. 1918, Air 1/1592/204/83/17; Slessor, *Air Power*, 165–9

14 Jones, *War in the Air*, VI, 436

15 Air Historical Board narrative, 111, 119, Air 1/677/21/13/1887; 9 Wing records, 7–8 Aug. 1918, Air 1/1533/204/176/14

16 No 57 Squadron, bomb dropping report no 136, 8 Aug. 1918, Air 1/958/204/5/1033; IX Brigade summary, 7–8 Aug. 1918, Air 1/977/204/5/1135; 107 Squadron, bomb dropping report no 21, 8 Aug. 1918, Air 1/1901/204/227/10; 205 SRB, 8 Aug. 1918, Air 1/2009/204/304/11

17 'No. 5 Squadrons Work under Command of Major C.H. Gardner, from July 1918, to November 11th 1918,' 3, Air 1/1313/204/13/96; HQ RAF, 'Notes on Corps Squadron Work during the Somme Offensive August 1918,' 1, Air 1/725/97/2

18 'Notes on Corps Squadron Work,' 1–2; '5 Squadrons Work ...' 1–3, 7, Air 1/1313/204/13/96; V Brigade, 'RAF Information for Ground Services for Forthcoming Operations,' 6 Aug. 1918, Air 1/1592/204/83/17

19 'No. 5 Squadrons Work ...' Air 1/1313/204/13/96; V Brigade summary, 7–8 Aug. 1918, Air 1/077/204/5/1135

20 Jones, *War in the Air*, VI, 464–5; T. Leigh-Mallory, 'History of Tank and Aeroplane Co-operation,' 31 Jan. 1919, 1–5, Air 1/725/97/10

21 Charlton to V Brigade, 14 Aug. 1918, Air 1/1592/204/83/17; Edmonds, *Military Operations: France and Belgium, 1918*, IV, 95

22 *Die Luftstreitkräfte*, 169, DHist SGR I 196, Set 70d

23 Bill Lambert, *Combat Report* (London 1973), 194–5

24 HQ RAF, 'Notes on Corps Squadron Work ...' 2–3, Air 1/725/97/2

25 No 8 SRB, 8 Aug. 1918, Air 1/1670/204/109/11; V Brigade summaries, 7–11 Aug. 1918, Air 1/977/204/5/1135

26 5th Canadian Infantry Battalion war diary, 8 Aug. 1918, PAC, RG 9 III, vol. 4916, folder 364; Slessor, *Air Power*, 169

27 V Brigade, annex to summary of work, 8 Aug. 1918, Air 1/977/204/5/1135; 24 Squadron air combat report, 8 Aug. 1918, Air 1/1221/204/5/2634/24

28 No 65 Squadron air combat report, 8 Aug. 1918, Air 1/1226/204/5/2634/65

29 V Brigade, annex to summary of work, 8 Aug. 1918, Air 1/977/204/5/1135; 84 SRB, 8 Aug. 1918, Air 1/1795/204/155/3; RAF war diary, 8 Aug. 1918, Air 1/1187/204/5/2595

30 V Brigade, annex to summary of work, 8 Aug. 1918, Air 1/977/204/5/1135; Jones, *War in the Air*, VI, 438

31 C.E.W. Bean, *The Official History of Australia in the War of 1914–1918*, VI: *The Australian Imperial Force in France during the Allied Offensive, 1918* (Sydney 1942), 600

32 Urquhart, *Currie*, 237

33 [E.] Ludendorff, *My War Memories* (London 1919), II, 680

34 *Die Luftstreitkräfte*, 158–9, 167, DHist SGR I 196, Set 70d

35 IX Brigade operation order (day) no 57, 8 Aug. 1918, Air 1/1057/204/5/1560

36 Air Historical Board narrative, 126, 138, Air 1/677/21/13/1887; Jones, *War in the Air*, VI, 442

37 Air Historical Board narrative, 122–3, Air 1/677/21/13/1887; 205 SRB, 8 Aug. 1918, Air 1/2009/204/304/11; IX Brigade summaries, 7–9 Aug. 1918, Air 1/977/204/5/1135

38 Air Historical Board narrative, 123, Air 1/677/21/13/1887; 98 Squadron bomb dropping report, 8 Aug. 1918, Air 1/958/204/5/1033; 'History of No. 98 Squadron,' Air 1/176/15/197/1; RAF war diary, 8 Aug. 1918, Air 1/1187/204/5/2595; 98 Squadron air combat reports, 8 Aug. 1918, Air 1/1227/204/5/2634/98

39 Air Historical Board narrative, 124–5, Air 1/677/21/13/1887

40 Ibid., 125–6; 73 SRB, 8 Aug. 1918, Air 1/1533/204/76/14; 73 Squadron air combat reports, 8 Aug. 1918, Air 1/1226/204/5/2634/73

41 IX Brigade operation order (night) no 14, 8 Aug. 1918, Air 1/1057/204/5/1560; 102 Squadron bomb raid report, 8–9 Aug. 1918, Air 1/958/204/5/1033; Air Historical Board narrative, 129, Air 1/677/21/13/1887

42 IX Brigade operation order (day) no 58, 8 Aug. 1918, Air 1/1057/204/5/1560

43 Ibid., Peter Robertson, 'W.J. Dalziel, Canadian Bomber Pilot – Western Front,' *CAHS Journal*, VIII, spring 1970, 4; Jones, *War in the Air*, VI, 446–7; Air Historical Board narrative, 130, Air 1/677/21/13/1887; IX Brigade summary, 8–9 Aug. 1918, Air 1/977/204/5/1135

44 Air Historical Board narrative, 130–1, Air 1/677/21/13/1887; IX Brigade summary, 8–9 Aug. 1918, Air 1/977/204/5/1135; 107 Squadron air combat report no 26, 9 Aug. 1918, Air 1/1901/204/227/10; 'History of No. 107 Squadron,' 2, 107 SRB, 9 Aug. 1918, Air 1/176/15/203/1

45 No 107 Squadron air combat report no 19, 9 Aug. 1918, Air 1/1901/204/227/10; Immediate Award table, Army Form W 3121, 14 Aug. 1918, Air 1/176/15/203/1

46 No 205 SRB, 9 Aug. 1918, Air 1/2009/204/304/11; III Brigade summary, 8–9 Aug. 1918, Air 1/977/204/5/1135; Air Historical Board narrative, 132–3, Air 1/677/21/13/1887

47 Air Historical Board narrative, 132; 205 SRB, 9 Aug. 1918, Air 1/2009/204/304/11

48 IX Brigade operation order (day) no 59, 9 Aug. 1918, Air 1/1057/204/5/1560; Air Historical Board narrative, 134–5, 139–40, Air 1/677/21/13/1887

49 Sir Archibald Montgomery-Massingberd, '8th August, 1918; a lecture delivered at the Royal Artillery Institution; Tuesday, 22 January, 1929,' *Journal of the Royal Artillery*, LV, 1929–30, 31; Montgomery, *Story of the Fourth Army*, 63–6

50 Air Historical Board narrative, 136–7, Air 1/677/21/13/1887

51 V Brigade, annex to summary of work, 8, 10 Aug. 1918, Air 1/977/204/5/1135

52 Ibid., 9–12, 17 Aug. 1918

53 No 65 Squadron air combat report, 9 Aug. 1918, Air 1/1226/204/5/2634/65

54 No 24 Squadron air combat reports, 10 Aug. 1918, Air 1/1221/204/5/2634/24; 84 Squadron air combat report nos 259 and 264, 11 Aug. 1918, Air 1/1227/204/5/2034/84

55 III Brigade summary, 9–10 Aug. 1918, Air 1/977/204/5/1135

56 No 56 Squadron air combat report nos 218 and 228, 10 Aug. 1918, Air 1/1224/204/5/2634/56

57 Ibid., no 220

58 IX Brigade operation order (day) no 60, 9 Aug. 1918, Air 1/1057/204/5/1560; Jones, *War in the Air*, VI, 452–3; 27 and 205 Squadron bomb dropping reports, 10 Aug. 1918, Air 1/958/204/5/1033; 205 SRB, 10 Aug. 1918, Air 1/2009/204/304/11; 32 Squadron air combat reports, 10 Aug. 1918, Air 1/1222/204/5/2634/32; 107 Squadron bomb dropping report, 10 Aug. 1918, Air 1/1901/204/227/10

59 No 57 SRB, 10 Aug. 1918, Air 1/1497/204/39/7; 103 Squadron bomb dropping report, 10 Aug. 1918, Air 1/958/204/5/1033; I Brigade and IX Brigade summaries, 10–11 Aug. 1918, Air 1/977/204/5/1135; 205 SRB, 11 Aug. 1918, Air 1/2009/204/304/11

60 Edmonds, *Military Operations: France and Belgium, 1918*, IV, 154–5

61 Slessor, *Air Power*, 164

62 Jones, *War in the Air*, VI, 452

63 Inter-Allied Transportation Council, 'Principle Affecting the Selection of Points of Attack on the Enemy's Railway Communications,' 2, Air 1/32/AH15/1/173; Andrew Boyle, *Trenchard* (London 1962), 308

64 F.H. Sykes, 'Remarks by the Air Staff on Two Papers Submitted by the Inter-Allied Transportation Council on the Subject of Aerial Bombardments of Enemy Railway Stations,' 13 Aug. 1918, Air 1/32/AH15/1/173

65 RAF war diary, 8 Aug. 1918, Air 1/1187/204/5/2595; Jones, *War in the Air*, VI, 445–6; *Die Luftstreitkräfte*, 198–9, DHist SGR 1 196, Set 70e

66 Jones, *War in the Air*, VI, 456; [Basil] Liddell Hart, *A History of the World War, 1914–1918* (London 1934), 549

CHAPTER 18: PERFECTING THE AIR WEAPON

1 Quoted in C.R.M.F. Cruttwell, *A History of the Great War, 1914–1918*, 2d ed. (Oxford 1936), 553; James E. Edmonds, *Military Operations: France and Belgium, 1918*, IV (London 1947), 173

2 J.F.C. Fuller, *Tanks in the Great War, 1914–1918* (London 1920), 226; Charlton to OC 15 Wing and OC 22 Wing, RAF, 14 Aug. 1918, Air 1/1592/204/83/17

3 T. Leigh-Mallory, 'Experiences on Active Service, 1914–1918,' 28 Sept. 1925, 15–16, Air 1/2388/228/11/80; Fuller, *Tanks in the Great War*, 247–8

4 Charlton to OC 15 Wing and OC 22 Wing, RAF, 14 Aug. 1918, Air 1/1592/204/83/17; H.A. Jones, *The War in the Air: being the Story of the Part played in the Great War by the Royal Air Force*, VI (London 1937), 474–5

5 Fuller, *Tanks in the Great War*, 244; Leigh-Mallory, 'Experiences,' 12–13. See also HQ RAF, 'Notes on Corps Squadron Work during the Somme Offensive, August 1918,' nd, Air 1/725/97/2.

6 RAF communiqué no 21, 19–25 Aug. 1918, DHist 75/414; 8 SRB, 21 Aug. 1918, Air 1/1670/201/109/12; Karl Bodenschatz, *Jagd in Flanderns Himmel* (München 1942), 131, 133

7 No 73 SRB, 21 Aug. 1918, Air 1/1533/204/76/14

8 Fuller, *Tanks in the Great War*, 253

9 H.H. Russell, 'A Brief History of No. 56 Squadron, RAF,' *Cross & Cockade Journal*, I, winter 1960, 1–15; 'A Copy of the 1918 Diary of Captain Henry John Burden, DSO, DFC,' Burden biographical file, DHist

10 OC 3 Squadron to OC 13 Wing, 1 Sept. 1918, Air 1/163/15/142/7; 3 SRB, 21 Aug. 1918, Air 1/166/15/142/19

11 No 60 Squadron, 'Report on Attack on Enemy Infantry,' 21 Aug. 1918, nos 9 and 17, Air 1/1555/204/79/60

12 Nos 27 and 107 Squadrons, bomb dropping reports, 21 Aug. 1918, Air 1/958/204/5/1033 and Air 1/1901/204/227/10

13 No 102 Squadron bomb raid report, 21–22 Aug. 1918, Air 1/958/204/5/1033

14 No 54 Squadron Air Combat reports, 22 Aug. 1918, Air 1/1901/204/227/10

15 RAF communiqué no 21, 19–25 Aug. 1918, DHist 75/414

16 *232 Reserve Regiment (107 Inf Div)*, 164, DHist SGR I 196, reproduction 73, Set 95 pt II; Edmonds, *Military Operations: France and Belgium, 1918*, IV, 213; 'Diary,' Burden biographical file, DHist

17 No 60 Squadron, 'Report on Attack on Enemy Infantry,' 24 Aug. 1918, no 26, Air 1/1555/204/79/60; Edmonds, *Military Operations: France and Belgium, 1918*, IV, 237

18 No 102 Squadron, 'Report of Machines which found Targets on Roads,' 24–25 Aug. 1918, Air 1/958/204/5/1033; *45 Infantry Regiment (221 Inf Div)*, 235–6, DHist SGR I 196, reproduction 56, Set 95 pt II

19 'Quex' [G.H.F. Nicholls], *Pushed and the Return Push* (Edinburgh and London 1919); Joseph Hayes, *The Eighty-Fifth in France and Flanders* (Halifax 1920), 136; RAF Staff College, 'The Employment of Aircraft in War,' nd, 52, Air 1/2385/228/10

20 Quoted in Edmonds, *Military Operations: France and Belgium, 1918*, IV, 260

21 Ibid., 280; 'Capt. E.J. Lussier, 73 Sqn.' in F.H. Hitchins, 'Canadian Airmen in World War I,' nd, DHist 73/1551

22 G. Knight, 'Canadian Corps War Records; No 5 Squadron's Work under Command of Major C.H. Gardner, from July 1918 to November 11th, 1918,' 12 Jan. 1919, PAC, RG 9 III, vol. 4611, folder 11, file 5

23 Jones, *War in the Air*, VI, 485–6; Edmonds, *Military Operations: France and Belgium, 1918*, IV, 306

24 Quoted in C.à C. Repington, *The First World War, 1914–1918* (London 1921), II, 362; Jones, *War in the Air*, VI, 486–7, 489

25 Jones, *War in the Air*, VI, 493–4

26 Hayes, *The Eighty-Fifth in France and Flanders*, 137; I and V Brigade war diary resumés, Aug.–Nov. 1918, PAC, RG 9 III, vol. 4614, folder 19, file 3, 8 SRB, 2 Sept. 1918, Air 1/1670/204/109/12

27 Jones, *War in the Air*, VI, 498–9; Deutschland, Oberkommandos des Heeres, *Der Weltkrieg 1914 bis 1918*, Band XIV *Beilagen: Die Kriegführung an der Westfront im Jahre 1918* (Berlin 1944), Beilage 40

28 R.C. Fetherstonhaugh, ed., *The Royal Montreal Regiment: 14th Battalion C.E.F., 1914–1925* (Montreal 1927), 242

29 J.A. MacDonald, ed., *Gun-Fire: an Historical Narrative of the 4th Bde. C.F.A. in the Great War (1914–18)* (Toronto 1929), 145

30 I and V Brigade resumés, PAC, RG 9 III, vol. 4614, folder 19, file 3

31 Ibid.; 8 SRB, 3 Sept. 1918, Air 1/1670/204/109/12; Edmonds, *Military Operations: France and Belgium, 1918*, IV, 416

32 Jones, *War in the Air*, VI, 501; *Der Weltkrieg 1914 bis 1918*, XIV *Beilagen*, Beilage 40

33 Quoted in Jones, *War in the Air*, VI, 500–1

34 No 20 Squadron air combat report, 5 Sept. 1918, Air 1/1220/204/5/2634/20

35 Ibid., 6 and 7 Sept. 1918

36 Donald Roderick MacLaren biographical file, DHist

37 'British Battles During 1918 (8th August to 11th Nov),' Jones, *War in the Air*, VI, facing 550

38 Ibid., 506; 84 Squadron air combat report, 20 Sept. 1918, Air 1/1227/204/5/2634/84

39 See RAF communiqué no 25, 16–22 Sept. 1918, DHist 75/414; 13 Squadron air combat report, 21 Sept. 1918, Air 1/1630/204/90/21; Jones, *War in the Air*, VI, 507.

40 H.D.G. Crerar, 'Organization and Procedure of Counter Battery Office, Canadian Corps Artillery,' 25 Jan. 1919, 11, DHist 72/13

41 Ibid., 20

42 No 83 Squadron reconnaissance reports, 20–21 Sept. 1918, Air 1/971/204/5/1113/1

43 No 102 Squadron reconnaissance reports, 21–22 Sept. 1918, Air 1/972/204/5/1113/2

44 Quoted in W.R. Puglisi, ed., 'Raesch of Jasta 43,' *Cross & Cockade Journal*, VIII, winter 1967, 322; 'Capt Reginald T.C. Hoidge, MC,' ibid., VII, winter 1966, 388

45 Fuller, *Tanks in the Great War*, 269; Jones, *War in the Air*, VI, 513

46 No 8 SRB, 27 Sept. 1918, Air 1/1670/204/109/12

47 Leigh-Mallory, 'Experiences,' 16; Fuller, *Tanks in the Great War*, 149, 269; DFC citation, W.H. Hubbard biographical file, DHist

48 I and V Brigade resumés, PAC, RG 9 III, vol. 4614, folder 19, file 3; Jones, *War in the Air*, VI, 520

49 'Lieut. W.A.W. Carter, 201 Sqn.' in Hitchins, 'Canadian Airmen'

50 'Work of Canadian Officers and Men with the Royal Air Force No. 5,' 5 Dec. 1918, CAF/–17–2–5, DHist 181.002 (D100)

51 Jones, *War in the Air*, VI, 523

52 Edmonds and R. Maxwell-Hyslop, *Military Operations: France and Belgium, 1918*, V (London 1974), 73, 143; *61 Infantry Regiment (35 Inf Div)*, 341, DHist SGR I 196, reproduction 79, Set 95 pt II; *176 Infantry Regiment (35 Inf Div)*, 290, ibid., reproduction 85; *119 Reserve Regiment (26 Res Div)*, 127, ibid., reproduction 69

53 RAF communiqué no 27, 30 Sept.–6 Oct. 1918, DHist 75/414

54 Quoted in Edmonds and Maxwell-Hyslop, *Military Operations: France and Belgium, 1918*, V, 186

55 Jones, *War in the Air*, VI, 535

56 W.S. Douglas, 'A Record of Experiences during the War, 1914–1918,' 41–2, Air 1/2386/228/11/13

57 *413 Infantry Regiment (204 Inf Div)*, 144, DHist SGR I 196, reproduction 88, Set 95 pt II

58 No 5 SRB, 15 Oct. 1918, Air 1/1480/204/36/141B; 'Record of Work Done by Canadian Officers and other Ranks serving in 1st (Corps) Wing, Royal Air Force,' month ending 31 Oct. 1918, Air 1/1485/204/36/162; 'Squadron "Canadian" Reports for October 1918,' quoted under 'Lieut. R.H. Schroeder, 4 Sqn.' in Hitchins, 'Canadian Airmen'

59 *413 Infantry Regiment (204 Inf Div)*, 142, DHist SGR I 196, reproduction 88, Set 95 pt II

60 Ibid.

61 No 46 Squadron air combat report, 26 Sept. 1918, Air 1/1223/204/5/2634/46

62 Jones, *War in the Air*, VI, 491

63 Copy of Air Ministry account on J.L.M. White biographical card, DHist

64 Barker to Lernan, 7 Nov. 1918, W.G. Barker Papers, PAC, MG 30 E 195, file 6; G.W.L. Nicholson, *The Canadian Expeditionary Force, 1914–1919* (Official History of the Canadian Army in the First World War; Ottawa 1964), 506n

65 Jones, *War in the Air*, VI, 545–6, 548

66 No 107 Squadron bomb-dropping report, 30 Oct. 1918, Air 1/972/204/5/114; IX (IIQ) Brigade and I Brigade work summaries, 30 Oct. 1918, Air 1/976/204/5/1132

67 X Brigade work summary, 30 Oct. 1918, ibid.

68 Nicholson, *The Canadian Expeditionary Force*, 473; Crerar, app. 12, DHist 72/13; I and V Brigade resumés, PAC, RG 9 III, vol. 4614, folder 19, file 3

69 No 8 Squadron war diary extracts, June-Nov. 1918, ibid., file 4

70 Knight, 'No. 5 Squadron's Working ...' PAC, RG 9 III, vol. 4611, folder 11, file 5; 5 SRB, 9 Nov. 1918, Air 1/1476/204/36/116

71 A.J. Lynch, 'An Interview with Lieutenant Richmond Viall, 46 Squadron RAF,' *Cross & Cockade Journal*, II, autumn 1961, 248–9

72 RAF communiqué no 32, 4–11 Nov. 1918, DHist 75/414

73 Douglas Haig, 1st Earl Haig, *Sir Douglas Haig's Despatches*, J.H. Boraston, ed. (London & Toronto 1919), 301–2

74 B.H. Liddell Hart, *Memoirs* (London 1965), II, 263

CHAPTER 19: TOWARDS THE ESTABLISHMENT OF A CANADIAN AIR FORCE

1 *Daily Mail and Empire* (Toronto), 27 April 1917, 6; *Toronto World*, 8 June 1917, 2; 23 June 1917, 6; 10 Sept. 1917, 6; *Toronto Star*, 26 July 1917, 8; *Globe* (Toronto), 19 Dec. 1917, 8

2 Morden to Perley, 26 Jan. 1917, Perley to Morden, 3 Feb. 1917, Morden to Gow, 26 Feb. 1917, P-5-94, PAC, RG 25, vol. 267

3 Morden to Perley, 26 Jan. 1917, ibid.; Carson to War Office, 2 Oct. 1916, Coade to Carson, 9 Oct. 1916, Morden to Carson, 16 Oct. 1916, HQ OMFC A–56–33, vol. 1, PAC, RG 9 III, vol. 2666

4 Letter to Gow, 14 Feb. 1917, Gow to Perley, 27 Feb. 1917, P–5–94, PAC, RG 25, vol. 267; Robert Laird Borden, *Robert Laird Borden: His Memoirs*, Henry Borden, ed. (Toronto 1938), II, 665, 679; F.H. Hitchins, 'Dominion Squadrons, 1915–1918,' 8, Hitchins Papers, DHist 75/514, file D1

5 Morden, 'Recommendation for the Establishment of Canadian Flying Corps,' nd, Hitchins Papers, file B1

6 DAS to HQ OMFC, 6 March 1917, Thacker to Turner, 7 March 1917, Gow to War Office, 8 March 1917, DAS to Overseas Ministry, 17 March 1917, OS 10–9–27, vol. 1, PAC, RG 9 III, vol. 80

7 'Notes on Australian-Canadian Conference,' 29 March 1917, ibid.; Perley to Henderson, 17 April 1917, P–5–94, PAC, RG 25, vol. 267

8 Dawson to Perley, 10 March 1917, Henderson to Perley, 19 May 1917, Kennedy to Hazen, 1 June 1917, Carson to Borden, 29 June 1917, P–5–94, PAC, RG 25, vol. 267; Perley to Borden, 14 June 1917, Borden to Perley, 19 June 1917, Perley Papers, PAC, MG 27 II D 12, vol. 9

9 Borden to Perley, 22 May 1917, OS 10–9–27, vol. 1, PAC, RG 9 III, vol. 80

10 Henderson to Perley, 26 May 1917, P–5–94, PAC, RG 25, vol. 267

11 Wanklyn to Perley, 29 May 1917, Henderson to Perley, 1 June 1917, ibid.

12 Henderson to Perley and enclosed statistical memorandum, 7 June 1917, ibid.

13 Perley to Borden, 12 June 1917, ibid.

14 Gwatkin, 'Memorandum Relating to the Proposed Formation of a Canadian Flying Corps,' nd, in Kemp to Borden, 22 June 1917, ibid.

15 Ibid.

16 Gwatkin to Hoare, 23 July 1917, Air 2/166/RU4116; Hoare quoted in Gwatkin to Kemp, 4 Aug. 1917, HQ OMFC 0–2–49, PAC, RG 9 III, vol. 3431

17 Kemp to Borden, 11 Aug. 1917, P–5–94, PAC, RG 25, vol. 267

18 *Daily Mail and Empire*, 5 Dec. 1916, 1

19 Turner to Perley, 13 July 1917, P–5–94, PAC, RG 25, vol. 267

20 Ibid.

21 Turner to Perley, 22 Sept. 1917, ibid.

22 McDonald to Perley, 5 June 1917, Perley to Mulock, 16 July 1917, Mulock to Perley, 22 July 1917, ibid.

23 McDonald, 'Memorandum on the Proposed Organization of a Canadian Flying Corps, Covering the Opinions Advanced by Flight-Commander Mulock, D.S.O., R.N.A.S.,' 26 July 1917, ibid.

24 Ibid.

25 Ibid.

26 Perley to Borden, 10 Aug. 1917, ibid.

27 Ibid.

28 Borden to Kemp, 14 July 1917, OS 10–9–27, vol. 1, PAC, RG 9 III, vol. 80

29 'Notes on Proposals for a Canadian Flying Corps,' [Aug. 1917], ibid.

30 Kemp to Perley, 22 Aug. 1917, Perley to Kemp, 2 Oct. 1917, P–5–94, PAC, RG 25, vol. 267

31 Perley to Borden, 7 Nov. 1917, Perley to Salmond, 6 Dec. 1917, Perley to Bell-Irving, 1 Jan. 1918, Perley to Kemp, 1 Jan. 1918, Warner to Perley, 9 Feb. 1918, Perley to Kemp, 11 Feb. 1918, Perley's minute on conversation with Kemp,

6 March 1918, ibid.; Turner to Kemp, 9 Feb. 1918, Turner Papers, PAC, MG 30 E 46, vol. 9, folder 59

32 Perley to Henderson, 31 Oct. 1916, Warner to Perley, 16 Nov. 1916, P-5-94, PAC, RG 25, vol. 267; Hitchins, 'Dominion Squadrons,' 11–12

33 Table on Canadians in RAF, 26 April 1918, Turner Papers, PAC, MG 30 E 46, vol. 9, folder 59

34 Hitchins, 'Dominion Squadrons,' 11

35 McAdams to Ewart, 14 July 1919, OS 10–9–27, vol. 3, PAC, RG 9 III, vol. 81; panel inscription, GAQ 10–20J, PAC, RG 24, vol. 1839

36 Panel inscription; Rudi Aksim, 'C.E.F. Transfers to the British Flying Services,' nd, 15, DHist 74/14

37 Aksim, 'C.E.F. Transfers,' 26–9

38 Ibid., 29–35

39 Turner to Kemp, 30 April 1918, 'Reasons for the Scheme,' [3 May 1918], Turner Papers, PAC, MG 30 E 46, vol. 9, folder 59

40 Ibid.

41 Kemp to Turner, 14 May 1918, ibid.; Turner to Kemp, 15 May 1918, HQ OMFC 0–2–49, PAC, RG 9 III, vol. 3431

42 Currie to Turner, 3 Nov. 1917, Turner Papers, PAC, MG 30 E 46, vol. 9, folder 59

43 Ibid.

44 Bishop to Morrison, 10 April 1918, ibid.

45 Critchley to Gibson, 26 April 1918, OS 10–9–27, vol. 1, PAC, RG 9 III, vol. 80

46 Kemp to Weir, 16 May 1918, Turner Papers, PAC, MG 30 E 46, vol. 9, folder 59

47 28th Air Council meeting, 23 May 1918, Air 6/12; Hitchins, 'Dominion Squadrons,' 13

48 Hitchins, 'Dominion Squadrons,' 14–15

49 Ibid., 15–16

50 Ibid., 16

51 Ibid.; Groves to CAS, 27 May 1918, Air 2/109A/19942

52 Groves to CAS, 27 May 1918, Air 2/109A/19942

53 Hitchins, 'Dominion Squadrons,' 17–18; memorandum of conference at the Air Ministry, 28 May 1918, Kemp Papers, PAC, MG 27 II D 9, vol. 157

54 Weir to Kemp, 29 May 1918, Kemp Papers, vol. 132

55 Ibid.

56 Kemp to Weir, 4 June 1918, ibid.

57 Memorandum of conference at Air Ministry, 5 June 1918, ibid., vol. 157; 'Minutes of Meeting held on June 5th on Manning of R.A.F. Squadrons with Canadian Personnel,' 5 June 1918, Air 2/109A/19942

58 Appendix 1 to minutes, 5 June 1918, Air 2/109A/19942

59 'Minutes of Conference on the Question of Formation of Canadian Air Force,' 27 June 1918, ibid.; McDonald to Secretary, Air Council, 28 June 1918, Robinson to GOC OMFC, 8 July 1918, OS 10–9–27, vol. 1, PAC, RG 9 III, vol. 80

60 Kemp to Borden, 16 May and 24 June 1918, Kemp Papers, PAC, MG 27 II D 9, vol. 132; Globe, 21 May 1918, 4; Toronto Star, 25 May 1918, 10; 12 July 1918, 10

61 Canada, Parliament, House of Commons, Debates, 24 April 1918 (J.E. Armstrong), 1114–16; 2 May 1918 (Sir Sam Hughes), 1417–18; 13 May 1918 (W.F. Nickle), 1906; PC 1984, 19 Sept. 1918

62 Memoranda on the Canadian Air Service, [May]–8 June 1918, Air 1/461/15/312/108

63 Ibid.

64 United States, Navy Department, *German Submarine Activities on the Atlantic Coast of the United States and Canada* (Washington 1920), 7, 22–3; Borden, *Robert Laird Borden*, II, 665; memorandum to Captain-in-Charge, Halifax Dockyard, 6 July 1915, Kingsmill to Crothers, 10 July 1915, NS 1062-13-4, PAC, RG 24, vol. 4022; Colonial Secretary to Governor General, 11 Nov. 1916, NS 1065-7-2, vol. 1, ibid., vol. 4031; Kingsmill to Minister and Deputy Minister Naval Service to Under Secretary External Affairs, 10 Feb. 1917, extracts from Interdepartmental Committee proceedings, 45th meeting, 10 Feb. 1917, 46th meeting, 12 Feb. 1917, Hazen to Naval Ottawa, 28 Feb. 1917, Seddon to Kingsmill, 21 and 25 March 1917, NS 1034-3-3, vol. 1, ibid., vol. 3894

65 Foster to Borden, 30 March 1917, ibid.; J.D.F. Kealy, 'Naval Aviation in Canada during the First World War,' 6–7, DHist 74/25

66 Admiralty minutes, 7 (signed 9) and 24–29 Jan. 1918, Air 1/272/15/226/123; Admiralty to Colonial Office, 3 Jan. 1918, Colonial Secretary to Governor General, 11 Jan. 1918, NS 1017-10-1, vol. 1, PAC, RG 24, vol. 3831; US Navy Department, *German Submarine Activities*, 23, 25; Operations Committee minutes, 18 Feb. 1918, Adm 1/8564, copy in Marder Papers, PRO 284, DHist M46

67 Operations Committee minutes, 2 March 1918, ibid.; Colonial Secretary to Governor General, 26 Feb. and 11 March 1918, NS 1034-3-4, vol. 1, PAC, RG 24, vol. 3894; Scarlett, 'Report on the Possibility of Establishing Aircraft Patrols for Anti-submarine Purposes on the Canadian Coast,' 1 March 1918, Colonial Secretary to Governor General, 11 March 1918, Air 1/272/15/226/123

68 Governor General to Colonial Secretary, 15 March 1918, Naval Ottawa to Admiralty, 20 April 1918, DAD to C-in-C NA & WI, 23 April 1918, ibid.; Admiral Superintendent Halifax to Secretary, Naval Service, 23 March 1918, NS 40-4-1, DHist 77/58, vol. 22; Stephen's memorandum, 6 May 1918, Admiralty to Kingsmill, 7 May 1918, NS 63-10-1, ibid., vol. 20; correspondence between C-in-C NA & WI, Naval Ottawa and Halifax, 1–30 April 1918, NS 1065-7-6, PAC, RG 24, vol. 4031; C-in-C NA & WI to Admiralty, 22 April 1918, Naval Service to Borden, 3 May 1918, Kingsmill to Ballantyne and Ballantyne's minute, 3 May 1918, NS 1034-3-4, vol. 1, ibid., vol. 3894

69 Admiralty to Paine, 29 April 1918, Barron to DAD, 24 May 1918, Air 1/272/15/226/123; F.H. Hitchins, 'The Royal Canadian Naval Air Service,' 4–5, Hitchins Papers, DHist 75/514, file D12

70 PC 1379, 5 June 1918; 'Air Service – Organization,' 8 May 1918, Fuller to Deputy Minister Public Works, 23 May 1918, NS 63-10-1, DHist 77/58, vol. 20

71 'Report on Selection of Sites for Proposed Air Stations at Halifax, N.S., and Sydney, C.B.,' [May 1918], Chief of Naval Operations USN to C-in-C NA & WI, 17 May 1918, Cull to Kingsmill, 11 July 1918, NS 1034-3-4, PAC, RG 24, vol. 3894; USN to C-in-C NA & WI, 27 July 1918, Cull to Kingsmill, 31 July 1918, C-in-C NA & WI to Kingsmill, 31 July 1918, Cull to Kingsmill, 3 Aug. 1918, NS 63-10-1, DHist 77/58, vol. 20

72 Hose to Admiral Superintendent Halifax, 28 Aug. 1918, NS ZZ 40-4-1, DHist 77/58, vol. 22; RCNAS weekly summaries, 1, 4, 7, and 11, 9 and 30 Sept., 21 Oct. and 18

Nov. 1918, NS 63–1–4, ibid., vol. 2; US Navy Department, *German Submarine Activities*, 7; Richard E. Byrd, *Skyward* (New York 1931), 64–5, 69–71

73 Letter to Cull [June 1918], Naval Ottawa to Admiralty, 11 July 1918, DAD to MGP, 12 July 1918, SO1 Air to DAD, 16 July 1918, DAD to Deputy First Sea Lord, 4 Sept. 1918, Air 1/272/15/226/123; Admiralty to Naval Ottawa, 18 July 1918, NS 63–10–1, DHist 77/58, vol. 20

74 Borden to Naval Ottawa, 31 July 1918, press release, 8 Aug. 1918, DHist 77/58, vol. 20

75 'Report of Formation and Future Policy of the Canadian Naval Air Service,' [27 Aug. 1918], Air 1/272/15/226/123

76 Ibid.; Borden, *Robert Laird Borden*, II, 847; Christie to Desbarats, 30 Aug. 1918, NS 63–1–1, PAC, RG 24, vol. 5666; PC 2154, 5 Sept. 1918

77 *Toronto Star*, 25 Oct. 1918, 6; RCNAS weekly summaries 2–9, 15 Sept.–4 Nov. 1918, NS 63–1–4, DHist 77/58, vol. 2

78 McDonald to Turner, 24 Sept. 1918, Bishop to Mewburn, 26 Sept. 1918, HQ OMFC A–6–36, vol. 1, PAC, RG 9 III, vol. 3068; McDonald to Turner, 1 Oct. 1918, Gow to Kemp, 2 Oct. 1918, Kemp to Turner, 26 Oct. 1918, Kemp Papers, PAC, MG 27 II D 9, vol. 143

79 Gibson to Minister, 26 July 1918, DAO order, 5 Aug. 1918, OS 10–9–27, vol. 1, PAC, RG 9 III, vol. 80

80 'Scheme for Canadian Air Force,' 3 May 1918, Kemp Papers, PAC, MG 27 II D 9, vol. 157; minutes of OMFC Council meeting, 16 July 1918, ibid., vol. 177; memorandum to Kemp, 6 Aug. 1918, HQ OMFC A–6–36, vol. 1, PAC, RG 9 III, vol. 3068; [Bishop] memorandum, 30 Sept. 1918, HQ OMFC D–2–49, ibid., vol. 3430; HQ OMFC to Air Ministry, 19 Nov. 1918, HQ OMFC S–10–49, ibid., vol. 3432

81 [Bishop] memorandum, 30 Sept. 1918, HQ OMFC D–2–49, ibid., vol. 3430; Gibson to Turner, 14 Oct. 1918, HQ OMFC O–2–49, ibid., vol. 3431; Gibson to Kemp, 28 Oct. 1918, OS 10–9–27, vol. 1, ibid., vol. 80; CAF memoranda and attached squadron lists, 11 and 16 Nov. 1918, HQ OMFC A–6–36, vol. 1, ibid., vol. 3068; OMFC to Air Ministry, 19 Nov. 1918, HQ OMFC S–10–49, ibid., vol. 3432

82 DAO order, 5 Aug. 1918, Air Ministry to Bishop, 28 Sept. 1918, Gibson to Minister, 28 Oct. 1918, OS 10–9–27, vol. 1, ibid., vol. 80; Lott to Gibson, 5 Dec. 1918, OS 10–9–27, vol. 2, ibid., vol. 81; HQ OMFC correspondence, 1–11 Aug. 1918, Air Ministry to HQ OMFC, 30 Oct. 1918, HQ OMFC R–1–49, ibid., vol. 3432

83 DAO order, 5 Aug. 1918, Lott memorandum, 21 Oct. 1918, Gibson to Minister, 28 Oct. 1918, OS 10–9–27, vol. 1, ibid., vol. 80; McCrimmon to HQ OMFC, 15 Oct. 1918, HQ OMFC O–285–33, ibid., vol. 2905

84 Brancker to Gibson, 16 Nov. 1918, Gibson to McDonald, 19 Nov. 1918, OS 10–9–27, vol. 1, ibid., vol. 80

85 Memorandum to McDonald, 12 Dec. 1918, McKeever to GS, 28 Dec. 1918, HQ OMFC O–2–49, ibid., vol. 3431; Air Ministry to HQ OMFC, 13 Dec. 1918, Marshall to Edwards, 28 Jan. 1919, HQ OMFC A–6–36, vol. 1, ibid., vol. 3068; McKeever memoranda, 7 and 12 Jan. 1919, HQ OMFC R–4–49, ibid., vol. 3432; McCrimmon to HQ OMFC, 7 Jan. 1919, Marshall to CAF Section, 25 Feb. and 13 March 1919, HQ OMFC D–2–49, ibid., vol. 3430

86 McKeever memorandum, 15 Dec. 1918, HQ OMFC to Air Ministry, 23 Dec. 1918, Lawson to GS, 28 Dec. 1918, McKeever to GS, 10 Feb. 1919, HQ OMFC E–5–49, HQ OMFC correspondence on Hounslow Flight, 16–28 Jan. 1919, HQ OMFC F–1–49, ibid., vol. 3430; OMFC conference on CAF [Feb. 1919], HQ OMFC O–2–49, ibid., vol. 3431; Canadian conference at Air Ministry, 21 March 1919, Air 2/109A/1990

87 McKeever memorandum, 28 Jan. 1919, HQ OMFC O–2–49, PAC, RG 9 III, vol. 3431; Edwards to Gibson, 31 Jan. 1919, HQ OMFC A–6–36, vol. 1, ibid., vol. 3068

88 Gibson to Edwards, 15 Jan. 1919, OMFC memoranda, 3–19 Feb. 1919, HQ OMFC A–6–36, vol. 1, ibid.; HQ OMFC to Air Ministry, 24 Feb. 1919, HQ OMFC O–2–49, ibid., vol. 3431; Lott to GSO1 and minute to AG, 26 Feb. 1919, Edwards to AG, 15 March 1919, HQ OMFC E–6–49, ibid., vol. 3430; Overseas Military Council meeting, 28 Feb. 1919, HQ OMFC E–289–33, ibid., vol. 2790; Sherwood to AG, 25 March 1919, HQ OMFC E–305–33, Overseas Military Council meeting, 30 April 1919, HQ OMFC E–304–33, ibid., vol. 2791; Canadian conference at Air Ministry, 21 March 1919, DAO order, 28 March 1919, Air 2/109A/1990

89 'Progress Report No. 2 – No. 1 Sqdn,' 31 Dec. 1918, HQ OMFC R–4–49, PAC, RG 9 III, vol. 3432; Warman to Air Ministry, 11 April 1919, HQ OMFC A–1–49, ibid., vol. 3428; Leckie to DAS, 12 April 1919, HQ OMFC P–12–49, Leckie to DAS, 14 April 1919, HQ OMFC P–6–49, ibid., vol. 3431; Warman to Air Ministry, 15 April 1919, Edwards to de Dombasle, 19 May 1919, de Dombasle to Air Ministry, 23 May 1919, HQ OMFC A–6–36, vol. 2, ibid., vol. 3068

90 Wing lists, April–May 1919, HQ OMFC P–8–49, squadron lists, April–May 1919, HQ OMFC P–12–49, ibid., vol. 3431

91 F.H. Hitchins, 'Gift Aircraft and Equipment,' 1–5, Hitchins Papers, DHist 75/514, file E5

92 Milner to Governor General, 4 June 1919, Turner Papers, PAC, MG 30 E 46, vol. 9, folder 59

93 F.H. Hitchins, *Air Board, Canadian Air Force and Royal Canadian Air Force* (Mercury Series, Canadian War Museum Paper No 2; Ottawa 1972), 5–6, 407

94 RCNAS weekly summary 11, 18 Nov. 1918, NS 63–1–4, DHist 77/58, vol. 2; Ballantyne to Borden, 22 Nov. 1918, Borden to Ballantyne, 24 Nov. 1918, NS 63–10–1, ibid., vol. 20; Ballantyne to Desbarats, 5 Dec. 1918, NS 63–9–1, ibid., vol. 19; PC 3009, 5 Dec. 1918

95 Hitchins, 'The Royal Canadian Naval Air Service,' 17–18; Desbarats to Ballantyne, 13 Dec. 1918, NS 63–1–1, PAC, RG 24, vol. 5666

96 Desbarats to Ballantyne, 13 Dec. 1918, NS 63–1–1, PAC, RG 24, vol. 5666

97 MacLaurin to Desbarats, 20 Aug. 1919, ibid.; Hitchins, 'The Royal Canadian Naval Air Service,' 18–19

98 Kemp to Mewburn, 8 Feb. 1919, Gwatkin to AG, 12 Feb. 1919, Mewburn to Kemp, 14 Feb. 1919, HQ C2841, vol. 5, DHist 77/57

99 Kemp to Mewburn, 19 Feb. 1919, OS 10–9–27, vol. 2, PAC, RG 9 III, vol. 81

100 Kemp to Borden, 19 Feb. 1919, Kemp Papers, PAC, MG 27 II D 9, vol. 132

101 Borden to Kemp, 24 Feb. 1919, ibid.; Mewburn to White, 23 Feb. 1919, Gwatkin to Military Secretary, 9 Jan. 1919, Gwatkin to Macallum, 8 Feb. 1919, HQ C2841, vol. 5, DHist 77/57

102 DCAS to DAO, 10 March 1919, Air 2/122/B9478; draft of paper 'Aerial Expansion with Particular Reference to Canada,' 10 March 1919, HQ OMFC O-2-49, PAC, RG 9 III, vol. 3431

103 Game to CAS, 17 March 1919, Air 2/122/B9478

104 Groves to Game, 19 March 1919, Gibson to CAS, 27 March 1919, ibid.

105 'Aerial Expansion with Particular Reference to Canada,' enclosed in Gibson to Kemp, 29 April 1919, Kemp Papers, PAC, MG 27 II D 9, vol. 132

106 Gibson to Kemp and enclosure 'Aviation in Canada,' 29 April 1919, ibid.; DCAS to DAO, 10 March 1919, HQ OMFC O-2-49, PAC, RG 9 III, vol. 3431

107 Gibson-Bristol correspondence, 20 and 26 May 1919, Turner Papers, PAC, MG 30 E 46, vol. 9, folder 59; Stevens' holographic minute no 55, 6 June 1919, Air 2/109 A/1990

108 Mewburn to Gwatkin and Gwatkin to Mulock, 30 May 1919, HQ C2841, vol. 5, DHist 77/57; Gwatkin to Hawksford, 31 May 1919, HQ 6978-2-131, vol. 10, PAC, RG 24, vol. 2043; Kemp to Gibson, 30 May 1919, Kemp to Borden, 30 May 1919, Kemp Papers, PAC, MG 27 II D 9, vol. 132

109 Gibson to Kemp, 5 June 1919, ibid.

110 Kemp to Gibson, 12 June 1919, ibid.

111 Gibson to Bristol, 24 June 1919, OS 10-9-27, vol. 3, PAC, RG 9 III, vol. 81; memorandum to Griffith, 8 Dec. 1921, letter to Frewin, 10 Feb. 1922, M-69-34, PAC, RG 25, vol. 232

112 MacAdams to OIC War Records, 14 and 15 July 1919, OS 10-9-27, vol. 3, PAC, RG 9 III, vol. 81

APPENDIX C

1 MacLaren to McBrien, 12 Aug. 1919, 0-285-33, PAC, RG 9 III, vol. 2907; McAdams to Deputy Minister, OMFC, 20 Aug. 1919, Kemp Papers, PAC, MG 27 II D 9, vol. 136

2 Interview with R.V. Dodds, DHist, 9 Dec. 1975

3 Canadian Bank of Commerce, *Letters from the Front: Being a Record of the Part Played by Officers of the Bank in the Great War*, C.L. Foster and W.S. Duthie, eds. (Toronto [1920-1]), II

4 Alan Sullivan, *Aviation in Canada, 1917-1918: Being a Brief Account of the Work of the Royal Air Force Canada, the Aviation Department of the Imperial Munitions Board and the Canadian Aeroplanes Limited* (Toronto 1919), 146

5 The analyses used here were the most useful of those presented in three preliminary reports. Andrew Johnson, 'Canadians in the British flying services: statistical report on the computer programme,' DHist 74/39; O.A. Cooke, 'Canadians in the British flying services: enlistments, manpower losses, honours and awards, operational service; analyses from the computer programme,' DHist 75/279; Jane Desbarats, 'Statistical study of Canadian participation in the British flying services in World War I,' DMS staff note, no 26/75, Directorate of Mathematics and Statistics paper, 1975, DHist 76/123

6 A. Fortescue Duguid, *Official History of the Canadian Forces in the Great War, 1914-1919* (Ottawa 1938), I, 51; G.W.L. Nicholson, *The Canadian Expeditionary*

Force, 1914–1919 (Official History of the Canadian Army in the First World War; Ottawa 1964), 343

7 Desmond Morton, 'French Canada and War, 1868–1917: the Military Background to the Conscription Crisis of 1917,' J.L. Granatstein and R.D. Cuff, *War and Society in North America* (Toronto 1971), 84–103; Robert Craig Brown and Ramsay Cook, *Canada, 1896–1921: a Nation Transformed* (The Canadian Centenary Series; Toronto 1974), 262–74

8 Duguid, *Official History*, I, 53

9 'Canadian volunteers and the Royal Naval Air Service,' nd, DHist 75/402

10 Recruiting advertisements for Royal Flying Corps Canada, DHist 77/18

11 Curtis Kinney and Dale M. Titler, *I Flew a Camel* (Philadelphia 1972), 16–17

12 Rudi Aksim, 'C.E.F. transfers to the British flying services,' 27–35, DHist 74/14

13 See 641–2.

14 Desbarats, 'Statistical Study,' 20

Index

Canadian airmen named in footnotes for the sole purpose of identifying their unit at a particular time are not included in this index.